# Handbook of
# Software Engineering
# &
# Knowledge Engineering

**Vol. 1**
**Fundamentals**

# Handbook of
# Software Engineering
# & 
# Knowledge Engineering

## Vol. 1
## Fundamentals

Editor

## S K Chang

*University of Pittsburgh, USA*
*and*
*Knowledge Systems Institute, USA*

**World Scientific**
*New Jersey • London • Singapore • Hong Kong • Bangalore*

*Published by*

World Scientific Publishing Co. Pte. Ltd.

P O Box 128, Farrer Road, Singapore 912805

*USA office:* Suite 1B, 1060 Main Street, River Edge, NJ 07661

*UK office:* 57 Shelton Street, Covent Garden, London WC2H 9HE

**British Library Cataloguing-in-Publication Data**
A catalogue record for this book is available from the British Library.

**HANDBOOK OF SOFTWARE ENGINEERING & KNOWLEDGE ENGINEERING, Vol. 1**
**Fundamentals**

ISBN 981-02-4973-X
ISBN 981-02-4514-9 (Set)

Printed in Singapore.

# PREFACE

The *Handbook of Software Engineering and Knowledge Engineering* is the first comprehensive handbook covering these two important areas that have become interwoven in recent years. Many international experts contribute to this Handbook. Each article is written in a way that a practitioner of software engineering and knowledge engineering can easily understand and obtain useful information. Each article covers one topic and can be read independently of other articles, providing both a general survey of the topic and an in-depth exposition of the state of the art. Practitioners will find this Handbook useful when looking for solutions to practical problems in software engineering and knowledge engineering. Researchers in turn can use the Handbook to quickly obtain background information, current trends and the most important references on a certain topic.

The Handbook consists of two volumes. Volume One covers the basic principles and applications of software engineering and knowledge engineering. Volume Two expands the coverage of basic principles and also contains many articles that specifically addresses visual and multimedia software engineering, and emerging topics in software engineering and knowledge engineering such as software patterns, data mining for software knowledge, etc. The two volumes form a complete set, but can be used separately for different purposes.

## Turning Knowledge into Software

There is a growing awareness that the central issue in software engineering and knowledge engineering is how to turn knowledge into software. Traditionally software engineering is concerned with the specification, design, coding, testing and maintenance of software. It also implicitly deals with the issues of transforming knowledge into software in the sense that the gathering of knowledge about the problem domain is incorporated into the requirements analysis phase of the software life cycle. Often, informal techniques of knowledge acquisition are used. Thus in the past, the role of knowledge engineering in the software process is an implicit one.

However it has long been recognized by many people that knowledge engineering plays an increasingly important role in software design. Indeed it is because of this conviction that the international conference series on Software Engineering and Knowledge Engineering (SEKE) was founded in 1988, followed by the publication of the *International Journal of Software Engineering and Knowledge Engineering* (*IJSEKE*) three years later. For both the SEKE conference series and the IJSEKE journal, the basic viewpoint is that the interdisciplinary area of software engineering and knowledge engineering is concerned with the interplay between software engineering and knowledge engineering — how software engineering can be applied to knowledge engineering, and how knowledge engineering can be applied to software engineering.

This viewpoint should now be modified and expanded because, both in theory and in practice, more and more software engineers and knowledge engineers are explicitly incorporating knowledge into the software process. In editing this two-volume handbook, this expanded viewpoint — that software engineering is concerned with the transformation of knowledge into software — has been carefully taken into consideration to conceptually organize the recent progresses in software engineering and knowledge engineering.

## Software Patterns

Let us start with two distinct, yet complementary, viewpoints on software engineering. The two viewpoints may seem completely different, but they are but different ways of viewing the "elephant" that is software engineering.

The first viewpoint, as stated above, is that software engineering is concerned with the transformation of knowledge into software. The second viewpoint is somewhat more technical. It says that software engineering is concerned with the specification, design, transformation, verification and validation of patterns.

Software is nothing but patterns. A program is constructed from some basic patterns, and the construction rules can in turn be expressed as other types of patterns. With grammars, formal languages and automata, there are many approaches to describe the basic patterns and how they are composed into programs.

Specifications are composed of patterns that are the basic building blocks of formal, informal or visual specifications. The specification, in the ideal case, can then be automatically transformed into programs, and verified and validated in the transformational process.

As mentioned above, knowledge used to be described informally, but now there are formal techniques and more precise ways of dealing with knowledge. With advances in object oriented methods, one comes to the inevitable conclusion that knowledge is also composed of patterns. Knowledge is first acquired, then transformed into formal/informal/visual specification, design and finally program.

Therefore, software engineering can now be viewed as the transformation of knowledge into software through the transformation of patterns. The central issue of software engineering is how to turn knowledge into software by means of the creation, composition and transformation of various types of patterns. A key question that can be asked repeatedly for any topic or sub-topic is the following: how to turn what-kind-of knowledge patterns into what-kind-of software patterns?

## Overview of Volume One

As mentioned above, the *Handbook of Software Engineering and Knowledge Engineering* is a comprehensive handbook providing readers with both useful overviews and detailed explanations of the methodologies, techniques and current research issues in software engineering and knowledge engineering. Volume One deals with the fundamentals of software engineering and knowledge engineering. Topics relevant to the traditional software life cycle are covered. Current research in software engineering and knowledge engineering are also surveyed.

The first group of articles deal with the basics in software engineering, including such topics as requirements engineering, domain engineering, object technology, software architecture, computer languages, program slicing techniques, incremental software development, technical reviews, formal verification, software maintenance, software reliability engineering, management of inconsistencies in software engineering, software configuration management, reengineering, software measurement, software metrics for identifying critical components in software projects, software engineering standards, engineering access control, usability issues in the software life cycle, software processes in software engineering and knowledge engineering, and message sequence charts in the software engineering process.

The second group of articles deal with the basics in knowledge engineering, including such topics as: conceptual modeling, case based reasoning, logical abduction in software engineering, knowledge-level models of knowledge systems, knowledge discovery and data mining, knowledge based Information access, machine learning for software engineering, and neural networks.

The third group of articles deal with the interplay of software engineering and knowledge engineering, including such topics as: pattern based software reengineering, agent-oriented software engineering, ontologies in software design, rationale management in software engineering, learning software organization, software engineering and learning theory, task models for interactive software systems, software engineering and knowledge engineering issues for web based education systems, and software engineering and knowledge engineering issues in bio-informatics.

## Overview of Volume Two

Volume Two expands the coverage of the basic principles of software engineering. However, this volume also addresses many current topics in software engineering and knowledge engineering such as visual patterns, multimedia software engineering, etc.

A central issue is how to turn knowledge patterns into visual software patterns and visual specifications such as UML. Techniques for knowledge acquisition, software visualization and knowledge visualization, are also of great interest.

The first group of articles deal with software engineering, including such topics as: formal description techniques, software specification and design, software inspections, component-based software engineering, versions of program integration, software reuse, assessing different testing strategies for software engineering and knowledge engineering, automated knowledge-based selection of suitable unit testing techniques, verification and validation, software cost estimation, data model metrics, uncertainty management, software project management, and reverse engineering,

The second group of articles deal with visual and multimedia software engineering, including such topics as: multimedia software engineering, web engineering, object-oriented modeling of multimedia applications, visual languages in software engineering, software engineering for visual programming languages, assessing visual programming languages, visual parallel programming, software visualization, and visualization of knowledge structures.

The third group of articles deal with emerging topics in software engineering and knowledge engineering, including such topics as: software patterns, supporting software processes using knowledge management, methods for knowledge elicitation, knowledge elicitation from software code, nonmonotonic reasoning and consistency management in software engineering, agent-oriented software construction with UML, improving UML designs using automatic design pattern detection, application of knowledge-based systems for supervision and control of machining processes, system-level design notations for embedded systems, situated computing for mobile users, and the synchronization of interactive web documents.

In a rapidly expanding area such as software engineering and knowledge engineering, no handbook can claim to cover all the subjects of interest. However it is hoped that this Handbook is comprehensive enough to serve as a useful and handy guide to both practitioners and researchers for a number of years to come.

Shi-Kuo Chang
*University of Pittsburgh and*
*Knowledge Systems Institute*

# CONTENTS

# COMPUTER LANGUAGE ADVANCES

DANIEL E. COOKE*,†,§, MICHAEL GELFOND*, and JOSEPH E. URBAN‡

*Computer Science Department, Texas Tech University,
P O Box 43104, Lubbock, TX 79409, USA
†NASA Ames Research Center
‡Computer Science and Engineering Department, Arizona State Univeristy
§E-mail: dcooke@coe.ttu.edu

Computer language research began with the advent of the von Neumann architecture and proceeds to the present day, with promise for further advances in the future. This paper reviews the history of language research, and includes distinctions between experimental and theoretical research in the area, as well as a distinction between evolutionary and revolutionary advances. Major language paradigms are introduced and language design experience in the development of SequenceL is presented.

*Keywords*: Computer language, procedural/object-oriented, Lisp, Prolog, ordinary science, extraordinary science, abstraction, syntax, semantics.

## 1. Introduction

The beginning of modern computer science can be marked by Alan Turing's paper, which among other advances, showed that there are unsolvable problems [1]. Within the infinite set of solvable problems there is a set of technically feasible and problems that are not technically feasible to solve (e.g. problems that it would take a supercomputer 10,000 years to solve). Thus, from the beginning, computer science has been viewed as *the science of problem solving using computers*.

One category of computer science research is devoted to outwardly encroaching upon the set of intractable problems. Advances in computer hardware, for example, lead to more powerful computers that execute faster and have larger stores of memory. Advances in hardware are meant to result in improvements in the raw computing power of the devices that can be brought to bear in order to solve more complex problems. Additionally, research efforts focusing on complexity and algorithms are also concerned with outwardly encroaching upon the set of intractable problems.

In general, this first category of computer science research is devoted to making complicated problems more **technically feasible** to solve. Problems that are technically feasible are those for which existing algorithms can obtain an answer in some reasonable time using currently available computer technology. The second major category of computer science research has to do with making it **humanly feasible** to solve more complicated problems. Human feasibility has to do with the level of difficulty one faces in finding a solution to a problem.

Some of the efforts in the second category of research focus on the development of approaches that delegate some of the complexity of certain activities to easy-to-use tools, such as database management systems, operating systems, networking tools. Other approaches to the second category focus on problem representation. These areas of research include artificial intelligence and software engineering. Central to all efforts to improve upon the human's ability to solve more complicated problems is computer language research.

This chapter focuses on language design from a scientific point of view. To do so, a scientific backdrop will be developed. Then the notions of language design from a theoretical and experimental point of view are outlined. From there, the history of language design efforts are reviewed, first from the evolutionary and then from the revolutionary vantages. The chapter ends with a brief introduction of recent results obtained by one of the authors.

## 1.1. *Scientific endeavors*

In most sciences, there are two organized research fronts: theoretical and experimental. Experiment provides a wealth of scientific observations that eventually must be distilled into a compact representation. The distilled, compact representation is a theory — a formulation of the body of knowledge gained by experiment that concisely represents the larger body of knowledge. Once formulated, the theory is employed in the design of future empirical studies to see if the theory predicts the outcomes of the experiments. Future experiments may **confirm** the theory — leading to greater confidence in it — or they may **falsify** the theory — indicating that the theory may be incorrect. Results existing between confirmatory and falsification may indicate that the theory needs some modification towards improvement.

Based upon the interaction between the theoretical and experimental communities of the physical sciences, Kuhn, in his now classic text *The Structure of Scientific Revolutions*, identified two types of theoretical science [2]. The first category of theoretical research (called **ordinary science**) attempts to modify, extend, and/or refine theories so that they do a better job of explaining empirical results that are not explained by the unrefined theories. The second category (called **extraordinary science**) takes place when a radically new view (or theory) is proposed and it is seen that the theory explains empirical evidence, subsuming the old theory and all of its subsequent refinements. Extraordinary science results in paradigm shifts and in scientific revolutions.

## 2. Theoretical Language Research

A programming language serves as the central part of a theory about how one best approaches problem solving with the aid of computers. The language is central to the theory because it is the basis for finding and communicating problem solutions to machines or other people. A language is meant to facilitate one's ability to state and structure problem solutions. Possibly the most important aspect of the language is the fact that it alone manifests the abstraction — or the approach to problem solving — provided by the theory. Wirth noted that "One of the most crucial steps in the design of a language is the choice of abstraction upon which programs are to base". [3] Abstraction is key to an understanding of language and language design.

## 2.1. *Abstraction*

An abstraction is commonly viewed as the act of taking away — the formation of an idea apart from the concrete existence or specification thereof. A computer abstraction can be viewed as the result of dropping out nonessential, complicating details. An abstraction defines that which is salient to the problem solution, and in doing so, identifies the extraneous details that can be ignored in previous abstractions.

The original model of computing required the physical rewiring of the CPU to alter the CPU's actions. A revolution in abstraction came with the advent of the stored program concept, also known as the Von Neumann architecture. The Von Neumann approach dropped out the original distinction between the storage of data and the storage of a program. Assembler languages quickly followed. These languages dropped out many nonessential details including the need to keep track of physical addresses. Macro definitions for oft-repeated functions such as input-output improved the assembler abstraction by removing many nonessential details from the programmer's concern. In the case of input-output on the IBM 360/370, the details hidden are those involved in executing channel programs. The GET and PUT macros essentially hide a surfeit of nonessential details: without these macros the programmer has to write programs that run on the I/O channel processors together with the mainframe program code required to initiate the I/O transfers.

FORTRAN was a major step in abstraction improvement because it provided a view of problem solving where one ignored many machine level details such as register usage and memory management. FORTRAN's abstraction moves the programmer away from machine operations — pointing the programmer towards algebraic operations. Languages like Algol and Pascal improved the FORTRAN abstraction in a significant way through the addition of prominent control structures and by placing data structure design on a level equal to algorithm design. In other words, with the newer abstractions the design of the data structure comes to be viewed as a critical element in problem solving. To illustrate the significance of the data structure, imagine trying to convert an arbitrary postfix expression into an equivalent prefix expression without the use of an advanced data structure. The Pascal abstraction eventually led to the view that the programmer's product is a data product rather than a program that produces that data product.

The object-oriented approach to programming is less of an abstraction change in that this approach adds, rather than deletes technical detail. From an historical viewpoint one might view the relationship between the procedural and object-oriented approaches as analogous to the relationship between the assembler and the macro-assembler languages. In other words, the following analogy may indeed be an appropriate one to consider: *macro-assembly* : *assembly* :: *object-oriented*: *procedural*.

The object-oriented approach was motivated by the fact that procedural languages lacked a "middle ground" between local and global variables. The lack of this middle ground led to technical difficulties in the implementation and reusability of data structures. The difficulty was addressed by Parnas's definitions of information hiding (a form of hiding variables beyond the hiding afforded by local variables) [4]. These problems were solved with the addition of features to encapsulate data structures. Once one encapsulates data structures, it is a logical step to encapsulate program structures. Reuse of the so-called objects is facilitated through an inheritance mechanism. Object-oriented programming is a natural, evolutionary step that adds features to the procedural language abstraction in order to solve technical problems that arise in the use and reuse of data and program structures.

Other changes to the procedural abstraction have been made in order to accommodate concurrent programming. Languages like Ada, Modula, and Linda have added some notion of multitasking in a manner that interacts with existent program structures for procedures and functions.

Java is considered by many to be the best designed object-oriented language. Java possesses an environment that provides one with the ability to develop graphical user interfaces, applets for web-based programming, concurrent processes, etc. As such, Java embodies a superset of the significant extensions and modifications that characterize the evolution of the procedural languages.

Apart from the evolution of procedural programming, completely new ways to view problem solving have arisen from work in functional [5], logic [6], and collection-oriented languages [7, 8]. These improvements have sought to change the view of programming altogether. They can be viewed more as revolutionary changes as opposed to the more characteristic evolutionary changes described above.

A programming language provides the fundamental level of abstraction for problem solving with a computer. It demarcates the point where the human leaves off and the architecture takes over, in the process of translating the problem solution into a set of actions to be performed by the computer. Language compilers or interpreters perform all further translation for us.

The fundamental level of abstraction is very important. It defines the basis for the way we organize our activities to solve problems, i.e. it is the basis for the software process model.

## 2.2. *What constitutes a computer language theory?*

As a theory for problem solving, a computer language should satisfy certain objective requirements. The requirements are important to know, because they form an important measure of the significance of a language as a theory. Before a community is willing to design and perform experiments related to a theory, the theory should satisfy requirements, which indicate that the experiments are warranted and worthwhile. In this section, requirements that a computer language should satisfy are presented.

One requirement of a computer language is that it be **unambiguous**. To satisfy this requirement there must be a mathematical definition of the syntax and semantics of the language. The **syntax** of a language provides a precise definition of the rules employed in order to construct grammatically correct (i.e., valid) sentences in the language. Backus-Naur Form is commonly used for simple syntax definitions. More complex syntactic features are frequently captured by attribute grammar, another form used in syntax definition. Attribute grammars permit the description of semantic constraints such as data typing constraints.

The **semantics** of a computer language should provide a precise definition of the meaning of a sentence stated in the language. Semantics can be stated using the denotational, axiomatic, or operational approaches, or through the use of other formal languages.

The Backus-Naur Form allows for the construction of a finite set of rules that define how any element of the infinite set is constructed. For example, the following finite set of recursive rules define an infinite set of elements:

$$T ::= \text{zero}|\text{succ}(T).$$

These rules define a set of syntactic objects, which belong to the language:

$$T = \{\text{zero}, \text{succ}(\text{zero}), \text{succ}(\text{succ}(\text{zero})), \ldots\}.$$

Now consider the set of natural numbers:

$$N = \{0, 1, 2, 3, \ldots\}.$$

Formal semantics are given in a function definition. The function maps from the syntactic set $T$, to the semantic set, $N$, i.e., $m : T \rightarrow N$. Equations define the function $m$. For example, consider the equations, which perform the simple mapping from elements of $T$ to elements of $N$:

$$m(\text{zero}) = 0 \tag{1}$$

$$m(\text{succ}(T)) = +(m(T), 1). \tag{2}$$

Using Eqs. (1) and (2), a precise (i.e., unambiguous) mapping can be developed from a syntactic to a semantic object:

$$m(\text{succ}(\text{succ}(\text{zero}))) = {}^{(2)}$$

$$+(m(\text{succ}(\text{zero})), 1) = {}^{(2)}$$

$$+(+(m(\text{zero}), 1), 1) = {}^{(1)}$$

$$+(+(0, 1), 1) = 2.$$

Notice that the lefthand side (LHS) of rules (1) and (2) refer to syntactic structures, while the righthand side (RHS) of the rules indicate the semantic of the syntactic structure. Once the rules have been developed they can be analyzed to determine if ambiguity exists in the language definition. For example, if there are two rules with the same LHS, but differing RHS's, then there are two meanings for one syntactic structure. Whenever multiple interpretations exist for the same syntactic structure, ambiguity exists in the language.

With the following modification to the Backus-Naur Form rule:

$$T ::= \text{zero}|\text{succ}(T)$$

$$T1 ::= T + T$$

together with additional semantic equations to define mappings from $T1$:

$$m(\text{zero} + \text{zero}) = 0 \tag{3}$$

$$m(\text{succ}(T) + \text{zero}) = m(\text{succ}(T)) \tag{4}$$

$$m(\text{zero} + \text{succ}(T)) = m(\text{succ}(T)) \tag{5}$$

$$m(\text{succ}(T1) + \text{succ}(T2)) = +(m(T1 + T2), 2) \tag{6}$$

one can provide for more sophisticated, yet equally precise mappings that specify the addition of natural numbers. Consider the expression $\text{succ}(\text{succ}(\text{zero})) + \text{succ}(\text{succ}(\text{zero}))$:

$$m(\text{succ}(\text{succ}(\text{zero})) + \text{succ}(\text{succ}(\text{zero}))) = {}^{(6)}$$

$$+(m(\text{succ}(\text{zero}) + \text{succ}(\text{zero})), 2) = {}^{(6)}$$

$$+(+(m(\text{zero} + \text{zero}), 2), 2) = {}^{(3)}$$

$$+(+(0, 2), 2) = 4.$$

Consider the expression $\text{succ}(\text{zero}) + \text{succ}(\text{succ}(\text{zero}))$:

$$m(\text{succ}(\text{zero}) + \text{succ}(\text{succ}(\text{zero}))) = {}^{(6)}$$

$$+(m(\text{zero} + \text{succ}(\text{zero})), 2) = {}^{(5)}$$

$$+(m(\text{succ}(\text{zero})), 2) = {}^{(2)}$$

$$+(+(m(\text{zero}), 1), 2) = {}^{(1)}$$

$$+(+(0, 1), 2) = 3.$$

The formal (i.e., unambiguous) syntax and semantic definitions of a computer language are objective requirements that a new language should satisfy.

Another desirable feature of a computer language has to do with size. A computer language should possess a small number of features that are easy to combine in any number of ways in order to produce complex problem solutions. Computer languages that possess a small number of combinable features are called **orthogonal**. Orthogonal languages allow a software developer to design solutions of complex problems through the interaction of a small set of language features. The syntax of a computer language provides important insight into the extent to which a software developer can claim that the language is orthogonal. Consider the grammar definitions below:

FOR ::= for id := E to E do?;

WHILE ::= while C do?;

IF ::= if C then? else?;

ASSIGN ::= id := E;

READ ::= readln(id);

WRITE ::= writeln(E);

STATE ::= FOR | WHILE | IF | ASSIGN | READ | WRITE | STATE; STATE

If one replaces all the ?'s above with the nonterminal STATE, the language has a good degree of orthogonality. The goodness is due to the fact that one is able to nest any control structure inside any other control structure.

The **writability** of a language has to do with how difficult it is to encode a problem solution. In general, an orthogonal language is arguably more writable than a nonorthogonal language. For the same reason, the **readability** of the orthogonal language — the ability to decipher the problem solution — is an improvement over nonorthogonal languages.

The **conciseness of the problem solutions** that can be developed in a language is often viewed to be an important feature of a good language. While it is certainly true that conciseness is an important criterion, conciseness must be considered within the context of a language's readability and writability. For example, one can imagine a language that has a unique one-character symbol for each problem solution known to humankind — obviously requiring an infinite supply of one-character symbols. Suppose, in this language, that the symbol # represents a heapsort program. The solution to the sort and any other problem in this language is definitely as concise as can be envisioned. The problem with the language has to do with its readability and writability. To be an effective problem solver, the programmer who writes or reads the program must recall that the # represents the heapsort program — and he/she must remember this fact as distinguished from the potentially infinite number of other pairings between a singular symbol and a problem solution.

The table-lookup quality to this hypothetical language would seem to go against the traditional efforts of computer scientists. Beginning with Alan Turing, computer scientists have focused on the identification of a small set of primitive elements that comprise problem solving. The design and choice of the primitives takes into consideration the degree to which the primitives chosen can be combined to "build up" complicated problem solutions. Thus, the conciseness of the language itself (rather than the size of the problem solutions written in the language), together with the degree to which the language constructs can be combined (i.e. the orthogonality of the language) would seem to be higher priority features of a language. If these features are met, then the conciseness of solutions becomes a reasonable criterion for a language.

Another desirable feature of a programming language is that it be capable of representing a Universal Turing Machine. Languages satisfying this requirement, are known as **Turing Computable**. A Turing Computable Language is one that can solve any problem that can be stated as an *algorithm, i.e., any effectively compatible function.* Simply put, an algorithm is a set of easy-to-follow instructions, that given an input, will produce a result [9]. Implied by the previous definition is the requirement that the algorithm will "halt". Given an arbitrary input, an algorithm must produce an answer (or result) in a finite amount of time. A language that can state any possible algorithm, is Turing Computable. A Turing Computable Language is capable of solving any algorithmically solvable problem (i.e., one for which there is an algorithmic solution). Therefore, a language should be Turing Computable.

**Coherence** is another desirable feature of a language [10]. Coherence requires that language features be drawn from the same abstraction level. Recall the quote seen earlier:

> One of the most crucial steps in the design of a language is the choice of abstraction upon which programs are to base.

Two sentences later, in the same text, one finds:

> [The language designer] should restrict his selection [of language features] from the same level which are in some sense compatible with each other [3].

Coherence of a language is an important feature insofar as one does not want the programmer to have to understand a given program on two differing levels of abstraction. Suppose there was a version of a procedural language like Pascal, which allowed the programmer to *dip* into the assembler level of representation. If a change is made to a program in this language, the programmer must understand the change at the Pascal and the assembler level. In other words, the programmer must understand the interaction of the machine code generated by the compiler and the assembler code that is embedded in the source program.

**Regularity** is yet another desirable feature in a language. Regularity requires that language features operate in a consistent and uniform manner, independent of context — regularity requires similar actions to have similar consequences. One way to view regularity is from the standpoint of a human interface. A computer system that has a "mouse" ought to have the mouse button(s) perform in a uniform manner at all times. Suppose a mouse has two buttons. If button **X** opens any available pop-up window at the operating system level, it should do the same for any application program one might enter from the operating system level. If button **X** performs function **A** in one application program and function **B** in another, the overall interface design is not consistent, not regular, and not particularly good. Here we begin to migrate away from objective requirements into the realm of nonobjective requirements.

A qualitative measure of a language is that it be **intuitive**. An intuitive language is one that allows the problem solver to follow instinct and intuition in solving the problem. Clearly, what one person views as intuitive is likely to be different from what the next person views to be intuitive. Since intuitiveness is a qualitative measure, a problem solver can only determine whether one language is more intuitive than another language through experimentation. Experimental computer science is costly and rarely done when it comes to language comparisons. However, if languages can be shown to meet some reasonable number of the qualities introduced in this section, it would be ideal if they could be compared experimentally for the more qualitative characteristics.

## 3. Experimental Science

There are at least two approaches to empirical language studies. The first approach involves the careful understanding and evaluation of a language and results in a value judgement on the part of the researcher. This first approach is not unlike the approach Wirth took in the Oberon project, see [11].

The formalisms developed to describe languages are analogous to differential equations, which are employed in describing and modeling physical phenomena. Just as the study of the models of physical phenomena have led to breakthroughs in Physics, the mathematical models describing language approaches should be carefully studied in order to advance the understanding of problem solving.

The second approach to empirical language studies involves the development of controlled experiments. The types of measurements that are required and the variables for which controls must be established need to be well understood. To some extent, computer scientists are like physicists attempting to study thermodynamics without a thermometer. Nonetheless, controlled experiments need to be undertaken.

If software advances are to keep pace with hardware advances, languages and other software tools must improve the productivity of software engineers (i.e., make problems more humanly feasible to solve). For a language to better facilitate productivity, it must provide a more *intuitive* approach to problem solving. The degree of intuitiveness of a language is a nonobjective consideration that may require controlled experimentation. To be effective, two major forms of experimentation are required. These forms are:

- to determine which languages are best suited for a given type of problem solver; and
- to determine which languages are best suited for a given type or domain of problems.

Ideally computer language research should be based upon a framework similar to that found in the physical sciences. In the physical sciences there is a healthy interaction between theory and experiment, where each drives the other. To a lesser extent the same is true in Computer Science. However, the organization of the theory and experimental communities is not as well developed in Computer Science.

Suppose one viewed a new language as a theory about how to best approach a certain type of problem solving. The language would be expected to meet certain criteria, like those listed in the previous section. Once the theory is accepted, the language would be subjected to experimental research where competing language approaches would be compared empirically. The experimental activity might require sociological and psychological testing to determine which language seems to provide the most intuitive approach.

## 4. Evolutionary versus Revolutionary

Recall the earlier discussion concerning Kuhn's ordinary and extraordinary science. There have been examples of extraordinary science in language research — beginning with the Von Neumann architecture, then FORTRAN, LISP, Algol/Pascal (to a lesser degree), SQL, and Prolog. The revolutionary approaches having had the greatest impact are the Von Neumann architecture and FORTRAN. Many will argue that the object-oriented approach was and is revolutionary. However, one can argue the other side as well — that the object-oriented approach is a refinement (and improvement) to the procedural approach and manifests an evolutionary, rather than revolutionary, impact.

### 4.1. *Evolution of computer languages*

The evolution of computer languages has been based upon the revolution brought about by the introduction of the Von Neumann computer architecture. This architecture was the basis for the computer language constructs. The stored program and the program counter permit the modification of the flow of control. These hardware capabilities have culminated in the sequence, selection, and iterative control constructs. The general-purpose registers — specialized memory locations between which arithmetic and logic circuitry exist — allow for the arithmetic and comparative capabilities. The arithmetic construct follows from these hardware features, as do the constructs — that when paired with the ability to alter the program counter — allow for the ability to perform conditional execution required for selection and iteration. Input/output ports on computers support the input-output constructs found in computer languages.

Because these architectural features are common to all computers and because languages allow us to tell computers what to do, the constructs are general constructs to all procedural, programming languages. The constructs form categories in which every procedural programming language has statements. Therefore, the constructs form a solid basis from which to learn a new programming language.

The evolution of languages is based upon the executable constructs — the constructs just mentioned that permit us to tell the computer what to do — and the nonexecutable commands to the language translator. The nonexecutable constructs provide for program and data structure definition.

FORTRAN, a true revolutionary approach to programming, provided the definitive version of the assignment statement and the arithmetic expression. No language since FORTRAN has altered the basic form of the arithmetic expression or the assignment statement. In other words, if one knows the operational semantics and basic syntactic forms of FORTRAN's assignment statement, then the problem solver will not need to relearn this type of statement or expression in any new language. The only differences will be syntactic nuances.

Likewise, languages like Algol and Pascal defined — for the most part — the remaining executable constructs. The input-output and the sequential control structures were established in a definitive way by the forms they took in Algol and Pascal. Pascal's stream I/O — as opposed to a strictly formatted I/O — has not been subsequently improved upon in any revolutionary way. Similarly, the block structured sequences, selective (e.g. *if-then-else* and *case* or *switch* statements), and the iterative (e.g. the *while* and the *for* statements) constructs have not been modified in a major way by subsequent languages. The only major changes in control constructs is in the addition of parallel control structures found in many languages, including Concurrent Pascal, Modula, Ada, and Java; and in the way in which encapsulated program structures are declared, instantiated, and invoked.

Encapsulation of program structures — though — is arguably less a change in control structures and more of a change in the commands a programmer gives to a language interpreter or compiler in order to establish data and program structures. The view taken here, is that in terms of the procedural paradigm (including the paradigm's Object-Oriented extensions), the declaration of program and data structures — the set of nonexecutable constructs — is the one area of a language that continues to undergo substantive evolutionary change.

## 4.2. *Revolution in computer languages*

Already mentioned are the revolutionary advances that accompanied FORTRAN's introduction. The dropping away of many machine details (e.g. memory and register usage) truly changed the ground upon which the programmer stands when solving problems. Algol and Pascal improved upon this ground in a semi-revolutionary way by having the programmer regard the data structure as being on par with the algorithm in problem solving.

LISP was a significant advance as well [12]. Problem solving was reduced to the interaction between two primitive features — recursion and the list. The simple elegance that ensued with LISP provided the programmer with a view of programming that is characterized by a simple and natural approach. The data structures that one composes in LISP are robust in terms of their growth and the fact that they can be heterogeneous. The revolution brought about by LISP allowed the programmer a view of programming based upon lambda calculus. Other significant advances in functional programming include the languages FP [5] and Haskell [13].

Prolog — another revolutionary language — allowed the programmer to view programming based upon First Order Predicate Calculus [6]. The language features allow for simple, concise, and elegant solutions to many problems. For example, one can implement a stack data structure with the simple clause:

$$\text{push}_{\text{pop}}(\text{Top, Stack, [Top|Stack]}).$$

Consider the following trace using this definition:

> Yes
>
> ?- $\text{push}_{\text{pop}}(9,[4,5,6,7], \text{Stack})$.
>
> Stack $= [9, 4, 5, 6, 7]$
>
> Yes
>
> ?- $\text{push}_{\text{pop}}(\text{Top, Stack, }[9,4,5,6,7])$.
>
> Top $= 9$
>
> Stack $= [4, 5, 6, 7]$
>
> Yes
>
> ?-

## 5. Concurrency and Parallelisms

Hoare's Communicating Sequential Processes provides a significant formal approach to concurrent and parallel programming [14]. Hoare's approach provides formalisms for loop unfolding and concurrent processing of other iterative structures as well as the ability to synchronize concurrent tasks by extending Djikstra' Guarded Commands and his Semaphores [15]. Communicating Sequential Processes led to languages like OCCAM and provided true insight into concurrent processing — influencing many subsequent languages.

Conventional approaches to concurrent programming (including Linda [16]) **add** features to the existing procedural and Object-Oriented approaches to programming. Adding features complicate these paradigms. Newer approaches to concurrent programming attempt to provide more intuitive approaches to parallelisms resulting in programs that are easier to write and easier to understand. Many of these approaches are based upon collection-oriented languages that provide for aggregation operators like those pioneered in [17, 18].

These newer approaches to parallel programming include [19, 8, 20, 21, 22, 23]. These approaches provide a way to indicate that functions being invoked are to execute concurrently. For example, suppose one wishes to compute the square of a list of numbers. In NESL one can specify this computation as follows [8, p. 90]:

$$\{a * a : a \text{ in } X\}$$

where $X$ is defined to be a list of numbers such as $[3, -4, -9, 5]$. NESL's computational model can be viewed architecturally as a Vector Random Access Machine (VRAM) [8]. The VRAM is a *virtual model* for computation consisting of an unlimited number of processors $\pi$ that have simultaneous access to a shared memory. The assignment of a computation $\chi(x)$ to a particular processor $\pi_i$ can be denoted as $\pi_i(\chi(x))$. In the NESL program statement above, the {}'s specify concurrent execution. The program statement above specifies the parallel computation of the square of each element of $X$:

$$\{a * a : a \text{ in } [3, -4, -9, 5]\}$$
$$= [\pi_i(3 * 3), \pi_{i+1}(-4 * -4), \pi_{i+2}(-9 * -9), \pi_{i+3}(5 * 5)] = [9, 16, 81, 25].$$

In the VRAM model, each processor obtains its data from and produces its result in the shared memory. Each processor $\pi_i$ is viewed as a conventional processor. NESL does provide an excellent language for the specification of data parallelism wherein a *divide and conquer* approach to problem solving is promoted. NESL provides for the specification of a data parallel approach to programming. *SequenceL*, presented below provides a more implicit approach to parallelisms. The problem above — in *SequenceL* can be specified as follows:

$$*([[3, -4, -9, 5], [3, -4, -9, 5]])$$

resulting in the following concurrent computations:

$$[*([3, 3])|| * ([-4, -4])|| * ([-9, -9])|| * ([5, 5])] = [9, 16, 81, 25].$$

Like NESL, the *SequenceL* language is based upon a shared memory architecture. In general, the history of language development has deeply affected the definition of *SequenceL*. Recall that one of the first major advances in Computer Language Design was the elimination of the distinction between program and memory. This advance eventually led to the paradigms where data is stored in named locations and algorithms can define the locations through the use of assignment and input-output statements. Advances also led to the development of the control flow constructs that are used to define and process data structures. These constructs are the **sequence**, **selection**, **iteration**, and **parallel** constructs.

The *SequenceL* paradigm provides no distinction between data and functions/operators. Furthermore, all data is considered to be nonscalar, i.e., sequences. *SequenceL* has an underlying control flow used in the evaluation of *SequenceL* operators. In the underlying **Consume-Simplify-Produce**-cycle (i.e., **CSP**-cycle), operators enabled for execution are **Consumed** (with their arguments) from the global memory, **Simplified** according to declarative constructs that operate on data, and the resulting simplified terms are then **Produced** in the global memory. This **CSP**-cycle, together with the declarative *SequenceL* constructs (applied during the simplification step) imply control flow structures that the programmer does not have to design or specify.

The elimination of the distinction between data and operators is achieved through the use of a global memory, called a tableau $T$, where *SequenceL* terms are placed:

$$[f^a1_1, f^a2_2, \ldots, f^an_n] \text{ where } n \geq 0$$

when $a_i = 0$, $f_i$ is a sequence and when $a_I > 0$, $f_i$ is a function or an operator. The arity $a_i$ of a function or operator $f_i$ indicates the number of arguments (i.e., sequences), $f_i$ requires for execution. There is no notion of assignment in *SequenceL*. Furthermore, there is no notion of input distinguished from the application of an operator to its operands. In this context, the word **operator** refers both to built-in and user-defined operators.

The underlying **CSP** control flow in *SequenceL* eliminates the need for the programmer to specify parallel and most of the specification of iterative and sequence-based operations. The control flow approach identifies operators that are enabled for execution. The enabling of operators is based upon the arity of the operator (which is derived from the operator's signature) matching the number of sequences following the operator. The global memory and the producer/consumer abstraction in *SequenceL* implements the basic ability to enable the Hoare/Djikstra concept of synchronized communication among processes. However, the *SequenceL* approach provides this ability without an additional language construct beyond its approach of enabling function execution through the data flow execution-based CSP execution strategy underlying *SequenceL*.

However, CSP alone will not achieve the desired effect. In order to derive finer-grained parallelisms and many iterative processes in an automated way, CSP must interact with advanced constructs for processing data. The desired interaction occurs in the **Simplification** step of the **CSP**-cycle. These advanced *SequenceL* constructs are the **regular**, **generative**, and **irregular** constructs. Among other capabilities, these constructs implement Hoare's loop unfolding constructs.

The regular construct applies an operator to corresponding elements of the normalized operand sequences. For example, $+([4, 4])$ distributes the plus sign among the corresponding elements of the two singleton sequences [4] and [4], resulting in [8]. Now consider the more complicated application:

$$T = [*([20, 30, 40], [2])].$$

In this case normalization results in the elements of the second operand sequence being repeated in the order they occur until it is the same length (and/or dimension in terms of nesting) as the larger:

$$T = [*([20, 30, 40], [2, 2, 2])].$$

Now the multiplication operator can be distributed among the corresponding elements of the operand sequences. The normalization/distribution is a single **simplification** step:

$$T' = [*([20, 2]), *([30, 2]), *([40, 2])].$$

As a result, in the next **CSP**-cycle there are three parallel operations that can take place (i.e., loop unfolding is implied by the regular construct). Thus, the interaction of the CSP execution cycle and the regular construct results in the identification of microparallelisms. The final result is:

$$T'' = [40, 60, 80].$$

The generative construct allows for the generation of sequences, e.g. $[1, \ldots, 5] = [1, 2, 3, 4, 5]$. The irregular construct allows for conditional execution:

$$T = [\text{Double-odds } (\text{Consume}(s\_1(n)), \text{Produce}(\textbf{next})) \textbf{ where next}$$
$$= [*([s\_1(i)2])\text{when} <> (\text{mod}([s\_1(i), 2]), 0) \text{ else } []]$$
$$\text{Taking } i \text{ from } [1, \ldots, n], [2, 3, 4, 5]].$$

See Fig. 1 for a trace of the function.

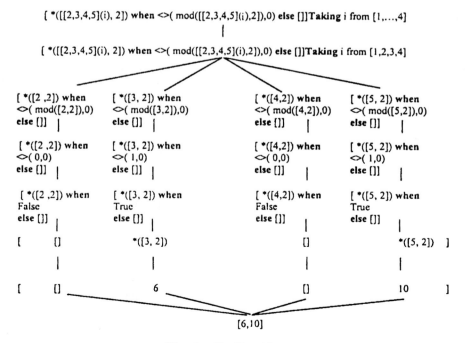

**Fig. 1.** Double-odds.

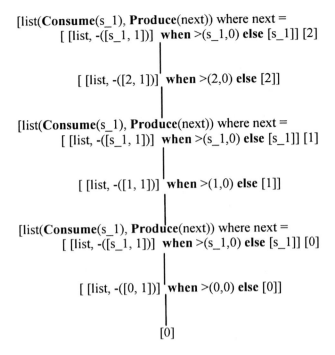

**Fig. 2.**   List function.

With the irregular construct one can, when necessary, produce recursive applications of a function:

$$T = [\text{list}(\text{Consume}(s\_1), \text{Produce}(\text{next})) \text{ where next}$$
$$= [[\text{list}, -([s\_1, 1])] \text{ when } > (s\_1, 0) \text{ else } [s\_1]][4].$$

Recursion involves a function placing itself back into $T$. See Fig. 2 for a trace of the function.

*SequenceL*, represents an attempt to develop a language abstraction in which control structures — sequential, iterative, and parallel — are implied.

In summary, the *SequenceL* abstraction presents a paradigm with the following aspects:

- A Global Memory that does not distinguish between operators and data, and whose state fully reflects the state of computation.
- All operands are sequences where atoms are represented by singleton sequences.
- Underlying **Consume-Simplify-Produce** execution strategy.
- High level constructs to process nonscalars, applied in the simplification step.

For more detail about *SequenceL* please see [7, 24]. Consider now a matrix multiply function as written in *SequenceL*:

**Function** matmul (**Consume** $(s\_1(n, *), s\_2(*, m),$ **Produce**(next)) **where** next
= {**compose** $([+([*(succ\_1(i, *), succ\_2(*, j))])])$}

    **Taking** $[i, j]$ **From** cartesian\_product([gen([1, \dots, n]), gen $([1, \dots, m])])$

    $([[2, 4, 6], [3, 5, 7], [1, 1, 1]], [[2, 4, 6], [3, 5, 7], [1, 1, 1]])$.

The term, $[[2, 4, 6], [3, 5, 7], [1, 1, 1]]$ is the sequence representation of a matrix. We will now trace the steps the *SequenceL* interpreter takes in order to evaluate the function above. Bear in mind the only information provided by the user is the function above, together with its arguments. The user does not specify any control structures — not even the parallel paths that can be followed in solving the problem. These parallel paths are implied in the solution and derived by the *SequenceL* semantic. The semantic is an interactions between the CSP-cycle and the *SequenceL* constructs applied in the **Simplify** step.

## 5.1. *Trace of the evaluation of the Sequencel matrix multiply*

For simplicity, let $T$ contain only the matrix multiply function and its input sequences as seen above. The first step is to instantiate the variables $s\_1$ and $s\_2$. At the same time, variables $n$ and $m$ obtain the cardinal values in the designated sequence dimensions:

    {compose $([+([*([[2, 4, 6], [3, 5, 7], [1, 1, 1]](i, *), [[2, 4, 6], [3, 5, 7], [1, 1, 1]](*, j))])])$}

    **Taking**$[i, j]$**From** cartesian\_product $([gen([1, \dots, 3]), gen([1, \dots, 3])])$.

Now *SequenceL*'s **generative construct** produces the values needed in the **Taking** clause. The simple form of the generative command is seen in this example. It simply fills in the integer values between the upper and lower bounds, i.e., from 1 to 3:

    {**compose**$([+([*([[2, 4, 6], [3, 5, 7], [1, 1, 1]](i, *), [[2, 4, 6], [3, 5, 7], [1, 1, 1]](*, j))])])$}

    **Taking** $[i, j]$ **From** cartesian\_product$([[1, 2, 3], [1, 2, 3]])$.

Next the *SequenceL* Cartesian Product generates the values for subscripts $i$ and $j$.

    {**compose**$([+([*([[2, 4, 6], [3, 5, 7], [1, 1, 1]](i, *), [[2, 4, 6], [3, 5, 7], [1, 1, 1]](*, j))])])$}

    **Taking** $[i, j]$ **From** [ [[1], [1]], [[1], [2]], [[1], [3]], [[2], [1]], [[2], [2]], [[2], [3]],

        [[3], [1]], [[3], [2]], [[3], [3]] ] .

Now that the simplification of the function is complete, the function's result is produced in $T$:

$$T = [\ [+([*([[2,4,6],[3,5,7],[1,1,1]](1,*),[[2,4,6],[3,5,7],[1,1,1]](*,1))]) \ ||$$
$$+([*([[2,4,6],[3,5,7],[1,1,1]](1,*),[[2,4,6],[3,5,7],[1,1,1]](*,2))]) \ ||$$
$$+([*([[2,4,6],[3,5,7],[1,1,1]](1,*),[[2,4,6],[3,5,7],[1,1,1]](*,3))])] \ ||$$
$$[+([*([[2,4,6],[3,5,7],[1,1,1]](2,*),[[2,4,6],[3,5,7],[1,1,1]](*,1))]) \ ||$$
$$+([*([[2,4,6],[3,5,7],[1,1,1]](2,*),[[2,4,6],[3,5,7],[1,1,1]](*,2))]) \ ||$$
$$+([*([[2,4,6],[3,5,7],[1,1,1]](2,*),[[2,4,6],[3,5,7],[1,1,1]](*,3))])] \ ||$$
$$[+([*([[2,4,6],[3,5,7],[1,1,1]](3,*),[[2,4,6],[3,5,7],[1,1,1]](*,1))]) \ ||$$
$$+([*([[2,4,6],[3,5,7],[1,1,1]](3,*),[[2,4,6],[3,5,7],[1,1,1]](*,2))]) \ ||$$
$$+([*([[2,4,6],[3,5,7],[1,1,1]](3,*),[[2,4,6],[3,5,7],[1,1,1]](*,3))])]\ ].$$

The next *Consume-Simplify-Produce* (CSP) step replaces the tableau above with the one below. This simplification step results in the parallel selection of the vectors to be multiplied. Concurrent evaluation is denoted by the $||$ symbol.

$$T = [\ [+([*([[2,4,6],[2,3,1]])]) \ || + ([*([[2,4,6],[4,5,1]])]) \ ||$$
$$+([*([[2,4,6],[6,7,1]])])] \ || [+([*([[3,5,7],[2,3,1]])]) \ ||$$
$$+([*([[3,5,7],[4,5,1]])]) \ || + ([*([[3,5,7],[6,7,1]])])] \ ||$$
$$[+([*([[1,1,1],[2,3,1]])]) \ || + ([*([[1,1,1],[4,5,1]])]) \ ||$$
$$+([*([[1,1,1],[6,7,1]])])]\ ].$$

In the next CSP step, the products are formed concurrently using *SequenceL*'s **regular construct**. The regular process distributes a built-in operator, e.g. the $*$ operation, among corresponding elements of the operands, resulting in 27 parallel multiplies:

$$T = [\ [+([*([[2],[2]])|| * ([[4],[3]])|| * ([[6],[1]])]) \ ||$$
$$+([*([[2],[4]])|| * ([[4],[5]])|| * ([[6],[1]])]) \ ||$$
$$+([*([[2],[6]])|| * ([[4],[7]])|| * ([[6],[1]])])] \ ||$$
$$[+([*([[3],[2]])|| * ([[5],[3]])|| * ([[7],[1]])]) \ ||$$
$$+([*([[3],[4]])|| * ([[5],[5]])|| * ([[7],[1]])]) \ ||$$
$$+([*([[3],[6]])|| * ([[5],[7]])|| * ([[7],[1]])])] \ ||$$
$$[+([*([[1],[2]])|| * ([[1],[3]])|| * ([[1],[1]])]) \ ||$$
$$+([*([[1],[4]])|| * ([[1],[5]])|| * ([[1],[1]])]) \ ||$$
$$+([*([[1],[6]])|| * ([[1],[7]])|| * ([[1],[1]])])]\ ].$$

Comparing the tableau above and the resulting tableau below, one can see that *SequenceL* handles nested parallelisms automatically. The final step of simplification involves the application of the regular construct to form the sums of the products.

$$T = [\ [+([4, 12, 6])\ ||\ +([8, 20, 6])\ ||$$
$$+([12, 28, 6])]\ ||\ [+([6, 15, 7])\ ||$$
$$+([12, 25, 7])\ ||\ +([18, 35, 7])]\ ||$$
$$[+([2, 3, 1])\ ||\ +([4, 5, 1])\ ||\ +([6, 7, 1])]\ ].$$

This regular process adds together corresponding elements of the operand sequences. E.G., $+([4, 12, 6]) = [4 + 12 + 6] = [22]$. The final result is:

$$[[22, 34, 46], [28, 44, 60], [6, 10, 14]].$$

Since no further simplification is possible, evaluation ends. There are three *SequenceL* constructs: the regular, irregular, and generative. The matrix multiply employed the regular and the generative. For more detailed explanation of these constructs, see [7, 24].

One important aspect of this language is that through the introduction of new language constructs, one can imply most control structures — even concurrent or parallel structures. Therefore, rather than producing an algorithm that implies a data product, one can come closer to specifying a data product that implies the algorithm that produces or processes it. The difficult part of traditional forms of programming seems to be centered around the fact that programmers have to somehow envision the elusive data product implied by their programs.

## 5.2. *Some additional language experiments involving SequenceL*

*SequenceL* is a Turing complete language. An interpreter exists that finds the parallel structures inherent in *SequenceL* problem solutions. The Matrix Multiply example represents a fairly straightforward problem solution insofar as the parallel paths behave independently of one another. In other words, once the parallelisms are known, the paths can be spawned and joined together with each path contributing its part of the final solution without knowledge of what the other paths have computed. Examples of problems where there are computed, intermediate results that need broadcasting have also been explored using the *SequenceL* interpreter.

For example, the Forward Processing in the Gaussian Elimination Solution of systems of linear equations has been executed with good results in terms of finding inherent parallelisms. With three or more equations, intermediate results must be known to all paths in order to produce the final result.

Finally, in terms of scheduling, both the matrix multiply and the Gaussian Codes are examples of problems for which static *a priori* schedules can be generated. The paths of execution can be determined based upon the dimensions of the matrix, in the matrix multiply, and the number of equations, in the Gaussian code. The

Quicksort problem was run as an example of a problem where dynamic scheduling is necessary [25].

## 6. Summary

In this chapter, an overview of computer language design was presented. A scientific backdrop was provided for the presentation from which it is easier to understand the exchange between theoretical and experimental language research. The backdrop also makes the distinction between ordinary and extraordinary language research easier to make. The impact of the scientific approach is then presented in the summary on the development of *SequenceL*.

## Acknowledgment

This research is sponsored, in part, by NASA NAG 5-9505.

## References

1. A. Turing, "On computable numbers, with an application to the Entscheidungs problem", *Proceedings of the London Mathematical Society* **2**, no. 42, 230–265.
2. T. Kuhn, *The Structure of Scientific Revolutions* (Chicago University Press, 1962).
3. N. Wirth, "On the design of programming languages", *Proceeding of the IFIP Congress 74* (North-Holland Publishing Co.) 386–393.
4. D. Parnas, "On criteria to be used in decomposing systems into modules", *CACM*, **14**, no. 1 (April 1972) 221–227.
5. J. Backus, "Can programming be liberated from the von Neumann Style? A functional style and its algebra of programs", *Communications of the ACM* **21**, no. 8 (August 1978) 613–641.
6. R. Kowalski, "Algorithm = logic + control", *Communications of the ACM* **22**, no. 7 (July 1979) 424–436.
7. D. Cooke, "An Introduction to *SequenceL*: A language to experiment with nonscalar constructs", *Software Practice and Experience* **26**, no. 11 (November 1996) 1205–1246.
8. G. Blelloch, "Programming parallel algorithms", *Communications of the ACM* **39**, no. 3 (March 1996) 85–97.
9. D. I. A. Cohen, *Introduction to Computing Theory* (John Wiley and Sons, Inc., New York, 1986).
10. P. Zave, "An insider's evaluation of PAISLey", *IEEE Transactions on Software Engineering* **17**, no. 3 (March 1991) 212–225.
11. N. Wirth and J. Gutknecht, *Project OBERON The Design of an Operating System and Compiler* (Addison-Wesley Publishing Company, Reading, MA, 1992).
12. J. McCarthy, "Recursive functions of symbolic expressions and their computation by machine", *Communications of the ACM* **3**, no. 4 (April 1960) 184–195.
13. P. Hudak, *The Haskell School of Expression: Learning Functional Programming through Multimedia* (Cambridge University Press, New York, 2000).
14. C.A.R. Hoare, "Communicating Sequential Processes", *Communications of the ACM* **21**, no. 8 (August, 1978) 666–677.
15. E. W. Dijkstra, "Guarded commands", *Communications of the ACM* **18**, no. 8, 453–457.

16. D. Gelernter, "Generative communications in Linda", *ACM Transactions on Programming Languages and Systems* **7**, no. 1 (1985), 80–112.

17. K. Iverson, *A Programming Language* (Wiley, New York, 1962).

18. K. Iverson, *Journal of the Introduction and Dictionary*, Iverson Software Inc. Toronto, 1994.

19. J. P. Banatre and D. Le Matayer, "Programming by multiset transformation", *Communications of the ACM* **36**, no. 1 (January 1993) 98–111.

20. V. Breazu-Tannen, P. Buneman and S. Naqvi, "Structural recursion as a query language," *Proceedings of 3rd International Conference on Database Programming Languages*, Nafplion, Greece (Morgan Kaufmann) 9–19.

21. C. Hankin, D. Le Metayer, and D. Sands, *A Calculus of Gamma Programs*, Publication Internet no 674, Juillet, IRISA, France, 1992.

22. J. Sipelstein and G. Blelloch, *Collection-Oriented Languages*, Report, School of Computer Science, Carnegie Mellon University, CMU-CS-90-127.

23. D. Suciu, *Parallel Programming Languages for Collections*, PhD Dissertation in Computer and Information Science, University of Pennsylvania, 1995.

24. D. Cooke, "SequenceL provides a different way to view programming", *Computer Languages* **24** (1998) 1–32.

25. D. E. Cooke and Per Andersen, "Automatic parallel control structures in sequenceL", Software Practice and Experience **30**, no. 14 (November 2000) 1541–1570.

# FORMAL VERIFICATION TECHNIQUES FOR COMPUTER COMMUNICATION SECURITY PROTOCOLS

LU MA and JEFFREY J. P. TSAI

*Department of Electrical Engineering and Computer Science, MC 154,*
*University of Illinois at Chicago, 851 S. Morgan ST, Chicago, IL 60607*
*E-mail: tsai@eecs.uic.edu*

Rapid development of networks and communications makes security a more and more crucial problem. To provide security for different systems, many communication security protocols are proposed. Such protocols must be proved correct before they can be used in practice. Formal verification techniques are promising methods to verify protocols and have been receiving a lot of attention recently. In this paper, we survey several security protocols and formal verification techniques to verify the protocols.

*Keywords*: Cryptography, authentication, formal verification, security.

## 1. Introduction

With the advances in computer and communication techniques, security has become more and more crucial for many systems. To guarantee security in computer communication, we must consider the possible actions of an intruder (or attacker, spy, enemy, etc). An intruder may be passive or active. As shown in Fig. 1, there may be four possibilities that an intruder can attack communication between two honest agents A and B. Among which, the first (eavesdrop) is a passive attack while the other three are active attacks. In the case of "Eavesdrop", an intruder R gets to know information sent by an honest party A to another honest party B without their notice. But the intruder doesn't modify the information. In the case of "Intercept", R intercepts the information from A without notice. A doesn't know such information hasn't reached B and B doesn't know that A sends some information to him. In the case of "Fake", R fakes as A and sends to B some information. B believes that it is A who sends this information, but A doesn't know anything at all. In the case of "Modificate", R intercepts the information from A to B first. After modifying the information, R sends the new information to B. Neither A nor B knows this information has been modified.

Certain protocols are proposed to provide protection for systems from those attacks. However, there may be some potential flaws in these protocols. An intruder may discover such flaws and thus breach the security through them. Examples include the Needham-Schroeder key distribution protocol [23] and a protocol in the CCITT X.509 draft standard [7]. According to Denning and Sacco [7], the former protocol allowed an intruder to pass off an old, compromised session key as a new

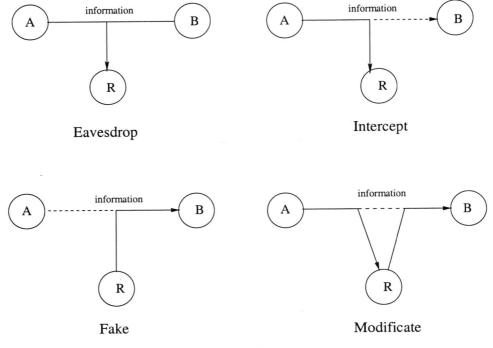

**Fig. 1.**  Possible attacks.

one. Burrows, Abadi and Needham showed that for the latter protocol, an intruder could cause an old session key as a new one [42]. Besides these two, numerous other flaws in protocols have been revealed.

So before the protocols are put into practice, their correctness and safety must be proved. To prove whether a protocol is secure or not, there are several options:

(1) One may exhaustively test the protocol to check if there is a flaw.
(2) One may test some particular scenarios and try to uncover a flaw.
(3) One may formally verify if the protocol is secure. That is to say, one may verify whether the specification of the protocol satisfies the desired security requirements.

Then what are the advantages and disadvantages of these options? For the first option, if a flaw does exist, exhaustive search will reveal it at last. But, it is not practical and feasible to generate and test all paths and situations for complex large-scale systems. For the second method, though test cases set becomes much smaller, a problem is that if the scenarios are not chosen correctly and appropriately, no flaw will be revealed. But this is only a false appearance.

Due to the drawbacks of the first two options, much research has focused on the third method. Formal methods have long been used in the analysis of communication protocols, and some promising work was done in the analysis of cryptographic protocols in the late 70's and early 80's [32]. Initially, Needham and Schroeder [46] attempted to use formal methods for security protocol analysis. However, Dolev and Yao [18] actually started the work in this area. And Dolev, Even and Karp [19] developed a set of algorithms for deciding the security of a restricted class of protocols. The application of formal methods to cryptographic protocols became more popular in the early 90's, when several researchers were able to find heretofore undiscovered security flaws in cryptographic protocols by using formal analysis techniquess. Several tools for the analysis of security protocols, such as Miller's Interrogator [45], Meadow's NRL Protocol Analyzer [9], and the Longley-Rigby tool, have been developed.

The goal of formal verification is to provide a rigid and thorough means to prove the security properties of a system. When various security protocols are concerned, different verification techniques may be employed. Formal verification techniques have several benefits:

- They remove ambiguity in the specification. Then no misunderstanding will occur.
- They identify precisely both the properties a certain protocol aims to satisfy and assumptions and environment under which they hold.
- They give a thorough insight of the strengths and weaknesses of protocols.
- They are systematic and exhaustive.
- They provide certification.
- They provide tools both at the specification level and at the implementation level.

This paper describes some security properties in Sec. 2. It presents some security protocols providing such properties and categorizes them in Sec. 3. It discusses main formal verification techniques in Sec. 4. We conclude this paper with some new research interests in this area.

## 2. Security Properties

Systems in different fields exhibit different security properties. In general, security properties include the following:

### 1) Confidentiality/Secrecy
Secret information exchanged should be restricted to honest parties of the communication. No one else is permitted to know secret information such as a session key used in encryption. This property is the most essential element for a security system.

### 2) Authentication
It should be guaranteed that an initiator of a session really communicates with the expected responder of the session. That is to say, a third party that intends to impersonate either side is not permitted. Authentication is provided by means of

ensuring the data source and destination, and it is usually achieved through digital signatures and certificates.

### 3) Date Integrity

Data sent during the process of a communication shouldn't be modifiable. Neither should it be modified while it is in storage.

### 4) Nonrepudiation

After a session, none of the parties involved should have the ability to deny that it has participated in the session. For example, the sender should not be able to deny the data it sent to the recipient.

### 5) Guaranteed Delivery

After a session, the sender should have the assurance that what it sent out can eventually reach the recipient.

### 6) NI(Non Interference) [50]

During the transmission of information, NI property requires that secret information won't leak to intruders. The communication system should have capabilities against all higher level potential interactions of other agents. This is achieved by controlling the whole flow of information directly instead of controlling over subjects to objects. Actually NI is also referred to as an approach for guaranteeing such security properties in computer systems.

All properties described above are general purpose properties required by almost all security protocols. With continuing growth of electronic commerce, some additional properties for electronic commerce protocols should be considered. Next, we introduce a couple of them.

### 7) Atomicity

Either all operations of an electronic transaction fully complete, or fully abort. Any intermediate state with only part of money or goods exchanged is not permitted. Moreover, the atomicity property should be preserved even if communication fails between some of the parties.

### 8) Fairness

Fairness property requires that no protocol participant gains an advantage over other participants. For example, for a protocol in which one party exchanges one item of its own for another item of the other party, if the protocol is fair, it must ensure that at the end of the exchanging process, only one of the following two cases is the result. The first case is that each party receives the item it wants and gives its own item to its counterpart. The second case is that none of the parties receives any information about the other's item or loses its own item.

## 3. Security Protocols

In order to provide the above security properties, a number of security protocols have been proposed. Most of them adopt some similar ideas and common techniques. In this section, we summarize several security protocols and categorize them according to certain criteria.

## 3.1. *Protocols based on cryptographic mechanisms*

A set of protocols are based on cryptography. We call such protocols *cryptographic protocols*. They aim to enable parties to communicate securely over an insecure network through cryptographic mechanisms, such as data encryption and decryption. A cryptographic protocol is precisely defined as a sequence of communication and computation steps. Generally speaking, cryptographic protocols require that two parties in a session first agree on keys related to their communication. Only after they both know the keys, is exchanging information between them enabled. They use these keys to encrypt/decrypt information. Some researchers also call such protocols *Key Exchange Protocols*. Depended on whether the keys used in encryption and decryption are the same, there are two catalogs of cryptography: symmetric cryptography and asymmetric cryptography.

### 3.1.1. *Symmetric cryptographic protocols*

Traditional cryptography applies symmetric algorithms (such as DES: Digital Encryption Standard), in which both encryption and decryption share a common key: shared-key. Some researchers also call symmetric cryptography protocols *shared-key protocols*.

The following graph illustrates symmetric cryptography. A Key Distribution Center (KDC) is often needed. It sends secret keys through secure channels to the Encrypt side, where cleartext is encrypted using the keys and becomes ciphertext. In the Decrypt side, ciphertext is decrypted using the same secret keys sent by KDC and becomes cleartext.

An example of shared-key protocol is Otway-Rees protocol. It includes four steps:

(1) $A \rightarrow B : N_a, A, B, \{N_a, A, B\}_{K_a}$
(2) $B \rightarrow S : N_a, A, B, \{N_a, A, B\}_{K_a}, N_b, \{N_a, A, B\}_{K_b}$
(3) $S \rightarrow B : N_a, \{N_a, K_{ab}\}_{K_a}, \{N_b, K_{ab}\}_{K_b}$
(4) $B \rightarrow A : N_a, \{N_a, K_{ab}\}_{K_a}$

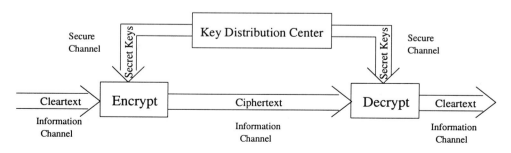

**Fig. 2.** Symmetric cryptography.

Here, $\{X\}_{K_a}$ stands for the ciphertext of $X$ encrypted using key $K_a$. $N_a, N_b$ are both nonces. A nonce is a randomly generated value originally known only by its generator. We will discuss nonces in more detail in Sec. 3.2.1. $K_a$, $K_b$, $K_{ab}$ are all keys. $A, B$ are identifiers of two sides.

$A$ initiates the session and generates a nonce $N_a$ to identify the run. $A$ uses his own key $K_a$ to encrypt $N_a$ together with identifiers of its own and its recipient, then sends this ciphertext and its corresponding cleartext to the other side $B$. After $B$ receives $A$'s message, he forwards it to the authentication server $S$, together with a nonce of his own and the ciphertext of $N_a, A, B$ encrypted with $K_b$. $S$ generates a new session key $K_{ab}$ and packages it separately for $A$ and $B$ with their own nonces, then sends the two packages and $N_a$ back to $B$. $B$ decrypts the last part of the message and checks whether the the nonce he received is the same as what he just sent out. If they are the same, he will accept the session key $K_{ab}$ and forward the rest to $A$. Similarly, $A$ also checks the nonce and if the answer is also "yes" he will accept that session key, too. Afterwards, both $A$ and $B$ can begin their communication with this common session key $K_{ab}$.

Such schemes provide confidentiality of information but little authentication. Neither do they validate the integrity of the data transmitted. Additionally, a drawback of such schemes is that they require large-scale distribution of the shared keys.

### 3.1.2. *Asymmetric cryptographic protocols*

An alternative method is asymmetric cryptography, or public-key cryptography. It applies two mathematically linked keys. If one of the two keys is used to encrypt some information, the other key must be used to decrypt the ciphertext. One of the two keys is kept secret by a certain agent and is referred to as the "private" key of this agent. This private key represents the identity of its owner. The second key, called the "public" key, is made available to the world.

There are several protocols in this category, such as IKE (Internet Key Exchange protocol), SET (Secure Electronic Transactions Protocol), TMN protocol, and the famous Needham-Schroeder public-key authentication protocol [23]. The last one has been taken as a paradigmatic example for analysis by many verification techniques, because of its simplicity and being well-known. The protocol aims to provide mutual authentication. After both agents involved in a communication session confirm the identity of the other side, they can exchange information.

We suppose that an agent A wants to establish a session with another agent B. A is the initiator while B is the recipient. S is the trusted key server. There are seven steps in the initial version of Needham-Schroeder public-key authentication protocol.

(1) $A \to S : A, B$
(2) $S \to A : \{K_b, B\}_{K_s^{-1}}$
(3) $A \to B : \{N_a, A\}_{K_b}$
(4) $B \to S : B, A$

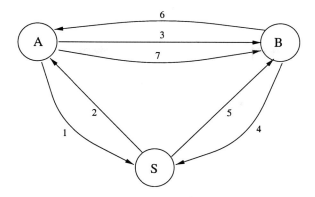

**Fig. 3.** Needham-Schroeder public-key authentication protocol.

(5) $S \to B : \{K_a, A\}_{K_s^{-1}}$

(6) $B \to A : \{N_a, N_b\}_{K_a}$

(7) $A \to B : \{N_b\}_{K_b}$

Here, $\{X\}_{K_a}$ is also the ciphertext of $X$ encrypted by $K_a$. $K_a$, $K_b$, $K_s$ are public keys of $A, B, S$ respectively. The inverse keys of them are private keys only known by their owner. It is assumed that every agent in the system knows $K_s$, so that each agent can decrypt the ciphertext encrypted by S using $K_s^{-1}$. When some agent wants another agent's public key, it should ask $S$ for it. $N_a$, $N_b$ are nonces generated by $A, B$ respectively.

Among those seven steps, steps 1, 2, 4, 5 are concerned with obtaining public keys, while steps 3, 6, 7 are concerned with the authentication of A and B. In step 3, $A$ sends out its nonce and identity encrypted with $K_b$. Because only $B$ has the private key $K_b^{-1}$, the inverse key of $K_b$, so A assumes that only $B$ can decrypt the information and obtain the clear form of $N_a$. So when $B$ returns this nonce (with $B$'s nonce) encrypted with $A$'s public key to $A$, $A$ can guarantee that it is really $B$ involved in their communication. The function of $N_b$ is the same.

Figure 3 illustrates these steps.

## 3.2. *Protocols based on main mechanisms to provide security*

To achieve a common security property, say, authentication property, different protocols use different mechanisms. Here, we categorize protocols according to the primary mechanisms. Protocols in one category may use techniques used in other categorizes as well.

### 3.2.1. *Protocols utilizing nonces*

A "nonce" is a randomly generated value originally known only by its generator. The main function of "nonce" is to verify "authentication". Authentication is the mechanism for proving identities over network systems. This goal is often achieved by possessing some particular information, or a "secret". The ISO/IEC 9798-1 states that "An entity to be authenticated proves its identity by showing its knowledge of a secret". Here, nonce plays the role of the secret.

When an agent $A$ wants to initialize a session with another agent $B$, $A$ may generate a nonce and encrypts it together with other information using some certain encryption method. Such method should guarantee that only $B$ can decrypt the message. Then $A$ sends the encrypted message to $B$ and waits for the response. If someone returns this nonce to $A$, $A$ will assume that the responder is really $B$ and can identify $B$'s authentication. This is the general idea of protocols based on nonces.

Many protocols use nonces, such as the Needham-Schroeder public-key authentication protocol introduced in Sec. 3.1.2.

### 3.2.2. *Protocols only utilizing session keys*

Some protocols only take advantage of session keys without nonces, such as TMN protocol [24]. TMN is a key distribution protocol for digital mobile communication systems, in which each user terminal in the network communicates with another user via a network center. The protocol employs the following two sorts of encryption:

**Standard** — An encryption function $E$ is used. Every initiator and responder knows how to produce $E(m)$ given a message $m$, but only the server knows how to decrypt the ciphertext to obtain the original $m$.

**Vernam** — The Vernam encryption of two keys $k_1$ and $k_2$, which is written as $V(k_1, k_2)$ is their bit-wise exclusive-or. Note that $V(k_1, V(k_1, k_2)) = k_2$, so if an agent knows $k_1$, then he can decrypt $V(k_1, k_2)$ to obtain $k_2$.

The TMN protocol for establishing a session key involves exchanging four messages. See Fig. 4:

(1) $A \rightarrow S : A.S.B.E(k_a)$

When the initiator $A$ wants to connect with the responder $B$, he chooses a key $k_a$, encrypts it using the function $E$, and sends it to the server.

(2) $S \rightarrow B : S.B.A$

The server sends a message to the responder $B$, telling it that $A$ wants to start a session with it.

**Fig. 4.** TMN protocol.

(3) $B \to S : B.S.A.E(k_b)$

   The responder $B$ acknowledges by choosing a session key $k_b$, encrypting it and sending it to the server.

(4) $S \to A : S.A.B.V(k_a, k_b)$

   The server forms the Vernam encryption of the two keys, and returns it to $A$.

   When $A$ receives this message, it can decrypt it using its own key $k_a$ to recover the session key $k_b$.

### 3.2.3. *Protocols utilizing time-stamp*

It is a principle that an old message used in a previous session, such as session key, can't be used in a new session. That is to say, the freshness property should be preserved. Kerberos is claimed as the first protocol using "time-stamp", which represents the current time to guarantee freshness.

   Figure 5 illustrates the basic Kerberos protocol [27].

   Kerberos is a shared-key protocol, which normally relies on a trusted third party. In fact, Kerberos relies on two. The first is the *Kerberos Authentication Server* (abbreviated as **Kas**), the second is the Ticket Granting Server (abbreviated as **Tgs**). The following steps describe the three phases of Kerberos Version IV.

   (i) Authentication

   (1) $A \to Kas : A, Tgs, Ta1$
   (2) $Kas \to A : \{AuthKey, Tgs, Tk, \underbrace{\{A, Tgs, AuthKey, Tk\}_{K_{tgs}}}_{AuthTicket}\}_{K_a}$

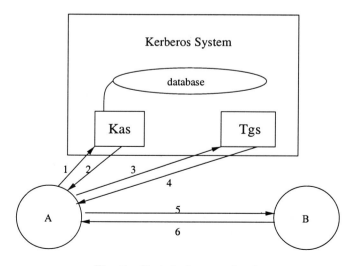

**Fig. 5.**   Basic kerberos protocol.

In this phase, $A$ logs onto the network. $A$ sends its identifier to $Kas$ and $Kas$ replys to it with a session key $Authkey$ and an encrypted ticket $Authticket$. They are encrypted using $A$'s shared key that $Kas$ retrieved from the database. The $Authkey$ has a lifetime of several hours. $A$ is automatically logged out when this key expires.

(ii) Authorization

(3) $A \rightarrow Tgs : \underbrace{\{A, Tgs, AuthKey, Tk\}_{K_{tgs}}}_{AuthTicket}, \underbrace{\{A, Ta2\}_{AuthKey}}_{authenticator}, B$

(4) $Tgs \rightarrow A : \{ServKey, B, Tt, \underbrace{\{A, B, ServKey, Tt\}_{K_b}\}}_{ServTicket}{}_{AuthKey}$

This phase occurs each time when $A$ wants to access the network resource $B$. $A$ presents the $Authticket$ to $Tgs$ together with an "*authenticator*" to show that the "*authenticator*" was issued to it. $Tgs$ issued $A$ with a new session key and a new ticket, respectively called "*ServKey*" and "*ServTicket*". The $ServKey$ has a short lifetime of few minutes.

(iii) Service

(5) $A \rightarrow B : \underbrace{\{A, B, ServKey, Tt\}_{K_b}}_{ServTicket}, \underbrace{\{A, Ta3\}_{ServKey}}_{authenticator}$

(6) $B \rightarrow A : \{Ta3 + 1\}_{ServKey}$

This phase follows each authorization phase. $A$ presents the $ServTicket$ to $B$ along with a new "*authenticator*". $B$'s reply is borrowed from the Needham-Schroeder public-key authentication protocol.

In Kerberos, there are four global constants for evaluating time-stamps: Auth-Life, ServLife, RecentAuth, and RecentResp. If a message in a session has a time-stamp "older" than the corresponding Lifetime constant, then most likely, the message will be judged to be faked.

## 3.3. *Protocols based on network environment*

Some protocols aim at providing security over a Local Area Network (LAN), such as the Kerberos mentioned above, while some others try to provide security over the Internet. With the development of electronic commerce, secure communication over the Internet is in great need. Both protocols protecting security at the web browser level and at the electronic transaction level are required.

### 3.3.1. *Protocols for security of web browser*

Many web browsers use the protocol SSL (Secure Sockets Layer). This protocol has several versions, the latest of which is called TLS (Transport Layer Security) [35]. This is a very complicated protocol.

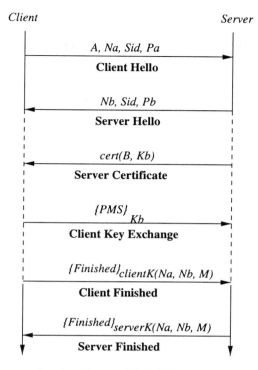

**Fig. 6.** The simplified TLS protocol.

The main concept in TLS is the *handshake*. A TLS *handshake* involves a client, such as a web browser $A$, and a web server $B$. Figure 6 illustrates a simplified version of TLS.

At the beginning of the handshake, $A$ contacts $B$, presenting a session identifier $Sid$, its public key certificate $P_a$ and a nonce $N_a$. B responds with another nonce $N_b$ and its public key certificate $P_b$ together with $Sid$, then certificate of B's identity and $K_b$. Then $A$ generates a *pre-master-secret*, a 48-byte random string, and sends it to $B$ encrypted with his public key. Now both parties calculate the master-secret $M$ from the nonces and the pre-master-secret, using a secure pseudo-random-number function (PRF). They also calculate session keys and MAC secrets from the nonces and master-secret. Each session involves a pair of symmetric keys: $A$ uses one of them and $B$ uses another. Before sending application data, both parties exchange **"finished"** messages to confirm all details of the handshake and to check that cleartext parts of messages have not been altered.

### 3.3.2. *Electronic commerce protocols*

Electronic commerce is potentially one of the most important Internet application areas. A number of protocols for electronic commerce have been proposed, such

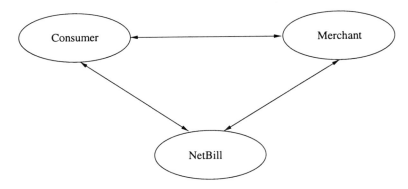

**Fig. 7.**   NetBill protocol.

as DigiCash, Open Market, CyberCash, First Virtual, and NetBill. They are all appropriate from medium to large transactions [58, 47].

But there are also some inexpensive transactions, 50 cents and less. If the protocols refered to above are used for them, the transaction cost will become a significant or even dominant component of the total purchase price. To solve this problem, some micro-payment protocols have been proposed, such as Eran Gabber's Agora, and Millicent.

We use NetBill and Millicent as two examples and introduce them as follows.

- NetBill

  NetBill is a dependable, secure and economical payment method for purchasing digital goods and services over the Internet. NetBill enables consumers and merchants to communicate directly with each other, using NetBill to confirm and ensure security for all transactions. See Fig. 7.

  A simplified version of NetBill protocol is given below. Here C stands for Customer, M stands for Merchant, B stands for Bank using NetBill.

  (1) $C \to M$: goods request
  (2) $M \to C$: goods, encrypted with a key K
  (3) $C \to M$: signed EPO (electronic payment order)
  (4) $M \to B$: endorsed signed EPO
  (5) $B \to M$: signed receipt
  (6) $M \to C$: signed receipt
  (7) $C \to B$: transaction inquiry
  (8) $B \to C$: signed receipt

- Millicent

  Millicent is designed to provide a mechanism for securing micro-payments when the cost of the protocol out-weights the cost of the transaction. Millicent addresses this problem by providing lightweight secure transactions. The trust model defines three roles: vendors, customers, and brokers. Brokers act as intermediaries between the vendors and the customers.

Millicent uses accounts based on "scrips". A scrip represents an account of a customer which is established with a vendor. The value of the scrip is the balance of the account. At any given time, a vendor keeps open accounts of the recently active customers. When the customer makes a purchase with a scrip, the cost of the purchase is deducted from the scrip's value and a new scrip with a new value is returned as change. When the customer has completed a series of transactions, he can "cash in" the remaining value of the scrip and close the account. Brokers serve as accounting intermediaries between customers and vendors.

There are also further categories for electronic commerce protocols. For example, fair exchange is proposed to provide fairness to both parties involved in an electronic transaction. There are two main types of this kind of protocol to solve the fair exchange problem.

- Gradual exchange protocol

  The idea of this method is that the parties release their items in small amounts, so that at any given moment, the amount of knowledge on both sides is approximately the same.
- Trusted third party

  In this method, a trusted third party supervises the communication between two parties and ensures that neither side can receive the item it wants before releasing its own item.

## 4. Formal Verification Techniques for System Security

The process of formally proving that the model of a system satisfies the specification of requirements, is called **formal verification**. Formal verification techniques play an important role in the field of security. Based on many researchers' work, we summarize three main research directions of formal methods in the field of security. One of them uses modal logic; another is based on state enumeration/exploration; the third is theorem proving. Next, we introduce these techniques with illustration using several real examples.

### 4.1. *Techniques using modal logic*

Modal logic consists of various statements about beliefs in or knowledge about messages in a system, as well as inference rules for deriving new beliefs from available beliefs and/or new knowledge from available knowledge and beliefs. The former corresponds to logic of belief, while the latter logic of knowledge. Logic of belief is useful in evaluating trustworthiness. So generally speaking, belief logic is limited to the analysis of the authentication property of protocols.

BAN logic, proposed by Burrows, Abadi, and Needham, is perhaps the best known and most influential modal logic [7]. It builds upon statements about messages sent and received throughout the process of a protocol run. It is designed specifically to reason about authentication protocols. When we intend to verify a certain protocol, first we should assume an initial set of beliefs and inference rules, as well as define the notions of adequacy using BAN. Then from the initial set of beliefs, using the inference rules, we can derived other beliefs. After all beliefs are generated, we check whether the set of beliefs is adequate based on the definition made before. If the answer is "yes", the protocol is correct. Otherwise, the protocol may have flaws. Compromises have to be made between precision and conciseness (or simplicity). It has been successfully used to find previously unknown flaws in a protocol that appeared in a draft recommendation for the CCITT X.509 standard.

Other logics and computation models like GNY [28], NPA, AT, VO, SVO [32] are all related to BAN logic to some extent. But they are restricted from the point of view of participants. Annette *et al* propose a new semantics for BAN logic [2]. The semantics enables reasoning about knowledge and, as a result, about the correctness of the participants' beliefs.

Bieber's CKT5 and Syverson's KPL are examples of logic of knowledge. Some researchers design logic which reasons about a hybrid of belief, knowledge and trust. For example, Rangan's logic is about trust and belief; Moser's logic reasons about knowledge and belief. They have different advantages and therefore different scopes of application.

Generally speaking, protocol verification based on a modal logic is a deductive reasoning process. Before a deduction process proceeds, rules of inference and axioms should be specified. Then the process proceeds in four steps [14]:

- Formally specify steps of a protocol in the language of the logic.
- Formally specify the desired protocol goals.
- Start with the initial protocol assumptions, build up logical statements after each protocol step using the logical axioms and inference rules.
- Compare these logical statements with the desired protocol goals to see if the goals are achieved.

Coffey and Saidha proposed a new logic of both knowledge and belief [14]. They used the logic to analyze the Needham-Schroeder protocol and revealed a known flaw. As illustrated in Sec. 3.1.2, the Needham-Schroeder protocol has seven steps. They used the proposed logic to formally state the protocol goals as follows first:

(1)  $K_{A,t2}(\exists t, t0 < t < t2, S(AS, t, d(\{K_B, B\}, K_{AS}^{-1})))$

(2)  $K_{B,t5}(\exists t, t0 < t < t5, S(AS, t, d(\{K_A, A\}, K_{AS}^{-1})))$

(3)  $K_{A,t6}(\exists t, t0 < t < t6, S(B, t, e(\{nA, nB\}, K_A)))$

(4)  $K_{B,t7}(\exists t, t0 < t < t7, S(A, t, e(\{nB\}, K_B)))$

$tn$ refers to the time at the end of protocol step $n$. $S(\Sigma, t, x)$ means $\Sigma$ sends message $x$ at time $t$. $K_{\sigma,t}\Phi$ means $\Sigma$ knows statement $\Phi$ at time $t$.

Then the initial assumptions related to the protocol participants are outlined:

(1) $L_{A,t0}(K_{AS})$

(2) $L_{B,t0}(K_{AS})$

(3) $L_{AS,t0}(K_A)$

(4) $L_{AS,t0}(K_B)$

(5) $K_{A,t0}(\forall i, i \in \{ENT\}, \forall t, t < t0, \neg L_{i,t}nA)$

(6) $K_{B,t0}(\forall i, i \in \{ENT\}, \forall t, t < t0, \neg L_{i,t}nB)$

$L_{\Sigma,t}x$ means $\Sigma$ knows and can reproduce object $x$ at time $t$. $ENT$ is the set of all possible entities.

Then they examined the message exchanges in order to verify the four desired protocol goals. Some axioms are used during the process. As a result, some conclusions are not compatible with the expected goals, which indicates that the protocol contains some security flaws and requires some additional steps in order to fulfil its objectives.

Since the initial protocol assumptions, protocol steps, inference rules and axioms are all finite and usually not large sets, the scale problem in using this technique is not a big problem. The first reason is that, quite often, after each protocol step, the set of logical statements doesn't grow sharply. The second reason is that once we find the desired protocol goals are included in the statements set, we don't need to continue the building statements process.

This technique requires translating a protocol into a set of logic formulas. This process is called idealization and is usually done manually. So it is error-prone and not systematic. This is a disadvantage of this method.

## 4.2. *Techniques using state enumeration/exploration*

State enumeration technique deals with systems with limited size. It models a certain protocol as a finite state system and verifies by exhaustive search that all reachable states satisfy some properties. Because verification is performed on a finite model, the process of verification can be automatic. Model checking is such a technique and has received a lot of attention recently.

Dolev and Yao's work forms the basis for this kind of method. Much research has been devoted to this direction. Miller uses Interrogator, a finite-state tool, to exhaustively search the state space and try to find a path from the initial state to the final state. The Longley-Rigby tool is similar to Interrogator but allows human intervention. Kemmerer models systems in a conventional formal specification language Ina Jo [49]. His method is modeling a protocol as a communication state machine and modeling security properties as state invariants and then trying to prove these invariants are preserved at each transition. Another well-known method is by Meadows *et al* [9]. Her tool is NRL Protocol Analyzer in which an insecure state might be specified and then efforts are made to construct a path to that state from the initial state. If such a path is found, then the protocol being tested is not secure. Lowe and Roscoe [24] have used CSP model checker FDR to perform finite-state analysis of cryptographic protocols. Dang [59] used ASTRAL, a high-level formal specification language for real-time systems, and its model checker to verify the Needham Schroeder Public Key Protocol and revealed the flaw already found. Marrero used Brutus, a special-purpose model checker, to verify fifteen classic authentication protocols and electronic commerce protocols, including 1KP, 2KP and NetBill.

Model checking attempts to check whether a property of a finite state machine holds. The property and the machine could be expressed in the same language or in different languages. In FDR, both of them are expressed in CSP. The protocol is described as a CSP process, say Prot. The property is another CSP process, Proc. In this case, in order to determine whether the property (one set of traces) holds for the machine (the second set of traces), we should test whether Prot's set of traces are a subset of Proc's set of traces. In other cases, the expression of the property and the machine could be in different languages. The property can be expressed using a logical formula and the machine can be described as a set of states and a state transition function. Since the machine has a finite number of states, an exhaustive search is done to check whether the logical formula holds at every state.

Next, we introduce an example of using CSP and FDR to verify NetBill [47].

Netbill is illustrated in Sec. 3.3.2. There are three agents in this protocol: the consumer, the merchant and the bank (using NetBill). In the CSP model, these three agents are described as three processes. A CSP process denotes a set of sequences of events, and an event represents a state transition. The following is the consumer process:

```
CONSUMER = ABORT || coutm ! goodsReq -> GOODS_REQ_SENT\\
GOODS_REQ_SENT = ABORT ||cinm ?x ->
                (if x==encryptedGoods then ENCRYPTED_GOODS_REC
                 else ERROR)
ENCRYPTED_GOODS_REC = ABORT || coutm !epo -> EPO_SENT
EPO_SENT = (cinm ?x -> (if (x==paymentSlip) then SUCCESS
                        else if (x==noPayment) then NO_FUNDS
                             else ERROR)) []
    (timeoutEvent -> coutb !transactionEnquiry -> BANK_QUERIED)
BANK_QUERIED = cinb ?x -> (if (x==paymentSlip) then SUCCESS
               else if (x==noPayment) then NO_FUNDS
                    else (if (x==noRecord) then NO_TRANSACTION
                          else ERROR))
```

The merchant and bank processes are expressed in the same way. The money automicity property can be specified as :

```
SPEC1 = STOP ||
  ((debitc -> creditM -> STOP) []
   (creitM -> debitC -> STOP))
```

We first combine the consumer, merchant, and the bank processes with an appropriate communication process, then hide all irrelevant events, and get a result system called "SYSTEM1".

Finally we use an FDR command to check whether the system satisfies the money automicity property.

```
Check1 ''SPEC1" ''SYSTEM1"
```

This technique has two benefits. It is completely automatic, and in addition, if the property being checked doesn't hold, a counterexample is produced.

For this technique, the complexity relies on the properties of the protocol. Since all reachable states are generated and an exhaustive search is to be done, if the state system corresponding to a protocol is not bounded or has a very large scale, the technique would not be appropriate for the analysis. In general, the state system of a security protocol is always bounded and not very large, so model checking the state space is not impractical.

## 4.3. *Theorem proving*

### 4.3.1. *General method*

Theorem proving is based on logic theories. Generally speaking, the proving process includes a deduction on a finite model rather than its generalization. Concerning the scale problem, these approaches further rely on the observation that logic used to reason about security protocols has a finite number of rules of inference that grow in a controlled manner. It is the small size of the number of entities in the model and the small size of the number of rules in any given logic that enable the checking to be performed fast.

Stated simply, the method is to build the entire theory, $Th$, given a logic and a model of the protocol. Since the model is finite and since the logic's rules always shrink or grow in a controlled manner, the theory generated is finite. Then we are expected to check whether a property, *phi*, of a protocol holds. The problem boils down to a simple membership test: Is *phi* in $Th$?

Here we give an example of Darrell and Jean [16]. Their technique, called "theory checking", consists of the following basic steps:

- Given a finite set of axioms and controlled-growth rules, their tool automatically generates a checker, $C$.
- Given the protocol, $P$, for which property *phi* will be checked, encode the initial assumptions and messages of $P$ as formulas; call this set $T^0$.
- Using $C$, exhaustively enumerate the theory, $T^*$, that is, the set of facts (formulas) derivable from the formulas in $T^0$.
- Determine whether a property *phi* holds by a simple membership test of whether the formula expression *phi* is in set $T^*$.

Another example which uses the general-purpose specification language Ina Jo and its execution tool Inatest is given by [49].

### 4.3.2. *Inductive techniques*

Unlike model checking approaches and general theorem proving techniques, Lawrence's inductive technique [26, 36–39] imposes no restrictions on finiteness. This techniques borrows the concept "trace" from model checking. A protocol is inductively defined as sets of traces, which may involve many interleaved protocol runs. Accidents and attacks can also be modeled. Properties are proved by induction on traces over the protocol. The aim of this method is to prove guarantees. But when the guarantees are absent, possible attacks may be indicated. Compared with modal logic, the logic in this method needs long and highly detailed proofs. The inductive technique uses higher-order logic (HOL) as a typed set theory and standard predicate calculus as well. A theorem prover Isabelle [25] is used.

This method applies similar idea to mathematical induction:

$$P(0) \text{ holds}$$

$$P(x) \Rightarrow P(Sucx)$$

To verify that $P(evs)$ holds for each trace $evs$, provided that a property $P$ is preserved under all the rules for creating traces, two steps are needed:

(i)  P covers empty trace.
(ii) For each of the other rules, try to prove $P(evs) \Rightarrow P(ev\#evs)$. ($ev\#evs$ is the trace that extends $evs$ with event $ev$.)

## 5. Some Future Research Areas

### 5.1. *Hybrid verification techniques*

Both proof-based techniques and model-checking techniques have their merits and demerits. Some researchers have taken advantage of both of them by combining them. One idea is to use proof-based technique as a general framework and use model-checking as a mechanism to achieve automation.

Dominique used such an approach [21]. He also used a certain version of the Needham-Schroeder public-key authentication protocol as an example. His approach includes three steps.

The first step is to formally specify the protocol. Different "principals" involved in the protocol will be identified. These principals can be trusted or not trusted such as an intruder. The formal specification contains the description of the trusted principals. The specification is in the form of a set of atomic actions. Because sending and receiving a piece of information is not synchronous, the Needham-Schroeder protocol which has seven steps will be identified by 14 different atomic actions. The whole system is represented as a pair $(s_0, r)$, in which $S_0$ is the initial global state and $r$ is a relation binding two global states before and after applying an action together.

The second step is to specify security properties. This approach employs a *filtering function* and an automaton. The former is to describe the visible actions and the latter is to specify the required sequencing of these visible actions. The filtering aims to focus on a certain session and the relevant actions for the chosen session; while the automaton is to place constraints on visible actions.

The third step is to automate. An abstraction function $h : B \to B_0$ is defined. $B_0$ is a finite subset of $B$, which is the set of basic data. Users can define different $B_0$ when different properties of the protocol are considered. Then we can derive some other abstraction functions from $h$, and based on the abstract model, the verification can go on in an automatic way using a model-checking technique.

## 5.2. *Methods to solve infinite state space problem*

During the process of generating the state space from an initial state of a protocol, the problem of infinite state space may occur if the system is not bounded. If any of the following occur, infinite state space will be generated [3].

(1) Some participants are able to perform unbounded steps in the protocol.
(2) Some participants may enter into infinitely many states.
(3) The set of participants is infinite.
(4) The set of messages received by a participant is infinite.

Antti *et al* [3] propose a new method and a tool HPA1 (Huima's Protocol Analyzer 1) based on symbolic state space search to deal with the analysis of an infinite state space if the infiniteness is only caused by (4). To reduce the complexity of space, Jeremy also proposes a method of embedding CSP trace theory within PVS [34].

Sometimes, even if the system itself is finite, infinite state space may be generated. When the size of a system increases linearly, the state space of it may increase exponentially. To keep the space under consideration finite, we must reduce the problem space according to a set of special concepts. Eric and Tsai [22] used compositional verification to tackle this problem. This technique makes use of the concepts of "composition" and "condensation" and aims to acquire an equivalent state space of much smaller size with respect to some properties. Then by analyzing a much smaller state space, conclusions about the properties of the original systems can be drawn. IOTA is a compositional verification tool designed and implemented by them. In [33], IOTA is compared with other model checkers such as SMC, SMV, SPIN, in verifying problems such as Client-Server, Reader-Writer, and Dining-Philosopher. Those problems all have state space scale problems. The experimental data shows excellent performance of IOTA. So compositional verification technique has a high potential of dealing with the state space exploration problem.

### 5.3. *Common specification languages*

The aim of this research is intended to provide a common specification interface for protocol analysis tools. If such an interface can be agreed on by most researchers, the cost of using different tools to analyze a certain protocol and the discrepancy in specification will be reduced.

## 6. Conclusion

This survey paper first introduces some standard security properties and a few specific security properties of electronic commerce protocols. Then several security protocols are categorized and illustrated. Because of the advantages of formal verification techniques in checking the correctness of security protocols, they are used widely to verify the security of a system. We describe three main methods and some realizing mechanisms.

Proof-based techniques use general or specific logics as the basis for the verification of a protocol and can provide deep insight into the nature of the protocol design. But they have the disadvantage of not being automatic. Model-checking techniques, on the contrary, can be used automatically but lack insight into a protocol. Some hybrid methods are proposed to combine the advantages of these two kinds of verification techniques. Finally, we introduce some research interests and directions in this area.

### Acknowledgments

This work is supported in part by the US National Science Foundation under Grants CCR-9988361 and CCR-0098120.

### References

1. A. Bhimani, "Securing the commercial internet", *Communications of the ACM* **39**, no. 6 (1996) 29–35.
2. A. Bleeker and L. Meertens, *A Semantics for BAN Logic* (Springer, Berlin, 1990).
3. A. Huima, "Efficient infinite-state analysis of security protocols", *http://netlib.bell-labs.com/who/nch/fmsp99/program.html.*
4. B. D. Decker and F. Piessens, "CryptoLog: A theorem prover for cryptographic protocols", *http://dimacs.rutgers.edu/Workshops/Security/program2/dedecker/paper.html*
5. M. J. Beeson, *Foundations of Constructive Mathematics* (Springer, Berlin, 1985).
6. C. E. Landwehr, "Security issues in networks with internet access", *Proceedings of the IEEE* **85**, no. 12 (December 1997) 2034–2051.
7. C. Meadows, "Formal verification of cryptographic protocols: A survey", *Advances in Cryptology — ASIACRYPT'94*, 135–150.
8. C. Meadows, "Analyzing the Needham-Schroeder public key protocol: A comparison of two approaches", *Proceedings of ESORICS* (Springer-Verlag), *http://chacs.nrl.navy.mil/publications/CHACS/CRYPTOindex.html.*
9. C. Meadows, "Language generation and verification in the NRL protocol analyzer", *http://chacs.nrl.navy.mil/publications/CHACS/CRYPTOindex.html.*

10. C. Meadows and P. Syverson, "A formal specification of requirements for payment transactions in the SET protocol", *Draft for Preproceedings of Financial Cryptography (FC98)* (February 1998).

11. C. Meadows, "A formal framework and evaluation method for network denial of service", *Proceedings of the IEEE Computer Security Foundations Workshop* (June 1999).

12. C. Meadows, "Analysis of the internet key exchange protocol using the NRL protocol analyzer", *Proceedings of the 1999 IEEE Symposium on Security and Privacy* (May 1999).

13. C. Meadows, "Open Issues in Formal Methods for Cryptographic Protocol Analysis", *Proceedings of DISCEX 2000, IEEE Computer Society Press* (January 2000) 237–250.

14. T. Coffey and P. Saidha, "Logic for Verifying Public-Key Cryptographic Protocols", *IEE Proceedings of the Computation Digital Technology* **144**, no. 1 (January 1997) 28–32.

15. C. Boyd, "Towards extensional goals in authentication protocols", *http://www.isrc. qut.edu.au/paper.htm*.

16. D. Kindred and J. M. Wing, "Fast, automatic checking of security protocols", *Proceedings of the Second USENIX Workshop on Electronic Commerce* (November 1996) 41–52.

17. M. Debbabi, M. Mejri, N. Tawbi and I. Yahmadi, "A new algorithm for the automatic verification of authentication protocols: From specification to flaws and attack scenarios".

18. D. Dolev and A. Yao, "On the security of public key protocols", *IEEE Transactions on Information Theory* **29**, no. 2 (1983) 198–208.

19. D. Dolev, S. Even and R. Karp, "On the security of ping-pong protocols", *Information and Control* (1982) 57–68.

20. D. Bolignano, "Towards a mechanization of cryptographic protocol verification", *CAV'97*, pp. 131–142.

21. D. Bolignano, "Integrating proof-based and model-checking techniques for the formal verification of cryptographic protocols", *CAV'98*, pp. 77–87.

22. E. Y. T. Juan, J. J. P. Tsai and T. Murata, "Compositional verification of concurrent systems using Petri-net-based condensation rules", *ACM Transactions on Programming Languages and Systems* **20**, no. 5 (September 1998) 917–979.

23. G. Lowe, "An attack on the Needham-Schroeder public-key authentication protocol", *Information Processing Letters* **56** (1995) 131–133.

24. G. Lowe and B. Roscoe, "Using CSP to detect errors in the TMN protocol", *IEEE Transactions on Software Engineering* **23**, no. 10 (October 1997) 659–669.

25. G. Bella and L. C. Paulson, "Using Isabelle to prove properties of the Kerberos authentication system", *DIMACS Workshop on Design and Formal Verification of Security Protocols* (September 1997).

26. G. Bella and L. C. Paulson, "Mechanising BAN Kerberos by the inductive method", *Tenth International Conference on Computer Aided Verification, CAV'98* (1998) 416–427.

27. G. Bella and L. C. Paulson, "Kerberos version IV: Inductive analysis of the secrecy goals", *ESORICS'98–European Symposium on Research in Computer Security* (1998) 361–375.

28. L. Gong, R. Needham and R. Yahalom, "Reasoning about belief in cryptographic protocols", *IEEE Computer Society Symposium in Security and Privacy* (May 2000) 234–248.

29. G. O'Shea, "On the specification, validation and verification of security in access control systems", *The Computer Journal* **37**, no. 5 (1994) 437–448.

30. J. F. Leathrum, Jr. R. M. B. E Morsi and T. E. Leathrum, "Formal verification of communication protocols", *http://www.ece.odu.edu/ leathrum/Formal-Methods/formal-methods.html*.

31. J. Esparza, A. Finkel and R. Mayr, "On the verification of broadcase protocols", *Proceedings of the 14th IEEE Symposium Logic in Computer Science (LICS'99)* (July 1999) 352–359.

32. J. M. Wing, "A symbiotic relationship between formal methods and security", *http://www.cs.cmu.edu/afs/cs/project/calder/www/needs.html*.

33. J. J. P. Tsai and K. Xu, "An empirical evaluation of deadlock detection in software architecture specifications", *Annals of Software Engineering (00)* (1999) 1–32.

34. J. Bryans and S. Schneider, "CSP, PVS and a recursive authentication protocol", *http://www.cs.rhbnc.ac.uk/research/formal/steve/publications.html*.

35. L. C. Paulson, "Inductive analysis of the internet protocol TLS", *http://www.cl.cam.ac.uk/users/lcp/papers/protocols.html*.

36. L. C. Paulson, "Proving properties of security protocols by induction", *Proceedings of the 10th Computer Security Foundations Workshop* (June 1997) 10–12.

37. L. C. Paulson, "Mechanized proofs for a recursive authentication protocolon", *Proceedings of the 10th Computer Security Foundations Workshop* (June 1997) 10–12.

38. L. C. Paulson, "Mechanized proofs of security protocols: Needham-Schroeder with public keys", Technical Report 413, University of Cambridge, Computer Laboratory (January 1997).

39. L. C. Paulson, "Relations between secrets: Two formal analyses of the yahalom protocol", *http://www.cl.cam.ac.uk/users/lcp/papers/protocols.html*.

40. L. C. Paulson, "The inductive approach to verifying cryptographic protocols", *Journal of the Computer Security* **6** (1998) 85–128.

41. R. Lorentz and D. B. Benson, "Deterministic and nondeterministic flow-chart interpretations", *Journal of Computer System Science* **27** (1983) 400–433.

42. M. Burrows, M. Abadi and R. Needham, "A logic of authentication", *ACM Transactions in Computer Systems* **8**, no. 1 (February 1990) 18–36.

43. M. Bellare and P. Rogaway, "Entity authentication and key distribution", *Advances in Cryptology-Crypto '93 Proceedings*.

44. M. Bellare, R. Canetti and H. Krawczyk, "A modular approach to the design and analysis of authentication and key exchange protocols", *Proceedings of the 30th Annual Symposium on the Theory of Computing* (1998).

45. J. K. Millen, S. C. Clark and S. B. Freedman, "The interrogator: Protocol security analysis", *IEEE Transactions on Software Engineering* **SE-13**(2) (1987).

46. R. M. Needham and M. D. Schroeder, "Using encryption for authentication in large networks of computers", *Communications of the ACM* **21**, no. 12 (1978) 993–999.

47. N. Heintze, J. D. Tygar, J. Wing and H. C. Wong, "Model checking electronic commerce protocols", *http://www.cs.cmu.edu/afs/cs.cmu.edu/project/venari/www/usenix96-submita.html*.

48. P. Syverson and C. Meadows, "A formal language for cryptographic protocol requirements", *Designs, Codes, and Cryptography* **7**, no. 1/2 (1996) 27–59.

49. R. A. Kemmerer, "Analyzing encryption protocols using formal verification techniques", *IEEE Journal of the Selected Areas in Communications* **7**, no. 4 (May 1989) 448–457.

50. R. Focardi, A. Ghelli and R. Gorrieri, "Using non interference for the analysis of security protocols", *http://www.dsi.unive.it/ focardi/biblio.html*.

51. R. Focardi and R. Gorrieri, "A classification of security properties for process algebra", *Journal of the Computer Security*, no. 30 (1994) 1–32.

52. R. Focardi and R. Gorrieri, "Automatic compositional verification of some security properties", *Proceedings of the TACAS'96*, pp. 111–130.

53. R. Focardi and R. Gorrieri, "The compositional security checker: A tool for the verification of information flow security properties", *IEEE Transactions on Software Engineering* **23**, no. 9 (September 1997) 550–570.

54. S. D. Stroller, "A reduction for automated verification of authentication protocols", *http://www.cs.indiana.edu/ stroller/*.

55. S. Nagono, Y. Kakuda and T. Kikuno, "A new verification method using virtual system states for responsive communication protocols and its application to a broadcasting protocol", *IEICE Transactions on Fundamentals* **E81-A**, no. 4 (April 1998).

56. S. Schneider, "Verifying authentication protocols in CSP", *IEEE Transactions on Software Engineering* **24**, no. 9 (Spetember 1998) 741–758.

57. S. Brackin, C. Meadows and J. Millen, "CAPSL interface for the NRL protocol analyzer", *Proceedings of ASSET 99* (March 1999).

58. T. Aslam, "Protocols for E-commerce", *Dr. Dobb's Journal* (December 1998) 52–58.

59. Z. Dang, "Using the ASTRAL model checker for cryptographic protocol analysis", *http://dimacs.rutgers.edu/Workshops/Security/program2/program.html*.

60. *Advances in Cryptology — AUSCRYPT '92, Lecture Notes in Computer Science 718*.

61. *Advances in Cryptology — ASIACRYPT '94, Lecture Notes in Computer Science 917*.

62. *Advances in Cryptology — ASIACRYPT '96, Lecture Notes in Computer Science 1163*.

63. *Automated Reasoning with Analytic Tableaux and Related Methods, Lecture Notes in Artificial Intelligence 1617*.

64. *Trends in Distributed Systems for Electronic Commerce, Lecture Notes in Computer Science 1402*.

65. *Security Protocols, Lecture Notes in Computer Science 1189*.

66. *Security Protocols, Lecture Notes in Computer Science 1361*.

67. D. W. Davies and W. L. Price, *Security for Computer Networks (Second edition)*.

68. *1993 IEEE Symposium on Research in Security and Privacy*.

69. *1994 IEEE Symposium on Research in Security and Privacy*.

70. *1993 IEEE Symposium on Security and Privacy*.

71. *10th Computer Security Foundations Workshop*.

# SOFTWARE ARCHITECTURE

RICK KAZMAN

*Software Engineering Institute, Carnegie Mellon University,*
*4500 Fifth Ave., Pittsburgh, PA 15213, USA*
*Email: kazman@sei.cmu.edu*

Software architecture is a rapidly growing sub-area of research and practice within software engineering. The foundation of any large software intensive system is its architecture. This artifact describes how the system will accomplish its tasks, how the development work will be broken down, how quality goals will be met, and much more. Because of its central importance, an architecture needs to be carefully designed and carefully analyzed, particularly in light of its ability to meet its quality requirements, such as performance, availability, security, and modifiability. The technical and business implications of an architecture need to be fully understood. And, in cases of legacy systems, the architecture of an existing system may need to be reverse engineered.

*Keywords*: Software architecture, architecture design, architecture analysis, architecture representation, reverse engineering.

## 1. Historical Introduction

Software architecture is a burgeoning field of research and practice within software engineering. Or, to be more precise, the architecture of large, software intensive *systems* has been the subject of increasing interest for the past decade. What accounts for this surge of interest in a field that, until about 1990, was unheard of?

To begin, the field did not spontaneously create itself in 1990. But that time-frame was when the term "software architecture" began to gain widespread acceptance and when the field first attracted substantial attention from both industry and the research community (e.g. [40, 34]). The field was created out of necessity. Software systems were growing larger: systems of hundreds of thousands or even millions of lines of code were becoming commonplace. Clearly the foundations of the ideas underlying the field that is today called "software architecture" were laid by Parnas, Brooks, Dijkstra and others in the 60's through the 80's ([4, 11, 13, 32, 33]) — but what changed is that by the 90's such large systems were becoming *common*. The pervasiveness of such huge systems meant that they needed to be understood and managed by ordinary skilled engineers. These systems were no longer solely the province of a select few virtuosos [39].

Fundamentally, there are three reasons why software architecture is important to large, complex, software intensive systems:

(1) *Communication among stakeholders.* Software architecture represents a common high-level abstraction of a system that most if not all of the

system's stakeholders can use as a basis for creating mutual understanding, forming consensus, and communicating with each other.

(2) *Early design*[a] *decisions.* The software architecture of a system is the earliest artifact that enables the priorities among competing concerns to be analyzed, and it is the artifact that manifests the concerns as system qualities. The trade-offs between performance and security, between maintainability and reliability, and between the cost of the current development effort and the cost of future developments are all manifested in the architecture.

(3) *Transferable abstraction of a system.* Software architecture constitutes a relatively small, intellectually graspable model for how a system is structured and how its components work together; this model is transferable across systems; in particular, it can be applied to other systems exhibiting similar requirements and can promote large-scale reuse.

These reasons will form the basis for the structure of this chapter. I will discuss how an architecture affects the stakeholders of a system, as well as an organization and its business goals. I will discuss how architecture is a vehicle for communication, and hence how it is documented and represented are of critical interest. And I will talk about how an architecture, as the repository of the first and deepest, most profound decisions about a system's structure, needs to be designed and analyzed with due diligence.

So what is a software architecture? Definitions abound (the Software Engineering Institute's web site [37], which collects definitions of software architecture, currently boasts over 60 of them), but I will use the one from [4], which represents a reasonably centrist view:

*The software architecture of a program or computing system is the structure or structures of the system, which comprise software components, the externally visible properties of those components, and the relationships among them.*

Note the key elements of this definition:

- Architecture is an abstraction of a system or systems. It represents systems in terms of abstract components which have externally visible properties and relationships (sometimes called connectors, although the notion of "relationships" is more general than connectors, and can include temporal relationships, dependencies, uses relationships, and so forth).
- Because architecture is about abstraction it suppresses purely local information; private component details are not architectural.

---

[a]It should be noted that I use the word "design" to mean any constructive creative process. Architecture is the application of this creative process at the highest level of abstraction.

- Systems are composed of *many* structures (commonly called views). Hence there is no such thing as "the" architecture of a system, and no single view can be appropriately represented anything but a trivial architecture. Furthermore, the set of views is not fixed or prescribed. An architecture should be described by a set of views that support its analysis and communication needs.

These points will be discussed in detail in the remainder of this chapter. For the moment, however, note that in almost every case where someone is interested in a software architecture, they are also interested in a system architecture.

## 1.1. *Related terms*

The term "architecture" is currently in vogue. People talk about their business architecture, the operational architecture, their information architecture, their process architecture. By these uses of the term architecture they typically mean "structure", or "organizing principles", and nothing more in much the same way that news reporters will refer to the "architect" of a crime. However, some uses of architecture *are* related to the definition above. For example, a "reference" architecture is commonly found in many domains. A reference architecture is a set of domain concepts mapped onto a standard set of software components and connectors. For example, the domain of compiler construction has a well-known reference architecture, which details the gross chunks of functionality (lexical analysis, syntactic analysis, code generation, optimization, etc) mapped onto a set of components arranged as a pipeline [39]. Modern information system architectures consist of a database, business logic, and a user interface mapped onto a 3-tier client-server structure.

## 2. Architecture and Its Effects on Stakeholders

Although an architecture is a technical description — an engineering blueprint — of a system, it affects everyone involved with the system. Each stakeholder of a system — customer, user, project manager, coder, tester, etc — is concerned with different characteristics of the system that are affected by its architecture. For example, the user is concerned that the system is usable, reliable and available; the customer is concerned that the architecture can be implemented on schedule and to budget; the manager is worried (in addition to cost and schedule) that the architecture will allow development teams to work largely independently, interacting in disciplined and controlled ways; the developer is worried about achieving all of those goals through coding; the tester wants to prove (or disprove) that these goals will be met.

Architecture provides a common language in which different concerns can be expressed, negotiated, and resolved at a level that is intellectually manageable even for large, complex systems. Without such a language, it is difficult to communicate and comprehend large systems sufficiently to make the early decisions that influence both quality and usefulness.

## 3. Architecture as Communication Vehicle

Architectures serve as a communication vehicle in two ways. The first way is that they are a common abstraction of the system, and so provide a convenient *lingua franca* — a language that all stakeholders can speak and understand. Stakeholders often have different backgrounds (they may be managers, users, customers, testers, implementors, administrators, operators, etc) and so have widely different views on what the system is or will be and how they perceive and interact with it. Many experiences with software architecture analysis have noted how reviewing a software architecture with a large number of different stakeholders allows their concerns to be aired in a common understandable language, often for the first time ([1, 5, 27]).

The second way that architecture serves as a communication vehicle is that it is a technical "blueprint" for the system that is to be built, modified, or analyzed [20]. While this aspect of architecture is not more important than the first, it is less obvious and intuitive, so I now turn to that in more detail.

### 3.1. *Architectural structures*

In a house, there are plans for the structure of the house, the layout of the rooms, for electrical wiring, plumbing, ventilation, and so forth. Each of these plans constitutes a "view" of the house. These views are used by different people. The electrician primarily uses the wiring view. The carpenter primarily uses the structural view.

Each specialist uses their own view to achieve different qualities in the house. The carpenter is primarily interested in making the walls straight and square and in assuring that joists are of sufficient strength to support the floors. The electrician is primarily concerned with providing appropriate electrical capacity in convenient locations, and in doing so in such a way as to safeguard the house's occupants. But each of the specialists may need to consult other views than their primary one: the electrician must ensure that when he drills a hole through a wall or joist that this hole doesn't compromise the structural properties of the house, or interfere with a location where a water pipe might need to run.

As with houses, architectural structures must be used as both a description and prescription, must be used by multiple stakeholders. While the architect designs the overall structure of a computational system, many specialists will refine and implement each of the views. Common architectural structures include (e.g. see [27] and [40]):

- functional (or logical) view;
- code view;
- development (or structural) view;
- concurrency (or process/thread) view; and
- physical (or deployment) view.

The precise number, names, and types of these views are still a subject of some debate, and not a particularly interesting debate at that. Some specific guidance on architectural documentation is beginning to appear (e.g. [3]). For the purposes of making architectural documentation concrete in this chapter, I will briefly illustrate each one. For each one I will say what its components and connectors (or relationships) are, who uses it, and what it's good for (what kind of reasoning it supports).

### 3.1.1. *Functional view*

The functional view is an abstraction of system functions and their relationships. The components of the functional view are: functions, key system abstractions, and domain elements. The connectors or relationships between components found in the view are dependencies and data flow.

The users of the view are domain engineers, product-line designers, and end users. These stakeholders think about this view in terms of what the functionality is, how data flows among the pieces, and what variability of functionality the architecture should support. The reasoning that supports it is, thus, decisions about what functionality should be in the architecture, the modifiability of the architecture (because part of modifiability depends on how functionality is partitioned with respect to the anticipated future changes [27]), product lines/reusability, tool support, and the allocation of work to various groups. For example, one might create a database group, or a transaction management group, or a user interface group in response to identifying such functionality as important in this view.

An example of a purely functional view is shown in Fig. 1. This is a decomposition of an interactive system into its functional elements.

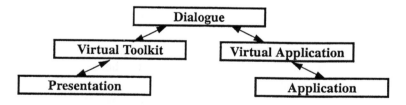

**Fig. 1.** Functional view example — The arch/slinky metamodel.

### 3.1.2. *Code view*

The code view is what the programmer sees. Thus the components of this view are things like classes, objects, procedures, and functions, and their abstraction/composition into things like subsystems, layers, and modules. The connectors/relationships are again what a programmer sees — calls and method invocation — as well as containment relations like is-a-sub-module-of.

The users of this view are programmers, designers, and reusers (who are also typically programmers and/or designers). They use this view to reason about

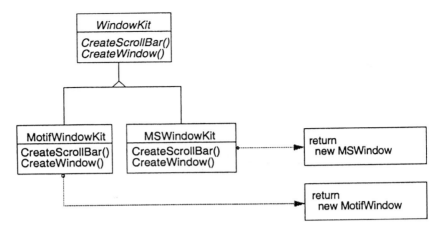

**Fig. 2.** Code view example — The abstract factory design pattern.

modifiability/maintainability, portability, and subsetability (the ability to field a subset of the system's functionality without making major changes to its code).

An example of a pure code view is found in design patterns [15], as exemplified in Fig. 2.

Pure code views are seldom found in practice. In fact, pure views of any sort are seldom found in practice. What is more useful is showing one view mapped onto another. Code views typically show the mapping of functionality onto code structures.

### 3.1.3. Development view

The development view is another view that the developer sees, but it is distinct from the code view. It is a view of the structure of the source code as a *repository* that various users (programmers and maintainers) create, modify, and manage. The components of this view are typically files, and directories (although other organizations are possible, such as keeping all source files in a database). The main relationship between these files and directories is containment. The users of the development view, in addition to programmers and maintainers are managers and configuration managers. These stakeholders use the view to reason about the modifiability/maintainability of the system (see [27] or [5] for examples of this), for dividing up the development and testing of the system, or for configuration management/version control.

An example of the development view is shown in Fig. 3. This view shows a greatly simplified view of the hierarchical structure of the directories and files comprising a physics simulation system. The top level directory is "Physics3D". Sub-directories are advection, chemistry, generator, etc. Each directory contains the source and the header files for that sub-system. This view provided a focus for

```
Physics3D                    hydro                    Wall.c
    advection                    CreateMatrix.c           Wall.h
        History.c                FormMatrix.c             ...
        Variables.c              Slide.c              parallel
        Faces.c                      ...                  Comm.c
        Zones.c          io                               Comm.h
        ...                      ChemInput.c              Elements.c
    chemistry                    ChemInput.h              ...
        Reaction.c               MatInput.c           slide
        Reaction.h                   ...                  InitSlide.c
        ReactionType.h       materials                    InitSlide.h
        ...                      AlumModel.c              PreProcess.c
    generator                    AlumModel.h              ...
        BuildObjs.c              ReactiveFlow.c       thermal
        BuildObjs.h                  ...                  HeatGen.c
        BuildSlide.c     obj                              HeatGen.h
        ...                      Boundary.c               ...
```

**Fig. 3.** Development view example — A physics simulation system.

the system's stakeholders in determining division of labor, testing, integration, and maintenance.

### 3.1.4. *Concurrency view*

When a complex system is deployed, it is typically packaged into a set of processes or threads which are deployed onto some computational resources. The concurrency view is a necessary step for reasoning about what processes or threads will be created and how they will communicate and share (or compete for) resources.

So the components of this view — processes and threads — interact with each other via data flow, events, and synchronization on shared resources. The users of this view are people who worry about deploying the system, who are concerned with the performance and availability of the system, as well as integrators and testers. This view is used to reason about performance, availability, and deployment.

An example of a concurrency view is given in Fig. 4. This view shows how a part of an air traffic control system is organized to provide high availability to the system [8]. Processes are triply replicated and clustered into groups of "operational units". As it happens, each process in an operational unit is allocated to a different processor, but that information is *intentionally* omitted in this view. Operational units are organized into client-server relationships. Operational units consist of PAS (primary address space) processes and SAS (standby address space) processes. The primary process sends data by data management messages to its secondaries so that they are synchronized with its state. In the event of a failure, one of the SASs is "promoted" to become PAS. Note that this view says nothing about what each operational unit's function is or how processes are allocated to processors. This separation of concerns is intentional.

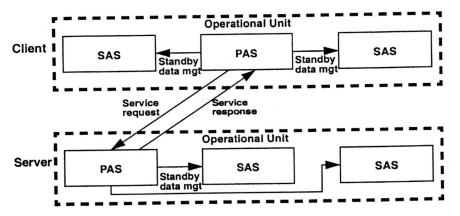

**Fig. 4.**   Concurrency view example — An air traffic control system.

### 3.1.5. *Physical view*

The physical view of a system describes how the system is deployed in terms of its hardware resources. For small, trivial systems this description is equally trivial: there is a single computer on which all processing is done. But for large, complex systems there may be a myriad of sensors, actuators, storage devices, networks, and computers.

The components are things like CPUs, sensors, actuators and storage. The connectors are typically networks or other communication devices (such as satellites or buses). The users of this view are hardware and system engineers who have to reason and worry about system delivery, installation, and upgrade (in some cases doing upgrades while the system is still running), as well as performance, availability, scalability, and security.

An example of a physical view, adapted from [9], is shown in Fig. 5. This figure shows a plethora of computers and interfaces to hardware devices (in this case sensors such as radar and actuators such as missiles) all connected by a LAN which is replicated to ensure that there isn't a single point of failure in the communications network.

### 3.2. *Scenarios*

In addition to the above views of a software/system architecture, many architects use scenarios to annotate the architecture by tying the views together, as suggested by Kruchten [30]. What are scenarios? Scenarios are a brief description of the use of a system or a change to a system. They are often divided thus into two sub-categories:

- use cases: sequences of responsibilities; and
- change cases: descriptions of proposed changes to the system.

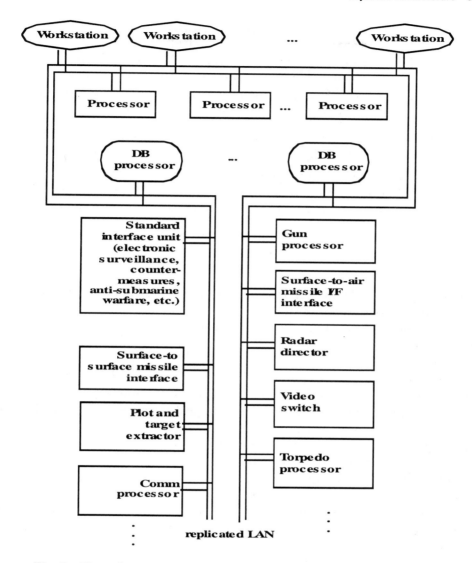

**Fig. 5.** Physical view example — An shipboard command and control system.

Scenarios are used:

- to understand and validate the architecture, by allowing architects, designers, and programmers to "walk through" the architecture as it is affected by a scenario;
- to communicate the architecture, particularly to those who have not had a major role in its creation;
- to tie the views together; as we have seen, views seldom occur in isolation. One view is typically mapped onto another view. Scenarios aid in this

mapping process by providing a need to concretely realize some aspect of the architecture; and

- to understand the limits of the architecture, by seeing where it is difficult for the architecture to satisfy or be adapted to satisfy a scenario.

So, for example, a maintainer might postulate a scenario like "Replace the middleware or communications infrastructure with one supplied by a different vendor" to understand the implications of this change on the code view and the process view. A systems engineer might suggest a scenario such as "Half of the processors or servers go down during operation" or "The network fails during operation" to understand the implications of these failures on the performance or availability of the system.

For example, here are some sample use cases for an embedded vehicle control system:

(1) Change performance and handling parameters in the field, via the service program.
(2) When the engine is not running, do not diagnose the presence of an engine oil pressure fault.
(3) Override pre-set carburation parameters at run-time.

These are anticipated uses of the system. In addition to these, the stakeholders will contribute a set of change cases, which represent their objectives for features and capabilities of the tool in the future:

(1) Change devices and hardware configurations, including doubling the memory map or making a harness change.
(2) Change the allocation of processes to processors, timing and priorities.
(3) Port the user interface to WIndows CE.

### 3.3. Architecture description languages

Hopefully by now you are convinced that architectural description is very important. It is central to an architecture's success in being communicated from one stakeholder to another, being analyzable by describing the right information, and being actually built from the blueprints that the architectural descriptions represent. Because architectural description is so important, there have been many attempts to design specific languages to support this task (see [31] for a survey of architecture description languages, or ADLs). In fact, architectural description languages have been both successes and failures.

They have been successes in that many ADLs have been created and employed in both academic and real-world projects. Each of these languages has concentrated on a different facet of architectural description and analysis (deadlock detection, consistency, completeness, real-time properties, etc). This success has brought with it its own problems: since there is a proliferation of ADLs, there has arisen a need to exchange information among them. From this need grew ACME [18], an ADL specifically designed to be an architecture interchange language — a means for the many disparate ADLs to jointly describe an architecture and to jointly support many different kinds of analysis that are unique to specific ADLs. For example, if one wanted to analyze an architecture with respect to deadlocks and the meeting of real-time deadlines, one might need to consult two different ADLs, each of which supports one of these analyses. But then the process of ensuring that the architectural descriptions in each ADL are consistent either requires human intervention, and the potential for human oversight, or it requires a special-purpose translator to be written to map from one ADL to the other.

The failure of ADLs is that none of them have been widely adopted. There have been some successes in specialized domains (see, for example, [4] where an ADL for describing object-oriented systems with real-time constraints is described), but these are limited islands of success.

All the discussion, however, might be moot. The Unified Modeling Language (UML) [36] is being widely adopted by organizations to describe their object-oriented designs and is being extended (frequently in an *ad hoc* fashion) to describe architectural constructs as well. If it truly becomes a *de facto* standard for architectural description then at least the interchange problem is trivially solved, and having a well understood, widely disseminated standard aids in the communication of designs using this language. The UML is certainly not a panacea however. It was originally construed as a language to support object-oriented design and analysis, not as an ADL. As such, it does not include architectural concepts as first-class entities. It does not naturally support the successive refinement of designs, from architectural abstractions to any level of hierarchical refinement. And while many of its facilities can be tailored to be used to represent architectures, it is a big complex language and can be used by different architects in dramatically different ways. FInally, it is a relatively abstract language and thus it is not easy to communicate UML designs to non-technical people. Despite these problems, it is receiving a great deal of attention from practicing architects. For a critical evaluation of UML as an ADL, see [16].

## 4. Architecture as Early Design Decisions

A software architecture is a coherent, justified collection of a system's earliest set of design decisions. These decisions, such as what style the system is composed of (client-server, pipe-and-filter, distributed objects, repository-centric, etc) will affect much of what the system will become.

These decisions will impose constraints on an implementation, e.g. all inter-process communication is to be done via TCP/IP. These decisions will affect how system resources are allocated and arbitrated. And they will affect the tradeoffs that any system must necessarily make.

The architecture will also affect the organization. There is almost always a strong correspondence between architectural structures and organizational ones. Why is this? Because architectural structures define coherent groupings of functionality and coherent sets of concerns. The concurrency view may suggest the need for a separate team that does performance planning, modeling, and tuning. Or it may suggest the need for a team that worries about how system failures are detected and managed. Each of these teams might do their own analyses and require specialized tools, training, and knowledge. The code and development views also dictate system structure in terms of modules, sub-systems, or layers. These once again influence organizational structure. A module, sub-system, or layer represents a highly coherent set of functionality which suggests high internal coupling and low coupling to external entities. Conway's law [12] states that this must match the organizational structure because otherwise you will have information flows in the system that don't match those of the organization. For example, the members of the database team typically know a great deal about each other's code and internal interfaces. They only likely see the externally published interfaces from the user interface team or the telecommunications team. Human separation of concerns must match the software separation of concerns. To do otherwise is to burden the development team with the need to know too much about the details of the system. Thus, organizational structure must match the architectural structures.

Early design decisions made in the architecture may result in constraints on an implementation. One such constraint is the choice of commercial components that can be easily integrated. Although interoperability protocols exist, for the most part choosing any commercial component will affect the choice of what other components may be employed. For example, choosing Microsoft's DNA (Distributed InterNet Architecture) set of components (Windows NT, MS Transaction Server, Wolfpack, Distributed COM, MS Message Queue, MS SQL Server, etc) will preclude, or at least make costly, the use of CORBA or Enterprise Java Beans compliant components [35]. Also the choice of an architectural style may make the use of some components difficult if they have widely divergent mechanisms for sharing data, passing control, etc [19].

An architecture's earliest design decisions should center around the forms of its infrastructure: how components communicate, how they pass or share data, how they initialize, shut down, self-test, report faults, etc. When the computational structure — sometimes called a framework — for supporting these activities is built first (as suggested in [4]) then many benefits accrue. For one thing, there can be a working version of the system very early in its life cycle. The earliest version may do little other than start up and hum to itself, but it provides all the infrastructure for the sub-systems to work together. Many of these sub-systems can be implemented initially as stubs; simply reading their data from a file or always outputting the same values, or looking up their results from a table. As the system is developed, these stubs can be replaced by their fully functioning versions. This means that, over time, the system increases in fidelity. But having an early working version of the system is wonderful for team morale, increases customer confidence, allows for better estimation of progress by management, and it means that integration and testing are continuous, rather than a risky "big-bang" activity late in the project.

## 4.1. *Architectural styles*

I have mentioned the term "architectural style" several times in this chapter. Just what are these exactly? Early research in software architecture was motivated, in part, by the observation that certain styles crop up over and over in practice in response to similar sets of demands. These styles, similar to object-oriented design patterns [15], but often higher abstraction capture a recurring solution to a recurring problem. A style:

- describes a class of architectures or significant architecture pieces;
- is found repeatedly in practice;
- is a coherent package of design decisions; and
- has known properties that permit reuse.

Shaw and Garlan first published a collection of architectural styles in [38]. Shaw and Garlan's initial list consisted of:

- independent components: communicating processes, implicit invocation, explicit invocation;
- data flow: batch sequential, pipe and filter;
- data-centered: repository, blackboard;
- virtual machine: interpreter, rule-based system; and
- call/return: main program and subroutine, object-oriented, layered.

Others, such as Buschmann *et al* have augmented this collection [10]. There is no complete list of styles and there is no unique, non-overlapping list. Complex systems can exhibit multiple styles at once: styles overlap or can contain one another hierarchically. But each architectural style consists of at least the following information:

- a set of component types (e.g. data repository, process, object);
- a set of connector types/interaction mechanisms (e.g. subroutine call, event, pipe);
- a topological layout of these components;
- a set of constraints on topology and behavior (e.g. a data repository is not allowed to change stored values, pipelines are acyclic); and
- an informal description of the costs and benefits of the style, e.g.: "Use the pipe and filter style when reuse is desired and performance is not a top priority.

More recently, the notion of Attribute-Based Architectural Styles (ABASs) [28] have added analysis reuse to design reuse, by joining together architectural styles and explicit analysis frameworks.

## 4.2. Architectures for product lines

Another way in which a software architecture is a repository of critical early design decisions is that it is a reusable model which can become the basis for a product line. A software architecture is an asset that an organization creates at considerable expense. This expense can and should be reused. In fact, while other forms of reuse have historically shown little success, architecture-based product lines are proving to be a significant commercial success for many organizations. In fact, economics dictates that products be built in different ways than they were 10 or 20 years ago ([22, 6]).

When creating a product line, new software engineering challenges are encountered that do not occur in single product developments. The creation and management of a set of core assets is both crucial to the success of the product line and is a major challenge, since a great deal of work goes into deciding which assets should be "core" and which should be "periphery". The other major challenge in creating a product line is using the core assets to create products. In particular, new products will frequently require new functionality, and it must be determined if and how this functionality gets folded back into the core assets.

The specific *architectural* challenges for a product line are twofold: managing the realization of quality attributes across instances of the product line and managing the variation in functionality while maintaining just a single architecture. The first problem challenges the architect to, for example, create a small, inexpensive, low-performance, uni-processor version of a product and a large, expensive, high-performance, multi-processor version using the same architecture. And the infrastructure to manage this variation cannot itself absorb too much of the system's processing power. The second problem forces the architect to be able to accommodate a wide variety of features or functions without changing the underlying model of how the system works.

While these issues are by no means solved, a great deal of research and practical industrial experience shows that architecture-based software product lines can be efficient and economical (e.g. [6, 9, 22]).

## 5. Architecture Design and Analysis

If we accept the idea that an architecture is a key to an organization's and a system's success and if we accept that we should design and document this artifact carefully as a set of engineering blueprints, then we should also recognize that we need to *analyze* the artifacts that we have designed. We do this for several reasons:

- to ensure that our design decisions are adequate to meet our quality attribute [21] goals;
- to predict the quality attributes that the eventual system will possess;
- to ensure that the system meets its stakeholders' needs; and
- to make sure that the design decisions that are proposed are cost effective and bring maximal benefit to the organization.

In short, we invest so much time and money in a software system that the architecture must be predictably competent. This is a characteristic of any mature engineering discipline: predictability.

How do we achieve predictability? How do they achieve it in other engineering disciplines? They achieve it through design reuse and through analysis reuse [39]. Design reuse at the architectural level currently takes two forms in today's practice: object-oriented design patterns ([15, 10]), and architectural styles [38]. As described above, the notion of Attribute-Based Architectural Styles (ABASs) [28] have added analysis reuse to design reuse, by joining together architectural styles and analysis frameworks.

## 5.1. *Architecture based design*

Using these building blocks, architecture based design can proceed as a true engineering effort, rather than as an *ad hoc* process. As an example of a first attempt at this, the Architecture-based Design (ABD) Method [2] proposes a method for transforming a set of customer requirements into an architecture for a system or a product-line, via a set of decompositions and refinements.

The ABD method begins, as do almost all software projects with a list of requirements relating to both functionality and quality attributes. It then recursively decomposes the architectural design to meet these requirements. Each time it decomposes the design it assigns some functional requirements to design elements. It meets quality attribute requirements by associating architectural styles with these requirements and realizing those styles in the architecture.

The design, as it evolves, concentrates on three architectural views: functional, concurrency, and physical. The creation of each of these views causes the architect to ask and answer questions of the design. These questions are typically posed as scenarios, which relate back to the requirements that spawned the process in the first place. The ABD method can be seen as a design-time realization of the ATAM, which will be presented next.

## 5.2. *Architecture based analysis*

However when an architecture design is done, it should be *analyzed* to ensure that the qualities the architect has planned for the architecture can actually be realized. Several architecture analysis methods have been proposed, such as SAAM [27], ATAM [26], and SAA [5]. These techniques are all *scenario* based. They are scenario based because without scenarios it is difficult to precisely characterize a set of quality attribute goals. The software engineering community does not understand, in any useful way, what it means to be modifiable, or available, or secure, or interoperable. So we substitute our lack of understanding of quality attributes with scenarios, which realize a specific quality attribute goals in a context: a stimulus, an environment, and a response.

These architecture analysis methods analyze and "test" the architecture by generating a set of scenarios, and applying them to the architecture in much the same way that actual systems are tested or benchmarked by using standard stimuli (a set of test cases as input), in the context of a standard operating environment (an execution platform, perhaps with a specified set of load or other environmental characteristics) that produce a set of responses (outputs) that are measured. The Architecture Tradeoff Analysis Method (ATAM), for example, realizes these activities with the following steps:

*Presentation:*

1) **Present the ATAM**: The method is described to the assembled stakeholders (typically customer representatives, the architect or architecture team, user representatives, maintainers, administrators, managers, testers, integrators, etc).

2) **Present business drivers**: The customer representative describes what business goals are motivating the development effort and hence what will be the primary architectural drivers (e.g. high availability or time to market or high security).

3) **Present architecture**: The architect will describe the proposed architecture, focussing on how it addresses the business drivers.

*Investigation and Analysis:*

4) **Map architecture to business goals**: The architect and other key project personnel such as project manager or marketing/customer representative detail how the system's quality attribute responses will map to value for the organization.

5) **Generate quality attribute utility tree**: The quality factors that comprise system "utility" (performance, availability, security, modifiability, etc) are elicited, sub-categorized, specified down to the level of scenarios, and prioritized.

6) **Analyze architecture approaches**: Based upon the high-priority scenarios identified in the utility tree generation step, the architectural approaches that address those scenarios are elicited and analyzed (for example, an architectural approach aimed at meeting performance goals will be subjected to a performance analysis). During this step architectural risks, sensitivity points, and tradeoff points are identified.

*Testing:*

7) **Brainstorm and prioritize scenarios**: Based upon the exemplar scenarios, a larger set of scenarios is elicited from the entire group of stakeholders. This set of scenarios is prioritized via a voting process involving the entire stakeholder group.

8) **Analyze architecture approaches**: This step reiterates step 6, but here the highly ranked scenarios from step 7 are analyzed as test cases for

the analysis of the architectural approaches determined thus far. These test case scenarios may uncover additional architectural risks, sensitivity points, and tradeoff points which are documented.

*Out-Briefing:*

9) **Present results**: Based upon the information collected in the ATAM (styles, scenarios, attribute-specific questions, the utility tree, risks, sensitivity points, tradeoffs) the ATAM team presents the results of the analysis to the assembled stakeholders detailing this information and any proposed mitigation strategies. The fine details of this method are described elsewhere (see [26] and especially [24] for more exhaustive descriptions). The point is that techniques exist to analyze and evaluate the ramifications of architectural design decisions before these decisions are committed to code and are extremely costly to change. These techniques are reasonably inexpensive and can be used at any point in the development life-cycle [1].

### 5.3. *Analyzing the business impacts of architectural decisions*

The benefits of a software system are only assessable relative to the business goals the system has been developed to serve. In turn, these benefits result from interactions between the system's functionality and its quality attributes. Its quality attributes are, in most cases, dictated by its architectural design decisions. The architecture is thus not only the crucial artifact to study in making design tradeoffs but also the crucial artifact to study in performing cost-benefit analyses. A substantial part of this analysis is in determining the level of uncertainty with which we estimate both costs and benefits.

A number of researchers have begun seriously considering how to link together business considerations with software analyses, employing methods from economics, such as portfolio theory and real-options theory ([42]). Although this kind of analysis is still in the early research stage, some methods and case studies already exist ([23]).

## 6. Architecture Reverse Engineering

In this chapter, I have discussed creating, documenting, and analyzing architectures. If these techniques are successful, then the architecture and the components that populate it will be one of an organization's key assets for many years. This means that architectural maintenance becomes an issue, and one that is even more pressing over time than was the original creation of the architecture itself. But, in fact, maintenance begins from the day that an architecture is first created. Why is this?

If an architecture is designed with some property in mind (say, high performance or high reliability), then does this property hold for a system created from the architecture? The answer is: *perhaps*. Why can I not be more definite about this? Because there is, in general, no way of ensuring that the architecture that was designed is the architecture that is actually implemented. For this reason, it is important to include architectural conformance exercises in any mature architecture development practice. To do conformance implies either that you never allow an architecture's realization to deviate from its specification, or (more likely) that you can *extract* an architecture from what you actually have built; to reverse engineer the system's architectural structures from the individual atoms that are realized in code (procedure calls, method invocations, class definitions, inter-process communication, etc).

There are additional reasons why you might want to reverse engineer a software architecture. An architecture's documentation may not exist, or is lost, or erodes over time:

- architectures may have never been documented, and the expertise needed for understanding the architecture lives only in the heads of employees who have left the organization;
- new products may be acquired for which no architectural documentation exists; and
- the individual efforts of programmers may wittingly or unwittingly "erode" the architecture, by bypassing the abstractions that the architect designed.

For these reasons, it is often necessary to reverse engineer an architectural description from its existing assets (typically code and build files). There is no automatic process for doing this. It is an interpretive process that is carried out as an interactive dialogue involving an architect (or someone who can at least conjecture architectural structures from knowledge of the system or an examination of existing documentation) and a reverse engineering toolset [29].

Several such toolsets exist currently, such as ManSART [43], Dali [25], and the Philips toolset [29], and the Software Bookshelf [14]. Each of these toolsets has four major functions: extracting architectural primitives from a code base, storing the extracted information in a repository, visualizing the contents of the repository to the user, and manipulating the contents of the repository to reflect the architecture's abstractions by applying a set of rules that map from the atomic extracted information to these abstractions.

## 7. The Future

Software architecture is rapidly becoming a respected sub-discipline of software engineering. Many commercial organizations have created their own architecture organizations which act as internal consultants to other parts of the company, aiding in architectural specification, documentation, analysis, and maintenance. This chapter has attempted to outline the highlights of the major software architecture practices. Of course, we cannot expect to do much more than quickly introduce a set of topics in such a brief format, and provide references to the reader for more information and motivation to want to go there. More exhaustive treatises on the subject exist (e.g. [4, 10, 22, 37, 38, 40]) and are being added to with increasing regularity.

There have also been a number of attempts at predicting the future of software architecture (e.g. [17, 4]). These have listed areas such as architecture for dynamic systems, reflective architectures, architecture migration, and others as hot topics of research and practice for the future. One thing is for certain, however: as long as people continue to build large, complex, software-intensive systems then software architecture will continue to be of critical importance to the success of such systems.

## References

1. G. Abowd, L. Bass, P. Clements, R. Kazman, L. Northrop and A. Zaremski, "Recommended best industrial practice for software architecture evaluation", Carnegie Mellon University, Software Engineering Institute Technical Report CMU/SEI-96-TR-025, 1996.
2. F. Bachmann, L. Bass, G. Chastek, P. Donohoe and F. Peruzzi, "The architecture based design method", Carnegie Mellon University, Software Engineering Institute Technical Report CMU/SEI-2000-TR-001, 2000.
3. F. Bachmann, L. Bass, J. Carriere, P. Clements, D. Garlan, J. Ivers, R. Nord and R. Little, "Software architecture documentation in practice: Documenting architectural layers", Carnegie Mellon University, Software Engineering Institute Special Report CMU/SEI-2000-SR-004, 2000.
4. L. Bass, P. Clements and R. Kazman, *Software Architecture in Practice* (Addison-Wesley, 1998).
5. P. Bengtsson, N. Lassing, J. Bosch and J. van Vliet, "Analyzing software architectures for modifiability", Hogskolan Karlskrona/Ronneby Research Report 2000:11, ISSN: 1103–1581.
6. J. Bosch, *Design and Use of Software Architectures* (Addison-Wesley, 2000).
7. F. Brooks, *The Mythical Man-Month — Essays on Software Engineering* (Addison-Wesley, 1975).
8. A. Brown, D. Carney, P. Clements, C. Meyers, D. Smith, N. Weiderman and W. Wood, "Assessing the quality of large, software intensive systems: A case study", *Proceedings of the European Conference on Software Engineering*, September 1995.
9. L. Brownsword and P. Clements, "A case study in successful product line development", Carnegie Mellon University, Software Engineering Institute Technical Report CMU/SEI 96-TR-016, Carnegie Mellon University, 1996.
10. F. Buschmann, R. Meunier, H. Rohnert, P. Sommerlad and M. Stal, *Pattern-Oriented Software Architecture: A System of Patterns* (Wiley & Sons, 1996).
11. P. Clements, D. Parnas and D. Weiss, "The modular structure of complex programs", *IEEE Transactions on Software Engineering* **SE-11**, no. 3, March 1985.
12. M. Conway, "How do committees invent?", Datamation, April 1968, 28–31.
13. E. W. Dijkstra, "The structure of the 'T.H.E.' multiprogramming system", *CACM* **18**, no. 8 (1968) 453–457.
14. P. Finnigan, R. Holt, I. Kalas, S. Kerr, K. Kontogiannis, H. Muller, J. Mylopoulos, S. Perelgut, M. Stanley and K. Wong, "The software bookshelf", *IBM Systems Journal* **36**, no. 4 (1997) 564–593.

15. E. Gamma, R. Helm, R. Johnson and J. Vlissides, *Design Patterns, Elements of Reusable Object-Oriented Software* (Addison-Wesley, 1995).
16. D. Garlan and A. Kompanek, "Reconciling the needs of architectural description with object-modeling notations", *Proceedings of the Third International Conference on the Unified Modeling Language*, October 2000.
17. D. Garlan, "Software architecture: A roadmap", *The Future of Software Engineering*, ed. A. Finkelstein (ACM Press, 2000).
18. D. Garlan, R. T. Monroe and D. Wile, "Acme: An architecture description interchange language", *Proceedings of CASCON '97*, November 1997.
19. D. Garlan, R. Allen and J. Ockerbloom, "Architectural mismatch: Why reuse is so hard", *IEEE Software*, November 1995, 17–26.
20. IEEE, 1999, Draft Recommended Practice for Architectural Description, P1471/5.2, December 1999.
21. International Organization for Standardization and International Electrotechnical Commission, Information technology — Software product evaluation — Quality characteristics and guidelines for their use, ISO/IEC 9216: 1991(E).
22. M. Jazayeri, A. Ran and F. van der Linden, *Software Architecture for Product Families* (Addison-Wesley, 2000).
23. R. Kazman, J. Asundi and M. Klein, "Quantifying the costs and benefits of architectural decisions", CMU/SEI-2000-TR-0??, Software Engineering Institute, Carnegie Mellon University, 2000.
24. R. Kazman, M. Klein and P. Clements, "ATAM: A method for architecture evaluation", Carnegie Mellon University, Software Engineering Institute Technical Report CMU/SEI-2000-TR-004, 2000.
25. R. Kazman and S. J. Carriere, "Playing detective: Reconstructing software architecture from available evidence", *Automated Software Engineering* **6**, no. 2 (April 1999) 107–138.
26. R. Kazman, M. Barbacci, M. Klein, S. J. Carriere and S. G. Woods, "Experience with performing architecture tradeoff analysis", *Proceedings of the 21st International Conference on Software Engineering (ICSE 21)* (Los Angeles, CA) May 1999, 54–63.
27. R. Kazman, G. Abowd, L. Bass and P. Clements, "Scenario-based analysis of software architecture", *IEEE Software*, November 1996.
28. M. Klein, R. Kazman, L. Bass, S. J. Carriere, M. Barbacci and H. Lipson, "Attribute-based architectural styles", *Software Architecture (Proceedings of the First Working IFIP Conference on Software Architecture (WICSA1))* (San Antonio, TX) February 1999, 225–243.
29. R. Krikhaar, A. Postma, A. Sellink, M. Stroucken and C. Verhoef, "A two-phase process for software architecture improvement", *Proceedings of ICSM'99*, Oxford, UK (September 1999).
30. P. Kruchten, "The 4+1 view model of architecture", *IEEE Software* **12**, no. 6 (November 1995).
31. N. Medvidovic and R. Taylor, "A classification and comparison framework for software architecture description languages", *IEEE Transactions on Software Engineering* **26**, no. 1 (January 2000) 70–93.
32. D. Parnas, "On a 'buzzword': Hierarchical structure," *Proceedings IFIP Congress 74*, 1974, 336–3390.
33. D. Parnas, "On the criteria to be used in decomposing systems into modules", *Communications of the ACM* **15**, no. 12 (December 1972) 1053–1058.
34. D. Perry and A. Wolf, "Foundations for the study of software architecture", *SIGSOFT Software Engineering Notes* **17**, no. 4 (October 1992) 40–52.

35. E. Roman, *Mastering Enterprise JavaBeans and the Java 2 Platform, Enterprise Edition* (Wiley, 1999).

36. J. Rumbaugh, I. Jacobson and G. Booch, The *Unified Modeling Language Reference Manual* (Addison-Wesley, 1998).

37. SEI Software Architecture, *http://www.sei.cmu.edu/ata/ata_init.html*.

38. M. Shaw and D. Garlan, *Software Architecture: Perspectives on an Emerging Discipline* (Prentice Hall, 1996).

39. M. Shaw, "Prospects for an engineering discipline of software", *IEEE Software* **7**, no. 6 (November 1990) 15–24.

40. M. Shaw, "Larger scale systems require higher-level abstractions", *Proceedings of Fifth International Workshop on Software Specification and Design*, IEEE Computer Society, 1989, 143–146.

41. D. Soni, R. Nord and C. Hofmeister, *Applied Software Architecture* (Addison-Wesley, 2000).

42. K. Sullivan, S. Chalasani and S. Jha, "Software design as an investment activity: A real options perspective", *Real Options and Business Strategy: Applications to Decision Making*, eds. L. Trigeorgis (Risk Books, December 1999).

43. A. Yeh, D. Harris and M. Chase, "Manipulating recovered software architecture views", *Proceedings of ICSE 19*, Boston, MA (May 1997) 184–194.

# ENGINEERING ACCESS CONTROL IN DISTRIBUTED APPLICATIONS

KONSTANTIN BEZNOSOV

*School of Computer Science,*
*Florida International University Miami, FL, 33199*
*E-mail: beznosov@cs.fiu.edu*

YI DENG*

*Department of Computer Science, School of Engineering and Computer Science,*
*University of Texas at Dallas, Richardson, TX 75083*
*E-mail: yideng@utdallas.edu*

This paper discusses issues of engineering access control solutions in distributed applications for enterprise computing environments. It reviews application-level access control available in existing middleware technologies, discusses open problems in these technologies, and surveys research efforts to address the problems.

*Keywords*: Software security, access control, authorization, distributed systems, software engineering, middleware.

## 1. Introduction

Computer system security is conventionally achieved via *protection* and *assurance*. The former is usually provided by some security subsystems or mechanisms, which are designed to protect the system from specific threats. A threat is any potential occurrence that can have an undesirable effect on the assets and resources associated with a computer system. Protection is based on the premise that it is possible to list most of the threats, which can happen, and to build mechanisms that can prevent the threats [13]. The protection mechanisms can be classified into three groups: accountability, availability and authorization. Accountability mechanisms make sure that users and other system active entities (conventionally called *subjects*) are held accountable for their actions towards the system resources and services. Availability mechanisms ensure either service continuity or service and resource recovery after interruption. Authorization mechanisms ensure that the rules governing the use of system resources and services are enforced. The mechanisms are further qualified as either access control or data protection ones.

Access control mechanisms allow system owner to enforce those rules when rules check and enforcement are possible. The term "authorization" also implies

---

*Contacting author.

the process of making access control decisions. When checking and enforcement of the rules are not possible, data protection mechanisms, such as data encryption, are used. A reference monitor is a part of the security subsystem, responsible for enforcing the rules via mediation of access by subjects to system resources (traditionally called *objects*).

Access control has been exercised at different places and levels of abstraction, e.g. network, database, operating system and middleware controls, each with different emphasis. Control to protected resources can also be addressed from a single system or an organization point of view. The objective of this paper, however, is to survey the design of access control mechanisms from an organization and application point of view. Modern information systems are increasingly interconnected to form information enterprise, which consists of many self-contained, heterogeneous and yet integrated application systems. The problem of access control in such an environment is to enforce organization-wide security policies across these applications. How to ensure the secure interoperation of interconnected software systems in an information enterprise is a complex task and emerges as a central issue in software development and operation. In this paper, we survey the issues, problems and solutions in engineering software to handle access control for enterprise-oriented application systems, and discuss future solutions and technology in this important area.

The rest of the paper is organized as follows. Section 2 provides background information on access control in application systems and defines evaluation criteria. We discuss problems of access control in distributed systems in Sec. 3. Section 4 discusses design approaches for application level access control in distributed environment. Section 5 surverys access control mechanisms supported by the mainstream middleware technologies. Summary and discussion are provided in Sec. 6.

## 2. Background and Evaluation Criteria

In this section, we give background information on access control, explain main concepts and terms, and then introduce the issue of application-level access control. In addition, we define criteria for evaluating existing technologies and research.

### 2.1. *Background*

The structure of traditional access control (AC) mechanisms can be viewed using the conceptual model of *reference monitor*. A reference monitor is a part of the security subsystem, responsible for mediating access by subjects to system resources (traditionally called *objects*), as illustrated in Fig. 1.

The mediation consists of making authorization decisions, by checking access requests against authorization rules from the authorization database — a storage of such rules — and enforcing them. A set of the rules is sometimes called a *policy*. Authorization rules commonly have a subject-action-object structure, which

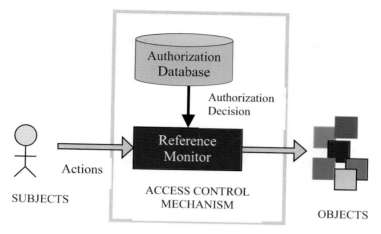

**Fig. 1.**   Conventional access control.

specifies what subject(s) can perform what action(s) on what object(s). Permitted actions are called *access rights*. Thus a subject has a particular access right to an object if it can perform the action towards that object. Furthermore, all authorization rules can be conceptualized into *access matrix* [39], where a row corresponds to a subject and a column to an object, and each cell specifies access rights granted to the subject for the corresponding object.

To make an authorization decision, a reference monitor takes authorization rules and three groups of information: (1) the access request, (2) the subject who made the request, and (3) the object to be accessed.

The information about access request usually carries the request type, for example "read". However, some application domains have a need for AC decisions based on additional attributes of the request. For instance, a banking system might deny a withdrawal request if its amount exceeds a pre-determined threshold.

Information about the subject can be divided into two types — related or unrelated to security. Originally, only security-related information was used in AC decisions. Controlled by security or user administrators, this information describes subject's identity, group membership, clearance, and other *security attributes*. Sometimes, the term *privilege attributes* is used to refer to those security attributes intended solely for the purpose of AC.

In some application domains, security-unrelated information about the subject needs to be taken into account. For example, access to rated materials in public libraries could be granted according to a person's age. Another example is information derived from organizational work-flow process. This information is not controlled by security or user administrators and it is not always provided to the reference monitor in the form of subject security attributes. The information about the object to be accessed can also be divided into categories related and unrelated to security. An example of an object security attribute is its security level.

Depending on the capabilities of a particular AC mechanism and the availability of information about the subject, request and object, either limited or elaborate information are available for making authorization decisions. This information availability will be used as a criterion for evaluating expressiveness (or power) of AC mechanisms.

AC mechanisms are part of most operating, database management (DBM) and middleware systems. They are also present in such control systems as firewalls, and many applications.

Application resources can be in the form of data processed by applications, their services (e.g. Telnet, SMTP or WWW servers), particular operations performed on them (e.g. GET access requested from a WWW server via HTTP protocol, operation invocation on a CORBA-based application server), or even menus of the application interface.

Some application resources, such as files, database records or network sockets, can be protected by an operating system, DBMS, or middleware system. However, there are resources that are application-specific and are recognized only by the application itself, for example the execution of particular parts of the application business logic. The granularity of application-specific resources is finer than of general purpose computing systems. This is one essential distinction between application-level and general purpose AC. Another vital difference is that authorization rules used for application-level AC require the use of such information about access operations, subjects, or objects, that is specific to the application domain or more elaborate (more expressive) than the information used by AC mechanisms of general purpose systems. In order to meet the requirements, applications commonly have their own AC mechanisms in addition to the use of those provided by the underlying general purpose systems. And this practice is increasingly common.

## 2.2. *Evaluation criteria*

There are a wide variety of technologies and techniques for handling AC, which differ from each other in various ways. To make meaningful comparisons, we define the following evaluation framework.

1) **Granularity of protected resources.** We will use the following granularity hierarchy: application, interface, method, arbitrary resource. If a solution does not allow authorization decisions on fine-grain resources, it cannot be used for protecting application resources.

2) **Support for policies specific to an organization or application domain.** There is a wide range of AC models and policies, as shown in Chap. 3. At one end are AC mechanisms that support only one model (and the corresponding policies), for example lattice-based mandatory AC (MAC). At the other end are solutions that allow implementation of any authorization logic and their support for policies is limited only by the interface to the logic. In general, the more AC policy types a

mechanism can support the easier it is to configure for required organizational policies. We will look at the range of supported AC models.

3) **Information used for making authorization decisions.** As we discussed above, authorization decisions are made based on information about the subject and object, as well as the operations to be performed. Some technologies allow obtaining only authenticated identity of the subject but not the information about group membership or activated roles, which ultimately limits the functional capabilities of the AC mechanism based on such a technology. We will look into what information is available and what information is used in authorization decisions.

4) **Use of application-specific information.** The use of information that is application-specific and becomes available only while the application processes the client request is critical for some application domains (e.g. healthcare). If a solution does not allow the use of such information, full automation of protecting application resources would not be possible.

5) **Support for consistency of policies across multiple applications.** It was discussed earlier that in the enterprise environment, the issue of consistent policy enforcement is a critical one. We will consider the support for enterprise-wide consistent AC policy enforcement while examining the available and proposed approaches.

6) **Support for changes.** No matter how functionally perfect the support for the AC is, if it is ineffective to accommodate changes, such as insertion or deletion of application systems and underlying computation environment, it is not suitable in enterprise settings. Most available approaches support the changes to some degree. Unfortunately, there is no objective quantitative criteria for determining the level of support. We will evaluate the level of support by comparing the solutions.

7) **Solution scalability.** Performance and administration scalability highly affects the utility of AC solutions. If a technology does not scale well it cannot be more then just an academic exercise. Since there is no benchmark available for evaluating the scalability of AC solutions, we will use common knowledge to reason about the scalability. For instance, we will examine the amount of data that needs to be modified, in order to accommodate a policy change. Another commonly known measure that we will use is the communication complexity, which is still regarded as a major factor in the performance of distributed systems.

## 3. Problems of Access Control in Distributed Systems

From software engineering point of view, design and implementation of software security in distributed enterprise environment must address several concerns. First, an information enterprise consists of many self-contained and yet interconnected or integrated application systems. The problem of access control is to enforce organization-wide security policies across these applications. Consequently, ways must be provided to ensure the consistency of enforcement across application boundaries. Second, changes occur frequently in enterprise environment. These may include changes to existing systems, insertion or deletion of applications, changes in business processes and security policies, changes in hardware/software platforms, etc. An attractive security system design must effectively support the evolution of enterprise systems. Last but certainly not least, the above qualities need to be achieved at reasonable cost during the development, operation, and evolution of application systems.

The industry has achieved considerable results on access control of operating system, databases and middleware in such a way to make the security mechanisms as relatively independent and self-contained components in the systems. Most of the operating systems implement authorization logic in the security part of their kernels [9, 18, 19, 23, 25, 30, 31, 35, 42, 44, 45, 48, 53, 54, 60, 64]. There are also special-purpose ad-on security software packages that furnish authorization decisions for operating systems [9, 15, 16, 32]. Abadi *et al* [1] and Lampson *et al* [39] developed a unified theory of authentication and access control in distributed systems. Practical implementations reflecting some results of the theory have been implemented in security architectures of some distributed environments [38, 47, 50, 51, 57]. However, fine-grain control of application resources, except when those resources are stored in a consolidated database, is done traditionally in *ad hoc* manner [65], and there are no automated means to ensure enterprise-wide consistency of such controls.

Generally speaking, current solutions to access control have two problems. First, access to protected resources is controlled at several points. They are network controls (e.g. firewall), middleware controls (access control mechanisms enforced by middleware environments such as CORBA [50], EJB [43], DCE [22], DCOM [46]), database and operating system controls. Making all these controls to work in concert and consistently enforce enterprise-wide access control policies is a daunting task, when there are hundreds of application and supporting systems (e.g. operating systems).

The second problem is that traditional access control mechanisms [61] provide limited capabilities for handling complex policies and authorization decisions that are based on factors specific to an application domain. The complexity of access control policies in some application areas, e.g. healthcare, requires exercising access control policies that are more sophisticated and of finer granularity than the general ones used in operating systems, databases, and security services of such distributed environments as Java [38], DCOM, DCE, SESAME [52], and CORBA. All but last types of access control points provide only coarse grain level of control. In addition, security requirements in some domains mandate domain-specific factors (e.g. relationship between the user and the patient [8], emergency context) to be used in access control policies. This complexity and granularity level often force application designers to embed domain-specific authorization logic inside their applications. Some even document patterns of designing "application security" [69]. As a result, it both increases the complexity of software design and makes it difficult to ensure system integrity and quality. It also significantly increases the difficulty and cost in system administration and management, especially in the face of rapidly changing business, technology, as well as system requirements and functionality. These problems are less severe in stand-alone systems. However, the distributed environments of enterprise systems with dozens of heterogeneous systems exacerbate them drastically.

## 4. Design Approaches to Application-Level Access Control

The research community has been working towards systematic ways of controlling access to resources in distributed and heterogeneous application systems. The three main research approaches are policy agents, interface proxies and interceptors, and enterprise-wide authorization services. They are discussed in this section.

### 4.1. *Policy agents*

The concept of policy agents [29] is motivated mainly by the goal of accommodating the existing body of products and technologies already deployed in organizations. The key idea is centralized AC management via rule translation into languages supported by local AC mechanisms, and distribution of the rules across the systems, as shown in Fig. 2. The distribution is achieved with the help of policy agents that

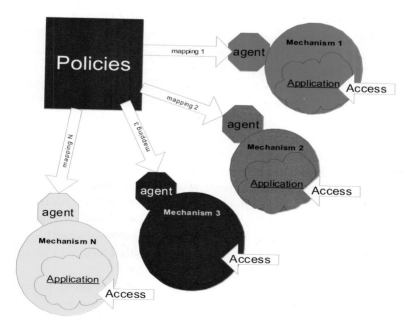

**Fig. 2.**   Policy agents.

reside on computers hosting applications. They could be the OS AC or add-on packages, AC provided by the middleware, by DBMS security layers, or even by the AC mechanisms integrated in the application. Consistency of authorization policies across application boundaries is achieved by the centralized AC management via translation of authorization rules into languages supported by local mechanisms through policy agents. The distributed management architecture based on such agents provides the infrastructure necessary to map domain-wide authorization rules into rules specific to particular mechanisms.

This approach have several advantages, including fault tolerance, compartmentalization of enterprise security without penalizing run-time performance. There is a high degree of run time autonomy between the local mechanisms.

The main problems of this approach are the difficulties in achieving the consistency of enforced global policy across different applications, and in automating the mapping of the global policy into the languages and representations specific to various AC mechanisms. This approach also suffers from some innate limitations. First, the granularity and expressiveness of domain-wide AC policies can be only as good as the policies supported by the most coarse-grain and least expressive mechanism in that domain. Second, the distribution of policy updates can be very slow, which could easily make policies based on periodic authorizations [10] unaffordable. However, this direction becomes irreplaceable if other approaches, such as proxies and interceptors, fail.

### 4.2. *Proxies and interceptors*

Solutions under this approach employ either interface proxies [28], role classes [8], security meta-objects [55, 56], or interceptors of intersystem communications, as in CORBA, DCOM, SafeBots [20, 21] and Legion system [26, 27, 67]. The idea is illustrated in Fig. 3. Access to an application is controlled externally and authorization decisions are made and enforced before an application gains control and/or after it dispatches an invocation to another system. Invocations are intercepted either in the communication, middleware, or application layers.

No changes to the application system are required in these solutions, which is their main advantage. The reference monitor is implemented externally to the application system. Security developers can control the behavior and size of the monitor. This makes it a good alternative to policy agents in controlling access to resources of already deployed applications. Moreover, if an existing application does not have any AC mechanism, proxies and interceptors become the only choice. Another advantage is the ability to make all the decisions locally to an application system, which improves performance scalability.

However, it is difficult to ensure the consistency of enforced policy and authorization data coherence because there are as many instances of access control proxies as applications. There are other significant limitations. First, the granularity of access control cannot be finer than (object) method and its arguments. Second,

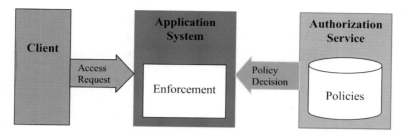

**Fig. 3.**   Authorization Services.

the decisions must always be made either before or after an application controls invocation execution. Third, variables, whose values become available at some point after the method is invoked but before an AC decision is made, cannot be used.

### 4.3. *Authorization servers*

When an application enforces its own access control policies, a reference monitor is embedded in the application. In this case, if an access control decision is performed by a dedicated authorization server external to the application system, the reference monitor spans the application and the authorization server. This allows decoupling of the reference monitor decision part from an application without losing the capability for an application to define its own space of protected resources and its semantics. This is the main idea behind solutions employing authorization services [63, 66, 67, 70].

The effort of developing a generalized framework for access control (GFAC) [2–5] at the MITRE Corporation is an early representative of this approach. The project endeavored to build a theoretical framework that explicitly recognizes the main information components for access control — subject and object (security-related) attributes, access context, authorities, and rules. They showed that "the rules for access control are an entity that is separate from, although necessarily related to, the model of the TCB (trusted computing base) interface" [40]. Moreover, La Padula suggests [40] that in a networking environment "one can conceive of an access control engine realized as a server, with access requests handled via a remote procedure čall mechanism".

The main advantages of this approach include:

- Logical centralization of access control rules, which supports inherent consistency and coherence of authorization policies enforced throughout a policy domain.
- Ease of policy change and update because authorizations are made at a (logically) single place.
- Since authorization logic is centralized and decoupled from the application logic, it is possible to change policy type without affecting application systems.

This approach can also significantly reduce the cost of access control administration. This is made possible by the centralized administration of authorization rules for all systems belonging to one policy domain.

Since an application system determines when to obtain an authorization decision from the server, it can do so right when such a decision is needed. The authorization service is to make authorization decisions for access to the application resources that cannot be protected by middleware AC mechanisms, as shown in Fig. 3. Authorization decisions on resources of any granularity level can be obtained from the server because an application uses the server while it is processing a request, as shown in Fig. 3. This lifts the limitation of the Proxies and Interceptors.

For this approach to be feasible, several issues must be addressed. First, it is much more challenging to design an authorization server so that it does not become a bottleneck in terms of performance. Second, if the server fails, all application systems served by it will have to resort to a simplistic and very limiting policy such as "always deny" or "always grant". This would render systems unoperational. Thus, the provision of high fault-tolerance degree needs to accompany such servers.

## 5. Application Access Control in Middleware

In this section, we review access control mechanisms provided by the mainstream middleware technologies, and discuss how these technologies can be used by distributed application systems, as well as what their limitations are.

### 5.1. *Java authentication and authorization service*

The release of Java 2 platform introduced a new security architecture [24] that uses a security policy to decide the granting of individual access permissions to running code. The Java Authentication and Authorization Service (JAAS) [38] is designed to provide a framework and standard API for authenticating and assigning privileges to users. Together with Java 2, an application can provide access control based on the attributes of code and its source (code-source-centric), or user (user-centric), or a combination of both. In JAAS, access control is enforced using proxies approach only on system resources, such as files, sockets, etc, whereas Java objects constituting an application system are not protected. Access control to these objects has to be implemented by application itself. Since JAAS specifies a flexible mechanism for defining application-specific protected resources of any granularity, an application can reuse these mechanisms for determining permissions granted to an invoking subject using JAAS decision logic as an authorization service. This would allow having a uniform interface to the authorization logic. JAAS also has a generic and extensible support for different authorization factors. Privilege attributes in JAAS need not be predefined.

New attributes can be easily defined via new classes, and this could introduce confusion because even semantically the same attributes are considered dissimilar by JAAS if they are implemented as different classes. A notion of attribute type, like in CORBA or SESAME, would address the problem.

JAAS supports authorization decisions based on the source code origination, the identity of the code signer, the value of a privilege attribute possessed by a subject. These are all used to determine permissions for a particular resource. An application system can retrieve permissions from Policy object and compare them with the required ones. In order for an application to enforce its own AC, it needs to determine the resource name and the required permissions. Afterwards, it would obtain from Policy permissions granted to the subject in question and make comparison for the final verdict. This is not much different from other middleware technologies such as CORBA, DCE, SESAME and DCOM. The flexibility comes from the way AC policies can be specified in JAAS. Since Policy is just an interface, behind which almost any functionality could be implemented, JAAS does not constrain implementers of AC policies to any particular mechanism.

## 5.2. *Distributed computing environment*

In the Open Software Foundation's (OSF) Distributed Computing Environment (DCE) [37], the service does not control access to applications or their resources. DCE applications are expected to enforce and provide administrative access to authorization policies on their own. To do so, an application has to implement AC functionality, including an access control list (ACL) manager and ACL storage, as shown in Fig. 4.

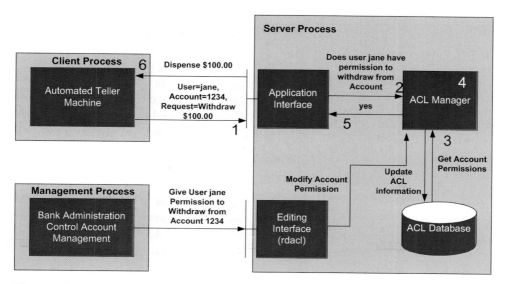

**Fig. 4.** Authorization process and ACL management in DCE-based application [17] systems (from [37]).

In order for an application to use DCE security service for AC, it needs (1) to determine the DCE object ID (OID) of the resource in question, and (2) to obtain authorization decision from its ACL manager using the OID.

If an application uses the DCE ACL model for authorization, it associates an ACL with a protected resource identified by the OIDs, which are used by the ACL manager to determine right ACLs. The exact definition of "resource" is entirely at the discretion of the application. For example, an object could be an item of stored data (such as a file), or could be a purely computational operation (such as matrix inversion). Thus, the concept of OIDs enables any granularity of protected resources.

DCE ACLs support a limited number of privilege attribute types — identities of the user, who is the resource owner, the owner group, and other group(s). DCE ACL language is also considerably limited allowing security administrators to either explicitly grant or deny rights to the subject based only on its identity or group attributes. The language capability to support policies specific to application or organization remains to be seen.

The following simple example from [17] illustrates (Fig. 4) how access control is expected to be implemented by an application system. User *jane* makes a request to withdraw $100.00 from her account number 1234. The application interface passes this information to the ACL manager asking for an authorization decision. The ACL manager retrieves the authorization policy for account 1234 from ACL database and applies the policy to derive the answer. If user *jane* is authorized, the withdrawal is performed. DCE security service does not provide transparent access control for application systems. If an application system needs to protect the resources it accesses, it has to implement access control functionality, including ACL manager and ACL storage shown in Fig. 4.

In terms of administration of ACL associated with application resources, the DCE applications are also expected to provide means for performing the task. They can implement DCE standard ACL administration interface (rdacl). When Jane's account is first set up, a bank employee would use an administrative tool to give user *jane* permission to withdraw money from account 1234. Rdacl interface seems to be the only means of ensuring the consistency of authorization policies across application boundaries unless access to the ACL database is implemented as a global service. In the latter case, policy and application changes could also be accommodated by the DCE environment easier than in the basic configuration shown in Fig. 4.

As seen from the discussion above, DCE security service provides rudimentary help to applications to make AC decisions, and it enforces no AC externally to an application. Compared to its predecessor, Kerberos [33, 49], it advances privilege attribute management by enabling attribute types other than subject identity. However, the expressiveness of DCE ACL language is fairly limited, and we could not determine how application-specific factors could be used in authorization decisions. It seems that the increase of the application client or server population would not drastically affect overall performance of the application systems in a DCE environment because AC decisions are made using local data. However, administration scalability is poor because policy changes have to be reflected in the ACL database for every application unless the database is centralized, in which case the performance scalability would suffer.

### 5.3. *Generic authorization and access control API*

Generic Authorization and Access Control API (GAA API) was published as an IETF Internet draft [59]. It defines a framework for application authorization. GAA API aims to address the lack of standard authorization API for applications using GSS API [41]. Kerberos [33, 49] was the first security technology providing GSS API functionality, and it did influence the model behind GSS API. It had only rudimentary authorization support for access control in networked applications. If a client does not have authenticated ticket for a particular network server, it will be denied access. This is why GAA API attempts to build an authorization model that would fit into the existing GSS API model.

It reuses security context from GSS API. Since the GSS API provided only subject identity, GAA API uses group membership service. GSS API provides very generic low-level abstraction. Its usage by application systems requires significant integration efforts. This prompted new generations of security technologies for distributed application systems such as CORBA and DCOM, in which an application can be developed without any notion of underlying security, including access control, unless it requires enforcement of complex security policies. However, if an application does use GSS API and it requires protection of fine grain resources or enforcement of complex access control policies, then GAA API gives more than most application systems would need for interfacing with an authorization service. However, the service, or at least its proxy, should be co-located in the same process because the only language binding, available as of May 2000, is defined in C language [58]. The main advantage of the API over the other models reviewed here is its support for very flexible and powerful concept of additional conditions that may need to be enforced by the application system or met by the client.

### 5.4. *Microsoft distributed component object model*

Since DCOM RPC is a derivation of DCE RPC, it is not surprising that its security model resembles DCE security. As with DCE, ACLs are used for coding authorization policies. In DCOM, they are named Discretionary ACLs to signify the default right of the owner to modify access control entries (ACE). However, this does not change the essence of the model. What it does, though, is the capability of enforcing policies outside of a DCOM object (proxies and interceptors approach) and a hierarchy of policies.

DCOM provides two choices for controlling access to applications and their resources. With "declarative security", DCOM can enforce AC without any cooperation on behalf of the object or the object's caller. The policies for an application can be externally configured and enforced. The declarative security policies can be divided into default policies and component-specific ones. A default policy specifies the default launch and access settings for all components running on the local machine that do not override these settings. Component security settings can be used to provide security for a specific component, thereby overriding the default security settings.

With "programmatic security", DCOM exposes its security infrastructure to a developer via security APIs[a] so that both clients and objects can enforce their own application-specific authorization policies of any granularity, and using any information as input for the decisions. Programmatic security can be used to override both default and component security settings in the registry.

Every invocation on a DCOM object is subject to control according to the policy hierarchy: (1) policy encoded in the component implementation, (2) the declarative process-specific policies, and (3) the declarative host-specific policies. Policies 2 and 3 are exercised before the call is dispatched to the object. This is a considerable advantage over DCE authorization model, where the security environment enforces no control and an application has to implement its own enforcement of the policies.

A significant hindrance of the authorization model is its granularity of "component-specific" policy (policy type 2). The granularity is per OS process, and there is no distinction among different object methods. That is, the policy uses the same discretionary access control list (DACL) to control access to all objects and their methods that a system process implements. Blakley [13] argues that OO security systems should let security administrators control access to individual methods of an object. Neither of DCOM process-wide or host-wide authorization policies supports such level of granularity.

Process-wide and host-wide policies (types 2 and 3) implicitly introduce the notion of access policy domains for DCOM objects. Unfortunately, the partitioning of objects is based only on their locations and not on their sensitivity or the value of other parameters. The limitation of authorization policy domains to the host boundaries restricts the administration scalability of DCOM-based distributed applications because it has to be performed individually on each host or even for each process.

As we have shown, no application-specific information can be used or application-specific policies are enforced when declarative AC is exercised. Declarative authorization policies and their changes have to be administered on a machine-by-machine basis, which hinders administration scalability and rules out automatic policy consistency across application boundaries unless applications are located on the same host.

---

[a]For example, calling subject identity can be obtained using methods `IObjectContext::IsCallerInRole()` and `ISecurityProperty:: GetCallerSID()`.

## 5.5. *SESAME security*

SESAME (a Secure European System for Applications in a Multi-vendor Environment) is a European project started in late 80's, and funded in part by the European Commission under its RACE program [34]. SESAME technology is not a middleware. Instead, it is an architecture for security services. It does not provide a means of communication such as ORB in CORBA, RPC layer in DCE or DCOM. Thus it cannot control pre/post invocation events. This is why access control and other security functionality has to be specifically invoked by an application system. This prevents SESAME from providing access control using proxies or interceptors approach. Instead, AC logic is provided, as an authorization service, to an application system by SESAME-compliant infrastructure, as opposed to DCE, where an application system has to implement ACL storage, as well as run-time and management functionality.

Another drawback of SESAME AC is the lack of capabilities, or at least there is no straightforward way, for applying one AC policy to several application systems. It means that AC policies have to be configured for applications individually.

The unit of AC check provided by SESAME is an application system. Therefore, either access is granted to the whole system or access is denied at all. For distributed application systems, which commonly expose their functionality via several operations with different AC requirements, such granularity is insufficient. Consequently an application system has to implement additional functionality to exercise peroperation AC. This makes SESAME less attractive then JAAS, DCE, DCOM or CORBA technologies discussed here from software engineering point of view. However, SESAME is neutral to the underlying communication protocols, and is known for its advanced model of privilege attributes management and propagation that is best suitable for large multi-domain heterogeneous environments [6]. This makes it suitable for building heterogeneous, multi-vendor distributed application systems that require authorization based on privilege attributes, other than user identity.

## 5.6. *CORBA security*

CORBA Security [50], like DCOM Security, strictly follows the direction of interceptors. Everything, including obtaining information necessary for making authorization decisions, is done before the method invocation is dispatched. The decisions are based on subject privilege attributes, required rights of the method, and the access control policy of the domains to which the object belongs. AC decisions can be specific for each object, if the object is located in a separate domain, or for a large group of objects associated with one policy domain. This means that the model scales very well without loosing fine granularity. Unlike DCOM, CORBA objects residing on different computers can be associated with the same domains.

The expressive power of CORBA access control mechanisms was analyzed by Karjoth [36], where it was shown to be capable of support lattice-based mandatory access control (MAC). Beznosov and Deng show [11] that it also possible to configure CORBA AC mechanisms to support role-based access control (RBAC0–RBAC3), which means that discretionary access control (DAC) models can be also implemented, as Sandhu and Munawer show in [62].

Because CORBA Security defines advanced concepts of privilege attributes, similar to SESAME, it enables AC policies based on roles, groups, clearance, and any other security-related attributes of subjects and their sessions, i.e., principals. User grouping via privilege attributes, object grouping via policy domains, and method grouping via the concept of required rights make CORBA Security highly scalable in terms of security administration, an important factor in object-oriented enterprise distributed environments.

Given the power and flexibility of CORBA Security AC mechanisms, there are still applications, in which additional access control needs to be exercised. If an application system is to enforce its own AC, it can do so with the help of CORBA Security interfaces. For enforcing conventional access control policies, an application system needs to know who wants to access what protected resource and in what way. CORBA Security interfaces, available to an application system, contain a method for obtaining subject security attributes, including privilege attributes. This information is sufficient for enforcing application-specific AC on application resources.

## 6. Summary and Discussion

There are two groups of technologies used for securing distributed software systems. One group merely provides party authentication, communication protection, and access control independently of the underlying communication technology, which includes Kerberos [33, 49], SESAME [34, 52] and GAA API [59]. This enables using and mixing any desired communication protocols and media, but developers are overburdened with significant efforts to integrate the security technology with the underlying communication mechanisms.

Another group is middleware technologies, such as CORBA [50], DCE [22], Java [38], and DCOM [46], which provide the underlying communication infrastructure along with the security subsystem. They enjoy reasonable integration of both and much more seamless use of the former by developers. Moreover, some of them enable basic access control completely outside of an application system because access decision and enforcement occur before the remote call is dispatched to the application server.

Access control in Java Authentication and Authorization Service (JAAS) is enforced only on system resources, such as files, sockets, etc, but not on Java objects and other application resources. JAAS has very generic and extensible support for different privilege attributes that can be easily defined via new classes. The source code base, the identity of the code signer, and the value of the subject privilege attribute are passed to the authorization code via `Policy` class interface for authorization decisions. JAAS allows any granularity of authorization decisions, and it does not constrain implementers of authorization policies to any particular mechanism or to the information used for the decisions. It also enables seamless change of policies. However, the architecture does not address the consistency of authorization policies across multiple applications. Nor does it have any provisions for achieving performance and administration scalability.

In the DCE, application systems are expected to enforce and provide administrative access to authorization policies themselves. An application system can use DCE access control list (ACL) but it has to implement most of the access control functionality, including ACL storage and manager, as well as its administration. DCE Security supplies an application with only the caller's subject and group identities. Cross-application administration of authorization logic is not directly supported although administrative interface for doing the administration on per-application basis is defined, yet it is not a scalable solution.

The security model of DCOM resembles DCE security. As with DCE, ACLs are used to code authorization policies. The main advance of DCOM is the capability of enforcing policies outside of objects with the presence of process and host-specific policies in addition to the capability for an application to use DCOM Security API for its own AC. The authorization model is hindered by the granularity of the so-called "component-specific" policy where there is no distinction among different objects and their methods in the same OS process. Component- and host-wide policies implicitly introduce the notion of access policy domains; still it is not clear if such domain partitioning is an administratively scalable and functionally successful solution. The administration has to be performed individually on each host or even for each process, which is better than the DCE solution but still limited. Although DCOM Security provides ways for application systems to exercise fine grain AC in an application-specific way, application-specific policies cannot be enforced and only security-related attributes of subjects and objects can serve as input for external AC.

SESAME is an architecture for security services which does not specify a communication layer. Thus it cannot control pre/post invocation events. This is why AC and other security functionality has to be specifically activated by an application. This prevents SESAME from providing AC externally to applications. Another drawback of SESAME authorization is the lack of support for applying one policy to several application systems located on separate hosts. The unit of authorization check is an application system. All these, especially the granularity of AC, make SESAME less attractive then JAAS, DCE, DCOM or CORBA technologies for providing access control to application resources. However, SESAME is neutral to the underlying communication protocols, and is known for its advanced model of privilege attributes management and propagation. This makes it indispensable for building heterogeneous, multi-technology and multi-organization distributed applications that require authorization based on privilege attributes, other than user identity, and the use of different communication technologies.

In CORBA Security, access control can be enforced completely outside of an application system. AC decisions are based on subject privilege attributes, required rights of the method, and the access control policies of the domains to which the object belongs. The AC model scales very well without losing fine granularity, for the decisions could be specific to each object or to a large group of objects associated with the same policy domain. Unlike DCOM, CORBA objects residing on different computers can be associated with the same policy domain. Because CORBA Security defines advanced concepts of privilege attributes, it enables AC policies based on roles, groups, clearance, and any other security-related attributes of subjects. User grouping via privilege attributes, object grouping via policy domains, and method grouping via the concept of required rights improve administration and performance scalability. If an application system is to enforce its own AC, it can do so with the help of CORBA Security API, which allows it to obtain subject security attributes, including privilege attributes. However, application-specific policies are difficult to enforce and the use of application-specific information in the CORBA AC is limited.

The Generic Authorization and Access Control API (GAA API) defines a framework for application authorization. The API aims to address the lack of standard authorization interfaces for those applications which use the generic security service (GSS) API. This is why GAA API's authorization model specifically fits into the existing GSS API. If an application uses GSS API, which provides very generic low-level abstraction, and it requires the protection of fine grain resources or the enforcement of complex authorization policies, GAA API defines interface with enough capabilities for most applications. The main advantage of the API over the other reviewed models is the support for the very flexible and powerful concept of additional conditions that can support application-specific policies. The drawbacks of the API are that it only defines the interface between an application and an authorization mechanism, and the model addresses neither administration scalability nor the consistency of authorization policies across multiple applications.

Ideally, all security functionality should be engineered outside of an application system, thereby allowing the application to be so called "security unaware". However, this is difficult to achieve for the majority of applications, where access control and other security policies are too complex, or require too fine-grain control, to be supported by the general-purpose middleware security technologies. This is an ongoing subject of research.

We expect that contemporary information enterprises with their dynamics and complexity to have application AC engineered at the middleware level as well as at the application level. For application-level access control, successful architectural solutions most probably will employ a combination of proxies and interceptors, policy agents, as well as authorization services because they complement each other. For systems with the existing AC mechanisms tightly integrated into applications, the approach of policy agents is the only choice. In those systems, where AC mechanisms are missing, weak, or too coarse grained, interceptors and proxies, combined with the ideas from policy agents and authorization services could cure the problem. New applications with requirements for fine-grain access control, complex or very dynamic AC policies, or to be deployed in organizations of different types (e.g. military, government, finance, healthcare, telecommunications) and sizes, will be best constructed with the use of authorization service.

# References

1. M. Abadi, M. Burrows, B. Lampson and G. Plotkin, "A calculus for access control in distributed systems", DEC, August 1991.
2. M. D. Abrams, A. B. Jeng and I. M. Olson, "Generalized framwork for access control: An informal description", The MITRE Corporation, Springfield, VA, USA MTR-89W00230, September 1989.
3. M. D. Abrams, K. W. Eggers, L. J. LaPadula and I. W. Olson, "A generalized framework for access control: An informal description", The MITRE Corporation, McLean, Virginia, USA MP-90W00043, August 1990.
4. M. D. Abrams, L. J. LaPadula and I. M. Olson, "Building generalized access control on UNIX", *Proceedings of UNIX Security II: USENIX Workshop Proceedings*, Portland, Oregon, USA (1990) 65–70.
5. M. Abrams, J. Heaney, O. King, L. J. LaPadula, M. Lazear and I. Olson, "A generalized framework for access control: Towards prototyping the orgcon policy", *Proceedings of National Computer Security Conference* (1991) 257–266.
6. P. Ashley, "Authorization for a large heterogeneous multi-domain system", *Proceedings of Australian Unix and Open Systems Gorup National Conference*, 1997.
7. J. Barkley, "Implementing role-based access control using object technology", *Proceedings of the First ACM Workshop on Role-Based Access Control*, Fairfax, Virginia, USA (1995) 93–98.
8. J. Barkley, K. Beznosov and J. Uppal, "Supporting relationships in access control using role based access control", *Proceedings of ACM Role-based Access Control Workshop*, Fairfax, Virginia, USA (1999) 55–65.
9. M. Benantar, R. Guski and K. M. Troidle, "Access control systems: From host-centric to network-centric computing", *IBM Systems Journal* **35**, no. 1 (1996) 94–112.
10. E. Bertino, C. Bettini, E. Ferrari and P. Samarati, "Supporting periodic authorizations and temporal reasoning in database access control", *Proceedings of 22th International Conference on Very Large Data Bases*, Mumbai (Bombay), India (1996) 472–483.
11. K. Beznosov and Y. Deng, "A framework for implementing role-based access control using CORBA security service", *Proceedings of Fourth ACM Workshop on Role-Based Access Control*, Fairfax, Virginia, USA (1999) 19–30.
12. K. Beznosov, Y. Deng, B. Blakley, C. Burt and J. Barkley, "A resource access decision service for CORBA-based distributed systems", *Proceedings of Annual Computer Security Applications Conference*, Phoenix, Arizona, USA (1999) 310–319.
13. B. Blakley, *CORBA Security: An Introduction to Safe Computing with Objects* (First edition, Addison-Wesley, Reading, 1999).
14. J. Bloomer, *Power Programming with RPC* (O'Reilly & Associates, Sebastopol, CA, 1992).
15. CA, "CA-ACF2 for OS/390", Computer Associates, 1998.
16. CA, "CA-top secret for OS/390", Computer Associates International, 1998.

17. D. L. Caswell, "An evolution of DCE authorization services", *Hewlett-Packard Journal: Technical Information from the Laboratories of Hewlett-Packard Company* **46**, no. 6 (1995) 49–54.

18. D. A. Curry, *UNIX System Security: A Guide for Users and System Administrators* (Addison-Wesley, 1992).

19. DEC, "Guide to VAX/VMS system security — Version 5.2", Digital Equipment Corporation, 1989.

20. R. Filman and T. Linden, "SafeBots: A paradigm for software security controls", *Proceedings of New Security Paradigms Workshop*, Lake Arrowhead, CA, USA (1996) 45–51.

21. R. Filman and T. Linden, "Communicating security agents", *Proceedings of the Fifth Workshop on Enabling Technologies: Infrastructure for Collaborative Enterprises*, Stanford, CA, USA (1996) 86–91.

22. F. Gittler and A. C. Hopkins, "The DCE security service", *Hewlett-Packard Journal* **46**, no. 6 (1995) 41–48.

23. V. Gligor, C. Burch, R. Chandersekaran, L. Chanpman, M. Hecht, W. Jiang, G. Luckenbaugh and N. Vasudevan, "On the design and the implementation of secure Xenix workstations", *Proceedings of IEEE Symposium on Security and Privacy*, Oakland, CA (1986) 102–117.

24. L. Gong, M. Mueller, H. Prafullchandra and R. Schemers, "Going beyond the sandbox: An overview of the new security architecture in the Java development kit 1.2", *Proceedings of the USENIX Symposium on Internet Technologies and Systems*, Monterey, CA (1997) 103–112.

25. F. T. Grampp and R. H. Morris, "UNIX operating system security", *AT & Bell Laboratories Technical Journal* **63**, no. 8 (1984) 1649–1672.

26. A. S. Grimshaw, M. J. Lewis, A. J. Ferrari and J. F. Karpovich, "Architectural support for extensibility and autonomy in wide-area distributed object systems", Department of Computer Science, University of Virginia CS-98-12, 1998.

27. A. S. Grimshaw and W. A. Wulf, "The legion vision of a worldwide virtual computer", *Communications of the ACM* **40**, no. 1 (1997) 39–45.

28. B. Hailpern and H. Ossher, "Extending objects to support multiple interfaces and access control", *IEEE Transactions on Software Engineering* **16**, no. 11 (1990) 1247–1257.

29. J. Hale, P. Galiasso, M. Papa and S. Shenoi, "Security policy coordination for heterogeneous information systems", *Proceedings of Annual Computer Security Applications Conference*, Phoenix, Arizona, USA (1999) 219–228.

30. A. Heydon and J. D. Tygar, "Specifying and checking UNIX security constraints", *Computing Systems* **7**, no. 1 (1994) 9–12.

31. R. Hommes, "VMS security architecture", *Proceedings of DECUS Europe Symposium*, Cannes, France, 1990.

32. IBM, *Resource Access Control Facility (RACF). General Information* (IBM Red Books, 1976).

33. IETF, "RFC 1510, The Kerberos Network Authentication Service, V5", 1993.

34. P. Kaijser, "A review of the SESAME development", *Lecture Notes in Computer Science* **1438** (1998) 1–8.

35. P. A. Karger, M. E. Zurko, D. W. Bonin, A. H. Mason and C. E. Kahn, "A retrospective on the VAX VMM security kernel", *IEEE Transactions on Software Engineering* **17**, no. 11 (1991) 1147–1165.

36. G. Karjoth, "Authorization in CORBA security", *Proceedings of Fifth European Symposium on Research in Computer Security (ESORICS)* (1998) 143–158.

37. M. M. Kong, "DCE: An environment for secure client/server computing," *Hewlett-Packard Journal* **46**, no. 6 (1995) 6–15.
38. C. Lai, L. Gong, L. Koved, A. Nadalin and R. Schemers, "User authentication and authorization in the Java platform", *Proceedings of Annual Computer Security Applications Conference*, Phoenix, Arizona, USA (1999) 285–290.
39. B. Lampson, M. Abadi, M. Burrows and E. Wobber, "Authentication in distributed systems: Theory and practices", *Proceedings of ACM Symposium on Operating Systems Principles*, Asilomar Conference Center, Pacific Grove, California (1991) 165–182.
40. L. J. LaPadula, "Formal modeling in a generalized framework for access control", *Proceedings of Computer Security Foundation Workshop III* (1990) 100–109.
41. J. Linn, "Generic security service application program interface", Internet Engineering Task Force, Internet Draft RFC 1508, September 1993.
42. G. L. Luckenbaugh, V. D. Gligor, L. J. Dotterer and C. S. Chandersekaran, "Interpretation of the Bell-LaPadula Model in secure Xenix", *Proceedings of DoD-NBS Conference on Computer Security*, 1986.
43. V. Matena and M. Hapner, "Enterprise JavaBeans", *Specification*, Sun Microsystems Inc., Palo Alto, CA., March 21, 1998.
44. E. J. McCauley and P. J. Drongowski, "KSOS — The design of a secure operating system", *Proceedings of National Computer Conference*, 1979.
45. M. J. McInerney, *Windows NT Security* (Prentice Hall, 1999).
46. Microsoft, "DCOM Architecture", Microsoft, 1998.
47. R. Monson-Haefel, *Enterprise JavaBeans* (O'Reilly and Associates, 1999).
48. S. J. Mullender, G. V. Rossum, A. S. Tanenbaum, R. V. Renesse and H. V. Staveren, "Amoeba: A distributed operating system for the 1990s", *Computer* **23**, no. 5 (1990) 44–53.
49. B. C. Neuman and T. Y. Ts'o, "Kerberos: An authentication service for computer networks", University of Southern California, Information Sciences Institute ISI/RS-94-399, 1994.
50. OMG, "Security service specification", *CORBAservices: Common Object Services Specification*, Object Management Group, 1996.
51. OSF, "Authentication and security services", Open Software Foundation, 1996.
52. T. Parker and D. Pinkas, "SESAME V4 — overview", SESAME, December 1995.
53. C. P. Pfleeger, *Security in Computing* (Prentice-Hall, 1989).
54. J. S. Quarterman, A. Silberschatz and J. L. Peterson, "4.2BSD and 4.3BSD as examples of the UNIX system", *ACM Computing Surveys* **17**, no. 4 (1985) 379–418.
55. T. Riechmann and F. J. Hauck, "Meta objects for access control: Extending capability-based security", *Proceedings of New Security Paradigms Workshop*, Langdale, Cumbria, UK (1997) 17–22.
56. T. Riechmann and F. J. Hauck, "Meta objects for access control: A formal model for role-based principals", *Proceedings of New Security Paradigms Workshop*, Charlottesville, VA, USA (1998) 30–38.
57. W. Rubin and M. Brain, *Understanding DCOM* (P T R Prentice Hall, 1999).
58. T. Ryutov and C. Neuman, "Access control framework for distributed applications (Work in progress)", Internet Engineering Task Force, Internet Draft draft-ietf-cat-acc-cntrl-frmw-03, March 9, 2000.
59. T. Ryutov and C. Neuman, "Generic authorization and access control application program interface: C-bindings", Internet Engineering Task Force, Internet Draft draft-ietf-cat-gaa-bind-03, March 9, 2000.

60. J. H. Saltzer, "Protection and the control of information sharing in multics", *Communications of the ACM* **17**, no. 7 (1974) 388–402.

61. R. Sandhu and P. Samarati, "Access control: Principles and practice", *IEEE Communications Magazine* **32**, no. 9 (1994) 40–48.

62. R. Sandhu and Q. Munawer, "How to do discretionary access control using roles", *Proceedings of ACM Workshop on Role-based Access Control*, Fairfax, Virginia, USA (1998) 47–54.

63. V. Varadharajan and C. C. A. J. Pato, "Authorization in enterprise-wide distributed system: A practical design and application", *Proceedings of 14th Annual Computer Security Applications Conference*, 1998.

64. B. J. Walker, R. A. Kemmerer and G. J. Popek, "Specification and verification of the UCLA unix security kernel", *Communications of the ACM* **23**, no. 2 (1980) 118.

65. W. Wilson and K. Beznosov, "CORBAmed security white paper", Object Management Group corbamed/97-11-03, November 1997.

66. T. Y. C. Woo and S. S. Lam, "Designing a distributed authorization service", University of Texas at Austin, Computer Sciences Department TR93-29, September 1993.

67. T. Y. C. Woo and S. S. Lam, "Designing a distributed authorization service", *Proceedings of IEEE INFOCOM*, San Francisco, 1998.

68. W. A. Wulf, C. Wang and D. Kienzle, "A new model of security for distributed systems", *Proceedings of New Security Paradigms Workshop*, Lake Arrowhead, CA, USA (1996) 34–43.

69. J. W. Yoder and J. Barcalow, "Architectural patterns for enabling application security", *Proceedings of Pattern Languages of Programming*, Monticello, Illinois, USA, 1997.

70. M. E. Zurko, R. Simon and T. Sanfilippo, "A user-centered, modular authorization service built on an RBAC foundation", *Proceedings of Annual Computer Security Applications Conference*, Phoenix, Arizona, 1998.

# SOFTWARE MAINTENANCE

GERARDO CANFORA* and ANIELLO CIMITILE[†]

*University of Sannio, Faculty of Engineering at Benevento,
Palazzo Bosco Lucarelli, Piazza Roma 82100, Benevento, Italy
Tel.: ++39 0824 305804; Fax.: ++39 0824 21866
* E-mail: gerardo.canfora@unisannio.it
[†] E-mail: cimitile@unisannio.it*

Software maintenance is widely recognised as a dominant factor for the high costs of large software systems. Whilst figures vary, a general agreement exists that 60% to 80% of a system's budget is spent on software maintenance.

Software maintenance is a very broad activity often defined as including all work made on a software system after it becomes operational. This covers the correction of errors, the enhancement, deletion and addition of capabilities, the adaptation to changes in data requirements and operation environments, the improvement of performance, usability, or any other quality attribute.

This article is an overview of software maintance, its relevance, the problems, and the available solutions. The focus is on the structure of the maintenance activity, including general models of the maintenance process, existing standards, and management practices and tools. The article also includes a discussion of related areas that support software maintenance, and particularly reverse engineering, reengineering, and legacy systems.

*Keywords*: Software maintenance, reverse engineering, reengineering, program comprehension, legacy systems.

## 1. Introduction

The term maintenance, when accompanied to software, assumes a meaning profoundly different from the meaning it assumes in any other engineering discipline. In fact, many engineering disciplines intend maintenance as the process of keeping something in working order, in repair. The key concept is the deterioration of an engineering artifact due to the use and the passing of time; the aim of maintenance is therefore to keep the artifact's functionality in line with that defined and registered at the time of release.

Of course, this view of maintenance does not apply to software, as software does not deteriorate with the use and the passing of time. Nevertheless, the need for modifying a piece of software after delivery has been with us since the very beginning of electronic computing. The Lehman's laws of evolution [50, 51] state that successful software systems are condemned to change over time. A predominant proportion of changes is to meet ever-changing user needs. This is captured by the first law of Lehman [50, 51]: "A program that is used in a real world environment necessarily must change or become progressively less useful in that environment".

Significant changes also derive from the need to adapt software to interact with external entities, including people, organizations, and artificial systems. In fact, software is infinitely malleable and, therefore, it is often perceived as the easiest part to change in a system [21].

This article overviews software maintenance, its relevance, the problems, and the available solutions; the underlying objective is to present software maintenance not as a problem, but in terms of solutions.

The remainder of the article is organized as follows. Section 2 defines software maintenance and Sec. 3 categorizes it. Costs and challenges of software maintenance are analyzed in Sec. 4. Sections 5–7 are devoted to the structure of the maintenance activity. In particular, Sec. 5 introduces general models of the maintenance process, while Sec. 6 discusses existing standards. Management of software maintenance is discussed in Sec. 7. Sections 8 and 9 deal with two related areas that support software maintenance, namely reverse engineering and reengineering. Section 10 is devoted to legacy systems, an issue that assumed an ever increasing economic relevance in the last decade. Concluding remarks and areas for further investigation are given in Sec. 11, while Sec. 12 provides resources for further reading.

## 2. Definitions

Software maintenance is a very broad activity often defined as including all work made on a software system after it becomes operational [56]. This covers the correction of errors, the enhancement, deletion and addition of capabilities, the adaptation to changes in data requirements and operation environments, the improvement of performance, usability, or any other quality attribute. The IEEE definition is as follows [40]:

> *"Software maintenance is the process of modifying a software system or component after delivery to correct faults, improve performances or other attributes, or adapt to a changed environment".*

This definition reflects the common view that software maintenance is a post-delivery activity: it starts when a system is released to the customer or user and encompasses all activities that keep the system operational and meet the user's needs. This view is well summarized by the classical waterfall models of the software life cycle, which generally comprise a final phase of operation and maintenance, as shown in Fig. 1.

Several authors disagree with this view and affirm that software maintenance should start well before a system becomes operational. Schneidewind [67] states that the myopic view that maintenance is strictly a post-delivery activity is one of the reasons that make maintenance hard. Osborne and Chikofsky [59] affirm that it is essential to adopt a life cycle approach to managing and changing software systems, one which looks at all aspects of the development process with an eye toward maintenance. Pigoski [62] captures the needs to begin maintenance when

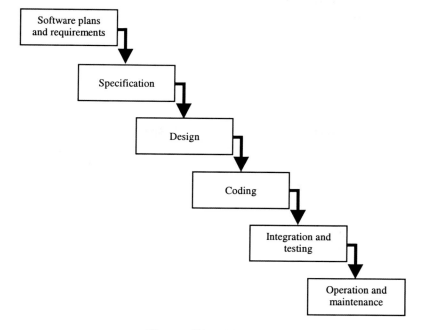

**Fig. 1.** Waterfall model.

development begins in a new definition:

> *"Software maintenance is the totality of activities required to provide cost-effective support to a software system. Activities are performed during the pre-delivery stage as well as the post-delivery stage. Pre-delivery activities include planning for post-delivery operations, supportability, and logistics determination. Post-delivery activities include software modification, training, and operating a help desk".*

This definition is consistent with the approach to software maintenance taken by ISO in its standard on software life cycle processes [44]. It definitively dispels the image that software maintenance is all about fixing bugs or mistakes.

## 3. Categories of Software Maintenance

Across the 70's and the 80's, several authors have studied the maintenance phenomenon with the aim of identifying the reasons that originate the needs for changes and their relative frequencies and costs. As a result of these studies, several classifications of maintenance activities have been defined; these classifications help to better understand the great significance of maintenance and its implications on the cost and the quality of the systems in use. Dividing the maintenance effort into categories has first made evident that software maintenance is more than correcting errors.

Lientz and Swanson [54] divide maintenance into three components: *corrective*, *adaptive*, and *perfective* maintenance. Corrective maintenance includes all the changes made to remove actual faults in the software. Adaptive maintenance encompasses the changes needed as a consequence of some mutation in the environment in which the system must operate, for instance, altering a system to make it running on a new hardware platform, operating system, DBMS, TP monitor, or network. Finally, perfective maintenance refers to changes that originate from user requests; examples include inserting, deleting, extending, and modifying functions, rewriting documentation, improving performances, or improving ease of use. Pigoski [62] suggests joining the adaptive and perfective categories and calling them *enhancements*, as these types of changes are not corrective in nature: they are improvements. As a matter of fact, some organizations use the term software maintenance to refer to the implementation of small changes, whereas software development is used to refer to all other modifications.

Ideally, maintenance operations should not degrade the reliability and the structure of the subject system, neither should they degrade its maintainability,[a] otherwise future changes will be progressively more difficult and costly to implement. Unfortunately, this is not the case for real-world maintenance, which often induces a phenomenon of aging of the subject system [60]; this is expressed by the second law of Lehman [50, 51]: "As an evolving program changes, its structure tends to become more complex. Extra resources must be devoted to preserving the semantics and simplifying the structure". Accordingly, several authors consider a fourth category of maintenance, named *preventive* maintenance, which includes all the modifications made to a piece of software to make it more maintainable [63].

ISO [43] introduces three categories of software maintenance: *problem resolution*, which involves the detection, analysis, and correction of software nonconformities causing operational problems; *interface modifications*, required when additions or changes are made to the hardware system controlled by the software; *functional expansion or performance improvement*, which may be required by the purchaser in the maintenance stage. A recommendation is that all changes should be made in accordance with the same procedures, as far as possible, used for the development of software. However, when resolving problems, it is possible to use temporary fixes to minimize downtime, and implement permanent changes later.

IEEE [41] redefines the Lientz and Swanson [54] categories of *corrective*, *adaptive*, and *perfective* maintenance, and adds *emergency maintenance* as a fourth category. The IEEE definitions are as follows [41]:

---

[a]The IEEE definition of maintainability reflects the definition of maintenance: the ease with which a software system or component can be modified to correct faults, improve performance or other attributes, or adapt to a changed environment [40]. ISO assumes maintainability as one of the six primary characteristics of its definition of software quality and suggests that it depends on four sub-characteristics: analyzability, changeability, stability, testability [42]; the new version of the standard, currently under development, adds compliance as a fifth sub-characteristic.

|  | Unscheduled | Scheduled |
|---|---|---|
| Reactive | Emergency | Corrective<br>Adaptive |
| Proactive |  | Perfective |

**Fig. 2.** IEEE categories of software maintenance.

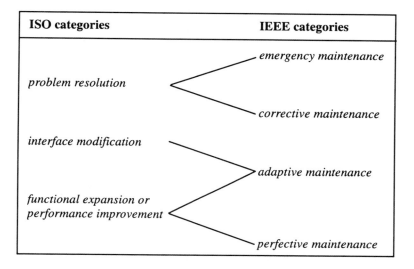

**Fig. 3.** Correspondences between ISO and IEEE maintenance categories.

"*Corrective maintenance*: *reactive modification of a software product performed after delivery to correct discovered faults.*
*Adaptive maintenance*: *modification of a software product performed after delivery to keep a computer program usable in a changed or changing environment.*
*Perfective maintenance*: *modification of a software product performed after delivery to improve performance or maintainability.*
*Emergency maintenance*: *unscheduled corrective maintenance performed to keep a system operational*".

These definitions introduce the idea that software maintenance can be either scheduled or unscheduled and reactive or proactive, as shown in Fig. 2. Figure 3 depicts the correspondences that exist between ISO and IEEE categories.

## 4. Costs and Challenges

However one decides to categorize the maintenance effort, it is still clear that software maintenance accounts for a huge amount of the overall software budget for an information system organization. Since 1972 [28], software maintenance was characterized as an "iceberg" to highlight the enormous mass of potential problems and costs that lie under the surface. Although figures vary, several surveys [1, 2, 7, 10, 34, 46, 54, 56, 58] indicate that software maintenance consumes 60% to 80% of the total life cycle costs; these surveys also report that maintenance costs are largely due to enhancements (often 75–80%), rather than corrections.

Several technical and managerial problems contribute to the costs of software maintenance. Among the most challenging problems of software maintenance are: *program comprehension*, *impact analysis*, and *regression testing*.

Whenever a change is made to a piece of software, it is important that the maintainer gains a complete understanding of the structure, behavior and functionality of the system being modified. It is on the basis of this understanding that modification proposals to accomplish the maintenance objectives can be generated. As a consequence, maintainers spend a large amount of their time reading the code and the accompanying documentation to comprehend its logic, purpose, and structure. Available estimates indicate that the percentage of maintenance time consumed on program comprehension ranges from 50% up to 90% [32, 55, 73]. Program comprehension is frequently compounded because the maintainer is rarely the author of the code (or a significant period of time has elapsed between development and maintenance) and a complete, up-to-date documentation is even more rarely available [26].

One of the major challenges in software maintenance is to determine the effects of a proposed modification on the rest of the system. Impact analysis [6, 64, 35, 81] is the activity of assessing the potential effects of a change with the aim of minimizing unexpected side effects. The task involves assessing the appropriateness of a proposed modification and evaluating the risks associated with its implementation, including estimates of the effects on resources, effort and scheduling. It also involves the identification of the system's parts that need to be modified as a consequence of the proposed modification. Of note is that although impact analysis plays a central role within the maintenance process, there is no agreement about its definition and the IEEE Glossary of Software Engineering Terminology [40] does not give a definition of impact analysis.

Once a change has been implemented, the software system has to be retested to gain confidence that it will perform according to the (possibly modified) specification. The process of testing a system after it has been modified is called regression testing [52]. The aim of regression testing is twofold: to establish confidence that changes are correct and to ensure that unchanged portions of the system have not been affected. Regression testing differs from the testing performed during development because a set of test cases may be available for reuse. Indeed, changes made during a maintenance process are usually small (major rewriting are a rather rare event in the history of a system) and, therefore, the simple approach of executing all test cases after each change may be excessively costly. Alternatively, several strategies for selective regression testing are available that attempt to select a subset of the available test cases without affecting test effectiveness [39, 66].

Most problems that are associated with software maintenance can be traced to deficiencies of the software development process. Sneidewind [67] affirms that "the main problem in doing maintenance is that we cannot do maintenance on a system which was not designed for maintenance". However, there are also essential difficulties, i.e., intrinsic characteristics of software and its production process, that contribute to make software maintenance an unequalled challenge. Brooks [21] identifies complexity, conformity, changeability, and invisibility as four essential difficulties of software and Rajlich [65] adds discontinuity to this list.

## 5. Models

A typical approach to software maintenance is to work on code first, and then making the necessary changes to the accompanying documentation, if any. This approach is captured by the quick-fix model, shown in Fig. 4, which demonstrates the flow of changes from the old to the new version of the system [8]. Ideally, after the code has been changed, the requirement, design, testing and any other form of available documents impacted by the modification should be updated. However, due to its perceived malleability, users expect software to be modified quickly and cost-effectively. Changes are often made on the fly, without proper planning, design, impact analysis, and regression testing. Documents may or may not be updated as the code is modified; time and budget pressure often entails that changes made to a program are not documented and this quickly degrades documentation. In addition, repeated changes may demolish the original design, thus making future modifications progressively more expensive to carry out.

Evolutionary life cycle models suggest an alternative approach to software maintenance. These models share the idea that the requirements of a system cannot be gathered and fully understood initially. Accordingly, systems are to be developed in builds each of which completes, corrects, and refines the requirements of

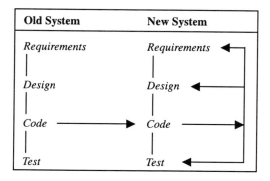

**Fig. 4.** The quick-fix model [8].

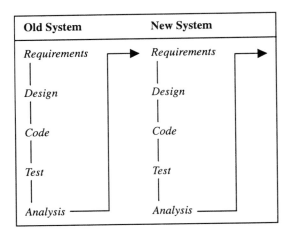

**Fig. 5.**  The iterative-enhancement model [8].

the previous builds based on the feedback of users [36]. An example is iterative enhancement [8], which suggests structuring a problem to ease the design and implementation of successively larger/refined solutions. Iterative enhancement explains maintenance too, as shown in Fig. 5. The construction of a new build (that is, maintenance) begins with the analysis of the existing system's requirements, design, code and test documentation and continues with the modification of the highest-level document affected by changes, propagating the changes down to the full set of documents. In short, at each step of the evolutionary process the system is redesigned based on an analysis of the existing system.

A key advantage of the iterative-enhancement model is that documentation is kept updated as the code changes. Visaggio [76] reports data from replicated controlled-experiments conducted to compare the quick-fix and the iterative-enhancement models and shows that the maintainability of a system degrades faster with the quick-fix model. The experiments also indicate that organizations adopting the iterative-enhancement model make maintenance changes faster than those applying the quick-fix model; the latter finding is counter-intuitive, as the most common reason for adopting the quick-fix model is time pressure.

Basili [8] suggests a model, the full-reuse model shown in Fig. 6, that views maintenance as a particular case of reuse-oriented software development. Full-reuse begins with the requirement analysis and design of a new system and reuses the appropriate requirements, design, code, and tests from earlier versions of the existing system. This is a major difference with the iterative enhancement, which starts with the analysis of the existing system. Central to the full-reuse model is the idea of a repository of documents and components defining earlier versions of the current system and other systems in the same application domain. This makes reuse explicit and documented. It also promotes the development of more reusable components.

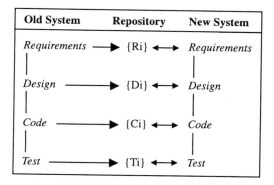

**Fig. 6.** The full-reuse model [8].

The iterative-enhancement model is well suited for systems that have a long life and evolve over time; it supports the evolution of the system in such a way to ease future modifications. On the contrary, the full-reuse model is more suited for the development of lines of related products. It tends to be more costly on the short run, whereas the advantages may be sensible in the long run; organizations that apply the full-reuse model accumulate reusable components of all kinds and at many different levels of abstractions and this makes future developments more cost effective.

## 6. Processes

Several authors have proposed process models for software maintenance. These models organize maintenance into a sequence of related activities, or phases, and define the order in which these phases are to be executed. Sometimes, they also suggest the deliverables that each phase must provide the following phases. An example of such a process is shown in Fig. 7 [82]. Although different authors identify different phases, they agree that there is a core set of activity that are indispensable for successful maintenance, namely the comprehension of the existing system, the assessment of the impact of a proposed change, and the regression testing.

IEEE and ISO have both addressed software maintenance, the first with a specific standard [41] and the latter as a part of its standard on life cycle processes [44]. The next two sections describe the maintenance processes defined by these two documents.

### 6.1. *IEEE*-1219

The IEEE standard organizes the maintenance process in seven phases, as demonstrated in Fig. 8. In addition to identifying the phases and their order of execution, for each phase the standard indicates input and output deliverables, the activities grouped, related and supporting processes, the control, and a set of metrics.

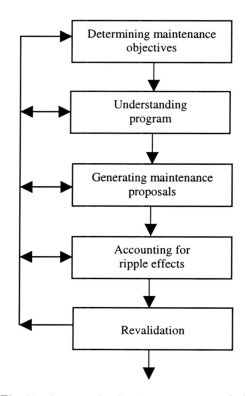

**Fig. 7.**   An example of maintenance process [82].

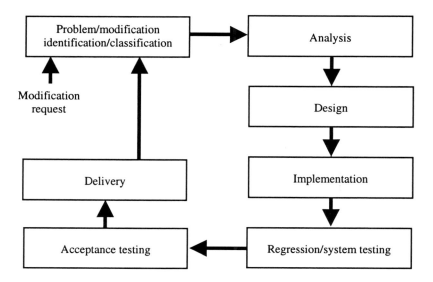

**Fig. 8.**   The IEEE maintenance process.

### Problem/modification identification, classification, and prioritization

This is the phase in which the request for change (MR — modification request) issued by a user, a customer, a programmer, or a manager is assigned a maintenance category (see Sec. 3 for maintenance categories definitions), a priority and a unique identifier. The phase also includes activities to determine whether to accept or reject the request and to assign it to a batch of modifications scheduled for implementation.

### Analysis

This phase devises a preliminary plan for design, implementation, test, and delivery. Analysis is conducted at two levels: feasibility analysis and detailed analysis. Feasibility analysis identifies alternative solutions and assess their impacts and costs, whereas detailed analysis defines the requirements for the modification, devises a test strategy, and develop an implementation plan.

### Design

The modification to the system is actually designed in this phase. This entails using all current system and project documentation, existing software and databases, and the output of the analysis phase. Activities include the identification of affected software modules, the modification of software module documentation, the creation of test cases for the new design, and the identification of regression tests.

### Implementation

This phase includes the activities of coding and unit testing, integration of the modified code, integration and regression testing, risk analysis, and review. The phase also includes a test-readiness review to assess preparedness fort system and regression testing.

### Regression/system testing

This is the phase in which the entire system is tested to ensure compliance to the original requirements plus the modifications. In addition to functional and interface testing, the phase includes regression testing to validate that no new faults have been added. Finally, this phase is responsible for verifying preparedness for acceptance testing.

### Acceptance testing

This level of testing is concerned with the fully integrated system and involves users, customers, or a third party designated by the customer. Acceptance testing comprises functional tests, interoperability tests, and regression tests.

## Delivery

This is the phase in which the modified systems is released for installation and operation. It includes the activity of notifying the user community, performing installation and training, and preparing and archival version for backup.

### 6.2. *ISO*-12207

While the standard IEEE-1219 [41] is specifically concerned with software maintenance, the standard ISO-12207 [44] deals with the totality of the processes comprised in the software life cycle. The standard identifies seventeen processes grouped into three broad classes: primary, supporting, and organizational processes. Processes are divided into constituent activities each of which is further organized in tasks. Figure 9 shows the processes and their distribution into classes. Maintenance is one of the five primary processes, i.e. one of the processes that provide for conducting major functions during the life cycle and initiate and exploit support and organizational processes. Figure 10 shows the activities of the maintenance processes; the positions do not indicate any-time dependent relationships.

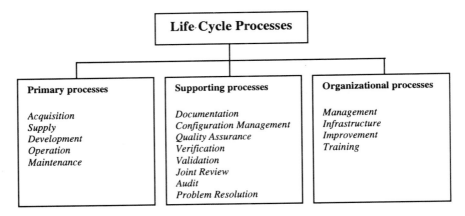

**Fig. 9.**   The ISO life cycle processes.

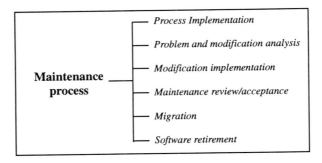

**Fig. 10.**   The ISO maintenance process.

## Process implementation

This activity includes the tasks for developing plans and procedures for software maintenance, creating procedures for receiving, recording, and tracking maintenance requests, and establishing an organizational interface with the configuration management process. Process implementation begins early in the system life cycle; Pigoski [62] affirms that maintenance plans should be prepared in parallel with the development plans. The activity entails the definition of the scope of maintenance and the identification and analysis of alternatives, including offloading to a third party; it also comprises organizing and staffing the maintenance team and assigning responsibilities and resources.

## Problem and modification analysis

The first task of this activity is concerned with the analysis of the maintenance request, either a problem report or a modification request, to classify it, to determine its scope in term of size, costs, and time required, and to assess its criticality. It is recommended that the maintenance organization replicates the problem or verifies the request. The other tasks regard the development and the documentation of alternatives for change implementation and the approval of the selected option as specified in the contract.

## Modification implementation

This activity entails the identification of the items that need to be modified and the invocation of the development process to actually implement the changes. Additional requirements of the development process are concerned with testing procedures to ensure that the new/modified requirements are completely and correctly implemented and the original unmodified requirements are not affected.

## Maintenance review/acceptance

The tasks of this activity are devoted to assessing the integrity of the modified system and end when the maintenance organization obtain the approval for the satisfactory completion of the maintenance request. Several supporting processes may be invoked, including the quality assurance process, the verification process, the validation process, and the joint review process.

## Migration

This activity happens when software systems are moved from one environment to another. It is required that migration plans be developed and the users/customers of the system be given visibility of them, the reasons why the old environment is no longer supported, and a description of the new environment and its date of availability. Other tasks are concerned with the parallel operations of the new and

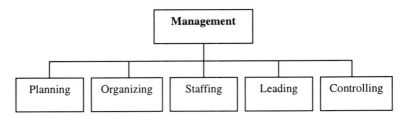

**Fig. 11.**    The functions of project management.

old environment and the post-operation review to assess the impact of moving to the new environment.

### Software retirement

The last maintenance activity consists of retiring a software system and requires the development of a retirement plan and its notification to users.

### 7. Maintenance Management

Management is "the process of designing and maintaining an environment in which individuals, working together in groups, accomplish efficiently selected aims" [79]. In the case of maintenance the key aim is to provide cost-effective support to a software system during its entire lifespan. Management is concerned with quality and productivity, that imply effectiveness and efficiency. Many authors [48, 79, 74] agree that management consists of five separate functions, as shown in Fig. 11. The functions are: planning, organizing, staffing, leading (sometimes also called directing), and controlling.

**Planning** consists of selecting missions and objectives and predetermining a course of actions for accomplishing them. Commitment of human and material resources and scheduling of actions are among the most critical activities in this function.

**Organizing** is the management function that establishes an intentional structure of roles for people to fill in an organization. This entails arranging the relationships among roles and granting the responsibilities and needed authority.

**Staffing** involves filling the positions in the organization by selecting and training people. Two key activities of this function are evaluating and appraising project personnel and providing for general development, i.e. improvement of knowledge, attitudes, and skills.

**Leading** is creating a working environment and an atmosphere that will assist and motivate people so that they will contribute to the achievement of organization and group goals.

1. Introduction
*Describes the purpose, goals, and scope of the software maintenance effort; determines deviations from the standard.*

2. References
*Identifies the documents that pose constraints on the maintenance effort and any other supporting documents.*

3. Definitions
*Defines or references all terms required to understand the plan.*

4. Software Maintenance Overview
*Describes organization, scheduling priorities, resources, responsibilities, tools, techniques, and methods used in the maintenance process.*

    4.1 Organization
    4.2 Scheduling Priorities
    4.3 Resource Summary
    4.4 Responsibilities
    4.5 Tools, Techniques, and Methods

5. Software Maintenance Process
*Identifies the actions to perform for each phase of the maintenance process; actions are to be defined in terms of input, output, process, and control.*

    5.1 Problem/modification identification/classification and prioritization
    5.2 Analysis
    5.3 Design
    5.4 Implementation
    5.5 System Testing
    5.6 Acceptance Testing
    5.7 Delivery

6. Software Maintenance Reporting Requirements
*Describes how information will be collected and provided to members of the maintenance organization.*

7. Software Maintenance Administrative Requirements
*Describes the standards, practices and rules for anomaly resolution and reporting.*

    7.1 Anomaly Resolution and Reporting
    7.2 Deviation Policy
    7.3 Control Procedures
    7.4 Standards, Practices, and Conventions
    7.5 Performance Tracking
    7.6 Quality Control of Plan

8. Software Maintenance Documentation Requirements
*Describes the procedures to be followed in recording and presenting the outputs of the maintenance process.*

**Fig. 12.** An example of a maintenance plan [41].

***Controlling*** measures actual performances against planned goals and, in case of deviations, devises corrective actions. This entails rewarding and disciplining project personnel.

The standard IEEE-1219 [41] suggests a template to guide the preparation of a software maintenance plan based on the standard itself; Fig. 12 shows an outline of this template. Pigoski [62] highlights that a particular care must be made to plan the transition of a system from the development team to the maintenance organization, as this is a very critical element of the life cycle of a system.

Software maintenance organizations can be designed and set up with three different organizational structures: functional, project, or matrix [74, 83].

***Functional organizations*** are hierarchical in nature, as shown in Fig. 13. The maintenance organization is broken down into different functional units, such as software modification, testing, documentation, quality assurance, etc. Functional organizations present the advantage of a centralized organization of similar special-ized resources. The main weakness is that interface problems may be difficult to solve: whenever a functional department is involved in more than a project con-flicts may arise over the relative priorities of these projects in the competition for resources. In addition, the lack of a central point of complete responsibility and authority for the project may entails that a functional department places more emphasis on its own specialty than on the goal of the project.

***Project organizations*** are the opposite of the functional organizations (see Fig. 14). In this case a manager is given the full responsibility and authority for con-ducting the project; all the resources needed for accomplishing the project goals are separated from the regular functional structure and organized into an autonomous, self-contained team. The project manager may possibly acquire additional resources from outside the overall organization. Advantages of this type of organization are

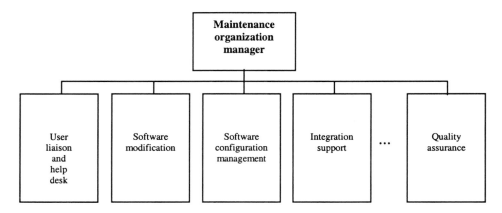

**Fig. 13.**   A functional organization.

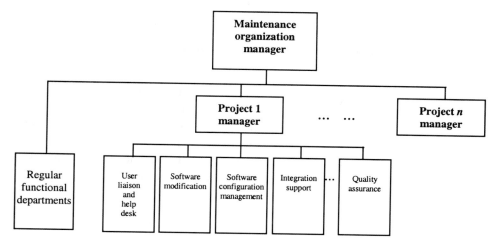

**Fig. 14.** A project organization.

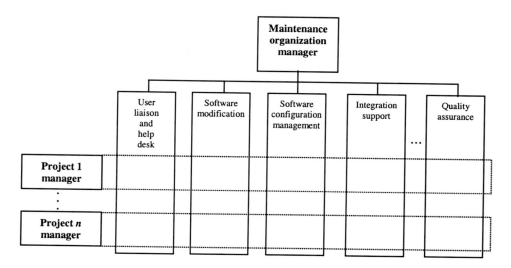

**Fig. 15.** A matrix organization.

a full control over the project, quick decision making, and a high motivation of project personnel. Weaknesses include the fact that there is a start-up time for forming the team, and there may be an inefficient use of resources.

*Matrix organizations* are a composition of functional and project organizations with the objective of maximizing the strengths and minimizing the weaknesses of both types of organizations. Figure 15 shows a matrix organization; the standard vertical hierarchical organization is combined with an horizontal organization for each project. The strongest point of this organization is that a balance is struck

| Decision | Manager | |
|---|---|---|
| | **Functional** | **Project** |
| Change the budget | Approves | Proposes |
| Commit resources | Approves | Proposes |
| Change requirements | Advises | Decides |
| Change release plan | Advises | Decides |

**Fig. 16.**   An example of conflict resolution table.

between the objectives of the functional departments and those of the projects. The main problem is that every person responds to two managers, and this can be a source of conflicts. A solution consists of specifying the roles, responsibility and authority of the functional and project managers for each type of decisions to be made, as shown in Fig. 16.

A common problem of software maintenance organizations is inexperienced personnel. Beath and Swanson [10] report that 25% of the people doing maintenance are students and up to 61% are new hires. Pigoski [62] confirms that 60% to 80% of the maintenance staff is newly hired personnel. Maintenance is still perceived by many organizations as a non-strategic issue, and this explain why it is staffed with students and new hired people. To compound the problem there is the fact that most universities do not teach software maintenance, and maintenance is very rarely though in corporate training and education programs, too. As an example, software maintenance is not listed within the 22 software courses of the software engineering curriculum sketched in [61]. The lack of appraisal of maintenance personnel generates other managerial problems, primarily high turnover and low morale.

## 8. Reverse Engineering

Reverse engineering as been defined as "the process of analyzing a subject system to identify the system's components and their interrelationships and to create representations of the system in another form or at a higher level of abstraction" [29]. Accordingly, reverse engineering is a process of examination, not a process of change, and therefore it does not involve changing the software under examination.

Although software reverse engineering originated in software maintenance, it is applicable to many problem areas. Chikofsky and Cross II [29] identify six key objectives of reverse engineering: coping with complexity, generating alternate views, recovering lost information, detecting side effects, synthesizing higher abstractions, and facilitating reuse. The standard IEEE-1219 [41] recommends reverse engineering as a key supporting technology to deal with systems that have the source code as the only reliable representation. Examples of problem areas where reverse engineering has been successfully applied include identifying reusable assets [23], finding objects in procedural programs [24, 37], discovering architectures [49], deriving conceptual data models [18], detecting duplications [47], transforming binary programs into source code [30], renewing user interfaces [57], parallelizing sequential programs [17], and translating [22], downsizing [70], migrating [27], and wrapping legacy code [72]. Reverse engineering principles have also been applied to business process re-engineering to create a model of an existing enterprise [45].

Reverse engineering as a process is difficult to define in rigorous terms because it is a new and rapidly evolving field. Traditionally, reverse engineering has been viewed as a two-step process: information extraction and abstraction. Information extraction analyses the subject system artifacts — primarily the source code — to gather row data, whereas information abstraction creates user-oriented documents and views. Tilley and Paul [75] propose a preliminary step that consists of constructing domain-specific models of the system using conceptual modeling techniques.

The IEEE Standard for Software Maintenance [41] suggests that the process of reverse engineering evolves through six steps: dissection of source code into formal units; semantic description of formal units and creation of functional units; description of links for each unit (input/output schematics of units); creation of a map of all units and successions of consecutively connected units (linear circuits); declaration and semantic description of system applications, and; creation of an anatomy of the system. The first three steps concern local analysis on a unit level (in the small), while the other three steps are for global analysis on a system level (in the large).

Benedusi *et al.* [12] advocate the need for a high-level organizational paradigm when setting up complex processes in a field, such as reverse engineering, in which methodologies and tools are not stable but continuously growing. The role of such a paradigm is not only to define a framework in which available methods and tools can be used, but also to allow the repetitions of processes and hence to learn from them. They propose a paradigm, called Goals/Models/Tools, that divides the setting up of a reverse engineering process into the following three sequential phases: Goals, Models, and Tools.

*Goals:* This is the phase in which the motivations for setting up the process are analyzed so as to identify the information needs and the abstractions to be produced.

*Models:* This is the phase in which the abstractions identified in the previous phase are analyzed so as to define representation models that capture the information needed for their production.

*Tools:* This is the phase for defining, acquiring, enhancing, integrating, or constructing:

- extraction tools and procedures, for the extraction from the system's artifacts of the row data required for instantiating the models defined in the model phase; and
- abstraction tools and procedures, for the transformation of the program models into the abstractions identified in the goal phase.

The Goals/Models/Tools paradigm has been extensively used to define and execute several real-world reverse engineering processes [11, 12].

## 9. Re-engineering

The practice of re-engineering a software system to better understand and maintain it has long been accepted within the software maintenance community. Chikofsky and Cross II taxonomy paper [29] defines re-engineering as "the examination and alteration of a subject system to reconstitute it in a new form and the subsequent implementation of the new form". The same paper indicates renovation and reclamation as possible synonyms; renewal is another commonly used term. Arnold [5] gives a more comprehensive definition as follows:

> "*Software Re-engineering is any activity that:* (1) *improves one's understanding of software, or* (2) *prepares or improves the software itself, usually for increased maintainability, reusability, or evolvability*".

It is evident that re-engineering entails some form of reverse engineering to create a more abstract view of a system, a regeneration of this abstract view followed by forward engineering activities to realize the system in the new form. This process is illustrated in Fig. 17. The presence of a reverse engineering step distinguishes re-engineering from restructuring, the latter consisting of transforming an artifact from one form to another at the same relative level of abstraction [29].

Software re-engineering has proven important for several reasons. Arnold [5] identifies seven main reasons that demonstrate the relevance of re-engineering:

> "*Re-engineering can help reduce an organization's evolution risk;*
> *Re-engineering can help an organization recoup its investment in software;*

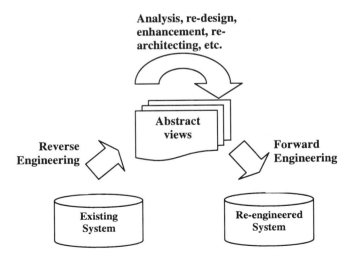

**Fig. 17.**   Reverse engineering and re-engineering.

*Re-engineering can make software easier to change;*
*Re-engineering is a big business;*
*Re-engineering capability extends CASE toolsets;*
*Re-engineering is a catalyst for automatic software maintenance;*
*Re-engineering is a catalyst for applying artificial intelligence techniques*
*to solve software re-engineering problems"*.

Examples of scenarios in which re-engineering has proven useful include migrating a system from one platform to another [19], downsizing [70], translating [22, 31], reducing maintenance costs [69], improving quality [4], and migrating and re-engineering data [3]. The standard IEEE-1219 [41] highlights that re-engineering cannot only revitalize a system, but also provide reusable material for future development, including frameworks for object-oriented environments.

Software re-engineering is a complex process that re-engineering tools can only support, not completely automate. There is a good deal of human intervention with any software re-engineering project. Re-engineering tools can provide help in moving a system to a new maintenance environment, for example one based on a repository, but they cannot define such an environment nor the optimal path along which to migrate the system to it. These are activities that only human beings can perform. Another problem that re-engineering tools only marginally tackle is the creation of an adequate testbed to prove that the end product of re-engineering is fully equivalent to the original system. This still involves much hand-checking, partially because very rarely an application is re-engineered without existing functions being changed and new functions being added. Finally, re-engineering tools often fail to take into account the unique aspects of a system, such as the use of a JCL or a TP-Monitor, the accesses to a particular DBMS or the presence of embedded calls to modules in other languages.

Success in software re-engineering requires much more than just buying one or more re-engineering tools. Defining the re-engineering goals and objectives, forming the team and training it, preparing a testbed to validate the re-engineered system, evaluating the degree to which the tools selected can be integrated and identifying the bridge technologies needed, preparing the subject system for re-engineering tools (for example, by stubbing DBMS accesses and calls to assembler routines) are only a few examples of activities that contribute to determining the success of a re-engineering project. Sneed [71] suggests that five steps should be considered when planning a re-engineering project: project justification, which entails determining the degree to which the business value of the system will be enhanced; portfolio analysis, that consists of prioritizing the applications to be re-engineered based on their technical quality and business value; cost estimation, that is the estimation of the costs of the project; cost-benefit analysis, in which costs and expected returns are compared, and; contracting, which entails the identification of tasks and the distribution of effort.

## 10.  Legacy Systems

A scenario that highlights the high cost of software maintenance is legacy systems. These are systems developed over the past 20/30 years (or even more) to meet a growing demand for new products and services. They have typically been conceived in a mainframe environment using non-standard development techniques and obsolete programming languages. The structure has often been degraded by a long history of changes and adaptations and neither consistent documentation nor adequate test suites are available. Nevertheless, these are crucial systems to the business they support (most legacy systems hold terabytes of live data) and encapsulate a great deal of knowledge and expertise of the application domain. Sometimes the legacy code is the only place where domain knowledge and business rules are recorded, and this entails that even the development of a new replacement system may have to rely on knowledge which is encapsulated in the old system. In short, legacy systems have been identified as "large software systems that we don't know how to cope with but that are vital to our organization" [14]. Similarly, Brodie and Stonebraker [20] define a legacy system as "an information system that significantly resists modifications and evolution to meet new and constantly changing business requirements".

There are a number of options available to manage legacy systems. Typical solutions include: discarding the legacy system and building a replacement system; freezing the system and using it as a component of a new larger system; carrying on maintaining the system for another period, and; modifying the system to give it another lease of life [15]. Modifications may range from a simplification of the system (reduction of size and complexity) to ordinary preventive maintenance (re-documentation, restructuring and re-engineering) or even to extraordinary processes of adaptive maintenance (interface modification, wrapping and migration). These possibilities are not alternative to each other and the decision on which approach, or a combination of approaches, is the most suitable for any particular legacy system which must be made based on an assessment of technical and business value of the system.

Four factors that have been successfully used to assess the value of a legacy system and make informed decisions are: obsolescence, deterioration, decomposability, and business value.

*Obsolescence* measures the ageing of a system due to the progress of software and data engineering and the evolution of hardware/software platforms. Obsolescence induces a cost which results from not taking advantage of modern methods and technologies which reduce the burden of maintaining a system.

*Deterioration* measures the decreases of the maintainability of a system (lack of analyzability, modifiability, stability, testability, etc) due to the maintenance operations the system has undergone in its lifespan. Deterioration directly affects the cost of maintaining a system.

*Decomposability* measures the identifiability and independence of the main components of a system. All systems can be considered as having three components: interfaces, domain functions, and data management services. The decomposability of a system indicates how well these components are reflected in its architecture.

*Business Value* measures the complexity of the business process and rules a system, or system's component, implements and their relevance to achieve efficiency and efficacy in the business operation.

Reference [25] suggests how these factors can be measured and introduces a life cycle model for legacy systems that uses these factors to drive decisions. Figure 18 gives an overview of the life cycle model. The model stresses the fact that a system is constantly under maintenance by means of the outermost maintenance loop; the figure also highlights three more loops which refer to ordinary maintenance, extraordinary maintenance, and replacement. Extraordinary maintenance differs from ordinary maintenance for the extent of the modifications and the impact

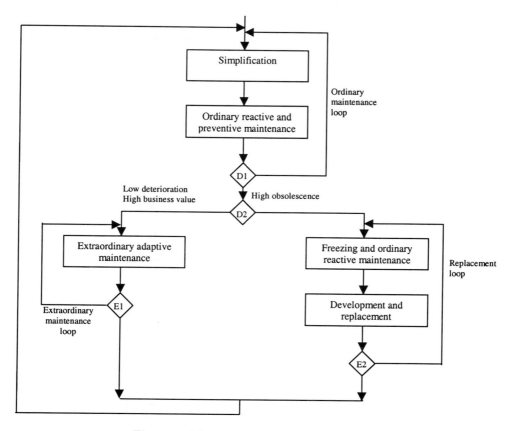

**Fig. 18.** A life cycle model for legacy systems.

that they have on the underlying business processes. New and replacement systems enter the ordinary maintenance loop; the decisions on whether or not a running system needs to enter an extraordinary maintenance loop or a replacement loop (decision points $D1$ and $D2$) requires that the system has been assessed based on the four factors discussed above. Returning to the ordinary maintenance loop (decision points $E1$ and $E2$) entails the evaluation of the progress/completion of the planned process.

Bennett *et al.* [15] stress the need to model the business strategy of an organization from a top-down perspective, including many stakeholders, to make informed decisions about legacy systems. They introduce a two-phase model, called SABA — Software as a Business Asset, that uses an organizational scenario tool to generate scenarios for the organization's future and a technology scenario tool to produce a prioritized set of solutions for the legacy system. Prioritization of solutions is achieved by comparing the current (legacy) system with the systems required by each scenario generated by the organizational scenario tool.

## 11.  Conclusions

This article has overviewed software maintenance, its strategic problems, and the available solutions. The underlying theme of the article has been to show that technical and managerial solutions exist that can support the application of high standards of engineering in the maintenance of software. Of course, there are open problems and more basic and applied research is needed both to gain a better understanding of software maintenance and to find better solutions.

Nowadays, the way in which software systems are designed and built is changing profoundly, and this will surely have a major impact on tomorrow's software maintenance. Object technology, commercial-off-the-shelf products, computer supported cooperative work, outsourcing and remote maintenance, Internet/Intranet enabled systems and infrastructures, user enhanceable systems, are a few examples of areas that will impact software maintenance.

Object technology has become increasingly popular in recent years and a majority of the new systems are currently being developed with an object-oriented approach. Among the main reasons for using object technology is enhanced modifiability, and hence easier maintenance. This is achieved through concepts such as classes, information hiding, inheritance, polymorphism, and dynamic binding. However, there is not enough data that empirically show the impact of object technology on maintenance [38, 68]. Wilde and Huitt [80] discuss some of the problems that may be expected in the maintenance of software developed with object technology and make recommendations for possible tool support. Among the recognized problems are the fact that inheritance may make the dependencies among classes harder to find and analyze [9, 33] and may cause an increase of rework [53]. Also, single changes may be more difficult to implement with object-oriented software compared to procedural software; however, object-oriented development typically results in fewer changes. In short, these findings suggest that object technology does not necessarily improve maintainability and more empirical studies are needed to understand its impact.

More and more organizations are replacing their in-house systems by acquiring and integrating commercial products and components; the main drivers are quicker time to market and lower development costs. However, commercial-off-the-shelf products have the effect of reducing the malleability of software and will have a major impact on the maintenance process [77, 78].

As software systems grow in size, complexity and age, their maintenance and evolution cease to be an individual task to require the combined efforts of groups of software engineers. The day-by-day work of these groups of software engineers produces a body of shared knowledge, expertise and experiences, a sort of rationale for the design of the system, that is precious to improve the productivity of the process of evolving the system over the time, and to reduce the chances of introducing errors at each maintenance operation. Whenever this agreed understanding is not available, software engineers have to develop it as a (preliminary) part of their maintenance assignment. This is a costly and time consuming activity: available figures indicate that 2/3 of the time of a software engineer in a maintenance team is spent looking at the code and the available documents to (re-)discover and process information which had probably been already derived several times during system lifetime [13]. Despite of its importance, this knowledge is seldom recorded in any systematic manner; usually, it is in the mind of engineers and is lost when engineers change their job (or duty). Hence, this is a great potential for improvement in the productivity of maintenance teams.

Outsourcing of software maintenance has grown in the past decade and is now a well established industry. The development of telecommunications, and the diffusion of Internet/Intranet infrastructures, are now pushing in the direction of telecommuting and remote maintenance; this will require a rethinking of the way in which maintenance organizations are designed and set up and processes are enacted.

Currently, there is a debate on the nature and the essence of software maintenance. Indubitably, the traditional vision of software maintenance as a post-delivery activity dates back to the seventies and is strictly related to the waterfall life cycle models. With the emerging of the iterative and evolutionary life cycle models the fact that maintenance is both a pre-delivery and a post-delivery activity has became apparent. However, there is still now a widespread opinion that software maintenance is all about fixing bugs or mistakes. That is why several authors prefer the term software evolution to refer to non-corrective maintenance. Recently, Bennett and Rajlich [16] have proposed a staged model of the software life cycle that partition the conventional maintenance phase of waterfall models in a more useful way. They retain initial development and add an explicit evolution stage during which functionality and capabilities are extended in a major way to meet user needs. Evolution is followed by a stage of servicing, in which the system is subject to defect repairs and simple changes in functions. Then, the system moves to a phase-out stage and finally to a close-down. The authors claim that evolution is different from servicing, from phase-out, and from close-down, and this difference has important technical and business consequences.

## 12. Resources

*The Journal of Software Maintenance*, published by John Wiley & Sons is the only periodical completely dedicated to software maintenance. Articles on software maintenance appear regularly also in *The Journal of Systems and Software*, published by Elsevier Science. Other journals that deliver software maintenance articles are: the *IEEE Transactions on Software Engineering*, the *International Journal of Software Engineering and Knowledge Engineering*, published by World Scientific, *Software Practice and Experience*, published by John Wiley & Sons, *Information and Software Technology*, published by Elsevier Science, *Empirical Software Engineering*, published by Kluwer Academic Publishers, and the *Journal of Automated Software Engineering*, published by Kluwer Academic Publishers.

The *International Conference on Software Maintenance* is the major annual venue in the area of software maintenance and evolution. Other conferences that address the theme of software maintenance are: the *Conference on Software Maintenance and Reengineering*, the *International Workshop on Program Comprehension*, the *Working Conference on Reverse Engineering*, the *Conference on Software Engineering and Knowledge Engineering*, the *Workshop on Software Change and Evolution*, and the *International Conference on Software Engineering*.

Pointers for further readings on software maintenance can be found in Chap. 6 of the *Guide to the Software Engineering Body of Knowledge* (www.swebok.org), whose purpose is to provide a consensually-validated characterization of the bounds of the software engineering discipline and to provide a topical access to the body of knowledge supporting that discipline. The chapter presents an overview of the knowledge area of software maintenance. Brief descriptions of the topics are provided so that the reader can select the appropriate reference material according to his/her needs.

## References

1. A. Abran and H. Nguyemkim, "Analysis of maintenance work categories tough measurement", *Proceedings of the Conference on Software Maintenance*, Sorrento, Italy (IEEE Computer Society Press, Los Alamitos, CA, 1991) 104–113.
2. G. Alkhatib, "The maintenance problem of application software: An empirical analysis", *Journal of Software Maintenance — Research and Practice* **4**, no. 2 (1992) 83–104.
3. A. Andrusiewicz, A. Berglas, J. Harrison and W. Ming Lim,, "Evalution of the ITOC information systems design recovery tool", *The Journal of Systems and Software* **44**, no. 3 (1999) 229–240.
4. P. Antonini, G. Canfora and A. Cimitile, "Re-engineering legacy systems to meet quality requirements: An experience report", *Proceedings of the International Conference*

*on Software Maintenance*, Victoria, British Columbia, Canada (IEEE Computer Society Press, Los Alamitos, CA, 1994) 146–153.

5. R. S. Arnold, "A road map to software re-engineering technology", Software re-engineering — A tutorial (IEEE Computer Society Press, Los Alamitos, CA, 1993) 3–22.

6. R. S. Arnold and S. A. Bohner, "Impact analysis — Toward a framework for comparison", *Proceedings of the Conference on Software Maintenance*, Montreal, Canada (IEEE Computer Society Press, Los Alamitos, CA, 1993) 292–301.

7. L. J. Artur, "Software evolution: The software maintenance challenge" (John Wiley & Sons, New York, 1988).

8. V. R. Basili, "Viewing maintenance as reuse-oriented software development", *IEEE Software* **7**, no. 1 (1990) 19–25.

9. V. R. Basili, L. C. Briand and W. L. Melo, "A validation of object-oriented design metrics as quality indicators", *IEEE Transactions on Software Engineering* **22**, no. 10 (1996) 651–661.

10. C. N. Beath and E. B. Swanson, *Maintaining Information Systems in Organizations* (John Wiley & Sons, New York, 1989).

11. P. Benedusi, A. Cimitile and U. De Carlini, "A reverse engineering methodology to reconstruct hierarchical data flow diagrams", *Proceedings of the Conference on Software Maintenance*, Miami, FL (IEEE Computer Society Press, Los Alamitos, CA, 1989) 180–189.

12. P. Benedusi, A. Cimitile and U. De Carlini, "Reverse engineering processes, document production and structure charts", *The Journal of Systems and Software* **16** (1992) 225–245.

13. K. H. Bennett and E. J. Younger, "Model-based tools to record program understanding", *Proceedings of the 2nd Workshop on Program Comprehension*, Capri, Napoli, Italy (IEEE Computer Society Press, Los Alamitos, CA, 1993) 87–95.

14. K. H. Bennett, "Legacy systems: Coping with success", *IEEE Software* **12**, no. 1 (1995) 19–23.

15. K. H. Bennett, M. Ramage and M. Munro, "Decision model for legacy systems", *IEE Proceedings on Software* **146**, no. 3 (1999) 153–159.

16. K. H. Bennett and V. Rajlich, "The staged model of the software lifetime: A new perspective on software maintenance", *IEEE Computer* (to appear, 2000).

17. S. Bhansali, J. R. Hagemeister, C. S. Raghavendra and H. Sivaraman, "Parallelizing sequential programs by algorithm-level transformations", *Proceedings of the 3rd Workshop on Program Comprehension*, Washington, DC (IEEE Computer Society Press, Los Alamitos, CA, 1994) 100–107.

18. M. R. Blaha and W. J. Premerlani, "An approach for reverse engineering of relational databases", *Communications of the ACM* **37**, no. 5 (1994) 42–49.

19. R. N. Britcher, "Re-engineering software: A case study", *IBM System Journal* **29**, no. 4 (1990) 551–567.

20. M. L. Brodie and M. Stonebraker, *Migrating Legacy Systems* (Morgan Kaufmann Publishers, San Mateo, CA, 1995).

21. F. P. Brooks, Jr., "No silver bullet", *IEEE Computer* **20**, no. 4 (1987) 10–19.

22. E. J. Byrne, "Software reverse engineering: A case study", Software — Practice and Experience **21**, no. 12 (1991) 1349–1364.

23. G. Canfora, A. Cimitile and M. Munro, "RE$^2$: Reverse engineering and reuse re-engineering", *Journal of Software Maintenance — Research and Practice* **6**, no. 2 (1994) 53–72.

24. G. Canfora, A. Cimitile and M. Munro, "An improved algorithm for identifying objects in code", *Software — Practice and Experience* **26**, no. 1 (1996) 25–48.

25. G. Canfora and A. Cimitile, "A reference life cycle for legacy systems", *Proceedings of ICSE'97 Workshop on Migration Strategies for Legacy Systems*, Technical Report TUV-1841-97-06, eds. A Cimitile, H. Muller and R. R. Klosch (1997).

26. G. Canfora and A. Cimitile, "Program comprehension", *Encyclopedia of Library and Information Science* **66**, supplement 29 (1999).

27. G. Canfora, A. De Lucia and G. A. Di Lucca, "An incremental object-oriented migration strategy for RPG legacy systems", *International Journal of Software Engineering and Knowledge Engineering* **9**, no. 1 (1999) 5–25.

28. R. Canning, "The maintenance iceberg", *EDP Analyzer* **10**, no. 10, 1972.

29. E. J. Chikofsky and J. H. Cross II, "Reverse engineering and design recovery: A taxonomy", *IEEE Software* **7**, no. 1 (1990) 13–17.

30. C. Cifuentes and K. J. Gough, "Decompilation of binary programs", *Software — Practice and Experience* **25**, no. 7 (1995) 811–829.

31. C. Cifuentes, D. Simon and A. Fraboulet, "Assembly to high-level language translation", *Proceedings of the International Conference on Software Maintenance*, Bethesda, Maryland (IEEE Computer Society Press, 1998) 228–237.

32. T. A. Corbi, "Program understanding: Challenge for the 1990s", *IBM System Journal* **28**, no. 2 (1989) 294–306.

33. J. Daly, A. Brooks, J. Miller, M. Roper and M. Wood, "Evaluating inheritance depth on the maintainability of object-oriented software", *Empirical Software Engineering, An International Journal* **1**, no. 2 (1996) 109–132.

34. J. R. Foster, "Cost factors in software maintenance", PhD Thesis, Computer Science Department, University of Durham, Durham, UK, 1993.

35. M. J. Fyson and C. Boldyreff, "Using application understanding to support impact analysis", *Journal of Software Maintenance — Research and Practice* **10**, no. 2 (1998) 93–110.

36. T. Gilb, *Principles of Software Engineering Management* (Addison-Wesley, Reading, MA, 1988).

37. J. F. Girard and R. Koschke, "A comparison of abstract data types and objects recovery techniques", *Science of Computer Programming* **36**, no. 2–3 (2000).

38. R. L. Glass, "The software research crisis", *IEEE Software* **11**, no. 6 (1994) 42–47.

39. J. Hartmann and D. J. Robson, "Techniques for selective revalidation", *IEEE Software* **16**, no. 1 (1990) 31–38.

40. IEEE Std. 610.12, "Standard glossary of software engineering terminology" (IEEE Computer Society Press, Los Alamitos, CA, 1990).

41. IEEE Std. 1219-1998, "Standard for software maintenance" (IEEE Computer Society Press, Los Alamitos, CA, 1998).

42. ISO/IEC 9126, "Information technology — Software product evaluation — quality characteristics and guidelines for their use", Geneva, Switzerland, 1991.

43. ISO/IEC 9000-3, "Quality management and quality assurance standards — Part 3: Guidelines for the application of ISO 9001 to the development, supply and maintenance of software", Geneva, Switzerland, 1991.

44. ISO/IEC 12207, "Information technology — software life cycle processes", Geneva, Switzerland, 1995.

45. I. Jacobson, M. Ericsson and A. Jacobson, *The object advantage — Business Process Re-engineering with Object Technology* (Addison-Wesley, Reading, MA, 1995).

46. C. Jones, *Assessment and Control of Software Risks* (Prentice Hall, Englewood Cliffs, NJ, 1994).

47. K. Kontogiannis, R. De Mori, E. Merlo, M. Galler and M. Bernstein, "Pattern matching for clone and concept detection", *Journal of Automated Software Engineering* **3** (1996) 77–108.

48. H. Koontz and C. O'Donnell, "Principles of management: An analysis of managerial functions" 5th ed. (McGraw-Hill, New York, 1972).

49. A. Lakhotia, "A unified framework for expressing software subsystem classification techniques", *The Journal of Systems and Software* **36** (1997) 211–231.

50. M. M. Lehman, "Lifecycles and the laws of software evolution", *Proceedings of the IEEE*, Special Issue on Software Engineering **19** (1980) 1060–1076.

51. M. M. Lehman, "Program evolution", *Journal of Information Processing Management* **19**, no. 1 (1984) 19–36.

52. H. K. N. Leung and L. J. White, "Insights into regression testing", *Proceedings of the Conference on Software Maintenance*, Miami, Florida (IEEE Computer Society Press, 1990) 60–69.

53. H. K. N. Leung, "The dark side of object-oriented software development", *Proceedings of the International Conference on Software Maintenance*, Victoria, British Columbia, Canada (IEEE Computer Society Press, Los Alamitos, CA, 1994) 438.

54. B. P. Lientz and B. E. Swanson, *Software Maintenance Management* (Addison-Wesley, Reading, MA, 1980).

55. P. E. Livadas and D. T. Small, "Understanding code containing preprocessor constructs", *Proceedings of the 3rd Workshop on Program Comprehension*, Washington, DC (IEEE Computer Society Press, Los Alamitos, CA, 1994) 89–97.

56. J. Martin and C. Mc Clure, *Software Maintenance — The Problem and Its Solutions* (Prentice Hall, Englewood Cliffs, NJ, 1983).

57. E. Merlo, P.-Y. Gagne, J.-F. Girard, K. Kontogiannis, L. Hendren, P. Panangaden and R. De Mori, "Re-engineering user interfaces", *IEEE Software* **12**, no. 1 (1995) 64–73.

58. J. T. Nosek and P. Prashant, "Software maintenance management: The changes in the last decade", *Journal of Software Maintenance — Research and Practice* **2**, no. 3 (1990) 157–174.

59. W. M. Osborne and E. J. Chikofsky, "Fitting pieces to the maintenance puzzle", *IEEE Software* **7**, no. 1 (1990) 11–12.

60. D. L. Parnas, "Software aging", *Proceedings of the 16th International Conference on Software Engineering*, Sorrento, Italy (IEEE Computer Society Press, Los Alamitos, CA, 1994) 279–287.

61. D. L. Parnas, "Software engineering programs are not computer science programs", *IEEE Software* **16**, no. 6 (1999) 19–30.

62. T. M. Pigoski, *Practical Software Maintenance — Best Practices for Managing Your Software Investment* (John Wiley & Sons, New York, 1997).

63. R. S. Pressman, *Software Engineering — A Practitioner's Approach* (McGraw-Hill, New York, 1992).

64. J. P. Queille, J. F. Voidrot, N. Wilde and M. Munro "The impact analysis task in software maintenance: A model and a case study", *Proceedings of the International Conference on Software Maintenance*, Victoria, Canada (IEEE Computer Society Press, Los Alamitos, CA, 1994) 234–242.

65. V. Rajlich, "Program reading and comprehension", *Proceedings of the Summer School on Engineering of Existing Software*, Monopoli, Bari, Italy, Giuseppe Laterza Editore, Bari, Italy (1994) 161–178.

66. G. Rothermel and M. J. Harrold, "A framework for evaluating regression test selection techniques", *Proceedings of the 16th International Conference on Software Engineering*, Sorrento, Italy (IEEE Computer Society Press, CA, 1994) 201–210.

67. N. F. Schneidewind, "The state of software maintenance", *IEEE Transactions on Software Engineering* **SE-13**, no. 3 (1987) 303–310.

68. J. Slonim, "Challenges and opportunities of maintaining object-oriented systems", *Proceedings of the International Conference on Software Maintenance*, Victoria, British Columbia, Canada (IEEE Computer Society Press, Los Alamitos, CA, 1994) 440–441.

69. M. Slovin and S. Malik, "Re-engineering to reduce system maintenance: A case study", *Software Engineering*, Research Institute of America, Inc. (1991) 14–24.

70. H. Sneed and E. Nyary, "Downsizing large application programs", *Proceedings of the International Conference on Software Maintenance*, Montreal, Quebec, Canada (IEEE Computer Society Press, Los Alamitos, CA, 1993) 110–119.

71. H. Sneed, "Planning the re-engineering of legcy systems", *IEEE Software* **12**, no. 1 (1995) 24–34.

72. H. Sneed, "Encapsulating legacy software for use in client/server systems", *Proceedings of the 3rd Working Conference on Reverse Engineering*, Monterey, CA (IEEE Computer Society Press, Los Alamitos, CA, 1996) 104–119.

73. T. A. Standish, "An essay on software reuse", *IEEE Transactions on Software Engineering* **SE-10**, no. 5 (1984) 494–497.

74. R. H. Thayer, "Software engineering project management", *Software Engineering Project Management*, 2nd edn., ed. R. H. Thayer (IEEE Computer Society Press, Los Alamitos, CA, 1997) 72–104.

75. S. R. Tilley and S. Paul, "Towards a framework for program understanding", *Proceedings of the 4th Workshop on Program Comprehension*, Berlin, Germany (IEEE Computer Society Press, Los Alamitos, CA, 1996) 19–28.

76. G. Visaggio, "Assessing the maintenance process through replicated controlled experiments", *The Journal of Systems and Software* **44**, no. 3 (1999) 187–197.

77. J. Voas, "Are COTS products and component packaging killing software malleability?", *Proceedings of the International Conference on Software Maintenance*, Bethesda, Maryland (IEEE Computer Society Press, 1998) 156–157.

78. J. Voas, "Maintaining component-based systems", *IEEE Software* **15**, no. 4 (1998) 22–27.

79. H. Weihrich, "Management: Science, theory, and practice", Software Engineering Project Management, 2nd edn., ed. R. H. Thayer (IEEE Computer Society Press, Los Alamitos, CA, 1997) 4–13.

80. N. Wilde and R. Huitt, "Maintenance support for object-oriented programs", *IEEE Transactions on Software Engineering* **18**, no. 12 (1992) 1038–1044.

81. S. S. Yau and J. S. Colleferro, "Some stability measures for software maintenance", *IEEE Transactions on Software Engineering* **SE-6**, no. 6 (1980) 545–552.

82. S. S. Yau, R. A. Nicholl, J. J. P. Tsai and S.-S. Liu, "An integrated life cycle model for software maintenance", *IEEE Transactions on Software Engineering* **SE-14**, no. 8 (1988) 1128–1144.

83. R. Youker, "Organization alternatives for project managers", *Project Management Quarterly*, The Project Management Institute **8**, no. 1 (1997).

# REQUIREMENTS ENGINEERING

ALFS T. BERZTISS

*University of Pittsburgh, Department of Computer Science,*
*Pittsburgh PA 15260, USA*
*and*
*SYSLAB, University of Stockholm, Sweden*
*E-mail: alpha@cs.pitt.edu*

Requirements gathering and analysis is the most important phase of software development. If done properly, it reduces future maintenance costs. It can also stop projects that
are unlikely to succeed before costs have become excessive. Different software systems
require different approaches to requirements engineering. A mature requirements process can be based on a generic requirements process from which specialized processes can
be adapted. We discuss such a generic process. The aim is to achieve for requirements
engineering a capability level that is comparable to Level 3 of the Capability Maturity
Model of SEI for the software process in general. We survey in some detail the parts of
the process that deal with project purpose and feasibility, the techniques of requirements
gathering, and the representation of requirements.

*Keywords*: Brainstorming, capability maturity, interview, questionnaire, requirements
engineering, stakeholder, UML.

## 1. Introduction

Every software system is to serve some purpose, and the first task of a software
or knowledge engineering team is to come to an understanding of the purpose of
the system in some detail. This is requirements engineering. In greater detail [1]:
"Requirements engineering can be characterized as an iterative process of discovery
and analysis, designed to produce an agreed-upon set of clear, complete, and consistent system requirements." We consider a requirement to be a verifiable statement
regarding some property that a software system is to possess. Thus, the statement that a traffic-light controlled by software is to be red for no longer than
two minutes is a requirement, but the unverifiable statement that the traffic lights
should be pedestrian-friendly is not. We refer to statements of the latter type as
wishes. Many requirements start out as wishes, but are converted into verifiable
statements. Those that are not may still appear in a requirements document as
a wish list — developers should try to satisfy them, but, because they cannot be
verified, there is no obligation to do so.

It has long been customary to claim that the purpose of requirements
engineering is to determine merely what is to be done, and that design is to
determine how the software system is to be built. This view was challenged as
early as 1982 by Swartout and Balzer [2] from a practical point of view, and more

recently by Zave and Jackson [3] on more theoretical grounds. The argument for the separation of requirements and design is that designers are not to be handicapped by having a particular approach forced on them. This may have some justification when requirements and design are carried out by different teams, but none at all when the same team has responsibility for the entire software process.

Some design must be part of the requirements process. Far too often software development suffers from excessive cost and schedule overruns. The primary reason for this is that design is left until far too late. Only if there is a detailed understanding of what components a software system is to have, how these components are to interact with each other, and how the system is to interact with its users and its wider environment does it become possible to arrive at reasonably accurate cost and schedule estimates. Without such estimates it is not possible to make even the most fundamental decision, namely whether the system is to be built at all.

Our survey is based on the assumption that the requirements engineering process includes some high-level design. This is to allow early cost and schedule estimation. We propose a generic process that is to be adapted to the specialized needs of particular projects. The motivation for such a process is given in Sec. 2. Section 3 is an outline of our generic process, and the sections that follow deal with phases of the process in some detail. As far as it is practicable, to avoid distraction, we have avoided introduction of references in the text of the survey. Section 10 surveys some of the literature — one criterion for the introduction of a reference was the extent to which it points to additional references; another was the need to arrive at a reasonably complete coverage of all of requirements engineering. The outline of the generic process of Sec. 3 is based on information extracted from the literature. About 300 items were consulted — only a few representative references will be given here.

## 2.  Requirements Engineering

The most influential work on the software process is the Capability Maturity Model (CMM) of the Software Engineering Institute [4]. It is not a process model as such, but a listing of the capabilities that an organization is to have to be effective in instituting a software process. Requirements management is a key process area of Level 2 of the CMM, the first level in a five-level sequence at which an organization has reached some degree of maturity. The explanation of requirements management in [4] is sketchy, stating little more than that requirements are to be documented, that there are to be adequate resources and training, that both the initial requirements and changes to requirements are to be reviewed, and that requirements are to be the basis for further development.

A Level 2 organization is to have the capability to control the development of a new software system on the basis of its experience with similar systems, and for this the sketchy recommendations are adequate. But a Level 3 organization is to be able to translate its past experience into a controlled process for development of software systems that may differ significantly from systems developed in the past, i.e., such an organization should base software development on a generic process that is adaptable to individual project needs. To assist in the requirements engineering phase of this process, several methods of requirements analysis form part of Level 3. They include functional decomposition, simulation, prototyping, and scenario generation. Still, this list does not provide guidance on how to define an explicit requirements process. The real contribution of the CMM is the identification of Level 3 with the capability to construct a specialized software process efficiently and effectively from a generic software process. Translating this line of thought to the present context, there has to be a generic requirements engineering process.

## 3. Generic Requirements Engineering

A generic software engineering process can be defined in terms of a set of natural-language task descriptions of 25–150 words each. In the definition of a specific instance of the process, these capsule descriptions are transformed into templates, still in natural language, but structured to some extent. The templates can be left in this form, or they can be translated into a program. The purpose of the program is to prompt the software development team into performing various actions — such a program defines what is essentially a workflow system.

The capsule-to-template approach is quite general in that it can be applied both to the requirements process and to its products. At the capsule stage tasks are defined with no regard of how they are to relate to each other. In a template the immediate predecessors and successors of a task are identified, as well as all data references and all human-performed activities. The latter are very important for workflow systems. We have found that such a two-stage approach is a very effective way of separating concerns: first define the tasks, then link them together and define the database for the application.

The capsules serve as checklists from which one selects those activities relevant for a particular instance of the requirements process. Here we can merely suggest the flavor of the approach. Even the capsules will not be written out in full. The capsules sometimes include design elements. As noted earlier, requirements and design are not all that easy to separate. Also, domain experts may not be able to express the "What" except in terms of the "How". We distinguish eleven tasks in the requirements process. Note that they do not necessarily follow the shown sequence. For example, *Stakeholder Identification* and *Task Identification* are likely to be concurrent with *Requirements Gathering*.

*Purpose and Environment Definition*. This establishes the type of the system and the environment in which the system is to operate. Control systems form one type, information systems another. A clear understanding of the environment is particularly important for control systems — for them the environment is the host into which they are embedded. Statements of purpose come from external clients or internal sponsors. For brevity we shall refer to both classes as clients.

*Feasibility Study.* An initial cost-risk estimation is performed. This requires an initial module or task identification, cost estimation for each such component, and hence for the entire project, possible cost reduction by use of COTS (Commercial Off-The-Shelf) software, consequences of schedule and cost overruns, and consequences of failure after delivery. A group decision support system may be used for the cost and risk estimation. A decision is made whether to proceed with the project.

*Requirements Gathering.* One way of gathering requirements for a software system is by a Joint Application Development (JAD) or Participatory Design (PD) workshop. The JAD approach is used when the views of developers and of the management of the client organization have the greatest weight; under PD greatest weight is attached to views of worker representatives, with emphasis on end-user satisfaction and avoidance of workplace disruption. Cost-benefit analyses may be used under both approaches, but they can differ significantly in their definition and ranking of benefits.

*Stakeholder Identification.* Because of the different emphases of JAD and PD, the selection of stakeholders for workshop participation will be influenced by the Requirements Gathering Format.

*Task Identification.* The input to this phase is the set of tasks that have been identified under *Feasibility Study*. However, as a result of the task identification step, the initial set may become modified.

*Task Refinement and Review.* Capsule descriptions of the tasks are to be produced, and subjected to a peer review, with the selection of participants in the review based on the type of the system. Particular attention is to be paid to completeness of the set of tasks and the activities in each task. The reuse potential of the tasks is to be determined, and the reuse of existing tasks investigated.

*Specialization of Tasks.* Each generic task is to be adapted for the specific project. The presentation is still in natural language, but a definite format is to be followed. It has three components: (1) *Triggered by*, which tells what initiates this task, and under what conditions; (2) *Activities*, which is an outline of the activities that constitute this task, the conditions under which they take place, and the data to be referenced by the activities (some activities are to be performed by people — the system is to remind such people of the tasks they need to perform); (3) *Affects*, which identifies all tasks initiated by this task, and the conditions under which the initiation is to take place.

*Review of the Specializations.* The set of elaborated tasks is to be subjected to a peer review. A special purpose of this review is to look for inconsistencies in the requirements. This is to be done throughout the requirements process, but a final concentrated effort is to be made here. This is particularly important when the tasks define corrective actions for dealing with exceptional situations in mission-critical systems. A separate safety review may be recommended.

*Formalization.* The tasks can be defined in a formal specification language. This may be mandated by authorities, or done to make possible the use of validation tools to establish that the system defined by the specification has particular properties.

*Specialized Requirements.* Some systems have highly special requirements, such as the need for better than average security, or the ability to be used by physically handicapped people. These special requirements need to be incorporated into the final requirements document, where appropriate.

*Change Control.* While in some systems liberal allowance can be made for changes, in other systems volatility even at the requirements stage cannot be tolerated — otherwise the project can get out of control.

## 4. Purpose and Feasibility

In order to clarify what we mean by the purpose of a software system, we introduce a taxonomy of software. Under this classification scheme, the primary partition of software is into procedural and transactional systems. Procedural systems are representations of algorithms that convert inputs into outputs, and a separate requirements phase does not really arise. Examples of such systems are heat transfer calculations, critical path analyses, and the like. Transactional systems are defined in terms of states and their changes. Note, though, that most systems are mixed. For example, a system that organizes a meeting is predominantly transactional, but the date and place may be selected by some optimizing algorithm.

One major type of transactional systems are information systems, which assist in the running of organizations. Control systems form another type. They control their environment, which may be machinery, or climatic conditions in a building, or the flow of traffic. A third type is made up of COTS software. Product lines form a subspecies of all three major types. An instance of a product line of information systems is based on a generic rental process, from which specific rental processes are derived, such as car rentals. The requirements process itself belongs to the product line category. Lift controllers, adaptable to the needs of different buildings, are an example of a control-system product line. A special concern with control systems is co-design. To reduce time to market, the hardware and the software that controls it should be designed concurrently. With COTS software, variability is caused by the need to make a system fit different platforms.

Requirements for information systems usually come from multiple sources, and it is important to establish their consistency. They also tend to be volatile, the volatility often being a consequence of better understanding by clients of their needs as discussions with developers progress. Volatility may also be shown by the requirements for control systems, but here the changes may be brought about by changes in the design of the host system into which the software is to be embedded. Because requirements for COTS software are formulated by the developers themselves, possibly guided by market research, they tend to be stable.

The main concern for some control systems is their correctness. Faults in software built into mass-produced TV-sets cannot be tolerated at all. The same holds for safety-critical systems. For some mission-critical systems in avionics or control of nuclear power stations the authorities may mandate the use of formal methods. The transition from an informal requirements definition to a formal specification is then to be part of the requirements process.

Completeness of requirements is very difficult to achieve. Transactional systems generally implement processes that are composed of tasks, e.g. workflow systems. A process consists of a normal sequence or network of tasks, and of exceptions. An example of a normal sequence is the situation in which a customer obtains money from a banking machine. Exceptional situations arise with use of a bank card that has been reported lost, withdrawal limits being exceeded, timeouts, etc. The normal sequence presents problems only when developers lack the skills to extract the required information from domain experts. The real problem arises with exceptions because in the requirements gathering phase many exceptions have not yet been recognized. It is therefore essential that minimal disruption will arise when new requirements that deal with exceptional situations have to be incorporated into the requirements document.

Besides the purpose of the system, it is also necessary to have a complete understanding of the environment in which the system is to operate. Examples: an interactive e-commerce system (the environment consists of a customer base); a shipping system for the same (here the environment is made up of carriers); portfolio management (stock markets make up the environment); embedded control system (its environment is the host of the control system).

In determining whether a project is feasible, several factors must be considered. They are formal feasibility, cost, schedule, and risk. Formal feasibility relates to algorithms — do algorithms exist for the tasks to be performed and, if so, are their time requirements acceptable? If an algorithmic solution cannot be generated within an acceptable time, are heuristic approaches acceptable? As regards cost, our interest lies in relating cost to benefits: how much are we willing to pay for the capabilities that we expect the system under consideration to provide? Not only do we need the capabilities, but we need them at the earliest possible time. The modern business environment changes so rapidly that software quality is often sacrificed in order to reduce the time it takes to bring a software system into service.

But this introduces risks. We distinguish between process risks and product risks. A process risk arises when actual software development cost or schedule exceeds its estimate. A product risk arises when a released software product fails in a way that causes major inconvenience or damage for the client to whom the product has been released. If the expected risk is too high, the project has to be abandoned. Such a decision has to be made before too many resources have been committed. An accurate risk estimate depends on fairly detailed understanding of the modular structure of the system, which explains our insistence that some high-level design is to be part of requirements engineering.

To prevent cost overruns, requirements should be prioritized, which again implies early modularization. For example, a controller of a set of lifts in a building can be designed as two components — a controller for each lift, and a dispatcher. The purpose of the dispatcher is to optimize the system, e.g. if somebody wants to go from floor 5 to floor 12, the dispatcher selects a particular lift that is to stop at floor 5. However, a simpler system can be developed without the dispatcher: every lift that reaches floor 5 in upward motion will stop there. The dispatcher is built only if cost and schedule allow it.

Estimation of parameters such as cost is very difficult in any case, but particularly so if a system is considered as a single monolithic entity. It is easier to arrive at the cost by combining estimated costs of modules. Group decision support systems can assist in estimating module costs. An early such system is Delphi, which has been used to estimate individual parameters and to rank items in order of importance. The basic procedure starts with a moderator sending out a problem description to a group of experts. The experts suggest a value for a parameter or a ranking of items, giving their reasons for this selection. The moderator collects this information, collates it, and sends it out again. When the experts see the reasoning for estimates different from their own, they tend to adjust their own estimates. The objective is to arrive at a consensus after several iterations. An important aspect of Delphi is that the estimates are anonymous. This is to prevent the so called "halo effect", which gives greater weight to opinions advanced by persons perceived to have greater expertise. If the greater expertise is in fact there, it should show in convincing arguments.

A problem with the early Delphi method was that it took a very long time. The time scale has been compressed by basing Delphi on modern group decision systems. One version has the experts sitting in a specially equipped room, and submitting their estimates (anonymously) to an electronic blackboard. The drawbacks of this scheme is that it requires the physical presence of the experts, and that not enough time may be given for them to carry out a thorough analysis of the problem. Distributed group decision systems allow the experts to interact asynchronously from different locations, which reduces the effect of both these negative features.

## 5. Stakeholder Identification

A number of different definitions of stakeholders in a software project have been advanced. They are surveyed and analyzed in [5]. These definitions can help to arrive at a detailed picture of what a stakeholder is. A good starting point is to consider a stakeholder to be "anyone whose job will be altered, who supplies or gains information..., or whose power or influence within the organization will increase or decrease" [6]. It should be noted that a stakeholder is nor necessarily a person — rather, it is a role that can be assumed by a person, a team, an organization, or even a software system. For financial systems a likely stakeholder is an auditing firm; for a control system used in a nuclear power plant it is a regulatory body. When the generic requirements process becomes a specialization, careful attention has to be given to the identification of the roles that relate to this particular specialization.

The definition from [6] is useful in two ways. It identifies three classes of stakeholders, and it suggests that there is a socio-political aspect to stakeholder selection. In an initial classification we call users those people whose jobs will be altered, domain experts those who supply or gain information, and managers those whose power or influence is affected. In addition, we have to consider developers and regulators.

*Users.* This role is perhaps the most important. A software system is to appeal to prospective users. Otherwise it will not be used at all, or it will be misused. It has to be realized that there may be different classes of users, such as frequent and infrequent users, users outside an organization (e.g. customers of an e-commerce company), users who merely retrieve information, and so forth.

*Domain experts.* The holders of this role are to supply developers with knowledge relating to the domain in which the application software system is to operate. Such knowledge consists of domain-related facts, business rules and conventions, and specialized algorithms. The identification of a *true* domain expert is not always straightforward. In this task peer evaluation of the suitability of candidate domain experts tends to be more accurate than management suggestions.

*Managers.* A system has a client who fills the central management role. The day-to-day supervision of the project is normally delegated to a lower-level manager. It is important to know the extent of the authority of the holder of the latter role, and the effect the software system under consideration will have on the power and influence of this manager. A very delicate situation can arise when this manager is not supportive of the project because it may diminish the manager's influence. In [6], it is suggested that one should be "very wary of changes which take power, influence or control from some stakeholders without returning something tangible in its place."

*Developers.* They are the team that will actually design the system, and supervise its implementation. A role that is often neglected is that of software librarian. The responsibility of this role is to advise what components of a proposed software product are available in the local reuse library, what components exist as COTS software, and what components of the new system are candidates for inclusion in the reuse library.

*Regulators.* The actual regulators are government agencies, standards organizations, and trade groups. Within the organization that develops the software the role of regulator is played by a person or group of persons familiar with the applicable regulations. This person or persons should be explicitly designated as the "regulator" for the given software project.

## 6. Requirements Gathering Format

Here we have to distinguish between requirements gathering activities and the representation of requirements. As requirements gathering progresses there is likely to be a shift in the preferred representation of requirements from textual to graphical. An advantage of diagrams is that they are two-dimensional. Hence they can highlight complex relationships more effectively than linear text. Still, it has also to be realized that some sections of the user community, particularly those with highly developed verbal skills, may prefer text throughout the requirements engineering phase. Moreover, many requirements that relate to properties of the software, such as descriptions of its environment, safety, security, usability, reusability, and reliability cannot be expressed in graphical form.

### 6.1. *Requirements gathering activities*

The requirements gathering subprocess has two phases. The first defines the parts of the application domain that are relevant for the application. This delimitation is achieved by means of questionnaires, interviews, and brainstorming. In the second phase, structured group sessions take over. The information gathered in the first phase allows the system developers to define a format for these group sessions.

**Questionnaires.** If an existing system, either manual or computer-based, is to be replaced, the virtues and deficiencies of the existing system can be obtained by questionnaires submitted to a well selected cross-section of users. The proper design of a questionnaire is very important because users tend to assume that they will find the good features in the new system no matter what. Positive identification of the good features of an existing system is essential because it indicates those characteristics of the old system that users will expect the new system to possess, and that the new system must therefore have. Otherwise, the users will be quite upset. If a list of deficiencies is short, a totally new system may not be needed.

In using questionnaires much attention has to be given to detail. A short checklist of what to consider:

- Send out a preliminary notice. Before sending out the questionnaire warn the sample group that the questionnaire is coming, and in a sentence or two explain its significance.
- Express all questions in short sentences, and try to make sure that the answer can also be short.
- Keep in mind that all recipients of questionnaires think that they would have formulated much better questions. Allow, therefore, ample space for the respondents' own comments.
- Test the questionnaire against a small group to determine that they understand the questions as you do.

- Make sure that a deadline is clearly stated, and make the period to the deadline short. Send out a reminder to all non-respondents the very next day after the deadline has passed.

**Interviews.** The basis for an interview is established by questionnaires or by an interviewer's understanding of the basic purpose of a system that is to be developed. However, for a totally new product, individual interviews may not be necessary. Proper interview techniques are crucial to the elicitation of reliable information from the people interviewed, whom we shall call responders. The use of individual interviews in requirements engineering has to be looked at from five angles. They are (1) selection of responders, (2) homework by the interviewer, (3) the mechanics of the interview, (4) interpretation of what a responder tells, (5) follow up.

*Selection of responders.* Here there are four sources. First, if a questionnaire was used, people who showed better than average care in answering the questions should be considered for interviews. The questionnaire, however, was sent out only to samples from various user groups. There is always the danger of some user group being left out. Also there can be stakeholders who are not actual users. The second pool of responders may be recruited by posting appeals for volunteers on bulletin boards. Gause and Weinberg [7] recount the story of an auditor who was the lone respondent to the bulletin-board appeal, but pointed out a flaw in the initial plan for a $20 million purchasing system so critical that the project had to be scrapped. Third, the responders already identified may suggest other responders. Fourth, very dependable information can sometimes be obtained from recently retired employees. Here the advantages are that a retiree has much experience, has the time to reflect on this experience, and is unlikely to be affected by office politics. While the interviews are going on, an organizational chart should be consulted to determine that some important constituency is not missed, and that no serious blunders regarding business manners are committed. Note that some responders may have to be interviewed more than once. As the interviewer's understanding of the system grows, the questioning can become a more probing coverage of the same material. The purpose of follow-up interviews is to resolve misunderstandings that may have arisen in earlier interviews.

*Homework by the interviewer.* This we give as a list of items to which the interviewer has to give special attention. The list is by no means exhaustive, and may have to be modified to take into account the corporate culture of the company at which the interviews are carried out. For example, the responder may be bound by some form of non-disclosure policy. Release from this restraint will be handled differently by different companies. The list of tasks for the interviewer:

- Get clearance from the supervisor of the prospective responder for the interview.
- Schedule an interview well ahead of time.

- Ask the prospective responder whether some co-workers should not be interviewed at the same time. People often work in closely integrated teams, and good reactions may be obtained when several members of a team are interviewed together.
- Define a list of areas to be covered. For each area have a few start-up questions ready. In later interviews these questions may be suggested by information obtained in previous interviews.

*Mechanics of the interview.* Here we shall again use a checklist, and again the list is very far from exhaustive. The most important principle of successful interviewing is to make the responder feel comfortable throughout the interview, and all the items in the list relate to this principle. It has to be faced that some people are better than others at putting responders at ease. Therefore, an important aspect of interviewing is the selection of the interviewer. A list of dos and don'ts for the interviewer:

- So that you can concentrate fully on the interaction with the responder, it may be a good idea to have a recorder present to take notes. You should not take notes yourself.
- This would have already been done when the responder was signed up, but explain again that the information the responder will provide is of crucial importance for coming up with a system to the liking of all users.
- Do not anticipate answers, i.e., hurry responders along by completing answers. This can lead responders to believe that you know all the answers anyway, and that the responders are not really needed.
- Avoid giving any indication that an answer is what you expected. If the trend in the answers leads you to suspect that the responder is giving "expected" answers, switch to a new area of questioning.
- Avoid questions that elicit short answers, particularly yes-no answers.
- Watch the responder very carefully. If there is a marked reluctance to answer a particular question, the reason for the reluctance should be probed, but not in a way to make the responder uneasy. Perhaps the follow up could go like this: "It seems to me that you expected a different question. What question did you expect?"

*Interpretation of responder responses.* Responders will rarely try to mislead the interviewer deliberately. But there is likely to be a cultural barrier between a user and a requirements engineer. Sometimes it shows as unrealistic assumptions about the capabilities of computerized systems. Users sometimes have great difficulty in formulating their real concerns. They may complain about screen layouts, although the real problem may be an indiscriminate use of clashing colors on the screen. Therefore, whatever responders can show, they should show rather than describe. Similarly, a responder may misinterpret an interviewer's question, the interviewer the responder's response, and both be unaware of this. The solution is to have follow-up interviews after a prototype of the new system has been built, and to concentrate in these interviews on actual interaction with the system. In expressing their dissatisfaction with some feature of a system, users are often preoccupied with observable symptoms rather than the causes of the symptoms. They should not be blamed for this — it is not their job to deduce the causes, but that of requirements engineers.

*Follow up.* Shortly after the interview a thank-you note should be sent to the responder. Future relations with the responder will be particularly helped if the requirements engineer itemizes what was learnt from the responder. When the requirements document is finished, all contributors (responders to questionnaires, participants in interviews) should be invited to look at it, and give additional comments. It should, however, be explained that all changes are now looked after by a change review committee.

**Brainstorming.** Brainstorming is a session in which a large group of participants urge each other on to come up with ideas for a software system. Brainstorming can be very fruitful in the development of a new product. In replacing an existing system there are the attributes of the old system to look at. In defining a totally new system a list of attributes has to be created. This creative effort is the function of brainstorming. Brainstorming has three distinct phases. The first is to identify groups that have or should have something to say about the new system. The second is to generate ideas. This is the real brainstorm. The third is to extract from the list generated in the second phase those attributes that are to be built into the new system.

In the first phase a convenor identifies stakeholders groups, selects a representative from each group, and sends out to the representatives (a) a brief description of the product to be developed; (b) a list of stakeholder groups, with the motivation of why each group has been selected; (c) a request to add to the list new groups, with motivation, and, if possible, to suggest a representative of the group; (d) a request to return the augmented list to the convenor.

A brainstorming team can be very large. In the second phase this team is assembled in a secluded comfortable room. The convenor explains the product that is to be developed, states the rules of the game, and starts the team off by suggesting a few attributes for the product. Some of these attributes must be outlandish, even downright silly, which introduces the first rule of brainstorming:

*Be creative.* Original ideas are to be encouraged, even when they seem silly. Many of the most familiar things we see around us started as outlandish ideas. It is a wonder there are automobiles — everyone knew that they were totally impracticable the way they scared horses. Creativity can be easily stifled, and the only function the convenor has after the initial introduction is to prevent such stifling, which takes us to the second rule:

*Do not criticize.* Both criticism and praise (which is implied criticism of ideas that are not being praised) must be avoided during brainstorming. There is plenty of time afterwards to sort out the ideas that are to be pursued from the ideas that will be quietly dropped. A ban on criticism does not mean that ideas that have already been presented cannot be modified. Hence, rule three:

*Build on what exists.* This is the feature that distinguishes brainstorming from other methods of requirements gathering. The group dynamics encourages participants to improve on what is already there, introduce variants, and combine ideas. This means that all the ideas already generated must be in full view of everybody. They may be written on blackboards or large sheets of paper, or made visible by some other means. Most of the ideas generated in a brainstorming session are discarded, but they must still be produced to help come up with the good ideas. An idea may be impracticable as is, but a mutation of it need not be.

The next stage is to "validate" the ideas. A mass of ideas is to be converted into a workable initial requirements statement. This process can be carried out by the same group that generated the ideas, preferably at a second meeting. Various voting schemes can be used to come up with a ranking of the ideas. An alternative is to apply previously established selection criteria to the ideas. If this is done, the selection can be made by a requirements engineer working alone.

**JAD workshops.** When we have a situation in which the system being built is not new or we have a good understanding of the purpose and key attributes of a new system, we still need input from different stakeholder groups, with emphasis on users. One technique to use in such a situation is JAD, short for Joint Application Development. Under JAD, users and other stakeholders meet system developers in a structured workshop that may last several days. These stakeholders should outnumber developers four to one or five to one. The task of getting the stakeholders together is handled by client representatives in cooperation with the moderator. There are several phases to JAD.

(1) The moderator establishes with high-level representatives of the client organization the purpose of the project, gets some understanding of the assumptions underlying the project, and defines the objectives of the JAD workshop. Participants for the workshop are also identified. Their number should be strictly limited to reduce cost and the problem of getting the participants together. JAD is based on intensive interaction, but in a structured manner, and this is difficult to achieve with a large number of participants.

(2) The moderator prepares workshop material. The most important component of the material is an initial system model, sketched out with no attention to detail. The purpose of the workshop is to refine this model by going through several iterations.

(3) The workshop takes place. The moderator presents the initial model, and detail gets added piece by piece by the participants. The main advantage of the JAD approach is that it can integrate inspections with

prototyping. If the result of a JAD workshop is a prototype, then it would have been built under constant scrutiny of representatives of the various stakeholder groups. They would speak up if they saw the prototype acquiring some unexpected features. But it is not often that the outcome of a JAD workshop is a working prototype. The product is more likely to be a well-inspected set of requirements.

The JAD format is used primarily in North America. An alternative is PD (Participatory Design), which is practiced primarily in Scandinavia and Great Britain. The PD approach puts much weight on social and ergonometric issues, such as job loss resulting from a proposed software system, and the effect of the system on stress levels of its users. PD tends to be less structured than JAD.

## 6.2. *Requirements representation*

A requirements document starts out as a collection of statements derived from questionnaires, interviews, and brainstorming. Part of this collection of statements can be transformed into a set of diagrams, but, as noted at the beginning of this section, some will remain as text. We shall assume that the target of the transformations is UML (Unified Modeling Language) because it has become the *de facto* standard for software development. Here we shall review applicable components of UML.

**Components of UML.** UML has seven components or diagram types that present different views of a software system, five of which are of interest for requirements representation, and will be discussed here. The main advantage of UML is that it is widely understood. This fosters communication: most software developers will interpret a UML diagram in more or less the same way. Another advantage is tool support. Tools are available for drawing UML diagrams and for checking consistency between different diagrams that relate to the same software elements.

*Use case diagrams.* They relate components of a software system and a set of actors. The actors may be users, or hardware units in the case of embedded systems, or other software systems. The software components are specific tasks, called use cases. A use case diagram shows interactions between actors and use cases, and between use cases themselves. Use case diagrams are used in early stages of requirements engineering. In the generic model of Sec. 3, they can support all the activities leading up to *Task Refinement and Review.*

*Class diagrams.* These diagrams are modernized Entity-Relationship diagrams. They define the object classes for an application by listing the attributes and methods that belong to a class, and showing how the object classes relate to each other. These diagrams complement use case diagrams.

*Sequence diagrams.* A sequence diagram shows in what sequence messages pass between members of a set of interacting elements that comprises actors and objects. Sequence diagrams are one version of interaction diagrams. Another version, called collaboration diagrams, is essentially equivalent to sequence diagrams.

*Statechart diagrams.* They represent the states that an object may assume, and show all permissible state transitions.

*Activity diagrams.* These diagrams show the process structure somewhat differently from statechart diagrams. They are essentially Petri nets.

Although we recognize the importance of UML as a means of standardizing representations, we find that the use of too many types of diagrams can be confusing. The diagrams have to be used in a disciplined way. If requirements are represented in UML, then use case and class diagrams are essential: use case diagrams show how a system is to interact with its environment, and the attributes of objects in class diagrams identify the data needs of the application. However, as regards the other three types listed above, just one may be sufficient to show the process structure.

We have found that the transition from a generic requirements model to a specialization of this model is done much more easily in a textual representation than by using UML. There is a place in requirements engineering for both diagrams and text. It remains to be determined under what conditions and for what classes of stakeholders each type of representation works best.

**A textual representation.** Step *Task Refinement and Review* of the requirements process of Sec. 3 introduces capsule descriptions of tasks, and these capsule descriptions are to be specialized in the next step of the requirements process. The task definitions in the process of Sec. 3 are themselves capsules, but they do not contain as much detail as a capsule normally would. A more realistic example relates to the reservation task for a generic rental process:

*Reservation.* A customer makes a reservation of a rental object for a length of time starting at an indicated date and/or time. Variants of the basic pattern include (a) group reservations, (b) indication of just the desired starting point and no indication of the length of rental, (c) no indication of a starting point, as in the case of a library book that is currently checked out to some other borrower, (d) confirmed reservation, (e) overbooking, in anticipation of a cancellation, (f) no prior reservation, with the arrival of a customer interpreted as a reservation, (g) in case of shortage of rental objects, a customer may be put into a wait line, and be encouraged to make a reservation if the shortage is no longer in effect, (h) for some applications, the rental site and the return site of a rental object may differ. The credit-worthiness of a customer may have to be established as part of this task.

As noted earlier, a capsule does not indicate how the task described in a capsule relates to other tasks. Neither is there much said about the data requirements of a task. Both of these concerns are addressed when the capsule description is refined into a specialization. The reservation capsule, when specialized into a template, becomes:

Template: *Reservation of rental car.*

- Triggered by: Customer communication, including the arrival of a customer at the rental desk, or the wait-line pattern.

- Activities:
  - — If customer requests a car of a particular type, check the availability of such a car for the requested period at the indicated rental site.
  - — If car of type requested by customer not available, or customer does not ask for a particular type, suggest a car of an available type.
  - — If triggered by the wait-line pattern, notify customer next in line of the possibility of making a reservation.
  - — If a reservation is made, encourage a customer to make this a confirmed reservation.
- Information base changes:
  - — If a reservation is made, enter customer details and car details into the information base.
  - — If the car is to be returned to a different site, make an appropriate entry in the information base for that site.

A subprocess in many applications is the assembling of a set of items $S$. We show two capsules that define this subprocess. Specializations include setting up a meeting in an office as soon as all participants are free, the assembly of a purchase order, and the assembly of parts from suppliers.

*Assemblage request.* A set of items $S$ is checked against a set of available items $AV$. If $S$ is a subset of $AV$, then $S$ becomes an assembly, and it is subtracted from $AV$ and added to a set *assembled*; otherwise $S$ is added to *requests*. Special cases arise when multiple copies of the items of $S$ are to enter an assembly, or when $S$ is required for a specific time period.

*Availability.* Whenever the supply of available items in $AV$ increases, elements of *requests* are tested against $AV$. How this supply increases is determined by the specific application. If there is now a set $S$ in *requests* such that $S$ is a subset of $AV$, then $S$ is subtracted from $AV$ and added to *assembled*.

## 7. The Task Structure

Under this heading, we shall first consider task identification. After the required tasks have been identified and their purpose established, generic capsule descriptions of the tasks are produced. The capsule descriptions should be subjected to peer reviews. When a specific application arises, the capsules are converted into formatted specializations. We realize that the approach of this section is only one of many that could be followed. Since a somewhat detailed outline of at least one approach should be part of this survey, we chose the one with which we have greatest familiarity. It effectiveness has been tested by means of student projects [8].

### 7.1. *Task identification*

Task identification begins in the *Feasibility Study* step of the requirements process of Sec. 3. However, at this stage no actual requirements have been defined. The real requirements gathering phase can start only after the format for the requirements gathering activities has been decided on, the stakeholders identified, and participation by representatives of the different stakeholder classes ensured. We noted at the start of Sec. 6.2 that the initial requirements document may be a collection of statements.

In order to impose some structure on this collection, the modules defined in the feasibility study can be interpreted as pigeonholes into which the individual statements are to be deposited. A statement may relate to more than one module. A decision has then to be made which of the pigeonholes is the most appropriate for it. In some cases, the most appropriate action may be to modify the modular structure. New modules certainly have to be defined if there are statements that do not relate to any of the modules of the initial structure. It is unlikely that the alteration of the modular structure will appreciably change initial cost and schedule estimates, but if it does, a review has to be undertaken that determines whether to proceed with the project.

An alternative is to start with an identification of agents, i.e., the people, hardware components, and other software systems that will interact with the system under consideration, and to define scenarios. A scenario is a step-by-step description of how a particular agent interacts with the system. For example, the customer of an e-commerce company orders an item, has the order confirmed if the item is available, selects a shipping option, selects a payment option, has the item delivered, and returns the item if dissatisfied with it.

All of these are use cases in the UML terminology, but the purpose here is not to construct a use case diagram. The purpose is merely to identify the use cases as a set of tasks. This identification of tasks can be carried out totally independently of what tasks were identified as part of the feasibility study, but at the end of scenario-based task identification the two sets of tasks are to be compared and, in case they differ, reconciled.

## 7.2. *Task refinement and review*

All that task identification had to accomplish was the determination of what tasks are needed. The tasks were given names, but the names merely convey an intuitive understanding of the purpose of each task. The next step is to produce for each task a brief outline of the activities that are to be part of the task. An important component of some task definitions is a list of special cases that can arise. For examples of such special cases, see the capsule for rental reservations of Sec. 6.2. The definition of a set of capsules is most likely motivated by a specific application. This application suggests what the text of the capsules is to be. The text is to be written with future reuse in mind, and this requires a generic formulation. We have found that even in cases where it is unlikely that a similar application will arise, an initial generic definition can be useful. It forces the essence of a task to be defined before details are added on.

The capsule descriptions should be subjected to a technical review. In this review, peers of the capsule designer inspect the capsules. They have four objectives, expressed as questions. First, is the set of tasks complete? There can be two types of incompleteness. As regards the specific application that motivates the development, not all tasks may have been identified. If there is reuse potential for the capsules, the set of tasks may be complete as regards to the present application, but incomplete for the general case. Second, are all the activities that should be part of a task listed in the capsule? Third, are the capsules truly generic? Here the objective is to establish that the capsules do not go into detail that may apply to the present application alone. However, specific aspects can be noted as special cases, as in the rental reservations capsule. Fourth, can we think of any special cases additional to those already listed in the capsules?

### 7.3. Task specialization

At this point there exists a set of capsules, either just developed or extracted from a reuse library. The capsules are to be adapted for the present application. Some of the capsules of the generic set may not be needed for the present application. Also, if the set of capsules has come from a reuse library, it may be incomplete as regards the present application. If this is the case, then additional capsules have to be constructed, for deposition in the reuse library and use in the present application.

In adapting the capsules for the present application, the list of special cases, which is part of at least some capsules, is of particular importance. It is to be hoped that the list includes all the special requirements of the present application. If it does not, it has to be appropriately extended. Task specialization then takes place. It produces formatted requirements of the tasks as a set of templates — an example is given in Sec. 6.2.

A technical review of the templates may be needed as well. It is to determine whether the templates truly express all needs and reasonable expectations of the stakeholder groups. In addition, the templates are to be checked for inconsistencies. The statements in an initial requirements document are usually too vague for there to be inconsistencies. The statements "Periodic summaries of sales activities are to be prepared" and "The sales manager is to receive summaries of sales activities periodically" are consistent. Inconsistency arises when further development leads to, say, "Summaries of sales activities are to be prepared once a month" and "The sales manager is to receive summaries of sales activities each Friday". Inconsistencies can be detected by means of indexes — the inconsistency of our example could be detected by looking up all statements in which some form of *summary of sales activities* appears.

We found that novice programmers (undergraduate students of computer science with no software engineering experience) were able to generate C++ code directly from templates. They were even able to carry out the earlier step of generating templates from capsules for a car rental process in one case, and a video rental process in another. Success in this may have been due to their familiarity with car and video rentals. In general, transformation of capsules into templates should be done by experienced personnel, but coding from templates does not require much experience.

## 8. Special Requirements

A demand by a regulatory agency that formal methods must be used for mission-critical systems is an example of a special requirement. The requirements document is then to be expressed as a formal specification, i.e., as expressions in logic. The main argument in favor of formal methods is that their use forces requirements engineers to think very carefully about the properties of the system to be developed. This is true, but the same effect can be achieved by technical reviews. Another argument is that formal proofs carried out on a specification can establish that the system defined by the specification will have certain properties. In particular, it should be possible to detect inconsistencies in a specification.

The author is in favor of the use of formal methods to prove that some critical components of mission-critical systems will perform as required, particularly components that are to respond to threatening situations with corrective actions — components that hopefully will never be executed during the lifetime of the system, but, if activated, must perform perfectly. All the tools that improve dependability must be applied to such components. We have found that the transformation of our templates into formal specifications is easier than the formalization of unformatted requirements.

In other situations advantages in the use of formal specifications is debatable. Hoare, who has done much work on formal methods, writes [9]: "Formal methods and proof play no greater role in large-scale programming than they do in any other branch of modern engineering". Briefly, the arguments against formal specifications are that it is very easy to introduce errors during the translation of natural language text into logic, that a very large number of logical expressions is required to specify a typical software system, that automated detection of inconsistencies in such a collection of expressions is impracticable, and that the proof that a system based on a set of requirements will have certain properties can be carried out informally, the way mathematicians normally carry out proofs.

Most special requirements relate to aspects other than functionality. They can come in a variety of forms. One of the most common relates to system performance, i.e., throughput or response time. For example, a telephone directory system may be required to respond to an enquiry within 500 msec. With current technology performance is rarely a serious issue. Delays can arise in access to servers, but this is not a problem to be solved by developers of an application system. In principle, unless unmanageable time demands result from algorithmic complexity, any performance problem can be solved by using a dedicated hardware system with all data stored in RAM.

Other special requirements can relate to security, special interfaces for handicapped users, and reliability. The latter is the concern of software reliability engineering. For example, a reliability requirement of 0.95 for 100 hours of execution of a software system states that the probability of failure in the next 100 hours of operation is to be no greater that 0.05. Testing and fault removal are to continue until this level of reliability is reached. Some ultrahigh reliability requirements that may be set by regulatory agencies are meaningless because the testing time to achieve such reliability is impossibly long [10].

## 9. Change Control

It is recognized that changes to operational software systems should be strictly controlled, but such discipline is rarely practiced during software development. The lack of discipline can result in what is known as requirements thrashing, which in the worst case means that a particular requirement is put into the requirements document several times, only to be taken out again. Volatility of requirements has resulted in some very large projects never reaching completion or reaching completion with excessive cost overruns.

Volatility is perfectly acceptable in early phases of requirements gathering. Initial interviews may result in an inconsistent wish list, and it may not be possible to determine how to resolve inconsistencies until the requirements process is well advanced. Resolution of inconsistencies results, of course, in changed requirements. This is normal, but at some point the requirements have to be frozen. The manager of the requirements engineering process determines, under consideration of local conditions, when disciplined change control is to begin. For example, if a JAD or PD workshop is part of the process, this could be at the end of the workshop.

After requirements have been frozen, any change to them must be approved by a Change Control Board (CCB). Although it is customary to talk of a board, it can be just one person, particularly in smaller organizations. The change proposal may come from a client, but it may originate from developers as well. In the latter case it may have to be approved by both the client and the CCB.

As a first step, the CCB examines the rationale for the change. The further advanced the project is, the more convincing does the rationale have to be. This also holds when concurrent engineering is practiced, i.e., hardware and embedded software are developed in parallel, or when a software system is developed in parallel with test plans and documentation — changes are more costly in such situations. If the change proposal passes this examination, the impact of the change on cost and schedule is analyzed. Hidden effects have to be included in the analysis, such as customer satisfaction (goodwill) and the impact of the change on future maintenance costs. If this examination is also passed, various adjustments have to be made to the process plan, but they are outside the scope of requirements engineering.

## 10. Bibliographic Notes

The Gause and Weinberg classic [7] deals with requirements for anything at all, not just software. It is an excellent survey of the attitudes that a requirements engineer should assume. A more recent text by Wiegers [11] is a general survey of current best practices; a book by Robertson and Robertson [12] is based on their Volere requirements engineering methodology. The journal *IEEE Software* has devoted its March 1994 and March/April 1998 issues to requirements engineering. The requirements process of Sec. 3 is discussed in [13]. Requirements must not only be carefully engineered. They must also be traced, which means that all accepted requirements and their changes must be satisfied by an implementation. The December 1998 issue of *Communications of the ACM* was devoted to requirements tracing.

Robinson and Pawlowski [1] identify three technical and three social problems that lead to requirements inconsistency. The technical problems are voluminous requirements, their change, and their complexity; the social problems are stakeholder conflicts, difficulty of identifying stakeholders, and changing expectations. With its 75 references this paper is a good starting point for further reading. It appeared in the November/December 1999 issue of *IEEE Transactions on Software Engineering*. This entire issue was devoted to inconsistencies in software development, as was the earlier November 1998 issue. Nuseibeh and Easterbrook [14] present a short but valuable outline of a process for inconsistency management — their main point is that this process must be an explicit part of the requirements process. Related to the inconsistency problem is the problem that it may be too costly to satisfy all consistent requirements. A cost-benefit prioritization approach is taken in [15]. Somewhat similar is the Win-Win process of Boehm *et al* [16].

A survey of different definitions of *stakeholder*, and an approach to stakeholder identification can be found in [5]. Their proper identification is essential for the success of JAD or PD workshops — on JAD, see [17], on PD, see [18]. A cross-cultural comparison of the two approaches is to be found in [19]. There are four critical issues that should be addressed in the workshops: effectiveness of scenarios, the extent to which UML is to be used, reuse of requirements, and the effect of the use of COTS software on requirements. The December 1998 issue of *IEEE Transactions on Software Engineering* is devoted to scenario management. The use of scenarios at 15 organizations is surveyed in a current-practices paper [20], and processes for the development and use of scenarios are defined in [21, 22]. Scenario-based analysis can lead to the use case diagrams of UML — for UML, see [23]. Reuse of requirements based on domain theory has been studied by Sutcliffe and Maiden [24]; for a similar approach, see [25], which should also give increased understanding of stakeholder identification. For the place of COTS software in requirements engineering, see [26, 27].

A method for software cost and risk estimation can be found in [28] — some use is made there of the Delphi approach. The approach based on capsules and templates can improve accuracy of cost estimation. All the capsules of the generic rental process and further examples of templates are to be found in [29]. For a survey of technical reviews see [30]. Arguments in favor of formal methods can be found in [31, 32].

# References

1. W. N. Robinson and S. D. Pawlowski, "Managing requirements inconsistency with development goal monitors", *IEEE Transactions on Software Engineering* **25** (1999) 816–835.
2. W. Swartout and R. Balzer, "On the inevitable intertwining of specification and implementation", *Communications of the ACM* **25** (1982) 438–440.
3. P. Zave and M. Jackson, "Four dark corners of requirements engineering", *ACM Transactions on Software Engineering Methodology* **6** (1997) 1–30.
4. M. C. Paulk *et al*, *The Capability Maturity Model: Guidelines for Improving the Software Process* (Addison-Wesley, 1995).
5. H. Sharp, A. Finkelstein and G. Galal, "Stakeholder identification in the requirements engineering process", *Proceedings of the Tenth International Workshop on Database and Expert Systems Applications* (1999) 387–391.
6. A. Dix, J. Finlay, G. Abowd and R. Beale, *Human-Computer Interaction* (Prentice-Hall, 1993).
7. D. C. Gause and G. M. Weinberg, *Exploring Requirements: Quality Before Design* (Dorset House, 1989).
8. A. T. Berztiss, "Failproof team projects in software engineering courses", *Proceedings of the 27th Frontiers in Education Conference* (IEEE CS Press, 1997) 1015–1019.
9. C.A.R. Hoare, "The role of formal techniques: past, current and future or how did software get so reliable without proof?" *Proceedings of the 18th International Conference Software Engineering* (1996) 233–234.
10. R. W. Butler and G. B. Finelli, "The infeasibility of experimental quantification of life-critical software reliability", *IEEE Transactions on Software Engineering* **19** (1993) 3–12.
11. K. Wiegers, *Software Requirements* (Microsoft Press, 1999).
12. S. Robertson and J. Robertson, *Mastering the Requirements Process* (Addison-Wesley, 1999).
13. A. T. Berztiss, "A flexible requirements process", *Proceedings of the 11th International Workshop Database Expert System Applications* (IEEE CS Press, 2000) 973–977.
14. B. Nuseibeh and S. Easterbrook, "The process of inconsistency management: A framework for understanding", *Proceedings of the 10th International Workshop Database Expert System Applications* (IEEE CS Press, 1999) 364–368.
15. J. Karlsson and K. Ryan, "A cost-value approach for prioritizing requirements", *IEEE Software* **14**, no. 5 (September/October 1997) 67–74.
16. B. Boehm, P. Bose, E. Horowitz and M. J. Lee, "Software requirements negotiation and renegotiation aids: A Theory-W based spiral approach", *Proceedings of the 17th International Conference Software Engineering* (1995) 243–253.
17. J. Wood and D. Silver, *Joint Application Development*, 2nd ed. (Wiley, 1995).
18. D. Schuler and A. Namioka (eds.), *Participatory Design: Principles and Practice* (Lawrence Earlbaum, 1993).
19. E. Carmel, R. D. Whitaker and J. F. George, "PD and joint application design: A transatlantic comparison", *Communications of the ACM* **36**, no. 6 (June 1993) 40–48.

20. K. Weidenhaupt, K. Pohl, M. Jarke and P. Haumer, Scenarios in system development: Current practice, *IEEE Software* **15**, no. 2 (March/April 1998) 34–45.

21. P. Hsia, J. Samuel, J. Gao, D. Kung, Y. Toyoshima and C. Chen, "Formal approach to scenario analysis", *IEEE Software* **11**, no. 2 (March 1994) 33–41.

22. C. Ben Achour, "Guiding scenario authoring", *Information Modelling and Knowledge Bases X* (IOS Press, 1999) 152–171.

23. G. Booch, J. Rumbaugh and I. Jacobson, *The Unified Modeling Language User Guide* (Addison-Wesley, 1999).

24. A. Sutcliffe and N. Maiden, "The domain theory for requirements engineering", *IEEE Transactions on Software Engineering* **24** (1998) 174–196.

25. M. Mannion, B. Keepence and D. Harper, "Using viewpoints to define domain requirements", *IEEE Software* **15**, no. 1 (January/February 1998) 95–102.

26. N.A.M. Maiden, C. Ncube and A. Moore, "Lessons learned during requirements acquisition for COTS systems", *Communications of the ACM* **40**, no. 12 (December 1997) 21–25.

27. N. A. Maiden and C. Ncube, "Acquiring COTS software selection requirements", *IEEE Software* **15**, no. 2 (March/April 1998) 46–56.

28. S. Chulani, B. Boehm and B. Steece, "Bayesian analysis of empirical software engineering cost models", *IEEE Transactions on Software Engineering* **25** (1999) 573–583.

29. A. T. Berztiss, "Domains and patterns in conceptual modeling", *Information Modelling and Knowledge Bases VIII* (IOS Press, 1997) 213–223.

30. A. T. Berztiss, Technical Reviews (this volume).

31. A. Hall, "Seven myths of formal methods", *IEEE Software* **7**, no. 5 (September 1990) 11–19.

32. J. P. Bowen and M. G. Hinchey, "Seven more myths of formal methods", *IEEE Software* **12**, no. 4 (July 1995) 34–41.

# SOFTWARE RELIABILITY ENGINEERING

ALFS T. BERZTISS

*University of Pittsburgh, Department of Computer Science,*
*Pittsburgh PA 15260, USA*
*and*
*SYSLAB, University of Stockholm, Sweden*
*E-mail: alpha@cs.pitt.edu*

The primary purpose of this brief nontechnical overview of software reliability engineering (SRE) is to clear up some misconceptions regarding SRE. We discuss several uses of SRE, and emphasize the importance of operational profiles in SRE. An SRE process is outlined in which several SRE models are applied simultaneously to failure data, and several versions of key components may be used to improve reliability.

*Keywords*: Operational profile, reliability growth, software reliability engineering.

## 1. Introduction

Software reliability engineering (SRE) is an adaptation of hardware reliability engineering (HRE). One area in which there is much interaction between hardware and software is telecommunications, and much of the early research on software reliability was carried out by telecommunications engineers. The first major text on SRE by Musa *et al* [1] was published in 1987; for a later (1996) survey by Musa and Ehrlich, see [2]. A more recent (1998) survey is by Tian [3]. A handbook of SRE [4] appeared in 1996. The handbook is a comprehensive survey of all aspects of SRE. We shall therefore limit ourselves to a brief nontechnical overview of the basic principles of SRE.

The SRE process has five main steps. (1) An operational profile is derived. This is a usage distribution, i.e., the extent to which each operation of the software system is expected to be exercised. (2) Test cases are selected in accordance with the operational profile. This is to ensure that system usage during testing is as close as can be to the usage patterns expected after release of the system. (3) Test cases are run. For each test case that results in failure the time of failure is noted, in terms of execution time, and the execution time clock is stopped. After repair the clock is started again, and testing resumes. (4) An appropriate statistical model is periodically applied to the distribution of the failure points over time, and an estimate of the reliability is determined. If an acceptable reliability level has been reached, the system is released. (5) Failure data continue to be gathered after system release.

Reliability is usually expressed in one of two ways, as a probability $R$, which is the probability that the system will not fail in the next $t$ units of execution time, or as MTTF, which stands for mean time to failure, and is an estimate of the length of time that will elapse before the next failure of the system occurs. Related to reliability are testability and trustability. Testability [5] is the probability that a program will fail if it contains at least one fault; trustability [6] is a measure of our confidence that a program is free of faults.

Section 2 contrasts hardware and software reliabilities, and defines several uses for SRE. Section 3 deals with the construction of operational profiles, and Sec. 4 outlines the SRE process. In Sec. 5, we discuss miscellaneous topics not covered earlier.

## 2. Development and Uses of SRE

Numerous differences between hardware and software affect reliability. Hardware failures result initially from failures of components or assemblies due to manufacturing faults, are relatively few after this initial period, but rise when wear-and-tear sets in. A plot of failure probability over time has a "bathtub" shape. With software, reliability continues to increase throughout the lifetime of the system — there is no wear-and-tear. Hence the statistical models used in SRE differ substantially from the models of HRE, and are called reliability *growth* models. It is true that early assembly language programs deteriorated very badly toward the end of their lifetimes because corrective patches destroyed whatever structure the programs might have had to begin with, but today the importance of well-structured software is fully understood, and then there is no software deterioration with time. Under adaptive and perfective maintenance there can occur deterioration, but the system resulting from such maintenance efforts can be regarded as a new system whose reliability estimation is to be started from scratch.

Another major difference is that hardware deteriorates even when not in use. For example, the reliability of an automobile with moderate use is higher than that of an automobile with no use at all. Software failures occur only when the software is being executed. Hence, SRE models are based on execution time instead of calendar time. Moreover, hardware is for the most part built from standardized interchangeable parts so that corrective action after a failure can consist of no more than the substitution of a new component for the failed one. With software it is often difficult to locate the fault that caused a failure, and removal of the fault may introduce new faults. In SRE, this is accounted for by a fault reduction factor $B$, which is 1.0 if fault removal is perfect. In practice, $B$ has been found to have a value around 0.95 [1], but it can be much worse for distributed systems in which fault location is very difficult because it may be impossible to recreate the state in which failure occurred.

The final difference relates to the hazard rate $z(t)$ — $z(t)dt$ is the probability that the system that has survived to time $t$ will fail in the interval between $t$ and

$t + dt$. Software failures can be traced back to individual faults, which has led to the use of per-fault hazard rates instead of the global hazard rate of HRE.

To summarize, the HRE approach has been modified by the introduction of different reliability growth models, and the use of execution time, fault reduction factors, and per-fault hazard rates in these models. These modifications have made SRE a practicable tool of software engineering, but one important difference remains. Hardware failures are for most part determined by the physical properties of the materials used in the hardware. Software failures arise because of human error, and the unpredictability of human behavior should invalidate statistical methods of prediction. Still, the methods work. We may have to apply more than one reliability growth model to a given set of failure data, but one of the models can be expected to represent the data quite well. There is still one proviso: statistical estimation requires fairly large numbers of failures, which means that SRE can be applied only to large systems.

The techniques of SRE have two main uses. First, SRE can give a quantitative estimate of the reliability of a software system at the time it is released. As a corollary, given a reliability goal, testing can stop when this goal has been reached. Second, SRE can reduce system development cost. The reliability of a system can be computed from the reliabilities of its components. Suppose a system has three components. Total reliability is the product of the three component reliabilities: $R = R_1 R_2 R_3$. If one of the $R_i$ is increased, another may be decreased without changing the value of $R$. Under system balancing [4, p. 261], given a required system reliability $R$, high reliability is aimed for in components in which this can be achieved at low cost, and lower reliability in high-cost components. Cost reduction can also be achieved by the use of COTS (Commercial Off-The-Shelf) software. However, if it is to be used in a SRE context, it has to be provided with reliability estimates. Berman and Cutler [7] discuss reliability of a system that uses components from a reuse library.

If only the total system reliability is of interest, system balancing can be applied to hardware as well as software components. There is a misconception that software failures are more likely than hardware failures. Actually hardware failures may be more likely [8], but locating faults and removing them is usually easier in hardware than in software.

## 3. The Operational Profile

A reliability estimate established by the SRE process is meaningful only if the conditions under which the software is tested closely correspond to the conditions under which it will be used in the field. This means that test cases are to have the same distribution according to type as the inputs after the system has been released. This distribution is called the operational profile. For example, if 20% of inputs to an information system are data updates and 80% are queries, then the test cases should have a 20–80 distribution in favor of queries. The construction of an operational profile is discussed in detail by Musa [9]; a later survey by Musa *et al* forms Chap. 5 of [4]. The development of an operational profile may take five steps, as follows.

- *Definition of client types.* This relates to product software, i.e., to software that is developed for a number of different clients. Consider a generic automated enquiry system that responds to telephone calls by customers. The system consists of prompts to the caller, call routing, canned responses, the possibility of speaking to a customer service representative, and wait lines. This structure is the same for all systems, only the content of the prompts and the canned responses differs from system to system. The systems for airlines will be more similar to each other than to a system that handles health insurance enquiries. Airlines and health insurance companies thus form two client types.
- *Definition of user types.* A user type consists of persons (or other software, as in automatic business-to-business e-commerce) who will use the system in the same way. In the case of the enquiry system, some users will update the canned response files, and this will happen more often for airlines than for health insurance companies. Other users will listen to responses, and still others will want to talk to customer representatives.
- *Definition of system modes.* These are the major operational modes of a system, such as system initialization, reboot after a failure, overload due to excessive wait line build-up, gathering of system usage statistics, monitoring of customer service representatives, selection of the language in which the customer will interact with the system.
- *Definition of functional profile.* In this step each system mode is broken down into the procedures or transactions that it will need, and the probability of use of each such component is estimated. The functional profile is developed during the design phase of the software process. (For a discussion of procedural and transactional computation, see [10].)
- *Definition of operational profile.* The functional profile relates to the abstractions produced as part of software design. The abstractions of the functional profile are now converted into actual operations, and the probabilities of the functional profile are converted into probabilities of the operations.

The five steps are actually part of any software development process. The operations have to be defined sooner or later in any case, and a process based on the five steps can be an effective way of defining operations. For example, user types can be identified with actors and system modes with use cases in use case diagrams of UML [11]. Identification of user types and system modes by means of use case diagrams can take place very early in the software process. What is specific to SRE and what is difficult is the association of probabilities with the operations.

Some of the difficulties are pointed out in [4, pp. 535–537]. They include the uncertainty of how a new software system will be used. Many systems are used in ways totally different from how the original developers envisaged their use — the Internet is the most famous example. Another problem is that requirements keep changing well after the initial design stage.

Fortunately, it has been shown that reliability models are rather insensitive to errors in the operational profile [12, 13]. Note that reliability is usually presented as a value together with a confidence interval associated with the value. Adams [14] shows how to calculate confidence intervals that take into account uncertainties associated with the operational profile — note that Adams defines reliability as the probability that the software will not fail for a test case randomly chosen in accordance with the operational profile.

One way of arriving at a more realistic operational profile is to combine expert opinions by the Delphi method [15]. Briefly, Delphi starts with a moderator sending out a problem description to a group of experts. The experts suggest probabilities for operations, giving their reasons for this. The moderator collects this information, collates it, and sends it out again. When the experts see the reasoning for estimates different from their own, they tend to adjust their estimates. The objective is to arrive at a consensus after several iterations. The early Delphi method took a very long time. The time scale has been compressed by basing Delphi on modern distributed group decision systems (see, e.g. [16]). Such systems allow the experts to interact asynchronously from different locations.

## 4. The SRE Process

In Sec. 1, it was noted that the SRE process is to have five steps. Step 1 was discussed in Sec. 3, and Steps 2 and 3 are straightforward. Here our concern will be Steps 4 and 5, but there is a question relating to software architecture that we have to look at first. In HRE very high reliability can be obtained by placing identical components in parallel — if there are $n$ such components and $n-1$ fail, one is still functioning. For $n$ parallel components, each with reliability $r$, the total reliability of the arrangement is

$$R = 1 - (1 - r)^n .$$

If $r = 0.9$ and $n = 3$, then $R = 0.999$.

Reliability improvement of software by means of redundancy is problematic. First, if we use identical implementations of the same operation, they will all fail identically, something that is very unlikely to happen with hardware. The solution is to create different implementations based on the same requirements. A second problem relates to common cause failures. If all the components were identical, all failures would be common cause. When components are not identical, we have $n$-version programming. The nature of failures in $n$-version programming has been examined by numerous authors [17–21]. Multiple versions have been found to give

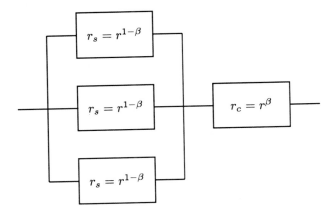

**Fig. 1.**    Parallel components and common cause failures.

better reliability than a single "good" version [22, 23]. But with multiple versions
their cost becomes a serious consideration — for an investigation of this, see [24].

Because of the cost, $n$-version programming is to be considered only for those
components of a mission-critical system whose failure would have serious consequences. Suppose that each of the $n$ components has been tested until its reliability
has become $r$. This has two components, $r_s$, which relates to failures specific to this
version, and $r_c$, which is the reliability with respect to common cause failures. Then
$r = r_s r_c = r^{1-\beta} r^\beta$, where the parameter $\beta$ $(0 \le \beta \le 1)$ indicates the strength of
the common cause effect. When $\beta = 0$, there are no common cause failures; when
$\beta = 1$, all failures are common cause. The reliability of the entire $n$-version critical
component is

$$R = r^\beta [1 - (1 - r^{1-\beta})^n].$$

Figure 1 shows the arrangement for $n = 3$.

This analysis is based on the assumption that in case of a common cause failure
all $n$ versions will fail rather than just $n - k$ of them. Justification for the assumption comes from the observation that practically all common cause failures in code
written by experienced programmers familiar with the domain of application are due
to faulty requirements [18], which, of course, are the same for all versions. A further
assumption is that the coordination mechanism for the different versions is fault-
free, or that $r_c$ absorbs the effect of failures of this mechanism. A major problem
is that the critical components are likely to be too small to give enough failures
for a meaningful reliability estimation for the replicated components. Techniques
for dealing with situations in which testing results in no failures can help in such a
case [25].

A complete software process that includes SRE is Cleanroom [26, 27]. It has
three phases after software design has taken place. First, each design unit is coded,
and the coder demonstrates by means of an informal mathematical proof that the

code satisfies the requirements for this unit. There is no unit testing at all. Proofs are not documented in order to keep down costs. Second, the individual units are integrated. Third, an independent team tests the integrated system using test cases selected on the basis of an operational profile, and testing continues until a required value of MTTF has been reached. Under this approach an appreciable percentage of statements in the software system will never have been executed before release of the software, which has led to criticism of Cleanroom [28]. However, it has been shown that the quality of Cleanroom products is higher than the industry norm [29]. Still, it is difficult to understand why unit testing is banned — intuitively one suspects that fewer system test cases would be needed to reach the required MTTF if unit testing had been performed. Therefore, unless this has already been done, it would be instructive to analyze failure data to determine which of the failures would have been avoided by unit testing, and on the basis of this, establish whether unit testing would have lowered total testing costs.

More serious than the construction of a truly representative operational profile is the selection of the appropriate reliability growth model. Experience shows that no model is appropriate for all software systems, even when the systems are similar and have been developed under similar conditions. An exception is provided by successive releases of the same system: the model that has worked for the first release works also for later releases [30]. Otherwise multiple models have to be used. For a full explanation of the problem and of the multiple-model approach, see [31]. The multiple-model approach has been made fully practicable by the very high speeds of modern computers. Moreover, the user of this approach does not have to be a professional statistician. Various SRE tools are available (see, e.g. [4, Appendix A]). A particularly interesting approach has been taken in the design of the Sorel tool [32]. This tool has two modules: one evaluates reliability on the basis of four reliability growth models, the other carries out a trend analysis. The latter draws attention to unexpected problems, such as an extended period during which reliability does not increase.

As discussed in [31], the main problem with reliability growth models is that reliability estimates are extrapolations of past experience into the future. Such extrapolations are not particularly safe even when the distribution of the data on which they are based is fairly smooth: the confidence range, i.e., the range in which an estimated value is expected to lie with probability 0.95, say, gets wider and wider the further we extrapolate, until it covers the entire range of possible values. This problem is made worse by the lack of smoothness in software failure data. There is an upward trend in the time between failures as testing progresses, but the pattern of the intervals between failures is very irregular. This has a negative effect on confidence intervals.

There have been claims that SRE can improve the accuracy of software process cost and schedule estimates. Advance estimates of the time required for testing, and of the expected number of failures coupled to estimates of the time required for repairs would give fairly accurate estimates of both cost and duration of the test phase. Unfortunately the extrapolation problem makes the accuracy of early reliability prediction highly questionable. The use of Bayesian techniques for early reliability estimation holds some promise. This will be discussed in Sec. 5.

Matters are quite different after the release of a software system, particularly in the case of product software that is distributed as a large number of copies. Operational use obviously follows a perfect operational profile, and, if there is no repair following failures, reliability is constant, which means that no complicated model is required for its estimation. It is common practice not to carry out repairs after failures, but save up all repairs for the next "minor" release, i.e., a release that has fault removal as its only purpose. The constant reliability value for this release is calculated, and so forth.

For an operating system running 24 hours a day at approximately 5000 installations, a failure intensity of no more than 0.9 failures per 1000 years of operation has been established [1, pp. 205–207]. Very high reliability has also been achieved in consumer products [33]; this can be attributed to the use of read-only memory. For a single-copy system the determination of ultra-high reliability would require an impossibly long testing phase [34]. It is therefore surprising that regulatory agencies impose such reliability requirements on safety-critical software — requirements that cannot possibly be verified. Schneidewind [35] combines risk analysis with SRE predictions to reduce the risk of failures of safety-critical systems. When there exists a software system with very high reliability, and such reliability is a major requirement, the best approach is not to replace the system or to carry out major changes on it.

A question that now arises is what level of reliability is reasonable. This is a social rather than a technical issue. It is customary to assume that the greatest risk is threat to human life. This is so in principle, but cost and convenience are also important. Otherwise automobiles, which constantly threaten human lives, would have been banned by consumer protection agencies. It has been estimated that the direct cost of the famous AT&T nine-hour breakdown was 60–70 million dollars [36]. Human life is rarely given this high a valuation in legal settlements. However, as pointed out in [37], a cost-benefit ratio, if made public, is not to outrage most members of the public. It is therefore important not to become cynical in a discussion on how to reduce testing costs.

## 5. Additional Topics

As noted above, a system tested according to the principles of SRE can contain code that has never been executed. Mitchell and Zeil [38] introduce an approach that combines representative and directed testing. Representative testing is based on an operational profile, directed testing uses a variety of approaches and criteria to uncover faults efficiently. One popular criterion for directed testing is statement coverage under which an attempt is made to execute as many statements of a program as possible. Combination of the two modes of testing is the subject matter of [39] as well. It should be noted that full 100% coverage is impossible to achieve. This is so because of some theoretical undecidability results, e.g. the non-existence of an algorithm for solving two non-linear inequalities. Hence, it is not always possible to find an input that will force control along a particular path in the software system. Actual statement coverage in system tests may be only 50–60%, although testers may guess it to be 90% or better [40]. If 100% statement coverage were possible, then, in principle, test cases could be generated automatically to achieve such coverage. This is impossible for even very simple cases. It should be realized that undecidability results indicate the non-existence of general algorithms. In unit testing full coverage is for the most part achievable by examination of the structure of the program unit.

An interesting development in SRE has been the use of Bayesian approaches to reliability prediction. In most cases statistical estimation is based on observations alone — this is a frequentist approach. However, if prior knowledge and beliefs are also taken into account in the estimation process, we have what is known as a Bayesian or subjectivist approach. Earlier work on this approach in SRE is surveyed in [4]. Some more recent research [41, 42] suggests that Bayesian techniques can give reasonable estimates of the cost of testing by analysis of early test data — see also [43, 44].

Nearly all the SRE literature deals with software composed of procedures written in languages such as Fortran or Pascal. The SRE approach can be applied also to logic programs [45], and to AI software [46–48]. We have used SRE techniques to estimate the level of completeness of data base schemas [49]. The approach is as follows. A set of queries likely to be put to a data base under construction is collected from prospective users, together with usage ratings. A usage rating is an integer between 1 and 5 that indicates the relative frequency with which a particular query will be put. A test suite is constructed in which each query has as many copies as its usage rating, and this collection of queries is randomized. The queries are put to the data base one after another, and if the data base base schema has to be extended to deal with a query, this is registered as a failure. The failure data are analyzed using SRE techniques, thus providing a quantitative estimate of the completeness of the schema.

## References

1. J. D. Musa, A. Iannino and K. Okumoto, *Software Reliability — Measurement, Prediction, Application* (McGraw-Hill, 1987).
2. J. D. Musa and W. Ehrlich, "Advances is software reliability engineering", *Advances in Computers* **42** (1996) 77–117.
3. J. Tian, "Reliability measurement, analysis, and improvement for large systems", *Advances in Computers* **46** (1998) 159–235.
4. M. R. Lyu (ed.), *Handbook of Software Reliability Engineering* (McGraw-Hill, 1996).
5. A. Bertolino and L. Strigini, "On the use of testability measures for dependability assessment", *IEEE Transactions on Software Engineering* **22** (1996) 97–108.

6. W. E. Howden and Y. Huang, "Software trustability analysis", *ACM Transactions on Software Engineering Methodology* **4** (1995) 36–64.

7. O. Berman and M. Cutler, "Choosing an optimal set of libraries", *IEEE Transactions on Reliability* **45** (1996) 303–307.

8. D. R. Kuhn, "Sources of failure in the public switched telephone network", *Computer* **30**, no. 4 (April 1997) 31–36.

9. J. D. Musa, "Operational profiles in software-reliability engineering", *IEEE Software* **10**, no. 2 (March 1993) 14–32.

10. A. T. Berztiss, "Transactional computation", *Database and Expert Systems Applications* (*Lecture Notes in Computer Science 1677*) (Springer, 1999) 521–530.

11. G. Booch, J. Rumbaugh and I. Jacobson, *The Unified Modeling Language User Guide* (Addison-Wesley, 1999).

12. A. Avritzer and B. Larson, "Load testing software using deterministic state testing", *Proceedings of the 1993 International Symposium on Software Testing and Analysis* [published as Software Engineering Notes **18**, no. 3 (July 1993)] 82–88.

13. A. Pasquini, A. N. Crespo and P. Matrella, "Sensitivity of reliability-growth models to operational profile errors vs testing accuracy", *IEEE Transactions on Reliability* **45** (1996) 531–540 (errata *ibid* 46, 1997, 68).

14. T. Adams, "Total variance approach to software reliability estimation", *IEEE Transactions on Software Engineering* **22** (1996) 687–688.

15. O. Helmer, *Social Technology* (Basic Books, 1966).

16. D. Kenis and L. Verhaegen, "The MacPolicy project: Developing a group decision support system based on the Delphi method", *Decision Support in Public Administration* (North-Holland, 1993) 159–170.

17. J. C. Knight and N. G. Leveson, "An experimental evaluation of the assumption of independence in multiversion programming", *IEEE Transactions on Software Engineering* **SE-12** (1986) 96–109.

18. P. G. Bishop, D. G. Esp, M. Barnes, P. Humphreys, G. Dahll and J. Lahti, "PODS — A project on diverse software", *IEEE Transactions on Software Engineering* **SE-12** (1986) 929–940.

19. S. S. Brilliant, J. C. Knight and N. G. Leveson, "The consistent comparison problem in *N*-version software", *IEEE Transactions on Software Engineering* **15** (1989) 1481–1485.

20. S. S. Brilliant, J. C. Knight and N. G. Leveson, "Analysis of faults in an *N*-version software experiment", *IEEE Transactions on Software Engineering* **16** (1990) 238–247.

21. D. E. Eckhardt, A. K. Caglayan, J. C. Knight, L. D. Lee, D. F. McAllister, M. A. Vouk and J. P. J. Kelly, "An experimental evaluation of software redundancy as a strategy for improving reliability", *IEEE Transactions on Software Engineering* **17** (1991) 692–702.

22. J. P. J. Kelly, T. I. McVittie and W. I. Yamamoto, "Implementing design diversity to achieve fault tolerance", *IEEE Software* **8**, no. 4 (July 1991) 61–71.

23. L. Hatton, "*N*-version design versus one good version", *IEEE Software* **14**, no. 6 (November/December 1997), 71–76.

24. R. K. Scott and D. F. McAllister, "Cost modeling of *N*-version fault-tolerant software systems for large *N*", *IEEE Transactions on Reliability* **45** (1996) 297–302.

25. K. W. Miller, L. J. Morell, R. E. Noonan, S. K. Park, D. M. Nicol, B. W. Murrill and J. M. Voas, "Estimating the probability of failure when testing reveals no failures", *IEEE Transactions on Software Engineering* **18** (1992) 33–42.

26. M. Dyer, *The Cleanroom Approach to Quality Software Development* (Wiley, 1992).
27. H. D. Mills, "Zero defect software: Cleanroom engineering", *Advances in Computers* **36** (1993) 1–41.
28. B. Beizer, "Cleanroom process model: A critical examination", *IEEE Software* **14**, no. 2 (March/April 1997) 14–16.
29. R. C. Linger, "Cleanroom software engineering for zero-defect software", *Proceedings of the 15th International Conference on Software Engineering* (1993) 2–13.
30. A. Wood, "Predicting software reliability", *Computer* **29**, no. 11 (November 1996) 69–77.
31. S. Brocklehurst and B. Littlewood, "Techniques for prediction analysis and recalibration", in [4], pp. 119–166.
32. K. Kanoun, M. Kaâniche and J.-C. Laprie, "Qualitative and quantitative reliability assessment", *IEEE Software* **14**, no. 2 (March/April 1997).
33. J. Rooijmans, H. Aerts and M. v. Genuchten, "Software quality in consumer electronics products", *IEEE Software* **13**, no. 1 (January 1996) 55–64.
34. R. W. Butler and G. B. Finelli, "The infeasibility of experimental quantification of life-critical software reliability", *IEEE Transactions on Software Engineering* **19** (1993) 3–12.
35. N. F. Schneidewind, "Reliability modeling for safety-critical software", *IEEE Transactions on Reliability* **46** (1997) 88–98.
36. T. C. K. Chou, "Beyond fault tolerance", *Computer* **30**, no. 4 (April 1997) 47–49.
37. W. R. Collins, K. W. Miller, B. J. Spielman and P. Wherry, "How good is good enough? An ethical analysis of software construction and use", *Communication of the ACM* **37**, no. 1 (January 1994) 81–91.
38. B. Mitchell and S. J. Zeil, "A reliability model combining representative and directed testing", *Proceedings of the 18th International Conferences on Software Engineering* (1996) 506–514.
39. J. R. Horgan and A. P. Mathur, "Software testing and reliability", in [4], pp. 531–566.
40. P. Piwowarski, M. Ohba and J. Caruso, "Coverage measurement experience during function test", *Proceedings of the 15th International Conferences on Software Engineering* (1993) 287–301.
41. J. M. Caruso and D. W. Desormeau, "Integrating prior knowledge with a software reliability growth model", *Proceedings of the 13th International Conferences on Software Engineering* (1991) 238–245.
42. C. Smidts, M. Stutzke and R. W. Stoddard, "Software reliability modeling: An approach to early reliability prediction", *IEEE Transactions on Reliability* **47** (1998) 268–278.
43. S. Campodonico and N. D. Singpurwalla, "A Bayesian analysis of the logarithmic-Poisson execution time model based on expert opinion and failure data", *IEEE Transactions on Software Engineering* **20** (1994) 677–683.
44. M.-A. El Aroui and J.-L. Soler, "A Bayes nonparametric framework for software-reliability analysis", *IEEE Transactions on Reliability* **45** (1996) 652–660.
45. A. Azem, *Software Reliability Determination for Conventional and Logic Programming* (Walter de Gruyter, 1995).
46. F. B. Bastani, I.-R. Chen and T.-W. Tsao, "A software reliability model for artificial intelligence programs", *International Journal of Software Engineering and Knowledge Engineering* **3** (1993) 99–114.
47. F. B. Bastani and I.-R. Chen, "The reliability of embedded AI systems", *IEEE Expert* **8**, no. 2 (April 1993) 72–78.

48. I.-R. Chen, F. B. Bastani and T.-W. Tsao, "On the reliability of AI planning software in real-time applications", *IEEE Transactions on Knowledge and Data Engineering* **7** (1995) 4–13.

49. A. T. Berztiss and K. J. Matjasko, "Queries and the incremental construction of conceptual models", *Information Modelling and Knowledge Bases VI* (IOS Press, 1995) 175–185.

# TECHNICAL REVIEWS

ALFS T. BERZTISS

*University of Pittsburgh, Department of Computer Science,*
*Pittsburgh PA 15260, USA*
*and*
*SYSLAB, University of Stockholm, Sweden*
*E-mail: alpha@cs.pitt.edu*

Reviews of software work products were introduced by Fagan in the 1970's. A review can be applied to any kind of software work product. A Fagan-type inspection is carried out in a meeting of four or five people who use checklists to help them locate problems in the product under review. Lately, the effectiveness of both inspection meetings and check-lists has been questioned. We examine Fagan-type inspections as well as alternatives to meetings and checklists.

*Keywords*: Checklist, Fagan-type inspection, inspection meeting.

## 1. Introduction

Technical reviews are a tool for validating the various artifacts or work products that arise during software development. They are also called peer reviews, inspections, and walkthroughs. We shall use the terms review and inspection interchangeably. The basic concept is that a group of people jointly examine a software requirements document, a specification, a design document, a piece of code, a test plan, a user manual, or a maintenance manual. Although here we shall discuss technical reviews in the context of software engineering, they can be part of the knowledge engineering process as well. The main advantage of technical reviews is that they can be applied at any stage of the software development process to any work product of that process. This means, for example, that misconceptions regarding requirements or user expectations can be cleared up early, when corrections are still relatively inexpensive. One estimate puts the savings in maintenance at 30 hours for each hour spent on a review of requirements [1]. Data relating to the Space Shuttle project put the cost of fixing a fault at 13 times greater during system test and 92 times greater after release [2, p. 106]. A second advantage is that reviews locate faults directly. In this a code inspection differs from testing: when a software test results in failure, considerable effort may still have to be applied to locate the fault that caused the failure. The third positive aspect is that technical reviews of a software work product extend the group of people familiar with this product. Even the author of the product gets a better understanding of it. Fourth, reviews do not look for actual faults alone; improvements in style and reduction of complexity can also be brought about by means of reviews. For this reason, we shall refer to the issues raised by reviews as problems rather than faults.

In terms of the Capability Maturity Model (CMM) of the Software Engineering Institute [2], peer reviews are one of the key process areas of Level 3 (Levels 2 through 5 represent increasing maturity of an organization with respect to software development). But reviews are easy to introduce, so that they are often used in organizations that have not even reached Level 2. The author of this survey has required the use of reviews in student projects. For full effectiveness, though, there has to be some specialized training in the conduct of reviews. Despite evidence of the positive effects of some form of inspection (see, e.g. [3]), it is estimated that inspections are used by only 20% of organizations [4].

The purpose of this chapter is to give an overview of technical reviews, but with special emphasis on recent innovations. Section 2 gives an outline of Fagan-type inspections. Empirical evidence has lately shown that Fagan-type inspections of code are not as effective as some more recently developed types of inspections. We discuss these innovations in Secs. 3 and 4. However, a basic Fagan-type inspection structure, possibly modified according to some of the suggestions of Secs. 3 and 4, can still be useful for reviews of work products other than code. This is because inspections can serve as an effective communication medium between software developers, and between developers and sponsors and users of software. Section 5 is a brief reading guide.

## 2. Fagan-type Inspections

Inspection methodology was introduced by Michael Fagan at IBM in the 1970's [5]. In describing the approach, we shall first identify the roles of the participants in an inspection meeting, and then consider the mechanics and rules of conduct for a meeting.

### 2.1. *Inspection participants*

The number of participants at a technical review of the Fagan type should not exceed four or five, but some of them will have to play multiple roles. Our view of inspections is that in addition to problem detection they should also serve as a means of communication between participants in different phases of software development and documentation. Hence, we include some roles that could have merely an observer status — observers should not be counted in the determination of the size of the inspection team. To distinguish active participants from observers, the former will be called reviewers. Supervisors of the author should not participate, not even as observers. The aim of inspections is to detect problems (sometimes called issues in the literature), not to evaluate the author. A supervisor may find it difficult to maintain this attitude.

*Moderator.* The moderator schedules an inspection meeting well in advance, but distributes the material for the meeting only a few days before the meeting in order not to extend unnecessarily the software development time. The distributed material consists of the work product to be examined, as well as a checklist of what to look for. The moderator should have received specialized training in group dynamics. The moderator is also responsible for checking that problems discovered in an inspection session get resolved. A member of the Software Quality Assurance group (SQA is a Level 2 key process area of the CMM) is a good candidate for the role of moderator.

*Author.* The author of the product, or, in case of a product developed by a team, a representative of the team, must be present to answer questions. The author also assists the moderator by indicating when a product is to be ready for inspection. This is to be approached with great care: a pessimistic estimate has a negative effect on the project schedule; an unsustainable optimistic estimate requires rescheduling of the inspection meeting.

*Presenter.* This role should not be filled by the author. If the presenter is not the author, then there will be at least one other person in the organization who is thoroughly familiar with the product. Also, conscious or unconscious attempts by authors to influence inspection teams in their favor are avoided.

*Secretary.* The secretary, sometimes called a scribe, records all problems identi-fied in the inspection session. Copies of the problem report go to the moderator and to the author. Some of the problems may have been detected by the participants while they examined the product in preparation for the meeting. Since some such "problems" may be false positives, i.e., issues that are not to be followed up, each such issue should be scrutinized in the meeting.

*Representation expert.* Somebody on the inspection team must be thoroughly familiar with the language in which the product under review is presented. This may be a programming language, a modeling language such as UML, or, as in the case of manuals, a natural language. One selection criterion for a moderator may be the ability of the moderator to fill the role of representation expert as well.

*Standards expert.* This role may be combined with that of the representation expert. In the case of code, the standards expert would check that extensions that do not belong to the standard for the programming language are not used, or, if used, explicitly identified as such — this is essential for portability of the code. Some organizations require additional internal standards to be followed, e.g. naming conventions for variables.

*Upstream representative.* For this we identify a sequence in the software process that consists of requirements collection and analysis, design, coding, testing, documentation. Unless the same team is responsible for the entire process sequence, there are handover points at which information loss can occur. To reduce such loss, a client representative should be present at an inspection of requirements, a member of the requirements engineering team at the inspection of design documents and of user manuals, and so forth.

*Downstream representative.* Members of the testing and the documentation teams should participate as observers at inspections of design and code, possibly also at requirements inspections. So should a member of the SQA group (which happens naturally when the moderator belongs to this group) and a member of the configuration management group.

## 2.2. *Inspection components*

At an inspection meeting the presenter goes through the product under inspection line by line or — in the case of diagrams — path by path through the diagram. Members of the inspection team are expected to have familiarized themselves with the product before the inspection session. How much time should be spent on this preparation is an open question. Now the participants use checklists to spot problems. The problems need not necessarily be faults. Opportunities for improvements of style or of clarity can also be pointed out.

*Checklists.* A checklist depends on the domain of the application, the type of work product under review, and the language in which the work product is expressed. For example, the types of faults in Java programs will differ from those in Lisp programs. For mission-critical software much attention has to be given to exception handling and fail-safe behavior. A by-product of an inspection session may be an improved checklist.

*Reports.* A problem report is generated by the secretary. No attempt is to be made to resolve problems during an inspection session, but some suggestions may be made on how best to deal with a problem, particularly by the representation expert and the standards expert. The nature of the problems listed in the problem report determines whether another inspection is needed after the author of the product has attempted to resolve the problems. Because a follow-up meeting may be difficult to arrange, and such a meeting can therefore substantially delay a project, follow-up meetings should be scheduled only in very exceptional cases. The secretary generates also a process report that should include at least the following information: participants, preparation time by each reviewer, size of the product inspected, length of the inspection session, types and counts of problems detected, including false positives. The effectiveness of each reviewer should also be indicated, in terms of the type of each problem detected by the reviewer, and whether it was detected during preparation or at the meeting. The moderator, who is to follow up on the resolution of the problems, adds to this report information of what percentage of each type of problem was resolved, and the effort needed for the resolution. An inspection meeting can be followed by "process brainstorming" [6]. The purpose of this is to try to determine the causes of the detected problems, and to suggest approaches to their elimination in the future. Results of the brainstorming session should be included in the process report.

*Length and intensity.* The length of an inspection session should not be below 60 or above 90 minutes. If the meeting is shorter, then the ratio of administrative overhead to productive work is too high; if longer, the attentiveness of participants goes down. Although this depends greatly on the complexity of the code, code inspection at the rate of 150 lines per hour appears to have the best cost-effectiveness [7].

*Team interaction.* The social atmosphere at a meeting should be relaxed, but not frivolous. Participants should not waste time on trivialities such as missing semicolons or spelling mistakes. When a problem is detected, it should be reported succinctly, and in a way that does not embarrass the author. Similarly, the author should not give excuses regarding the problem.

*Inspections and tests.* Robert Glass [8] claims that there is consistent evidence that 90% of faults in code can be found by inspections before the first test case is run. This suggests that code inspections should precede unit testing. Indeed, if unit testing precedes inspections, the reviewers of the code can become negatively influenced to the extent that they regard inspections as superfluous. There have been suggestions that code inspections can replace most unit testing altogether [9, 10].

*Global results.* At Hewlett-Packard, the role of Chief Moderator was created to serve as the owner of the entire inspection process [3]. The Chief Moderator receives all process reports and uses them to monitor the effectiveness and efficiency of the inspection process. The aim is to improve this process. In addition, the effectiveness of the reviewers is to be monitored. If some reviewers are found to be ineffective, then they should undergo additional training or be removed from the pool of reviewers. The training may be in code reading — von Mayrhauser and Vans [11] survey program understanding, which is important for all reviewers during preparation for a code inspection, and for the presenter at the code inspection itself. The ultimate objective of the Chief Moderator is to lead the organization toward Level 5 on an inspection-maturity scale that is a specialization of the CMM adapted for the inspection process [3].

## 3. Are Inspection Meetings Needed?

The IBM Cleanroom methodology (see, e.g. [12]) uses neither unit testing nor code inspection meetings. Instead, the author of a code unit carries out an informal mathematical proof of correctness of the code unit. Only integration testing is performed, and statistical software reliability engineering is used to estimate the mean time to failure of the software system at the time of its release. The use of informal proofs can be regarded as highly systematized one-person code inspections. There now exists a large amount of experimental evidence that questions the effectiveness of code inspections performed by large teams. As regards Cleanroom, failure rates of Cleanroom products are significantly lower than industry norms [13], and this can be traced back to what we have called one-person code inspections.

Although the effectiveness of inspections as such is not being questioned, the use of meetings for code inspections has come under criticism. The criticism has two components. First, meetings are said to increase project completion time. For one of AT&T's products with a base size of 5,000,000 lines of code, and 10% of this added or changed at each release, inspection meetings are said to increase the process time for each release from 60 weeks to 70 [14]. The growing rate of change that characterizes our information age has made time to market of a product a critical concern for software developers. It is therefore essential to try and eliminate process components that add to this time unnecessarily.

Second, several experiments have indicated that most problems are detected during individual preparation for a meeting, with very few additional problems detected at the meeting itself [14]. This suggests that group meetings can be eliminated with no appreciable effect on problem detection. However, it has not been established how the time spent on preparation relates to the cost-effectiveness of a meeting. In other words, if preparation time were merely familiarization with the product to be inspected, with little attempt to detect problems, would meetings then still be cost-ineffective? Differences in problem detection rates have been studied for cases in which preparation was with and without problem detection [15], but no time-dependence analysis appears to have been carried out. Since the experiments reported in [15] showed that meetings have some positive aspects, the question remains open whether Fagan-type meetings should or should not be retained.

Several alternatives to a formal meeting have been tried. One is to have just two reviewers, the author and one other person [16]. This can cut costs significantly, but the other person has to be good at spotting problems. Unfortunately the variability in reviewer performance is high [17]. It has also been established that fewer problems are reported when reviewers are more familiar with each other [18]. Care must therefore be exercised in selecting the second reviewer.

Another approach is to abolish the review meeting, but keep a fairly large number of reviewers. In a technologically unsophisticated version reviewers submit problem lists to a moderator who collates the reports and hands the composite report to the author of the work product. A more efficient version can be based on an electronic blackboard. As soon as reviewers identify problems, they display them on the blackboard. Other reviewers may attach their comments, which helps a moderator decide whether an issue is to be followed up. If this is the case, the author can immediately start appropriate repair. The advantages of this approach are that it does not require geographic proximity of reviewers, that problem identification is an asynchronous process, that reviewers can make suggestions on how to resolve a problem, and that problem identification and resolution can overlap. The electronic "meeting" becomes particularly attractive when a large number of reviewers is required, which is the case with user manuals — representatives of every class of potential users must participate in the review.

## 4. Are Checklists Adequate?

Reviewers need some guidance on how to look for problems in a work product. One approach is to provide them with checklists, which are collections of questions that can be asked regarding the product. As we noted earlier, the contents of a checklist are determined by the application domain, and the type and language of the work product. Examples: Are system initiation procedures defined by the requirements? Is the exit test for every loop correct? Is the vocabulary in the user manual sufficiently basic for foreign users? Although one would expect the use of checklists to be straightforward, that is not so. One problem is the size of the checklist. For it to be useful, it should cover many eventualities. On the other hand, a large checklist becomes unwieldy. A general fault classification given as an appendix to a book on testing covers 15 pages [19]. A second problem is that it is far from clear how to determine that a checklist item is being satisfied, e.g. how to establish that loop exits are correct.

The problem of size can be dealt with by partitioning a checklist into several separate checklists, with reviewers assuming primary responsibility for just those items that are on their individual checklists. Another approach is to use phased inspections [20]. The basic concept here is that instead of a single inspection, there are several inspections, each of which concentrates on just one feature of the work product. There are no more than two reviewers for each phase, and this keeps the costs low. Resolution of problems relating to one phase is supposed to take place before the next phase begins. This has the advantage that reviewers are not distracted by unresolved problems that relate to earlier phases, but may make the inspection phase unnecessarily long.

Inspection scenarios [21] are an alternative to checklists. The purpose of a scenario is to convert a checklist question into an explicit procedure for finding an answer to the question. For example, to show that exit from a loop will eventually occur, define a positive parameter $t$ such that $t$ decreases in every iteration of the loop, but that $t$ is guaranteed to be greater than zero as long as control remains in the loop. Eventually a state has to be reached where $t$ is less than or equal zero, which means that exit from the loop will have taken place. The correctness of the loop is established by means of a loop invariant. Gries [22] can be consulted for details. The loop invariant concept is the basis for the informal proofs required by Cleanroom. Cleanroom is primarily used in the development of information systems for which a useful loop invariant is easily found. For such system, it is also easy to define $t$.

Some examples of scenarios for the inspection of software requirements are to be found in [21], which also describes experiments that established the greater effectiveness of scenarios over checklists — problem detection rate increased by about 35%. Some questions remain. First, how are scenarios to be designed, and what is their construction cost? Second, how general are scenarios, i.e., what is their reuse potential? In particular, in constructing scenarios for code inspections, to what extent is it necessary to consider differences between programming languages? But the scenario method can be recommended irrespective of what the answers to these questions turn out to be. In [21], it is also reported that there was no difference in problem detection rates between the use of checklists and *ad hoc* inspections, i.e., inspections with no systematic guidance at all. It is therefore unlikely that the use of scenarios, however rudimentary, will have worse detection rates than an *ad hoc* method, as long as it is realized that scenarios may not cover all problem types, so that reviewers cannot depend on scenarios alone, but have to include some *ad hoc* detection as well.

Chernak [23] introduces a design for checklists that is similar to scenarios, but does not require as much effort as scenario construction. A checklist item now has two components: "Where to look" and "How to detect". For example, when the "Where to look" component is *Variable Declaration*, the "How to detect" component has three parts, which relate, respectively, to variable type correctness, variable name consistency, and variable name uniqueness. Chernak's second contribution is the ranking of checklist items according to their effectiveness in problem detection — the items that have led to the detection of the greatest number of problems are moved to the top of the list.

## 5. A Reading Guide

P. Johnson has established an Internet Formal Technical Review archive, which contains an online bibliography of several hundred entries [24]. The reading guide here will therefore be very brief. A 1996 review by Porter, Siy, and Votta [14] contains 50 references, and a more recent research program outline by Sauer *et al* [25] has 88 references. The latter paper is interesting in its own right in that the research program it outlines is to be based on behavioral theory of group performance. The importance of social aspects was recognized earlier by Seaman and Basili [18].

A survey of advances relating to Fagan-style inspections was prepared by Fagan himself [26]. Detailed discussion of inspections of this type can be found in four books [6, 27–29]. Weller [10] presents metrics derived from more than 6000 inspection meetings. Electronic meetings are discussed in [30–32]. Ebrahimi [33] shows how to estimate the number of faults remaining in a software design document after its inspection.

## References

1. E. P. Doolan, "Experience with Fagan's inspection method", *Software — Practice & Experience* **22** (1992) 173–182.
2. M. C. Paulk *et al.*, *The Capability Maturity Model: Guidelines for Improving the Software Process* (Addison-Wesley, 1995).
3. R. B. Grady and T. Van Slack, "Key lessons in achieving widespread inspection use", *IEEE Software* **11**, no. 4 (July 1994) 46–57.
4. P. M. Johnson, "Reengineering inspection", *Communications of the ACM* **41**, no. 2 (February 1998) 49–52.
5. M. E. Fagan, "Design and code inspections to reduce errors in program development", *IBM Systems Journal* **15** (1976) 182–211.
6. T. Gilb and D. Graham, *Software Inspection* (Addison-Wesley, 1993).

7. G. W. Russell, "Experience with inspection in ultralarge-scale developments", *IEEE Software* **8**, no. 1 (January 1991) 25–31.

8. R. L. Glass, "Inspections — Some surprising findings", *Communications of the ACM* **42**, no. 4 (April 1999) 17–19.

9. A. F. Ackerman, L. S. Buchwald and F. H. Lewski, "Software inspections: An effective verification process", *IEEE Software* **6**, no. 3 (May 1989) 31–36.

10. E. F. Weller, "Lessons from three years of inspection data", *IEEE Software* **10**, no. 5 (September 1993) 38–45.

11. A. von Mayrhauser and A. M. Vans, "Program understanding: Models and experiments", *Advances in Computers* **40** (1995) 1–38.

12. H. D. Mills, "Zero defect software: Cleanroom engineering", *Advances in Computers* **36** (1993) 1–41.

13. R. C. Linger, "Cleanroom software engineering for zero-defect software", *Proceedings of the 15th International Conference on Software Engineering* (1993) 2–13.

14. A. Porter, H. Siy and L. G. Votta, "A review of software inspections", *Advances in Computers* **42** (1996) 40–76.

15. A. A. Porter and P. M. Johnson, "Assessing software review meetings: Results of a comparative analysis of two experimental studies", *IEEE Transactions on Software Engineering* **23** (1997) 129–145.

16. D. B. Bisant and J. R. Lyle, "A two-person inspection model to improve programming productivity", *IEEE Transactions on Software Engineering* **15** (1989) 1294–1304.

17. A. Porter, H. Siy, A. Mockus and L. G. Votta, "Understanding the sources of variation in software inspections", *ACM Transactions on Software Engineering Methodology* **7** (1998) 41–79.

18. C. B. Seaman and V. R. Basili, "Communication and organization: An empirical study of discussion in inspection meetings", *IEEE Transactions on Software Engineering* **24** (1998) 559–572.

19. B. Beizer, *Software Testing Techniques*, 2nd ed. (Van Nostrand Reinhold, 1990).

20. J. C. Knight and E. A. Myers, "An improved inspection technique", *Communications of the ACM* **36**, no. 11 (November 1993) 51–61.

21. A. A. Porter, L. G. Votta and V. R. Basili, "Comparing detection methods for software requirements inspections: A replicated experiment", *IEEE Transactions on Software Engineering* **21** (1995) 563–575.

22. D. Gries, *The Science of Programming* (Springer-Verlag, 1981).

23. Y. Chernak, "A statistical approach to the inspection checklist formal synthesis and improvement", *IEEE Transactions on Software Engineering* **22** (1996) 866–874.

24. *http://www.ics.hawaii.edu/~johnson/FTR/*

25. C. Sauer, D. R. Jeffery, L. Land and P. Yetton, "The effectiveness of software development technical reviews: A behaviorally motivated program of research", *IEEE Transactions on Software Engineering* **26** (2000) 1–14.

26. M. E. Fagan, "Advances in software inspections", *IEEE Transactions on Software Engineering* **SE-12** (1986) 744–751.

27. D. P. Freedman and G. M. Weinberg, *Handbook of Walkthroughs, Inspections, and Technical Reviews*, 3rd ed., (Little, Brown, 1982). [Reprinted: Dorset House, 1990].

28. C. P. Hollocker, *Software Reviews and Audits Handbook* (Wiley, 1990).

29. R. G. Strauss and R. G. Ebenau, *Software Inspection Process* (McGraw-Hill, 1994).

30. V. Mashayekhi, J. M. Drake, W.-T. Tsai and J. Riedl, "Distributed, collaborative, software inspection", *IEEE Software* **10**, no. 5 (September 1993) 66–75.

31. V. Mashayekhi, C. Feulner and J. Riedl, "CAIS: Collaborative asynchronous inspection of software", *Proceedings of the 2nd ACM SIGSOFT Symposium*

*Foundations of Software Engineering* [published as *Software Engineering Notes* **19**, no. 5, December 1994] 21–34.

32. P. M. Johnson, "An instrumented approach to improving software quality through formal technical reviews", *Proceedings of the 16th International Conferences on Software Engineering* (1994) 113–122.

33. N. B. Ebrahimi, "On the statistical analysis of the number of errors remaining in a software design document after inspection", *IEEE Transactions on Software Engineering* **23** (1997) 529–532.

# REENGINEERING AND PROCESSES

ALFS T. BERZTISS

*University of Pittsburgh, Department of Computer Science,*
*Pittsburgh PA 15260, USA*
*and*
*SYSLAB, University of Stockholm, Sweden*
*E-mail: alpha@cs.pitt.edu*

In this survey we look at two classes of reengineering, of software systems and of organizations. The latter is known as business reengineering. The purpose of reengineering is to improve the structure of a software system or organization by use of an engineering approach. Part of the survey is therefore a listing of engineering principles. An important principle is that there be well-planned processes — we define a process for reengineering. We put particular emphasis on the reengineering of organizations that develop software. Our main purpose is to define a business reengineering process that is to introduce the Capability Maturity Model of the Software Engineering Institute into a software organization.

*Keywords*: Business reengineering, capability maturity, engineering principles, software engineering.

## 1. Introduction

The word reengineering is composed of two parts: re- and -engineering. It means that something is to be done again, and that engineering principles are to be followed in this task. Reengineering arises in two contexts. In software engineering it is the giving of a new representation to an existing software system that in some way improves or standardizes the existing system. This is software reengineering (SRE). In a broader sense reengineering is the reorganization of an entire enterprise. This latter form is generally referred to as business process reengineering or simply as business reengineering (BRE). We have an interest in BRE here because the processes that are the result of BRE tend to be supported by software. Moreover, software developing organizations, to be called just software organizations in what follows, must themselves follow sound engineering principles, and have to be reengineered if they do not. This is what makes BRE highly relevant in the software and knowledge engineering contexts.

We shall take a uniform approach to reengineering, both SRE and BRE, by putting emphasis on processes. A process is a structured set of tasks, performed to achieve an objective. Most commonly the objective is to add value: manufacturing processes convert raw materials into more valuable products, the software development process converts requirements into a software system that represents value to a client, a business process contributes to the profitability of an enterprise. Sometimes the added value is hidden. For example, if in the performance of risk analysis a decision is made to discontinue a project, the cost of the project to this point is value lost. However, if the project were permitted to continue, losses would be much higher, and the avoidance of these losses is the value added by risk analysis. Under reengineering, the value adding potential of every task in a process is to be examined, and tasks that do not support the value-generating objective of a process or of an enterprise as a whole should be eliminated. In software such tasks represent features that are costly to implement and are of little interest to a client.

BRE is to result in the definition of an enterprise as a set of processes, but a process structure may have to be the result of SRE as well, and reengineering itself is to follow a well-defined process. We thus have four processes to consider. First, there is the process that reorganizes an enterprise, where our interest is in enterprises that develop software. This is BRE. Second, there are the processes that define the enterprise. In particular, as regards software, there is a software development process, which is generally called the software process. Third, the purpose of the software process is to develop software systems that may take the form of processes. These we call product processes. Fourth, a product process may have to be reengineered — this is done by the SRE process.

This survey is organized as follows. Section 2 gives an overview of the engineering principles that should be followed by a software organization. In Sec. 3, SRE is reviewed, and in Sec. 4, we look at a BRE process. Section 5 presents an outline of a process for introducing the concepts of the Capability Maturity Model (CMM) of the Software Engineering Institute [1] into a software organization. Section 6 contains bibliographic pointers, including references to some specialized instances of SRE.

## 2. Engineering Principles

We define engineering practice in terms of 12 principles that are discussed in greater detail in [2]. Reengineering of a software organization should aim at introducing these principles into the organization. The principles constitute a very general statement of what engineers do. If software and knowledge engineering are to become fully accepted by the rest of the engineering community, the practitioners of software and knowledge engineering should follow these principles. The principles are consistent with the capabilities that CMM recognizes as supportive of the development of high quality software.

Principle 1: Engineering development follows a plan in accordance with requirements, which may be functional or non-functional. The requirements must be verifiable, i.e., they must be stated in quantitative terms.

Principle 2: Requirements are ranked according to cost-effectiveness, and the development plan provides for their incremental implementation. Requirements are often contradictory. For example, a high reliability requirement is in conflict with a low cost requirement. It is therefore essential to develop quantitative estimates of trade-offs between requirements.

Principle 3: Standards are used where available and applicable, with every departure from applicable standards explicitly justified. Standards were established to allow engineered objects or their parts to be readily interchanged, thus reducing maintenance costs. Also, the initial cost of an object is reduced if the object can be constructed from standard parts. As a rule of thumb, standardization should be limited to terminology, or to entities that can be patented or copyrighted. As an example, our terminology will be kept "standard" by following as closely as possible the reengineering terminology of [3].

Principle 4: Future changes are anticipated, and engineering design minimizes the cost of modifications. The design of a software system should have a modular structure that allows easy modification.

Principle 5: Fault- and failure-tolerance are built into engineering designs. Not all conditions can be anticipated. Engineers try to minimize the effects of unexpected conditions by fault-tolerant and failure-tolerant design.

Principle 6: Findings of mathematics and the sciences are applied in the solution of engineering problems. In software engineering, this can be the use of formal methods and of statistical reliability estimation techniques. In knowledge engineering, it can be the use of fuzzy logic and of rough sets.

Principle 7: Efficient techniques are used to scale up size or production. Engineering often starts with a model, such as a scaled-down version of the target object, e.g. a laboratory model of a chemical plant, or a prototype, which is a full-scale version of a product to be manufactured.

Principle 8: Quality control techniques are used to maintain quality at predetermined levels. An engineering ideal is to produce objects with zero faults, i.e., objects that fully conform to requirements, both functional and non-functional. This goal may not be cost-effective. Instead, statistical quality control and reliability engineering are used to impose strict control on quality levels.

Principle 9: Tools are used to improve productivity. The nature of tools in engineering has changed dramatically over the past twenty years with the introduction of computer-based tools, but as yet no tool has replaced human creativity.

Principle 10: Contributors from many disciplines participate in engineering tasks. Engineering practice is not individual-oriented. However, engineers accept full individual responsibility for the consequences of their actions or their failure to act.

Principle 11: Effective engineering management is based on a collection of skills acquired by an extensive process of learning. Because of the cooperative nature of engineering, not every engineer has to become a manager, but every engineer should have an appreciation of the nature of engineering management. Cost and risk estimation, the matching up of design tasks with personnel, constant monitoring of the progress of a project, and the timely identification of problems require a good grasp of management principles and people skills, and broad knowledge of the technical aspects of engineering.

Principle 12: Technological adventure is good engineering, provided the aim is to add to engineering knowledge. When a technology for an area has not yet been developed, engineers are not afraid to move ahead, and in so doing develop the technology. Many areas of software and knowledge engineering are still in a technological adventure stage.

## 3. Software Reengineering

No matter what software process is used to develop a software system, four activities are common to all. First, objectives are stated. These may be very general business goals, e.g. improvement of customer satisfaction, or fairly narrow technical aims, e.g. greater use of embedded software in a line of products. This activity justifies the development of a software system, but is not strictly part of a software process. Second, a set of requirements is developed. The requirements describe a software system that is to assist in achieving the objectives. The formulation of requirements is part of any software process, but there can be major differences in what this activity is to include. Sometimes the requirements are expressed as a formal specification. The third stage is software design, in which the requirements are made more precise and more explicit. For many applications the requirements define a process, e.g. a workflow system in a business environment. Under software reengineering such a process may have to be redesigned, or several processes merged into a single process. At the design stage there has to be a full understanding of how the functionality of a system is to be distributed between people, software, and machines. Fourth, the software components of the total system become implemented. Of course, verification and validation have to be an integral part of the entire software process.

The boundaries between the phases are by no means firm. For example, software design can be distributed throughout the software process. The process is then essentially the refinement of design. We recommend that modularization of the system, which is part of design, begin with requirements because a partitioning of requirements statements into modular groups gives structure to the requirements document. Also, early modularization allows more reliable cost and schedule estimation, which in turn allows an early decision of whether a project should be continued as planned.

The four steps of objectives, requirements, design, and implementation define a forward engineering process. Reverse engineering tries to recover the design from an implementation, requirements from design, perhaps even objectives from requirements. Reverse engineering is essentially an attempt to improve understanding — generally an implementation is harder to understand than requirements, and the easiest to understand are the objectives.

An example is an algorithm that determines when and for how long manufacturing runs should be scheduled to keep inventory at a desired level. Suppose that lately inventory requirements have been underestimated, so that the algorithm needs to be adjusted. Suppose further that the code is the only documentation there is. To carry out this maintenance task, the algorithm has to be recovered from the code, i.e., we are to derive the design from the implementation, and this is reverse engineering. After the algorithm has been modified, it has to be reimplemented in a forward engineering step.

The simplest class of software reengineering is at the implementation level. It can take two forms. In the simpler form, which is variously called code restructuring or source-to-source transformation, one implementation is changed into another, and both implementations are in the same programming language. We shall use the term code-to-code *transformation*. The second form involves a change of language, e.g. an existing program has to be translated into Java. This we call code-to-code *translation*. Translation even between similar languages can be more complicated than expected, as has been seen in C to C++ translation [4]. Some indication of the ease or difficulty of it can be obtained by comparing the ratios of the number of source statements in a program to a count of its function points. Since code-to-code translation does not change program complexity as measured in terms of function points, the ratios give some indication of language complexity. For function points, see [5], where on p. 76 the expansion factor in terms of number of source statements per function point is estimated as 320 for assembly language, 128 for C, 105 for Fortran 77, 91 for ANSI Cobol 85, and 71 for Ada.

Our interest in reengineering relates to the two cases shown in Fig. 1. In both cases, we have an existing system (subscripts 1), and a changed system (subscripts 2). The drawing on the left depicts what we call SRE driven by objectives. Objectives for a software system may change because the environments in which software systems operate tend to change, sometimes quite dramatically. If

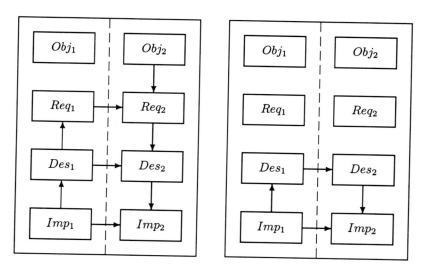

**Fig. 1.** From objectives to implementation.

the software system has not been well designed, then the implementation of changes necessitated by changes in objectives cannot be carried out unless the design is improved.

In both diagrams upward arrows indicate reverse engineering, downward arrows forward engineering, and arrows that go from left to right suggest reuse potential. If there is a change of objectives, the system undergoes radical change, but there is possibility of reuse of some components of the existing system. Unless the existing system has been well documented, and been subject to effective configuration management, reverse engineering is needed to establish what can be reused. Here we have an instance of maintenance, but of a form that Basili [6] interprets as reuse-oriented new development.

Another reason for software reengineering is fault removal, and the drawing on the right in Fig. 1 relates to it. If a software system is not well designed, then, on detection of a failure, the determination in the software of the fault responsible for the failure can be very difficult, and it is even more difficult to remove the fault without introducing new faults. This provides an economical justification for the redesign of a software system. Not only will the present fault be easier to detect and remove, future fault removal will also be easier. Reengineering in anticipation of future needs is known as preventive maintenance. Many companies carried out extensive preventive maintenance as part of their Y2K activities, and the benefits derived from this have in most cases outweighed the costs of Y2K compliance. Here we have a reverse engineering step that recovers design from implementation, the modular structure of the system is improved, i.e., it is redesigned, and the new design is transformed into code, with some reuse of the old code.

A special case of software reengineering arises with the merging of companies. Until the merger, the companies have probably followed different procedures, e.g. for payroll and for order fulfillment, and their data base schemas and user interfaces are likely to be quite different. Three approaches can be followed. First, one of the systems is selected as the standard, and the user community of the other system is required to adapt itself to this standard. Second, a system structure is selected that consists of the best features of the two systems, and reengineering adapts one of the systems so that it corresponds to this ideal. Third, a totally new design is defined. This, however, is closer to BRE that to the more limited software reengineering.

Whichever of the three approaches is taken, the data bases of the two companies have to be merged and this is where trouble starts. Data base merging requires data base schema integration, which is a difficult problem. As a result, merger of data bases may still not have taken place years after the merger of the companies, which means that the new company continues to use two sets of programs to refer to the data bases. This easily leads to degradation of data quality, and overall inefficient operation. It is therefore essential to understand early in merger negotiations that sizable resources will be needed for software integration.

Reverse engineering has been surveyed in [7], and the entire SRE process in [8]. To this we add a selection of later work. Gall *et al* [9] use domain models to assist in the transformation of a conventional system into an object-oriented system. Recovery of design of distributed systems is discussed in [10]. The reuse aspect of SRE is considered in [11]. For an experience report on a major reengineering project, see [12]. One of the lessons learned in this project was that reengineering tools do not take care of themselves; there has to be a dedicated "toolsmith" in charge of them. A critical attitude to reverse engineering is taken in [13] — not only is its cost-effectiveness being questioned, but also the practicability of reengineering tools and whether the organization that carries out the SRE effort is mature enough to really improve the structure of a system. Sneed [14] outlines a technique for estimating the cost-effectiveness of SRE projects.

## 4. A Business Reengineering Process

Business reengineering has often been misunderstood. Unfortunately this has resulted is a somewhat negative image of BRE. Some managers have equated BRE with vigorous downsizing, i.e., reduction of personnel, even the most essential personnel. Some consultants have created chaos by ripping apart business processes that were performing perfectly. After the consultants had completed their destructive work, and tight labor markets in the United States made it impossible to re-hire badly needed key personnel, blame for the disaster was put on BRE.

BRE is neither downsizing nor indiscriminate reorganization. It has precisely one aim: to define an enterprise in terms of a set of processes, and to define each process as a set of tasks, such that each task adds value. Software and knowledge engineers who define software support for these processes must keep the value-added aspect constantly in mind, realizing that intangibles, such as staff and customer satisfaction also add value. Now, the replacement of inefficient manual or semi-automated procedures by a well-defined software-driven process can result in personnel redundancy, particularly at the middle management level, but recognition that there is value in staff satisfaction will often lead to reassignment of staff within the organization instead of termination — since BRE, properly applied, should stimulate business growth, the personnel may be of much use elsewhere in the organization.

We have a special reason for being interested in BRE: a software organization is a business, and it should be reengineered if it is not already based on well-defined processes, where each process has a value-adding function. In [2], we define a 16-step BRE process. In our context the purpose of such a process is to improve the software development capability of a software organization in accordance with the engineering principles of Sec. 2. Here we have drastically compressed the BRE process of [2], and have adapted it to suit the specialized needs of a software organization. A software organization is to be defined by six processes, which we discuss in Sec. 5, and our compressed BRE process is to introduce these six processes into the organization. The BRE process itself has five steps, as follows.

- *Management Structure.* A special BRE manager should be designated. The function of the manager is to see that the BRE process progresses smoothly. In other businesses, special reengineering teams have to be established. Since software developers have a familiarity with processes, the entire software organization participates in the BRE effort. Specific role assignments will, however, be necessary from time to time.

- *Education.* Everybody in the company is to become acquainted with the aims of the BRE process. As reengineering progresses, specialized education relating to the processes that are being created has to be provided. A continuing training program is one of the processes of Sec. 5. Training can be general or very specific. An example of the latter is a course on color theory for developers of user interfaces.
- *Process Specification.* The six processes of Sec. 5 are to be defined in detail. Each process is to be partitioned into tasks, and a timeframe established for the introduction of each task. A particular concern is the creation of a software process data base of measurements relating to the software process.
- *Cost-benefit Analysis.* The purpose of this step is to define priorities for the tasks of the processes. Normally several alternative designs would have been developed for each process, and evaluation of competing designs would be a major part of this step. By basing our processes on the CMM, we have restricted ourselves to a single design.
- *Infrastructure Definition.* This step deals with support facilities, especially software tools. The tools are to assist in software development, software maintenance, documentation, and cooperative work. Specialized tools for the gathering of process measurements should be acquired or developed.

## 5. Toward Capability Maturity

The biggest impact on the quality of software and the cost and schedule of its development results from the adoption of a detailed and well-defined software process, such as advocated by the Software Engineering Institute by means of its CMM. Capabilities of the CMM are organized as 18 Key Process Areas (KPAs), distributed over four levels (Levels 2 through 5). Very few organizations have reached Level 5, and not even Level 2 has been reached by very many organizations. We now define six processes as the target of the BRE process of Sec. 4. Two major processes relate to software products and the software process — they are, respectively, Project Management and Process Management. Four additional processes deal with quality control, training, infrastructure and technological change, and external interactions.

Each of the processes relates to some KPAs. The correspondences are not exact in that the activities associated with a particular KPA may be allocated to several processes during the Process Specification phase of the BRE process, but the overall structure defines a disciplined incremental introduction of CMM into a software organization. In the listing below the CMM level is given in parentheses for each KPA assigned to a process. Note that we have added contract negotiations to our model. The failure of many software projects has been due to too optimistic an attitude by management. Projects have been started without a proper estimation of their likelihood of success. Contract negotiations should be based on thorough risk analysis (Activity 10 of the Level 3 KPA of Integrated Software Management).

- *Project Management*

  Requirements management (2)
  Software project planning (2)
  Software project tracking and oversight (2)
  Software configuration management (2)
  Software product engineering (3)

- *Process Management*

  Organization process focus (3)
  Organization process definition (3)
  Integrated software management (3)
  Intergroup coordination (3)
  Quantitative process management (4)
  Process change management (5)

- *Quality Control*

  Software quality assurance (2)
  Peer reviews (3)
  Software quality management (4)
  Defect prevention (5)

- *Training*

  Training program (3)

- *External Interaction*

  Contract negotiation (–)
  Software subcontract management (2)

- *Infrastructure and Technology*

  Technology change management (5)

## 6. Additional Bibliographic Pointers

A bibliography on reverse engineering in SRE has been compiled by v. d. Brand, Klint, and Verhoef [15] — this bibliography contains 110 items, and the authors are continuing to update it. Reverse engineering requires an understanding of a program. For a survey of this task, see [16]. Program understanding is aided by program slicing, which automatically decomposes a program by analysis of its control flow and data flow. A slice relates to a specific variable $v$ at a specific place $p$ in a program, and consists of all statements in the program that can affect the value of $v$ at $p$. Binkley and Gallager [17] survey program slicing. Weide, Heym, and Hollingsworth [13] have shown that a program analysis tool has at least exponential complexity; Woods and Yang [18] show that program understanding is NP-hard. It should be noted that reverse engineering of COTS (Commercial-Off-The-Shelf) software can have legal implications [19]. Examples of source-to-source transformations are to be found in [20, 21]. Experience with the reengineering of a configuration management system is reported in [22], and of a control system in [23]. For reengineering of user interfaces, see [24, 25]. The most influential books on BRE were by Chompy and Hammer [26] and by Davenport [27], where the latter expresses the more moderate view; [2] deals with software support of BRE, and can be consulted for further references on BRE. Workflows provide a way of modeling processes — see [28, 29].

## References

1. M. C. Paulk *et al*, *The Capability Maturity Model: Guidelines for Improving the Software Process* (Addison-Wesley, 1995).
2. A. Berztiss, *Software Methods for Business Reengineering* (Springer, 1996).
3. E. J. Chikofsky and J. H. Cross, "Reverse engineering and design recovery: A taxonomy", *IEEE Software* **7**, no. 1 (1990) 13–17.
4. A. Quilici, "A memory-based approach to recognizing programming plans", *Communications of the ACM* **37**, no. 5 (1994) 84–93.
5. C. Jones, *Applied Software Measurement* (McGraw-Hill, 1991).
6. V. R. Basili, "Viewing maintenance as reuse-oriented software development", *IEEE Software* **7**, no. 1 (1990) 19–25.
7. J. H. Cross, E. J. Chikofsky and C. H. May, "Reverse engineering", *Advances in Computers* **35** (1992) 295–353.
8. A. T. Berztiss, "Reverse engineering, reengineering, and concurrent engineering of software", *International Journal of Software Engineering and Knowledge Engineering* **5** (1995) 299–324.
9. H. C. Gall, R. R. Klösch and R. T. Mittermeir, "Using domain knowledge to improve reverse engineering", *International Journal of Software Engineering and Knowledge Engineering* **6** (1996) 477–505.
10. L. J. Holtzblatt, R. L. Piazza, H. B. Reubenstein, S. N. Roberts and D. R. Harris, "Design recovery for distributed systems", *IEEE Transactionns on Software Engineering* **23** (1997) 461–472.
11. R. Thomson, K. E. Huff and J. W. Gish, "Maximizing reuse during reengineering", *Proceedings of the 3nd International Conference on Software Reusability* (1994) 16–23.
12. W. S. Adolph, "Cash cow in the tar pit: Reengineering a legacy system", *IEEE Software* **13**, no. 3 (May 1996) 41–47.
13. B. W. Weide, W. D. Heym and J. E. Hollingsworth, "Reverse engineering of legacy code exposed", *Proceedings of the 17th International Conference on Software Engineering* (1995) 327–331.
14. H. M. Sneed, "Planning the reengineering of legacy systems", *IEEE Software* **12**, no. 1 (January 1995) 24–34.
15. M. G. J. v. d. Brand, P. Klint and C. Verhoef, "Reverse engineering and system renovation — An annotated bibliography", *Software Engineering Notes* **22**, no. 1 (January 1997) 57–68.
16. A. v. Mayrhauser and A. M. Vans, "Program understanding: models and experiments", *Advances in Computers* **40** (1995) 1–38.

17. D. W. Binkley and B. Gallagher, "Program slicing", *Advances in Computers* **43** (1996) 1–50.
18. S. Woods and Q. Yang, "The program understanding problem: Analysis and a heuristic approach", *Proceedings of the 18th International Conference on Software Engineering* (1996) 6–15.
19. B. C. Behrens and R. R. Levary, "Practical legal aspects of software reverse engineering", *Communications of the ACM* **41**, no. 2 (February 1998) 27–29.
20. P. A. Bailes, S. Atkinson, M. Chapman, D. Johnston and I. Peake, "Towards an open software conversion architecture", *International Journal of Software Engineering and Knowledge Engineering* **5** (1995) 423–444.
21. U. Geske and M. Nitsche, "Representing Cobol in Prolog — Comprehension and reengineering", *International Journal of Software Engineering and Knowledge Engineering* **6** (1996) 113–133.
22. O. Bray and M. M. Hess, "Reengineering a configuration-management system", *IEEE Software* **12**, no. 1 (January 1995) 55–63.
23. L. R. Welch, G. Yu, B. Ravindran, F. Kurfess, J. Henriques, M. Wilson, A. L. Samuel and M. W. Masters, "Reverse engineering of computer-based control systems", *International Journal of Software Engineering and Knowledge Engineering* **6** (1996) 531–547.
24. E. Merlo, P.-Y. Gagné, J.-F. Girard, K. Kontogiannis, L. Hendren, P. Panangaden and R. De Mori, "Reengineering user interfaces", *IEEE Software* **12**, no. 1 (January 1995) 64–73.
25. C. Plaisant, A. Rose, B. Shneiderman and A. J. Vanniamparampil, "Low-effort, high-payout user interface reengineering", *IEEE Software* **14**, no. 4 (July/August 1997), 66–72.
26. M. Hammer and J. Champy, *Reengineering the Corporation: A Manifesto for Business Revolution* (Harper Business, 1993).
27. T. H. Davenport, *Process Innovation: Reengineering Work Through Information Technology* (Harvard Business School Press, 1993).
28. T. Schael, *Workflow Management Systems for Process Organization*, (*Lecture Notes in Computer Science, 1096*), 2nd ed. (Springer, 1998).
29. M. Jackson and G. Twaddle, *Business Process Implementation: Building Workflow Systems* (Addison-Wesley, 1997).

# USABILITY IN THE SOFTWARE LIFE CYCLE

MARIA FRANCESCA COSTABILE

*Dipartimento di Informatica, Università di Bari, Via Orabona 4, 70125 Bari, Italy*
*E-mail: costabile@di.uniba.it*

The objective of this chapter is to clarify the role of usability processes and methods within the software life cycle. After discussing the concept of usability as quality factor and providing various definitions, including those in ISO standards, it presents the user-centered design methodology for designing usable systems and provides indications on how to include usability in the software life cycle.

*Keywords*: Usability, software life cycle, user-centered design.

## 1. Introduction

"People are required to conform to technology. It is time to reverse this trend, time to make technology conform to people" Donald A. Norman says in the article "Designing the Future", published in Scientific American in September 1995. This is particularly true for the computer technology, which nowadays is providing everybody with the possibility of using a computer, and directly interacting with software systems and exploring information resources. For too long we have designed software systems that require a lot of effort by users. Many computer users experience frustration and anxiety, and this phenomenon is even growing, due to the huge amount of data that are becoming available on networked information systems, such as the WWW. As a consequence, current software systems must provide enhanced user interfaces that support this intensive interaction with users.

Referring to any software product, from the users' point of view the user interface is the most important component, since it is what the users see and work with when using a product. We need to create successful user interfaces, whose quality is primarily evaluated from the point of view of the users. A good design of the user interface results when designers understand people as well as technology. The designers must understand who will be the users of their products, their personal characteristics, their physical capabilities, their goals and the tasks they need to accomplish, the circumstances under which they work.

Unfortunately, very little attention has been devoted to the user interface by software engineers, with the unavoidable result that most software systems are very hard to use. The user interface has been considered a detail to be added at the end of the development of the system. This is not possible anymore with interactive systems, for which it is estimated that about 50% of the code is devoted to the user interface [1].

Since the late 70's, within the software engineering discipline quality factors have been introduced as part of software quality measurements frameworks that have been developed to provide a measurement approach for software engineering. In [2], McCall says that quality factors "represent attributes or characteristics of the software that a user, or customer of the software product, would relate to its overall quality". Pionering work on quality factors was performed by Boehm [3], and by McCall *et al* [4]. Interestingly, already at that time one of these factors was *usability*, defined as the "effort required to learn, operate, prepare input, and interpret output of a program" [2, 4].

The fact that it was already included as a quality factor did not really mean that software engineers have put so far much attention on it. Traditionally, they are trained to judge their work by criteria that may have little to do with the needs and constraints of the end users. They are more sensitive to other factors, such as efficiency of code or flexibility of the programs, which are certainly important engineering goals, but have little or nothing to do with creating a computer system accessible to and supportive for a particular type of user. The need of improving the user interface is now emerging, and more recent books on software engineering (e.g. [5]) devote more attention to the user interface design. Software engineers are starting to appreciate the importance of high-quality users interfaces, but more has to be done. In particular, we need to insert the notions developed in the Human-Computer Interaction (HCI) discipline into the software professional training. HCI is now a consolidated discipline and there is a fast accumulating body of knowledge regarding user interface design that must be taken into account to guide software developers into their design decisions, thus avoiding to repeat bad designs. More importantly, we must integrate user interface design methods and techniques into the standard software development methodologies and adopt for interface testing and quality control procedures analogous to those already accepted for testing other aspects of software design [6, 7].

This chapter aims at clarifying the role of usability processes and methods within the software life cycle. The organization of the chapter is the following. Section 2 discusses the concept of usability and provides various definitions, including those in ISO standards. Section 3 presents the main features of the user-centered design methodology whose main objective is to design usable software systems. Section 4 provides indications on how the software life cycle can be augmented to include usability, while Sec. 5 discusses different usability evaluation methods and their applicability at the various steps of the software life cycle. Finally, the conclusions are provided.

## 2. Definition of Usability

Regardless of the scarce attention devoted so far to usability by software engineers, it is now widely acknowledged that usability is a crucial factor of the overall quality of interactive applications. Several definitions of usability have been proposed. We report here those we consider the most representative. The first one is proposed by J. Nielsen and provides a detailed description of the usability attributes [8]. The second definition is provided in the standard ISO/IEC 9126 and reflects the software engineering perspective over the quality of software products [9]. As it will be shown in the discussion, from a certain point of view, the latter definition is similar to the one given in the ISO 9241 standard [10], that is the standard of the ergonomic and HCI communities.

Nielsen proposes a model in which usability is presented as one of the aspects that characterizes a global feature of a system that is *acceptability* by the end users, reflecting whether the system is good enough to satisfy the needs and the requirements of the users. In Nielsen's model, usability is not a one-dimensional property of a system, rather it has multiple components. It can be decomposed into five attributes: *learnability*, i.e., the ease of learning the functionality and the behavior of the system; *efficiency*, i.e., the level of attainable productivity, once the user has learned the system; *memorability*, i.e., the ease of remembering the system functionality, so that the casual user can return to the system after a period of non-use, without needing to learn again how to use it; *low error rate*, i.e., the capability of the system to support users in making less errors during the use of the system, and in case they make errors, to let them easily recover; *user's satisfaction*, i.e., the measure in which the users like the system. The latter attribute must not be underestimated, since finding a system pleasant to use increases user's productivity.

These attributes can be objectively and empirically verified through different evaluation methods. Defining the abstract concept of usability in terms of more precise and measurable components is an important step towards the definition of usability engineering as a discipline, where usability is not just argued, but is systematically approached, evaluated, and improved [8].

We already said in the introduction that usability has been so far neglected by software engineers. Nevertheless, it was even mentioned in the original definition of the standard for software product evaluation ISO/IEC 9126. In a more recent formulation, the standard ISO/IEC 9126-1 (*Information-Technology Software Product Quality*) emphasizes the importance of designing for quality, focusing on intrinsic system features which can help create products which are effective, efficient and satisfying for the intended users [9]. The overall quality of a software product is given by its internal and external capability to support the achievement of the goal of users and their organizations, thus improving productivity and human health. The standard describes a model for software product quality, which includes internal quality, external quality and quality in use. Usability is defined as one of the six characteristics of software quality. Specifically, it is the "capability of the software product to be understood, learned, used and attractive to the user, when used under specified conditions". It is further subdivided into five subcharacteristics: *understandability*, i.e., the intrinsic capability of the software product of showing to the users its appropriateness to the tasks to be accomplished and to the context of use; *learnability*, i.e., the intrinsic capability of the software product to help users to easily learn its functionality; *operability*, i.e., the intrinsic capability of the software product to make possible for the users the execution and the control of its functionality; *attractiveness*, i.e., the intrinsic capability of the software product to be pleasant for users; *compliance*, i.e., the capability of the software product to adhere to standards, conventions, style guides about usability.

The standard then introduces the concept of *quality in use*, as a feature of the interaction between user and software product, which is measurable only in the context of a real and observable task, also taking into consideration different relevant internal attributes, such as usability. Quality in use is defined in terms of factors that represent the user's view of the software quality, i.e., *effectiveness*, *productivity*, *safety*, and *satisfaction*. These factors are very much related to those defining usability in another standard, the ISO 9241 (*Ergonomic Requirements for Office Work with Visual Display Terminals*), and the concept of quality in use, as described in ISO/IEC 9126-1, is closer to that of usability given in Part 11 of ISO 9241 (*Guidance on Usability*), where it is defined as "the extent to which a product can be used by specified users to achieve specified goals with *effectiveness*, *efficiency* and *satisfaction* in a specified context of use". *Effectiveness* is defined as the accuracy and the completeness with which specified users achieve specified goals in particular environments. *Efficiency* refers to the resources expended in relation to the accuracy and completeness of goals achieved (it is similar to the productivity factor that characterizes quality in use in the ISO/IEC 9621-1). *Satisfaction* is defined as the comfort and the acceptability of the system for its users and other people affected by its use. Usability is therefore intended as a high level goal of system design. We may conclude that both concepts of quality in use and usability, as defined in ISO 9241, incorporate the most significant aspects generally associated to usability by the HCI community.

The overall standard ISO 9241 contains guidance on user interface design, and provides requirements and recommendations which can be used during the design and evaluation of user interfaces [10]. The standard consists of 17 parts. The first nine parts are concerned with hardware issues (requirements for visual display, colors and non-keyboard input devices), the others are devoted to software issues such as the design of different styles of the dialog between the user and the computer (dialog principles, menu dialogs, presentation of information, user guidance, command dialogs, direct manipulation dialogs, and form-filling dialogs).

Usability is strictly dependent on the particular circumstances in which a product is used, i.e., the nature of the users, the tasks they perform, and the physical and social environments in which they operate. Special attention must be devoted to usability of software products used in stress conditions by the user, e.g. safety critical systems like those for *air traffic* control.

The HCI discipline is devoting a lot of emphasis on defining methods for ensuring usability of interactive systems. Much attention on usability is currently paid by industry, which is recognizing the importance of adopting usability methods during product development, for verifying the usability of new products before they are put on the market [11]. Some studies have in fact demonstrated how the use of such methods enables cost saving, with a high cost-benefit ratio [12, 13].

## 3. System-Centered vs User-Centered Design

As discussed in [14], one of the reasons why many high-tech products, including computer-based systems as well as electronic equipment and every day appliances, are so hard to use is that, during the development of a product, the emphasis and focus have been on the system, not on the people who will be the ultimate end-user. Maybe developers counted on the fact that humans are flexible and adaptable, they can better adapt to the machine rather than vice versa. Human needs have been neglected in the past also because engineers were developing products for end users who were very much like themselves. With the large spreading of computers everywhere, the target audience has changed dramatically and keeps changing every day. One of the main requirements of the information technology society is to design for universal access, i.e., computer systems must be accessible by any kind of users. What has been done in the past does not work for today's users and technology. Designers must allow the human users to focus on the task at hand and not on the means for doing that task. We need methods and techniques to help designers change the way they view and design products, methods that work for the users' needs and abilities.

One of the approaches in this direction is user-centered design, which has already proven as a key factor for leading towards the development of successful interfaces [14–16]. User-centered design implies that final users are involved from the very beginning of the planning stage, and identifying user requirements becomes a crucial phase. Early involvement of users has the potential for preventing serious mistakes when designing innovative systems. Indeed, it compels designers to think in terms of utility and usability of the system they are going to develop. Benefits of the user-centered approach are mainly related to completeness of system functionality, repair effort saving, as well as user satisfaction. Involving users from early stages allows basing the system core on what is effectively needed. Poor or inadequate requirement specifications can determine interaction difficulties, including lack of facilities and usability problems. Even if late evaluations are useful to assess the usability of final systems, it is unrealistic to expect that these results bring about a complete redesign.

The basic principles of user-centered design are: (1) analyze users and task; (2) design and implement the system iteratively through prototypes of increasing complexity; (3) evaluate design choices and prototypes with users. User-centered approach requires understanding reality: who will use the system, where, how, and to do what. Then, the system is designed iterating a design-implementation-evaluation cycle. In this way it is possible to avoid serious mistakes and to save re-implementation time, since the first design is based on empirical knowledge of user behavior, needs, and expectations. Collecting user information is not an easy task, even discussing with users, since users often neglect aspects that they erroneously consider not important.

Many different techniques can be applied for collecting user information, among them direct observation, interviews and questionnaires [13, 15, 16]. Direct observation means observing the users while they carry out their tasks at their workplace. It is the most reliable and precise method for collecting data about users, especially valuable for identifying user classes and related tasks. Moreover, it allows identifying critical factors, like social pressure, that can have a strong effect on user behavior when the system will be used in the field. Unfortunately, direct observation is very expensive because it requires experimenters to observe each user individually. For this reason, it is useful when a reduced number of observations is enough to generalize behavioral predictions or when hypotheses have to be tested rather than generated. Interviews collect self-reported experience, opinion, and behavioral motivations. They are essential to finding out procedural knowledge as well as problems with currently used tools. Interviews cost a bit less than direct observations, because they can be shorter and easier to code. However, they still require skilled experimenters to be effective. By contrast, self-administered questionnaires can be handed out and collected by untrained personnel allowing to gather from various users a huge quantity of data at low cost. They allow statistical analyses and stronger generalizations than interviews.

Questionnaires provide an overview on the current situation as well as specific answers. Which combination of these methods is worth applying depends both on requirements and budget. By elaborating the outcome of the knowledge phase, designers define a first version of the system. At this stage, design techniques (e.g. task-centered [17] or scenario-based [16]) provide satisfying solutions. The goal is to explore different design alternatives before settling on a single proposal to be further developed. Possibly, in this way designers will propose different solutions and different interaction strategies. Techniques like paper mock-ups and prototyping can be applied. Paper mock-ups are the cheapest: pieces of the system interface are drawn on paper and the interaction with a user is simulated by an experimenter. Despite its trivial appearance, this technique allows collecting reliable data which can be used for parallel reviewing. Prototyping allows testing some functionalities in depth (vertical prototyping) or the whole interface (horizontal prototyping). Then, one or more solutions can be evaluated with or without users. This step, called formative evaluation, aims at checking some choices and getting hints for revising the design.

At the end of the design cycle, summative evaluations are run. They test of the final system with actual users performing real tasks in their working environment. Therefore, a summative evaluation should be considered as the very last confirmation of the correctness of the hypotheses stated during the design process.

## 4. Modifying the Software Life Cycle to Include Usability

Software production process is a way to call the process followed to build, deliver, and evolve a software product [18]. By acknowledging the fact that software, like any other industrial product, has a life cycle that spans from the initial concept formation of a software system up to its retirement, this process is generally called *software life cycle*. Several models of the software life cycle have been proposed, with the aim of controlling the life cycle and therefore producing high quality software products reliably, predictably and efficiently. Our intent is not to discuss the various models, but to raise some issues that affect the usability of interactive systems and are relevant within all activities of the software life cycle. To this aim, we take into account the standard *waterfall model*, in which each activity naturally leads into the next: the requirements are collected at the beginning, and then this information is processed and converted into a general design that drives next phases of detailed design of modules, which are then coded, integrated and tested. Then the product is completed, tested and maintained for the rest of its life. The activities of the classical waterfall model are the blocks without shadow in Fig. 1.

In this cycle, which is system-centered, usability is not addressed. Moreover, there are some further drawbacks. For instance, the system is tested only at the end of the cycle, when unfortunately is too late for going through radical design modifications to cope with possible discrepancies with the requirements. Another problem is that these requirements are collected with customers, who often are different from the people who will use the system. We call customers the people who negotiate with designers the features of the intended system, while users or end users are those people that will actually use the designed systems. As an example, customers may be company managers that request and buy the new system, while users will be the company employees who will work with the new system. Furthermore, requirements are usually restricted to functional requirements, i.e., services the system must provide in the work domain, and do not take into account features of the system more directly related to the manner in which these services must be provided, such as easy to learn, easy to use, safety, etc.

A direct consequence of the restricted nature of the requirement specifications is that, usually, system testing not only performs late in the development cycle, but is also limited to some of its functional aspects, thus neglecting system usability. Hopefully, the health and safety regulations now available and the ISO standards mentioned in the previous section will then make necessary to certify the final system according to usability as well.

In order to create usable interactive systems, it is therefore necessary to augment the standard life cycle to explicitly address usability issues. The shadowed boxes in Fig. 1 indicate some activities to be performed in order to shift from the system-centered design typical of the classical waterfall model to user-centered design that may lead to designing usable systems. The shadowed box denoted by 1 indicates that it is mandatory to integrate the requirement phase with a careful analysis of the users, meaning the people who will actually use the system, the tasks they perform and the environments in which they work. The best way to collect this information is by visiting users at their workplace, observe the way they carry out their tasks, and talk to them through different types of interviews [13]. The user analysis will also affect the general design of the system. Moreover, the classical phases of architectural design and detailed design should explicitly include the design of the user interface, that is not anymore deferred to the end of the system development. Indeed, the user interface is the most relevant part of the system from the users' point of view, and its design should be discussed by the designers directly with the users since the very beginning of the life cycle. As indicated in the shadowed box 2, use scenarios [16], that is a sequence of steps describing an interaction between a user and the system, may help figuring out the design of a usable interface.

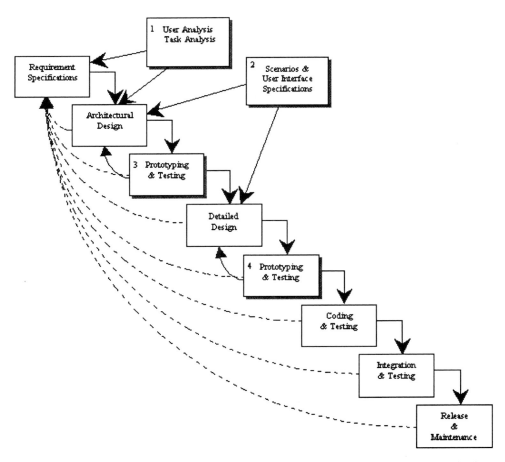

**Fig. 1.** The revised waterfall life cycle. Boxes without shadow refer to the classical model, while shadowed boxes are added to include usability.

As discussed in the previous section, the user-centered design methodology stresses the iteration of the design-implementation-evaluation cycle. We therefore inserted shadowed boxes 3 and 4 in the waterfall model in order to make explicit that both the architectural and detailed design of software modules must be carried out through the development of prototypes that are evaluated with users to check if they meet the intended requirements. If not, a new prototype is developed and then evaluated again, and this iterative process ends when the specified requirements are satisfied; only at this point we may proceed to the development of a more advanced prototype, that includes new functionalities. Moreover, the iterative approach actually implies that from each phase of the software life cycle it is possible to go back to any of the previous phases, in particular to go back and update the requirement specifications, as indicated by the dotted arrows in Fig. 1. Paper mock-ups may be used as early prototypes, since they are very easy to develop and can then save time still giving the possibility of checking the important ideas with users. Prototypes developed with languages such as Visual Basic™ are the next phase after paper prototypes, and are used by many developers.

The key principles of the user-centered design methodology, namely the focus on users, the task they perform and the context in which they work, and the iterative development through prototypes of increasing complexity that are evaluated with the users, have been captured in the standard ISO 13407 (Human-centered design process for interactive systems), that is shown in Fig. 2 [19]. The design solutions mentioned in block 4 of Fig. 2 are implemented through prototypes that are evaluated, and if they do not meet the specified requirements, the process is iterated and goes again through a revision of the specifications and a proposal of a new prototype. The iterative process is stopped when requirements are met.

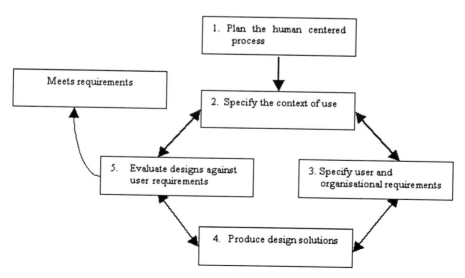

**Fig. 2.**   The ISO 13407 Human-centered design process for interactive systems.

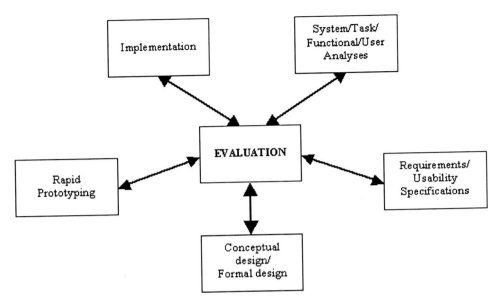

**Fig. 3.**   The star life cycle model [20].

From our discussion above, it follows that evaluation represents the central phase in the development cycle. For this reason, within the HCI community, Hartson and Hix have developed the star life cycle model shown in Fig. 3 [20]. While the waterfall model suggests a top-down (analytic) approach, the star model recognizes that this approach needs to be complemented by a bottom-up (synthetic) approach, and can start from any point in the star (as shown by the entry arrows), followed by any other stage (as shown by the double arrows). In this way, the requirements, the design, and the product gradually evolve, becoming step by step well defined.

## 5. Applying Usability Evaluation Methods in the Software Life Cycle

In order to design usable systems, we have seen that in the software life cycle usability evaluation plays the fundamental role. The HCI research has provided several principles and guidelines that can drive the designers in taking their decisions. However, applying available design guidelines is a good start, but there are no "cookbooks", and therefore no substitute for system evaluation.

Different methods can be used for evaluating systems at the different phases of their development: the most commonly adopted are user-based methods and inspection methods. User-based methods mainly consist of user testing, in which usability properties are assessed by observing how the system, or a prototype of the system, is actually used by some representative of real users performing real tasks [15, 16, 21]. Usability inspection methods involve expert evaluators only, who inspect the user interface in order to find out possible usability problems, provide judgements based on their knowledge, and make recommendations for fixing the problems and improving the usability of the application [22].

User-based evaluation provides a trusty evaluation, because it assesses usability through samples of real users. However, it has a number of drawbacks, such as the difficulty to properly select a correct sample of the user community, and to train it to manage not only the main application features but also the most sophisticated and advanced facilities of an interactive system.

With respect to user-based evaluation, usability inspection methods are more subjective, having heavy dependence upon the inspector skills. Among the inspection methods, we may include heuristic evaluation, cognitive walkthrough, formal usability inspection, guidelines reviews [22]. Heuristic evaluation is the most informal method; it involves a usability expert who analyses the dialogue elements of the user interface to check if they conform to usability principles, usually referred as heuristics, hence the name of this method. In a cognitive walkthrough, the expert uses some detailed procedures to simulate users' problem solving processes during the user-computer dialogue, in order to see if the functionalities provided by the system are efficient for users and lead to the correct actions. Formal usability inspection is a review of users' potential task performance with a product. It was designed to help engineers to review a product and find a large number of usability defects. It is very similar to the code inspection methods with which software developers are familiar. It is carried out by the engineer designing the product and a team of peers, looking for defects. Finally, in a guidelines review, the expert inspects the interface to check if it is conformed to a list of usability guidelines. The method can be considered as a cross between heuristic evaluation and standard inspection, the latter is another kind of inspection to check the compliance of the interface to some interface standards. A detailed description of these and other inspection methods is in [22].

The main advantage of inspection methods is however the cost saving: they do not involve users nor require any special equipment or lab facilities [8, 22]. In addition, experts can detect a wide range of problems and possible faults of a complex system in a limited amount of time. For these reasons, inspection methods have achieved widespread use in the last years, especially in the industrial environments [23], since industry is very much interested in effective methods that can provide good results yet being cost-effective.

Inspection methods aim at finding usability problems in an existing user interface, and making recommendations for fixing these problems. Hence, they can be applied at various steps of the software development, and are certainly used for evaluating the design of the system in a prototype form, even a paper prototype, so that possible defects can be fixed as soon as possible. When a system implementation is available, user-based evaluation is often recommended. It includes experimental methods, observational methods, and survey techniques. Among experimental methods, controlled experiments are very valuable, as they provide empirical evidence to support specific hypotheses. They allow a comparative evaluation, very useful when alternative prototypes or versions of the same system are available. An experiment consists of the following steps: formulation of the hypotheses to be tested, definition of the experimental conditions that differ only in the values of some controlled variables, execution of the experiment, analysis of collected data. In order to verify the usability of a single prototype, we can observe users working with it. A valid technique is the thinking aloud, in which users are asked to think aloud when they use the system or prototype. In this way, evaluators can detect users misconceptions and the system elements that cause them. Both experimental and observational methods are used for collecting data about system and user performance; they do not provide data about users' satisfaction, that is a subjective measure that can be obtained by survey techniques, such as interviews and questionnaires that we mentioned in Sec. 3, since they are also used for requirement gathering. For further details, the reader is referred to [15, 16].

By considering the industry's interest for cheap but effective methods, heuristic evaluation plays an important role. It prescribes having a small set of experts analyzing the system, and evaluating its interface against a list of recognized usability principles, the heuristics. Some researches have shown that heuristic evaluation is a very efficient usability engineering technique [24], with a high benefit cost-ratio [23], and therefore it falls within the so-called discount usability methods.

In principle, only one evaluator can conduct heuristic evaluation. However, in an analysis of six studies, it has been assessed that single evaluators are able to find only the 35% of the total number of the existent usability problems [8, 22]. Different evaluators tend to find different problems. Therefore, the more experts are involved in the evaluation, the more problems it is possible to find. The mathematical model defined in [12] shows that reasonable results can be obtained by having only five evaluators.

Heuristics evaluation, and in general the inspection methods proposed so far are not systematic, and lack methodological frameworks. In some recent papers, the User Action Framework (UAF) has been proposed, as a unifying and organizing framework, supporting usability inspection, design guidelines, classification and reporting of usability problems [25]. It provides a knowledge base, in which different usability problems are organized according to the Interaction Cycle model — an extension of the Norman's theory of actions [26]. Following such a model, problems are organized taking into account how user interaction is affected by the application design, at various points where users must accomplish cognitive or physical actions. The knowledge base is a notable contribution of the UAF methodology, which tries to provide a solution to the need for more focused usability inspection methods, and more readable and comparable inspection reports.

Classifying problems, and organizing them in a knowledge base, is also a way to keep track of the large number of problems found in different usability studies, thus capitalizing on past experiences. Reusing the past evaluation experience, and making it available to less experienced people is also one of the basic goals of a new inspection technique described in [27, 28], which introduces the use of evaluation patterns for guiding the inspector activity. The patterns precisely describe which objects to look for and which actions to perform in order to analyze such objects. Such evaluation patterns are called *Abstract Tasks* for the following reasons: *Task*, because each one describes a task the evaluator must perform during inspection in order to detect usability problems; *Abstract*, because it describes the operations for accomplishing the task, without any reference to a specific application, providing instead a description that is independent from any application. Their formulation is the reflection of the experiences of some skilled evaluators. They allow even less experienced evaluators to come out with good results. The major effectiveness and efficiency of the inspection based on the use of Abstract Tasks, with respect to the traditional heuristic evaluation, has been verified through a comparative study described in [29].

## 6. Conclusions

In the chapter, we have stressed the importance of a good user interface for today's interactive systems. The quality of the interface must be evaluated especially from the users' point of view, by taking into account the users that will actually use the system. Usability, a quality that has been neglected by the software engineering community for a too long time, becomes a crucial factor for judging the quality of the user interface. The user-centered design methodology for designing usable systems has been discussed, and indications on how to include usability in the software life cycle have been provided.

## References

1. B. Myers and M. B. Rosson, "Survey on user interface programming", *Proceedings of the CHI'92* (ACM Press) 195–202.
2. J. A. McCall, "Quality factors", *Encyclopedia of Software Engineering*, ed. J. J. Marciniak (John Wiley & Sons, New York, 1994) 958–969.
3. B. Boehm, *Characteristics of Software Quality* (North Holland Publishing Co., New York, 1978).
4. J. McCall, P. Richards and G. Walters, *Factors in Software Quality*, 3 Vols., NTIS AD-A049-015, 015, 055, November 1977.
5. R. S. Pressman, *Software Engineering: A Practitioner's Approach*, 4th ed. (McGraw-Hill Companies, New York, 1997).
6. D. J. Mayhew, *Principles and Guidelines in Software User Interface Design* (Prentice Hall, Englewood Cliffs, 1992).
7. D. J. Mayhew, *The Usability Engineering Lifecycle: A Practitioner's Handbook for User Interface Design* (Morgan Kaufmann Publishers, CA, 1999).
8. J. Nielsen, *Usability Engineering* (Academic Press, Cambridge, MA, 1993).
9. ISO/IEC (International Organization for Standardization and International Electrotechnical Commision), ISO/IEC 9126-1: Information Technology — Software Product Quality, 1998.
10. ISO (International Organization for Standardization), ISO 9241: Ergonomics Requirements for Office Work with Visual Display Terminal (VDT) — Parts 1–17, 1997.

11. K. H. Madsen, Special issue on "The diversity of usability", *Communications of the ACM* **42**, no. 5, 1999.

12. J. Nielsen and T. K. Landauer, "A mathematical model of the finding of usability problems", *Proceedings of the ACM INTERCHI'93 — International Conference on Human Factors in Computing Systems* (ACM Press, Amsterdam NL, 1993) 296–313.

13. J. Hackos and J. C. Redish, *User and Task Analysis for Interface Design* (John Wiley & Sons, 1998).

14. J. Rubin, *Handbook of Usability Testing* (John Wiley & Sons, 1994).

15. Dix, J. Finlay, G. Abowd and R. Beale, *Human Computer Interaction* (Prentice Hall, 1998).

16. J. Preece, Y. Rogers, H. Sharp, D. Beyon, S. Holland and T. Carey, *Human-Computer Interaction* (Addison Wesley, 1994).

17. F. Paterno, "Task models for interactive software systems" (in this volume).

18. C. Ghezzi, M. Jazayeri and D. Mandrioli, *Fundamentals of Software Engineering* (Prentice Hall International, 1991).

19. ISO (International Organization for Standardization), ISO 13407: Human-Centered Design Process for Interactive Systems, 1998.

20. H. R. Hartson and D. Hix, *Developing User Interfaces* (John Wiley, New York, 1993).

21. J. Whiteside, J. Bennet and K. Holtzblatt, "Usability enginnering our experience and evolution", *Handbook of Human-Computer Interaction*, ed. M. Helander (Elsevier Science, 1988) 791–817.

22. J. Nielsen and R. L. Mack, *Usability Inspection Methods* (John Wiley & Sons, New York, 1994).

23. J. Nielsen, "Guerrilla HCI: Using discount usability engineering to penetrate intimidation barrier", *Cost-Justifying, Usability*, eds. R. G. Bias, D. J. Mayhew (Academic Press) Also available at the URL *http://www.useit.com/papers/guerilla_hci.html*, 1994.

24. R. Jeffries and H. W. Desurvire, "Usability testing vs heuristic evaluation: Was there a context?" *ACM SIGCHI Bulletin* **24**, no. 4 (1992) 39–41.

25. H. R. Hartson, T. S. Andre, R. C. Willges and L. van Rens, "The user action framework: A theory-based foundation for inspection and classification of usability problems", *Proceedings of the HCII '99*, Munich, Germany **I** (August 1999) 1058–1062.

26. D. A. Norman, *The Psychology of Everyday Things* (Basic Books, 1988).

27. M. Matera, "SUE: A systematic methodology for evaluating hypermedia usability", PhD Thesis, Dipartimento di Elettronica e Informazione, Politecnico di Milano, 2000.

28. M. F. Costabile and M. Matera, "Proposing guidelines for usability inspection", *Proceedings of the TFWWG'2000*, Biarritz, France (Springer, October 7–8, 2000) 283–292.

29. De Angeli, M. Matera, M. F. Costabile, F. Garzotto and P. Paolini, "Evaluating the SUE inspection technique", *Proc. AVI'2000 — International Conference on Advanced Visual Interfaces*, Palermo, Italy (ACM press, May 24–27, 2000) 143–150.

# THE SOFTWARE PROCESS: MODELING, EVALUATION AND IMPROVEMENT

SILVIA T. ACUÑA

*Departamento de Informática, Universidad Nacional de Santiago del Estero,*
*Avenida Belgrano (S) 1912, 4200 Santiago del Estero, Argentina*
*E-mail: silvac@unse.edu.ar*

ANGÉLICA DE ANTONIO, XAVIER FERRÉ and LUIS MATÉ

*Facultad de Informática, Universidad Politécnica de Madrid, Campus de Montegancedo,*
*28660 Boadilla del Monte, Spain*
*E-mail: {angelica,xavier,jlmate}@fi.upm.es*

MARTA LÓPEZ

*Software Engineering Institute Carnegie Mellon University, Pittsburgh,*
*PA 15213-3890, USA*
*E-mail: mlopez@sei.cmu.edu*

Two different research fields work on the issue of software process: software process modeling on one hand and software process evaluation and improvement on the other. In this paper, the most relevant results of both approaches are presented and, despite they have evolved independently, the relation between them is highlighted. Software process modeling tries to capture the main characteristics of the set of activities performed to obtain a software product, and a variety of models have been created for this purpose. A process model can be used either to represent the existing process in an organization, or to define a recommended software process. Software process evaluation assesses the quality of the software process used in a software development organization, being the SCE and ISO/IEC 15504 the two most commonly used evaluation methods. Software process evaluation can be the starting point of a software process improvement effort. This effort aims to direct the organization's current practices to a state where the software process is continuously evaluated and improved.

*Keywords*: Software process, software process modeling, software process evaluation, software process improvement.

## 1. Introduction

The software process is a critical factor for delivering quality software systems, as it aims to manage and transform the user need into a software product that meets this need. In this context, software process means the set of activities required to produce a software system, executed by a group of people organized according to a given organizational structure and counting on the support of techno-conceptual tools. General concepts about software process are presented in this chapter and some specific approaches are highlighted.

The ultimate goal of research into the software process is to improve software development practice through [87]: (a) better ways of organizational design at the level of individual processes and the organization as a whole, (b) accompanying innovations in technological support. Hence, there are two lines of research into the software process.

(1) *Software process modeling* describes the creation of software development process models. A software process model is an abstract representation of the architecture, design or definition of the software process [50]. Each representation describes, at different detail levels, an organization of the elements of a finished, ongoing or proposed process and it provides a definition of the process to be used for evaluation and improvement. A process model can be analyzed, validated and simulated, if executable. The process models are used mainly for software process control (evaluation and improvement) in an organization, but they can be also used for experimenting with software process theory and to ease process automation.

(2) *Software process evaluation and improvement* by means of which to judge and decide on the quality of the object under analysis or the evaluand, that is, the software process of a given organization, and propose a process improvement strategy. The efforts of the scientific community in this field have led to quite a number of maturity models and standards, such as ISO 9000 [78, 79, 120], CMM (Capability Maturity Model) [108], ISO/IEC 15504 [77] and Bootstrap [91]. All these models have two goals: (a) determine the aspects for improvement in a software development organization; and (b) reach an agreement of what a good process is. This goal stems from the very nature of the evaluation process, as it is essential to use a reference model or yardstick against which to compare the software process of the organization under evaluation. Therefore, it involves modeling the above process by identifying what sorts of activities have to be carried out by an organization to assure the quality of the production process and, ultimately, the end product. The existing methods include models focused on the management process, encompassing quality management [112]. Methods of this sort evaluate the maturity of the software process, that is, how well defined, managed, measured and controlled a given process is and determine an organization's software production capability. The findings of this evaluation can include a software process improvement strategy, as the reference standard is really an evolutionary framework for improving management activities. This group includes the CMM-based appraisals (SCE (Software Capability Evaluation) and CBA IPI (CMM Based Appraisal for Internal Process Improvement)) [108] and methods like Bootstrap [91].

These are the two aspects of the software development process that are going to be addressed in this paper (Secs. 3 and 4 deal with software process modeling, Secs. 5 and 6 with evaluation and Sec. 7 with improvement). Firstly, some basic concepts related to this subject are presented in Sec. 2.

## 2. Software Process Basics

### 2.1. *What is the software process?*

Originally, the term life cycle was employed in every software development project [39]. Even though the notion of software process was present in these projects, the concept of software process was not clearly identified [16, 99]. As software and software construction were further investigated, the software process acquired an identity in its own right and has been the subject of research and investigation in recent years [52, 65]. The concepts of life cycle and process are so closely related that confusion often arises, calling for a clarification of these concepts. The view taken of these concepts is as follows [2].

(1) *Life cycle*: All the **states** through which the software evolves. The life cycle centres on the product, defining the states through which the product passes from the start of construction (the initial state is the user need) until the software is in operation (this product state is the deployed system) and finally retired (the state is the retired system) [119, 43]. A *life cycle model* is an abstract representation of the software life cycle. In the case of the software product, there is no one life cycle. A product can pass through different states, depending on the specific circumstances of each project. For example, if the problem is well defined and well understood and the user need is practically invariable, a *short*, waterfall-like life cycle is likely to be sufficient. However, when we come up against a poorly defined and poorly understood problem and a highly volatile user need, we can hardly expect to output a full requirements specification at the start. In this case, we have to opt for *longer* and more complex life cycles, like the spiral life cycle [18]; prototyping, where the first state will be a prototype [100, 58]; or an incremental life cycle, where the first state will be the specification of the system kernel, followed by the kernel design and finally implementation, then going back to specify the next system increment and so on [66]. So, there are different life cycles for different project circumstances. A method for selecting a model from several alternative life cycle models is presented in [6]. Descriptions of the life cycle models that represent the main life cycles are given in [119, 29, 111, 110]. Software engineering and knowledge engineering life cycle models are compared in [135] and software engineering models in [38, 29].

(2) *Software process*: A partially ordered set of **activities** undertaken to manage, develop and maintain software systems, that is, the software process centres on the construction process rather than on the product(s) output. The definition of a software process usually specifies the actors executing the activities, their roles and the artefacts produced. An organization can define its own way to produce software. However, some activities are common to all software processes. The set of processes that form a software process should be called subprocesses, but we will follow in this chapter the IEEE's terminology, calling them processes too. A *software process model* is an abstract representation of the software process. The two key international standards that prescribe processes for developing and maintaining software are IEEE 1974-1991 [75] and ISO/IEC 12207 [81]. Both standards determine a set of essential, albeit unordered activities, which have to be completed to obtain a software product. They do not prescribe a specific life cycle. Each organization that uses the standard must instantiate the prescribed process as a specific process. ISO/IEC 12207 presents a process of adaptation that defines the activities required to tailor the standard to an individual software project. A variety of software process models have been designed to structure, describe and prescribe the software system construction process. These models are considered in Sec. 4.

This paper deals with the software process and not the life cycle.

## 2.2. *Software engineering and knowledge engineering software process*

The prescription of the software construction process is a subject that has been studied in software engineering for quite some years now. The IEEE published a qualitative, informal and prescriptive model in 1991. As mentioned above, many other proposals have emerged since then, seeking to formalize and automate the construction process. The situation in knowledge engineering, however, is quite a different kettle of fish. The issue of the technical activities to be performed to build a Knowledge-Based System (KBS) was debated in the 80's [25, 134, 5, 62, 45], but knowledge engineering has never taken an interest in fully defining all the activities to be performed to build a knowledge-based system, including management and support activities.

Although knowledge engineering has not focused efforts on outputting a full definition of its development process, it is true that the process definitions made in software engineering are not so far removed. This is because the process models are highly abstract, thus hiding differences in the development techniques required to build different types of software. The software process defines how the development is organized, managed, measured, supported and improved, irrespective of the techniques and methods used for development [41]. Therefore, even admitting the underlying differences between traditional and knowledge-based software, the work carried out in software engineering on software process definition, modeling, evaluation and improvement can be interesting for knowledge engineering.

[2] includes a discussion of the software engineering activities applicable to knowledge engineering and vice versa, and it also includes a software process model to be used in both disciplines. This model prescribes a set of processes, activities, products, roles, and abilities of the people participating in the development process of both traditional and knowledge-based systems.

## 2.3. *Software process modeling, evaluation and improvement*

Today, there are three main actions that can be taken with respect to the software process: define or model, evaluate and improve. The *definition of the software process* refers to the definition of the processes as models, plus any optional automated support available for modeling and for executing the models during the software process. Finkelstein *et al* [52] define a process model as the description of a process expressed in a suitable process modeling language. There are other possible uses of software process models that will not be considered, such as the introduction of a new process in an organization and personnel training/motivation.

Curtis *et al* present some of the specific goals and benefits of the software process modeling [36].

(1) *Ease of understanding and communication*: Requiring a process model containing enough information for its representation. It formalizes the process, thus providing a basis for training.

(2) *Process management support and control*: Requiring a project-specific software process and monitoring, management and coordination.

(3) *Provision for automated orientations for process performance*: Requiring an effective software development environment, providing user orientations, instructions and reference material.

(4) *Provision for automated execution support*: Requiring automated process parts, cooperative work support, a compilation of metrics and process integrity assurance.

(5) *Process improvement support*: Requiring the reuse of well-defined and effective software processes, the comparison of alternative processes and process development support.

Different process models can define different points of view. For example, one model may define the agents involved in each activity, while another may centre on the relationship between activities. There is a model that addresses the organizational culture and focuses on the behavioural capabilities or duties of the roles involved in the software process [3, 4]. This means that each model observes, focuses on or gives priority to particular points of such a complex world as software construction [42, 50]. A model is always an abstraction of the reality and, as such, represents a partial and simplified description of the reality; that is, not all the parts or aspects of the process are taken into account in the model. Generally, a process model can be divided into several sub-models expressing different viewpoints or perspectives. Additionally, there is a variety of notations for defining the process models as described in Sec. 3.2. The results achieved so far in software process modeling research are reviewed in [7].

*Software process evaluation* involves analyzing the activities carried out in an organization to produce software. The ultimate goal of process evaluation is to improve software production. Development process evaluation and improvement works under the hypothesis that the quality of the software product is determined by the quality of its development process. This strategy is equivalent to the one implemented in other branches of engineering and industries, where the quality of the resulting product is increased by controlling the process used in its production [70].

Software process evaluation methods introduced innovative concepts that have changed the way in which software production activities are perceived. The new process standards and maturity models developed for use as yardsticks in the assessments are the most important innovation. However, agreement has not been reached on what a good process is and what characteristics of the process are to be evaluated.

*Software process improvement* studies the way of improving the software development practices in an organization, once software process evaluation has made clear what the current state of the process is. Software process improvement is not planned in a single step to excellence, but it is performed gradually by transitions between specific maturity levels. Due to the unstable nature of software development technologies, it is necessary to continuously evaluate and improve the software process. Thus, a capable and mature software development organization institutionalizes the improvement effort.

Software process research is comprehensively reviewed in [41], while [57] presents an overall critical evaluation and possible directions for future research.

## 3. Concepts and Approaches of Software Process Modeling

Firstly, we are going to deal with the basic process-related elements, as well as their possible interrelationships. Then the different approaches to modeling from the viewpoint of the information they can address, and the diverse process environments will be presented.

### 3.1. *Basic process modeling elements*

The software process basically consists of two interrelated processes: the production process and the management process. The first is related to the construction and maintenance of the software product, whereas the second is responsible for estimating, planning and controlling the necessary resources (people, time, technological, ...) to be able to carry out and control the production process. This control makes it possible to generate information about the production process, which can be used later on by the management process with a view to improving the software process and increasing the quality of the developed software. There are two main submodels in process modeling: the management process model and the production process model [41].

Different elements of a process, for example, activities, products (artefacts), resources (personnel and tools) and roles, can be modelled [68]. There are several classifications concerning the main elements of a process model [94, 50, 31]. The elements most commonly modelled are presented below [14, 52, 99, 56]. Figure 1 shows these elements and their interrelationships. Other possible elements like project/organization, workspace (repository), user viewpoint, model of cooperation, versioning, transactions, quality, etc will not be considered.

- *Agent* or *Actor*: is an entity that executes a process. Actors can be divided into two groups as regards to their close relationship with the computer: (a) human actors, who are the people who develop software or are involved in the software process and are possibly organized as teams; (b) system actors or system tools, which are the computer software or hardware components. An actor is characterized by the properties of its role and its availability. An actor, person or system can play several roles, which are composed of consistent sets of activities. A role can be judged by several cooperative actors.
- *Role*: describes a set of agent or group responsibilities, rights and skills required to perform a specific software process activity. This is an association between agents and activities in terms of a defined set of responsibilities executed by agents.
- *Activity*: is the stage of a process that produces externally visible changes of state in the software product. An activity can have an input, an output and some intermediate results, generically termed products (they can be software products, requirements specification documents, database schemata, etc). The activity includes and implements procedures, rules, policies and goals to generate and modify a set of given artefacts. This activity can be performed by a human agent or using a tool. The activities can be divided into more elementary activities; that is, there are elementary or compound activities. The activities can be organized in networks with both horizontal (chained) and vertical (decomposition) dimensions. The activities are associated with roles, other activities and artefacts.
- *Artefact* or *Product*: is the (sub)product and the "raw material" of a process. An artefact produced by a process can be used later as raw material for the same or another process to produce other artefacts. An artefact or software product is developed and maintained in a process. An artefact can have a long lifetime, and there may be different versions of each artefact as the software process evolves. The (sub)products can be created, accessed

or modified during a process activity. A set of software artefacts to be delivered to a user is named software product. Therefore, a relationship "composed of" can appear between the products.

- *Event*: is a noteworthy occurrence happening at a specific moment in time. Event-based models provide a different view (not represented in Fig. 1) of the activities by which the dynamic nature of the process is made evident.

The relationships between these elements, such as activity/role/actor interaction, activity-activity interaction, product-activity interaction, product-product interaction, are described in [14]. Definitions of the process modeling concepts are found in [30, 94] and the main software process models that use these concepts are described in [52].

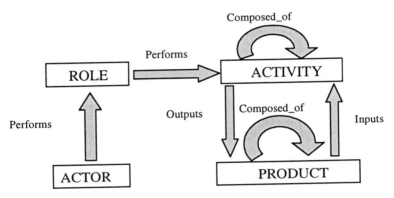

**Fig. 1.**    Basic process modeling components.

### 3.2. *Modeling approaches*

There are different types of process modeling. Processes can be modelled at different levels of abstraction (for example, generic models vs tailored models) and they can also be modelled with different goals (descriptive models vs prescriptive models). The distinguishing features of these models have been described in [70, 96, 99, 110]. The types of information in a process model can be structured from different viewpoints. Curtis presents the following list of *information perspectives* commonly found in the literature [36]:

- *Functional*: represents which process elements are being implemented and which information entity flows are important for the above process elements.
- *Behavioural*: represents when (that is, sequentiality) and under which conditions the process elements are implemented.
- *Organizational*: represents where and by whom in the organization the process elements are implemented.

- *Informative*: represents the information entities output or manipulated by a process, including their structure and relationships.

The models are built according to the languages, abstractions or formalisms created for representing the specific information about these characteristics. The most used language in practice is (structured) natural language due to its flexibility. Table 1 presents a list of representation abstractions (excluding natural language) organized according to the above-mentioned viewpoints. These abstractions are the most popular in software process research. None of these abstractions covers all the classes of information. Therefore, most of the models found in the literature present languages based on more than one of these abstractions. These models consider the need to integrate multiple representation paradigms (that is, different process models), although this generally makes the model more complex to define [132].

**Table 1.** Perspectives for process information and applicable language bases.

| Language Base | Information Perspectives |
| --- | --- |
| Procedural programming language [114] | Functional |
| | Behavioural |
| | Informative |
| Systems analysis and design, including data flow diagram [55] and structured analysis and design technique (SADT) [102] | Functional |
| | Organizational |
| | Informative |
| Artificial intelligence languages and approaches, including rules and pre-/post-conditions [12] | Functional |
| | Behavioural |
| Events and triggers // Control flow [52] | Behavioural |
| State transition and Petri nets [40, 11] // Statecharts [88, 89, 61, 113] | Functional |
| | Behavioural |
| | Organizational |
| Functional languages // Formal languages [36, 68] | Functional |
| Data modeling, including entity-relationship diagrams, structured data and relationship declarations [109] | Informative |
| Object modeling, including types of classes and instances, hierarchy and inheritance [49] | Organizational |
| | Informative |
| Quantitative modeling, including quantitative operational research and systems dynamic techniques [1] | Behavioural |
| Precedence networks, including actor dependency modeling [138, 20] | Behavioural |
| | Organizational |

On the one hand, as shown in Table 1, a wide variety of notations have been used to model processes. A text that describes different notations for modeling the process is [128]. A good overview over the concepts used in some of the various modeling notations mentioned is given in [116]. There are no data on which of the available notations are more useful or easier to use under given conditions.

On the other hand, as mentioned above, a variety of multi-paradigm approaches have been proposed for modeling software processes. These approaches have two main characteristics. Firstly, excepting mainly Petri net-based approaches, they all use textual representations. Secondly, most of them are already at a programming language level of abstraction. Thus, they make it difficult to model a problematic situation directly, whereas they force the engineer or process manager to take into account many technical aspects of the modeling formalism [49].

### 3.3. *Process environments*

Software process models can exploit contributions, concepts and factors from three interrelated environments: organizational, cultural and scientific/technological.

- The *Organizational Environment* reflects if the model deals with organizational issues such as the organizational culture, behaviour, the design and evolution of the organization, and the abilities of the people and organizations involved.
- The *Cultural Environment* of a model deals with the three essential characteristics of the organizational culture: creative ability, social interaction and flexibility with the environment. *Creative ability* is about the development of new organizational and software process models. *Social interaction* is based on the relation between the different reasoning structures one can found in each discipline, in each profession and even in each person. *Flexibility with the environment* considers the organization's position regarding socio-cultural and scientific/technological environments and generic software process models, where social interaction and creative ability dimensions are developed.
- The *Scientific/Technological Environment* of a model shows that it points towards the tools, infrastructure, software environments and methodologies to be used for software production and also for software process management, improvement and control.

Viewing software development as a process has significantly helped identify the different dimensions of software development and the problems that need to be addressed in order to establish effective practices. This vision has evolved from "software processes are software too" [106] to "software processes are processes too" [57]. Indeed, addressing the problems and issues of software development is not just a matter of introducing some effective tool and software environment. It is not sufficient to select a reasonable lifecycle strategy either. Rather, we must pay attention to the complex interrelation of a number of organizational, cultural, and scientific/technological factors.

## 4. Overview of Software Process Models

In this section, the main software process models are presented, divided according to their approach into descriptive and prescriptive.

In case the reader is interested just in basic modeling concepts and not in particular models, he or she can skip this section.

### 4.1. *Descriptive models*

The goal of descriptive modeling is to make a process now used in an organization explicit, or to represent a proposed process so as to predict some process characteristics [99]. Software process models that go by the name of *descriptive models* answer the questions "how is software now developed?" or "how has software been developed?" [94]. A descriptive model can uncover many previously hidden problems in the organization's software development process, and knowing what is actually being done is the first step to be able to improve it. McChesney [99] divides this group of models into two main categories (informal descriptive models and formal descriptive models), depending on the goal of the descriptions.

The goal of *informal descriptive models* is simply to provide an informal and qualitative model. Examples of informal models are the process cycle model [96]; the stratified behaviour model [35]; Bendifallah & Scacchi's model [15]; and Cain and Coplien's model [22]. *Formal descriptive models* of the software process can be related to process assessment, process improvement and/or process prediction. This category includes: the Systems Dynamics Based model [1]; the FUNSOFT network-based model [40]; the PRISM change model [98]; the STATEMATE model [89]; the TAME model [13]; the Amadeus model [124]; the actor dependency model [138]; and the Wolf & Rosenblum's event-based model [136].

Each of these classes are addressed below from the viewpoint of model criteria, representation criteria and methodological criteria in order to identify the elements that represent the software process and, therefore, model the process in question. Figure 2 lists some of the most important descriptive models [92, 8, 99], belonging to each of these classes. These models are characterized in Table 2 according to the above-mentioned criteria. If they meet a table characteristic, the respective table cell is marked with X; otherwise the space is left blank.

The stratified behaviour model and the process cycle model are qualitative and are orthogonal to existing process models. Although they are extremely informal and have no modeling procedure, they do address the question of the human agents involved in the software process. With regard to formal models, Madhavji provides a methodological perspective of process cycle evolution [96], proposes the PRISM methodology [97] for building and adapting generic software process models and provides a process-centred environment for managing changes in the PRISM

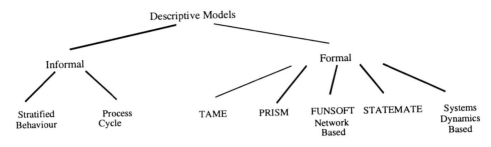

**Fig. 2.**   Descriptive models.

model [98]. Basili and Rombach [13] formalize the Goal-Question-Metric paradigm for the following tasks: characterization of the current state of the project environment and planning, construction, analysis, learning and project feedback. Each of these tasks is addressed in the TAME model from the constructive and analytical viewpoint; that is, the model integrates methods and tools to build the products (constructive viewpoint) and methods and tools to analyze the construction processes and products output (analytical viewpoint). Additionally, STATEMATE covers the four information perspectives, as it integrates three graphical representation languages (state diagrams, activities diagrams, modules diagrams) [89] to analyze and predict the behaviour of the process models.

As shown in Table 2, the FUNSOFT network-based model focuses on a formal and graphic notation. It addresses neither organizational issues nor aspects related to the people involved in the process, it merely deals with the scientific/technological environment, which is reflected under the column labelled *Process environments addressed by the model*. The systems dynamics approach to process modeling is used as a means for simulating proposed processes, predicting dynamic software process behaviour and reporting the administration or management of the right policies and procedures. Abdel-Hamid and Madnick [1] develop a comprehensive automated systems dynamics model of the software development process. It is the only descriptive model that includes both the organizational environment and people's creative ability, which is reflected under the columns labelled *Process environments addressed by the model* and *cultural environment*.

However, as shown in Table 2, none of these models examine all the components of software process models that we consider to be desirable, which is evidenced under the column labelled *Procedure coverage (partial)*. Sufficient model coverage specifies whether the procedure proposed by each model, if any, covers all the objects and characteristics of the software process model we consider desirable; that is, whether the content of the model considers all the environments, processes, activities, agents, products, roles and relationships between the elements involved in the process. With respect to the environments, sufficient coverage indicates whether the procedure models the organizational, cultural and scientific/technological environments with their related aspects. As far as processes and activities are concerned, it

**Table 2.** Characterization of descriptive models.

*Model Criteria* — Process elements represented by the model; Process environments addressed by the model (*cultural*). *Representation Criteria* — Information perspectives; Notation characteristics (from the viewpoint of information quality; from the viewpoint of formal notation). *Methodological Criteria* — Modelling procedure; Procedure coverage; Procedure definition.

| MODEL | agent | activity | artefact | role | event | organisational | creative ability | social interaction | environment flexibility | scientific / technological | functional | behavioural | organisational | informative | informal | formal | automated | text | graphic | non-developed | developed | partial | sufficient | undefined | semi-defined | defined |
|---|---|---|---|---|---|---|---|---|---|---|---|---|---|---|---|---|---|---|---|---|---|---|---|---|---|---|
| Stratified Behaviour | X | | | | | X | | | | | | | | | | | | | | | | | | | | |
| Process Cycle | X | X | | X | | | | | | | X | | | | X | | | | | X | | | | | | |
| TAME | X | X | X | | | X | | | | | X | X | X | | | X | X | | | | X | X | X | | X | |
| PRISM | X | X | X | | | X | | | | | X | X | X | X | | X | X | | | | X | X | X | | X | |
| FUNSOFT Network Based | X | X | X | | | X | | | | | X | X | X | X | | X | | X | X | X | | X | X | X | | |
| STATEMATE | X | X | X | X | X | | | | | | X | X | X | X | | X | | X | X | | | X | X | X | | |
| Systems Dynamics Based | X | X | | | | X | X | | | | X | | | | X | | | X | X | | | X | X | X | | |

denotes whether the procedure models organizational, management, technical and process support processes and their respective activities. With regard to people and their roles, it shows whether the procedure models the roles of designer, manager and developer (including software engineer, planning engineer, monitoring and control engineer, analyst, designer, knowledge engineer) and the capabilities of the people who play these roles. With reference to products, sufficient coverage specifies whether the procedure models all the documents generated by the activities of each process.

Furthermore, none of the models considered provides a series of fully defined activities for process modeling, as shown under the column labelled *Procedure definition (defined)*. There are two models, TAME and PRISM, with a semi-defined modeling procedure, as shown under *Procedure modeling (developed)* and *Procedure definition (semi-defined)* columns and the column labelled *From the viewpoint of information quality (formal and automated)*. Finally, the models are found to provide nowhere near enough information for guiding the engineer in the process of building descriptive process models.

## 4.2. *Prescriptive models*

Prescriptive models are the outputs of prescriptive modeling. The goal of prescriptive modeling is to define the required or recommended means of executing the process [99]. The software process models that go by the name of *prescriptive models* answer the question, "how should the software be developed?" [94]. McChesney [99] divides this group of models into two categories (manual prescriptive models and automated prescriptive models), depending on the goal of the prescriptions.

*Manual prescriptive models* can be standards, methodologies and methods centred on management, development, evaluation and software life cycle and organizational life cycle support processes. The models belonging to this category include:

- Traditional structured methodologies.
- Object-oriented methodologies.
- Knowledge engineering methodologies.
- Organizational design methodologies, which are considered as some of the most representative in the field of socio-cultural systems [53, 115].
- Software life cycle development process standards (like IEEE 1074-1991 and ISO 12207).
- Software process evaluation standard- or model-based methods.

The *automated prescriptive models* perform activities related to assistance, support, management and/or computer-assisted software production techniques. The models belonging to this category include: ALF [23]; IPSE 2.5 [133]; Marvel [84]; PMDB [109]; SOCCA [49]; SPADE [10]; TRIAD [114]; Conversation Builder [85]; EPOS [32]; GRAPPLE [67]; HFSP [86]; MERLIN [83]; and the Unified Software Development Process or Unified Process [82].

These models are computerized specifications of software process standards. Their main aim is to act as a guide for the software modeling process; that is, they are directed at aiding process agents by mechanically interpreting software process models [95]. The automated prescriptive models can be divided into two categories, depending on the guiding criterion selected to address software process modeling: (a) activity-oriented models and (b) people-oriented models.

Activity-oriented models focus on the functions, activities of and information about parts of the management, development and software life-cycle support processes. These include TRIAD, Marvel, IPSE 2.5 and SPADE, for example. People-oriented models focus on the specifications of the people involved in the software process and their relationships. They include SOCCA, ALF, PMDB and the Unified Process. People are the least formalized factor in existing software process models. Their importance, however, is patent [127]: their behaviour is non-deterministic and subjective and has a decisive impact on the results of software production, which is basically an intellectual and social activity [59]. Additionally, the non-specification of human resources means that the process does not reflect the actual status of the software process of the modelled organization, having the added risk of processes not suited to the capability of the organization's human resources being executed [123, 138, 48].

As mentioned above, a variety of multi-paradigm software process modeling approaches have been proposed. Most focus on one main paradigm, like rules

(Marvel, for example), imperative programs (TRIAD/CML, for example), activity-oriented programs (IPSE 2.5) or Petri nets (SPADE, for example). The integration of formalisms to describe both the software process and the members of the process and their relationships, which explicitly includes the human components and any interaction in which they are involved, has been proposed by approaches such as SOCCA, ALF and PMDB. The chapter by Kneuper in this handbook deals with this issue, considering the process models as support for developers. The complexity of the resulting software, which over-stretches both the technical and organizational management, can be better dealt with in this manner.

Each of these classes is addressed below from the viewpoint of model criteria, representation criteria and methodological criteria in order to identify the elements that represent the software process and, therefore, model the process in question. The prescriptive models considered are shown in Fig. 3. Just two process definition standards were considered for manual models. The most important automated models were chosen [92, 8, 95, 99, 57]. These prescriptive models are characterized according to the above-mentioned criteria in Table 3. If they meet a table characteristic, the respective table cell is marked with X, otherwise the space is left blank.

In relation to the manual prescriptive models, the software life cycle process standards are informal and consider only the functional perspective of the information in the model, as shown under the columns labelled *Notation characteristics — From the viewpoint of the information quality* (informal) and *Information perspectives* (functional).

The table shows that the representations of prescriptive software process models, except the Unified Process, have focused on three elementary process features: the activity, the artefact and the agent (human and computerized) [99]. However, other characteristics, like human and organizational roles, have been empirically proven to have a big impact on the production process [17, 34, 63, 60, 131, 72, 126]. Most of the existing software process models deal with roles and related issues partially [93, 52],

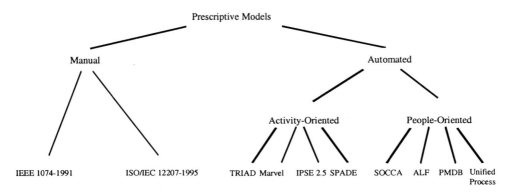

**Fig. 3.** Prescriptive models.

**Table 3.** Characterisation of prescriptive models.

| MODEL | Model Criteria — Process elements represented by the model | | | | | Model Criteria — Process environments addressed by the model (cultural) | | | | | Representation Criteria — Information perspectives | | | | Representation Criteria — Notation characteristics (from the viewpoint of information quality) | | | Representation Criteria — Notation characteristics (from the viewpoint of formal notation) | | Methodological Criteria — Modelling procedure | | Methodological Criteria — Procedure coverage | | Methodological Criteria — Procedure definition | | |
|---|---|---|---|---|---|---|---|---|---|---|---|---|---|---|---|---|---|---|---|---|---|---|---|---|---|---|
| | agent | activity | artefact | role | event | organisational | creative ability | social interaction | environment flexibility | scientific / technological | functional | behavioural | organisational | informative | informal | formal | automated | text | graphic | non-developed | developed | partial | sufficient | undefined | semi-defined | defined |
| IEEE 1074 - 1991 | | X | X | | | | | | | | X | X | | | X | | | | | X | | | | | | |
| ISO/IEC 12207 - 1995 | X | X | X | | | X | X | | | | X | X | | | X | | | | | | X | X | | | | X |
| TRIAD | X | X | | X | | | | | | | X | X | X | X | | X | X | | | X | | | | | | |
| Marvel | X | X | | | | | | | | | X | X | X | | | X | X | | | X | | | | | | |
| IPSE 2.5 | X | X | X | X | | | | | | | X | | X | X | X | | X | | | X | | | | | | |
| SPADE | X | X | X | | X | | | | | | X | X | X | X | | X | | X | X | X | | | | | | |
| SOCCA | X | X | X | X | | X | X | | | | X | X | X | X | X | X | | X | X | | X | X | | | | X |
| ALF | X | X | X | | | X | X | | | | X | X | X | X | X | X | | X | X | X | | | | | | |
| PMDB | X | | X | | | | | | | | X | | X | X | | X | | X | X | X | | | | | | |
| Unified Process | X | X | X | X | X | X | | | | | X | X | X | X | X | X | | X | X | | X | X | | | | X |

while the organization (organizational behaviour, culture and individual abilities) is considered as separate from the characteristics applied for modeling the software process [103] or it is ignored [49]. This is because the organization is the software process environment and is not, therefore, explicitly modelled. Therefore, these software process models are not integral and joint modeling approaches to the technical and organizational characteristics of the software process.

According to Table 3, the most applicable models are SOCCA and the Unified Process, as the models formally address human resources and the software process interactions in which they are involved and specify a procedure for building and adapting generic software process models, as reflected under the columns labelled *Modeling procedure (developed) and Procedure definition (defined)*. However, the proposed guides do not cover all the desired concepts, objects, characteristics and software process environments nor is there a fully comprehensive and formal modelling process [95], as observed under the column *Procedure coverage (partial)*.

Owing to the complexity of and the requirements for modeling the software process, the best thing appears to be for each low-level modeling or software process implementation to be derived from a high-level specification step, where all the information perspectives can be modelled: (a) separately and (b) as integrated components of a full specification. Such a modular specification reduces the complexity of the modeling activity and increases the possibility of software process model change and evolution. SOCCA, ALF and PMDB consider these aspects, generally taken into account from the software engineering viewpoint. The Unified Process is iterative, incremental and it is centred in the software architecture. This design based in the software architecture serves as a solid basis over which to plan and manage the development of component-based software. These are the four most advanced and complete models. They model the software project life cycle process and investigate the use of a process model, in this case SOCCA, ALF, PMDB or the Unified Process, as a conceptual and user interaction model and as a framework for integrating tools and/or agents and roles. The approach is incremental, as the whole life cycle is long and complex. Special emphasis is placed on process formalization, large project support, generalization and extendibility. The Unified Process includes a formal prescription of the process, where all the process elements are specified using the UML (Unified Modeling Language). Additionally, as mentioned above, SOCCA and the Unified Process give directions on an aspect that is often neglected in software engineering: the problem of the specification under development having to describe not only the technical but also the human parts of the software process, or better still, the human resources, the software process and all classes of interaction between the different non-human and human parts. However, SOCCA and the Unified Process do not deal with the cultural software process modeling questions, absent as well in the other models analyzed or considered informally in the socio-cultural models [53, 115], as observed under the *creative capability, social interaction and environment flexibility* columns of the *cultural environment* of the process addressed by the model. Table 3 shows that the organizational, cultural and scientific/technological environments are not integrated in the models in question (as shown under the columns of the same name).

Finally, Table 3 evidences one of the main limitations of existing models: the lack of proposed guides for identifying and defining all the essential organizational and software process conceptual modeling process components. In other words, it confirms that all the prescriptive models considered lack a *defined and fully comprehensive software process modeling procedure.* This procedure should provide a formally integrated model of both the software processes and the organizational environments [49, 23, 103, 132].

## 5. Software Process Evaluation

There are now several software process evaluation methods, each of which is associated with a standard or maturity model used as a reference model or yardstick in the appraisal. The descriptions of these evaluation methods found in the literature tend to match the original definition given by the method developers. However, we will describe the software process evaluation methods according to a set of six basic components, common to any type of evaluation irrespective of the discipline, field or evaluand considered. These components are derived from Evaluation Theory and the progress made in other non-software fields concerning evaluation [122, 121, 137]. These components are described in subsec. 5.2, after reviewing current software process evaluation methods (subsec. 5.1). Finally, the components of an evaluation will be used to describe the two most commonly used methods in Sec. 6: SCE [21] and ISO/IEC 15504 [77].[a]

### 5.1. *Review of evaluation methods*

Organizations that want to improve their software process now have the possibility of choosing from several software process evaluation methods. This choice will depend on the model or standard to be used as a yardstick for evaluating and improving the software process applied in the organization. Nowadays, there are plenty of standards and models [125]. However, not all the standards/models were generated for evaluation purposes, which is why they do not feed any method of evaluation. An example of this are the standards mentioned in Sec. 4.2, IEEE 1074-1991 and ISO 12207. On the other hand, we can find models applied in evaluations, like the Software Capability Maturity Model (CMM hereinafter) [108] which is used as a yardstick in two appraisal methods: Software Capability Evaluation (SCE) [21] and CMM-Based Appraisal for Internal Process Improvement [44]. Indeed, process modeling and evaluation came into being independently and ran parallel, without much (if any) interaction. They are, however, two sides of the same coin and two steps taken on the same object: the software process.

Focusing exclusively on software process evaluation, Fig. 4 shows a classification of the best-known software process evaluation methods. Depending on the yardstick for application, organizations can use one of the developed evaluation/assessment methods or prepare the evaluation components according to the requirements for performing an assessment and developing a compatible reference model described in ISO/IEC standard 15504 (formerly known as SPICE, Software Process Improvement and Capability dEtermination). A distinction can be made between the developed evaluation/assessment methods, depending on the type of yardstick used. Hence, ISO 9000 Certification and TickIT [129] are audits of the organization's quality system based on the ISO 9000 series, and specifically ISO 9001 and/or ISO 9000-3. Evaluations of this kind are always run by a team from outside the organization for the purpose of certifying that the organization's quality system meets the requirements specified in these standards, applying the guidelines for auditing quality systems described in ISO standard 10011 [76]. On the other hand, if the organization wants to use a maturity model as its software process improvement guide, it can use the CMM-based appraisals CBA IPI; or BOOTSTRAP [91], a software process assessment and improvement method developed by a European research project within the ESPRIT programme.

---

[a]To date, ISO 15504 is a Technical Report of type 2. This implies that it is still in draft form. Only Technical Reports of type 3 can be considered as International Standards.

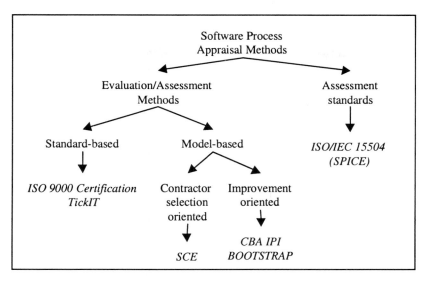

**Fig. 4.** Software process evaluation methods.

One requirement of most of the methods shown in Fig. 4 is that the team of evaluators is composed of authorized evaluators from outside the organization whose software process or quality system is to be evaluated. However, software process improvement efforts can be based on the findings of an internal self-assessment (for example, an internal CBA IPI) or on the results of an in-house instantiation of the assessment process according to ISO/IEC 15504. Therefore, the set of evaluation methods shown in Fig. 4 are the seed that organizations can use to start to improve their software process on the basis of the results yielded by an evaluation applying a given yardstick. Some of these evaluation methods can be used with other yardsticks. The most noteworthy case is Trillium [130], a telecommunications product development and support capability model that can be used in a capability evaluation, performed according to recognized auditing practices such as ISO 10011; in a capability joint-assessment; and in a capability self-assessment, following the Software Process Assessment method (SPA), the forerunner of the CBA IPI [105]. After having outlined the set of evaluation components, the SCE method and ISO 15504 standard will be described in the next section to illustrate the efforts made in the evaluation area.

However, irrespective of the selected evaluation method, the output of an evaluation is not a single digit to label an organization at a specific maturity level: the most relevant output is the discovery of the problems with the current process and the recommendations to fix them [139]. This is the ideal purpose of the software process evaluation and improvement activities. However, this ideal purpose can be sometimes distorted because some managers think about evaluation only as a way to label the organization within a maturity level but without involving in a real software process improvement (SPI) effort. Although it is possible to initiate an SPI program without management commitment, the success of the program will depend on the commitment of the managers. As a consequence, the organization's management plays an important role: its attitude will motivate the organization's professionals to accept the changes to the software process and assure that the necessary resources, time and personnel are available to undertake the evaluation and improvement efforts. A software process evaluation is a critical process but it is not the only activity for enhancing the way software products are constructed.

### 5.2. *Basic components of an evaluation*

The basic components of an evaluation can be applied: (a) to design an evaluation method, developing all the components involved in the evaluation; (b) to develop and/or adapt these components in each instantiation of the evaluation method when it is run. The basic components of an evaluation are defined as follows.

- Target or evaluand: the object under evaluation.
- Criteria: the characteristics of the target for assessment.
- Yardstick: the ideal target against which the real target is to be compared.
- Gathering techniques: the techniques needed to gather data or information for each criterion under analysis. This information will be used by the synthesis techniques to judge each criterion.
- Synthesis techniques: techniques used to organize and synthesize the information obtained with the gathering techniques and judge each criterion comparing the data obtained with the yardstick. The output of these techniques is the results of the evaluation.
- Evaluation process: series of activities and tasks by means of which an evaluation is performed.

These components are closely interrelated, as shown in Fig. 5. A software process evaluation method should identify and explicitly delimit the target in question to find out the primary software process factors to be considered in the evaluation (process, technological resources, etc). A specific set of characteristics, or evaluation criteria, should be identified to make it easier to adapt the yardstick, if necessary, and select the gathering techniques to be applied. Also, explicit definition and development of the synthesis techniques is an aid for minimizing the variability in the final results of the evaluation. All these components are linked by the evaluation process, because the activities and tasks describe the order of application of the preceding components. Also, the evaluation process includes tasks focused on: the definition of the scope and extent of the evaluation; and the development of the criteria, yardstick and techniques. When some of these components are already developed, it is necessary to analyze if they have to be adapted or not. All software process evaluation methods apply these components, although some are described implicitly: normally target delimitation and criteria identification are implicit in the yardstick

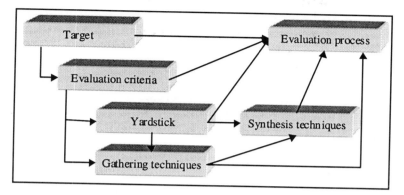

**Fig. 5.**   Components of an evaluation and their interrelationships.

or reference model/standard used, and the gathering and synthesis techniques are described in the activities and tasks in which they have to be developed and applied. However, if the evaluation components used in the software process evaluation methods are explicitly identified, it will be possible to find out how formally described the method is, how well developed each component is and how much effort it will take to make the evaluators apply the method. Thus, if the method does not provide the gathering techniques, the evaluation team will have to develop these techniques before visiting the organization whose software process is to be evaluated.

### 5.3. *Software process evaluation and knowledge engineering*

Software process evaluation is an activity performed in software engineering since the late 80's, having a great influence in this community because an evaluation is an aid to establish management processes in an organization and to institutionalize a documented, controlled and matured way to produce software. And vice versa, organizations can enhance the yardsticks to apply in the evaluation; for example, including new processes needed to control other processes or develop the software product. Nevertheless, there is no correspondence of this relevant process in the knowledge engineering community. In knowledge engineering we can find diverse methodologies but there are not software process definitions of management and support processes similar as those applied in software engineering. In this sense, knowledge engineering can be considered more immature than software engineering because it has no way to manage the basic knowledge engineering activities.

However, it could be possible to apply the evaluation in knowledge engineering taking into account the hypothesis and evaluation methods considered in software engineering. We can evaluate the knowledge engineering process under the hypothesis that the quality of the software product obtained is determined by the quality of its development process. This implies the identification and description of the management processes needed to control the basic knowledge engineering activities.

But to develop a complete evaluation method, we have to elaborate all the evaluation components: with regard to the evaluation process, the main processes and activities performed in the software engineering field could be applicable, but the target, criteria, yardstick, and gathering and synthesis techniques have to be developed. Analogous to software engineering, it could be possible to define a specific knowledge engineering maturity model with KPAs (see Sec. 6.1 below) associated with each maturity level. However, there is no experience with the application of management processes in knowledge engineering and consequently, although we can try to apply software engineering management activities in knowledge engineering field, it could be better to discuss first and pilot the potential application of the different software engineering processes, their implications in the knowledge engineering basic activities, the potential alternatives practices to be considered, synthesis techniques to apply, and so on. But despite the great work needed to implement and institutionalize all these management processes, the effort would be worthwhile whether the evaluation could help to mature the knowledge engineering field.

## 6. Process Evaluation Methods

The two most popular process evaluation methods, SCE and ISO/IEC 15504, are presented in this section, along with related methods. If the reader is not interested in specific evaluation methods, he or she can skip this section.

### 6.1. *Software Capability Evaluation (SCE) and other CMM-based methods*

SCE is the method developed by the Software Engineering Institute (SEI) for evaluating the software process of an organization for the purpose of using the results of the evaluation for: supplier selection, as a discriminator to select suppliers; process monitoring, between the sponsoring organization and the development organization; and internal evaluation, to provide independent evaluations of the internal processes applied in one organization. An external group applies the SCE in all the above cases. An SCE evaluation focuses on the analysis of the implementation and institutionalization of certain key process areas by analyzing if the organization's software processes satisfy the requirements specified in the yardstick. The SCE evaluation process is composed of three phases: plan and preparation; conduct evaluation (during the visit of the evaluation team to the evaluated organization); and report results.

The *target* considered in a SCE evaluation is delimited by the yardstick applied: SCE uses the CMM as the reference model. The general target of SCE evaluations is the software process, defined as a set of activities, methods, practices and transformations that people use to develop and maintain software and associated products. In particular, the SCE's target is a set of processes (or key process areas, KPAs) divided into three categories: organizational processes, which contain a set of KPAs focused on software process issues and organizational management; project processes, which include a set of KPAs focused on software projects management, such as project planning and tracking; and engineering processes, or the set of KPAs which provides product building operational support, such as requirements management, product engineering or peer reviews. Although the CMM refers to the technical production processes, these are not evaluated in a SCE evaluation.

The CMM provides requirements that good processes will meet [125]. These requirements are organized in a structure based on the concept of software process maturity, defined as the extent to which a specific process is explicitly defined, managed, measured, controlled and effective [108]. Based on this concept, the CMM describes five maturity levels that define an ordinal scale corresponding to the evolution of the software process from an "*ad hoc*" (unpredictable and unmanaged), through an intuitive (basic management of the processes and capability of repetition of some projects), qualitative (well-defined and institutionalized processes) and quantitative (measured and controlled processes), up to the optimized state in which the processes are continuously improved, thanks to their quantitative control. The five maturity levels and the KPAs associated with each level, except the first level that has no KPAs, are shown in Fig. 6.

All the characteristics of each process that will be analyzed make up the *evaluation criteria*. These criteria are implicit in the structure of the maturity levels and in the description of each KPA. The structure of the CMM at each maturity level is shown on the left-hand side of Fig. 7. Each KPA is described in terms of the

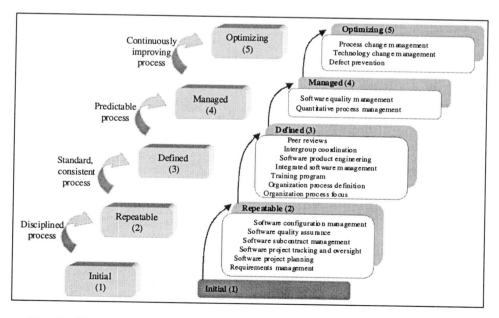

**Fig. 6.** Target of a SCE evaluation: KPAs associated with different levels of maturity.

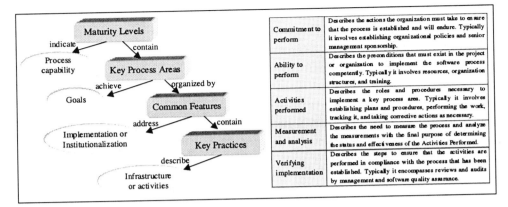

**Fig. 7.**  CMM structure and general criteria of a SCE evaluation: common features.

key practices (KP) organized by a set of common features. The common features, described on the right-hand side of Fig. 7, provide a structure for describing each KPA, using the same general criteria. The specific criteria will depend on each KPA, as each KPA will necessarily have to deal with all the characteristics described in the common features. Therefore, the set of generic criteria (common features and characteristics considered in each of these categories) of an SCE evaluation can be obtained taking the general description of the CMM. The CMM model, shaped according to Evaluation Theory, is detailed below.

As mentioned above, the yardstick or reference model of a SCE evaluation is the CMM. This maturity model contains the description of the goals of each KPA and all the KPs of each KPA under consideration, apart from the subpractices and supplementary information which usually accompanies some KPs. Table 4 shows an extract from the model for the KPA Software Quality Assurance (maturity level 2) and the common feature Ability to Perform. The specific criterion under consideration is associated with each KP in the left-hand column of Table 4. The information obtained from the application of the gathering techniques will be compared against the CMM (the reference model). This maturity model will be applied to analyze the software process applied in the organization as a whole: the evaluation team evaluates the organization's software project development practices against the KPAs in order to determine whether the organization follows a stable, predictable software process. The results are always related to the organization, not to a specific project or projects.

The *gathering techniques* applied in a SCE evaluation are interviews, document review and presentations. These techniques are applied during the visit to the organization to gather the information required to judge the target.

Interviews can be used to find out how the processes are implemented in practice and show the extent to which processes are internalized and understood by the staff. There are two types of interviews: exploratory, used to gather information about

**Table 4.** Yardstick of a SCE evaluation: example of key practices for a KPA considered in the CMM.

*Maturity Level*: 2. *Key Process Area*: Software Quality Assurance
*Common Feature*: Ability to perform

| Criteria | Key Practices |
|---|---|
| Responsibility | A group that is responsible for coordinating and implementing SQA for the project (i.e., the SQA group) exists. |
| Resources and Funding | Adequate resources and funding are provided for performing the SQA activities. |
| Training | Members of the SQA group are trained to perform their SQA activities. |
| Orientation | The members of the software project receive orientation on the role, responsibilities, authority and value of the SQA group. |

the actual processes practised and guide the team to the supporting documentation; and consolidation, focusing on corroboration and clarification of evidence.

Document review provides objective evidence of the processes used. This technique is complementary to the above and is based on the review of product artefacts (both intermediate and end products) obtained in the execution of a process to determine the extent of implementation across a site.

Finally, presentations provide both additional data (when the organization presents to the team and when participants react to team presentations) and validation of data (when participants react to preliminary observations of the SCE final results).

An important aspect is data consolidation, necessary for organizing the information obtained after applying the gathering techniques and combining it into a manageable summary of data; determining whether or not the information provides a sufficient basis for making judgements concerning an organization's process capability; and, if not, determining any revisions that should be made to the gathering techniques to obtain the additional information required to make judgements.

However, to be able to apply the gathering techniques, the evaluation must be delimited during a previous "plan and prepare" phase. Scope (how much of the reference model will be investigated) and coverage (amount of detail with which data within the scope must be collected) must be defined, and the areas in need of more detailed analysis must be also determined by applying instruments like the maturity, project, and organization questionnaires, among others [140]. The maturity questionnaire was the main gathering technique in the first version of the SCE method [69]. As of SCE version 1.5, the maturity questionnaire is no longer a gathering technique, because data from the questionnaire could not be used as part of the consolidation and judgement process [21].

The information obtained after applying the gathering techniques will be used to get the results of the evaluation, by applying the *synthesis techniques*. These techniques output the analysis and judgements made taking into account the validated observations (findings) collected by the gathering techniques. In general, the rating process always proceeds in a bottom up manner: key practices and common features will be rated first; goals are then rated, and the results are rolled up into KPA and maturity level ratings. However, rating the key practices, common features and maturity level are optional outputs of the evaluation. The decision to rate these components of the CMM must be made during the evaluation planning activity. A typical output of an SCE evaluation only includes the ratings for the goals and KPAs. To judge each KPA's goal satisfaction in an organization, both the activities (implementation) and other common features (institutionalization) must be satisfied. All of the goals of a KPA must be achieved in order for the KPA to be satisfied, and all KPAs within a maturity level and each lower maturity level must be rated to determine whether the maturity level has been attained. The rating values used to rate each reference model component (KP, common features, goals, KPAs) are: satisfied, not satisfied, not applicable and not rated. A "satisfied" rating is assigned if a reference model component is implemented and institutionalized either as defined in the CMM or with an adequate alternative. A reference model component will be rated as "not satisfied" when there are significant weaknesses in the implementation or institutionalization of the item, as defined in the CMM, or no adequate alternative is in place. When the reference model component does not apply in the organization's environment, it will be rated as "not applicable". Lastly, a component is "not rated" if the evaluation data do not meet coverage requirements or the item is outside the appraisal scope. All the ratings will be used to develop the final results of an SCE evaluation: strengths, weaknesses, improvement activities, and graphical representations of the rating values for each KPA and maturity level.

Finally, the SCE evaluation process indicates when to apply and/or use the preceding components of an evaluation. Figure 8 shows the phases and main activities to be carried out in a SCE evaluation. The "plan and prepare for evaluation" phase encompasses the activities required to delimit the evaluation, select the evaluation team and prepare for data collection; all these activities will be completed before visiting the organization. The "Conduct evaluation" phase and "Deliver final findings" activity, focused on the application of the gathering and synthesis techniques, will be performed during this visit. The visit ends when the results of the evaluation are obtained. Later, the evaluation team will produce the reports and support follow-on activities.

The components of the evaluation of a CBA IPI assessment are very similar to a SCE evaluation. The main differences lie in the orientation of the appraisal, as it is an improvement-oriented assessment; the formation of the assessment team, which will be either a mixed or an internal team, formed by professionals from the evaluated organization; and the allotted time, as a SCE takes on average

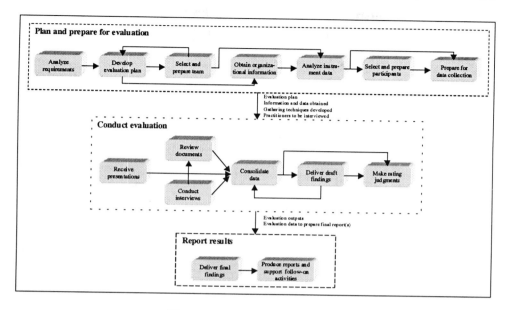

**Fig. 8.** SCE evaluation process.

some 176 hours, approximately, including the four-day visit to the evaluated organization [21], whereas as CBA IPI is run in a time frame of 4 months [44]. The CBA IPI assessments and CMM maturity model are used by organizations from all over the world to assess their software processes. The results obtained from CMM-based appraisals can be used to verify the underlying hypothesis for developing CMM and its associated evaluation and improvement methods [64].

Diverse criticisms and comments about CMM and its related methods have been made since their introduction at the end of the 80's. For example, Bollinger and McGowan [19] criticize the gathering and synthesis techniques used in the first versions of the evaluation methods based on the CMM; they criticize the application of a questionnaire with just two possible answers ("Yes" or "No") and the simplicity of the algorithm to obtain the final value of the organization's maturity level. Bach [9] centers his analysis on the CMM model emphasis: its focus on process (ignoring people) and its lack of theoretical basis. The CMM authors' rebuttals to Bollinger's and Bach's criticisms can be found in [71, 37], respectively. Some other criticisms are focused on the evaluation process; for example, Saiedian and Kuzara highlight the lack of rigorous definition of the process applied; the results variability; and the non-comparability of the findings of more than one assessment, even when applying the same method [117]. Other criticisms and comments can be found in [24, 26, 33, 104].

The recent release of the CMMI models [27, 28] has been accompanied by a new assessment method, the SCAMPI method (Standard CMMI Assessment Method for Process Improvement) [141], based on the CBA IPI V1.1 and the Electronic

Industries Alliance/Interim Standard (EIA/IS) 731.2 Appraisal Method [142]. One of the driving forces in the definition of SCAMPI has been emphasizing the confidence in the appraisal findings despite the cost of the assessment.

## 6.2. *ISO/IEC* 15504

ISO/IEC 15504 is a framework for assessing an organization's software processes for the purpose of using the results for process improvement or process capability determination [77]. This framework defines a reference model of processes and process capability that forms the basis for any model to be used for the (singular, no plural) purpose of process assessment [46]. The composition of the assessment team will depend on the purpose and specific circumstances of the assessment. ISO/IEC 15504 does not provide a fully developed assessment process, it sets the minimum set of requirements for performing an assessment, thus increasing the likelihood that results are objective, impartial, consistent, repeatable, representative of the processes assessed and comparable with the results of future assessments. Similarly, the ISO/IEC 15504 reference model specifies the requirements to be met in order for a model(s) used in an assessment to be compatible with the reference model of the standard. The assessors can use other standards and/or models for developing the assessment model to be applied in a specific assessment of the software process of a particular organization.

The *target* of the ISO/IEC 15504 is the software process and specifically a set of processes strongly related to those defined in ISO 12207. The total set of processes are divided into five categories (customer-supplier, engineering, support, management and organization), which are grouped into three life cycle processes: primary, supporting and organization, shown in Fig. 9. The primary life cycle process includes the categories: customer-supplier, which contains the set of processes that directly affect the customer, support development and transition of the software to the customer and provide for the correct operation and use of the software product and/or service; and engineering, or the set processes that directly specify, implement or maintain the software product, its relation to the system and its customer documentation. On the other hand, the supporting life cycle process is composed of the support category, which contains the set of processes that can be employed by any of the other processes (including other supporting processes) at various points in the software life cycle. Finally, the organizational life cycle process is composed of two categories: (a) management, or the set of processes which contain practices of a generic nature that can be used by anyone who manages any type of project or process within a software life cycle; and (b) organization, which includes the set of processes that establish the business goals of the organization and develop process, product and resource assets, which, when used by the projects in the organization, will help the organization to achieve its business goals.

The ISO/IEC 15504 *evaluation criteria* are several measurable characteristics defined to analyze any of the processes identified in the target. Each criterion

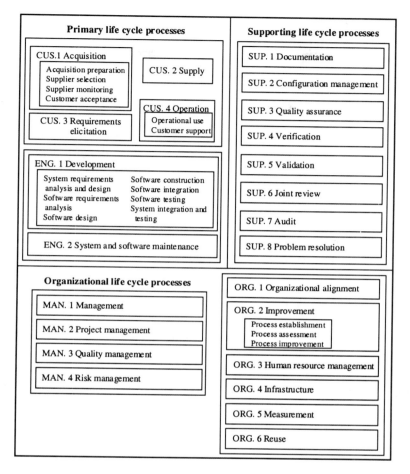

**Fig. 9.** Target of ISO/IEC 15504.

is associated with one of the six process capability levels that define a scale for a well-defined route for improvement for each individual process. Table 5 shows the different levels, general criteria associated with each level (denoted as process attributes in ISO/IEC 15504) and the description of each criterion. However, these general criteria have to be broken down into specific criteria or indicators when running an assessment. An indicator is defined as an objective attribute or characteristic of a practice or work product that supports the judgement of the extent of achievement of a particular process attribute. For example, the specific criteria for process performance are: identify input and output work products; ensure that the scope of work is identified for process execution and for the work products to be used and produced by the process; and ensure that basic practices are implemented, producing work products which support achievement of the defined process outcomes.

**Table 5.**  Process capability levels and criteria associated with each level.

| Levels | General Criteria | Definition |
|---|---|---|
| 0 — Incomplete | — | — |
| 1 — Performed | Process performance | The extent to which the process achieves the process outcomes by transforming identifiable input work products to produce identifiable output work products. |
| 2 — Managed | Performance management | The extent to which the performance of the process is managed to produce work products that meet the defined objectives. |
| | Work product management | The extent to which the performance of the process is managed to produce work products that are appropriately documented, controlled, and verified. |
| 3 — Established | Process definition | The extent to which the performance of the process uses a process definition based upon a standard process to achieve the process outcomes. |
| | Process resource | The extent to which the process draws upon suitable resources (for example, human resources and process infrastructure) that is appropriately allocated to deploy the defined process. |
| 4 — Predictable | Measurement | The extent to which product and process goals and measures are used to ensure that performance of the process supports the achievement of the defined goals in support of the relevant business goals. |
| | Process control | The extent to which the process is controlled through the collection, analysis and use of product and process measures to correct, when necessary, the performance of the process to achieve the defined product and process goals. |
| 5 — Optimizing | Process change | The extent to which changes to the definition, management and performance of the process are controlled to achieve the relevant business goals of the organization. |
| | Continuous improvement | The extent to which changes to the process are identified and implemented to ensure continuous improvement in the fulfilment of the relevant business goals of the organization. |

ISO/IEC 15504 does not provide a *yardstick* that is directly applicable in an evaluation. The standard only provides a reference model that defines what processes can be considered in the evaluation, with the definition of each process purpose (denoted as process dimension and corresponding to the target); and the capability levels and process attributes (denoted as capability dimension and corresponding

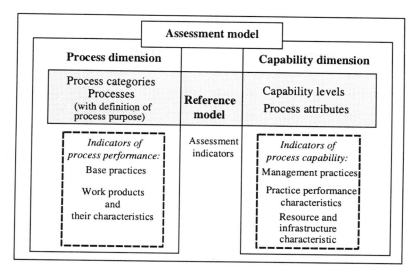

**Fig. 10.**   Structure of the reference and assessment model.

to criteria). The yardstick for application (denoted as assessment model) has to be developed on the basis of the above two components (target and criteria) and the structure defined by ISO/IEC 15504, as shown in Fig. 10, to run a software process assessment.[b] For this purpose, the assessors will have to complete the definition of each process for assessment, including a set of base practices for each process, providing a definition of the tasks and activities needed to accomplish the process purpose and fulfil the process outcomes; a number of input and output work products, associated with each process; and characteristics associated with each work product. Figure 11 includes an example of an instantiation of the yardstick for the "Software design process", showing the reference model definitions in italics. The base practices, process inputs and outputs and characteristics of an output (high level software design) are shown under the process purpose. The yardstick to be applied in a specific assessment would be formed by this detailed description for all the processes to be assessed.

ISO/IEC 15504 does not provide a developed set of *gathering techniques* to be applied in the assessment. It merely specifies that "the documented assessment process should provide guidance on data collection mechanisms, such as interview techniques and document reviewing instruments", that the information gathered must be validated, and that validated data should sufficiently cover the assessment scope.

---

[b]The reference model is described in a normative part of the Technical Report (Part 2. A reference model for processes and process capability).
An example of an assessment model can be found in Part 5 (An assessment model and indicator guidance), which is informative.

---

**ENG. 1.3. *Software design process***
*Component process of ENG. 1 Development process*

*The purpose of the Software Design Process is to define a design for the software that implements the requirements and can be tested against them. As a result of succesful implementation of the process:*
- *An architectural design, will be developed that describes the major software components that will implement the software requirements.*
- *Internal and external interfaces of each software component will be defined.*
- *A detailed design will be developed that describes software units that can be built and tested.*
- *Consistency will be established between software requirements and software designs.*

Base practices:

ENG.1.3.BP1. Develop software architectural design. Transform the software requirements into a software architecture that describes the top-level structure and identifies its major components.

ENG.1.3.BP2. Design interfaces. Develop and document a design for the external and internal interfaces.

ENG.1.3.BP3. Verify the software design. Verify that the software design satisfies related software requirements.

ENG.1.3.BP4. Develop detailed design. Decompose the top level design into a detailed design for each software component. The software components are refined into lower levels containing software units. The result of this base practice is a documented software design document, which describes the position of each document unit in the software architectures.

NOTE: The detailed design includes the specification of interfaces between the software units.

ENG.1.3.BP5. Establish traceability. Establish traceability between the software requirements and the software design.

| ENG.1.3. Software design process. Associated Work Products | |
|---|---|
| Input | Output |
| 2) Life cycle model | 54) High level software design |
| 33) Reuse strategy/plan | 55) Low level software design |
| 52) Requirement specification (software) | 58) Traceability record/mapping |
| 53) System design/architecture | 63) Unit test strategy/plan |
| 59) Test strategy/plan | 101) Database design |
| | 105) Customer documentation |

54) High level software design
- Describes the overall software structure
- Identifies the required software components
- Identifies the relationship between software components.
- Consideration is given to:
  - Any required software performance characteristics
  - Any required software interfaces
  - Any required security characteristics
  - Any database design requirements
  - Any required error handling & recovery attributes

**Fig. 11.**   Example of an instantiation of the ISO/IEC 15504 yardstick.

*Synthesis techniques* correspond to the process rating for each criterion (process attribute). The rating scale applied is a percentage scale from zero to one hundred that represents the extent of achievement of the criteria. This scale has the following values: (a) not achieved (N, 0%–15%), which means that there is little or no evidence of achievement of the defined attribute in the assessed process; (b) partially achieved (P, 16%–50%), to indicate that there is evidence of a sound systematic approach to and achievement of the defined attribute in the assessed process; (c) largely achieved (L, 51%–85%), when there is evidence of a sound systematic approach to and significant achievement of the defined attribute in the assessed process; and (d) fully achieved (F, 85%–100%), when there is evidence of a complete and systematic approach to and full achievement of the defined attribute in the assessed process, and therefore no significant weaknesses exist across the defined organizational unit. The set of the criteria rated for each process forms the process profile for that process. These values yield the capability level associated with each assessed process, taking into account that the value of the criteria associated with the above $n-1$ levels must be "$F$" (Fully achieved) and the value of the criteria for the level $n$ must be "$L$" (Largely achieved) or "$F$" to satisfy a

**Table 6.**  Assessment process of ISO/IEC 15504.

| | |
|---|---|
| 1. Planning | A plan for the assessment shall be developed and documented, specifying at least:<br>(1) The required inputs defined in the standard (assessment purpose, scope, constraints and model(s) used, among others).<br>(2) The activities to be performed in conducting the assessment.<br>(3) The resources and schedule assigned to these activities.<br>(4) The selection and defined responsibilities of the assessors and organization's participants in the assessment.<br>(5) The criteria for verification of the performance of the requirements, and<br>(6) A description of the planned assessment outputs. |
| 2. Data collection | Data required for evaluating the processes within the scope of the assessment shall be collected in a systematic and ordered manner, applying at least the following:<br>(1) The strategy and techniques for the selection, collection and analysis of data and justification of the ratings shall be explicitly identified and shall be demonstrable.<br>(2) Correspondence shall be established between the organizational unit's processes specified in the assessment scope through the compatible model(s) used for assessment to the processes defined in the reference model.<br>(3) Each process identified in the assessment scope shall be assessed on the basis of objective evidence.<br>(4) The objective evidence gathered for each attribute for each process assessed shall be sufficient to meet the assessment purpose and scope.<br>(5) Objective evidence, based on the indicators, that supports the assessor's judgement of process attribute ratings shall be recorded and maintained to provide the basis for verification of the ratings. |
| 3. Data validation | The data collected shall be validated. Actions shall be taken to ensure that the validated data sufficiently cover the assessment scope. |
| 4. Process rating | A rating shall be assigned based on validated data for each process attribute<br>(1) The set of process attribute ratings shall be recorded as the process profile for the defined organization unit.<br>(2) In order to provide the basis for repeatability across assessments, the defined set or assessment indicators in the compatible model(s) shall be used during the assessment to support the assessors' judgement in rating process attributes.<br>(3) The decision-making process (e.g. consensus of the assessment team or majority vote) that is used to derive rating judgements shall be recorded. |
| 5. Reporting | The assessment results, including at least the outputs specified in the standard (data, inputs, objective evidence gathered and set of process profiles, among others) shall be documented and reported to the Assessment Sponsor. |

capability level $n$. The final result of the assessment will generally contain the set of process profiles for all assessed processes and the capability levels associated with the assessed processes.

With regard to the *assessment process*, ISO/IEC 15504 only specifies the requirements to be met by a software process assessment to ensure that the assessment output is self-consistent and provides evidence to substantiate the ratings [47]. The assessors will have to develop and document the process to be applied which must contain at least the activities shown in Table 6.

## 7. Software Process Improvement

Software process evaluation should be only the first step for an organization on its way to raising maturity levels. As soon as the current state of the organization is known, it is possible to plan and start the transition to the desired state. But, what is the desired state? Looking, for example, at the SEI's CMM maturity levels, an organization that continuously improves its software processes is considered to be at the highest maturity level. So, the goal of an organization should be to institutionalise the improvement effort.

A capable and mature software development organization is one that is never completely satisfied with the actual results, no matter how good they are; one that is able to recognize the limitations and pitfalls of its software processes as they are actually defined and implemented; one that is able to identify candidate changes to the software processes, or technologies to be adopted, and to evaluate their possible impact on the organization's performance; and one that is able to manage the adoption of the new technologies and the process changes so as to make the most of them at minimum cost. Therefore, software process improvement is a way of life in a capable and mature organization.

What is the next step for an organization that has gone through a software process evaluation and the results show that they are still far from the desired state? First, they should realize that improvement is a long and difficult job, and it has been proven that it is better to do it incrementally. This means that they should set priorities among the many different goals, and they should select a limited set of goals for the first increment. The prioritization and selection of improvement goals is one of the most important and critical issues.

Looking at the most popular frameworks for the evaluation of software processes, ISO/IEC 15504 and the SEI's CMM, there is a fundamental difference in the way they help to set improvement goals. While ISO/IEC 15504 deals with processes separately, the CMM organizes the processes in a levelled representation that defines a reasonable sequence for improvement. As mentioned above, each level in the CMM groups a set of KPAs, and each KPA groups a set of related activities that, when performed collectively, help to achieve goals that are considered important for establishing the capability of the software process at the given maturity level. If an organization is, for instance, at level 2, the CMM recommends that their immediate improvement efforts should be directed towards level 3 KPAs. ISO/IEC 15504, on the other hand, provides a detailed snapshot of the current state of each process through process profiles, but makes no suggestions as to how to improve on that state.

The new integrated version of the CMM, the CMMI, which has been recently released by the SEI [27, 28], aims to combine both approaches and provides two alternative representations, a continuous and a staged representation. The staged representation clearly orders the maturity levels, while the continuous representation focuses on separate process areas and provides achievement profiles (a list of process areas and their respective capability levels) as a result of the evaluation. Using the continuous approach, the improvement should be planned as target staging, that is, a sequence of target profiles to be achieved by the organization. An equivalence has been defined between the maturity levels of the staged representation and some target profiles. Thus, the continuous approach allows organizations to set their own improvement goals more flexibly, while staging is a more guided and restricted approach, although it allows for benchmarking between organizations or projects.

Complementary to the CMM, the SEI has defined an improvement model called IDEAL [101] that divides the improvement process into five stages: Initiation, Diagnosing, Establishing, Acting and Leveraging. The initiation stage is prior to software process evaluation. It is the stage at which the senior management first realizes the need to improve the organization's software processes and sets the context for and makes a commitment to the improvement program. Sustained senior management commitment is vital for the success of the improvement program. The elementary infrastructure for improvement is established at this stage, including a Management Steering Group (MSG) and a Software Engineering Process Group (SEPG).

The concept of SEPG has been used extensively by improving organizations and has proven to be extremely useful for sustaining the support and commitment of a continuously changing and unstable organization to the Software Process Improvement (SPI) program. This group is responsible for coordinating and nurturing the activities of the different improvement teams that work simultaneously on specific improvements. It is also responsible for creating and maintaining a repository of software process assets. This repository should contain the organization's standard software processes, guidelines and criteria for tailoring the standard processes for individual projects, the description of possible life cycles for software development, a software process library and a software process database, which contains measurements and data about the observed performance of defined processes on given projects. A post-mortem analysis of projects that have failed can shed new light over the weaknesses of current software processes. Thus, maintaining a software process database is fundamental for the identification of possible improvements. A mature organization with a repository of standard processes has captured and made explicit the organizational best practices, and therefore it is able to maintain a uniform level of performance independently of the performance of the individuals.

Coming back to the IDEAL model, the Diagnosing stage is the one that is most related to the evaluation of the current software processes. The objective of this stage is to set a baseline for the current state. This baseline will help identify the deficiencies to be overcome and, later on, to measure the degree of improvement that has been achieved.

The next step is to Establish the goals for the improvement program. The MSG should produce a Strategic Action Plan for the next three to five years, setting the short and long-term goals, according to the baseline and the organization's business needs. A Tactical Action Plan is also sketched for the first improvement cycle and organizational arrangement are made, including one or more Technical Working Groups (TWG). Each TWG will be in charge of building and implementing solutions for one of the selected improvement areas.

During the Acting stage, the TWG searches for solutions to the problems identified at baseline. The main steps to be followed are: (a) analyze in detail the current or "as is" state; (b) define the desired or "to be" state; (c) evaluate possible solutions and select the most appropriate one; (d) launch one or more pilot projects and refine the solution; (e) plan the institutionalization process; and (f) wrap up and dissolve the team. The roll-on and institutionalization of solutions across the organization is the responsibility of the MSG and the SEPG.

The current improvement cycle finishes with a Leveraging stage in which the organization analyses what happened in this cycle and prepares for the next cycle, revising the goals of the improvement effort and verifying that the necessary commitment and resources are still there. The results of the improvement are compared to the baseline and communicated throughout the organization, and the improvement process itself is improved for the next iteration.

Other improvement models and solutions have also been defined, like the Business Improvement Guides (BIGs) developed by the European Software Institute (ESI) [118, 107, 51] or the Process Improvement Guide (PIG) developed by the ISO/IEC 15504 project [80] (called "Software Process Assessment — Part 7: Guide for use in process improvement", working draft V1.00). The methodology proposed in the PIG comprises the following steps: examine organization's needs; initiate process improvement; prepare and conduct process assessment; analyze results and derive action plan; implement improvements; confirm the improvement; sustain improvement gains; and monitor performance. It is also a cyclic model, and the approach is very similar to that of IDEAL, although the PIG is much less detailed than IDEAL. The most noteworthy difference from IDEAL is perhaps the "sustain improvement gains" step that recognizes the complexity of deploying and institutionalizing the improved process throughout the organization.

The ESI's BIG guides are also based on ISO/IEC 15504. However, they are specially oriented towards small and medium-sized enterprises (SMEs), and their objective is to help SMEs to develop their own improvement plans with limited resources. Starting from a generic business need, the ESI derives a staged model from the continuous ISO/IEC 15504 model, by selecting the most important ISO/IEC

15504 processes for that business need and defining an appropriate capability level for each process. The staged model is included within an improvement guide, together with the steps to be taken to get a customised staged model for a specific company. Three BIGs have been developed. The business needs they address are: reducing Time To Market (TTM), attaining ISO 9001 certification, and achieving repeatability of project results through CMM level 2 activities. The BIG project started in 1997 and is still in progress.

Software process improvement in SMEs deserves a special mention. A SPI program is typically very high cost, and costs for a small organization cannot be expected to be cut in proportion to the smaller number of affected employees, making SPI almost prohibitively expensive. Moreover, the cultural issues in a small organization are usually completely different. As Kelly [90] states, small organizations tend to be creative, dynamic and innovative, and their software engineers are used to being involved in all aspects of the software engineering process. SPI is perceived as leading to increased bureaucracy and decreased freedom. Kelly advises getting as many people as possible involved in the SPI effort, because solutions imposed by a small group might not be accepted.

The cultural issues in both SMEs and in big companies are crucial to the success of the improvement effort. [54] suggests that SPI should be dealt with like a technology transfer problem. Studying the affected people and the culture of the organization may be as important in the adoption of a new technology or process as having in-depth knowledge of the new technology. The ISO/IEC 15504 PIG also stresses the importance of cultural issues and identifies some of the most significant questions, like staff motivation, senior management leadership, middle management commitment, confidentiality of the assessment results, an appropriate recognition and reward system, education and training and communication of progress.

While recognizing the importance of cultural and people-related issues, all of the above mentioned models and methods for software process improvement have an organizational focus. They are top-down approaches that require the commitment of top-level management and the establishment of an organizational infrastructure for process improvement. A radically different approach was proposed by Watts S. Humphrey in 1995 with his Personal Software Process (PSP) [72, 73]. The PSP is a bottom-up approach focused on the individual software engineers, that provides them with a framework to measure and analyze their current software development processes and to identify and implement process improvements for a better individual performance.

The PSP is organized as a course with fifteen lessons and ten programming exercises. Starting with the establishment of a baseline of the current process (called PSP0), six additional processes are progressively introduced and applied, with incremental improvements.

The rationale behind PSP is that the quality of a software system is determined by the quality of its worst component, and the quality of a software component is determined by the quality of the engineer that developed it. Therefore, by improving the "quality" of individual software engineers an improvement in the quality of software systems can be expected. Two fundamental improvement areas are considered in PSP: the estimation and planning of individual work and the quality of software products.

Filling the gap between the CMM (an organization-centred approach) and the PSP (an individual-centred approach) the Team Software Process (TSP) [74] came to address the software process improvement problem at the team level. The goal of the TSP is to help in the establishment of self-directed teams that are able to plan and track their own work, to set goals and that own their processes and plans, with a strong motivation for maintaining top-level performance.

Despite the many approaches to software process improvement, there are no magic recipes. Improvement is a long and hard effort and any organization that embarks on a SPI program should realize that the main benefits will be perceived in the long term.

## 8. Summary

We have tried to offer in a single chapter a joint view of research on software process modeling with research on evaluation and improvement. Process modeling serves the purpose of defining the current process under evaluation, or defining the desired process to attain in an improvement effort. In fact, the first level of the maturity levels considered in process evaluation, is usually called "defined". Anyway, process definition is not an easy task, as the diversity of process models presented in Sec. 4 emphasizes. Despite these difficulties, software process evaluation and improvement offer a way to work on and improve the software process in a software development organization, even if it is required a substantial and sustained effort in order to reach and maintain a high maturity level in terms of software process practices.

## References

1. T. Abdel-Hamid and S. Madnick, *Software Project Dynamics: An Integrated Approach* (Prentice-Hall, 1991).
2. S. T. Acuña, M. Lopez, N. Juristo and A. Moreno, "A process model applicable to software engineering and knowledge engineering", *International Journal of Software Engineering and Knowledge Engineering* **9**, no. 5 (1999) 663–687.
3. S. T. Acuña, G. Barchini and M. Sosa, "A culture-centered multilevel software process cycle model", *Proceedings of the 22nd International Conference on Software Engineering* (June 2000).
4. S. T. Acuña, G. Barchini, C. Laserre, A. Silva, M. Sosa and V. Quincoces, "Software engineering and knowledge engineering software process: Formalizing the who's who", *Proceedings of the 12th International Conference on Software Engineering and Knowledge Engineeering* (July 2000) 221–230.
5. R. Alberico and M. Micco, *Expert Systems for Reference and Information Retrieval* (Mockler Corporation, 1990).
6. L. Alexander and A. Davis, "Criteria for selecting software process models", *Proceedings of COMPSAC'91* (1991) 521–528.

7. V. Ambriola, R. Conradi and A. Fuggetta, "Assessing process-centered software engineering environments", *ACM Transactions on Software Engineering and Methodology* **6**, no. 3 (1997) 283–328.

8. P. Armenise, S. Bandinelli, C. Ghezzi and A. Morzenti, "A survey and assessment of software process representation formalisms", *International Journal of Software Engineering and Knowledge Engineering* **3**, no. 3 (1993) 401–426.

9. J. Bach, "The Immaturity of the CMM", *American Programmer* **7**, no. 9 (September 1994) 13–18.

10. S. C. Bandinelli, A. Fuggetta, C. Ghezzi and L. Lavazza, "SPADE: An environment for software process analysis, design, and enactment", *Software Process Modeling and Technology*, Chap. 9 (Research Studies Press, 1994) 223–247.

11. S. Bandinelli, A. Fuggetta, L. Lavazza, M. Loi and G. Picco, "Modeling and improving an industrial software process", *IEEE Transactions on Software Engineering* **21**, no. 5 (1995) 440–454.

12. N. Barghouti, D. Rosenblum, D. Belanger and C. Alliegro, "Two case studies in modeling real, corporate processes", *Software Process — Improvement and Practice* (Pilot Issue, 1995) 17–32.

13. V. R. Basili and H. D. Rombach, "The TAME project: Towards improvement-oriented software environments", *IEEE Transactions on Software Engineering* **14**, no. 6 (June 1988) 758–773.

14. K. Benali and J. C. Derniame, "Software processes modeling: What, who, and when", *Proceedings of the Second European Workshop on Software Process Technology* (September 1992).

15. S. Bendifallah and W. Scacchi, "Work structures and shifts: An empirical analysis of software specification teamwork", *Proceedings of the 11th International Conference on Software Engineering* (May 1989) 260–270.

16. B. I. Blum, *Software Engineering: A Holistic View* (Oxford University Press, 1992).

17. B. W. Boehm, *Software Engineering Economics* (Prentice-Hall, Englewood Cliffs, 1981).

18. B. W. Boehm, "A spiral model of software development and enhancement", *Computer* (May 1988) 61–72.

19. T. B. Bollinger and C. McGowan, "A critical look at software capability evaluations", *IEEE Software* **8**, no. 4 (July 1991) 25–41.

20. L. Briand, W. Melo, C. Seaman and V. Basili, "Characterizing and assessing a large-scale software maintenance organization", *Proceedings of the 17th International Conference on Software Engineering* (1995).

21. P. Byrnes and M. Phillips, "Software capability evaluation", Version 3.0. Method Description, Technical Report, CMU/SEI-96-TR-002, Carnegie Mellon University, Pittsburgh (1996).

22. B. G. Cain and J. O. Coplien, "A role-based empirical process modeling environment", *Proceedings of the Second International Conference on Software Process* (February 1993) 125–133.

23. G. Canals, N. Boudjlida, J. C. Derniame, C. Godart and J. Lonchamp, "ALF: A framework for building process-centred software engineering environments", *Software Process Modeling and Technology*, Chap. 7 (Research Studies Press, 1994) 153–185.

24. D. N. Card, "Understanding process improvement", *IEEE Software* **8**, no. 4 (July 1991) 102–103.

25. M. A. Carrico, J. E. Girard and J. P. Jones, *Building Knowledge Systems: Developing and Managing Rule-based Applications* (McGraw-Hill, 1989).

26. F. Cattaneo, A. Fuggetta and L. Lavazza "An experience in process assessment", *Proceedings of the 17th International Conference on Software Engineering* (ACM Press, 1995) 115–121.

27. CMMI Product Development Team, CMMI for Systems Engineering/Software Engineering/Integrated Product and Process Development, Version 1.01 (CMMI-SE/SW/IPPD, V1.01) Staged Representation, Technical Report, CMU/SEI-2000-TR-030 ESC-TR-2000-095, Carnegie Mellon University, Pittsburgh (2000).

28. CMMI Product Development Team, CMMI for Systems Engineering/Software Engineering/Integrated Product and Process Development, Version 1.01 (CMMI-SE/SW/IPPD, V1.01) Continuous Representation, Technical Report CMU/SEI-2000-TR-031 ESC-TR-2000-096, Carnegie Mellon University, Pittsburgh (2000).

29. E. Comer, "Alternative software life cycle models", *Software Engineering* (IEEE CS Press, 1997).

30. R. Conradi, C. Fernström, A. Fuggetta and R. Snowdon, "Towards a reference framework for process concepts", *Proceedings of the Second European Workshop on Software Process Technology* (September 1992) 3–17.

31. R. Conradi, C. Fernström and A. Fuggetta, "Concepts for evolving software processes", *Software Process Modeling and Technology*, Chap. 2 (Research Studies Press, 1994) 9–31.

32. R. Conradi, M. Hagaseth, J.-O. Larsen, M. N. Nguyen, B. P. Munch, P. H. Westby, W. Zhu, M. L. Jaccheri and C. Liu, "EPOS: Object-oriented cooperative process modeling", *Software Process Modeling and Technology*, Chap. 3 (Research Studies Press, 1994) 33–70.

33. D. A. Cook, "Confusing process and product: Why the quality is not there yet", *CrossTalk* (July 1999) 27–29.

34. B. Curtis, *Human Factors in Software Development* (IEEE Computer Society, 1985).

35. B. Curtis, H. Krasner and N. Iscoe, "A field study of the software design process for large systems", *Communications of the ACM* **31**, no. 11 (November 1988) 1268–1287.

36. B. Curtis, M. Kellner and J. Over, "Process modeling", *Communications of the ACM* **35**, no. 9 (September 1992) 75–90.

37. B. Curtis, "A mature view of the CMM", *American Programmer* **7**, no. 9 (September 1994) 19–28.

38. A. Davis, E. Bersoff and E. Comer, "A strategy for comparing alternative software development life cycle models", *IEEE Transactions on Software Engineering* **14**, no. 10 (1988) 1453–1461.

39. A. Davis, "Software specification", *Events, Objects and Functions* (Prentice Hall, 1993).

40. W. Deiters and V. Gruhn, "Software process analysis based on FUNSOFT nets", *Systems Analysis Modeling Simulation* **8**, nos. 4-5 (1991) 315–325.

41. J. C. Derniame, B. A. Kaba and D. Wastell, "Software process: Principles, methodology and technology", *Lecture Notes in Computer Science 1500* (Springer, 1999).

42. M. Dowson, B. Nejmeh and W. Riddle, "Concepts for process definition and support", *Proceedings of the Sixth International Software Process Workshop* (October 1990).

43. M. Dowson, B. Nejmeh and W. Riddle, "Fundamental software process concepts", *Proceedings of the First European Workshop on Software Process Modeling* (May 1991).

44. D. K. Dunaway and S. Masters, "CMM SM-Based Appraisal for Internal Process Improvement (CBA IPI): Method Description", Technical Report CMU/SEI-96-TR-007, Carnegie Mellon University, Pittsburgh (1996).

45. J. S. Edwards, "Building knowledge-based systems", *Towards a Methodology* (Biddles Ltd., 1991).
46. K. E. El Emam, J.-N. Drouin and W. Melo, *SPICE: The Theory and Practice of Software Process Improvement* (IEEE Computer Society Press, 1998).
47. K. El Emam and N. H. Madhavji, *Elements of Software Process Assessment and Improvement* (IEEE Computer Society Press, 1999).
48. E. Ellmer, "Extending process-centered environments with organizational competence", *Lecture Notes in Computer Science 1149, Software Process Technology: Proceedings of the 5th European Workshop* (Springer-Verlag, 1996) 271–275.
49. G. Engels and L. Groenewegen, "SOCCA: Specifications of coordinated and cooperative activities", *Software Process Modeling and Technology*, Chap. 4 (Research Studies Press, 1994) 71–102.
50. P. H. Feiler and W. S. Humphrey, "Software process development and enactment: Concepts and definitions", *Proceedings of the Second International Conference on Software Process* (February 1993) 28–40.
51. P. Ferrer, J. M. Sanz, E. Gallo, M. Vergara and G. Satriani, Business Improvement Guide: BIG-CMM — Part A; User Manual, Technical Report, ESI-1999-TR-007 European Software Institute (February 1999).
52. A. Finkelstein, J. Kramer and B. Nuseibeh, *Software Process Modeling and Technology* (Research Studies Press, 1994).
53. R. Flood and M. Jackson, *Creative Problem Solving: Total Systems Intervention* (John Wiley & Sons, 1991).
54. P. Fowler and M. Patrick, "Transition packages for expediting technology adoption: The prototype requirements management transition package", SEI Technical Report, CMU/SEI-98-TR-004, Carnegie Mellon University, Pittsburgh (1998).
55. D. Frailey, "Defining a corporate-wide software process", *Proceedings of the First International Conference on the Software Process* (1991) 113–121.
56. A. Fuggetta and A. Wolf, *Software Process* (John Wiley & Sons, 1996).
57. A. Fuggetta, "Software process: A roadmap", *The Future of Software Engineering*, ed. A. Finkelstein (ACM Press, 2000) 27–34.
58. H. Gomaa, "The impact of rapid prototyping on specifying user requirements", *ACM Software Engineering Notes* **8**, no. 2 (1983) 17–28.
59. V. Gruhn, "Software processes are social processes", Technical Report, University of Dortmund (February 1992).
60. R. Guindon and B. Curtis, "Control of cognitive processes during design: What tools would support software designers?", *Proceedings of the CHI88, Human Factors in Computing Systems* (1988) 263–268.
61. D. Harel and M. Politi, *Modeling Reactive Systems with Statecharts: The Statemate Approach* (McGraw-Hill, 1998).
62. P. Harmon and B. Sawyer, *Creating Expert Systems for Business and Industry* (John Wiley & Sons, 1990).
63. R. Hastie, "Experimental evidence on group accuracy", *Information Processing and Group Decision-Making*, eds. G. Owen and B. Grofman (JAI Press, 1987) 129–157.
64. J. Herbsleb, D. Zubrow, D. Goldenson, W. Hayes and M. Paulk, "Software quality and the capability maturity model", *Communications of the ACM* **40**, no. 6 (1997) 30–40.
65. D. S. Hinley, "Software evolution management: A process-oriented perspective", *Information and Software Technology* **38**, no. 11 (November 1996) 723–730.
66. E. Hirsch, "Evolutionary acquisition of command and control systems", *Program Manager* (November/December 1985) 18–22.

67. K. E. Huff and V. R. Lesser, "A plan-based intelligent assistant that supports the software development process", *ACM SIGSOFT Software Engineering Notes* **13**, no. 5 (November 1988) 97–106.

68. K. Huff, "Software process modeling", *Software Process* (John Wiley & Sons, 1996).

69. W. Humphrey and W. Sweet, "A method for assessing the software engineering capability of contractors", Technical Report, CMU/SEI-87-TR-023, Carnegie Mellon University, Pittsburgh (1987).

70. W. Humphrey, *Managing the Software Process* (Addison Wesley, 1989).

71. W. Humphrey and B. Curtis, "Comments on 'A Critical Look'", *IEEE Software* (July 1991) 42–46.

72. W. Humphrey, *A Discipline for Software Engineering* (Addison Wesley, 1995).

73. W. S. Humphrey, *Introduction to the Personal Software Process, SEI Series in Software Engineering* (Addison-Wesley, 1997).

74. W. S. Humphrey, "Three dimensions of process improvement — Part III: The team software process", *Crosstalk* (April 1998).

75. IEEE Standard for Developing Software Life Cycle Processes, IEEE Standard, 1074–1991.

76. ISO 10011, Guidelines for Auditing Quality Systems, 1994.

77. ISO/IEC TR 15504, Information technology — Software process assessment, International Organization for Standardization, International Electrotechnical Commission, 1998. *http://wwwsel.iit.nrc.ca/spice*

78. ISO, ISO 9001:1994, Quality systems — Model for quality assurance in design, development, production, installation and servicing, International Organization for Standardization, ISO (1994).

79. ISO, ISO 9000-3:1997, Quality management and quality assurance standards — Part 3: Guidelines for the application of ISO 9001: 1994 to the development, supply, installation and maintenance of computer software, International Organization for Standardization, ISO (1997).

80. SPICE project web site. *http://www-sqi.cit.gu.edu.au/spice*

81. ISO/IEC International Standard: Information Technology, Software Life Cycle Processes, ISO/IEC Standard 12207-1995.

82. I. Jacobson, G. Booch and J. Rumbaugh, *The Unified Software Development Process* (Addison Wesley, 1999).

83. G. Junkermann, B. Peuschel, W. Schäfer and S. Wolf, "MERLIN: Supporting cooperation in software development through a knowledge-based environment", *Software Process Modeling and Technology*, Chap. 5 (Research Studies Press, 1994) 103–129.

84. G. E. Kaiser, P. H. Feiler and S. S. Popovich, "Intelligent assistance for software development and maintenance", *IEEE Software* (May 1988) 40–49.

85. S. M. Kaplan, W. J. Tolone, A. M. Carroll, D. P. Bogia and C. Bignoli, "Supporting collaborative software development with conversation-builder", *Proceedings of the 5th ACM SIGSOFT Symposium Software Development Environments, ACM SIGSOFT Software Engineering Notes* **17**, no. 5 (December 1992) 11–20.

86. T. Katayama, "A hierarchical and functional software process description and its enaction", *Proceedings of the 11th International Conference on Software Engineering* (May 1989) 343–352.

87. P. Kawalek and D. G. Wastell, "Organizational design for software development: A cybernetic perspective", *Lecture Notes in Computer Science 1149, Software Process Technology: Proceedings of the 5th European Workshop* (Springer-Verlag, 1996) 258–270.

88. M. Kellner and G. Hansen, "Software process modeling: A case study", *Proceedings of the 22nd International Conference on the System Sciences* (1989).

89. M. I. Kellner, "Software process modeling support for management planning and control", *Proceedings of the First International Conference on Software Process* (October 1991) 8–28.

90. D. P. Kelly and B. Culleton, "Process improvement for small organizations", *IEEE Computer*, **32**, no. 10 (October 1999) 41–47.

91. P. Kuvaja, J. Similä, L. Krzanik, A. Bicego, G. Koch and S. Saukkonen, *Software Process Assessment and Improvement, The BOOTSTRAP Approach* (Blackwell Publishers, 1994).

92. J. Lonchamp, K. Benali, C. Godart and J. C. Derniame, "Modeling and enacting software processes: An analysis", *Proceedings of the 14th Annual International Computer Software and Applications Conference* (October/November 1990) 727–736.

93. J. Lonchamp, "Supporting social interaction activities of software processes", *Proceedings of the Second European Workshop on Software Process Technology, EWSPT92* (September 1992) 34–54.

94. J. Lonchamp, "A structured conceptual and terminological framework for software process engineering", *Proceedings of the Second International Conference on Software Process* (February 1993) 41–53.

95. J. Lonchamp, "An assessment exercise", *Software Process Modeling and Technology*, Chap. 13 (Research Studies Press, 1994) 335–356.

96. N. H. Madhavji, "The process cycle", *Software Engineering Journal* **6**, no. 5 (September 1991) 234–242.

97. N. H. Madhavji and W. Schäfer, "Prism — Methodology and process-oriented environment", *IEEE Transactions on Software Engineering* **17**, no. 12 (December 1991) 1270–1283.

98. N. H. Madhavji, "Environment evolution: The Prism model of changes", *IEEE Transaction on Software Engineering* **18**, no. 5 (May 1992) 380–392.

99. R. McChesney, "Toward a classification scheme for software process modeling approaches", *Information and Software Technology* **37**, no. 7 (1995) 363–374.

100. D. McCracken and M. Jackson, "Life cycle concept considered harmful", *ACM SIGSOFT Software Engineering Notes* **7**, no. 2 (April 1982) 29–32.

101. B. McFeeley, *IDEAL: A User's Guide for Software Process Improvement*, Handbook CMU/SEI-96-HB-001, Carnegie Mellon University, Pittsburgh (February 1996).

102. C. McGowan and S. Bohner, "Model based process assessments", *Proceedings of the 15th International Conference on Software Engineering* (1993) 202–211.

103. S.-Y. Min and D.-H. Bae, "MAM nets: A Petri-net based approach to software process modeling, analysis and management", *Proceedings of the 9th International Conference on Software Engineering and Knowledge Engineering* (June 1997) 78–86.

104. O'Connell and H. Saiedian, "Can you trust software capability evaluations?", *IEEE Computer* **33**, no. 2 (February 2000) 28–35.

105. T. Olson, W. Humphrey and D. Kitson, "Conducting SEI-assisted software process assessments", Technical Report, CMU/SEI-89-TR-007, Carnegie Mellon University, Pittsburgh (1989).

106. L. J. Osterweil, "Software processes are software too", *Proceedings of the 9th International Conference on Software Engineering* (1987).

107. E. Ostolaza, E. Gallo, M. L. Escalante and G. Benguria, Business Improvement Guide: BIG-TTM Version 1.0, Technical Report, ESI-1999-TR-012, European Software Institute (February 1999).

108. M. C. Paulk, C. V. Weber and M. B. Chrissis, *The Capability Maturity Model: Guidelines for Improving the Software Process* (Addison-Wesley, 1995).

109. M. H. Penedo and C. Shu, "Acquiring experiences with the modeling and implementation of the project life-cycle process: The PMDB work", *Software Engineering Journal* **6**, no. 5 (September 1991) 259–274.

110. S-L. Pfleeger, *Software Engineering: Theory and Practice* (Prentice-Hall, 1998).

111. R. Pressman, *Software Engineering: A Practitioner's Approach* (McGraw-Hill, 1997).

112. A. Rae, P. Robert and H-L. Hausen, *Software Evaluation for Certification. Principles, Practice and Legal liability, International Software Quality Assurance Series* (McGraw-Hill, 1995).

113. D. Raffo and M. Kellner, "Modeling software processes quantitatively and evaluating the performance of process alternatives", *Elements of Software Process Assessment and Improvement*, eds. K. El Emam and N. Madhavji (IEEE CS Press, 1999).

114. J. Ramanathan and S. Sarkar, "Providing customized assistance for software lifecycle approaches", *IEEE Transactions on Software Engineering* **14**, no. 6 (June 1988) 749–757.

115. R. A. R. Ulloa, "Strategic management and control processes in the Peruvian culture: The systemic methodology for strategic management (SM: SM)", PhD Thesis, University of Lancaster, Lancaster (1991).

116. H. D. Rombach and M. Verlage, "Directions in software process research", *Advances in Computers* **41** (1995) 1–63.

117. H. Saiedian and R. Kuzara, "SEI capability maturity model's impact on contractors", *IEEE Computer* **8**, no. 1 (January 1995) 16–26.

118. G. Satriani, A. Andrés, M. L. Escalante and L. Marcaida, "Business improvement guide: SPICE — ISO 9001", Version 1.0, Technical Report, ESI-1998-TR-007, European Software Institute (May 1998).

119. W. Scacchi, "Models of software evolution: Life cycle and process", Carnegie Mellon University, Software Engineering Institute, SEI Curriculum Modules, SEI-CM-10-1.0 (1987).

120. H. Schmauch, *ISO 9000 for Software Developers* (ASQC Quality Press, 1995).

121. M. Scriven, *Evaluation Thesaurus* (Sage Publications, 1991).

122. M. Scriven, Evaluation Core Courses Notes, Claremont Graduate University (2000). *http://eval.cgu.edu/lectures/lecturen.htm*

123. B. Seaman and V. R. Basili, "OPT: An approach to organizational and process improvement", *Proceedings of AAAI Symposium on Computational Organizational Design* (March 1994).

124. R. W. Selby, A. A. Porter, D. C. Schmidt and J. Berney, "Metric-driven analysis and feedback systems for enabling empirically guided software development", *Proceedings of the 13th International Conference on Software Engineering* (May 1991) 288–298.

125. S. A. Sheard, "The frameworks quagmire, a brief look", *Proceedings of the 7th Annual International INCOSE Symposium (INCOSE97)* (August 1997) 3–7. *http://stsc.hill.af.mil/CrossTalk/1997/sep/frameworks.asp*; *http://www.software.org/quagmire/frampapr*

126. K. Sherdil and N. H. Madhavji, "Human-oriented improvement in the software process", *Lecture Notes in Computer Science 1149, Software Process Technology: Proceedings of the 5th European Workshop* (Springer-Verlag, 1996) 145–166.

127. I. Sommerville and T. Rodden, "Human, social and organizational influences on the software process", Lancaster University, Computing Department, Cooperative Systems Engineering Group, Technical Report, CSEG/2/1995 (1995) 1–21.

128. SPC, "Process definition and modeling guidebook", Software Productivity Consortium, SPC-92041-CMC (1992).
129. The TickIT Guide (4.0). A Guide to Software Quality Management System Construction and Certification to ISO 9001, British Standards Institution (1998).
130. Trillium, Model for Telecom Product Development and Support Process Capability, Version 3.0 (Bell Canada, 1994).
131. J. D. Valett and F. E. McGarry, "A summary of software measurement experiences in the software engineering laboratory", *Journal of Systems and Software* 9, no. 2 (1989) 137–148.
132. M. de Vasconcelos Jr. and C. M. L. Werner, "Software development process reuse based on patterns", *Proceedings of the 9th International Conference on Software Engineering and Knowledge Engineering* (June 1997) 97–104.
133. B. Warboys, "The IPSE 2.5 project: Process modeling as the basis for a support environment", *Proceedings of the First International Conference on System Development Environments and Factories* (May 1989).
134. B. J. Wielinga, A. Th. Schrieber and P. de Greef, *KADS: Synthesis*, Document Y3, Project ESPRIT KADS, Amsterdam University (1989).
135. M. Wilson, D. Duce and D. Simpson, Life cycles in software and knowledge engineering: A comparative review, *The Knowledge Engineering Review* 4, no. 3 (1989) 189–204.
136. L. Wolf and D. S. Rosenblum, "A study in software process data capture and analysis", *Proceedings of the Second International Conference on Software Process* (February 1993) 115–124.
137. B. Worthen, J. Sanders and J. Fitzpatrick, *Program Evaluation. Alternative Approaches and Practical Guidelines* (Addison Wesley, Longman, 1997).
138. S. K. Yu and J. Mylopoulos, "Understanding "why" in software process modeling, analysis, and design", *Proceedings of the 16th International Conference on Software Engineering*, IEEE Computer Society (May 1994) 1–10.
139. S. Zahran, *Software Process Improvement, Practical Guidelines of Business Success* (Addison Wesley, Longman, 1998).
140. D. Zubrow, W. Hayes, J. Siegel and D. Goldenson, *Maturity Questionnaire*, Special Report, CMU/SEI-94-SR-7, Carnegie Mellon University, Pittsburgh (1994).
141. CMMI Product Development Team, SCAMPI V1.0. Standard CMMI SM Assessment Method for Process Improvement: Method Description, Version 1.0. Technical Report, CMU/SEI-2000-TR-009 ESC-TR-2000-009, Carnegie Mellon University, Pittsburgh (2000).
142. Electronic Industries Association, Systems Engineering Capability Model EIA/IS 731 (Electronic Industries Association, Washington, D.C, 1998). *http://www.geia.org/eoc/G47/page6.htm*

# SOFTWARE MEASUREMENT

SANDRO MORASCA

*Università dell'Insubria, Dipartimento di Scienze Chimiche,*
*Fisiche e Matematiche, Sede di Como, Via Valleggio 11, Como, I-22100, Italy*
*Email: morasca@uninsubria.it*

This article provides an overview of the basic concepts and state of the art of software measurement. Software measurement is an emerging field of software engineering, since it may provide support for planning, controlling, and improving the software development process, as needed in any industrial development process. Due to the human-intensive nature of software development and its relative novelty, some aspects of software measurement are probably closer to measurement for the social sciences than measurement for the hard sciences. Therefore, software measurement faces a number of challenges whose solution requires both innovative techniques and borrowings from other disciplines. Over the years, a number of techniques and measures have been proposed and assessed via theoretical and empirical analyses. This shows the theoretical and practical interest of the software measurement field, which is constantly evolving to provide new, better techniques to support existing and more recent software engineering development methods.

*Keywords*: Software measurement, software metrics, theoretical validation, empirical validation.

## 1. Introduction

Measurement permeates everyday life and is an essential part in every scientific and engineering discipline. Measurement allows the acquisition of information that can be used for developing theories and models, and devising, assessing, and using methods and techniques. Practical application of engineering in the industry would not have been possible without measurement, which allows and supports

- production planning, from a qualitative and quantitative viewpoint;
- production monitoring and control, from a qualitative and quantitative viewpoint;
- decision making;
- cost/benefit analysis, especially when new techniques are proposed or introduced;
- post-mortem analysis of projects; and
- learning from experience.

Like in all other engineering branches, industrial software development requires the application of software engineering methods and techniques that are effective, i.e., they allow software organizations to develop quality software products, and efficient, i.e., they allow software organizations to optimize the use of their production resources. However, software engineering differs from other engineering disciplines in a number of aspects that have important consequences on software measurement. First, software engineering is a young discipline, so its theories, methods, models, and techniques still need to be fully developed and assessed. Other engineering branches rely on older, well-consolidated scientific disciplines. These disciplines have developed a large number of deep mathematical models and theories over the centuries and have long identified the important concepts (e.g. length, mass) that need to be studied and have long developed suitable tools to measure them. Second, software engineering is a very human-intensive discipline, while other engineering branches are based on the so-called hard sciences (e.g. Physics, Chemistry). Therefore, some aspects of software measurement are more similar to measurement in the social sciences than measurement in the hard sciences. For instance, in a number of software measurement applications, repeatability of results may not be achieved. As a consequence, one cannot expect software engineering measurement models and theories to be necessarily of the same nature, precision, and accuracy as those developed for more traditional branches of engineering. Third, there are several different types of software development, for different application areas and purposes, so, software measurement models may not be valid on a general basis, like those used in other engineering branches.

However, the very nature of software engineering makes measurement a necessity, because more rigorous methods for production planning, monitoring, and control are needed. Otherwise, the amount of risk of software projects may become excessive, and software production may easily get out of industrial control. This would produce obvious damages to both software producers (e.g. higher costs, schedule slippage) and users (e.g. poor quality products, late product delivery, high prices). To be effective and make good use of the resources devoted to it, software measurement should address important development issues, i.e., it should be carried out within a precise goal of industrial interest. In this context, software measurement may serve several purposes, depending on the level of knowledge about a process or product. Here, we list some of these purposes, from one that can be used when a limited or no amount of knowledge is available to one that requires an extensive amount of knowledge.

- Characterization, i.e., the gathering of information about some characteristic of software processes and products, with the goal of acquiring a better idea of "what's going on".
- Tracking, i.e., the (possibly constant and regular) acquisition of information on some characteristic of software processes and products over time, to understand if those characteristics are under control in on-going projects.
- Evaluation, i.e., judging some characteristic of a software process or product, for instance based on historical data in the same development environment or data available from external sources.

- Prediction, i.e., identifying a cause-effect relationship among product and process characteristics.
- Improvement, i.e., using a cause-effect relationship to identify parts of the process or product that can be changed to obtain positive effects on some characteristic of interest, and collecting data after the changes have been made to confirm or disconfirm whether the effect was positive and assess its extent.

Therefore, the goal of software measurement is certainly not limited to deriving measures. In addition to the above practical goals, one may say that, from a more abstract point of view, the goal of software measurement is to build and validate hypotheses and increase the body of knowledge about software engineering. This body of knowledge can be used to understand, monitor, control, and improve software processes and products. Therefore, building measures is a necessary part of measurement, but not its final goal.

Software measurement poses a number of challenges, from both a theoretical and practical points of view. To face these challenges, we can use a number of techniques that have been developed over the years and/or have been borrowed from other fields.

First, we need to identify, characterize, and measure the characteristics of software processes and products that are believed to be relevant and should be studied. This is very different from other engineering branches, where researchers and practitioners directly use measures without further thought. In those disciplines, there no longer is a debate on what the relevant characteristics are, what their properties are, and how to measure these characteristics. In software engineering measurement, instead, we still need to reach that stage. There is not as much intuition about software product and process characteristics (e.g. software cohesion or complexity) as there is about the important characteristics of other disciplines. Therefore, it is important that we make sure that we are measuring the right thing, i.e., it is important to define measures that truly quantify the characteristic they purport to measure. This step — called theoretical validation — is a difficult one, in that it involves formalizing intuitive ideas around which there is limited consensus. To this end, one can use Measurement Theory, which has been developed in the social sciences mainly in the last 60 years, or property-based approaches, which have been used in mathematics for a long time.

Second, we need to show that measuring these characteristics is really useful, via the so-called empirical validation of measures. For instance, we need to show if and to what extent these characteristics influence other characteristics of industrial interest, such as product reliability or process cost. It is worthwhile to measure them and use them to guide the software development process only if they have a sufficiently large impact. To this end, experiments must be carried out and threats to their internal and external validity must be carefully studied.

In addition, the identification and assessment of measures may not be valid in general. Nothing guarantees that measures that are valid and useful in one context and for some specified goal are as valid and useful for another context and goal. Goal-oriented frameworks that have been defined for software measurement can be used.

Before illustrating the various aspects of software measurement, we would like to explain that the term "metric" has been often used instead of "measure" in the software measurement field in the past. As it has been pointed out, "metric" has a more specialized meaning, i.e., distance, while "measure" is the general term. Therefore, we use "measure" in the remainder of this article.

The remainder of this article is organized as follows. Section 2 describes a framework for goal-oriented measurement (the Goal/Question/Metric paradigm). Sections 3 and 4 introduce the basic concepts of software measurement. Sections 5 and 6 illustrate how Measurement Theory and axiomatic approaches can be used to carry out the so-called theoretical validation of software measures, i.e., to show that a measure actually quantifies the attribute it purports to measure. Section 7 describes some of the measures that have been defined for the intrinsic attributes (e.g. size, structural complexity) of the artifacts produces during software development. Section 8 concisely reports on external software attributes (e.g. reliability, maintainability), i.e., those that refer to the way software relates to its development or operational environment. Process attributes are discussed in Sec. 9. Remarks on the practical application of software measurement are in Sec. 10. Possible future developments are discussed in Sec. 11.

Good surveys of the state of the art and on-going research can be found in [1, 2].

## 2. Goal-Oriented Measurement

It is fundamental that all measurement activities be carried out in the context of a well-defined measurement goal. In turn, the measurement goal should be clearly connected with an industrial goal, so the measurement program responds to a software organization's needs. The Goal/Question/Metric (GQM) paradigm [3, 4] provides a framework for deriving measures from measurement goals. The idea is to define a measurement goal, with five dimensions, as follows:

- *Object of Study*: the entity or set of entities that should be studied, e.g. a software specification, or a testing process.
- *Purpose*: the reason/the type of result that should be obtained: e.g. one may want to carry out/obtain a characterization, evaluation, prediction, or improvement.
- *Quality Focus*: the attribute or set of attributes that should be studied, e.g. size (for the software specification, or effectiveness (for the testing process).
- *Point of View*: the person or organization for whose benefit measurement is carried out, e.g. the designers (for the software specification), or the testers (for the testing process); and

- *Environment*: the context (e.g. the specific project or environment) in which measurement is carried out.

The following is an example of a GQM goal:

*Analyze* the testing process (object of study) *for the purpose of* evaluation (purpose) *with respect to* the effectiveness of causing failures (quality focus) *from the point of view of* the testing team (point of view) *in the environment of* project X (environment).

GQM goals help clarify what needs to be studied, why, and where. Based on the goal, the relevant attributes are identified via a set of questions (an intermediate document between the goal and the questions, the Abstraction Sheet, has been recently introduced to provide a higher-level view of the questions). As a simple example, a question related to the study of testing effectiveness may ask: How much is defect density? Each question is then refined into measures that can be collected on the field. For instance, defect density may be defined as the ratio of the number of defects found to the number of lines of code. Figure 1 shows this top-down refinement of goals into measures. Figure 1 also shows that several measurement goals may be pursued at the same time, and questions and measures may be reused across goals, thus decreasing the effort for adding further goals to an existing set of goals, questions, and measures. Conversely, interpretation of results proceeds bottom-up, i.e., the measures collected are used and interpreted in the context and for the objectives that have been initially defined. The GQM paradigm has been successfully used in many industrial environments to increase the knowledge of software organizations about their own practices and lay the quantitative foundations for improvement of software processes and products.

The GQM paradigm is a part of an organized approach to the improvement of software products and processes, the Quality Improvement Paradigm (QIP), which can be concisely described as an instantiation of the scientific method tailored for the needs of Software Engineering. The QIP is based on the idea that improvement can be achieved and quantified via the acquisition of knowledge on software

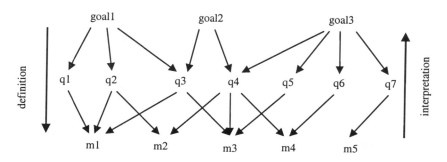

**Fig. 1.**   A sample GQM.

processes and products over time. The Experience Factory (EF) is another central aspect of the QIP. The EF is the organizational unit that collects, stores, analyzes, generalizes, and tailors information from software development projects, so it can be used in future ones.

## 3. Entities and Attributes

We now introduce the basic concepts of measurement. First, we identify the object of measurement. To this end, measurement is based on the following two concepts [1].

*Entity.* An entity may be a physical object (e.g. a program), an event that occurs at a specified instant (e.g. a milestone) or an action that spans over a time interval (e.g. the testing phase of a software project).

*Attribute.* An attribute is a characteristic or property of an entity (e.g. the size of a program, the time required during testing).

Both the entity and the attribute to be measured must be specified, because measurement should not be used for entities or attributes alone. For instance, it does not make sense to "measure a program", since the attribute to be measured is not specified (it could be size, complexity, maintainability, etc), or to "measure size", since the entity whose size is to be measured is not specified (it could be a specification, a program, a development team, etc). Instead, one can "measure the size of a program".

Entities in software measurement can be divided into two categories: products and processes. Product and process entities may be of different kinds. For instance, requirements, specifications, designs, code, test sets are all product entities and their parts are product entities as well. On the other hand, single phases, activities, and resources used during a project are process entities. Product and process entities have specific attributes. For instance, product attributes include size, complexity, cohesion, coupling, reliability, etc. Process attributes include time, effort, cost, etc.

Attributes are usually divided into internal and external attributes. An internal attribute of an entity depends only on the entity. For instance, the size of a program may be considered an internal attribute, since it depends only on the program. An external attribute of an entity depends on the entity and its context. For instance, the reliability of a program depends on both the program and the environment in which the program is used. As for product attributes, external attributes are usually the ones whose measures have industrial interest. For instance, it is important to measure the reliability of a program during its operational use, so as to assess whether its quality is sufficiently high. However, external attributes are usually difficult to measure directly, since they depend on the environment of the entity. Internal product attributes are easier to measure, but their measurement is seldom interesting *per se*, at least from a practical point of view. Internal product attributes are measured because they are believed to influence the external attributes (e.g. coupling is believed to influence maintainability) or process attributes (e.g. program complexity is believed to influence cost).

## 4. Measurement and Measure

We introduce a distinction between measurement and measure, as follows.

*Measurement.* Measurement is the process through which values are assigned to attributes of entities of the real world.

*Measure.* A measure is the result of the measurement process, so it is the assignment of a value to an entity with the goal of characterizing a specified attribute.

Therefore, a measure is not just a value, but it is a function that associates a value with an entity. In addition, the notion of value is by no means restricted to real or integer numbers, i.e., a measure may associate a symbol with an entity. For instance, a measure for the size of programs may associate the values "small", "medium", and "large" with programs. These values cannot be used for arithmetic or algebraic manipulations, but they can be used to obtain useful results through a variety of statistical techniques.

Because of the distinction between internal and external attributes, measures for internal attributes of an entity can be computed based only on the knowledge of the entity, while measures for external attributes also require the knowledge of the context of the entity.

Not all functions that associate a value with an entity are sensible measures for an attribute of that entity. For instance, if we intuitively rank a program $P'$ as longer than another program $P''$, we expect that a sensible measure of program size gives program $P'$ a value greater than the value it gives program $P''$.

Measures that make sense on an intuitive level are an obvious precondition in every measurement application. The measures used in many scientific fields (especially in the hard sciences) are usually taken for granted, i.e., they are considered intuitively valid for the attributes they purport to measure. For instance, there is no debate about the measures used to quantify the volume of an object. The reason is that there is a consolidated consensus about which measures can be considered intuitively valid. This consensus has been built over centuries and is so well established that the question hardly ever arises whether a measure is a sensible one for an attribute. However, this is not the case in software engineering measurement. Because of the novelty of the field, a sufficient degree of consensus still needs to be reached about which measures make sense on an intuitive level. Moreover, there is no widespread agreement on the attributes themselves, i.e., how can we define attributes unambiguously? Which attributes are really relevant?

These questions are important from an engineering point of view, because methods and techniques are devised with reference to attributes of software entities. For instance, it is commonly accepted that software systems should be composed of modules (entities) with high levels of inner cohesion (attribute) and low levels of coupling (attribute) among them. These software systems (entities) are believed to have, for instance, a high degree of maintainability (attribute). This is one of the reasons why object-oriented programming is believed to lead to better software systems than other techniques. However, this hypothesis (i.e., there is an influence of module cohesion and coupling on the maintainability of a software system) cannot undergo a real scientific examination until unambiguous definitions are provided for cohesion, coupling, and maintainability, and until measures are defined that are consistent with these definitions when applied to software modules and systems. This is not to say that module cohesion and coupling have no impact on software system maintainability or that object-oriented programming has not been beneficial in software development. However, in a sound engineering approach, we need to ascertain

- whether the evidence is sufficient for us to draw reliable conclusions (e.g. is the evidence only anecdotal or do statistical procedures such as the test of hypotheses confirm the hypothesis?)
- the absence of other influencing factors (e.g. has maintainability improved because of the adoption of object-oriented programming, or because of the improvement in the education of programmers, or the adoption of CASE tools?)
- the extent of the impact of the influencing attributes on the influenced attribute (e.g. does module cohesion influence software maintainability more than module coupling does? What is the impact of a variation in module coupling on maintainability?)

If we had information on these three points above, we would be able to use software techniques more effectively.

We now describe two approaches (Representational Measurement Theory and property-based approaches) that help identify those measures that make sense. It is to be borne in mind that, in both cases, we are actually modeling intuition, and intuition may vary across different people. For instance, one person may not agree with another person on how programs should be ranked according to their size. However, the value added by either approach is to spell out one's own intuition in mathematical, unambiguous terms, which can be used as a basis for discussion about the measures for an attribute and, eventually, to reach widespread consensus.

## 5. Representational Measurement Theory

Representational Measurement Theory [5] (see also [1, 6]) formalizes the "intuitive", empirical knowledge about an attribute of a set of entities and the "quantitative", numerical knowledge about the attribute. The intuitive knowledge is captured via the so-called empirical relational system (described in Sec. 5.1), and the quantitative knowledge via the so-called numerical relational system (Sec. 5.2). Both the empirical and the numerical relational systems are built by means of set algebra. A measure (Sec. 5.3) links the empirical relational system with the numerical relational system in such a way that no inconsistencies are possible, as formalized by the Representation Condition. In general, many measures may exist that quantify equally well one's intuition about an attribute of an entity (e.g. weight can be measured in kilograms, grams, pounds, ounces, etc). The relationships among the admissible measures for an attribute of an entity are illustrated in Sec. 5.4. As we will see, this leads to classifying measures into different categories, as described in Sec. 5.5. "Objectivity" and "subjectivity" of measures are discussed in Sec. 5.6.

### 5.1. *Empirical relational system*

An empirical relational system for an attribute of a set of entities is defined through the concepts of set of entities, relations among entities, and operations among entities. Therefore, an empirical relational system is defined as an ordered tuple $ERS = \langle E, R_1, \ldots, R_n, o_1, \ldots, o_m \rangle$, as we now explain.

- $E$ is the set of entities, i.e., the set of objects of interest that are subject to measurement with respect to that attribute.
- $R_1, \ldots, R_n$ are empirical relations: each empirical relation $R_i$ has an *arity* $n_i$, so $R_i \subseteq E^{n_i}$, i.e., $R_i$ is a subset of the cartesian product of the set of entities $E \times E \times \cdots \times E$ $n_i$ times.
- $o_1, \ldots, o_m$ are binary operations among entities: each binary operation $o_j$ is a function $o_j : E \times E \to E$. Therefore, its result is an entity, so we have $e_3 = e_1 o_j e_2$ (infix notation is usually used for these operations). As an additional assumption, all binary operations $o_j$'s are closed, i.e., they are defined for any pair of entities $\langle e_1, e_2 \rangle$.

As an example, suppose that we want to study the size (attribute) of program segments (set of entities). A program segment is defined as a sequence of statements. To characterize the size attribute, we may define the binary relation "longer than", i.e., $longer\_than \subseteq E \times E$. Therefore, given two program segments $e_1$ and $e_2$, we may have $\langle e_1, e_2 \rangle \in longer\_than$ (i.e., our intuitive knowledge is that $e_1$ is longer than $e_2$) or $\langle e_1, e_2 \rangle \notin longer\_than$ (i.e., our intuitive knowledge is that $e_1$ is not longer than $e_2$). If we were interested in another attribute, e.g. complexity, we would characterize the complexity attribute via a different relation, e.g. $more\_complex\_than \subseteq E \times E$. A binary operation may specify how program segments may be built based on other program segments, e.g. by concatenating program segments. For instance, $e_3 = e_1 \oplus e_2$ may represent the fact that program segment $e_3$ is built by concatenating program segments $e_1$ and $e_2$.

The empirical relations do not involve any values or numbers. We are not comparing the values obtained by measuring $e_1$'s and $e_2$'s sizes, but we are just stating our intuitive understanding and knowledge on $e_1$'s and $e_2$'s sizes and that $e_3$ is the concatenation of $e_1$ and $e_2$. Since this knowledge is intuitive, empirical relational systems are built in a somewhat subjective way, as intuition may very well vary across different individuals.

## 5.2. *Numerical relational system*

The intuitive knowledge of the empirical relational system is translated into the numerical relational system, which predicates about values. A numerical relational system is defined as an ordered tuple $NRS = \langle V, S_1, \ldots, S_n, \bullet_1, \ldots, \bullet_m \rangle$, as we show.

- $V$ is the set of values that can be obtained as results of measures.
- $S_1, \ldots, S_n$ are numerical relations: each numerical relation $S_i$ has the same *arity* $n_i$ of the empirical relation $R_i$, so $S_i \subseteq V^{n_i}$, i.e., $S_i$ is a subset of the $n_i$-times cartesian product of the set of values.
- $\bullet_1, \ldots, \bullet_m$ are binary operations among values: each binary operation $\bullet_j$ is a function $\bullet_j : V \times V \to V$. Therefore, its result is a value, so we have $\nu_3 = \nu_1 \bullet_j \nu_2$ (infix notation is usually used for these operations). As an additional assumption, all binary operations $\bullet_j$'s are closed, i.e., they are defined for any pair of values $\langle \nu_1, \nu_2 \rangle$.

For instance, the set $V$ may be the set of nonnegative integer numbers. A binary relation may be "greater than", i.e., $>$, so $> \subseteq V \times V$. A binary operation may be the sum between two integer values, i.e., $\nu_3 = \nu_1 + \nu_2$. Therefore, the numerical relational system in itself does not describe anything about the entities and the attribute.

## 5.3. *Measure*

The link from the empirical relational system and the numerical relational system is provided by the definition of measure, which associates entities and values, and scale, which associates the elements of the tuple of the empirical relational system with elements of the numerical relational system. A measure is a function $m : E \to V$ that associates a value with each entity.

As defined above, a measure establishes a link between the set of entities and the set of values, regardless of the relations and operations in the empirical and numerical relational system. Therefore, a measure for the size of program segments may be inconsistent with our intuitive knowledge about size as described by the relation *longer_than*. For instance, we may have three program segments $e_1, e_2$, and $e_3$ such that $\langle e_1, e_2 \rangle \in longer\_than$, $\langle e_2, e_3 \rangle \in longer\_than$, $m(e_1) < m(e_2)$, and $m(e_2) > m(e_3)$. This shows that not all measures are sensible ways for quantifying intuitive knowledge. The Representation Condition places a constraint on measures, so they do not exhibit this kind of counterintuitive behavior.

*Representation Condition.* A measure $m : E \to V$ must satisfy these conditions

$$\forall i \in 1..n \forall \langle e_1, \dots, e_{n_i} \rangle \in E^{n_i} (R_i(e_1, \dots, e_{n_i}) \Leftrightarrow S_i(m(e_1), \dots, m(e_{n_i})))$$

$$\forall j \in 1..m \forall \langle e_1, e_2 \rangle \in E \times E(m(e_1 o_j e_2) = m(e_1) \bullet_j m(e_2)).$$

The first condition requires that a tuple of entities be in the relation $R_i$ if and only if the tuple of measures computed on those entities is in the relation $S_i$ that corresponds to $R_i$. Therefore, if the relation $>$ is the one that corresponds to *longer_than* we have $\langle e_1, e_2 \rangle \in longer\_than$ if and only if $m(e_1) > m(e_2)$, as one would intuitively expect. The second condition requires that the measure of an entity obtained with the binary operation $o_j$ from two entities be obtained by computing the corresponding binary operation $\bullet_j$ on the measures computed on those two entities.

*Scale.* A scale is a triple $\langle ERS, NRS, m \rangle$, where $ERS = (E, R_1, \dots, R_n, o_1, \dots, o_m)$ is an empirical relational system, $NRS = (V, S_1, \dots, S_n, \bullet_1, \dots, \bullet_m)$ is a numerical relational system, and $m : E \to V$ is a measure that satisfies the Representation Condition.

For simplicity, we also refer to $m$ as a scale in what follows.

## 5.4. *Uniqueness of a scale*

Given an empirical relational system and a numerical relational system, two issues naturally arise, i.e., existence and uniqueness of a scale that maps the empirical relational system into the numerical relational system. We do not deal with the existence issue here, so we assume that a scale exists that links an empirical relational system and a numerical relational system. As for uniqueness, many different scales can be used given an empirical relational system and a numerical relational system. This is well known in everyday life or scientific or engineering disciplines. For instance, the distance between two points may be measured with different scales, e.g. kilometers, centimeters, miles, etc. All of these are legitimate scales, i.e., they satisfy the representation condition, so it does not really matter which scale we choose. Using one instead of another is just a matter of convenience, since there exists a transformation of scale (multiplication by a suitable proportionality coefficient) from a scale to another scale. However, multiplication by a suitable proportionality coefficient is also the only kind of transformation that can be applied to a distance scale to obtain another distance scale. Other transformations would not lead to a distance scale, since they would "distort" the original distance scale. For instance, given a distance scale $m$, using $m' = m^2$ as a distance measure would distort the original distance scale, so we cannot use $m^2$ as a legitimate distance measure.

In general, this leads to the notion of admissible transformation, i.e., a transformation that leads from one scale to another scale.

*Admissible Transformation.* Given a scale $\langle ERS, NRS, m \rangle$, a transformation $f$ is admissible if $\langle ERS, NRS, m' \rangle$ is a scale, where $m' = f \circ m$ is the composition of $f$ and $m$.

As a different example, suppose that we want to study failure severity, whose empirical relational system is defined by the set of failures $F$ and the relationship *more_severe_than*. Suppose we have a scale $m$, with values 1, 2, and 3. In this case, we can obtain a new measure $m'$ by simply mapping these three values into any three values, provided that an order is defined among them and that the measure preserves that order. For instance, we can use the numeric triples 2, 4, 6, or 6, 15, 91, to obtain a new scale. The set of admissible transformations in this case is broader than the set of admissible transformations for the distance between two points, since we are not forced to using only proportional transformations to obtain new scales. We could even use the triples a, b, c, or e, r, w, with the usual alphabetical ordering, or the three values low, medium, high, with the obvious ordering among them.

A broader set of admissible transformations means a broader choice of measures, but this comes with a price. All that our knowledge on failure severity allows us to tell is whether a failure is more severe than another, but nothing about the relative magnitude of severity. Therefore, it does not make sense to say that a failure is twice as severe as another failure, since the truth value of this statement depends on the specific scale used. For instance, one could say that medium severity failures are twice as severe as low severity ones according to the scale with values 1, 2, 3, or even the scale with values 2, 4, 6, but this would no longer be true according to the scale with values 6, 15, 91, let alone the scales with values a, b, c, or e, r, w. Instead, it makes sense to say that the distance between two points is twice as much as the distance between two other points. This statement does not change its truth value regardless of the scale chosen. This is a meaningful statement, according to the following definition.

*Meaningful Statement.* A statement about the values of a scale is meaningful if its truth value does not change if the scale is transformed according to any of its admissible transformations.

As an additional price to pay, we cannot use the values of the measure for failure severity as we would use the values we obtain for the distance between two points. For instance, we can sum the values we compute for distance measures, but it does not make sense to sum the values we obtain for failure severity.

### 5.5. *Scale types*

The set of admissible transformations, the set of meaningful statements, and the set of operations that can be used on the values are related to each other. Specifically, the set of admissible transformation defines the *measurement level* of a scale. In general, the narrower the set of admissible transformations, the smaller the number of scales, and the more informative the scale we choose. In Measurement Theory,

**Table 1.** Scale types and their properties.

| Scale Type | Admissible Transformations | Examples | Indicators of Central Tendency |
|---|---|---|---|
| Nominal | Bijections | Name of programming language (attribute: "programming language") | Mode |
| Ordinal | Monotonically increasing | A ranking of failures (as a measure of failure severity) | Mode + Median |
| Interval | Positive linear | Beginning date, end date of activities (as measures of time) | Mode + Median + Arithmetic Mean |
| Ratio | Proportionality | LOC (as a measure for program size) | Mode + Median + Arithmetic Mean + Geometric Mean |
| Absolute | Identity | LOC (as a measure of the attribute "number of lines of code") | Mode + Median + Arithmetic Mean + Geometric Mean |

five measurement levels are usually used. Here, we describe them, from the least to the most informative one. They are summarized in Table 1 along with their properties.

### 5.5.1. *Nominal scale*

A scale is a nominal one if it divides the set of entities into categories, with no particular ordering among them. For instance, the programming language used for a program is a nominal measure, since it allows programs to be classified into different categories, and no ordering among them is available. The set of admissible transformations is the set of all one-to-one transformations, since the specific values of the measures do not convey any particular information, other than the fact that they are different, so they can be used as labels for the different classes. For instance, a transformation that changed all the names of the programming languages would be acceptable, as long as different names are transformed into different names. We could have also used numbers to identify the programming languages, as long as different programming languages are encoded with different numbers. It is obvious that we cannot carry out any arithmetic operations on these numbers, since it makes no sense to sum or multiply them, and it does not make sense to order them, since there is no ordering of programming languages.

Nominal scales are the least informative ones, but they may well provide important information. For instance, a scale for the gender of people is a nominal one. However, scientific research has shown that gender may be related to diseases (e.g. the people of one gender may be more likely to have a disease than the people of the other gender) or to immunity to diseases. Therefore, nominal measures do provide important pieces of information. For instance, the programming language used is fundamental in interpreting models built on the number of lines of code.

### 5.5.2. Ordinal scale

A scale is an ordinal one if it divides the set of entities into categories that are ordered. For instance, an ordinal scale is the one that divides programs into small, medium, and large ones. The difference with the nominal scale is therefore that we have an additional piece of information, i.e., we know how to order the values of the measure. The set of admissible transformations is the set of strictly monotonic functions, i.e., those functions that preserve the ordering among the values of the measure, since we do not want to lose this piece of information. These functions are a subset of the one-to-one transformations, which are admissible for nominal scales. For instance, we can use the values a, b, and c with the usual alphabetical ordering instead of small, medium, and large. We might as well use the values 1, 2, and 3, with the usual, trivial ordering of integers. However, these values must then be used with caution. Unlike in the nominal case, we can compare these values, but we still cannot use them for arithmetic operations. For instance it would make no sense to sum the values 1 and 1 to obtain 2 and claim that 2 is the value of the size of a program segment obtained by putting together the two program segments whose values are 1 and 1. (Just imagine summing 3 and 3: the result would not even be defined.)

### 5.5.3. Interval scale

In an interval scale, the distance between two values is the basis for meaningful statements. For instance, it makes sense to say that the distance in time between the start of a software project and its completion is three times as much as the distance between the start and the end of the implementation phase. This statement makes sense regardless of the origin of time we adopt (e.g. foundation of Rome, first Olympic games) and the unit used (e.g. seconds, hours). The set of admissible transformations is a subset of the monotonic functions that are admissible for ordinal scales, the set of functions of the kind $m' = am + b$, where $b$ is any number (i.e., we can change the origin of the measure) and $a > 0$ (i.e., we can change the unit of the measure). Thus, not only can we order these distances, but we can establish truly numerical relations on them that are meaningful. What we cannot do is establish numerical statements of the same kind on the values of the measures. For instance, it does not make sense to say that the time at which a software project ended was twice as much as the time the project started. However, it makes sense to subtract values of an interval measure.

### 5.5.4. Ratio scale

A ratio scale allows the definition of meaningful statements of the kind "twice as much" on the single values of the measure. For instance one can say that a program segment is twice as long as another program segment. In this case, we can no longer choose the reference origin arbitrarily, as in the interval scale case. The reference origin is fixed, and its value is 0. On the other hand, we may change the unit without changing the meaningfulness of statements. For instance, when measuring the volume of objects, we can use liters, centiliters, gallons, etc. The truth value of a statement that says that the volume of an object is twice as much as the volume of another object does not change depending on the unit adopted. The set of admissible transformations is therefore a subset of the set of admissible transformations for the interval case, as the origin is now fixed. The set of admissible transformations is of the kind $m' = am$, where $a > 0$, since we can only change the unit of the measure. It makes sense to add and subtract ratio measures, and to multiply and divide them by constants.

### 5.5.5. *Absolute scale*

Absolute scales are the most informative ones, but they are also seldom used in practice. For instance, consider the attribute "number of lines of code" of a program segment. (This attribute is *not* the same as size, since we may want to measure size through different measures.) There is only one possible measure for this attribute, i.e., LOC, so there is only one admissible transformation, i.e., the identity transformation. Therefore, the set of admissible transformation, $m' = m$, is a subset of the admissible transformations for ratio measures.

### 5.5.6. *Scale types and statistics*

The above classification of scales has a very important impact on their practical use, in particular on the statistical techniques and indices that can be used. For instance, as an indicator of "central tendency" of a distribution of values, we can use the following different statistics, depending on the measurement level of the scale. For nominal scales, we can use the mode, i.e., the most frequent value of the distribution. (Several modes may exist.) For ordinal scales, we can use the median, i.e., the value such that not more than 50% of the values of the distribution are less than the median and not more than 50% of the values of the distribution are greater than the median. In addition, we can still use the mode. (There may be one or two-adjacent-medians.) For interval scales, in addition to the median and the mode, we can use the arithmetic mean. For ratio and absolute scales, in addition to the arithmetic mean, the median, and the mode, we can use the geometric mean. Therefore, the higher the level of measurement of a scale, the richer the set of indicators of central tendency. More importantly, the higher the level of measurement, the more powerful the statistical techniques that can be used, for instance, for ascertaining the presence of statistical relationships between measures [7]. In particular, parametric statistical techniques may be used only with interval, ratio, and absolute scales, while only nonparametric statistical techniques may be used with nominal and ordinal scales. Without going into the details of these two kinds of statistical techniques, we can say that parametric statistical techniques may use additional information than nonparametric ones, specifically information about the distance between values that is available in interval, ratio, and absolute scales, but that cannot be derived in ordinal or nominal scales. Thus, fewer data are needed to reach a statistically-based conclusion with parametric techniques than nonparametric ones.

### 5.6. *Objective vs subjective measures*

A distinction is sometimes made between "objective" and "subjective" measures. The distinction is based on the way measures are defined and collected. Objective measures are defined in a totally unambiguous way and may be collected through automated tools, while subjective measures may leave some room for interpretation and may require human intervention. For instance, ranking a failure as catastrophic, severe, non-critical, or cosmetic may be done based on human judgment. As a consequence, subjective measures are believed to be of lower quality than objective ones. However, there are a number of cases in which objective measures cannot be collected, so subjective measures are the only way to collect pieces of information that may be important and useful. Efforts must be made to keep the discrepancies among the values that are provided by different people as small as possible. Guidelines can be provided for limiting the amount of variability in the values that different people can give to a measure. As an example, the definition of values for an ordinal measure should be accompanied by an explanation of what those values really mean. So, if we have a size measure with values, small, medium, and large, we need to explain what we mean by each of the three values. Otherwise, different people with different intuitions may provide totally different values when ranking a program according to that measure.

## 6. Property-based Approaches

Representational Measurement Theory is not the only way the properties of the measures for software attributes have been modeled. In recent years, a few studies have proposed to describe the characteristics of the measures for software attributes via mathematical properties, in the same way as other concepts have been described in the past (e.g. distance). Based on an abstract description of a software artifact, each attribute is associated with a set of properties that its measure should satisfy. A few sets of properties have been defined [8,9], which address single software attributes, e.g. complexity, or general properties for software measures [10]. Here, we summarize the proposal of [11] because it addresses several different software product attributes. The proposal is based on a graph-theoretic model of a software artifact, which is seen as a set of elements linked by relationships. The idea is to characterize the properties for the measures of a given software attribute via a set of mathematical properties, based on this graph-theoretic model. We describe the

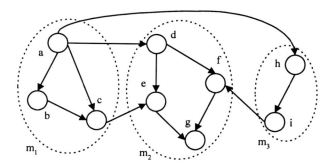

**Fig. 2.**   A modular system.

basic concepts of the approach and the sets of properties for the measures of four internal software attributes of interest.

*System, Module,* and *Modular System.* A software artifact is modeled by a graph $S = \langle E, R \rangle$, called system, where the elements of a software artifact are modeled by the nodes, and the relationships by the edges. The subgraph that represents the elements and relationships of a portion of the artifact is called a module. So, $m = \langle E_m, R_m \rangle$ is a module of S if and only if $E_m \subseteq E$, $R_m \subseteq E_m \times E_m$, and $R_m \subseteq R$. A module is connected to the rest of the system by external relationships, whose set is defined as $OuterR(m) = \{\langle e_1, e_2 \rangle | (e_1 \in E_m \wedge e_2 \notin E_m) \vee (e_1 \notin E_m \wedge e_2 \in E_m)\}$. A modular system is one where all the elements of the system have been partitioned into different modules. Therefore, the modules of a modular system do not share elements, but there may be relationships across modules.

Figure 2 shows a modular system with three modules $m_1$, $m_2$, $m_3$.

Because of its generality, this graph-based model may be applied to several different kinds of software artifacts, including specifications, designs, code, etc. For instance, when modeling software code, elements may represent statements, relationships transfers of control from one statement to another, and modules functions.

A few additional definitions of operations and properties of modules have been defined, as follows ($m_1 = \langle E_{m1}, R_{m1} \rangle$, $m_2 = \langle E_{m2}, R_{m2} \rangle$, and $m = \langle E_m, R_m \rangle$).

- *Inclusion.* Module $m_1$ is included $m_2$ (notation $m_1 \subseteq m_2$) if and only if $E_{m1} \subseteq E_{m2}$ and $R_{m1} \subseteq R_{m2}$.
- *Union.* Module $m$ is the union of modules $m_1$ and $m_2$ (notation $m = m_1 \cup m_2$) if and only if $E = E_{m1} \cup E_{m2}$ and $R = R_{m1} \cup R_{m2}$.
- *Intersection.* Module $m$ is the intersection of modules $m_1$ and $m_2$ (notation $m = m_1 \cap m_2$) if and only if $E = E_{m1} \cap E_{m2}$ and $R = R_{m1} \cap R_{m2}$.
- *Empty module.* Module $m$ (notation $m = \oslash$) is empty if and only if $m = \langle \oslash, \oslash \rangle$. The empty module is the "null" element of this small algebra.
- *Disjoint modules.* Modules $m_1$ and $m_2$ are disjoint if and only if $m_1 \cap m_2 = \oslash$.

We describe the properties for the internal attributes size, complexity, cohesion and coupling. Size and complexity may be defined for entire systems or modules of entire systems. Cohesion and coupling may be defined for entire modular systems or modules in a modular system. For simplicity, we only show the properties for the measures of cohesion and coupling of modules, and not of entire modular systems.

*Size.* The basic idea is that size depends on the elements of the system. A measure $Size(S)$ of the size of a system $S = \langle E, R \rangle$ is

- non-negative: $Size(S) \geq 0$
- null if $E$ is empty: $E = \emptyset \Rightarrow Size(S) = 0$
- equal to the sum of the sizes of any two of its modules $m_1 = \langle E_{m1}, R_{m1} \rangle$, $m_2 = \langle E_{m2}, R_{m2} \rangle$ such that $\{E_{m1}, E_{m2}\}$ is a partition of $E : E = E_{m1} \cup E_{m2} \wedge E_{m1} \cap E_{m2} = \emptyset \Rightarrow Size(S) = Size(m_1) + Size(m_2)$

*Complexity.* Complexity depends on the relationships between elements. A measure $Complexity(S)$ of the complexity of a system $S = \langle E, R \rangle$ is

- non-negative: $Complexity(S) \geq 0$
- null if $R$ is empty: $R = \emptyset \Rightarrow Complexity(S) = 0$
- not less than the sum of the complexities of any two of its modules $m_1 = \langle E_{m1}, R_{m1} \rangle$, $m_2 = \langle E_{m2}, R_{m2} \rangle$ without common relationships: $R_{m1} \cap R_{m2} = \emptyset \Rightarrow Complexity(S) \geq Complexity(m_1) + Complexity(m_2)$
- equal to the sum of the complexities of two disjoint modules: $m_1 \cap m_2 = \emptyset \Rightarrow Complexity(S) = Complexity(m_1) + Complexity(m_2)$

*Cohesion.* Cohesion is based on the internal relationships of modules. A measure $Cohesion(m)$ of the cohesion of a module $m = \langle E_m, R_m \rangle$ of a modular system is

- non-negative and with an upper bound: $0 \leq Cohesion(m) \leq Max$
- null if $R_m$ is empty: $R_m = \emptyset \Rightarrow Cohesion(m) = 0$
- non-decreasing if relationships are added to the set of relationships of a module: given two modules $m_1 = \langle E_{m1}, R_{m1} \rangle$, $m_2 = \langle E_{m2}, R_{m2} \rangle$, we have $R_1 \subseteq R_2 \Rightarrow Cohesion(m_1) \leq Cohesion(m_2)$
- non-increasing if two modules that are not linked by any relationships are grouped in a single module: $OuterR(m_1) \cap OuterR(m_2) = \emptyset \Rightarrow Cohesion(m_1 \cup m_2) \leq Cohesion(m_1) + Cohesion(m_2)$

*Coupling.* Coupling depends on the relationships that link a module to the rest of the system. A measure $Coupling(m)$ of the coupling of a module $m = \langle E_m, R_m \rangle$ of a modular system is

- non-negative: $Coupling(m) \geq 0$
- null if $OuterR(m)$ is empty: $OuterR(m) = \emptyset \Rightarrow Coupling(m) = 0$
- non-decreasing if relationships are added to the set of external relationships of a module: $OuterR(m_1) \subseteq OuterR(m_2) \Rightarrow Coupling(m_1) \leq Coupling(m_2)$

- not less than the sum of the couplings of any two of its modules $m_1 = \langle E_{m1}, R_{m1} \rangle$, $m_2 = \langle E_{m2}, R_{m2} \rangle$ : $Coupling(m_1 \cup m_2) \leq Coupling(m_1) + Coupling(m_2)$
- equal to the sum of the couplings of two modules that are not linked by any relationships: $OuterR(m_1) \cap OuterR(m_2) = \oslash \Rightarrow Coupling(m_1 \cup m_2) = Coupling(m_1) + Coupling(m_2)$

Sets of properties such as the one described above may be used to

- model intuition about the properties that measures for an attribute should possess;
- show similarities and differences among the measures for different attributes;
- check whether a given measure is consistent with intuition: the fact that a measure satisfies the set of properties for an attribute does not imply that the measure is valid for the attribute it purports to measure, but as supporting evidence. On the other hand, if a measure does not satisfy the set of properties for the attribute it purports to measure, then it is not a measure for that attribute.

## 7. Measures for Internal Product Attributes

Many software measures have been defined over the last few years, mainly for programs. There are two reasons for this. Programs are the main products of software development, so they are always built during software development. The other artifacts may not always exist or they may not be explicitly and completely recorded. The second reason is that software code is a totally formal artifact, so it can be automatically processed to extract measures. Instead, the other software artifacts (e.g. requirements, specifications, etc) are seldom fully formal, so they cannot usually be processed as easily in an automated way. In addition, human intervention may be required, so the measures obtained are more subjective than those for software code. Nevertheless, measures for artifacts other than software code exist, since measurement should be used in all phases of the software process, especially in the early ones, which are believed to have the biggest influence on the entire software process.

In what follows, we concisely describe a number of measures that have been defined for different software artifacts to measure a number of software attributes. Before proceeding, it is necessary to say that these measure have been seldom defined according to the concepts of Measurement Theory or the property-based approaches. This makes their adherence to intuition questionable in some cases.

### 7.1. *Requirements*

Measures for the early development phases would be the most useful ones, since the early phases and the artifacts they produce are believed to have the largest impact on the entire software development process and the final product. However, few measures have been defined for the artifacts produced during the early phases. One of the reasons is that these artifacts are hardly ever formal in nature, and, therefore, it is hardly ever possible to analyze them in an automated fashion. Nevertheless, due to the need for early measures, measures for requirements have been defined.

### 7.1.1. *Requirements count*

A widely used measure is the requirements count, which is intended to measure the size of a software application. As such, it can be used to come up with at least a rough estimate of the size of the final product and, more importantly, time and effort required for developing the software product. This latter estimation may be carried out through mathematical estimation models (e.g. based on the average productivity in previous projects, interpreted, for instance, as the average time required for coding a requirement), or based on personal experience. The variations in the requirements count over time has also been used to quantify the volatility of requirements, which is a frequent phenomenon in industrial software development. Good definition and practical application of requirements count require that all requirements be of the "same size", i.e., there shouldn't be requirements with intuitively different sizes, or, alternatively, requirements with intuitively different sizes should be given different "weights".

### 7.1.2. *Function points*

Another measure has emerged over the years and is commonly used: Function Points. The aim of Function Points (FP) [12] is to measure software functionality. On an intuitive level, the more functionality in a program, the higher the number of Function Points. The attribute "functionality", however, is quite elusive, so Function Points have often been taken as an *operational* definition of a measure for functionality, without much formal consideration on the intrinsic characteristics of the functionality attribute.

Function Points abstract from the specific languages used to specify, design, and implement a software system, so they are not a measure of the size of the final product. Due to the informal nature of requirements, Function Points are a subjective measure. Function Points are now used for several purposes, including contracts and pricing.

The computation of FP is carried out in two steps. First, Unadjusted Function Points (UFP) are computed. Second, a correction factor, Technical Correction Factor (TCF), is computed. The value of FP is the product $FP = UFP \cdot TCF$.

Unadjusted Function Points are computed based on element types belonging to the five categories below, which are used to summarize the input/output behavior of the software system and the internally handled data:

- external input types: each unique (different format or different processing logic) user data or control input type that enters the external boundary of the application and adds or changes data in a logical internal file type (include transactions from other applications);
- external output types: each unique user data or control output type that leaves the external boundary of the application (include reports and messages to the user or to other applications);
- logical internal file types: each major logical (from the viewpoint of the user) group of user data or control information that is generated, used, maintained by the application;
- external interface file types: files (major logical group of user data or control information) passed or shared between applications (outgoing external interface file types are also counted as logical internal file types);
- external inquiry types: each unique input/output combination, where an input causes and generates an immediate output (the input data is entered only to direct the search and no update of logical internal file type occurs).

Each element type of the software system (e.g. each different external inquiry type) is ranked on a three-valued complexity scale with values low, medium, high. A weight $W_{i,j}$ is associated with each element type $i$ and complexity value $j$. Table 2 shows the values, which were determined by "trial and error". Each element type therefore contributes to UFP according to its weight, so the value of UFP is obtained by summing all the products given by the number of elements types of kind $i$ and complexity $j$ times $W_{i,j}$

$$UFP = \sum_{i \in 1..5} \sum_{j \in 1..3} \#Element\ Types_{i,j} W_{i,j}$$

The value of UFP is multiplied by a correction factor called Technical Complexity Factor (TCF), which accounts for 14 different General System Characteristics $GSC_k$ of the software system: data recovery and back-up, data communication, distributed processing, performance issues, heavily used configuration, advanced data entry and lookup, online data entry, online update of master files, complex

**Table 2.** Weights for the computation of Unadjusted Function Points.

| Complexity<br>Function Types | Low | Average | High |
| --- | --- | --- | --- |
| External inputs | 3 | 4 | 6 |
| External outputs | 4 | 5 | 7 |
| Internal logical files | 7 | 10 | 15 |
| External interface files | 5 | 7 | 10 |
| External inquiries | 3 | 4 | 6 |

functionality, internal processing complexity, reusability, installation ease, multiple sites, modifiability. These characteristics are ranked according to their degree of influence $DegGSC_k$ from "None" to "Essential" and are accordingly associated with a value in the 0–5 range. The value of TCF is obtained as follows:

$$TCF = 0.65 + 0.01 \sum_{k \in 1..14} DegGSC_k$$

The idea is that the impact of each $GSC_k$ on FP has a 5% range, since the sum of the $DegGSC_k$'s is multiplied by 0.01 (i.e., 1%). In addition, if the influence of all $GSC_k$'s is rated as "Essential" the value of $0.01 \sum_{k \in 1..14} DegGSC_k$ is 0.7. At the other extreme, if all the influence of all $GSC_k$'s is rated as "None" the value of $0.01 \sum_{k \in 1..14} DegGSC_k$ is 0. Therefore, there is a 70% oscillation interval, which explains the number 0.65 in the formula for TCF, since TCF varies in the [0.65, 1.35] range.

Function Points are therefore computed based on subjective considerations. The extent of the discrepancies in the counting of Function Points by different people has been studied in a few works (e.g. [13]). At any rate, the International Function Points Users Group (IFPUG), an international organization with local chapters, periodically provides and refines existing guidelines to reduce the extent of subjectivity.

Several variants of Function Points have been defined. Among them, Feature Points [14] introduce Algorithmic Complexity as an additional element type and modify some values of the original complexity weights. Mark II Function Points [15] simplify the set of element types. A system is viewed as a set of "transaction types", composed of input, processing, and output, used to compute the Unadjusted Function Points. Then, Mark II Function Points are computed by multiplying the Unadjusted Function Points by a correction factor which takes into account 19 General System Characteristics.

The original justifications of Function Points were founded on Halstead's Software Science (see Sec. 7.4.2). Over the years, Function Points have been used as a measure of several attributes [16], including, size, productivity, complexity, functionality, user deliverables, overall behavior, or as a dimensionless number. Despite these theoretical problems, Function Points are widely spread and used as a *de facto* standard.

## 7.2. *Specifications*

Few measures exist for the attributes of software specifications. However, it would be important to have an early quantitative evaluation of the attributes of a software specification, since the early phases and artifacts are commonly believed to be the most influential ones during software development. The lack of measures for specifications is mainly due to the fact that specifications are usually written in plain text, so it is difficult to build "objective" measures that can be computed automatically. Measures have been defined for formal or semi-formal specifications, since the measures can be defined in an "objective" way (i.e., no subjective assessments are required) and computations can be automated. As an example, a preliminary study was carried out on software specifications written in TRIO+ [17], a formal object-oriented specification language. Another application of software measurement to specifications is in [18].

## 7.3. *Designs*

A few measures have been defined for high-level and low-level design.

### 7.3.1. *High-level design measures*

In [19], measures have been defined for cohesion and coupling of the high-level design of an object-based system, which differs from a full-fledged object oriented system because objects are instances of types that are exported by modules, i.e., there is no real syntactic concept of class, and inheritance is not allowed.

At the high-level design stage, only the interfaces of modules of the system (functions types, variables, and constants defined in the module interfaces) are known.

The measures are based on two kinds of interactions, which may relate data to data or data to functions. There is an interaction between two data (DD-interaction) if one appears in the definition of the other (e.g. a type appears in the definition of another type, variable, constant, or function parameter). There is an interaction between a piece of data and a function as a whole (DF-interaction) if the piece of data appears in the definition of the function (e.g. a type appears as the type returned by the function or as the type of a parameter). The notions of interaction are also transitive, so, for instance, data A and C also interact if A interacts with a third piece of data B that interacts with C. Some interactions contribute to cohesion, others to coupling. The interactions between data and functions of a module and the interactions between data of a module (excluding the parameters of functions) are considered cohesive. The interactions between data of a module and data of other modules are believed to contribute to coupling. More specifically, some interactions contribute to import coupling of a module (those in which data from some other module appears in the data definitions of a module) and others to export coupling (those in which data from the module appear in the data definitions of some other module).

Among the measures defined for cohesion, the Ratio of Cohesive Interactions is the ratio of cohesive interactions existing in a module to the maximum number possible of cohesive interactions for that module, based on its data. Among the coupling measures, Import Coupling is the number of interactions that link data from other modules to data in a module. These measures are consistent with the properties shown in Sec. 6 for cohesion and coupling measures. In addition, it was shown that they could be used as a part of models for fault-proneness of the final software.

Among recent developments, measures have been proposed for object-oriented systems [20, 21], some of which may be applied to software designs and software code. The measures defined in [20] are explained in more detail in Sec. 7.4.4.

### 7.3.2. *Low-level design measures*

Based on the modularization of high-level design, low level design takes care of designing the parts of the single modules. Information Flow Complexity [22] is probably the best-known measure for low-level design. The measure is based on the communication flows to and from a function. The input parameters and the global data structures from which the function retrieves information are called the fan-in. The output parameters and the global data structures that the function updates are called the fan-out. Information Flow Complexity is defined as follows:

$$InformationFlowComplexity = length \cdot (fanIn \cdot fanOut)^2$$

where *length* is a suitable size measure, and *fanIn* and *fanOut* are the number of parameters and data of the fan-in and fan-out, respectively.

## 7.4. *Code*

A very large number of measures have been defined for software code. Here, we report on some of the best-known and widely used ones.

### 7.4.1. *Lines of code*

The number of Lines of Code (abbreviated as LOC) is the oldest and most widely used measure of size. It is commonly used to give an indication about the size of a program and in several models for the prediction of effort, fault-proneness, etc. The success of LOC is due to the fact that it is easy to understand and to measure. A few variations exist, though. For instance, one needs to decide whether to count only executable lines, as was done when LOC was first introduced, or declaration lines as well. Also, one needs to decide whether comment lines and blank lines should be counted. However, in the vast majority of cases, there is a very high linear correlation between the values of LOC obtained with or without comment and blank lines. Therefore, the predictive power is not really affected by these decisions. Nevertheless, it is sensible, in a specified development environment, to define a consistent mechanism for counting LOC, so the measures collected are comparable.

### 7.4.2. *Halstead's software science*

Halstead's Software Science [23] was an attempt to build a comprehensive theory for defining measures for several attributes of software code. The idea was to identify a set of basic elements of programs and measure them to build measures for a number of attributes of software code. Software Science argues that a program is composed of two basic types of elements, i.e., operators and operands. Operands are variables and constants. Operators are symbols or combinations of symbols that affect the values of operands. The basic measures computed on a program, on top of which Software Science was built, are:

- $\eta_1$: the number of distinct operators that appear in the program.
- $\eta_2$: the number of distinct operands that appear in the program.
- $N_1$: the total number of occurrences of operators in the program.
- $N_2$: the total number of occurrences of operands in the program.
- $\eta_2^*$: the number of conceptual input/output operands of in the program, i.e., the input and output parameters that would be needed if the program was represented as a function.

Therefore, the main assumption of Software Science is that all measures for several attributes can be obtained based on these five measures. Through considerations deriving from a number of sources, including Information Theory and Thermodynamics, a number of measures are defined, as follows.

*Program Length.* A program is made only of operators and operands, so its length is given by the total number of occurrences of operators and operands, $N = N_1 + N_2$.

*Length Estimator.* Program length is known only upon program completion. However, it is useful to know or estimate the length of a program at the beginning of coding for prediction purposes, for instance to estimate the effort needed. Under the assumption that the number of distinct operators and operands of a program can be estimated early during coding, an estimator of length is derived as $\hat{N} = \eta_1 \log_2 \eta_1 + \eta_2 \log_2 \eta_2$.

*Volume.* The volume of a program is the number of bits needed to represent it, so it is another measure of size. It is computed as $V = N \log_2(\eta_1 + \eta_2)$.

*Potential Volume.* This is the minimal number of bits required to represent a program, which would be attained if the function implemented by the program was already available. In that case, it is argued that the number of operators would be two (the name of the function and a mechanism to group the function's parameters), the number of operands would be $\eta_2^*$, and each operator and operand would appear only once, so the potential volume is $V^* = (2 + \eta_2^*) \log_2(2 + n_2^*)$.

*Program Level.* The level of the program (L) is an indicator of how close a program is to its potential volume, so $L = V/V^*$.

*Estimator of Program Level.* Since the value of $\eta_2^*$ may be difficult to compute, the following estimator is introduced for $L : \hat{L} = 2\eta_2/(\eta_1 N_2)$.

*Effort.* Effort is measured as the number of elementary discriminations (of the kind yes/no) that a programmer must make to write a program. It is argued that this

| | Operators | Occurrencies | Operands | Occurrencies |
|---|---|---|---|---|
| begin | begin ... end | 2 | max | 4 |
|   max:=0; | := | 2 | 0 | 2 |
|   read(x); | ; | 5 | x | 5 |
|   while x<>0 do | read | 2 | | |
|   begin | (...) | 3 | | |
|     if x>max | while ... do | 1 | | |
|     then max:=x; | <> | 1 | | |
|     read(x) | if ... then | 1 | | |
|   end; | > | 1 | | |
|   write(max); | write | 1 | | |
| end; | | | | |
| $\eta_2^* = 2$ (x and max) | $\eta_1 = 10$ | $N_1 = 19$ | $\eta_2 = 3$ | $N_2 = 11$ |

$N = 30$, $\hat{N} = 38$, $V = 112$, $V^* = 11.61$, $L = 0.1037$, $\hat{L} = 0.0545$, $E = 1568$, $\hat{T} = 87.1$

**Fig. 3.**  Example of computations for Halstead's Software Science.

number is $E = V^2/V^* = V/L$. Since $L$ may be difficult to obtain, due to the fact that it is computed based on $\eta_2^*$, $\hat{L}$ may be used in the formula.

*Time.* The time (in seconds) needed to write a program is given by the number of elementary discriminations divided by the number of elementary discriminations that a programmer makes every second, assumed to be 18, so $\hat{T} = E/18$.

The example in Fig. 3 (in a Pascal-like language) shows how the computations are carried out.

Halstead's Software Science's theoretical foundations and derivations of measures are somewhat shaky, and it is fair to say that not all of the above measures have been widely used in practice. However, due to their popularity and the availability of automated tools for computing them, some of the above measures are being used. As an example, a value $V \leq 4000$ would be considered desirable for maintainability purposes in some environments.

### 7.4.3. *Cyclomatic complexity*

The Cyclomatic Complexity [24] of a program is a measure for the complexity of the control flow graph of the program. The basic assumption is that the higher the number of paths in a program, the higher its control flow complexity. Since the number of paths in a control flow graph is infinite if the program has at least one loop, Cyclomatic Complexity only counts the so-called base paths, i.e., those paths from the start point to the end point of a program whose linear combinations provide all the paths in the program. Based on graph theory results, the number of base paths in a program is computed as $\nu(G) = e - n + 2$, where $e$ and $n$ are

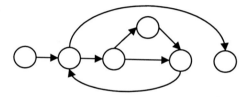

**Fig. 4.**  Control flow graph for the program of Fig. 3.

the number of edges and nodes in the control flow graph, respectively. If a program has one main routine and $(p-1)$ subroutines, the value of $\nu(G)$ is computed as $\nu(G) = e - n + 2p$.

It is not necessary to build the control flow graph of a program to compute its Cyclomatic Complexity. Mills' theorem shows that $\nu(G) = d + p$, where $d$ is the number of decision points in the program including its subroutines (an $n$-way decision point is counted $n-1$).

Figure 4 contains the control flow graph for the software code in Fig. 3, for which $\nu(G) = 7 - 6 + 2 = 3$.

"Rules of thumb" are sometimes used to curb the control flow complexity of software modules. In different application environments, upper limits ranging between 7 and 15 have been suggested.

### 7.4.4. *Object-oriented measures*

Following the success of Object-Oriented techniques, several measures have been proposed. The measures that have been most widely discussed and accepted are those defined in [20], which we now concisely describe. Some of these measures can also be used on object-oriented designs. We also provide a rough idea of the median values for them, based on the systems studied in [20, 25].

- *Weighted Methods per Class (WMC)*. It is the sum of the complexities of the methods of a class. Any complexity measure can be taken as the one to be used for the single methods, i.e., it is not fixed in the definition of the measure. By assuming each method has a unit weight, median values range between 5 and 10.
- *Number Of Children of a class (NOC)*, computed as the number of classes that directly inherit from a class in the inheritance hierarchy. Median values are around 0.
- *Depth of Inheritance Tree (DIT)*, which is the length of the longest path starting from the root of the inheritance hierarchy to the terminal classes. Median values range between 0 and 3.
- *Coupling Between Object classes (CBO)*, which is the number of classes to which a class is coupled, i.e., those classes that use that class or are used by that class. Median values may range around 5.

- *Response For a Class (RFC)*, defined as the number of methods of a class that can be executed when a class receives a message. Median values range between 15 and 20.
- *Lack of COhesion in Methods (LCOM)*, computed as the difference between the number of pairs of methods that do not share class variables (e.g. member data) and the number of pairs of methods that share class variables, if this difference is non-negative, otherwise LCOM is 0. Median values range between 0 and 1.

Although their theoretical validation is not fully convincing, the above measures (except LCOM) have been found generally useful in building models for various attributes. Many other measures have been defined. A comprehensive set is proposed in [21]. Surveys can be found in [26, 27].

### 7.4.5. *Functional cohesion*

Three measures for functional cohesion are introduced in [28], based on the *data tokens* (i.e., the occurrences of a definition or use of a variable or a constant) that appear in a procedure, function, or main program. Each data token is on at least one *data slice*, i.e., a sequence of data tokens belonging to those statements that can influence the statement in which the data token appears, or can be influenced by that statement. Those data tokens that belong to more than one data slice are called *glue tokens*, and those that belong to all data slices are called *super-glue tokens*. Given a procedure, function, or main program p, the following measures SFC(p) (Strong Functional Cohesion), WFC(p) (Weak Functional Cohesion), and A(p) (adhesiveness) are introduced for all the data slices that refer to the results of the computations

$$SFC(p) = \frac{\#SuperGlueTokens}{\#AllTokens} \qquad WFC(p) = \frac{\#GlueTokens}{\#AllTokens}$$

$$A(p) = \frac{\sum_{GT \in GlueTokens} \#SlicesContainingGlueTokenGT}{\#AllTokens \; \#DataSlices}$$

It can be shown that $SFC(p) \leq A(p) \leq WFC(p)$, so the measures for cohesion define a range with lower bound $SFC(p)$ and upper bound $WFC(p)$ and "central value" $A(p)$. As an example, consider the function in Fig. 5, which computes the minimum and the maximum values of a series of n integer numbers (with $n \geq 1$). The procedure computes two outputs (min and max), so we are interested in the data slices for those two outputs. For each data token in the procedure, the table in Fig. 5 shows the occurrence number and whether it belongs to the min or the max data slice (YES or NO in the corresponding column). There are two data slices, so all glue tokens are also super-glue ones and the values for the three cohesion measures coincide, i.e., $SFC(p) = A(p) = WFC(p) = 8/22 = 0.36$.

```
procedure minmax
        (n: integer;
          var min, max: integer);
    var i: integer;
        temp: integer;
begin
  read(temp);
  min:=temp;
  max:=temp;
  for i:=2 to n do
  begin
    read(temp);
    if temp<min
      then min:=temp;
    if temp>max
      then max:=temp
  end
end;
```

| Data Token | Occurrence | min | max |
|---|---|---|---|
| n | 1 | YES | YES |
| min | 1 | YES | NO |
| max | 1 | NO | YES |
| i | 1 | YES | YES |
| temp | 1 | YES | YES |
| temp | 2 | YES | YES |
| min | 2 | YES | NO |
| temp | 3 | YES | NO |
| max | 2 | NO | YES |
| temp | 4 | NO | YES |
| i | 2 | YES | YES |
| 2 | 1 | YES | YES |
| n | 2 | YES | YES |
| temp | 5 | YES | YES |
| temp | 6 | YES | NO |
| min | 3 | YES | NO |
| min | 4 | YES | NO |
| temp | 7 | YES | NO |
| temp | 8 | NO | YES |
| max | 3 | NO | YES |
| max | 4 | NO | YES |
| temp | 9 | NO | YES |

**Fig. 5.** Example of computations for cohesion measures.

## 7.5. *Verification*

Measures have been defined for the artifacts used during the verification phase. Among these, the best known ones are coverage measures, which are used during software testing to assess how thoroughly a program is exercised by a set of test data. Coverage measures provide the percentage of elements of interest that have been exercised during software testing. Below, we list a few coverage measures that can be defined based on a given program $P$ and a given set of test data $TD$.

- *Statement coverage* (also called *C0* coverage), i.e., the percentage of statements of $P$ that are executed by at least one test in $TD$.
- *Branch coverage* (also called *C1* coverage), i.e., the percentage of branches of $P$ that are executed by at least one test in $TD$.
- *Base path coverage*, i.e., the percentage of base paths (see Sec. 7.4.3) of $P$ that are executed by at least one test in $TD$. Path coverage measures cannot be used effectively, since the number of paths of the control flow graph of a non-trivial program (i.e., one that contains at least one loop) is infinite. Therefore, base path coverage or other measures are used instead.

- *Definition-use path coverage*, i.e., the percentage of definition-use paths of $P$ that are executed by at least one test in $TD$. A definition-use path is defined as the path between the statement in which a variable receives a value and the statement in which that variable's value is used.

## 8. Measures for External Product Attributes

Several external attributes have been studied and quantified through measures. External product attributes are usually attributes of industrial interest, since they are related to the interaction between software entities and their environment. Examples of these attributes are reliability, maintainability, and portability. Despite their practical interest, these attributes are often the least well-understood ones. One of the reasons is that they have several facets, i.e., there are several different ways to interpret them.

Reliability is one of the external software attributes that have received the most attention, because it is probably one of the best-understood one, and the one for which it is easiest to use for mathematical concepts. Reliability as an attribute has been studied in several other fields, including computer hardware. Therefore, a vast literature was available when software reliability studies began and an accepted definition of reliability was available. For software engineering applications, reliability may be defined as the probability that a specified program behaves correctly in a specified environment in a specified period of time. As such, reliability depends on the environment in which the program is used. For instance, it is to be expected that a program's reliability is different during testing than it is during operational use. There is an important difference between software and other traditional fields in which reliability has been studied. Software does not wear out, as does hardware, for instance. Thus, software reliability studies have devised new reliability models that can be used in the software field. Most of these models [29] provide an estimate of reliability based on the time series of the failures, i.e., the times at which failures have occurred.

Another important product attribute is the detectability of faults in a software artifact. It is an external attribute in that it depends on the environment (e.g. techniques) and the time span in which the software artifact is examined. Therefore, it is not to be confused with the presence of faults in a software artifact. Faults may be detected in all software artifacts, and the nature of the specific artifact at hand influences the type of methods used to uncover faults. For instance, testing may be used to uncover faults on formal artifacts, such as programs, but executable specifications as well. As another example, inspections may be used with most sorts of artifacts. The simplest measure of the detectability of faults is the number of faults uncovered in a software artifact. This number may provide an idea of the quality of the artifact. However, it is usually useful to identify different categories of faults, which can be for instance classified according to their criticality from the user's viewpoint or the software developers' viewpoint. A problem may be the definition itself of a fault. For instance, suppose that a variable is used in several points of a program instead of another one. Does the program contain one fault or is every occurrence of the incorrect variable to be considered a single fault? Unambiguous guidelines should be provided and consistently applied to prevent these problems. A related attribute is the detectability of software failures in software products.

## 9. Measures for Process Attributes

A number of process attributes are well understood, because they are closer to intuition than product attributes. For instance, these attributes include development effort, cost, and time. Process attributes often have an industrial interest. Building measures for these attributes is not a problem, as long as some consistent criterion is used, so measures are reliable and comparable across projects or environments. Process attributes are also used for tracking software project progress and checking whether there are problems with its schedule and resources. A number of derived attributes are of industrial attributes. For instance, productivity is a popular attribute and may have different facets depending on the process phase in which it is applied. As an example, in the coding phase, one may interpret productivity in terms of the amount of product or functionality delivered per unit time; in the verification phase, productivity may be interpreted in terms of the failures caused per unit time. These derived attributes may pose a definition problem. For instance, measuring coding productivity as the number of lines of code produced in the unit time may unjustly reward long programs. A more general problem that involves many process attributes is prediction, i.e., managing to link their measures with measures for internal product and process attributes, especially those that are available in the early development phases. Examples on how measures for process attributes may be used are shown in Sec. 10.3.

Software process measurement is an important part of improvement and maturity assessment frameworks. An example of improvement framework is the QIP, as briefly mentioned in Sec. 2. Several maturity assessment framework exist, among which the Capability Maturity Model (CMM) [30] is probably the best known one. The CMM defines five maturity levels at which a software organization may be classified. At each level, the CMM defines a number of Key Problem Areas (KPAs), i.e., issues that a software organization needs to address to progress up to the next maturity level. Process measurement is one of the KPAs addressed at the CMM level 3 (Defined Level), so the software organization may reach the CMM level 4 (Managed Level). The reader may refer to [31] for further information on software process measurement.

## 10. Practical Application of Measurement

There are several important aspects in the practical application of measurement, all of which derive from the fact that measurement should be seen as an activity that provides value added to the development process.

## 10.1. *Experimental design*

The measurement goals also determine the specific "experimental design" to be used. We have put "experimental design" in quotes, because that is the term used by the scientific literature, but application of software measurement does not necessarily entail carrying out a full-fledged scientific experiment, i.e., one where hypotheses are confirmed or disconfirmed. What we mean here is that the measures to be defined, the data to be collected, and the results that can be expected should be clearly specified, and that a suitable measurement process should be put in place. At any rate, it is not the goal of this paper to describe the various experimental designs that can be used in software measurement even when one wants to carry out a real scientific experiment. We simply want to highlight that it is important to identify an experimental design that is consistent with the defined goals and the expected results. This might seem obvious, but problems sometimes have arisen in the scientific literature and practical applications for a variety of reasons, e.g. the measures were not the right ones for the quantification of the attributes, the specific experimental design could not lead to the stated conclusions, other reasons could be found for the results obtained, hidden assumptions were present, etc.

## 10.2. *Data collection*

Data collection is not a trivial part of software measurement, and may well take a large amount of time and effort. Therefore, data collection should be designed and planned carefully. Based on the measures that have been defined, data collection requires the identification of

- all the points of the process at which data can and should be collected;
- the artifacts that need to be analyzed;
- who is responsible for collecting data;
- who should provide data; and
- the ways in which data can/should be collected (e.g. via questionnaires, interviews, automated tools, manual inspection).

Data collection should be as little invasive as possible, i.e., it should not perturb the software development process and distract developers from their primary goals. Therefore, all activities that can be automated should be automated indeed. This can be done by building automated analyzers for software code, to obtain data for the measures of internal software attributes.

More importantly, the collection of data that involves human intervention should be automated to the extent possible. For instance, electronic data forms should be used to collect project data from the software developers and managers, instead of other kinds of data collection. These forms should be

- complete but concise, i.e., ask for only the information that is necessary to collect from developers and managers so that they should not use much time filling the forms out;

- clear, i.e., the meaning of the information that is required should be straightforward to developers and managers, so they can provide accurate and precise answers in little time.

Automated collection has also the positive effect of feeding the data directly into the database that contains the values, so they can be used for interpretation and analysis.

Data collection should be timely. Sometimes, data are reconstructed *a posteriori*. Though this procedure may provide useful pieces of information, there is a danger that these data are not reliable.

Not all the collected data can be used. Some data may be incomplete (e.g. some important pieces of information are missing), inconsistent (e.g. they conflict with each other), or incorrect (e.g. some values may be out of the admissible range). Before the data analysis, all these data should be removed from the database and lessons should be learned to prevent — to the extent possible — the reoccurrence of such problems.

## 10.3. *Data analysis*

Data analysis can be used to carry out the so-called empirical validation of software measures, i.e., show that a measure is useful towards some parameter of industrial interest (as opposed to the so-called theoretical validation of measures as described in Secs. 5 and 6, which entails providing sufficient evidence that a measure really quantifies the attribute it purports to measure). This is obtained through the building of models, based on a number of techniques.

It would be well beyond the scope of this article to provide a thorough examination of the techniques that can be used to analyze software measurement data, since a vast literature is available about data analysis. At any rate, we would like to point out that, besides well-known and well-established statistical techniques such as linear regression or principal component analysis [32], there are a number of other techniques that have been used for data analysis in software engineering measurement. However, it is necessary to point out a few problems of statistical analyses (e.g. see [33]). For instance, the existence of a statistical correlation between two variables does not show the existence of causal relation between them. In addition, given a large number of variables, there is a high likelihood that at least two of them are linked by a statistical correlation. Therefore, some care should be used in interpreting a statistical correlation relation between variables.

New statistical techniques have been borrowed from other disciplines. For instance, Logistic Regression [34] has been used originally in medicine. In its simplest form, Logistic Regression estimates the probability that an object belongs to either of two classes, based on the values of measures of attributes of the object. Based on a threshold value on the estimated probability, objects are classified as belonging to either class. For instance, Logistic Regression has been used in software measurement to predict whether a software module is faulty based on the values of measures collected on the module.

Machine-learning based techniques have been borrowed from artificial intelligence, e.g. classification trees [35]. Other machine-learning techniques, e.g. Optimized Set Reduction [36] have been defined in the context of software measurement. These techniques divide a set of objects into subsets in a stepwise fashion based on the values of measures for classification purposes. The goal is to obtain subsets that are homogeneous with respect to the values of a measure for some attribute of interest. For instance, these techniques can be used to predict which modules are faulty.

Models have been built that relate measures for internal product attributes and process attributes, on the one side, to measures for external product attributes or process attributes, on the other side. For instance, models have been defined that relate a number of measures such as LOC, v(G), etc to software fault-proneness, cost, etc (a review can be found in [1]). Among the best known ones, COnstructive COst MOdel (COCOMO) [37] defines a family of models that allow for the estimation of software cost based on LOC and a number of attributes belonging to four categories, i.e., product attributes, computer attributes, personnel attributes, and project attributes. The measures for these attributes are computed in a subjective way. COCOMO has undergone several changes over the years, with the new COCOMO 2 [38].

At any rate, the derivation and use of sophisticated models may not be justified in various application cases. For instance, suppose that software measurement is used in a software project for tracking purposes and the focus is on elapsed time, to check whether the project is being carried out according to the original schedule. A simple comparison between the original schedule and the actual one will be probably sufficient for identifying schedule slippage. Figure 6 shows the comparison between two simple GANTT diagrams of a project that is running behind its original schedule.

As another example, Fig. 7 shows the number of failures (divided according to their criticality level) found in a series of consecutive baselines (i.e., intermediate releases) through which a software product goes during coding and testing.

The data in Fig. 7 may be used during coding and verification to monitor, evaluate, and control the software process. For instance, Fig. 7 shows that the number of failures decreases in the last baselines, which suggests that the number

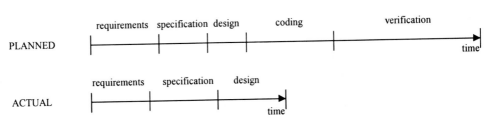

**Fig. 6.**  Simple GANTT diagrams for a project.

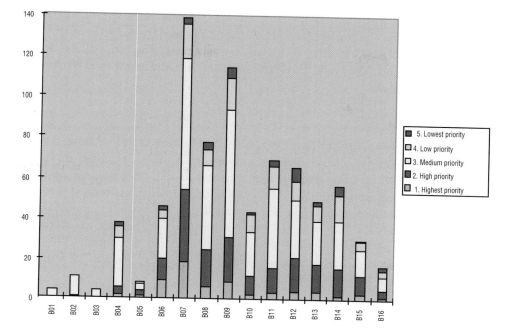

**Fig. 7.** Failures per priority per baseline.

of faults in the software is decreasing too. The figure also shows that the number of highest priority failures is kept under control. More information on the topic may be found in [39, 40].

## 10.4. *Interpretation and use of results*

The final goal of measurement in industrial environments is not to validate measures or build models, but to make the results obtained available to software practitioners, who can use them in future projects. First, measurement results should be interpreted by the software developers and managers of the environment(s) in which the data have been collected. They are the ones that have the necessary knowledge to understand and explain the phenomena that have been studied through measurement. Researchers might provide tentative explanations and interpretations, but these can hardly be conclusive if they are not validated by software practitioners. For instance, only the knowledge of the software process and the specific project may explain why there are few failures before baseline 4 in the project whose data are shown in Fig. 7 and there is a peak for baseline 7.

Second, it is imperative to understand how the measurement results are to be used. It should be clear from the start of a measurement program that measurement will not be used to judge people, but to help them. If this is not clear, the measurement program is doomed to failure, because a measurement program should always be seen as a part of an improvement process, which entails providing better ways for software practitioners to carry out their duties. In addition, there is a danger that software practitioners will not cooperate in data collection or, if they do, provide reliable information. Thus, the measurement program will be doubly unsuccessful, in that it provides bad data and results that are not used to improve software development [39].

## 10.5. *Standards*

Standards for software quality have been defined. The best known of these is probably ISO/IEC 9126 [41], which defines software quality as composed of six external attributes of interest, namely, functionality, reliability, efficiency, usability, maintainability, and portability. In turn, each of these qualities is refined into sub-attributes. For instance, maintainability is refined into analyzability, modifiability, stability, and testability. The "weights" of the external attributes and sub-attributes may vary according to the product whose quality is under evaluation. The main problems with this standard and other quality models (e.g. see McCall's quality model [42]) are that it is not clear

- whether the set of attributes is complete;
- whether an attribute should be such or it should be a sub-attribute, and whether a sub-attribute should be an attribute, instead; and
- what the definitions are for the attributes and their measures (as explained in Secs. 5 and 6).

## 11. Future Developments

Future work on software measurement will encompass both theoretical and practical activities. On the theoretical side, studies are needed to better characterize the relevant attributes to be studied and the properties of their measures. On the application side, measurement needs to be introduced in traditional development environments and in new ones, such as web-based applications.

## References

1. N. E. Fenton and S. L. Pfleeger, *Software Metrics: A Rigorous and Practical Approach*, 2nd ed. (International Thomson Publishing, London, 1996).
2. IEEE Software, Special Issue on Measurement **14** (1997).
3. V. R. Basili and D. Weiss, "A methodology for collecting valid software engineering data", *IEEE Transactions on Software Engineering* **10** (1984) 728–738.
4. V. R. Basili and H. D. Rombach, "The tame project: Towards improvement-oriented software environments", *IEEE Transactions on Software Engineering* **14** (1988) 758–773.
5. F. S. Roberts, *Measurement Theory with Applications to Decisionmaking, Utility, and the Social Sciences* (Addison-Wesley, Reading, MA, 1979).
6. H. Zuse, *A Framework of Software Measurement* (Walter de Gruyter, Berlin, 1998).
7. M. Kendall and A. Stuart, *The Advanced Theory of Statistics*, 4th ed. (Charles Griffin & Co., London, UK, 1977).

8. R. E. Prather, "An axiomatic theory of software complexity measure", *The Computer Journal* **27** (1984) 340–346.

9. E. J. Weyuker, "Evaluating software complexity measures", *IEEE Transactions on Software Engineering* **14** (1988) 1357–1365.

10. J. Tian and M. V. Zelkowitz, "A formal program complexity model and its application", *Journal of System Software* **17** (1992) 253–266.

11. L. C. Briand, S. Morasca and V. R. Basili, "Property-based software engineering measurement", *IEEE Transactions on Software Engineering* **22** (1996) 68–86.

12. A. J. Albrecht and J. Gaffney, "Software function, source lines of code and development effort prediction", *IEEE Transactions on Software Engineering* **9** (1983) 639–648.

13. D. R. Jeffery, G. C. Low and M. Barnes, "A comparison of function point counting techniques", *IEEE Transactions on Software Engineering* **19** (1993) 529–532.

14. C. Jones, *Programmer Productivity* (McGraw-Hill, New York, 1986).

15. C. R. Symons, "Function point analysis: Difficulties and improvements", *IEEE Transactions on Software Engineering* **14** (1988) 2–11.

16. A. Abran and P. N. Robillard, "Function points: A study of their measurement processes and scale transformations", *Journal of System and Software* **25** (1994) 171–184.

17. L. C. Briand and S. Morasca, "Software measurement and formal methods: A case study centered on TRIO+ specifications", *Proceedings of ICFEM'97*, Hiroshima, Japan (November 1997) pp. 315–325.

18. K. Finney, K. Rennolls and A. Fedorec, "Measuring the comprehensibility of Z specifications", *Journal of System. and Software* **42** (1998) 3–15.

19. L. C. Briand, S. Morasca and V. R. Basili, "Defining and validating measures for object-based high-level design", *IEEE Transactions on Software Engineering* **25** (1999) 722–741.

20. S. R. Chidamber and C. F. Kemerer, "A metrics suite for object oriented design", *IEEE Transactions on Software Engineering* **20** (1994) 476–498.

21. F. B. Abreu and R. Carapuca, "Candidate metrics for object-oriented software within a taxonomy framework", *Journal of System and Software* **23** (1994) 87–96.

22. S. Henry and D. Kafura, "Software structure metrics based on information flow", *IEEE Transactions on Software Enginering* **7** (1981) 510–518.

23. M. Halstead, *Elements of Software Science* (Elsevier, North Holland, New York, 1977).

24. T. J. McCabe, "A complexity measure", *IEEE Transactions on Software Enginering* **2** (1976) 308–320.

25. V. R. Basili, L. C. Briand and W. L. Melo, "A validation of object-oriented design metrics as quality indicators", *IEEE Transactions on Software Engineering* **22** (1996) 751–761.

26. L. Briand, J. Daly and J. Wuest, "A unified framework for cohesion measurement in object-oriented systems", *Empirical Software Engineering — An International Journal* (1998).

27. L. Briand, J. Daly and J. Wuest, "A unified framework for coupling measurement in object-oriented systems", *IEEE Transactions on Software Engineering* (1999).

28. J. Bieman and L. M. Ott, "Measuring functional cohesion", *IEEE Transactions on Software Engineering* **20** (1994) 644–657.

29. J. D. Musa, A. Iannino and K. Okumoto, *Software Reliability: Prediction and Application* (McGraw-Hill, New York, 1987).

30. M. C. Paulk, C. V. Weber and B. Curtis, *The Capability Maturity Model: Guidelines for Improving the Software Process* (Addison-Wesley, 1995).

31. IEEE Software, Special Issue on Measurement-Based Process Improvement **11** (1994).

32. J. C. Munson and T. M Khoshgoftaar, "The detection of fault-prone programs", *IEEE Transactions on Software Engineering* **18** (1992) 423–433.
33. R. E. Courtney and D. A.Gustafson, "Shotgun correlations in software measures", *Software Engineering Journal* (January 1993) 5–13.
34. D. W. Hosmer and S. Lemeshow, *Applied Logistic Regression* (John Wiley & Sons, Inc., New York, 1989).
35. R. W. Selby and A. A. Porter, "Learning from examples: Generation and evaluation of decision trees for software resource analysis", *IEEE Transactions on Software Engineering* **14** (1988) 1743–1757.
36. L. C. Briand, V. R. Basili and W. M. Thomas, "A pattern recognition approach for software engineering data analysis", *IEEE Transactions on Software Engineering* **18** (1992) 931–942.
37. B. W. Boehm, *Software Engineering Economics* (Prentice-Hall, Englewood Cliffs, 1981).
38. B. W. Boehm, B. Clark, E. Horowitz *et al*, "Cost models for future life cycle processes: COCOMO 2.0", *Annals of Software Engineering* **1** (1995) 1–24.
39. R. B. Grady, *Practical Software Metrics for Project Management and Process Improvement* (Prentice-Hall, Englewood Cliffs, 1992).
40. W. Royce, *Software Project Management: A Unified Framework* (Addison-Wesley, 1998).
41. International Standards Organization, Information Technology — Software Product Evaluation — Quality Characteristics and Guidelines for Their Use, ISO/IEC9126, Geneva, Switzerland (1991).
42. J. A. McCall, P. K. Richards and G. F. Walters, "Factors in software quality", RADC TR-77-369, Rome Air Development Center, 1977.

# SOFTWARE ENGINEERING STANDARDS: REVIEW AND PERSPECTIVES

YINGXU WANG

*Department of Electrical and Computer Engineering, University of Calgary,*
*Room ENA206B, 2500 University Drive, NW, Calgary, Alberta, Canada T2N 1N4*
*E-mail: wangyx@enel.ucalgary.ca*

Standardization in software engineering plays an important role for integrating, regulating, and optimizing existing best practices and fundamental theories in software development and organization. An idiom says that one can "gain new knowledge by reviewing the past". This chapter reviews current software engineering and software quality related standards and the history of their development. Usability and open issues in applications of the major software engineering standards are discussed. Future trends and research topics considered significant and worthy of being explored are suggested in this chapter.

*Keywords*: Software engineering, processes, quality, standards, models, best practices, foundations, trends, process-based software engineering.

## 1. Introduction

Along with the rapid growth of the software industry in the last decades, software engineering has been an increasingly important discipline. For the most dynamic and innovative discipline, standardization is an attempt to integrate, regulate, and optimize existing best practices and theories developed in research and adopted in the industry. Software engineering standardization is covered by the research inherent to ISO/IEC/JTC1 Software Engineering Subcommittee (SC7) and ISO Technical Committee 176 (TC176) on quality management and quality assurance.

Major software engineering standards developed in ISO/IEC JTC1/SC7 recently are ISO/IEC 12207 (1995) [49] — Software Life Cycle Processes, and ISO/IEC TR 15504 (1999) [51–59] — Software Process Assessment. In addition, ISO/IEC CD 15288 (1999) [50] — System Life Cycle Processes is under development.

A number of international standards on generic quality systems have been developed, such as ISO 9126 — Quality Characteristics and Guidelines for Their Use [46], ISO 10011 — Guidelines for Auditing Quality Systems [47], and ISO 10013 — Guidelines for Developing Quality Manuals [48]. A major serial standard developed by ISO TC176 is ISO 9000 [34–38]. ISO 9000 has been recognized worldwide for establishing quality systems. Within ISO 9000, ISO 9001 [34, 39, 40] and ISO 9000-3 [42] are applicable to software quality systems for certifying the processes, products and services within a software development organization according to the ISO 9000 model.

This chapter reviews major software engineering and software quality standards, and philosophies behind them. The usability of current standards in applications is evaluated, and open issues of them are discussed by using the body of empirical and theoretical studies [66, 83, 86, 89–94]. Perspectives on trends and future development in software engineering standardization are provided.

## 2. A Brief History of Standardization in Software Engineering

There are two main historical threads in tracing the emergence of software engineering standards. They are software engineering itself and applications of management science in software engineering.

Research into the engineering processes and management principles in management sciences began in the 60's [1, 62, 63, 78, 81]. In the 70's and 80's, management science was well established in almost all branches. Worthy of particular note are Crosby, Juran and Deming who developed the approach of quality conformity to requirements and specifications [16, 17, 63] and proposed a number of agendas that must be carried out in order to deliver total quality. These concepts have largely influenced software engineering processes and software quality assurance technology. In 1982, the Deming Circle, Plan-Do-Check-Act (PDCA), was proposed [17] and received much attention in software process modeling and analysis. Then, a project designated ISO TC176 in 1987 to develop an international standard for quality systems [34–38] was implemented. The ISO 9000 standards are applicable to a wide range of engineering systems, with ISO 9001 particularly focusing on software engineering [15, 34, 39, 40].

In the software engineering sector, studies on the software engineering process can be traced to as early as 1965 in Weinwurm and Zagorski's work. However, interest in the software process was initiated in the 70's after the so called "software crisis" [3, 14, 69]. The software process as a recognized branch of software engineering was formed in the 80's following the work of Basili [4], Aron [2], Evans [23], Boehm [7–9], Gilb [26], Humphrey [27–29]. These works led to the development of the capability maturity model (CMM) [27, 70–72] and several other models, such as the IEEE Software Engineering Standards [32, 33] and British Standard BS 5750 [15] in the late 80's. Since then, the software engineering process has attracted much interest and recognition in software engineering research, practices, and standardization.

### 2.1. *Software engineering process standardization*

In 1987, a Software Engineering Subcommittee (SC7) was established by the ISO/IEC Joint Technical Committee-1 (JTC1) in order to recognize the importance and requirements for a set of software engineering standards. Since then, a dozen working groups (WGs) have been founded to cover specific software engineering areas such as, *inter alia*:

- WG7: Life cycle management.
- WG8: Support of software life cycle processes.
- WG9: Software integrity.
- WG10: Software process assessment.
- WG11: Software engineering data definition and representation.
- WG13: Software measurement framework.

The major outputs of ISO/IEC JTC1/SC7 WG8 are ISO/IEC 12207 (1995) — Software Life Cycle Processes [49], and ISO/IEC CD 15288 (1999) — System Life Cycle Processes (Draft) [50]. ISO/IEC JTC1/SC7 WG10 focuses on ISO/IEC 15504 (1998/1999) — Software Process Assessment [51–59]. A recent trend of ISO/IEC TR 15504 is to align its process dimension to ISO/IEC 12207. In addition, extensions of ISO/IEC TR 15504 have been proposed to cover broader system life cycle processes such as acquisition processes and system environment processes [20].

The list of JTC1/SC7 working groups is still expanding. As software engineering theory, methodologies, and practices evolve, we may expect more areas to be covered in software engineering standardization, such as system requirement definition, domain knowledge infrastructure, software architecture and frameworks, software engineering notations, etc.

## 2.2. *Software quality standardization*

Software quality system standardization is carried out by the ISO Technical Committee 176 (TC176) on quality management and quality assurance. ISO TC176 was initiated in 1979 with subcommittees working on generic quality systems and supporting technologies.

Major standards developed by ISO TC176 are the ISO 9000 family [34–45], and ISO 9126 software quality characteristics [46]. Within ISO 9000, ISO 9001 [34, 39, 40] and ISO 9000-3 [37] are specially oriented to software quality systems for certifying the processes, products, and services within a software development organization. For absorbing the experience in developing process-based software engineering standards, ISO 9000/9001 are under revision currently [34], and this will be described in Sec. 4.6.

All current software quality and software process standards are based on generic quality system principles developed in management sciences, such as the following:

- Statistical quality control.
- Total quality management (TQM).
- Continuous improvement.

These principles are considered to benefit from the pioneering work of Walter Shewhart (1939) [80], Joseph Juran (1962) [62], Philip Crosby (1979) [16], W. Edwards Deming (1982) [17] and others.

### 2.3. *Interrelationship between current software engineering standards*

A number of software engineering standards and models have been developed in the last decade, such as TickIT [22, 84, 85], ISO 9001 [34, 39, 40], CMM [27–29, 70–73], ISO/IEC 12207 [49], ISO/IEC 15504 (SPICE) [51–59]. In addition, a number of regional and internal models [6, 15] have been adopted. According to a recent worldwide survey [86, 89, 91], the ISO 9001 standard are the most popular in software engineering, followed by CMM and ISO/IEC TR 15504. Some regional, internal, and industry sectors' process models, such as Trillium, also share a significant part of application in the software industry.

The SEI Capability Maturity Model (CMM) was initially developed as an assessment model for software engineering management capabilities of software providers [27, 28]. As such it was expected that it would provide useful measurement for organizations bidding or tendering for software contracts. It was soon found that the concept of "process" for software engineering has more utility than that of capability assessment, and that software development organizations may use the process model for internal process improvement. As a result of this deeper understanding, new practices in process-based software engineering have been emerging in the last decade. This is considered as one of the important inspirations arising from CMM and related research.

From another angle of management sciences looking at software engineering, ISO 9001 and ISO 9000-3 were developed. ISO 9001 (Quality Systems — Model for Quality Assurance in Design, Development, Production, Installation, and Servicing) [34, 39, 40], and ISO 9000-3 (Quality Management and Quality Assurance Standards Part 3 — Guidelines for the Application of ISO 9000 to the Development, Supply, and Maintenance of Software) [37] are important parts of ISO 9000, and are designed for software engineering.

In 1992, the ISO/IEC JTC1 software engineering committee recognized a need to develop a new international standard for software process assessment and improvement. Then, after a six-year international collaborative project (SPICE) within the ISO/IEC JTC1/SC7/WG10, an ISO 15504 Technical Report suite was completed. Inspired by a European research project, BOOTSTRAP [12, 67], ISO/IEC 15504 has recognized the value inherent in separating the "process" dimension from the "capability" dimension in a software engineering process model. As a result, a true two-dimensional process system model was developed for the first time. However, what is interesting is that in the ISO/IEC TR 15504 model, the activities for the process dimension and the attributes for the capability dimension at some points overlap. This means that there is still a need to further distinguish the process activities and the measurement attributes as well as their indicators in the two dimensions.

## 3. Review of Current Software Engineering Standards and Models

According to a number of worldwide surveys in the software industry, widely accepted software engineering standards are ISO 9001, CMM, ISO 9126, and ISO/IEC 15504 [66, 86, 89, 91]. This section reviews the four major software engineering standards and models. The technical frameworks and usability of these standards are described and evaluated based on industrial trial experience and reports [83, 86, 88, 90–94].

### 3.1. *CMM*

The capability maturity model (CMM) was the first process methodology that tried to model software engineering process systems. CMM [27–29, 70–73] was initially developed in the Software Engineering Institute (SEI) at Carnegie-Mellon University in 1987. The current version of CMM (Version 1.1) was released in 1993.

The requirements for distinguishing and selecting matured software providers led to the development of the SEI method for assessing software project contractors [28, 29] and the SEI capability maturity model (CMM) for software [70–73]. A set of important concepts and successful experience, such as process, quality, and management techniques, have been introduced into software engineering from management sciences.

However, in addition to the initial goals of CMM for software engineering management capability modeling and software organization maturity measurement, researchers and the software industry soon realized that the concept of software process introduced in CMM is a universal model for organizing software engineering. This led to the studies in a new approach to *process-based software engineering* [87] and the development of a number of new software process models and standards.

CMM (V.1.1) was developed by Paulk and his colleagues [70] with the supplement of a set of detailed key practices in Paulk *et al* [71], and a questionnaire in Zubrow *et al* [95]. A summary of differences between Version 1.0 and Version 1.1 is provided in [72]. For more background and related work that led to the development of CMM, see Humphrey and his colleagues [27–29].

Applications and case studies of CMM were reported in Humphrey *et al* [31], Kitson and Masters [64], and Saiedian and Kuzara [77]. For looking at relationships of CMM with other process models, see Paulk *et al* [74], Kitson [65], Wang *et al* [86, 88–94]. Criticism on CMM may be referred to Bollinger and McGowan [11], Brodman and Johnson [13], and Fayad and Laitinen [24, 25]. Readers may also be interested in reading the counterpoint comments on Bollinger and McGowan's article by Humphrey and Curtis [30].

### 3.1.1. *Framework of the CMM process model*

CMM models 18 key practice areas and 150 key practices. These key practices and key practice areas are grouped into a 5-level process capability maturity scale known as the initial, repeatable, defined, managed, and optimizing levels. What is significant is the systematic breakdown of software engineering activities, and the analytical judgement of process capability levels that the model allows.

A hierarchical structure of the CMM framework is shown in Table 1.

**Table 1.**   Structure of the CMM framework.

| ID. | Level | Key Practice Area (KPA) | Identified Key Practices |
|---|---|---|---|
| $CL_1$ | Initial | | 0 |
| $CL_2$ | Repeated | | 62 |
| $KPA_{2.1}$ | | Requirement management | 3 |
| $KPA_{2.2}$ | | Software project planning | 15 |
| $KPA_{2.3}$ | | Software project tracking and oversight | 13 |
| $KPA_{2.4}$ | | Software subcontract management | 13 |
| $KPA_{2.5}$ | | Software quality assurance | 8 |
| $KPA_{2.6}$ | | Software configuration management | 10 |
| $CL_3$ | Defined | | 50 |
| $KPA_{3.1}$ | | Organization process focus | 7 |
| $KPA_{3.2}$ | | Organization process definition | 6 |
| $KPA_{3.3}$ | | Training program | 6 |
| $KPA_{3.4}$ | | Integrated software management | 11 |
| $KPA_{3.5}$ | | Software product engineering | 10 |
| $KPA_{3.6}$ | | Intergroup coordination | 7 |
| $KPA_{3.7}$ | | Peer reviews | 3 |
| $CL_4$ | Managed | | 12 |
| $KPA_{4.1}$ | | Quantitative process management | 7 |
| $KPA_{4.2}$ | | Software quality management | 5 |
| $CL_5$ | Optimizing | | 26 |
| $KPA_{5.1}$ | | Defect prevention | 8 |
| $KPA_{5.2}$ | | Technology change management | 8 |
| $KPA_{5.3}$ | | Process change management | 10 |

### 3.1.2. *Process capability scale*

CMM develops a five-level software process capability model as shown in Table 2 [70]. Each capability level is defined in the table with supplemental description of capability performance indicators in the last column.

**Table 2.** The CMM process capability model.

| Capability Level | Title | Description | Performance Indicator |
|---|---|---|---|
| $CL_1$ | Initial | At this level, the software process is characterized as *ad hoc*, and occasionally even chaotic. Few processes are defined, and success depends on individual effort. | Schedule and cost targets are typically overrun. |
| $CL_2$ | Repeated | At this level, basic project management processes are established to track cost, schedule, and functionality. The necessary process discipline is in place to repeat earlier successes on projects with similar applications. | Plans based on past performance are more realistic. |
| $CL_3$ | Defined | At this level, the software process for both management and engineering activities is documented, standardized, and integrate into a standard software process for the organization. All projects use an approved, tailored version of the organization's standard software process for developing and maintaining software. | Performance improves with well-defined processes. |
| $CL_4$ | Managed | At this level, detailed measures of the software process and product quality are collected. Both the software process and products are quantitatively understood and controlled. | Performance continues to improve based on quantitative understanding of process and product. |
| $CL_5$ | Optimizing | At this level, continuous process improvement is enabled by quantitative feedback from the process and from piloting innovative ideas and technologies. | Performance continuously improves to increase process efficiency, eliminate costly rework, and allow development time to be shortened. |

### 3.1.3. *Evaluation of CMM*

The design philosophy behind CMM is a software project contractor's perception on the organizational and managerial capacity of a software development organization. It has been noted, however, that interpretations of CMM have been shifted from the original second-party point of view to the third-party and first-party-oriented applications in the software industry.

Despite the fact that programming had been a profession for almost half a century, it is noteworthy that the software industry is still relatively young, and the discipline of software engineering is still being built. Because of the systematic studies in developing CMM, the process approach as an overarching methodology to software engineering is widely accepted by researchers and the software industry. CMM has developed a stepwise software engineering process assessment and improvement methodology. It is relatively easy in application and has intensive adoption in the software industry worldwide.

However, CMM is a 1-D process model and there is no distinction between the dimensions of process and capability. This inherent limitation of CMM results in a number of structural arguments about whether CMM provided a process dimension or a capability dimension in process system modeling. There were also logical arguments about CMM concerning whether we would recommend the implementation of only a subset of a whole process system for a software organization each time if all processes in the system were considered essential for producing quality software [86].

## 3.2. *ISO* 9001

ISO 9000 [34–45] is a set of international standards for quality systems. It is designed for quality management and assurance, and specifies the basic requirements for the development, production, installation, and servicing at system and product levels. ISO 9000 provides a quality-system-oriented approach to the organization and management of production and service industries. ISO 9000 was first published in 1987 and revised in 1994, and is updating again currently [34].

Within the ISO 9000 suite, ISO 9001 [34, 39, 40] and ISO 9000-3 [37] are applicable to the software process and quality systems for a software development organization. ISO 9001 aims to set minimum requirements for a general quality management system. The ISO 9001 model is generic, simple, and it has been accepted and supported worldwide.

There are a number of derived versions of ISO 9000 standards adopted by national or regional standardization bodies, such as: ANSI/ASQC 9001 in the USA, EN29001 in Europe, BS/EN29001 in the UK, and AS/NZS 9001 in Australia and New Zealand. Some variation or extension of ISO 9000 standards also exist, such as IEEE 1298 [33] and TickIT [84, 85].

In Jenner's work [61], a set of 177 management issues was identified in the ISO 9001 conformance checklist for assessors based on the ISO 9001 revised version in 1994. Wang *et al* [86, 88–94] presented a series of comparative analyses of relationships and mutual mappings between major process models including ISO 9001. According to Wang *et al* [86], those organizations that may pass the threshold of ISO 9001 assessment are equivalent to CMM capability levels 2–3. Referring to Zubrow's statistics [95], this implies that about 38% of those CMM-assessed organizations are technically at or above the ISO 9001 requirement level.

Seddon [79] set out 10 arguments against ISO 9000. He argued that the command-and-control ethos that pervades the ISO 9000 way of thinking — an inflexible compliance to a rigid set of written rules — is precisely what most companies do not need. He showed how real quality can be achieved by viewing the organization as a system and focusing on continuous improvement as the best means to create higher quality products and services.

### 3.2.1. *Framework of ISO 9001*

ISO 9001 models a basic set of requirements for establishing and maintaining a quality management and assurance system for software engineering. It identifies 20 main topic areas (MTAs) and 177 management issues (MIs), and categorized them into three subsystems known as management, product management, and development management. Perhaps because of its simplicity, ISO 9001 has been the most popular process model that is adopted in the software industry [68, 86, 89, 91]. An important characteristic of ISO 9001 is the underlying notion of a threshold standard and pass/fail criteria.

A hierarchical structure of the ISO 9001 framework is shown in Table 3.

**Table 3.**   Structure of the ISO 9001 framework.

| ID. | Subsystem | Main Topic Area (MTA) | Identified Management Issues |
|-----|-----------|-----------------------|------------------------------|
| $SS_1$ | Organization management | | 53 |
| $MTA_{1.1}$ | | Management responsibility | 15 |
| $MTA_{1.2}$ | | Quality system | 7 |
| $MTA_{1.3}$ | | Document and data control | 8 |
| $MTA_{1.4}$ | | Internal quality audits | 6 |
| $MTA_{1.5}$ | | Corrective and preventive action | 6 |
| $MTA_{1.6}$ | | Quality system records | 7 |
| $MTA_{1.7}$ | | Training | 4 |
| $SS_2$ | Product management | | 31 |
| $MTA_{2.1}$ | | Product management | 4 |
| $MTA_{2.2}$ | | Control of customer-supplied product | 4 |

**Table 3.** (*Continued*)

| ID. | Subsystem | Main Topic Area (MTA) | Identified Management Issues |
|---|---|---|---|
| MTA$_{2.3}$ | | Purchasing | 8 |
| MTA$_{2.4}$ | | Handling, storage, packaging, preservation, and delivery | 9 |
| MTA$_{2.5}$ | | Control of nonconforming product | 6 |
| SS$_3$ | Development management | | 93 |
| MTA$_{3.1}$ | | Contract reviews | 9 |
| MTA$_{3.2}$ | | Process control | 23 |
| MTA$_{3.3}$ | | Design and development control | 30 |
| MTA$_{3.4}$ | | Inspection and testing | 11 |
| MTA$_{3.5}$ | | Inspection and test status | 2 |
| MTA$_{3.6}$ | | Control of inspection, measuring, and test equipment | 12 |
| MTA$_{3.7}$ | | Statistical techniques | 2 |
| MTA$_{3.8}$ | | Servicing and software maintenance | 4 |

### 3.2.2. *Evaluation of ISO 9001*

The design philosophy behind ISO 9001 is a generic quality system perception on software engineering. Although this philosophy has been proven successful in the conventional manufacturing industries, there is still a need for supporting evidence of its effectiveness and impact on the design-intensive software engineering and nonconventional software industries. It appears likely that software engineering is sufficiently unique as an engineering discipline in that it relies upon special foundations and applies a different philosophy [86]. Therefore, further studies on common features and differences between conventional mass manufacturing and software engineering are still expected.

ISO 9001 has developed a straightforward checklist-based process methodology for a quality management system of a software development organization. Because of its simplicity, ISO 9001 has been widely accepted and applied in the software industry. While, it is noteworthy that ISO 9001 lacks a staged process capability framework for software engineering process assessment and improvement. As a result, all software organizations that pass the ISO 9001 registration assessment may lost their motivation and identification of differences in long-term continued software engineering process improvement.

### 3.3. *ISO 9126*

Another key international software quality standard is ISO 9126 — Software Product Evaluation — Quality Characteristics and Guidelines for Their Use [46].

ISO 9126 extends principles of quality control to software engineering and summarizes the major characteristics and attributes of software quality.

### 3.3.1. *Framework of ISO 9126*

What is software quality and how to measure it? This is a significant issue in software engineering that we are still seeking solutions. Usually, quality software is perceived as the software that meets users' needs. However, for the same application system, users' needs may be different and informally described. Therefore, the quality of software is difficult to be verified according to this definition. Another definition perceives quality software as the software that contains fewer bugs. While, bugs as an internal feature of software, are difficult to identify and measure in practice.

The author defined software quality as a software system's inherent internal and external characteristics that show relative advantages over similar systems or indicate a conformance to a standard [86]. The central idea of this definition is to recognize that the quality of software (not quality software) is a relative concept. That is why we usually refer to the quality of a product as "higher" or "better".

ISO 9126 develops a collective way to perceive software quality. According to the philosophy of ISO 9126, software quality is a set of quantitative or qualitative characteristics and attributes. ISO 9126 provides a software quality model by defining 6 software quality characteristics and 20 attributes, which are intended to be exhaustive. An overview of ISO 9126 software quality model is shown in Table 4.

The major quality characteristics identified in ISO 9126, as shown in Table 4, are described below:

- **Functionality:** The characteristics that a system can provide specified services that meet users' requirements.
- **Reliability:** The probability that a system will fulfil the service during a given period whenever a user demands.
- **Usability:** The characteristics that a system is ready and easy for use when a user needs its service.
- **Efficiency:** The characteristics that a system uses minimum resources and provides timely response to an application.
- **Maintainability:** The probability that a system can be restored, within a given time after a failure, to provide the originally specified services.
- **Portability:** The characteristics that a system is capable of running on different target machines, operating systems, and network platforms.

### 3.3.2. *Evaluation of ISO 9126*

Software quality may be characterized by external and internal attributes. External quality characteristics are those which can be evaluated when executing the software; and internal quality characteristics are those which are evaluated by inspecting the internal features of the software. The former is user-oriented and

**Table 4.**    ISO 9126 software quality model.

| No. | Quality characteristics | Quality attributes |
|---|---|---|
| 1 | Functionality | |
| 1.1 | | Suitability |
| 1.2 | | Accuracy |
| 1.3 | | Interoperability |
| 1.4 | | Security |
| 2 | Reliability | |
| 2.1 | | Maturity |
| 2.2 | | Fault tolerance |
| 2.3 | | Recoverability |
| 3 | Usability | |
| 3.1 | | Understandability |
| 3.2 | | Learnability |
| 3.3 | | Operability |
| 4 | Efficiency | |
| 4.1 | | Time behavior |
| 4.2 | | Resource behavior |
| 5 | Maintainability | |
| 5.1 | | Analyzability |
| 5.2 | | Changeability |
| 5.3 | | Stability |
| 5.4 | | Testability |
| 6 | Portability | |
| 6.1 | | Adaptability |
| 6.2 | | Installability |
| 6.3 | | Conformance |
| 6.4 | | Replaceability |

may be verified by black-box testing techniques. While, the latter is oriented to developers and maintainers, and may be verified by white-box testing techniques.

ISO 9126 adopts a philosophy of the black-box that represents user's view on quality of software products and systems. Recent investigations [21, 75] argue that the ISO 9126 model focuses only on external characteristics of software quality. Substantial internal attributes of software quality, such as of architecture, reuse description, coding styles, test completeness, run-time efficiency, resource usage efficiency, and exception handling, have not been modeled. Another gap in ISO 9126's quality characteristic set is the lack of exception handling capability requirements for software [86]. The exception handling capability is an important attribute of software quality that identifies the unexpected circumstances and conditions of a system, and specifies how the system should behave under such conditions. Design for exception handling capability of software is recognized as a good sign to distinguish naive and professional software engineers and system analysts, even that a customer has not explicitly required for this kind of built-in software quality.

Further, it is found that the concept of software quality might be different between vendor-specified (common system) software and user-specified (applications) software. For the former, quality refers to the software that provides much more usability and higher dependability at a comparable price. While, for the latter, quality means the software that meets the user's requirements and runs with less failures. Also, it is considered that we need to distinguish the quality of software according to its developing processes. For example, we may identify the design quality, implementation quality, test quality, and maintenance quality of a software system, rather than pursuing a hybrid concept of the quality of software.

Generally, in a broad view, it is recognized that internal quality attributes of software can be measured and assured by software process standards and models. In this way, an interesting connection between software product quality standards (ISO 9126/ISO 9001) and software engineering process standards (ISO 15504/ISO 12207) may be established.

## 3.4. *ISO/IEC* 15504(*SPICE*)

ISO/IEC TR 15504 is an emerging international standard for software engineering process system assessment and improvement. SPICE, software process improvement and capability determination, is the name of the international project for the development of this standard.

The design philosophy behind ISO/IEC TR 15504 is to develop a set of structured capability measurements for all software lifecycle processes and for all parties, such as software developers, acquirers, contractors, and customers. ISO/IEC TR 15504 is a result of an international collaborative effort working towards developing an ISO software process assessment standard. ISO/IEC TR 15504 has incorporated experience and the improved understanding of software engineering processes gained in the development of CMM, BOOTSTRAP, ISO 9001, Trillium, and other models.

An ISO/IEC standard development is usually divided into three phases:

- DTR — Draft technical report.
- TR — Technical report.
- STD — Formal standard.

The international project SPICE was initiated in 1991. An ISO/IEC 15004 technical report (TR) was released in 1999 [51–59] as a final step before publishing as an international standard. Now ISO/IEC TR 15504 is in the third phase of user trials.

ISO/IEC TR 15504 develops a 2-D process capability assessment model with both a process and a process capability dimension based on the technology advances. ISO/IEC TR 15504 assesses a software development organization in the process dimension against the process attributes in the capability dimension. The 2-D framework of ISO/IEC TR 15504 provides a refined process assessment approach and a process improvement platform for process-based software engineering.

Dorling [18, 19] reviewed the initiative and history of the SPICE project and the early development phases of ISO/IEC TR 15504. Rout [76] highlighted the technical issues in ISO/IEC TR 15504 development. Kitson [65] related the ISO/IEC TR 15504 framework and ESI approach to software process assessment. Wang *et al* [86, 88–94] presented a series of comparative analyses of relationships and mutual mappings between major process models including ISO/IEC TR 15504. Wang *et al* [90] reported a conformance analysis case study between a tailored CMM and ISO/IEC TR 15504. For industrial experience reports on ISO/IEC TR 15504, see SPICE Phase 2 Trial Report [83]. For the latest development of ISO/IEC TR 15504 extensions for acquisition processes, see Dorling and Wang *et al* [20].

### 3.4.1. *Framework of ISO/IEC TR 15504*

ISO/IEC TR 15504 models 5 process categories, 35 processes, and 201 base practices. The processes are measured at 6 levels with 9 attributes. A hierarchical structure of the ISO/IEC TR 15504 framework is shown in Table 5.

**Table 5.**   Structure of the ISO/IEC TR 15504 framework.

| ID. | Process Category | Process | Identified Base Practices |
|-----|------------------|---------|---------------------------|
| CUS | Customer-supplier | | 39 |
| CUS.1 | | Acquire software product | 5 |
| CUS.2 | | Establish contract | 4 |
| CUS.3 | | Identify customer needs | 3 |
| CUS.4 | | Perform joint audits and reviews | 6 |
| CUS.5 | | Package, deliver and install software | 7 |
| CUS.6 | | Support operation of software | 7 |
| CUS.7 | | Provide customer service | 4 |
| CUS.8 | | Assess customer satisfaction | 3 |
| ENG | Engineering | | 32 |
| ENG.1 | | Develop system requirements | 4 |
| ENG.2 | | Develop software requirements | 5 |
| ENG.3 | | Develop software design | 4 |
| ENG.4 | | Implement software design | 3 |

**Table 5.** (*Continued*)

| ID. | Process Category | Process | Identified Base Practices |
|---|---|---|---|
| ENG.5 | | Integrate and test software | 6 |
| ENG.6 | | Integrate and test system | 5 |
| ENG.7 | | Maintain system and software | 5 |
| PRO | Project | | 50 |
| PRO.1 | | Plan project life cycle | 5 |
| PRO.2 | | Establish project plan | 10 |
| PRO.3 | | Build project teams | 4 |
| PRO.4 | | Manage requirements | 5 |
| PRO.5 | | Manage quality | 6 |
| PRO.6 | | Manage risks | 8 |
| PRO.7 | | Manage resources and schedule | 5 |
| PRO.8 | | Manage subcontractors | 7 |
| SUP | Support | | 32 |
| SUP.1 | | Develop documentation | 5 |
| SUP.2 | | Perform configuration management | 8 |
| SUP.3 | | Perform quality assurance | 5 |
| SUP.4 | | Perform problem resolution | 6 |
| SUP.5 | | Perform peer reviews | 8 |
| ORG | Organization | | 48 |
| ORG.1 | | Engineer the business | 6 |
| ORG.2 | | Define the process | 13 |
| ORG.3 | | Improve the process | 9 |
| ORG.4 | | Perform training | 4 |
| ORG.5 | | Enable reuse | 7 |
| ORG.6 | | Provide software engineering environment | 4 |
| ORG.7 | | Provide work facilities | 5 |
| Total | 5 | 35 | 201 |

### 3.4.2. *ISO/IEC TR* 15504 *process capability scale*

In the ISO/IEC TR 15504 capability dimension [52], a process capability scale is defined by capability levels with generic measurement aids known as process attributes. Process attributes are features of a process that can be evaluated on a scale of achievement that provides a measure of the capability of the process. The process attributes are designed as a set of generic measures of process capability, or as refinement of the given capability levels.

The process capability scale of ISO/IEC TR 15504 is defined at six levels with nine process attributes as shown in Table 6. The ISO/IEC TR 15504 capability levels generally consist of two process attributes except Level 1 (one attribute) and Level 0 (no attribute).

### 3.4.3. *Evaluation of ISO/IEC TR* 15504

Technically and historically, ISO/IEC TR 15504 has absorbed the basic capability rating scale from CMM; the software engineering process activities identified in ISO/IEC 12207, Trillium, and CMM; the attribute-based profile representation for process capability from BOOTSTRAP; and the general quality system management experience from ISO 9001. Major contributions of ISO/IEC TR 15504 are considered as follows:

- It is the first 2-D software engineering process model with a fully independent process dimension and capability dimension. As a result, the processes and/or practices have no longer been assigned a pre-allocated and fixed priority as those in CMM.
- A process assessment result may be represented by a 2-D process profile.
- There is a refined process capability scale with a set of nine generic process attributes at six capability levels.
- A set of conformance criteria has been defined for enabling external process models to be compared and to meet common requirements.

Open issues on ISO/IEC TR 15504 methodology and framework have been identified as follows [86]:

- It is found that the domain of ISO/IEC TR 15504 processes may need to be expanded significantly in order to provide a broader coverage and to increase compatibility with the existing process models.
- In ISO/IEC TR 15504 development and applications, there were difficulties in making the nine process attributes universally generic for all processes and base practices (BPs). As a result, it is often found that some of the attributes used as a rating scale were not suitable or applicable to some of the processes and BPs in assessment.
- The capability dimension of ISO/IEC TR 15504 has grown relatively complicated. It also introduced some extent of overlaps with the process

**Table 6.**  The ISO/IEC TR 15504 process capability model.

| ID. | Capability Level | Process Attribute | Description |
|---|---|---|---|
| CL[0] | Incomplete | | There is general failure to attain the purpose of the process. There are little or no easily identifiable work products or outputs of the process. |
| CL[1] | Performed | | The purpose of the process is generally achieved. The achievement may not be rigorously planned and tracked. Individuals within the organization recognize that an action should be performed, and there is general agreement that this action is performed as and when required. There are identifiable work products for the process, and these testify to the achievement of the purpose. |
| PA$_{11}$ | | Process performance | |
| CL[2] | Managed | | The process delivers work products according to specified procedures and is planned and tracked. Work products conform to specified standards and requirements. The primary distinction from the Performed Level is that the performance of the process now delivers work products that fulfil expressed quality requirements within defined timescales and resource needs. |
| PA$_{21}$ | | Performance management | |
| PA$_{22}$ | | Work product management | |
| CL[3] | Established | | The process is performed and managed using a defined process based upon good software engineering principles. Individual implementations of the process use approved, tailored versions of standard, documented processes to achieve the process outcomes. The resources necessary to establish the process definition are also in place. The primary distinction from the Managed Level is that the process of the Established Level is using a defined process that is capable of achieving its process outcomes. |
| PA$_{31}$ | | Process definition | |
| PA$_{32}$ | | Process resource | |

**Table 6.** (*Continued*)

| ID. | Capability Level | Process Attribute | Description |
|---|---|---|---|
| CL[4] | Predictable | | The defined process is performed consistently in practice within defined control limits to achieve its defined process goals. Detailed measures of performance are collected and analyzed. This leads to a quantitative understanding of process capability and an improved ability to predict and manage performance. Performance is quantitatively managed. The quality of work products is quantitatively known. The primary distinction from the Established Level is that the defined process is now performed consistently within defined limits to achieve its process outcomes. |
| PA$_{41}$ | | Process measurement | |
| PA$_{42}$ | | Process resource | |
| CL[5] | Optimizing | | Performance of the process is optimized to meet current and future business needs, and the process achieves repeatability in meeting its defined business goals. Quantitative process effectiveness and efficiency goals (targets) for performance are established based on the business goals of the organization. Continuous process monitoring against these goals is enabled by obtaining quantitative feedback, and improvement is achieved by analysis of the results. Optimizing a process involves piloting innovative ideas and technologies and changing noneffective processes to meet defined goals or objectives. The primary distinction from the Predictable Level is that the defined and standard processes now dynamically change and adapt to effectively meet current and future business goals. |
| PA$_{51}$ | | Process change | |
| PA$_{52}$ | | Continuous improvement | |

dimension. This indicates there is a need to further explore the roles and relationships of the two dimensions in process system modeling.

- The assessment complexity of ISO/IEC TR 15504 is quite high with regard to the other process models. This means the cost of an ISO/IEC TR 15504 assessment would be much higher than that of the other process models.

# 4. Perspectives on Trends in Software Engineering Standardization

This section presents perspectives on current trends and future development of software engineering standardization. Some areas for future research are suggested which the author considers significant and worthy of being explored.

## 4.1. *Integration of process-related standards*

A number of process-related standards have been developed or are under development within the international and professional standardization organizations such as the ISO/IEC JTC1/SC7 software engineering subcommittee and the IEEE. Significant standards coming forward are, *inter alia*: ISO/IEC 12207 [49] on software life cycle processes, ISO/IEC CD 15288 [50] on system life cycle processes, and ISO/IEC TR 15504 [51–59] on software process assessment and capability determination.

Major trends in software engineering process standardization have been considered to integrate the existing process-related standards and models, but standardization may also cover new process areas in software engineering.

## 4.2. *Requirements for new standards*

The list of ISO/IEC JTC1/SC7 working groups is continuously expanding. As the evolution of software engineering theories, methodologies, and practices gets faster, more and more areas are expected to be covered by efforts in software engineering standardization. Candidate examples, as the author forecasts, might be new standards as follows:

- Standard for system requirement definition.
- Standard for domain knowledge infrastructure.
- Standard for software architecture and frameworks.
- Standard for software engineering notations.
- Standard for reference software design samples.

## 4.3. *Standardization of software engineering notations*

Almost all mature science and engineering disciplines have a common notation system. A requirement for establishing standard software engineering notations independent of languages and methodologies is beneficial to mainstream software development efforts.

Various software notations have been developed and adopted in software engineering, from graphical to symbolic notations, or from visual to formal (mathematical) notations. The existing software notations can be classified into five categories: the formal (algebraic and logical) notations, state-machine-based notations, data-flow-based notations, object-oriented notations, and process notations.

The international standardization community (e.g. IEEE SNP) is now investigating the feasibility of developing and unifying software engineering notations. The central concept of this effort is to develop a notation standard that is a primary independent entity built on a life-cycle-based framework for the description of software archetypes. Archetypes may be described in different languages or meta-languages using the same core set of notations and a limited set of its extensions. The standard notation should be flexible enough to accommodate recent languages and implementations as well as those of the future.

## 4.4. *Development of new subdomain process models*

It is recognized that software engineering is a discipline requiring inter-disciplinary domain knowledge. A number of subdomain process models have been developed recently in order to provide a more detailed process methodology for a specific application and/or process area in software engineering. Examples of subdomain process models are those below:

- Requirement engineering processes [82].
- System engineering processes [5].
- Software and IT acquisition processes [20].
- The Spiral software processes [10].
- The Rational software development processes [60].

For details, readers may wish to consult the references provided above.

## 4.5. *Process-based software engineering*

In the software industry, the software engineering process systems have been seen as a fundamental infrastructure for software engineering [86, 87]. Process-based development has been proven a successful approach not only in software engineering, but also in other, long matured engineering disciplines.

A trend in software engineering process system modeling is to adopt an operating system technology known as "plug-ins". A plug-in is an extended process module that can be easily adapted to a host process system infrastructure. The plug-in process module usually has a conformant structure and identical syntax as those of the host process system model.

Process reengineering is another attractive technology that adapts and reorganizes an existing software engineering process system. Process reengineering has been found benefit-providing in the software industry. For instance, in one of the pilot projects the author advised a software organization to shift its test design process from postcoding to parallel with system specification and design processes. By this simple reengineering of the whole processes, a large proportion of the requirement specification gaps and system design defects are found long before the software implementation processes begin. As a result, the postcoding defect rate has been reduced dramatically. Further, and much more significantly, the project showed that the defects injected and revealed in different processes were not equivalent in terms of significance, scope of impact, and/or the costs to removal. Almost all of the defects found in the reengineered test design process were significant problems that would impact all following processes if they had not been removed at an early stage.

## 4.6. *Trends in ISO* 9000/9001 *evolution*

On the basis of feedback from both industries and researchers, a significant trend in current ISO 9000/9001 revision [34] is to shift from a check-list based quality system standard to a process-oriented one. The new version of ISO 9001 will include a process model based on Deming's Plan-Do-Check-Act cycle for product, service, and management processes. Also, ISO 9001:2000 will merge the 1994 versions of ISO 9001, ISO 9002, and ISO 9003 into a single and integrated standard.

The 20 MTAs of ISO 9001 as shown in Table 3 will be re-organized into 21 processes which are categorized in four primary processes: management responsibility, resource management, product realization, and measurement, analysis and improvement. New requirements in ISO 9001:2000, such as customer focus, establishment of measurable objectives, continual improvement, and evaluation of training effectiveness, are added for enabling quality process assessment and improvement.

## 4.7. *Trends in ISO/IEC* 15504/12207 *evolution*

ISO/IEC TR 15504 is currently undergoing a transition process from technical report (TR) to full international standard (IS). A set of requirements has been specified and the new base documents are well under way. The document set of ISO/IEC 15504 standard will be reduced from 9 parts to 5 parts. The new 15504-2 is already prepared for ballot.

Part of a structural evolution of ISO/IEC TR 15504 is the shift from a self-contained software process and process assessment model to a standard software process assessment model with an open infrastructure for incorporating any existing or future process models with unified definitions and descriptions. This would mean that the future ISO/IEC 15504 might only provide a standard process assessment methodology and defined compliance requirements for any external software processes. Therefore, the existing and/or innovative software engineering processes compliant to the standard will be defined and developed by any process model providers who so wish.

One of the most important new features is that ISO/IEC 15504 will align to ISO/IEC 12207. This means, at the high level, ISO/IEC 15504 will provide a conceptual process reference model (PRM), [86] and describe how a process provider can achieve conformance to the requirements of the PRM. The overall reference model concept [86, 94] for ISO/IEC 15504 will allow other PRMs to be defined. For instance, there could be an ISO 9001 PRM defined for software or an ISO/IEC

15288 PRM defined for systems. In fact, although the scope of ISO/IEC 15504 is defined within the domain of Software Engineering, the name of ISO/IEC 15504 is being changed to Process Assessment. There is the possibility therefore to use a future ISO/IEC 15504 with a PRM outside the domain of Software Engineering.

Secondly, ISO/IEC 12207 is planning for continuously evolution by amendments and revisions towards year 2020. The first such amendment is already underway and is currently out on ballot by national standardization bodies. This Amendment provides an interim revision to ISO/IEC 12207 that establishes a coordinated set of software process information that can be used for process definition and process assessment and improvement. The amendment accommodates the requirements of current and developing ISO/IEC SC7 standards and technical reports, notably ISO/IEC 12207 and ISO/IEC TR 15504, and considers other standards, i.e., ISO/IEC 14598 and ISO/IEC 15939. The overall result of this amendment will provide a set of process definitions with process purpose and outcome statements that can be used as a basis for an ISO/IEC 12207 Process Reference Model in conjunction with ISO/IEC 15504 capability dimension to assess software processes. When ISO/IEC 15504 is published, it will contain an exemplar assessment model related to an ISO/IEC 12207 PRM.

## 5. Conclusions

A variety of software engineering standard and models, international, regional, and internal, have been developed in the last decade. This chapter has reviewed the major international software engineering standards, especially their emergence, history of development, inter-relationships, and principles and philosophies behind the standards and models for software engineering.

It is recognized that almost all current software engineering standards is based on a generic quality system perception on software development. Although this philosophy has been proven successful in conventional manufacturing industry, there is still a need for supporting evidence of its effectiveness and impact on the design-intensive software engineering and the non-conventional software industry. Further research on common features and differences between conventional mass manufacturing and software development is still expected.

Considering that the software engineering process system seems to be one of the most complicated engineering systems, the search and integration of useful and valid processes and best practices have much further to go. Also, it is noteworthy that as long as the fast development of software engineering methodologies remains viable, software engineering standards and models will need to evolve quickly, especially in the important areas for future software engineering standardization as identified in this chapter.

## Acknowledgments

This chapter is developed based on the author's work in ISO/IEC JTC1/SC7, IEEE SESC, IEEE SNP, and The Canadian Advisory Committee for ISO JTC1

(CAC/JTC1). It resulted from many interesting discussions with colleagues in the working groups. The author would like to thank the referees and colleagues for their valuable comments that have improved the quality of this chapter.

## References

1. R. N. Anthony, "Planning and control systems: A framework for analysis", Harvard University Graduate School of Business Administration, Cambridge, MA (1965).
2. J. D. Aron, *The Program Development Process — The Programming Team*, Part 2 (Addison-Wesley, Reading, MA, 1983).
3. F. T. Baker, "Chief programmer team management of production programming", *IBM Systems Journal* **11**, no. 1 (1972) 56–73.
4. V. Basili, *Models and Metrics for Software Management and Engineering* (IEEE Computer Society Press, Los Alamitos, CA, 1980).
5. R. Bate *et al*, "A system engineering capability maturity model", Version 1.1, CMU/SEI-95-MM-03, Software Engineering Institute, Pittsburgh, PA, 841993, 1993.
6. Bell Canada, "TRILLIUM — Model for telecom product development and support process capability (Internet ed.)", Release 3.0 (December 1994) 1–118.
7. B. W. Boehm, *Software Engineering Economics* (Prentice-Hall, Englewood Cliffs, NJ, 1981).
8. B. W. Boehm and M. H. Penedo *et al*, "A software development environment for improving productivity", *IEEE Computer* **17**, no. 6 (1986) 30.
9. B. W. Boehm, "Improving software productivity", *IEEE Computer* **20**, no. 9 (1987) 43.
10. B. Boehm and P. Bose, "A collaborative spiral software process model based on theory W", *Proceedings of the 3rd International Conference on the Software Process* (IEEE Computer Society Press, Reston, VA, October 1994) 59–68.
11. T. B. Bollinger and C. McGrowan, "A critical look at software capability evaluations", *IEEE Software* (July 1991) 25–41.
12. BOOTSTRAP Team, "BOOTSTRAP: Europe's assessment method", *IEEE Software* (May 1993) 93–95.
13. J. G. Brodman and D. L. Johnson, "What small business and small organization say about the CMM", *Proceedings of the 16th International Conference on Software Engineering (ICSE16)* (1994) 331–340.
14. F. P. Brooks, *The Mythical Man Month* (Addison-Wesley, 1975).
15. BSI, *BS 5750: Quality Systems* (BSI, London, 1987).
16. P. B. Crosby, *Quality is Free* (McGraw Hill, New York, 1979).
17. W. E. Deming, "Methods for management of productivity and quality", George Washington University, Washington, D.C. (1982).
18. A. Dorling, "SPICE: Software process improvement and capability determination", *Information and Software Technology* **35**, no. 6/7 (June/July 1993).
19. A. Dorling, "History of the SPICE project, *Proceedings of the 2nd International SPICE Symposium*, Brisbane, Australia (1995) 1–7.
20. A. Dorling and Y. Wang *et al*, "Reference model extensions to ISO/IEC TR 15504-2 for acquirer processes", ISO/IEC JTC1/SC7/WG10, Curitiba, Brazil (May 1999) 1–34.
21. R. G. Dromey, "Cornering the chimera", *IEEE Software* **13**, no. 1 (January 1996) 33–43.
22. DTI, *The TickIT Guide*, Department of Trade and Industry, London (1987).
23. M. W. Evans and J. J. Marciniak, *Software Quality Assurance and Management* (Wiley-Interscience, New York, 1987).

24. M. E. Fayad, "Software development process: The necessary evil?" *Communications of the ACM* **40**, no. 9 (September 1997).

25. M. E. Fayad and M. Laitinen, "Process assessment: Considered wasteful", *Communications of the ACM* **40**, no. 11 (November 1997).

26. T. Gilb, *Principles of Software Engineering Management* (Addison-Wesley, Reading, MA, 1988).

27. W. S. Humphrey and W. L. Sweet, "A method for assessing the software engineering capability of contractors", Technical Report CMU/SEI-87-TR-23, Software Engineering Institute, Pittsburgh, PA (1987).

28. W. S. Humphrey, "Characterizing the software process: A maturity framework", *IEEE Software* (March 1988) 73–79.

29. W. S. Humphrey, *Managing the Software Process* (Addison-Wesley Longman, Reading, MA, 1989).

30. W. S. Humphrey and B. Curtis, "Comment on 'a critical look'", *IEEE Software* **8**, no. 4 (1991) 42–47.

31. W. S. Humphrey, T. R. Snyder and R. R. Willis, "Software process improvement at Hughes aircraft", *IEEE Software* (July 1991) 11–23.

32. IEEE, *Software Engineering Standards, 1983 Collection* (IEEE Computer Society Press, Los Alamitos, CA, 1983).

33. IEEE, *Software Engineering Standards, 1988 Collection* (IEEE Computer Society Press, Los Alamitos, CA, 1988).

34. ISO 9001, *Outline of ISO 9001:2000 Draft International Standard,* http://www.iso-9000-2000/ (2000).

35. ISO 9000-1, "Quality management and quality assurance standards (Part 1) — Guidelines for selection and use", International Organization for Standardization, Geneva (1994).

36. ISO 9000-2, "Quality management and quality assurance standards (Part 2) — Generic guidelines for application of ISO 9001, ISO 9002 and ISO 9003", International Organization for Standardization, Geneva (1994).

37. ISO 9000-3, "Quality management and quality assurance standards (Part 3) — Quality management and quality assurance standards (Part 3) — Guidelines to apply ISO 9001 for development, supply and maintenance of software", International Organization for Standardization, Geneva (1991).

38. ISO 9000-4, "Quality management and quality system (Part 4) — Guidelines for dependability programme management", International Organization for Standardization, Geneva (1993).

39. ISO 9001, "Quality systems — Model for quality assurance in design, development, production, installation and servicing", International Organization for Standardization, Geneva (1989).

40. ISO 9001, "Quality systems — Model for quality assurance in design, development, production, installation and servicing, revised edition", International Organization for Standardization, Geneva (1994).

41. ISO 9002, "Quality systems — Model for quality assurance in production, installation and servicing", International Organization for Standardization, Geneva (1994).

42. ISO 9003, "Quality systems — Model for quality assurance in final inspection and test", International Organization for Standardization, Geneva (1994).

43. ISO 9004-1, "Quality management and quality system elements (Part 1) — Guidelines", International Organization for Standardization, Geneva (1994).

44. ISO 9004-2, "Quality management and quality system elements (Part 4) — Guidelines for quality management and quality systems elements for services", International Organization for Standardization, Geneva (1991).

45. ISO 9004-4, "Quality management and quality system elements (Part 2) — Guidelines for quality improvement", International Organization for Standardization, Geneva (1993).
46. ISO 9126, "Information technology — Software product evaluation — Quality characteristics and guidelines for their use", International Organization for Standardization, Geneva (1991).
47. ISO 10011, "Guidelines for auditing quality systems", International Organization for Standardization, Geneva (1988).
48. ISO 10013, "Guidelines for developing quality manuals", International Organization for Standardization, Geneva (1992).
49. ISO/IEC 12207, "Information technology — Software life cycle processes", International Organization for Standardization, Geneva (1995).
50. ISO/IEC CD 15288, "Information technology — Life cycle management — System life cycle processes", ISO/IEC JTC1/SC7 Draft N2184, Geneva (1999) 1–42.
51. ISO/IEC TR 15504-1, "Information technology — Software process assessment — Part 1: Concept and introduction guide", ISO/IEC, Geneva (1999) 1–11.
52. ISO/IEC TR 15504-2, "Information technology — Software process assessment — Part 2: A reference model for processes and process capability", ISO/IEC, Geneva (1999) 1–39.
53. ISO/IEC TR 15504-3, "Information technology — Software process assessment — Part 3: Performing an assessment", ISO/IEC, Geneva (1999) 1–4.
54. ISO/IEC TR 15504-4, "Information technology — Software process assessment — Part 4: Guide to performing assessments", ISO/IEC, Geneva (1999) 1–18.
55. ISO/IEC TR 15504-5, "Information technology — Software process assessment — Part 5: An assessment model and indicator guidance", ISO/IEC, Geneva (1999) 1–132.
56. ISO/IEC TR 15504-6, "Information technology — Software process assessment — Part 6: Guide to qualification of assessors", ISO/IEC, Geneva (1999) 1–23.
57. ISO/IEC TR 15504-7, "Information technology — Software process assessment — Part 7: Guide for use in process improvement", ISO/IEC, Geneva (1999) 1–36.
58. ISO/IEC TR 15504-8, "Information technology — Software process assessment — Part 8: Guide for use in determining supplier process capability", ISO/IEC, Geneva (1999) 1–17.
59. ISO/IEC TR 15504-9, "Information technology — Software process assessment — Part 9: Vocabulary", ISO/IEC, Geneva (1999) 1–11.
60. I. Jacobson, G. Booch and J. Rumbaugh, *The Unified Software Development Process* (Addison Wesley Longman, Reading, MA, 1998).
61. M. J. Jenner, *Software Quality Management and ISO 9001* (John Wiley & Sons, Inc., New York, 1995).
62. J. M. Juran, L. A. Seder and F. M. Gryna, *Quality Control Handbook*, 2nd ed. (McGraw-Hill, New York, 1962).
63. J. M. Juran and F. M. Gryna, *Quality Planning and Analysis* (McGraw-Hill, New York, 1980).
64. D. H. Kitson and S. Masters, "An analysis of SEI software process assessment results: 1987–1991", Technical Report CMU/SEI-92-TR-24, Software Engineering Institute, Pittsburgh (1992).
65. D. H. Kitson, "Relating the SPICE framework and SEI approach to software process assessment", *Proceedings of the International Conference on Software Quality Management (SQM'96)* (MEP Press, London, 1996) 37–49.
66. H. J. Kugler and S. Rementeria, "Software engineering trends in Europe", ESI Research Report, Spain (1995) 1–5.

67. P. Kuvaja and A. Bicego, "BOOTSTRAP — A European assessment methodology", *Software Quality Journal* (June 1994).
68. Mobil Europe Ltd, "The Mobil survey of ISO 9000 certificates awarded worldwide (4th Cycle)", *Quality System Update* **5**, no. 9 (1995).
69. P. Naur and B. Randell, Software Engineering: A Report on a Conference Sponsored by the NATO Science Committee, NATO (1969).
70. M. C. Paulk, B. Curtis, M. B. Chrissis and C. V. Weber, "Capability maturity model for software", Version 1.1, CMU/SEI-93-TR-24 Software Engineering Institute (February, 1993).
71. M. C. Paulk, C. V. Weber, S. Garcia, M. B. Chrissis and M. Bush, "Key practices of the capacity maturity model", Version 1.1, Technical Report CMU/SEI-93-TR-25, Software Engineering Institute, Pittsburgh, PA (1993).
72. M. C. Paulk, B. Curtis, M. B. Chrissis and C. V. Weber, "Capability maturity model", Version 1.1, *IEEE Software* **10**, no. 4 (July 1993) 18–27.
73. M. C. Paulk, C. V. Weber and B. Curtis, "The capability maturity model: Guidelines for improving the software process", *SEI Series in Software Engineering* (Addison-Wesley, 1995).
74. M. C. Paulk, "How ISO 9001 compares with the CMM", *IEEE Software* (January 1995) 74–83.
75. S. L. Pfleeger, *Software Engineering: Theory and Practice* (Prentice-Hall, Englewood Cliffs, NJ, 1998).
76. T. Rout, "SPICE: A framework for software process assessment", *Software Processes: Improvement and Practice* **1**, no. 1 (1995).
77. H. Saiedian and R. Kuzara, "SEI capability maturity model's impact on contractors", *IEEE Computer* **28**, no. 1 (1995) 16–26.
78. E. H. Schein, "Management development as a process at influence", *Industrial Management Review* **2**, no. 2 (Spring, 1961) 59–77.
79. J. Seddon, *In Pursuit of Quality: The Cases Against ISO 9000* (Oak Tree Press, Oxford, UK, 1997).
80. W. A. Shewhart, "Statistical method from the viewpoint of quality control", The Graduate School, George Washington University, Washington, D.C. (1939).
81. H. A. Simon, *The New Science of Management Decision* (Harper & Row, New York, 1960).
82. I. Sommerville and P. Sawyer, *Requirements Engineering — A Good Practice Guide* (John Wiley & Sons, New York, 1997).
83. SPICE Project, "SPICE phase II trials interim report", ISO/IEC JTCI/SC7/WG10 (1998) 1–175.
84. TickIT Project Office, "Guide to software quality management system construction and certification using EN29001", Issue 1.0, UK Department of Trade and Industry and BCS, UK (1987).
85. TickIT Project Office, "Guide to software quality management system construction and certification using EN29001", Issue 2.0, UK Department of Trade and Industry and BCS, UK (1992).
86. Y. Wang and G. King, *Software Engineering Processes: Principles and Applications*, ISBN: 0849323665 (CRC Press, USA, April 2000) 1–752.
87. Y. Wang and A. Bryant, "Process-based software engineering", CFP, *International Journal of Annals of Software Engineering* **14** (2002), *http://manta.cs.vt.edu/ase/vol14call.html*.
88. Y. Wang, G. King, A. Doling and H. Wickberg, "A unified framework of the software engineering process system standards and models", *Proceedings of the 4th IEEE*

*International Software Engineering Standards Symposium* (*IEEE ISESS99*) (IEEE CS Press, Brazil, May 1999) 132–141.

89. Y. Wang, I. Court, M. Ross, G. Staples, G. King and A. Dorling, "Towards software process excellence: A survey report on the best practices in the software industry", *ASQ Journal of Software Quality Professional* **2**, no. 1 (December 1999) 34–43.

90. Y. Wang, A. Dorling, J. Brodman and D. Johnson, "Conformance analysis of the tailored CMM with ISO/IEC 15504", *Proceedings of the International Conference on Product Focused Software Process Improvement* (*PROFES99*), Oulu, Finland (June 1999) 237–259.

91. Y. Wang, G. King, A. Dorling, D. Patel, I. Court, G. Staples and M. Ross, "A worldwide survey on software engineering process excellence", *Proceedings of the IEEE 20th International Conference on Software Engineering* (*ICSE98*), Kyoto (IEEE Press, April 1998) 439–442.

92. Y. Wang, I. Court, M. Ross, G. Staples, G. King and A. Dorling, "Quantitative analysis of compatibility and correlation of the current SPA models", *Proceedings of the IEEE International Symposium on Software Engineering Standards* (*IEEE ISESS97*), USA (June 1997) 36–56.

93. Y. Wang, I. Court, M. Ross, G. Staples, G. King and A. Dorling, "Quantitative evaluation of the SPICE, CMM, ISO9000 and BOOTSTRAP", *Proceedings of the IEEE International Symposium on Software Engineering Standards* (*IEEE ISESS97*), USA (June 1997) 57–68.

94. Y. Wang, I. Court, M. Ross and G. Staples, "Towards a software process reference model (SPRM)", *Proceedings of the International Conference on Software Process Improvement* (*SPI96*), Brighton, UK (November 1996) 145–166.

95. D. Zubrow, "The software community process maturity profile", Software Engineering Institute, Pittsburgh (1997).

# DOMAIN ENGINEERING

J. L. DÍAZ–HERRERA

*Department of Computer Science, Southern Polytechnic State University,*
*1100 South Marietta Parkway, Marietta, GA 30060-2896*
*E-mail: jdiaz@spsu.edu*

Software reuse has remained an elusive goal. A promising approach is to separate asset creation, a process commonly known as domain engineering, from their application to derive concrete products. We contend that this causal relationship provides a sound basis for industrial-strength software engineering, a prerequisite for successful systematic software reuse. A fundamental notion is to be able to de-couple software technology from the asset generation and the application building processes. We provide an illustration of the impact of object-oriented technological advances and construction technology as a roadmap to help organizations decide which are better for what aspects and how the various advancements fit together in a coherent way. We conclude with adoption guidelines and a discussion of the work that lies ahead.

*Keywords*: Software reuse, component-based development, software architectures, domain analysis, reusable components, product lines.

## 1. Introduction

For quite some time now there has been an explicit recognition of the need for building software based on "reusable components" [1]. Despite the amount of work to date focusing on software technology to achieve high levels of reuse, most notably object-oriented approaches, software reuse has remained an elusive goal. Quite simply, the great majority of software practitioners today still develop applications according to the *standard stovepipe approach*, whereby applications are created from first principles repeatedly, from scratch. Such practices have a number of drawbacks and shortcomings [2, 3]. We need to move our focus from engineering single systems to *engineering families of systems* by identifying "reusable" solutions.

Why hasn't there been a more widespread acceptance of software reuse? Why do we care?

Systematic reuse needs to be planned for and it does mean more work at front. It requires a consolidation of understanding of software systems in a domain in order to *exploit commonality* and *anticipate diversity*, a process known as domain engineering. Domain engineering primarily involves efforts to create assets for future software development, i.e., an investment for future work. By creating assets, that support the future development of multiple systems, an organization

- reduces cycle time and cost of new applications by eliminating redundancy and by producing applications from common assets;

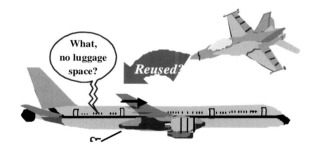

- reduces risk and improves quality by using trusted components;
- manages its legacy assets more efficiently;
- evolves a common marketing strategy and strengthens core competency around strategic business interests and goals; and
- makes decisions based on an asset-base and strategic goals.

However, before all this can happen, we must first plan ahead. For example, taking a product that was built for a specific customer and adapting it for a new customer, would likely result in an inferior product: *one that contains undesirable features while lacking other desired features*. This is not systematic reuse, but *ad hoc reuse* (see Fig. 1 above).

Systematic reuse on the other hand, occurs when reusable assets are planned and created as a separate activity from application development. It is clear that two sets of complementary activities are required: modeling generic solutions, a process known as domain engineering, and product development by applying these solution models. This formal interaction between asset producing and asset utilization activities, whereby applications are assembled from prefabricated artifacts, is known as systematic reuse. The goal of systematic reuse is to produce quality software products consistently and predictably by moving toward an asset-supported, component-based development approach.

Although there are technical difficulties, technology alone is not enough for achieving systematic reuse. It requires making reuse an organization-wide strategy, not a project-centered one. The entire organization may need to be redesigned to fall in harmony with the "domain-model building and application construction processes" that are needed to support reuse [4]. Currently, organizations are emphasizing *component-based development* (CBD) in the hope that this will bring about the elusive goal of systematic reuse. The idea has had certain amount of success in commercial products, such as OMG's CORBA, Microsoft's COM, and Sun's JavaBeans [5], mainly due to "flexibility through a capability of composition" and not necessarily due to technological developments.

In this chapter, we discuss *domain engineering* — a way of institutionalizing systematic reuse — its motivation and benefits, and in conjunction with object-oriented technical support for the modeling and development processes involved. The chapter is divided into five sections. This introductory section continues with motivational aspects for institutionalizing systematic reuse. Section 2 introduces some basic reuse terminology.[a] Section 3 presents domain engineering in its constituents parts, namely process, technology and artifacts. Section 4 presents a framework incorporating current technological advancements. Section 5 outlines implementation guidelines accompanied with some examples. We conclude with a discussion of the effort that lies ahead.

## 1.1. *Motivation: The hope for systematic reuse*

In today's post-PC era, new artifacts and systems are increasingly more software-driven. Software gets bigger all the time, and very costly to create and modify. The software industry is very large, and growing at unprecedented rates. The enormous demand for software is fundamentally based on two aspects; namely, the critical nature of software for today's well-functioning world, and the poor state-of-the-practice in software development. Plummeting hardware costs are leading to rapid growth in many new application areas requiring more software being built in shorter time frames. Many artifacts, from consumer electronics (e.g. smart phones, personal digital assistants, set-top boxes), transportation systems (including automotive, avionics, trains, etc), to industrial plants, and corporations, all depend on well-engineered software for their continuing functioning.

Another critical reality is the poor record of accomplishment in software construction: software seldom performs as expected, and cost/schedule overruns are very common even in the most sophisticated organizations. This further increases demand. Furthermore, it is quite typical that for many such systems each time a new application is built, *routine functionality is custom-written repeatedly from scratch*. This also contributes to higher demands for more software.

Concomitant with these problems, there is a shortage of qualified software professionals [6].

For these software intensive systems, a reuse-driven approach will potentially reduce time-to-market, while improving product quality and reducing uncertainty on cost and schedule estimates. The approach would allow engineers to come up with the "right" solution quickly and effectively by assembling applications out of "proven" components. The quality of products is maintained through rigorous analysis and prediction, continuous improvement and refinement, and through designed experimentation and feedback from observations of actual systems. This represents a main motivation for domain engineering: a desire to modularize a system in such a way that there is a high probability that significant portions of the system can be built from standard parts.

---

[a]Object-oriented concepts are well known and will not be defined here.

## 1.2. *Domain engineering*: *Industrial-strength software engineering*

Systematic reuse requires more "original" engineering design work, first by focusing on identifying as much commonality and flexibility as possible; these are then optimized out by reducing unnecessary variation, and by providing specific variability control mechanisms. Analysis is different from conventional development: we must conduct a special, more comprehensive study of the applications in the domain. We do this to identify the components that are typically "present" in those applications, and particularly, the way that these components vary from one application to another. That is, we must *anticipate change* and *build adaptation capabilities* into "standard" components.

Within the duality of modeling and development, products are created by instantiating models and by integrating prefabricated artifacts. Thus, the developing process becomes more of a routine activity mapping from needs to solutions rather than a synthesis activity of building from scratch. This, as shown graphically in Fig. 2 below, where the causal relationship between building *model solutions*, on the one hand, and constructing actual products from these models, on the other, provides a sound basis for industrial-strength software engineering. We can observe this phenomenon in more traditional engineering disciplines where an explicit distinction is commonly made between original engineering (e.g. R&D) and routine practice [7]. In the field of software engineering, we are beginning to see an increased focus on this duality too. This move, we believe, is in the right direction toward the more encompassing aim of attaining industrial-strength software engineering, a necessary condition that naturally leads to systematic reuse [8]. As Shaw has put it (the underlining added)

"Engineering relies on *codifying knowledge* about a technological problem domain in a form that is directly useful to the practitioner, thereby

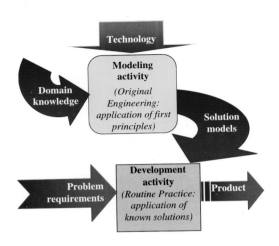

**Fig. 2.** Modeling/development duality.

providing answers for questions *that commonly occur in practice....* Engineers of ordinary talent can then apply this knowledge to solve problems far faster that they otherwise could"[9].

Shaw's notion of engineering directly supports the modeling first-develop second duality, whereby development focuses on setting problems in terms of known solutions, not building products from first principles. Fundamentally, reuse has the effect of reducing variance and increasing homogeneity, two essential aspects observed from disciplines that have moved into industrialization. Modeling is an important practice in increasing homogeneity. Statistical process control, for example, has worked successfully in environments characterized by low variance.

The term **Domain Engineering (DE)** is used to refer to a development-for-reuse process of creating reusable software assets. This is like performing *original engineering*, and refers to new tasks and problems that are realized by synthesizing new solution principles (using first principles) and sometimes by inventing completely new technology. This process requires careful technical and economic analyses and usually goes through all of the development phases.

The complementary term of **Application Engineering (AE)** refers to a development-with-reuse process to create specific systems with these prefabricated assets. In common engineering this is referred to as *routine practice*, and it involves the application of known solutions to solve reoccurring problems. This process requires original design effort only once, and it can be applied in two ways:

(1) *Adaptive design*: use known, established solution principles adapting the embodiment to the requirements. It may be necessary to perform original design on some individual parts.
(2) *Variant design*: arrangements of parts and other product properties (size, etc) are varied within the limits set by a previously designed product structure during original engineering.

The engineering practice concepts of variant design and adaptive design map directly into our definition of systematic software reuse.

## 2. Systematic Reuse: Some Terminology and Concepts

Earlier definitions of *software reuse* include the following:

"Re-use is considered as a means to support the construction of new programs using in a systematical way existing designs, design fragments, program texts, documentation, or other forms of program representation" [10].

And,

"Reusability is the extent to which a software component can be used (with or without adaptation) in multiple problem solutions"[11]. See also [12].

From these definitions, we highlight three important aspects:

- reuse is not an end in itself but a means to an end;
- reusable assets are not limited to code components but include any artifact produced during the development cycle; and
- software components may need adaptation to particular problem solutions at reuse time.

A good definition of **systematic software reuse** is as follows:

"The organized creation of common parts or assets with controlled variability that forms the basis for systematically building systems in a domain of expertise by assembling them from these reusable assets".

Earlier definitions of an *asset* focused more on code. There are several problems with this view. Yes, code from one project can be saved in a "reuse" library in the hope that it will be useful in the future; but unplanned, miscellaneous collections of code components will fail to achieve high-leverage reuse. They would be difficult to locate, understand, and modify, since typically, design information is unavailable and adaptability is not designed-in. Assets serve as templates for the generation of the various work-products during product development. To assure higher probability of success, assets should be organized around ongoing business activities or domains, such as specific mission areas, domain of expertise, or core competencies (e.g. command and control, automotive, web development, etc).

Assets emphasize *design-for-commonality*. **Design-for-Commonality** forms the basis for standardizing assets to build products in a domain of expertise by encapsulating common features of related products, and by defining a common architecture for related products. In this way, design-for-commonality translates into the following:

- common structure of related products;
- specific design created by instantiating a common design;
- clearly coordinated role in meeting a common need; and
- product implemented by the identified reusable components.

**Control-of-Variability** is the basis for providing flexibility in the assets to meet requirements for a variety of products without compromising commonality; it requires careful design to include appropriate levels of parameterization, generalization and specialization, and extension. Like commonality, adaptability must be engineered *a priori*, and thus, analysis must explicitly identify variations that anticipate adaptations. Control-of-variability results into:

- specification of optional components;
- clearly specified alternate structures; and
- parameterized context dependencies.

This need for design-for-commonality and for control-of-variability results in the introduction of **product lines** [13]. When product lines are designed to support an organization's objective or mission, we are institutionalizing reuse. Here is a common definition of product line:

"A product line is a collection of applications sharing a common, managed set of features that satisfy the specific needs of a selected market to fulfill an organization's mission" [14].

From this discussion we can see that *reuse actually occurs both within a product line and across product lines*, a notion discovered earlier and associated with the concepts of horizontal and vertical reuse. Assets that cross several systems take advantage of "economies of scope", a benefit that comes from developing one asset used in multiple contexts [15]. **Horizontal reuse** refers to the use of an asset across several distinct product lines; typically, assets reused in this way tend to be general (i.e., they are application domain-independent), and with a very specific set of functionality. Horizontal reuse solely focuses on specifying components as independent as possible of any domain-specific product decisions.

**Vertical reuse** refers to the use of assets specially designed for a given product line; these assets are therefore more specific to a set of products (i.e., they are application domain-specific). Vertical reuse focuses on defining product-line specific components whose specification is constrained by the product line architectural decisions. Economies of scale are achieved through the recognition of product lines.

## 3. Systematic Reuse Process

The achievement of Design-for-commonality and control-of-variability requires the establishment of a reuse infrastructure. There is a need for an overall framework that integrates the corresponding set of modeling, planning, and asset construction activities necessary for systematic reuse, and that, at the same time, allows the assimilation of technology effectively.

There are three basic phases in the overall systematic reuse process: Domain Modeling, Product Line Design and Implementation, and Product Development [16]. In Fig. 3 below, we illustrate the interrelations between these three phases. We use the formalism introduced by Gunter *et al* [17] in their reference model for requirements engineering to label the arrows.

The primary information elements manipulated are in the Domain Knowledge {W}, which encompasses known facts about the domain environment or outside *W*orld. The domain modeling activity is constrained by the chosen scope {d} thus sub-setting the domain knowledge to the specific set of products {Wd} based on strategic goals and organizational mission. The *R*equirements {R} define needs from an end-user point of view. The specification {S} is produced as a precise description of {Wd} from where an optimal *P*roduct {P} can be built. The Target Platform, or *M*achine {M} provides the specific computing environment(s) on which the delivered products and assets will execute.

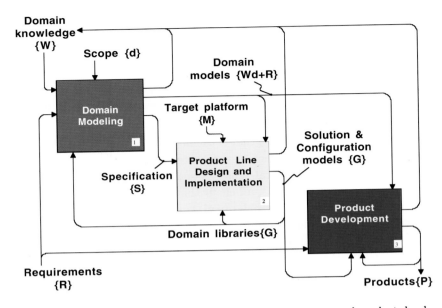

**Fig. 3.**  The relationship between domain modeling, implementation and product development.

The various representations of W, R, and S contain models from different viewpoints. Each of these models highlights different aspects of the world, needs, and requirements, and are collectively referred to as *domain models*. A Domain Model formalizes knowledge about existing systems and requirements for new systems, all represented using information modeling techniques such as object models (use cases are very useful here) and feature models. They may also form the basis for business process reengineering.

Models are subject to validation and verification before being baselined. Model validation and verification as well as product validation and verification is carried out through a continuous cycle. One of the most critical questions is to be able to define correct, unambiguous and useful mappings between all these sets of conceptual elements and generated artifacts. For example, it follows that $S \subseteq R \subseteq Wd$, and that $S \leftrightarrow M * P$, where $\{W + R\}$ = abstract problem model, $\{S + M\}$ = concrete problem model, $G$ = generic solution model, and $P$ = concrete solution model. A complete analysis of these equations is beyond the scope of our current discussions. Interested readers should look at [17].

The focus is thus one of analysis and design of variability within a set of products and the analysis and design of commonality across products. This takes special consideration of contextual differences to allow an asset to cater for the variability found in the various products, while designing for commonality across products (see Fig. 4). Domain models describe typical systems features, including functional and non-functional, as well as mandatory and optional features. Design models describe the generic *solutions* that are the result of PL design and implementation.

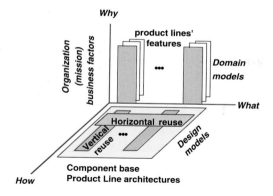

**Fig. 4.** Software product lines.

Design models also include *configuration* models with specific information to support adaptation.

*Solution models* represent both software and hardware architectures (i.e., components and their interfaces) suitable for solving typical problems in the domain. Product line architectures depicts the structure for the design of related products and provide models for integrating optional/alternative components. Component Designs specify the structure for the explicit variability of components across products and product lines; they serve as models for specifying and encapsulating commonality. A *configuration model* maps between the problem models and solution models in terms of product construction rules, which translate capabilities into implementation components. These rules describe legal *feature* combinations, default settings, etc. For example, certain combinations of features may be not allowed; also, if a product does specify certain features, some reasonable defaults may be assumed and other defaults can be computed based on some other features. The configuration model isolates abstract requirements into specific configurations of components in a product line architecture.

Optional parts are very important. Possible combinations of optional features must be supported by the product line architectural design and the flexibility incorporated in the component design, otherwise it may be impossible to reuse an asset "as-is" because commonality and specificity are mixed. This would make it necessary to modify the asset when reused in the new context, and this should obviously be voided whenever feasible. Configuration models help here.

### 3.1. *Domain modeling*

The domain modeling process primarily includes *domain analysis* and *architectural design* to produce a generic problem description. Figure 4 illustrates the various subprocesses and products of the modeling activity, and the techniques and technologies used. To address the question of what components are needed requires special, broad analyses of the problem domain to identify the components "present" in the products of a given domain, a process known as **domain analysis**. Domain Analysis strives for the identification of commonalties across applications in a domain, and results in the definition of *product line features* documented by *domain models*. Domain analysis is a top-down activity considering only applications in a domain of discourse. See [18] for a survey of DA methods.

A method specifically designed for DA is the Feature Oriented Domain Analysis (FODA) method developed at the SEI [19]. This method defines a process for domain analysis that supports the discovery, analysis, and documentation of commonality and differences within a domain. The feature-oriented concept is based on the emphasis the method places on finding the capabilities that are usually expected or desired in applications in a given domain.

The FODA domain model captures the similarities and differences among domain assets in terms of a set of related features. A feature is a distinctive aspect, quality, or characteristic of the domain asset. The features identified by the FODA method can be used to parameterize the system (product line) architectures and implementations of the domain assets. The features differentiating domain entities arise from differences in capabilities, operating environments, domain technology, implementation techniques, etc, i.e., a range of possible implementations within the domain. A specific implementation consists of a consistent set of feature values describing its capabilities.

**Architecture modeling** focuses on a common architecture of related systems in such a way that design models become the means for system construction and for incremental growth. New capabilities offered to the user can be introduced through prototyping of new system components (possibly utilizing different implementation technology). Such prototypes coexist alongside the operational system and may get hardened through incremental reengineering.

*The* architectural design process produces architectures that specify products and components. It refers to "modularizing" for component-based development; it focuses on design-for-commonality and control-of-variability. It increases the probability that significant portions of the products can be built from standard parts (components) as specified in the design model. The resulting designs make trade-offs iteration between function (domain model) and form (domain design), between generality vs specificity. The architectural model proposes a "best fit" high-level architectural style(s) for the kind of problems in hand. The specification contains details of specific behavior and systems properties (e.g. timeliness, and other SWaP[b] constraints) complete enough that can be subject to analytical tools.

### 3.2. *Product line design and implementation*

The *Design* activity fine-tunes the high level architectural design with detailed common and flexible product and component structures. These detailed designs

---

[b]Size, weight, and power.

correspond to *product line architectures* and *component designs*, respectively, documented as *design models*. The design activities are supported by system/software architecture technology, most notably Architecture Description Languages or ADLs [20]. Component design is supported by Interface Definition Languages or IDLs.

The *domain implementation* includes selection of suitable target platforms, the partitioning and allocation of functionality among hardware/software components, and the implementation of the various components populating the system architecture. The implementation activities define the *solution space* with all their possible combinations. Domain Implementation also includes a process for the creation of reusable software components and their storage and retrieval in the domain library. Domain Implementation is supported by component composition technology, most notably Module Interconnection Languages [21] such as Ada and Java.[c] The *domain libraries* contain generic solutions and components that for a given target platform $M$ satisfies the set of needs described by {W, R, S}. It involves the use of domain-specific languages, code generators and component libraries.

*Product line architectures* capture common high-level structures of related products (design-for-commonality) for building products, identifying common assets, and defining the means for connecting these assets. They allow integration of optional/alternative components (control-of-variability). There is a strong relationship between a component model and architectural constraints [2]. Implementation decisions are outside the scope of the architectural design. They belong in the detailed design of the components and the connectors, which together form the component base.

*The Component base* specifies common functionality across families of systems with direct control of variability. There are different ways to control variability, e.g. class hierarchies, generators, generic parameters (templates), libraries, configurations, etc. Components,[d] through design-for-commonality, implement those *crosscutting aspects* that are typically present in the majority of the applications in a domain. Components also capture the way that these aspects may vary from one product to another, and provide plug-in compatibility via standard interfaces — control-of-variability.

### 3.3. *Product development*

The Product development process is multiplexed to correspond to the various product lines. Generative application development can be applied, whereby the application engineer states requirements in abstract terms and the generator

---

[c]Non modular languages such as C and C++ make use of environment provided capabilities such as UNIX header files to support "composability".
[d]We use the term *components* in its most widely form to include requirements, software and hardware architectures as well as blocks (both hardware and software code modules) and their test harnesses.

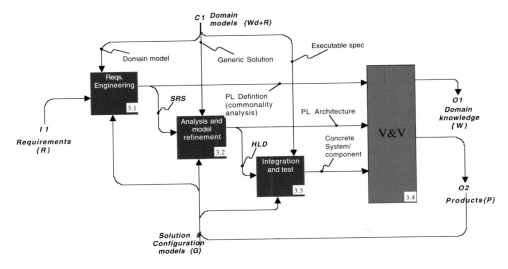

**Fig. 5.** Product Development activities.

produces the desired system or component. The actual development process follows any software development established framework, as for example the one illustrated below in Fig. 5.

## 4. Software Technology for Systematic Reuse

In this section, we describe in some detail the technological aspects of the systematic reuse processes. Due to space constraints, we do not discuss specific technology in detail. Rather, we suggest a roadmap for its application in the various phases, and outline some problems that have surfaced, especially in relation to object-oriented technology and systematic reuse. We explicitly show the different kinds of models needed during modeling and development, at the same time that we show each of the different levels of abstraction needed for PLs. The former, i.e., kinds of models, represents the different stages of product development ranging from requirements to implementation, whereas the latter indicates the degree of domain information incorporated in the artifact being reused. In general, we need modeling methods and specification languages, architectural styles, frameworks, and architectural description languages, and component metamodels, patterns, and component description languages. All these models then serve as the basis for requirements and design analysis for a specific product, and they support creation of component libraries.

We illustrate this as shown in Fig. 6. In this figure, we juxtaposition software technology representing the various product artifacts — the $x$-axis, against product generation stages — the $y$-axis. The $x$-axis "product's artifacts" plots software technology used to model the different product artifacts generated during the production process; these models go from high-level artifacts such as requirement models to more specific implementations such as components and systems. Thus, product

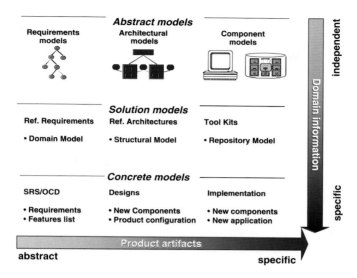

**Fig. 6.** Integrated-MBSE [25]: the relationship between the modeling and development activities is driven by technology and models, respectively. The former runs down from domain-independent models (top) to domain specific artifacts (bottom). Product development proceeds from high-level specifications (left), to the concrete realization of application systems (right).

artifacts fall into three kinds, namely requirements models, architectural models, and component models.

At the same time, the $y$-axis indicates the level of abstraction of these models with respect to domain-information-dependency. That is, each product artifact model exists at various levels of abstraction ranging from abstract domain-independent models (for Horizontal reuse) and generic solution product line models (for Vertical reuse), to specific product configuration and implementation models (for system delivery).

These models are generated during domain engineering, and it is useful to distinguish two levels, namely *abstract models* and generic *solution models*. Abstract models provide basic modeling concepts in the domain, and include things like, reference requirements, product lines architectures, and specific problem solutions (e.g. patterns). Analysis models include artifacts such as object and data models, whereas design models include architectural representations, patterns, and frameworks. The solution models become reusable assets that serve as templates for the generation of the various work-products required during actual product development.

There are also *concrete models*, which result from the application of the abstract models to a concrete set of requirements by adding specific domain information.

### 4.1. *Architectures and components in systematic reuse*

Software architectures and reusable component-based designs are becoming the dominant themes. The term *software architecture* has been defined as:

"The components into which a system is divided at the level of system organization, and the way in which these components communicate, interact, and coordinate with each other" [9].

In this way, *architectural components* encapsulate specific functionality specified by *interfaces*. Components in this way imply some form of code, and, from this viewpoint, architectural components are relevant at two levels: at the static or source-management level, and at the dynamic or execution level. Quite explicitly, the term component is being used to refer to this static nature as the "unit of software deployment", whereas "objects" capture software's runtime behavior; thus, "components and objects together enable the construction of next generation software" [22]. Several definitions of this kind of components abound [2, 5]; they address granularity, contextual dependencies and explicit, as well as implicit, interfaces.

Components interact via *architectural connections*, which are specified by protocols. Thus, connections are relations among components. This happens also at two levels, namely at the static level as context dependencies, and at the dynamic level for control and data flow. Rapide [23] makes this distinction explicit as follows: an Object Connection Architecture specifies collaborations as run-time message exchanges, whereas an Interface Connection Architecture defines connections between the components of a system using only the interfaces.

An *architectural style* is a description of component types and a pattern of their interaction. A style can be thought of as a set of constraints (on the component types and on the interaction patterns) in an architecture, e.g. in the client-server style, clients are anonymous. Architecture styles are not architectures, however they represent, in a very high level sense, families of related systems. A related concept is that of a *reference model, which specifies a division of functionality into conceptual components*, i.e., a standard decomposition of a known problem into parts that cooperatively solve the problem. They are characteristic of matured domains (e.g., compilers). A reference software architecture is a reference model mapped onto software components and their relations (i.e., mapping of functionality onto software components).

## 4.2. *Object-oriented support for reuse*

In terms of actual software components, we can identify two kinds of object-oriented components, namely class hierarchies and frameworks. **Class hierarchies (or class libraries)** are application domain-independent components; they provide direct support for horizontal reuse and typically consist of a number of classes associated by inheritance. These domain-independent components are useful building blocks for different applications and even in different domains, but they are not easily adaptable and when reused, they may carry extra baggage, i.e., extra functionality, due to their general nature.

**Object-oriented frameworks** on the other hand, represent domain-specific (partially complete) solutions to concrete, hopefully sharable, sub-problems in the domain; they provide direct support for vertical reuse and typically consist of a number of abstract classes associated by message passing. They specify how to implement an application or a part of it by extending the framework with appropriate instantiations of some specific "plug-ins" and "hot-spots"; the latter refers to variability identified in the requirements. More recently, the focus has been on higher level abstractions called object-oriented **patterns** (specially design patterns); these are abstract descriptions of solutions that work within a given context, allowing developers to reuse successful "working principles". In this sense, frameworks are concrete realizations of patterns and patterns are abstract descriptions of frameworks. Collections of interrelated patterns form pattern languages, an "informal" communication tool to share architectural knowledge relating how the various individual solutions may work together to solve a larger problem. Variation points can be explicitly identified as abstract classes.

The notions of vertical and horizontal reuse have been formally incorporated in important software construction technology such as CORBA [24]. The top layers of the CORBA architecture specify standard objects that can be shared by applications across domains; they are known as the Horizontal CORBA Facilities. Standard objects that are reusable within products in a given product line are referred to as the Vertical (Domain) CORBA Facilities.

Although the principle of reuse is at the center of object-oriented development, and the technology *does* provide superior technical support for *code* reuse, object-oriented programming is simply not enough for large-scale systematic reuse [25]. Reusing code artifacts has the least amount of reuse payoff [26]. Also, object hierarchies do not directly support the definition of families of systems [27]. A more fundamental problem is that systems are not being designed for reuse; thus, because of object-orientation focus on code, it is not easy to design the system architecture *a priori*, i.e., before components (e.g. classes) are built. For instance, architectural patterns and frameworks cannot be created before the actual components (classes) that they connect do exist! This, however, may not be a serious problem since we expect to have a library of components to begin with. The real question is the identification of the components in the first place and the way they fit together in an architecture. Also, objects in a class library are potentially reusable, but problems arise when we try to interface them with the outside world.

Object-oriented systems are typically monolithic pieces with difficult to detach "components". Current object-oriented component technology (including JavaBeans, ActiveX, COM, etc) imposes severe constraints on the components, tightly coupling them to implementation infrastructure. Truly reusable components must be specified as free of constraints as possible.

In summary, object technology is in fact neither necessary nor sufficient for systematic reuse. The properties of adaptability and composability are not yet automatically achieved by applying object-oriented concepts. Identifying flexibility and designing mechanisms that control this flexibility is the real issue.

## 5.  Adoption Guidelines and Illustration

Two fundamental component features that affect composition ability and reuse-payoff are *scope* and *granularity*. A component's scope can be domain-independent, domain-specific, or product-specific. The second component feature of granularity has two dimensions, namely fine-grained (small-scale) and coarse-grain (large-scale) granularity. The former is typically found in domain-independent components, whereas the latter are typical of application subsystems, or semi-finished applications (such as frameworks). Component functionality is less with the size of it, but reuse profit is directly proportional with size.

### 5.1.  *Types of components*

A *domain-independent* component has a general purpose with broad applicability used in many domains. Components of this type are almost entirely abstract data types such as list managers, mathematical functions, user-interface toolkits and database management systems. The term horizontal reuse is commonly used to refer to domain-independent components. More recently, these issues have reached the programming level with the notion of "adapters" and aspect-oriented programming as in AspecJ (from Xerox [28]), Hyper/J (from IBM [29]), and Demeter [30].

*Domain-specific* components have more limited applicability, and are especially reusable within a specific application domain. The term vertical reuse is commonly used to refer to these components. The semantics of the component are domain-dependent, and hence have little or no use outside its domain, and are things like packages that compute taxes, flight control laws, scheduling routines, etc. Such domain-specific components make certain assumptions about how they will be used, reducing generality but increasing its usability.[e]

*Product-specific* components are reusable within a specific product line. The semantics of the component are bound to a specific application type. The product line may dictate a generic architecture, and component roles will be developed to fit it. Typical product-specific components are entire architectures developed internally or in-house — this means that the organization is developing for reuse and providing services internally; and hence it does not have a company barrier between service providers and customers. There are also externally developed product-line components — this means that the organization is developing for reuse and providing services on the external market, and hence it does have a company barrier between service providers and customers, which complicates communication.

### 5.2.  *Heuristics*

One problem in design is the management of complexity. Design principles deal with complexity and are also important for component-based development; these

---

[e]The traditional conflict between design-for-reuse and design-with-reuse [31].

include decomposition and hierarchical structuring to increase understanding, cohesion/coupling to allow aggregation, encapsulation to support optional parts, and abstraction/hiding to support modifiability. High cohesion and low coupling are desirable properties in any system. Optional parts are very important for component-based development within a product line. The product line architectural design and the component-base design must support possible combinations of optional features. It is almost impossible to reuse a component as-is when commonalties and specifics are mixed. This makes it necessary to modify the component when reused in the new context.

Heuristics deal with design issues that cannot be specified exactly in algorithmic form. Here are some guidelines to address many of the issues discussed above.

**During analysis**: the greatest impact on the preliminary system definition (or product line specification) is at the interfaces. This focus allows us to highlight important distinctions with conventional development. These are:

- analysis identifies, most notably, the variability in the set of systems in the product line;
- separate nice-to-have features from the essential ones (no unnecessary features), but at the same time anticipate new requirements;
- no feature redundancy but provide alternate uses of needed features; and
- implementation features not imposed on existing technology.

**During design**: design produces architectures to specify products and components. This phase provides a software solution in the form of a high-level design of the application. An architecture model, also known as a reference model, is developed; detailed design and component construction can be done from this model; a high-level design for applications in the domain is produced. The focus is on modularizing for a product line, i.e., design for commonality and control of variability. This increases the probability that significant portions of the products can be built from standard parts as specified in the design model:

- Avoid constraining design unnecessarily; e.g. hierarchies that are too shallow do not allow sharing (commonality suffers).
- Avoid simplifying design unnecessarily; e.g. hierarchies that are too deep do not control variability effectively and also lose commonality.
- Iteration between function (domain model) and form (domain design): form follows function in the sense that product line analysis is feature-based whereas design is form-based. Product lines are designed from the top down, driven by function instead of form.
- Enforce strict layering: objects enforce encapsulation through the hiding of local variables and local functions, the idea is to permit changes to an object's implementation without triggering changes to other objects (by keeping its specification "clean"). Design encapsulation, on the other hand, is the form of encapsulation that is required for software component

technology! It is the hiding of design decisions within "layers". Unlike object encapsulation, design encapsulation is not (currently) enforceable by language processing tools. Interfaces across levels make the distinction between design encapsulation and object encapsulation clear; higher level components utilize lower level ones, hence users of higher level component reuse the lower level ones.

- Regardles of its type, each component is a means of achieving one or more reusability features. They must have syntactically and semantically clear specification (separate from implementation) and independence from environment (e.g. parametric coupling). A component specification captures its functional description and operability (parameters, conditions, etc). A description of the connections among the interface elements and level of parameterization and kind of extension (e.g. parametric polymorphism vs inheritance) enhance adaptability. Users of higher-level components may instead develop their own lower-level components to create the parameters needed to instantiate the higher-level component.

The tradeoff between generality vs specificity is also related to complexity and specificity. The fundamental problem is to reduce complexity to a manageable degree, and to produce generic models that are useful, to the point where routine engineering can be brought to bear. The focus is in reducing complexity, uncertainty, and ambiguity at the same time that we strive to produce specifiable adaptable concepts. The difficulty is in making feasible concepts work, resolving conflicts and making all the pieces fit.

Appendix A contains a small example of a product line analysis of the domain of traffic management [32], and following the three axes model (see Fig. 4).

## 6. Conclusions

In this paper, we have argued establishing a causal relationship between models representing reusable assets, created by applying first principles, and the application of these models to actually develop the delivered application, by the routine application of solution models. We conjecture that the separation of models and product artifacts provides a suitable framework for integrating technology in the pursuit of systematic reuse. It is increasingly clear that developers require software models to be able to build new systems as variations of "old" systems. A prime example of this promising technology can be observed in the development of CORBA and its recent focus on domain technology. There are currently eight vertical-domain task forces and special groups, a wealth of information can be found at OMG's web-site [33], and this in turn promotes the development of new, higher-level domains as illustrated in Fig. 7. With these important efforts, we are at the brink of finally beginning to have domain-specific engineering handbooks, a most critical component of an industrial-strength engineering discipline for software.

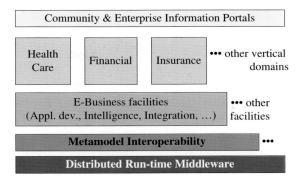

**Fig. 7.** OMG E-Business Integration high-level architecture (modified from [33]).

Organizations must invest in creating models of the common capabilities of related software applications, a process commonly known as **domain engineering**. Organizations use these models as software assets supporting the creation of products that meet increasingly changing requirements, a process also commonly known as **application engineering**. Domain engineering is a *development-for-reuse* process to create software assets, whereas application engineering is a *development-with-reuse* process to create specific systems with these prefabricated assets.

Object-oriented technology does provide superior technical support for code reuse, however it by itself is not enough for institutionalized systematic reuse. Interestingly enough, claims are being made that object technology is neither necessary nor sufficient for systematic component-based development. (It is worth emphasizing that component-based development seems to work with and without objects [2, 3], for additional examples visit the SEI web page on experiences [34]). One problem with object-oriented development is the low level of granularity of the assets being reused. Furthermore, the perceived benefits of reusing patterns and frameworks will not be materialized unless they are taken into account by the application development process. The reason for this is that, in contrast with functionally decomposed systems, object-oriented systems will not have high-level functions that map directly to the functional requirements. This information is not easily extracted from the code either since the focus there is on inheritance. The development process for domain-specific components (frameworks) should follow the traditional domain analysis process. An important change in the traditional object-oriented analysis process to accommodate for systematic reuse is the need for a more formal variability analysis. Product line domain analysis must be done (not just domain analysis of one application domain) with emphasis on variability analysis. It is also important to keep domain-independent, domain-specific, and product-specific components apart and possibly physically separate.

An important aspect to secure institutionalization of systematic reuse is the attainment of "economies of scope". Component-based development focuses on structure of a set of components, embodying features within a domain, leveraging prior investment to maximum degree in support of developing multiple products. Components, objects, and architectures will all be important parts of the next generation of software development technologies.

## APPENDIX A: A Product Line Analysis Example

The following example of product lines is based on the Universal Traffic Management Society of Japan established in 1993 for the achievement of a safe, comfortable and environment friendly automotive society. The following subsections refer to Fig. 4 above.

### A.1.  *WHY: Mission and strategic goals*

The traffic management needs can be grouped as follows, each serving a different constituency:

- law enforcement and education;
- managing traffic accidents or emergency cases;
- managing traffic in large scale disasters;
- managing drivers and driving licenses;
- managing road usage (e.g. freight); and
- managing non-traffic police activities.

Traffic management dimension defines various business objectives or strategic goals. These include secure satisfactory traveling circumstances, optimum resource distribution, and public welfare. These translate into optimum allocation of traffic related resources (e.g. traffic demand management), arrangement of rights of way in time division (e.g. traffic signaling), arrangement of rights of way in space division (e.g. route guidance or regulation), protection of people (e.g. pedestrians, physically impaired and the aged), etc.

### A.2.  *WHAT: Product lines*

The achievement of the strategic goals can be met by the definition of the following products grouped into three product lines:

Product line 1: Safety

- DSSS: Driving Safety Support Systems
- HELP: Help system for Emergency Life saving and Public safety
  A. FAST: Fast Emergency Vehicle Preemption systems

Product line 2: Control

- DRGS: Dynamic Route Guidance Systems
- MOCS: Mobile Operation Control Systems
- ITCS: Integrated Traffic Control Systems
- PTPS: Public Transportation Priority Systems

Product line 3: Information management

- Environment Protection Management Systems
- IIIS: Intelligent Integrated ITV Systems
- AMIS: Advanced Mobile Information Systems
- PICS: Pedestrian Information and Communication Systems

## A.3.  *HOW: Asset base*

These products share the following common elements:

| Actors | |
|---|---|
| walking people | outside people (operators & administrators) |
| driving people | roads |

| Traffic Information Features | |
|---|---|
| Information acquisition | Information dissemination |
| vehicle detectors | traffic information to drivers |
| whether and environment | traffic information to pre-trip drivers |
| travel time | travel information to all travelers |
| traffic information from video image | public transport information to travelers |
| traffic information from still image | Warning information |
| police communication | hazard information at dangerous places |
| strategy | warning information at roads |
| traffic planning | driving information about neighboring |
| tactics | Vehicles |
| control parameters | driving information on high-speed traffic |

| Traffic Management Features | |
|---|---|
| Controlling elements | Controlled elements |
| route guidance | pedestrians (including wheel chairs) |
| arterial/wide area traffic control | the environment |
| intersection traffic control | public transportation (include. taxis) |
| lane oriented traffic control | commercial vehicles |
| zone oriented traffic control | emergency vehicles |
| | grade crossing |
| | special vehicles (governor's, pope's) |

Domain analysis will identify the various systems features, commonalities and differences. The domain design will identify a high-level architecture with an explicit identification of the points of variation (hot-spots) and corresponding component flexibility.

# References

1. D. McIlroy, "Mass produced software components", *NATO Conference on Software Engineering* (1968) 138–155.
2. A. W. Brown and K. C. Wallnau, "The current state of CBSE", *IEEE Software* (1998).
3. L. Brownsword and P. Clements, *A Case Study in Successful Product Line Management*, CMU/SEI-96-TR-016, Software Engineering Institute, Pittsburgh, PA, Carnegie Mellon University (1996).
4. I. Jacobson, "Succeeding with objects: Reuse in reality", *Object Magazine* (July 1996) 94–96.
5. G. T. Leavens and M. Sitaraman, *Foundations of Component-Based Systems* (Cambridge University Press, Cambridge, UK, 2000).
6. P. Freeman and W. Aspray, "The supply of IT workers in the US", Computer Research Association, Special Report, 1999.
7. G. Pahl and W. Beitz, *Engineering Design: A Systematic Approach* (Springer-Verlag, Berlin, 1996).
8. J. L. Diaz-Herrera, S. Coehn and J. Withey, "Institutionalizing systematic reuse: A model-based approach", *Proceedings of the Seventh Workshop on Institutionalizing Software Reuse* (Chicago, 1995).
9. M. Shaw and D. Garlan, *Software Architectures: Perspectives on an Emerging Discipline* (Prentice-Hall, Upper Saddle River, NJ, 1996).
10. E. M. Dusink and J. van Katwijk, "Reflections on reusable software and software components", Ada Components: Libraries and Tools, *Proceedings of the Ada-Europe Conference*, Stockholm, ed. S. Tafvelin (Cambridge University Press, Cambridge, UK, 1987) 113–126.
11. J. W. Hooper and R. O. Chester, *Software Reuse, Guidelines and Methods* (Plenum Press, New York, 1991).
12. S. Katz, *et al*, *Glossary of Software Reuse Terms*, National Institute of Standards and Technology, Gaithersburg, MD (1994).
13. D. M. Weiss and C. T. R. Lai, *Software Product-Line Engineering* (Addison-Wesley, Reading MA, 1999).
14. S. Cohen, L. Friedman, L. Martin, L. Solderitsch and L. Webster, *Product Line Identification for ESC-Hanscom* CMU/SEI-95-SR-024, Software Engineering Institute, Pittsburgh, PA, Carnegie Mellon University (1995).
15. J. Withey, *Investment Analysis of Software Assets for Product Lines* CMU/SEI-96-TR-010, Software Engineering Institute, Pittsburgh, PA, Carnegie Mellon University (1996).
16. J. L. Diaz-Herrera and V. Madissetti, "Embedded systems product lines", *Software Product Lines, ICSE Workshop* (Limerick, Ireland, June 2000).
17. C. A. Gunter, E. L. Gunter, M. Jackson and P. Zave, *A Reference Model for Requirements and Specifications, IEEE Software* (May/June 2000) 37–43.
18. G. Arango, "Domain analysis methods", *Software Reusability* (Ellis Horwood, Chichester, UK, 1994) 17–49.
19. K. Kang, *et al*, *Feature-Oriented Domain Analysis (FODA) Feasibility Study*, CMU/SEI-90-TR-21, Software Engineering Institute, Pittsburgh, PA, Carnegie Mellon University (1990).
20. F. Hayes-Roth, *Architecture-Based Acquisition and Development of Software*, ARPA Domain-Specific Software Architecture Program, Teknowledge Federal Systems, Palo Alto, CA (1994).
21. R. Prieto-Diaz and J. Neighbors, "Module interconnection languages", *Journal of Systems and Software* **6** (November 1986) 307–334.

22. C. Szyperski, *Component Software: Beyond Object-Oriented Programming* (Addison-Wesley, Harlow, UK, 1998).

23. D. Luckham, J. J. Kenney, L. M. Augustin, J. Vera, D. Bryan and D. Mann, "Specification and analysis of system architecture using rapide", *IEEE Transactions on Software Engineering* **21**, no. 4 (April 1995) 336–355.

24. Siegel OMG Overview: CORBA and the OMA in Enterprise Computing, *Communications of the ACM* **41**, no. 10 (1998) 37–43.

25. J. L. Diaz-Herrera and B. Thomas, "Model-based systematic reuse: An Analysis of OOT support", OOPSLA Workshop #18 "Object Technology, Architecture and Domain Analysis" (1998).

26. I. Jacobson, M. Griss and P. Jonsson, *Software Reuse: Architecture, Process, and Organization for Business Success* (Addison-Wesley, New York, 1997).

27. R. T. Monroe, *Rapid Development of Custom Software Design Environments*, PhD Thesis, Carnegie Mellon University (July 1999).

28. G. Kiczales, J. Lamping, A. Mendhekar, C. Maeda, C. Videira Lopes, J-M. Loingtier and J. Irwin, "Aspect-oriented programming", *Proceedings of the European Conference on Object-Oriented Programming, Lecture Notes in Computer Science 1241*, Finland (Springer-Verlag, June 1997).

29. P. Tarr, H. Ossher, W. Harrison and S. M. Sutton, Jr., "*N* Degrees of separation: Multi-dimensional separation of concerns", *Proceedings of the International Conference on Software Engineering* (May 1999).

30. K. Lieberherr, *Adaptive Object-Oriented Software: The Demeter Method with Propagation Patterns* (PWS Publishing Company, 1996).

31. M. Becker and J. L. Díaz-Herrera, *Creating Domain-Specific Libraries: A Methodology and Design Guidelines, IEEE International Conference in Software Reuse* (Rio de Janeiro, Brazil, November 1–4, 1994).

32. M. Mochizuki, A. Suzuki and T. Tajima, "UTMS system architecture", *Sixth Annual World Congress on ITS* (Toronto, November 8–12, 1999).

33. OMG CORBABusiness Objects: http://www.omg.org/homepages/bodtf/

34. Product LINE Case Studies: *http://www.sei.cmu.edu/plp/plp_case_studies.html*

# INCONSISTENCY MANAGEMENT IN SOFTWARE ENGINEERING: SURVEY AND OPEN RESEARCH ISSUES

GEORGE SPANOUDAKIS and ANDREA ZISMAN

*Department of Computing, City University Northampton Square,*
*London EC1V 0HB, UK*
*E-mail: {gespan, a. zisman}@soi.city.ac.uk*

The development of complex software systems is a complex and lengthy activity that involves the participation and collaboration of many stakeholders (e.g. customers, users, analysts, designers, and developers). This results in many partial models of the developing system. These models can be inconsistent with each other since they describe the system from different perspectives and reflect the views of the stakeholders involved in their construction. Inconsistent software models can have negative and positive effects in the software development life-cycle. On the negative side, inconsistencies can delay and increase the cost of system development; do not guarantee some properties of the system, such as safety and reliability; and generate difficulties on system maintenance. On the positive side, inconsistencies can facilitate identification of some aspects of the system that need further analysis, assist with the specification of alternatives for the development of the system, and support elicitation of information about it.

The software engineering community has proposed many techniques and methods to support the management of inconsistencies in various software models. In this paper, we present a survey of these techniques and methods. The survey is organized according to a conceptual framework which views inconsistency management as a process composed of six activities. These activities are the *detection of overlaps, detection of inconsistencies, diagnosis of inconsistencies, handling of inconsistencies, tracking of inconsistencies,* and *specification* and *application of a management policy for inconsistencies.* This paper also presents the main contributions of the research work that has been conducted to support each of the above activities and identifies the issues which are still open to further research.

*Keywords*: Software specification, overlaps detection, detection and handling of inconsistencies.

## 1. Introduction

The construction of complex software systems is characterized by the distribution of roles and responsibilities among autonomous or semi-autonomous *stakeholders* (e.g. customers, users, analysts, designers, developers, third parties). These roles and responsibilities may be organizationally defined, be the result of the advocated system development process, follow some separation of concerns about the system under development, or be in line and reflect the different capabilities of the stakeholders involved in the process. The distribution of responsibilities and roles often results in the construction of many partial models of the developing system (referred to as "software models" in the following). These models may be requirement specifications and domain analysis models, system architecture models, structural and behavioural system design models, models of the implementation structure of the system, and/or models of the deployment of the components of the system.

Software models normally describe the system from different angles and in different levels of abstraction, granularity and formality. They may also be constructed using different notations and they are likely to reflect the perspectives and the goals of the stakeholders involved in their construction. Very often, these dimensions of heterogeneity lead to inconsistencies among the models. Inconsistencies arise because the models overlap — that is they incorporate elements which refer to common aspects of the system under development — and make assertions about these aspects which are not jointly satisfiable as they stand, or under certain conditions.

Inconsistencies may have both positive and negative effects on the system development life-cycle. On the negative side, they may delay and, therefore, increase the cost of the system development process, jeopardize properties related to the quality of the system (e.g. reliability, safety), and make it more difficult to maintain the system. On the positive side, inconsistencies highlight conflicts between the views, perceptions, and goals of the stakeholders involved in the development process (which must be dealt with in an accountable way or, otherwise, they may put in risk the acceptance and usability of the system), indicate aspects of the system which deserve further analysis, and facilitate the exploration of alternatives in system development and the elicitation of information about the system.

The above benefits of inconsistencies have not been only the wisdom of academic researchers; they have also been confirmed by empirical studies [5, 25, 55, 78]. It has, however, to be appreciated that these benefits arise only if inconsistencies are allowed to emerge as models evolve, tolerated for at least some period and used as drivers of managed interactions among the stakeholders that can deliver the above benefits [55]. However, more important perhaps than any of these positive consequences is the fact that inconsistencies are the inevitable result of the need to describe complex systems from different perspectives, distribute responsibilities to different stakeholders in the software development life cycle, and allow them to work autonomously without requiring a continual reconciliation of their models and views for, at least, certain periods of time. These benefits and needs indicate that inconsistencies need to be "managed", that is detected, analyzed, recorded and possibly resolved.

The software engineering community has been concerned with the problem of inconsistencies in software models since the late 80's and has developed techniques, methods and tools which support the identification, analysis, and treatment of various forms of inconsistencies in models expressed in a wide range of modelling languages and notations, including:

- formal specification languages including first-order logic [22, 30, 59, 23, 24, 74], Z [9, 8, 80], LOTOS [9], KAOS [76, 77];

- structured requirements templates [4, 18, 49, 66, 67];
- state transition diagrams [37] and state-based languages [41, 11];
- conceptual graphs [16]; and
- object-oriented languages [12, 26, 72, 73, 75, 80].

The objectives of this paper are: (a) to clarify the issues which arise in connection with the problem of inconsistencies in software models, (b) to survey the research work that has been conducted to address this problem (with the exception of work concerned with inconsistencies in the specification and enactment of software process models), (c) to identify which of the arising issues have been addressed by the research work in this area so far, and (d) to identify current research trends and establish the issues which are still open to further research. Note, that this paper does not cover research work related to inconsistencies in the modelling and execution of software processes (e.g. [14]).

The paper is organized according to a conceptual framework which views the management of inconsistency as a process that involves six major activities, namely the detection of overlaps between software models, the detection of inconsistencies between software models, the diagnosis of inconsistencies, the handling of inconsistencies, the tracking of the findings, the decisions made and the actions taken in the process, and the specification and application of an inconsistency management policy.

The rest of this paper is organized as follows. Section 2 contains definitions of the main phenomena, which arise in inconsistency management, and describe each of the activities of this process in detail. Section 3 presents the research work concerned with the identification of overlaps. Section 4 describes work related to the detection of inconsistencies. Section 5 is concerned with the work about diagnosis of inconsistencies. Section 6 presents work on handling of inconsistencies. Section 7 explores work related to tracking of the inconsistency management process. Section 8 presents work regarding specification and application of the inconsistency management process. Section 9 discusses open issues for further research. Finally, Sec. 10 summarizes existing work and presents the conclusions of the survey.

## 2. Inconsistency Management: Basic Definitions and Process

One of the factors that make it hard to understand and contrast the findings and contributions of the various strands of research and techniques developed to address the problem of inconsistencies in software models has been the lack of a commonly used terminology by the various researchers in this area [81]. In this section, we attempt to overcome this problem by establishing a framework which:

(a) defines the main phenomena which relate to inconsistencies in software models, and

(b) describes the main activities of the process of managing inconsistencies.

## 2.1. *Main definitions*

In Sec. 1, we informally described inconsistency as a state in which two or more overlapping elements of different software models make assertions about the aspects of the system they describe which are not jointly satisfiable. In this section, we define *overlaps* and *inconsistencies* in more precise terms. However, our definitions are still deliberately broad in order to accommodate the different ways in which these phenomena of overlaps and inconsistencies have been realized in the literature.

Following [74], we define overlaps as relations between *interpretations* ascribed to software models by specific *agents*. An agent in this setting may be a person or a computational mechanism.

An interpretation is defined as follows:

**Definition 1.** The interpretation of a software model $S$ specified as a set of interrelated elements $E$ is a pair $(I, U)$ where:

- $U$ is a non-empty set of sets of individuals, called the *domain* of the interpretation of the model.
- $I$ is a total morphism which maps each element $e$ of $E$ onto a relation $R$ of degree $n$ ($R \subseteq U^n$) called the extension of $e$ ($n = 1, 2, \ldots, |U|$).

According to this definition, an interpretation maps each element of a model onto the set of individuals or the relationships between these individuals in a given domain which are denoted by the element. Thus, an interpretation reflects how an agent understands a software model in reference to a given domain.

Given the previous definition of an interpretation, overlaps between software models are defined as follows:

**Definition 2.** Given a pair of elements $e_i$ and $e_j$ of two software models $S_i$ and $S_j$ and two interpretations $T_{iA} = (I_{iA}, U_{iA})$ and $T_{jB} = (I_{jB}, U_{jB})$ of $S_i$ and $S_j$ ascribed to them by the agents $A$ and $B$, respectively:

- $e_i$ and $e_j$ will be said not to overlap at all with respect to $T_{iA}$ and $T_{jB}$ if $I_{iA}(e_i) \neq \emptyset$, $I_{jB}(e_j) \neq \emptyset$, and $I_{iA}(e_i) \cap I_{jB}(e_j) = \emptyset$.[a]
- $e_i$ and $e_j$ will be said to overlap totally with respect to $T_{iA}$ and $T_{jB}$ if $I_{iA}(e_i) \neq \emptyset$, $I_{jB}(e_j) \neq \emptyset$, and $I_{iA}(e_i) = I_{jB}(e_j)$.
- $e_i$ will be said to overlap inclusively with $e_j$ with respect to $T_{iA}$ and $T_{jB}$ if $I_{iA}(e_i) \neq \emptyset$, $I_{jB}(e_j) \neq \emptyset$, and $I_{jB}(e_j) \subset I_{iA}(e_i)$.
- $e_i$ will be said to overlap partially with $e_j$ with respect to $T_{iA}$ and $T_{jB}$ if $I_{iA}(e_i) \neq \emptyset$, $I_{jB}(e_j) \neq \emptyset$, $I_{iA}(e_i) \cap I_{jB}(e_j) \neq \emptyset$, $I_{iA}(e_i) - I_{jB}(e_j) \neq \emptyset$, and $I_{jB}(e_j) - I_{iA}(e_i) \neq \emptyset$.

---

[a]The symbols $\cap, \cup$ and $-$ denote the set intersection, union and difference operations, respectively.

According to this definition, two model elements overlap totally if they have identical interpretations, overlap partially if they have non-identical but overlapping interpretations, overlap inclusively if the interpretation of one of the elements includes the interpretation of the other, and do not overlap if they have disjoint interpretations.

As Spanoudakis *et al* have pointed out in [74], in reality, it is impossible to enumerate the domains of interpretations with sufficient completeness for establishing the interpretations of the models and identifying overlaps on the basis of these interpretations. This is because in many cases these domains are not of bounded size or change frequently. To overcome this problem, overlaps can be represented as relations between the sets of elements $E_i$ and $E_j$ of two software models $S_i$ and $S_j$, the set of the agents who can identify them ($A$), and the set of overlap kinds ($O_T$):

$$OV \subset E_i \times E_j \times A \times O_T{}^{\text{b}}.$$

An element of this relation $ov(c_i, c_j, a, t)$ denotes that there is an overlap of type $t$ between the elements $c_i$ and $c_j$ of two models $S_i$ and $S_j$ given the interpretation of $S_i$ and $S_j$ that is assumed by the agent $a$. The set of overlap kinds $O_T$ includes the following elements: *no* (null overlap); *to* (total overlap); *po* (partial overlap); and *io* (inclusive overlap — $c_i$ overlaps inclusively with $c_j$). Agents can identify overlap relations without having to define the interpretations underlying these relations. However, if an agent $A$ identifies that a model element $e_i$ overlaps inclusively with a model element $e_j$, this agent essentially confirms that $I_A(e_j) \subset I_A(e_i)$ without having to define $I_A(e_j)$ and $I_A(e_j)$. Thus, the identity of the agent becomes a substitute for a precise account of the interpretation underlying the relation and the agent who asserted an overlap relation can be traced when this relation is involved in the derivation of an inconsistency.

An inconsistency is then defined in terms of overlaps as follows:

**Definition 3.** Assume a set of *software models* $S_1 \cdots S_n$, the sets of *overlap relations* between them $O_a(S_i, S_j)(i = 1, \ldots, n$ and $j = 1, \ldots, n)$, a *domain theory* $D$, and a *consistency rule* $CR$. $S_1, \ldots, S_n$ will be said to be inconsistent with $CR$ given the overlaps between them as expressed by the sets $O_a(S_i, S_j)$ and the domain theory $D$ if it can be shown that the rule $CR$ is not satisfied by the models.

The domain theory $D$ in this definition may express some general knowledge about the domain of the system that is described by the models as in [76] and/or some general software engineering knowledge (e.g. interactions between quality system features and architectural system design patterns [4, 6]).

---

[b]This representation of overlap relations is a simplification of the scheme proposed by Spanoudakis *et al* in [74].

A consistency rule may be:

- A *well-formedness* rule — These are rules which must be satisfied by the models for them to be legitimate models of the language in which they have been expressed. An example of a rule of this kind is a well-formedness rule specified in the semantic definition of the Unified Modelling Language (UML) which requires that the graph formed by the generalization relations in UML models must be acyclic [62].
- A *description identity* rule — These are rules which require the different elements of software models which totally overlap to have identical descriptions [12, 16, 72].
- An *application domain* rule — These are rules that specify relations between the individuals in the domain of the system which are denoted by the model elements connected by the rule. An example of such a relation for a resource management software system could be that every user who has requested a resource will get it, even if this will happen some time after the request [76].
- A *development compatibility* rule — These are rules which require that it must be possible to construct at least one model that develops further two or more other models or model elements and conforms to the restrictions which apply to both of them. This model, depending on the assumed development relation, might be an implementation model [9]. An example of such a rule is the existence of a common unification of two abstract data types used in [8]. Similar rules are also used in [1].
- A *development process compliance* rule — These are rules which require the compliance of software models with specific software engineering practices or standards followed in a project. Emmerich *et al* in [27] give examples of numerous such rules for the case of the PSS-05 standard [82]. As an example, consider one of these rules which requires that each user requirement must have an associated measure of priority in a model that describes a system that is to be delivered incrementally [27].

## 2.2. *The inconsistency management process*

Inconsistency management has been defined by Finkelstein *et al,* [29] as the process by which inconsistencies between software models are handled to support the goals of the stakeholders concerned. In the literature, there have been proposed two general frameworks describing the activities that constitute this process: one by Finkelstein *et al,* [29] and one by Nuseibeh *et al,* [56, 61]. Both these frameworks share the premise that an inconsistency in software models has to be established in relation to a specific consistency rule (as in Definition 3) and that the process of managing inconsistencies includes activities for detecting, diagnosing and handling them. These core activities are supplemented by other activities which are not shared by both frameworks such as the specification and application of inconsistency management policies in [29].

In this article, we propose a set of activities which unifies the above frameworks and amends them in a way which, as far as we are concerned, reflects more accurately the operationalization of the inconsistency management process by the various techniques and methods which have been developed to support it. These activities are:

(1) *Detection of overlaps* — This activity is performed to identify overlaps between the software models. The identification of overlaps is a crucial part of the overall process since models with no overlapping elements cannot be inconsistent [8, 16, 18, 29, 46, 50, 79, 74]. The identification of overlaps is carried out by agents which are specified in the inconsistency management policy (see below).

(2) *Detection of inconsistencies* — This activity is performed to check for violations of the consistency rules by the software models. The consistency rules to be checked are established by the adopted inconsistency management policy (see below). This policy also specifies the circumstances which will trigger the checks.

(3) *Diagnosis of inconsistencies* — This activity is concerned with the identification of the *source*, the *cause* and the *impact* of an inconsistency. The source of an inconsistency is the set of elements of software models which have been used in the construction of the argument that shows that the models violate a consistency rule [61]. The cause of an inconsistency in our framework is defined as the conflict(s) in the perspectives and/or the goals of the stakeholders, which are expressed by the elements of the models that give rise to the inconsistency (a survey of studies of conflict in computer-supported cooperative work is given in [19]). The impact of an inconsistency is defined as the consequences that an inconsistency has for a system. The source and the cause of an inconsistency have a very important role in the inconsistency management process since they can be used to determine what options are available for resolving or ameliorating an inconsistency, as well as the cost and the benefits of the application of each of these options (see handling of inconsistencies below). Establishing the impact of an inconsistency in qualitative or quantitative terms is also necessary for deciding with what priority the inconsistency has to be handled, and for evaluating the risks associated with the actions for handling the inconsistency which do not fully resolve it (see handling of inconsistencies below).

(4) *Handling of inconsistencies* — The handling of inconsistencies has been considered as a central activity in inconsistency management [76, 68]. This activity is concerned with:

    (i) the identification of the possible *actions* for dealing with an inconsistency;

    (ii) the evaluation of the *cost* and the *benefits* that would arise from the application of each of these actions;

    (iii) the evaluation of the *risks* that would arise from not resolving the inconsistency; and

    (iv) the selection of one of the actions to execute.

(5) *Tracking* — This activity is concerned with the recording of: (a) the reasoning underpinning the detection of an inconsistency, (b) the source, cause and impact of it, (c) the handling actions that were considered in connection with it, and (d) the arguments underpinning the decision to select one of these options and reject the other. Keeping track of what has happened in the process makes the understanding of the findings, the decisions, and the actions taken by those who might need to use or refer to the software models in subsequent stages of the development life-cycle of the system easier. This is especially true for those who may not have been involved in the development of the system and/or the process of managing the inconsistencies detected in it. However, a detailed tracking of this sort certainly imposes an information management overhead to the process of inconsistency management and the software development process. This overhead has to be carefully evaluated in relation to the expected benefits.

(6) *Specification and application of an inconsistency management policy* — There are numerous questions that need to be answered before and during the application of an inconsistency management process. These are questions about the agent that should be used to identify overlaps between particular kinds of software models, questions about when and how often inconsistencies should be detected, questions about the diagnostic checks that should be applied to breaches of specific consistency rules, questions about the techniques that should be applied to evaluate the cost, benefits and risks associated with inconsistency handling options, and questions about the stakeholders who will undertake responsibility for handling inconsistencies. The answers to these questions depend on the kind of the software models that the inconsistency management process will have to deal with, the general software development process advocated in a specific project [61] and the particular standards that this process wants to observe [27], as well as the characteristics of the software development team (for example availability of stakeholders during particular inconsistency management activities, willingness of stakeholders to engage in resolution negotiations).

Clearly to provide coherent and effective answers to the above questions it is necessary to have a *policy* about the inconsistency management that should be applied to a particular project [29]. This policy must specify:

   (i) the agent(s) that should be used to identify the overlaps among the partial models;

   (ii) the consistency rules that should be checked against the models;

   (iii) the circumstances that will trigger the detection of the overlaps and the inconsistencies;

   (iv) the mechanisms that should be used for diagnosing inconsistencies and the circumstances that should trigger this activity;

   (v) the mechanisms that should be used for assessing the impact of inconsistencies and the circumstances that should trigger this activity;

   (vi) the mechanisms that should be used for assessing the cost, benefits and risks associated with different inconsistency handling options; and

   (vii) the stakeholders who would have responsibility for handling inconsistencies.

This activity also establishes the mechanisms for applying an inconsistency management policy in a project and for monitoring this application to ensure that progress is being made with regards to the general objectives that the policy should achieve [29].

In the subsequent sections of this paper, we present the main ways in which the various methods and techniques which have been developed to handle inconsistencies in software models support the above inconsistency management activities. In the end of each section, we present a table summarizing the existing techniques.

## 3. Detection of Overlaps

The methods and techniques that have been developed to support the management of inconsistencies in software models detect overlaps based on representation conventions, shared ontologies, human inspection, and forms of similarity analysis of the models involved.

The different ways in which each of these approaches has been realized are discussed after presenting the properties of the different types of overlap relations defined in Sec. 2.1. Spanoudakis *et al*, in [74] have shown that according to Definition 2:

   — total overlap is a reflexive, symmetric and transitive relation,

   — inclusive overlap is an irreflexive, antisymmetric and transitive relation, and

   — partial overlap is an irreflexive and symmetric relation.

These properties give us a basis for establishing the exact type of the overlap relations that each of the approaches in the literature can identify.

### 3.1. *Representation conventions*

The simplest and most common representation convention is to assume the existence of a total overlap between model elements with identical names and no overlap between any other pair of elements. This convention is widely deployed by model checking [11, 40] and other specialized model analysis methods and techniques [12].

The same convention also forms the basis of the classical unification algorithms (see [47] for a survey) and predicate matching process which are used to detect overlaps in all the logic-based methods and techniques for inconsistency management [1, 8, 22, 27, 30, 55, 69, 76]. The classical unification algorithms find the *most general unifier* (if one exists) between terms expressed in some first-order logical language. A term in such a language is either a constant or a variable symbol, or a function symbol followed by a series of other terms separated by commas.

The unification algorithms perform a syntactic matching between the terms that they are given to unify. For terms which start with a function symbol the matching is successful only if these symbols are the same in both terms, the terms have the same number of subterms (arity), and the matching of their corresponding subterms is also successful. Variable symbols can be matched freely with constant or other variable symbols, or terms which start with function symbols provided that the latter do not contain the variable symbol that they are matched with in any of their subterms (i.e., the *occur* check [47]). This matching process returns a mapping of the variables of the terms onto other terms, called *substitution*. The most general unifier is a substitution $\sigma$ between two terms $t_1$ and $t_2$ for which there is always another substitution $\tau$ that can be applied to $\sigma$ in order to translate it to any other unifier $\theta$ of $t_1$ and $t_2$, that is $\tau(\sigma) = \theta$.[c]

As an example of classical term unification consider the predicates *student* and *project_supervisor* below:

- *student*$(x)$,
- *student*$(a)$,
- *student*$(y)$,
- *project_supervisor*$(x, personal\_tutor(x))$,
- *project_supervisor*$(y, x)$, and
- *project_supervisor*$(a, personal\_tutor(a))$

where "student" and "project_supervisor" are predicate symbols, "personal_tutor" is a function symbol, $x$ and $y$ are variable symbols, and $a$ is a constant symbol. In this example, the most general unifier of *student*$(x)$ and *student*$(a)$ is $\{x/a\}$, the most general unifier of *student*$(x)$ and *student*$(y)$ is $\{x/y\}$ and the most general unifier of *project_supervisor*$(x, personal\_tutor(x))$ and *project_supervisor* $(a, personal\_tutor(a))$ is $\{x/a\}$.[d]

It has to be appreciated that unification makes a number of matching assumptions which turn out to be weak given the forms of heterogeneity which may appear in independently constructed software models (see Sec. 1). These weak assumptions

---

[c]$\tau(\sigma)$ denotes the application of the substitution $\tau$ onto the result of the application of the substitution $\sigma$.
[d]The symbol "/" means "is replaced by".

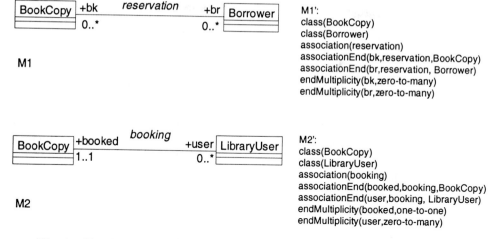

**Fig. 1.** Two UML class diagrams and their translations into a first-order language.

are: (a) that only terms with the same function symbol can be matched, (b) that only terms with the same arity can be matched, and (c) that only subterms which appear in the same relative position in the structure of a term can be matched. Assumptions analogous to (a), (b) and (c) are also used in matching predicates while making inferences using the standard inference rules of classical logic. In this process, unification is attempted only between predicates with the same predicate symbol and arity, and only between the corresponding terms in the structures of two predicates. The assumption (a) in both predicate matching and term unification has been the subject of extensive criticism by many researchers in this area, including Zave and Jackson [79], Jackson [46], Spanoudakis *et al* [74] and Boiten *et al* [8]. This is because the assumption (a) turns out to be inadequate even for simple forms of heterogeneity between models such as the presence of synonyms and homonyms.

To give an example, consider for instance the two UML class diagrams $M1$ and $M2$ and their translations $M1'$ and $M2'$ into the first-order logical language shown in Fig. 1[e] and the consistency rule $CR1$ below:

$$CR1: \quad (\forall x_1)(\forall x_2)(\forall x_3)(\forall x_4)(\forall x_5) : \text{associationEnd}(x_1, x_2, x_3) \wedge$$
$$\text{endMultiplicity}(x_1, x_4) \wedge \text{endMultiplicity}(x_1, x_5) \rightarrow (x_4 = x_5).$$

$CR1$ requires all the assertions about the multiplicity of an association end in one or more models to be the same (i.e., a *description identity* rule). The models

---

[e]The first-order representation of the class diagram in Fig. 1 follows a commonly suggested scheme for translating diagrammatic models into a first-order language (see for example [23, 30]). According-ing to this scheme, the name of an element of the diagram becomes a constant that denotes the element and appears as an argument of a predicate that denotes the construct of the language that is instantiated by the element.

$M1$' and $M2$' are not inconsistent with respect to $CR1$ if the overlaps between their elements are detected using unification. Clearly, $M1$' and $M2$' would not satisfy $CR1$ if the association ends "bk" and "booked" in them were known to overlap totally. Note, however, that standard unification would not be able to detect this total overlap since the non-identical constants "bk" and "booked" cannot be unified. Possible ways of overcoming this problem in the framework of first-order logic are discussed in Sec. 4.1.

In the case of first-order languages with function symbols, classical unification gives rise to a reflexive and symmetric, but not transitive relation between predicates. In the above example, for instance, although the predicate $project\_supervisor(x, personal\_tutor(x))$ can be unified with the predicate $project\_supervisor(a, personal\_tutor(a))$ (mgu = $\{x/a\}$) and the predicate $project\_supervisor(a, personal\_tutor(a))$ can be unified with the predicate $project\_supervisor(y, x)$ (mgu = $\{y/a, x/personal\_tutor(a)\}$) there is no unifier for the predicates $project\_supervisor(x, personal\_tutor(x))$ and $project\_supervisor(y, x)$. Thus, in the case of such languages, it is not possible to classify the overlap relation between a pair of unified predicates in terms of the overlap types of [74] (a unification relation may be a total or a partial overlap). Note, however, that transitivity is guaranteed when unification is applied to models expressed in first-order languages with no function symbols as those used in [22, 30, 74, 76, 79]. Thus, in the case of such languages, it can be argued that unification detects total overlap relations.

## 3.2. *Shared ontologies*

An alternative approach for the identification of overlaps is to use shared ontologies. This approach requires the authors of the models to tag the elements in them with items in a shared ontology. The tag of a model element is taken to denote its interpretation in the domain described by the ontology and, therefore, it is used to identify overlaps between elements of different models. A total overlap in this approach is assumed when two model elements are "tagged" with the same item in the ontology [6, 50, 66, 67].

The ontologies used by Robinson [66], and Robinson and Fickas [67] in their Oz system are domain models which prescribe detailed hierarchies of domain objects, relationships between them, goals that may be held by the stakeholders, and operators which achieve these goals. The software models which can be handled by their techniques are constructed by instantiating the common domain models they propose. In searching for inconsistencies their techniques assume total overlaps between model elements which instantiate the same goal in the domain model. The ontology used by the QARCC system [6] is a decomposition taxonomy of software system quality attributes. This ontology also relates quality attributes with software architectures and development processes that can be used to achieve or inhibit these attributes. For example, there is a quality attribute called "portability" in QARCC's ontology which is decomposed into the quality attributes "scalability" and "modifiability". Portability, according to QARCC's ontology can be achieved through a "layered" system architecture and a "prototyping" approach to system development. The software requirements models that QARCC analyses for inconsistencies are described through "Win" conditions which are connected to quality attributes. An overlap between two Win conditions is established if the quality attribute that these conditions refer to can be realized or inhibited by a common architecture or system development process.

It has to be appreciated that in order to facilitate communication between stakeholders about a specific domain of discourse, without necessarily assuming the existence of a global shared theory amongst the stakeholders, ontologies have to provide definitions of the items they include and be general. Furthermore, the stakeholders need to "commit" themselves to the ontology. Commitment in this setting means that the observable actions of the stakeholders are consistent with the definitions of the items in the ontology [35, 36]. As a consequence of the generality of ontologies, software models have to add a lot of details to them to describe a complex system with a reasonable degree of completeness. Inevitably this leads to associations of many model elements with the same item in the ontology and as a result only coarse-grain overlaps can be identified by using these items. Furthermore, since ontologies incorporate item definitions, they are models themselves and as such they might be interpreted in different ways by different stakeholders! Thus, the same ontology item may be used for ascribing different meanings to different model elements. As a consequence, the existence of overlaps between elements associated with the same item in an ontology cannot be assumed with safety unless there is evidence that the stakeholders understood the ontology in the same way and committed themselves to it.

### 3.3. *Human inspection*

A third general approach is to get the stakeholders to identify the overlap relations. Numerous methods and techniques rely on this approach including [8, 9, 16, 18, 28, 46, 79].

*Synoptic* [18], for instance, expects stakeholders to identify "strong" and "weak" correspondences between models which correspond to total and partial overlaps in our framework. The support provided by this tool takes the form of visual aid for browsing, graphically selecting and recording of overlaps. Delugach [16] requires stakeholders to specify "counterpart" relationships between model elements. These relationships correspond to total overlaps.

Zave and Jackson [79] suggest the use of "description" graphs to relate the predicate symbols in the "signatures" of different software models. A model signature includes the symbols of the predicates in the model which cannot be defined in terms of other predicates. The decision about which predicates should become part of the signature of a model is language-dependent. For example, in the case of representing a state-transition diagram in a first-order language, if the predicates which represent the states of this diagram become members of the signature of the model, then the predicates which represent the transitions of the diagram will not become part of this signature and vice versa [79]. A relation between two predicates in the description graph can be created only if there is an overlap between them and both models include assertions which incorporate the predicates. The relations specified in description graphs do not distinguish between different types of overlaps.

Jackson [46] suggests the identification of overlaps by virtue of "designations". Designations constitute a way of associating non-ground terms in formal models with ground terms which are known to have reliable and unambiguous interpretations (called "phenomena"). A designation associates a non-ground term with a recognition rule which identifies the phenomena designated by it. The rule is specified in natural language. Designations can certainly help stakeholders in identifying overlaps but should not be used as definitive indications of them. The reason is that the recognition rules of the designations might themselves admit different interpretations.

Boiten *et al* [8] expect the authors of the $Z$ schemas that their techniques are dealing with to identify "correspondence" relations between the variables which appear in these schemas (but not the predicates). These relations correspond to total overlaps and are subsequently used in constructing possible compositions of two or more $Z$ schemas (i.e., the basic way of exploring and handling inconsistencies in their approach). A similar approach is taken in [9] for the Open Distributed Processing models expressed in LOTOS.

Fiadeiro and Maibaum [28] suggest the representation of overlap relations between model elements using the formal framework of the category theory [34]. They formalize models as categories (directed graphs with a composition and identity structure) and use functors between these categories (i.e., functional mappings between the nodes and edges of the categories) to interconnect them. The functors are then checked if they preserve the structures and therefore the properties of the category elements that they interconnect. This check in our framework constitutes the detection of inconsistencies. The idea to use functors to represent overlaps has been supported by other authors [21] who, nevertheless, have criticized the stance that it should be checked whether functors preserve the structures of the parts of the models they interconnect. This criticism has been on the grounds that such a check would be too strict in the development of large software systems.

Spanoudakis *et al* in [74] have also acknowledged the need to check the consistency of overlap relations but they propose a less strict check. According to them, a set of asserted overlap relations should be checked if they satisfy certain properties which arise from the formal definition of overlaps given in Sec. 2.1. For example, if it has been asserted that a model element $a$ inclusively overlaps with a model element $b$ but has no overlap with a third element $c$, it should be checked that there is no total, inclusive or partial overlap between $b$ and $c$. In their view, this check should be performed before checking the consistency of the models involved. This check would be particularly useful in cases of overlaps asserted by humans.

The main difficulty with the identification of overlaps using inspections by humans is that this kind of identification becomes extremely time consuming even for models of moderate complexity.

### 3.4. *Similarity analysis*

The fourth general approach is to identify overlaps by automated comparisons between the models. This approach exploits the fact that modelling languages incorporate constructs which imply or strongly suggest the existence of overlap relations. For instance, the "Is-a" relation in various object-oriented modelling languages is a statement of either an inclusive overlap or a total overlap. This is because "Is-a" relations normally have a set-inclusion semantics, that is the subtype designates a proper (or not proper) subset of the instances of the supertype. Similarly, the implication ($\rightarrow$) between two predicates of the same arity constitutes a statement of inclusive overlap in a first-order language.

The comparison methods that have been deployed to realize this approach search for structural and semantic similarities either between the models themselves [72] or between each model and abstract structures that constitute parts of domain specific ontologies [52]. In the "reconciliation" method of Spanoudakis and Finkelstein [72, 73] the detection of overlaps is formulated as an instance of the *weighted bipartite graph matching problem* [63]. The nodes in the two partitions of the graph in their method denote the elements of the models being compared, the edges of the graph represent the possible overlap relations between these elements, and the weights of the edges are computed by distance functions which measure modelling discrepancies in the specifications of the elements connected by the edge, with respect to different semantic modelling abstractions. The method detects partial overlaps between the elements of the two models by selecting the morphism between the two partitions of the overlap graph that has the lowest aggregate distance. Palmer and Fields [83] also identify overlaps between software requirements models expressed in multimedia documents by using indexing and clustering techniques.

Overall, it should be noted that similarity analysis techniques tend to be sensitive to extensive heterogeneity in model representation, granularity and levels of abstraction.

### 3.5. *Summary*

A summary of the assumptions, and the main positive features and limitations of the various approaches to the identification of overlaps is given in Table 1.

**Table 1.**   Summary of different approaches to identification of overlap.

| Approach | Main Assumptions | Positive Features | Main Limitations |
|---|---|---|---|
| Representation Conventions | • models expressed in some formal language | • relatively inexpensive way of overlap identification | • sensitive to simple forms of model heterogeneity<br>• applicable only to models expressed in the same language |
| Shared Ontologies | • existence of well-defined ontologies<br>• models need to be related to the ontologies | • applicable to models expressed in different languages | • stakeholders may understand an ontology differently<br>• identification of only coarse-grain overlaps |
| Human Inspection | • stakeholders need to identify overlap relations | • certainty in overlap identification<br>• applicable to models expressed in different languages | • labour intensive |
| Similarity Analysis | • models need to be related through a common meta-model | • automatic identification of overlaps<br>• applicable to models expressed in different languages | • sensitive to model heterogeneity<br>• resulting overlaps are not always accurate |

## 4. Detection of Inconsistencies

Our survey has indicated that, there have been four broad approaches to the detection of inconsistencies in software models. These are:

— the logic-based approach,
— the model checking approach,
— the specialized model analysis approach, and
— the human-centered collaborative exploration approach.

The basic mechanisms used by each of these approaches and their merit are discussed next.

### 4.1. *Logic-based detection*

The logic-based approach to the detection of inconsistencies is characterized by the use of some formal inference technique to derive inconsistencies from software models expressed in a formal modelling language (e.g. first-order classical logic [22, 23, 30, 59, 74], real-time temporal logic [76, 77], Quasi-Classical (QC) logic [45], Object Constraint Language [75], assertional language of O-Telos [55], Z [1, 9]).

The methods and techniques which adopt this approach use the following reformulation of the definition of inconsistencies given in Sec. 2.1:

**Definition 4.** Assume a set of software models $S_1 \cdots S_n$, sets of overlap relations between their elements $O_a(S_i, S_j)(i = 1, \ldots, n$ and $j = 1, \ldots, n)$ and a *consistency rule* $CR$. $S_1, \ldots, S_n$ are inconsistent with respect to the rule $CR$ when they overlap as indicated by the sets $O_a(S_i, S_j)$ if and only if:

$$\{F(G_1(S_1), \ldots, G_n(S_n), O_a), D\} \vdash_L \neg CR$$

where

- $O_a$ is the set of all the overlap relations asserted by an agent $a$: $O_a \equiv \cup_{\{i=1,\ldots,n\}\{j=1,\ldots,n\}} O_a(S_i, S_j)$.
- $G_i$ is a transformation that translates the model $S_i$ from the original language in which it was expressed into the formal language assumed by the technique $(i = 1, \ldots, n)$.
- $F$ is a transformation from the vocabularies of the translated models (these are the sets of their predicate, function, variable and constant symbols) into a new common vocabulary which is used to represent the overlap relations between these symbols.
- $D$ are the axioms of some domain theory (see Sec. 2.1).
- $\vdash_L$ is a consequence relation based on a particular set of inference rules $L$.

Definition 4 constitutes a parametrized re-formulation of definitions of inconsistencies in [9, 30, 45, 55, 74, 60]. It is also a special case of the Craig and Robinson's theorem of joint consistency. According to this theorem, two theories $T_i$ and $T_j$ are inconsistent if and only if there is a formula $A$ such that $T_i \vdash A$ and $T_j \vdash \neg A$ (see p. 79 in [70]).

Examples of transformations that could be used in the place of $G$ for different non logic-based software modelling languages are given in [30, 79].

Note also that, $F$ becomes the *identity* transformation (and therefore can be ignored) if the overlaps between the models are identified by standard unification (see Sec. 3.1). Spanoudakis *et al* in [74] have proposed a transformation $F$ that gets as input two models expressed in a first-order logical language (with no function symbols) and a set of overlap relations between their constant and predicate symbols asserted by some agent, and translates them into a single model that can then be checked by normal theorem proving and unification for inconsistencies. Using this transformation a total overlap relation between the constants "bk" and "booked" in the models $M1'$ and $M2'$ of Fig. 1, $ov(bk, booked, a, to)$, would be translated into the fact (bk = booked) (assuming the application of the intra-overlap algorithm presented in [74]). Then given the following translation of the rule $CR1$ (see

Sec. 4.2):

$$CR1' : (\forall x_1)(\forall x_2)(\forall x_3)(\forall x_4)(\forall x_5) : \text{associationEnd}(x_1, x_2, x_3) \wedge,$$
$$\text{associationEnd}(x_6, x_7, x_8) \wedge \text{endMultiplicity}(x_1, x_4) \wedge,$$
$$\text{endMultiplicity}(x_6, x_5) \wedge (x_1 = x_6) \rightarrow (x_4 = x_5),$$

the inconsistency between $M1'$ and $M2'$, and $CR1'$ that we discussed in Sec. 4.2 would be detectable (if the formulas of $M1'$ and $M2'$ are expanded by the set of *equality* axioms [84]). It should be noted, however, that one of the limitations of this re-writing scheme is that it does not handle inclusive or partial overlaps between constant symbols and cannot handle overlaps relations between predicates of different arities.

Most of the techniques which advocate the logic-based approach operationalize the consequence relation $\vdash_L$ by using theorem proving based on the standard inference rules of classical logic such as resolution, conjunct and negation elimination, instantiation of universally quantified formulas, and other rules for introducing negative information in the models such as the closed-word-assumption (CWA) (see [42]). These techniques include [22, 23, 30, 59, 74]. A theorem proving facility is also incorporated in a technique that checks whether a common unifying abstract data type (ADT) exists for two ADTs which are expressed in $Z$ described in [8]. A similar technique is described in [1]. A similar approach, in terms of the inference mechanism used, is also taken in [27, 55, 69, 75].

Nissen *et al* [55] assume software models and consistency rules expressed in $O$-Telos. $O$-Telos is a variant of Telos [54], an object-oriented knowledge representation language that allows the specification of integrity constraints and deductive rules using its own assertion sub-language. Integrity constraints and deductive rules in $O$-Telos are associated with specific classes (or meta-classes) to restrict the relationships of their instances with other objects and to deduce information about these instances, respectively. The adequacy and efficiency of Telos in representing a wide range of software models has been demonstrated in research and industrial projects [13]. Nissen *et al* [55] specify consistency rules as "query classes". A query class in $O$-Telos is an object class defined as a subclass of one or more normal classes with detectable class membership. This means that the objects which are instances of all the superclasses of a query class become instances of it only if their description satisfies an integrity constraint that has been specified for the query class. Thus, if $CR$ is a consistency rule that must be checked against specific kinds of software model elements in $O$-Telos, a query class may be created as a subclass of the classes that represent these kinds of elements having $\neg CR$ as its associated integrity constraint. Robinson and Pawlowski [69] also use $O$-Telos query classes to express development process compliance rules and check the compliance of requirements models against these rules as described above.

Spanoudakis and Kassis [75] adopt a very similar approach in checking whether UML models satisfy certain well-formedness consistency rules. In their framework, the consistency rules are specified as *invariants* in the Object Constraint

Language [62] and are associated with meta-classes in the UML meta-model. These meta-classes represent the various types of UML model elements and the relationships between them. An invariant is checked against all the elements of a model which are instances of the UML meta-class that it is associated with. The approach taken by Emmerich *et al* [27] is also similar to it. Their system checks the compliance of structured requirements documents against consistency rules which determine relationships that should hold between them. The contents of documents are expressed as sets of relations. The rules expressible in their tool are expressed in AP5, an extension of Common Lisp, which supports the specification and checking of formulas similar to those that can be expressed in first-order logic. These rules can make references to the relations used to represent the documents.

One of the criticisms against reasoning using a consequence relation ($\vdash L$) based on the standard inference rules of classical logic is that reasoning is trivialized in the case of inconsistent information [45]. This is the result of allowing the introduction of arbitrary disjuncts in formulas in the inference process: if a formula $\alpha$ is known then $\alpha \vee \beta$ is valid consequence of it according to the standard set of inference rules of classical logic [45]. Thus, in the case where both $\alpha$ and $\neg \alpha$ are part of a model then any formula $\beta$ can be derived from this model (first by obtaining $\alpha \vee \beta$ and then by resolving $\alpha \vee \beta$ with $\neg \alpha$). This problem of having arbitrary trivial inferences following from inconsistent information (termed as "ex falso quodlibet" in [70]) is significant in software engineering settings. Its significance comes from the fact that software models — especially those developed in the early stages of the software development life-cycle when the stakeholders may have a vague understanding of the system under construction and its domain — are likely to incorporate inconsistent information [15, 48, 78, 61].

To address this problem Hunter and Nuseibeh in [44, 45] have suggested the use of QC-logic [2]. QC-logic overcomes the above problem by allowing no further inferences after the introduction of an arbitrary disjunct in a formula during theorem proving.

The major advantage that theorem proving has over its competitors as a reasoning mechanism for deriving inconsistencies is the fact that the reasoning rules that it deploys have an extensively studied, well-defined and sound semantics. In addition, theorem proving can, in principle, be used to derive inconsistencies against any kind of consistency rule. Note, however, that theorem proving also has two major disadvantages. The first disadvantage is that first-order logic is semidecidable (if a formula does not hold in a first-order model the process of trying to prove it using theorem proving may never terminate). The second disadvantage is that theorem proving is computationally inefficient. These two disadvantages have been the basis of criticism against this approach [79].

Finally, two more formal techniques are proposed for the detection of inconsistencies. These are the derivation of "boundary conditions" by goal regression and the detection of inconsistencies using patterns of divergences. Both these techniques have been used to detect "divergences" in models of requirements expressed in the

KAOS language [76, 77]. The KAOS language advocates a goal-oriented approach to requirements specification. The modelling of a system starts by specifying the goals that the system should meet. Goals are refined into successive layers of sub-goals by AND/OR refinements until the fulfillment of these subgoals may become the responsibility of an individual agent(s), for example, a software agent, or an agent in the environment of the system. KAOS incorporates a real-time temporal logical language to specify goals formally.

A divergence in KAOS is a special kind of inconsistency. It is defined as a state where some goal about a system cannot be satisfied given other goals about the system, the overlap relations which exist between these goals, some domain theory about the system, and a boundary condition which arises due to some feasible agent behaviour [76].

Goal regression is used in KAOS to identify boundary conditions that give rise to divergences. The technique is based on backward chaining and assumes that the goals and the domain theory relevant to a system are all specified as formulas of the form $A \to C$. Backward chaining starts by taking the negation $B$ of a goal $G(B = \neg G)$ and tries to unify any subformula $L$ in $B$ with the implication part $C$ of some formula in the domain theory or the other goals (the latter are tried first). If such a formula is found the most general unifier of $L$ and $C$, mgu$(L, C)$, is applied to the premises of the implication $A$, and the resulting formula replaces $L$ in $B$. This procedure is repeated until no more unifications can be found or until the stakeholders recognize the new form of formula $B$ as a boundary condition that may arise under some scenario regarding the operation of the system. This scenario is an interaction with the system that can produce a behaviour $H$ which entails $B, H \models B$ [77]. The identification of such a scenario as suggested in [77] can be done manually, by planning or by model checking (see Sec. 5.2). In [77], van Lamsweerde and Letier present a variant of goal regression that can be used to identify boundary conditions which are consistent with a domain theory and which together with this theory entail the negation of a goal. These conditions are called "obstacles" [77].

Goal regression is useful in cases where the objective is to explore the potential for inconsistencies rather than to identify existing inconsistencies. In the special case of searching for obstacles which can obstruct the achievement of individual goals, the technique in effect explores exceptional behaviours and is used to "derive more complete and realistic goals, requirements and assumptions" [77]. The main difficulty that we envisage in practical applications of goal regression is the lack of heuristic criteria that could direct the search for boundary conditions towards goals and domain formulas whose sub-formulas would be more likely to appear in prominent scenarios. This could certainly speed up the regression process for large complex domain theories and goal hierarchies. The developers of the technique admit this weakness [76].

van Lamsweerde *et al* [76] have also identified a number of frequent patterns of divergence which they have formally described and used to detect divergences in goal-oriented models. A divergence pattern associates the abstract syntactic forms of two goals with an abstract syntactic form of the boundary condition that gives rise to a divergence between them. Each pattern is matched against goals in the models and if the match is successful the pattern is instantiated to generate the boundary condition that gives rise to the divergence.

Consider, for example, the divergence pattern called "retraction" which is shown in Fig. 2 and the goal $(G1)$ and the domain assertion $(D1)$ shown below (the formulas include operators of temporal logic whose semantics are informally explained in Fig. 2):

$$(G1) \ \text{Fire} \rightarrow \Diamond\text{Fire-Alarm-Rings},$$

$$(D1) \ \text{Fire-Alarm-Rings} \rightarrow \text{Fire}.$$

The goal $G1$ specifies that if there is a fire the fire alarm of a system will ring at some point after it. The domain assertion $(D1)$ specifies that when the fire alarm rings there is a fire. $G1$ and $D1$ match with the syntactic form of the divergent assertions in the "retraction" pattern of Fig. 2: "Fire" matches with $P$ and "Fire-Alarm-Rings" matches with $Q$. These matches are used in the following instantiation of the boundary condition of the pattern:

$$\Diamond \ [\text{Fire} \ \wedge \ (\neg \ \text{Fire-Alarm-Rings} \ \upsilon \ \Box \ \neg \ \text{Fire})].$$

This formula represents a potential state where there will be a fire but the fire alarm will not ring until the fire is off.

Patterns of goals and obstacles that can obstruct them are also given in [77]. Divergence and obstacle patterns have been proved to be sound (i.e., the boundary condition or obstacle that they specify always entails the negation of the goal(s) of the pattern [76, 77]). The main benefit arising from the use of divergence patterns is that they can detect boundary conditions for certain combinations of goals more

### RETRACTION PATTERN

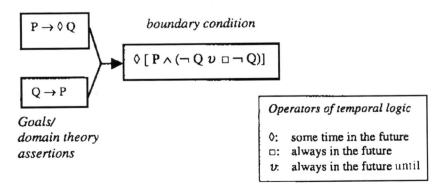

**Fig. 2.** The retraction divergence pattern (based on [76]).

efficiently than goal regression. However, as admitted in [76], the current set of patterns has to be expanded to capture a larger part of the range of divergences that can be found in goal specifications for complex systems.

## 4.2. *Detection based on model checking*

Model checking methods and techniques deploy, as indicated by their name, specialized model checking algorithms, for example, SMV [53] and Spin [43]. Model checking algorithms were originally developed for, and have been proved to be, effective means of detecting errors in hardware designs. Their use for checking the compliance of software models with consistency rules started in the mid-nineties. Two of the techniques that we surveyed deploy model checking algorithms. The first of these techniques was developed to check the consistency of software models expressed in the notations used by the SCR (Software Cost Reduction) method [3, 40, 41]. The second technique [11] was developed to analyze requirements specification models expressed in the RSML (Requirements State Machine Language [39]).

In the SCR method, a software system is described through a set of variables that take values in specific ranges. A SCR software model describes how the values of these variables change as the system moves from one state to another. A state is defined as a set of assignments of specific values to the variables. The system moves from one state to another when specific events occur in its environment. A SCR model is specified using a tabular representation scheme that constitutes an extension of state transition diagrams (STD). Models represented in this scheme may be checked against a variety of both well-formedness and application domain rules called "invariants" (see Sec. 2.1). Well-formedness rules in this case are concerned with the syntactic and type correctness of SCR models, the absence of circular definitions, and undesired non-determinism. These rules are checked using forms of analysis that pertain to the particular model specification language of SCR. Invariants in this case determine legitimate combinations of values of variables at any state of the system (*state invariants*) or legitimate changes of values of variables after state transitions (*transition invariants*). Model checking is used to establish whether state invariants hold on all the possible states of a system and whether transition invariants hold after the transitions they are associated with [3]. The application of model checking requires the translation of SCR models into the languages used by the deployed model checker. SCR provides automatic translation of its models into the languages used by SMV and Spin.

Chan *et al* [11] have also developed a scheme which translates a requirements specification expressed in RSML into the language of the symbolic model verifier SMV. This language is based on binary decision diagrams.

The main problem with model checking arises with systems which have a non-finite number of states. Model checking is also inefficient due to the explosion of the sequences of the state transitions that must be generated when checking consistency rules against systems specified by complex state transition diagrams [20]. Recent research tries to address this problem by using abstraction techniques such as *variable restriction and variable elimination* [3].

### 4.3. *Detection of inconsistencies based on specialized forms of automated analysis*

Numerous inconsistency management methods and techniques use specialized ways of checking the consistency of software models including [12, 16, 26, 37, 67, 72, 73, 80, 85]. Most of these techniques check the satisfiability of specific consistency rules.

The "reconciliation" method [72, 73] developed by Spanoudakis and Finkelstein checks the consistency of UML models against rules which require the totally overlapping elements in them to have identical descriptions. This method uses distance functions to compare model elements, and to identify and quantify the discrepancies in their descriptions as described in [71]. The technique developed by Clarke *et al* [12] also checks whether or not overlapping elements of UML class diagrams have identical descriptions but is based on a much simpler matching mechanism. Delugach's technique [16] checks whether totally overlapping elements of requirements models expressed as conceptual graphs have: (1) identical descriptions, or (2) any parts in their descriptions that can be mutually disproved. His technique is based on comparisons of conceptual graphs. In Oz [67], inconsistencies are detected between identical goals in different stakeholder perspectives which are to be realized by different design plans.

Glinz [37] has developed a technique that checks behavioural software models expressed as statecharts [38] for deadlocks, reachability and mutual exclusiveness of states. Cheung *et al* [85] have developed a technique that checks whether the sequence of the execution of operations that is implied by a UML statechart diagram is compliant with the sequence of the executions of operations implied by a UML sequence diagram. Their approach is based on the transformation of these diagrams into Petri-nets [64].

Ellmer *et al* [26] have developed a technique for detecting inconsistencies in distributed documents with overlapping content. The documents represent either software models generated during software systems development life cycle, or general business documents (e.g. financial documents). The technique is based on the eXtensible Markup Language (XML) [10] and related technologies and uses consistency rules to describe the relationships that are required to hold among the documents. Zisman *et al* [80] present a language based on XML and related technologies to express these consistency rules. A consistency link generator has been developed to check the various consistency rules through the participating documents and associate related elements. The result of this checking is specified by "consistency links", represented in XLink [17]. A consistency link can be either "inconsistent" or "consistent" depending on whether or not the related consistency rule has failed. The technique has been tested for UML and $Z$ software models.

## 4.4. Detection of inconsistencies based on human-centered collaborative exploration

Many of the techniques and methods that have been developed to support the management of inconsistencies between software models assume models or parts of models expressed in informal modelling languages (mainly supporting forms of structured text). These techniques include Synoptic [18], QARCC [6], DealScribe [69], and VORD [49]. In these techniques, the detection of inconsistencies is assumed to be the result of a collaborative inspection of the models by the stakeholders. A similar approach is also used as an option in the technique for divergence and obstacle management developed by van Lamsweerde et al [76, 77].

In Synoptic stakeholders are expected to fill the so-called "conflict forms" to describe a conflict that in their view exists between the overlapping model elements which are referenced in the form. A conflict in Synoptic may relate to non-identical descriptions of the same situation or the design of a system, or non-identical terms which have been used to denote the same aspect of the system.

As we discussed in Sec. 3.2, in QARCC a potential conflict is identified between "Win" conditions which are connected to a pair of quality attributes $a$ and $b$, if the attribute $a$ is realized by an architecture or system development process that inhibits $b$, or vice versa. A potential inconsistency becomes the subject of further analysis only if the stakeholders who own the involved "Win" conditions decide to create an "issue" which confirms and explains the nature of the identified conflict.

In DealScribe [69], the stakeholders are expected to identify conflicts between the so-called "root requirements" in their models. Root requirements are identified for each concept that is represented in the software models and have the property of being the most general requirements defined for these concepts (requirements in DealScribe are organized in generalization hierarchies). The stakeholders are expected to explore the interactions between all the possible pairs of root requirements in the models and indicate for each pair the nature of the interaction between its requirements elements. An interaction may be characterized as "very conflicting", "conflicting", "neutral", "supporting", or "very supporting". The former two characterizations need to be accompanied by a subjective measure of the probability that the envisaged conflict will occur during the operation of the system. Kotonya and Sommerville [49] also expect the stakeholders to identify conflicts between requirements for system services in their VORD method. These conflicts may be related to constraints associated with the provision of these services.

The detection of inconsistencies may also be left to the stakeholders in the techniques developed by van Lamsweerde and his colleagues [76, 77]. Note that, although these techniques have been developed to detect inconsistencies between formal models, their developers realize that in large models the detection of inconsistencies using their goal-regression method and their divergence or obstacles patterns may turn out to be inefficient. To address this problem, van Lamsweerde and his colleagues have developed a number of heuristics that could be used by the stakeholders to explore the possibility of divergences and obstacles (see Sec. 4.1) in connection with certain types of goals. Thus, for example, in the case of a goal regarding the confidentiality of a chunk of information and a second goal regarding the provision of some information, the stakeholders are advised to check if the particular pieces of information which are referenced by the two goals are the same. If they are, the goals are divergent.

**Table 2.** Summary of different approaches to the detection of inconsistencies.

| Approach | Main Assumptions | Positive Features | Limitations |
|---|---|---|---|
| Logic-Based | • models expressed in some formal language | • well-defined inconsistency detection procedures with sound semantics <br> • applicable to arbitrary consistency rules | • first-order logic is semi-decidable <br> • theorem proving is computationally inefficient |
| Model Checking | • it must be possible to express or translate models in the particular state-oriented language used by the model checker | • well-defined inconsistency detection procedures with sound semantics | • not efficient due to explosion of states <br> • only specific kinds of consistency rules (e.g. reachability of states) can be checked |
| Special Forms of Analysis | • models need to be expressed in a specific common language (e.g. conceptual graphs, UML, Petri Nets, XML) or be translated into it | • well-defined inconsistency detection procedures | • only specific kinds of consistency rules can be checked |
| Human-Based Collaborative Exploration | • models (or parts of models) expressed in informal modelling languages | • only method for informal models | • labour intensive and difficult to use with large models |

## 4.5. *Summary*

A summary of the assumptions, and the main positive features and limitations of the various approaches to the detection of inconsistencies is given in Table 2.

## 5. Diagnosis of Inconsistencies

In Sec. 2.2, we described the diagnosis of inconsistencies as an activity whose objective is to establish the source, cause and impact of an inconsistency. Most of the techniques and methods for inconsistency management provide little or no support for this activity. Notable exceptions to this is the work of Hunter and Nuseibeh [45] on QC-logic, and the significance diagnosis framework of Spanoudakis and Kassis [75]. The former work provides a mechanism for identifying the source of inconsistencies detected in formal software models and the latter provides a configurable framework for assessing the impact of inconsistencies detected in UML models. The DealScribe system developed by Robinson and Pawlowski [69] and the VORD method [49] also provide schemes for making a quantitative assessment of the impact of inconsistencies detected in goal-oriented requirements models.

As part of their work on using QC–Logic to support reasoning from software models in the presence of inconsistencies, Hunter and Nuseibeh [45] have also addressed the problem of identifying the "possible sources" of an inconsistency. In their work, this source is defined in terms of the set $\Delta$ of the original formulas in the software model(s) and the set $P$ of the formulas used in the proof of the inconsistency (i.e., the derivation of the empty clause ($\perp$) from the formulas in $\Delta$). More specifically, a possible source of an inconsistency is defined as any subset $S$ of $P$ whose formulas belong to $\Delta$ and for which the set of formulas $(\Delta \cap P) - S$ is a set of consistent formulas.[f] As an example (the example is taken from [45]) consider the following set of labeled formulas $\Delta$:

$$\{a\} : \alpha \qquad \{b\} : \neg\alpha \vee \neg\beta \qquad \{c\} : \beta \qquad \{d\} : \gamma$$

The empty clause can be obtained from the above formulas by resolving the formula labeled by $\{a\}$ with the formula labeled by $\{b\}$ to get the formula $\{a, b\}$[g] : $\neg\beta$ and then the formula labeled by $\{a, b\}$ with the formula labeled by $\{c\}$ to get the formula $\{a, b, c\}$ : $\perp$. In the above example, $\Delta = \{a, b, c, d\}$, $P = \{a, b, c\}$ and the subsets of $P$ which belong to $\Delta$ are $\{a\}, \{b\}, \{c\}$. The complements of these subsets with respect to $(\Delta \cap P)$ are $\{b, c\}, \{a, c\}$, and $\{a, b\}$, respectively. All these complement sets are consistent. Therefore, the possible sources of the inconsistency are the formulas $\{a\}, \{b\}$ and $\{c\}$.

---

[f]The definition of a possible source in this paper is a simplification of the definition of a possible source given in [45] which is equivalent to it when the formulas in $\Delta$ have single labels.
[g]Recall from Sec. 3.1 that Hunter and Nuseibeh in [45] keep track of the formulas used in a proof by labeling the formulas in the original models, and taking as the label of a formula derived by the application of the resolution rule of inference the union of the labels of the formulas which were resolved.

Hunter and Nuseibeh suggest that some ordering of the formulas in the original models (i.e., the set $\Delta$) could be used to order the different possible sources and thus to identify the most likely resource of an inconsistency. The ordering of the formulas in $\Delta$ may be one that reflects the belief of the stakeholders in the validity of the formulas in this set. They also suggest that the labels may be used to identify the stakeholders who provided the formulas. In this case, the identification of the possible source could also identify the stakeholders involved in the inconsistency. These stakeholders can subsequently be consulted to check whether there is a deeper conflict underpinning the inconsistency manifested in the models.

The framework of Spanoudakis and Kassis defines a set of "characteristics" that indicate the significance of the main types of elements in UML models (i.e., classes, attributes, operations, associations and messages) and incorporates belief functions which measure the extent to which it may be believed from a model that an element has a characteristic. Examples of the characteristics used in this framework are the "co-ordination capacity" of a class in a model (i.e., the capacity of a class in co-ordinating other classes in specific interactions within a system) and the "functional dominance" of a message (i.e., the ability of a message to trigger an entire interaction within a system). The framework provides a formal language (based on OCL) that can be used to specify criteria of significance and associate them with specific consistency rules. These criteria of significance are defined as logical combinations of the characteristics of the framework using a formal language called *S-expressions*. Consider, for example, a consistency rule requiring that for every message which appears in an interaction (sequence) diagram of a UML model there must be an association or an attribute defined from the class of the object that sends the message to the class of the objects that receives the message (this condition guarantees that the message can be dispatched). A criterion that could be defined and associated with this rule is that the message must have functional dominance in the interaction that it appears and the class of the object that sends it must have a co-ordinating capacity in that interaction. The framework in this case would calculate beliefs for the satisfiability of the significance criterion by the messages which breach the rule, and subsequently rank the inconsistencies caused by each of these messages in descending order of the computed beliefs.

Robinson and Pawlowski [69] suggest the use of two simple measures as estimates of the impact of conflicting requirement statements, namely the requirement "contention" and "average potential conflict". As we discussed in Sec. 4, the root requirements statements, which can be expressed in DealScribe, are related to each other as conflicting, very conflicting, neutral, supporting and very supporting. The contention of a requirement statement is computed as the ratio of the number of the very conflicting or conflicting relations over the total number of relations that this statement has with other requirements statements. The average potential conflict of a statement is measured as the average of the subjective probabilities of conflict that have been associated with all the conflicting and very conflicting

**Table 3.**   Summary of inconsistency diagnosis techniques.

| Technique | Main Assumptions | Positive Features | Limitations |
|---|---|---|---|
| QC-Logic [45] | • applied to formal software models <br> • formulas in models must be labeled | • automatic identification of possible source(s) of inconsistencies | • computationally expensive |
| *S*-Expressions [75] | • models expressed in UML <br> • stakeholders specify criteria to diagnose significance of inconsistencies | • fine-grain distinctions of significance based on reasoning with well-defined semantics <br> • relatively inexpensive computations | • not possible to differentiate the significance of violations of different consistency rules |
| DealScribe [69] | • requirements models expressed in a goal-oriented proprietary language <br> • based on subjective probabilities of conflicts identified by the stakeholders | • effective in ranking conflicting requirements | • scalability due to the need to provide subjective probabilities of all conflicts |
| VORD [49] | • informal requirements models <br> • based on weights indicating the importance of requirements | • applicable to informal requirements models | • differentiation of requirements importance is not always possible |

relations that have been asserted for it. Robinson and Pawlowski claim that their contention measure has been found to be very effective in ranking conflicting requirements in terms of significance and attempting the resolution of conflicts in the derived order. Kotonya and Sommerville in their VORD method [49] also expect the stakeholders to provide weights that indicate the order of importance of their requirements. These weights are subsequently used to establish the importance of conflicts between these requirements.

A summary of the assumptions, and the main positive features and limitations of the various approaches to the diagnosis of inconsistencies is given in Table 3.

## 6. Handling of Inconsistencies

The handling of inconsistencies is concerned with the questions of *how* to deal with inconsistencies, *what* are the impacts and consequences of specific ways of dealing with inconsistencies, and *when* to deal with inconsistencies. Inconsistencies may be handled through actions, which may be taken under certain conditions. The actions to be taken depend on the type of an inconsistency [61] and can be of two kinds. Actions of the first kind can modify the models, the overlap relations or the violated rules to restore or ameliorate inconsistencies. Actions of the second kind may notify stakeholders about inconsistencies, or perform sorts of analysis that would make further reasoning from models safe without however changing the models, the overlaps or the rules. Thus, we call actions of the first kind *changing actions* and actions of the second kind *non-changing actions*. Changing actions can be further divided into *partial* and *full resolution* actions. The former are actions that ameliorate the inconsistencies, but do not fully resolve them. The latter are actions that resolve the inconsistencies. Both these kinds of actions can be automatically executed or executed only if selected by the stakeholders. The application of an action has a cost and certain benefits which need to be established before the action is taken, especially in cases where the stakeholders are expected to select one action from a pool of possible actions.

Many of the surveyed techniques provide some support for handling inconsistencies. Based on the type of the actions that they support these techniques may be distinguished into (a) those which support changing actions, and (b) those which support non-changing actions. In the following, we present the ways in which these techniques deal with handling based on the above classification.

### 6.1. *Changing actions*

Most of the techniques classified in this group use human interaction to support inconsistency handling. These techniques expect the stakeholders to define and select handling actions by evaluating the inconsistencies, and execute these actions. Examples of these techniques are described below.

Easterbrook in [18] proposed a general framework for comparing and resolving inconsistencies (viz. conflicts) to integrate software models. His method is interactive. The stakeholders get involved in the generation of solutions for handling inconsistencies after they have explored the overlaps between models and identify the inconsistencies between them. This phase is called "generative phase" in Synoptic. No guidance for generating resolutions is offered. The result of the generative phase is a list of options for resolution. The main goal in Synoptic is to identify the options that best resolve the issues related to the inconsistencies and link them together. The process of linking the options to the inconsistencies is performed by either displaying an option and asking the user to select related issues, or by displaying an issue and allowing the user to select the options. The resolution chosen is represented as a new model.

In an evolving software development process, it is not possible to guarantee that an inconsistency that was resolved at a particular stage will not be re-introduced at other stages of the process. Easterbrook and Nuseibeh [23, 24] suggested an approach for handling inconsistencies in evolving specifications. The method is demonstrated through the ViewPoints framework (see Sec. 8) developed by Nuseibeh and Finkelstein [57]. The method requires the specification of various actions to change software models called ViewPoints when a specific consistency rule is violated. The set of actions is defined by the method designer, as part of the process of specifying consistency rules. Some actions will repair the inconsistency, while other actions will only ameliorate it by taking steps towards a resolution. Actions are selected by the stakeholder who owns the ViewPoint(s) that breach the rule. The actions taken are recorded.

The Oz tool [67] is able to detect and characterize inconsistencies, generate resolutions, and derive a final integrated model. The resolutions are generated using a small set of domain independent strategies, such as patching, re-planning, relaxation, reformulation, and augmentation, together with a domain specific model. The system has a component named Conflict Resolver that proposes actions which can resolve a conflict. Actions are identified using an analytic method which establishes trade-offs between weighted issues related to the inconsistency (the issues and their weights are defined by the stakeholders) or heuristics. The heuristic method uses abstraction hierarchies to find substitute or additional issues. Using a graphical interface, a stakeholder selects intermediate alternatives and automated negotiation methods. Following this idea, Robinson in [68] suggested two ways of resolving inconsistencies: structured-oriented resolution and value-oriented resolution. The former is related to the modification of the context in order to remove conflict. The latter modifies attribute values of objects in order to reduce the degree of inconsistency.

The "reconciliation" method [72, 73] generates and proposes to the stakeholders actions that can partially resolve the different types of the modelling discrepancies (inconsistencies) which have been detected in UML models. The generation process is driven by distance measures that the method computes between the two models. These distance measures indicate the type and the extent of the inconsistencies. The actions generated can resolve inconsistencies of specific types (e.g. inconsistencies in the classification of model elements) and are associated with measures which indicate the extent to which they can ameliorate an inconsistency. The stakeholders are free to select or disregard the actions proposed by the method.

van Lamsweerde *et al* [76] have developed techniques and heuristics for conflict resolution by transforming software models and/or consistency rules (called "goals" in their KAOS framework) which give rise to "divergences" (see Sec. 4.1). Divergences in their framework can be resolved: (a) by introducing new goals, (b) by weakening (i.e., dropping conditions of) one or more of the existing goals that caused the divergence, (c) by refining goals to subgoals that are no longer divergent, or (d) by transforming goals into new goals that no longer cause a conflict. Their approach is based on divergence resolution patterns and heuristics.

Another approach has been proposed by Nuseibeh and Russo to allow inconsistency management in evolving specifications based on abduction [60]. Their approach uses abductive reasoning to identify changes that have to be executed in inconsistent requirements specifications specified in QC logic [45]. Abductive reasoning generates a list of actions to be executed in a specification in order to bring it to a consistent state. The generated actions eliminate literals from the formulas of the models. The literal to be removed can be the one causing the inconsistency, or a literal involved in the inference process that derives the literal causing the inconsistency, or both. Nuseibeh and Russo do not mention how and when to perform the elimination of literals neither propose how to select a specific change out of all the possible changes. Providing support for the selection of the change is important for large models where there are numerous alternative literals that could be removed. In such case, it would be necessary to evaluate the impact of each literal removal [60].

## 6.2. *Non-changing actions*

Inconsistencies do not necessarily have to be resolved or ameliorated (see [32, 33] for a similar perspective regarding inconsistencies in databases specified in temporal logic). The actions which may be taken in response to an inconsistency can be a reference to a user or an attempt to obtain more data or some sort of further analysis over the models.

This approach has been adopted by Finkelstein *et al* [30] who use meta-level axioms to specify how to act on the inconsistency in the ViewPoint framework [31]. The actions in their approach are expressed by action rules, which are triggered when inconsistencies are detected between two ViewPoints. These actions may invoke a truth maintenance system, request information from a user, or invoke an external tool. To give an example of handling in the approach, when an identified inconsistency is due to typographical error, the user is notified about the problem and is asked to deal with it.

Hunter and Nuseibeh [45] suggest that in certain cases the handling that is required for inconsistencies should take the form of further analysis to identify the parts of the models that it would be safe to continue reasoning from in the presence of an inconsistency. They propose a specific form of such analysis which is based on QC logic. This analysis identifies maximally consistent subsets of formulas in inconsistent software models and qualifies inferences depending on the consistent subsets that they were made from (see Sec. 5). The result of this analysis is specified in a report, which is used to assist with the identification of possible actions that can be taken in the presence of inconsistencies.

In the approach proposed by Boehm and In [6], the stakeholders are responsible to evaluate and select the potential attribute requirements conflicts and resolution options, identified by the QARCC tool. A similar approach is advocated by Clarke *et al* [12]. Their system supports conflict resolution in UML class models. Handling in their system takes the form of presenting the designer of the model with a dialog displaying a conflict and the source of it.

Another technique which handles inconsistencies through non-changing actions approach is that developed by Ellmer *et al* [26]. This technique represents

**Table 4.**   Summary of techniques for handling inconsistencies.

| Technique | Main Assumptions | Positive Features | Limitations |
|---|---|---|---|
| Synoptic [18] | • stakeholders are expected to define and select handling actions | • complete freedom to the stakeholders <br> • support for informal models | • inconsistencies are handled by stakeholders <br> • no support for generating handling actions |
| OZ System [67] | • use of set of domain independent strategies to generate handling actions | • identification of resolution actions | • high human interaction |
| Reconciliation Method [72,73] | • use of distance metrics to indicate the type and extent of inconsistencies in proposing handling actions | • stakeholders have control of the handling activity <br> • support for partial resolution <br> • automatic generation of handling actions | • no support for automating application of actions |
| KAOS [76, 77] | • use of divergence resolution patterns | • stakeholders have control of the handling activity <br> • sound semantics | • only specific kinds of divergences can be handled |
| ViewPoint Framework [30] | • stakeholders may specify the handling actions to be taken in violations of specific rules | • automatic, partial or full resolution | • stakeholders not in full control of the process but may de-activate handling rules |
| QC-Logic [45] | • analysis to identify maximally consistent parts of the models that are safe to continue reasoning | • useful analysis in cases of partial resolutions <br> • sound semantics | • manual identification of related actions <br> • computationally expensive |

the existence of inconsistencies through "consistency links". Consistency links are generated after checking "consistency rules", as described in Sec. 5. In order to leave the original documents intact, the consistency links are stored in different documents. The users are expected to identify inconsistent elements in the participating documents (software models) by navigating through the consistency links. At the current stage of its development, this technique does not suggest which actions should be taken when a consistent link of type "inconsistent" is identified.

A summary of the assumptions, and the main positive features and limitations of the various approaches to inconsistency handling is given in Table 4.

## 7. Tracking

As outlined in Sec. 2, this activity is concerned with the recording of information about the consistency management process. The kinds of information which are tracked by various techniques and the structures used to do it are described below.

Most of the techniques for inconsistency management which are based on the ViewPoints framework including [23, 24, 30] have a structure to record information about the process. This structure is provided by what has been termed as "ViewPoint work record" which stores the trace of the development process of a ViewPoint.[h] Easterbrook in [18] suggested also the use of a map with information about ViewPoints overlaps and conflicts, a list of options to resolve the inconsistencies, and links between the map and options. In their approach for consistency checking and conflict resolution using decentralized process models Leonhardt *et al* [51] also store the results of consistency checks in the work record slots of the ViewPoints which participate the process. Hunter and Nuseibeh also proposed the use of a "report" with the results of their inconsistency diagnosis analysis [45].

When checking for standards compliance in [27], a diagnostic of non-compliant document elements and range of possible repairs that can be performed in order to guarantee the compliance is produced. This diagnostic is specified as functions and used by the users to assess the importance and difficulty of making the document compliant. The approach implements three such diagnostic functions: LIST, which generates a list of non-compliant elements; STAT, which generates a statistical analysis on non-compliant elements; and TRAV, which generates a filtered document with all non-compliant elements after traversing a document.

The approach proposed by Ellmer *et al* [26] keeps information about consistency management in various XML documents. This approach uses different XML documents for the consistency rules and for the consistency links [80].

One of the goals of the requirements dialog meta-model (DMM) in DealScribe [69] is to allow tracking and reporting on development issues. DealScribe is composed of two tools: HyperNews and ConceptBase. The first tool has a World

[h]The inconsistency management process is seen as part of the overall ViewPoint development process in this approach as we discuss in Sec. 8.

Wide Web interface and provides access to a discussion system like Usenet News. ConceptBase is a deductive database based on *O*-Telos (see Sec. 4.1) that defines the dialog meta-model and stores the dialog history as instances of DMM. DealScribe contains a dialog goal model composed of set of goals specified by logical conditions. The dialog goal model is used to automatically check the history for compliance.

Tracking is also supported by the "reconciliation" method [73]. When using this method, it is possible to keep a trace of the enactment of the software process model incorporated in it to describe the activity of reconciling models. This process model provides a structure for holding information about overlap relations,

**Table 5.**   Summary of techniques for tracking.

| Technique | Main Assumptions | Positive Features | Limitations |
|---|---|---|---|
| ViewPoint Framework [30] | • models expressed according to instantiated ViewPoint template(s) | • automatic recording of all information related to detection and handling of inconsistencies | • strongly related to the ViewPoint development process<br>• may generate a vast amount of information |
| Standards Compliance [27] | • informal requirements models expressed in proprietary format | • generates a report of all the model elements which violate consistency rules | • does not keep track of the entire inconsistency management process |
| XML Technique [26] | • models expressed in or translated to XML | • use of special XML documents and hyperlinks | • requires knowledge of XML |
| DealScribe [69] | • goal-oriented requirements models expressed in proprietary format | • automatic check of the history of models compliance | |
| QARCC [6] | • informal models | • provides a structure for recording conflicts, their handling and the alternative handling options considered | • the record has to be created manually by the stakeholders |
| Reconciliation Method [73] | • models expressed in UML | • keeps a record of the enactment of the built-in model of the process of reconciliation | • may generate a vast amount of information |

inconsistencies, and actions taken by the stakeholders to resolve these inconsistencies. Boehm and In [6] also use a specific structure for storing information about inconsistencies (called "issues"), possible ways of resolving them (called "options") and the decisions made about their resolutions (called "agreements").

A summary of the assumptions, and the main positive features and limitations of the various techniques in keeping track of the inconsistency management process is given in Table 5.

## 8. Specification and Application of Inconsistency Management Policies

In Sec. 2.2, we argued about the need to have an inconsistency management policy that specifies the techniques that could be used to carry out the activities of overlap and inconsistency detection, diagnosing and assessing the impact of inconsistencies, and handling inconsistencies. The variety of the possible ways which may be used to carry out each of these inconsistency management activities that were presented in Secs. 4–7 must have reinforced this point. Each of these ways is applicable under certain conditions, works best in settings which satisfy its own assumptions and has its own advantages and disadvantages. Thus, the stakeholders are faced with numerous options to select from and need guidance for making mutually coherent decisions which serve best the objectives of the overall process.

In this section, we discuss the support that is available for the specification and monitoring of an inconsistency management policy by the methods and techniques that we have surveyed. More specifically, we examine whether the reviewed techniques and methods:

(i) have an implicit or explicit inconsistency management process specification and in the latter case how this process is specified;

(ii) allow the modification of their inconsistency management process by the stakeholders;

(iii) enforce their inconsistency management processes or guide the stakeholders in enacting them; and

(iv) embed their inconsistency management process within a broader software development process or method.

In the techniques built upon or derived from the ViewPoints[i] framework [22, 23, 30, 59], the inconsistency management process is seen as part of the overall ViewPoints development process. This process is expressed in process rules of the form [<situation><action>]. The meaning of these rules is that the <action>

---

[i]A ViewPoint is defined in [59] as a locally managed software model that can be created by instantiating a template which encapsulates the specification of the language in which its instances are described (called "style") and the process by which these instances can be developed (called "work plan"). Each ViewPoint also keeps a record of the actions that have been applied to it or taken in connection with it in its development history (called "work record").

may be taken if the <situation> is satisfied. Process rules of this kind are generally used to define ViewPoints development actions and the situations under which these actions can be applied [58]. In the case of inconsistency management, rules of the same kind may be used to define: (a) when the consistency rules should be checked (the <action> in this case becomes the consistency rule to check and the <situation> defines the conditions under which the check should be triggered); or (b) the actions that may be executed when a consistency rule is violated (the <situation> in this case refers to the event of having detected the violation of the rule). The action in the latter case may be a handling action, an inconsistency diagnosis action, or an action that assesses the impact of an inconsistency.

Leonhardt *et al* [51] describe a scheme that supports a decentralized enactment of inconsistency management process models in the ViewPoints framework. In their operationalization of the approach, a <situation> is defined by a regular expression which refers to events in the development history of a software model that is encapsulated within a ViewPoint. An <action> in this case may be an "execute", "display" or "recommend" action. "Execute" actions are used by a model which wishes to check a consistency rule to request from another model (also encapsulated in a ViewPoint) whose parts are referenced by the consistency rule to supply information about these parts. This information is required for the execution of the check. The model which receives the request event may accept it and send the necessary information, or reject it. Its reaction depends on whether it has a process rule that enables it to recognize and act upon the request event. If it accepts and responds to the request, the model that issued it will check the rule, inform its collaborating model about the result of the check, and will finally append the result of the check to its work record. This model of enacting the inconsistency management process clearly requires some compatibility between the process models held in the different software models. Leonhardt *et al* admit this requirement but offer no general advise on how to construct compliant local process models that could lead to effectively coordinating software models.

The method developed by Emmerich *et al* [27] advocates a similar approach to that taken in the ViewPoints framework. This method has a number of explicit and modifiable inconsistency management process models (called "policies") which cover the activities of inconsistency detection, diagnosis, significance assessment and handling. The check of groups of consistency rules in policies is triggered by the recognition of events which occur in the models referenced by the rules. These events are specified by the policy in terms of actions that can be performed in models. An event occurs when there is an attempt to perform the action(s) that the event references in a specific model. Events are specified using the event specification language of FLEA which is also used to monitor the events. When the check of a consistency rule fails, a "diagnostic" which is associated with it in a policy is executed. A diagnostic is a script that produces information that could help the stakeholders to handle the inconsistencies. This information may refer to the source of the inconsistency, the significance of the inconsistency or the actions that could be taken to resolve it. Policies in this method may be executed in three different modes, namely the "error", "warning" and "guideline" mode. When executed in the "error" mode the policy is enforced, that is the consistency rules are automatically checked and the model changing actions that triggered the check are aborted if they would breach the rules. In the "warning" mode, the checks are again automatically triggered but the stakeholders are allowed to perform the actions that triggered the checks even if the rules would be violated. Finally, in the "guideline" mode the stakeholders are advised but not forced to execute a check if the events that should trigger it have occurred. The inconsistency management process of this method is not embedded within a broader software development process or method.

DealScribe [69] has an explicit and modifiable inconsistency management process which covers the activities of inconsistency detection and handling. The stakeholders can define process compliance development rules (called goals), the operations that should be executed to monitor them, the operations that should be executed to handle their violations, and the conditions under which each of these operations should be invoked. These goals and operations are defined as $O$-Telos objects and the conditions as $O$-Telos constraints (see Sec. 4.1). The stakeholders can instruct DealScribe to create and start monitors that check the goals and handle their violations as defined by the operations associated with them. When a monitor is started it acts according to the operations defined for the goal it is meant to monitor. The stakeholders cannot intervene in this process. However, they can instruct the system to deactivate any of the created monitors (by issuing a stop monitor statement). The inconsistency management process of DealScribe is not embedded within a broader software development process or method.

The "reconciliation" method [73] also has an explicit, non-modifiable model of its process of inconsistency management specified using the contextual process modelling approach described in [65]. This process model describes the ways of carrying out the activities of overlap and inconsistency detection, and the activity of inconsistency handling. The enactment of the process is performed by a process enactment engine which monitors the state of the inconsistency management process and proposes to the stakeholders the actions that they are allowed to take at the current state of the process. The stakeholders have the right to reject all the suggested actions and take a different action. The inconsistency management process of "reconciliation" is not embedded within a broader software development process or method.

Oz [67] and QARCC [6] have implicit models of their inconsistency management processes which cover the activities of overlap and inconsistency detection, and inconsistency handling. None of these models is enforced. The inconsistency management process in QARCC is part of the WinWin spiral model of software development [7]. van Lamsweerde and his colleagues [76, 77] suggest that their divergence and obstacle management techniques should be used as part of the goal elaboration phase of their goal-driven requirements engineering process but provide no explicit fine-grain process model for the use of these techniques.

**Table 6.**   Summary of techniques with respect to process specification and application.

| Technique | Main Assumptions | Positive Features | Limitations |
|---|---|---|---|
| ViewPoint Framework [30,51] | • the inconsistency management process is part of the overall ViewPoint development process<br>• the process is specified by rules of the form *if <situation> then <action>* | • explicit and modifiable model of the process<br>• decentralized enactment of the process | • requires compatibility between the process models held in different software models |
| Standards Compliance [27] | • use of explicit process models called "policies" | • explicit and modifiable model of the process<br>• covers inconsistency detection, diagnosis, and handling | • process not embedded within a broader software development process or method |
| DealScribe [69] | • the stakeholders can define goals, operations to monitor the goals, operations to handle violations, and conditions to invoke the operations | • explicit and modifiable model of the process<br>• covers detection and handling inconsistencies | • process not embedded within a broader software development process or method |
| Reconciliation Method [72,73] | • explicit specification of the inconsistency management process using the "contextual" software process modelling approach<br>• execution and tracking of the process through a process enactment engine | • explicit model of the process which is not enforced<br>• covers overlap identification and detection, diagnosis, and handling inconsistencies | • process not embedded within a broader software development process or method |
| OZ System [67] | • use of implicit process | • the process is not enforced<br>• covers overlap identification, inconsistency detection and handling | • implicit model of the process<br>• process not embedded within a broader software development process or method |
| QARCC [6] | • use of implicit process | • the process is not enforced<br>• the process is part of the spiral WinWin model of software development | • implicit model |

The rest of the techniques and methods that we surveyed do not have an explicit model of the inconsistency management process. In [12], there is an acknowledgement of the need to describe the overlap detection and the inconsistency handling activity through a set of explicitly defined overlap detection and inconsistency resolution rules but this is left to future work.

A summary of the assumptions, and the main positive features and limitations of the various techniques in specifying and applying an inconsistency management process is given in Table 6.

## 9. Open Research Issues

As presented in this survey, in the last decade there has been a substantial body of research that has tackled a number of significant problems and issues, which arise in the context of managing inconsistencies in software models. A summary of the techniques discussed in this survey is shown in the Tables 7(a) and 7(b). In these tables, the rows represent the techniques, the columns represent the different activities, and the cells summarize the support that each of these techniques offers for the respective activity. An empty cell indicates that a technique does not support the relevant activity.

Despite the considerable work that has been concerned with the problem of inconsistency management in software models, important issues need to be studied further and addressed in all the six individual activities of the inconsistency management process. These issues are discussed in the following subsections.

### 9.1. *Open issues in the detection of overlaps*

In our view, there are issues, which deserve further research in the detection, synthesis, representation and management of overlaps.

The detection of overlap is complicated by software models expressed in different languages, being at different levels of abstraction, granularity and formality, and deploying different terminologies. Stakeholders certainly cannot be expected to carry this activity without support and representation conventions fail when models are constructed independently. Our work on similarity analysis [71, 72, 73] clearly reflects our assumption that effective overlap identification is possible by developing specialized methods or algorithms for software models expressed in specific modelling languages. Forms of automated analysis can be used as "quick and dirty" identification mechanisms whose results should be subsequently confirmed by human inspection. For large models, this inspection will not be feasible unless it is focused on specific sets of overlap relations. The identification of these sets is an open research issue. Possibilities that may be explored in this direction include the inspection of overlap relations which have given rise to significant inconsistencies and/or overlap relations which are referenced by consistency rules expressing critical properties of a system (e.g. safety critical properties, reliability properties).

**Table 7a.**   Summary of inconsistency management techniques.

| Technique | Overlap Detection | Inconsistency Detection | Diagnosis | Handling | Tracking | Policy |
|---|---|---|---|---|---|---|
| Model Checking [40, 11] | elements with the same name | use of specialized model checking algorithms | | | | |
| Specialized Techniques [12] | elements with the same name | checking of specific rules concerned with UML class models | | conflict resolution in UML class models | | |
| OZ System [66, 67] | elements associated with the same goal in a domain model | checks for identical goals in different stakeholder perspectives | | use of domain independent strategies (e.g. patching, relaxation) | | covers the activities of overlap and inconsistency detection and handling |
| QARCC [6] | based on common "Win" conditions | responsibility of stakeholders analysis and explanation of the nature of a conflict | | generation of resolution options; guidance in selecting from them | | |
| Synoptic [18] | human inspection (visual aids are provided) | responsibility of stakeholders | | generation of handling options by the stakeholders | | |
| Reconciliation Method [72, 73] | based on weighted bipartite graph matching | use of distance functions to detect modelling discrepancies | | generation of resolution options; guidance in selecting from them | tracking of the enactment of the process model of the method | explicit model covering the activities of overlap and inconsistency detection, and handling |

**Table 7a.** (*Continued*)

| Technique | Overlap Detection | Inconsistency Detection | Diagnosis | Handling | Tracking | Policy |
|---|---|---|---|---|---|---|
| ViewPoint Framework [30] | unification | based on theorem proving | | automatic handling based on action rules | tracking of rules checked, and executed handling actions | covers the activities of inconsistency detection and handling |
| Delugach [16] | human inspection | based on comparison of conceptual graphs | | | | |
| QC-Logic [45] | unification | theorem proving (special set of inference rules) | detection of source of inconsistencies | detection of consistent subsets of models | | |

**Table 7b.** Summary of inconsistency management techniques.

| Technique | Overlap Detection | Inconsistency Detection | Diagnosis | Handling | Tracking | Policy |
|---|---|---|---|---|---|---|
| O-Telos [55] | unification | checking of integrity constraints | | | | |
| XML Technique [26] | matching similar to unification | special algorithm for checking rules expressed in XML syntax | | navigation through *consistency links* | use of special XML documents and hyperlinks | |
| S-Expressions [75] | matching similar to unification | check of OCL rules against UML models | based on criteria formally defined by the stakeholders | | | |

**Table 7b.**    *(Continued)*

| Technique | Overlap Detection | Inconsistency Detection | Diagnosis | Handling | Tracking | Policy |
|---|---|---|---|---|---|---|
| Standard Compliance [27] | matching similar to standard unification | special algorithm for checking rules expressed in proprietary format | diagnostics of compliance | | | covers the activities of inconsistency detection, diagnosis, and handling |
| KAOS [76, 77] | unification | derivation of boundary conditions by goal regression use of patterns of divergence | | resolution based on patterns and heuristics | | |
| DealScribe [69] | unification | stakeholders identify conflicts between "root requirements"; goal monitoring | based on "contention" and "average potential conflict" | | use of HyperNews and ConceptBase | covers the activities of inconsistency detection and handling |
| VORD [49] | | by the stakeholders | based on measures of importance provided by the stakeholders | | | |
| Abduction [60] | | | | generation of handling actions based on abduction | | |

We also envisage that in many settings a combination of different overlap identification techniques will be required, and overlap relations identified by different
agents will need to be synthesized in an attempt to reduce the cost and complexity
of overlap identification. For instance, in cases where a shared ontology has been
evidently used in a coherent way for some time, it makes sense to use it for
identifying coarse-grain overlaps and then refine them using some other method
(e.g. specification matching or inspection). In cases where overlap relations have
been identified by different agents, it is necessary to be able to check if these relations are consistent, and to synthesize them in a coherent and systematic way prior
to using them in consistency checks. It is also necessary to be able to assess the
confidence of the agents in consistency checking based on these relations.

Finally, to facilitate consistency checking with respect to different sets of overlap
relations, these relations need to be represented in forms suitable for consistency
checking and separately from the software models that they relate [74]. Easterbrook
*et al* in [21] have suggested the use of category theory as a means of representing
and reasoning about overlaps between models. This is certainly a direction worth
pursuing especially in cases where the overlap relations connect models specified
in different languages. However, representing overlaps separately from the models
that they relate raises interesting questions about what happens to these relations
when the models change, and especially in cases where the agents that identified
these relations are not those who made the changes.

## 9.2. *Open research issues in the detection of inconsistencies*

The most important open research issues regarding the detection of inconsistencies
are related to the efficiency and scalability of this process. The detection of inconsistencies has to be efficient and scalable because in real projects it has to deal
with a large number of complex software models and many consistency rules. None
of the current approaches to detection including theorem proving, model checking, special forms of automated analysis and collaborative exploration can really
claim that it sufficiently addresses the issues of scalability and efficiency as far as
we are concerned. One possible way of tackling this problem is to try to reduce
the original models into versions that could be safely used to reason about specific
consistency rules. This approach of model reduction has been explored in the context of techniques which employ model checking algorithms and has been termed
as "abstraction" [3]. The most difficult aspect of model reduction is the ability to
prove that the reduced model is equivalent to the original one with regards to the
inferences that may be made from it in connection with a specific consistency rule.

Efficiency and scalability become even more important when inconsistencies
need to be detected in evolving software models. Obviously, changes in software
models may make it necessary to go through another inconsistency detection cycle.
In such circumstances, it is important to be able to identify the parts of the models
that have been changed and the rules that refer directly or indirectly to these parts

in order to avoid unnecessary checks. This is particularly crucial for techniques which detect inconsistencies based on inspections by the stakeholders.

## 9.3. *Open research issues in diagnosis*

It must have been clear from the discussion in Secs. 5 and 6 that although diagnostic information about the source, the cause and the impact of an inconsistency is essential for deciding how and when to handle inconsistencies the support which is available for this activity is limited.

The approach taken in [45] regarding the identification of the source of an inconsistency is interesting but computationally expensive (since all the consistent subsets of the model formulas that have been used in the derivation of an inconsistency need to be computed). To this end, the developers of this technique have suggested that diagnosis should try to identify the most likely source(s) of an inconsistency rather than all the possible sources. We fully agree with them that this is a direction worth pursuing. Possible issues to explore in this direction include the use of schemes for reasoning on the basis of: (a) beliefs that the stakeholders may have about the validity of the information provided by the different formulas (model elements), and/or (b) beliefs about the validity of a certain formula computed from the use of the formula in other forms of reasoning with the model.

The approach taken in [75] for the assessment of the impact of an inconsistency in object-oriented models is also a direction that could be pursued for non object-oriented models. In that case, however, the stakeholders would need concrete guidelines about the sorts of the significance criteria that they should associate with specific consistency rules. Research in this direction should also explore whether or not the significance predictions that may be made on the basis of evolving software models are confirmed in later stages of the software development life-cycle.

Finally, substantial research is required to support the stakeholders in establishing the cause of an inconsistency. This research could certainly benefit from work on requirements traceability which provides schemes for annotating model elements with the stakeholders who contributed to their construction [86, 87]. Schemes of this sort could be used to locate the stakeholders who have constructed the relevant model elements or whose perspectives are expressed in them. However, this would be only one step towards the final objective which is to identify if there is a conflict between the model contributors that has been manifested as an inconsistency in the models. Work in this direction should start from an empirical investigation of the circumstances under which stakeholder conflicts are manifested as inconsistencies between models (see for example [5]).

## 9.4. *Open research issues in handling*

Most of the approaches proposed for handling inconsistencies assume that stakeholders will be responsible for selecting a handling action without however supporting them in making this selection. In most cases, the information presented to the stakeholders is a list of possible actions to be taken. Normally, the stakeholders select an action from the list intuitively, based on their experience and knowledge about the system being developed. This lack of support becomes a problem in cases where the stakeholders are given a large number of actions to select form.

As we argued in Sec. 2.2, a selection should be based on the cost, risk and benefit of applying an action and therefore it is essential to develop ways of evaluating or measuring these factors. This evaluation relates to the diagnosis of the inconsistencies but even those techniques which support diagnosis do not relate their findings with the above selection factors. The estimation of the risk and benefits associated with an action can also be based on an analysis of the effects that the application of an action may have on the satisfiability of consistency rules other than those that the action is meant to satisfy. In handling, it is also necessary to be able to identify the optimal time to perform the various actions associated to the different types of inconsistencies.

Another issue in handling that needs further investigation is related to languages that may be used to specify actions [45]. Existing techniques seem to be using informal schemes with not well-defined semantics to specify handling actions and actions that do not change the models. Finally, handling has to address the issue of efficient generation of actions.

## 9.5. *Open research issues in tracking*

Only few of the approaches for managing inconsistencies support tracking of the whole process. Tracking information is a very important activity for the management process and should be performed for the activities of overlap and inconsistency detection, inconsistency diagnosis, and handling. It is also necessary to have efficient mechanisms for managing the vast amount of information collected during the process.

Another important issue in tracking relates to the ability to represent the context in which certain actions were taken in the process. Context information is important for the stakeholders and could provide a basis for performing more advanced forms of analysis connected to activities of the inconsistency management process such as the handling of inconsistencies.

## 9.6. *Open research issues in the specification and monitoring of the inconsistency management process*

The research in the area of software process modelling has generated many alternative schemes that can be used to specify and enact processes for inconsistency management (see [65] for an overview). Some of these schemes, as we discussed in Sec. 8, have already been successfully used by inconsistency management techniques to represent their underpinning processes (e.g. [73]). Other techniques have opted for more light-weight schemes (e.g. [51]). Overall, the way of representing processes in this area seems to be a relatively well-understood issue with the exception of the schemes for defining inconsistency handling actions which do not change the models (see Sec. 9.4 above).

In our view, the two most important issues which have to be investigated for this activity include: (a) the relationship between the inconsistency management process with the more general software development process followed in a project, and (b) the construction of efficient process monitoring mechanisms. A process for inconsistency management can be effective and relatively easy to follow only if it is properly embedded in a general software development process. A deep understanding of the roles of the participants, procedures, phases and milestones used by the general software development process in a project is required before trying to integrate an inconsistency management process into it. Existing research on inconsistency management appears to have neglected this issue.

The second issue relates to the way that an inconsistency management process is being monitored. It seems to us that this monitoring needs to be both decentralized and centralized at different stages of the software development life-cycle. For instance, decentralized monitoring will be probably required when the stakeholders work on their models independently. Centralized monitoring will be required during group activities whose objective will be to establish overlaps and/or handle inconsistencies. In the former case, the construction of compliant, distributed, local inconsistency management process models is necessary although not well-understood yet [51].

## 10. Conclusions

In this paper, we have presented a survey of the research work that has been conducted to deal with the problem of managing inconsistencies in software models. This survey has been presented according to a conceptual framework that views inconsistency management as a process which incorporates activities for detecting overlaps and inconsistencies between software models, diagnosing and handling inconsistencies, tracking the information generated along the way, and specifying and monitoring the exact way of carrying out each of these activities.

We have tried to survey all the research work that has been brought to our attention, identify which of the issues that arise in the process of managing inconsistencies have been addressed by this work, which are the main contributions that have been made, and what are the issues which seem to be open to further research for the time being. We have attempted to be unbiased in our discussion but have probably failed! To this end, the readers of this paper are certainly advised to study the literature on the subject themselves and use this survey only as roadmap to this literature if they wish.

Our overall conclusion from this survey is that the management of inconsistency in software models has been an active and still rapidly evolving field in the more general area of software engineering. Existing research has certainly made significant contributions to the clarification of the issues which arise in this field and has delivered techniques which address a considerable number of these issues. However, it has to be appreciated that managing inconsistency is by no means an easy problem. This is because it needs to deal with models expressed in different modelling languages (ranging from completely informal to formal), constructed through different software development processes, and developed to describe systems in different domains. Most of the techniques that have been developed are aimed at dealing only with particular manifestations of this problem and do not address all the issues of it. To this end, we believe that more research is required. The arguments underpinning this claim are those that we discussed in the section on the open research issues.

## Acknowledgements

The research that led to this survey article has been partially funded by the British Engineering and Physical Sciences Research Council (EPRSC) under the grant IMOOSD (GR/M57422). We also wish to thank Dr. Stephen Morris whose comments have helped us to improve this paper both in content and presentation.

## References

1. M. Ainsworth, S. Riddle and P. Wallis, "Formal validation of viewpoint specifications", *IEE Software Engineering Journal* **11**, no. 1 (1996), 58–66.
2. P. Besnard and A. Hunter, "Quasi-classical logic: Non-trivialisable reasoning from inconsistent information", *Symbolic and Quantitative Approaches to Uncertainty*, eds. C. Froidevaux and J. Kohlas, *Lecture Notes in Computer Science 946* (Springer-Verlag, 1995) 44–51.
3. R. Bharadwaj and C. Heitmeyer, "Model checking complete requirements specifications using abstraction", *Automated Software Engineering* **6** (1999) 37–68.
4. B. Boehm, P. Bose, E. Horowitz and M. J. Lee, "Software requirements negotiation and renegotiation aids: A theory-w based spiral approach", *Proceedings of the 17th International Conference on Software Engineering* (IEEE CS Press, Los Alamitos, CA, 1995) 243–253.
5. B. Boehm and A. Egyed, "Software requirements negotiation: Some lessons learned", *Proceedings of the 20th International Conference on Software Engineering* (1998).
6. B. Boehm and H. In, "Identifying quality requirements conflicts", *IEEE Software* (March 1996) 25–35.
7. B. Boehm and R. Ross, "Theory w software project management: Principles and example", *IEEE Transactions on Software Engineering* (1989) 902–916.
8. E. Boiten, J. Derrick, H. Bowman and M. Steen, "Constructive consistency checking for partial specification in Z", *Science of Computer Programming* **35**, no. 1 (September 1999) 29–75.
9. H. Bowman, J. Derrick, P. Linington and M. Steen, "Cross-viewpoint consistency in open distributed processing", *IEE Software Engineering Journal* **11**, no. 11 (1996) 44–57.
10. T. Bray, J. Paoli and C. M. Sperberg-McQueen, "Extensible Markup Language (XML) 1.0 Specification", World Wide Web Consortium (1998) *http://www.w3.org/TR/1998/REC-xml-19980210*.

11. W. Chan *et al*, "Model checking large software specifications", *IEEE Transactions on Software Engineering* **24**, no. 7 (1998) 498–520.

12. S. Clarke, J. Murphy and M. Roantree, "Composition of UML design models: A tool to support the resolution of conflicts, *Proceedings of the International Conference on Object-Oriented Information Systems* (1998) 464–479

13. P. Constantopoulos, M. Jarke, J. Mylopoulos and Y. Vassiliou, "The software information base: A server for reuse", *VLDB Journal* **4**, no. 1 (1995) 1–43.

14. G. Cugola, E. Di Nitto, A. Fuggetta and C. Ghezzi, "A framework for formalizing inconsistencies and deviations in human-centered systems", *ACM Transactions on Software Engineering and Methodology* **3**, no. 5 (1996).

15. B. Curtis, H. Krasner and N. Iscoe, "A field study of the software design process for large systems", *Communications of the ACM* **31**, no. 11 (1988) 1268–1287.

16. H. Delugach, "Analyzing multiple views of software requirements", *Conceptual Structures: Current Research and Practice*, eds. P. Eklund, T. Nagle, J. Nagle and L. Gerholz (Ellis Horwood, New York, 1992) 391–410.

17. S. De Rose, E. Maler, D. Orchard and B. Trafford, XML Linking Language (XLink), World Wide Web Consortium (2000), Working Draft *http://www.w3.org/TR/WD-xlink-20000119*.

18. S. Easterbrook, "Handling conflict between domain descriptions with computer-supported negotiation", *Knowledge Acquisition* **3** (1991) 255–289.

19. S. Easterbrook, "A survey of empirical studies of conflict", *CSCW: Cooperation or Conflict?*, eds. S. Easterbrook (Springer-Verlag, 1993) 1–68.

20. S. Easterbrook, "Model checking software specifications: An experience report", NASA/WVU Software Research Laboratory (available from *http://research.ivv.nasa.gov*) (1997).

21. S. Easterbrook, J. Callahan and V. Wiels, "V & V through inconsistency tracking and analysis", *Proceedings of the International Workshop on Software Specification and Design*, Kyoto, Japan (1998).

22. S. Easterbrook, A. Finkelstein, J. Kramer and B. Nuseibeh, "Co-ordinating distributed viewpoints: The anatomy of a consistency check", *International Journal on Concurrent Engineering: Research & Applications*, CERA Institute, USA **2**, no. 3 (1994) 209–222.

23. S. Easterbrook and B. Nuseibeh, "Using viewpoints for inconsistency management", *IEE Software Engineering Journal* **11**, no. 1 (1995) 31–43.

24. S. Easterbrook and B. Nuseibeh, "Managing inconsistencies in an evolving specification", *Proceedings of the 2nd International Symposium on Requirements Engineering* (IEEE Press, 1995) 48–55.

25. A. Egyed and B. Boehm, "Comparing software system requirements negotiation patterns", *Journal for Systems Engineering* (2000) (to appear).

26. E. Ellmer, W. Emmerich, A. Finkelstein, D. Smolko and A. Zisman, "Consistency management of distributed document using XML and related technologies", UCL-CS Research Note 99/94 (1999) (submitted for publication).

27. W. Emmerich, F. Finkelstein, C. Montangero, S. Antonelli and S. Armitage, "Managing standards compliance", *IEEE Transactions on Software Engineering* **25**, no. 6 (1999).

28. J. Fiadeiro and T. Maibaum, "Interconnecting formalisms: Supporting modularity, reuse and incrementality", *Proceedings of the Symposium on the Foundations of Software Engineering (FSE 95)* (ACM Press, 1995) 1–8.

29. A. Finkelstein, G. Spanoudakis and D. Till, "Managing interference", *Joint Proceedings of the Sigsoft '96 Workshops — Viewpoints '96* (ACM Press, 1996) 172–174.

30. A. Finkelstein, D. Gabbay, A. Hunter, J. Kramer and B. Nuseibeh, "Inconsistency handling in multi-perspective specifications", *IEEE Transactions on Software Engineering* **20**, no. 8 (1994) 569–578.

31. A. Finkelstein, J. Kramer, B. Nuseibeh, L. Finkelstein and M. Goedicke, "Viewpoints: A framework for integrating multiple perspectives in system development", *International Journal of Software Engineering and Knowledge Engineering* **2**, no. 1 (1992) 31–58.

32. D. Gabbay and A. Hunter, "Making inconsistency respectable 1: A logical framework for inconsistency in reasoning", *Foundations of Artificial Intelligence Research, Lecture Notes in Computer Science 535* (1991) 19–32.

33. D. Gabbay and A. Hunter, "Making inconsistency respectable: Part 2 — Meta-level handling of inconsistency", *Symbolic and Qualitative Approaches to Reasoning and Uncertainty (ECSQARU 93), Lecture Notes in Computer Science 746* (Springer-Verlag, 1993) 129–136.

34. J. Goguen and S. Ginali, "A categorical approach to general systems theory", *Applied General Systems Research*, ed G. Klir (Plenum, 1978) 257–270.

35. T. Gruber, "Towards principles for the design of shared ontologies used for knowledge sharing", *Proceedings of the International Workshop on Formal Ontology*, Padova, Italy (1993) (also available as Technical Report KSL 93-04, Knowledge Systems Laboratory, Stanford University).

36. N. Guarino, "The ontological level", *Philosophy and the Cognitive Sciences*, eds. R. Casati, B. Smith and G. White, Holder-Pichler-Tempsky, Vienna (1994).

37. M. Glinz, "An integrated formal model of scenarios based on statecharts", *Proceedings of the 5th European Software Engineering Conference (ESEC 95), Lecture Notes in Computer Science 989* (Springer-Verlag, 1995) 254–271.

38. D. Harel, "Statecharts: A visual formalism for complex systems", *Science of Computer Programming* **8** (1987) 231–274.

39. M.P.E. Heimdahl and N. Leveson, "Completeness and consistency in hierarchical state-based requirements", *IEEE Transactions in Software Engineering* **22**, no. 6 (1996) 363–377.

40. C. Heitmeyer, B. Labaw and D. Kiskis, "Consistency checking of SCR-style requirements specifications", *Proceedings of the 2nd International Symposium on Requirements Engineering (RE 95)* (IEEE CS Press, 1995) 56–63.

41. C. Heitmeyer, R. Jeffords and D. Kiskis, "Automated consistency checking requirements specifications", *ACM Transactions on Software Engineering and Methodology* **5**, no. 3 (1996) 231–261.

42. C. Hogger, *Essential of Logic Programming, Graduate Texts in Computer Science Series* (Clarendon Press, Oxford, 1990) ISBN 0-19-853832-4.

43. J. Holzmann, "The model checker SPIN", *IEEE Transactions on Software Engineering* **23**, no. 5 (1997) 279–295.

44. A. Hunter and B. Nuseibeh, "Analysing inconsistent specifications", *Proceedings of the 3rd International Symposium on Requirements Engineering (RE 97)*, Annapolis, USA, January (IEEE CS Press, 1997) 78–86.

45. A. Hunter and B. Nuseibeh, "Managing inconsistent specifications: Reasoning, analysis and action", *ACM Transactions on Software Engineering and Methodology* **7**, no. 4 (1998) 335–367.

46. M. Jackson, "The meaning of requirements", *Annals of Software Engineering* **3** (1997) 5–21.

47. K. Knight, "Unification: A multidisciplinary survey", *ACM Computing Surveys* **21**, no. 1 (1989) 93–124.

48. H. Krasner, B. Curtis and N. Iscoe, "Communication breakdowns and boundary spanning activities on large programming projects", *2nd Workshop of the Empirical Studies of Programmers*, eds. G. Olson, S. Sheppard, E. Soloway (Ablex Publishing Corporation, 1987).

49. G. Kotonya and I. Sommerville, "Requirements engineering with viewpoints", *Software Engineering Journal* **11**, no. 1 (January, 1999) 5–18.

50. J. Leite and P. A. Freeman, "Requirements validation through viewpoint resolution", *IEEE Transactions on Software Engineering* **12**, no. 12 (1991) 1253–1269.

51. U. Leonhardt, A. Finkelstein, J. Kramer and B. Nuseibeh, "Decentralised process enactment in a multi-perspective development environment", *Proceedings of 17th International Conference on Software Engineering (ICSE 17)*, Seattle, Washington, USA (1995).

52. N. Maiden, P. Assenova, M. Jarke, G. Spanoudakis *et al*, "Computational mechanisms for distributed requirements engineering", *Proceedings of the 7th International Conference on Software Engineering & Knowledge Engineering (SEKE 95)*, Pittsburgh, Maryland, USA (1995) 8–16.

53. L. McMillan, *Symbolic Model Checking* (Kluwer Academic Publishers, 1993).

54. J. Mylopoulos, "Telos: Representing knowledge about information systems", *ACM Transactions on Information Systems* (1990) 325–362.

55. H. Nissen, M. Jeusfeld, M. Jarke, G. Zemanek and H. Huber, "Managing multiple requirements perspectives with metamodels", *IEEE Software* (1996) 37–47.

56. B. Nuseibeh, "Towards a framework for managing inconsistency between multiple views", *Proceedings Viewpoints 96: International Workshop on Multi-Perspective Software Development* (ACM Press, 1996) 184–186.

57. B. Nuseibeh and A. Finkelstein, "Viewpoints: A vehicle for method and tool integration", *Proceedings of the 5th International Workshop on CASE — CASE 92* (IEEE CS Press, 1992) 50–60.

58. B. Nuseibeh, A. Finkelstein and J. Kramer, "Method engineering for multi-perspective software development", *Information and Software Technology Journal* **38**, no. 4 (1996) 267–274.

59. B. Nuseibeh, J. Kramer and A. Finkelstein, "A framework for expressing the relationships between multiple views in requirements specification", *IEEE Transactions on Software Engineering* **20**, no. 10 (1994) 760–773.

60. B. Nuseibeh and A. Russo, "Using abduction to evolve inconsistent requirements specifications", *Australian Journal of Information Systems* **7**, no. 1 (Special issue on Requirements Engineering, 1999) 1039–7841.

61. B. Nuseibeh, S. Easterbrook and A. Russo, "Leveraging inconsistency in software development", *IEEE Computer* **33**, no. 4 (2000) 24–29.

62. OMG, OMG Unified Modelling Language Specification, V. 1.3a. Available from: *ftp://ftp.omg.org/pub/docs/ad/99-06-08.pdf* (1999).

63. C. Papadimitriou and K. Steiglitz, *Combinatorial Optimisation: Algorithms and Complexity* (Prentice-Hall Inc., Englewood Cliffs, NJ 1982).

64. J. Peterson, *Petri Net Theory and the Modelling of Systems* (Prentice Hall, 1981).

65. K. Pohl, "Process-centered requirements engineering", *Advanced Software Development Series*, ed. J. Krammer (Research Studies Press, London, 1996) ISBN 0-86380-193-5.

66. W. Robinson, "Interactive decision support for requirements negotiation", *Concurrent Engineering: Research & Applications* **2** (1994) 237–252.

67. W. Robinson and S. Fickas, "Supporting multiple perspective requirements engineering", *Proceedings of the 1st International Conference on Requirements Engineering (ICRE 94)* (IEEE Computer Society Press, 1994) 206–215.

68. W. Robinson, "I didn't know my requirements were consistent until I talked to my analyst", *Proceedings of the 19th International Conference on Software Engineering (ICSE 97)* (IEEE Computer Society Press, Boston, USA, 1997) 17–24.

69. W. Robinson and S. Pawlowski, "Managing requirements inconsistency with development goal monitors", *IEEE Transactions on Software Engineering* (Special issue on Managing Inconsistency in Software Development, 1999).

70. J. Shoenfield, *Mathematical Logic* (Addison Wesley, 1967).

71. G. Spanoudakis and P. Constantopoulos, "Integrating specifications: A similarity reasoning approach", *Automated Software Engineering Journal*, **2**, no. 4 (1995) 311–342.

72. G. Spanoudakis and A. Finkelstein, "Reconciling requirements: A method for managing interference, inconsistency and conflict", *Annals of Software Engineering* **3**, no. 1 [Special issue on Software Requirements Engineering (1997) 433–457].

73. G. Spanoudakis and A. Finkelstein, "A semi-automatic process of identifying overlaps and inconsistencies between requirement specifications", *Proceedings of the 5th International Conference on Object-Oriented Information Systems (OOIS 98)* (1998) 405–424.

74. G. Spanoudakis, A. Finkelstein and D. Till, "Overlaps in requirements engineering", *Automated Software Engineering Journal* **6** (1999) 171–198.

75. G. Spanoudakis and K. Kassis, "An evidential framework for diagnosing the significance of inconsistencies in UML models", *Proceedings of the International Conference on Software: Theory and Practice, World Computer Congress 2000*, Beijing, China (2000) 152–163

76. A. van Lamsweerde, R. Darimont and E. Letier, "Managing conflicts in goal-driven requirements engineering", *IEEE Transactions on Software Engineering* (Special issue on Managing Inconsistency in Software Development, 1999).

77. A van Lamsweerde and E. Letier, "Handling obstacles in goal-oriented requirements engineering", *IEEE Transactions on Software Engineering* **6** (Special issue on Exception Handling, 2000).

78. B. Walz, J. Elam and B. Curtis, "Inside a software design team: Knowledge acquisition, sharing and integration", *Communications of the ACM* **36**, no. 10 (1993) 63–77.

79. P. Zave and M. Jackson, "Conjunction as composition", *ACM Transactions on Software Engineering and Methodology* **2**, no. 4 (1993) 379–411.

80. A. Zisman, W. Emmerich and A. Finkelstein, "Using XML to specify consistency rules for distributed documents", *10th International Workshop on Software Specification and Design (IWWSD 10)*, Shelter Island, San Diego, California (November 2000).

81. G. Spanoudakis, A. Finkelstein and W. Emmerich: "Viewpoints 96: International workshop on multiple perspectives in software development — workshop report", *Software Engineering Notes* **22**, no. 1 (1997) 39–41.

82. C. Mazza, J. Fairclough, B. Melton, D. de Pablo, A. Scheffer and R. Stevens, *Software Engineering Standards* (Prentice Hall, Hertfordshire, Britain, 1994) ISBN 0-13-106568-8.

83. J. Palmer and A. Fields, "An integrated environment for requirements engineering", *IEEE Software* (March 1992) 80–85.

84. J. C. Shepherdson, "Negation in logic programming", *Foundations of Deductive Databases and Logic Programming*, ed. J. Minker, (Morgan Kaufmann, 1988) 19–89.
85. K. Cheung, K. Chow and T. Cheung, "Consistency analysis on lifecycle model and interaction model", *Proceedings of the International Conference on Object-Oriented Information Systems (OOIS 98)* (1998) 427–441.
86. O. Gotel and A. Finkelstein, "Contribution structures", *Proceedings of the 2nd International Symposium on Requirements Engineering (RE 95)* (1995) 100–107.
87. O. Gotel and A. Finkelstein, "An analysis of the requirements traceability problem", *Proceedings 1st International Conference on Requirements Engineering* (1994) 94–101.

# INCREMENTAL DEVELOPMENT — TERMINOLOGY AND GUIDELINES

EVEN-ANDRÉ KARLSSON

*Q-Labs AB, Ideon Research Park, S-22 370 Lund, Sweden*
*E-mail: eak@q-labs.se*

Many software producing organizations are using alternatives to the traditional waterfall software development model, e.g. evolutionary delivery, concurrent software engineering, time boxing, spiral model, iterative development, phased development, versioned implementation, short interval scheduling, or as we prefer to call it — incremental development. The confusion of terminology in this area is large. The proposed methods are also not very precise on how to apply them, i.e., providing practical guidelines and examples. This article tries to outline the design space within incremental development, and provide guidelines from our experience where we have worked with or studied a dozen medium to large (20–1000 kilo man-hours) incremental development projects. We also relate this to Microsoft's approach to incremental development.

*Keywords*: Incremental development, iterative development.

## 1. Introduction

Many software producing organizations are using alternatives to the traditional waterfall model to software development, e.g. evolutionary delivery [1, 12], concurrent software engineering, time boxing [2], spiral model [3], iterative development, phased development, versioned implementation, short interval scheduling [4], or as we prefer to call it — incremental development [5]. These models are usually called life-cycle models.

The confusion of terminology in this area is large. This is confusing for practitioners who want to compare and evaluate different approaches to decide how to implement it in their organization, as well as for researchers who want to understand and compare what these companies are doing.

The proposed methods are also not very precise on how to apply them, i.e., they provide few practical guidelines and examples, e.g. when should you do increments of this or that type, and what are the pitfalls of these type of increments?

In this article, we outline the design space within incremental development, and provide guidelines from our experience. This work is based on industrial experience from consultancy and studies of over a dozen medium to large (20–1000 kilo man-hours) incremental development projects in the telecommunication and other domains over the last 7 years, e.g. [18–21]. These guidelines and terminology are successfully applied in these projects to structure their approach to incremental development, and evaluate their choice of increments.

In this article we do not go into the reasons that organizations have to depart from the waterfall model, as our aim is not to advocate incremental development. The advantages promised by this and other alternatives are often astonishing — and are well covered in other sources, e.g. [1, 6, 13–17]. We do also not cover the process of planning increments e.g. [22], nor the requirements on configuration management, build and test [20, 23].

The essence of incremental development is illustrated in Fig. 1.

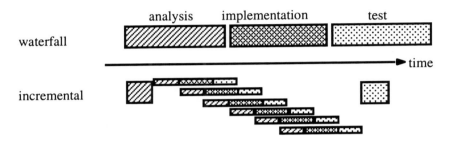

**Fig. 1.**   Waterfall vs incremental development.

As we see here the idea is to divide the development into smaller increments, which are gradually accumulated to become the complete system. The remaining sequential analysis and test activities are discussed in Chap. 4.

The concept of incremental development is independent of the development process, i.e., after the project it is not possible to see how many increments the project used, if any. For this article, we will use a simple three phase development process with analysis, implementation and test. The artifacts produced to document the system during these phases are called design items, e.g. specification, design, code and test cases. The plan of the increments is called the construction plan.

Note that an increment is an abstract concept, and can have several instantiations within software development. Some examples are:

- For a product line each release of the product is an increment. The product strategy (if any) is the construction plan. These increments are delivered to the customers.
- Within a project there can be several increments, each adding to the functionality of the earlier. These project level increments can be system tested and demonstrated to customers. Larger systems are usually structured in subsystems, where a sub-project or team could be responsible for each subsystem. Thus each sub-project and subsystem has to participate in the delivery of the project level increments.
- Each sub-project or team can divide their work within one project level increment into several smaller increments, which could be tested in a simulated environment.

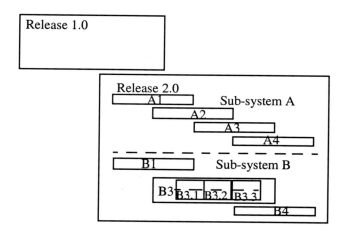

**Fig. 2.** Increments on different levels.

One example of a possible situation is shown in Fig. 2. Here we have two releases of the product (1.0 and 2.0). Release 2.0 has two sub-systems (A and B) and is developed in 4 increments. Sub-system A contributes to all increments (with A1 to A4), whereas sub-system B only contributes to system increment 1, 3 and 4 (with B1, B3 and B4). The second increment of sub-system B (B3) contains 3 sequential increments (B3.1–B3.3). Within each of B3.1–B3.3, there could be 2 different teams involved in delivering functionality (shown with a dashed line inside increment B3).

The parts from sub-systems A and B which contribute to the system increments could be dependent or independent, e.g. either A3 and B3 are separately testable and are only delivered to integration at the same time for convenience or they are functionally dependent on each other. Based on this distinction we have found it useful to distinguish between two different kinds of increments:

- Integration increments are executable and testable. These are the real increments.
- Design increments are parts of integration increments and are not executable and testable without other design increments. A design increment can be seen as a projection of an integration increment onto a subset of design items. A team or sub-project usually handles these design items.

Note that this distinction depends on which environment we want to execute and test the increments (from simulated to customer environment). We could thus have an interleaved hierarchy and aggregation of increments. Referring back to the example in Fig. 2, assuming we have two test environments, simulated (for subsystems) and target (for system), we could get the following:

- Each team contributes with a design increment to each of the three integration increments (B3.1 to B3.3) for simulated test of increment B3 of sub-system B.

- Sub-system B contributes with three design increment (B1, B3 and B4) to integration increment 1, 3 and 4 for target test on system level. Note that from the figure we cannot see if there are any dependencies between A1 and B1, etc. If there are no dependencies they are integration increments by themselves, and are only synchronized for convenience.

Another very important fact about increments is that there are an accumulation of functionality, e.g. Release 2.0 builds on Release 1.0.

The terminology and guidelines we discuss here are equally applicable, independent of where one chooses to apply increments.

The rest of this article is organized as follows:

- Section 2 outlines the design alternatives when doing a project in increments and the terminology use.
- Sections 3–6 discuss different alternatives within each of the areas, with advantages, disadvantages and examples.
- Section 7 contains a discussion of Microsoft's approach to incremental development.
- Section 8 contains a conclusion and a comparison to related work.

## 2. Increment Alternatives

In this section, we introduce four different but interrelated questions which have to be answered when one wants to apply incremental development. These four questions can be easily explained with the help of Fig. 3:

- What is the functionality of increments? The functionality of increments is what is developed in each increment, i.e., what can the system do at the end of each of the 5 increments in Fig. 3.

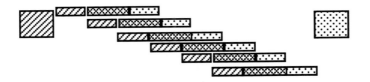

**Fig. 3.**   Incremental development alternatives.

- Which phases do the increments span? Thus, how much of the development process is done in increments vs before the increments start and after all increments are completed. In Fig. 3, the span is from the middle of analysis to the middle of test.
- What is the duration of increments and how are they scheduled? The duration is the lead-time of each increment, and scheduling how they are

allocated in time. In Fig. 3, the duration is fixed and quite long, and the increments are partly overlapping.

- How is work allocated? Work allocation is how we organize the people, e.g. either per increment (horizontally in Fig. 3) or per phase (vertically in Fig. 3 with responsibility for specific development phases).

There is no right answer to any of these questions. It depends on the context of the project and the product to be developed. In Secs. 3 to 6, we will discuss some of the alternatives we have seen, and some advantages and disadvantages of each.

## 3. What is the Functionality of Increments

This question concerns the type of functionality we develop in each increment, i.e., the type of increment. For this question, there are several different possibilities. Some of the ones that we have encountered are:

(1) Separate user functions are added in different increments. The choice of when to add which functions can be made based on e.g.:

- basic — advanced (from a user point of view);
- simple — complex (from an implementation point of view);
- critical — non-critical (from a safety point of view);
- stability of requirements; and
- cost benefit ratio for customer.

Whatever choice is made the architecture and the interdependency between the functions has to be taken into account.

For each function the complete function is implemented, i.e., everything that is needed for the function to work, all error handling, etc. We call this alternative feature increment. Note that several features can be developed in parallel for one increment.

(2) Simple normal cases, more complex normal cases, without error handling and then addition of error handling of different types. We call this alternative normal/error increment.

(3) Separate system functionality, where for instance start, restart, dynamic size alteration, commands and traffic handling are examples from the telecommunication domain. We call this alternative system function increment.

These three alternatives are not exclusive, as we can use a combination of them, i.e., we can use feature increments on an overall level, within each feature we use normal/error increments, and within each normal/error increment we use system function increments. In the example shown in Fig. 2, the top-level increments within Release 2.0 could be of feature type, whereas the B3.1–B3.3 increments could be normal/error type.

There is some confusion about the difference between prototyping and incremental development. In our opinion, there are two main differences:

- The increments are not to be thrown away. Each increment provides code and documentation which is supposed to go as untouched as possible into the complete system.
- Incremental development requires a thorough plan for what functionality to develop, when, and how it fits together.

There are also similarities, e.g. both approaches have the ability to take user feedback into account.

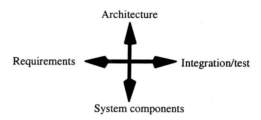

**Fig. 4.**   Technical factors influencing the choice of increments.

When we select the increments, we need to find a suitable balance between several potentially conflicting factors as illustrated in Fig. 4.

- Architecture means increments to ensure that we have the right architecture, thus we might want to select functionality, which establishes the backbone of the architecture as soon as possible. The architecture is also usually the bearer of the non-functional requirements of the system, e.g. performance, fault tolerance, and restart. We have found that a focus on non-functional requirements when defining the increments is crucial. This is also a key point in Gilb's method [1]. One practical example is to establish performance goals for each increment.
- System components mean increments to establish the usability of certain system components to reduce the risks with such components, e.g. hardware, reusable components, etc. In this case it can be good to integrate the risky component in an early increment where we only have made limited commitments to the component in the design. If the component is found useless, we can still switch to an alternative solution without too much rework.
- Requirements mean increments to compensate for unstable or unknown requirements. It could also mean to choose the increments based on customer priorities.
- Integration/test means increments to ensure the quality of the system or to optimize the testing.

There are also other factors influencing the choice of increments, e.g. competence where we can use small and isolated early increments to build up competence in the domain. All of these factors have to do with controlling the risks in the project with an active use of incremental development.

Risk management is actually the main driver in one of the alternative incremental development models, the Spiral model [3].

In the case of development of a system from scratch a sufficiently small first increment is usually difficult to find. In this case we can use a combination of feature and normal/error increments, i.e., we select a minimal set of features and for these we implement the normal cases first. Other feature increments can then build on the normal cases in parallel with the addition of error cases for the first feature increment.

In the case of development from scratch or large restructuring we have often seen design increments used. Another alternative when developing from scratch is to base the increments on system functionality. These two alternatives are further elaborated in connection with the anatomy and Fig. 6.

In most projects we have seen a combination of an inside out and outside in approach to find the increments:

- Outside in: How far can the functionality be split and still be meaningful? If we can split the functionality in more pieces than the number of increments which we want to end up with; it will be easier to find suitable larger increments as combinations of these smaller functionalities. One example of this was a project where each requirement items, i.e., each paragraph in each requirements specification, was seen as a potential increment, with associated costs and dependencies on other requirement items.
- Inside out: For the complex part of the system, how is it possible to break up the implementation, and what is needed around this break-up to provide user functionality. Thus here we will look inside the system at the "kernel" part to see how it can be implemented in increments. Usually the key to the increments is in splitting the part, which seems the most monolithic.

This distinction relates to the two dimensions discussed in relation with Fig. 4, i.e., outside in is connected to Requirements and Integration/test, whereas Inside out is connected to architecture and system components.

A concept known as the system anatomy, or anatomy only, has proved helpful in working out possible increments. The anatomy is a visualization of the interconnection of the different functionality in the system, where the most basic functionality is shown at the bottom. A simplified example of an anatomy is shown in Fig. 5. Here each box represents some functionality of a telecommunication system, e.g. phone traffic. The anatomy can help us to find increments by pointing out the dependencies between the functionality in the system. It also helps us to get a better understanding and visualization of the system. Note that the increments need not

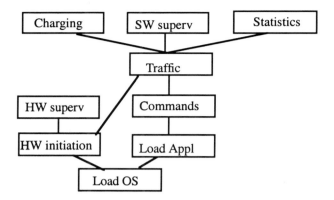

**Fig. 5.**   Example anatomy of telecom system.

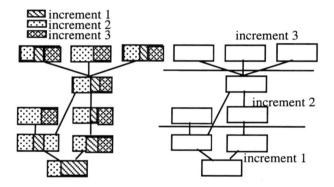

**Fig. 6.**   Two alternatives for increments from an anatomy.

be chosen according to the elements in the anatomy, we could as well provide a thread through the anatomy in the first increment, and then extending this thread in later increments. These two alternatives are shown in Fig. 6. The left alternative is a more feature type increments or increments chosen from a requirements point of view (see Fig. 4), i.e., we will only build what is needed of the lower level boxes in the anatomy (support functions) for the user functionality we will provide. The alternative on the right is more system function type increments chosen from an integration/test point of view.

These two alternatives have different advantages and disadvantages:

- Feature increments tests all the parts of the system at an early stage, thus we can see if they really fit together. We also only construct the support functions that are really necessary for the user functionality.
- Feature increments can lead to reopening of the same design items several times to add new functionality. This is an advantage for learning, but can lead to more regression testing and possibly unstructured design items.

Note that the anatomy is different from the product structure, i.e., the division of the system into sub-systems and code modules (design items). The anatomy provides a functional view, whereas the system structure is an implementation view.

The majority of software development is not development from scratch but enhancements or restructuring of existing systems. In this case each enhancement can form a natural feature increment. The remaining problem is to split large enhancements and restructuring into smaller parts. In our experience large restructuring is the most difficult to do incrementally as we have all the old code present.

For enhancement projects the total system anatomy can provide an understanding of how the enhancements affect the existing system and generally how they depend on each other. But an internal anatomy of each enhancement, e.g. feature, is necessary to provide insight into possible increments for the feature and detailed dependencies between features.

## 4. Which Phases Do the Increments Span

This question concerns which phases of the development process the increments cover. Here we need to consider when the increments

- Split, i.e., when in the development process do we stop doing development breath first and start doing depth first.
- Merge, i.e., when in the development process do we end the increments and deliver a whole product to the next phase.

We call the phases of the development process (from split to merge) the span of the increment. Both the split and the merge can be at virtually any point in the development process, and we can even have several splitting and merging points, either for the complete product or some increment.

Some of the most common splitting points that we have encountered are (referring to the development process depicted in Fig. 1):

- During analysis. Here only an overall understanding of the total requirements and architecture of the total system is developed before the first increments are defined. After each increment the overall plan and architecture is updated. This early split is also used for enhancement projects where the features are grouped in increments according to customer priority.
- After analysis. Here the complete set of requirements and architecture are known, but the design is not started. It is not necessary that all requirements are completely stable, but at least we know which ones are and which ones are not, and for the unstable requirements we have some idea of the range of variation so that this can be taken into account in the architecture.

- During implementation. Here the design of the system is more complete, but the detailed design and implementation is still to be completed.

The decision when to do the splitting is naturally influenced by two factors:

- Early splitting: Less is known about the total requirements and necessary architecture. There is an increased risk of wrong initial design decisions that can lead to a badly structured system and considerable rework.
- Late splitting: Long time spent in the waterfall model reduces the advantages that we want to achieve with increments.

As for most other choices regarding incremental development there is no right answer. It has to be considered for each project.

There is also some freedom in choosing the merging point:

- Before each separate test phase. This means that all testing after the merging point is executed when all increments are accumulated. The test phases could be module test, sub-system test or system test. Note that we could even define a final review of the design items in a development phase as a test, and end the increments there.
- Before release to customer. Here the increments are tested to completion as the final system, and the system can in principle be delivered to the customer after each increment.
- Released to customer in increments. This is the most radical alternative where the customer starts to use the earlier increments.

Here it is also a trade-off between early and late merging:

- Late merging: This requires more planning to ensure that the functionality of all increments can be effectively and completely tested in the later test phases without writing a lot of dummy code. Thus there is a natural latest possible merging point depending on the natural testability of the increments. Late merging also implies additional synchronization problems between error correction in one increment and development of the next.
- Early merging. Long time spent at the later phases in a waterfall mode reduces the advantages that we wanted to achieve with incremental development, e.g. reduced lead-time by overlapping test and implementation, early integration and feedback etc.

We can combine different alternatives for which phases each increment spans with alternative types of functionality of each increment (discussed in Sec. 3). If we continue the example from Fig. 2 where we had a project with a combination of increments, we can have

- feature increments spanning from during analysis to delivery to customer;
- normal/error increments spanning from after analysis to function test; and

- finally system function increments spanning from during design to some test phase (e.g. simulated testing).

The situation is shown in Fig. 7. Note that we here only show one increment in each group. The existence of several increments means that the start and end of increments within each group is displaced. This is another view of Fig. 2, which shows increments on different levels.

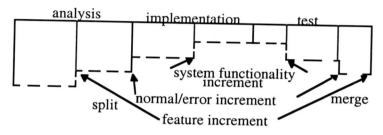

**Fig. 7.** Relation between different increment types.

## 5. How Long Are the Increments and How Are They Scheduled

The third question concerns three aspects:

- The duration of increments, i.e., how long should an increment last from start to completion.
- Fixed or variable duration of increments.
- The scheduling of increments, i.e., should they be done in sequence with all personnel focused on one increment or should we allow parallelism between the increments.

The duration of increments is connected to the type and span of increments, but within a given type and span we have some freedom with regards to the duration.

- Short increments keep up the focus and pressure on the organization, but can result in a focus on code, and neglecting the other documentation, i.e., developers can be tempted to wait with documentation to the next increment as they are anyway extending the documents for that later increment.
- Too long increments bring us back to the problems of the waterfall model.

Some organizations have tried very short increments. In the case of HP [7], increments have been down to one week. Here there is one-day planning, two-three days implementation and one-two days test. Microsoft [8] is going even further with daily builds. These increments are in our opinion only feasible during the later stages of implementation. In extreme programming [15], the recommend increments should last for hours, not days. Increments from three to six weeks spanning implementation and test and four to 20 weeks spanning analysis to test are the most common in our experience. Our recommendation is 8–10 weeks for feature like increments, but shorter for other types of increments. We have also experience from "increments" which were longer, but they have seldom worked as well as the shorter ones.

Fixed or variable duration of increments also has advantages and disadvantages:

- Fixed duration makes planning and follow up easier. The schedules are fixed, and everyone knows what is the goal, e.g. integration the first working day of every month. Splitting the functionality into suitable increments that make sense to integrate can however be a problem.
- Variable duration increments require more planning and coordination, but the splitting of increments can be done more based on natural functionality.

The last part of this question concerns scheduling of increments. Here there are in principle two different alternatives:

- Sequential, i.e., all resources are focused on one increment. The advantages here are the focus and no need for coordination between parallel increments.
- Parallel, i.e., several partially overlapping increments. The advantages here are the longer continuous execution of all phases, the opportunity to spend longer time with each increment which can be necessary to understand the functionality and the better utilization of scarce resources, e.g. design items, test environments.

Often projects have chosen to do analysis and implementation in sequence and in parallel with test.

Three schematic example projects both with fixed duration increments spanning analysis to test are shown in Fig. 8. The first project has 8 increments that are $2 \times 4$ displaced parallel increments. The second has three displaced increments. Note that the project with 8 increments has more opportunities for feedback and learning than the one with 3 increments. The total lead-time is also shorter since there is more overlap between the different phases. The project with 8 increments will however require better planning and coordination to define and execute more and smaller increments. The last project has 4 increments. The overlap between the increments is less compared to the others. This has the advantage that more feedback from the previous increment can be taken into account in the next, and there is less synchronization between parallel increments. The disadvantage is that the lead-time will be longer, but if we have only two types of competence, e.g. combined analysis and implementation vs test, and we can utilize all fully — this is a good alternative.

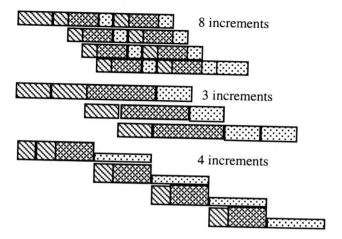

8 increments

3 increments

4 increments

**Fig. 8.** Three example projects.

There is an intrinsic time that is needed to understand and make a good solution to a problem or function, and this needs to be taken into account when we select the functionality, span and duration of the increments. This applies for all phases of development (e.g. analysis of a function and specification of a solution, design and implementation of a central piece of the system or test of interacting functions). The strategy of incremental development for attacking a complex problem is to split the problem into a simple version that is gradually enhanced in later increments in parallel with the other activities for earlier and later increments. This would in practice mean:

- Split a complex feature into several increments so that a simple version can be analyzed in the first, and then extended.
- Split implementation of a complex design item over several increments so that we can gradually enhance it by adding functionality.
- Split complex testing over several increments.

This does however require that we have a fairly good understanding of the totality of the problem, so that we choose suitable increments.

## 6. How is Work Allocated?

There are basically two different strategies for allocation of work in a project using increments:

- Design item responsibility. People are assigned to design items or development phases, and they deliver the functionality necessary for each increment.
- Increment responsibility. People are assigned to increments, and they do the necessary functionality in each design item affected by the increment.

The kind of responsibility used is connected to the type of increments (Sec. 3), i.e.:

- Increment responsibility is the most natural with feature increments. Here the responsibility is for complete user functionality, and the design items are seen as means to achieve this goal. In particular for enhancement projects this is a natural choice [18, 21]; i.e., the project is responsible for a new release (Fig. 2).
- Design item responsibility is more natural for normal/error increments and some cases of system functionality. For normal/error increments it is not natural that different persons implement the simple normal case and the error cases in a design item.

In the choice between design item or increment responsibility, we must take into account whether the complexity is in

- communication, i.e., the interaction between the design items participating in the functionality of one increment is complex, or
- design items, i.e., the interaction of the impacts of different increments on single design items are complex.

Complex communication points towards increment responsibility whereas complex design items point towards design item responsibility.

The advantages of design item responsibility are:

- Clear design item responsibility and ownership.
- Better knowledge of the design item.
- No cost to "open" and understand the design item.
- Specialist on design item and phase of the process.
- May give better solution in design items as consistency between increments can be maintained.

The advantages of increment responsibility are:

- Responsibility for some complete and understandable user functionality that is usually more rewarding than being responsible for a small piece which contributes to different functions. It is also easier for customers and developers to keep in touch, as both are working on the same level.
- System understanding, even if not an expert on any particular design item.
- Improved overall solution, i.e., one understands the whole functionality and can make global decisions.
- Understanding of the overall development process as one increment is followed through different phases (the span of the increment).
- No hand over of intermediate results between different phases of the development process. No need to learn the functionality.

We have often used a role called design item coordinator in connection with increment responsibility to get the advantages of both worlds. The design item coordinator is then responsible for following the design item through the increments, e.g. participating in reviews, approving solutions, ensuring that it stays consistent and is not misused. The person doing the most work on the design item during the project or the maintenance responsible usually fills this role. It is usually so that even if a design item by itself is complex and affected by many increments, most of its complexity is allocated to one increment, and the other increments are only doing minor extensions. In this case the person working on the increment with the major impact is a natural choice for the design item coordinator.

Note that design item responsibility and increment responsibility are independent of design and integration increments as described in Sec. 1. The design increment is just the projection of one increment on a subset of the design items. These design items can be taken over by someone else in the next increment, where they also can be split into other design increments.

In the following, we discuss some examples of how work has been allocated in incremental projects.

One example is increment responsibility in connection with team work (teams of 4–5 persons) for feature type increments spanning from analysis to test [18, 21]. The team has a very concrete common goal (analyze, implement and test the feature), they have different design items to work with (ability to split the work), but all design items must work together to achieve the goal.

Another example is a team of people doing analysis, implementation and test in displaced parallelism. This can be exemplified by the two projects with 3 and 8 increments in Fig. 8, assuming we have two separate implementation phases, e.g. design and coding. Here the analysis people are handing the analysis of the first increment over to implementation as they start on the analysis of the next increment. Thus, we have a pipeline. This of course requires fixed duration for each increment as well as development phase.

It is possible to use a mix of responsibility in different stages, e.g. start the project with design item responsibility to learn the design items and then move over to increment responsibility for later increments when the architecture is more stable. In connection with teamwork this could mean teams responsible for design items in the first increment, then splitting these to teams responsible for increments so that competence from design items is properly spread.

A mix of design item and increment responsibility can be used throughout the same project, e.g. a few central and complex design items can be developed with design item responsibility whereas the majority of the functionality is developed with increment responsibility [21]. Thus the increment responsible can implement everything needed for the functionality except the impacts on a few complex design items, where all impacts are handled by design item responsible.

## 7. Microsoft's Approach to Incremental Development

Microsoft has been applying incremental development quite heavily and with good results [8, 11]. In this section we will briefly describe Microsoft's approach using the terminology introduced in this article.

Microsoft does incremental development on two levels. Each project is a collection of new features, which are organized into three groups of equal size. Each group then becomes one top-level increment, which is completed before the next is started. The duration of each of these increments is 3–4 months. On the lower level increments are on daily basis, i.e., the developer is coding something which is integrated every day to a complete executable system. The general idea is shown in Fig. 9.

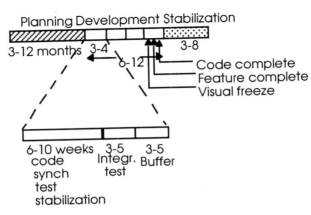

**Fig. 9.**   Incremental development at Microsoft.

Thus, using our terminology the top-level increments can be classified as:

- Feature type.
- Rather short span (mainly coding and test), i.e., there is a quite substantial start-up (Planning) and completion (Stabilization) phase which is run waterfall.
- Fixed duration of 3–4 months, and increments are sequential, i.e., one set of features is completed before the next is started.
- Increment responsibility, as each developer is responsible for one or more features. Design items (code modules) are shared between developers on an *ad hoc* basis with merging through the CM system.

The lower level increments can be classified as:

- Unidentified type, as it is up to each designer to develop the code in increments, but a guess is that some form of normal/error case increments are used.

- Very short span, only coding. The reason that this short span can be used without having a lot of documentation that is not up to date is that Microsoft does not use much design documentation apart from the code. Thus the developer is basing the development on the functional specification of the feature which is developed in the planning phase before the increments start.
- Fixed/variable duration, i.e., integration every day, but developers can choose whether to check their code in or not. Since there is no planned evolution of the design items, not checking in regularly is a big risk for the designer as the system might evolve so that he must do a large merge job to get the code in later. The increments are overlapping as each developer has a buddy tester, which is doing testing in parallel with new development on the feature the day after synchronization.
- Increment responsibility as each designer is doing the necessary updates to all code modules impacted by his feature.

As can be seen Microsoft's approach to incremental development is quite aggressive, but there is not that much structure in the selection and planning of increments. The grouping of features on the top level is rather easy for a stable system with a set of relatively independent new functional features. The selection of features can mainly be done based on the requirement viewpoint (Fig. 4). The lower level increments can be developed rather independently because of the frequent synchronization and that no change to the system is so large that it cannot be done within a couple of days. The operating system development in Microsoft is operating under totally different conditions with major reconstructions or new large subsystems in each new release. To introduce incremental development in this environment would require a different approach with much better up front planning of increments.

## 8. Conclusion

In this article, we have tried to provide some consistent terminology and practical guidelines for incremental development. We have elaborated on four fundamental questions:

- Type.
- Span.
- Duration and scheduling.
- Work allocation.

Since there is a large freedom in implementing incremental development it is necessary that we get some more precision in the description of projects which have applied it. It is also important that we relate the chosen increments to the development process, as well as the type of project, i.e., development from scratch, enhancements or restructuring. Thus, when describing incremental development projects, we recommend to use the following structure:

- Description of project (size, type, constraints).
- Description of development process (major phases).
- Description of increments, i.e., type, span, duration, scheduling and work allocation.

There is limited related work in this area. Most of the work only explains the advantages of incremental development, advocates one specific approach, or is very generic, e.g. the Spiral model [3]. A good overview of incremental development from a Cleanroom Software Engineering point of view is provided by Trammel et al. [13]. They have the Cleanroom view of increments, i.e., increments spanning from a complete specification of the system to complete certification, and do not discuss different alternatives to incremental development. Tom Gilb [1] discuss evolutionary development, but also here the choices of increments are discussed very briefly. However, one main point in Gilb's work is to focus on non-functional requirements in early increments. Extreme Programming [15] applies extremely short increments (or iterations), but also here there is a lack of guidelines for how to choose the right increments. Redmill [14] provides a good book on managing incremental software projects, but is also weak on the different choices.

In MIL-STD-498 [9], program strategies are explained in Appendix G. The different approaches are shown in the table below.

| Strategy | Define all Requirements First | Multiple Development Cycles | Filed Interim Software |
|---|---|---|---|
| Grand Design (waterfall) | Yes | No | No |
| Incremental (Preplanned Product Improvements) | Yes | Yes | Maybe |
| Evolutionary | No | Yes | Yes |

This is quite a coarse classification, which mainly focus on the span of the increments.

Davis [10] describes a comparison based on how the development model satisfies the user needs as illustrated in Fig. 10. The concepts in the figure are:

- Shortfall: Difference between user requirements and system capabilities at any time.
- Lateness is the lead-time of implementation of a requirement.

- Adaptability is the rate at which we can incorporate new requirements.
- Longevity is the time between replacements of systems (the vertical line represents a replacement).
- Inappropriateness is the integration of the shortfall.

This characterization focuses on the behavior of the development model and is rather orthogonal to our discussion, which focuses more at the internal properties, and how to apply them.

The concept of increments is related to configuration management concepts in the following way:

- An increment will constitute a release of the product.
- A release consists of a version of each design item.
- For parallel increments, the need to handle variants during the project arises.

## References

1. T. Gilb, *The Principles of Software Engineering Management* (Addison–Wesley, 1988).
2. J. Martin, *Information Engineering Book III* (Prentice Hall, 1990).
3. B. Boehm, "A spiral model of software development and enhancement", *IEEE Computer* (May 1988).
4. *Navigator System Series Overview Monograph* (Ernest & Young International Ltd., 1991).
5. H. D. Mills, M. Dyer and R. C. Linger, "Cleanroom software engineering", *IEEE Software* (September 1987) 19–24.
6. P. A. Hausler, R. C. Linger and C. J. Trammel, "Adopting cleanroom software engineering with a phased approach", *IBM Systems Journal* **33**, no. 1 (1994).
7. G. Head, "Can cleanroom thrive in a chaotic world"?, *2nd European Industrial Symposium on Cleanroom Software Engineering*, Berlin (1995).
8. C. Anderson, "An operating system development: Windows 3", Industrial Experiences Presentation at ICSE 18.
9. MIL-STD-498 (Draft, June 29, 1994), Appendix G, Fig. 7.
10. A. M. Davis, E. H. Bersoff and E. R. Comer, "A strategy for comparing alternative software development life cycle models", *IEEE Transactions on Software Engineering* **14**, no. 10 (October 1988).
11. M. Cosumano and R. Selby, *Microsoft Secrets* (Free Press, 1995).
12. D. McCracken and M. Jackson, "Life-cycle concepts considered harmful", *ACM Software Engineering Notes* (April 1982) 29–32.
13. C. Trammel, M. Pleszkoch, R. Linger and A. Hevner, "The incremental development process in cleanroom software engineering", *Decision Support Systems* **17**, no. 1 (1996) 55–71.
14. F. Redmill, *Software Projects — Evolutionary vs Big-Bang Delivery* (John Wiley, 1997).
15. K. Beck, *Extreme Programming Explained, Embrace Change* (Addison-Wesley, 2000).
16. Department of Defense, "Report on the Defense Science Board Task Force on Military Software" (September 1987).

17. F. Brooks, "No silver bullet: Essence and accidents of software engineering", *Computer* (April 1987) 10–19.
18. Ø. Johansen and E. A. Karlsson, "Experiences from using cleanroom at Ericsson in Arendal, Norway", *2nd European Industrial Symposium on Cleanroom Software Engineering*, Berlin (March 1995) 27–29.
19. G. Allen, L. Davies, G. Lindmark and E. A. Karlsson, "TTM15 — A large multi-site improvement project", *6th European Software Engineering Conference*, Zurich (September 1997).
20. E. A. Karlsson and L. Taxen, "Incremental development for AXE 10", *6th European Software Engineering Conference*, Zurich (September 1997).
21. E. A. Karlsson, L. G. Andersson and P. Leion, "Daily build and feature development in large distributed projects", *International Conference on Software Engineering*, Limerick, Ireland (June 2000).
22. E. A. Karlsson, "A construction planning process", *3rd Annual International Conference on Cleanroom Software Engineering Practices*, College Park, Maryland, USA (October 1996) 9–11.
23. E. A. Karlsson and L. G. Andersson, "XP and large distributed projects", XP 2000, Calgari, Italy (June 2000).

# METRICS FOR IDENTIFYING
# CRITICAL COMPONENTS IN SOFTWARE PROJECTS

CHRISTOF EBERT

*Alcatel, Switching and Routing Division,*
*Fr. Wellesplein 1, B-2018 Antwerpen, Belgium*
*E-mail: christof.ebert@alcatel.be*

Improving field performance of telecommunication systems is a key objective of both telecom suppliers and operators, as an increasing amount of business critical systems worldwide are relying on dependable telecommunication. Early defect detection improves field performance in terms of reduced field failure rates and reduced intrinsic downtime. Cost-effective software project management will focus resources towards intensive validation of those areas with highest criticality. This article outlines techniques for identifying such critical areas in software systems. It concentrates on the practical application of criticality-based predictions in industrial development projects, namely the selection of a classification technique and the use of the results in directing management decisions. The first part is comprehensively comparing and evaluating five common classification techniques (Pareto classification, classification trees, factor-based discriminant analysis, fuzzy classification, neural networks) for identifying critical components. Results from a large-scale industrial switching project are included to show the practical benefits. Knowing which technique should be applied to the second area gains even more attention: What are the impacts for practical project management within given resource and time constraints? Several selection criteria based on the results of a combined criticality and history analysis are provided together with concrete implementation decisions.

*Keywords*: Telecommunication, classification techniques, quality model, software quality, software metrics, fuzzy classification.

## 1. Introduction

*The danger of computer is not that they will eventually get as smart as men, but that we will meanwhile agree to meet them halfway.*

*Bernard Aviskai.*

With a growing impact of software on almost all products and services such as traffic or telecommunication, it is of primary concern to manage software quality and to control software development cost. To better manage quality and reduce development cost of globally available products, various validation techniques are applied. A large share of defects is however still detected too late in the project, thus creating danger to the public and far too high cost of rework. This article will focus on how

- to detect source code defects early in the development process by means of code reviews and unit testing; and

- to focus defect detection on those areas that are error-prone instead of wasting effort by random or scattered reviews.

In order to achieve an early indication of software quality, software is subjected to measurement. It would be of great benefit to predict early in the development process those components of a software system that are likely to have a high error rate or that need high development effort. Though the search for underlying structures and rules in a set of observations is performed in many scientific fields and effective solutions to refine forecasting methods based on past data have been suggested, their applicability to software development has been restricted [1, 2]. Few references give insight that attention has been paid to a systematic analysis of empirical data (e.g. [3–6]).

This article compares different classification techniques as a basis for constructing quality models that can identify outlying software components that might cause potential quality problems. For example, when distinguishing modules that are more error-prone than others, a metric vector consisting of few metrics such as module size, cohesiveness and data fan-in can be determined during the design phase. Now, the goal is to determine those modules that belong to the rather small group of modules that potentially cause most of the errors, costs, and rework. Obviously, the best solution would be to filter out exactly the specific high-risk components in order to improve their design or start again from scratch.

Such classification models are based on the experience that typically a rather small number of components has a high failure rate and is most difficult to test and maintain. Our own project experiences for instance just recently showed that 20% of all modules in large telecommunication projects were the origin of over 40% of all field failures with high priority (Fig. 1). Even worse is the fact that we could also show that it is not so difficult to identify these modules in advance — either by asking designers and testers and grouping their subjective ratings, or by applying classification rules based on simple structural software metrics [7].

In this context the article addresses typical questions often asked in software engineering projects:

- How can I early identify the relatively small number of critical components that make significant contribution to faults identified later in the life cycle?
- Which modules should be redesigned because their maintainability is bad and their overall criticality to the project's success is high?
- Are there structural properties that can be measured early in the code to predict quality attributes?
- If so, what is the benefit of introducing a metrics program that investigates structural properties of software?
- Can I use the — often heuristic — design and test know-how on trouble identification and risk assessment to build up a knowledge base to identify critical components early in the development process?

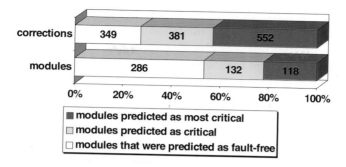

| | | | |
|---|---|---|---|
| corrections | 349 | 381 | 552 |
| modules | 286 | 132 | 118 |

0%  20%  40%  60%  80%  100%

■ modules predicted as most critical
□ modules predicted as critical
□ modules that were predicted as fault-free

**Fig. 1.** Benefits of using early criticality prediction in a telecommunication project.

Beyond addressing such questions the article compares different approaches for identifying critical components and provides insight into the most common techniques for complexity-based classification of software modules. Quantitative data both from literature (in order to provide easy access to some quality data and thus to do own experiments and to validate results) and from telecommunication software development is used to show in two concrete situations how classification techniques can be applied and what results to expect.

The effects of applying complexity-based criticality prediction to a new project can be summarized based on results from telecommunication projects (Fig. 1):

- 20% of all modules in the project were predicted as most critical (after coding);
- these modules contained over 40% of all faults (up to release time). Knowing from these and many other projects that [11, 23];
- 60% of all faults can theoretically be detected until the end of module test; and
- fault correction during module test and code reading costs less than 10% compared to fault correction during system test.

It can be calculated that 24% of all faults can be detected early by investigating 20% of all modules more intensively with 10% of effort compared to fault correction during system test, therefore yielding a 20% total cost reduction for fault correction. Additional costs for providing the statistical analysis are in the range of two person days per project. Necessary tools are off the shelf and account for even less per project.

The article is organized as follows. Section 2 presents a brief summary of background and problems associated with metric-based decision models. Section 3 introduces common classification methodologies and their applicability to software quality models, covering Pareto classification, crisp classification trees, factor-based discriminant analysis, neural network approaches, and fuzzy classification. Due to size limits we will concentrate on brief qualitative introductions with references on archive materials. Section 4 describes the construction of a classification system for software quality management (see also Appendix 1 for more practical details on software quality assurance and validation techniques). Section 5 provides the experimental setup to investigate classification for error and change prediction. It summarizes the environment from which the data has been taken as well as the type of study that supports the data evaluation and validity of described observations.

Two projects from the area of real-time systems are introduced for comparing classification results within Sec. 5. Project A is based on already published metric data, which permits easy access for further (third party) studies. Project B is a collection of 451 modules from a large Alcatel telecommunication switching system.

Section 6 provides the results of these experiments and Sec. 7 discusses these results in the context of applicability to other projects from a pragmatic viewpoint. Finally, Sec. 8 gives an outlook on future research.

There are two appendices included at the end of this chapter. A first appendix introduces to validation techniques within software engineering. All those who are interested to get some more background why classification techniques are necessary for validation efficiency and effectiveness should read this appendix. It outlines how classification techniques best fit into the development life cycle.

A second appendix summarizes concepts of fuzzy classification. Since fuzzy classification are not yet as popular for multidimensional classification as other techniques used in this article, this part is helpful in underlining the key concepts and the practical relevance once heuristic knowledge is available.

As such we should conclude this introduction by stating that the selection of feasible classification techniques and their evaluation always needs profound understanding of underlying data sets and environmental conditions. We will come back to this observation quite frequently.

## 2. Metric-Based Quality Models

Although striving to reach high quality standards, only a few organizations apply true quality management. Quality management consists of proactively comparing observed quality with expected quality, hence minimizing the effort expended on correcting the sources of defect. In order to achieve software quality, it must be developed in an organized form by using defined methods and techniques and applying them consistently. In order to achieve an indication of software quality, software must be subjected to measurement. This is accomplished through the use of metrics and statistical evaluation techniques that relate specific quantified product requirements to some attributes of quality.

### 2.1. *Quality modeling with metrics*

The approach of integrating software metrics and statistical techniques is shown in Fig. 2. The CASE environment provides defined methods and process, and holds descriptions of different products developed during the software life cycle. Multivariate statistical techniques provide feedback about relationships between components

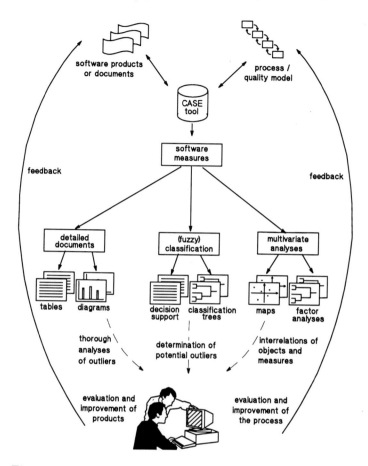

**Fig. 2.**    Measures and statistical techniques in software engineering.

(e.g. factor analysis [8], principal component analysis [4]). Classification techniques help determining outliers (e.g. error-prone components) [2, 3, 9]. Finally, detailed diagrams and tables provide insight into the reasons why distinct components are potential outliers and how to improve them [8, 10].

Quality or productivity factors to be predicted during the development of a software system are affected by many product and process attributes, e.g. software design characteristics or the underlying development process and its environment.

In order to achieve a distinct quality goal that is often only measurable at delivery time, quality criteria are derived that allow *In Process Quality Checks*. Such quality criteria if measured are indirect quality metrics because they do not directly measure the related quality factor (Fig. 3). However, being available early in the development process they can be used to set up immediate targets for project tracking. Quality criteria are measurable during the development process. An example is given in Fig. 3. The quality factor reliability that is contracted based on the failure

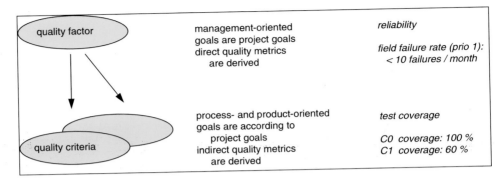

**Fig. 3.**   Quality factors, quality criteria and metrics.

rate of 10 failures per month can only be measured after the product is deployed to the field.

The associated quality criteria, for instance test coverage, can be measured early and they can be kept within a distinct range if experience suggests so [10]. These quality criteria are part of the development quality plan and can rather easily be checked at appropriate milestones.

## 2.2.  *Quality prediction and classification*

Quality prediction models try to give an early indication on achieving quality goals in terms of quality factors. They are based upon former project experiences and combine quantitative quality criteria with a framework of rules (e.g. limits for metrics, appropriate ranges etc.).

For instance, the distribution of defects among modules in a software system is not even. An analysis of several recent projects revealed the applicability of the Pareto rule: 20% of the modules are responsible for 80% of the malfunctions of the whole project [26].

An example for such a distribution is provided in Fig. 4 that accumulates history data for several frequently used subsystems of switching software over several years. These critical components need to be identified as early as possible, i.e., in the case of legacy systems at start of detailed design and for new software during coding. By concentrating on these components the effectiveness of code-inspections and module test is increased and less faults have to be found during test phases.

It is of great benefit toward improved quality management to be able to predict early in the development process those components of a software system that are likely to have a high fault rate or those requiring additional development effort. This chapter describes the selection and application of techniques for identifying such critical modules in the context of large switching systems software. Criticality prediction is based on selecting a distinct small share of modules that incorporate sets of properties which would typically cause defects to be introduced during design more often than in modules that do not possess such attributes. Criticality prediction is thus a technique for risk analysis during the design process. Compared

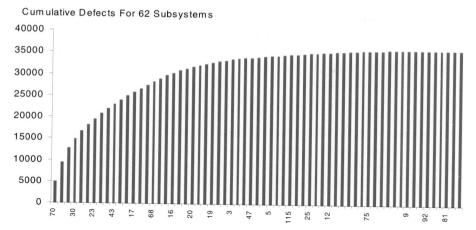

**Fig. 4.** Criticality prediction and the Pareto rule: 20% of all sub-systems contain 80% of all defects.

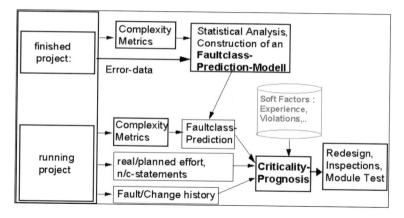

**Fig. 5.** Criticality classification during software development.

to previous studies [26], we took not only complexity metrics and defect numbers (i.e., hard factors) into consideration, but also the processes contributing to fault injection, namely staffing, designers' experiences with the legacy code (i.e., soft factors). In addition, the best ranking technique, namely fuzzy classification was further enhanced with genetic algorithms to improve rule identification for optimal prediction effectiveness.

Figure 5 shows the typical approach of metric-based classification in a project environment. They are generated by combination and statistical analysis of product metrics (e.g. complexity metrics) and product or process attributes (e.g. quality characteristics, effort, etc) [3, 5, 6, 10, 11].

These models are evaluated by applying and comparing exactly those invariant figures they want to predict the quality factors (e.g. error rate). Iterative repetition of this process can refine the quality models, hence allowing the use of them as predictors for similar environments and projects. Typical problems connected to data collection, analysis, and quality modeling are addressed and discussed comprehensively in [1, 11, 23].

One of the few examples for a metric-based decision environment with expert rules has been suggested by Behrendt *et al* [13]. This tool is based on a factorial quality taxonomy that classifies the above mentioned quality factors (e.g. reusability) and related sub-factors (e.g. modularity) into linguistic categories (e.g. "not acceptable"). The proposed classification system takes measurable and non-measurable attributes as input, such as design of control structures or number of system parameters. Another tool system for assessing risk factors of software components has been developed by Porter and Selby [2, 9]. The proposed method generates metric-based models of high-risk components automatically, based on metrics from previous releases or projects.

These models are built according to a classification tree with binary and multi-value decision nodes. While the first approach permits the use of linguistic descriptions and qualitative reasoning without describing how the classes had been created, the latter is based on history-based crisp decisions that do not indicate any intuition. Thus, both approaches try to solve the problem of metric-based decision support; however, it is often not clear how to justify the decisions. The most serious constraint imposed by classification trees and other crisp clustering techniques is their goal to identify *mutually exclusive subsets*, thus not allowing fuzzy memberships to several classes.

It must be emphasized that criticality prediction techniques being used do not attempt to detect all faults. Instead they belong to the set of managerial instruments that try to optimize resource allocation by focusing them on areas with many faults that would affect the utility of the delivered product. The trade-off of applying complexity-based predictive quality models is estimated based on:

- limited resources are assigned to high-risk jobs or components;
- impact analysis and risk assessment of changes is feasible based on affected or changed complexity;
- gray-box testing strategies are applied to identified high-risk components; and
- fewer customer reported failures.

Criticality predictions surely go well beyond component-oriented validation activities, such as inspections or module test. Especially testing procedures, which look on units or the entire system, can gain a lot from not only testing randomly as it is typically done. Random testing is effective only when defects are distributed uniformly throughout a system.

## 3. Classification Techniques

Classification and clustering algorithms are mathematical tools for detecting similarities between members of a collection of objects. Metric vectors assigned to the same cluster are in some sense similar to each other, more so than they are to other metric vectors not assigned to that cluster. Instead of predicting number of errors or changes (i.e., algorithmic relationships) we are considering assignments to groups (e.g. "change-prone"). While the first goal has been achieved more or less with regression models or neural networks predominantly for finished projects, the latter goal seems to be adequate for predicting potential outliers in running projects, where precision is too expensive and unnecessary for decision support.

Of course, the primary concern with the use of a classification algorithm is how well it has actually identified underlying structures that are present in the data (cluster validity). Classification algorithms may be constructed manually or automatically. Manual construction reflects intuitive knowledge about underlying structures and relations or influences of metrics on distinct factors to be predicted; automatic construction is applied to large data sets where unknown structures and a variety of interdependencies are to be considered. Because it is a difficult task to try all combinations of ranges of (input) metrics and determine their individual influence on the classification algorithm to predict quality factors, such automated techniques have been developed that solve this problem [9, 19, 20].

### 3.1. Pareto classification

*Pareto analysis* is included as a classification technique that is common for quick quality analyses. The goal of a Pareto analysis is to identify those 20% of all components that contribute heavily to all troubles. The principle is nicknamed "80:20 *rule*" because it assumes that the 20% share is responsible for 80% of the problems. It is amazing that this simple approach holds in most application domains. Software quality management methods, such as root cause analysis, typically also start by applying a Pareto analysis and identify the small amount of problems (20%) that provide the biggest return on effort when resolved.

We apply simple Pareto analysis based on the software size (i.e., the top 20% of all modules ranked according to module size are selected). In our comparison this type of analysis clearly performed well with volume as the only input metric for selecting the top 20%. We thus suggest applying Pareto classification as a quick rule of thumb to decide on further activities. The difference to crisp classification trees that could easily provide similar results is that the classification rule is not connected to static boundaries, but to a static rule of thumb with dynamic boundaries in terms of values.

### 3.2. Crisp classification trees

*Classification trees* have been widely used in many areas, for example in image recognition, taxonomy, or decision table programming. The trees are based on a set of metrics that are used to classify components according to how likely they are to have certain high-risk properties. They consist of several leaf nodes that contain binary or multi-value decisions to indicate whether a component is likely to be in a certain class based on historical data. Because each leaf describes values of a distinct metric, such trees might be composed from a set of production rules.

Several methods for automatic tree generation have been described and used for real projects [9]. Each rule imposes crisp boundaries with the result being exclusively allocated to one set based on the values of the input metrics. They are all based on automatic learning from examples with distinct approaches for optimizing, controlling and supervising the learning process (e.g. pattern recognition). Features with more values can lead to decision trees that are unintelligible to human experts and require a larger increase in computation.

### 3.3. *Factor-based discriminant analysis*

*Factor-based discriminant analysis* is an instrument to identify structures and suggest possible organizations of the data into meaningful groups [21, 8, 3]. Any given metric vector can be considered as a multidimensional space where each software component (e.g. a module) is represented as a point with distinct coordinates. We identify as a cluster any subset of the points which is internally well connected and externally poorly connected (i.e., components of a cluster are closely related to each other based on some similarities within the related input metrics). The underlying assumption is that objects under investigation may be grouped such that elements residing in a particular group or cluster are, in some sense, more similar to each other than to elements belonging to other groups.

Typically the classification consists of two steps. First, factor analysis or principal-components procedure is used for reducing the dimensionality of the metric vector to fewer metrics with orthogonal complexity domains. Discriminant analysis is then used to separate groups of software components according to one selected quality attribute (i.e., changes, error rate).

### 3.4. *Neural network classification*

To avoid unnecessary crispness while dealing with approximate knowledge, some recent research has focused towards employing *artificial neural networks* for metric-based decision support [17]. The multilayer perceptron is the most widely applied neural network architecture today. Neural network theory showed that only three layers of neurons are sufficient for learning any (non) linear function combining input data to output data. The input layer consists of one neuron for each complexity metric, while the output layer has one neuron for each quality metric to be predicted.

Because neural network based approaches are predominantly result-driven, not dealing with design heuristics and intuitive rules for modeling the development process and its products, and because their trained information is not accessible from outside, they are even less suitable for providing reasons for any result. To our point of view, any decision support system should contain the maximum amount of expert knowledge that is available. Neural networks can be applied when there are only input vectors (software metric data) and results (quality or productivity data), while no intuitive connections are known between the two sets (e.g. pattern recognition approaches in complicated decision situations).

However, neural networks can currently not provide any insight *why* they arrived at a certain decision besides providing result-driven connection weights. It is interesting to note that feedforward neural nets can be approximated to any degree of accuracy by fuzzy expert systems [22], hence offering a new approach for classification based on neural fuzzy hybrids that can be trained and pre-populated with expert rules.

### 3.5. *Fuzzy classification*

In the above mentioned classification techniques, expert rules are either completely ignored or not adequately covered because neither predicate logic nor probability-based methods provide a systematic basis for dealing with them [5, 2, 6]. Only recently, fuzzy classification techniques had been introduced to software quality management [12, 18].

Most fuzzy expert systems are using production rules (as opposed to semantic nets or frames) that represent procedural knowledge. Such production rules are used to capture both heuristic rules of thumb and formally known relations among the facts in the domain. These rules are represented as if-then-rules that associate conclusions to given antecedents. To arrive at a conclusion, the fuzzy implication and the underlying premise have to be interpreted by a compositional rule of inference. If there are many fuzzy production rules, their individual results can be superimposed. More details are summarized in the appendix.

## 4. Developing a Metric-Based Classification System

The development of a classification system for software quality management consists of the following steps:

(1) Describe an exactly defined development process environment from which the software products under investigation are selected.

(2) Select a group of expert development staff who will be asked to develop a consensus concerning distinct quality factors. Of course, this jury should consist of people with respected knowledge in the areas that influence those projects being ranked (e.g. database or real-time experts for projects determined by such problem domains). If the selected quality factors include maintain-ability or testing effort, staff members that are assigned to such areas must be considered in the jury.

(3) Select a random, however representative sample of software components of past projects from the environment (e.g. modules, procedures, classes) which is used as training and validating data.

(4) Measure these components with respect to a metric vector $M = \{m1, \ldots, mn\}$ based on $n$ selected direct software product metrics that are available during the development process (e.g. cyclomatic complexity or number of input data to a module).

(5) Measure or have the jury cluster these software components with respect to quality or productivity factors in a quality vector $F$ by comparing and evaluating them. Typically $F$ considers aspects such as reliability, error-count, maintainability, or effort. It can have values such as number of errors or MTTF of a given group of software components. Usually $F$ is unknown during the project development and therefore highest interest lies in its early and accurate prediction. To support accurate prediction is actually the task of the classification system. Because $F$ is used for training and validation purposes, an associated metric vector $M$ from the same past projects is required. The result of this step is a data set $\{M; F\}$ for each software module or component. If construction and validation of the prediction model is required, the associated data sets $M$ and $F$ need to be divided into two mutually exclusive sets $\{M'; F'\}$ and $\{M''; F''\}$ before the classification process takes place. One is the set used for training or construction of a distinct classification scheme, while the other one will be used to validate the scheme [5].

(6) Assign the elements of the set $\{M; F\}$ to appropriate linguistic variables. Usually one linguistic variable is assigned to each metric and quality element of the vectors.

(7) Define values for each linguistic variable. Place membership functions for mapping the scale and (usually numeric) range of metrics or quality factors to membership degrees of these values.

(8) For construction of a rule-based system (e.g. pre-populated classification trees, neural-fuzzy hybrids, fuzzy classification) let the experts condense their design knowledge to a set of recursively refined predictive expert rules. The rules are usually dominated by fuzzy linguistic and qualitative descriptions in opposition to quantitative selection formulas that might be preferable on the first sight. Each rule must be explained exactly in order to permit a repeatable classification. When expert knowledge is not available or too expensive algorithmic fuzzy classification approaches may be used for the training data sets. Integrate this set of rules to a classification scheme that can be applied automatically to analyze other software components. Test the resulting set of production rules in terms of completeness (boundaries of ranges) and inconsistencies (several rules with similar antecedents, or similar consequences with contradictive antecedents, etc).

(9) Validate the classification system by classifying the test data sets $\{M''; F''\}$.

(10) The final step is to improve the model by adjusting its properties to optimization goals (e.g. adjusting weights in neural networks, shifting membership functions in fuzzy classification systems, condensing classification trees). Such goals include reducing chi-square values, which is equal to reducing misclassification errors (see Secs. 5 and 6). Parameter tuning is measured by separating misclassification errors, either type I errors ("change-prone components" classified as "uncritical components") or type II errors ("uncritical components" classified as "change-prone components"; also called False Positives). The goal must be to reduce type I errors at the cost of type II errors because it is less expensive to investigate some components despite the fact that they are not critical compared to labeling critical components as harmless without probing further.

## 5. Practical Application: Predicting Changes Based on Complexity Data

It is relatively easy to construct metric-based quality models that happen to classify data of past projects well, because all such models can be calibrated according to quality of fit. The difficulty lies in improving and stabilizing models based on historic data that are of value for use in anticipating future outcomes. While working on software for large real-time systems, we had the task of developing a quality model with predictive accuracy. The main interest of these quality models for metric-based software development was in detecting change-prone modules during the design. Changes include both corrective and additive maintenance; in any case they indicate components requiring more effort than others do. The following subsections summarize results from several experiments that had been conducted to investigate two hypotheses:

- Fuzzy classification applied to criticality prediction provides better results than other classification techniques that have been used in this area in the past.
- Fuzzy classification as introduced here does not necessarily need training (i.e., it could start completely untrained based on design heuristics), thus being more portable to other systems and easier to understand than other classification techniques.

Obviously the purpose of this section is not to evaluate or challenge hypotheses, but rather to give insight into practical results, leading to conclusions that will later be summarized for general applicability.

Subsection 5.1 describes the study setting. Subsection 5.2 investigates already published data (thus providing access for further studies and validations) by applying the classification techniques introduced in Secs. 3 and 4. The last subsection shows how to use metric-based classification in an ongoing industrial project.

Both hypotheses have been tested with the Chi-Square Test. Based on this test a hypothesis is rejected if the calculated $\chi^2$ is bigger than the respective value of $\chi^2_{1;a}$ from $\chi^2$-tables [25]. The population size was in both experiments sufficiently high to employ this test. An additional experiment for the investigation of the different classification techniques was performed based on a random selection of test sets that were then classified. Numbers of type I errors and type II errors are also used for evaluation. The success criteria are in all cases oriented towards low overall misclassification, sufficiently high $\chi^2$-value and low number of type I errors. Due to outliers it is intrinsically impossible to optimize one classification method for both types of misclassification errors. Residual analysis was not performed because our goal was to predict change-prone modules and not number of changes. A sound statistical analysis of change or fault numbers would require a much larger data set with more modules and is usually not requested in practice.

## 5.1. *Study setting*

The *Alcatel* 1000 *S12* is a digital switching system that is currently used in over 40 countries worldwide with over 130 million installed lines. It provides a wide range of functionality (small local exchanges, transit exchanges, international exchanges, network service centers, or intelligent networks) and scalability (from small remote exchanges to large local exchanges). Its typical size is over 2.5 million source statements of which a big portion is customized for local network operators. The code used for *S12* is realized in Assembler, C and CHILL. Recently object-oriented paradigms supported by C++ and Java are increasingly used for new components. Within this study, we focus on modules coded in the CHILL programming language, although the concepts apply equally for other languages. CHILL is a Pascal-like language with dedicated elements to better describe telecommunication systems.

In terms of functionality, *S12* covers almost all areas of software and computer engineering. This includes operating systems, database management and distributed real-time software.

The organization responsible for development and integration is registered for the ISO 9001 standard. Most locations are ranked on capability maturity model (CMM) Level 2, while few have already achieved CMM Level 3. Development staff is distributed over the whole world in over 20 development centers with the majority in Europe and US. Projects within the product line are developed typically within only few centers with a focus on high collocation of engineers involved in one project and a high allocation degree to one specific project at a time. In terms of effort or cost, the share of software is increasing continuously and is currently in the range of over 80%.

A product line concept has been introduced which is based on few core releases that are further customized according to specific market requirements around the world. The structuring of a system into product families allows the sharing of design effort within a product family and as such, counters the impact of ever growing complexity. This makes it possible to better sustain the rate of product evolution and introduction to new markets. There is a clear trade-off between coherent development of functionality vs the various specific features of that functionality in different countries. Not only standards are different (e.g. Signaling or ISDN in the USA vs Europe) but also the implementation of dedicated functionality (e.g. supplementary services or test routines) and finally the user interfaces (e.g. screen layout, charging records).

Project size in terms of effort ranges between 10 and 500 person years with around four million new or changed statements in total. Each of those projects was built on around 2500 KStmt legacy code depending on the degree of reused functionality and underlying base release. The field performance metrics used in this study cover altogether several thousand years of execution time.

The data for this study was collected between 1995 and 1997. Metrics are collected automatically (e.g. size) or semi-automatically derived from operational databases (e.g. faults, elapse time, effort). They are typically first stored in operational databases related to the respective development process, and later extracted and aggregated for the project history database. Since the projects are typically developed in a timeframe of several months and then deployed to the field again over a period of several months, the timestamp for each project in time series was the handover date. This is the contractually fixed date when the first product is delivered to the customer for acceptance testing. Customer detected faults, which is one of the dependent variables, are counted from that date onwards.

Fault accounting is per activity to allow for overlapping development activities and incremental development. This means that the major activities of the entire development process are taken for reporting of both faults and effort, even if they overlap with a follow-on activity. If for instance a correction was inspected before regression testing, the faults found during that code inspection would be reported an inspection fault, rather than a test fault.

The described results within this paper result from the Software Process Improvement program, which Alcatel heavily pushes since 1995. This process improvement program is based on the Capability Maturity Model (CMM) [26] and initially looks into improving quality and predictability of projects. One core part of this program in the first years was to improve reliability for the reasons mentioned in the introduction. The improvement program is based on the CMM, and although this framework would not go to so much detail as prescribing specific reliability engineering techniques, it's clear focus in the beginning is on better software quality and improved project management, both closely related to a managed reliability of the delivered system [26]. At the beginning of our approach to improve reliability the focus was thus on two measurable objectives closely related to Alcatel's business goals:

- improving the customer-perceived quality; and
- reducing the total cost of non-quality.

Improving customer perceived quality can be broken down to one major improvement target, namely to dramatically reduce customer detected faults. This sounds superficial given the many dimensions of quality. There was however, at the start of this SPI program, strong indication in several markets that above all, field failures had to be reduced. Such targets are quite common in telecommunication systems and often contracts fix upper limits of failures and downtime with respect to priorities and calendar time or execution time.

## 5.2. *Project A*

To investigate the effectiveness of different classification techniques we applied them to data originally published by Kitchenham *et al* [1]. Given two sets of metrics from modules of the ICL general-purpose operating system VME, complexity-based classification was performed to estimate change-proneness of the modules. Both sets of data came from two different implementations of the same sub-system with identical functional requirements. As each program was coded, it was placed under formal configuration control and subsequent changes to modules were recorded. It was not distinguished between corrective and additive changes' intentions. Ten different software complexity metrics are provided together with change rates for 67 modules altogether. The complexity metrics' set includes machine code instructions, lines of code (executable), modules called (calls to external modules), data items (access to static data items by a program module), parameters, Halstead's unique operator count, Halstead's unique operand count, total operators in a module, total operands in a module, and McCabe's cyclomatic complexity.

Since these data sets had been investigated and used for other studies [4], we will only summarize some explorative outcomes. The given software complexity metrics are highly correlated, most Spearman rank correlation coefficients are above 0.5. For example, the volume of the code in executable lines of code (without comments and without empty lines) is correlated with the cyclomatic complexity (0.90), and with unique operands (0.93) for all modules. Such relations between metrics are typical and were studied extensively [11]. Factor analysis was performed for reducing dimensions of the metric space resulting in three almost orthogonal factors: volume, control and parameterization. Based on these results, we selected five complexity metrics as input values for the prediction models that are most common in complexity metrics application, namely lines of code (tvol), modules called (func), data items (data), unique operands (uopd), and cyclomatic complexity (cycl).

Two VME sub-systems had been described within the Kitchenham study with sub-system 1 containing 27 modules and sub-system 2 containing 40 modules. Since all changes to each module had been provided together with several complexity metrics, we first divided both sub-systems in two classes for each sub-system containing around 80% of modules with few changes and the remaining 20% with many changes. Then one sub-system was treated as the data set for training, while the other one was tested for validation purposes after having trained the classification system. For testing the robustness of different classification methods we treated the sets equally despite knowing about the presence of outliers. Compared to other studies [4], we did not eliminate outliers because no common agreement for such filtering exists [11].

Factor-based discriminant analysis could be performed rather easily because it only requires factor analysis for reducing metrics' dimensionality and afterwards discriminant analysis which needs just one learning cycle. This approach hence is the fastest way for classification. Both classification tree and neural network predictions need several thousand training cycles for optimization that are performed automatically on workstations or PCs. It was interesting to realize that classification tree results were similar to results from crisp cluster analysis with ten classes, although the latter approach takes almost no computational effort. For neural network classification, a three layer perceptron (5, 12, 1 nodes) with backpropagation learning (100,000 training cycles; learning rate: 0.5; momentum between 0 and 0.5) showed best results.

Fuzzy classification was a short cut to only one given rule system without further optimization (as presented in Fig. 6). Therefore the rules (weights = 1) and membership functions (trapezoid and symmetrical) provide good comprehension and portability. Optimizing the fuzzy classification resulted in the reduction of misclassification errors by one or two (not presented here). However, rules and membership functions looked very strange (i.e., asymmetric membership functions with overly precise boundaries, increasing the number of rules with individual weight factors). We, hence, discarded those results.

### 5.3. *Project B*

The second experiment was for portability of the classification methods to bigger projects. Training data was taken from several real-time telecommunication projects that had been developed according to a similar design approach. We will describe classification results for one telecommunication project in the area of switching systems called "Project B" that was used for testing purposes. We investigated a selection of 451 modules that had been placed under configuration control since the start of coding. The overall size of these modules is in the area of 1 million lines of executable code. The specific project had been in field use for over a year thus showing stability in terms of features and failures. Software changes (comparative to those in project A) are given for each module together with several complexity metrics [24].

Complexity metrics used in this project include number of (executable) statements, statement complexity, expression complexity, data complexity, depth of nesting (control flow), and data base access (number and complexity of data base accesses). Statement complexity, expression complexity and data complexity are simple metrics that count the use of distinct statements (e.g. different data types and their use is considered data complexity) according to given hierarchies

## Membership Functions:

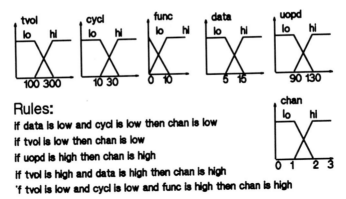

## Rules:

If data is low and cycl is low then chan is low

If tvol is low then chan is low

If uopd is high then chan is high

If tvol is high and data is high then chan is high

'f tvol is low and cycl is low and func is high then chan is high

**Fig. 6.**   Fuzzy membership functions and inference rules for module design.

of individual complexity assignments. Again Spearman rank correlation among different complexity metrics was considerably high. For all selected metrics they were above 0.8. Complexity metrics also correlated with the number of changes (average over 0.4).

The second hypothesis being tested is that using fuzzy classification as introduced here does *not necessarily* need training (i.e., it could start completely untrained based on design heuristics), thus being more portable to other systems and easier to understand than the other methods. We tested this hypothesis in a third experiment for project B in order to achieve insight in portability of classification techniques without further training. Based on an earlier project that had been designed similarly, we provided few expert rules for the fuzzy classification. The rules were as follows:

- if statement count is high then changes are high;
- if data complexity is high then changes are high;
- if expression complexity is high then changes are high;
- if data base access is high then changes are high;
- if depth of nesting is high then changes are high;
- if data complexity is low then changes are low; and
- if statement count is low then changes are low.

Membership functions remained unchanged from the former project that allows application of these expert rules as design heuristics or vice versa.

## 6.  Results and Discussion

Table 1 shows a portfolio of predictions vs reality for both sub-systems of project A. Notions in quotation marks (in the first column) are the predictions. The upper half of the table investigates sub-system I, while the lower half analyses sub-system II.

**Table 1.**   Classification results for Project A with five classification methods.

| Project A: Two Subsystems with 67 Modules. | Pareto Classification by Volume (top 20%) | Crisp Classification Tree | Factor-Based Discriminant Analysis | Neural Network Classification | Non-Optimized Fuzzy Classification |
|---|---|---|---|---|---|
| VME sub-system 1 (27 modules) used for testing (sub-system 2 for training) | | | | | |
| reality: $\leq 5$ changes: 21 modules (77%) | | | | | |
| prediction: "few changes" | 19 | 19 | 20 | 19 | 20 |
| prediction: "change-prone" (type II) | 2 | 2 | 1 | 2 | 1 |
| reality: $> 5$ changes: 6 modules (23%) | | | | | |
| prediction: "few changes" (type I) | 2 | 2 | 5 | 3 | 0 |
| prediction: "change-prone" | 4 | 4 | 1 | 3 | 6 |
| $\chi^2$ | 8.82 | 8.82 | 0.96 | 5.06 | 22.0 |
| VME sub-system 2 (40 modules) used for testing (sub-system 1 for training) | | | | | |
| reality: $\leq 4$ changes: 31 modules (78%) | | | | | |
| prediction: "few changes" | 28 | 30 | 28 | 30 | 30 |
| prediction: "change-prone" (type II) | 3 | 1 | 3 | 1 | 1 |
| reality: $> 4$ changes: 9 modules (22%) | | | | | |
| prediction: "few changes" (type I) | 3 | 4 | 1 | 4 | 3 |
| prediction: "change-prone" | 6 | 5 | 8 | 5 | 6 |
| $\chi^2$ | 13.0 | 15.0 | 15.5 | 15.0 | 19.4 |
| random selection of test sets (percentage of overall correct classification) | 83.0% | 78.3% | 73.2% | 80.7% | 92.5% |

Instead of common portfolio tables the four values for predictions vs reality are put into single line entries. For example sub-system I consists of 27 modules. 21 of these modules (77%) contain 5 changes or less, while 6 modules (23%) contain more than 5 changes. This share reflects approximately the 80:20 ratio that is useful for predictions that require rework in terms of redesign or other approaches to improve maintainability. Applying the Pareto classification (second column) results in a selection of 6 modules that have the biggest volume (i.e., top 20%). The remaining 21 modules are predicted as having "few changes". Now these two groups are compared with reality. Nineteen modules with few changes and 4 change-prone modules were classified correctly. Two modules were misclassified as having few changes (type I error) and 2 modules were predicted as change-prone, while belonging to the class of modules with few changes (type II error). Taking these values gives the chi-square result of 8.82.

The last line of Table 1 provides the average percentage of correct classifications for several runs when all data sets (both sub-systems) were mixed and then half of them were randomly selected for training or testing, respectively.

Classification seems to be more difficult for sub-system 1, which contains more outlying data sets (i.e., complexity metrics and number of changes do not fit together). Fuzzy classification performed best in terms of $\chi^2$ and overall misclassifications were altogether at a minimum. Figure 7 shows a scatterplot of the complete Kitchenham data set (both sub-systems) with changes (horizontal axis), lines of code (vertical axis), and cyclomatic complexity (shape). Outliers with small complexity and high change-rate can be clearly identified. It is obviously impossible to strive for zero misclassifications because several data sets are overlapping in a sense that they belong to the, intuitively, wrong group according to the delivered error count.

Applying the five different classification techniques to the switching system data of project B showed almost identical results in terms of overall correct classification of the modules (Table 2). Results showed highest overall correct classification for crisp classification trees (85% of all modules). Pareto classification (83% of all modules) and neural network classification (82.5%) performed slightly worse. Factor-based discriminant analysis and non-optimized fuzzy classification finally

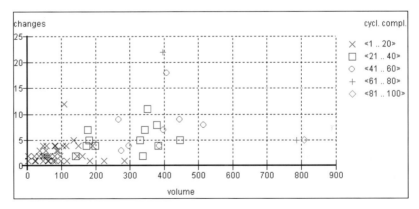

**Fig. 7.** Scatterplot of number of changes with volume and cyclomatic complexity for project A (both sub-systems).

**Table 2.**  Classification results for project B with five classification methods.

| Project B: 200 Modules Used for Testing (163 Modules with Zero or One Faults; 37 Modules with More Than One Fault) | Pareto Classification by Volume (Top 20%) | Crisp Classification Tree | Factor-Based Discriminant Analysis | Neural Network Classification | Non-Optimized Fuzzy Classification |
|---|---|---|---|---|---|
| reality: $\leq 1$ fault: 163 modules (81.5%) | | | | | |
| prediction: "few changes" | 146 | 149 | 137 | 149 | 133 |
| prediction: "change-prone" (type II) | 17 | 14 | 26 | 14 | 30 |
| reality: $> 1$ faults: 37 modules (18.5%) | | | | | |
| prediction: "few changes" (type I) | 17 | 16 | 12 | 21 | 8 |
| prediction: "change-prone" | 20 | 21 | 25 | 16 | 29 |
| $\chi_2$ | 38.1 | 48.9 | 42.3 | 28.4 | 52.2 |

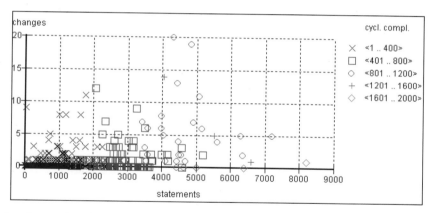

**Fig. 8.**  Scatterplot of number of changes with volume and cyclomatic complexity for project B.

achieved 81% correct classifications. Obviously there is no clear winner given this ranking which is due to a number of outliers that either increase types I or II misclassifications when optimization of the other area is achieved (Fig. 8).

A better indicator for comparing classification techniques is the number of type I misclassifications. Table 2 provides these results. Fuzzy classification shows lowest misclassification results with only 8 modules indicated as having few changes while they actually were change-prone. Chi-square analysis also indicates that fuzzy classification is performing better than the other techniques ($\chi^2 = 52.2$). Automatic optimization of rules (e.g. more than two input values in one rule) and membership functions improved these results, however due to desired intuitiveness of rules we won't discuss such techniques.

Results of the third experiment on portability of classification techniques without further training are as follows: fuzzy classification with data from a follow-on project provided $\chi^2 = 46.1$ for 200 modules. Pareto classification performed slightly worse ($\chi^2 = 35.7$), while the three remaining classification techniques had a $\chi^2$ below 30.

A comparison of different classification approaches suitable for metric-based decision support is presented in Tables 3. Results as presented in this table are based on various applications of the four classification techniques to data sets from switching systems. Pareto classification is left out because this mere analytical technique needs neither training nor does it provide any constructive guidelines during design and coding. The upper part of this table presents a summary on

**Table 3.**    Comparison of different classification methods (without Pareto classification).

| | Crisp Classifica-tion Tree | Factor-Based Discriminant Analysis | Neural Network Classification | Fuzzy Classification |
|---|---|---|---|---|
| crisp data values as metric data values | x | x | x | x |
| fuzzy, vague, linguistic data values | | | | x |
| algorithmic knowledge representation | (x) | x | (x) | (x) |
| rule-based knowledge representation | x | | | x |
| information represented by *intuitive* rules | | | | x |
| *learning* is result-driven (as opposed to design heuristics) | x | x | (x)* | |
| learning can be performed automatically (0, +, ++) | ++ | 0 | ++ | + |
| reasons for decisions are given (0, +, ++) | ++ | 0 | 0 | ++ |
| effects of highly correlated metrics in input training data (0, +, ++) | ++ | ++ | + | ++ |
| effects of uncorrelated metrics in input training data (0, +, ++) | + | + | 0 | ++ |
| robustness to outlying data sets during training (0, +, ++) | ++* | + | 0 | ++* |
| portability to data sets from other projects with same design methodology (0, +, ++) | + | + | 0 | ++ |
| bibliography for applications and theory | [2,9,19,23] | [4,21] | [17] | [12,15,18,22] |

* dependent on learning approach or classification algorithm
0 bad results
+ medium results
++ good results

learning and knowledge representation. The lower part gives the effects of using manipulated data values (i.e., two metrics are highly correlated, one metric is almost random; several data sets contain random values). The remaining two parts of Table 3 provide portability results and, again, a short bibliography for improved orientation.

Based on the described experiments, fuzzy classification clearly performed best. Since there are some guiding principles for decision support available, we emphasize on utilizing expert-derived, however vague, knowledge that we included in a fuzzy expert system-type classification scheme. For the same reason (i.e., software engineering expert knowledge is available) we strongly oppose using learning strategies that are only result-driven (e.g. classification trees or mere neural network approaches). However, we see the necessity of such approaches when only few guiding principles are available and sufficient project data can be utilized for supervised learning.

## 7. Conclusions

The choice of the proper approach to automatic decision support depends on the problem. To software classification problems, multibranching fuzzy classification provides a more comprehensive solution than crisp decision trees. Such multi-branching decision support is based on structures that are not necessarily trees but also networks that resemble expert systems' structures. When these classification schemes are applied to new data sets, the best solution is to provide not only a binary result, but fuzzy attributes that consider those results that lie in between a clear "yes" or "no". We emphasize the necessity of applying fuzzy concepts to the areas of metric-based software project and quality management because subjective and qualitative judgment plays an important role in this area.

We can conclude out of the comparison of the different techniques the following:

- If it comes to fast and simple identification of critical modules, a simple Pareto classification is the choice.
- Compared with other classification methods fuzzy classification shows best results in terms of both chi-square and reduction of type I misclassification errors.
- Expert rules that are already available (e.g. design heuristics, coding guidelines) can be directly included in the classification scheme.
- Rules can be used independent of the projects because membership functions may be tuned according to project environments without violating the rules.
- Derived classification schemes can be combined with CASE tools and automatic metrics generation for integrated design support.

The impacts of this study for other applications in software development projects are as follows:

- Complexity metrics together with history data sets of past projects must be utilized for criticality prediction of modules. They help to identify those few critical components that later are responsible for most of the faults that show up in integration and in the field.
- Criticality predictions are most effective before the start of system integration.
- For a quick overview, for instance in a project review, Pareto analysis should be applied to identify few highly critical modules.
- The best classification technique among five techniques that are currently applicable for complexity-based criticality prediction is fuzzy classification. This technique can easily be applied because tool environments are available off the shelf.
- The outcome of each criticality prediction must be an intensive investigation of the identified modules in order to find out whether they indeed contain not-yet-detected errors.

## 8. Summary and Further Research

We have evaluated several classification techniques as an approach for predicting faults based on code complexity metrics. Given complexity metrics and quality data (fault rates) of several different real-time systems best results were achieved with fuzzy classification. Pareto analysis ("80:20 rule") generally showed good results which clearly underlie its importance as a rule of thumb for easy identification of the top 20% of critical modules. Complexity-based classification has been applied to the design and testing of telecommunication systems. Its practical use was showed for detecting fault-prone components and assigning additional fault-detection effort.

As such the technique proves to be effective in early identification of critical components. It must be emphasized that criticality prediction techniques being used do not attempt to detect all faults. Instead they belong to the set of managerial instruments that try to optimize resource allocation by focusing them on areas with many faults that would affect the utility of the delivered product.

The trade-off of applying complexity-based predictive quality models is estimated based on:

- limited resources are assigned to high-risk jobs or components;
- impact analysis and risk assessment of changes is feasible based on affected or changed complexity;
- gray-box testing strategies are applied to identified high-risk components; and
- less customer reported failures.

Especially the mentioned levels for reaction and the appropriate measure how to react most effectively must be subject to continuous evaluation. They will improve over time with more projects being applied. Further research in the area of predictive quality models should focus on the areas:

- Investigation of more projects from different application areas in order to provide fundamental insight in the development of quality models and their influence on different project types. This should include analyses of different approaches for constructing classification schemes (e.g. decision trees) and optimizing their accuracy, intelligibility, and reproducibility.
- Model the processes contributing to fault injection, detection and correction (look for example on staffing, late feature changes, corrections affecting complex components, testing strategies and their coverage and distribution over the whole system).
- Coping with noisy data sets for constructing predictive classification systems. Solutions to this problem include robust feature selection and error-estimation during the induction of classification schemes.
- Application to practical software project management based on predictive and dynamic classification models. Derived classification schemes must be combined with IPSE and CM thus providing automatic metric generation for integrated design and test management support.

## Appendix 1: Validation within Software Development Projects

Quality improvement such as increased reliability and maintainability are of utmost importance in software development. In this field, which was previously *ad hoc* and unpredictable rather than customer oriented, increasing competition and decreasing customer satisfaction have motivated many companies to put more emphasis on quality. Failures in telecommunication systems, such as a nation-wide switching circuit failure in 1992, show that low software quality in such a sensible field has much more effect than defects in many other applications. Compared to other products with high software complexity (e.g. scientific computing, real-time systems) telecommunication systems provide manifold risks (based on the product of probability and effect) due to the high coupling of various components, which lets failures being distributed rapidly within the entire network. Criticality of telecommunication systems is multiplied by the fact that numerous other applications, such as stock exchange or electronic commerce, dependent on correct functionality of real-time information supply.

Competition, along with the customer's willingness to change providers whenever he is dissatisfied has resulted in huge efforts to provide switching software on time and with *exactly* the quality the customer has specified and expects to pay for. A study by the Strategic Planning Institute shows that customer-perceived quality is amongst the three factors with the strongest influence on long-term profitability of a company. Customers typically view achieving the right balance among reliability, delivery date, and cost as having the greatest effect on their long-term link to a company. Engineering for improved reliability as described in this paper is to achieve this balance in software-based systems.

Since defects can never be entirely avoided, several techniques have been suggested for detecting defects early in the development life cycle:

- design reviews;
- code inspections with checklists based on typical fault situations or critical areas in the software;
- enforced reviews and testing of critical areas (in terms of complexity, former failures, expected fault density, individual change history, customer's risk and occurrence probability);
- tracking the effort spent for analyses, reviews, and inspections and separating according to requirements to find out areas not sufficiently covered;
- test coverage metrics (e.g. C0 and C1);
- dynamic execution already applied during integration test;
- application of protocol testing machines to increase level of automatic testing; and
- application of operational profiles/usage specifications from start of system test.

We will further focus on several selected approaches that are applied for improved defect detection before starting with integration and system test.

One important tool for effectively reducing defects and improving reliability is to track all faults that are detected independently of development process. Counting faults is one of the most widely applied and accepted methods used to determine software quality. Typically development views quality on the basis of faults, while it is failures that reflect the customer's satisfaction with a product. Counting faults during the complete project helps to estimate the end of distinct phases (e.g. module test or sub-system test) and improves the underlying processes. Failure prediction is used to manage release time of software. This ensures that neither too much time nor money is spent on unnecessary testing that could possibly result in late delivery, nor that early release occurs which might jeopardize customer satisfaction due to undetected faults. More advanced techniques in failure prediction focus on typical user operations and therefore avoid wasting time and effort on wrong test strategies. Failures reported during system test or field application must be traced back to their primary causes and specific faults in the design (e.g. design decisions or lack of design reviews).

An example of good reporting is when a customer provides adequate data and is interested in detecting as many faults as possible in order to get them corrected. Obviously the same quality of defect reporting must be achieved during the entire development process to achieve liable prediction and criticality results. Based on fault reports since module test, predictive models have been developed on the basis of complexity metrics and on the basis of reliability prediction models. As a result, it was possible to determine defective modules already during design and field failure rates during test!

Figure 9 shows that in organizations with rather low maturity (i.e., ranked according to the capability maturity model) faults are often detected at the end of the development process despite the fact that they had been present since the design phase. Late fault detection results in costly and time consuming correction efforts, especially when the requirements were misunderstood or a design flaw occurred. Organizations with higher maturity obviously move defect detection towards the phases where they have been introduced.

The single most relevant techniques for early and cost-effective defect detection so far are inspections and module test. Detecting faults in architecture and design documents has considerable benefit from a cost perspective, because these defects are expensive to correct. Major yields in terms of reliability however can be attributed to better code, for the simple reason that there are much more defects residing in code that were also inserted during the coding activity. We therefore provide more depth on techniques that help to improve quality of code, namely code reviews (i.e., code reading and code inspections) and module test.

There are six possible paths between delivery of a module from design until start of integration test (Fig. 10). They indicate the permutations of doing code reading alone, performing code inspections and applying module test.

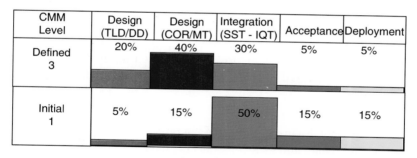

| CMM Level | Design (TLD/DD) | Design (COR/MT) | Integration (SST - IQT) | Acceptance | Deployment |
|---|---|---|---|---|---|
| Defined 3 | 20% | 40% | 30% | 5% | 5% |
| Initial 1 | 5% | 15% | 50% | 15% | 15% |

**Fig. 9.** Typical benchmark effects of detecting faults earlier in the life cycle, the higher the maturity of the respective organization.

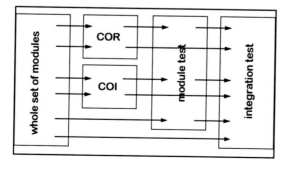

**Fig. 10.** Six possible paths for modules between end of coding and start of integration test (COR: code reviews; COI: formal code inspections).

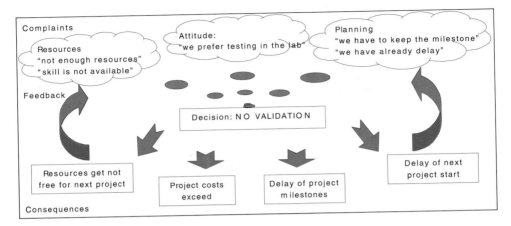

**Fig. 11.**   The vicious cycle of not reviewing results in due time.

Although the best approach surely is from a mere defect detection perspective to apply inspections and module test, cost considerations and the objective to reduce elapse time and thus improve throughput, suggested to carefully evaluate which path to go in order to most efficiently and effectively detect and remove faults. To our experience code reading is the cheapest detection technique, while module test is the most expensive. Code inspections lie somewhat in between.

Module test however, combined with C0 coverage targets has the highest effectiveness for regression testing of existing functionality. Inspections on the other hand help in detecting distinct fault classes that can only be found under load in the field.

There is nevertheless a tendency not to perform these inexpensive validation techniques adequately. Figure 11 indicates the typical vicious circle of not validating when it's the right time, and as a consequence, having to detect defects at a much higher cost thus again taking away resources unexpectedly during the next design activity of a project.

The target must be to find the right balance between efficiency (time to be spent per item) and effectiveness (ratio of detected faults compared to remaining faults) by making the right decisions to spend the budget for the most appropriate quality assurance methods. In addition, overall efficiency and effectiveness have to be optimized. It must be therefore carefully decided which method should be applied on which work product to guarantee high efficiency and effectiveness of code reading (i.e., done by one checker) and code inspections (i.e., done by multiple checkers in a controlled setting). Wrong decisions can mainly have two impacts:

- Proposed method to be performed is too "weak": faults that could have been found with a stronger method are not detected in the early phase. Too little effort would be spend in the early phase. Typically in this case, efficiency is high and effectiveness is low.

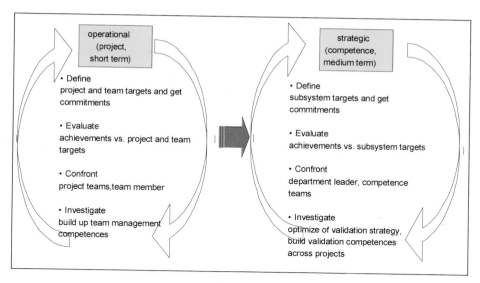

**Fig. 12.** Validation needs to derive operational targets from strategic product related objectives.

- Proposed method to be performed is too "strong": if the fault density is low from the very beginning, even an effective method will not discover many faults. This leads to a low efficiency, compared to the average effort, which has to be spent to detect one fault. This holds especially for small changes in legacy code.

Obviously, specific targets must be set covering both operational and strategic perspectives to introduce validation activities in projects (operational) and products (strategic). Figure 12 shows their mutual influence.

Knowing about the difficulties in introducing and maintaining a good level of early validation activities implies for most organizations a major cultural change. Not many projects or product lines adequately manage to defect detection according to optimizing cost of non-quality. Such process change means that not only a process has to be defined and trained, but also that continuous coaching is available (Fig. 13).

Faults are not distributed homogeneously through new or changed code. By concentrating on fault-prone modules both, effectiveness and efficiency are improved. Our main approach to identify fault-prone software-modules is a criticality prediction taking into account several criteria. One criterion is the analysis of module complexity based on complexity metrics. Other criteria concern the amount of new or changed code in a module, and the amount of field faults a module had in the predecessor project.

The main input parameters for planning code inspections are:

- General availability of an inspection leader: only a trained and internally certified inspection leader is allowed to plan and perform inspections to

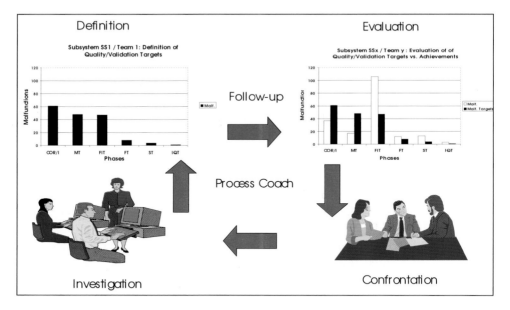

**Fig. 13.** Successfully introducing and sustaining validation activities is a culture change requesting adequate process management.

ensure adherence to the formal rules and achievement of efficiency targets. The number of certified inspection leaders and their availability limits the number of performed inspections for a particular project.

- Module design effort (planned/actually spent): the actual design effort per module can already give an early impression on how much code will be new or changed. This indicates the effort that will be necessary for verification tasks like inspections.

- Know-how of the checker: if specific know-how is necessary to check particular parts of the software the availability of correspondingly skilled persons will have an impact on the planning of code reviews and code inspections.

- Checking rate: based on the program language and historic experiences in previous projects, the optimal checking rate determines the necessary effort to be planned.

- Size of new or changed statements: relating to the checking rate the total amount of the target size to be inspected defines the necessary effort.

- Quality targets: if high-risk areas are identified (e.g. unexpected changes to previously stable components or unstable inputs from a previous project) exhaustive inspections must be considered.

- Achieving the entry criteria: the inspection or review can start earliest if entry criteria for these procedures can be matched. Typically, at least error-free compilable sources have to be available.

The intention is to apply code inspections on heavily changed modules first, to optimize payback of the additional effort that has to be spent compared to the lower effort for code reading. Code reading is recommended to be performed by the author himself for very small changes with a checking time shorter than two hours in order to profit from a good efficiency of code reading. The effort for know-how transfer to another designer can be saved.

For module test some additional parameters have to be considered:

- Optimal sequence of modules to be tested before start of integration test: start-up tests typically can start without having the entire new features implemented for all modules. Therefore the schedule for module test has to consider individual participation of modules in start-up tests. Later increments of the new design are added to integration test related to their respective functionality.
- Availability of reusable module test environments: effort for setting-up sophisticated test environments for the module test must be considered during planning. This holds especially for legacy code where often the module test environments and test cases for the necessary high C0 coverage are not available.
- Distribution of code changes over all modules of one project: the number of items to be tested has a heavy impact on the whole planning and on the time, which has to be planned for performing module test. The same amount of code to be tested can be distributed over a small number of modules (small initialization effort) or over a wide distribution of small changes throughout a lot of modules (high initialization effort).
- Completion date of planned code reviews and code inspections: overlap of code reviews or code inspections with module test should be avoided as much as possible in order to ensure high overall efficiency. Obviously, it is not reasonable to test in parallel to inspections of the same portion of code, as corrections must be tested again.
- Achieving the entry criteria: the readiness of validated test lists is a mandatory prerequisite for starting the module test.

The intention is to avoid spending high initialization effort by setting-up module test environments in order to test only a few number of changed statements. If on the other side, reusable module test environments are available, this effort will be small enough to be appropriate. For modules identified as potentially critical module test must be performed independent of the effort which is necessary to initialize the module test environment.

During test the correction of faults is typically the bottleneck for the project progress (not the detection of faults). It's no problem to add testers to a test phase in order to increase the number of detected faults within a given time schedule, but it's impossible to increase the correction rate by the same time if many corrections have to be made in a small group of modules.

Therefore, a criticality prediction performed upfront should help to identify error-prone modules in advance to avoid a small number of designers having to correct the majority of the faults. For this group of modules early quality assurance activities should be performed preferably to cut peaks for the number of faults in error-prone areas.

The result of a multi-linear discriminant analysis based on complexity metrics for a criticality prediction was taken into account for the planning of code inspections and module tests (especially modules identified as critical had to be inspected and module tested mandatory). It was expected that corrections from integration test onwards will be distributed over a larger set of modules. Our experiences clearly demonstrate that the impacts of the bottleneck in getting corrections could be reduced by performing additional quality assurance activities before the start of integration. Instead of the 80–20 distribution, after these activities the bottleneck was widened: we achieved an 81–40 distribution (i.e., 81% of the faults are distributed over 40% of the modules), and a 63–20 distribution.

## Appendix 2: Fuzzy Classification

Often, fuzzy facts and rules are generally manipulated as if they were non-fuzzy; leading to conclusions whose validity is open to question. As a simple illustration of this point, consider the fact [2]: *"If data bindings are between 6 and 10 and cyclomatic complexity is greater than 18 the software component is likely to have errors of a distinct type"*. Obviously the meaning of this — automatically generated — fact is less precise than stated and might be provided by a maintenance expert as a fuzzy fact: *"If data bindings are medium and cyclomatic complexity is large then the software component is likely to have errors of a distinct type"*. Of course, the latter fact requires the determination of the fuzzy attributes "medium" or "large" in the context of the linguistic variables they are associated with (i.e., data bindings and cyclomatic complexity).

### Fuzzy Sets and Fuzzy Logic

Fuzzy logic provides a method for representing the meaning of both fuzzy and non-fuzzy predicate modifiers or hedges (e.g. *not, very, much, slightly, extremely*) which permits a system for computing with linguistic variables, that is, variables whose values are words in a natural language [15]. For example, cyclomatic complexity is a linguistic variable when its values are assumed to be: *high, small, medium, very high, rather small*, etc, where each value can be interpreted as a possibility distribution over all integers. In order to permit rule-based approximate reasoning based on external input data from software products or documents and vague knowledge about the underlying process that produced the software components to be classified, it is necessary to permit the formulation of fuzzy (expert) rules. Fuzzy classification has been introduced to complexity-based criticality prediction in [18].

While in two-valued logic systems a proposition may be qualified by associating it with a truth value (i.e., true or false) or a modal value (e.g. impossible), in fuzzy logic, these qualifications are either truth (possibility) qualifications expressed as a real value $\tau \in [0,1]$ or probability qualifications with a qualifier $\lambda \in [0,1]$. A fuzzy set $A$ of a given universe of discourse $U$ which is associated with its base variable $y$ is described by its membership function $\mu_A : U \rightarrow [0,1]$ which represents each element $y$ of discourse $U$ as a number $\mu_A$ in the interval $[0,1]$ that represents the grade of membership of $y$ in $A$. In other words, the value of the membership function indicates the possibility or certainty with which $y$ belongs to the fuzzy set $A$. Because both, possibility distributions and probability distributions may be associated with $y$, it is necessary to distinguish exactly between the two interpretations.

As an example let $A$ be a linguistic variable with the label "cyclomatic complexity" with $y \in U = [1,100]$. The terms of this linguistic variable, which are fuzzy sets, are labeled "high", "small", and so on. The base variable $y$ of $A$ is the number of decisions in a software component plus one. $\mu_A : U \rightarrow [0,1]$ is the representation rule that assigns a meaning, that is, a fuzzy set, to the terms. Though different shapes of membership functions have been described, practical applications usually describe fuzzy numbers with a triangular membership function (i.e., the degree of membership of a distinct value to a fuzzy set is of triangular shape starting with 0, indicating non-membership, to 1, indicating full membership, and back to 0, hence allowing various degrees of membership for the elements of the given set).

## Fuzzy Decision Support

In order to permit rule-based approximate reasoning based on external input data from software products or documents and vague knowledge about the underlying process that produced the software components to be classified, it is necessary to permit the formulation of fuzzy (expert) rules. The combination of interacting fuzzy rules derived from expert knowledge is called a fuzzy expert system, because it is supposed to model an expert and make his or her knowledge available for non-experts for the purposes of diagnosis or decision making. The declarative knowledge of fuzzy expert systems is represented as fuzzy sets and data.

Let $M = \{M_1, \ldots, M_m\}$ be a set of $m$ metric vectors in $\mathfrak{R}^n$, representing $n$ measures applied on $m$ software components. Fuzzy clustering of the $m$ software components $M_i$ into $c$ clusters results in functions $\mu_1, \ldots, \mu_c$ where $\mu_i : M \rightarrow [0,1]$ and $\sum_i \mu_i(M_j) = 1, \forall M_j \in M$ which corresponds to the full membership of each component in $M$. As already described, these functions are called membership functions that can have as values any real number between 0 and 1. Zadeh proposed that rather than describe a set by its membership, to describe it by a membership function and allow the function to have values between 0 and 1 to represent ambiguity that might be present in the set. A cyclomatic complexity of 20 might be assigned a membership of 0.8 in the set labeled *"medium"* and a membership of 0.2 in the set labeled *"high"*, while a cyclomatic complexity of 30 has a membership degree of 0.3 in the set labeled *"medium"* and a membership of 0.7 in the set labeled *"high"*. The clusters of a fuzzy classification are hence the membership functions themselves. They indicate structure of the input data in a way that two components $M_i$ and $M_j$ with membership functions close to one for the same label can be considered equal to each other. If several components have their individual maximum membership for the same membership function, that component with the highest membership is classified best by the clustering.

Most fuzzy expert systems are using production rules (as opposed to semantic nets or frames) that represent procedural knowledge. Such production rules are used to capture both heuristic rules of thumb and formally known relations among the facts in the domain (Fig. 6). These rules are represented as if-then-rules that associate conclusions to given antecedents. An example for a production rule that we use is *"if cyclomatic complexity is medium and statement count is medium then the component is error-prone"*. The advantage of production rules obviously lies in the fact that there is a convenient way to represent one's domain knowledge and that they can be augmented easily by adding further rules. The inference engine that controls the application of fitting rules to given data is based on an extension of set-theoretic operators (e.g. and, or, then). Originally the following three operators were proposed by Zadeh for intersection, union and complement:

$$\mu_A \cap B(y) = \min(\mu_A(y), \mu_B(y)), y \in U$$

$$\mu_A \cup B(y) = \max(\mu_A(y), \mu_B(y)), y \in U$$

$$\mu_{\neg A}(y) = 1 - \mu_A(y), y \in U.$$

Although other operators have been introduced, we will stick to these definitions since they are most common and simple to deal with.

One of the most important inference rules in traditional logic is the *modus ponens* that has also been generalized to be applicable to fuzzy sets. Let $A$, $A'$, $B$, $B'$ be fuzzy sets, then the generalized modus ponens states:

Premise : $x$ is $A'$

Implication : If $x$ is $A$ then $y$ is $B$

Conclusion : $y$ is $B'$.

Of course, it is possible that different conclusions can be arrived at by using the same implication if the premises vary. Fuzzy inference finally is based on the concepts of fuzzy implication and a compositional rule of inference. Fuzzy implication is represented as $A \to B$, where $A$ and $B$ are fuzzy sets. The most common implications have already been introduced (e.g. fuzzy union $\mu_{A \cup B}(y)$).

To arrive at a conclusion, the fuzzy implication and the underlying premise have to be interpreted by a compositional rule of inference. If there are many fuzzy production rules their individual results can be superimposed. The conclusion of all rules may be derived by using the centroid of the area under the resulting fuzzy membership curve. This process of ending with a crisp value, called defuzzification, is of course not necessary when the curves can be associated with fuzzy sets of result variables on nominal scales, and thus provide qualitative decision support.

# References

1. B. A. Kitchenham and L. Pickard, "Towards a constructive quality model", *Software Engineering Journal* **2**, no. 7 (July 1987) S. 114–126.
2. A. A. Porter and R. W. Selby, "Empirically guided software development using metric-based classification trees", *IEEE Software* **7**, no. 3 (March 1990) S. 46–54.
3. M. Pighin and R. Zamolo, "A predictive metric based on discriminant statistical analysis", *Proceedings of the International Conference on Software Engineering ICSE'97* (IEEE Computer Society Press Los Alamitos, CA, 1997) 262–270.
4. J. C. Munson and T. M. Khoshgoftaar, "Regression modelling of software quality: Empirical investigation", *Information and Software Technology* **32**, no. 2 (1990) 106–114.
5. N. F. Schneidewind, "Validating metrics for ensuring space shuttle flight software quality" *IEEE Computer* **27**, no. 8 (1994) 50–57.
6. R. W. Selby and V. R. Basili, "Analyzing error-prone system structure", *IEEE Transactions on Software Engineering* **17**, no. 2 (1991) 141–152.
7. C. Ebert and T. Liedtke, "An integrated approach for criticality prediction", *Proceedings of the 6th International Symposium on Software Reliability Engineering ISSRE'95* (IEEE Computer Society Press Los Alamitos, CA, 1995).
8. C. Ebert, "Visualization techniques for analyzing and evaluating software measures", *IEEE Transactions on Software Engineering* **18**, no. 11 (November 1992) 1029–1034.
9. R. W. Selby and A. A. Porter, "Learning from examples: Generation and evaluation of decision trees for software resource analysis", *IEEE Transactions on Software Engineering* **14**, no. 12 (1988) 1743–1757.
10. M. R. Lyu, "Reliability-oriented software engineering: Design, testing and evaluation techniques", *IEE Proceedings on Software* (December 1998) 191–196.
11. N. E. Fenton and S. L. Pfleeger, *Software Metrics: A Practical and Rigorous Approach* (Chapman & Hall, London, UK, 1997).
12. W. Pedrycz and J. Waletzky, "Fuzzy clustering in software reusability", *Software — Practice and Experience* **27**, no. 3 (March 1997) 245–270.
13. W. Behrendt, S. C. Lambert *et al*, "A metrication framework for knowledge-based systems", *Proceedings of the Eurometrics '92*, Comm. of the E.C.: Eureka, Brussels, April 1992, 197–210.
14. A. C. Zimmer, "Verbal versus numerical processing", *Individual Decision Making Under Uncertainty*, ed. R. Scholz (North-Holland, Amsterdam, NL, 1983).
15. H.-J. Zimmermann, *Fuzzy Set Theory and its Applications*, 2nd ed. (Kluwer, Boston, 1991).
16. C. V. Negoita, *Expert Systems and Fuzzy Systems* (Benjamin/Cummings, Menlo Park, USA, 1985).
17. T. Khoshgoftaar and D. L. Lanning, "A neural network approach for early detection of program modules having high risk in the maintenance phase", *Journal of the Systems and Software* **29** (1995) 85–91.
18. C. Ebert, "Rule-based fuzzy classification for software quality control", *Fuzzy Sets and Systems* **63** (1994) 349–358.

19. L. Breiman, J. H. Friedman, R. A. Olshen and C. J. Stone, *Classification and Regression Trees* (Wadsworth, Belmont, CA, 1984).
20. J. J. Shann and H. C. Fu, "A fuzzy neural network for rule acquiring on fuzzy control systems", *Fuzzy Sets and Systems* **71** (1995) 345–357.
21. W. R. Dillon and M. Goldstein, *Multivariate Analysis-Methods and Applications* (John Wiley & Sons, New York, 1984).
22. J. J. Buckley and Y. Hayashi, "Neural nets for fuzzy systems", *Fuzzy Sets and Systems* **71** (1995) 265–276.
23. R. B. Grady, *Practical Software Metrics for Project Management and Process Improvement* (Prentice Hall, Englewood Cliffs, 1992).
24. C. Debou, N. Fuchs and H. Saria, "Selling believable technology", *IEEE Software*, November 1993.
25. M. G. Kendall and A. Stuart, *The Advanced Theory of Statistics*, Vol. II (Griffin, London, 1961).
26. C. Ebert, "Improving the validation process for a better field quality in a product line architecture", *Proceedings Informatik 2000*, ed. K. Mehlhorn u. G. Snelting (Springer, Berlin, September 2000) 372–388.

## Basic Readings

- N. E. Fenton and S. L. Pfleeger, *Software Metrics: A Practical and Rigorous Approach* (Chapman & Hall, London, UK, 1997). Good introduction and thorough overview on software metrics theory and application.
- C. Ebert, "Rule-based fuzzy classification for software quality control", *Fuzzy Sets and Systems* **63** (1994) 349–358. The classic introductory article on fuzzy classification in software metrics. Although it provides an earlier stage than the material given above, this article outlines the whole field and contrasts its advantages towards other approaches.
- R. B. Grady, *Successful Software Process Improvement* (Prentice Hall, Upper Saddle River, 1997). The best introduction available on practically introducing a process improvement program. A lot of insight is provided on how to introduce validation techniques and stimulate engineers to focus on early quality improvement.

# MESSAGE SEQUENCE CHARTS IN THE SOFTWARE ENGINEERING PROCESS

S. MAUW, M. A. RENIERS and T.A.C. WILLEMSE

*Department of Mathematics and Computer Science,*
*Eindhoven University of Technology,*
*P.O. Box 513, NL-5600 MB Eindhoven, The Netherlands*

The software development process benefits from the use of Message Sequence Charts (MSC), which is a graphical language for displaying the interaction behaviour of a system. We describe canonical applications of MSC independent of any software development methodology. We illustrate the use of MSC with a case study: the *Meeting Scheduler.*

*Keywords*: Message Sequence Chart, software engineering process, groupware.

## 1. Introduction

The common agreement is that software engineering is a difficult discipline. Despite the methodologies that describe the partitioning of the software engineering process into phases including the deliverables for each phase and techniques that can be applied in these phases, a great number of industrial software engineering projects encounter unanticipated problems. Unfortunately, pinpointing the exact causes for these problems is not always possible, but there are a few well-known issues that give rise to these problems. Among these issues are the transitions between subsequent phases and version-management of documentation and software, but also the more basic communication problems between the client and the engineering team. In this chapter, we will explain how the language Message Sequence Chart can assist in dealing with such problems.

The language *Message Sequence Chart* (MSC) is a graphical language, initially developed to support the SDL (Specification and Description Language) methodology for describing possible scenarios of systems and is standardized by the ITU (International Telecommunication Union). In the past decade, many features have been added to the core language. This has culminated in the most recent version, MSC 2000. The syntax, semantics and conventions of MSC2000 are described in [1].

Traditionally, MSC has been used in the area of telecom oriented applications. There, it has earned its medals for visualizing and validating dynamic behaviour (see the SDL Forum proceedings [2–6]). Alongside the increase in expressiveness of the language, specifying dynamic behaviour in MSC has also become a major topic of research and practice, both within and outside the telecommunication community. Apart from the language MSC, many other techniques for visualizing behaviour have emerged, e.g. sequence diagrams in UML [7] or interaction diagrams in Objectory [8]. There is a great overlap between these techniques, most notably in their basic concepts and constructs. Effectively, this means that in many applications of MSC, sketched in this chapter, the language MSC could have been replaced with any of the other languages. However, one of the main advantages of MSC over comparable languages is that it has been standardized and formalized. Moreover, the language is understandable both by the specialist and a layman, i.e. it can serve as a medium for communication between groups with different backgrounds. This is particularly useful in the setting of software engineering.

In this chapter, we will give an overview of the canonical applications of MSC within the software engineering process, without focusing on one particular methodology. This is done by identifying the commonly occurring phases in a number of software engineering methodologies, and explaining the applications of MSC in and between each phase, based upon this identification. Some of these applications are already much used, while other applications are not that straightforward. Wherever possible, references to literature or ongoing research are provided.

In order to present more than an abstract framework, in this chapter a relatively trivial case study is presented. Using this case study, several applications of the language MSC are shown in practice, thereby providing a more profound understanding of the canonical applications of MSCs and of the language itself. The case study we will discuss is an application that is part of an *Inter Business Communication Support System* software suite, called the *Meeting Scheduler*.

We will start by introducing the language MSC in a nutshell in Sec. 2 for the common understanding of the diagrams presented in this chapter. The application of MSCs in the software engineering process is subsequently discussed in Sec. 3. There, the canonical applications in each phase, and between different phases, are presented. Using the Meeting Scheduler as a running example, in Sec. 4, some of the canonical uses of MSC are presented, thus providing a concrete example of both the applications of MSC and the language itself. At the end of this chapter, in Sec. 5, some concluding remarks are made.

## 2. Message Sequence Charts

MSC (Message Sequence Charts) is a graphical specification language standardized by the ITU (International Telecommunication Union). In this section, we will give an overview of the main features of the MSC language. For a more detailed introduction the reader may consult [9, 10].

MSC is a member of a large class of similar drawing techniques which more or less independently arose in different application areas, such as object-oriented design, real-time design, simulation and testing methodology.

The main virtue of these languages is their intuitive nature. Basically, an MSC describes the communication behaviour of a number of logically or physically

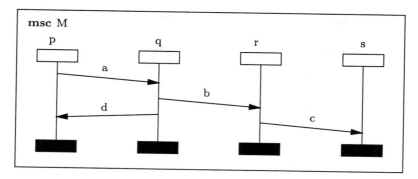

**Fig. 1.**   A basic MSC.

distributed entities, displaying the order in which messages are exchanged. Graphically, the life-line of an entity is represented by a vertical axis, while the messages are drawn as arrows connecting these life-lines. A simple MSC (such as the one in Fig. 1), can be easily understood by a non-trained user, which makes the MSC language very suitable for communication with, e.g. clients.

The MSC language used in this chapter stems from the telecommunication world. The popularity of MSC in this area is explained by the fact that typical telecom applications can be characterized as distributed reactive systems with real-time demands, that can be well understood by a scenario based description with MSC. While the application of MSC in the telecom world dates back to the seventies, the first official ITU recommendation was issued in 1992. Since then, the language has been maintained actively by an international user community and has been supported by commercially available design tools (e.g. [11, 12]).

Over the years, the small and informal MSC92 language developed into a powerful and formalized language, of which the current version is called MSC2000 ([1]).

The choice for using MSC2000 in this chapter is motivated by these factors: MSC is a formal, standardized and well supported language. Although, in the context of the ITU, MSC is embedded in the SDL design methodology for distributed telecom applications ([13–17]), this does not impose any restrictions on its use in a different methodological context. We consider MSC as a generally applicable tool which can be used to strengthen the software development process independent of the adopted methodology.

The remainder of this section will be devoted to explaining the main constructs from the MSC language.

## 2.1. *Basic Message Sequence Charts*

As explained above, a basic MSC consists of vertical axes representing the life-lines of entities and arrows connecting these lines, which represent messages. MSC M from Fig. 1 contains four entities, p, q, r, and s (in this section we will introduce MSC with meaningless abc-examples. More useful MSCs are given when discussing the case study in Sec. 4). Instance **p** first sends message **a** to instance **q**, which subsequently receives this message. Messages in an MSC are considered asynchronous, which means that the act of sending a message is separate from the reception of a message. Of course the sending of a message must occur before the reception of this same message, but between these two events, other events may take place. We say that the sending and reception of a message are causally related events.

After reception of message **a** by instance **q**, instance **q** will send message **b**. The reception of **a** and the sending of **b** are causally related, because they occur in the given order on the same instance axis. After sending **b**, we come into a state where two events are enabled: the reception of **b** and the sending of **d**. Since in the diagram no causal dependency between these two events is expressed there is no implied order of execution. Continuing this line of reasoning, we find that a basic MSC diagram defines a number of execution orders of simple communication events.

This interpretation is worked out in mathematical detail in the official MSC semantics (see [18–22]). In this chapter, we will not pursue the path of formality, but we will restrict ourselves to intuitive explanations.

In Fig. 2, we have extended the simple MSC with additional information. First, we see that the events of sending **a** and receiving **d** are vertically connected by a two-way arrow. This means that we have put a time constraint on the occurrence of these two events: the reception of **d** must occur within 3 time units after the sending of **a**.

Apart from the expression of relative time requirements, MSC also supports the observation of absolute time stamps. This is denoted by the timing attribute connected to the reception of message **c**. Therefore, this event occurs at time 8.

Next, observe that the life-line of instance **q** is partly dashed. This means that the events on this part of the instance axis are not causally ordered. The sending

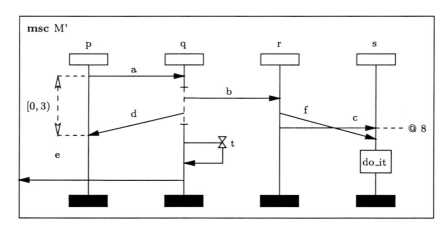

**Fig. 2.**   An extended basic MSC.

of b may occur before or after the sending of d. This allows to reduce determinacy of the specification. This construct is called a *coregion*.

Message e is a special kind of message, namely a message to the environment. Such messages are needed to specify open systems. Message f is added to show that messages are allowed to overlap. This means that there is no *a priori* assumption about the type of message buffering.

At the end of instance q we have added an example of the use of timers. This example denotes the setting of a timer with name t, followed by the subsequent time-out signal of this timer. So, this symbol represents two separate events. These events should be interpreted in a purely symbolic way. They express the observation that these two timer events occur in the given order, and that message e is sent after the reception of the time-out. It is allowed to detach the time-out event from the setting of the timer. In that case, the hour glass symbol and the attached timer name must be repeated.

Finally, notice the small box at the end of instance s. This stands for a local action, performed by instance s. This is simply an action event of which we know the name (do_it), which must occur after the reception of f.

## 2.2. *Structured Message Sequence Charts*

Although basic MSCs yield quite clear descriptions of simple scenarios, structuring mechanisms are needed to nicely express more complex behaviour. There are three ways of defining substructure within an MSC: MSC references, instance decomposition and inline expressions (see Fig. 3).

This example shows a reference to MSC A, which must be defined elsewhere. MSC A is simply thought to replace the area of the MSC reference which covers the instances p and q. The diagram also shows that we expect that a message x is leaving the MSC reference. This implies that within MSC A a message x to the environment must be defined.

Instance decomposition is similar to MSC references. Rather than abstracting from the internals of a region within an MSC, it serves to abstract from the internals of an instance. In the example instance t is labelled as a decomposed instance, which means that the reader must refer to an MSC named t to find the description of the internal behaviour of this instance. MSC t will in general contain a number of (new) instances, which cooperate to obtain the external behaviour of instance t. This clearly implies that MSC t must contain at least a message u sent to the environment and a message v received from the environment.

The main difference between MSC references and instance decomposition comes from the fact that a decomposed instance is not allowed to occur in the referenced MSC, while the instances covered by an MSC reference are allowed to occur in the referenced MSC. This makes instance decomposition particularly suited for hierarchical decomposition of the system's components, whereas MSC references are more often used for behavioural abstraction and reuse.

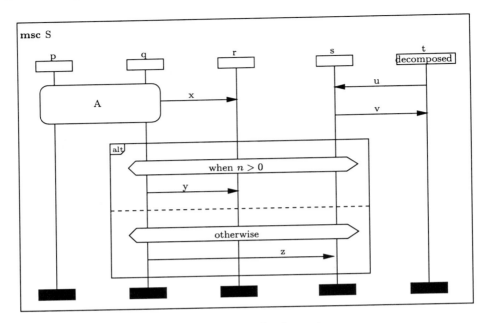

**Fig. 3.** An MSC with sub-structure.

The third structuring mechanism in Fig. 3 is the *inline expression*. An inline expression consists of a framed region of the MSC with in the upper left corner the name of an operator. The operands to which the operator applies are separated by a dashed horizontal line. In this case, the operator is the **alt** operator which stands for *alternative*. The two operands which are considered alternatives consist of message y and message z, respectively. In its general appearance, all alternatives in a choice context are possible continuations. However, by using *conditions* the selection criterion can be made explicit. In this case, the alternatives are preceded by conditions (represented by stretched hexagons) testing the value of some variable $n$. Please notice that such a condition does not represent a synchronization of the involved instances. It merely expresses that the instances reach agreement on the continuation, possibly not exactly at the same moment of time. In the case that more than one condition is enabled in a choice context, all enabled alternatives are considered as possible continuations. Whenever none of the conditions are enabled this essentially models a deadlock.

The conditions as used in this example also hint at the use of data variables in an MSC. Since we do not need data in our examples, we will not discuss this issue in greater detail. A condition without a data expression serves as a symbolic condition. This means that the name of the condition represents a Boolean value. If the keyword **when** occurs before the name of the condition, this implies that the condition is tested and that it can be used to guard continuation of the execution. If the condition is not preceded by **when**, it means that the implicitly associated

Boolean variable is set to true. In practice, conditions are often used in an informal way, in which case they should be read as comments.

In its general appearance an inline expression may contain other operators than the **alt** operator, such as **loop** to express repetition and **par** to describe (interleaved) parallelism. The allowed number of operands depends upon the operator used.

### 2.3. *High-level Message Sequence Charts*

A different construct which supports modularization of MSC specifications is a High-level MSC (HMSC). An HMSC serves as a kind of road-map linking the MSCs together. In Fig. 4, we see the relation between three MSC references, A, B, and C. The upside down triangle indicates the start point. Then, following the arrow we arrive at a condition, which states a requirement about the state the system is in (idle). Then, we encounter the first MSC to be executed, MSC A. After executing A there is a choice between continuation: B, preceded by the condition ok, and C, preceded by condition retry. After selecting the left branch, B is executed which is followed by another triangle, indicating the end of the HMSC. If we would have selected the right branch, MSC C is executed, after which we restart at MSC A.

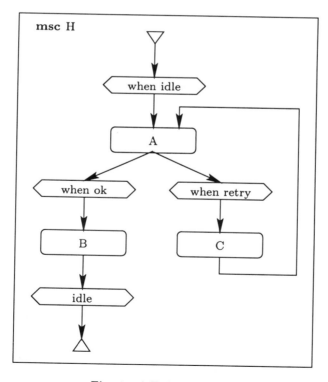

**Fig. 4.**  A High-level MSC.

## 2.4. *Additional MSC constructs*

Until now we have discussed all MSC language constructs needed to understand the remainder of this chapter. There are other useful constructs, but we will only mention these briefly.

An *MSC document* is a collection of MSCs, and declarations of instances, variables and other objects. In an MSC document a distinction is made between *public* and *private* MSCs so as to control visibility to the outside world. Also, the decomposition hierarchy which emerges when using the decomposition construct iteratively is reflected in the use of MSC documents.

Finally, we mention special syntax for expressing a more rigid order on the contained events, for the creation and stopping of instances, for describing method calls and replies, and for defining messages that do not arrive at their destination.

## 3. The Application of MSCs in Software Engineering

In this section, a simplified view of the software engineering process is presented. This view is subsequently used as a framework for explaining the canonical uses of MSC in the software engineering process.

## 3.1. *Software engineering*

There are many models that prescribe the software engineering process. We mention the waterfall model [23], the incremental delivery model [24], the spiral model [25], the V-model [26], and the cluster model [27]. In general, these models prescribe the same types of activity, but differ in the way these activities are partitioned into phases, the order in which the phases are executed, and the deliverables. We will not focus on one of these models specifically. Instead, we will pay attention to a number of frequently occurring phases in these models. These are requirements engineering, specification, design, and implementation. Summarizing, these phases can be characterized as follows.

In the *requirements engineering* phase it is clarified what the system is supposed to do and in which way it is dependent on the environment of the system. This not only refers to the functional requirements the system should satisfy, but also includes non-functional requirements like timeliness, dependability, fault-tolerance, etc.

In the *specification* phase the user requirements are analyzed and a set of software requirements is produced that is as complete, consistent and correct as possible. In contrast with the user requirements, the software requirements are the developer's view of the system and not the user's view. The result of this phase is a specification of the system in natural language, a formal specification language, or possibly a combination of both.

In the *design* phase decisions are taken as to the partitioning of the system into subsystems and interfaces with a well-understood and well-specified behaviour. Also the interaction of the subsystems is considered carefully. The design will serve as a blueprint for the structure of the implementation.

In the *implementation* phase the design from the design phase is realized in terms of software and hardware. Typical validation activities are acceptance, conformance and integration testing.

In each of the abovementioned phases verification and validation activities are performed. These activities are intended to verify the results of a phase with respect to the results of other phases (or with respect to requirements not mentioned before). We will not make any assumptions about the order in which phases are executed, the overlapping of phases, or the number of iterations. Based on the distinction of phases, discussed in this section, the use of MSC will be described in the next section.

### 3.2. *MSCs in the software engineering phases*

Thus far, we have mentioned some frequently occurring phases in the software engineering process.

An overview of the relations between these phases and the use of MSCs in these phases is visualized in Fig. 5. To each phase (denoted by a squared box), MSC products (denoted by a round box) are linked via a right arrow. The MSC products that again serve as input for subsequent phases are denoted by a left arrow. Validation activities that can be performed on the level of the MSC products are denoted by a dashed arrow. In the course of this section, these relations will be explained in greater detail.

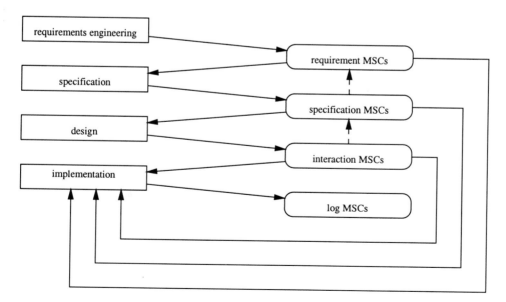

**Fig. 5.** Overview of the use of MSC in the software engineering process.

### 3.2.1. *Requirements engineering*

In the requirements engineering phase of the software engineering process, we consider two tasks in more detail. These are *requirements capturing* and *requirements analysis*.

The objective of requirements capturing is to obtain a view of the client's wishes. Unfortunately, clients are not always clear in what their wishes are; hence, the user requirements are not straightforwardly obtained. Often employed techniques involve interviews, confrontations with prototypes and conversations with the engineering team. Although the experienced requirements engineer is trained in abstraction and deduction, still, tools are necessary for documenting requirements in a clear and concise manner. Message Sequence Charts can very much assist the process of converting informal ideas into more formal requirements; moreover, MSC eases communications with clients whenever difficult parts of system's behaviour and implications of a combination of requirements are discussed.

Basically, in every interview with a client, various causal relations are indicated. From these relations, one can derive scenarios or use cases, describing parts of the desired system's behaviour. Such a use case describes (part of) the external behaviour of the system placed in its environment. The descriptions can include resource constraints, timeliness constraints, performance constraints, etc. In this chapter, we will assume that the result of the requirements capturing phase among others consists of a set of use cases.

The language MSC can be used to clarify use cases in which one or more actors and the system are involved. The roles that appear in use cases are represented by instances in MSCs. Also the system is represented by an instance. MSCs are suited for this purpose as they emphasize the interaction between instances. The interactions between the roles and the system are described by means of messages. Conditional behaviour can be expressed by means of conditions and alternatives.

Consider the user requirement that the system must react within 15 seconds on a request from an initiator by means of an acknowledgement. In Fig. 6, the corresponding MSC is given.

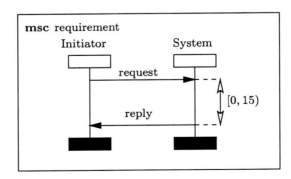

**Fig. 6.**   A simple user requirement.

Scenarios are not always considered to be *true requirements*, as they describe the system's behaviour in a very operational manner, possibly containing redundancy. However, the skilled requirements engineer is capable of turning these scenarios into real requirements by abstraction, deduction and combination. This process is called *requirements analysis*.

MSCs can be of use in the requirements analysis phase by aiding communication between the engineering team and the client. By the mere task of collecting all user requirements and combining them, system behaviour, foreseen or not foreseen by the client can be derived. Being of a more complex nature than simple user requirements, these composed behaviours are often hard to explain to the client. The concepts of the language MSC can be employed to visualize these more complex behaviours. In this way, communication between the engineering team and the client is eased.

If use cases described by MSCs tend to be large and have overlapping parts, re-occurring parts can be isolated in separate MSCs and be referred to by means of MSC references. The relation between the auxiliary MSCs obtained in this way can be defined in an HMSC. The MSC document allows the separation of *defining MSCs* from *auxiliary MSCs*. Especially in an incremental or iterative software engineering process, the MSC document enables one to maintain a good overall view of the MSCs and their relations.

Although MSC does not really add new ways to finding requirements, the benefit of using MSC may be clear: abstracting and deducting information is eased by the overview that is achieved by explicitly focusing on the causal relationships that would otherwise remain hidden in text. References to the use of MSC for use case description are [28, 29].

The MSCs, produced in the requirements engineering phase serve various purposes. On the one hand, they can be used for validating the specification and the specification MSCs. On the other hand, they can also be used as descriptions of the test purposes or test cases for acceptance testing during the implementation phase.

### 3.2.2. *Specification*

The specification of the system is not necessarily described by means of formal methods. Often prototypes are built, only parts of the system are described by means of formal methods, or even only natural language is used. The MSCs derived in the requirements engineering phase can be used to serve as the basis for writing a more complete specification of the system. In theory, MSC can also be used for writing specifications. In the literature, several papers deal with the generation of a formal specification from a set of (requirement) MSCs: in [30–32] SDL descriptions are generated, in [33] statecharts are generated, and in [34] ROOM models are generated.

However, here, we will focus on the use of MSC for visualizing traces, or *runs* of the system. In essence, as long as a specification has been written in a formalism that allows the execution of the specification, MSC can be used to visualise the system runs. A (sub)set of these execution traces are then the set of specification MSCs. If the language used is less formal, still, it might be possible to extract MSCs based on informal reasoning and a good understanding of the specification. If a prototype of the system is developed, MSCs can be obtained from logging and interpreting execution traces of the prototype. In [35], MSCs are used to visualize the execution sequences that result from partial order simulations of SDL descriptions. In several commercially available SDL tools [11, 12], simulation runs of SDL descriptions are represented by MSCs.

MSCs that result from the specification in the ways described above are useful for validating the specification against the user requirements. At the right level of abstraction each of the MSCs representing a user requirement should be contained in the MSCs obtained from the specification. Alternatively, the MSCs that represent the user requirements can be used as a monitor for executable specifications such as Promela programs in the Spin tool [36] and SDL specifications in the SDT tool [11].

The MSCs produced in the specification phase are used to validate the MSCs produced in the design phase, as will be explained in Sec. 3.2.3. Moreover, the products of the specification phase can also be used for conformance testing in the verification and validation part of the implementation phase.

### 3.2.3. *Design*

The activities carried out in the design phase must lead to a physical and/or logical decomposition of the system into interacting subsystems in such a way that the external behaviour of this collection of subsystems "implements" the specification. As a consequence, the interaction between the subsystems must be specified in a clear and unambiguous way. Message Sequence Charts are especially useful in the description of the interactions in the form of communication protocols, method calls and procedure invocations.

If a physical decomposition of the system is envisioned, the relation between the system and the subsystems is represented in MSC by means of instance refinement (decomposition). In logical decompositions the relation between the different MSCs can be made clear in an HMSC.

As in the specification phase, MSCs can be generated, based on the specification of the subsystems and the interactions between these. These MSCs then also display the internal events. Various well-established mathematical techniques allow for validating a design against a specification. These techniques involve abstracting from the internal events, i.e. hiding them from their environment. A prerequisite for using such mathematical techniques is a formal semantics of the language. Since MSC has a formal semantics, this implies that these techniques can also be used to validate a design MSC against a specification MSC.

MSCs describing forms of interaction can later be used for integration testing. If the interaction between system components is based on the buffering of messages, it is possible to determine if this interaction can be realized with a given communication model [37].

### 3.2.4. *Implementation*

The implementation phase amounts to the realization of the design in terms of hardware and executable software. Message Sequence Charts can be used in this phase to log execution traces of the implementation. If performance is of relevance, typically all events in such MSCs have a time stamp. In Fig. 12, an example of such an execution MSC is given.

These traces can be inspected manually for unexpected situations or can be compared with Message Sequence Charts defined earlier in the software engineering process. For example, after applying the appropriate abstractions it is useful to compare the traces to MSCs generated by the specification (if any), or to the MSCs issued in the requirements engineering phase.

If errors are detected in the implementation the MSC that logs the trace leading to the error can be used to locate the error in the implementation.

In the verification and validation part of the implementation phase, by means of acceptance, conformance and integration testing the confidence in the systems performance (both functional and non-functional) is validated against the user requirements, the specification and the design, respectively. We explain the use of MSC in conformance testing in some detail. The use of MSC in acceptance and integration testing is similar.

In conformance testing, the behaviour of the implementation is validated against the expected behaviour as described in the specification. In the literature several authors have indicated that the use of MSCs in conformance testing is valuable [38–42]. In conformance testing the expected behaviour, in terms of observable events of the implementation, is described in a test suite, i.e. a set of test cases. A test case describes a tree of observable events and to each path in the tree it assigns a verdict which specifies whether the described behaviour is correct or incorrect. Execution of a test case results in feeding the implementation with inputs and observing the generated observable events. This execution sequence of the implementation is then compared with the test case. The verdict of the corresponding path in the test tree is the outcome of the test execution.

The use of MSC for the identification of test purposes is advocated by the method SaMsTaG [43–46]. In the SaMsTaG method a complete test case can be generated from a system specification in SDL and a test purpose description in MSC. The test case is described in the Tree and Tabular Combined Notation (TTCN) [47]. A similar approach is followed by the HARPO toolkit [48, 49].

Among others the papers [50–52] use MSC for the description of test cases. In [53], synchronous sequence charts, i.e., Interworkings [54], are used for this purpose.

## 4. Case: The Meeting Scheduler

We will illustrate the use of Message Sequence Charts with a simple case study, baptized *The Meeting Scheduler*. This is an internet application which supports the scheduling of a meeting. In this section, we give an explanation of the Meeting Scheduler, but before doing so, we will give the context of its use.

### 4.1. *Communication support*

The Meeting Scheduler is part of a software suite that supports the communication between people of different enterprises (an *Inter Business Communication Support System*, IBCSS). The main difference with existing packages, such as ERP (Enterprise Resource Planning) packages and business support systems such as Outlook, is that IBCSS focuses on the communication between different enterprises. This reflects current trends in business operation, such as lean production and concentration on core business. The consequence of this development is that production is no longer performed mainly within one enterprise, but within a cooperation of several independent enterprises. Each of these enterprises contribute their share to the final product. The clear cut distinction between customer and producer becomes ever more blurred; both consumer and producer cooperate to achieve a common goal. As a consequence, the spectrum of communication shifts from the intra-business perspective to the inter-business perspective.

Current communication support tools are often not suited to support the interbusiness communication process. For instance, these tools assume that every user has the same software environment. It is evident that inter-business support tools must be based on established internet technology, such as web browsers.

Examples of such internet based applications are a blackboard system or even a shared repository, where users can share and manipulate electronic documents (such as the BSCW server [55], which allows access via normal web browser software). Other tools one could imagine are project management tools taking care of e.g. resource planning and decision support systems.

A very simple example of such a communication support system is the aforementioned *Meeting Scheduler*, which we have chosen to demonstrate the use of MSCs.

### 4.2. *Informal description*

Scheduling a meeting can be a rather time consuming activity. Dependent on how many people are involved, a number of telephone calls or e-mails are necessary in order to come to a date and time that is convenient to all, or at least to the majority of the participants. The Meeting Scheduler is tailor-made to support the administration of relevant information and communication with the intended participants.

The Meeting Scheduler runs on some internet server and people communicate with the server via e-mail, simple web pages and web forms. The working of the Meeting Scheduler is best explained by giving the basic scenario of usage.

Two roles can be distinguished: the *initiator* of the meeting and the *invitees*. The initiator takes the initiative of setting up the meeting. He provides the system with the initial information, such as purpose of the meeting, the list of invitees and the list of possible dates and times. Next, the Meeting Scheduler informs the invitees about the meeting and collects information from the participants with respect to the suitability of the proposed dates. If all participants have provided their information (or if some deadline is met), the system reports back to the initiator and suggests the best possible date. After confirmation by the initiator, the final invitation is sent to the participants.

This very basic description can be easily extended with many features. In fact, very advanced tools which support the scheduling of meetings already exist, but these are often platform dependent, and require participants to maintain an on-line agenda.

In the subsequent section some of the uses that are mentioned in Sec. 3.2 are explained using the Meeting Scheduler. Note that this is not done extensively for all phases. Most notably, no examples are given for the implementation phase. Since the use of MSC for validation is discussed extensively in the literature, only brief remarks are added wherever possible.

## 4.3. *User requirements*

The techniques for requirements capturing mentioned in Sec. 3.2.1 can very well be applied to the Meeting Scheduler. For instance, the use of MSC in an interview can be illustrated by transforming the following phrases, taken from an interview, into MSC: "... the initiator feeds the system with the necessary information to send out meeting requests to all potential participants of a certain meeting. These participants should be allowed ample time to respond to these invitations. Eventually, the system will send the current information about potential dates to the initiator who will then decide on a date for the meeting to take place. The system will subsequently inform all participants of the decision of the initiator. Finally, a confirmation of this operation is sent to the initiator ...".

The scenario obtained by projecting on the behaviour of the interactions between the initiator and the system is rather straightforwardly deduced from the above sentence (see Fig. 7). Here, the initiator is represented by an instance initiator and the system is represented by a single instance system, thereby portraying the black-box approach. The meeting_info message is used by the initiator to send information vital for the scheduling of the meeting by the system. The message collected_info represents the collected information for the meeting that is communicated between the system and the initiator; the messages decision and confirmation are self-explanatory. The conditions that are introduced can be read as comments, denoting the (required) state of the system.

One can imagine that various scenarios for the Meeting Scheduler describe the causal relationship between the reception of information for a meeting to be

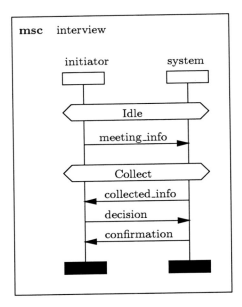

**Fig. 7.** Scenario deduced from a part of an interview.

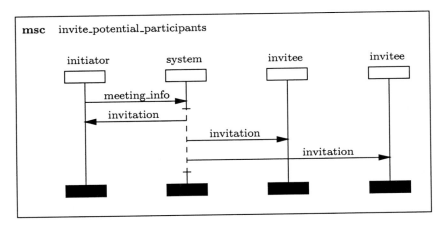

**Fig. 8.** Requirement deduced from interviews.

scheduled (denoted by a message meeting_info) and the sending of meeting requests to potential participants of this meeting (denoted by a message invitation). The true (functional) requirement that can be distilled from these scenarios would be one that focuses on exactly that causal relationship (see Fig. 8).

Note that this still is a scenario, and therefore portrays only parts of a system's behaviour. The fact that in this scenario the initiator is also informed about the meeting means that in this case the initiator is himself considered as an invitee, but this is not necessarily always the case.

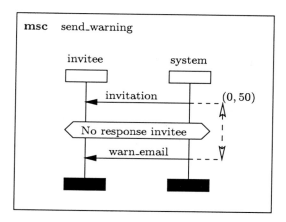

**Fig. 9.** Requirement deduced from a scenario.

As the discussion in Sec. 3.1 pointed out, not all requirements can be classified as functional requirements; hence, a language supporting only functional requirements would not suffice. Using MSC, also non-functional requirements, such as the need for time-outs under certain conditions can be illustrated. For example, a non-functional requirement in the Meeting Scheduler would be the sending of a warning message to participants that did not yet respond to the meeting call (denoted by a message warn_email) *before* a deadline (50) is reached. Such a requirement can be elegantly formulated in MSC as Fig. 9 shows.

Thus far, we have focussed on the more trivial user requirements and the scenarios belonging to them. As already mentioned in Sec. 3.2.1, the combination of requirements may lead to an intricate interplay of causal relations. Finding out these relations already is part of the requirements analysis phase. As an example, a less basic interaction scheme between the initiator and the system for the Meeting Scheduler is considered (see Fig. 10). Overview diagrams such as these assist the communication between the engineering team and the client.

Basically, in Fig. 10, a blueprint for the logical structure for distinguishing between the two options the initiator is confronted with can be read. The information returned by the Meeting Scheduler may or may not be according to the wishes of the initiator. Worst case information may even mean that the invitees for a meeting could not agree on a date for the meeting. Hence, the initiator is confronted with the dilemma of having to decide to cancel the meeting altogether or decide on a date, represented by the MSC reference conclude, or retry to schedule the meeting (possibly using different dates), represented by the MSC reference retry.

The MSC conclude is depicted in Fig. 11; if the invitees could not agree on a date and the initiator decides to cancel the meeting, a cancel_meeting message is sent to the system; the system then subsequently responds with a confirmation, using a confirmation message. In case a date is found for the meeting, the system is informed by the initiator about this using a convene_meeting message, and again,

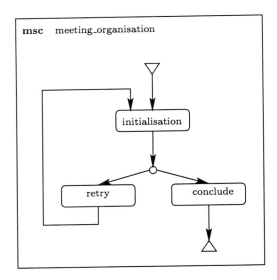

**Fig. 10.**   Combination of user requirements may lead to more complex behaviour.

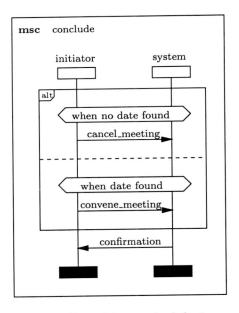

**Fig. 11.**   Part of the complex behaviour.

the system responds with a confirmation. A similar MSC can be written for the MSC reference retry (not shown here).

A careful comparison of MSC interview (Fig. 7) and HMSC meeting_organisation (Fig. 10) learns that the MSC interview is one of the possible scenarios described by the HMSC meeting_organisation.

## 4.4. *Specification*

Although the language MSC can even be utilized for specifying systems, (see Sec. 3.2.2), we will adopt the language only for validation and visualization purposes in this phase. Since MSC was also devised for this purpose, we feel it is strongest in this respect. As already mentioned in Sec. 3.2.2, the ways in which one can obtain scenarios in this phase are plenty; the size and complexity of the Meeting Scheduler would allow for a formal specification, and hence, the generation of traces, or *runs* from this specification is, dependent on the method used, rather straightforward. It would be outside the scope of this chapter to give a specification for the Meeting Scheduler, hence, we adopt the operational description of Sec. 4.2 as a reference for a possible specification for this system.

As an example trace for the Meeting Scheduler, one can think of the scenario depicted in Fig. 12. Basically, this scenario is a combination of some user requirements listed in the previous section and some requirements not yet mentioned, such as the appearance of a sorry_email. Here, this message is used to notify an invitee that the deadline for responding has expired and that he is assumed not to participate in the meeting.

The MSC depicted in Fig. 12 can be validated against the user requirements. For instance, one can observe that the functional and non-functional requirements

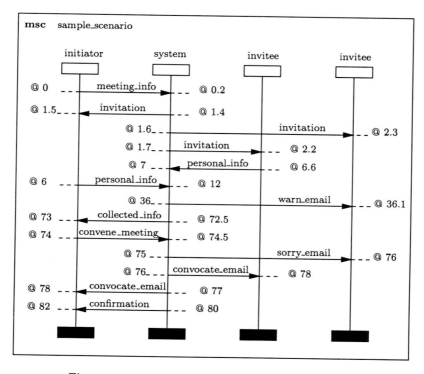

**Fig. 12.** A typical scenario obtained by a specification.

of Sec. 4.3 are met. As already mentioned in Sec. 3.2.2, the scenarios generated in the specification phase are again needed for validating the products of the implementation phase.

## 4.5. *Design*

The design phase prescribes as one of its main activities the decomposition of the system into subsystems. More concretely, this means that choices have to be made with respect to the desired properties of the system under construction. For the Meeting Scheduler, this boils down to finding logical and/or physical decompositions of the black-box which are chosen in such a way that the requirements of Sec. 4.2 are fulfilled. Note that the (part of the) design that is discussed here is based on the operational description of the Meeting Scheduler.

The obvious choice for a physical decomposition for the Meeting Scheduler is to consider a decomposition in two subsystems, a front-end and a database. The front-end is a system that deals with the interactions between users of the Meeting Scheduler and as such is the intermediate between the users and the database, whereas the database primarily stores the information posted by users concerning possible dates and times for the meeting.

The interactions between all subsystems involved for the Meeting Scheduler can be grouped, based on a logical decomposition of the global state of the system. The change of state is again, like in Sec. 4.3, a more complex concept, typically expressed in HMSC (see Fig. 13). Closer observation of Fig. 13 reveals the expected structure of an *initialising*, a *collecting* and a *deciding* phase. In each of these phases, basic MSCs can be used to explain the interactions between various subsystems.

To highlight some of the interactions between the subsystems for the Meeting Scheduler, the MSC references initialise, collect and warn_invitees are highlighted.

The basic MSC initialise (see Fig. 14) describes the essence of which interactions can typically be expected in the initialising phase. Most notably, parts of the interactions identified in the requirements engineering phase (see Figs. 8–11) reappear in this scenario. Basically, the scenario describes the interaction between the initiator and the front-end of the Meeting Scheduler, in which information for the scheduling of a meeting is communicated using a message meeting_info. Subsequently, the front-end updates the database, and only then it starts sending calls to all invitees for this meeting in random order, (using invitation messages). In order to meet the non-functional requirements (see Fig. 9), two timers are initialised, one for sending a warning message and one for keeping track of the deadline for responding to the invitation.

Collecting information of the invitees is illustrative for typical update interactions occurring between the front-end system and the database, as a reaction to messages from the users of the system (see Fig. 15). Using the message personal_info, the invitees inform the Meeting Scheduler of their preferred dates and times for the

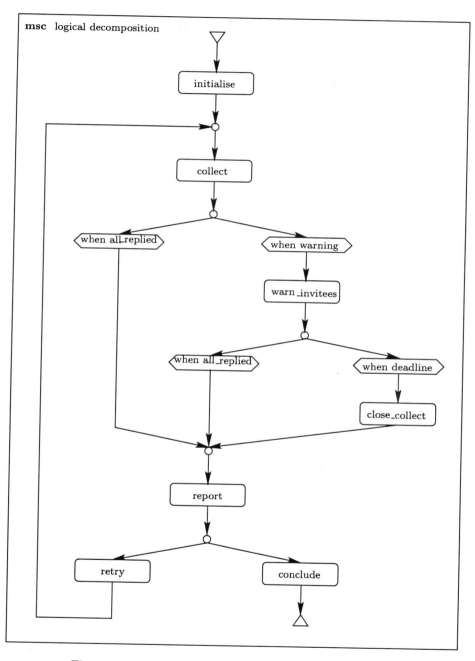

**Fig. 13.** The global change of state for the Meeting Scheduler.

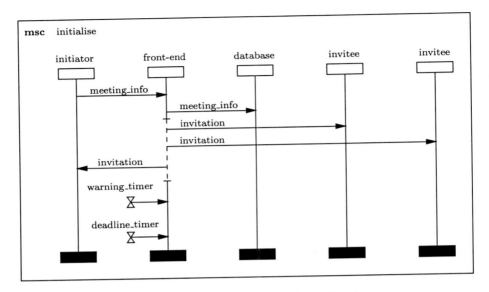

**Fig. 14.**    The initialisation of the Meeting Scheduler.

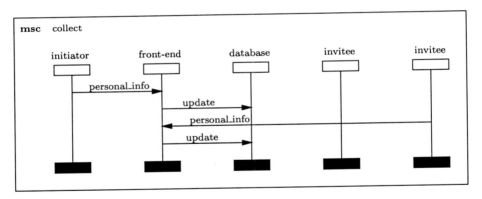

**Fig. 15.**    Collecting of information.

meeting to take place. The front-end of the system uses this information to update the database via an **update** message.

As an example of how non-functional requirements are captured in this phase, the MSC **warn_invitees** is illustrated in Fig. 16. When a warning time-out is reported to the front-end system, the front-end system consults the database for information about who responded and who did not yet respond to the meeting announcement. This figure also shows an example of the informal use of conditions by explicitly mentioning which invitee responded and which invitee did not respond. Those invitees that did not yet respond, are warned (expressed by the message **warn_email**) by the front-end subsystem. Note that in this example, the initiator is also an invitee.

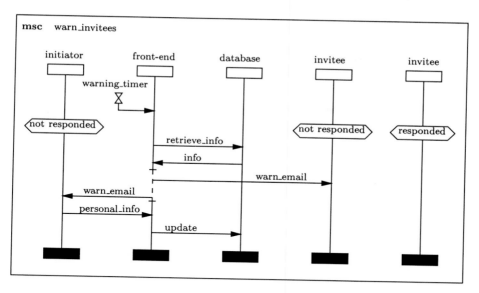

**Fig. 16.** Warning of invitees.

Validation in this phase boils down to checking whether the MSC scenarios described in this phase refine the MSC scenarios generated in the specification phase. For the Meeting Scheduler, the interactions left after abstracting from the interactions between the different subsystems of the Meeting Scheduler should also be allowed scenarios of the specification.

## 5. Concluding Remarks

This chapter presents an overview of the canonical applications of the language *Message Sequence Chart* (MSC) in the area of software engineering. These applications have been sketched independent of any particular software engineering methodology (e.g. ESA PSS 5 Software Engineering standard) or model (e.g. the incremental delivery model, the waterfall model). Alongside a more abstract framework, describing these applications, a more concrete example, in the form of a case study has been discussed. This allowed for relating the more practical aspects to the abstract framework.

The MSC language constructs used and indicated in this chapter belong to the more common constructs. In particular, the case study is of a simple nature; hardly any need for structuring mechanisms exists nor does data play a role in this case study. Yet, for illustrating some of the canonical applications of MSC a simple example is vital. In general, the full set of language constructs does allow for dealing with substantially more complex applications than the ones sketched in this chapter. In dealing with such applications, it is recommended (and often necessary) to choose those language constructs necessary for describing exactly what is relevant for the particular application.

Some aspects of the applications mentioned in the preceding sections are quite orthogonal with respect to others, e.g. in simulating an executable specification absolute time stamps are commonly used, whereas in writing requirements for a system, relative time is often employed. This illustrates the broad spectrum of applications for MSC we have sketched in this chapter. Given this broad spectrum, it is common sense to select which purposes are best served using MSC (e.g. using MSC only during the requirements engineering phase and validation of these requirements).

As mentioned before, the formal semantics of the language MSC allows for performing validation and verification. These activities have been described without going into too much detail. Wherever possible, references to illustrative works on this area have been added.

## Acknowledgements

We like to thank Victor Bos, André Engels and Marc Voorhoeve for their efforts and we thank Lies Kwikkers and Jan Roelof de Pijper for their work on the case study.

## References

1. ITU-T, "Recommendation Z.120: Message Sequence Chart (MSC)", ITU-T, Geneva, 2000.
2. O. Færgemand and R. Reed, *SDL'91 — Evolving Methods* (North-Holland, 1991).
3. O. Færgemand and A. Sarma, *SDL'93 — Using Objects* (North-Holland, 1993).
4. R. Bræk and A. Sarma, *SDL'95 — with MSC in CASE* (North-Holland, 1995).
5. A. Cavalli and A. Sarma, *SDL'97: Time for Testing — SDL, MSC and Trends* (North-Holland, 1997).
6. R. Dssouli, G. von Bochmann and Y. Lahav, *SDL'99: The Next Millenium, Proceedings of the Ninth SDL Forum* (North-Holland, 1999).
7. J. Rumbaugh, I. Jacobson and G. Booch, *The Unified Modeling Language Reference Manual* (Addison-Wesley, 1999).
8. I. Jacobson, M. Christerson, P. Jonsson and G. Overgaard, *Object-Oriented Software Engineering — A Use Case Driven Approach* (Addison-Wesley, Reading, MA, 1992).
9. E. Rudolph, P. Graubmann and J. Grabowski, "Tutorial on Message Sequence Charts", *Computer Networks and ISDN Systems* **28**, no. 12 (1996) 1629–1641. Special issue on SDL and MSC, guest editor, Ø. Haugen.
10. Ø. Haugen, "MSC-2000 interaction diagrams for the new millenium", *Computer Networks* **35**, no. 6 (2001) 721–732.
11. Telelogic AB, "SDT 3.1 reference manual", Malmö, Sweden (1996).
12. Verilog, "ObjectGEODE toolset documentation" (1996).
13. ITU-T, "Recommendation Z.100: Specification and Description Language (SDL)", ITU-T, Geneva (June 1994).
14. R. Saracco, R. Reed and J.R.W. Smith, *Telecommunications Systems Engineering Using SDL* (North-Holland, Amsterdam, 1989).
15. F. Belina, D. Hogrefe and A. Sarma, *SDL — With applications from protocol specification*, The BCS Practitioners Series (Prentice-Hall International, London/Englewood Cliffs, 1991).

16. R. Bræk and Haugen Ø, *Engineering Real-time Systems with an Object-oriented Methodology Based on SDL* (Prentice-Hall International, London, 1993).

17. A. Olsen, O. Færgemand, B. Møller-Pedersen, R. Reed and J.R.W. Smith, *Systems Engineering Using SDL-92* (Elsevier Science Publishers B.V., Amsterdam, 1994).

18. ITU-T, "Recommendation Z.120 Annex B: Algebraic semantics of Message Sequence Charts", ITU-T, Geneva (1998).

19. S. Mauw and M. A. Reniers, "An algebraic semantics of Basic Message Sequence Charts", *The Computer Journal* **37**, no. 4 (1994) 269–277.

20. S. Mauw, "The formalization of Message Sequence Charts", *Computer Networks and ISDN Systems* **28**, no. 12 (1996) 1643–1657. Special issue on SDL and MSC, guest editor Ø. Haugen.

21. S. Mauw and M. A. Reniers, "High-level Message Sequence Charts", eds. A. Cavalli and A. Sarma, *SDL'97: Time for Testing — SDL, MSC and Trends, Proceedings of the Eighth SDL Forum*, Evry, France, (Amsterdam, North-Holland, September 23–26, 1997) 291–306.

22. M. A. Reniers, *Message Sequence Chart: Syntax and Semantics*, PhD Thesis, Eindhoven University of Technology (June 1999).

23. W. W. Royce, "Managing the development of large software systems", *Proceedings of the IEEE WESCON* (1970).

24. R. T. Yeh, "An alternate paradigm for software evolution", eds. P. A. I. Ng and R. T. Yeh, *Modern Software Engineering: Foundations and Perspectives* (Van Nostrand Reinhold, New York, 1990).

25. B. W. Boehm, "A spiral model of software development and enhancement", *IEEE Computer* **21**, no. 5 (1988) 61–72.

26. Ministry of the Interior, Ottobrunn, Germany, "Software life-cycle process model (V-model)" (1992).

27. C. Gindre and F. Sada, "A development in Eiffel: Design and implementation of a network simulator", *Journal of Object-Oriented Programming* **2**, no. 2 (May 1989) 27–33.

28. M. Andersson and J. Bergstrand, "Formalizing use cases with Message Sequence Charts", Master's Thesis, Lund Institute of Technology (1995).

29. E. Rudolph, J. Grabowski and P. Graubmann, "Towards a harmonization of UML-sequence diagrams and MSC", eds. R. Dssouli, G. von Bochmann and Y. Lahav, *SDL'99: The Next Millenium, Proceedings of the Ninth SDL Forum* (North-Holland, 1999).

30. G. Robert, F. Khendek and P. Grogono, "Deriving an SDL specification with a given architecture from a set of MSCs", eds. A. Cavalli and A. Sarma, *SDL'97: Time for Testing — SDL, MSC and Trends*, Evry, France (Elsevier Science Publishers B.V., 1997) 197–212.

31. S. Somé and R. Dssouli, "Using a logical approach for specification generation from Message Sequence Charts", Publication Départementale 1064, Département IRO, Université de Montréal (April 1997).

32. L. M. G. Feijs, "Generating FSMs from interworkings", *Distributed Computing* **12**, no. 1 (1999) 31–40.

33. I. Krüger, R. Grosu, P. Scholz and M. Broy, "From MSCs to statecharts", ed. F. J. Rammig, *Distributed and Parallel Embedded Systems* (Kluwer Bedrijfswetenschappen B.V., 1999) 61–71.

34. S. Leue, L. Mehrmann and M. Rezai, "Synthesizing room models from Message Sequence Chart specifications", Technical Report 98-06, Department of Electrical and Computer Engineering, University of Waterloo (April 1998).

35. D. Toggweiler, J. Grabowski and D. Hogrefe, "Partial order simulation of SDL specifications", eds. R. Bræk and A. Sarma, *SDL'95 — with MSC in CASE, Proceedings of the Seventh SDL Forum*, Oslo (North-Holland, Amsterdam, 1995) 293–306.

36. G. J. Holzmann, "The model checker Spin", *IEEE Transactions on Software Engineering*, **23**, no. 5 (1997) 279–295.

37. A. Engels, S. Mauw and M. A. Reniers, "A hierarchy of communication models for Message Sequence Charts", eds. T. Mizuno, N. Shiratori, T. Higashino and A. Togashi, *Formal Description Techniques and Protocol Specification, Testing and Verification, Proceedings of FORTE X and PSTV XVII '97*, Osaka, Japan (Chapman & Hall, November 1997) 75–90.

38. B. Takacs, "Use of SDL in an object oriented design process during the development of a prototype switching system", eds. O. Færgemand and A. Sarma, *SDL'93 — Using Objects, Proceedings of the Sixth SDL Forum*, Darmstadt (North-Holland, Amsterdam, 1993) 79–88.

39. Ø. Haugen, R. Bræk and G. Melby, "The SISU project", eds. O. Færgemand and A. Sarma, *SDL'93 — Using Objects, Proceedings of the Sixth SDL Forum*, Darmstadt (North-Holland, Amsterdam, 1993) 479–489.

40. Ø. Haugen, "Using MSC-92 effectively", eds. R. Bræk and A. Sarma, *SDL'95 — With MSC in CASE, Proceedings of the Seventh SDL Forum*, Oslo (North-Holland, Amsterdam, 1995) 37–49.

41. G. Amsjø and A. Nyeng, "SDL-based software development in Siemens A/S — Experience of introducing rigorous use of SDL and MSC", eds. R. Bræk and A. Sarma, *SDL'95 — With MSC in CASE, Proceedings of the Seventh SDL Forum*, Oslo (North-Holland, Amsterdam, 1995) 339–348.

42. L. M. G. Feijs, F. A. C. Meijs, J. R. Moonen and J. J. van Wamel, "Conformance testing of a multimedia chip using PHACT", eds. A. Petrenko and N. Yevtushenko, *Testing of Communicating Systems* (1998) 193–210.

43. J. Grabowski, D. Hogrefe and R. Nahm, "Test case generation with test purpose specification by MSCs", eds. O. Færgemand and A. Sarma, *SDL'93 — Using Objects, Proceedings of the Sixth SDL Forum*, Darmstadt (North-Holland, Amsterdam, 1993) 253–265.

44. J. Grabowski, "Test case generation and test case specification with Message Sequence Charts", PhD Thesis, Universität Bern (1994).

45. R. Nahm, "Conformance testing based on formal description techniques and Message Sequence Charts", PhD Thesis, Universität Bern (1994).

46. J. Grabowski, R. Scheuer, Z. R. Dai and D. Hogrefe, "Applying SaMsTaG to the B-ISDN protocol SSCOP", eds. M. Kim, S. Kang and K. Hong, *Testing of Communicating Systems, Tenth International Workshop on Testing of Communicating Systems, IFIP TC6*, Cheju Island, Korea (Chapman & Hall, September 1997) 397–415.

47. ISO, *TTCN: ISO/IEC JTC 1/SC 21: Information Technolgy — Open Systems Interconnection — Conformance Testing Methodology and Framework — The Tree and Tabular Combined Notation*, Part 3, Volume ISO 9646-3, ISO/IEC, 1991.

48. E. Algaba, M. Monedero, E. Pérez and O. Valcárel, "HARPO: Testing tools development", eds. M. Kim, S. Kang and K. Hong, *Testing of Communicating Systems, Tenth International Workshop on Testing of Communicating Systems, IFIP TC6*, Cheju Island, Korea (Chapman & Hall, September 1997) 318–323.

49. E. Pérez, E. Algaba and M. Monedero, "A pragmatic approach to test generation", eds. M. Kim, S. Kang and K. Hong, *Testing of Communicating Systems, Tenth International Workshop on Testing of Communicating Systems, IFIP TC6*, Cheju Island, Korea (Chapman & Hall, September 1997) 365–380.

50. J. Grabowski, D. Hogrefe, I. Nussbaumer and A. Spichiger, "Test case specification based on MSCs and ASN.1", eds. R. Bræk and A. Sarma, *SDL'95 — With MSC in CASE, Proceedings of the Seventh SDL Forum*, Oslo (North-Holland, Amsterdam, 1995) 307–322.

51. L. M. G. Feijs and M. Jumelet, "A rigorous and practical approach to service testing", eds. B. Baumgarten, H. Burkhardt and A. Giessler, *Testing of Communicating Systems, Nineth International Workshop on Testing of Communicating Systems, IFIP TC6* (Chapman & Hall, 1996) 175–190.

52. A. Cavalli, B. Lee and T. Macavei, "Test generation for the SSCOP-ATM networks protocol", eds. A. Cavalli and A. Sarma, *SDL'97: Time for Testing — SDL, MSC and Trends, Proceedings of the Eighth SDL Forum*, Evry (North-Holland, Amsterdam, 1997) 277–288.

53. A. Engels, L.M.G. Feijs and S. Mauw, "Test generation for intelligent networks using model checking", ed. E. Brinksma, *Proceedings of the Third International Workshop on Tools and Algorithms for the Construction and Analysis of Systems, Lecture Notes in Computer Science, 1217* (Springer-Verlag, 1997) 384–398.

54. S. Mauw and M. A. Reniers, "A process algebra for interworkings", eds. J. A. Bergstra, A. Ponse and S. Smolka, *Handbook of Process Algebra* (Elsevier Science B.V., 2001).

55. R. Bentley, W. Appelt, U. Busbach, E. Hinrichs, D. Kerr, S. Sikkel, J. Trevor and G. Woetzel, "Basic support for cooperative work on the world wide web", *International Journal of Human-Computer Studies* **46**, no. 6 (1997) 827–846.

# PROGRAM SLICING:
# PRECISE CHOPS EXTRACTION APPROACHES

TAHAR KHAMMACI

*University of Nantes, Institut de Recherche en Informatique de Nantes,*
*2, Rue de la Houssinière, B.P. 92208, F-44300, Nantes, France*
*E-mail: khammaci@irin.univ-nantes.fr*


ZINE E. BOURAS

*University of Annaba, Department of Computer Science,*
*P.O. Box 12, DZ-23000, Annaba, Algeria*
*E-mail: bourasz@yahoo.com*


SAID GHOUL

*Philadelphia University, Department of Computer Science, Sweilah, Jordan*
*E-mail: said_ghoul@yahoo.com*

Program understanding is an important task in software maintenance. It consists of understanding the concepts linked to execution behaviour and their relationships which are implicit in source code. Program slicing technique can aid this task by an automatic extraction of precise fragments or chops, whose execution behaviour is identical to the original program with respect to a given point. Researchers in the program slicing domain face two problems: identification of a dependence model with an adequate granularity and extraction of precise chops. In this chapter, we discuss the state-of-art in program slicing approaches in order to represent explicitly a program and to extract precise chops. Chops precision depends on the granularity level of the program element and on the existence of unrealizable paths that are unfeasible paths with respect to program execution.

*Keywords*: Software maintenance, program understanding, program slicing, program chopping, system dependence graph, relational expression, chop extraction algorithms.

## 1. Introduction

Software maintenance represents the most expensive task in the life cycle of a software. In this context, program understanding consists of identifying the concepts linked to execution behaviour and their relationships which are implicit in source code [1]. Current program understanding approaches are based on *slice concept* [24, 19, 21].

The concept of *slice* is related to program execution behavior and can be automatically extracted. *Program slice*, originally introduced by Mark Weiser [24] consists of finding all statements in a program that directly affect the value of a variable occurrence. *Program slicing* is a program decomposition technique useful for several maintenance task [9]. It has applications to program debugging [14, 16], program testing [4, 10], program integration [4, 3], program analysis [5], program comprehension [11, 7], parallel program execution [24], reuse [6] and software maintenance [9]. A survey about program slicing techniques and their applications can be found in [23].

Program execution behaviour is defined as the set of variable values generated by the program execution at a given point [24]. The purpose of execution behaviour analysis is automatic extraction of precise fragments, called *chops*, whose behaviour is identical to the original program with respect to a given point. With their reduced size, *chops* are useful in understanding and transforming complex and large programs [9, 19]. Jackson and Rollins [15] have introduced the *chop concept* while generalizing the *slice concept* [24]. A *program chop* is composed of all the instructions which transmit data or control flows from an instruction $s$ to another $t$.

Behaviour analysis requires an explicit representation of data and control flows, called *dependencies relationships*. The *program dependence graphs* are good candidates for this representation [13]. In these graphs, vertices represent program elements and edges their dependencies. *Chopping* is therefore a graph traversal. However, the use of graphs implies two problems: (1) identification of an *appropriate granularity level* of the program element and (2) suppression of *unrealizable paths* from the graphs. In the case where the element is an instruction, dependencies between variables are not captured. *Chops* are then imprecises because they include "extra" instructions. *Unrealizable paths* are unfeasible paths with respect to program execution. They are generated by many calls to the same procedure and correspond to one or many incorrect "call-return" links. Thus, researchers in this domain face the problems of identifying a dependence representation [8, 13] and determining adequate chopping operations [15, 20].

Some approaches have particularly contributed to the resolution of these problems. These approaches can be grouped into two families: approaches based on System Dependence Graphs (SDG) and approaches based on relational expressions. In the first one, Jackson and Rollins [15] have developed a dependence representation where the element is a variable action. In spite of a good granularity level of the program element, this model provides *chopping* relative only to one procedure. Therefore, the problem of *unrealizable paths* has not been addressed. By another way, Reps and Rosay [20] have introduced a dependence representation where the element is an instruction. In order to eliminate *unrealizable paths*, their graph edges are labelled and their *chopping algorithms* operate in two passes. This model allows the extraction of four types of *precise chops* which are relative to many procedures. However, the element granularity is coarse and *chops* cannot be relative to different call points to the same procedure. The second approach, introduced by [2], is based on a dependence model with a fine-grained program element: a variable action. This model allows the extraction of the above four types of precise chops extracted by the Reps and Rosay approach and a new *chop* type which is relative to many call points to the same procedure. However, this approach allows to extract all types of *chops* by a single algorithm operating in one pass.

The chapter is organized as follows. In Sec. 2.5 we present the System Dependence Graph based approach that includes Jackson *et al* [15] and Reps *et al* [20] works. Section 3 describes the relational expressions approach defined by [2] with some guidance on when this approach is preferred. We study in Sec. 4, spatial and temporal complexities of the relational expressions approach and a comparative study of complexity between the two families of approaches presented above. Section 5 presents a CASE tool called PUT (Program Understanding Tool), based on the relational expressions approach which automatically extracts from a given PASCAL program all chops types. Section 6 concludes this chapter and Sec. 7 provides some resources for further reading.

## 2. System Dependence Graphs Based Approach

### 2.1. *System dependence graphs*

Instructions in a program, are linked by *data and control flow dependencies* [4, 2]. Two instructions have a *data dependencies* if they cannot be executed simultaneously because of a data conflict. *Data dependencies* can be flow dependencies, iteration dependencies, output dependencies or anti-dependencies. There are a *control dependencies* between two instructions $e_1$ and $e_2$, when $e_1$ specifies whether $e_2$ will be executed [4, 2].

For a *monolithic program*, without procedures, dependencies are represented by a directed graph named *Program Dependence Graph* (PDG) [8]. In this type of graphs, the vertex represents the instructions, and the edges their *data and control dependencies*. The root of PDG is a particular vertex called *Entry* representing the program title.

For a *multi-procedure program*, there are two other dependence forms: *call dependencies* and *summary dependencies*. The first modelizes call statement and parameter passing. The second dependence form represents the execution effect of the input effective parameters on the output effective parameters, by abstracting the called procedure [4]. In this kind of program, dependencies are represented by a *System Dependence Graph* (SDG) [13, 18]. It is composed of a set of PDG linked by connecting edges which depict *call and summary dependencies* [4, 20]. A *call dependence* is represented either by an edge linking a call vertex to an entry vertex, or by edges linking actual vertex to formal vertex. There is an actual-in vertex (resp. actual-out vertex) for each actual-in parameter (resp. actual-out vertex). There is a formal-in vertex (resp. formal-out vertex) for each formal-in parameter (resp. formal-out vertex). Global variables are in general treated as "extra" actual parameters. The *summary edges* are represented by edges linking actual-in vertices to actual-out vertices. Their construction consists in identifying a path between actual-in and actual-out and avoid *unrealizable paths*. Figure 1(a) shows a multi-procedure example program and Fig. 2 shows its corresponding *system dependence graph*.

| a. **Example** program | b. **Backward slice** $C_r = \langle 13, I \rangle$ | c. **Forward slice** $C_r = \langle 2, I \rangle$ | d. **Program chop** $C_r = \langle 2, 13 \rangle$ |
|---|---|---|---|
| [1] Program Product; | [1] Program Product; | | |
| [2] I:Integer; | [2] I:Integer; | **[2] I:Integer;** | **[2] I:Integer;** |
| [3] S:Integer | | | |
| [4] K:Integer; | | | |
| [5] Procedure Add(A,B:Integer); | [5] Procedure Add(A,B:Integer); | [5] Procedure Add(A,B:Integer); | [5] Procedure Add(A,B:Integer); |
| Begin | Begin | Begin | Begin |
| [6] A:=A + B | [6] A:=A + B | [6] A:=A + B | [6] A:=A + B |
| end | end | end | end |
| begin; | begin; | begin; | begin; |
| [7] I:=1; | [7] I:=1; | [7] I:=1; | [7] I:=1; |
| [8] S:=0; | | | |
| [9] While I < 11 Do; | [9] While I < 11 Do; | [9] While I < 11 Do; | [9] While I < 11 Do; |
| [10] Add(S,I); | | | |
| [11] Add(I,1); | [11] Add(I,1); | [11] Add(I,1); | [11] Add(I,1); |
| od; | od; | od; | od; |
| [12] K:=S/I; | | | |
| [13] Write(I); | **[13] Write(I);** | [13] Write(I); | **[13] Write(I);** |
| [14] Write(K); | | | |
| end; | | end; | |

**Fig. 1.** An example program and the results reported by backward slice, forward slice and program chop.

## 2.2. *Program slicing*

The *slice* of a program with respect to program point $p$ and variable $x$ consists of all statements and predicates of the program that might affect the values of $x$ at point $p$ [13]. It has been introduced by Weiser [24] as a powerful method for automatically decomposing a program by analyzing its control and data flow. This concept has many applications. A survey about program slicing techniques and their applications can be found in [23].

A *program slice* is a minimum fragment for which the execution behavior is identical to the initial program behavior with respect to a given point [24, 19]. Program execution behavior with respect to a given point is defined as the set of all variable values generated by the program execution in this point [24].

In Weiser's terminology, a *slicing criterion* of a program $P$ is a pair $\langle p, x \rangle$ where $p$ is a program point and $x$ is a subset of variables in $P$. In other words, a *program slice* is a program with an execution behavior identical to one of the initial program with respect to a given criterion, but may have a reduced size.

Weiser [24] has introduced *backward slice*. A *backward slice* with respect to a program variable $x$ and a given point $p$ is composed of all instructions and predicates from which depends the computation of the value of $x$ at point $p$. Binkley *et al* [4] have proposed *forward slice*. A *forward slice* with respect to a variable $x$ and point $p$ is composed by all the instructions and predicates which may depend on the value of $x$ at point $p$. In other words, *forward slice* is the dual of *backward slice*.

*Slices* are automatically extracted by a traversal of a graph which represents explicitly program data and control flows [8, 19, 13]. For instance, Fig. 1(b) shows a *backward slice* and Fig. 1c shows *forward slice* of the example program, with respectively criterion $\langle [13], I \rangle$ and $\langle [2], I \rangle$.

Suppose that the comprehender wants to know for instance which instructions have an effect on the printed value by the instruction "[13] *Write(I)*". The *backward slice* on criterion $\langle [13], I \rangle$ allows the automatic extraction of these instructions [Fig. 1(b)]. Likewise, if the comprehender wants to know the effect of any modification of the variable $I$ in instruction "[2] $I := Integer$" on the rest of the program, *forward slice* with criterion $\langle [2], I \rangle$ identifies all the instructions which may be affected by this modification [Fig. 1(c)].

By its reduced size and automatic extraction, the *slice concept* is helpful to the maintainer for understanding programs. However, there is nearly as many slices as program instructions, making this concept inadequate for the maintenance of large software. In addition, two or more slices can share one or more instructions, making any program modification unforeseen and difficult to accomplish.

### 2.3. *Program chopping*

Jackson and Rollins [15] have introduced the *chop* concept by generalization of the *slice concept*. A *program chop* is composed of all the instructions which transmit data or control flows from a variable $v_s$ in site $s$ to another $v_t$ in site $t$. The parameters $Source = \langle s, v_s \rangle$ and $Target = \langle t, v_t \rangle$ specify the *chop criterion*, noted $C_r = \langle Source, Target \rangle$ [15]. It is possible with this criterion, to obtain chops on a set of variables by specifying the symbol $*$ instead of a variable name. For example, the last column of Fig. 1 represents a *chop* between the instructions [2] and [13] of the example program. This *program chop* is composed of all instructions which have an effect on the value of $I$ at point [13].

Depending on the nature of the program, we distinguish *intraprocedural chops* and *interprocedural chops*. *Intraprocedural chopping* is a PDG traversal, whereas *interprocedural chopping* is an identification of paths in the SDG. If the SDG facilitates chopping, it poses the problem of extracting imprecise chops. A *chop* is precise if it does not contain "extra" instructions. *Chop* precision depends on the *granularity level* of the program element and on the existence of *unrealizable paths*.

### 2.4. *Granularity level of the program element*

If the program element is an instruction, extracted chops will be imprecises because dependencies between variables are not captured. On the other hand, if the program element is an action on a variable, extracted chops are more precises. Jackson and Rollins [15] approach allows to extract *precises chops*. In their dependence representation the program element is an action on a variable and call instructions are represented by *summary edges*. To each program instruction corresponds a box composed of input nodes (output nodes) which represent used variables (defined variables). In addition to user variables, there are three types of temporary variables: $\tau$ and $\epsilon$ depicting control flow and $\gamma$ representing a constant. Data and control flows are represented by three types of edges: internal, external and control edges. This model does not provide a System Dependence Graph, but gives a Program Dependence Graph for each procedure augmented by *summary edges*. For example, Fig. 3 presents the example program PDG according to the Jackson and Rollins approach.

Note that the call instruction [10] $Add(S, I)$ is represented by the three summary edges between input and output effective parameters. Suppose that the user is interested by the instructions which have an effect by data or control flows not on all the instruction [12] $K := S/I$ but only on the value of variable $I$. This can be obtained by the extraction of the chop with criterion $C_r = \langle ([1], *), ([12], I) \rangle$.

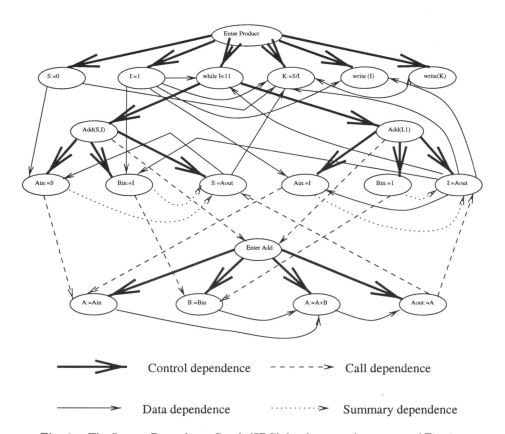

**Fig. 2.**   The System Dependence Graph (SDG) for the example program of Fig. 1a.

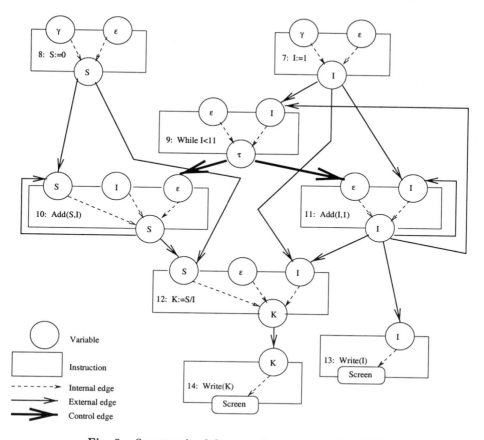

**Fig. 3.**   Source code of the example program and its GDP.

Using the GDS of Fig. 2, the set of instructions [3, 4, 5, 8] and [10] have an effect on instruction [12] and particularly on variables $S$ and $K$. However they have no effect on variable $I$. These instructions are included in the extracted *chop* and make it imprecise. On the other hand, using the augmented GDP of Fig. 3, there is a precise *chop* composed by the instructions [7, 9, 11] and [12].

### 2.5. *Unrealizable paths*

*Unrealizable paths* are unfeasible paths with respect to program execution. Every path, in the SDG, which goes through an incorrect call-return link is unrealizable [20]. *Unrealizable paths* imply imprecise *interprocedural chopping* [12]. For example in the SDG of Fig. 2, where we have two calls to the same procedure *Add*, there are two incorrect call-return links.

The first one is composed by the edges $(A_{in} := S, A := A_{in})$ and $(A_{out} := A, I := A_{out})$ which are related respectively to the enter of the first call and the exit of the second one. The second link is composed by the edges $(A_{in} := I, A := A_{in})$ and

$(A_{out} := A, S := A_{out})$. In the chop $C_1 = \langle ([8], S), ([13], I) \rangle$, the path crossing vertices $S := 0$, $A_{in} := S$, $A := A_{in}$, $A := A + B$, $A_{out} := A$, $I := A_{out}$, and $Write(I)$ is incorrect because it includes the first incorrect call-return link. Thus instructions [10] $Add(S, I)$ and [11] $Add(I, 1)$ are incorrectly linked implying the inclusion of "extra" instructions ([8, 10, 11] and [13]) in chop $C_1$. By avoiding unrealizable paths of the GDS, we found no link between vertices $S := 0$ and $Write(I)$; the chop $C_1$ is empty.

Reps and Rosay [20] approach allows to enhance the SDG by labelling its edges. Their chopping algorithm operates in two passes in order to avoid *unrealizable paths*. This approach have identified four types of precise interprocedural chops: truncated, non-truncated, same-level and unrestricted. A *chop* is truncated if between *Source* and *Target* sets we make an abstraction on called procedures. A *chop* is same-level if *Source* and *Target* sets belongs to the same procedure. The *chop* concept initially defined by Jackson and Rollins is a truncated same-level interprocedural chop.

### 2.6. Call chop

The *call chop* is a chop where *Target* and/or *Source* belongs to a procedure which is called from many points $m$. The criterion $C_r$ of a *call chop* has another parameter, *NumCall*, which specifies the call point, $C_r = \langle Source, Target, NumCall \rangle$.

For example, given a procedure $P_1$ which calls many times another procedure $P_2$ in call points $\mu_1, \mu_2, \ldots, \mu_n$ and given a chop $C$ defined between *Source* and *Target* belonging respectively to $P_1$ and $P_2$ [Fig. 4(a)]. Using Reps and Rosay approach, chop $C$ corresponds to the path between *Source* and *Target* crossing all the call points [Fig. 4(b)].

However, there are $m$ call chops $C_1, C_2, \ldots, C_m$. Call chop $C_1$ is defined by the criterion $C_r = \langle Source, Target, \mu_1 \rangle$. It represents the path between *Source* and *Target* crossing only $\mu_1$ [Fig. 4(c)]. The criterion of $C_2$ is equal to $C_r = \langle Source, Target, \mu_2 \rangle$ which represents the path between *Source* and *Target* crossing only $\mu_1$ and $\mu_2$ [Fig. 4(d)]. The criterion of $C_m$ is equal to $C_r = \langle Source, Target, \mu_m \rangle$ which represents the path between *Source* and *Target* crossing all the call points $\mu_1, \mu_2, \ldots, \mu_n$. In fact, *call chop* $C_m$ is the *unrestricted interprocedural chop* defined by Reps and Rosay [20].

To highlight *call chop* usefulness, suppose that a maintainer, after he has modified a variable $v_s$ at point $s$ of procedure $P_1$ containing $m$ calls to $P_2$, notes an anomaly of the value of variable $v_t$ at point $t$ of procedure $P_2$. This anomaly can be caused by one of the $m$ call points; "but which one?". Reps and Rosay's algorithm cannot assist the maintainer to answer this question, because it provides only call chop $C_m$. By construction itself this algorithm cannot provide the other *call chops* $C_1, C_2, \ldots, C_{m-1}$.

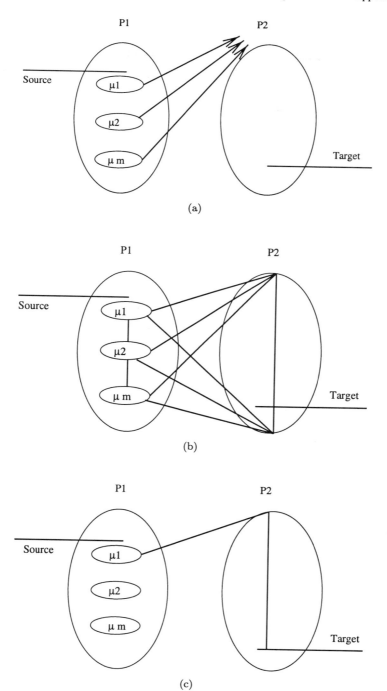

**Fig. 4.** Examples of call chops. (a) P1 calls m times P2, (b) Reps and Rosay chop, (c) call chop C1 and (d) call chop C2.

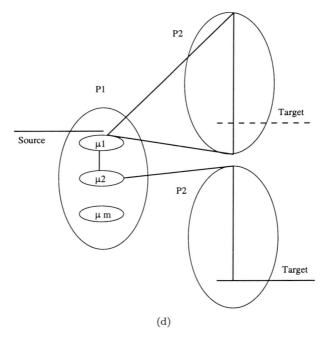

(d)

**Fig. 4.**    (*Continued*)

## 3.  Relational Expressions Based Approach

This approach represents a program by an explicit model of data and control flows between its instructions. Each instruction is decomposed into a set of elementary actions corresponding to the involved variables. It is represented by a dependence between its elementary actions. This dependence is an *intra-instruction dependence* and the relation between actions of different instructions defines an *inter-instruction dependence*. A unique identifier, noted *IdDep*, which represents the site of the related instruction is associated to each *intra-instruction dependence*.

This approach concerns imperative languages with the following constructions: assignment (:=), input (Read), conditional (If), loop (While), output (Write), procedure declaration (Procedure) and procedure invocation instructions (Call). For these constructions, four types of elementary actions are identified: assignment (*Assign*), input (*Read*), reference (*Value*) and output (*Write*) of value. Two types of variables which represent the control structure of the program have also introduced: $\mu_i$ for call instructions ($\mu_0$ for the program head) and $\zeta$ for control instructions (If, While). In the following, the examples are in general extracted from the example program of Fig. 1(a).

On adopting a formal specification modelling in terms of relational expressions [22], this approach allows the use of a variety of implementation algorithms and a direct transcription of analysis code.

## 3.1. *Formalization of the dependence model*

A program is represented by a set of triplets, named *System Internal Form* (SIF), that represents explicitly dependencies between elementary actions. Every automated processing of a given source statement is carried on the SIF form. A dependence represents a link between elementary action *Atarget* and *Asource* according to semantic *Sem*. The triplet is formally noted as:

$$\langle Atarget, Sem, Asource \rangle$$

It means that target actions *Atarget* and source actions *Asource* have a dependence relationship *Sem*. The dependence relationship *Sem* can be a flow dependence (FD), control dependence (CD), flow and control dependence (FCD), loop-carried dependence (LCD), call dependence (CALD), enter dependence (IND) and output dependence (OUTD).

The cartesian product formally defines elementary actions *Atarget* and *Asource* is $Var \times Act \times IdDep$, where:

- *Var* can be a program variable, a control variable, a call variable or a formal parameter:

$$-Var = PgmVar \cup CtrlVar \cup CallVar \cup ProcPrm$$

$$*CtrlVar = \{\zeta_1, \zeta_2, \ldots, \zeta_n\}$$

$$*CallVar = \{\mu_1, \mu_2, \ldots, \mu_m\}$$

- *Act* can be a definition action or a reference action to a variable:

$$-Act = Def \cup Ref$$

$$*Def = \{Assign, Read, Write\}$$

$$*Ref = \{Value\}$$

- *IdDep* is a unique identifier corresponding to an instruction site (*Pgm StmtId*), an effective parameter (*EffPrmId*) or a formal parameter (*FormPrmId*):

$$-IdDep = PgmStmtId \cup EffPrmId \cup FormPrmId$$

Thus an *intra-instruction dependence* is expressed by:

$$\{\langle\langle Y, A_y, i\rangle, Sem, \{\langle X, Value, i\rangle*\}\rangle / A_y \in Def\}$$

where $X$ and $Y$ are program variables and $i$ is an instruction site identifier.

For example the instruction [12] $K := S/I$ of the example program of Fig. 1(a) is composed of four elementary actions: *K.Assign*, *S.Value*, $\mu_0$. *Value* and *I.Value*. This instruction is represented by the following *intra-instruction dependence*:

$$\langle\langle K, Assign, [12]\rangle, FD, \{\langle S, Value, [12]\rangle, \langle I, Value, [12]\rangle,$$

$$\langle \mu_0, Value, [12]\rangle\}\rangle$$

On the other hand, *inter-instruction dependence* is expressed by:

$$\{\langle\langle X, Value_x, i\rangle, Sem, \{\langle X, A_x, j\rangle\}\rangle / A_x \in Def\}$$

For example the reference action $K.Value$ of instruction [14] $Write(K)$ depends on the definition action $K.Assign$ of the same variable of instruction [12] $K := S/I$. This relationship is represented by the *inter-instruction dependence*:

$$\langle\langle K, Value, [14]\rangle, FD, \{\langle K, Assign, [12]\rangle\}\rangle$$

The set of System Internal Form triplets constitutes in this model an internal representation of a given source code on which every automated processing is carried. The construction of SIF is given in the following subsection.


### 3.2. *System Internal Form construction*

The construction of SIF is composed of two steps. The first one constructs from the source code a set of triplets $SP$ which represent the dependencies of program procedures linked by *call dependencies*. The second step identifies the set of triplets $SR$ which depict *summary dependencies*. Thus, $SP$ augmented by $SR$ constitute SIF. The set $SP$ is constructed by syntactic and semantic analysis of source code. In addition to $SP$, a table is constructed in order to memorize all recursive call points of the program [2].

The identification of $SR$ is made by examining dependencies of the main program ($Main$). If $Main$ does not include any call point, there are no *summary dependencies*. The set SIF is equal to $SP$ and the construction is terminated. If $Main$ includes call points, *summary dependencies* are constructed for each one. This task is not obvious and cannot be done by a simple graph traversal because of *unrealizable paths*.

Two methods have been proposed in the literature for this task. The first one, defined by Weiser [24] supposes that each argument is both an input and output parameter for procedures whose body is not available (library functions). Therefore there is a *summary edge* for each argument. In the second method, Horwitz *et al* [13] propose to construct *summary dependencies* by unfolding PDG of called procedures until a fixed point (a procedure without call points).

In the relational expressions based approach, the PDG is not associated to recursive call points. Weiser's method has been used for identifying *summary dependencies* of recursive calls and Horwitz's one for no recursive calls. The same treatment applied to $Main$, is done recursively for each procedure. In addition, the set SIF allows to generate the System Dependence Graph (SDG). The vertices of the SDG symbolize elementary actions and the edges symbolize their dependencies. Notice that this SDG can include *unrealizable paths*. Avoiding *unrealizable paths* depend on the nature of chop criterion. It is treated in the next section.

### 3.3. *Chop extraction*

The program representation model allows the extraction of all chop types by using a single function, named $CHOP$. This function has five parameters where the last two are optional:

$$CHOP(G, Source, Target, [Type], [NumCall])$$

The parameter $Type$ specifies whether the extracted chop should be truncated whereas parameter $NumCall$ specifies the identifier of the *call chop*. $CHOP$ function operates in three steps as it is described by Fig. 5.

```
Step 1. We accomplish a graph traversal, C₁, in graph G between
        Source and Target;
        % C₁ is specified in Sec. 3.3.1 %
        If in C₁ there is at most a call point by procedure
          Then C₂ = C₁;
            Goto Step 3;
          Else Goto Step 2;
          % we have unrealizable paths %
        Endif;
Step 2. We accomplish another graph traversal, C₂, in graph G₂
        between Source S₂ and Target T₂;
        % G₂, S₂, T₂ and C₂ are given in Sec. 3.3.2 %

Step 3. If Type = truncated
          Then CHOP = C₂ without call dependencies;
          % the chop should be truncated %
          Else CHOP = C₂;
        Endif;
        Return;
```

**Fig. 5.** Chop extraction algorithm.

The four chop types defined by Reps and Rosay [20], as well as *call chops* defined in Sec. 2.6, are obtained by a traversal of the SDG using only $CHOP$ function. The way they are chopped is given in Sec. 3.4.

### 3.3.1. *Graph traversal*

Inspired by Jackson and Rollins's approach [15], the transitive closure $(G \circ G) *$ is used instead of giving algorithms of graph traversal of $G$. This closure includes all the possible dependencies. The set of paths $C_1$ in $G$ between $Source$ and $Target$ is given by the following equation:

$$C_1 = (G \circ G)^*(Target) \triangleleft G \triangleright ((G \circ G)^*)\tilde{\ }(Source), \text{where:}$$

$$s \triangleleft p = \{\langle a, b, c \rangle \in p/a \in s\} \text{ and } p \triangleright s = \{\langle a, b, c \rangle \in p/c \in s\}$$

The term $(G \circ G)^*(Target)$ defines all the elementary actions which affect $Target$ and $((G \circ G)^* \check{)}(Source)$ defines all elementary actions which are affected by $Source$ [15].

### 3.3.2. *Construction mechanism*

The construction mechanism of graph $G_2$ and the identification of $S_2$ and $T_2$ uses the table of recursive call points and the parameter $NumCall$. It modifies graph traversal $C_1$ by duplicating GDP of each procedure which is invoked not recursively $m$ times. In the opposite of SDG, $G_2$ is constructed and memorized only during a chop extraction operation. The construction of $G_2$ generates two problems: (1) an ambiguity in identifying dependencies of the $m$ PDG and (2) combinatory explosion of their number.

In order to resolve the ambiguity problem, the $m$ PDG is considered as being graphs of different procedures. Previous designation ambiguity is then eliminated by concatenation of the call point number with the identifier of each dependence of the corresponding PDG. The duplication generates a combinatory explosion of the PDG number for recursive calls as well as for the absence of recursive calls. For recursive calls, Hwang [14] propose an approach based on a computation of a fixed point. However, Reps *et al* [20] have shown that this computation needs an exponential temporal complexity implied by the combinatory explosion of the call numbers. For a recursive call, the PDG of the called procedure is the same as the calling procedure. Notice that it is useless, for data and control flows understanding, to represent it more than once. Thus, only in *summary dependencies* there are no PDG attached to them, and are associated to recursive calls (mutual or not).

If $Source$ and/or $Target$ belong to a procedure which is called by $m$ points then there are different call chops. In this case, depending on the value $k$ of $NumCall$, the corresponding PDG is identified in order to compute $S_2 = Source_k$ and/or $T_2 = Target_k$. When $NumCall$ is absent, $S_2 = Source_m$ and/or $T_2 = Target_m$ correspond to the *call chop* $C_m$. Thus:

$$C_2 = (G_2 \circ G_2)^*(T_2) \triangleleft G_2 \triangleright (G_2 \circ G_2)^*)\check{}(S_2)$$

## 3.4. *Extraction of different chop types*

- *Intraprocedural chop.* Intraprocedural chop ($IntraChop$) is a chop where $Source$ and $Target$ belong to a monolithic program. We have:

$$IntraChop = CHOP(GDP, Source, Target)$$

- *Same-level interprocedural chops.* A truncated same-level interprocedural chop ($TrunSameChop$) or untruncated ($SameChop$) is a chop where $Source$ and $Target$ belong to the same procedure. Thus:

$$TrunSameChop = CHOP(GDS, Source, Target, Truncated)$$

$$SameChop = CHOP(GDS, Source, Target, Untruncated)$$

- *Unrestricted interprocedural chops.* A truncated unrestricted interprocedural chop ($TrunDiffChop$) or untruncated ($DiffChop$) is a chop where *Source* and *Target* belong to different procedures. We have:

$$TrunDiffChop = CHOP(GDS, Source, Target, Truncated)$$

$$DiffChop = CHOP(GDS, Source, Target, Untruncated)$$

- *Call chops.* A truncated call chop ($TrunCallChop$) or untruncated ($CallChop$) with respect to a call $k$ is a chop where *Source* and/or *Target* belong to a procedure called many times. Thus:

$$TrunCallChop = CHOP(GDS, Source, Target, Truncated, k)$$

$$CallChop = CHOP(GDS, Source, Target, Untrucated, k)$$

## 4. Complexity Study

Spatial and temporal complexities with respect to the representation and the processing of dependence relationships of a program are expressed according to its size by the parameters of Fig. 6. Since the formal specification model is based on an explicit representation of dependence relationships, the study of the complexity will be mainly on edges. Sections 4.1 and 4.2 show that the complexity of the SIF construction and the chop operations are polynomial with respect to the size of the source code. In addition, Sec. 4.3 presents a complexity comparison between the system dependence graphs based approach and the relational expressions based approach.

### 4.1. *System Internal Form construction complexity*

The construction complexity of SIF depends on two costs: (1) the construction cost of each PDG procedure and (2) the computation cost of summary edges. The construction cost of PDG of procedure $p$ depends on the number of instructions in

| P | The number of procedures in the program |
|---|---|
| **Call** | The number of call sites in the program |
| **Callp** | The maximum number of call sites in procedure p |
| **M** | The number of call sites concerned by a chop |
| **Prmp** | The maximum number of call arguments in p |
| **Instp** | The maximum number of instructions in p (other than call instruction) |
| **Varp** | The maximum number of reference actions in an instruction |
| **Refp** | The maximum number of data flow dependencies with respect to the same variable |
| **Nodep** | The number of vertices in PDG of p |
| **Edgep** | The number of edges in PDG of p |

**Fig. 6.** Parameters defining program size.

*p* [20]. It is bounded by $O(Callp + Instp)$. The parameters $Callp$ and $Instp$ are defined in Fig. 6.

The cost of summary edges depends on the spatial complexity of edge traversal of the PDG and the summary edges in the called procedure. In the worst case, we have a summary edge for each output effective parameter. The number of its vertices ($Nodep$) and the number of its edges ($Edgep$) express the spatial complexity of a PDG [20]. As the program element is a variable action, $Nodep$ and $Edgep$ are polynomialy bounded, in addition to the number of instructions, by the number of variable invocations in each instruction:

$$Nodep \leq O(Instp \times Varp + Callp \times 2 \times Prmp)$$

$$Edgep \leq O(Instp \times Varp \times Refp + Callp \times Prmp \times Refp)$$

Then, the cost of computing summary edges for a single call is equal to the number of output effective parameters (bounded by $Prmp$) times the number of edges ($Edgep$) and the number of summary edges of the called procedure ($Callp \times Prmp$).

The cost of computing summary edges for a single call and the cost of computing summary edges for all calls in the program are bounded respectively by:

$$O((Prmp \times Edgep) + (Callp \times Prmp^2)) \text{ and}$$

$$O((Call \times Prmp \times Edgep) + (Call \times Callp \times Prmp^2))$$

Therefore, the SIF construction complexity is polynomial, and its cost is bounded by:

$$O(P \times (Instp + Callp) + (Call \times Prmp \times Edgep + Call \times Callp \times Prmp^2))$$

### 4.2. *Chop extraction complexity*

The complexity of different chop extraction depend on the complexity of function $CHOP$. In case where there is at most one call for each procedure between *Source* and *Target*, the extraction complexity (i.e. $C_1$) is polynomial with respect to the instruction number and is bounded by:

$$O(P \times Edgep + Call \times Prmp)$$

If between *Source* and *Target*, there are $m_i$ calls ($m_i < 1$) to a same procedure $i$, the extraction complexity needs extra costs relative to traversal $C_2$. Given $M = m_1 + m_2 + \cdots + m_n$ the total number of duplicated PDG, the cost of traversal $C_2$ is bounded by:

$$O(M \times (Edgep + Callp \times Prmp))$$

Therefore, the extraction complexity is polynomial and its cost is given by:

$$O(P \times (Edgep + Callp \times Prmp) + (M \times (Edgep + Callp \times Prmp)))$$

## 4.3. *Comparative study of complexity*

We present a comparative study of complexity relative to present approaches which resolve *element granularity level* and *unrealizable paths* problems. This comparative study is between the system dependence graphs based approach [15, 20, 14] presented in Sec. 2 and the relational expressions based approach [2] described in Sec. 3.

The spatial complexity of PDG proposed by Jackson and Rollins is polynomial with respect to the number of variable invocation in the program:

$$Nodep \leq O(Instp \times Varp + Callp \times 2 \times Prmp)$$

$$Edgep \leq O(Instp \times Varp_2 \times Refp + Callp \times Prmp^2 \times Refp)$$

The number of vertices in their PDG is identical to ours. However, their number of edges is more important with the following quantity "$P \times Varp + Call \times Prmp$". This is due to their *element granularity level*. The spatial complexity of PDG proposed by Reps *et al* is polynomial with respect to the number of instructions other than the call instructions and the number of effective parameters:

$$Nodep \leq O(Instp + Callp \times 2 \times Prmp)$$

$$Edgep \leq O(Instp \times Varp \times Refp + Callp \times Prmp^2 \times Refp)$$

The number of vertices and edges in their PDG is less important than in the relational expressions based approach respectively with the linear quantities "$P \times Varp$" and "$P \times Instp$". This is due to our *element granularity*. The temporal complexity of SDG proposed by Reps *et al* is more important than ours because of their summary edges construction cost. This cost is bounded by:

$$O((P + Call) \times Prmp \times (Instp + Edgep))$$

Likewise, the chop extraction cost, $O((P \times Edgep \times Prmp) + (Call \times Prmp^3))$, proposed by Reps *et al* is more important than ours. Thus, when we have for each procedure at most a call point, our cost is bounded by:

$$O(P \times Edgep + Call \times Prmp)$$

On the other hand, when we have many call points to the same procedure, our cost is bounded by:

$$O(P \times (Edgep + Callp \times Prmp) + (M \times (Edgep + Callp \times Prmp)))$$

However, the relational expressions based approach is less speedy only if the number of call points $m$, in the chop, is more important than the number of procedures in the program. The temporal complexity of slice extraction proposed by Hwang *et al* is exponential with respect to the program size. It is bounded by $O(2^k)$ where $k$ is the number of recursive call points to reach a fixed point [20]. In our approach, the temporal complexity of chop extraction is polynomial with respect to $C_2$ size.

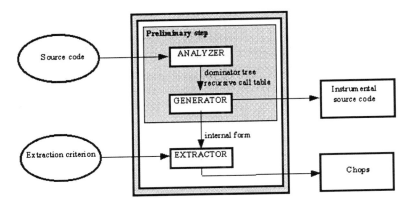

**Fig. 7.**   Architecture of PUT tool.

## 5. PUT: A CASE Tool for Program Understanding

We have designed and implemented a CASE tool [17] based on the relational expressions based approaches [2], named PUT (Program Understanding Tool). It extracts automatically from a given PASCAL program all *chop types*. This CASE tool has been developed in a C++ environment. Its global architecture is shown in Fig. 7.

PUT is composed of three main modules: *Analyzer, Generator* and *Extractor*. The *analyzer module* makes lexical, syntactic and semantic analysis and provides a dominator tree for each procedure, a table of definitions and references for each variable and a table of recursive call points. The *generator module* provides the system internal form SIF, shows the instrumented source code (where each instruction is labelled by a unique number) and gives statistic measurement of the program. The execution of these two modules constitutes the preliminary phase. Finally, the *extractor module*, which implements the function *CHOP*, is used in interactive mode and provides to the maintainer the extraction of all *chop types*. The maintainer selects from the instrumented source code the instruction numbers and variables of the desired chop criterion. The result can be shown in graphical or textual (source code) form. For example, chop on the instrumented program of Fig. 8 with criterion $C_r = \langle 1, 10 \rangle$ is given in source code form in Fig. 9.

## 6. Conclusion

Automatic chop extraction is a support for program understanding indeed software maintenance. Chop extraction depend on identification of a dependence model with adequate granularity and precise extraction (realizable path). In this chapter, we have presented the actual approaches which resolve these problems. In the first one, Jackson and Rollins [15] propose a model where the element is a variable action. In spite of a good granularity of the program element this model provides chopping relative to one procedure. Therefore, the problem of *unrealizable paths* has not been

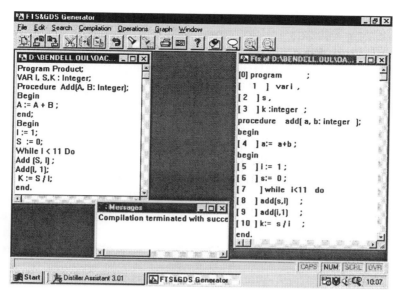

**Fig. 8.** Preliminary phase of PUT tool for the example program.

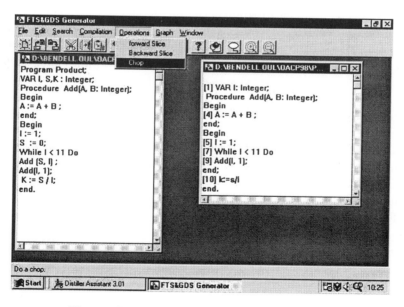

**Fig. 9.** Result in source code of $C_r = \langle 1, 10 \rangle$ chop.

addressed. By another way, Reps and Rosay [20] propose a model where the program element is an instruction. The problem of *unrealizable paths* have been resolved by labelling edges of their graph. Also their chopping algorithms operate in two passes. However, the *element granularity* is coarse and chops cannot be relative to different call points to the same procedure. The second approach proposed by [2] is based on a model with adequate granularity and *chops* are relative to many procedures. Its *chopping algorithms* operate in one pass. In addition, this approach permits to extract a new *chop type* which is relative to many call points of the same procedure and gives to the maintainer more precision on the effect of each of the call points to the same procedure.

## 7. Resources

There is no journals or conferences completely dedicated to program slicing. Therefore, as program slicing is a software maintenance sub-area, the International Conference on Software Maintenance (ICSM) is the major annual venue in this theme. Other conferences that address the theme of program slicing are: the International Conference on Software Engineering and Knowledge Engineering (SEKE), the International Conference on Software Engineering (ICSE), the Working Conference on Reverse Engineering (WCRE), the International Workshop on Program Comprehension (IWPC), and the ACM SIGPLAN/SIGSOFT Workshop on Program Analysis for Software Tools and Engineering (PASTE).

The Information and Software Technology Journal (Elsevier Science) has published a Special Issue on Program slicing in December 1998. This special issue was forwarded by M. Weiser and introduced by M. Harman and K. Gallagher. Other journals that edit articles on program slicing are: the Journal of Automated Software Engineering (Kluwer Academic Publishers), the International Journal of Software Engineering and Knowledge Engineering (Word Scientific), the Journal of Systems and Software (Elsevier Science), the ACM Transactions on Programming Languages and Systems and the IEEE Transactions on Software Engineering.

Some projects on program slicing are: the Wisconsin Program Slicing Project at the University of Wisconsin-Madison, the GUSTT Project (GUided Slicing and Targeted Transformation at Goldsmiths College (UK), the Unravel at the Loyola College is a prototype Computer Aided Software Engineering tool that can be used to statically evaluate ANSI C source code using program slicing, the VALSOFT (Validating Software Controlled System by Program Slicing and Constraint) project at the University of Passau (Germany), analyses ANCI C programs and calculates slices and path conditions via a graphical user interface, the Spyder project originated at Purdue University, involves reseach into advanced methods of software debugging, including exploration of new methods of bounded backtracking, dynamic program slicing and slice heuristics, the tkXSurgeon is a new project at the Loyola College, the Project project at the University of North London (UK) is about slicing and transformation.

Finally, some program slicing tools are: the CodeSurfer tool is the enhanced commercial version of the Wisconsin Slicer (available from GrammaTech), the Menagerie developed by the Program Analysis Transformation and Vizualization group at the IBM T. J. Watson Research Center, is an interactive tool for computing constrained program slices of C programs, the Microsoft's slicing tool from Advanced Programming Language Group at Microsoft Research is about static program analysis and transformation, the Linz Oberon Slicing System at the University of Linz (Austria) is a intermodular slicing tool for the Language Oberon, the Ghinsu environment developed at the Software Engineering Research Center (SERC) is an Integrated Software Maintenance Environment, the ChopShop tool originated at the Carnegie Mellon University is a reverse engineering tool to help programmers understand unfamiliar C code.

# References

1. R. S. Arnold, *Software Reengineering* (IEEE Computer Society Press, Los Alamitos, 1993).
2. M. S. Bendelloul, Z. E. Bouras, S. Ghoul and T. Khammaci, "Program understanding assistance: A model and a fragmentation algorithm", *Software Engineering Review* **45** (1997) 13–23. (In French).
3. V. Berzins, *Software Merging and Slicing* (IEEE Computer Society Press, Los Alamitos, 1995).
4. D. Binkley *et al*, "Program integration for languages with procedure calls", *ACM Transactions on Software Engineering and Methodology* **4**, no. 1 (1995) 3–35.
5. D. Binkley and J. R. Lyle, "Application of the pointer state subgraph to static program slicing", *Journal of Systems Software* no. 40 (1998) 17–27.
6. A. Cimitile, A. De Lucia and M. Munro, "A specification driven slicing process for identifying reusable functions", *Journal of Software Maintenance: Research and Practice* **3**, no. 3 (1996) 145–178.
7. A. De Lucia, A. R. Fasolino and M. Munro, "Understanding function behaviors through program slicing", *Proceedings of the Fourth Workshop on Program Comprehension*, Berlin, Germany (March 1996).
8. J. Ferrante *et al*, "The program dependence graph and its use in optimization", *ACM Transactions on Programming Languages and Systems* **9**, no. 3 (1987) 319–349.
9. K. Gallagher and J. Lyle, "Using program slicing in software maintenance", *IEEE Transactions on Software Engineering* **17**, no. 8 (1991) 751–761.
10. R. J. Hall, "Automatic extraction of executable program subsets by simultaneous program slicing", *Journal of Automated Software Engineering* **2**, no. 1 (March 1995) 33–53.
11. M. Harman, "Program comprehension assisted by slicing and transformation", *Proceedings of the First UK Program Comprehension Workshop*, CSM, University of Durham (July 1995).
12. S. Horwitz, J. Prins and T. Reps, "Integration non-interfering versions of programs", *ACM Transaction on Programming Languages and Systems* **11**, no. 3 (1989) 345–387.
13. S. Horwitz, T. Reps and D. Binkley, "Interprocedural slicing using dependence graphs", *ACM Transaction on Programming Languages and Systems* **12**, no. 1 (1990), 26–60.
14. M. Hwang, M. W. Du and C. R. Chou, "Finding program slices for recursive procedures", *Proceedings of the Twelfth COMPSAC*, Chicago, IL, USA (October 1988) 220–227.
15. D. Jackson and E. J. Rollins, "A new model of program dependencies for reverse engineering", *IEEE ACM SIGSOFT, Software Engineering Notes* **19**, no. 5 (1994) 2–10.

16. M. Kamkar, "Application of program slicing in algorithm debugging", *Information and Software Technology* **40**, no. 11 (1998).

17. T. Khammaci, "A CASE tool to assisting intelligently software developement process", *Journal of Computing and Information* **2**, no. 1 (November 1996) 1217–1232, ISSN 1201-8511.

18. K. J. Ottenstein and L. M. Ottenstein, "The program dependence graph in software development environment", *Proceedings of the ACM SIGSOFT/SIGPLAN Software Engineering Symposium on Practical Software Development Environments*, Piitsburg, PA, USA (1984) 177–184, and *Software Engineering Notes* **9**, no. 3.

19. T. Reps *et al*, "Speeding up Slicing", *ACM SIGSOFT Software Engineering Notes* **19**, no. 5 (1994) 11–20.

20. T. Reps and G. Rosay, "Precise interprocedural chopping", *ACM SIGSOFT Software Engineering Notes* **20**, no. 4 (1995) 41–52.

21. S. Sinha, M. J. Harrold and G. Rothermel, "System dependence graph based slicing of programs with arbitrary interprocedural control flow", *Proceedings of the ACM ICSE'99*, Los Angeles, CA, USA (1999).

22. J. M. Spivey, *Understanding Z: A Specification Language and Its Formal Semantics* (Cambridge University Press, UK, 1988).

23. F. Tip, "A survey of program slicing techniques", *Journal of Programming Languages* **3**, no. 5 (1995) 121–189.

24. M. Weiser, "Program slicing", *IEEE Transactions on Software Engineering* **10**, no. 4 (1984) 352–357.

# A LARGE SCALE NEURAL NETWORK AND ITS APPLICATIONS

DANIEL GRAUPE

*University of Illinoris at Chicago, EECS Department,*
*851 South Morgan Street, Chicago IL 60607-7053, USA*
*E-mail: graupe@eecs.uic.edu*


HUBERT KORDYLEWSKI

*Knowledge Systems Institute 3420 Main Street Skokie, Illinois 60076, USA*
*E-mail: hkordyl@ksi.edu*

This chapter discusses an artificial neural network (ANN) specifically designed for large-scale memory strorage and retriecal of information. The chapter discusses applications of ANN to retrieval, diagnosis, classification, prediction and decision problems. The network is based on Minsky's knowledge-lines theory of memory storage and retrieval. It employs arrays of SOM modules, such that the "k-lines" are implemented via link weights (address-correlations) that are being updated by learning.

*Keywords*: Neural networks, SOM, LAMSTAR, adaptive learning, classification, prediction, diagnosis, large-scale memory, interpolation/extrapolation.

## 1. General Introduction

Neural Networks have been developed since the 40's [1] in order to model and to grossly simulate the biological central nervous system (CNS) on the one hand, and in order to develop computational tools that can take advantage of the remarkable computational capabilities and efficiency of the CNS on the other hand. When observing a simple housefly, with only a few hundred neural cells, with signal propagation speeds averaging 3 meters/second and with bit rates of the order of 100 Hz can compute flight trajectories to evade a human hand trying to catch the fly, then one can understand the potential involved in imitating the biological computation system. This computational ability is achieved even while the average housefly probably holds no PhD in mathematics or in computer science. Indeed, the biological neural network is strikingly efficient in its recognition and retrieval capabilities. Its abilities of generalization, and of dealing with non-analytical and incomplete while huge data bases, within a virtually fixed architecture that involves no reprogramming when moving from one class of tasks to another, is well beyond those of any other computational architecture. The latter computational tasks involving huge databases with partly missing data sets and where data is in part non-analytical and/or fuzzy and/or stochastic, are the main challenges for today's

487

computer science. This is indeed the motivation for presenting the large-scale neural network of the present article.

The major principles of neural networks (NN's) are common to practically all NN approaches, including the LAMSTAR NN on which we focus below.

Considering major common principles, we first consider the model of the elementary unit or cell (neuron) employed in all NNs. This is nothing but a simplified mathematical model of the biological neuron, which was first formulated by Rosenblatt [2]. Accordingly, if the $N$ inputs into a given neuron (from other neurons or from sensors or transducers at the input to the whole or part of the whole network are denoted as $x(i)$; $i = 1, 2, \ldots, N$, and if the (single) output of that neuron is denoted as $y$, then

$$y = f \left[ \sum_{i=1}^{N} w_i x_i \right] \tag{1}$$

where $f[\cdot]$ is a nonlinear function denoted as Activation Function, that can be considered as a (hard or soft) binary (or bipolar) switch [3]. The weights $w(i)$ of Eq. (1) are the weights assigned to the neuron's inputs and whose setting is the learning action of the $NN$. The model of Eq. (1) is often known as the Perceptron model [2]. It is a simplified model of the biological neuron in which the inputs are trains of electrical impulses that are input to the neuron's dendrites, whereas the neuron's (single) output is an output all-or-nothing output at the pre-synaptic region of the same neuron. The weights $w(i)$ are input-weights whose embodiment is in terms of the chemistry at the dendrites and over the very narrow gap that separates the dendrites from the pre-synaptic region of another neuron whose output forms the input in question. Each neuron thus constitutes $N$ inputs ($N$ not being fixed per all neurons) and a single output which is being transferred from the given neuron to many other neurons (not to all), thus forming the neural networking structure.

The other main principles of networking are that neural firing (output production) is of all-or-nothing nature, and that the weights $\underline{w}(i)$ often constitute the memory itself. Hence, a vector $\underline{x}(j)$ of memory (of input to be stored, say, for further computation), will be stored in weights $\underline{w}(ij)$ of vector $w(j)$ relating to a $j$th neuron, if the distance $d(ij)$ satisfies:

$$d(j, j) = \|\underline{x}_j - \underline{w}_j\| \leq \|\underline{x}_j - \underline{w}_{k=1}\| \triangleq d(j, k) \tag{2}$$

such storage is known as BAM (Bidirectional Associative Memory) storage [4]. Also, a WTA (Winner-Take-All) principle is often employed [5], such that an output (firing) is produced only at the winning neuron (say, neuron $j$, satisfying Eq. (2) above), whose weights are closest to vector $x(j)$ when being applied to several neurons during a memory search/retrieval task). Another principle, derivable from Hebb's Law [6] and which is related to Hebb's observation of the Pavlov Dog's phenomenon, is that there are interconnecting weights (link weights) that adjust and serve to establish flow of neuronal signal traffic between groups of neurons, such that when a certain neuron fires very often (regarding a given situation/task), then the interconnecting link-weights (not the memory-storage weights) relating to that traffic, increase as compared to other interconnections [3, 7].

The above principles of BAM, WTA and link-weights are observable in biological networks to at least some degree. However, not all NN architectures employ all of them. Of the classical NN's, we briefly comment on the following:

(1) The Back-Propagation NN (BP) is essentially a multi-layer Perceptron. It employs a Dynamic-Programming-based algorithm [8] for weight setting that is not a BMA or WTA setting, nor does it employ link-weights. This NN is mathematically rigorous and well suited for well formulated analytical problems. Like Dynamic Programming, it suffers from the curse of dimensionality and requires full data sets.

(2) Hopfield Nets (HN) [9] are fully-connected recurrent NN's, using BAM, but no WTA, nor do they employ traffic-based link weights. They are also rigorous but suffer from the curse of dimensionality regarding number of categories they can handle efficiently, and are sensitive to incomplete data sets.

(3) Counter Propagation NN's (CP) [10] are BAM-based WTA networks. They are fast to compute. They employ no traffic-based weights. They play an important role in the LAMSTAR neural network described below.

## 2. Introduction to the LAMSTAR Neural Network

This chapter discusses a neural network specifically designed for application to retrieval, diagnosis, classification, prediction and decision problems which involve a very large number of categories. The resulting LAMSTAR (LArge Memory STorage And Retrieval) neural network [3, 11–13] is designed to store and retrieve patterns in a computationally efficient manner, using tools of neural networks, especially SOM (Self Organizing Map)-based network modules [5], combined with statistical decision tools. By its structure as described in Sec. 3, the LAMSTAR network is uniquely suited to deal with analytical and non-analytical problems [11–13] in which data are of many vastly different categories and which some may be missing, where data are both exact and fuzzy and where the vastness of data requires very fast algorithms. These features are rare to find, especially when coming together, in other neural networks. The network can be viewed as an intelligent expert system, where expert information is continuously being ranked for each case through learning and correlation. What is unique about the LAMSTAR network is its capability to deal with non-analytical data, which may be exact or fuzzy and where some categories may be missing. These characteristics are facilitated by the network's features of forgetting, interpolation and extrapolation. These allow the network to zoom out of stored information via forgetting and still being able to approximate forgotten information by extrapolation or interpolation. We shall show below that the LAMSTAR is equally powerful in many other decision and recognition applications in a wide range of areas.

The basic processing modules of the LAMSTAR network are modified Kohonen SOM modules [5] that are BAM-based WTA, as discussed in Sec. 1 above. In the LAMSTAR network, the information is stored and processed via correlation links between individual neurons in separate SOM modules. Its ability to deal with a large number of categories is partly due to its use of very simple calculation of link weights and by its use of forgetting features and features of recovery from forgetting. The link weights are the main engine of the network, connecting many layers of SOM modules such that the emphasis is on (co)relation of link weights between atoms of memory, not on the memory atoms (BAM weights of the SOM modules) themselves. In this manner, the design becomes closer to knowledge processing in the biological central nervous system than is the practice in most conventional artificial neural networks. The forgetting feature too, is a basic feature of biological networks whose efficiency depends on it, as is the ability to deal with incomplete data sets.

The input word is a coded real vector $\underline{X}$ given by:

$$\underline{X} = [\underline{x}_1^T, \underline{x}_2^T, \ldots, \underline{x}_N^T]^T \tag{3}$$

where $T$ denotes transposition, $\underline{x}_i^T$ being subvectors (subwords describing categories or attributes of the input word).

In the training phase, the input word is augmented by a subset of subwords that represents the desired output of the network (diagnosis/decision). Each subword $\underline{x}_i$ is channeled to a corresponding $i$th SOM module that stores data concerning the $i$th category of the input word. The network is organized to find a neuron in a set of neurons of a class (namely, in one SOM module) that best matches (correlates) the input pattern in WTA-manner.

## 3. An Outline of the LAMSTAR Network

### 3.1. *Basic structural elements*

The SOM structure employed in the LAMSTAR system adheres to fundamentals of the SOM structure but it differs in details. Whereas in Kohonen's networks [5] all neurons of an SOM module are checked, in the LAMSTAR network only a finite group of $p$ neurons is checked at a time due to the huge number of neurons involved (the large memory involved). The final set of $p$ neurons is determined by the weights $(N_i)$ as shown in Figs. 1 and 2.

A winning neuron is determined for each input based on the similarity between the input (vector $X$ in Fig. 2) and a weight vector $W$ (stored information). For an input subword $x_i$, the winning neuron is determined by minimization of a distance norm $\| * \|$ given by:

$$\|\underline{x}_i - \underline{w}_{i,m}\| = \min \|\underline{x}_i - \underline{w}_{i,k}\|, \quad \forall k \in \langle l, l+p \rangle; \, l \sim \{N_{i,j}\} \tag{4}$$

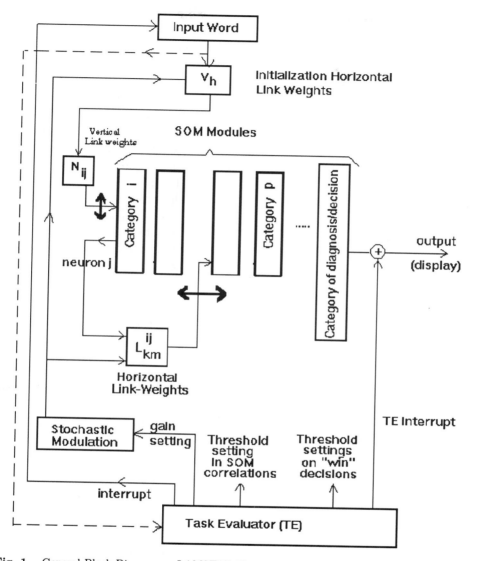

**Fig. 1.** General Block Diagram — LAMSTAR Network. Task Evaluation unit provides highest hierarchy of control — to modify tolerances and thresholds. Stochastic Modulation Unit introduces modulation noise to all settings of weights.

where

$m$: is the winning unit in $i$th SOM module (WTA).

$(N_{i,j})$: denoting of the weights to determine the neighborhood of top priority in SOM module $i$.

$L$: denoting the first neuron to be scanned (determined by weights $N_{i,j}$): $\sim$ denoting proportionality.

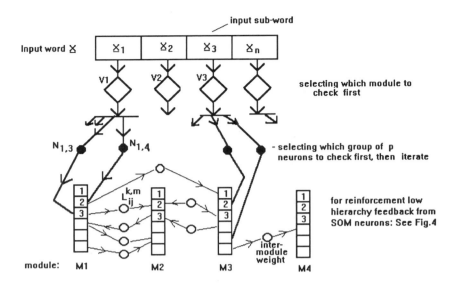

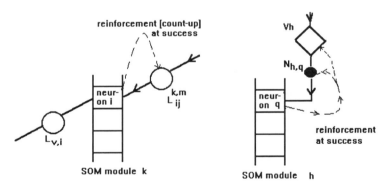

**Fig. 2.**   Details of Fig. 1. Top: Links between SOM modules. Bottom: Low-Hierarchy feedbacks from neurons that control weights $N$, $V$ and $L$ used in the LAMSTAR.

### 3.2. *Adjustment of resolution in SOM modules*

Equation (4), which serves to determine the winning neuron, does not deal effectively with the resolution of close clusters/patterns. This may lead to degraded accuracy in the decision making process when decision depends on local and closely related patterns/clusters which lead to different diagnosis/decision. The local sensitivity of neuron in SOM modules can be adjusted by incorporating an adjustable maximal Hamming distance function $d_{\max}$ as in Eq. (5)

$$d_{\max} = \max[d(\underline{x}_i \underline{w}_i)] \,. \tag{5}$$

Consequently if the number of subwords stored in a given neuron (of the appropriate module) exceeds a threshold value, then storage is divided into two adjacent storage neurons (i.e. a new-neighbor neuron is set) and $d_{max}$ is reduced accordingly.

### 3.3. *Links between SOM modules (L-weights)*

Information in the LAMSTAR system in encoded via correlation links $L_{i,j}$ (Figs. 1 and 2) between individual neurons in different SOM modules. The LAMSTAR system does not create neurons for an entire input word. Instead, only individual subwords are stored in BAM-like manner in SOM modules ($W$ weights), and correlations between subwords are stored in terms of creating/adjusting $L$-links ($L_{i,j}$ in Figs. 1 and 2) that connect neurons in different SOM modules. This allows the LAMSTAR network to be trained with partially incomplete data sets. The $L$-links are fundamental to allow interpolation and extrapolation of patterns (when a neuron in an SOM model does not correspond to an input subword but is highly linked to other modules which serve as an interpolated estimate).

When the new input word is presented to the system during the training phase, the LAMSTAR network inspects all weight vectors ($w_i$) in SOM module $i$ that corresponds to an input subword $\underline{x}_i$ that is to be stored. If any stored pattern matches the input subword $\underline{x}_i$ within a preset tolerance, the system updates weights $W$ according to the following procedure:

$$\underline{w}_{i,m}(t+1) = \underline{w}_{i,m}(t) + \alpha_i(\underline{x}_i(t) - \underline{w}_{i,m}(t)), \quad \text{for} \quad m : \varepsilon_m < \varepsilon_i \text{ (const)} \quad (6)$$

where

$w_{i,m}(t+1)$: modified weights in module $i$ for neuron $m$.
$\quad\quad \alpha_i$: learning coefficient for module $i$.
$\quad\quad \varepsilon_m$: minimum error of all weight vectors $W_i$ in module $i$ (Eq. (2)).
$\quad\quad t$: denotes the sequential number of the iteration (time equivalent).

If no match was found, the system creates a new pattern in the SOM module. It stores input subword $\underline{x}_i$ as a new pattern $\underline{w}_{in}$, where subscript $n$ denotes the first unused neuron in $i$th SOM module. We repeat the above storage procedure for every input subword $\underline{x}_i$ to be stored.

Link weight values $L$ are then set such that for a given input word, after determining a winning $k$th neuron in module $i$ and a winning $m$th neuron in module $j$, then the link weight $L_{i,j}^{k,m}$ is counted up by an increment $\Delta L$, whereas, all other links $L_{i,j}^{s,y}$ are reduced by a very small forgetting increment. (Fig. 2) [3, 7, 14]. The values of $L$-links are modified according to:

$$L_{i,j}^{k,m}(t+1) = L_{i,j}^{k,m}(t) + \Delta L : L_{i,j}^{k,m} \leq L_{max} \quad (7a)$$

$$L_{i,j}^{s,y}(t+1) = L_{i,j}^{s,y}(t) - f(t) : \quad L_{i,j} \geq 0 \quad (7b)$$

where:

$L_{i,j}^{k,m}$: links between winning neuron $i$ in $k$th module and winning neuron $j$ in
   $m$th module.

$\Delta L$: increment value.

$L_{\max}$: maximal links value.

   $f(t)$: some low increment value, that determines forgetting rate as function of
   time.

The link weights then serve as address correlations [7] to evaluate traffic rates
between neurons [3, 14]. (See Fig. 2).

### 3.4. *Forgetting and recovery from forgetting*

As a result of the learning formula of Eqs. (7a) and (7b) link weights $L_{i,j}$ de-
cay over time. Hence, if not chosen successfully, the appropriate $L_{i,j}$ will drop
towards zero. Therefore, correlation links $L$ which do not participate in successful
diagnosis/decision over time, or lead to an incorrect diagnosis/decision are gradually forgotten. The forgetting feature allows the network to rapidly retrieve very
recent information. Since the value of these links decreases only gradually and does
not drop immediately to zero, the network can re-retrieve information associated
with those links. The forgetting feature of the LAMSTAR network helps to avoid
the need to consider a very large number of links, thus contributing to the network
efficiency.

### 3.5. *Retrieval of information in the LAMSTAR network*

#### 3.5.1. *Input word for training and information retrieval*

In applications such as medical diagnosis, the LAMSTAR system is trained by entering the symptoms/diagnosis pairs (or diagnosis/medication pairs). The training
input vectors $\underline{X}$ are of the following form:

$$\underline{X} = [\underline{x}_1^T, \underline{x}_2^T, \dots, \underline{x}_n^T, \underline{d}_1^T, \dots, \underline{d}_k^T]^T \tag{8}$$

where $x_i$ are input subwords and $d_i$ are subwords representing the output of the
network (diagnosis/decision).

   In the processing of data (storage and retrieval), the diagnosis subwords ($\underline{d}$
in Eq. (8)) are processed in the same manner as other subwords, namely, all
punishment/reward feedbacks also apply to the diagnosis subwords. Therefore,
one or more SOM module serve as output modules to output the LAMSTAR's
decision/diagnosis.

   The input word of Eqs. (3) and (8) is set to be a coded word (Sec. 3.1),
comprising coded vector-subwords ($\underline{x}_i$) that relate to various categories (input
dimensions). Also, each SOM module of the LAMSTAR network corresponds to
one of the categories of $\underline{x}_i$ such that the number of SOM modules equals the number of subvectors (subwords) $\underline{x}_n$ and $\underline{d}$ in $\underline{X}$ defined by Eq. (8).

### 3.5.2. *Channeling of weights for fast retrieval*

An input subword $x_i$ is channeled to only one SOM module at a time. To speed up the search process, a two stage channeling process is employed. First, weight $V_j$ (as in Figs. 1 and 2) determine which subword of any input word is to be the first examined, noting that from then on, the inter-module links $L_{i,j}$ will take over to consider other subwords. In applications were input-word categories are *a priori* assumed to be of equal importance, or when no *a priori* information about input work categories is available, $V_j$ weights should be modified (in similarity to the modification of the $L_{ij}$ weight) by simple increment (reward) or decrement (punishment) functions, as follow:

$$V_i(t+1) = \begin{cases} V_i(t) + \xi, & \text{for} \quad V_i(t) < V_{\max} \\ V_i(t), & \text{for} \quad V_i(t) \geq V_{\max} \end{cases} \tag{9}$$

where

$\xi$: denotes a small increment/decrement.
$V$: weights for determining priority of subwords in the input vector.
$t$: denotes the sequential number of the iteration (time equivalent).
$V_{\max}$: maximum value for weights $V$.

The selection of the first SOM module is pseudo-randomly set according to a Probability Distribution Function (PDF) that is determined via weights $V_j$, according to the following rule:

$$P_i = \frac{V_i}{\sum_{n=1}^{k} V_n} \tag{10}$$

where

$P_i$: probability of choosing $i$th SOM module for initial search.
$V_i$: weighs associated with the $i$th SOM module.
$K$: number of SOM modules with active inputs.

Furthermore, and as is most important for speeding up the search, weights $N_{ih}$ as in Figs. 1 and 2 serve to assign priorities to certain neurons of the same SOM module. This is also accomplished by traffic counting (rewarding) of past successes, as displayed in details in Fig. 2, to increase weights $N_{ij}$ accordingly or to reduce it, if a "drought" has been observed in utilizing a certain memory, the latter being a forgetting feature.

### 3.5.3. *The SOM correlations links, interpolation and wandering searches*

The winning neuron of an SOM module is determined by Eq. (4) above. This winner connects to a neuron in another SOM module (relating to another subword) via $L_{i,j}^{k,m}$ link-weights, according to the following Eq. (7).

The role of the $L$ weights between SOM modules other than the output (decision) modules serves for retrieval and data analysis. These weights also serve to eliminate redundant input subwords (categories), namely categories that are fully correlated to other categories. Furthermore, as stated in Sec. 3.3, they allow interpolation and extrapolation in cases of missing categories. The resulting retrieval is subsequently checked at the SOM level concerning correlations between stored subwords and input subwords. The links are then reinforced in cases of a successful retrieval to "strengthen" the weights of such links according to Eq. (8).

Therefore, if for a given SOM module, a winning neuron has been determined (for its corresponding input-subword), then first the highest $L$-valued links to a subword relating to another subword of the input word (and which is or may be stored in another SOM module) is being examined.

Furthermore, through the $L_{ij}$ links, the LAMSTAR network facilitates extrapolation and interpolation to previous related subwords that were missed in input word. Extrapolation/interpolation is accomplished such that if no subword exists in the input word for SOM category $p$, then a neuron $q$ in SOM module $p$ will be declared as an interpolation/extrapolation estimated subword in $p$ is the sum of the $L$-links from winning neurons of all other subwords to that neuron in module $p$ is the highest and exceeds a threshold value.

### 3.5.4. *Determination of winning decision at output modules*

The diagnosis/decision at the output SOM modules is found by analyzing correlation links $L$ between diagnosis/decision neurons in the output SOM modules and neurons in all input SOM modules selected and accepted by process outlined in Sec 3.5.

The winning neuron (diagnosis/decision) from the output SOM module is a neuron with the highest cumulative value of links $L$ connecting to the selected (winning) input neurons in the input modules. The diagnosis/detection formula for output SOM module $i$ is given by:

$$\sum_{kw}^{M} L_{kw}^{i,n} \geq \sum_{kw}^{M} L_{kw}^{i,j} \quad \forall k, j, n; \ i \neq n \tag{11}$$

where

$i$: $i$th output module.

$n$: winning neuron in the $i$th output module.

$kw$: winning neuron in the $k$th input module.

$M$: number of input modules.

$L_{kw}^{i,j}$: link weight between winning neuron in input module $k$ and neuron $j$ in $i$th output module.

The $L$ weights above are derived in the same manner as $L$ weights between the input SOM modules, while success/failure is now being trained (and updated) by the task-evaluation unit.

## 3.6. *LAMSTAR processing algorithm for data analysis*

Since all information in the LAMSTAR network is encoded in the correlation links, the LAMSTAR can be utilized as a data analysis tool. In this case, the system provides analysis of input data such as evaluating the importance of input subwords, the strengths of correlation between categories, or the strengths of correlation of between individual neurons.

The system's analysis of the input data involves two phases:

(1) Training of the system (as outlined in Sec. 3).
(2) Analysis of the values of correlation links created after the training.

Since the correlation links connecting clusters (patterns) among categories are modified (increased/decreased) in the training phase, it is possible to single out the links with the highest values. Therefore, the clusters connected by the links with the highest values determine the trends in the input data. In contrast to using data averaging methods, isolated cases of the input data will not affect the LAMSTAR results, noting its forgetting feature. Furthermore, the LAMSTAR structure makes it very robust to missing input subwords.

After the training phase is completed, the LAMSTAR system finds the highest correlation links and reports messages associated with the clusters in SOM modules connected by these links. The links can be chosen by two methods: (1) links with value exceeding a pre-defined threshold, (2) a pre-defined number of links with the highest value. An example to this analysis capability is given in Sec. 4.5 (College-Course Evaluation Application).

## 4. Applications of the LAMSTAR Network

### 4.1. *General discussion*

The decisions of the LAMSTAR neural network are based on many categories of data, where often some categories are fuzzy while some are exact, and often categories pieces are missing (incomplete data sets). As mentioned in Sec. 3.2, the LAMSTAR network can be trained with incomplete data or category sets. Therefore, due to its features, the LAMSTAR neural network is a very effective tool in just such situations. The knowledge base of the system contains a mathematical extract of a series of cases with known outcome that are input into the system in the training phase. As an input, the system accepts data defined by the user, such as, system state, system parameters, or very specific data as it is shown in the application examples presented below. Then, the system builds a model (based on data from past experience and training) and searches the stored knowledge to find the best approximation/description to the features/parameters given as input data. The input data could be automatically sent through an interface to the LAMSTAR's input from sensors in the system to be diagnosed, say, an aircraft into which the network is built in.

The LAMSTAR system can be utilized as:

(1) a computer-based medical diagnosis system.
(2) a teaching aid.
(3) a tool for industrial maintenance and fault diagnosis.
(4) a tool for data analysis, classification, browsing, and prediction.

In addition to diagnosis features, the LAMSTAR network can provide multidimensional analysis of input variables that can, for example, assign different weights (importance) to the items of data, find correlation among input variables, or perform identification, recognition and clustering of patterns. Being a neural network algorithm, the LAMSTAR system can do all this without re-programming for each diagnostic problem.

The following sub-sections discuss the application of the LAMSTAR network to various problems and compare performance with other neural networks applied to the same problems, using the same data. The examples considered below are:

(1) patient diagnosis after removal of kidney stones.
(2) renal cancer diagnosis.
(3) diagnosis of drug abuse in emergency room situation (unconscious patient).
(4) college-course evaluation analysis.
(5) load balancing in distributed computations.
(6) speech recognition.

The examples presented below illustrate the scope of applications of the LAMSTAR network.

## 4.2. *Case study of ESWL medical diagnosis problem*

In this example, the LAMSTAR system is applied to aid in a typical urological diagnosis problem that is in fact, a prediction problem [12, 13]. It evaluates a patient's condition and provides long term forecasting after removal of renal stones via Extracorporeal Shock Wave Lithotripsy (denoted as ESWL). The ESWL procedure breaks very large renal stones into small pieces that are then naturally removed from the kidney with the urine. Unfortunately, the large kidney stones appear again in 10% to 50% of patients (1–4 years after surgery). It is difficult to predict with reasonable accuracy (more than 50%) if the surgery was a success or a failure, due to the large number of analyzed variables.

In this particular example, the input data (denoted as a "word" for each analyzed case, namely, for each patient) are divided into 16 subwords (categories). The length in bytes for each subword in this example varies from 1 to 6 bytes. The subwords describe patient's physical and physiological characteristics, such as patient demographics, stone's chemical composition, stone location, laboratory assays, follow-up, re-treatments, medical therapy, etc.

**Table 1.** Performance comparison of the LAMSTAR network and the BP network for the renal cancer and the ESWL diagnosis.

| | Renal Cancer Diagnosis | | ESWL Diagnosis | |
| --- | --- | --- | --- | --- |
| | LAMSTAR Network | BP Network | LAMSTAR Network | BP Network |
| Training time | 0.08 sec | 65 sec | 0.15 sec | 177 sec |
| Test accuracy | 83.15% | 89.23% | 85.6% | 78.79% |
| Negative specificity | 0.818 | 0.909 | 0.53 | 0.68 |
| Positive predictive value | 0.95 | 0.85 | 1 | 0.65 |
| Negative predictive value | 0.714 | 0.81 | 0.82 | 0.86 |
| Positive specificity | 0.95 | 0.85 | 1 | 0.83 |
| Wilks' Test computation time | <15 mins | weeks | <15 mins | weeks |

**Comments:**

*Positive/negative predictive values* — ratio of the positive/negative cases that are correctly diagnosed to the positive/negative cases diagnosed as negative/positive.

*Positive/negative specificity* — the ratio of the positive/negative cases that are correctly diagnosed to the negative/positive cases that are incorrectly diagnosed as positive/negative.

Table 1 compares results for the LAMSTAR network and for a Back-Propagation (BP) neural network [15], as applied to exactly the same training and test data sets [13]. While both networks model the problems with high accuracy, the results show that the LAMSTAR network is over 1000 times faster in this case. The difference in training time is due to the incorporation of an unsupervised learning scheme in the LAMSTAR network, while the BP network training is based on error minimization in a 37-dimensional space (when counting elements of subword vectors) which requires over 1000 iterations. Both networks were used to perform the Wilks' Lambda test [16, 17] which serves to determine which input variables are meaningful with regard to system performance. In clinical settings, the test is used to determine the importance of specific parameters in order to limit the number of patient's examination procedures.

### 4.3. *Renal cancer diagnosis problem*

In this case study, we attempted to predict if patients will develop a metastatic disease after surgery for the removal of renal-cell-tumors. The input variables were grouped into sub-words describing patient's demographics, bone metastases, histologic subtype, tumor characteristics, and tumor stage [13]. In this case study we used 232 data sets (patient record), 100 sets for training and 132 for testing. The performance comparison of the LAMSTAR network vs the BP network are also summarized in Table 1 below. As we observe, the LAMSTAR network is not only much faster to train (over 1000 times), but clearly gives better prediction accuracy (85% as compared to 78% for BP networks) with less sensitivity.

## 4.4. *Diagnosis of drug abuse for emergency cases*

In this case study, the LAMSTAR network is used as a decision support system to identify the type of drug used by an unconscious patient who is brought to an emergency-room (data obtained from Maha Noujeime, University of Illinois at Chicago [18, 19]). A correct and very rapid identification of the drug type, will provide the emergency room physician with the immediate treatment required under critical conditions, whereas wrong or delayed identification may prove fatal and when no time can be lost, while the patient is unconscious and cannot help in identifying the drug. The LAMSTAR system can diagnose to distinguish between five groups of drugs: alcohol, cannabis (marijuana), opiates (heroin, morphine, etc), hallucinogens (LSD), and CNS stimulants (cocaine) [18]. In the drug abuse identification problem diagnosis cannot be based on one or two symptoms since in most cases the symptoms overlap. The drug abuse identification is a very complex problem since most of the drugs can cause opposite symptoms depending on additional factors like: regular/periodic use, high/low dose, time of intake [18]. The diagnosis is based on a complex relation between 21 input variables arranged in 4 categories (subword vectors) representing drug abuse symptoms. Most of these variables are easily detectable in an emergency-room setting by simple evaluation (Table 2). The large number of variables makes it often difficult for a doctor to properly interrelate them under emergency room conditions for a correct diagnosis. An incorrect diagnosis, and a subsequent incorrect treatments may be lethal to a patient. For example, while cannabis and cocaine require different treatment, when analyzing only mental state of the patient, both cannabis and large doses of cocaine can result in the same mental state classified as mild panic and paranoia. Furthermore, often not all variables can be evaluated for a given patient. In emergency-room setting it is impossible to determine all 21 symptoms, and there is no time for urine test or other drug tests.

The LAMSTAR network was trained with 300 sets of simulated input data of the kind considered in actual emergency room situations [13]. The testing of the network was performed with 300 data sets (patient cases), some of which have incomplete data (in emergency-room setting there is no time for urine or other drug tests). Because of the specific requirements of the drug abuse identification problem (abuse of cannabis should never be mistakenly identified as any other drug), the training of the system consisted of two phases. In the first phase, 200 training sets were used for unsupervised training, followed by the second phase where 100 training sets were used in on-line supervised training with punishment [coefficients of Eqs. (7a), (7b) and (9) increased when cannabis was incorrectly] identified.

The LAMSTAR network successfully recognized 100% of cannabis cases, 97% of CNS stimulants, and hallucinogens (in all incorrect identification cases both drugs were mistaken with alcohol), 98% of alcohol abuse (2% incorrectly recognized as opiates), and 96% of opiates cases (4% was incorrectly recognized as alcohol).

## 4.5. *College-course evaluation analysis*

In this application example, the LAMSTAR system is utilized not as a diagnostic tool, but as a tool for multidimensional analysis of input variables. The prototype system for course evaluation is implemented at the Knowledge System Institute — Graduate School at Skokie, IL [20]. The results generated by the system will identify the strengths and weaknesses of the course. This will further assist the dean or the administration personnel in evaluating the performance of the faculty members in an objective manner. The components of the entire evaluation system are: data entry forms, LAMSTAR network, and evaluation results forms. The system is implemented in a secure environment through the Internet Web Pages. Table 2 shows the input data grouped into pre-defined categories. These categories serve as subwords in the LAMSTAR network. All the entries are stored into a database for easy retrieval and analysis of data. The results generated by LAMSTAR are: (1) list of categories with strengths/weaknesses, (2) numerical score for each category. These results are subsequently mapped into pre-defined sentences that should be included into the evaluation letters to the faculty. The processing algorithm of the LAMSTAR Network utilized in this example is outlined in Sec. 3.5.

## 4.6. *Load balancing in distributed computing*

In this example the LAMSTAR system is utilized for balancing in a distributed network computing [21]. The LAMSTAR network controls a system with $N$ computers, where computer can be a member of distributed system or a networked computer (as shown on Fig. 3) interchanging services or data. The LAMSTAR system is used to redirect services from client computers to servers that provide the fastest and most reliable services. The on-line training of the system is based

**Table 2.** Symptoms divided into four categories for drug abuse diagnosis problem.

| Category 1 | Category 2 | Category 3 | Category 4 |
|---|---|---|---|
| Respiration | Pulse | Euphoria | Physical Dependence |
| Temperature | Appetite | Conscious Level | Psychological Dependence |
| Cardiac Arhythmia | Vision | Activity Status | Duration of action |
| Reflexes | Hearing | Violent Behavior | Method of Administration |
| Saliva Secretion | Constipation | Convulsions | Urine Drug Screen |

**Table 3.**  Categories associated with questions from the evaluation form.

| Category | Variable (Associated with a question) |
| --- | --- |
| Course | 1. Was the course taught too fast or too slow? |
| | 2. Was this course too easy or too difficult? |
| | 3. Was the the course poorly organized or well organized? |
| | 4. Was the course boring or exciting? |
| Teacher | 1. Did the teacher give out informative handouts? |
| | 2. Was the teacher enthusiastic? |
| | 3. Did the teacher review the materials enough before the exam? |
| | 4. Did the teacher help you learn? |
| Communication with the teacher | 1. Could you talk to the teacher before or after class? |
| | 2. Did the teacher answer your questions? |
| | 3. Did you have difficulty communicating with the teacher? |
| | 4. Did you feel comfortable asking questions in class? |
| Textbook and quizes and homeworks | 1. Was the textbook too easy or too difficult? |
| | 2. Was the the amount of home work too little or too much? |
| | 3. Was the quizzes and exams fair? |
| | 4. Was the homework based upon materials covered in class? |
| General | 1. Did you learn a lot in this course? |
| | 2. Will you recommend this course to other students? |

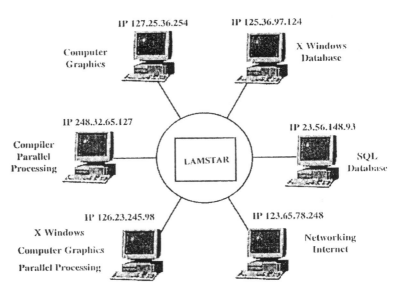

**Fig. 3.**  The LAMSTAR Network implemented as a look-up table with load balancing for distributed computers network.

on the following criteria: (1) finding the nearest server to the client, (2) finding a server that will not be overloaded while providing the service, (3) finding an appropriate server while keeping the cost of communication between computers to minimum. The input data to the system consists of a type of service requested (data, or application type) along with information about the requested/projected computational load. The LAMSTAR system is trained by providing information about available servers, such as: database, type/speed of the connection, operating system, processors type/speed, available services.

## 4.7. Speech recognition

In this example the LAMSTAR system is utilized as a limited-dictionary word recognition system. The system's categories (subwords) represent the frequency bins of the FFT of the analyzed words (with cuf-off at 3.5 kHz). The output of the network is an integer index describing which word was detected. After the system is trained, the correlation links (as described in Sec. 2) define relationship between the frequency bins for each word. The network recognizes close to 99% of words for speaker dependent word recognition, and 83% for speaker independet recognition.

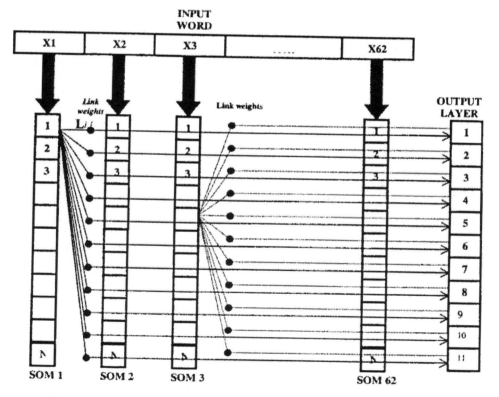

**Fig. 4.** The LAMSTAR neural network used for speech recognition problem.

In both cases a noise was added to the input. The results for recognizing 10 words for a case involving speech control of electrical stimulation for paraplegics has yielded 98.7% correct recognition using the LAMSTAR against 92% with Counter Propagation network [10, 22], when emplying exactly the same pre-processing of the speech signals in both cases, and the same amount of training.

Figure 4 shows LAMSTAR neural network used for speech recognition.

## References

1. W. S. McCulloch and W. Pitts, "A logical calculus of the ideas imminent in nervous activity", *Bulletin of the Mathematical Biophysics* **5** (1943) 115–133.
2. F. Rosenblatt, "The perceptron, a probabilistic model for information storage and organization in the brain", *Psychological Review* **65** (1958) 386–408.
3. D. Graupe, *Principles of Artificial Neural Networks* (World Scientific Publishing Co., Singapore and River Edge, NJ, 1997) (especially Chap. 13 thereof).
4. T. Longuett-Higgins, "Holographic memory of recall", *Nature* **217** (1968) 104.
5. T. Kohonen, *Self-Organizing and Associative Memory*, 2nd ed. (Springer-Verlag, New York, 1988).
6. D. Hebb, *The Organization of Behaviour* (John Wiley, New York, 1949).
7. D. Graupe and W. J. Lynn, "Some aspects regarding mechanistic modeling of recognition and memory", *Cybernetica* **3** (1970) 119–141.
8. R. Bellman, *Dynamic Programming* (Princeton University Press, Princeton, NJ, 1961).
9. J. J. Hopfield, "Neural networks and physical systems with emergent collective computational capabilities", *Proceedings of the National Acadermy of Sciencies* **79** (1982) 2554–2558.
10. R. Hecht-Nielsen, "Counter propagation networks", *Applied Optics* **26** (1987) 4979–4984.
11. D. Graupe and H. Kordylewski, "A large memory storage and retrieval neural network for adaptive retrieval and diagnosis", *International Journal of Software Engineering and Knowledge Engineering* **8**, no. 1 (1998) 115–138.
12. H. Kordylewski and D. Graupe, "Applications of the LAMSTAR neural network to medical and engineering diagnosis/fault detection", *Proceedings of 7th ANNIE Conference*, St. Louis, MO (1997).
13. H. Kordylewski, D. Graupe and K. Liu, "Medical diagnosis applications of the LAMSTAR neural network", *Proceedings of Biological Signal Interpretation Conference* (BSI-99), Chicago, IL, 1999.
14. M. L. Minsky, "K-Lines: A theory of memory", *Cognitive Science* **4** (1980) 117–133.
15. CS Niederberger, *et al*, "A neural computational model of stone recurrence after ESWL", *International Conference on Engineering Application of Neural Networks* (*EANN '96*) 423–426.
16. D. F. Morrison, *Multivariate Statistical Methods* (McGraw-Hill, 1996) 222.
17. S. Wilks, "The large sample distribution of the likelihood ration for testing composite hypothesis", *Annals of Mathematical Statistics* **9** (1938) 2–60.
18. L. J. Bierut, *et al*, "Familiar transmission of substance dependence: Alcohol, marijuana, cocaine, and habitual smoking", *Archives of General Psychiatry* **55**, no. 11 (1998) 982–988.
19. M. Noujeime, "Primary diagnosis of drug abuse for emergency case", Project Report, EECS Department, University of Illinois, Chicago (1997).

20. H. Kordylewski, "A large memory storage and retrieval neural network for medical and industrial diagnosis", PhD Thesis, EECS Department, University of Illinois, Chicago (1998).
21. V. Todorovic, "Load balancing in distributed computing", Project Report, EECS Department, University. of Illinois, Chicago (1998).
22. T. S. Patel, "LAMSTAR NN for real time speech recognition to control functional electrical stimulation for ambulation by paraplegics", MS Project Report, EECS Department, University of Illinois, Chicago (2000).

# AGENT-ORIENTED SOFTWARE ENGINEERING

MICHAEL WOOLDRIDGE

*Department of Computer Science, University of Liverpool,*
*Liverpool L69 7ZF, UK*


PAOLO CIANCARINI

*Dipartimento di Scienze dell'Informazione, University of Bologna,*
*47127 Bologna, Italy*

Software and knowledge engineers continually strive to develop tools and techniques to manage the complexity that is inherent in the systems they have to build. In this article, we argue that *intelligent agents* and *agent-based systems* offer novel opportunities for developing effective tools and techniques. Following a discussion on the classic subject of what makes software complex, we introduce intelligent agents as software structures capable of making "rational decisions". Such rational decision-makers are well-suited to the construction of certain types of software, which mainstream software engineering has had little success with. We then go on to examine a number of prototype techniques proposed for engineering agent systems, including formal specification and verification methods for agent systems, and techniques for implementing agent specifications.

*Keywords*: Autonomous agents, multi-agent systems.

## 1. Introduction

Over the past three decades, software engineers have derived a progressively better understanding of the characteristics of complexity in software. It is now widely recognized that *interaction* is probably the most important single characteristic of complex software (see, e.g. [21]). Software architectures that contain many network-aware, dynamically interacting components, each with their own thread of control, and engaging in complex coordination protocols to get or offer a plethora of services to other components, are typically orders of magnitude more complex to correctly and efficiently engineer than those that simply compute a function of some input through a single thread of control.

Unfortunately, it turns out that many (if not most) real-world applications have precisely these characteristics. As a consequence, a major research topic in Computer Science over at least the past two decades has been the development of tools and techniques to model, understand, and implement systems in which interaction is the norm. The advent of global computing platforms, like the Internet and the World Wide Web, has only increased the requirement of designing systems including complex interactions.

Many researchers now believe that in future, computation itself will be understood as chiefly as a process of interaction [23]. This has in turn led to the search for new computational abstractions, models, and tools with which to conceptualize and implement interacting systems.

Since the 80's, software agents and multi-agent systems have grown into what is now one of the most active areas of research and development activity in computing generally. There are many reasons for the current intensity of interest, but certainly one of the most important is that the concept of an agent as an autonomous system, capable of interacting with other agents in order to satisfy its design objectives, is a natural one for software designers. Just as we can understand many systems as being composed of essentially passive objects, which have state, and upon which we can perform operations, so we can understand many others as being made up of interacting, semi-autonomous agents which offer services.

This paper has the following structure: Section 2 defines what we mean by the term "agent", and summarizes why such agents might be appropriate for engineering certain complex software systems. We then describe some typical application domains for multi-agent systems. In Sec. 4, we describe agent-oriented specification techniques, focussing in particular on the requirements that an agent-oriented specification framework will have. In Sec. 5, we discuss how such specifications can be implemented, either by directly executing them, or else by automatically synthesizing executable systems from specifications. Section 6 discusses how implemented systems may be verified, to determine whether or not they satisfy their specifications. Finally, in Sec. 7, we conclude with some comments on future issues for agent-oriented software engineering.

Note that Sec. 4 through to 6 include some material from [55], where a fuller examination of, in particular, the specification, implementation, and verification of agent-based systems may be found.

## 2. Agent-Based Systems

By an *agent-based system*, we mean one in which the key abstraction used is that of an *agent*. By an *agent*, we mean an abstraction that enjoys the following properties [58, pp. 116–118]:

- *autonomy*: agents encapsulate some state (which is not accessible to other agents), and make decisions about what to do based on this state, without the direct intervention of humans or others;
- *reactivity*: agents are *situated* in an environment (which may be the physical world, a user via a graphical user interface, a collection of other agents, the Internet, or perhaps many of these combined), are able to *perceive* this environment (through the use of potentially imperfect sensors), and are able to respond in a timely fashion to changes that occur in it;
- *pro-activeness*: agents do not simply act in response to their environment, they are able to exhibit goal-directed behaviour by *taking the initiative*; and

- *social ability*: agents interact with other agents (and possibly humans) via some kind of *agent-communication language*, and typically have the ability to engage in social activities (such as cooperative problem solving or negotiation) in order to achieve their goals.

A *multi-agent system* is a system composed of a number of such agents, which typically interact with one-another in order to satisfy their goals.

An obvious question to ask is why agents and multi-agent systems are seen as an important new direction in software engineering. There are several reasons [27, pp. 6–10]:

- *Natural metaphor*
  Just as the many domains can be conceived of consisting of a number of interacting but essentially passive *objects*, so many others can be conceived as interacting, active, purposeful *agents*. For example, a scenario currently driving much research and development activity in the agents field is that of software agents that buy and sell goods via the Internet on behalf of some users. It is natural to view the software participants in such transactions as (semi-)autonomous agents.
- *Distribution of data or control*
  For many software systems, it is not possible to identify a single locus of control: instead, overall control of the systems is distributed across a number computing nodes, which are frequently geographically distributed. In order to make such systems work effectively, these nodes must be capable of autonomously interacting with each other — they must agents.
- *Legacy systems*
  A natural way of incorporating legacy systems into modern distributed information systems is to *agentify* them: to "wrap" them with an agent layer, that will enable them to interact with other agents.
- *Open systems*
  Many systems are *open* in the sense that it is impossible to know at design time exactly what components or services the system will be comprised of, and how they will be able to interact with one-another. To operate effectively in such systems, the ability to engage in flexible autonomous decision-making is critical. An important example of this kind of systems are middleware platforms like OMG's CORBA [40] or Sun's Jini [38]. These platforms include some concept of agenthood, which helps in designing some specific types of component or service.

Now that we have defined what an agent is, we can look at some example applications of agent technology.

## 3. Some Applications of Agent Technology

Agents have been applied in several application domains, amongst the most important of which have been the following.

**Agents and Distributed Systems.** In distributed systems, the idea of an agent is often seen as a natural metaphor, and, by some, as a development of the concurrent object programming paradigm [1]. Specifically, multi-agent systems have been applied in the following domains:

- *Air traffic control*
  Air-traffic control systems are among the oldest application areas in multi-agent systems [49, 15]. A recent example is OASIS (*O*ptimal *A*ircraft *S*equencing using *I*ntelligent *S*cheduling), a system that is currently undergoing field trials at Sydney airport in Australia [33]. The specific aim of OASIS is to assist an air-traffic controller in managing the flow of aircraft at an airport: it offers estimates of aircraft arrival times, monitors aircraft progress against previously derived estimates, informs the air-traffic controller of any errors, and perhaps most importantly, finds the optimal sequence in which to land aircraft. OASIS contains two types of agents: *global* agents, which perform generic domain functions (for example, there is a "sequencer agent", which is responsible for arranging aircraft into a least-cost sequence), and *aircraft agents*, one for each aircraft in the system airspace.

- *Business process management*
  Workflow and business process control systems are an area of increasing importance in computer science. Workflow systems aim to automate the processes of a business, ensuring that different business tasks are expedited by the appropriate people at the right time, typically ensuring that a particular document flow is maintained and managed within an organization. The ADEPT system is a current example of an agent-based business process management system [25, 26]. In ADEPT, a business organization is modelled as a society of negotiating, service providing agents. ADEPT is currently being tested on a British Telecom (BT) business process which involves some nine departments and 200 different tasks.

- *Industrial systems management*
  The largest and probably best-known European multi-agent system development project to date was ARCHON [24]. This project developed and deployed multi-agent technology in several industrial domains. The most significant of these domains was a power distribution system, which was installed and is currently operational in Northern Spain. Agents in ARCHON have two main parts: a *domain* component, which realizes the domain-specific functionality of the agent, and a *wrapper* component, which provides the agent functionality, enabling the system to plan its actions, and to represent and communicate with other agents. The ARCHON technology has subsequently been deployed in several other domains, including particle accelerator control.

- *Distributed sensing*

  The classic application of multi-agent technology was in distributed sensing [32, 11]. The broad idea is to have a system constructed as a network of spatially distributed sensors. The sensors may, for example, be acoustic sensors on a battlefield, or radars distributed across some airspace. The global goal of the system is to monitor and track all vehicles that pass within range of the sensors. This task can be made simpler if the sensor nodes in the network *cooperate* with one-another, for example by exchanging predictions about when a vehicle will pass from the region of one sensor to the region of another. This apparently simple domain has yielded surprising richness as an environment for experimentation into multi-agent systems: Lesser's well known *Distributed Vehicle onitoring Testbed* (DVMT) provided the proving ground for many of today's multi-agent system development techniques [32].

- *Space shuttle fault diagnosis*

  It is difficult to imagine a domain with harder real-time constraints than that of in-flight diagnosis of faults on a spacecraft. Yet one of the earliest applications of the PRS architecture was precisely this [18]. In brief, the procedures that an astronaut would use to diagnose faults in the space shuttle's reaction control systems were directly coded as PRS plans, and the PRS architecture was used to interpret these plans, and provide real-time advice to astronauts in the event of failure or malfunction in this system.

- *Factory process control*

  Organizations can be modelled as societies of interacting agents. Factories are no exception, and an agent-based approach to modelling and managing factories has been taken up by several researchers. This work began largely with Parunak [50], who, in YAMS (*Yet Another Manufacturing System*) used the Contract Net protocol [48] for manufacturing control. More recently, Mori *et al* have used a multi-agent approach to controlling steel coil processing plant [36], and Wooldridge *et al* have described how the process of determining an optimal production sequence for some factory can naturally be viewed as a problem of negotiation between the various production cells within the factory [57].

**Agents in the Internet.** Much of the hyperbole that currently surrounds all things agent-like is related to the phenomenal growth of the Internet [12, 5]. In particular, there is a lot of interest in *mobile* agents, that can move themselves around the Internet operating on a user's behalf. This kind of functionality is achieved in the TELESCRIPT language developed by General Magic, Inc., for *remote programming* [52]; related functionality is provided in languages such as Java. There are a number of rationales for this type of agent:

- *Electronic commerce*
  Currently, commercial activity is driven primarily by humans making decisions about what goods to buy at what price, and so on. However, it is not difficult to see that certain types of commerce might usefully be automated. A standard motivating example is that of a "travel agent". Suppose I want to travel from Manchester to San Francisco. There are many different airlines, price structures and routes that I could choose for such a journey. I may not mind about the route, as long as the aircraft involved is not "fly-by-wire"; I may insist on a dietary option not available with some airlines; or I may not want to fly with Ruritanian airlines after I had a bad experience once. Trying to find the best flight *manually* given these preferences is a tedious business, but a fairly straightforward one. It seems entirely plausible that this kind of service will in future be provided by agents, who take a specification of your desired flight and preferences, and, after checking through a range of on-line flight information databases, will return with a list of the best options.

- *Hand-held PDAs with limited bandwidth*
  Hand-held "personal digital assistants" are seen by many as a next step in the laptop computer market. Such PDAs are often provided with limited-bandwidth links to telecommunications networks. If a PDA has a query that needs to be resolved, that will require network information resources, it may be more efficient to send out an agent across the network whose purpose is to resolve this query remotely. The searching process is done by the agent at a remote site, and only the final result of the query need be sent back to the PDA that originated the query.

- *Information gathering*
  The widespread provision of distributed, semi-structured information resources such as the world-wide web obviously presents enormous potential; but it also presents a number of difficulties (such as "information overload"); agents are seen as a natural tool to perform tasks such as searching distributed information resources, and filtering out unwanted news and email [34, 31].

At the time of writing, most interest in mobile agents is centred around the Java programming language, which, in the form of applets (portable downloadable programs embedded within WWW pages), already provides a very widely used mobile object framework. Also of relevance is the work of the Object Management Group (OMG), a consortium of computer manufacturers who are developing, amongst other things, a mobile agent framework based on their well known CORBA (*Common Object Request Broker Architecture*) distributed object standard [40].

**Agents in Interfaces.** Another area of much current interest is the use of agent in *interfaces*. The idea here is that of the agent as an *assistant* to a user in some task. The rationale is that current interfaces are in no sense *pro-active*: things only happen when some user initiates a task. The idea of an agent acting in the way that a good assistant would, by *anticipating* our requirements, seems very attractive. Nicholas Negroponte, director of the MIT Media Lab, sees the ultimate development of such agents as follows [37]:

> "The "agent" answers the phone, recognizes the callers, disturbs you when appropriate, and may even tell a white lie on your behalf. The same agent is well trained in timing, versed in finding opportune moments, and respectful of idiosyncrasies". (p. 150)

> "If you have somebody who knows you well and shares much of your information, that person can act on your behalf very effectively. If your secretary falls ill, it would make no difference if the temping agency could send you Albert Einstein. This issue is not about IQ. It is shared knowledge and the practice of using it in your best interests". (p. 151)

> "Like an army commander sending a scout ahead ... you will dispatch agents to collect information on your behalf. Agents will dispatch agents. The process multiplies. But [this process] started at the interface where you delegated your desires". (p. 158)

Some prototypical interface agents of this type are described in [34].

In the remainder of this article, we consider what it means to *specify, implement,* and *verify* agent-based systems.

## 4. Specification

In this section, we consider the problem of *specifying* an agent system. What are the requirements for an agent specification framework? What sort of properties must it be capable of representing? The predominant approach to specifying agents has involved treating them as *intentional systems* that may be understood by attributing to them *mental states* such as beliefs, desires, and intentions [9, 58]; see [56] for a detailed justification of this idea. Using this idea, a number of approaches for formally specifying agents have been developed, which are capable of representing the following aspects of an agent-based system:

- The *beliefs* that agents have — The information they have about their environment, which may be incomplete or incorrect.
- The *goals* that agents will try to achieve.
- The *actions* that agents perform and the effects of these actions.
- The *ongoing interaction* that agents have — How agents interact with each other and their environment over time.

We use the term *agent theory* to refer to a theory which explains how these aspects of agency interact to generate the behaviour of an agent. The most successful approach to (formal) agent theory appears to be the use of a *temporal modal logic* (space restrictions prevent a detailed technical discussion on such logics — see, e.g. [58] for extensive references). Two of the best known such logical frameworks are the Cohen–Levesque theory of intention [8], and the Rao–Georgeff belief-desire-intention model [43, 56]. The Cohen–Levesque model takes as primitive just two attitudes: beliefs and goals. Other attitudes (in particular, the notion of *intention*) are built up from these. In contrast, Rao–Georgeff take intentions as primitives, in addition to beliefs and goals. The key technical problem faced by agent theorists is developing a formal model that gives a good account of the interrelationships between the various attitudes that together comprise an agents internal state [58]. Comparatively few serious attempts have been made to specify real agent systems using such logics — see, e.g. [17] for one such attempt.

## 5. Implementation

Once given a specification, we must implement a system that is correct with respect to this specification. The next issue we consider is this move from abstract specification to concrete computational system. There are at least two possibilities for achieving this transformation that we consider here:

(1) Somehow directly execute or animate the abstract specification.
(2) Somehow translate or compile the specification into a concrete computational form using an automatic translation technique.

In the sub-sections that follow, we shall investigate each of these possibilities in turn.

### 5.1. *Directly executing agent specifications*

Suppose we are given a system specification, $\phi$, which is expressed in some logical language $L$. One way of obtaining a concrete system from $\phi$ is to treat it as an *executable specification*, and *interpret* the specification directly in order to generate the agent's behaviour. Interpreting an agent specification can be viewed as a kind of constructive proof of satisfiability, whereby we show that the specification $\phi$ is satisfiable by *building a model* (in the logical sense) for it. If models for the specification language $L$ can be given a computational interpretation, then model building can be viewed as executing the specification. To make this discussion concrete, consider the Concurrent METATEM programming language [16]. In this language, agents are programmed by giving them a temporal logic specification of the behaviour it is intended they should exhibit; this specification is directly executed to generate each agent's behaviour. Models for the temporal logic in which Concurrent METATEM agents are specified are linear discrete sequences of states: executing a Concurrent METATEM agent specification is thus a process of constructing such a sequence of states. Since such state sequences can be viewed as the histories traced out by programs as they execute, the temporal logic upon which Concurrent METATEM is based has a computational interpretation; the actual execution algorithm is described in [2].

Note that executing Concurrent METATEM agent specifications is possible primarily because the models upon which the Concurrent METATEM temporal logic is based are comparatively simple, with an obvious and intuitive computational interpretation. However, agent specification languages in general (e.g. the BDI formalisms of Rao and Georgeff [43]) are based on considerably more complex logics. In particular, they are usually based on a semantic framework known as *possible worlds* [6]. The technical details are somewhat involved for the purposes of this article: the main point is that, *in general*, possible worlds semantics do not have a computational interpretation in the way that Concurrent METATEM semantics do. Hence it is not clear what "executing" a logic based on such semantics might mean. In response to this, a number of researchers have attempted to develop executable agent specification languages with a simplified semantic basis, that has a computational interpretation. An example is Rao's AgentSpeak(L) language, which although essentially a BDI system, has a simple computational semantics [42].

## 5.2. *Compiling agent specifications*

An alternative to direct execution is *compilation*. In this scheme, we take our abstract specification, and transform it into a concrete computational model via some automatic synthesis process. The main perceived advantages of compilation over direct execution are in run-time efficiency. Direct execution of an agent specification, as in Concurrent METATEM, above, typically involves manipulating a symbolic representation of the specification at run time. This manipulation generally corresponds to reasoning of some form, which is computationally costly. Compilation approaches aim to reduce abstract symbolic specifications to a much simpler computational model, which requires no symbolic representation. The "reasoning" work is thus done off-line, at compile-time; execution of the compiled system can then be done with little or no run-time symbolic reasoning.

Compilation approaches usually depend upon the close relationship between models for temporal/modal logic (which are typically labeled graphs of some kind), and automata-like finite state machines. For example, Pnueli and Rosner [41] synthesize reactive systems from branching temporal logic specifications. Similar techniques have also been used to develop concurrent system skeletons from temporal logic specifications. Perhaps the best-known example of this approach to agent development is the *situated automata* paradigm of Rosenschein and Kaelbling [46]. They use a epistemic logic (i.e., a logic of *knowledge* [13]) to specify the perception component of intelligent agent systems. They then used a technique based on constructive proof to directly synthesize automata from these specifications [45].

The general approach of automatic synthesis, although theoretically appealing, is limited in a number of important respects. First, as the agent specification language becomes more expressive, then even offline reasoning becomes too expensive to carry out. Second, the systems generated in this way are not capable of *learning*, (i.e., they are not capable of adapting their "program" at run-time). Finally, as with direct execution approaches, agent specification frameworks tend to have no concrete computational interpretation, making such a synthesis impossible.

## 6. Verification

Once we have developed a concrete system, we need to show that this system is correct with respect to our original specification. This process is known as *verification*, and it is particularly important if we have introduced any informality into the development process. We can divide approaches to the verification of systems into two broad classes: (1) *axiomatic*; and (2) *semantic* (model checking). In the subsections that follow, we shall look at the way in which these two approaches have evidenced themselves in agent-based systems.

### 6.1. *Axiomatic approaches*

Axiomatic approaches to program verification were the first to enter the main-stream of computer science, with the work of Hoare in the late 60's [20]. Axiomatic verification requires that we can take our concrete program, and from this program systematically derive a logical theory that represents the behaviour of the program. Call this the program theory. If the program theory is expressed in the same logical language as the original specification, then verification reduces to a proof problem: show that the specification is a theorem of (equivalently, is a logical consequence of) the program theory. The development of a program theory is made feasible by *axiomatizing* the programming language in which the system is implemented. For example, Hoare logic gives us more or less an axiom for every statement type in a simple PASCAL-like language. Once given the axiomatization, the program theory can be derived from the program text in a systematic way.

Perhaps the most relevant work from mainstream computer science is the specification and verification of reactive systems using temporal logic, in the way pioneered by Pnueli, Manna, and colleagues [35]. The idea is that the computations of reactive systems are infinite sequences, which correspond to models for linear temporal logic. Temporal logic can be used both to develop a system specification, and to axiomatize a programming language. This axiomatization can then be used to systematically derive the theory of a program from the program text. Both the specification and the program theory will then be encoded in temporal logic, and verification hence becomes a proof problem in temporal logic.

Comparatively little work has been carried out within the agent-based systems community on axiomatizing multi-agent environments. We shall review just one approach. In [54], an axiomatic approach to the verification of multi-agent systems was proposed. Essentially, the idea was to use a temporal belief logic to axiomatize the properties of two multi-agent programming languages. Given such an axiomatization, a program theory representing the properties of the system could be systematically derived in the way indicated above. A temporal belief logic was used for two reasons. First, a temporal component was required because, as we observed above, we need to capture the ongoing behaviour of a multi-agent system. A belief component was used because the agents we wish to verify are each symbolic AI systems in their own right. That is, each agent is a symbolic reasoning system, which includes a representation of its environment and desired behaviour. A belief component in the logic allows us to capture the symbolic representations present within each agent. The two multi-agent programming languages that were axiomatized in the temporal belief logic were Shoham's AGENT0 [47], and Fisher's Concurrent METATEM (see above). Note that this approach relies on the operation of agents being sufficiently simple that their properties can be axiomatized in the logic. It works for Shoham's AGENT0 and Fisher's Concurrent METATEM largely because these languages have a simple semantics, closely related to rule-based systems, which in turn have a simple logical semantics. For more complex agents, an axiomatization is not so straightforward. Also, capturing the semantics of concurrent execution of agents is not easy (it is, of course, an area of ongoing research in computer science generally).

## 6.2. *Semantic approaches: model checking*

Ultimately, axiomatic verification reduces to a proof problem. Axiomatic approaches to verification are thus inherently limited by the difficulty of this proof problem. Proofs are hard enough, even in classical logic; the addition of temporal and modal connectives to a logic makes the problem considerably harder. For this reason, more efficient approaches to verification have been sought. One particularly successful approach is that of *model checking* [7]. As the name suggests, whereas axiomatic approaches generally rely on syntactic proof, model checking approaches are based on the semantics of the specification language.

The model checking problem, in abstract, is quite simple: given a formula $\phi$ of language $L$, and a model $M$ for $L$, determine whether or not $\phi$ is valid in $M$, i.e. whether or not $M \models_L \phi$. Model checking-based verification has been studied in connection with temporal logic. The technique once again relies upon the close relationship between models for temporal logic and finite-state machines. Suppose that $\phi$ is the specification for some system, and $\pi$ is a program that claims to implement $\phi$. Then, to determine whether or not $\pi$ truly implements $\phi$, we take $\pi$, and from it generate a model $M_\pi$ that corresponds to $\pi$, in the sense that $M_\pi$ encodes all the possible computations of $\pi$; determine whether or not $M_\pi \models \phi$, i.e. whether the specification formula $\phi$ is valid in $M_\pi$; the program $\pi$ satisfies the specification $\phi$ just in case the answer is "yes". The main advantage of model checking over axiomatic verification is in complexity: model checking using the branching time temporal logic CTL ([7]) can be done in polynomial time, whereas the proof problem for most modal logics is quite complex.

In [44], Rao and Georgeff present an algorithm for model checking agent systems. More precisely, they give an algorithm for taking a logical model for their (propositional) BDI agent specification language, and a formula of the language, and determining whether the formula is valid in the model. The technique is closely based on model checking algorithms for normal modal logics [19]. They show that despite the inclusion of three extra modalities (for beliefs, desires, and intentions), into the CTL branching time framework, the algorithm is still quite efficient, running in polynomial time. So the second step of the two-stage model checking process described above can still be done efficiently. However, it is not clear how the first step might be realized for BDI logics. Where does the logical model characterizing an agent actually comes from — can it be derived from an arbitrary program $\pi$, as in mainstream computer science? To do this, we would need to take a program implemented in, say, PASCAL, and from it derive the belief, desire, and intention accessibility relations that are used to give a semantics to the BDI component of the logic. Because, as we noted earlier, there is no clear relationship between the BDI logic and the concrete computational models used to implement agents, it is not clear how such a model could be derived.

## 7. Conclusions

In this article, we have given a summary of why agents should be perceived to be a significant technology for software engineering, and also of the main techniques for the specification, implementation, and verification of agent systems. Software engineering for agent systems is at an early stage of development, and yet the widespread acceptance of the concept of an agent implies that agents have a significant future in software engineering. If the technology is to be a success, then its software engineering aspects will need to be taken seriously. Probably the most important outstanding issues for agent-based software engineering are: (i) an understanding of the situations in which agent solutions are appropriate; and (ii) principled but *informal* development techniques for agent systems. While some attention has been given to the latter (in the form of analysis and design methodologies for agent systems [30, 60, 39, 10, 3, 29, 53]), almost no attention has been given to the former (but see [59]).

## 8. How to Find Out More About Agents

There are now many introductions to intelligent agents and multiagent systems. Ferber [14] is an undergraduate textbook, although as its name suggests, this volume focussed on multiagent aspects rather than on the theory and practice of individual agents. A first-rate collection of articles introducing agent and multiagent systems is Weiß [51]. Two collections of research articles provide a comprehensive introduction to the field of autonomous rational agents and multiagent systems: Bond and Gasser's 1988 collection, *Readings in Distributed Artificial Intelligence*, introduces almost all the basic problems in the multiagent systems field, and although some of the papers it contains are now rather dated, it remains essential reading [4]; Huhns and Singh's more recent collection sets itself the ambitious goal of providing a survey of the whole of the agent field, and succeeds in this respect very well [22]. For a general introduction to the theory and practice of intelligent agents, see Wooldridge and Jennings [58], which focuses primarily on the theory of agents, but also contains an extensive review of agent architectures and programming languages. For a collection of articles on the applications of agent technology, see [28]. A comprehensive roadmap of agent technology was published as [27].

# References

1. G. Agha, P. Wegner and A. Yonezawa, *Research Directions in Concurrent Object-Oriented Programming* (The MIT Press, Cambridge, MA, 1993).
2. H. Barringer, M. Fisher, D. Gabbay, G. Gough and R. Owens, "METATEM: A framework for programming in temporal logic", *REX Workshop on Stepwise Refinement of Distributed Systems: Models, Formalisms, Correctness Lecture Notes in Computer Science 430* (Springer-Verlag, Berlin, Germany, June 1989) 94–129.
3. B. Bauer, J. P. Müller and J. Odell, "Agent UML: A formalism for specifying multiagent software systems", eds. P. Ciancarini and M. Wooldridge, *Agent-Oriented Software Engineering, Proceedings of the First International Workshop (AOSE'2000)* (Springer-Verlag, Berlin, Germany, 2000).
4. A. H. Bond and L. Gasser, *Readings in Distributed Artificial Intelligence* (Morgan Kaufmann Publishers, San Mateo, CA, 1988).
5. C. Brown, L. Gasser, D. E. O'Leary and Alan Sangster, "AI on the WWW: Supply and demand agents", *IEEE Expert* **10**, no. 4 (August 1995) 44–49.
6. B. Chellas, *Modal Logic: An Introduction* (Cambridge University Press, Cambridge, England, 1980).
7. E. M. Clarke, O. Grumberg and D. A. Peled, *Model Checking* (The MIT Press, Cambridge, MA, 2000).
8. P. R. Cohen and H. J. Levesque, "Intention is choice with commitment", *Artificial Intelligence* **42** (1990) 213–261.
9. D. C. Dennett, *The Intentional Stance* (The MIT Press, Cambridge, MA, 1987).
10. R. Depke, R. Heckel and J. M. Kuester, "Requirement specification and design of agent-based systems with graph transformation, roles, and uml", eds. P. Ciancarini and M. Wooldridge, *Agent-Oriented Software Engineering, Proceedings of the First International Workshop (AOSE'2000)*. (Springer-Verlag, Berlin, Germany, 2000).
11. E. H. Durfee, *Coordination of Distributed Problem Solvers* (Kluwer Academic Publishers, Boston, MA, 1988).
12. O. Etzioni and D. S. Weld, "Intelligent agents on the internet: Fact, fiction, and forecast", *IEEE Expert* **10**, no. 4 (August 1995) 44–49.
13. R. Fagin, J. Y. Halpern, Y. Moses and M. Y. Vardi, *Reasoning About Knowledge* (The MIT Press, Cambridge, MA, 1995).
14. J. Ferber, *Multi-Agent Systems* (Addison-Wesley, Reading, MA, 1999).
15. N. V. Findler and R. Lo, "An examination of distributed planning in the world of air traffic control", *Journal of Parallel and Distributed Computing* **3** (1986).
16. M. Fisher, "A survey of concurrent METATEM — The language and its applications", eds. D. M. Gabbay and H. J. Ohlbach, *Temporal Logic, Proceedings of the First International Conference (LNAI Volume 827)* (Springer-Verlag, Berlin, Germany, July 1994) 480–505.

17. M. Fisher and M. Wooldridge, "On the formal specification and verification of multi-agent systems", *International Journal of Cooperative Information Systems* **6**, no. 1 (1997) 37–65.

18. M. P. Georgeff and A. L. Lansky, "Reactive reasoning and planning", *Proceedings of the Sixth National Conference on Artificial Intelligence (AAAI'87)* Seattle, WA (1987) 677–682.

19. J. Y. Halpern and M. Y. Vardi, "Model checking versus theorem proving: A manifesto", eds. V. Lifschitz, *AI and Mathematical Theory of Computation — Papers in Honor of John McCarthy* (The Academic Press, London, England, 1991) 151–176.

20. C. A. R. Hoare, "An axiomatic basis for computer programming", *Communications of the ACM* **12**, no. 10 (1969) 576–583.

21. C. A. R. Hoare, "Communicating sequential processes", *Communications of the ACM* **21** (1978) 666–677.

22. M. Huhns and M. P. Singh, *Readings in Agents* (Morgan Kaufmann Publishers, San Mateo, CA, 1998).

23. N. R. Jennings, "On agent-base software engineering", *Artificial Intelligence* **117** (2000) 277–296.

24. N. R. Jennings, J. M. Corera and I. Laresgoiti, "Developing industrial multi-agent systems", *Proceedings of the First International Conference on Multi-Agent Systems (ICMAS'95)*, San Francisco, CA (June 1995) 423–430.

25. N. R. Jennings, T. J. Norman, P. Faratin, P. O'Brien and B. Odgers, "Autonomous agents for business process management", *Applied Artificial Intelligence Journal* **14** no. 2 (2000) 145–190.

26. N. R. Jennings, T. J. Norman, P. Faratin, P. O'Brien and B. Odgers, "Implementing a business process management system using ADEPT: A real-world case study", *Applied Artificial Intelligence Journal* **14**, no. 5 (2000) 421–490.

27. N. R. Jennings, K. Sycara and M. Wooldridge, "A roadmap of agent research and development", *Autonomous Agents and Multi-Agent Systems* **1**, no. 1 (1998) 7–38.

28. N. R. Jennings and M. Wooldridge, *Agent Technology: Foundations, Applications and Markets* (Springer-Verlag, Berlin, Germany, 1998).

29. E. A. Kendall, "Agent software engineering with role modelling", eds. P. Ciancarini and M. Wooldridge, *Agent-Oriented Software Engineering, Proceedings of the First International Workshop (AOSE'2000)* (Springer-Verlag, Berlin, Germany, 2000).

30. D. Kinny and M. Georgeff, "Modelling and design of multi-agent systems", eds. J. P. Müller, M. Wooldridge and N. R. Jennings, *Intelligent Agents III, Lecture Notes in Artificial Intelligence 1193* (Springer-Verlag, Berlin, Germany, 1997).

31. M. Klusch, *Intelligent Information Agents* (Springer-Verlag, Berlin, Germany, 1999).

32. V. R. Lesser and L. D. Erman, "Distributed interpretation: A model and experiment", *IEEE Transactions on Computers* **C-29**, no. 12 (1980) 1144–1163.

33. M. Ljunberg and A. Lucas, "The OASIS air traffic management system", *Proceedings of the Second Pacific Rim International Conference on AI (PRICAI'92)*, Seoul, Korea (1992).

34. P. Maes, "Agents that reduce work and information overload", *Communications of the ACM* **37**, no. 7 (July 1994) 31–40.

35. Z. Manna and A. Pnueli, *Temporal Verification of Reactive Systems — Safety* (Springer-Verlag, Berlin, Germany, 1995).

36. K. Mori, H. Torikoshi, K. Nakai and T. Masuda, "Computer control system for iron and steel plants", *Hitachi Review* **37**, no. 4 (1988) 251–258.

37. N. Negroponte, *Being Digital* (Hodder and Stoughton, 1995).

38. S. Oaks and H. Wong, *Jini in a Nutshell* (O'Reilly & Associates, Inc., 2000).

39. J. Odell, H. van D. Parunak and B. Bauer, "Representing agent interaction protocols in UML", eds. P. Ciancarini and M. Wooldridge, *Agent-Oriented Software Engineering, Proceedings of the First International Workshop (AOSE'2000)* (Springer-Verlag, Berlin, Germany, 2000).

40. The Object Management Group (OMG), *http://www.omg.org/*

41. A. Pnueli and R. Rosner, "On the synthesis of a reactive module, *Proceedings of the Sixteenth ACM Symposium on the Principles of Programming Languages (POPL)* (January 1989) 179–190.

42. A. S. Rao, "AgentSpeak(L): BDI agents speak out in a logical computable language", eds. W. Van de Velde and J. W. Perram, *Agents Breaking Away, Proceedings of the Seventh European Workshop on Modelling Autonomous Agents in a Multi-Agent World, Lecture Notes in Artificial Intelligence 1038* (Springer-Verlag, Berlin, Germany, 1996) 42–55.

43. A. S. Rao and M. Georgeff, "BDI Agents: From theory to practice", *Proceedings of the First International Conference on Multi-Agent Systems (ICMAS'95)* San Francisco, CA (June 1995) 312–319.

44. A. S. Rao and M. P. Georgeff, "A model-theoretic approach to the verification of situated reasoning systems", *Proceedings of the Thirteenth International Joint Conference on Artificial Intelligence (IJCAI'93)*, Chambéry, France (1993) 318–324.

45. S. Rosenschein and L. P. Kaelbling, "The synthesis of digital machines with provable epistemic properties", ed. J. Y. Halpern, *Proceedings of the 1986 Conference on Theoretical Aspects of Reasoning About Knowledge* (Morgan Kaufmann Publishers, San Mateo, CA, 1986) 83–98.

46. S. J. Rosenschein and L. P. Kaelbling, "A situated view of representation and control", eds. P. E. Agre and S. J. Rosenschein, *Computational Theories of Interaction and Agency* (The MIT Press, Cambridge, MA, 1996) 515–540.

47. Y. Shoham, "Agent-oriented programming", *Artificial Intelligence* **60**, no. 1 (1993) 51–92.

48. R. G. Smith, *A Framework for Distributed Problem Solving* (UMI Research Press, 1980).

49. R. Steeb, S. Cammarata, F. A. Hayes-Roth, P. W. Thorndyke and R. B. Wesson, "Distributed intelligence for air fleet control", eds. A. H. Bond and L. Gasser, *Readings in Distributed Artificial Intelligence* (Morgan Kaufmann Publishers, San Mateo, CA, 1988) 90–101.

50. H. van D. Parunak, "Manufacturing experience with the contract net", ed. M. Huhns, *Distributed Artificial Intelligence* (Pitman Publishing, London and Morgan Kaufmann, San Mateo, CA, 1987) 285–310.

51. G. Weiß, *Multi-Agent Systems* (The MIT Press, Cambridge, MA, 1999).

52. J. E. White, "Telescript technology: The foundation for the electronic marketplace", White Paper (General Magic, Inc., 2465 Latham Street, Mountain View, CA 94040, 1994).

53. M. Wood and S. A. DeLoach, "An overview of the multiagent systems engineering methodology", eds. P. Ciancarini and M. Wooldridge, *Agent-Oriented Software Engineering, Proceedings of the First International Workshop (AOSE'2000)* (Springer-Verlag, Berlin, Germany, 2000).

54. M. Wooldridge, *The Logical Modelling of Computational Multi-Agent Systems*, PhD Thesis, Department of Computation, UMIST, Manchester, UK (October 1992).

55. M. Wooldridge, "Agent-based software engineering", *IEE Proceedings on Software Engineering* **144**, no. 1 (February 1997) 26–37.

56. M. Wooldridge, *Reasoning About Rational Agents* (The MIT Press, Cambridge, MA, 2000).

57. M. Wooldridge, S. Bussmann and M. Klosterberg, "Production sequencing as negotiation", *Proceedings of the First International Conference on the Practical Application of Intelligent Agents and Multi-Agent Technology (PAAM'96)*, London, UK (April 1996) 709–726.

58. M. Wooldridge and N. R. Jennings, "Intelligent agents: Theory and practice", *The Knowledge Engineering Review* **10**, no. 2 (1995) 115–152.

59. M. Wooldridge and N. R. Jennings, "Pitfalls of agent-oriented development", *Proceedings of the Second International Conference on Autonomous Agents (Agents'98)*, Minneapolis/St Paul, MN (May 1998) 385–391.

60. M. Wooldridge, N. R. Jennings and D. Kinny, "A methodology for agent-oriented analysis and design", *Proceedings of the Third International Conference on Autonomous Agents (Agents'99)*, Seattle, WA (May 1999) 69–76.

# SOFTWARE CONFIGURATION MANAGEMENT IN SOFTWARE AND HYPERMEDIA ENGINEERING: A SURVEY

L. BENDIX

*Department of Computer Science,*
*Aalborg University, Fredrik Bajers Vej 7E, 9220 Aalborg Øst, Denmark*
*E-mail: bendix@cs.auc.dk*


A. DATTOLO

*Dipartimento di Matematica ed Applicazioni, Università di Napoli "Federico II",*
*via Cinthia, Monte Sant'Angelo, 80126 Napoli, Italy*
*E-mail: antonina.dattolo@dma.unina.it*


F. VITALI

*Department of Computer Science,*
*University of Bologna, Mura A. Zamboni, 7, 40127 Bologna, Italy*
*E-mail: fabio@cs.unibo.it*

Software configuration management (SCM) is a very important feature in the software development area and in many authoring fields. The main purpose of this survey is to introduce readers to SCM in software and hypermedia engineering, presenting general concepts, principles and techniques and considering advantages and open issues. The new challenges proposed by World Wide Web (WWW), which can be seen both as a complex distributed hypermedia system and as a software development environment, are discussed.

*Keywords*: Configuration management, version control, build management, version, maintenance, traceability, coordination, referential integrity.

## 1. Introduction

In software development, the evolution process is characterized by continuous changes. Typically, a team of people produces, changes and exchanges common and individual software parts, working together towards a common goal. Often, the goal is not a single static object, but a dynamic collection of components designed to work with each other. Not all assemblies may result in a complete and consistent product, and the collection is often composed of a large number of components, with several persons at different sites maintaining and changing them; the entire development process often becomes a continuous history of changes, revisions and improvements. To keep all multi-version, multi-people activities under control, it is fundamental to introduce the concepts collectively called "software configuration management" (SCM).

*SCM is the discipline of organizing, controlling and managing the development and evolution of software systems.*

The goal of using SCM is to ensure the integrity of a software artefact and to make its evolution more manageable; this objective is obtained by identifying the configuration of the software at discrete points in time and systematically controlling changes to the identified configuration for the purpose of maintaining software integrity, traceability and accountability throughout the software life cycle [1].

Naturally, the use of SCM implies an additional overhead in time, resources, and other aspects of the software lifecycle. However it is generally agreed that the consequences of not using SCM can lead to many problems and inefficiencies [2]. SCM is important for any design task, including software development, word processing, spreadsheet applications, hypermedia authoring, computer-aided design and manufacturing, databases and many other applications in which data is entered and revised frequently.

SCM has been particularly investigated in software engineering [3] and computer-aided design databases [4]. More recently, the advent of the WWW [5] and the possibility to use it as shared virtual workspace by a team of people have encouraged SCM research in hypermedia engineering.

The term "hypermedia engineering" [6] is quite recent; but it is defined using a similar definition as for software engineering [7], as the "employment of a systematic, disciplined, quantifiable approach to the development, operation and maintenance of hypermedia applications".

The goal of this survey is to introduce readers to SCM in software engineering, showing general existing and proven techniques and explaining their main features. The second step is to deepen the discussion on SCM in hypermedia engineering.

The rationale of this choice is in the important roles played on the one hand by hypermedia systems in software engineering, and on the other hand, by configuration management concepts in hypermedia authoring. This is due in part to the explosion of WWW, that is at the same time the widest known hypermedia system, the largest and most complex software system, and the "meeting point" for distributed and collaborative workgroups. An additional reason to discuss SCM in hypermedia engineering is the strong interdependence that links software engineering and hypermedia engineering; in fact, several tools and concepts of software engineering are applied to the development, use and maintenance of hypermedia systems.

In Sec. 2, we introduce SCM, providing a set of preliminary definitions and discussing traditional approaches to it. Section 3 presents general concepts, principles and techniques of SCM, considering advantages and open issues. Section 4 deepens the discussion on SCM in hypermedia engineering, presenting specific advantages and issues, and a brief history of existing hypermedia supporting SCM and highlighting the new challenges introduced in SCM by the advent of the World Wide Web. Finally, Sec. 5 ends the paper with an account of the contributions of academic research and a look to the future perspectives.

## 2. Introduction to SCM

This section provides an introduction to SCM. In order to make it easier for the reader and avoid confusion, Subsec. 2.1 provides some preliminary definitions.

### 2.1. *Some preliminary definitions*

SCM has been investigated in many software development areas; in part due to this reason, there is a tremendous amount of overloading of terminology. Some attempts of unification have been proposed [4, 8, 9], but, to assure there is no confusion in the reading of this paper, we provide the following definitions:

- **Configuration item:** A configuration item is each single software item that is individually identifiable as a logical entity. A configuration item can be atomic, like documents and modules, or composed, like libraries and systems.
- **Version:** A version is one specific instance of a configuration item. It provides a stable referencing mechanism for the management of configuration items. All versions but working versions are frozen, i.e. they cannot be changed without creating a new version.
- **Revision:** A revision is the kind of version that is a step in the evolution of a configuration item; it supersedes an earlier version and may contain arbitrary changes compared with its predecessor. Typically, it is created to fix bugs or to support permanent changes [10].
- **Variant:** Variants are alternative versions of a configuration item. They remain valid at a given instant in time and are typically created to handle environmental differences. A collection of variants of configuration items taken from specified revision levels defines the **version-set**.
- **Release:** A release is a version set that passed some defined quality assurance measures and is ready for a customer [11].

Versions, revisions, .variants and releases are typically organized in a version graph, as in Fig. 1, where the boxes represent the single configuration items.

A software product is in version 3.0 for Windows (3.0 WIN). Horizontal arrows represent revisions (3.1 WIN — 3.2 WIN — 3.3 WIN — 3.4 WIN), while diagonal arrows represent variants (1.0 UNIX). A succession of revisions (1.1 UNIX — 1.2 UNIX) can produce a new release (2.0 UNIX).

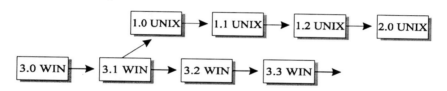

**Fig. 1.** Configuration items, versions, variants, revisions, releases.

We have defined SCM as the discipline for organizing, controlling and managing the development and evolution of software systems. In this paper, we will use interchangeably the terms SCM and versioning, although the second term, versioning, will be principally used in the discussion of hypermedia engineering aspects.

## 2.2. *Configuration management and version control*

The timely and orderly development of quality software is both a challenging and difficult task. Software systems tend to grow ever bigger and the complexity of their development and maintenance becomes very hard to handle. Complex software systems such as the space-shuttle software or air-traffic control systems are amongst the most complex things ever constructed by man. They are the result of the cooperation of many people who have worked together as a large team, each person or group managing just a small part of the complete system. We thus need methods and mechanisms to be able to divide a large system up into manageable parts and, even more important, to put those parts back together again to form a whole system.

In other situations, such as for telephone switchboard systems the management of the development of the system is further complicated by the fact that such systems are developed and maintained in many different versions and variants. The development of these different versions and variants must proceed in a controlled fashion and all versions and variants must be preserved for back-up purposes. Furthermore, since each part of a system may exist in several versions, we must have ways to control, record and query exactly which version of each part went into the final product.

These are some of the problems dealt with in the discipline, which was named "software engineering" at a NATO conference in 1968.

Configuration management and version control are two very important and fundamental activities in the software development process [12], and we believe that, together with results from fields like programming languages, development methodologies, and programming environments in general, configuration management leads to a distinct improvement in the general capability to produce high-quality software.

Some of the major problems in managing the development of large software systems are related to *the size of the system* (in lines of code), *the size of the project* (in number of people), and *the number of versions* of both the system and its components. Most modern programming languages contain a modularization concept to help divide up a big system into smaller parts. This leads to the problem of having to assemble these parts to obtain a complete system, which, together with deriving object-code from source-code, is one of the problems dealt with by configuration management.

A multitude of different versions of the same item will come into existence during the lifetime of a project. This is due to the fact that bugs will be corrected and functionality will be changed or extended. We need to record information as to what has changed, why and by whom the change was made in order to be able to control the evolution of objects. Version control deals with all these problems.

Traditional approaches to configuration management and version control tend to view people as working in isolation and as such they give very little support for cooperation. A good support for cooperation will have impact on the way version control is performed and a proper integration between configuration management and version control becomes a mandatory requirement.

Today's systems tend to be long-lived and therefore most of the effort and money will go into actually maintaining the system. This implies that many changes — corrective as well as perfective — will be carried out during its lifetime, and it is therefore of the utmost importance to have good models, methods and tools for configuration management and version control such that good change control can be exercised.

Traditionally configuration management and version control have been seen as rather bureaucratic tasks (for instance in [13, 14]), where clerical paperwork and standards are the main preoccupation. Other authors, like [15, 16], looking at configuration management as a practical problem having a practical solution, have a strong tool perspective and focus much on the basic mechanisms and capabilities the programming environment must have in order to provide support for configuration management and version control [17].

## 3. Configuration Management Concepts and Principles

SCM was born out of the 1968 NATO conference and specific military needs for much better control over software development efforts; it is an evolution of traditional configuration management. Configuration management was not something new, as it was practised in most other industries. However, to apply its principles to software development was — and still is to some extent — something new. For this reason, the military and its needs were the driving forces behind transferring and adapting configuration management to software development. Later on it was recognized that also non-military software development could benefit from exercising configuration management. This led to a shift in focus away from bureaucratic paperwork and control towards productivity and coordination.

According to [2], SCM is more complex than the traditional configuration management due to the malleability of the software: changes are easy to perform and occur more often that in traditional configuration management areas, software is simple to duplicate, which obliges SCM to manage multiple copies of a software component, some private, some public, each having its individual set of changes which may diverge in time, and, most importantly, the application of a change in a single component may induce hard-to-trace failures in other components due to non-evident dependencies among modules. On the other hand, SCM can be widely automated, since all the components are under computer control. This partly compensates for the added complexity.

The two single most important principles of SCM are the *immutability* of components and unique *identification* of components. Immutability of components is needed to ensure that no part of the development history — and thus traceability — of a component is lost. Once a component has been created and "published" it must remain unaltered and accessible forever. If need occurs to change the component, a copy must be taken, modified and subsequently added to the pool of immutable components. Once we apply this principle it is easy to see why we need unique identification too. If we cannot directly change a component, we will soon have several almost identical copies of it and thus we need to uniquely identify each of these copies.

The evolution of SCM is reflected in the structure of this section. First, we explain the concepts and principles behind traditional SCM as defined by the military standards. Then we present how SCM is considered in a more pragmatic approach where military rigor is not needed.

## 3.1. *Traditional configuration management*

In the traditional perspective, which favours management needs, the objectives of performing SCM are to maintain product integrity, to obtain traceability, and to ensure accountability in software development.

The exposition in this subsection is based on approaches like [13, 14] that show the connection from hardware configuration management to SCM. In particular, we highlight four operational aspects: configuration identification, control, status accounting and audit.

### 3.1.1. *Configuration identification*

One of the fundamental principles of SCM is unique identification. The configuration identification activity covers both the identification of what things have to be covered and how they are named. This activity should ideally be carried out at the beginning of a project as a part of the planning phase.

We need to choose what should be put under control in the project. This includes far more than just the source code that will be produced. Things such as requirements, design, documentation, test cases are among the candidates to be put under control depending on the nature of the project. Each single entity that is individually identifiable is called a configuration item. Configuration items can be either atomic or composed; examples of the latter are configurations or sub-systems. Composed configuration items are, however, considered atomic entities at a higher level.

For each type of configuration item we have to plan how we want to structure configuration items belonging to that type. This structure will become part of identifying the configuration items. This is, however, not enough to uniquely identify items. For each type of configuration items we must decide on a naming scheme that allows us to identify it more precisely. Furthermore, we have to deal with the different versions of each single configuration item. Numbering schemes will have to be defined for versions, variants and releases.

### 3.1.2. *Configuration control*

Configuration control addresses the old wisdom "if it ain't broken, don't fix it". Changes to a system are made because it is broken in some way or some functionality is missing. This means that the central points for this activity are change requests and how they are handled from birth to implementation. Having this controlled and documented contributes towards the objectives of traceability and accountability.

Not all change requests should be implemented and not all changes are equally important. In order to decide what should be implemented and to prioritize changes we must form a committee. This is known as the configuration (or change) control board and consists of representatives of both supplier and customer. The board makes its decisions based on information that may be provided by people outside of the board. Each change request must be documented, it has to be analyzed and the impact of carrying it out has to be estimated. The configuration control board approves all changes before they are implemented and it also follows the implementation status of approved changes.

Another part of the configuration control activity has to do with the creation of a safe repository for all the configuration items of a project. The easy part of this is to find reliable storage; the more difficult part has to do with defining and enforcing access rules to the items. It must be defined who has access to what and how the access is performed. Usually access happens through a checkout operation that locks the item, in order to avoid that other people work on it; when the user has finished working on the item he releases the new version through a checkin operation.

### 3.1.3. *Configuration status accounting*

Configuration status accounting is the activity of keeping historical records of what has happened as far as Configuration Management is involved, and of using them in the CM process itself. Data must be collected and it must be reported. Usually the information is used by management and by the configuration control board.

Loads of data are created by the other activities during the development process and unless this data is organized in a way that we can analyze and act upon, it is of no use. The activity can be broken down into data capture, data processing, and data reporting. Reports must be written in such a way that they can be used. The number, type and form of reports needed will depend or the specific organization's needs. Statistics is another type of data that is usually recorded as part of this configuration management activity.

Management use the status accounting reports to keep track of the current state of the system. Without this information it will not be able to know if the project is on track and what to do if it is not. Furthermore, management can assess the effects of the SCM process through the information available in the reports. This is a fact that is often overlooked by configuration managers who find a hard time justifying the resources spent on the configuration management process and tools. The change control board will need a different kind of reports from the status accounting activity. In order to perform their job they will need reports of proposed and approved changes and of problem reports. Furthermore, they will need information that enables them to follow the implementation status of approved changes such that problems can be discovered early and acted upon quickly.

### 3.1.4. *Configuration audit*

The main purpose of this activity is to ensure the quality and maintain the integrity of both the product that is being built and the information that are being collected. Configuration audit is the activity of verifying and validating the fact that a proposed configuration is complete, accurate and consistent. It is also the activity where it is ensured that the recorded information is reliable and that the designated processes were followed and that they work properly. It usually consists of functional configuration audits, physical configuration audits and configuration verification audits.

The functional configuration audit is conducted on the engineering prototype and its purpose is to assure that tests have been conducted to verify that each requirement has been met by the design. Even if formal tests cannot be carried out for some requirements, at least an error analysis must be performed to verify compliance. Physical configuration audit is started after the completion of the functional configuration audit. During physical configuration audit, software components (implemented modules) are verified by comparing them with the design units. Furthermore, revisions must be compared and verified. At the end of this activity an acceptance test is carried out to assure that the examined components are the same as those that passed the functional configuration audit. The configuration verification audit is conducted on both the entire configuration (system) and on the single components to ensure that integrity has been maintained after changes. It is important to verify that changes have been documented so that there is traceability between change requests and modified components. Furthermore, it is important to document and record the way in which components and configurations have been built. This is often done by recording bill of materials that state exactly how and from what a system — or subsystem — was constructed.

## 3.2. *Practical configuration management*

The early objectives of configuration management were to maintain product integrity and to ensure complete control and accountability of its development, which led to configuration management being practised as described above. This is, however, far too expensive an approach for small and medium size projects and in general for projects that do not need total control and accountability. Furthermore, traditional configuration management has very little help to offer the developer in his daily work, as its focus is on management needs. Emphasis has thus changed and more focus has been put on the coordination for team productivity [15], putting SCM into a wider perspective [18], and best configuration management practices [16] based on the traditional model. This has led to a different focus where the sub-division is: version control, coordination support, build management and configuration control [19].

### 3.2.1. *Version control*

For many reasons it is convenient to keep, or to be able to recreate, a component. Version control is the activity that allows us to do this, and it has to address several problems. It has to minimize the storage space needed to keep all versions of a file. It has to impose a structure on how versions can develop from each other. And, finally, it has to keep track of all information about the different versions. This could be done manually, but using a tool, these tasks are automated and are not prone to human errors.

Each single components of a given system will undergo many changes during the development and maintenance of that system. The set of changes that transform one version of a component into a new version is called a *delta* and represents the difference between the two versions. In addition to the actual changes, we are also interested in keeping other useful information about the change such as who did it, when, for what reason. This information is called the *log entry* for a version. Together with the delta, the log entry constitutes one history step in the development history of a component.

The structure that a version control tool imposes on the development of history steps is called a *version graph* and is basically linear (Fig. 2(a)). One version follows the other and a new version is always created from the end of the line, as is the case for the tool SCCS [20]. For simple development needs this model is sufficient even though limited. However, it cannot support maintenance (i.e., further development of) older versions, it does not handle parallel development (for instance, additional development and maintenance going on in parallel) and thus variants of the same component cannot be represented in this model. To solve that problem most tools allow branches to be created from older versions and thus support the tree model (Fig. 2(b)) that was introduced in RCS [21]. In this model, several branches can exist in parallel to reflect either maintenance of older versions, parallel work or

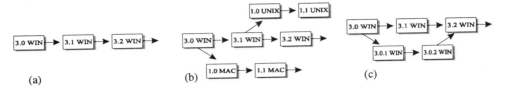

**Fig. 2.**   Version graph structures: linear (a), tree (b) and acyclic graph(c) models.

variants. Other models support acyclic graphs (Fig. 2(c)); in this way, a version may have two or more predecessors, for example, in order to express that a bug fix in an old version is merged with the currently developed version.

The degree to which it is possible to represent information about versions varies between tools. Most tools, however, have the possibility to save textual information about a version, which means that any information could be represented that way. The drawback of having information represented as text is that it becomes difficult to search for information. Most tools have a number of attributes connected with each version and these attributes can be used whenever we want to retrieve a version from the repository.

### 3.2.2. *Coordination support*

Today all but the smallest projects are carried out as group efforts. Many people work together on the same product towards a common goal. We need to coordinate the effort of these people such that they do not interfere with each other's work. On the other hand, we should also allow them to be as productive as possible.

Many problems can happen when people share things and want to change them, as pointed out by [15]. The core of the problem is that we really do not want people to share things that are being changed, even though their parts go towards the common system. If something that is under my control is changed by someone else, I might not be aware of it and I might be misled to believe that I introduced an error, when in reality it was introduced by their change. So it is important to work isolated from the changes that other people make. Sometimes people may share documents and may want to change the shared document. If that is not coordinated properly, the change of one authors may be lost, as it gets overwritten by the other changes. To have identical copies of shared documents is not a viable solution, as it will soon become even more difficult to keep the copies identical.

In order to solve these problems we can try to keep the components as small as possible to make sure that there is no need to share components. This is often not possible and we have to allow some degree of sharing of components. If components are shared we will have to deal with the fact that there might be the need to carry out changes in parallel. Two different strategies are used here: one is to forbid it, the other to support it. When it is forbidden changes have to be sequentialized. This is done by locking components before they can be changed, the lock making sure that only one person at a time can change the component. Tools that allow components to be changed in parallel simply create a branch to reflect that two parallel changes are going on, as is the case using CVS [22]. Most tools are also able to merge the two branches together back into one version to get the composite of the two changes.

The problem of other people's changes having an impact on the system without us being aware of it is handled differently. What we would like to obtain are periods where we work in isolation from other changes, and periods where we want to integrate our own changes with those of other people. We can use the workspace for that purpose. The central repository handles stable versions of the configuration items. In the workspace we copy (check-out) the items we intend to work on, and also a copy of all components of the system. When a change is checked into the repository by someone else, the copy in our workspace will remain the same. When we check in the contents of our own workspace, we will check in only those components that we have actually changed. Furthermore, as most tools allow parallel work, there is the possibility that someone else has made a change to a component that we have changed too and the two changes have to be merged. If this is the case the later person to check in has the responsibility to make sure that the merge has been carried out correctly and that all conflicts are resolved.

### 3.2.3. *Build management*

Build management handles the problems created by following the good programming advice to divide large programs into modules [23]. These modules have to be put back together and compiled in order to create a running system. The number of modules or components in a system is increased by the fact that we might want to keep them as small as possible to avoid sharing conflicts.

To build a system from its components we need both a description of the structure of the system and information about how to derive object code from the source code modules. The description is called a *system model* and is used to instantiate specific systems. In early tools like make [24] both the *system model* and the information about how to derive object code and link it together was given in one single resource — the makefile. This automates the build process and avoids errors from human intervention. Furthermore, make implements a minimal build as it only recompiles source modules that are out-of-date with respect to existing object code. This can lead to huge savings in compile time for big systems, if only a small part of the system has been changed.

Further improvements have been made to build tools to remove the limitations of the original. The most severe problem with the original make is that it keeps no data of its own. To decide whether an object module is up-to-date or not it uses timestamps from the file system. This can be very unsafe especially in distributed environments where there is no global clock. Furthermore, make does not remember the way a given object module was created. This means that source modules do not get recompiled if such things as compilation options are changed or another version of the compiler is used, and this may create several problems. Additionally, the successors of make take advantage of the fact that todays computers are networked and support for compilation in heterogeneous environments is common as is the support for parallel compilation.

### 3.2.4. *Configuration control*

The build management we just described has no notion of versions of modules. Each module that has to go into the system, described by the system model, is assumed to exist in only one version and the task managed by them is only to compile and link these modules as efficiently as possible. This works quite well for projects without version control — and in the case of working in a workspace that has all the needed modules locally. However, when we take a more global look some weaknesses of this approach become evident.

If we add versions to the modules this has to be reflected in the system model. For each node in our dependency graph we now have a version group instead of a single file. This is much the same we have when we look at the repository and want to check some (or all) modules out into our workspace. This means that the build tool must be extended with the ability to select from the repository. Unfortunately, not all queries to the repository are unambiguous. In the case of a human being checking something out, this is not a problem as he can refine the query to become unambiguous. However, a tool does not have that capacity. This means that we have to be very careful about how we write our selections. Most tools have opted for the rather unsafe solution to automatically (without user intervention) solve all ambiguities by choosing the latest version. However, once the selection has been made we are back to normal build management.

In the absence of versions (in our workspace) we can still run into troubles. If the structure of the system changes, this will have to be reflected in the system model. This implies that we will have to create a new system model for each change in the structure. So we will have to perform version control not just on the single modules, but also on the system model. Even worse we will have to make sure that the system model that is used to construct the system is also the same that was used to create our workspace. No existing tool does that automatically, so it all has to be done manually — exercising extreme care. Fortunately, most systems do not change structure very often, but if rapid prototyping is used as development model this issue may become prominent, and currently there is little help from existing tools.

## 4. Versioning Hypermedia and the Web

In the hypermedia field, the problems connected to configuration management have been frequently examined and discussed [25]. Of course, most of the problems that apply to other authoring or software development environments also apply to hypermedia. Yet, there are peculiarities in versioning inter-linked content, that at the same time pose some new problems, and propose an elegant solution to an important issue, referential integrity of links [26], that is specific of hypermedia. This may in part be the reason traditional approaches to versioning have been customized to the requirements specific of hypermedia.

Several important systems throughout the long history of hypermedia have discussed, implemented, or even relied on versioning functionalities, from Nelson's Xanadu [27] to the current IETF standardization effort WebDAV [28], ranging through well-known systems such as SEPIA ([29, 30]), Hyperform [31], and Microcosm [32]. One most important hypermedia system, the World Wide Web, has further exacerbated the complexity, the vastity and the diversity of the issues involved. In this section, we will first introduce the basic issues of versioning hypermedia, then a brief roundup of the systems and proposals that have made the history of this field, and then we will concentrate in considering the issues of versioning specifically to the World Wide Web, which can be seen both as an overly complex, anarchistic distributed hypertext system, and as the environment of choice for the sexiest software applications lately.

### 4.1. *Versioning hypermedia*

The versioning is considered as one of the relevant issues in modelling and building of hypermedia systems and its importance has been emphasized in [33] as regards its relationships with software engineering.

In situations where the hypermedia authoring is managed and controlled both within and outside of a workflow, the accounting and verification of the authoring activities provide important motivations for versioning; just like in the software engineering process, it is useful to compare the evolving states of the same resource in order to:

- determine the changes;
- evaluate the progress of the development;
- preserve former states and save them from destruction;
- reuse intermediate states;
- preserve the historical perspective of work done;
- maintain the consistency of the distributed resources [10]; and
- provide effective solutions to multi-user concurrency control [34].

Of course, versioning will only be accepted by the user if the effort spent on configuration management is out-weighed by the benefits. This imposes that the versioning must be carried out automatically, according to the session-based schema, instead of the user-decided approach that is required to let the user free to adopt the choices he prefers [29].

### 4.1.1. *Advantages*

The advantages deriving from applying version management benefit many aspects of the authoring process:

- *Exploratory authoring* is helped by versioning, since keeping a good and reliable baseline version makes authors more confident in trying out new development paths with their documents, even if these paths eventually turn out to be unviable or unacceptable.

- *Distributed and collaborative authoring* may profit the most from version support: verification and evaluation of others' contribution is eased by the possibility to compare their work with previous baseline versions of the resource; furthermore, if the chain of subsequent versions is allowed to fork into independent branches, then multiple authors can work on the same resource at the same time with no risk of overwriting.

- *Long transactions.* It has been noted (for instance see [34]) that in many creative authoring situations (including hypermedia) long transactions are crucial, because operations in authoring environments are often long-lived. In these situations of collaborative authoring efforts, especially if distributed geographically, it becomes fruitful to use *locking*, that prevents other users but the first to access and modify a resource, and *branching*, that forks the single flow of versions into two or more independent sequences, possibly later merged back together. Branching versions could even encourage emergent unplanned collaboration [35], whereby even simple readers of a published resource, if providing interesting suggestions, modifications, or additional links, could be accepted and published side-by-side with the main version of the resource.

- *Referential integrity of links.* Versioning constitutes an additional advantage for hypermedia, providing an easy solution to the old problem referred to as referential integrity of links [26], which can be shortly described as the problem of automatically updating references to positions in documents that have changed. In many situations, it is useful to link not just whole documents, but specific locations within them (the so-called point-to-point links). There are very good reasons to store links outside of the documents they connect, rather than embedded inside them *à la* HTML. For instance, external links allow linking into resources that we have no write access to, that are stored in a read-only medium, or that have been heavily linked to by other users for other purposes we are not interested in. Furthermore, external links allow private links, specialized trails, and multiple independent link sets to be created for the same document set. It is interesting to note that the W3C is proposing with XLink [36] a way to create external links on Web documents. Whenever a linked document changes, external links risk to point to the wrong place because of the changes themselves: whatever method is used for referring to a specific location of a document (e.g. counting, searching or naming), there exists a type of change that messes up the reference. To summarize, the referential integrity of links is at stake whenever the modification of a document does not update at the same time all the existing references to it, and especially when these references point to a specific location of the document. When no update is performed, we end up with dangling links, i.e., links that do not point to the correct destination. Automatically fixing dangling references can be performed either by applying a *"best bet"* *heuristics*, whereby the current link end-point is determined by finding the most similar content to the old end-point, or by *position tracking*, that is, by following change after change the evolution of the references, thus determining their current positions. Of these solutions, only position tracking guarantees a correct solution in all cases. Position tracking, on the other hand, requires fine-grained versioning, i.e., it requires the changes to a document to be correctly and orderly recorded, since it is by comparing them in a sufficiently fine-grained detail that it is possible, following version after version, to track the evolution of the relevant positions.

### 4.1.2. *Structural and cognitive issues*

The adoption of a versioning mechanism within a hypermedia system raises some important structural and cognitive issues:

- *Version models.* In [37], two basic version models were identified:
  - *State-based versioning* maintain the version of an individual resource; does not support the tracking of a set of changes involving several components of a hypertext network.
  - *Task-based versioning* focus on tracking versions of complex systems as a whole; it provides system support for maintaining the relationships between versions of resources that have been changed in a coordinated manner during the performance of a task. Holistic, task-based approaches to versioning are especially sensible in hypermedia, given the complex, multi-dimensional aspects of modifying a complex hypermedia network.

  These concepts are similar to those of state-based and change-based versioning as known in software engineering [38].
- *Immutability of frozen versions.* As discussed in [39], it represents an important structural problem. Intrinsic to any version model is the fact that older versions of a resource are frozen, that is, they cannot be changed without creating a new version of the resource. Yet it may be useful to allow frozen versions to have new links (for instance, annotations or comments) coming from and going to them without necessarily creating a new version of the resource. At the same time, some links are substantially

part of the resource itself, and thus their modification should definitely require the creation of a new version of the whole resource. Depending on their meaning and their role, therefore, the creation of some new links may or may not imply the creation of a new version of the resource. External link sets may seem a solution to this problem: when creating a new version of a resource, the author would also specify the set of substantial links (the ones that if modified would create a new version of the resource), while all other links would be considered as annotation links (and would not require a new version of the resource if changed or incremented).

## 4.2. *Hypermedia systems supporting versioning*

Version management is intrinsic and fundamental to the inner workings of the Xanadu system [27], one of the oldest proposals for hypermedia system. Xanadu proposes a peculiar way to organize the data, called the Xanalogical storage [40], where the documents (the minimal structure of the system) either actually contain their content (native bytes), or refer to it by inclusion from other documents (included bytes). In Xanadu, versioning is at the same time an immediate functionality of the system (a new version of a document is a new document that includes all the parts of a document that were present also in the previous version, and that has as native bytes all the new data) and a fundamental requirement for it to work: in Xanadu inclusions refer to their end-points by offsets, so that any change to the content of a document would corrupt the very structure of the inclusions unless exact tracking of the documents' evolution is activated through versioning. Later in time, both RHYTHM [41] and Palimpsest [42] proposed solutions similar to the Xanalogical storage, heavily relying on versioning for the management of correct inclusions.

Open hypermedia systems are largely used to address the complexity and heterogeneity of large-scale software development [43]. A body of research has been developed over the past two decades that has explored the effectiveness of this approach in supporting software engineering tasks; hypermedia was first used to support the construction of software systems in Neptune [44]. Neptune was built on top of the Hypertext Abstract Machine (HAM) [45] and featured integrated support for hypermedia within custom-built CAD applications. The elaboration of these first approaches has conducted towards interesting research that has been performed on:

- integrating hypermedia functionality [46] into all the tools of an integrated development environment (IDE) [47];
- examining how hypermedia services can influence the act of programming itself [48];
- developing and creating hypermedia-enabled programming environments [49, 50]; and

- using hypermedia in an attempt to raise the level of abstraction at which software engineers perform their software development tasks [51].

After the experience of the PIE system [52] and Halasz's powerful keynote address to the Hypertext '87 Conference [33], where versioning was mentioned as one of the main open issues in the hypermedia field, many researchers set out to study the subject: CoVer ([29, 30]) is a contextual version server that can provide both state-based and task-based version models for the SEPIA hypermedia authoring system; within HB3 [53] and Hyperform [31] researchers concentrated instead on abstracting the concept of version management from the actual hypertext systems they were going to provide such service for. An analytical approach to version management is presented in [54], where structural and cognitive issues are managed in a Petri net based hypermedia model.

In 1994 and 1995, two versioning workshops ([55, 56]) helped to further shape the field, examining aspects such as link selection, conceptual overhead in version freezing, and support for collaboration in distributed hypermedia. Among the hypertext systems that discussed the implementation of some kind of version support we will also include Microcosm [32] and Chimera [57].

A first attempt to manage versioning by means of a fully distributed and cooperative approach based on autonomous actors is proposed in [58] and successively extended with HyDe [59]. The formal model at the basis of HyDe is constituted by populations of independent and autonomous actors that work in a distributed and concurrent universe in order to reach the common goal of configuration management. It represents a first step in the definition of a reference model for the World Wide Web that, given its importance and diffusion, is discussed more in detail in the next section.

## 4.3. *Versioning the World Wide Web*

Even considering the WWW just as a distributed hypermedia systems, then the issues discussed previously also apply: the WWW is being provided with an external linking mechanism called XLink [36], which will provide sophisticated linking mechanism to XML [60] documents, and that will most prominently face the problem of referential integrity of its links. Furthermore, inclusion mechanisms for whole documents and parts thereof are already available even in HTML 4.0, and probably the lack of any position tracking mechanism for the end-points of the inclusions will hinder their use. An early proposal to deal with these issues was VTML (Versioned Text Markup Language) [61], a markup language to express change operations for WWW documents, in particular HTML. It should be noted that already HTML 4.0 [62] includes two tags, INS and DEL, that are meant to express changes from previous versions of the same document (e.g. in legal texts); unfortunately these tags, being part of the markup language, cannot express changes in the markup itself (e.g. that two paragraphs have been joined, that a link destination has been changed, etc) or changes that disrupt the correct nesting of the markup.

But the WWW is much more than a distributed hypermedia system: it is more and more the target platform of choice for software development, content provision, e-commerce, etc. As noted in [61], creating successful web sites requires the knowledge of a wide array of diverse and non-conventional tools, technologies and languages, by a large number of different authors with different skills, background, professional skills, few of which will probably have a background in change management and design. Other problems in the development of web sites can be found in the pace of development for Internet sites, which hinders the adoption of mature, process-driven development techniques, the number of slightly but not quite compatible client environments to build for, that forces the management of a very large number of variants of the same solutions, and the problems connected with the outsourcing and parcelization of the development and deployment, which, although in general a positive trend, may also add delays, misunderstandings, and incoherence in the development of web solutions. Even if no software applications are involved, but just content production, the potentials for corporate embarrassments or legal liabilities do exist in the production of any web site that does not provide a formalized process for change management and testing.

WebDAV ([63, 64]) is an IETF working group devoted to extend the HTTP protocol in order to provide a general, standardized framework for distributed authoring and versioning management for Web sites. The current specifications deal with distributed authoring, defining new methods, new headers and response codes for HTTP, a workable formalization of the existing PUT method, as well as the definition of "properties", meta-information parcels associated to editable resources. Two further working groups have been established within the main WebDAV activities, DASL (DAV Searching & Locating Working Group) [65] to provide querying mechanism for WebDAV-enabled sites, and Delta-V [66] to further extend the protocol for version management of web resources.

The WebDAV protocol provides concurrency control for write access to the same resources, allowing locks to be set and unset on shared resources. It provides a way to add, modify, delete and access arbitrary metadata of Web resources, so that the mere content of resources is enriched by an open set of properties, name-values pairs that can be freely associated with Web resources. It provides support for content independent links and relationships between resources. It provides support for server-side namespace manipulation, allowing authors to move, rename and copy web resources on a server. It provides support for collections, containers of resources allowing grouping, navigation, query, etc. Finally, the WebDAV protocol has set as a fundamental requirement that of providing the aforementioned services to all Web resources, regardless of their data type. This helps to make the HTTP protocol a truly interoperable distributed environment for collaboration and authoring.

Within this framework, the Delta-V group is providing further extensions in terms of methods, properties, response codes and headers, so as to provide version management for Web resources. The WebDAV versioning model includes the management of multiple versions of the same resources, independent access to each revision, parallel access and modification of the same versioned resources (branching) and the subsequent reunification of branches (merge), configuration management and collection versioning, under the same set of global requirements that WebDAV already has.

WebDAV does not provide direct support for the design and activation of change management processes, which are seen as fundamental to bring some order in the current chaos of web development. Furthermore, it does not provide direct support for small-granularity change tracking mechanisms, necessary for the automatic maintenance of the referential integrity of links. Unfortunately, these mechanisms are inherently content-type dependent and therefore outside of the scope of the WebDAV protocol.

Nonetheless, this protocol represents a fundamental step forward for the evolution of the Web towards a real distributed collaborative environment, and a necessary platform for these missing features and practices to be built.

## 5. Configuration Management Research and Concluding Remarks

Over the past twenty years, SCM has been largely investigated and it has become an indispensable support for the development and authoring of software products. The majority of research related to SCM is found in software engineering, but many issues encountered in this area are relevant to the hypermedia engineering, including version control, storage management or object identification [67]. The field of hypermedia has dealt with versioning issues for a long time, since Xanadu considered it a fundamental mechanism for its inner workings. The main difference in these two research areas is in the hypermedia management of explicit relationships among the resources being managed.

Versioning hypermedia presents a few new problems because of the management of *ad hoc* relationships among versioned resources. On the other hand, besides many more advantages, versioning provides an easy and safe solution to the well-known problem of referential integrity of links.

On the basis of this and similar observations on the reciprocal support provided by software engineering to hypermedia engineering and vice versa, and principally in consideration of the new challenges proposed by the WWW, this paper has been focused on SCM not only in software engineering but also in hypermedia engineering.

This survey has presented general concepts, principles and techniques, considering advantages and open issues; in this concluding section, we want to look into the research achievements of configuration management, both past and present. Furthermore we will point to what we anticipate to be the future problems of configuration management that have to be solved by new research. Academics and academic research has been and still is rather absent from what is happening in the configuration management world. The military started the field of SCM because of their need to control their development of software. Large companies and tool vendors followed after as the drivers of further progress. Academic research has, though, made some substantial contributions on the technical level, which has brought significant improvements in the tools and models used for configuration management today. However, the practise of configuration management (its activities and process) also today continues to be dominated by companies, practitioners and tool vendors. The problem with this approach is that results are rarely widely published and improvements thus spread very slowly.

## 5.1. *Past*

The following are some of the achievements from past academic research. The most basic requirement to a configuration management system is that it must provide an efficient and secure storage. Today's SCM tools provide secure storage, even though some tools have occasional corruptions caused by the rather complex structures that have to be maintained. The efficient use of space to save multiple versions is assured by the use of delta techniques [20, 21]; these techniques have even been refined to be applicable to binary formats too [68]. Workspaces have been provided to ease moving back and forth files by allowing to group them in hierarchically structured projects [22]. Furthermore, mechanisms exist to coordinate groups of people by letting them work in parallel and in isolation from each other, and only synchronize and automatically merge their work when they are ready [22]. For the production of systems, automation is provided by tools like make [24], distributed and parallel builds on heterogeneous platforms were provided by [69, 70], and before that reproducibility and traceability from a system to its components was supported by bill of materials in [71]. Flexible and powerful system models have been proposed by both [71, 72]. Support for specifying process aspects of the configuration management activities was investigated in [73].

## 5.2. *Present*

Several problems are presently being worked on in the academic world and are giving insight that will mature into results to be adopted in the next few years. In today's reality for software development, teams that work on the same system are often distributed around the world. There are even companies that have "around-the-clock" software development, where one team picks up the development work when another goes home after its day of work. This leads to high demands for a SCM tool's capability to synchronize people that are located far from each other and that might have only slow modem lines to transfer files and to check in their work [74]. The same situation occurs when people want to work from home. Many companies are discovering the benefits of performing configuration management, but are not quite sure how to do it. Work is being done on collecting experience and best practices from companies that have already implemented configuration management [75]. Likewise, teaching of configuration management concepts and principles has been neglected at many universities with the result that people working in industry have little or no knowledge of what SCM is or how to perform it. There is the need for a huge education effort here [76]. The fact that a configuration management system collects information about the components being developed has led to research into whether software configuration management tools and product data management (PDM) tools can and should be integrated [77].

## 5.3. *Future*

There are still enough problems around to keep configuration management research alive for many years to come. Just as the connections between SCM and PDM are being researched, also the connections between software configuration management (system models) and software architecture should be researched. Principally thanks to the support of the WWW, it is becoming more frequent to see that people are working in integrated teams that are physically distributed. Such teams need ways to create awareness about what is going on and how the project is progressing. Furthermore, we need ways to be able to synchronize and merge work that is not based on lines of text. Component-based software development has been proposed as a way to improve software productivity. If components are to be substitutable also at runtime, we need SCM tools that are capable of handling dynamic configurations. Many companies are discovering that they are producing many different products that are alike. It is tempting to try to reuse as much of the commonality between these products as possible go gain in productivity and time to market. This, however, means that they have to handle many variants of the same component and to keep track of which variant of a component went into what product. Variant handling has already been researched, but no satisfactory solution has been provided yet. Especially not a solution that covers all aspects from variation in the small (like running on different operating systems) to variation in the big (like different graphical user interfaces). More research should also be done to document the effects of configuration management. So far only one experiment on the return of investment of introducing configuration management has been reported [78].

Finally, there is the eternal problem of how to get configuration management functionality properly and transparently integrated with the rest of the tools in an environment, such that it is "invisible" for the user under "normal" circumstances. In DSEE [71] that was actually the case, as all calls to read and write in the operating system were intercepted by the configuration management functionality. Unfortunately, this approached seems to have been abandoned by tool vendors.

## References

1. A. Leon, *A Guide to Software Configuration Management* (Artech House Publishers, April 2000).
2. A. Zeller, "Configuration management with versions sets", PhD Thesis, Technical University of Braunschweig (April 1997). *http://www.cs.tu-bs.de/softech/papers/zeller-phd/*

3. S. Dart, "Concepts in configuration management", *Proceedings of the 3rd International Workshop on Software Configuration Management*, Trondheim, Norway (June 12–14, 1991) 1–18.

4. R. H. Katz, "Toward a unified framework for version modeling in engineering databases", *ACM Computing Surveys* **22**, no. 4 (1990) 375–408.

5. T. Berners-Lee, R. Cailiau, A. Luotonen, H. F. Nielsen and A. Secret, "The world wide web", *Communications of the ACM* **37** (1994) 76–82.

6. D. Lowe and W. Hall, *Hypermedia and the Web. An Engineering Approach* (John Wiley & Sons Ltd, 1998).

7. IEEE, *IEEE Standard Glossary of Software Engineering Terminology* (Spring edition, 1991).

8. W. F. Tichy, "Tools for software configuration management", *Proceedings of the International Workshop on Software Version and Configuration Control*, Grassau, Germany, January 27–29, 1988 (Teubner Verlag, 1988).

9. K. Meiser, "Software configuration management terminology", *http://www.stsc.hill.af.mil/crosstalk/1995/jan/terms.asp*

10. B. Magnusson, "Fine-grained revision control for collaborative software development", *SIGSOFT'93* (1993) 33–41.

11. S. A. MacKay, "The state of the art in concurrent, distributed configuration management, software configuration management", *Selected Papers SCM-4 and SCM-5*, ed. J. Estublier, *Lecture Notes in Computer Science 1005*, Seattle, WA (April) (Springer-Verlag, 1995) 180–194.

12. M. C. Paulk, B. Curtis, M. B. Chrissis and C. V. Weber, "Capability maturity model", Version 1.1, *IEEE Software* (July 1993).

13. E. H. Bersoff, V. D. Henderson and S. G. Siegel, *Software Configuration Management: An Investment in Product Integrity* (Prentice-Hall, Inc., 1980).

14. F. J. Buckley, "Implementing configuration management: Hardware, software, and firmware", *IEEE Computer* (Society Press, 1993).

15. W. A. Babich, *Software Configuration Management — Coordination for Team Productivity* (Addison-Wesley Publishing Company, 1986).

16. D. D. Lyon, *Practical CM — Best Configuration Management Practices* (Butterworth-Heinemann, 2000).

17. V. Ambriola, L. Bendix and P. Ciancarini, "The evolution of configuration management and version control", *Software Engineering Journal* **5**, no. 6 (November 1990), reprinted in "Software Engineering: A European Perspective", eds. R. H. Thayer, and A. D. McGettrick (IEEE Computer Press, Los Alamitos, USA, June 1993) 389–401.

18. M. Kelly, *Configuration Management — The Changing Image* (McGraw-Hill Book Company Europe, 1996).

19. L. Bendix, "Fundamental tasks in software development environments", *INFORMATICA — An International Journal of Computing and Informatics* **19**, no. 3 (September 1995).

20. M. J. Rochkind, "The source code control system", *IEEE Transactions on Software Engineering*, **SE-1**, no. 4 (December 1975).

21. W. F. Tichy, "RCS — A system for version control", *Software — Practice and Experience* **15**, no. 7 (July 1985).

22. B. Berliner, "CVS II: Parallelizing software development", *Proc. of USENIX Winter*, Washington D.C. (1990).

23. D. L. Parnas, "On the criteria to be used in decomposing systems into modules", *Communications of the ACM* **15**, no. 12 (December 1972).

24. S. I. Feldman, "Make — A program for maintaining computer programs", *Software — Practice and Experience* **9** (April 1979).

25. F. Vitali, "Versioning hypermedia", *ACM Computing Surveys*, 1999.

26. H. C. Davis, "Hypertext link integrity", *ACM Computing Surveys*, 1999.

27. T. H. Nelson, *Literary Machines*, edition 87.1 (Sausalito Press, 1987).

28. J. Slein, F. Vitali., E. J. Whitehead Jr. and D. Durand, "Requirements for distributed authoring and versioning on the world wide web", *ACM Standard-View* **5**, no. 1 (1997) 17–24. Also published as RFC 2291 (February 1998) IETF, *http://www.ics.uci.edu/pub/ietf/webdav/requirements/rfc2291.txt*.

29. A. Haake, "CoVer: A contextual version server for hypertext applications", *ECHT '92 Conference*, Milan, I (ACM Press, New York, 1992) 43–52.

30. A. Haake, "Under CoVer: The implementation of a contextual version server for hypertext applications", *ECHT '94 Proceedings*, Edinburgh, UK (ACM Press, New York, 1994) 81–93.

31. U. K. Wiil and J. J. Leggett, "Hyperform: Using extensibility to develop dynamic, open and distributed hypertext systems", *Proceedings of ECHT '92 Conference*, Milan, I (ACM Press, New York, 1992) 251–261.

32. M. Melly and W. Hall, "Version control in microcosm", *Proceedings of ECSCW '95 Workshop on the Role of Version Control in CSCW Applications*, Stockholm, Sweden (1995).

33. F. G. Halasz, "Reflections on notecards: Seven issues for the next generation of hypermedia systems", *Communications of the ACM* **31**, no. 7 (1988) 836–852.

34. U. K. Wiil and J. J. Leggett, "Concurrency control in collaborative hypertext systems", *Hypertext '93 Proceedings*, Seattle, WA (ACM Press, New York, 1993) 14–24.

35. C. Maioli, S. Sola and F. Vitali, "The support for emergence of collaboration in a hypertext document system", *CSCW'94 Workshop on Collaborative Hypermedia Systems*, Chapel Hill, NC, GMD Studien n. 239 (1994).

36. S. De Rose, D. Orchard and B. Trafford, "XML Linking Language (XLink)", W3C Working Draft (1999), *http://www.w3.org/TR/WD-xlink*

37. A. Haake and D. Hicks, "VerSE: Towards hypertext versioning styles", *Hypertext '96 Proceedings*, Washington DC (ACM Press, New York, 1996) 224–234.

38. R. Conradi and B. Westfechtel, "Version models in software configuration management", *ACM Computing Surveys* **30**, no. 2 (1998) 232–282.

39. K. Østerbye, "Structural and cognitive problems in providing version control for hypertext", *Proceedings of ECHT '92 Conference*, Milan, I (ACM Press, New York, 1992) 33–42.

40. T. H. Nelson, "Xanalogical media: Needed now more than ever", *ACM Computing Surveys* (1999).

41. C. Maioli, S. Sola and F. Vitali, "Wide-area distribution issues in hypertext systems", *SIGDOC '93 Proceedings*, Kitchener, Canada (ACM Press, 1993) 185–197.

42. D. Durand, "Cooperative editing without synchronization", *Proceedings of Hypertext '93 Workshop on Hyperbase Systems*, Seattle, WA, Technical Report TAMU-HRL 93-009, Hypertext Research Lab, Texas A & M University, College Station TX (1993).

43. K. A. Anderson, "Supporting software engineering with open hypermedia", *ACM Computing Surveys* **31**, no. 4 (December 1999).

44. N. M. Delisle and M. D. Schwartz, "Neptune: A hypertext system for CAD applications", *Proceedings of ACM SIGMOD'86*, Washington DC (May 1986) 134–142.

45. B. Campbell and J. M. Goodman, "HAM: A general-purpose hypertext abstract machine", *Proceedings of ACM Hypertext'87*, Chapel Hill, NC (November 1987) 21–32.

46. M. Bieber, H. Oinas-Kukkonen and V. Balasubramanian, "Hypertext functionality", *ACM Computing Surveys Symposium on Hypertext and Hypermedia* (2000).

47. H. Oinas-Kukkonen, "Flexible CASE and hypertext", *ACM Computing Surveys Symposium on Hypertext and Hypermedia* (2000).

48. K. Østerbye, "Literate smalltalk programming using hypertext", *IEEE Transactions on Software Engineering* **21**, no. 2 (1995) 138–145.

49. A. Dattolo and V. Loia, "Active distributed framework for adaptive hypermedia", *International Journal of Human-Computer Studies* **26** (1997) 605–626.

50. M. Amsellem, "ChyPro: A hypermedia programming environment for smalltalk-80", *Proceedings of ECOOP'95*, Aarhus, Denmark (August, 1995).

51. M. L. Creech, D. F. Freeze and M. L. Griss, "Using hypertext in selecting reusable software components", *Proceedings of ACM Hypertext'91*, San Antonio, TX (December 1991) 25–38.

52. I. Goldstein and D. Bobrow, "A layered approach to software design", eds. D. Barstow, H. Shrobe, E. Sandewell, *Interactive Programming Environments* (McGraw Hill, 1984) 387–413.

53. D. Hicks, *A Version Control Architecture for Advanced Hypermedia Environments*, Dissertation Department of Computer Science, Texas A & M University, College Station TX (1993).

54. A. Dattolo and A. Gisolfi, "Analytical version control management in a hypertext system", *Proceedings of the 3th International Conference on Information and Knowledge Management* (November 29–December 1, 1994), Caithersburg, MD, USA (1994) 132–139.

55. D. Durand, A. Haake, D. Hicks and F. Vitali, *Proceedings of the ECHT '94 Workshop on Versioning in Hypertext Systems*, Technical Report of the Computer Science Department, Boston University 95–01, *http://www.cs.bu.edu/techreports/95-001/Home.html* and Arbeitspapiere der GMD 894, GMD-IPSI, Darmstadt, Germany (1994).

56. D. Hicks, A. Haake, D. Durand and F. Vitali, *Proceedings of the ECSCW '95 Workshop on the Role of Version Control in CSCW Applications*, Technical Report of the Computer Science Department, Boston University 96–06 (1995). *http://www.cs.bu.edu/techreports/96-009-ecscw95-proceedings/Book/proceedings_txt.html*

57. J. E. Whitehead, "A proposal for versioning support for the chimera system", *ECHT '94 Workshop on Versioning in Hypertext Systems*, Edinburgh, UK (1994).

58. A. Dattolo and V. Loia, "Collaborative version control in an agent-based hypertext environment", *Information Systems*, **21**, no. 2 (1996) 127–145.

59. A. Dattolo and V. Loia, "Distributed information and control in a concurrent hypermedia-oriented architecture", *International Journal of Software Engineering and Knowledge Engineering* **10**, no. 3 (2000) 345–369.

60. XML — Extensible Markup Language, *http://www.w3.org/XML/*

61. F. Vitali and D. Durand, "Using versioning to provide collaboration on the WWW", *The World Wide Web Journal* **1**, no. 1 (1995) 37–50.

62. D. Raggett, A. Le Hors and I. Jacobs, *HTML 4.0 Specification*, W3C Recommendation (1998), *http://www.w3.org/TR/PR-html40/*

63. J. Whitehead and M. Wiggins, "WEBDAV: IETF standard for collaborative authoring on the web", *IEEE Internet Computing* (September/October 1998) 34–40.

64. T. Ellison, "WEBDAV Versioning scenario", *INTERNET-DRAFT draft-ietf-deltav-scenarios-00.1* (February 10, 2000). *http://www.webdav.org/deltav/scenarios/scenarios-00-1.htm*

65. DASL (DAV Searching & Locating Working Group), *http://www.webdav.org/dasl/*

66. J. Whitehead, "The future of distributed software development on the internet", From CVS to WebDAV to Delta-V (1999). *http://www.webtechniques.com/archives/1999/10/whitehead/*.

67. D. L. Hicks, J. J. Leggett, P. J. Nrnberg and J. L. Schnase, "A hypermedia version control framework", *ACM Transactions on Information Systems* **16**, no. 2 (1998) 127–160.

68. C. Reichenberger, "Delta storage for arbitrary non-text files", *Proceedings of the 3rd International Workshop on Software Configuration Management*, Trondheim Norway (June 12–14, 1991).

69. D. B. Leblang, R. P. Chase Jr. and H. Spilke, "Increasing productivity with a parallel configuration manager", *Proceedings of the International Workshop on Software Version and Configuration Control*, Grassau, Germany (January 27–29, 1988) (Teubner Verlag, January 1988).

70. D. Lubkin, "Heterogeneous configuration management with DSEE", *Proceedings of the 3rd International Workshop on Software Configuration Management*, Trondheim, Norway (June 12–14, 1991).

71. D. B. Leblang and R. P. Chase Jr., "Computer-aided software engineering in a distributed workstation environment", *Proceedings of the ACM SIGSOFT/SIGPLAN Software Engineering Symposium on Practical Software Development Environments* (April 1984), ACM SIGPLAN Notices **19**, no. 5 (May 1984).

72. J. Estublier, S. Ghoul and S. Krakowiak, "Preliminary experience with a configuration control system for modular programs", *Proceedings of the ACM SIGSOFT/SIGPLAN Software Engineering Symposium on Practical Software Development Environments*, May 1984, ACM SIGPLAN Notices **19**, no. 5 (May 1984).

73. J. Estublier, S. Dami and M. Amiour, "High level process modelling for SCM systems", *Proceedings of the 7th International Workshop on Software Configuration Management*, *Springer Lecture Notes in Computer Science 1235*, Boston, Massachusetts (May 18–19, 1997).

74. U. Asklund, B. Magnusson and A. Persson "Experiences: Distributed development and software configuration management", *Proceedings of the 8th International Symposium on System Configuration Management*, *Springer Notes in Computer Science 1439*, Brussels, Belgium (July 20-21, 1998).

75. L. Wingerd and C. Seiwald, "High-level best practices in software configuration management", *Proceedings of the 8th International Symposium on System Configuration Management*, *Springer Lecture Notes in Computer Science 1439*, Brussels, Belgium (July 20–21, 1998).

76. L. Bendix, "Continuous improvement of the configuration management process", *Proceedings of the Conference Views on Software Development in the New Millennium*, Reykjavik, Iceland (August 31–September 1, 2000).

77. J. Estublier, J.-M. Favre and P. Morat, "Towards SCM/PDM integration?, *Proceedings of the 8th International Symposium on System Configuration Management*, *Springer Lecture Notes in Computer Science 1439*, Brussels, Belgium (July 20–21, 1998).

78. J.-O. Larsen and H. M. Roald, "Introducing clearcase as a process improvement experiment", *Proceedings of the 8th International Symposium on System Configuration Management*, *Springer Lecture Notes in Computer Science 1439*, Brussels, Belgium (July 20–21, 1998).

# CASE-BASED REASONING

KLAUS-DIETER ALTHOFF

*Fraunhofer Institute for Experimental Software Engineering (IESE),*
*Sauerwiesen 6, D-67661 Kaiserslautern, Germany*
*E-mail: althoff@iese.fhg.de*

Case-Based Reasoning (CBR) is an Artificial Intelligence approach to learning and problem solving based on past experience. CBR combines aspects from the knowledge-based systems as well as from the machine learning field. In this chapter, we present the main characteristics of CBR technology, describe the main CBR subtasks and methods, and the main underlying principles. CBR is presented more from the user and usage point of view: we consider different application types, survey CBR applications up to now, and briefly present methodologies for developing and evaluating CBR systems. Finally, important issues concerning the past, present, and future of CBR overview the field for the reader. A huge number of references supports the reader with information where to get more detailed technical descriptions on various CBR related topics of interest.

*Keywords*: Process model, knowledge model, organizational model, knowledge-container model, case-based classification, case-based diagnosis, case-based decision support, case-based knowledge management, usage of CBR technology, applications, application development, evaluation, past-present-future.

## 1. Introduction

Case-Based Reasoning (CBR) is an approach to learning and problem solving based on past experience. A past experience is stored in the form of solved problems ("cases") in a so-called case base. A new problem is solved based on adapting solutions of known similar problems (see Fig. 1) to this new problem.

For solving a new problem, a query is submitted to a CBR system to retrieve the solutions of the most similar problems/cases in the case base. The query is considered as a potential new case. The classical view on a case imposes that it consists of a problem description and a described solution to this problem. Recent applications have shown that this view is too restrictive [63]. A more general view on cases is that a case consists of a characterization (a more or less structured set of information entities) and, optionally, one or more artifacts [31, 32]. The characterization part is mandatory and usually contains both formal parts, which can be interpreted by the CBR system, and informal parts, which can be understood by the user only. The characterization can be completed by links to any kind of artifact. Examples for artifacts are web pages, pictures, audio-visual media, or formally described pieces of knowledge. During the retrieval a part of the formal characterization of the new case is specified. The CBR system uses this for matching against the characterizations of the other cases in the case base. The most similar cases

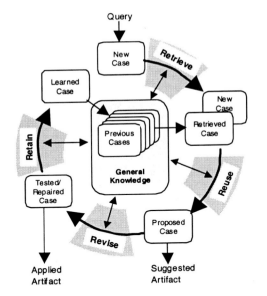

**Case** := Problem (characterization)/Solution (artifact) Pair

**Query:** Query at hand defines new case (problem without solution)

**Retrieve:** New case is used to find most similar case among the known (previous) cases

**Reuse:** New and retrieved case are combined to a proposed case including the suggested artifact

**Revise:** Suggested artifact is applied and evaluated

**Retain:** Useful experiences from applying the artifact are retained by adapting the case base and the conceptual knowledge

**Fig. 1.**   Case-based reasoning process model.

are retrieved and parts of their characterizations and associated artifacts are combined to yield a proposed case. Applying the suggested artifact(s) associated with the proposed case results usually in a repaired case and validated and/or revised artifact(s). The repaired case with its applied artifact(s) can be stored as a learned case, merged with previously available cases, and/or only extracted parts of it are stored. These problem solving steps are also known as the CBR cycle and/or CBR process model [7].

CBR has been used to create numerous applications in a wide range of domains including

- financial analysis,
- risk assessment,
- technical maintenance,
- process control,
- quality control,
- medical diagnosis,
- software support systems,
- forecasting,
- planning,
- design,
- classification of objects,
- photo-interpretation,
- real estate appraisal,

- electronic commerce,
- customer support,
- knowledge management,
- software engineering,
- etc [23, 26, 52, 51].

The underlying idea of CBR is simple: do not solve problems from scratch but remember how you (or someone else) solved a similar problem and apply this knowledge to solve your current problem. The notion of *case-based reasoning* was introduced by Roger Schank. The motivation of his work was based on a cognitive science perspective and one early application area was the cognitive oriented research on story understanding. Another root of current CBR research was the motivation to use knowledge-based methods for legal reasoning, initiated by Edwina Rissland [154]. A third root for current CBR might be found in research on analogical reasoning (e.g. [83]), though early work on CBR and analogical reasoning were quite independent from each other for many years.

After more then twenty years of existence "modern CBR" still consists of work done in the areas mentioned above. However, it has also become an engineering discipline for using knowledge and software engineering methods to develop real-life applications. In the beginning of the 90's, the first commercial CBR tools appeared and, since then, more mature tools have been developed [23, 173]. While for some years the strong focus on various real-life applications seemed to separate current CBR research and development activities from its origins, in the most recent years methods and ideas from the more humanities oriented parts of CBR again become very important. Complex application domains like knowledge management, education and training, and continuous quality improvement require broadly applicable techniques. It is one of the biggest challenges of current CBR research and development to not only develop solutions for very specific (small) problems but also to develop more general solution strategies that allow, for instance, an integration of computer and human based methods.

To give you a glimpse of what CBR covers, we introduce some of the most important aspects. They already make some basic characteristics of CBR obvious.

(1) CBR is an approach for developing knowledge-based systems (e.g. [38], [2]).
Through CBR, knowledge in the form of cases can be formally represented and used for automated problem solving, for instance, to aid some decision-maker [108], to solve diagnostic as well as planning or design problems [37, 73, 122, 181, 53, 127, 58]. Besides case-specific knowledge, CBR systems also exploit general domain knowledge (e.g. a set of rules) to support retrieval, similarity judgment, case adaptation,

as well as learning.[a] Thus, CBR can be viewed as an approach for developing knowledge-based systems (see also [131]).

(2) CBR is an approach for learning from experience (examples, cases) [9, 100, 84, 38].

Learning from cases can be implemented using CBR. The learning result then is the whole CBR system including its case base. This result can, for example, be incrementally improved through adding new cases.

(3) CBR is an explanation model for human problem solving and learning [157, 104, 105, 158, 115].

This is, in part, the origin of CBR.

(4) CBR is a very natural approach for the development of knowledge, especially in the context of teaching and tutoring [159, 186, 187, 139, 164].

Of course, here is some strong relationship to 3.

(5) CBR is a knowledge based extension of the nearest neighbor classifier paradigm known from pattern recognition [17, 11, 98, 60].

On an abstract level nearest neighbor classification is very similar to CBR. However, CBR enables also to use explicit knowledge to improve retrieval and reuse. In addition, it offers an approach to combine quantitative and qualitative approaches because both kinds of knowledge can be easily integrated within a CBR system [174].

(6) CBR is a holistic system approach [26, 93].

Here CBR is different, for instance, from many approaches in the machine learning community that are more oriented towards developing optimized algorithms for specific problems and, therefore, do not consider requirements (for building software systems) from knowledge/software engineering very much.

This is also a very important aspect to be considered if learning (knowledge-based) *systems* have to be developed.

(7) CBR is an organizational[b] approach for experience management [40, 175, 185, 130].

Recent work on knowledge management and continuous quality improvement in software engineering [102, 95, 119, 112] made it very obvious that due to CBR's various relations to work in the humanities, some of CBR's underlying principles can be successfully applied to the human (and organizational) aspects of experience management [143, Tautz 2000, 176, 75, 156].

(8) CBR is an open environment for integrating different kinds of techniques. It is a matter of fact that various hybrid systems have been

---

[a]Some explanations for differentiating case-specific from general domain knowledge can be found in the Sections on *Case-Based Reasoning Task-Method Decomposition Model*, *Case-Based Reasoning Systems*, and *Case-Based Reasoning Knowledge Container Model*.

[b]as well as technical

built with the use of CBR [16, 120, 12, 138, 4, 5, 80, 21]. In addition, methods from other disciplines have been successfully integrated into CBR approaches (e.g. *similarity measures*: [64, 55]; *object-centered representation*: [56, 177]; *inductive learning*: [128, 166, 61, 71]; *databases*: [165, 190, 66, 163]; etc).

(9) Knowledge based information retrieval [100, 126, 190, 155].

CBR can also be viewed as an approach to retrieve relevant information from some information base. Here CBR offers opportunities to integrate knowledge into the retrieval process, to improve the retrieval system through learning, and to adapt the retrieval results to the current problem at hand.

In the next section, CBR is described from various perspectives that reflect the current state of the art/practice. We then present one introductory CBR application example and give a short overview on already existing/documented CBR real-life applications, present approaches on the evaluation of CBR systems and applications, and describe some basic aspects on systematic development of CBR applications. Finally, a historical overview on the development of CBR is given, current CBR information resources are briefly surveyed, and some future directions are outlined.

## 2. Description of CBR

We shall describe CBR from various points of view. First we shall introduce the task-method decomposition model of CBR by Aamodt & Plaza [7], which details the CBR process model described above. Since CBR is very much concerned with developing software *systems* we shall contrast CBR systems to database systems as well as (other) knowledge-based systems. This will be completed with a briefly described organizational model for running CBR systems, which includes basic roles involved as well as a goal-oriented procedure of how to develop knowledge for CBR systems. The knowledge container model — first introduced by Michael Richter [149] — is an explanation model for some basic characteristics of CBR systems, which is widely accepted in the CBR community and should not be left out in a handbook chapter like this. Finally, in this section, some case-based reasoning methods are introduced for different kinds of application tasks, namely classification, diagnosis, decision support, and knowledge management.

## 2.1. *Case-based reasoning task-method decomposition model*

At the highest level of generality, a general CBR cycle may be described by four tasks [7]: *Retrieve* the most similar case or cases, *reuse* the information and knowledge in that case to solve the problem (a process called "solution transfer"), *revise* the proposed solution, and *retain* the parts of this experience likely to be useful for future problem solving (Fig. 1).

Note that the tasks referred to here are internal reasoning tasks, and differ from application problem tasks like diagnosis, planning, scheduling, etc. The four CBR tasks each involve a number of more specific subtasks. An initial description of a problem (top of Fig. 1) defines a new case. In the *retrieve* task this new case is used to find a matching case from the collection of previous cases. The retrieved case is combined with the input case — in the *reuse* task — into a solved case, that is, a proposed solution to the initial problem. The *revise* task tests this solution for success, for example, by applying it to the real-life environment or having it evaluated by a teacher, and repaired if failed. This task is important for learning, since the system needs feedback on how successful its proposed solution actually was. *Retain* is the main learning task, where useful experience is retained for future reuse, by updating the case base and possibly also the general domain knowledge.

As indicated in Fig. 1, general knowledge usually plays a part in this cycle, by supporting the CBR processes. This support may range from very weak to very strong, depending on the type of CBR method. By general knowledge we here mean general domain-dependent knowledge, as opposed to the specific domain knowledge embodied by cases. For example, in diagnosing a patient by retrieving and reusing the case of a previous patient, a model of anatomy together with causal relationships between pathological and other physiological states may constitute the general knowledge used by a CBR system. A set of rules may have the same role.

The tasks from Fig. 1 are further decomposed in Fig. 2 [7, 22]. The tasks have node names in bold letters, while methods are written in plain text. The links between task nodes (bold lines) are task decompositions, that is, part-of relations. The links between tasks and methods (stippled lines) identify alternative methods

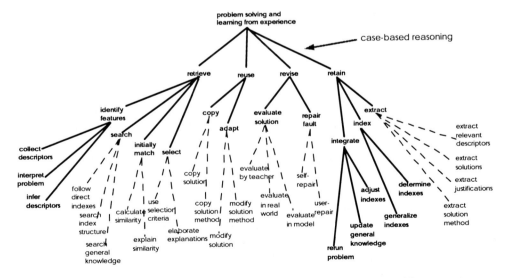

**Fig. 2.**   Task-method decomposition of case-based reasoning [7].

applicable for solving a task. The top-level task is *problem solving and learning from experience* and the method to accomplish the task is a *case-based reasoning* method. This splits the top-level task into the four major CBR tasks corresponding to Fig. 1. All the four tasks are necessary in order to perform the top-level task. The *retrieve* task is, in turn, partitioned in the same manner (by a retrieval method) into the tasks *identify features*, *search* (to find a set of past cases), *initially match* (the relevant descriptors to past cases), and *select* (the most similar case(s)). All task partitions in the figure are considered complete; that is, the set of subtasks of a task are intended to be sufficient to accomplish the task, at this level of description. The figure does not show any control structure over the subtasks. Control is specified as part of the problem-solving method. The retrieval method, for example (not explicitly indicated in the figure), specifies the sequence and loop-backs for the subtasks of *retrieve*. A method specifies the algorithm that identifies and controls the execution of subtasks, or solves the task directly, while accessing and utilizing the domain knowledge needed to do this. The methods shown in the figure are high level method classes, from which one or more specific methods should be chosen. The method set as shown is incomplete; that is, one of the methods indicated may be sufficient to solve the task, several methods may be combined, or there may be other methods that have not been mentioned.

This structure provides the basis for an analytic framework. It needs to be elaborated and described in more detail. Characterizations of domain knowledge types need to be added, and dependencies between the various knowledge types need to be identified (see [22, 21]).

## 2.2. *Case-based reasoning systems*

In general, the decision how much general knowledge is needed for an application and whether it should be used to complete a CBR system or, vice versa, whether it should be used to build a (general) knowledge-based system, depends on the available knowledge sources that are related to given application, their degree of availability, as well as the respective reliability of the knowledge sources. General knowledge used within a CBR system can help to reduce the number of cases necessary for problem solving, to improve the reliability of potential solutions, to make the overall system more efficient in the handling of routine situations, to exploit *known* generalizations, and to immediately adapt to a changing environment. CBR offers a flexible intermediate position between database systems containing mostly informal knowledge, which can only be interpreted by the user, and knowledge-based systems including widely formalized knowledge, which can be automatically processed by the computer. The advantage offered here by a CBR system is that it can start from a very simple database-system-like situation and can use increasingly more formal knowledge depending on the respective application (Fig. 3).

From the perspective of continuous learning from experience CBR systems can be embedded in industrial and other kinds of organizations as roughly shown in

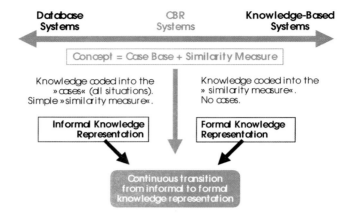

**Fig. 3.** Case-based reasoning knowledge model.

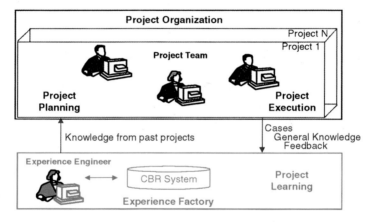

**Fig. 4.** Organizational model for running CBR systems.

Fig. 4. As first mentioned by Henninger [94] and later explained in detail by Althoff and Wilke [40] and Tautz and Althoff [175], CBR and *experience factory* [48, 59, 156] share many similar assumptions and are to some degree complementary. While CBR provides an approach to learning from experience on the technical system implementation level, an experience factory — together with its underlying *quality improvement paradigm* (QIP) ([48], Fig. 5 [156]) — supports it as a physical and/or logical infrastructure on a technology-independent organizational level. Various research institutions, groups, and people have already started to benefit from the synergy of these two approaches [40, 175, 52, 44, 99, 174].

By adopting an experience factory approach for running CBR systems in organizations, two immediate benefits are available. First, project learning can be facilitated through goal-oriented knowledge development based on the QIP (Fig. 5,

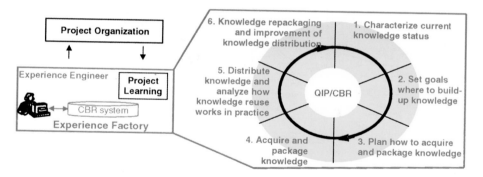

**Fig. 5.** Goal-oriented knowledge development for CBR systems.

[156]). Second, some basic roles necessary to operationalize CBR systems in practice can be described as follows:

- The *manager* provides resources, defines strategic goals, and initiates improvement programs. He defines the structure of the case base and controls its quality.
- The *supporter* is responsible for documenting new experiences and supporting the project teams. He collects and qualifies artifacts from projects according to the reuse criteria and goals of the experience engineer. He supports the project team on request for retrieving cases and/or adapting them to the current project situation.
- The *experience engineer* is responsible for packaging and analyzing existing cases. Together with the manager he identifies new reuse criteria and acquires new cases based on these criteria. He analyzes the case base to discover further improvement potential.
- The *librarian* is responsible for technical tasks like development and maintenance of the case base. He stores and publishes new cases.

## 2.3. *Case-based reasoning knowledge container model*

Richter [151] has introduced a helpful explanation model or view on CBR systems (Fig. 6). He identified four knowledge containers for a CBR system. Besides the underlying vocabulary, these are the similarity measure, the solution transformation, and the cases. While the first three represent compiled knowledge (i.e., more stable knowledge is assigned to these containers), the cases are interpreted knowledge.[c] As a consequence, newly added cases can be used directly. Therefore, the cases enable a CBR system to deal with dynamic knowledge more efficiently and effectively. In addition, knowledge can be shifted from one container to another when this knowledge

---

[c]Of course, knowledge for solution transformation or similarity assessment can be captured and represented as cases. Thus, a "small" CBR system is used, for instance, for transforming a case's solution. However, we would like to avoid this recursive view in an explanation model.

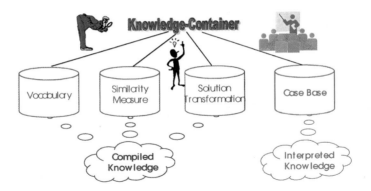

**Fig. 6.** The distribution of knowledge in a CBR system (Richter, 1998).

has become more stable. For instance, in the beginning a simple vocabulary, a rough similarity measure, and no knowledge on solution transformation are used. However, a large number of cases are collected. Over time, the vocabulary can be refined and the similarity measure defined in higher accordance with the underlying domain. In addition, it may be possible to reduce the number of cases because the improved knowledge within the other containers now enables the CBR system to better differentiate between the available cases. If knowledge about solution transformation also becomes available, it may be possible to further reduce the number of available cases, because then a number of solutions can be derived from one case.

## 2.4. *Different degrees of user involvement in solution development*

CBR is a technology that usually involves the user in solution development. In the following we briefly present three different types of (basic) CBR systems, where the degree of user involvement increases (Fig. 7). In addition, one more complicated application task is presented that requires the integration of basic reasoning methods to support the processes available in the underlying application context.

### 2.4.1. *Case-based classification*

The basic classification process maps objects or situations to a given set of classes. We assume that all necessary information is available to carry out the mapping process (Fig. 8). Examples of classification tasks are risk assessment of cars, determination of biological objects, analysis of client data, or cost estimation [79]. For basic classification tasks CBR is in competition with many other approaches. While inductive machine learning approaches normally reason with generalized knowledge and, by contrast, databases store all the case data, CBR is more flexible in the sense that it distributes its competence on both the cases and the similarity measure (Fig. 3 [194, 150, 84]). Depending on the specific requirements of an application a simple or a well-informed measure can be used. The better the similarity measure

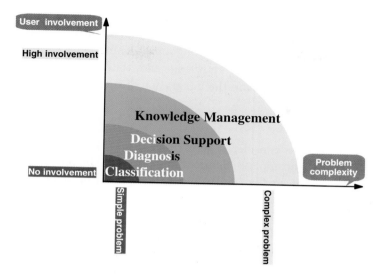

**Fig. 7.** More user involvement enables solution development for more complex problems.

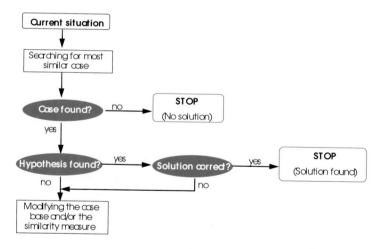

**Fig. 8.** Basic reasoning method for case-based classification.

is suited for a given task, the fewer cases must be stored. In principle, the CBR approach offers the flexibility to decide this at a very late stage in system development. Always when this flexibility is wanted, CBR is a good choice. Comparing CBR with approaches based on generalized knowledge results in similar advantages and disadvantages like those associated with (case) interpretation and (case) compilation.

CBR systems (e.g. PATDEX: [37, 189]; INRECA: [21, 190] often use at least one similarity measure per class, which can be of high value for certain classification problems. Additionally, both systems can learn the relevance of certain attributes for the respective classes (e.g. [148]). Aamodt and Nygård [6] pointed out that depending on their role in decision making and learning by experience, cases may be viewed as data, information, or knowledge and, thus, the CBR approach maybe helpful for certain domains where the integration of such issues is important.

### 2.4.2. Case-based diagnosis

Diagnostic processes, as considered here, differ from basic classification processes by the problem of incomplete information. That is, before carrying out the classification process normally (much) more information must be acquired. Thus, the diagnosis task includes, in addition to the classification task, the task of selecting the best test(s) to acquire the missing information as cheaply, fast, and securely as possible. Examples are fault diagnosis of a car motor, a CNC[d] machine tool (see section on Application Example: Fault Diagnosis of Technical Equipment), or an aircraft engine.

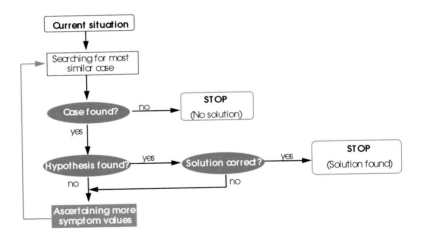

**Fig. 9.**   Basic reasoning method for case-based diagnosis.

   The additional test selection subtask makes the diagnosis task a very specific one (Fig. 9). Often general domain knowledge is required to reasonably guide the selection process. For some application tasks (e.g. fault diagnoses of CNC machines) the degree of incomplete information can be very high (> 90%). Therefore, approaches based on induction have serious difficulties in coping with such problems in an efficient way. This is again due to the interpretation/compilation contrast we mentioned in the previous section. CBR can also offer a solution to the test selection problem itself by using an additional kind of cases or by structuring its

---

[d]Computerized Numerical Control.

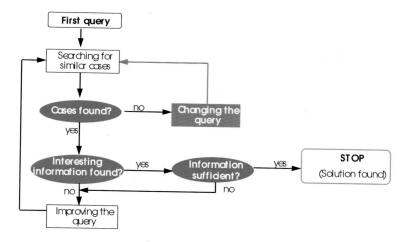

**Fig. 10.** Basic reasoning method for case-based decision support.

retrieval according to explicitly specified retrieval goals [86]. In principle, general knowledge about the biological or the engineering system can be used to adapt the diagnostic class in the case description.

### 2.4.3. *Case-based decision support*

Decision support processes differ from classification processes by the necessity of representing more general knowledge and allowing user-computer interaction to a very high degree [122, 190, 26]. While the classification goal is clearly defined for the classification and the diagnosis processes (static target definition), decision support processes must cope with (more explorative) problems where the classification goal is defined during the problem solving process (dynamic target definition). Examples are looking for a house to buy, looking for a last-minute trip without clearly defining the location and the kind of travel, and looking for a well-suited used or new truck for a company.

To support a basic algorithm for case-based decision support as given in Fig. 10, usually more domain knowledge [122, 190], efficient and effective retrieval structures [42, 191, 123, 21], as well as improved similarity assessment is necessary [148, 190, 195, 21, 86].

### 2.4.4. *Case-based knowledge management*

A much more complicated application task than the three already mentioned ones is knowledge management. It is used here just as an example. Other complicated tasks include most planning and design problems [183, 137].

For knowledge management no basic reasoning method is directly applicable. Instead various reasoning methods are relevant to support knowledge management

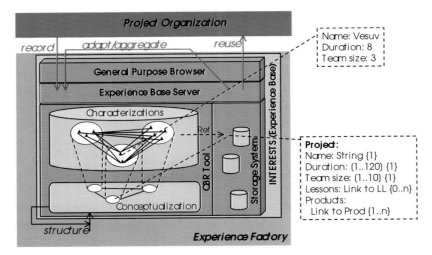

**Fig. 11.**   Intelligent retrieval and storage system supporting some high-level experience factory processes.

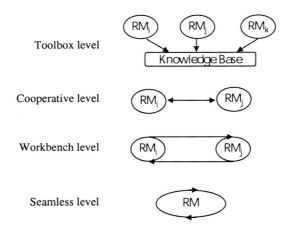

**Fig. 12.**   Integration of different reasoning methods.

processes[e] including the ones mentioned above (e.g. [75, 8, 143, 88]). Figure 11 presents an example of a CBR architecture for knowledge management [32], which also shows the high-level processes of structuring knowledge, recording knowledge in the experience base, and reusing/adapting/aggregating it. Since more complex application tasks require the integration of different reasoning methods, we present four different levels of how to integrate them in principle (Fig. 12).

---

[e] According to Probst and Romhardt [144] there are at least processes for knowledge goal definition, knowledge acquisition, knowledge processing, knowledge preservation, knowledge distribution, knowledge utilization, and knowledge valuation (see also [34]).

These integration levels depend on the degree of interactiveness between certain reasoning methods [23, 21, 15, 132]:

- *Toolbox level.* Here the integration is restricted to the common use of parts of the knowledge base. Reasoning is done by only one method. Exchange of reasoning results is not possible.
- *Cooperative level.* During the reasoning process different reasoning methods can be used. The exchange of intermediate results is possible using a common representation formalism [128].
- *Workbench level.* Beyond switching between available reasoning methods, they can also be aggregated into a combined reasoning method. For instance, a diagnostic system can carry out its classification subtask using a rule-based module, and the test selection subtask using a CBR component [19].
- *Seamless level.* This is the highest level of integration. Different reasoning methods have been integrated within a new algorithm based on an integrating element. Thus, the change of reasoning methods is hidden from the user [2].

## 2.5. *Usage of case-based reasoning technology*

CBR is an approach to develop knowledge-based systems. It provides a huge number of formal computer science techniques for executing, among others, the subtasks mentioned in the CBR task-method decomposition model in Fig. 2. Some of the characteristics of a domain that indicate whether a CBR approach would be suitable are [23]:

(1) there exist records of previously solved problems;
(2) historical cases are viewed as an asset that ought to be preserved;
(3) if there is no case history, it is intuitively clear that remembering previous experiences would be useful;
(4) specialists talk about their domain by giving examples;
(5) experience is at least as valuable as textbook knowledge;
(6) approximate solutions are acceptable.

While the first five indicators need not to be fulfilled all, of course, the sixth indicator is more like a requirement or an assumption. It is aiming at the very "heart of CBR" as a "nearest neighbor" technology [152], which provides solutions that are more or less appropriate (similar). In some sense CBR is an approximation approach like Fuzzy technology. If no approximate solution is requested but one that is 100% correct, for instance, a logic based approach is better suited than CBR. Here perhaps other problem solving methods are more appropriate [131].

However real-life applications very often require that not only one approach is used. The integration of different reasoning methods [106, 29], as for instance described in the section above, is one important solution to this problem. For the integrated development of knowledge systems (see also section on CBR Application Development), the contribution of CBR is — besides integrating knowledge technologies with learning and approximation — the introduction of some "locality principle" for knowledge. Cases can be understood, communicated, and validated as they are, that is (to a high degree) independent from the rest of the CBR system. Cases are especially independent from each other. For example, if one important case is missing in a case base, this would only result in an answer of the CBR system where this case might be missing as a similar one. The other similar cases can still be provided to the user. This is different, for instance, than in rule-based or other kinds of knowledge-based systems where rules or other kinds of knowledge usually interact in a much more complicated way. Thus, CBR and cases introduce more transparency into knowledge-based systems [131]. How the different kinds of knowledge interact within a CBR system has partly been described in the section on the Case-Based Reasoning Knowledge Container Model.

The issues of competence and maintenance of CBR systems are currently hot research topics. Among others, Mark Keane and especially Barry Smyth, together with people working in his group, already started to look deeper into the issue of competence of a CBR system [168, 169, 197, 118]. In the recent past several research efforts on the maintenance of CBR systems have been started [82, 92, 117, 147, 134]. Open research issues include a comparison of competence development and maintenance effort of CBR systems and other knowledge-based systems, the influence of machine learning techniques on competence development and maintenance effort of CBR systems, as well as the competence development and maintenance effort of hybrid knowledge-based systems [2, 5, 120] that also include a CBR part.

## 3. CBR Applications

We shall first present a simple application example on fault diagnosis for technical equipment, which hopefully demonstrates some basic and informative features of CBR systems. Then we give an overview of past and present CBR applications. In addition, both subsections include various links to CBR applications described in the literature.

### 3.1. *Application example: fault diagnosis of technical equipment*

We shall briefly present a simple example of a CBR application from the domain of fault diagnosis of technical equipment. More concretely, the application task of diagnosing a CNC[f] machining center is chosen, briefly called *CNC domain*. This application was developed in the second half of the 80's and is based on real-life data but remains a research prototype: the PATDEX system. However, it was the starting point for many other CBR systems and applications [21].

---

[f]Computerized Numerical Control.

The CNC domain is difficult to handle because of the huge amount of unknown values. In addition, the overall number of attributes and classes is very high. This domain also illustrates the necessity of having integrated systems [140, 19], even if treated as a more closed domain, that is, ignoring influences outside of the machine like vibrations of the workshop floor. However, it is not possible to view it as a static domain [37, 19, 74]. One reasonable approach here is to use/view cases as exceptions [37, 19].

The CNC domain is a good example for the need of having a well-suited and flexible test selection component that includes, among others, the following features:

- Asking for the next symptom value.
- Accepting any symptom value at any step in the user-system interaction.
- Accepting any number of symptom values.
- Accepting user hypotheses [33].

The PATDEX system [189] was originally designed for the CNC domain. Though PATDEX's similarity measure is well-suited for it, in the similarity assessment scenario below it will retrieve the wrong case (CaseIncorrect). However, it is able to improve this situation by its test selection component (asking for symptom values to improve the given information) and/or by the application of causal and/or heuristic rules that allow the derivation of additional symptom values based on known ones. In addition, PATDEX can use weights for the relative importance of the given attributes for the respective classes (diagnoses). These weights can be automatically updated to avoid misclassifications [189, 148]. The use of default values for symptoms and its special handling of pathologic/abnormal symptom values also allow an improved treatment of situations similar to that given in the similarity assessment scenario below. Later extensions of PATDEX also allowed using a deep model of the underlying CNC machine's behavior to improve the similarity measure [54].

Let us consider the following scenario. The CNC machine has stopped with an error message code "i59". In addition, the maintenance technician knows that some specific input/output status "IN32" has the value "logical-1" and that the valve 5Y2 is not switched. He formulates a query to the PATDEX system that includes this information (right column of Table 1). We assume that PATDEX's case base consists of two cases, namely CaseCorrect (left column of Table 1) and CaseIncorrect (middle column of Table 1), and both cases consist of a number attributes with attribute values (for a diagnostic problem solving situation also called symptom and symptom value). Some of these attribute values are not known ("?"), because they have not been recorded for this case (e.g. because they have been considered as irrelevant). As can be derived from the respective names, CaseCorrect reflects the underlying fault situation, that is, for this scenario it is assumed that the values included in CaseCorrect are correct and that the correct diagnosis is "IOCardDefect".

**Table 1.** CaseCorrect, CaseIncorrect, the Query case, and the respective similarities.

| CaseCorrect | CaseIncorrect | Query |
|---|---|---|
| ErrorCode = i59 | ErrorCode = i59 | ErrorCode = i59 |
| I/OStateOut7 = logical-1 | ? | ? |
| Valve5Y1 = switched | Valve5Y1 = not-switched | ? |
| I/OStateOut24 = logical-0 | ? | ? |
| Valve5Y2 = not-switched | ? | Valve5Y2 = not-switched |
| PipesClampingReleaseDevice = ok | ? | ? |
| I/OStateIn32 = logical-1 | I/OStateIn32 = logical-1 | I/OStateIn32 = logical-1 |
| DIAGNOSIS = IOCardDefect | DIAGNOSIS = Magnetic-SwitchDefect | ? |
| SIM(Query, CaseCorrect) = $\dfrac{1 \cdot 3}{1 \cdot 3 + 0.5 \cdot 4} = 0.6$ | SIM(Query, CaseIncorrect) = $\dfrac{1 \cdot 2}{1 \cdot 2 + 0.5 \cdot 2} = 0.67$ | |

We assume that the underlying similarity measure is as follows [33]:
$$\text{SIM}(\text{Case}_1, \text{Case}_2) = \frac{a \cdot \text{card}(E)}{a \cdot \text{card}(E) + b \cdot \text{card}(D) + c \cdot \text{card}(U_1) + d \cdot \text{card}(U_2)}$$

- $E$ set of symptoms with the *same* values for Case$_1$ and Case$_2$
- $D$ set of symptoms with *different* values for Case$_1$ and Case$_2$
- $U_1$ set of symptoms with *known values for Case$_1$* but not for Case$_2$
- $U_2$ set of symptoms with *known values for Case$_2$* but not for Case$_1$
- $a = 1$, $b = 2$, $c = 1/2$, $d = 1/2$ (the default weights used by PATDEX)
- card cardinality of sets.

Given the above defined Query case, PATDEX comes up with the wrong diagnosis (because the similarity between CaseIncorrect and the Query case is higher than that between CaseCorrect and the Query case, see Table 1). The reason for this is that PATDEX uses its well-informed similarity measure based on Tversky's contrast model [180] and explicitly considers unknown symptom values. However, the first wrong judgment (Table 1) can be improved (Table 2) by the use of general domain knowledge, namely the application of causal or heuristic rules:

- Applying a causal rule for deriving additional symptom values based on the already known symptom values
- For instance, the following causal rule could be applied:
  IF ErrorCode = i59 & Valve5Y2 = not-switched
  THEN I/OStateOut24 = logical-0.

**Table 2.** Situation after applying rule R1.

| CaseCorrect | CaseIncorrect | Query-2[g] |
|---|---|---|
| ErrorCode = i59 | ErrorCode = i59 | ErrorCode = i59 |
| I/OStateOut7 = logical-1 | ? | ? |
| Valve5Y1 = switched | Valve5Y1 = not-switched | ? |
| I/OStateOut24 = logical-0 | ? | I/OStateOut24 = logical-0 |
| Valve5Y2 = not-switched | ? | Valve5Y2 = not-switched |
| PipesClampingReleaseDevice = ok | ? | ? |
| I/OStateIn32 = logical-1 | I/OStateIn32 = logical-1 | I/OStateIn32 = logical-1 |
| DIAGNOSIS = IOCardDefect | DIAGNOSIS = Magnetic-SwitchDefect | ? |
| SIM(Query, CaseCorrect) = $\dfrac{1 \cdot 4}{1 \cdot 4 + 0.5 \cdot 3} = 0.73$ | SIM(Query, CaseIncorrect) = $\dfrac{1 \cdot 2}{1 \cdot 2 + 0.5 \cdot 3} = 0.57$ | |

Table 2 shows the outcome of applying the causal rule. Now the similarity between the (automatically improved) Query-2 case and CaseCorrect is higher (0.73) than the similarity between CaseIncorrect and Query-2 (0.57). Thus, the application of the rule adapts the result of PATDEX in the right way.

The above improvement is based on the availability of the causal (or heuristic) rules. An alternative improvement strategy (results in Table 3), which is not necessarily based on the availability of such knowledge, is the acquisition of further information using a complete test selection subcomponent:

- Applying test selection to extend and thereby improve the available information.
- For instance, the following test could be carried out:
  Test 5Y1: "What is the status of Valve5Y1?"
  Result of Test5Y1: "Valve5Y1 = switched".

The reason to ask such a question is to carry out some kind of differential diagnosis as known from medical diagnostics, because CaseCorrect and CaseIncorrect have different values for this attribute. Table 3 shows that the outcome of knowing one attribute value more is that now the similarity between CaseCorrect and

---

[g] "Query-2" is the improvement of "Query" that has been achieved by automatically applying the mentioned causal rule.

**Table 3.**   Situation after ascertaining status of Valve5Y2.

| CaseCorrect | CaseIncorrect | Query-38[h] |
|---|---|---|
| ErrorCode = i59 | ErrorCode = i59 | ErrorCode = i59 |
| I/OStateOut7 = logical-1 | ? | ? |
| Valve5Y1 = switched | Valve5Y1 = not-switched | Valve5Y1 = switched |
| I/OStateOut24 = logical-0 | ? | ? |
| Valve5Y2 = not-switched | ? | Valve5Y2 = not-switched |
| PipesClampingReleaseDevice = ok | ? | ? |
| I/OStateIn32 = logical-1 | I/OStateIn32 = logical-1 | I/OStateIn32 = logical-1 |
| DIAGNOSIS = IOCardDefect | DIAGNOSIS = Magnetic-SwitchDefect | ? |
| $\text{SIM(Query, CaseCorrect)} = \dfrac{1 \cdot 4}{1 \cdot 4 + 0.5 \cdot 3} = 0.73$ | $\text{SIM(Query, CaseIncorrect)} = \dfrac{1 \cdot 2}{1 \cdot 2 + 2 \cdot 1 + 0.5 \cdot 1} = 0.44$ | |

the Query-3 case is much higher than the similarity between CaseIncorrect and Query-3.

Important problems that need to be handled in the CNC domain are system-guided and/or user-guided completion of available information, the handling of a huge number of attributes, classes, cases, and unknown values ($> 90\%$). An attribute-value based case representation using symbolic value ranges was sufficient for this application task. Tolerating the high number of unknown symptom values required a Tversky-like similarity measure (e.g. the one presented above). In addition, general domain knowledge is helpful (but not necessary) for supporting both the test selection and the similarity measure.

### 3.2. Overview on CBR applications[i]

Real-life applications have shown that CBR is a practically important technology. Many researchers and practitioners view CBR technology as one of the most successful artificial intelligence technologies [47]. This is documented through many application oriented books that appeared during the last few years. Althoff [21]

---

[h] "Query-3" is an alternative improvement of "Query". Here one additional attribute value is entered by the maintenance technician (PATDEX has asked for that value).
[i] It is far beyond the scope of this chapter to give a complete overview on this. Instead, a few exemplary applications are presented.

describes four applications carried out in the INRECA[j] project in the years 1992–1995:

- a help-desk on robot diagnosis;
- a maintenance support system for troubleshooting jet engines;
- a system for assessing wind risk factors in Irish forests; and
- a research prototype system for supporting the reuse of object-oriented software.

Overviews on CBR applications in design [137], planning [183], and in diagnosis and decision support [124] appeared in a special issue of the AI Communications. More detailed descriptions are presented in [122], which also describes application domains like software engineering, medicine, tutoring, and help systems. Bergmann *et al* [52] briefly summarize more than a dozen applications carried out by the partners of the INRECA-2[k] consortium (1996–1999). The special issue on CBR of the International Journal of Engineering Applications of Artificial Intelligence [51] includes, among others, applications on image processing. While Stolpmann and Wess [173] focus on customer relationship management in detail, Wilke [196] and Cunningham [72] concentrate on electronic commerce applications. Althoff *et al* [23] report on a number of early CBR applications on planning and design (including Lockheed's CLAVIER application on the configuration of autoclave loads, one of the first (1990) breakthrough applications for CBR technology like AcknoSoft's application on troubleshooting aircraft engines at CFM International in 1992), especially on classification like application tasks. Cheetham & Graf [69], Finnie *et al* [79], Jarmulak [98], and Azuaje *et al* [41] focus on specific classification and data interpretation tasks. Schulz [162] describes the use of CBR in corporate decision processes.

A very recent but popular application domain is knowledge management [88, 31, 13, 14, 77, 87, 85, 32, 178, 75]. See also the section on Case-Based Knowledge Management above.

## 4. Evaluation of CBR Systems and Applications

An important part of systematically developing software systems is the evaluation of developed applications, of different candidate software tools, and/or candidate development methodologies (Fig. 13). In the CBR community the second kind of evaluation was treated first and in most detail. Based on the motivation of evaluating industrial CBR applications using commercial CBR tools, which was underlying

---

[j]The INRECA project lasted from 1992–1995 and was funded by the Commission of the European Union (Esprit III P6322). The partners of INRECA were AcknoSoft (coordinating partner, France), tec:inno (Germany), IMS (Ireland), and the University of Kaiserslautern (Germany).

[k]The European Union funded INRECA-2 project lasted from 1996–1999. The partners of INRECA-2 were AcknoSoft (coordinating partner, France), tec:inno (Germany), IMS (Ireland), DaimlerChrysler (Germany), and the University of Kaiserslautern (Germany).

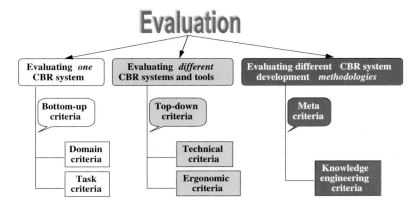

**Fig. 13.** Different views on evaluating CBR systems.

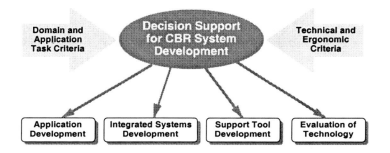

**Fig. 14.** Decision support criteria for CBR system development.

the INRECA project, Traphöner *et al* [179] presented a first criteria catalogue. Althoff *et al* [25] started with a subset of these criteria, further extended and modified them, and refined them in a way that they could be used for detailed comparison of five well-known commercial CBR tools.[1] A revised version of this was made available for a broader public [23].

Within the INRECA project the tool comparison was used to define the final architecture of the INRECA tool to be developed within the project. This tool was compared to commercial tools based on the same criteria [21]. In addition, a more general framework for evaluating CBR systems was established [22]. This was used to compare the INRECA system with many other CBR research systems. The key idea of this framework was to combine different kinds of criteria — technical and ergonomic criteria, and domain and task criteria — to relate "CBR tools" and "CBR applications" with one another (Fig. 14). For example, describing a CBR application with technical criteria, namely those to be fulfilled if the application should be developed, enables us to compare the application with different CBR

---

[1]CBR Express, Esteem, Kate tools, Remind, S3-Case (1994 versions).

tools. That is, to decide which is the most appropriate (e.g. in the sense of most similar) CBR tool.

Of course, this works also the other way round: associating CBR tools with domain and application task criteria, to decide which tool can be applied for which application domain and/or task. In practice such associated criteria are not very detailed. However, they are already valuable on a more general level. For instance, such criteria were used for an implementation of a case-based information system on CBR tools and applications called CBR-PEB (CBR Product Experience Base[m]; [26, 46, 36].

The criteria set described in Althoff [21] is not only helpful for comparing tools and defining goals for new tool development, but it also supports the evaluation of CBR technology in a more general sense, as for instance posed by Cohen [70], and systematic application development. Based on this, two different methodologies for building CBR applications have been developed (see next section on CBR Application Development).

In the scope of building one of these methodologies, it turned out that the *goal-question-metric* paradigm [49, 170, 156] known from experimental software engineering, is a good candidate technology for evaluating one (single) CBR application. Experiences were gathered during the development (and evaluation) of the CBR-PEB application [135]. Currently, the combination of evaluation with maintenance is an interesting topic for research ([134], see section on Usage of Case-Based Reasoning Technology).

An in-depth description of all important evaluation issues of CBR technology will appear in Althoff & Nick [35].

## 5. CBR Application Development

On the basis of the process model described in Fig. 1, it is already possible to identify the key issues in building a useful and usable CBR system [26]:

- First of all, it is necessary to have or to be able to acquire enough[n] cases to achieve a representative coverage of the application domain.
- Next, it is essential to represent the cases in a way that is storable in a computer memory, accessible by a software program and capable to capture the true meaning of a case.
- In order to do efficient case retrieval, it is important to have or to develop an indexing procedure that works automatically and brings back a certain number of similar cases in a rather short time.

---

[m]CBR-PEB is available via www: http://demolab.iese.fhg.de:8080/.
[n]Leake & Wilson [118] point out that unlike a rule-based system, which needs to cover the space of *possible* domain problems, CBR systems only need cases for a representative sample of the problems that actually arise. This may be a small subset of the full application domain, which can make the task much easier (if no user ever asks a particular question, the system won't need a case for answering that question).

- The program that assesses the similarity between the actual and the stored cases' problem description has to be both precise and robust enough to enable the transfer of solutions without too much risk.
- If the domain is of a kind where it makes sense to adapt suggested solutions to the actual situation then another key issue is the ability of the CBR system to carry out the necessary adaptation steps.
- Last but not least, CBR systems usually come together with organizational changes. Therefore, it is of major importance to achieve a proper integration of the system into mostly new or changed business processes and to get the CBR system accepted and properly used by all persons in an organization that are expected to benefit from its use.

Meanwhile a number of development strategies and methodologies of how to develop CBR systems have been presented. The DISER methodology [174, 176, 29] describes how to systematically develop experience factory applications based on CBR technology. DISER's methods for case base design include the definition of the objectives and the respective subject areas underlying the CBR system to be developed. In addition, all scenarios concerned with the case base have to be identified. Based on this information the case base conceptualization is detailed (Fig. 15). When this information is available it can be defined how the recording of the cases shall work to fill the case base (Fig. 16).

The INRECA-2 methodology [52, 50] is based on the experiences collected by project partners. Here the basic organizational background is also an experience factory (Fig. 17). Application development is supported on three different levels: a common generic level, a cookbook level, and a specific project level (Fig. 18).

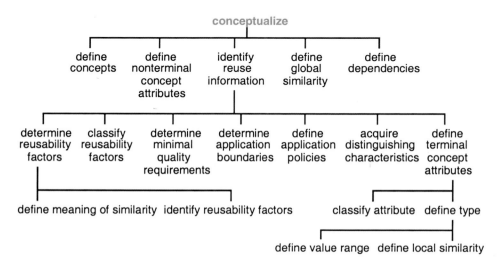

**Fig. 15.**  Developing the conceptual structure for a CBR system.

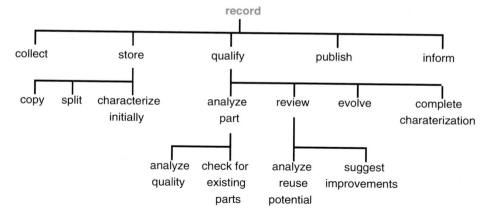

**Fig. 16.** Case acquisition and case base development.

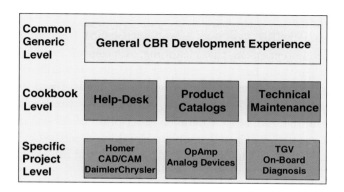

**Fig. 17.** Experience factory for developing CBR applications (adapted from [50]).

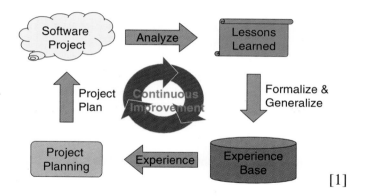

**Fig. 18.** INRECA experience base (adapted from [50]).

## 6. Case-Based Reasoning: Past, Present, and Future

CBR has its roots in Roger Schank's work on scripts [160] and dynamic memory [157]. The notion of *case-based reasoning* dates back to the beginning of the 80's [103, 157]. The underlying motivation was to model human learning and problem solving behavior. In the sequel, several exemplary research prototypes were built that made the underlying ideas more concrete (some overviews can be found in [109]). Based on these early experiences, CBR became an interesting approach for several different reasons:

- CBR offers the possibility of modeling and analyzing human learning and problem solving behavior.
- CBR supports, in an intuitively reasonable and understandable way, the handling of application domains where the notion of a case is already naturally existing (law, medicine, etc).
- CBR integrates learning and problem solving "per construction".

In Europe, CBR research started a few years later (an overview can be found in [7]). Compared to the USA it has been more focused towards knowledge-based systems development, and to the integration of case-based and other approaches (e.g. [45, 33, 1, 171, 141, 2, 37]. Research efforts on CBR were considerably focused — especially in the USA — by the DARPA workshops in 1988, 1989, and 1991 [107, 89, 43]. A similar effect was achieved by comparable national and European events [39, 97, 193, 101].

From 1995 on — based on the successful experiences of the European Workshops on Case-Based Reasoning EWCBR in Otzenhausen/Kaiserslautern 1993 (organized by Michael Richter, Klaus-Dieter Althoff, and Stefan Wess) and Chantilly 1994 (organized by Mark Keane, Michel Manago, and Jean-Paul Haton) the North American and the European CBR communities decided to join their efforts and start a biennial International Conference on Case-Based Reasoning [182, 116, 27], alternating with EWCBR° [78, 167, 57]. This process of building a real international CBR community was additionally supported by the development of a number of web repositories and email lists [18, 67, 68, 96].

For many years, CBR has been a well established topic of many regularly held scientific conferences. In the meantime, a basis of knowledge, principles, methods, and algorithms has been achieved that most researchers seem to agree on. Thus, this can be seen as the core of the field. Besides the usual introductory articles [108, 38, 7, 114, 136, 47], introductory textbooks are available [153, 192, 109, 113, 184, 125, 173]. A detailed description of several interesting early systems is given in [192], being well completed by those described in Kolodner [109], and Aamodt & Plaza [7]. The books also describe several interesting systems and approaches.

---

°Starting in 2002, the European Workshop on CBR will turned into a conference.

From a technological point of view, CBR has achieved a certain degree of maturity. This is documented by both the applications that have been carried out up to now (see section on CBR Applications) and the commercial tools currently available on the market. In 1991, the first CBR tools were offered. Though the market was completely dominated by American products at that time, the situation has been considerably changed by the introduction of new European CBR tools. An overview of early commercial tools is given by Harmon [91]. More recently, a detailed evaluation of a selection of the most important CBR tools was carried out [23]. Currently, in October 2000, more than two dozen CBR tools exist.

CBR has started to play a role in knowledge and software engineering (as can be seen by this book chapter), business informatics [162], and knowledge management. One reason here is the enormous amount of applications available [173] especially on help-desk and service support applications. And CBR will play an important role in e-commerce, customer-relationship management, and corporate knowledge management. To embed CBR technology in the business processes of various organizations, it appears to be very beneficial to view and run CBR applications as experience factories [99, 44, 30, 174]. This creates a direct link between CBR and software and knowledge engineering, for instance with topics like maintenance and meta-knowledge [129]. In addition, roles, tasks, and methods (e.g. goal-oriented measurement and evaluation) available from experience factory can be used for running real-life applications on knowledge management.

While CBR can be viewed as an approach for putting (some kind of) knowledge-based systems into practice either as implementation or as plug-in technology, the relationship to another artificial intelligence subfield will become important soon: Machine Learning.[p] One interesting issue here is the use of CBR systems as an intelligent platform for machine learning procedures, for instance, learning of retrieval structures (e.g. based on decision trees: [61, 21]; Kohonen networks: [76]; index learning: [89, 81, 62, 146, 121, 198], learning of similarity assessments procedures (e.g. adaptation of importance degrees of case features: [133, 195], learning of case structure/contents from databases and/or textual descriptions (e.g. textual CBR, text mining: [121]), or learning of user-adapted access structures ($n$-step CBR: [188, 152]).

In addition, machine learning techniques for knowledge discovery in case bases will probably be used more and more to support systematic knowledge development, a task of increasing importance for knowledge management applications and the running of lessons-learned systems. The back of knowledge development is the task of knowledge maintenance. Both tasks can be supported with goal-oriented measurement and evaluation [134]. So, techniques from experimental software engineering, machine learning, and CBR should be combined to strengthen the knowledge management method spectrum. Here the positive experience with using CBR as a plug-in technology can be reused. In addition, knowledge

[p]This supplements CBR being already a machine learning method, namely through case learning.

engineering approaches could be integrated here for knowledge elicitation and modeling.

A big challenge for CBR, and also for other information technologies, will be the possibility to represent interrelated case bases of different granularities and subject areas within, for example, an internationally operating company or a group of related companies that use the same knowledge. Here a huge knowledge network has to be built that can be accessed from various points of view, on different levels of abstraction, and on related subject areas.

An advantage of CBR could be to offer an "open environment" for integrating different kinds of approaches. This already happened very often in the past and could be a key issue to develop integrated solutions for complicated real-life problems [4, 21, 16]. For example, experience reuse is a very general task that can definitely be supported by CBR and that is of importance for nearly every application area and research field.

One example of a mutual benefit of integrating CBR with other technologies has already been mentioned above: combining CBR with the experience factory (EF) approach [175, 174]. While CBR can offer a technology for implementing the experience repository included in an experience factory, it can in addition be used as a strategy on an organizational level [31]. Vice versa, an experience factory offers a physical and/or logical infrastructure for operationalizing a CBR system in

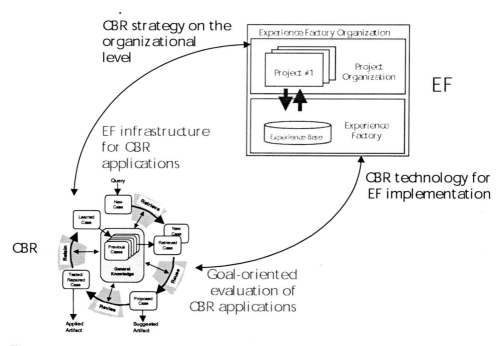

**Fig. 19.**   Mutual benefits of integrating CBR with other technologies: the experience factory example.

an organization's environment and technologies like goal-oriented measurement to evaluate CBR applications (Fig. 19).

What has to happen or to be guaranteed is that CBR remains a research field that brings up new, innovative research methods and tools helpful for information technology or, even broader, the information society?

- The collaboration and scientific communication between humanities oriented and engineering oriented research groups/practitioners within the CBR community should be preserved and/or revitalized.
- CBR should remain a community that is open for people from outside. By this, integrations as shown in Fig. 19 should be possible with various communities, among others knowledge management, knowledge engineering, software engineering, machine learning, statistics, information retrieval, decision theory, pattern recognition, neural networks, and fuzzy technologies.
- It should be possible to use CBR more and more as a plug-in technology [47].
- The current advantage of being a community that integrates "real-life applications" and "basic research" should be preserved. It is one very characteristic feature of the CBR community that has worked well during the past years. It also provides integration with other technologies will take place (through applications) and become an integrated part of the community (through basic research).

## Acknowledgment

The ideas and concepts presented here have been influenced by many persons. I am especially grateful, among others, to Agnar Aamodt, Brigitte Bartsch-Spörl, Ralph Bergmann, Christiane Gresse von Wangenheim, Markus Nick, Michael M. Richter, Dieter Rombach, Ralph Traphöner, Carsten Tautz, and Stefan Wess. Thanks go also to David Aha, Matthias Brandt, Brigitte Bartsch-Spörl, Ralph Bergmann, Hans-Dieter Burkhard, Padraig Cunningham, Werner Dubitzky, Christiane Gresse von Wangenheim, David Leake, Markus Nick, Enric Plaza, Michael M. Richter, Barry Smyth, Carsten Tautz, Ian Watson, and Gerhard Weber as well as the anonymous reviewers for commenting on an earlier version of this chapter.

## References

1. A. Aamodt, "Towards robust expert systems that learn from experience — An architectural framework", eds. J. Boose, B. Gaines and J.-G. Ganascia, *Proceedings of the EKAW'89* (1989) 311–326.
2. A. Aamodt, "A knowledge-intensive, integrated approach to problem solving and sustained learning", PhD Thesis, University of Trondheim, 1991.
3. A. Aamodt, "A case-based answer to some problems of knowledge-based systems", eds. E. Sandewall and G. Jansson, *Proceedings of the Scandinavian Conference on Artificial Intelligence* (IOS Press, 1993).

4. A. Aamodt, "Explanation-based case-based reasoning", eds. S. Wess, K.-D. Althoff and M. M. Richter (1994) 274–288.

5. A. Aamodt, Knowledge acquisition and learning by experience the role of case-specific knowledge, eds. Kodratoff and Tecuci (1995) 197–245.

6. A. Aamodt and M. Nygård, "Different roles and mutual dependencies of data, information, and knowledge — An AI perspective on their integration", *Data and Knowledge Enigneering* **16** (1995) 191–222.

7. A. Aamodt and E. Plaza, "Case-based reasoning: Foundational issues, methodological variations and system approaches", *AI Communications* **7**, no. 1 (1994) 39–59.

8. A. Abecker, A. Bernardi and M. Sintek, "Proactive knowledge delivery for enterprise knowledge management", eds. G. Ruhe and F. Bomarius, *Learning Software Organizations — Methodology and Applications Lecture Notes in Computer Science* (Springer-Verlag, 2000).

9. D. W. Aha, "Case-based learning algorithms", ed. R. Bareiss (1991) 147–158.

10. D. W. Aha, *Proceedings of the Case-Based Reasoning Workshop, AAAI'1994*, AAAI Technical Report, 1994.

11. D. W. Aha, "Editorial on lazy learning", *Artificial Intelligence Review* **11** (1997) 7–10.

12. D. W. Aha, "The omnipresence of case-based reasoning in science and application", *Knowledge-Based Systems* **11**, nos. 5–6 (1998) 261–273.

13. D. W. Aha, "The AAAI-99 KM/CBR workshop: Summary of contributions", eds. G. von Wangenheim and C. Tautz (1999) II-37–II-44.

14. D. W. Aha, I. Becerra-Fernandez, F. Maurer and H. Muñoz-Avila (eds.), *Exploring Synergies of Knowledge Management and Case-Based Reasoning: Papers from the AAAI 1999 Workshop*, Technical Report WS-99-10 (AAAI Press, Menlo Park, CA, 1999).

15. D. W. Aha, L. A. Breslow and H. Muñoz-Avila, "Conversational case-based reasoning" *Applied Intelligence*, 2000 (To appear in).

16. D. W. Aha and J. Daniels (eds.), *Case-Based Reasoning Integrations: Papers from the AAAI 1998 Workshop*.

17. D. W. Aha, D. Kibler and M. K. Albert, "Instance-based learning algorithms", *Machine Learning* **6** (1991) 37–66.

18. AI-CBR: *http://www.ai-cbr.org/*.

19. K.-D. Althoff, *Eine fallbasierte Lernkomponente als integrierter Bestandteil der MOLTKE-Werkbank zur Diagnose technischer Systeme*, Doctoral Dissertation, University of Kaiserslautern; also Sankt Augustin, Germany (infix Verlag, 1992).

20. K.-D. Althoff, "Evaluating case-based reasoning systems", *Proceedings of the Workshop on Case-Based Reasoning: A New Force in Advanced Systems Development*, S. 48–61 (published by Unicom Seminars Ltd., Brunel Science Park, Cleveland Road, Uxbridge, Middlesex UB8 3P, UK, 1995).

21. K.-D. Althoff, *Evaluating Case-Based Reasoning Systems: The INRECA Case Study*, Habilitationsschrift (Postdoctoral Thesis), Department of Computer Science, University of Kaiserslautern, July 9, 1997.

22. K.-D. Althoff and A. Aamodt, "Relating case-based problem solving and learning methods to task and domain characteristics: Towards an analytic framework, *AI Communications* **9**, no. 3 (1996) 1–8.

23. K.-D. Althoff, E. Auriol, R. Barletta and M. Manago, *A Review of Industrial Case-Based Reasoning Tools* (AI Intelligence, Oxford, UK, 1995a).

24. K.-D. Althoff, E. Auriol, R. Bergmann, S. Breen, S. Dittrich, R. Johnston, M. Manago, R. Traphöner and S. Wess, "Case-based reasoning for decision support

and diagnostic problem solving: The INRECA approach", eds. B. Bartsch-Spörl, D. Janetzko and S. Wess, XPS-95-Workshop: Fallbasiertes Schließen — Grundlagen and Anwendungen, *3rd German Workshop on CBR (GWCBR'99)*, LSA-REPORT 95-02, Centre for Learning Systems and Applications, Department of Computer Science, University of Kaiserslautern, Germany, 1995b.

25. K.-D. Althoff, E. Auriol, H. Holz, M. Manago, A. Meissonnier, C. Priebisch, S. Wess and W. Wilke, *An Evaluation of Commercial Case-Based Reasoning Tools*, INRECA (Esprit P6322), Deliverable D5, 1994.

26. K.-D. Althoff and B. Bartsch-Spörl, "Decision support for case-based applications", *Wirtschaftsinformatik 1/96*, Special Issue on Case-Based Decision Support, ed. D. Ehrenberg (1996) 8–16.

27. K.-D. Althoff, R. Bergmann and L. K. Branting (eds.), *Case-Based Reasoning Research and Development, Proceedings of the Third International Conference on Case-Based Reasoning (ICCBR'99)*, Seeon Monastery, Germany, July 27–30, *Lecture Notes in Artificial Intelligence 1650* (Springer-Verlag, 1999a).

28. K.-D. Althoff, A. Birk, G. von Wangenheim and C. Tautz, "Case-based reasoning for experimental software engineering", eds. Lenz *et al* (1998a) 235–254.

29. K.-D. Althoff, A. Birk, S. Hartkopf, W. Müller, M. Nick, D. Surmann and C. Tautz, "Managing software engineering experience for comprehensive reuse", *Proceedings of the 11th International Conference on Software Engineering and Knowledge Engineering (SEKE'99)* (1999c).

30. K.-D. Althoff, F. Bomarius, W. Müller and M. Nick, "Using a case-based reasoning for supporting continuous improvement processes", ed. P. Perner, *Proceedings of the German Workshop on Machine Learning*, Technical Report, Institute for Image Processing and Applied Informatics, Leipzig (1999d) 8.

31. K.-D. Althoff, F. Bomarius and C. Tautz, "Using case-based reasoning technology to build learning software organizations", *Proceedings of the 13th Biennial European Conference on Artificial Intelligence (ECAI'98) Workshop on Building, Maintaining, and Using Organizational Memories (OM'98)* (1998b).

32. K.-D. Althoff, F. Bomarius and C. Tautz, "Knowledge management for building learning software organizations", (*Accepted for The Information System Frontiers Journal*, 2000a).

33. K.-D. Althoff, S. Kockskämper, F. Maurer, M. Stadler and S. Wess, Ein System zur fallbasierten Wissensverarbeitung in technischen Diagnosesituationen, eds. J. Retti and K. Leidlmeier, *5th Austrian Artificial Intelligence Conference* (Springer Verlag, 1989) 65–70.

34. K.-D. Althoff, W. Müller, M. Nick and B. Snoek, "KM-PEB: An online experience base on knowledge management technology", eds. E. Blanzieri and L. Portinale, *Advances in Case-Based Reasoning — Proceedings of the 5th European Workshop on Case-Based Reasoning (EWCBR'00)* (to appear, 2000b).

35. K.-D. Althoff and M. Nick, *Evaluating Case-Based Reasoning Systems* (Springer Verlag) (to appear, 2001).

36. K.-D. Althoff, M. Nick and C. Tautz, "CBR-PEB: A tool for implementing reuse concepts of the experience factory for CBR-system development", *Proc. 5th German Conference on Knowledge-Based Systems (XPS'99) Workshop on Case-Based Reasoning (GWCBR'99)*, CBR-PEB is publicly accessible via *http://demolab.iese.fhg.de:8080/*.

37. K.-D. Althoff and S. Wess, "Case-based knowledge acquisition, learning and problem solving in diagnostic real world tasks", *Proceedings of the EKAW'91*, Glasgow and Crieff, ed. D. Smeed; also [published in *Proceedings of the European Knowledge*

*Acquisition Workshop (EKAW'91)*, eds. M. Linster and B. Gaines], GMD-Studien Nr. 211 (September 1992) 48–67.

38. K.-D. Althoff and S. Wess, "Case-based reasoning and expert system development", eds. F. Schmalhofer, G. Strube and T. Wetter, *Contemporary Knowledge Engineering and Cognition* (Springer Verlag) 146–158.

39. K.-D. Althoff, S. Wess, B. Bartsch-Spörl and D. Janetzko (eds.), Ähnlichkeit von Fällen beim fallbasierten Schließen, *Proceedings of the 1st Meeting of the German Working Group on Case-Based Reasoning*, University of Kaiserslautern, June 1992.

40. K.-D. Althoff and W. Wilke, "Potential uses of case-based reasoning in experience based construction of software systems and business process support", eds. R. Bergmann and W. Wilke, *Proceedings of the Fifth German Workshop on Case-Based Reasoning*, Centre for Learning Systems and Applications, University of Kaiserslautern, LSA-97-01E (1997) 31–38.

41. F. Azuaje, W. Dubitzky, N. Black and K. Adamson, "Improving clinical decision support through case-based fusion", *IEEE Transactions on Biomedical Engineering*, Special Issue on *Biomedical Data Fusion* **46**, no. 10 (1999) 1181–1185.

42. F. Azuaje, W. Dubitzky, N. Black and K. Adamson, "Case retrieval strategies for CBR: A categorised bibliography", *The Knowledge Engineering Review* (in press, 2000).

43. R. Bareiss (ed.), *Proceedings of the 3rd DARPA Workshop on Case-Based Reasoning* (Morgan Kaufmann, 1991).

44. K. Bartlmae, "An experience factory approach for data mining", *Proceedings of the LWA'99*, University of Magdeburg, Germany (1999) 5–14.

45. B. Bartsch-Spörl, Ansätze zur Behandlung von fallorientiertem Erfahrungswissen in Expertensystemen, *KI* **4** (1987) 32–36.

46. B. Bartsch-Spörl, K.-D. Althoff and A. Meissonnier, "Learning from and reasoning about case-based reasoning systems", eds. P. Mertens and H. Voß, *Expertensystem 1997 (XPS'97) — Proceedings of the 4th German Conference on Knowledge-Based Systems* (infix Verlag, 1997).

47. B. Bartsch-Spörl, M. Lenz and A. Hübner, "Case-based reasoning — Survey and future directions", ed. F. Puppe, *Knowledge-Based Systems — Survey and Future Directions (XPS'99) — Proceedings of the 5th German Biennial Conference on Knowledge-Based Systems* (Springer Verlag, 1999) 67–89.

48. V. R. Basili, G. Caldiera and D. Rombach, "Experience factory", ed. J. J. Marciniak, *Encyclopedia of Software Engineering* **1** (John Wiley & Sons, 1994a) 469–476.

49. V. R. Basili, G. Caldiera and D. Rombach, "Goal-question-metric paradigm", ed. J. J. Marciniak, *Encyclopedia of Software Engineering* **1** (John Wiley & Sons, 1994b).

50. R. Bergmann, "Developing industrial case-based reasoning applications using the INRECA methodology", *IJCAI 1999 Workshop on Automating the Construction of Case-Based Reasoners*, Slide Copies, Invited Talk, 1999a.

51. R. Bergmann, Preface to the special issue on "Engineering applications of case-based reasoning", Special Issue of the *International Journal Engineering Applications of Artificial Intelligence* **12**, no. 6 (Elsevier, 1999b) 661–663.

52. R. Bergmann, S. Breen, M. Göker, M. Manago and S. Wess, *Developing Industrial CBR Applications, The INRECA — Methodology, Lecture Notes in Artificial Intelligence, 1612* (Springer Verlag, 1999).

53. R. Bergmann, H. Muñoz-Avila, M. Veloso and E. Melis, "Case-based reasoning applied to planning tasks", ed. M. Lenz *et al* (1998a) 169–200.

54. R. Bergmann, G. Pews and W. Wilke, "Explanation-based similarity: A unifying approach for integrating domain knowledge into case-based reasoning for diagnosis and planning tasks", eds. S. Wess, K.-D. Althoff and M. M. Richter (1994) 182–196.

55. R. Bergmann and A. Stahl, "Similarity measures for object-oriented case representations", eds. B. Smyth and P. Cunningham (1998) 25–36.

56. R. Bergmann, W. Wilke, I. Vollrath and S. Wess, "Integrating general knowledge with object-oriented case representation and reasoning", *Proceedings 4th German Workshop on Case-Based Reasoning (GWCBR-96)*, 1996.

57. E. Blanzieri and L. Portinale (eds.), *Advances in Case-Based Reasoning: Proceedings of the Fifth European Workshop on Case-Based Reasoning* (Springer-Verlag, 2000).

58. K. Börner, "CBR for design", eds. M. Lenz *et al* (1998a) 201–234.

59. F. Bomarius, K.-D. Althoff and W. Müller, "Knowledge management for learning software organizations", *Software Process — Improvement and Practice 4* (1998, printed 1999) 89–93.

60. M. Brandt, *Fallbasierte Aufwandsschätzung von Softwareentwicklungsprojekten*, Technical Report No. 33, Institute for Business Informatics, University of Leipzig, Germany, 2000.

61. L. A. Breslow and D. W. Aha, "Simplifying decision trees: A survey", *Knowledge Engineering Review* 1 (1997) 1–40.

62. H.-D. Burkhard, *Case Retrieval Nets*, Technical Report, Humboldt University Berlin, 1995.

63. H.-D. Burkhard, "Extending some concepts of CBR — Foundations of case retrieval nets", ed. M. Lenz *et al* (1998a) 17–50.

64. H.-D. Burkhard and M. M. Richter, On the notion of similarity in case-based reasoning and fuzzy theory, ed. S. K. Pal *et al* (2000).

65. J. G. Carbonell (eds.), "Special volume on machine learning", *Artificial Intelligence* 40 (1989).

66. C. Carrick and Q. Yang, "Activating CBR systems through autonomous information gathering", *Proceedings of the International Joint Conference on Artificial Intelligence 1999 (IJCAI'99)*, 1999.

67. CBR-Web: *http://www.cbr-web.org/*.

68. CBR-PEB: *http://demolab.iese.fhg.de:8080/*.

69. W. Cheetham and J. Graf, "Case-based reasoning in color matching", eds. D. B. Leake and E. Plaza (1997) 1–12.

70. P. R. Cohen, "Evaluation and case-based reasoning", ed. K. Hammond (1989b) 168–172.

71. S. Craw, N. Wiratunga and R. Rowe, "Case-based design for tablet formulation", eds. B. Smyth and P. Cunningham (1998) 358–369.

72. P. Cunningham, *Intelligent Systems in Electronic Commerce*, Keynote speech at the *Third International Conference on Case-Based Reasoning (ICCBR'99)*, 1999.

73. P. Cunningham and B. Smyth, "A Comparison of model-based and incremental case-based approaches to electronic fault diagnosis", D. W. Aha, *Proceedings of the Case-Based Reasoning Workshop at AAAI 1994*, 1994.

74. A. De la Ossa, "Knowledge adaptation: Analogical transfer of empirical knowledge across domains for case-based problem solving", Doctoral Dissertation, University of Kaiserslautern, 1992.

75. S. Decker and S. Staab, *AI Techniques for Knowledge Management*, ECAI-2000 tutorial, *http://kmtutorial.aifb.uni-karlsruhe.de/*, 2000.

76. W. Dubitzky and F. Azuaje, "A genetic algorithm and a growing cell structures approach to learning case retrieval structures", ed. S. K. Pal *et al* (2000) 115–146.

77. W. Dubitzky, A. Büchner and F. Azuaje, "Viewing knowledge management as a case-based application", *Proceedings of the AAAI'99 Workshop on Knowledge Management and CBR Synergy*, Technical Report WS-99-10 (AAAI Press, 1999) 23–27.

78. B. Faltings and I. Smith, *Advances in Case-Based Reasoning: Proceedings of the Third European Workshop on Case-Based Reasoning* (Springer-Verlag, 1996).

79. G. R. Finnie, G. E. Wittig and J.-M. Desharnais, Estimating software development effort with case-based reasoning, eds. D. B. Leake and E. Plaza (1997).

80. S. E. Fox, "A unified CBR architecture for robot navigation", eds. B. Blanzieri and L. Portinale (2000) 406–417.

81. S. E. Fox and D. B. Leake, "Modeling case-based planning for repairing reasoning failures", *Proceedings of the 1995 AAAI Spring Symposium on Representing Mental States and Mechanisms* (AAAI Press, 1995) 31–38.

82. P. Funk, M. Minor, T. Roth-Berghofer and D. Wilson (eds.), "Flexible strategies for maintaining knowledge containers", *Proceedings of a Workshop at the 14th European Conference on Artificial Intelligence (ECAI 2000)*, 2000.

83. M. L. Gick and K. J. Holyoak, "Analogical problem solving", *Cognitive Psychology* **12** (1980) 306–355.

84. C. Globig and S. Lange, "On case-based representability and learnability of languages", eds. S. Arikawa and K. P. Jantke, *Proceedings of the 4th International Workshop on Analogical and Inductive Inference (AII'94), Lecture Notes in Artifical Intelligence, 872* (Springer-Verlag, 1994) 106–121.

85. M. Göker and T. Roth-Berghofer, *Workshop on The Integration of Case-Based Reasoning in Business Processes*, eds. S. Schmidt and I. Vollrath (1999).

86. C. G. von Wangenheim, K.-D. Althoff and Barcia, "Intelligent retrieval of software engineering experienceware", *Proceedings of the 11th International Conference on Software Engineering and Knowledge Engineering (SEKE'99)*, 1999.

87. C. G. von Wangenheim and C. Tautz, *Workshop on Practical Case-Based Reasoning Strategies for Building and Maintaining Corporate Memories*, eds. S. Schmidt and I. Vollrath (1999), 1999.

88. K. M. Gupta, "Case base engineering for large scale industrial applications", *Proceedings of AAAI Spring Symposium on Artificial Intelligence in Knowledge Management, http://ksi.cpsc.ucalgary.ca/AIKM97/AIKM97Proc.html*, 1997.

89. K. Hammond, *Case-Based Planning* (Academic Press, London, 1989a).

90. K. Hammond, *Proceedings of the 2nd Darpa Workshop on Case-Based Reasoning*, Holiday Inn (Morgan Kaufmann, Pensacola Beach, 1989b).

91. P. Harmon, "Overview: Commercial case-based reasoning products", *Intelligent Software Strategies* (January 1992).

92. F. Heister and W. Wilke, "An architecture for maintaining case-based reasoning systems", eds. B. Smyth and P. Cunningham (1998), 1998.

93. J. Hendler, Experimental AI systems, in *Journal of Experimental and Theoretical AI* **7** (1995) 1–5.

94. S. Henninger, "Developing domain knowledge through the reuse of project experiences", *Proceedings of the Symposium on Software Reusability (SSR'95)*, Seattle WA (April 1995).

95. S. Henninger, "Capturing and formalizing best practices in a software development organization", *Proceedings of the 9th International Conference on Software Engineering and Knowledge Engineering (SEKE'97)*, 1997.

96. ICCBR: *http://www.iccbr.org/*.

97. D. Janetzko and T. Schult, *Fälle in hybriden Systemen, Proceedings of the Second German Workshop on CBR*, University of Freiburg, Germany, 1993.

98. J. Jarmulak, *Case-Based Reasoning for NDT Data Interpretation*, PhD Thesis, Delft University of Technology, The Netherlands, 1999.

99. Y. Kalfoglou and D. Robertson, "Applying experienceware to support ontology deployment", *Proceedings of the International Conference on Software Engineering and Knowledge Engineering*, 2000.

100. G. Kamp, S. Lange and C. Globig, "Related areas", eds. M. Lenz *et al* (1998a) 327–352.

101. M. Keane, J.-P. Haton and M. Manago, *Advances in Case-Based Reasoning: Proceedings of the Second European Workshop on Case-Based Reasoning* (Springer-Verlag, 1995).

102. H. Kitano and H. Shimazu, "The experience sharing architecture: A case study in corporate-wide case-based software quality control", ed. D. B. Leake (1996a), 1996.

103. J. L. Kolodner, "Retrieval and organizational strategies in conceptual memory: A computer model", PhD Thesis, Yale University, 1980.

104. J. L. Kolodner, "Maintaining organization in a dynamic long-term memory", *Cognitive Science* **7** (1983a) 243–280.

105. J. L. Kolodner, "Reconstructive memory: A computer model", *Cognitive Science* **7** (1983b) 281–328.

106. J. L. Kolodner, "Extending problem solver capabilities through case-based inference", *Proceedings of the 4th International Workshop on Machine Learning* (1987) 167–178.

107. J. L. Kolodner, *Proceedings of the 1st Darpa Workshop on Case-Based Reasoning* (Morgan Kaufmann, Holiday Inn, Clearwater Beach, 1988).

108. J. L. Kolodner, "Improving human decision making through case-based decision aiding", *AI Magazine* **91**, no. 2 (1991) 52–68.

109. J. L. Kolodner, *Case-Based Reasoning* (Morgan Kaufmann, 1993).

110. J. L. Kolodner, R. L. Simpson and K. P. Sycara, "A process model of case-based reasoning in problem solving", *Proceedings of the IJCAI'85* (Morgan Kaufmann, Los Angeles, CA, 1985) 284–290.

111. P. Koton, Reasoning about evidence in causal explanations, *Proceedings of the AAAI'88* (1988) 256–261.

112. W. Lam and V. Shankararaman, "Managing change during software development: An incremental, knowledge-based approach", *Proceedings of 10th International Conference on Software Engineering and Knowledge Engineering*, San Francisco Bay, California, 1998.

113. D. B. Leake, *Case-based Reasoning — Experiences, Lessons and Future Directions* (AAAI Press, 1996a).

114. D. B. Leake, "CBR in Context: The present and the future", Leake (1996a), 1996b.

115. D. B. Leake, "Cognition as case-based reasoning", *The Blackwell Companion to Cognitive Science*, 1998.

116. D. B. Leake and E. Plaza, "Case-based reasoning research and development", *Proceedings of the Second International Conference on Case-Based Reasoning (ICCBR'97)* (Springer-Verlag, 1997).

117. D. B. Leake and D. C. Wilson, "Categorizing case-base maintenance: Dimensions and directions", eds. B. Smyth and P. Cunningham (1998) 196–207.

118. D. B. Leake and D. C. Wilson, "Remembering why to remember: Performance-guided case-base maintenance", eds. E. L. Blanzieri and Portinale (2000), 2000.

119. B. Lees, M. Hamza and C. Irgens, "Applying case-based reasoning to software quality management", eds. D. B. Leake and E. Plaza (1997), 1997.

120. B. Lees, *Workshop on Hybrid Case-Based Reasoning Systems*, eds. S. Schmidt and I. Vollrath (1999), 1999.

121. M. Lenz, *Case Retrieval Nets as a Model for Building Flexible Information Systems*, Sankt Augustin, Germany, DISKI 236 (influx Verlag, 2000).
122. M. Lenz, E. Auriol and M. Manago, "Diagnosis and decision support", Lenz *et al* (1998a), (1988c) 51–90.
123. M. Lenz and H.-D. Burkhard, "Case retrieval nets: Basic ideas and extensions", *Advances in Artificial Intelligence (KI'96) — Proceedings of the 20th Annual German Conference on Artificial Intelligence, Lecture Notes in Artificial Intelligence, 1137* (Springer-Verlag, 1996) 227–239.
124. M. Lenz, H.-D. Burkhard, P. Pirk, E. Auriol and M. Manago, CBR for diagnosis and decision support, *AI Communications* **9**, no. 3 (September 1996) 138–146.
125. M. Lenz, B. Bartsch-Spörl, H.-D. Burkhard and S. Wess, "Case-based reasoning technology: From foundations to applications", *Lecture Notes in Artificial Intelligence, 1400* (Springer-Verlag, 1998a).
126. M. Lenz, A. Hübner and M. Kunze, Textual CBR, Lenz *et al* (1998a), 1998b.
127. M. L. Maher, B. Balachandran and D. M. Zhang, *Case-Based Reasoning in Design* (Lawrence Erlbaum Associates, 1995).
128. M. Manago, K.-D. Althoff, E. Auriol, R. Traphöner, S. Wess, N. Conruyt and F. Maurer, "Induction and reasoning from cases", eds. M. M. Richter, S. Wess, K.-D. Althoff and F. Maurer, *Proceedings of the First European Workshop on Case-Based Reasoning (EWCBR'93)*, SEKI-REPORT SR-93-12, Universität Kaiserslautern, 313–318, 1993.
129. T. Menzies, K.-D. Althoff, Y. Kalfoglou and E. Motta, "Issues with meta-knowledge", Accepted for the *International Journal of Software Engineering and Knowledge Engineering (IJSEKE)*, 2000.
130. M. Minor and A. Hanft, "The life cycle of test cases in a CBR system", eds. E. Blanzieri and L. Portinale (2000) 455–466.
131. E. Motta, "Knowledge level modelling", (in this volume, 2000).
132. H. Muñoz-Avila, J. A. Hendler and D. W. Aha, "Conversational case-based planning", *Review of Applied Expert Systems* **5** (1999) 163–174.
133. H. Muñoz-Avila and J. Hüllen, "Feature weighting by explaining case-base planning episodes", eds. B. Faltings and I. Smith (1996) 280–294.
134. M. Nick and K.-D. Althoff, "Systematic evaluation and maintenance of experience bases", ed. P. Funk *et al* (2000), 2000.
135. M. Nick, K.-D. Althoff and C. Tautz, "Facilitating the practical evaluation of organizational memories using the goal-question-metric technique", *Proceedings of the Twelfth Workshop on Knowledge Acquisition, Modeling and Management (KAW'99)*, Banff (October 1999) 16–21.
136. L. S. Ong and A. D. Narasimhalu, "Case-based reasoning", ed. J. Liebowitz, *The Handbook of Applied Expert Systems* (CRC Press, 1998) 11-1–11-16.
137. R. Oxman and A. Voß, "CBR in design", *AI Communications* **9**, no. 3 (September 1996) 117–127.
138. S. K. Pal, T. S. Dillon and D. S. Yeung, *Soft Computing in Case-Based Reasoning* (Springer-Verlag, London, 2000).
139. M. Papagni, V. Cirillo and A. Micarelli, "Ocram-CBR — A shell for case-based educational systems", eds. D. Leake and E. Plaza (1997) 104–113.
140. T. Pfeifer and M. M. Richter, *Diagnose von technischen Systemen — Grundlagen, Methoden und Perspektiven der Fehlerdiagnose* (Deutscher Universitäts-Verlag, 1993).
141. E. Plaza and R. López de Mántaras, "A case-based apprentice that learns from fuzzy examples", eds. Ras, Zemankova and Emrich, *Methodologies for Intelligent Systems* **5** (North Holland, 1990) 420–427.

142. B. W. Porter, R. Bareiss and R. C. Holte, "Concept learning and heuristic classification in weak-theory domains", *Artificial Intelligence* **45** (1990).

143. N. V. N. Prased and E. Plaza, "Corporate memories as distributed case libraries", *Proceedings of the 10th Banff Knowledge Acquisition for Knowledge-based Systems Workshop*, Banff, Canada **2** (1996) 40: 1–19.

144. G. Probst and Romhardt, "The components of knowledge management — A practical approach", URL: *www.cck.uni-kl.de/wmk/papers/public/Bausteine/*, 1998 (in German).

145. F. Puppe and A. Günter, "Expertensysteme 93", *Proceedings of the 2nd German Conference on Expert Systems* (Springer-Verlag, 1993).

146. K. Racine and Q. Yang, "Maintaining unstructured case bases", eds. D. B. Leake and E. Plaza (1997) 553–564.

147. T. Reinartz, I. Iglezakis and T. Roth-Berghofer, "On quality measures for case base maintenance", eds. E. Blanzieri and L. Portinale (2000) 247–259.

148. M. M. Richter, "Classification and learning of similarity measures", *Proceedings of the 16th Annual Conference of the German Society for Classification* (Springer-Verlag, 1992).

149. M. M. Richter, "The knowledge contained in similarity measures", *First International Conference on Case-Based Reasoning (ICCBR'95)*, Invited talk, Sesimbra, Portugal, 1995a.

150. M. M. Richter, "Some elementary remarks on case-based reasoning", (*Unpublished manuscript*, 1995b).

151. M. M. Richter, "Introduction to case-based reasoning", ed. M. Lenz *et al* (1998a) 1–16.

152. M. M. Richter, Personal communication, 2000.

153. C. K. Riesbeck and R. C. Schank, *Inside Case-Based Reasoning* (Lawrence Erlbaum Associates, Hillsdale, NJ, 1989).

154. E. L. Rissland, "Examples in legal reasoning: Legal hypotheticals", *Proceedings of the IJCAI'93*, 1983.

155. E. L. Rissland and J. J. Daniels, "Using CBR to Drive IR", ed. C. S. Mellish, *Proceedings of the IJCAI'95* (1995) 400–408.

156. G. Ruhe, "Learning software organizations", *in this volume*, 2000.

157. R. C. Schank, *Dynamic Memory: A Theory of Learning in Computers and People* (Cambridge University Press, 1982).

158. R. C. Schank, "Case-based explanation", ed. J. G. Carbonell (1989) 353–385.

159. R. C. Schank, *Inside Multi-Media Case Based Instruction* (Lawrence Erlbaum Associates, 1998).

160. R. C. Schank and R. Abelson, *Scripts, Plans, Goals, and Understanding* (Lawrence Erlbaum Associates, Hillsdale, NJ, 1977).

161. S. Schmidt and I. Vollrath, "Challenges for case-based reasoning", *Proceedings of the ICCBR'99 Workshops*, LSA-Report LSA-99-03E, University of Kaiserslautern, Germany, 1999.

162. R. Schulz, *Fallbasierte Entscheidungsunterstützende Systeme — ein Ansatz zu Lösung betrieblicher Entscheidungsprobleme*, Doctoral Dissertation, Faculty of Economics, University of Leipzig, Germany, 1998.

163. J. Schumacher and R. Bergmann, "An efficient approach to similarity-based retrieval on top of relational databases", eds. E. Blanzieri and L. Portinale (2000) 273–284.

164. A. Seitz, "A case-based methodology for planning individualized case oriented tutoring", ed. K.-D. Althoff *et al* (1999) 318–328.

165. H. Shimazu, H. Kitano and A. Shibata, "Retrieving cases from relational data-bases: Another stride towards corporate-wide case base systems", ed. R. Bajcsy, *Proceedings of the 13th IJCAI* (1993) 909–914.

166. B. Smyth and P. Cunningham, "A comparison of incremental case-based reasoning and inductive learning", ed. M. Keane *et al*, 1995.

167. B. Smyth and P. Cunningham, *Advances in Case-Based Reasoning: Proceedings of the Fourth European Workshop on Case-Based Reasoning* (Springer-Verlag, 1998).

168. B. Smyth and M. Keane, "Remembering to forget: A competence-preserving case deletion policy for case-based reasoning systems", ed. C. S. Mellish, *Proceedings of the IJCAI'95* (1995) 377–383.

169. B. Smyth and E. McKenna, "Modelling the competence of case-bases", eds. B. Smyth and P. Cunningham (1998) 196–207.

170. R. van Solingen and E. Berghout, *The goal/question/metric method, a practical method for quality improvement of software development* (McGraw-Hill, 1999).

171. M. van Someren, L. L. Zheng and W. Post, "Cases, models, or compiled knowledge? A cooperative analysis and proposed integration", eds. B. Wielinga and J. Boose *et al*, *Current Trends in Knowledge Acquisition* (IOS Press, 1990) 339–355.

172. C. Stanfill and D. L. Waltz, "Towards memory based reasoning", *Communications of the ACM* **29** (1986) 1213–1229.

173. M. Stolpmann and S. S. Wess, *Optimierung der Kundenbeziehung mit CBR-Systemen, Intelligente Systeme für E-Commerce und Support* (Addison Wesley, 1998).

174. C. Tautz, *Customizing Software Engineering Experience Management Systems to Organizational Needs*, Doctoral Dissertation, Departmant of Computer Science, University of Kaiserslautern, Germany, 2000.

175. C. Tautz and K.-D. Althoff, "Using case-based reasoning for reusing software knowledge", eds. D. B. Leake and E. Plaza (1997) 156–165.

176. C. Tautz and K.-D. Althoff, "A case study on engineering ontologies and related processes for sharing software engineering experience", *Proceedings of the 12th International Conference on Software Engineering and Knowledge Engineering (SEKE'00)*, 2000.

177. C. Tautz and C. G. von Wangenheim, *A Representation Formalism for Supporting Reuse of Software Engineering Knowledge*, IESE-Report 051.98/E, Fraunhofer IESE, Kaiserslautern, Germany, 1998.

178. R. Traphöner, "Worth writing home about: Some notes on methodology in a big software organisation", eds. K.-D. Althoff and W. Müller, *Proceedings of the 2nd International Workshop on Learning Software Organisations*, Fraunhofer IESE, Kaiserslautern, Germany, 2000.

179. R. Traphöner, M. Manago, N. Conruyt and S. Dittrich, *Industrial Criteria for Comparing the Technologies of INRECA*, INRECA (Esprit P6322), Deliverable D4, 1992.

180. A. Tversky, "Features of similarity", *Psychological Review* **84** (1977) 327–362.

181. M. Veloso, *Planning and Learning by Analogical Reasoning* (Springer-Verlag, 1994).

182. M. Veloso and A. Aamodt, *Case-Based Reasoning Research and Development, Proceedings of the First International Conference on Case-Based Reasoning (ICCBR'99)* (Springer-Verlag, 1995).

183. M. Veloso, H. Munoz-Avila and R. Bergmann, "Case-based planning: selected methods and systems", *AI Communications* **9**, no. 3 (September 1996) 128–137.

184. I. Watson, *Applying Case-Based Reasoning — Techniques for Enterprise Systems* (Morgan Kaufmann, 1997).

185. I. Watson, "CBR is a methodology not a technology", eds. R. Miles, M. Moulton and M. Bramer, *Research and Development in Expert Systems XV* (Springer, London, 1998) 213–223.

186. G. Weber, "Episodic learner modeling", *Cognitive Science* **20** (1996) 195–236.

187. G. Weber and T. J. Schult, "CBR for tutoring and help systems", ed. M. Lenz *et al* (1998a) 255–271.

188. S. Weibelzahl and G. Weber, Benutzermodellierung von Kundenwßnschen durch Fallbasiertes Schließen, *Proceedings of the LWA'1999*, University of Magdeburg, Germany (1999) 295–300.

189. S. Wess, PATDEX — ein Ansatz zur wissensbasierten und inkrementellen Verbesserung von Åhnlichkeitsbewertungen in der fallbasierten Diagnostik, eds. F. Puppe and A. Günter (1993) 42–55.

190. S. Wess, *Fallbasiertes Schließen in wissensbasierten Systemen zur Entscheidungsunterstützung und Diagnostik*, Doctoral Dissertation, University of Kaiserslautern, Germany, 1995.

191. S. Wess, K.-D. Althoff and G. Derwand, Using k-d trees to improve the retrieval step in case-based reasoning, eds. S. Wess, K.-D. Althoff and M. M. Richter (1994) 167–181.

192. S. Wess, K.-D. Althoff, F. Maurer, R. Paulokat, R. Praeger, and O. Wendel (eds.), *Fallbasiertes Schließen — Eine Übersicht, Bände 1-3*, SEKI-REPORT SWP-92-08/09/10, University of Kaiserslautern, Germany (1992) 425.

193. S. Wess, K.-D. Althoff and M. M. Richter, *Topics in Case-Based Reasoning* (Springer-Verlag, 1994b).

194. S. Wess and C. Globig, "Case-based and symbolic classification algorithms — A case study using version space", eds. S. Wess, K.-D. Althoff and M. M. Richter (1994) 77–91.

195. D. Wettschereck, D. W. Aha and T. Mohri, "A review and empirical evaluation of feature weighting methods for a class of lazy learning algorithms", *Artificial Intelligence Review* **11** (1997) 273–314.

196. W. Wilke, *Knowledge Management for Intelligent Sales Support in Electronic Commerce*, Doctoral Dissertation, University of Kaiserslautern, Germany, 1999.

197. J. Zhu and Q. Yang, "Remembering to add: Competence-preserving case addition policies for case base maintenance, *Proceedings of the International Joint Conference in Artificial Intelligence (IJCAI'99)* August 1999.

198. P. Perner, "Different learning strategies in a case-based reasoning system for image interpretation", eds. B. Smyth and P. Cummingham, *Advances in Case-Based Reasoning* (Springer-Verlag, 1998) 251–261.

# THE KNOWLEDGE MODELING PARADIGM
# IN KNOWLEDGE ENGINEERING

ENRICO MOTTA

*Knowledge Media Institute, The Open University Walton Hall,*
*Milton Keynes, MK7 6AA, UK*
*E-mail: e.motta@open.ac.uk*

The essence of *knowledge-level modeling* (henceforth *knowledge modeling*) is to represent a system at a level which abstracts from implementation considerations and focuses instead on its competence: what does the system know? how does the system use its knowledge? The system in question is not necessarily a software artifact: it can be an organization, a human being, an artificial agent. For instance, modern methodologies for knowledge-based system development, such as CommonKADS, prescribe the development of abstract problem solving and domain models, prior to their implementation in a particular tool. In a knowledge management scenario, a knowledge modeling approach can be used to develop a model of the competence of an organization, which can then support a variety of decision-making scenarios. The recent social and technological changes (i.e., the rise of the knowledge-creating company, the rapid growth of the Internet) have also emphasized the need for effective methods and formalisms for acquiring, representing, sharing and maintaining knowledge, independently of its use in performance systems. In this paper, I will provide an overview of research in knowledge modeling. Specifically, I will first characterize the main tenets of the knowledge modeling paradigm, as formulated by a number of researchers in knowledge-based systems, and I will then present the state-of-the-art in knowledge modeling research, with particular emphasis on the application of knowledge modeling technology to knowledge engineering, knowledge management and knowledge sharing and reuse.

*Keywords*: Knowledge modeling, knowledge engineering, problem solving methods, ontologies, task models.

## 1. Introduction

As discussed in some detail by Stutt and Motta [1] our own time is unique not perhaps in its concentration on knowledge but in its appropriation of the term "knowledge" and its cognates (intelligence, expertise, smartness). The examples are legion: knowledge management, knowledge workers, knowledge-creating company, knowledge systems, knowledge engineering, knowledge media, intelligent machines, expert systems, smart bombs, smart buildings. In the aforementioned paper, Arthur Stutt and I use the expression *the epistemification of technology*, to emphasize the changing nature of the technology surrounding us (i.e., things are becoming "smarter", they exhibit "knowledge") and we point out that in the new knowledge-centred scenarios which characterize the emerging *knowledge age*, technologies such as *knowledge-level modeling* [2–5] will play a crucial, almost *organic* (i.e., essential, integral and natural) role. If knowledge is everywhere (e.g. in software, in people, in organizations, in devices), we need methods and techniques for acquiring, representing, sharing and maintaining it, independently of its particular embodiment — i.e., whether it resides in a database, in a person, in a tacitly shared organizational practice, or in a robot.

The term *knowledge-level modeling* (henceforth, *knowledge modeling*) denotes a representation of a system at a level which abstracts from implementation considerations and focuses instead on its competence: "What does the system know?", "How does the system use its knowledge?". Such a system is not necessarily a software artefact: it can be an organization, a human being, an artificial agent. In addition, knowledge modeling activities can target a variety of domains, can be performed in a variety of contexts and for a variety of purposes. For instance, modern methodologies for knowledge-based system development, such as CommonKADS [6], prescribe the development of abstract problem solving and domain models, prior to their implementation in a particular tool. In a knowledge management scenario, a knowledge modeling approach can be used to develop a model of the competence of an organization [7, 8], which can then support a variety of decision-making scenarios. Researchers on knowledge sharing and reuse [9, 10, 5, 11, 6] know that abstractions (i.e., knowledge models) are needed to allow selection and configuration of reusable components for a specific application.

The recent social and technological changes (i.e., the rise of the knowledge-creating company, the rapid growth of the Internet) have also emphasized the need for effective methods and formalisms for acquiring, representing, sharing and maintaining knowledge, independently of its use in performance systems. In a nutshell, knowledge modeling technologies, in their various forms (e.g. ontologies, problem solving methods, domain models), are now becoming ubiquitous. In this paper, I will provide an overview of research in knowledge modeling. Specifically, I will first characterize the main tenets of the knowledge modeling paradigm, as formulated by a number of researchers in knowledge-based systems, and I will then present the state-of-the-art in knowledge modeling research, with particular emphasis on the application of knowledge modeling technology to knowledge engineering, knowledge management and knowledge sharing and reuse.

## 2. The Knowledge Modeling Paradigm

Although the term "knowledge modeling" can be used loosely to describe any implementation-independent model of competence, this term can also be given a strict interpretation: it refers to a precise research paradigm, which emerged in knowledge engineering as a reaction to the *mining view of knowledge acquisition* [12, 13], which was prevalent in the early days of expert systems and still permeates (more or less consciously) much expert system research. In a nutshell, the mining view assumes that discrete and distinct "gems of expertise" can be elicited one by one from a domain expert and encoded in a system. This approach

**Table 1.** Characterization of the mining approach to rule-based system development.

| | |
|---|---|
| Knowledge Categories | Facts and Heuristic Problem Solving Rules |
| KA Methodology | Acquisition process is driven by the computational model underlying the chosen implementation shell (typically a rule-based one) |
| Levels of Descriptions | Only one, in terms of the rule-based representation |
| KA Paradigm | Transfer of expertise |
| Cognitive Paradigm | Production systems as general problem solving architectures for intelligence |
| Reusable Components | Inference engine |

is typically supported by rule-based shells, such as Emycin [14], which provide a generic inference engine and rule editing facilities, to support the codification and operationalization of knowledge expressed as inference rules. The aim here is to built a virtual expert, i.e., a system which can emulate the problem solving behaviour of an expert by relying on the same body of knowledge. Hence, the mining approach strongly relies on the assumption that expertise does in fact consist of (or can be at least reformulated as) a set of rules. The cognitive basis for such an assumption can be traced back to Newell and Simon [15], who proposed production systems as a general computational paradigm for describing intelligent behaviour. Table 1 summarizes the main tenets of the mining approach, as applied to rule-based system development.

A practical problem with this style of expert system development was recognized early on and dubbed the *knowledge acquisition bottleneck* [16]. The expression refers to the fact that the expert system development process was often hindered by the difficulties associated with eliciting knowledge from an expert and coding it into the system. It is easy to see that this problem is an obvious consequence of the approach chosen. The "knowledge acquisition as mining" development scenario is one in which (i) system development is essentially incremental rule acquisition and (ii) knowledge acquisition (KA) consists of an interactive transfer of expertise from expert to system — Buchanan and Shortliffe [17] refer to this process as *knowledge programming*. Therefore, in this scenario the expert is not just one of the players involved in a subset of the system development life-cycle but the person who is central to the whole process — i.e., the main bottleneck.

The knowledge acquisition bottleneck seemed to provide evidence to the arguments put forward by those researchers [18, 19], who rejected the idea that "true expertise" could be transferred from an expert to a software system and reduced to a rule-based representation. These authors argue that expertise is by its nature *tacit* (i.e., not all human expertise is amenable to verbalization and formalization) and *situated* (human knowledge is context-dependent and this context cannot necessarily be shared with a computer program). As a result, enterprises such as expert systems are misguided in principle and the knowledge acquisition bottleneck an inevitable side effect of a reductionist view of expertise.

A paradigm shift was therefore needed, in order to address these problems. Clancey's analysis of first generation rule-based systems [3, 20] provided the research breakthrough which eventually led to the formulation of the modeling paradigm in knowledge engineering. I will briefly discuss this work below.

## 2.1. *Abstract models of problem solving*

The mining approach, as exemplified by Mycin [17], a system which diagnoses pulmonary infections, considers expert knowledge and rule-based representation as essentially equivalent — knowledge acquisition is an interactive transfer of if-then associations. This uniform approach to representation was criticized by Clancey [20], who showed that, at least in the case of the Mycin's knowledge base, it fails to capture important conceptual distinctions in the acquired knowledge. The competence of the Mycin system should not be analyzed in terms of its rule-based behaviour but in terms of the knowledge types it uses and the conceptual tasks it carries out. In particular, Clancey pointed out that Mycin's problem solving behaviour could be characterized in terms of a generic *heuristic classification* model, shown in Fig. 1. This model consists of three problem solving inferences which (i) generate abstractions from the given data (e.g. infer an abstract characterization of a patient, such as "immunosuppressed", from the available data, e.g. low white blood count); (ii) match these data abstractions to possible solution types (e.g. classes of diseases) and then (iii) refine these to produce one or more solutions (e.g. a

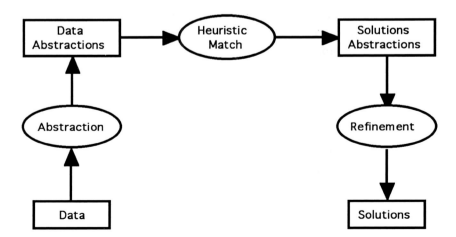

**Fig. 1.**   Clancey's heuristic classification model.

specific diagnosis). An important feature of the model shown in Fig. 1 is that it is *generic*; Clancey [3] analyzed the behaviour of a dozen rule-based systems tackling problems in various domains and found that in all cases their problem solving behaviour could be characterized in terms of the heuristic classification model. Hence, Clancey showed not only that it was possible to uncover from Mycin-like systems their knowledge-level (and implicit in the design) problem solving structures, but also that these structures were common to different systems, i.e., *generic*.

Clancey's analysis of rule-based systems provided an important milestone in knowledge engineering. He showed that a *knowledge-level analysis* [2] makes it possible to focus on *what* a system actually does, rather than *how* it does it. In other words we have a shift from an emphasis on the *symbol level* (Mycin is a rule-based system that reasons by means of backward-chaining) to the *knowledge level* (Mycin carries out medical diagnosis using a heuristic classification approach). Moreover, by showing that the heuristic classification model is generic, Clancey uncovered the principle of *role differentiation*, which has subsequently informed much knowledge engineering research [4, 21, 22]. Role differentiation means that it is possible to describe problem solving agents in terms of generic models, which impose specific *problem solving roles* on the domain knowledge. For example, domain structures in different application domains, such as diseases and book classes, actually play the same role (e.g. solution abstraction) when a heuristic classification model is used to describe the problem solving behaviour of a pulmonary infection or a book selection system.

## 2.2. *Knowledge acquisition as modeling*

Wielinga and Breuker [23, 24] were among the first to apply to knowledge acquisition the lessons drawn from the work carried out by Clancey. In particular, they argued that the so-called bottleneck was caused by the fact that "the mapping between the verbal data on expertise and the implementation formalisms is not a simple, one to one correspondence". Therefore, in developing the KADS methodology [4], they proposed an approach in which expertise modeling and design are clearly separated. First, "in an analysis stage, the knowledge engineer develops an abstract model of the expertise from the data ... this model is (then) transformed into an architecture for the KBS" [25]. Thus, they made the case for the development of conceptual modeling frameworks, addressing the issue of characterizing expertise at a level independent from implementation. A similar approach was also taken by my colleagues and I working on the KEATS project [26], in which we distinguished between modeling "overt behaviour" (i.e., understanding problem solving behaviour) and "internal representation" which was concerned with the realization of this behaviour on a computer system.

Other researchers [21, 27] set to the task of putting the role differentiation principle into practice, by developing knowledge acquisition tools based on task-specific, but application-independent problems solving models.

Of course there are differences between the approaches followed by all these researchers. Nevertheless, it is possible to group all these efforts around a common paradigm, which considers knowledge acquisition and engineering as a *modeling activity*. Below I list the main features of the modeling paradigm.

- Knowledge engineering is not about cognitive modeling (i.e., "reproducing" expert reasoning) but about developing systems which perform knowledge-based problem solving and which can be judged on task-oriented performance criteria.
- There are enough similarities between classes of applications, which make it possible to build generic models of problem solving.
- Knowledge acquisition should not be characterized as a process of mapping expert knowledge to a computational representation, but it is *a model-building process*, in which application-specific knowledge is configured according to the available problem solving technology. In the words of Ford et al. [28], "The mining analogy notwithstanding, expertise is not like a natural resource which can be harvested, transferred, or captured, but rather it is constructed by the expert and *reconstructed* by the knowledge engineer".
- It is useful to describe such a model of problem solving behaviour at a level which abstracts from implementation considerations (the knowledge level). This approach has the advantage of separating problem solving from implementation-related issues.
- Given that (i) knowledge acquisition is about model construction and that (ii) models can be application-generic, it follows that these generic models can be used to provide the interpretation context for the knowledge acquisition process (i.e., the knowledge acquisition process can be *model-based*). In this scenario, much of the knowledge acquisition task can be reduced to acquiring the domain knowledge required to instantiate generic problem solving roles [29].

Table 2 characterizes the modeling approach according to the same template used to describe the mining approach. In particular, the table shows a paradigm shift from an implementation-oriented to a knowledge-oriented view of knowledge acquisition. Multiple levels of descriptions are introduced and, as a result, the choice of implementation-level formalisms becomes less important. The knowledge categories are characterized at a conceptual, rather than computational level. The goal is no longer to emulate an expert by means of some kind of "expertise mapping", but to acquire the domain knowledge required to configure a generic problem solving model. Thus, the knowledge acquisition process becomes less amenable to the cognitively-motivated criticisms aimed at the mining approach. Researchers subscribing to the modeling approach no longer make claims of building rule-based cognitive models of experts and acquiring expertise by "direct transfer". The cognitive paradigm underlying the modeling approach can be characterized

**Table 2.** Characterization of the modeling approach.

| | |
|---|---|
| Knowledge Categories | Differentiation is Driven by Generic Knowledge Roles |
| KA Methodology | Acquisition is driven by a knowledge-level model of problem solving, which is independent of the chosen computational platform |
| Levels of Descriptions | Multiple (e.g. knowledge vs symbol level) |
| KA Paradigm | Model construction |
| Cognitive Paradigm | Functional view of knowledge |
| Reusable Components | Generic task, generic problem solving model, generic domain model |

as a pragmatic one, which is based on a *functional view of knowledge*. Knowledge is functionally described as whatever an observer attributes to an agent to explain its problem solving behaviour [2]. A knowledge-level description characterizes knowledge neither as a symbol-level data structure, nor as "stuff" in the mind of an expert: it is simply what enables a knowledge-based system to handle complexity. Such knowledge can be represented in different ways — e.g. as plain text, in some logical formalism, as a set of rules, but the representation should not be confused with the knowledge itself (i.e., the competence expressed by a knowledge model of problem solving is not a function of the chosen representation). The advantage of this approach is that it makes it possible to characterize knowledge modeling as a distinct technology, which focuses on knowledge-based behaviour *per se*, independently of cognitive or machine-centred biases. In other words, as researchers in knowledge modeling (and I dare say, in knowledge engineering) we are not interested in transferring expertise, we are interested in building models of intelligent behaviour.

The adoption of a knowledge modeling paradigm introduces a number of important research avenues.

- The emphasis on knowledge-level modeling and the separation between knowledge-level and symbol-level analysis opens the way to structured development processes in knowledge engineering, characterized by distinct analysis and design phases, each supported by different languages, tools and guidelines. In the next section, I will show how these ideas have shaped the CommonKADS methodology, which relies on multiple models to break down the complexity of a knowledge management or engineering project.
- We have seen that Clancey's analysis uncovered the existence of generic, knowledge-level models of problem solving. This raises interesting issues with respect to both the theory and practice of knowledge engineering. From a theoretical point of view, interesting questions concern the

space of these reusable models, "What are the main classes of reusable models?", "Is it feasible to hypothesize that future knowledge engineering handbooks will provide comprehensive lists of reusable models?". To answer these questions we have to devise sound typologies of reusable problem solving models, based on clear theoretical foundations. The engineering questions concern the use of these models in a specific project: "What tools do we need to support model-based knowledge acquisition?", "Is it feasible to imagine automatic configuration of these reusable models for specific domains?". In Sec. 5, I will briefly discuss ongoing work on the IBROW project, which is developing a range of advanced technologies to support the specification and the reuse of library components.

Thus, an important aspect of the knowledge modeling paradigm is that it creates a framework in which new research issues can be addressed, which concern robust knowledge engineering. In other words, while knowledge-based system development used to be seen as "an art" [16], the adoption of a knowledge modeling paradigm allows us to construct what can essentially be seen as a practical theory of knowledge engineering: an enquiry into the space of problem solving behaviours which are of interest to researchers in knowledge engineering. The domain is intelligent problem solving, the approach is knowledge-level analysis. In the next section, I will show how these ideas have been used to devise a comprehensive methodology for knowledge engineering and management.

## 3. The CommonKADS Methodology

The modeling paradigm in knowledge engineering informs many approaches to knowledge-based system development, e.g. KADS [4], CommonKADS [6], VITAL [30, 31], Mike [32], Generic Tasks [22], Components of Expertise [33], Role-limiting Methods [21] and Protégé [34]. Clearly, there is not enough room in this paper for a detailed survey and the reader is referred to the given references for more details on the various approaches. Here, I will briefly illustrate the main features of the CommonKADS methodology, which is the best established and the most comprehensive of all current approaches to knowledge engineering.

The CommonKADS methodology has evolved over almost two decades. It was originally conceived as the KADS approach to knowledge acquisition [23] and it has been extended, adapted and revised over the years until its most recent formulation by Schreiber *et al.* [6]. The Common KADS methodology provides a comprehensive framework in which both "traditional" knowledge engineering projects (i.e., projects whose main goal is the development of a performance system) and "modern" knowledge management projects can be situated. Indeed, an important contribution by the CommonKADS authors is the provision of an integrated framework for knowledge management, which also encapsulates knowledge engineering activities. In [6], the authors explicitly stress this point, by stating that "knowledge engineering has several different applications. The construction of knowledge systems is only one of them, albeit an important one. In all applications of knowledge engineering the conceptual modeling of knowledge at different levels of details is a central topic" (pp. 82). In other words, Schreiber *et al.* emphasize that the role of a methodology based on the knowledge modeling paradigm is to provide a suite of techniques to support knowledge analysis in an organization, in a wide range of scenarios. In some cases, the goal may be to develop and integrate a knowledge-based system in the organizational workflow; in other cases it may be simply to develop a competence model of an organization, or to provide a knowledge management solution to support knowledge creation and sharing.

An important aspect of the CommonKADS methodology is its reliance on multiple models to address the complexity of a knowledge management or knowledge engineering project. These models are briefly illustrated in the next subsections.

## 3.1. *Organization model*

An organization model provides a model of the organization in which the knowledge management or engineering project is going to be situated. This model typically describes the organizational structure (e.g. divisions, relations between divisions, "power structures"), the broader environment in which the project is taking place (e.g. the organizational goals), and an explicit preliminary description of the possible solutions to the problem in hand. Indeed, an important aspect of organizational analysis in CommonKADS is the emphasis on analyzing both the current scenario and future ones, as they may be implied by the proposed solutions.

## 3.2. *Task model*

This model is strictly related to the organization model. It lists the relevant "subparts of a business process" [6], their "inputs and outputs, preconditions and performance criteria, as well as needed resources and competences". In a nutshell, it provides a detailed task analysis for the business processes identified in the organization model.

## 3.3. *Agent model*

The task model specifies what needs to be done. The agent model specifies who does it. That is, it describes "the characteristics of agents, ... their competences, authority to act, and constraints in this respect". The term "agent" in Common KADS has a generic connotation: an agent can be a human being, a robot (e.g. in a manufacturing plant), or a software program.

## 3.4. *Knowledge model*

A knowledge model provides a knowledge-centred perspective on a task: "What are the main types of knowledge required?", "What reasoning steps need to be taken to carry out a task?". A knowledge model in CommonKADS distinguishes between *task*, *inference* and *domain* (sub-)models. An inference model in CommonKADS is similar to the heuristic classification model shown in Fig. 1: it describes the main knowledge categories and inference actions, needed to achieve a task. The term "task model" in the context of a knowledge model (not to be confused with the class of task models described above) specifies a possible control structure over an inference model.[a] Both task-control and inference models are represented in domain-independent terms. A domain model specifies the application domain on which task-control and inference models are going to be applied. For instance, it may describe the specific medical domain on which a heuristic classification model can be applied to perform medical diagnosis. A knowledge model is the current incarnation of the original interpretation models used in KADS. The fact that knowledge models are "just another class of models" in the CommonKADS suite of models shows the evolution of the methodology from the early days in which the focus was knowledge acquisition to the scenario today, in which CommonKADS provides a comprehensive framework, integrating knowledge engineering techniques in the context of generic knowledge management projects.

### 3.5. *Communication model*

The CommonKADS methodology caters for the design of multi-agent systems by means of task and agent models. The communication model structures the dialogue between agents at three levels, in terms of the overall *communication plan*, *individual transactions* and detailed *information exchange specifications*. The latter define the content and the form of individual messages, as well as their communication type. This makes it possible to specify the intention of a message, in terms of a number of predefined types (request, require, order, propose, offer, ask, reply, etc).

### 3.6. *Design model*

This model maps the conceptual analysis made explicit in the knowledge and communication models to a specific implementation. The model specifies the target software and hardware platform, the various software modules included in the target system, their functional and technical specifications and the mapping between these modules and the conceptual components identified during the analysis phase.

### 3.7. *Concluding remarks*

Thus, the CommonKADS methodology implements many of the ideas informing the knowledge modeling paradigm and provides an integrated framework in which

---

[a]To avoid confusion between the two different types of task models listed in the CommonKADS methodology I will use the expression *task-control model* to refer to a task model in the context of a knowledge model.

to carry out knowledge engineering and management projects. The emphasis is very much on *knowledge-level analysis through reusable problem solving models*. CommonKADS is supported by a library of reusable models [35], which provide support for a wide range of knowledge engineering tasks, such as monitoring, planning, diagnosis, etc. These models are defined rather informally, although a number of formal languages for KADS models exist, which can be used to specify Common KADS models in a rigorous way [36].

I will address issues of knowledge sharing and reuse in more detail in the next section, where I will discuss recent work on libraries of reusable components for knowledge models.

## 4. Knowledge Sharing and Reuse

As discussed at length in [5], there is a strong relationship between research in knowledge modeling and research in knowledge sharing and reuse. As Krueger points out [37], "all approaches to software reuse use some form of abstraction for software artefacts. Abstraction is the essential feature in any reuse technique. Without abstractions, software developers would be forced to sift through a collection of reusable artefacts trying to figure out what each artefact did, when it could be reused, and how to reuse it". In the case of components for knowledge systems, these abstractions can be characterized as knowledge-level models. In other words, reuse implies modeling: we cannot figure out what an artefact does, unless we have a model of its competence. At the same time, we have also seen that the identification of generic models of problem solving is an essential aspect of the knowledge modeling paradigm. That is, modeling implies reuse.

### 4.1. *What gets reused*

Given the "organic" relationship between modeling and knowledge sharing and reuse it is not surprising that the knowledge modeling community has developed very sophisticated frameworks and technologies to support reuse-centred approaches to knowledge management and engineering. We have already seen that CommonKADS distinguishes between task, domain and inference models. Each of these models provides a distinct focus for reuse. Recent work on knowledge sharing and reuse [38, 5, 39, 40] has moved beyond CommonKADS and devised sophisticated frameworks for reuse, which are based on clear theoretical foundations and support the development of sound and comprehensive libraries of components for knowledge modeling. These libraries rely on two main technologies developed by the knowledge modeling community to support knowledge sharing and reuse: *ontologies* [41–45] and *problem solving methods* [46].

An ontology is a partial specification of a conceptual vocabulary to be used for formulating knowledge-level theories about a domain of discourse. For instance, Fig. 2 shows a partial graphical view of an ontology, which specifies the

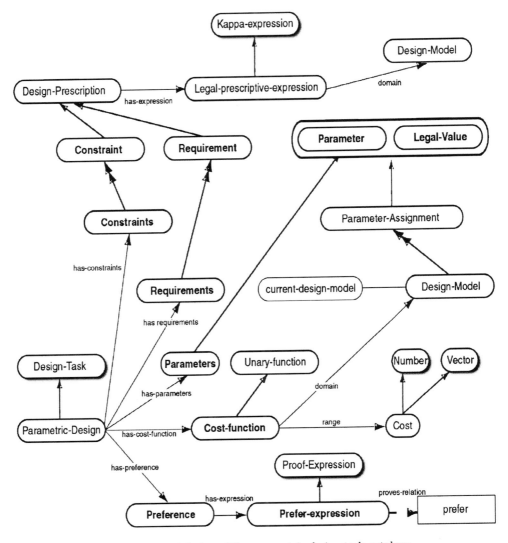

**Fig. 2.**   A partial view of the parametric design task ontology.

various concepts and relations required to model parametric design problems —
e.g. parameters, constraints, requirements, design model, etc. Various ontology specification languages have been proposed in the literature [47, 5, 48]. As an illustrative
example, I show the definition of relation `design-model-suitable` in the parametric design specification, which is expressed in the OCML language [5]. The definition
states that a design model, `?dm`, is suitable with respect to a set of requirements,
`?reqs`, if and only if it satisfies all of them.

Several surveys on research on ontologies exist in the literature [49, 50] and the interested reader is referred to these for more details.

```
(def-relation DESIGN-MODEL-SUITABLE (?dm ?reqs)
 "A design model is suitable is all requirements are
  applicable and satisfied. ?dm is assumed to be complete"
 :constraint (design-model-complete ?dm ?reqs)
 :iff-def (every ?reqs
                 (kappa (?req)
                        (and (design-prescription-applies
                              ?req ?dm)
                             (design-model-satisfies
                              ?dm ?req)))))
```

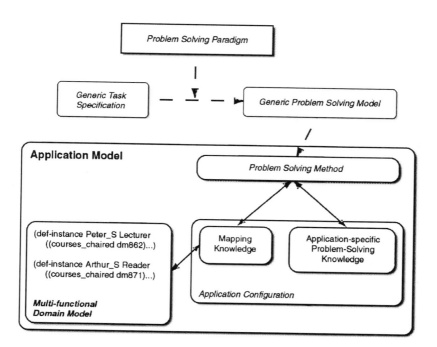

**Fig. 3.**  Overall modeling framework.

The second important technology to support knowledge reuse is *problem solving methods*. A problem solving method is a partial, domain-independent specification of a pattern of behaviour which can be reused across applications. For instance, the graphical model given in Fig. 1 can be seen as a partial and informal specification of a classification problem solving method. Recent research on problem solving methods is trying to answer a number of theoretical and engineering questions:

"How best to model problem solving methods?", "What is the relationship between problem solving and domain knowledge?", "What principles should be used to develop libraries of problem solving methods?", etc. In what follows, I will illustrate some of the answers that have been proposed to these questions, by describing recent work on libraries of problem solving methods.

Figure 3, taken from [5] shows the framework I used to develop a library of reusable components for parametric design problem solving [38]. The components of this framework, which is called *TMDA* (the acronym stands for *Task-Method-Domain-Application*), are described in the next subsections.

### 4.2. *Generic task specification*

This model provides a knowledge-level specification of a class of knowledge engineering problems (e.g. fault diagnosis, parametric design, classification). The specification is independent of both domain and problem solving considerations. That is, it specifies what needs to be achieved, independently of where and how. As shown in Fig. 2, ontologies are often used to provide these specifications.

### 4.3. *Problem solving paradigm*

Research in artificial intelligence has uncovered generic *problem solving paradigms*, which can be used to describe a large range of algorithms. Indeed, a long-standing hypothesis in artificial intelligence is that all intelligent behaviour can be characterized as search in a state space [51]. Thus, I used the search model of problem solving to provide a foundation to the various problem solving methods in the library. The advantage of this approach is that the resulting library is not simply a collection of reasoning modules, but it is based on a clear theoretical foundation.

### 4.4. *Generic problem solving model*

By instantiating the generic problem solving paradigm in terms of the generic task specification (say, instantiating a search model of problem solving in terms of a parametric design task specification), we can (i) move from a perspective centred on a problem specification to a problem solving one and we can (ii) acquire a task-specific foundation for a library of problem solving components. The generic problem solving model can be seen as a highly generic problem solving method, which subsumes all possible reasoning behaviours associated with a class of tasks. Figure 4 shows the main *task-method hierarchy* defining the generic model of parametric design problem solving. The ovals represents *generic tasks* to be carried out when solving parametric design problems and the arrows define *subtask-of* relationships. For example, in order to achieve task `evaluate-design-state`, four subtasks need to be carried out, to evaluate the consistency of the current design model, its cost, its feasibility (does it satisfy the stated design requirements?), and its completeness (are there any parameters still unbound?).

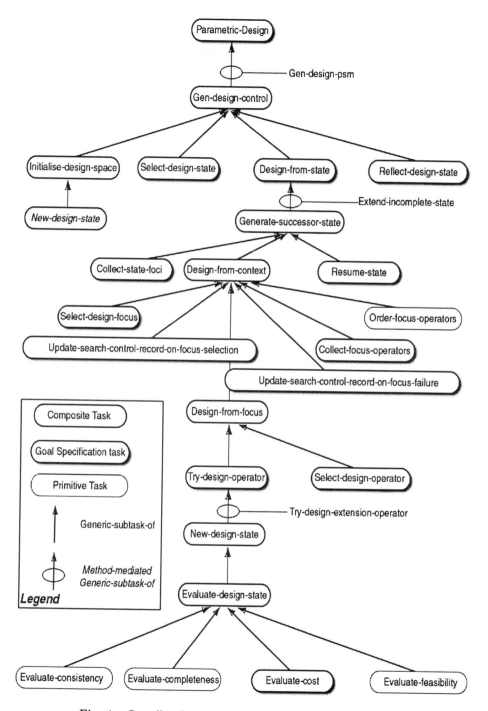

**Fig. 4.** Overall task-method hierarchy in generic design model.

Some of these *task-subtask* decompositions are mediated by the selection of a problem solving method. For instance, the topmost task-subtask decomposition in the figure, from task `parametric-design` to task `gen-design-control` is mediated by the selection of a (highly generic) problem solving method, called `gen-design-psm`. In total, the model comprises about forty problem solving methods and tasks and can be seen as a high-level shell for building parametric design problem solvers. However, in contrast with other work on task-specific shells — e.g. DIDS [10], this model has a clear theoretical foundation. It is based on an explicitly defined model of the class of problems under exam (the generic task specification) and it is grounded on a generic model of problem solving, based on the search paradigm, whose properties have been extensively studied in the artificial intelligence literature. In addition, in contrast with the work on role-limiting methods [21], this model is not meant to be used directly to solve applications. Its role is to provide a generic problem solving template, which can then be configured to develop specific problem solving methods.

Clearly, an endless number of concrete problem solving methods can be defined as specializations of this model. To date, we have defined and tried out 18 problem solving methods, including problem solving methods derived from general-purpose problem solving techniques, such as case-based reasoning and search algorithms, as well as knowledge-based problem solving methods, such as *Propose & Revise* [52], *Propose & Backtrack* [53] and *Propose & Exchange* [54]. This approach has resulted in both analytical and engineering advantages.

Analytically, because all these problem solving methods are defined as specializations of a common generic model, we can easily compare both their knowledge assumptions (i.e., what knowledge is required from the underlying domain) and their problem solving behaviour. Specifically, we showed that the plethora of behaviours exhibited by the various problem solving methods could be classified according to three classes: (i) some problem solving methods pursue a cost-minimization strategy — i.e., they look for the cheapest design; (ii) some pursue a consistency-centred strategy — i.e., their overarching criterion is to maintain consistency; (iii) some pursue a completion-centred strategy — they try to home in on a complete model early on in the design process and only later they deal with inconsistencies. Full details can be found in [5, 38].

From an engineering point of view the advantages had to do with minimal development cost. Because problem solving methods were not built from scratch but developed as specializations of a comprehensive model of parametric design problem solving, it was possible to achieve high levels of reuse. Specifically, all problem solving methods could be specified by adding no more than 20% extra components to the generic model. In practice, this means that even when we carried out rational reconstructions of complex problem solving methods described in the literature, such as Propose & Revise, very little development effort was required. In addition, because our reconstructions were based on a comprehensive, method-generic problem solving model, we were able to focus on the essential properties of the problem solving method in question and abstract from the various idiosyncrasies associated with each specific implementation. In particular, in the case of Propose & Revise, we were able to abstract from the original specification [52] and define several alternative variations of this class of methods, which avoided the brittleness exhibited by the original proposal — see [55] for details.

Clearly, in this approach problem solving methods have a strong commitment to a task model. However, this does not necessarily need to be the case. Recent work on the *UPML framework* [39, 40] generalizes this approach and allows for both strong (task-specific) and weak (task-independent) problem solving methods to be integrated in the same library — see also discussion on the IBROW project in Sec. 5.

### 4.5. *Multi-functional domain model*

A *multi-functional domain model* provides a representation of a domain of discourse, which is independent from its possible use in applications. For instance data about employees in an organization can be represented independently of whether this information is going to be used by the organizational payroll system or by an office allocation system, brought in to support a move to a different building. A well-known example of a multi-functional knowledge base is Cyc [56], which comprises the millions of notions which make up "consensus reality". These include common-sense notions, e.g. time and space; knowledge about the organization of human institutions, e.g. family, school; naive physics and biology, e.g. things fall and organisms die; and innumerable other concepts which human beings use routinely to make sense of phenomena in the world.

### 4.6. *Application configuration knowledge*

Given the framework shown in Fig. 3, building systems by reuse consists of selecting (or developing) the relevant task, method and domain models and then configuring them according to specific application needs. This application configuration activity can be done in two ways: either *mapping knowledge* is used to connect domain concepts to task and/or problem solving method concepts, or the knowledge requirements imposed by a task or problem solving method are satisfied by acquiring the relevant application-specific problem solving knowledge in a task-driven or method-driven way. I'll clarify this point with an example taken from a real-world application.

An office allocation problem (i.e., the problem of allocating members of an organization to offices in a building) can be modeled as a parametric design problem [57, 5], by considering employees as parameters and offices as possible parameter values. Let's suppose (i) we are given the task of developing an office allocation system for a particular group, say the Knowledge Media Institute (KMi), and (ii) we already have available a database of employees, which we can reuse as

our domain model. The first thing to do is then to instantiate the generic parametric design task model available from the library for our domain. To do this,
we need to define the design parameters and acquire the relevant constraints, requirements, preferences and (in case we are looking for optimal solutions) a cost
criterion. Because we assume the availability of a domain model we can integrate
this with the task model by mapping the concept of parameter in the task ontology with the concept of employee in the domain ontology. These mappings can be
represented by means of the mapping constructs provided by the OCML language.

```
(def-upward-class-mapping kmi-member parameter)
```

The above definition specifies that a *class mapping* should be created between the class kmi-member (members of the Knowledge Media Institute) and
the class of parameters. In practice this means that for each instance of the class
kmi-member a meta-level referent is created as an instance of class parameter. The
three *relation mappings* below connect relation current-design model defined in
the generic problem solving model to relation in-room, which specifies whether
an employee is allocated to a particular room. The three mappings specify how
to retrieve the current design model (:up), how to reflect a new assertion to the
domain (:down :add) and what to do when an instance of the relation is removed
(:down :remove).

```
(def-relation-mapping current-design-model :up
   ((current-design-model ?dm)
    if
    (= ?dm (setofall (?p . ?v)
                     (and (in-room ?X ?v)
                          (maps-to ?p ?x))))))
```

```
(def-relation-mapping current-design-model (:down :add)
   (lambda (?x)
     (loop for ?pair in ?x
           do
           (if (maps-to (first ?pair) ?z)
               (tell (in-room ?z (rest ?pair)))))))

(def-relation-mapping current-design-model (:down :remove)
   (lambda (?x)(unassert (in-room ?x ?y))))
```

The other knowledge types required by the task model (i.e., constraints, requirements, preferences and cost function) will not normally be part of a task-
independent domain model and therefore are acquired on an application-specific
basis.

Having instantiated the task model, we can then select a problem solving method from the library, which may in turn impose additional knowledge requirements. In particular, all problem solving methods in the parametric design library inherit the notion of *design operator* from the generic problem solving model, so application-specific design operators need to be acquired. A design operator defines a move in the space of possible design models. Design operators can be defined by operationalizing constraints, requirements or preferences acquired during the task model instantiation phase (e.g. a professor should go into a single-person office), or by using additional heuristic knowledge.

An important advantage of this approach is that because much of the application configuration effort consists of instantiating the generic task model (which is independent from any problem solving method) in a particular domain, it is feasible to try out several problem solving methods, rather than one. For instance, in the case of the KMi office allocation model we experimented with a number of problem solving methods and eventually we found that, given the dense nature of the solution space (i.e., several alternative solutions were possible) and the impossibility to define a monotonic cost function, a Propose & Improve problem solving method performed best.

The parametric design library has been tested on several application domains, which include, in addition to the KMi and Sisyphus-I [58] office allocation problems, the VT elevator design problem [59], sliding bearing design, initial vehicle design and design of casting technology for manufacturing mechanical parts [60]. All these applications were tackled successfully, using different problem solving methods and achieving significant amount of reuse. Typically very little method customization was needed, in addition to the effort required to elicit and formalize the knowledge required by the task model and by individual problem solving methods.

### 4.7. *The usability vs reusability trade-off*

The approach described here tries to reconcile the trade-off between *usability* and *reusability* [61]. The more generic a model, the more reusable it is; the more specific a model, the more usable it is, although in a restricted space of applications. The proposed framework addresses these issues at the knowledge level, i.e., in terms of modeling solutions, rather than efficiency considerations. At the knowledge level, the problem can be reduced to one of different degrees of coupling between the different components of a knowledge model. In particular, the framework makes the following assumptions:

- **Strong coupling between generic tasks and problem solving methods.** Problem solving methods are designed to perform efficient problem solving and they are typically designed with a class of tasks in mind. A close coupling between a generic method and a generic task is therefore not so much a requirement, as a consequence of the *raison d'être* of problem solving methods.

- **Weak coupling between generic problem solving models and multi-functional domain knowledge.** By definition, multi-functional knowledge is domain knowledge which characterizes the task-independent aspects of a domain, i.e., domain knowledge which can be used in many different ways. For the sake of reusability this knowledge is modelled in a task and method independent way. It follows that only weak coupling of multi-functional and problem solving knowledge can be supported. This weak coupling is expressed by means of mapping mechanisms.

The TMDA framework also tries to address the *knowledge interaction problem* [62], which states that both the type of knowledge required by an application and its representation are strongly determined by the chosen task and/or method. In the proposed approach the knowledge interaction problem is tackled by introducing an application-configuration component. In particular, the assumption here is that the interaction problem can be tackled in terms of the activities of acquiring application-specific knowledge and establishing the appropriate mappings between the problem solving and domain components.

## 5. Open Issues and Recent Developments

There is a certain amount of consensus in the knowledge modeling community that many important questions concerning knowledge sharing and reuse have now been answered to a significant extent. We now have comprehensive frameworks for devising libraries of problem solving methods, which subsume both weak and strong methods and provide mechanisms for managing very large libraries [40]. Several libraries are available online, which are doing a good job in fostering knowledge sharing and reuse [47, 63]. We also have sophisticated modeling languages for problem solving methods [40] and ontologies [47, 5, 48]. Although it would be too optimistic to say that there is consensus on the "right" language for ontology specification, existing proposals provide sufficient engineering leverage to support large initiatives centred on modeling technology. It is also possible to flag a number of success stories reported in the literature, which show the value of these technologies in the workplace — see for instance [64, 65] for ontologies and [66, 67] for problem solving methods. Nevertheless, a number of issues are still open. In particular, there is a need for a support infrastructure, which can facilitate access to libraries of reusable components and support their configuration for specific applications. The IBROW project [68] is tackling this issue and aims to provide a comprehensive set of technologies to support the development and use of reusable knowledge components. The project has developed the UPML architecture [39, 40], which provides a powerful framework and modeling support for developing libraries of reusable components. In addition a number of web-based tools will make it possible to access and configure IBROW-compliant libraries online. These tools include a *brokering agent* [69], whose aim is to identify the "right" components for a particular application and to help the users configure and integrate them with pre-existing domain models.

Another important area of research is the application of knowledge modeling technology to support "smart" retrieval on the Internet [70, 71, 8]. Efforts in this area are using ontologies to support "intelligent" query parsing and information retrieval. There is also much activity aimed at devising XML-compliant knowledge representation functionalities [48], which will be used to enable semantic markup of web pages, thus supporting semantic search engines and agent interoperability (for instance in e-commerce applications).

In conclusion, knowledge technologies have come a long way since the early days of expert systems and we now have a wide range of methods, tools and languages to perform knowledge analysis and system development activities in a wide range of contexts and domains. In this paper, I have provided an overview of the knowledge modeling paradigm in knowledge engineering and emphasized the important role that it has played in establishing solid theoretical and engineering foundations for knowledge systems. It is important to emphasize that this paradigm is situated at a different level from the various generic problem solving paradigms available in Artificial Intelligence, e.g. search, case-based reasoning [72], neural networks [73]. Knowledge modeling does not define a class of algorithms or a specific computational paradigm but (i) proposes a framework to analyze and engineer knowledge-based problem solving, which is based on a number of basic epistemological distinctions in knowledge systems, such as tasks, problem solving methods and domain knowledge, and (ii) relies on technologies such as problem solving methods and ontologies for its realization. Hence, it does not provide, for instance, an alternative to a case-based reasoning approach: it provides a framework which, for instance, can be used to characterize the epistemology and the competence of a case-based reasoning system.

The current dramatic changes in the communication and economic infrastructure are generating massive demand for "smart" technologies and for knowledge-based solutions. In this "brave new world", knowledge modeling technologies provide us with the analytic and engineering tools to help us shape these exciting developments.

# References

1. A. Stutt and E. Motta, "Knowledge modeling: An organic technology for the knowledge age", eds. M. Eisenstadt and T. Vincent, *The Knowledge Web*, Kogan Page (1998) 211–224.
2. A. Newell, "The knowledge level", *Artificial Intelligence* **18**, no. 1 (1982) 87–127.
3. W. J. Clancey, "Heuristic classification", *Artificial Intelligence* **27** (1985) 289–350.
4. B. J. Wielinga, A. T. Schreiber and J. Breuker, "KADS: A modeling approach to knowledge engineering", *Knowledge Acquisition* **4**, no. 1 (1992) 5–53.
5. E. Motta, *Reusable Components for Knowledge Models* (IOS Press, Amsterdam, The Netherlands, 1999).

6. G. Schreiber, H. Akkermans, A. Anjewierden, R. de Hoog, N. Shadbolt, W. van de Velde and B. Wielinga, *Knowledge Engineering and Management* (MIT Press, Cambridge, MA, 2000).

7. P.-H. Speel, N. Shadbolt, W. de Vries, P. H. van Dam and K. O'Hara, "Knowledge mapping for industrial purposes", eds. B. Gaines, R. Kremer and M. Musen, *Proceedings of the 12th Banff Workshop on Knowledge Acquisition, Modeling and Management — KAW-99*, Banff, Canada (1999). Paper available online at *http://sern.ucalgary.ca/KSI/KAW/KAW99/papers/Speel1/index.html*.

8. J. B. Domingue and E. Motta, "Planet-onto: From news publishing to integrated knowledge management support", *IEEE Intelligent Systems* **15**, no. 3 (2000) 26–32.

9. R. Neches, R. Fikes, T. Finin, T. Gruber, R. Patil, T. Senator and W. Swartout, "Enabling technology for knowledge sharing", *AI Magazine* **12**, no. 3 (1991) 37–56.

10. J. T. Runkel, W. P. Birmingham, T. P. Darr, B. R. Maxim and I. D. Tommelein, "Domain-independent design system", ed. J. S. Gero, *Artificial Intelligence in Design '92* (Kluwer Academic Publishers, 1992) 21–40.

11. E. Motta, D. Fensel, M. Gaspari and R. Benjamins, "Specifications of knowledge components for reuse", *Proceedings of the 11th International Conference on Software Engineering and Knowledge Engineering (SEKE'99)* Kaiserslautern, Germany (1999) 36–43. Published by the Knowledge Systems Institute, 3240 Main Street, Skokie, IL, 60076 USA.

12. R. Davis, "Interactive transfer of expertise: Acquisition of new inference rules", *Artificial Intelligence* **12** (1979) 121–158.

13. A. Kidd, *Knowledge Acquisition for Expert Systems* (Plenum Press, New York, 1987).

14. W. van Melle, E. H. Shortliffe and B. G. Buchanan, "EMYCIN: A knowledge engineer's tool for constructing rule-based expert systems", eds. B. G. Buchanan and E. H. Shortliffe, *Rule-Based Expert Systems* (Addison-Wesley, Reading, MA, 1984).

15. A. Newell and H. A. Simon, *Human Problem Solving* (Prentice Hall, Englewood, NJ, 1972).

16. E. A. Feigenbaum, "The art of artificial intelligence: Themes and case studies of knowledge engineering", *Proceedings of the Fifth International Joint Conference on Artificial Intelligence* (Cambridge, MA, 1977).

17. B. G. Buchanan and E. H. Shortliffe, *Rule-Based Expert Systems* (Addison-Wesley, Reading, MA, 1984).

18. T. Winograd and F. Flores, *Understanding Computers and Cognition* (Ablex Publishing, 1986).

19. H. Dreyfus, *What Computers Can't do: A Critique of Artificial Reason* (Freeman, 1979).

20. W. J. Clancey, "The epistemology of a rule-based expert system: A framework for explanation", *Artificial Intelligence* **20**, no. 3 (1983) 215–251.

21. J. McDermott, "Preliminary steps toward a taxonomy of problem-solving methods", ed. S. Marcus, *Automating Knowledge Acquisition for Expert Systems* (Kluwer Academic, 1988).

22. B. Chandrasekaran, T. R. Johnson, and J. W. Smith, "Task-structure analysis for knowledge modeling", *Communications of the ACM* **35**, no. 9 (1992) 124–137.

23. B. J. Wielinga and J. A. Breuker, "Interpretation models for knowledge acquisition", ed. T. O'Shea, *Advances in Artificial Intelligence (ECAI'84, Pisa)* (North-Holland, Amsterdam, 1984).

24. B. J. Wielinga and J. A. Breuker, "Models of expertise", eds. B. du Boulay, D. Hoggs and L. Steels, *Advances in Artificial Intelligence (ECAI'86, Brighton)* (North-Holland, Amsterdam, 1986).

25. J. Breuker and B. J. Wielinga, "Models of expertise in knowledge acquisition", eds. G. Guida and C. Tasso, *Topics in Expert Systems Design* (North-Holland, 1989).

26. E. Motta, T. Rajan and M. Eisenstadt, "A methodology and tool for knowledge acquisition in KEATS-2", eds. G. Guida and C. Tasso, *Topics in Expert Systems Design* (North-Holland, 1989).

27. M. A. Musen, L. M. Fagan, D. M. Combs and E. H. Shortliffe, "Use of a domain model to drive an interactive knowledge-editing tool", *International Journal of Man-Machine Studies* **26** (1987) 105–121.

28. K. Ford, H. Stahl, J. Adams-Webber, J. Novak, A. Canas and J. Jones, "ICONKAT: A constructivist knowledge acquisition tool", *Proceedings of the 5th Banff Knowledge Acquisition Workshop*, Banff, Canada (1990) 7-1–7.20.

29. S. Marcus, *Automatic Knowledge Acquisition for Expert Systems* (Kluwer Academic, Boston, MA, 1988).

30. N. Shadbolt, E. Motta and A. Rouge, "Constructing knowledge based systems", *IEEE Software* **10**, no. 6 (1990) 34–38.

31. E. Motta, K. O'Hara, N. Shadbolt, A. Stutt and Z. Zdrahal, "Solving VT in VITAL: A study in model construction and knowledge reuse", *International Journal of Human-Computer Studies* **44**, no. 3–4 (1996) 333–371.

32. J. Angele, D. Fensel, D. Landes and R. Studer, "Developing knowledge-based systems with MIKE", *Journal of Automated Software Engineering* **5**, no. 4 (1998) 389–418.

33. L. Steels, "Components of expertise", *AI Magazine* **11**, no. 2 (1990) 29–49.

34. A. R. Puerta, J. W. Egar, S. W. Tu and M. A. Musen, "A multiple-method knowledge-acquisition shell for the automatic generation of knowledge-acquisition tools", *Knowledge Acquisition* **4**, no. 2 (1992) 171–196.

35. J. A. Breuker and W. van de Velde, *CommonKADS Library for Expertise Modeling* (IOS Press, Amsterdam, The Netherlands, 1994).

36. D. Fensel and F. van Harmelen, "A comparison of languages which operationalize and formalize KADS models of expertise", *The Knowledge Engineering Review* **9**, no. 2 (1994).

37. C. W. Krueger, "Software reuse", *ACM Computing Surveys* **24**, no. 2 (1992) 131–183.

38. E. Motta and Z. Zdrahal, "An approach to the organization of a library of problem solving methods which integrates the search paradigm with task and method ontologies", *International Journal of Human-Computer Studies* **49**, no. 4 (1998) 437–470.

39. D. Fensel, V. R. Benjamins, E. Motta and B. J. Wielinga, "A framework for knowledge system reuse", *Proceedings of the International Joint Conference on Artificial Intelligence (IJCAI'99)*, Stockholm, Sweden (July 31–August 5, 1999).

40. D. Fensel and E. Motta, "Structured development of problem solving methods" (in press) (to appear in *IEEE Transactions on Knowledge and Data Engineering*).

41. N. Guarino and P. Giaretta, "Ontologies and knowledge bases: Towards a terminological clarification", ed. N. Mars, *Towards Very Large Knowledge Bases: Knowledge Building and Knowledge Sharing* (IOS Press, Amsterdam, 1995) 25–32.

42. A. Valente and J. A. Breuker, "Towards principled core ontologies", eds. B. Gaines and M. Musen, *Proceedings of the 10th Banff Knowledge Acquisition for Knowledge-Based Systems Workshop*, Banff, Alberta, Canada (1996).

43. T. R. Gruber, "A translation approach to portable ontology specifications", *Knowledge Acquisition* **5**, no. 2 (1993).

44. T. R. Gruber, "Toward principles for the design of ontologies used for knowledge sharing", *International Journal of Human-Computer Studies* **43**, no. 5–6 (1995) 907–928.

45. G. van Heijst, A. T. Schreiber and B. J. Wielinga, "Using explicit ontologies for KBS development", *International Journal of Human-Computer Studies* **46**, no. 2–3 (1997) 183–292.

46. V. R. Benjamins and D. Fensel, "Special issue on problem solving methods", *International Journal of Human Computer Studies* **49**, no. 4 (1998).

47. A. Farquhar, R. Fikes and J. Rice, "The ontolingua server: A tool for collaborative ontology construction", eds. B. Gaines and M. Musen, *Proceedings of the 10th Banff Knowledge Acquisition for Knowledge-Based Systems Workshop*, Banff, Alberta, Canada (1996).

48. D. Fensel, I. Horrocks, F. van Harmelen, S. Decker, M. Erdmann and M. Klein, "OIL in a Nutshell", eds. R. Dieng *et al.*, *Proceedings of the European Conference on Knowledge Acquisition, Modeling and Management (EKAW'2000)*, *Lecture Notes in Artificial Intelligence* (Springer-Verlag, October 2000).

49. N. Fridman Noy and C. D. Hafner, "The state of the art in ontology design", *AI Magazine* **18**, no. 3 (1997) 53–74.

50. M. Uschold and M. Gruninger, "Ontologies: Principles, methods and applications", *Knowledge Engineering Review* **11**, no. 2 (1996) 93–136.

51. A. Newell, "Reasoning, problem solving, and decision processes: The problem space as a fundamental category", ed. R. S. Nickerson, *Attention and Performance VIII* (Lawrence Erlbaum Associates, Hillsdale, NJ, 1980).

52. S. Marcus and J. McDermott, "SALT: A knowledge acquisition language for propose and revise systems", *Journal of Artificial Intelligence* **39**, no. 1 (1989) 1–37.

53. J. T. Runkel, W. B. Birmingham, A. Balkany, "Solving VT by reuse", *International Journal of Human-Computer Studies* **44**, no. 3–4 (1996) 403–433.

54. K. Poeck and F. Puppe, "COKE: Efficient solving of complex assignment problems with the propose-and-exchange method", *5th International Conference on Tools with Artificial Intelligence*, Arlington, Virginia (1992).

55. Z. Zdrahal and E. Motta "An in-depth analysis of propose & revise problem solving methods", eds. B. R. Gaines and M. Musen, *Proceedings of the 9th Banff Knowledge Acquisition for Knowledge-Based Systems Workshop* (1995) 38-1–38-20.

56. D. B. Lenat and R. V. Guha, *Building Large Knowledge-Based Systems: Representation and Inference in the Cyc Project* (Addison-Wesley, Reading, MA, 1990).

57. A. Balkany, W. P. Birmingham and J. Runkel, "Solving sisyphus by design", *International Journal of Human-Computer Studies* **40**, no. 2 (1994) 221–241.

58. M. Linster, "Problem statement for sisyphus: Models of problem solving", *International Journal of Human-Computer Studies* **40**, no. 2 (1994) 187–192.

59. M. Valasek and Z. Zdrahal, "Experiments with applying knowledge based techniques to parametric design", ed. A. Riitahuhta, *Proceedings of the International Conference on Engineering Design (ICED'97)*, Tampere University of Technology, Finland **1** (1997) 277–280.

60. G. R. Yost and T. R. Rothenfluh, "Configuring elevator systems", *International Journal of Human-Computer Studies* **44**, no. 3–4 (1996) 521–568.

61. G. Klinker, C. Bhola, G. Dallemagne, D. Marques and J. McDermott, "Usable and reusable programming constructs", *Knowledge Acquisition* **3** (1991) 117–136.

62. T. Bylander and B. Chandrasekaran, "Generic tasks in knowledge-based reasoning: The right level of abstraction for knowledge acquisition", eds. B. Gaines and J. Boose, *Knowledge Acquisition for Knowledge-Based Systems*, Vol. 1 (Academic Press, London, 1988) 65–77.

63. J. Domingue, "Tadzebao and webonto: Discussing, browsing, and editing ontologies on the web", eds. B. Gaines and M. Musen, *Proceedings of the 11th Knowledge Acquisition for Knowledge-Based Systems Workshop*, Banff, Canada (April 18–23, 1998).

64. D. L. McGuinness, "Ontology-enhanced search for primary care medical literature", *Proceedings of the International Medical Informatics Association (Working Group 6 — Medical Concept Representation and Natural Language Processing) Conference*, Phoenix, Arizona (December 16–19, 1999). Paper available online at URL *http://ksl.stanford.edu/people/dlm/papers/imia-dlm-final.doc*.

65. P. Mulholland, Z. Zdrahal and J. Domingue and M. Hatala, "Integrating working and learning: A document enrichment approach", *Behaviour and Information Technology* **19**, no. 3 (2000) 171–180.

66. P.-H. Speel and M. Aben, "Applying a library of problem solving methods on a real-life task", *International Journal of Human-Computer Studies* **46** (1997) 627–652.

67. M. Hori and T. Yoshida, "A domain-oriented library of scheduling methods: Design principles and real-life applications", *International Journal of Human Computer Studies* **49**, no. 4 (1998) 601–626.

68. V. R. Benjamins, E. Plaza, E. Motta, D. Fensel, R. Studer, B. Wielinga, G. Schreiber and Z. Zdrahal, "IBROW3 — An intelligent brokering service for knowledge-component reuse on the world wide web", eds. B. Gaines and M. Musen, *Proceedings of the 11th Workshop on Knowledge Acquisition, Modeling and Management (KAW'98)*, Banff, Canada (April 18–23, 1998). Paper available online at *http://www.swi.psy.uva.nl/projects/IBROW3/docs/papers/kaw-ibrow.ps*.

69. R. Benjamins, B. J. Wielinga, J. Wielemaker and D. Fensel, "Brokering problem-solving knowledge on the internet", eds. D. Fensel and R. Studer, *11th European Workshop on Knowledge Acquisition, Modeling, and Management (EKAW'99)*, *Lecture Notes in Artificial Intelligence 1621* (Springer-Verlag, 1999).

70. D. McGuinness, "Ontological issues for knowledge-enhanced search", eds. N. Guarino, *Formal Ontologies in Information Systems* (IOS Press, 1998).

71. N. Guarino, C. Masolo and G. Vetere, "Ontoseek: Using large linguistic ontologies for accessing on-line yellow pages and product catalogs", *IEEE Intelligent Systems* **14**, no. 3 (1999) 70–80.

72. K.-D. Althoff, "Case-based reasoning", ed. S. K. Chang, *Handbook of Software Engineering and Knowledge Engineering, Volume 1* (World Scientific Publishing Co., 2001).

73. D. Graupe, "Large scale neural networks and their applications", ed. S. K. Chang, *Handbook of Software Engineering and Knowledge Engineering, Volume 1* (World Scientific Publishing Co., 2001).

# KNOWLEDGE DISCOVERY AND DATA MINING IN DATABASES

VLADAN DEVEDZIC

*Department of Information Systems, FON — School of Business Administration,
University of Belgrade, POB 52, Jove Ilica 154, 11 000 Belgrade, Yugoslavia
E-mail: devedzic@fon.fon.bg.ac.yu*

*Knowledge Discovery in Databases (KDD)* is the process of automatic discovery of previously unknown patterns, rules, and other regular contents implicitly present in large volumes of data. *Data Mining (DM)* denotes discovery of patterns in a data set previously prepared in a specific way. DM is often used as a synonym for KDD. However, strictly speaking, DM is just a central phase of the entire process of KDD.

The purpose of this chapter is to gradually introduce the process of KDD and typical DM tasks. The idea of automatic knowledge discovery in large databases is first presented informally, by describing some practical needs of users of modern database systems. Several important concepts are then formally defined and the typical context and resources for KDD are discussed. Then the scope of KDD and DM is briefly presented in terms of classification of KDD/DM problems and common points between KDD and several other scientific and technical disciplines that have well-developed methodologies and techniques used in the field of KDD. After that, the chapter describes the typical KDD process, DM tasks and some algorithms that are most frequently used to carry out such tasks. Some other important aspects of KDD are covered as well, such as using domain knowledge in the KDD process and evaluating discovered patterns. Finally, the chapter briefly surveys some important KDD application domains and practical KDD/DM systems, and discusses several hot topics and research problems in the field that are of interest to software industry.

*Keywords*: Knowledge discovery, data mining, patterns, measure of interestingness, data mining tasks, data mining algorithms.

## 1. Introduction

As a result of constant increase of business needs, the amount of data in current database systems grows extremely fast. Since the cost of data storage keeps on dropping, users store all the information they need in databases. Moreover, people believe that by storing data in databases they may save some information that might turn up to be potentially useful in the future, despite the fact that it is not of direct value at the moment [13].

### 1.1. *The key idea of KDD and DM*

Raw data stored in databases are seldom of direct use. In practical applications, data are usually presented to the users in a modified form, tailored to satisfy specific business needs. Even then, people must analyze data more or less manually, acting as sophisticated "query processors". This may be satisfactory if the total amount of data being analyzed is relatively small, but is unacceptable for large amounts of data. What is needed in such a case is an *automation of data analysis tasks*. That's exactly what KDD and DM provide. They help people improve efficiency of the data analysis they perform. They also make possible for people to become aware of some useful facts and relations that hold among the data they analyze and that could not be known otherwise, simply because of the overload caused by heaps of data. Once such facts and relations become known, people can greatly improve their business in terms of savings, efficiency, quality, and simplicity.

Typically, KDD/DM systems are not general-purpose software systems. They are rather developed for specific users to help them automate data analysis in precisely defined, specific application domains.

## 1.2. *Definitions*

*Knowledge discovery* is the process of nontrivial extraction of information from data, information that is implicitly present in that data, previously unknown and potentially useful for the user [13]. The information must be in the form of patterns that are comprehensible to the user (such as, for example, If-Then rules).

For a data set $F$, represented in a language $L$, if $F_S$ is a subset of $F$ and $c$ denotes certainty measure, then a *pattern* is an expression $S$ in the language $L$ with the certainty $c$ about some relation(s) among the data in $F_s$. In order for the expression $S$ to really be a pattern, it must be simpler than merely counting all the data in $F$.

*Knowledge* is a pattern that is sufficiently interesting to the user and sufficiently certain. The user specifies the measure of interestingness (see below) and the certainty criterion. *Discovered knowledge* is the output from a program that analyzes a data set and generates patterns. A pattern's *certainty* is the measure of confidence in discovered knowledge represented by the pattern. Discovered knowledge is seldom valid for all the data in the data set considered. Pattern's certainty is higher if data in the data set considered are good representatives of data in the database, if they contain little or no noise at all, if they are valid, reliable, complete, precise, and contain no contradictions.

A pattern's *measure of interestingness* is a quantitative indicator used in pattern evaluation. Only interesting patterns are knowledge. A pattern is interesting if it is new, non-trivial, and useful.

*Data mining* is the process of pattern discovery in a data set from which noise has been previously eliminated and which has been transformed in such a way to enable the pattern discovery process. Data mining is always based on a data-mining algorithm.

## 1.3. *The context and resources for KDD*

Figure 1 illustrates the context and computational resources needed to perform KDD [20]. The necessary assumptions are that there exists a database with its

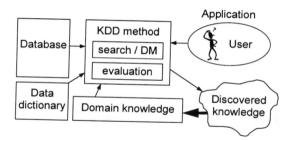

**Fig. 1.** The context and resources for KDD (after [20]).

data dictionary, and that the user wants to discover some patterns in it. There must also exist an application through which the user can select (from the database) and prepare a data set for KDD, adjust DM parameters, start and run the KDD process, and access and manipulate discovered patterns. KDD/DM systems usually let the user choose among several *KDD methods*. Each method enables preparation of a data set for automatic analysis, searching that set in order to discover/generate patterns (i.e., applying a certain kind of DM over that set), as well as pattern evaluation in terms of certainty and interestingness. KDD methods often make possible to use domain knowledge to guide and control the process and to help evaluate the patterns. In such cases domain knowledge must be represented using an appropriate knowledge representation technique (such as rules, frames, decision trees, and the like). Discovered knowledge may be used directly for database query from the application, or it may be included into another knowledge-based program (e.g. an expert system in that domain), or the user may just save it in a desired form. Discovered patterns mostly represent some previously unknown facts from the domain knowledge. Hence they can be combined with previously existing and represented domain knowledge in order to better support subsequent runs of the KDD process.

## 1.4. *Examples*

Some airlines companies use databases of their passengers to discover patterns in the way they fly (embarkation and destination ports, return flights, routes, frequency of flying to a specific destination, etc). Exceptional passengers get promotional prizes, which attracts more customers to the company's Frequent Flyer program.

Another example is the way many banks use KDD/DM systems to explore their databases of credits and loans. Based on the patterns they discover from such databases, the patterns' certainties, and the measures of the discovered patterns' interestingness, the banks can more successfully predict the outcome and possible consequences of approving a loan to certain customers, thus increasing the quality of their business decisions.

Marketing agencies use KDD/DM systems to discover patterns in the way customers buy retail products. Once they discover that many people buy product

A simultaneously with product B, they can easily create an appropriate and potentially successful commercial or marketing announcement.

## 2. The Scope of KDD/DM and Typical Problems

The fields of KDD and DM were developed quite gradually, and different names were used for them in the past (such as data archeology, knowledge extraction, information discovery, information harvesting, and pattern processing). The concept of DM has been known in the field of statistics long before database professionals have started to develop and use KDD. It is only in the late 80's and early 90's that the database community has shown its interest in KDD and DM. However, since mid-90's both fields have gone through a rapid expansion, due to an extraordinary support and attention of software industry.

### 2.1. *Classification of KDD/DM problems*

Being the central activity of KDD, DM certainly represents the most challenging problem of KDD. However, KDD covers not only DM, but also many other problems and related concepts, topics, activities, and processes as well [1, 11–26]. They include (but are not limited to) the following.

*Integration of different methods of machine learning and knowledge discovery.* Machine learning provides a number of algorithms for learning general concepts from specific examples, learning by analogy, learning classification rules, and so on, which are all useful in the KDD process for pattern discovery.

*Integration of knowledge-based systems and statistics.* Knowledge-based systems provide a rich spectrum of knowledge-representation techniques, some of which are used for representing the patterns discovered by applying KDD processes. For example, discovered patterns are often represented in the form of rules or decision trees. Also, many KDD/DM systems nowadays are based on neural networks, since neural networks can also be used to identify patterns and to eliminate noise from data. Statistical measures are always necessary in KDD, because they help select and prepare data for KDD, as well as quantify the importance, certainty, inter-dependencies, and other features of discovered patterns.

*Discovering dependencies among the data.* A change of a data item in a large database can sometimes result in other data changing as well, and it is often useful to be able to predict them.

*Using domain knowledge in the KDD process.* Domain knowledge can dramatically improve the efficiency of the KDD process (see the dedicated section below).

*Interpreting and evaluating discovered knowledge.* Once some patterns are discovered using an appropriate DM algorithm, it is important to determine whether they have an important meaning for the user, or just represent useless relations among the data.

*Including discovered knowledge into previously represented domain knowledge.* The idea here is to use the knowledge discovered in the KDD process along with the other facts and rules from the domain that help guide the process, and thus further improve the process efficiency.

*Query transformation and optimization.* Discovering useful patterns in data can help modify database queries accordingly and hence improve data access efficiency.

*Discovery of data evolution.* Data analysts often benefit from getting an insight into possible patterns of changes of certain data in the past.

*Discovery of inexact concepts in structured data.* Highly structured data (such as data records in relational databases) sometimes hide some previously unknown concepts which do make sense to domain experts, although they often cannot define the meanings of such concepts exactly; such concepts can be discovered by appropriate combinations of fields in data records, groupings of subsets of data in larger data sets, and so on.

*Process, data, and knowledge visualization.* In some applications, patterns and activities in the KDD process are best described by means of various graphs, shading, clusters of data and animation. Selecting the most appropriate visualization technique is an important problem in KDD.

*Error handling in databases.* Unfortunately, real-world databases are full of inconsistencies, erroneous data, imprecision, and other kinds of noise. Handling such data properly can be the key to success for the entire KDD process.

*Representing and processing uncertainty.* Discovered patterns are never absolutely certain, and there are various ways to represent their certainty.

*Integrating object-oriented and multimedia technologies.* Most KDD systems today work with relational databases. It is only since recently that KDD and DM extend to object-oriented and multimedia databases.

*Various ethical, social, psychological and legal aspects.* Although KDD applications are useful, not all of them are 100% ethical. For example, mining various kinds of race-dependent data, some medical records, as well as some tax-payment databases, can sometimes provoke unwanted interpretations such as jeopardy of privacy. There are also examples of giving up a KDD project because of possible legal consequences.

There is another kind of classification that is often used in describing KDD/DM systems. It is based on typical kinds of knowledge that the DM process mines for, and on the corresponding types of DM activities (such as cluster identification, mining association rules, or deviation detection — see the dedicated section on DM tasks).

## 2.2. *KDD/DM and other scientific and technical disciplines*

It follows from the above classification of KDD/DM problems that many other scientific and technical disciplines have some points in common with KDD and DM. KDD/DM specialists apply (possibly with some adaptation) many useful algorithms, techniques and approaches originally developed and used in other fields. Summing up the above list and a number of discussions on influences from other fields on KDD/DM [11, 14, 21] one may note that the other fields that have much to do with KDD and DM are database technology itself, statistics, pattern recognition, knowledge acquisition and representation, intelligent reasoning, expert systems, and machine learning. All of these fields except of database technology and statistics are also about identifying, representing and processing knowledge. Hence, it is no wonder that they go together well with KDD.

One other field of computer science and engineering requires a special note, because it is the one that probably most largely overlaps with KDD/DM. It is data warehousing, since data warehouses provide much of data preprocessing used in the KDD process as well (see the section on KDD as a process, later on in this chapter).

A further comment is also necessary on the relation between KDD/DM and statistics. Although KDD and DM heavily rely on techniques from statistics and probability theory [15, 26], it is important to stress that statistics alone is not sufficient for KDD. It certainly *does* enable some data analysis, but it necessarily requires the user to take part in it. The goal of KDD/DM is automated data analysis. Statistics often gives results that are hard to interpret, and cannot handle non-numerical, structured data. It also doesn't enable the use of domain knowledge in data analysis.

## 3. KDD as a Process

Knowledge discovery is a *process*, and not a one-time response of the KDD system to a user's action. As any other process, it has its environment, phases, and runs under certain assumptions and constraints.

Figure 2 shows typical data sets, activities, and phases in the KDD process [12]. Its principal resource is a *database* containing a large amount of data to be searched for possible patterns. KDD is never done over the entire database, but over a representative *target data set*, generated from the large database. In most practical cases, data in the database and in the target data set contain noise, i.e., erroneous, inexact, imprecise, conflicting, exceptional and missing values, as well as ambiguities. By eliminating such noise from the target data set, one gets the set of *preprocessed data*. The set of *transformed data*, generated from the preprocessed

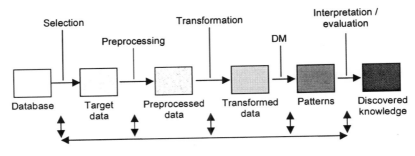

**Fig. 2.**  Phases in the KDD process (after [12]).

data set, is used directly for DM. The output of DM is, in general, a *set of patterns*, some of which possibly represent *discovered knowledge*.

The phases of the process are as follows. *Selection* is an appropriate procedure for generating the target data set from the database. Its major goal is to select *typical* data from the database, in order to make the target data set as representative as possible. The phase of *preprocessing* eliminates noise from the target data set and possibly generates specific data sequences in the set of preprocessed data. Such sequences are needed by some DM tasks (e.g. sequence analysis; see the next section for more detailed explanation). The next phase is *transformation* of the preprocessed data into a suitable form for performing the desired *DM task*. DM tasks are specific kinds of activities that are carried out over the set of transformed data in search of patterns, guided by the kind of knowledge that should be discovered. The kinds of transformations of the preprocessed data depend on the DM task. Typically, transformations include some appropriate reduction of the number of fields in the data records, since each DM task focuses only on a subset of data record fields. Also, some further modifications and combinations of the remaining data record fields can be done in order to map the original data onto a data space more suitable for the DM task that will be carried out in the next phase, the DM.

In the DM phase, a procedure is run that executes the desired DM task and generates a set of patterns. However, not all of the patterns are useful. The goal of *interpreting and evaluating* all the patterns discovered is to keep only those patterns that are interesting and useful to the user and discard the rest. Those patterns that remain represent the discovered knowledge.

In practice, the KDD process never runs smoothly. On the contrary, it is a time-consuming, incremental, and iterative process by its very nature, hence many repetition and feedback loops in Fig. 2. Individual phases can be repeated alone, and the entire process is usually repeated for different data sets.

Discovered patterns are usually represented using a certain well-known knowledge representation technique, including inference rules (If-Then rules), decision trees, tables, diagrams, images, analytical expressions, and so on [1, 24]. If-Then rules are the most frequently used technique [12, 21]. The following example is a pattern from financial domain, discovered by applying the MKS system described in [3]:

| | |
|---|---|
| IF | Home_Loan = Yes |
| THEN | Post_Code = POST_RURAL and |
| | Gender = MALE and |
| | Marital_Status = MARRIED and |
| | Access_Card = Yes and |
| | Credit_Turnover = 4000_GTR and |
| | Account_Type = CURRENT and |
| | Credit_Amount = 4500_GTR |
| WITH | certainty = 23.75%, support = 23.75%, interestingness = 0.806 |

Decision trees are a suitable alternative for If-Then rules, since with many machine learning algorithms the concepts the program learns are represented in the form of decision trees. Transformations between decision trees and inference rules are easy and straightforward. Rules are often dependent on each other, so the discovered knowledge often has the form of causal chains or networks of rules.

KDD systems usually apply some probabilistic technique to represent uncertainty in discovered patterns. Some form of certainty factors often goes well with inference rules (see the *certainty* and *support* indicators in the above example). Probability distribution is easy to compute statistically, since databases that KDD systems start from are sufficiently large. Probability distribution is especially suitable for modeling noise in data. Fuzzy sets and fuzzy logic are also used sometimes. However, it is important to note that an important factor in modeling uncertainty is the effort to actually *eliminate* sources of uncertainty (such as noisy and missing data) in early phases of the process.

The advantage of representing patterns in textual form, such as If-Then rules, is that it is simple to implement and well understood, since it reflects human cognitive processing. The main disadvantages are that textual patterns may be hard to follow and interpret (they may be rather complex), and that some patterns are very hard to express as text [13, 28]. Graphical forms of pattern representation, such as diagrams, images and shading, are visually rich and exploit human perceptual and cognitive abilities for pattern interpretation [10, 18]. For example, a shaded region on the map of a certain country may denote the country's region where the KDD/DM system discovers that some increase of sale can be expected under certain conditions. As another example, domain experts may be capable of easily interpreting peaks on a diagram representing a pattern discovered in a patient database about the effects of a certain drug applied over a number of patients. However, patterns represented graphically are harder to implement and require more complex interfaces and supporting software.

What technique exactly should be used to represent discovered knowledge depends on the goals of the discovery process. If discovered knowledge is for the users only, then natural language representation of rules or some graphically rich form is most suitable. Alternatively, discovered knowledge may be used in the knowledge base of another intelligent application, such as an expert system in the same domain. In that case, discovered knowledge should be translated into the form used by that other application. Finally, discovered knowledge may be used along with the previously used domain knowledge to guide the next cycle of the KDD process. That requires representing discovered patterns in the same way the other domain knowledge is represented in the KDD system.

## 4. Data Mining Tasks

DM tasks depend on the kind of knowledge that the KDD/DM system looks for. Each DM task has its specific features and follows specific steps in the discovery process. The following DM tasks are among the most frequently used ones in nowadays KDD/DM application [1, 11–21, 24, 26].

*Classification.* The task is to discover whether an item from the database belongs to one of some previously defined classes. The main problem, however, is how to define classes. In practice, classes are often defined using specific values of certain fields in the data records or some derivatives of such values. For example, if a data record contains the field *Region*, then some of the field's typical values (e.g. *North*, *South*, *West*, *East*) may define the classes.

*Cluster identification.* In this task the goal is to *generate* descriptions of classes of data (clusters), as opposed to classification, in which the classes are known beforehand. When identifying clusters, various Euclidean distance measures are used to compute how close are data items to each other in an $n$-dimensional space defined by the fields in data records. For example, densely distributed points on a section of a 2-D graph can be interpreted as a cluster.

*Summarization.* This is the task of discovering common and/or essential characteristics of groups of data in a compact form (e.g. "all Olympics winners of 100 m race were *black* and under 28"). Typically, the compact form is summarization rules, and more sophisticated techniques make possible to generate functional dependencies among data items.

*Dependency modeling.* The goal of this task is to describe important dependencies among the data in a data set. Dependency means that the value of a data item can be predicted with some certainty if the value of another data item is known (e.g. A → B, CF = 0.93). A collection of interrelated dependencies forms a dependency graph. It shows cascaded dependencies (dependency propagation).

*Change and deviation detection.* One form of knowledge that can be discovered in a data set is related to specific deviations and changes of data values with respect to some expected values (e.g. the change in mean value, standard deviation, probability density, gradient, and other statistical indicators, as well as detection of outliers, changes of data values over time, and difference between expected and observed data values).

*Discrimination.* In the context of KDD, discrimination means identification of distinct features that make possible to differentiate among two classes of data. For example, "truly ascetic people are *thin*". Discrimination is naturally done before cluster identification, classification, change and deviation detection, and discovering reference values and attributes.

*Discovering reference values and attributes.* In order to perform some other DM tasks, such as change and deviation detection, it is necessary to discover reference values and attributes first and then use them for comparisons with other data. For example, "soldiers on duty wear *uniforms* and carry *weapons*".

*Sequence analysis.* Some data have their full-blown meanings and exhibit some correlation's only if they are considered within a regular series (e.g. time series data). Selection and preprocessing phases of the KDD process are quite critical in this task, since data sets must represent a regular sequence of data.

*Mining association rules.* This is a frequently used DM task. It detects correlations between two or more fields in a data record, or among sets of values in a single field. The correlations are represented as rules, such as "From all data records that contain A, B, and C, 72% also contain D and E". This is important if the task is, for example, to discover what items consumers usually buy together in retail shopping ("shopping patterns").

*Link analysis.* It means detecting correlations among different data records, usually in the form of rules with certainty factors. It is similar to mining association rules, but here the correlations are between different records, not between different fields.

*Spatial dependency analysis.* This task discovers patterns of spatial data in geographical information systems, astro-physical systems, ecological systems, and so on. For example, "The price of real estate at location $X$ always raises in September and drops in May".

*Discovering path traversal patterns.* Sometimes dependencies among data items can be suitably modeled using graphs. In such cases it may be interesting to discover some paths in the graph that are important in a certain sense, and are not explicitly known. A typical example is discovering path traversal patterns in accessing WWW pages. Knowing such patterns can help design Web-based applications better [8, 9].

## 5. Data Mining Algorithms

DM algorithms are procedures for pattern extraction from a set of cleaned, preprocessed, transformed data. Many DM algorithms are not used in DM exclusively, but have been adopted from other disciplines and adapted for DM. However, some DM algorithms have been originally developed by DM experts.

There is no such a thing as a universally good DM algorithm. While each DM algorithm corresponds to one specific DM task, there are usually several popular algorithms for performing each DM task. DM experts continue to invent new algorithms and improve existing ones.

Two main aspects of each DM algorithm are pattern identification and pattern representation and description.

*Pattern identification* is the process of discovering collections (classes) of data items that have something in common. Numerical DM algorithms are often used for pattern identification. All of them are based on maximizing similarities between the data within a class and minimizing that similarity between the classes themselves. Euclidean distance measures are used to compute the similarities. However, numerical DM algorithms work well only with essentially numerical data. For structured data, such as records and objects, numerical DM algorithms are not easy to apply. Moreover, it is hard to use domain knowledge with numerical algorithms (e.g. the knowledge about the shape of a cluster).

Another kind of algorithms for pattern identification is algorithms for discovering conceptual clusters. They use similarities among the attributes of data items, as well as conceptual cohesion of data in the items. Conceptual cohesion is defined by domain knowledge. Such algorithms work well for both numerical and structured data.

Finally, it is possible to identify patterns and clusters interactively, i.e., with an active participation of the user. The idea is to combine the computing power of the KDD/DM system with the knowledge and visual capabilities of the user. The system presents data sets to the user in a suitable graphical form, along various dimensions, and the user herself/himself defines the patterns and the clusters and guides the KDD/DM process in a desired direction.

*Pattern representation and description* is a transformation of the procedure defined by a DM algorithm and the results obtained by applying the algorithm into the space of universally known algorithms, methods and techniques that are used in other disciplines as well. There are two ideas behind it. The first one is to transform the results obtained by applying a DM algorithm into a form that the user easily understands and in which it is easy for the user to tell the meaning of discovered patterns. DM algorithms in their basic form usually generate patterns that are suitable in terms of their representation in the computer and/or processing efficiency. However, the user needs patterns in the form that she/he is used to, such as rules, decision trees, linear models, or diagrams. The other idea is to use some algorithms that are already used in other disciplines for pattern identification, cluster description, computation of probability density and correlation, etc. and apply them to DM. In that sense, DM systems use numerous well-established algorithms and techniques, such as statistical methods, neural networks, genetic algorithms, $k$-nearest neighbor algorithm, various techniques of using domain knowledge, case-based reasoning, Bayesian networks, and so on.

In order to get a feeling of how a typical DM algorithm works, consider the famous Apriori algorithm for mining association rules [2, 8]. The purpose of the algorithm is to discover association rules of the following form:

$$P \Rightarrow Q, \quad \text{i.e.,} \ P_1 \wedge P_2 \wedge \cdots \wedge P_m \Rightarrow Q_1 \wedge Q_2 \wedge \cdots \wedge Q_n$$

The meaning of this expression is that if a data record or one of its attributes contains the item set $P$, then it also contains the item set $Q$, and $P \cap Q = \varnothing$. In fact, Apriori discovers patterns in the form of so-called *large k-itemsets* ($k = 1, 2, \ldots$), which are essentially the sets of items that are often associated (often go together) within individual data records in the database. "Often" means that there is a sufficient support $s$ (above a predefined threshold) for large $k$-itemsets in the database. For example, if $\{AB\}$ is a large 2-itemset, then at least $s\%$ of the data records in the database contains both $A$ and $B$. The corresponding association rules are $A \Rightarrow B$ and $B \Rightarrow A$. In other words, there is usually no one-to-one correspondence between large itemsets and association rules, but the transformation from large itemsets to association rules is straightforward. The rules that correspond to the large 4-itemset $\{ABCD\}$ are $A, B, C \Rightarrow A$, or $A, B \Rightarrow C, D$, or $A, C \Rightarrow B, D$, and so on. Apriori discovers large $k$-itemsets for all $k$ such that the number of large $k$-itemsets is greater than zero.

| ID | elements |
|----|----------|
| 10 | A C D    |
| 20 | B C E    |
| 30 | A B C E  |
| 40 | B E      |

**Fig. 3.**   An example database (as in [8]).

**Fig. 4.**   An example of different levels of abstraction.

The complete description of the algorithm is beyond the scope of this chapter, but the basic ideas can be easily understood from an example. Figure 3 shows a simple database. If the required support factor is $s = 50\%$, then each large $k$-itemset must be present in at least 2 records. Large 1-itemsets are $\{A\}$, $\{B\}$, $\{C\}$, and $\{E\}$ (but not $\{D\}$, since it exists only in the record with ID $= 10$). Large 2-itemsets are $\{AC\}$, $\{BC\}$, $\{BE\}$, and $\{CE\}$ (but not $\{AB\}$, $\{AD\}$, and so on, for similar reasons). There is only one large 3-itemset, $\{BCE\}$.

There are numerous variants, modifications and improvements of the original Apriori algorithm. One of the best known is proposed within the DHP algorithm (Dynamic Hashing and Pruning) that uses hash functions and hash tables in order to increase the efficiency of discovering large $k$-itemsets [8, 23]. Another interesting improvement is illustrated in Fig. 4. It is concerned with the idea of introducing different *levels of abstraction* in the process of discovering association rules. Recall that mining association rules is often used to discover shopping patterns from shopping data records. If the idea is to discover what articles people often buy together in newsstands, a discovered rule might be:

buy NBA News $\Rightarrow$ buy Camel cigarettes

However, it is highly likely that such a rule would have a small support factor. On the other hand, the rule:

buy sport-related newspaper $\Rightarrow$ buy strong cigarettes would probably have a larger support. Finally, the rule:

buy newspaper ⇒ buy cigarettes

would have even larger support. It all comes from different levels of abstraction. In general, associations on higher levels of abstraction are stronger but less concrete. Moreover, associations are easy to see only on higher levels of abstraction. Hence it makes sense to explore lower levels of abstraction only if the associations at the higher levels are strong enough. Different thresholds for support factor can be used at different levels of abstraction. The lower the level of abstraction, the more concrete the entities considered and the lower the threshold to be adopted.

## 6. Using Domain Knowledge in KDD

Along with raw data, additional information is also useful in any KDD process, such as information about data themselves, links between them, their meanings, and their constraints. The data dictionary contains parts of that information — links between data and internal organization of data within the database. In order to use the other parts of that information in a KDD process, it is necessary to include domain knowledge in the process (see Fig. 1).

Domain knowledge in the KDD process is the knowledge about the contents of data in the database, the application domain, and the context and goals of the KDD process. It facilitates focusing of activities in all phases of the process from selection to DM, focusing of the search process (see Fig. 1), and more accurate evaluation of discovered knowledge. However, users should take care of the fact that search focusing can result in failing to discover some useful knowledge that happens to lie out of the focus.

KDD systems today typically use domain knowledge in the forms of data dictionary, field correlations (e.g. body height and weight are correlated), heuristic rules, and procedures and functions.

It is usually a domain expert who provides domain knowledge, but it is also possible to *discover* it through KDD. In other words, newly discovered knowledge is also a part of domain knowledge. Moreover, it is sometimes possible to represent that newly discovered knowledge in a suitable machine-readable form (e.g. rules) and use them as input to other programs, such as an expert system and a query optimizer.

Using domain knowledge in KDD enables data set reduction in performing search activities in the DM phase of the process, hypothesis optimization in various DM tasks, query optimization, and testing validity and accuracy of knowledge discovered in the KDD process [22]. For a simple example, if the task is to discover from a database of medical records whether a certain drug has effects on pregnant patients, domain knowledge can reduce the data set by using the fact that only records of *female* patients within some age boundaries should be searched.

Similarly, domain knowledge can help eliminate redundant clauses from the hypothesis stated as the following rule (and thereby optimize the hypothesis):

| IF | age >= 30 | AND | |
| | gender = FEMALE | AND | //redundant! |
| | pregnancy = YES | AND | |
| | . . . | | |
| THEN | effect of drug X = POSITIVE | | |

The way domain knowledge helps in query optimization is easy to see from the following example that uses the fact that search hypotheses are usually easy to convert directly into a query:

| IF | age >= 70 | AND | //a hypothesis |
| | physical condition = BAD | AND | |
| | therapy for other diseases = YES | AND | |
| | insurance = NO | | |
| THEN | operation = NO | | |
| | | | |
| SELECT | age, physical condition, therapy for | //the corresponding | |
| | other diseases, insurance | //query | |
| FROM | Patients, Operations | | |
| WHERE | operation = NO | | |
| | Patients.P# = Operations.P# | | |

The meaning of the above IF-THEN hypothesis is, obviously, that operation is not suggested for patients above a certain age limit, in a bad physical condition, who suffer from other diseases, and have no adequate insurance coverage. The above query corresponds to the hypothesis directly. However, if a domain rule built in the system says "hemophilia = YES ⇒ operation = NO", then an optimized query might be [22]:

| SELECT | age, physical condition, therapy for other diseases, insurance |
| FROM | Patients |
| WHERE | hemophilia = YES |

When testing validity and accuracy of knowledge discovered in the KDD process, it might happen that the knowledge contains redundant facts and contradictions. Redundancies are not a serious problem, but contradictions are. Testing discovered knowledge by applying valid and accurate domain knowledge can help determine whether contradictory patterns are really contradictory, or they just appear to be contradictory. For example, a KDD system may discover that in, say, 1998 the increase in selling beverages in the place X was 2%, while in 1999 it was 20%. At the first glance, this may appear to be contradictory. However, domain knowledge may tell the user that the place X is actually a small, tiny village in which the first store selling beverages has been open in early 1999, and hence the significant difference in the percents. On the other hand, an appropriate care should be taken when drawing conclusions about the validity of discovered knowledge, since *that* knowledge may be correct, and the domain knowledge used in the process may be out of date and inaccurate.

## 7. Pattern Evaluation

In order to express how important a discovered pattern is for the user, various measures of pattern's interestingness have been proposed. They combine pattern's validity (certainty), novelty, usability and simplicity to specify the pattern's interestingness quantitatively. Pattern's *validity* is usually a number (on some prespecified scale) showing to what extent the discovered pattern holds for the data in the database. *Novelty* shows quantitatively how new is the pattern for the user. *Usability* is the feature describing how and to what degree the user can use the discovered pattern. *Simplicity* is best understood from the following example: if the pattern is represented as an If-Then rule, then the fewer the If-and Then-clauses in the rule, the simpler the pattern is. Simple patterns are easier to interpret and use than complicated ones.

Some measures are *objective*. They show pattern's accuracy and precision, and rely on applying some statistical indicators (e.g. support and certainty factors), probability theory, and/or domain knowledge when evaluating a pattern's interestingness. For example, a KDD system using the summarization DM task may discover the following two patterns: "sale increase in region 1 is 5%" and "sale increase in region 2 is 50%". In this example domain knowledge might contain the fact that 1,000.000 people live in region 1 and only 15.000 in region 2, hence the system will evaluate the first pattern to be more important than the second one.

There are also *subjective* measures of interestingness. They are often heuristic and depend on the user, hence can be different for different users. Fortunately, all discovered patterns have some important features that help create subjective measures of interestingness in spite of the fact that different users will use them with different subjective bias.

As an illustration, consider the measure proposed by Silberschatz [25]. It relies on pattern's *unexpectedness* and *actionability*. Unexpectedness means that a pattern is interesting and important if it surprises the user. For example, if sale increase is more-or-less equal in all regions but one, that might be a surprise for the user who may have expected equal increase in all the regions considered. Actionability is the possibility to translate a discovered pattern into an appropriate action, i.e., to "do something" when the pattern is discovered. It is directly related to the usability feature described above. After discovering an exceptionally low increase of sale in a certain region, the user can undertake, for example, some marketing actions to improve the sale in that region. Both unexpectedness and actionability are subjective in nature. While actionability is extremely difficult to quantify, there *are* ways to quantify unexpectedness. An important assumption here is that unexpected patterns are also actionable. If that is so, then measuring pattern's unexpectedness alone is sufficient to measure its interestingness.

One way to measure pattern's unexpectedness is to describe and apply the user's *system of beliefs*, since unexpected patterns contradict the user's beliefs. If the system of beliefs is represented as a set of logical expressions $b$, then the conditional probability $d(b|E)$ can denote the strength of some belief $b$, based on some previous evidence $E$. *Strong beliefs* have a high value of $d(b|E)$. A pattern that contradicts such beliefs is unexpected and is always interesting. *Variable beliefs* have lower values of $d(b|E)$. The higher the effect of a pattern on variable beliefs, the more interesting the pattern is to the user.

Different beliefs have different importance. If $b_i$ is a belief in a system of beliefs $B$, let $w_i$ denote the importance (weight) of $b_i$ in $B$. Let also:

$$\sum_{b_i \in B} w_i = 1$$

Then, according to [25], the interestingness of pattern $p$ for the system of beliefs $B$ is the sum:

$$I(p, B, E) = \sum_{b_i \in B} w_i |d(b_i|p, E) - d(b_i|E)|$$

The interpretation of the above sum is as follows. If we assume that each belief $b_i$ can change upon the discovery of $p$, then the change of belief $b_i$ can be measured as the absolute value of the difference between the strengths of the belief before and after the discovery of $p$. The importance of the change for the system of beliefs $B$ can be higher or lower, hence the difference is multiplied by $w_i$. Then the sum $I(p, B, E)$ actually shows how much the entire system of beliefs changes when the pattern $p$ is discovered, hence it is a good measure for evaluating the pattern $p$.

Intuitively, adding new data to a database can result in changes of some beliefs about the data in the database. It can be shown from the above expression for computing $I(p, B, E)$ that for the old data $D$ and the newly added $\Delta D$ it holds:

$$(d(b_i|\Delta D, D) \neq d(b_i|D)) \Rightarrow \exists p, I(p, B, E) \neq 0$$

This means that when new data are added to a database, the strengths of beliefs $d(b_i|D)$ in the user's system of beliefs generally change. If the change is above a predefined threshold, it makes sense to start a search for new patterns. That process is called *belief-driven DM*.

## 8. Systems and Applications

KDD/DM systems and various systems that support the KDD process are being developed intensively since mid-90's. Table 1 shows some important application domains and typical problems that KDD/DM systems are used for in these domains [11, 13, 20, 21, 24].

**Table 1.** KDD/DM application domains and typical problems.

| Domain | Problem |
|---|---|
| Medicine | Discovering side-effects of drugs, genetic sequence analysis, treatment costs analysis |
| Finance | Credit/Loan approval, bankruptcy prediction, stock market analysis, fraud detection, unauthorized account access detection, investment selection |
| Social sciences | Demographic data analysis, prediction of election results, voting trends analysis |
| Astronomy | Analysis of satellite images |
| Law | Tax fraud detection, identification of stolen cars, fingerprints recognition |
| Marketing | Sale prediction, identification of consumer and product groups, frequent-flyer patterns |
| Engineering | Discovering patterns in VLSI circuit layouts, predicting aircraft-component failures |
| Insurance | Detection of extremely high or chained claims |
| Agriculture | Classification of plant diseases |
| Publishing | Discovering reader profiles for special issues of journals and magazines |

The following brief descriptions illustrate the variety of current KDD/DM systems and applications.

*Recon.* Lockheed Martin Research Center has developed Recon, a KDD/DM-based stock-selection advisor [18]. It analyzes a database of over 1000 most successful companies in USA, where data are stored for each quarter from 1987 to date. For each company in the database the data change historically, and each data record in the database contains over 1000 fields, such as the stock price for that company, the trend of price and profit change, the number of analysts monitoring the company's business, etc. Recon predicts return on investment after three months of buying some stock and recommends whether to buy the stock or not. The results of the analysis are patterns in the form of rules that classify stock as exceptional and non-exceptional. Recon recommends to buy the stock if its return on investment can be classified as exceptional. Since the users are financial experts, not computer ones, Recon has a rich, easy-to-use graphical user interface. Pattern evaluation is done interactively, letting the users analyze and manually fine-tune the rules detected in the analysis.

*CiteSeer.* There are huge amounts of scientific literature on the Web. In that sense, the Web makes up a massive, noisy, disorganized, and ever-growing database. It is not easy to quickly find useful and relevant literature in such a database. CiteSeer is a custom-digital-library generator that performs information filtering and KDD functions that keep users up-to-date on relevant research [5]. It downloads Web publications in a general research area (e.g. computer architectures), creates a specific digital library, extracts features from each source in the library, and automatically discovers those publications that match the user's needs.

*JAM.* The growing number of credit card transactions on the Internet increases the risks of credit card numbers being stolen and subsequently used to commit fraud. The JAM (Java Agents for Metalearning) system provides distributed DM capabilities to analyze huge numbers of credit card transactions processed on the Internet each day, in search of fraudulent transactions [7]. Many more transactions are legitimate than fraudulent. JAM divides a large data set of labeled transactions (either fraudulent or legitimate) into smaller subsets and applies DM techniques to generate classifiers and subsequently generate a metaclassifier. It uses a variety of learning algorithms in generating the classifiers.

*Subdue.* It is possible to search graphs and discover common substructures in them. That is the basis of Subdue, the system developed to perform substructure discovery DM on various databases represented as graphs [10]. Subdue performs two key DM techniques, called unsupervised pattern discovery and supervised concept learning from examples. The system has been successfully used in discovering substructures in CAD circuit layouts, structures of some protein categories, program source code, and aviation data. Experts in the corresponding domains ranked all of the substructures that have been discovered by Subdue highly useful.

*Advanced Scout.* The purpose of the KDD/DM system Advanced Scout is discovering patterns in the basketball game [4]. It helps coaches of the NBA basketball teams in analyzing their decisions brought during the games. Advanced Scout lets a coach select, filter, and transform data from a common database of all the games in the current NBA season, the database that is accessible to all NBA coaches. The database contains huge amounts of data per game, all time-stamped, and showing everything about individual players, their roles, shooting scores, blocks, rebounds, etc. The coach uses his domain knowledge (of the game and of his team) and can ask Advanced Scout DM-queries about the shooting performance, optimal playset, and so on. An example of patterns that Advanced Scout discovers is "When Price was the guard, Williams' shooting score was 100%". Video records of each game facilitate interactive pattern evaluation process.

## 9. Research Issues

Recent research efforts and trends in KDD/DM roughly belong to the following avenues:

- *Improving efficiency of mining association rules.* Apriori remains the fundamental algorithm for mining association rules, but its efficiency is constantly being under further investigation. Apart from the already mentioned DHP improvment [8, 23], most notable other attempts to increase Apriori's efficiency are the CD, DD, IDD and HD algorithms that parallelize Apriori for execution by multiple processors [16]. Zaki has proposed several new algorithms based on organizing items into a subset lattice search space, which is decomposed into small independent chunks or sublattices which can be solved in memory [31].

- *Mining object-oriented databases.* One general criticism to KDD/DM technology is that until very recently it has been applicable only to mining for patterns in relational databases. Knowledge discovery in object-oriented databases has just started to emerge, and there are still many open research problems in that direction. An example of research attempts in that direction is trying to mine for structural similarities in a collection of objects [29].

- *Mining multimedia databases.* This is another research and application area of KDD and DM in which research has only started. Multimedia databases are structurally much different from relational databases, but also much richer in terms of the information they contain. KDD/DM challenges in multimedia databases include mining correlations between segments of text and images, between speech and images or faces, finding common patterns in multiple images, and the like [17].

- *Mining distributed and heterogeneous databases.* Currently, KDD/DM tools work mainly on centralized databases. This is an important limitation, given the fact that many applications work combining raw data from multiple databases in distributed and heterogeneous environments. The question is how to apply KDD/DM tools to distributed, heterogenous databases. One possible way is to first apply KDD process on each database and generate partial patterns, and then to use either a central coordinator or various other tools to integrate these patterns and generate complete results [28]. The various tools have to communicate with each other to provide a complete picture. Another idea is to first integrate multiple databases by creating a data warehouse, and then mine the warehouse for patterns using a centralized KDD/DM tool [27]. In that case, KDD/DM techniques can be used for mining integration knowledge. Examples of such knowledge include rules for comparing two objects from different databases in order to determine whether they represent the same real-world entity. Another example would be rules to determine the attribute values in the integrated database.

- *Text mining.* Mining textual databases is tightly coupled with natural language processing, hence it is inherently very hard to fully automate. It requires large amounts of formally codified knowledge (knowledge about words, parts of speech, grammar, word meanings, phonetics, text structure), and the world itself [19]. However, interesting though simple applications are still possible in this area. For example, any online English text can be treated as a database containing a large collection of article usage or phrase structuring (parsing) knowledge. It is possible to automatically extract such kinds of knowledge about natural languages by text mining. One other important goal of text mining is automatic classification of electronic documents and contents-based association between them [30].

- *Using discovered knowledge in subsequent iterations of the KDD process.* This is another shortcoming of current KDD/DM technology that has to be investigated further, in spite of some solutions that have been proposed [10, 28]. Automating the use of discovered knowledge is not easy and requires necessary translations, since the form used to represent discovered knowledge is usually not suitable for storing and processing the same knowledge by the same tool.

- *Knowledge discovery in semistructured data.* Semistructured data are data that are structured similarly, but not identically. Traditional data mining frameworks are inapplicable for semistructured data. On the other hand, semistructured data still have some structural features. For example, different person-related records and objects may have different structures and fields (attributes), but *most* of them will have a *Name* field, an *Address* field, and so on. Such structural features of semistructured data make it possible to extract knowledge of common substructures in data. Wang and Liu have proposed a solution for this discovery task based on the idea of finding typical (sub)structures that occur in a minimum number of observed objects [29]. Discovery of common substructures in graphs, such as in the above mentioned Subdue system, is another example of this kind of discovery task [10].

*Web mining* is a KDD/DM-related issue that attracts much attention in recent years [5, 6]. Although the World Wide Web is not a database in the classical sense, it is itself an enormously large resource of data. It puts much challenge to KDD/DM system developers, since data on the Web are highly unstructured and stored in a number of different formats. However, some minimum structure still exists and is represented by various linguistic and typographic conventions, standard HTML tags, search engines, indices and directories, as well as many classes of semi-structured documents, such as technical papers and product catalogues. This minimum structure creates realistic opportunities for Web mining through resource discovery, information extraction from discovered resources, and pattern discovery on certain locations and groups of locations on the Web. In that sense, Web mining is related to mining semistructured data.

## 10. Discussion and Summary

Building a KDD/DM application in practice requires a lot of efforts. To an extent, using an integrated software environment for developing KDD/DM applications can alleviate these efforts. Such environments usually have a number of built-in techniques that facilitate going through all phases of the KDD process, and also support several DM tasks and algorithms. Moreover, some of them can be even downloaded for free from the Internet (see the first two sites mentioned in the final section). Still, KDD/DM systems are expensive to develop and it is risky to start such a project before conducting a detailed feasibility study. Generally, if data can be analyzed manually or just by applying some statistical techniques, then developing a KDD/DM system may be too expensive. There must be at least an expectation in the organization that the KDD/DM system will bring some positive financial effects, otherwise organizational support in developing the system is likely to be missing [13]. Likewise, the amount of available data must be large enough and domain knowledge must be available in some form. The likelihood of success of a KDD/DM application is higher if available data are noise-free and if at least some domain knowledge already exists (KDD will upgrade it!).

In spite of many open problems, the number of KDD/DM applications grows rapidly and the application domains constantly multiply. Perhaps the most important driving forces for future KDD/DM applications are the Internet and the Web. KDD and DM over the Internet will most likely be reality once the Internet technology, services, protocols, and management get improved through ongoing projects such as Internet 2 and Next Generation Internet (NGI).

## 11. KDD and DM on the Web

There are many KDD and DM resources on the Web. The short list of URLs shown below has been composed according to the following criteria:

- the number of useful links following from that URL;
- how comprehensive the site is; and
- how interesting the URL is for researchers.

As for the first two criteria, the KD Mine site is the most useful starting point for everyone who wants to mine himself/herself for KDD/DM resources. Knowledge Discovery Mine is also a very useful general KDD/DM site. Researchers would probably be most interested in what's new in the field. In that sense, the two KDD Conferences sites shown are only two in a series of such sites dedicated to the most important annual KDD/DM conference. The most relevant dedicated journal in the field, launched in 1997, is Data Mining and Knowledge Discovery (the last URL shown).

(1) KD Mine:                              http://www.kdnuggets.com/
(2) Knowledge Discovery Mine   http://info.gte.com/~kdd/
(3) KDD Conferences               http://www-aig.jpl.nasa.gov/kdd98/
                                              ttp://research.microsoft.com/datamine/kdd99/
(4) Data Mining and Knowledge Discovery (journal)
                                              www.research.microsoft.com/research/
                                                         datamine/

# References

1. P. Adriaans and D. Zanintge, *Data Mining* (Addison-Wesley, Reading, 1996).
2. R. Agrawal *et al.*, "Fast discovery of association rules", *Advances in Knowledge Discovery and Data Mining* eds. U. M. Fayyad *et al* (AAAI/MIT Press, Menlo Park, 1996) 307–328.
3. S. S. Anand, B. W. Scotney, M. G. Tan, S. I. McClean, D. A. Bell, J. G. Hughes and I. C. Magill, "Designing a kernel for data mining", *IEEE Expert* **12** (March/April 1997) 65–74.
4. I. Bhandari, E. Colet, J. Parker, Z. Pines, R. Pratap and K. Ramanujam, "Advanced Scout: Data mining and knowledge discovery in NBA data", *Data Mining and Knowledge Discovery* **1** (1997) 121–125.
5. K. D. Bollacker, S. Lawrence and C. Lee Giles, "Discovering relevant scientific literature on the Web", *IEEE Intelligent Systems* **15** (March/April 2000) 42–47.
6. Chakrabarti *et al.*, "Mining the web's link structure", *IEEE Computer* (August 1999) 50–57.
7. P. K. Chan, W. Fan, A. Prodromidis, and S. J. Stolfo, "Distributed data mining in credit card fraud detection", *IEEE Intelligent Systems* **14** (November–December 1999) 67–74.
8. M.-S. Chen, J. Han and P. S. Yu, "Data mining: An overview from a database perspective", *IEEE Transactions on Knowledge and Data Engineering* **8** (1996) 866–883.
9. M.-S. Chen, J. S. Park and P. S. Yu, "Efficient data mining for path traversal patterns", *IEEE Transactions on Knowledge and Data Engineering* **10** (1998) 209–221.
10. D. J. Cook and L. B. Holder, Graph-based data mining, *IEEE Intelligent Systems* **15** (March/April 2000) 32–41.
11. U. M. Fayyad, "Data mining and knowledge discovery: Making sense out of data, *IEEE Expert* **11** (October 1996) 20–25.
12. U. Fayyad, G. Piatetsky-Shapiro and P. Smyth, "The KDD process for extracting useful knowledge from volumes of data", *Communications of the ACM* **39** (November 1996) 27–34.
13. W. J. Frawley, G. Piatetsky-Shapiro, and C. J. Matheus, "Knowledge discovery in databases: An overview", *AI Magazine* (Fall 1992) 57–70.
14. V. Ganti, J. Gehrke and R. Ramakrishnan, "Mining very large databases", *IEEE Computer* **32** (August 1999) 38–45.
15. C. Glymour, D. Madigan, D. Pregibon and P. Smyth, "Statistical themes and lessons for data mining", *Data Mining and Knowledge Discovery* **1** (1997) 11–28.
16. E.-H. Han, G. Karypis and V. Kumar, "Scalable parallel data mining for association rules", *IEEE Transactions on Knowledge and Data Engineering* **12** (2000) 337–352.
17. A. G. Hauptmann, "Integrating and using large databases of text, images, video, and audio", *IEEE Intelligent Systems* **14** (1999) 34–35.
18. G. H. John, P. Miller and R. Kerber, "Stock selection using rule induction", *IEEE Expert* **11** (October 1996) 52–58.
19. K. Knight, "Mining online text", *Communications of the ACM* **42** (November 1999) 58–61.
20. C. J. Matheus, P. C. Chan and G. Piatetsky-Shapiro, "Systems for knowledge discovery in databases", *IEEE Transactions on Knowledge and Data Engineering* **5** (1993) 903–913.
21. T. Munakata, "Knowledge discovery", *Communications of the ACM* **42** (November 1999) 26–29.

22. M. M. Owrang and F. H. Grupe, "Using domain dnowledge to guide database knowledge discovery", *Expert Systems with Applications* **10** (1996) 173–180.

23. J. S. Park, M.-S. Chen and P. S. Yu, "Using a hash-based method with transaction trimming for mining association rules", *IEEE Transactions on Knowledge and Data Engineering* **9** (1997) 813–825.

24. N. Ramakrishnan and A. Y. Grama, "Data mining: From serendipity to science", *IEEE Computer* **32** (August 1999) 34–37.

25. A. Silberschatz, "What makes patterns interesting in knowledge discovery systems", *IEEE Transactions on Knowledge and Data Engineering* **8** (1996) 970–974.

26. E. Simoudis, Reality check for data mining, *IEEE Expert* **11** (October 1996) 26–33.

27. J. Srivastava and P.-Y. Chen, "Warehouse creation — A potential roadblock to data warehousing", *IEEE Transactions on Knowledge and Data Engineering* **11** (1999) 118–126.

28. B. Thuraisingham, "A primer for understanding and applying data mining", *IEEE IT Professional* (January/February 2000) 28–31.

29. K. Wang and H. Liu, "Discovering structural association of semistructured data", *IEEE Transactions on Knowledge and Data Engineering* **12** (2000) 353–371.

30. S. M. Weiss, *et al.*, "Maximizing text-mining performance", *IEEE Intelligent Systems* **14** (July/August 1999) 63–69.

31. M. J. Zaki, "Scalable algorithms for association mining", *IEEE Transactions on Knowledge and Data Engineering* **12** (2000) 372–390.

# KNOWLEDGE-BASED INFORMATION ACCESS

AMY K. KARLSON,* RALPH D. SEMMEL† and DAVID P. SILBERBERG

*The Johns Hopkins University Applied Physics Laboratory,
11100 Johns Hopkins Road, Laurel, MD 20723-6099*
*\*E-mail: amy.karlson@jhuapl.edu*
*†E-mail: rds@aplcomm.jhuapl.edu*

Current data storage, retrieval, and management mechanisms are inherently complex, perpetuating the need for intuitive access to stored data. The Internet has complicated the situation further by vastly increasing the quantity, types, and availability of data. In a distributed environment, data storage, retrieval, and management must coordinate among multiple heterogeneous sources. In this article, we present approaches to simplifying access to data sources. We begin by presenting automated query generation as a means to provide high-level access to a single database. We then present an overview of architectures that support the interoperability of multiple distributed heterogeneous data sources, including an architecture which generalizes an automated query formulation technique to support multiple distributed heterogeneous sources. We conclude by discussing the role of distributed object and agent technologies in distributed information access.

*Keywords*: Automated query formulation, distributed databases, heterogeneous databases, entity-relationship models, knowledge-based architecture.

## 1. Introduction

Data management technology has not kept pace with the demand to effectively and efficiently store, manage, and access unprecedented quantities and types of data, stressing current data management systems and architectures. Several factors have exacerbated the technology lag. First, data itself is complex: organizations may store terabytes of data containing thousands of attributes which are spread across hundreds of tables or objects, potentially surpassing any individual's ability to comprehend the structure and population of a database. Second, data storage is complex: in our increasingly network-centric economy, staying competitive requires distributing, integrating, and sharing data resources, resulting in related data that can be stored across multiple, geographically distributed, heterogeneous databases. Finally, data access is complex: database access has remained primarily low-level and knowledge-intensive, requiring users to understand the details of the database design to retrieve data. As new databases are added to a system and existing databases are modified, the complexity of maintaining and integrating design details increases dramatically.

Facilitating management of and access to data requires providing an interface to databases that abstracts the essence of *what* data the user requires from the details of *how* the data is stored or even *where* the data is located. It also requires providing architectures and approaches to enable the integration and interoperability of distributed heterogeneous databases. Finally, it requires acknowledging the trend toward distributed resources and embracing internet-based, open-architecture, and intelligent-agent solutions.

## 2. A Motivating Example

Let us look at an example to demonstrate some issues. Imagine that you need to make a request for data in an environment that provides no preconstructed views, such as when making an internet query to a search engine. As in the search engine scenario, you may not even know where the data is stored. Intuitively, however, you know that you want buyers who bought expensive watches in 1999, and that the data you want can be represented by the following request.

```
SHOW     buyer_name,
         buyer_id
WHERE    date >= '01/01/1999' AND
         date < '01/01/2000' AND
         product_type = "watch" AND
         cost_bracket = "expensive"
```

**Example 1.** An intuitive request.

Suppose, however, that for the appropriate data source to satisfy your request, you would have to issue the following SQL statement.

```
SELECT   CONCAT(BUYER.fname, BUYER.lname),
         BUYER.b_id
FROM     BUYER,
         TRANSACTION,
         TRANSACTION_PRODUCT,
         PRODUCT
WHERE    TRANSACTION.date >= '01/01/1999' AND
         TRANSACTION.date < '01/01/2000' AND
         PRODUCT.type = "watch" AND
         PRODUCT.price >= 1000 AND
         BUYER.b_id = TRANSACTION.b_id AND
         TRANSACTION.trans_id =
         TRANSACTION_PRODUCT.trans_id AND
         TRANSACTION_PRODUCT.p_id = PRODUCT.p_id
```

**Example 2.** A database-specific query.

The fact that the query in Example 2 is significantly more detailed than that of Example 1 illustrates one of the fundamental complexities of data retrieval: most database management systems provide only low-level data manipulation and retrieval support that requires users to be familiar with the underlying structure of the database. Intuitively, users know the data they want to retrieve and the constraints to impose. Ideally, retrieving the data would be as straightforward as passing those requirements on to the database management system. In practice, query formulation is tightly coupled to the conceptual and implementation models of the database and thus requires the user to be familiar with detailed aspects of the target database. For example, the target database in the previous examples supported access via queries in SQL [1], the standard query language for relational databases. SQL requires even the simplest queries to include the table names from which the data will be drawn. More involved queries require programmers to include not only the table *names*, but the precise table *navigation* by specifying how tables are to be associated via join criteria.

## 3. Conceptual Modeling

Given that you conceptually want to issue the request in Example 1, how would you know how to formulate the corresponding query in Example 2 that is required to retrieve the results? Often, the conceptual schema of the target database can be used to infer the appropriate database-level query. Early in the database lifecycle, designers develop the conceptual schema to capture the structure of the database as suggested by the user requirements [4]. The schema is defined using a high-level conceptual data model, which provides the notation for declaring and relating such database abstractions as entities, relationships, and constraints. Because the model provides an abstract representation for expressing high-level database properties, the development of the conceptual model is independent of any particular target platform or database implementation. Conceptual models therefore provide the basis for documenting and understanding the architecture of any database.

Assume the database that can satisfy your request is structured as shown in Fig. 1, where Fig. 1 describes the conceptual schema for a simple on-line store in entity-relationship (ER) model [6] notation. As the *de facto* standard for modeling large and complex database systems, the ER model is both easy to use and understand. For the purpose of this example, buyers purchase products by generating transactions, and can maintain multiple shopping carts that represent categories of items to be bought at a later date. The BUYER, TRANSACTION, SHOPPING_CART and PRODUCT entities are represented as rectangles in the schema diagram, with associated attributes represented as text joined to the entity by lines. Underlined attributes represent key attributes, which are those that uniquely identify entities. Diamonds represent the relationships between entities. The numbers and letters that label the connections between relationships and entities represent the cardinalities of the relationships. For example, the BUYER_TRANSACTION relationship is a

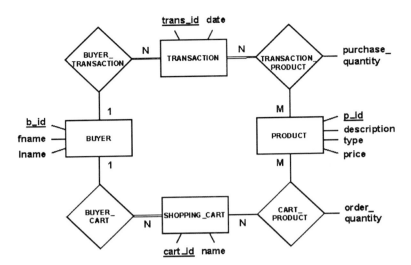

**Fig. 1.**    The conceptual model for an on-line store.

one-to-many $(1 : N)$ relationship between BUYER and TRANSACTION, indicating that each buyer can be associated with many transactions, but that each transaction is associated with only one buyer. A double line connecting a relationship to an entity indicates that the entity is required to participate in the relationship. For example, the double line connecting BUYER_CART to SHOPPING_CART indicates that a shopping cart must be associated with a buyer, whereas a buyer need not be associated with a shopping cart.

## 4. Conceptual to Implementation Model Mapping

A question that remains is how the conceptual model, which is a generic representation of the database, can be used to construct a database-specific query? Although the conceptual model is implementation-independent, it supports straightforward transformation to the relational and other implementation models, and thus to the database-level schema. The relational implementation schema for the on-line store is shown in Fig. 2, and expresses the tables that comprise the on-line store database. Each row represents a table descriptor, displaying each table name to the left of the cells that represent the table attributes. As in the conceptual model, the underlined attributes represent the table keys.

The relational implementation schema for the on-line store was generated from the conceptual schema in Fig. 1 through the application of well-defined transformation rules [11]. For example, one such rule dictates that each entity in the conceptual model is represented as a table in the implementation model. Notice that each entity in Fig. 1 is represented as a table of the same name in Fig. 2, with each entity attribute preserved as a corresponding table attribute. Just as conceptual-model relationships serve to relate entities to one another, their representations

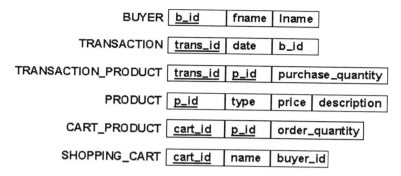

**Fig. 2.** The implementation model for an on-line store.

in the implementation model serve to relate tables to one another. The mechanism by which one table is related to another table is by including one table's key attributes in the other table as a *foreign key*. Depending upon the cardinality and participation constraints of participating entities, a conceptual model relationship can be represented either as a distinct table that includes the keys of the participating entities as foreign keys, or by including the keys of all participating entities as foreign keys in the table associated with one of the participating entities. For example, the many-to-many TRANSACTION_PRODUCT relationship is represented in the implementation model as the TRANSACTION_PRODUCT table, and in addition to including its associated attribute purchase_quantity, includes the keys of its participating entities as foreign keys: trans_id from the TRANSACTION entity and p_id from the PRODUCT entity. The one-to-many BUYER_CART relationship, on the other hand, is represented in the implementation model by drawing the key (b_id) from the table representing the entity on the "one" side of the relationship (BUYER_ID) into the table corresponding to the entity on the "many" side of the relationship (SHOPPING_CART) as the foreign key buyer_id. We assume that the renaming of b_id to buyer_id has been dictated by the designer, illustrating that foreign key attributes need not retain the names of their associated primary key attributes.

Significant design information is lost in mapping from the conceptual model to the implementation model. Notice, for example, that Fig. 2 does not express the mandatory participation of TRANSACTION in its relationship with TRANSACTION_PRODUCT. In fact, the relationship between the two tables is not explicitly expressed in the schema and must be inferred from the fact that the identical attribute name (i.e. trans_id) appears in both tables. In practice, however, related attributes between tables can be referred to by different names. As in the conceptual-to-implementation mapping from above in which b_id from BUYER is represented as buyer_id in SHOPPING_CART, it is not obvious from the implementation representation, as it is in the conceptual representation, that the two tables are related.

Because notation at the implementation level is not rich enough to express important design details of a database, reasoning about how to navigate a database to retrieve desired data should occur at the conceptual rather than the implementation level. Unfortunately, if the conceptual model is not maintained after database implementation, as is often the case, users who wish to formulate queries to the database must perform significant research to reconstruct the conceptual model. Even users that have access to the conceptual design may find it difficult to digest the notational details and associated implications that would allow them to formulate semantically reasonable queries to complex databases. This issue suggests that typical database users would benefit from intelligent interfaces that assume the burden of formulating complex database-level queries and that provide the user with intuitive, high-level access to desired data.

## 5. Automated Query Generation

Various approaches to providing high-level query mechanisms have been explored. Early on, the problem was addressed by the Universal Relation (UR) theory [16, 21, 39], which provides programmers and users with a single-table view of the database. High-level queries are formulated to the "database table", while an underlying query engine creates a database-level query based on the relationships defined by the conceptual representations of the databases. Unfortunately, many of the UR systems rely upon abstractions not typically used by database designers, further complicating the design process by requiring an additional UR design component. Other approaches that use the more common ER models either present a graphical user interface for selecting subgraphs which correspond to requests [18, 42], or use universal relation concepts directly [23, 40]. Others attempted to create automated query generators [22] which resolve the shortcomings of the universal relation model, but still failed to provide the richness of expression needed for generalized queries. Although many variations on intelligent interfaces have been explored and implemented, we will refer to the QUICK intelligent database access system [27] in our examples.

QUICK uses knowledge extracted from the conceptual model to automate query generation, effectively eliminating the requirement that users be intimately familiar with the databases from which they retrieve data. QUICK relies on an extended entity-relationship (EER) [4, 10, 22, 37] model notation to conceptually describe a database. The extensions are drawn from semantic data modeling, object-oriented, and knowledge representation approaches [14, 26] to extend the expressive power of the ER model. QUICK supports intuitive high-level user requests similar to the request presented in Example 1. Specifically, QUICK accepts requests in USQL [9], a high-level version of SQL that allows users to specify only the attributes they desire and the associated constraints. USQL does not require users to specify the tables or objects the attributes are stored in, or the joins that relate tables or objects to one another.

Presented with only attribute names, the query generator must determine a reasonable navigation of the database tables to formulate the actual database query. For example, if you were interested in all transaction dates for all buyers, you might request fname, lname and b_id, which would be retrieved from the BUYER table, and date, which would be retrieved from the TRANSACTION table. But how would the query generator know to relate BUYER and TRANSACTION via the BUYER → TRANSACTION path, rather than via the BUYER → SHOPPING_CART → CART_PRODUCT → PRODUCT → TRANSACTION_PRODUCT → TRANSACTION path? The first navigation path would return the results you intended, whereas the second would return the buyer and transaction information for all buyers that intend to buy products they have bought in the past. Although the navigation path for the query we intended happens to be shorter, this is not always the case, and in general, complex databases demand a more sophisticated approach than shortest-path determination to guide the decision. Indeed, the query generator must draw upon hints embedded in the conceptual model notation to identify the path or paths that represent likely user intent.

Query generators recognize that some conceptual objects are more strongly related than others and that more intuitive queries can be generated by following paths that span strongly-related objects. For example, the UR model's representation of a database as a single table suggests that all database objects are strongly related, which can lead to incorrect interpretations of user queries. The introduction of the concept of *maximal objects* allowed the UR model to support the generation of intuitively correct interpretations of user queries [20]. Other query generators used ER based techniques to accomplish similar goals [22]. For illustrative purposes, we present the grouping mechanism used by QUICK, which can be considered an extension of maximal objects to EER objects.

## 6. Contexts

QUICK analyzes the conceptual model to identify *contexts*, which are sets of strongly associated conceptual model objects [39], including entities, attributes, and relationships [27]. The strengths of the associations are determined heuristically from the model notation, but conceptually represent the designer's intent with respect to the interrelationships among objects. Figure 3 shows the contexts for the on-line store as two rounded rectangles enclosing two subsets of objects. The first context relates BUYER, BUYER_TRANSACTION, TRANSACTION, TRANSACTION_PRODUCT, and PRODUCT objects, and essentially represents the notion that buyers purchase products by conducting transactions. The second context relates BUYER, BUYER_CART, SHOPPING_CART, CART_PRODUCT, and PRODUCT, representing the notion that buyers maintain lists of products they wish to purchase at a future date. That there exists no obvious relationship between the products a buyer has already purchased and those he intends to purchase is indicated by the TRANSACTION and SHOPPING_CART entities belonging to different contexts.

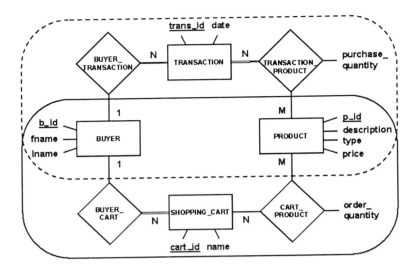

**Fig. 3.**   Contexts for the on-line store.

## 7.  Query Generation Using Contexts

Heuristically-driven algorithms [29] identify contexts within a database's conceptual model representation. For example, every relationship belongs to the same context as its associated entities, while cardinality constraints determine whether relationships adjacent to those entities are included in the same context. Once the contexts have been identified, all conceptual model objects will belong to at least one context, and possibly multiple distinct contexts.

The query generator uses the heuristically extracted contexts as knowledge for inferring user intent from high-level queries. A high-level query is composed of a set of attributes, each of which is associated with a conceptual model object. If the set of model objects associated with the requested attributes form a subset of a context, the query generator formulates the corresponding SQL query using knowledge of the join paths defined by the conceptual model and the enclosing context as well as knowledge of the conceptual-to-implementation mapping for the target database. For example, a user who wants to retrieve buyer, product and date information for all buyer transactions might pose the following USQL query to the query generator:

SELECT    fname,

lname,

date,

p_id

The query generator first identifies the EER objects that contain each requested attribute, in this case BUYER, TRANSACTION, and PRODUCT. Because BUYER,

TRANSACTION, and PRODUCT are contained solely by the top context in Fig. 3, the top context is assumed to reflect the user's intent. The identified context dictates the table navigation whereas the conceptual-to-implementation mapping knowledge determines the resulting SQL query:

```
SELECT    BUYER.fname,
          BUYER.lname,
          TRANSACTION.date,
          PRODUCT.p_id
  FROM    BUYER,
          TRANSACTION,
          TRANSACTION_PRODUCT,
          PRODUCT
 WHERE    BUYER.b_id = TRANSACTION.b_id AND
          TRANSACTION.trans_id =
          TRANSACTION_PRODUCT.trans_id AND
          TRANSACTION_PRODUCT.p_id = PRODUCT.p_id
```

The identified context represents the query generator's best estimation of the user's intent with respect to the posed high-level query, and provides the information necessary to generate the database-level query. However, had attributes from both TRANSACTION and SHOPPING_CART been requested, say date and cart_id, the query generator would not have been able to identify a single context that contains the requested attributes and would thus conclude that the database designer never intended for such a query to be posed. On the other hand, if the requested attributes had been completely contained within multiple contexts, such as if only fname, lname and p_id had been requested, the query generator would not be able to determine which of the two possible meanings defined by the top and bottom contexts was intended. In the latter case, the query generator would generate the query that is the UNION of the queries generated by each context by default.

That users cannot specify which of multiple contexts reflect the intended meaning of a high-level query illustrates limitations of the context paradigm. Even when a high-level query maps to a unique context, there is no guarantee that the generated query matches the user's intent. However, similar grouping techniqes, for example, maximal objects, suffer from similar shortfalls, and QUICK's deployment in real-world software applications indicates that it performs well in generating reasonable queries [32, 28].

Researchers have explored the use of role-based queries to provide guidance to the context selection process [33] when data requests can be satisfied by more than one context. To support role-based queries, the EER notation is augmented to include the assignment of role names to relationships. For example, imagine that the relationship BUYER_TRANSACTION between BUYER and TRANSACTION, included in the top context in Fig. 3, is assigned the role of `purchase`, whereas the `BUYER_CART` relationship between `BUYER` and `CART`, included in the bottom context in Fig. 3, is assigned the role of `order`. The `purchase` role specifies that any attribute "to the right of" `purchase` within its context assumes the role of `purchase` with respect to all context attributes "to the left". Similarly, the `order` role specifies that any attribute "to the right of" `order` within its context assumes the role of `order` with respect to all context attributes "to the left".

Recall from above that if a user requests only `BUYER` and `PRODUCT` attributes, the objects associated with the attributes will be completely contained within both the top and the bottom contexts, preventing the query generator from identifying the context which uniquely represents the intended request. That is, the query generator will not be able to determine whether the user intends to retrieve `BUYER` and `PRODUCT` information through `TRANSACTION` for purchased products or through `SHOPPING_CART` for ordered products, and will therefore return the UNION of the two possible queries. Role-based queries allow the user to augment a high-level query with role names to communicate the intended query. Thus, a user who issues the role-based query:

```
SELECT    fname,
          lname,
          b_id,
          purchase.p_id
```

communicates to the query generator that he intends the query defined by the top context, even though the conceptual objects that contain the requested attributes belong to both the top and the bottom contexts. Similarly, the role-based query:

```
SELECT    fname,
          lname,
          b_id,
          order.p_id
```

guides the query generator in formulating the query defined by the bottom context.

This type of query generator succeeds in recycling valuable database engineering products to provide a knowledge-based automated query formulation service to a single database. Central to the query generator's success is the recognition that conceptual data models contain knowledge that can be used to infer the meaning of high-level queries, expressed in terms of the associated contexts. An interpretation of a high-level query can thus be inferred from contexts that contain attributes of the query, and corresponding database-level queries can be generated. In this capacity, automated query generators can address the issue of tedious low-level data access by allowing users to specify their data needs at a high level, independent of the target data source architecture.

## 8. Accessing Multiple Databases

In practice, data retrieval over multiple sources is often more complicated than single database access. Consider, for example, that the on-line store actually maintains product data and customer data in separate databases. The resulting database models might look like those in Fig. 4. The circle in the Customer database model identifies TRANSACTION as a generalization of the associated specialized entities COMMITTED_TRANSACTION and INTENDED_TRANSACTION. That is, according to the Customer database, customer shopping carts can be thought of as intended transactions, and customer purchases can be thought of as committed transactions, both of which can be considered specialized transactions. Although the two database designs do not preserve the structure or terminology of the conceptual on-line store design of Fig. 1, together the two database models preserve the original intent of what comprises the on-line store database. That is, all concepts within the envisioned on-line store model of Fig. 1 can be expressed in one or the other of the Customer and Product databases, and relationships between the data in each database can be made through the product_id attribute of each database.

Although the conceptual model in Fig. 1 represents the unified conceptual structure of an on-line store, it is certainly not how a buyer, customer service representative, or marketer perceives the data. A buyer would be aware of the products available and those he intends to buy, but not likely his entire transaction history. A customer service representative, on the other hand, would not be interested in a buyer's intended purchases, but would be interested in a buyer's purchase history to address questions or problems concerning past purchases. Finally, marketing software may be used to determine which advertisements are displayed to buyers and may use past and future purchase criteria to distinguish extravagant buyers from thrifty buyers and alter the advertisements accordingly. The Buyer, Customer Service, and Marketing domains can be expressed as the conceptual models in Fig. 5.

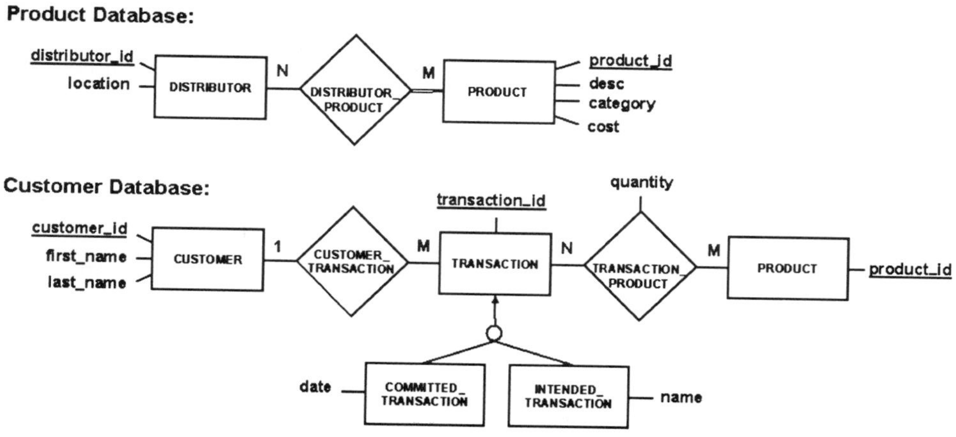

**Fig. 4.** Database domain conceptual models.

Note that a user domain conceptual model corresponds to an external view, which is a more general concept than an SQL view [4]. Although each user domain employs unique terminology that reflects how a user of that domain perceives the on-line store data, all user domain concepts can be expressed in the original design of Fig. 1. Many user domain concepts can be mapped directly to the original model's concepts, such as buyer_id of the Marketing domain to b_id of Fig. 1, while other concepts such as buyer_name of the Marketing domain involve a more complicated transformation, in this case the concatenation of fname and lname of Fig. 1.

## 9. Achieving Heterogeneous Database Access

With the scenario sufficiently more complicated, how will user queries from multiple domains be supported to multiple databases? Many systems have been developed to simplify access to distributed and heterogeneous databases. In general, there exist four categories of approaches by which database interoperability is achieved [25]:

(1) Require all databases to be implemented with the same conceptual schemas.
(2) Require systems to communicate via a single, global interface schema, while allowing them to implement local data schemas independently.
(3) Require systems to communicate via a single, global abstract interface schema. This abstraction eliminates underlying schema representation details.
(4) Allow systems to communicate through explicit correspondences between separately developed interface schemas.

The first approach is exemplified by AMASE [5], an astrophysics system which combines the catalogs and archives of two missions, IRAS and ROSAT, into a single, homogeneous catalog. Although IRAS is an infrared mission and ROSAT is an X-ray mission, the scientists in these areas of astrophysics "speak" a common domain language. In addition, scientists and the underlying database share the same domain of discourse. Thus, the application programmers did not need to translate queries and results among domain vocabularies. Rather, they tightly coupled the user interface to the underlying database model. Since the underlying database is an object-oriented DBMS, the architecture is scaleable within the astrophysics domain. However, it cannot be readily ported to other domains. Furthermore, other applications that wish to access the AMASE catalog must become intimately familiar with its database schema and terminology.

The Master Environment Library (MEL) [8], which provides one-stop shopping for all Department of Defense (DoD) environmental data archives, is another example of the first approach. MEL imposes a unified view of the distributed metadatabase catalogs by insisting that the participating archives standardize on the FGDC [12] data standard. Unfortunately, each participating archive must force their metadata into the FGDC format whether or not it is the best representation for the archived data. Furthermore, if other applications wish to access catalogs associated with the MEL, they must interpret the FGDC format. Finally, the architecture does little to provide assistance to users and databases that use different vocabulary sets.

The second approach is represented by NASA's Master Directory (MD) [38], which is a meta-catalog for finding both space and environment data archives. It is one of the earliest attempts to provide content-based search capabilities for distributed data archives. The MD has a central database catalog that stores the description of contents of distributed data archives. Participating archives, which supply Directory Interchange Format (DIF) entries that describe their data holdings, populate it. The success of the system depends heavily on the right choice of common terminology. The DIF keyword values are descriptors that have been standardized by an international scientific committee over the period of more than ten years. Even after ten years of standards meetings, there is still discussion concerning which are the "correct" keywords to use in which circumstances. Such an approach takes much time, effort, and expense. In addition, application designers that want to access the MD must become familiar with the nomenclature arrived upon by the international committee.

Systems using the third approach present underlying databases through an abstract global schema. Typically, they use mediators to translate queries from the application domains to the catalog domains. The SIMS architecture [3] provides interoperability among distributed, heterogeneous databases. Central to the architecture is a knowledge base that integrates the schemas of underlying databases within a single domain. Users are not presumed to know about how data is distributed over the data- and knowledge-bases to which SIMS has access. Rather, they query underlying databases as if they were a single, unified database. Unfortunately, users are required to be familiar with standard terminology of the domain. In addition, users must query the databases using the Loom query language [19], which is not generally familiar and requires some understanding of the conceptual classes of the knowledge base.

HERMES [35, 2] also provides a mediated approach for integrating distributed information systems. Knowledge engineers define the domain mappings with a declarative, rule-based language. A mediator compiler defines the semantic database integration to the system in an automated way. HERMES also provides a "yellow pages" facility to assist the mediator author in locating data sources. Unfortunately, applications must still be familiar with a common domain language and they must be somewhat familiar with the underlying database schemas to formulate queries.

Systems using the fourth approach communicate via explicit schema mappings. Tsimmis [13] integrates heterogeneous information systems by placing translators (or wrappers) around all information servers. Translators are written to convert the domain-specific database representations to a common model. Domain applications call mediators, which are at a level above the translators, to resolve queries. Mediators send queries to translators, assemble results, and return responses to applications. An excellent feature of this approach is that the knowledge base is not centralized. Rather, it consists of the set of system translators and mediators, which are usable by any application. However, writing both translators and mediators is a manually intensive task. While the authors of Tsimmis believe that these tasks can be automated, they agree that creating such a tool is a difficult task. Furthermore, mediators tend to implement database views, which implies that *ad hoc* queries are not easily answered.

Carnot [7] provides a layered, service-oriented approach to achieving and managing integrated databases. Integral to Carnot is an enterprise modeling and integration facility and a knowledge discovery facility. The core knowledge base of Carnot is Cyc [16], which is semantic network that describes the global context of the domain of query discourse. (To be precise, the purpose of Cyc is to describe the entire domain of human discourse.) The model integration facility automates the integration of disparate data models and then represents them in Cyc. Carnot, therefore, allows applications to query information using vocabulary in their own domain of discourse. However, Carnot does not provide capabilities for formulating complex *ad hoc* queries across distributed databases. It also does not provide adequate data fusion capabilities.

IMPACT [36] is an agent-based platform that supports multiple agent applications. Its focus is on coordinating the tasks of many independent application program and database agents. It provides an agent infrastructure for language-independent API agent functions, action constraints, concurrency, and integrity constraints. However, agents must be aware of both the information that other agents offer and the implicit relationships among the information sources. Furthermore, for complicated requests of a data source, calling agents must have an explicit understanding of its ontology or schema.

## 10. An Architecture for Distributed Information Access

Given the numbers and types of systems that have been built, each with its own advantages and disadvangages, it is clear that achieving heterogeneous database access is a hard problem. To illustrate an approach in more detail, we present a knowledge-based Architecture for Distributed INformation Access (ADINA) [34] that combines the functionality of QUICK's automated query generation with concept mappings between data representation levels to provide high-level access from unique user domains to multiple unique databases. Users specify only the values to be retrieved and the constraints of the search, using their own vocabulary and using a familiar query language interface. Underlying databases do not conform to any particular standards. The architecture automatically locates relevant underlying databases and formulates queries according to the structure and vocabularies of their schemas. The architecture also fuses the results and presents the results back to the application in the language of the application domain.

In this architecture, each user domain is associated with an implicit data model that represents the user view of the domain data, analogous to the Buyer, Customer

**Customer Service Domain:**

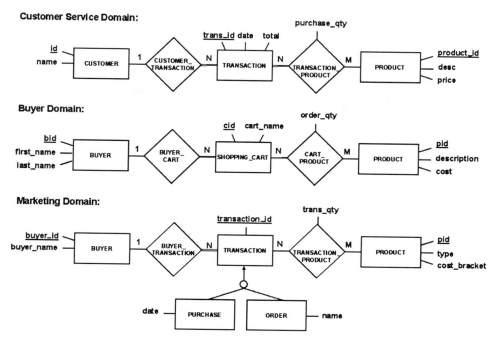

**Fig. 5.** User domain conceptual models.

Service, and Marketing user models of Fig. 5. Additionally, each database is associated with an explicit data model, such as the Customer and Product databases of Fig. 4. Finally, a generic conceptual model is developed for the particular domain of discourse, which captures all concepts that are expressed in the user and database conceptual models. In our example, the on-line store model from Fig. 1 represents the generic on-line store domain.

As shown in Fig. 6, the architecture includes three tiers — an Application Layer, Database Layer, Generic Layer and a Knowledge Base. Each tier, in conjunction with the Knowledge Base, is responsible for mapping high-level queries of one conceptual model to high-level queries of another model according to the concept mappings defined between layers.

## 10.1. *Concept mapping*

Because all concepts in the user and database domain models are expressible in the generic model, user domain concepts can be expressed as database domain concepts by transformation through associated generic model concepts. To achieve this transformation, concept mappings must be defined between adjacent architecture abstraction layers and stored in the Knowledge Base for use by the system. A concept can be defined as a conceptually atomic data item. Concepts at each abstraction level essentially correspond to the conceptual model attributes at that

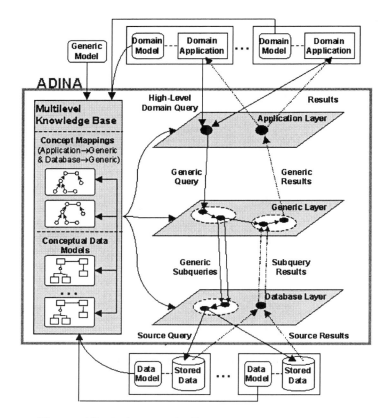

**Fig. 6.** The Architecture for Distributed INformation Access.

level. However, a conceptually atomic data item at one abstraction level does not necessarily correspond to an atomic data item at another abstraction level. For example, recall that buyer_name at the Buyer user domain level, is represented as the concatenation of fname and lname at the Generic domain level. Significantly, it has been shown that concept mappings preserve the meanings of query representations as well as concepts between abstraction levels [34].

### 10.2. *Application Layer*

The Application Layer serves as the interface that allows users to request data from several databases using local terminology. The Application Layer is responsible for the conversion of queries and their responses between their Application domain representation and their Generic domain representation, including concept mapping for queries and data unit and format conversion for responses. Suppose the query in Example 1 actually represents a marketing software request for expensive watch buyers in 1999, where an expensive watch is defined at the generic layer as a watch that costs at least $1,000. The software would formulate the high-level query in its

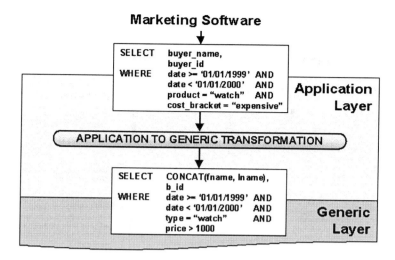

**Fig. 7.** Application to generic layer transformation.

own domain terminology and submit it to the Application Layer of the architecture. The Application Layer would apply concept mappings from the Knowledge Base as well as perform any manipulation needed to maintain proper USQL form to produce the generic representation of the query, which it would then pass on to the Generic Layer as shown in Fig. 7.

### 10.3. *Generic Layer*

The Generic Layer receives the high-level query in the terminology of the generic model and is responsible for partitioning the query into sub-queries for multiple databases and merging the multiple results to form a single result set. The Generic Layer first extracts query concepts to be mapped to corresponding Database Layer concepts. The Knowledge Base is consulted to determine which data sources can satisfy the query, and concepts are then grouped according to the target databases to which they map. Each concept grouping is transformed into a high-level sub-query over its respective database. Because sub-queries are only meaningful insofar as they relate to the original high-level query and hence to each other, the system must derive relationships between the sub-queries. Using contexts generated from the generic conceptual model, the system identifies additional attributes and constraints that bridge the sub-queries and inserts them into the sub-queries. Any attributes inserted into the queries for the purpose of relating sub-queries to one another are removed when the results are merged to ensure the results reflect only the data originally requested. For example, when the original request is divided into two subqueries in Fig. 8, p_id is inserted into each query in order to relate the results from each subquery. Since the original request did not include p_id, it would be inappropriate and confusing to include p_id in the results returned to the user.

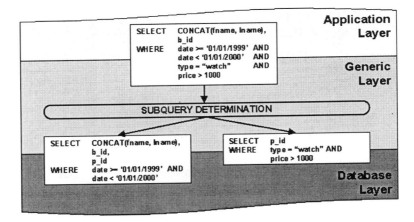

**Fig. 8.**   Generic sub-query formation.

Hence, when the subquery results are returned to the Generic Layer in Fig. 10, the p_id values are used to fuse the multiple results into a unified result, but are then discarded from the result set.

### 10.4. *Database Layer*

The Database Layer is responsible for converting the high-level generic sub-queries into valid database queries over each database. Concept mappings in the Knowledge Base are used to transform the generic sub-queries into database-specific high-level sub-queries. The sub-queries are then passed to the QUICK automated query generator to infer the complete database-level queries that include the navigational details necessary to retrieve the data from the target databases. The system then submits each query to its target database. The Database Layer query submission process is illustrated in Fig. 9.

### 10.5. *Knowledge Base*

The Knowledge Base captures the knowledge used by the system to perform query transformation, expansion, and fusion. It contains the Application, Generic, and Database conceptual models, the contexts derived from the models, and the data types, formats and units needed for data fusion. The Knowledge Base also contains the inter-domain concept mappings which support the high-level query transformation between domain layers, as well as the database location information for issuing the complete database-level subqueries.

### 10.6. *Returning query results*

As each database returns results to the architecture's Database Layer, the Knowledge Base is used to convert attribute data units and formats to corresponding

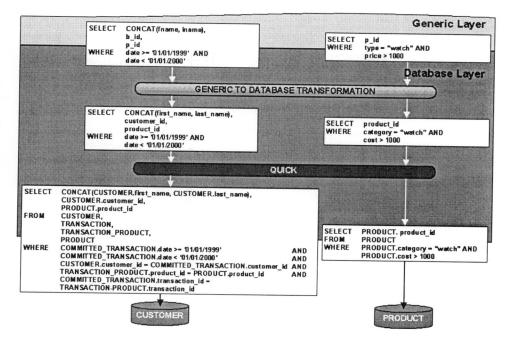

**Fig. 9.** Generic to database transformation.

units and formats defined for the attributes at the Generic Layer. The results are passed to the Generic Layer, where the Knowledge Base is again consulted to fuse the sub-results into a single result employing the same knowledge that was used to partition the original query. For example, the results from the Customer database are joined with the results from the Product database on p_id, and only those buyers that bought watches that cost at least $1,000 in 1999 are returned to the Application Layer. Finally, the fused results are passed to the Application Layer where they undergo a final data unit and format conversion to their Application Layer representation before they are presented to the user. The transformation process is shown in Fig. 10.

## 10.7. *Real-world application*

The architecture above has been applied to the Objective Defense Satellite Communications System (DSCS) Operations Control System (ODOCS) project, which is an effort to re-engineer an existing system that supports Department of Defense communication users of the military's Super High Frequency satellites. The current system plans and schedules satellite and ground resources and was designed in the early 80's, consisting of standalone subsystems that contain incompatible operating systems. ODOCS has been mandated to provide interoperability with other communication planning/scheduling and controlling/monitoring systems and to use

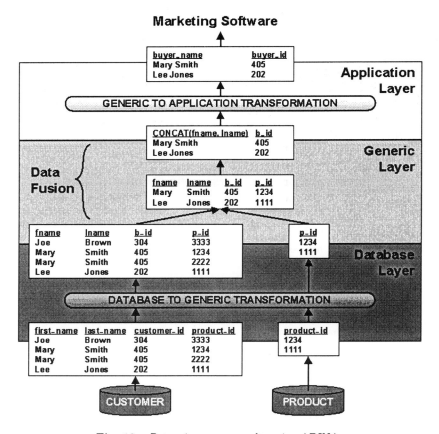

**Fig. 10.** Returning query results using ADINA.

common architecture standards to provide a distributed open software and database environment. The architecture was used to support the ODOCS Data Management Service (ODMS) [15], which is intended as a mechanism to support data reuse and interoperability among various mission applications and external systems. A "proof-of-concept" version of the ODMS has been implemented which supports the feasibility of both the ODMS and the underlying Architecture for Distributed INformation Access. High-level queries based on an application's terminology have successfully been transformed and expanded into queries required by each of the underlying databases, the queries have been issued to multiple databases in a networked environment, and the query results have been returned as expected.

By combining automated query generation functionality with a supporting architecture, the system described above is able to provide high-level access to multiple databases from multiple user domains. In providing this functionality, the system relies on a Knowledge Base that includes conceptual models, standard database engineering products from which it extracts knowledge about user intent given high-level queries. The system supports autonomy of diverse user and database domains, allowing users and database domain engineers complete design and implementation freedom. Finally, the system is flexible and extensible, allowing users and databases to dynamically join the architecture by providing their domain conceptual model and concept mappings to the generic unified model.

## 11. Directions

In the increasingly networked business environment, a growing area of research is that of intelligent software agents [24]. Although the precise definition of an agent is somewhat elusive, an agent is generally agreed to be an autonomous software entity that has the ability to collaborate with other software agents to meet users' needs. Agents are expected to play a major role in the future of the Internet and hence will naturally be important in the area of distributed information management. Agents are central to the IMPACT system described earlier, and many existing architectures can themselves be intuitively transformed into agent-based systems by distributing architectural modules, and assigning an agent to each. As such, each agent would be responsible for receiving and responding to external requests to each module, and dynamically adapting to network topology changes to provide appropriate and efficient responses to user requests. Furthermore, multiple information access architectures that support distinct data domains may exist on a network and may each be associated with an agent. If a query is posed to an architecture which can answer only part of or none of the query, its agent can enlist the help of the other architecture agents in an attempt to satisfy the request.

In general, autonomous software systems cannot intrinsically communicate and collaborate with one other, and information access architectures do not magically solve this problem. Fortunately, many development communities have recognized the value of open architectures and infrastructures, such as OMG's Common Object Request Broker Architecture (CORBA) [30], which allow diverse applications to work together over a network. CORBA allows proprietary applications to communicate with one another by providing a standard transport protocol and a standard by which applications define and publish their interfaces. Similarly, industry-standard database access Application Programming Interfaces (APIs), such as Open Database Connectivity (ODBC) [31] and Java Database Connectivity (JDBC) [41], allow diverse database applications to communicate with diverse databases in a standardized manner. The flexibility and scalability of production versions of information access architectures will rely on interfacing and communicating with user applications and databases that employ such standard distributed object technologies and database access APIs.

## Summary and Conclusions

We have presented an overview of data access approaches, from high-level access to a single database, to generalized access to multiple, distributed, heterogeneous databases. Database designers expend significant energy in developing a high-level conceptual schema that captures crucial structural knowledge for determining how queries to that database must be formulated. If the conceptual schema is not maintained or is discarded, users who wish to formulate queries to the database face the burden of reverse-engineering the database to guess its structure. Automated query generators bridge the knowledge gap between the rich conceptual database design and the typical database user. By capturing, processing, and reasoning over conceptual design knowledge, automated query generators are able to provide high-level, intuitive access to a single complex database. Several database interoperablility architectures have been developed to extend high-level access to a single database to include access to multiple, distributed heterogeneous databases. Among the successful architectures will be those that employ distributed agent technologies for efficiency and adaptability, support standard interfaces for maximal interoperability, and will support many types of real-world databases, including relational-, frame, XML-, and object-based systems.

## References

1. American National Standards Institute, "The database language SQL", Document ANSI X3.135, 1986.
2. S. Adali and R. Emery, "A uniform framework for integrating knowledge in heterogeneous knowledge systems", *Proceedings of the 11th International Conference on Data Engineering* (IEEE Computer Society Press, 1995) 513–521.
3. Y. Arens, C. Y. Chee, C. Hsu and C. A. Knoblock, "Retrieving and integrating data from multiple information sources", *International Journal of Intelligent and Cooperative Information Systems* **2**, no. 2 (1993) 127–158.
4. C. Batini, S. Certi and S. B. Navathe, *Conceptual Database Design: An Entity-Relationship Approach* (Benjamin/Cummings Publishing Co., 1992).
5. C. Cheung, N. Roussopoulos, D. Leisawitz, D. Silberberg, S. Kelley, G. Reichert and J. Wang, "AMASE: An object-oriented metadatabase catalog for accessing multimission astrophysics data", *Proceedings of the Science Information Systems Interoperability Conference (SISIC)*, College Park, Maryland (1995).
6. P. P. Chen, "The entity-relationship model — Toward a unified view on data", *ACM Transactions on Database Systems* **1**, no. 1 (1976) 9–36.
7. C. Collet, M. Huhns and W.-M. Shen, "Resource integrating using a large knowledge base in Carnot", *IEEE Computer* **24**, no. 12 (1991) 55–64.
8. Defense Modeling and Simulation Office, "Master Environmental Library (MEL) Technical Reference" (2000), *http://mel.dmso.mil/docs/trg/trg.pdf*.
9. S. D. Diamond, "The universal SQL processor", Internal Johns Hopkins University Applied Physics Laboratory Communication, RMI-95-005 (1995).
10. R. Elmasri, J. Weeldreyer and A. Hevner, "The category concept: An extension to the entity-relationship model", *International Journal on Data and Knowledge Engineering* **1**, no. 1 (1985) 75–116.
11. R. Elmasri and S. B. Navathe, *Fundamentals of Database Systems* (Addison-Wesley, 2000).
12. Federal Geographic Data Committee, "Content Standard for Digital Geospatial Metadata" (1998), *http://www.fgdc.gov/metadata/contstan.html*.
13. H. Garcia-Molina, Y. Papakonstantinou, D. Quass, A. Rajararnan, Y. Sagiv, J. Ullman, V. Vassalos and J. Widom, "The TSIMMIS approach to mediation:

Data models and languages", *Journal of Intelligent Information Systems* **2** (1997) 117–132.

14. R. Hull and R. King, "Semantic database modeling: Survey, applications and research issues", *ACM Transactions on Database Systems* **6**, no. 3 (1981) 351–386.

15. The Johns Hopkins University Applied Physics Laboratory, *Software Specification for the ODOCS Data Management Service (ODMS)* — Version 1, VS-99-038 (April 1999).

16. D. B. Lenat and R. V. Guha, *Building Large Knowledge-Based Systems: Representation and Inference in the CYC Project* (Addison-Wesley, 1990).

17. F. Leymann, "A survey of the universal relation model", *Data and Knowledge Engineering* **4**, no. 4 (1989) 305–320.

18. Y. E. Lien, "On the semantics of the entity-relationship model", *Entity-Relationship Approach to System Analysis and Design*, ed. P. P. Chen (North-Holland, 1980) 155–167.

19. R. M. MacGregor, "A description classifier for the predicate calculus", *Proceedings of the Twelfth National Conference on Artificial Intelligence*, Seattle, Washington (1994) 213–220.

20. D. Maier and J. D. Ullman "Maximal objects and the semantics of universal relation databases", *ACM Transactions on Database System* **8**, no. 1 (1983) 1–14.

21. D. Maier, J. D. Ullman and M. Y. Vardi, "On the foundations of the universal relation model", *ACM Transactions on Database System* **9**, no. 2 (1984) 283–308.

22. V. M. Markowitz and A. Shoshani, "Abbreviated query interpretation in extended entity-relationship oriented databases", *Entity-Relationship Approach to Database Design and Querying*, ed. F. H. Lochovsky (North-Holland, 1990) 325–343.

23. A. Pahwa and A. K. Arora, "Automatic database navigation: Towards a high level user interface", *Proceedings of the 4th International Conference on Entity-Relationship Approach*, ed. P. P. Chen (IEEE Computer Society Press, 1985) 36–43.

24. D. Reicken, "Intelligent agents: Introduction to special issue", *Communications of the ACM* **37**, no. 7 (1994) 18–21.

25. A. Rosenthal, E. Sciore and S. Renner, "Toward unified metadata for the department of defense", *Proceedings of the Second IEEE Metadata Conference*, Silver Spring, Maryland (September 1997).

26. R. D. Semmel and D. P. Silberberg, "Extended entity-relationship model for automatic query generation", *Telematics and Informatics* **10**, no. 3 (1993) 301–317.

27. R. D. Semmel, "Discovering context in an entity relationship conceptual schema", *Journal of Computer and Software Engineering* **2**, no. 1 (1994) 47–63.

28. R. D. Semmel, "Integrating reengineered databases to support data fusion", *Journal of Systems Software* **30** (1995) 127–135.

29. R. D. Semmel, "Automated query formulation using an entity-relationship conceptual schema", *Journal of Intelligent Information Systems* **8** (1997) 267–290.

30. J. Siegel, *CORBA Fundamentals and Programming* (John Wiley & Sons, Inc., 1996).

31. R. Signore, J. Creamer and M. O. Stegman, *The Odbc Solution: Open Database Connectivity in Distributed Environments* (McGraw-Hill, 1995).

32. D. P. Silberberg and R. D. Semmel, "The starview flexible query mechanism", *Astronomical Data Analysis Software and Systems III*, eds. D. R. Crabtree, R. J. Hanisch and J. Barnes, Astronomical Society of the Pacific **61** (1994) 92–95.

33. D. P. Silberberg and R. D. Semmel, "Role-based semantics for conceptual-level queries", *Proceedings of the 5th KRDB Workshop*, eds. A. Borgida, V. Chaudhri and M. Staudt (1998), <*http://sunsite.informatik.rwth-aachen.de/Publications/CEUR-WS/Vol-10/*>.

34. D. P. Silberberg, J. R. Schneider, A. K. Karlson and G. A. Collins, "Supporting universal data query and data fusion for network-centric warfare", *Proceedings of the Federal Database Colloquium and Exposition* (AFCEA Press, 1999) 155–168.

35. V. S. Subrahmanian, S. Adali, A. Brink, R. Emery, J. J. Lu, A. Rajput, T. J. Rogers, R. Ross and C. Ward, "HERMES: A heterogeneous reasoning and mediator system" (1995), <*http://www.cs.umd.edu//projects/hermes/overview/paper/index.html*>.

36. V. S. Subrahmanian, P. Bonatti, J. Dix, T. Eiter, S. Kraus, F. Ozcan and R. Ross, *Heterogeneous Agent Systems* (The MIT Press, 2000).

37. T. J. Teorey, D. Yang and J. P. Fry, "A logical design methodology for relational databases using the extended entity-relationship model", *ACM Computing Surveys* **18**, no. 2 (1986) 197–222.

38. J. R. Thieman, E. Bell, S. Conroy, L. Sprayregen and D. P. Silberberg, "NASA master directory, a world wide web space science information source", The XXI General Assembly of the International Union of Geodesy and Geophysics, American Geophysical Union, Washington, D.C., 1995.

39. J. D. Ullman, *Principles of Database and Knowledge-Base Systems* **2** (Computer Science Press, 1989).

40. J. A. Wald and P. G. Sorenson, "Resolving the query interface problem using Steiner trees", *ACM Transactions on Database Systems* **9**, no. 3 (1984) 348–368.

41. S. White, M. Fisher, R. Cattel, G. Hamilton and M. Hapner, *JDBC (TM) API Tutorial and Reference, Universal Data Access for the Java (TM) 2 Platform*, 2nd ed. (Addison-Wesley Pub., Co., 1999).

42. Z. Zhang and A. O. Mendelzon, "A graphical query language for entity-relationship databases", *Proceedings of the 3rd International Conference on Entity-Relationship Approach* (1983) 441–448.

# LEARNING SOFTWARE ORGANIZATIONS

GÜNTHER RUHE

*Fraunhofer Institute for Experimental Software Engineering (IESE),*
*Sauerwiesen 6, D-67661 Kaiserslautern, Germany*
*E-mail: ruhe@iese.fhg.de*

A Learning Software Organization (LSO) is an organization that learns within the domain of software development, evolution and application. In the context of LSO, knowledge management and learning approaches are complementary views on knowledge handling processes. Learning is based on knowledge and experiences related to the different processes, products, tools, techniques and methods applied to the software development process. The overall objective of an LSO is to improve software processes and products according to the strategic goals of the organization.

Knowledge is considered a crucial resource of each organization and, therefore, needs to be managed carefully. The knowledge management literature usually deals with the mechanisms of knowledge handling, while learning approaches address the process how to gain knowledge. This can be done on an individual, group, or organizational level.

Learning extends knowledge and enables decision making for individuals as well as for groups and entire organizations. LSO can only be understood from the interplay between its organizational, content, technology, and methodology dimension.

In this chapter, KM as a prerequisite for organizational learning is described. The basic terminology and core principles of an LSO are characterized in the same way as its enabling techniques: experimentation, modeling, measurement, reuse and collaborative learning.

*Keywords*: Learning software organization, knowledge management, quality improvement paradigm, explicit knowledge, tacit knowledge, experience factory, experimentation, modeling, measurement, reuse, collaborative learning.

## 1. Introduction

Knowledge is considered a crucial resource of each organization and, therefore needs to be managed carefully. Systematic management of knowledge is of particular importance in fast-changing, knowledge-intensive business areas. Knowledge is a mandatory source of business success. Sustained knowledge management is a prerequisite to maintaining a competitive advantage.

In the fast moving area of software development, which is characterized by a particularly rapid technological change and uncertainty, the most successful companies are those that systematically and continuously create new knowledge, disseminate it throughout the organization and embody it in new products and services. The contribution of software development cost to total development costs of products and services has increased to more than 70% in several of the most important European industries. Software implements the majority of the latest and, from a marketing point of view, most important features of new products and services. While software is of paramount importance for market success in all high-tech and service domains, Software Engineering practice does not always live up to this challenge and requires tremendous efforts to increase its maturity. The need for further development of software engineering practices within companies adds to the demand for systematic knowledge management.

In order to become and remain competitive in software development, there is no alternative than to become a Learning Software Organization (LSO). A LSO is a continuous endeavour of actively identifying, securing, disseminating and employing knowledge in the software development organization. Building and running corporate-wide knowledge management systems in the domain of Software Engineering is an idea that was initiated about 20 years ago [7] with a more limited scope and strong emphasis on explicit knowledge. This idea has now gained widespread attention and software companies are more striving to implement Learning Software Organizations. The new dimension of LSO is to handle both explicit and tacit knowledge, to better support knowledge creation processes, and to broaden the scope of learning [15].

## 2. Knowledge Management and its Contribution to Organizational Learning

### 2.1. *Basic terminology*

Data is a set of discrete, objective facts about events. It says nothing about its own importance or irrelevance. It is essential raw material for the creation of information.

Information can be described as a message, usually in the form of a document or an audible or visible communication. It has a sender and a receiver. Information is meant to change the way the receiver perceives something, to have an impact on his judgement and behavior. Information moves within an organization through both hard and soft networks. Data becomes information when its creator or receiver adds meaning.

Experience describes results from historical, controlled or observational experiments. Experiments can be devoted to any kind of method, technique or tool for any stage of the software development process.

Knowledge is information combined with experience, context, interpretation and reflection. It is a high-value form of information. It is ready to be applied in decision-making and action taking. Knowledge can be classified along a spectrum from tacit to explicit, ranging from knowledge the holder might not even be aware of to knowledge s/he is very well aware of (i.e., has a structured view onto this knowledge) or has even made available through writing, graphs, models etc.

Tacit knowledge is personal knowledge embedded in personal experience and is shared and exchanged through direct, face-to-face contact. Subjective insights, intuitions, and hunches fall into this category of knowledge. It is hard to formalize and is generally in the heads of individuals and teams. On the other side, it is often assumed to be the most valuable and untapped knowledge.

Explicit knowledge is formal or semi-formal knowledge that can be packaged as information. It can be found in the documents of an organization: reports, articles, manuals, models, lessons learned. It can also be found in the representations that an organization has of itself: organizational charts, process models, mission statements, domains of expertise.

Models are formalized representations of knowledge, often in the form of mathematical formulae, graphs, causal relationship networks, etc.

Baselines are data sets or models that provide "typical" values, trends, mathematical dependencies, etc. from past projects in the environment under investigation against which a current project in the same environment can compare itself. Baselines are a result of systematic capturing of experiences (often through measurement programs).

Knowledge management (KM) is the formal management of knowledge for facilitating creation, access, reuse of knowledge, and learning from its application, typically using advanced technology. KM deals with tacit as well as explicit knowledge. A very broad definition of KM also includes human resources management activities, such as hiring new staff or to train staff in order to increase the company's capacities. If not stated otherwise, we will use the term KM for handling both knowledge and experience.

## 2.2. *Content of knowledge bases*

The knowledge (and experience) base of an LSO typically includes different kinds of knowledge (know-how, know-why, know-what), models, experiences or lessons learned. Examples are:

- Change and defect models.
- Resource models and baselines.
- Process definitions and models.
- Lessons learned for usage of methods and techniques.
- Experience from application of methods, techniques, or tools.

Depending on the maturity of the organization or the project, and also depending on the underlying objectives of the corresponding analysis and interpretation of data, the content of the knowledge and experience base of an LSO can be used for the following purposes:

- Characterize and understand.
  Which project characteristics affect the choice of optimal selection of processes, methods, and techniques?
- Characterize and understand.
  Does the inspection process reduce rework effort?

- Predict and control.
  Given a set of project characteristics (size, reuse), what is the expected cost and reliability, based upon our history?
- Motivate and improve.
  Which reading technique for performing software inspections is most effective and which techniques is most efficient for the different types of defects and for the different degrees of experience of the reader?

### 2.3. *Knowledge management processes*

The goal of KM is to improve the organizational skills of all levels of the organization (individual, group, division, organization) by better usage of the resource knowledge. It is a management activity and as such goal oriented, planned and monitored.

Knowledge Management at the organization level requires a clear definition in which context and for what purpose the knowledge is intended to be used. These so-called knowledge goals are closely related to the organizational goals. The storage and representation of the knowledge goals requires a clear definition of the repositories for this knowledge. For instance this can be a new employee, acquisition of new technologies or acquisition of another company to increase and complement existing knowledge in a specific field. An instrument to consolidate knowledge goals at the individual level is the definition of education plans for employees.

Success of KM activities is strongly influenced by appropriate tool support based on advanced information and communication technology. Typical KM tools are based on internet, intranet or commercial environments such as Lotus Notes. AI developments such as intelligent agents, case-based reasoning [1], knowledge discovery/machine learning [10] or ontologies play an important role in KM systems. An evaluation of 21 well-known KM tools is given in [2].

For Knowledge Management in organizations, seven core processes can be identified at the individual and organizational levels [2, 8]:

- Knowledge identification.
- Knowledge acquisition.
- Knowledge development.
- Knowledge dissemination.
- Knowledge usage.
- Knowledge preservation.
- Knowledge evaluation.

In the following paragraphs, these processes are described in more detail.

### 2.3.1. *Knowledge identification*

The objective of knowledge identification is to achieve transparency over already existing knowledge in the organization. One instrument to achieve this is a knowledge map for structuring and visualization of knowledge and to facilitate the access to this knowledge.

### 2.3.2. *Knowledge acquisition*

The knowledge acquisition process can be subdivided into the acquisition of external knowledge and the acquisition of knowledge within the organization. For instance, education and learning at the workplace, hiring new employees and their knowledge and acquisition or cooperation with other companies to be more competitive in the global market are concrete means for knowledge acquisition.

### 2.3.3. *Knowledge development*

Knowledge development involves the generation of new ideas, models, skills and product innovations. Knowledge management has to support knowledge development by providing a framework, which encourage knowledge growth in the organization. This framework should provide answers to questions like "How can employees be supported during their daily work?". Some instruments to solve this problem are collaboration tools (chats, email, video conferencing software), group-ware applications for document management and replication management), web-based learning environments or computer based learning tools.

### 2.3.4. *Knowledge dissemination*

Knowledge dissemination addresses the question of how people can be motivated to share knowledge. An instrument for such motivation is the creation and support of personal networks. These networks can be informal meetings (peer networks) or regular meetings of experts. They provide a forum where dialogue and knowledge exchange is enforced. This can be supported by technologies like Newsgroups and building of communities to a specific interest field in the Internet/Intranet. The success of knowledge dissemination can be supported by technology but ultimately it depends on the policies in the organization. which consists of people with their beliefs, their behavior and goals.

### 2.3.5. *Knowledge usage*

Improved knowledge usage can be achieved by context-sensitive and customer-oriented representation of information and knowledge. For instance, these processes include the improvement of the layout and look of documents, visualization of complex facts and figures, text analysis, automatical generation of summaries and reports, and push and pull technologies for personalization of information and knowledge that is delivered directly to the desk of the knowledge searcher.

### 2.3.6. *Knowledge preservation*

The objective of knowledge preservation is to avoid the knowledge loss in the organization. For example, this can happen when employees left the organization. How can the employees implicit knowledge could be preserved? One possible instrument is the implementation of a buddy system. A specialist that wants to leave the company gets an assistant at his side. The specialist will provide the assistant with his experience and knowledge and the assistant learns while working with the specialist. Within this process, implicit knowledge based on experience is transferred. Project documentation in which the key lessons learned are documented is an instrument for preservation of explicit knowledge and it should be combined with a knowledge management systems which can provide the requested information in the right context.

### 2.3.7. *Knowledge evaluation*

For the evaluation and benchmarking of the achieved knowledge in the organization, indicators are necessary. Indicators for the education field are the result of tests, which are performed by the employees. They assess the qualification of the employee in a specific field. The result of knowledge evaluation should consequently result in a modification of knowledge goals. One important evaluation criteria is the degree to what extend knowledge can be used at the workplace, i.e., during software development.

## 3. Learning Software Organizations

### 3.1. *Basic terminology*

LSO is a new and by no means established domain. It is composed of influences and ideas from many disciplines. In order to understand the contributions of this chapter, we try to define the most important terminology in a pragmatic way.

Learning extends knowledge and enables decision making for individuals as well as for groups and entire organizations. In the context of LSO knowledge management and learning approaches are complementary views on knowledge handling processes. The knowledge management literature usually deals with the mechanisms of knowledge handling, while learning approaches address the process how to gain knowledge. This can be done on an individual, group, or organizational level.

A learning organization is defined as a group of people who systematically extend their capacities so as to accomplish organizational goals. Organizational learning (OL) is the process of learning by individuals and groups in an organization. OL aims at a general increase of the organization's problem solving capability. From an organizational perspective, "organizational learning" is the learning process that results from the creation, maintenance, dissemination and exploitation of knowledge within an organization.

A learning software organization is an organization that learns within the domain of software development, evolution and application. Objects of learning can consist of models, knowledge and lessons learned related to the different processes, products, tools, techniques and methods applied during the different stages of the software development process.

## 3.2. *The quality improvement paradigm*

The Quality Improvement Paradigm (QIP) is the underlying methodological framework for systematic improvement [4]. As such, it guides the activities and goals of the LSO. QIP is essentially based on an appropriate characterization of the environment. The paradigm provides a context for goal definition and is essentially based on the systematic reuse of obtained experiences by packaging them in structured knowledge. The improvement process due to QIP is defined as an iterative process that repeatedly performs a sequence of basic activities. QIP can be applied to quality improvement in two different ways. One cycle through the QIP can be seen as a step towards project related improvement (project level). Simultaneously, it is a step towards long-term learning and improvement in an organization (strategic level).

For each of the two applications, a specialized version of the QIP has been defined. They are described in Table 1. The project level improvement process is integrated in the strategic-level improvement process, because achieving a long-term

**Table 1.**   Project level and strategic level activities of the QIP.

| QIP Step | Project Level Activities | Strategic Level Activities |
|---|---|---|
| Characterize | Characterize project and identify relevant models to be reused. | Characterize organization and identify future trends. |
| Set Goals | Define project goals in measurable terms and derive related metrics. | Define improvement goals and add hypotheses in measurable terms. |
| Choose Models | Choose appropriate processes and develop project plan. | Identify projects or pilots for investigating the hypotheses. |
| Execute | Perform project according to plan, collect data, and provide on-line feedback for project guidance. | Perform projects or pilots and collect data. |
| Analyze | Analyze project and collected data and suggest improvements. | Analyze projects and pilots and evaluation hypotheses. |
| Package | Package analysis results into improved reusable models. | Package experiences for use in future projects. |

improvement goal is typically done by means of improvement in multiple projects or pilot studies.

### 3.3. *Organizational knowledge creation*

Establishing learning software organizations is not just a technical issue — it involves a cultural change within an organization. All the different roles and perspectives of the software development process have to be included for this objective. Organizations are composed of multiple interacting communities. Each community has a highly specialized knowledge, skills, and technologies. To become a LO requires that these diverse communities bridge their differences and integrate their knowledge and skills in order to create a new, shared perspective.

Social sharing is not a passive process but an active one. It is often complicated by the fact that a community's shared vocabulary or domain model is often tacit, making it non-inspectable and difficult for another community to understand. The social processes necessary to continuously create and share tacit as well as explicit knowledge are not sufficiently covered by current KM approaches. Nonaka and Takeuchi [12] have pointed out with their knowledge spiral (socialization, externalization, combination and internalization) that knowledge creation derives from a balance in the processing (creation and sharing) of tacit as well as explicit knowledge. In this process both types of knowledge are of equal importance and can be transformed into each other. Socialization, externalization, combination, and internalization are the core activities of a knowledge management system and must therefore be accommodated. Their mutual relationship is described in Fig. 1.

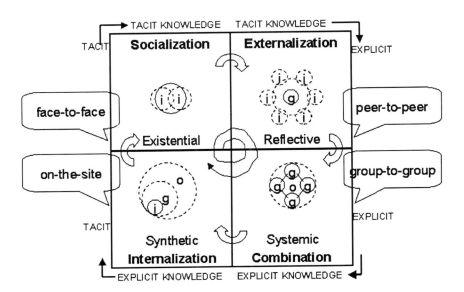

**Fig. 1.**  The four phases of organizational knowledge creation [11].

During socialization, individuals (i) share experiences through collaboration, observation or imitation. Examples are project-touch down meetings, inspection meetings or quality circles. This is also called learning by sharing. One of the keys to sharing individual knowledge is having the appropriate incentive system for sharing knowledge.

Externalization (or: learning by reflection) is the transformation of the individuals tacit knowledge into explicit knowledge that can be documented and thereby understood by groups (g). Dialogue, listening, and collective reflection as performed in project post mortems are examples for how to support externalization [3].

Combination (or: learning by integration) is the integration of different kinds of explicit knowledge from inside or outside the company (o) for the purpose of delivering appropriate knowledge at the right time to the right groups of people. Experience or knowledge bases, technical reports, quality handbooks or mathematical models are example results of combination.

Finally, internalization (or: learning by doing) addresses the exploitation of knowledge in order to perform concrete actions. Individuals identify and access the relevant knowledge and learn by adapting the knowledge to the relevant context of groups or organizations. The participation and integration of novices in inspections is an example therefor.

## 3.4. *Enabling techniques for learning software organizations*

The evolution of scientific knowledge involves learning by observing, formulating theories, and performing experiments. Many fields like physics, medicine and manufacturing use experimentation as a means to encapsulate as well as to verify and validate knowledge. Learning is essentially based on modeling. We need appropriate abstractions from the reality of software development to learn how to improve skills and competencies. For that purpose, process, product and quality models are developed. If learning comes through experience, it follows that the more one plans guided experiences, the more one can learn. But how to make the effects of experimentation transparent? Application of goal-oriented measurement facilitates to gain new insights into the phenomena under investigation.

### 3.4.1. *Experimentation*

Experimentation in software engineering concerns the building of empirical software engineering models (e.g. efficiency models for inspections), and the validating the software engineering hypotheses (e.g. impact of object-oriented designs on maintainability) [14]. The experimental process of iterative definition, testing, and enhancing model-based hypotheses provides a powerful scientific tool for the necessary advancement in knowledge and understanding. Three categories with related subcategories of experimental approaches can be identified [17]:

- Historical:
  - — Examine previously published studies (Literature search).
  - — Examine qualitative data from completed projects (Lessons learned).
  - — Examine the structure of the developed product (Static analysis).
- Controlled:
  - — Develop multiple versions of the product (Replicated).
  - — Replicate one factor in a laboratory setting (Synthetic).
  - — Execute the developed product for performance (Dynamic analysis).
  - — Execute the product with artificial data (Simulation).
- Observational:
  - — Collect development data (Project monitoring).
  - — Monitor the project in depth (Case study).
  - — Use *ad hoc* validation techniques (Assertion).
  - — Monitor multiple projects (Field study).

The challenge is to find the most appropriate technique for a given situation. Typically, a sequence and/or combination of techniques will be applied.

### 3.4.2. *Measurement*

The motivation for performing measurement in the context of an LSO initially stems from the objective to accompany the process of knowledge asset creation. Measurement can also be used for:

- Evaluation of knowledge assets with respect to the intellectual capital of an organization for survival, renewal and growth.
- Evaluation of the performance of an organization, to get the right things to the attention of managers (for short-term and long-term decision making).
- Controlling performance of the knowledge-related activities by continuously measuring performance indicators of these activities and quality indicators of the knowledge handled as well as of the results created with the help of the knowledge.

The Goal-Question-Metrics (GQM) approach [5] is a flexible and effectively applicable approach to perform measurement of software processes, products and projects. By applying GQM, information is identified that is relevant to solve specific problems (goals), and that can be represented in a practical, applicable and interpretable way. Main features of the GQM approach are:

- Goal-orientation through top-down definition of metrics via questions.
- Careful characterization of essential environmental which influence underlying knowledge processes.
- Guiding the bottom-up analysis and interpretation of measured data.

• Active participation of staff in definition, collection, analysis and interpretation of measured data.

Figure 2 illustrates the essential features of GQM. The goal is formulated as a 5-tuple. The refinement of the goal into questions is supported by elicitating the implicit models of related experts (viewpoint). The questions are the guideline to find appropriate metrics to answer them.

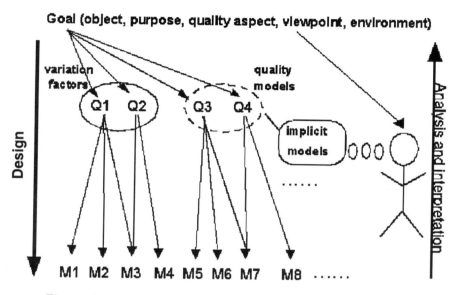

**Fig. 2.** Structure of the GQM approach to goal-oriented measurement.

### 3.4.3. *Modeling*

Models are abstract and simplified descriptions of reality. In the context of software development, a model is an idealized representation of a process, product, or an abstract description of quality. The different kinds of models to support individual and organizational learning are contained in an experience base of a LSO. Modeling forms the basis for understanding and improving software processes. This is especially true because of the fact that software development is a human and team-based activity.

Without a process model it is difficult to see what happens (or should happen) in a process and how to communicate this to others. Without a product model of requirements, specification, design, test plan, etc., it is difficult to charcterize what is (or should be) developed or produced at the different stages of the life cycle. Without a quality model (of effort, effectiveness, efficiency, cost, etc) it is difficult to see how good something is developed or produced. The different kinds of models as result of an abstraction of reality are described in Fig. 3.

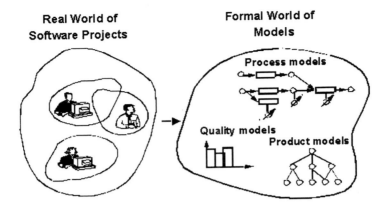

**Fig. 3.**  Abstraction from real world to model world.

There are two types of modeling activities: descriptive and prescriptive. The purpose of descriptive models is to describe the actual status or behaviour of a system. The purpose of a prescriptive model is to describe the intended or optimal status or behaviour of a system.

The task of descriptive process modeling is to capture the current software development practices and organizational issues of a software-producing unit as a descriptive process model.

The content of a descriptive process model is mainly based on collecting knowledge from process experts and software development practitioners, i.e., the actual processes are represented, not the official ones. Entities and relationships between entities, e.g. input/output relations, activity sequences, reporting channels between roles, and role assignments to activities represent relevant real-world aspects. Entities are formalized in an operational way through attributes, which characterize the entities. Examples of attributes are size, complexity, status, time, and effort.

The task of prescriptive process modeling is to design a new process or to define an intended process improvement for the purpose of assistance. The conformance of process implementation to the prescriptive process model may be enforced through the support of a tool-based software engineering environment.

Modeling is also applied to describe the different competencies of a (learning) organization, how they are structured and how they are related to each other. For further details on knowledge modeling we refer to [12].

### 3.4.4.  *Reuse of know-how and the experience factory organization*

Projects and organizations as a whole have different aims: projects develop software products fulfilling predefined requirements. This has to be done within predefined time, cost and with fixed quality criteria.

Organizations are encouraged to improve over time. Projects cannot be expected to manage corporate experiences. An organizational infrastructure has to

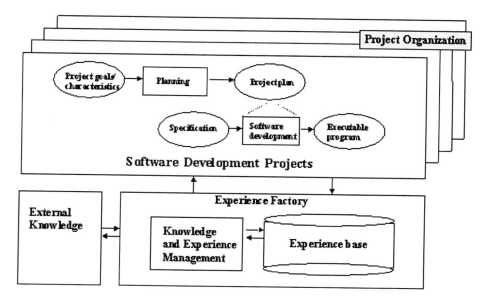

**Fig. 4.** Experience factory and its interaction with project organization.

be established to perform the role of knowledge management from an organizational and also from a more long-term perspective. This infrastructure is constituted by the experience factory [4] as illustrated in Fig. 4.

The experience factory is an organizational learning infrastructure for software development. Its main part is the experience base, a corporate repository for storing relevant software engineering experience. It distinguishes the project organization in which the software development activities are performed, from the organizational improvement infrastructure, where analysis and packaging activities are carried out for project support and for maintenance and continuous evolution of the experience base.

There is a general need for reuse of know-how in all companies; however, there are strong differences about what to reuse and how to reuse. Typically, software reuse needs some kind of modification or adaptation to the new environment. The degree of modification depends on how many, and to what degree, existing object characteristics differ from those required [6]. There are a variety of artefacts that are candidates for reuse: requirement models and specifications, components, architectures and designs, checklists, scenarios, source code, user and technical documentation, human interfaces, data, test cases, project plans or cost and effort estimates.

### 3.4.5. *Computer Supported Collaborative Learning (CSCL)*

Since the learning needs of the participating software developers change rapidly and significantly it is important that the learning/teaching environment is flexible enough that new topics can be easily added and discussed. It would be desirable to connect the individual software developers in a way that they get aware of other people within the company who work on similar problems, technologies, projects, etc. The potential benefits for the individuals are

- to add new insights and experiences with certain methods and technologies to the information space;
- to access general training material to specific topics and technologies;
- to communicate about the knowledge and experience with their peers;
- to access "examples" of how their peers used the new method/technology within their projects; and
- to develop a "best practice" description of the use for their specific part of the company they are in.

CSCL is an emerging learning paradigm that focuses on the use of information and communications technology as a tool within collaborative methods (e.g. peer learning and tutoring, reciprocal teaching, project or problem-based learning, simulations) of learning [16]. Collaborative learning provides an environment to enliven and enrich the learning process. Introducing interactive partners into an educational system creates more realistic social contexts, thereby increasing the effectiveness of learning.

A collaborative learning system concentrates on refining and integrating the learning process and the subject knowledge of the learner with the help of the collaborative partners. The promise of collaborative learning is to allow learning in relatively realistic, cognitively motivating and socially enriched learning contexts, compared to other tutoring paradigms like socratic learning, discovery learning, integrated learning, etc. With CSCL the learner can discuss these strategies with a group of fellow students who advise, motivate, criticize, compete, and direct the student towards better understanding of the subject matter [9].

## Acknowledgement

The ideas of the paper are partially based on publicly funded projects PERFECT (Esprit project #9090), PROFES (Esprit project #23239), SOFTQUALI (BMBF project 01 IS 518C), and CORONET (IST-1999-11634). In addition, the author especially acknowledges the fruitful discussions with Andreas Birk, Frank Bomarius and Dieter Rombach as well as the anonymous reviewers for commenting on an earlier version of this chapter.

## References

1. K. D. Althoff, "Case-based reasoning", *Handbook of Software Engineering and Knowledge Engineering* (World Scientific Publishing Co., Inc., 2001).
2. K. D. Althoff, W. Müller, M. Nick and B. Snoek, "KM-PEB: An online experience base on knowledge management technology", eds. E. Blanzieri and L. Portinale, "Advances in case-based reasoning", *Proceedings of the 5th European Workshop on Case-Based Reasoning (EWCBR'00)* (Springer, 2000).

3. J. Arent, J. Norbjerg and M. D. Petersen, "Creating organizational knowledge in software process improvement", *Proceedings of the 2nd International Workshop on Learning Software Organizations*, Oulu, Finland (June 2000) 81–92.

4. V. R. Basili, G. Caldiera and H. D. Rombach, "Experience factory", *Journal of Marciniak: Encyclopedia of Software Engineering* 1 (1994) 469–476.

5. V. R. Basili, G. Caldiera and H. D. Rombach, "Goal-question-metric paradigm", *Journal of Marciniak: Encyclopedia of Software Engineering* 1 (1994), 528–532.

6. V. R. Basili and H. D. Rombach, "Support for comprehensive reuse", *Software Engineering Journal* (September 1991) 301–318.

7. V. R. Basili, M. V. Zelkowitz, F. McGarry, J. Page, S. Waligora and R. Pajerski, "SEL's software process improvement program", *IEEE Software* 12 (November 1995) 83–87.

8. Corporate Software Engineering Knowledge Networks for Improved Training of the Work Force, 5th Framework Project of the European Commission, IST-1999-11634.

9. V. S. Kumar, "Computer-supported collaborative learning — Issues for Research", *Eighth Annual Graduate Symposium on Computer Science*, University of Saskatchewan (1996).

10. T. Menzies, "Practical machine learning for software engineering", *Handbook of Software Engineering and Knowledge Engineering* (World Scientific Publishing Co., Inc., 2001).

11. I. Nonaka and N. Konno, "The concept of 'Ba', Building a foundation for knowledge creation", *California Management Review* 40, no. 3 (Springer, 1998) 40–54.

12. I. Nonaka and H. Takeuchi, *The Knowledge-Creating Company: How Japanese Companies Create the Dynamics of Innovation* (Oxford University Press, 1995).

13. G. Probst, S. Raub and K. Romhardt, Wissen managen, Wie Unternehmen ihre wertvollste Ressource optimal nutzen, Wiesbaden, Gabler/FAZ (1998).

14. H. D. Rombach, V. R. Basili and R. W. Selby, "Experimental software engineering issues: A critical assessment and future directions", *Lecture Notes in Computer Science 706* (Springer, 1993).

15. G. Ruhe and F. Bomarius, "Learning software organizations — Methodology and applications", *Lecture Notes in Computer Science 1756* (Springer, 2000).

16. B. Wasson, "Computer supported collaborative learning; An overview", *Lecture Notes from IVP 482*, University of Bergen (Spring, 1998).

17. M. V. Zelkowitz and D. R. Wallace, "Experimental models for validating technology", *IEEE Computer* (May 1998) 23–31.

# ON SOFTWARE ENGINEERING AND LEARNING THEORY FACILITATING LEARNING IN SOFTWARE QUALITY IMPROVEMENT PROGRAMS

RINI VAN SOLINGEN

*CMG TTI/RTSE1, P. O. Box 8566, 3009 AN Rotterdam, The Netherlands*
*E-mail: rini.van.solingen@cmg.nl*

EGON BERGHOUT

*Delft University of Technology, The Netherlands*
*E-mail: e.w.berghout@its.tudelft.nl*

"Knowledge" is one of the main results of software engineering, software projects and software process improvement. During software engineering projects, developers learn to apply certain technologies and how to solve particular development problems. During the process of software improvement developers and managers learn how effective and efficient their development processes are, and how to improve these processes. As "learning" is so important in software practice, it is logical to examine it more closely. What is learning? How does learning take place? Is it possible to improve the conditions of learning?

This chapter presents an overview of learning theories and the application of these theories in the software-engineering domain. It is not our intention to be complete; our objective is to show how established learning theories can help to facilitate learning in software development practice.

*Keywords*: Learning, learning organization, software quality, process improvement, enabling learning.

## 1. Introduction

The importance of human factors to the success of software development seems widely accepted. The success of a software project is primarily determined by having the right people on the right place at the right time. As software development is knowledge intensive, the knowledge and skills of software engineers primarily determine their "quality", and as a consequence these also determine the quality of the resulting product.

Knowledge and skills are important input for a software development project; however, they are also important output, because they are continuously enhanced over time through experience. To some extent people always learn during software projects and learning is also an important prerequisite to improve software development practices. Creating an organizational structure in which effective learning is established is a major challenge for organizations in the software domain [2]. In this chapter, we illustrate that this is not a repeatable process for which a procedure or manual can be written. On the contrary, managing the learning process during software development appears to be a difficult and complex task, for which a specific management style is required.

This chapter presents an overview of learning theory, which is summarized into a conceptual model of nine "learning enablers" to facilitate learning. Furthermore, a model is presented that illustrates the learning process of a software project team and the measurement/quality support team.

## 2. Learning Theory

In this section learning theory is investigated. However, only the most essential elements are mentioned. Given the limited space in this chapter, it is impossible to be complete.

Learning is the process by which existing knowledge is enriched or new knowledge is created [36]. Learning deals with expanding knowledge. Knowledge is the personal ability that enables a person to perform a certain task. This ability is the product of information ($I$), experience ($E$), skill ($S$) and attitude ($A$) of a person at a certain time ($K = I \cdot ESA$) [36]. Several classifications of the learning process are described in the literature. For example: cognitive vs motoric learning [7], declarative vs procedural learning [4], explicit vs implicit learning [33], or rationalistic vs empirical learning [36]. Nonaka and Takeuchi distinguish four learning processes [27]:

- "socializing": a learning process between people in which implicit (tacit) knowledge is transferred by copying, imitating, master/pupil relationships, and experiencing by trial and error;
- "externalizing": a learning process, individual or between people, in which implicit knowledge is made explicit by, for example, model building, dialogues, and hypothesis formulation;
- "combining": a learning process in which explicit knowledge from different sources is combined by, for example: studying, analyzing, reconfiguring, and integrating; and
- "internalizing": an individual learning process in which explicit knowledge is made implicit through learning by doing a particular task, creating routines, and enlarging operational efficiencies.

Although all four learning processes are present during software development and relevant to it, we focus on the explicit learning processes in this chapter: externalizing and combining. Given this decision, this chapter continues with an exploration of learning theory. First, individual learning will be considered, followed by group learning.

## 2.1. *Individual learning*

In individual learning, the knowledge of a single person enhances. Experiential Learning theory [21] defines an explicit learning process as a process in which experiences are transformed into knowledge through model building and model testing.

Furthermore, it divides experiences into concrete experiences: observations like seeing, feeling or hearing, and abstract conceptualizations: theories and models about observations and their relationships. The process of transformations is divided into reflective observations: analyzing observations and developing new models and theories, and active experiments: testing models and theories in practice. According to Experiential Learning theory, neither the experience nor the process of transforming it alone is a sufficient condition to achieve learning.

Following the different classes of experience and transformation, four particular modes of learning are distinguished. These modes are:

- "divergent learning", during which observations are analyzed;
- "assimilative learning", during which models are built;
- "convergent learning", during which models are tested in practice; and
- "accommodative learning", during which experiments are observed.

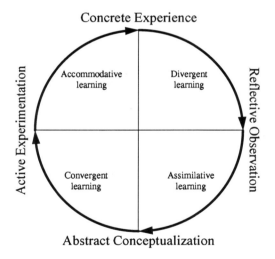

**Fig. 1.**   Experiential Learning [21].

According to Kolb, the combination of these four modes of learning results in the highest level of learning [21]. This combination requires that the learning process includes the observation of phenomena, analyzing them, developing models and theories about them and testing these theories and models in practice. The understanding of processes requires understanding of details as well as of the overall process.

All activities involved in learning take place with respect to an existing frame of reference [33]: people start with a certain amount of knowledge and experience. It is often argued that learning requires relating new knowledge to existing knowledge [20]. Therefore, it is important to make explicit the knowledge people already possess explicitly, before introducing new knowledge. This way, links can be created between new and existing knowledge so that people can interpret the unfamiliar using the familiar.

## 2.2. *Group learning*

Software is developed within teams, projects, departments and companies; it always concerns groups of people. The development processes and improvement objectives are shared. Not only should individual learning take place but organizational learning as well. In such a situation, the knowledge gained is shared among colleagues and contributes to synergy in the organization [23]. A learning process, therefore, demands "group learning".

The term group learning indicates that over a period of time a set of people, share the same learning goals and learning processes. In such a situation, knowledge has to be shared among organizational members and it has to contribute to the synergy of the organization [20]. This is also referred to as "organizational learning". Organizational learning is defined as a skilled process in which knowledge is created, acquired, and transferred, and through which behavior is modified based on the new knowledge and insights [16]. It is important to note that organizations cannot learn: the individual people can learn and learn together [36].

This definition reflects that learning happens when new insights arise. Such new insights alone are, however, insufficient. Without accompanying changes in the work processes, only a potential for improvement exists [16]. Similarly, George Huber states that learning takes place when "the potential behaviors are changed" [17]. Behavior does not need to be changed for every situation, however, the potential ways in which one can work need to be expanded. So effective learning results in potentially) changed behavior. If behavior remains unchanged, apparently no learning has taken place. Argyris and Schön identify two modes of learning [5]:

- Single loop learning. This is learning in which the actor only learns within the confines of the theory he/she already uses. There is a focus on the operational level: learning is based on detecting and correcting errors, competencies and routines.
- Double loop learning. Double loop learning starts when an event is diagnosed as incompatible with the actors' current theory. With double loop learning this current theory and models are altered and, for example, new strategies enabling more efficient learning are identified.

In practice, most organizations only focus on single loop learning [6]. Optimization is only done within the current working method. This is not wrong in itself. Through repetitive experiences, employees became skilled in their work, and create competitive advantages based on these skills. However, occasionally new approaches become available with which an organization has no experience. In such a case, switching to a new approach might be better. Challenging the existing way of working refers to double loop learning. Many organizations tend to regard double loop learning as a threat because it conflicts with existing and established habits.

It is also dangerous for an organization to constantly adopt new ways of working, because all knowledge gained up to then might immediately become outdated. "The known can in many situations be preferred over the unknown" [25]. A balance should be found between optimizing current processes (single loop learning) and experimenting with new approaches (double loop learning). Learning theory promotes a parallel application of optimization of current practices and experimentation with new ones. The skills and capabilities required for learning in an organization are [28]:

- "aspiration": the capacity of individuals, teams, and eventually larger organizations to focus on what they consider important, and to improve because they want to, not just because they need to;
- "reflection and conversation": the capacity to reflect on patterns of behavior and assumptions deeply hidden in a person's behavior, both individually and collectively; and
- "conceptualization": the capacity to see larger systems and forces at play and to construct public, testable ways of expressing these views.

According to Senge, three categories of learning skills exist [28]. Firstly, there is the motivation to learn and improve. This includes having time for learning, learning objectives, interest in learning, etc. Management commitment to learning tasks is also one of the aspects that falls under aspiration. Secondly, there is the willingness to discuss the underlying assumptions. This is what Argyris and Schön call "double loop learning". Finally, there is conceptualization, which corresponds to model building and testing of the experiential learning theory [21]. These three conditions to establish learning need to be addressed in software development.

Learning theory states that a learning method should include making explicit the goals for learning [16]. Defining these goals is often difficult, however, in a business environment it makes sense to base them on business goals. These goals will be different for different organizations. Differences are for example: the market in which an organization operates, the type of product it makes the organization of the development teams, or the country in which the products will be used. Learning practices should be directed to the goals of the organization [16].

The last aspect of organizational learning relevant to this review is based on a phenomenon called "creative tension" [28]. This is the difference between current reality and a desired future. The gap between the current reality and the desired future should not be too great, because the objectives become too abstract and it is not clear which concrete actions will lead towards improvement. On the other hand, the gap between current reality and the desired future should not be too small either, because this will result in no action at all, since the need for action seems unnecessary. This creative tension principle shows that reachable objectives should be set for learning.

### 2.3. *Learning model of student-teacher interaction*

The above ideas about for integrating learning objectives with industrial software projects have been validated in several case studies [32]. In seven software projects in two industrial organizations we integrated explicit learning goals and learning processes with the day-to-day software projects, targets and deadlines. During these industrial case studies we learned that during quality improvement and measurement programs the main benefit was gained in so-called "feedback sessions". In a feedback session, a software development team looks at their own performance as expressed by a set of collected data: defect measurements, process maturity measurements, product quality measurements, etc. During these feedback sessions, the developers interpret their measurements, draw conclusions and define actions.

Although the literature confirms the importance of this feedback process, no models are available to support the interpretation process. In our research we tried to find an explanation of positive and negative experiences with feedback, and to find guidelines to further improve feedback sessions. Learning theory already identified the main advantage of a feedback session: improved understanding by the project team, or in other words: learning. Therefore our research focussed on developing a model for feedback sessions based on learning theory.

An important element of learning is the student-teacher interaction. In this section, we describe the Entwistle model of student-teacher interaction to introduce the elements involving [15]. This model is shown in Fig. 2. The Entwistle model of influencing factors describes two loops. One loop reflects learning of a student; the other one the teaching of a teacher. Both loops have a short-term and a long-term impact. A teacher has specific personal characteristics, and defines the learning tasks. The student (who also has specific personal characteristics) has a *perception* of these learning tasks, and learns in one or more learning style. Both student and teacher influence the outcome of the learning process.

### 2.3.1. *Student characteristics*

The characteristics of the student play an important role in his/her perception of the task to be performed. Several different aspects can be discerned. First, there is prior knowledge. All activities involved in learning are accomplished against an existing frame of reference [37]: people already have a lot of knowledge and experience, gathered throughout their lives. It is often argued that learning requires

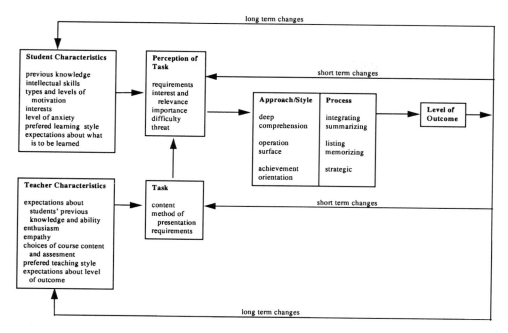

**Fig. 2.**  Model of learning processes [15].

relating new knowledge to existing knowledge [15]. Therefore, it is important to make existing knowledge explicit, before introducing new knowledge. In this way, links can be created between new and existing knowledge, allowing students to learn the unfamiliar by using the familiar. The degree to which the previous knowledge can be applied to new problems is determined by someone's intellectual skill [11].

Motivation is defined as the psychological drive for executing a task. "Adults want to learn and learn effectively when they have a strong inner motivation. Intrinsic motivation is a key factor in effective learning" [34]. "Intrinsic motivation is defined as performing a task for no other reason than the positive feeling or satisfaction inherent in task participation and completion ... Extrinsic motivation occurs when some reward or punishment is used which lies outside the task itself" [15]. "Most theorists believe that intrinsic motivation is undoubtedly the most powerful means towards learning and development ..." [3].

Interest can be described as the degree to which new knowledge is perceived as being useful in pursuit of a goal. In this perspective, interest will be especially high when no plans are available in the pursuit of particular goals. Otherwise, when plans are available, two motivational drives can be discerned: hope of success and fear of failure. "Subjects motivated by hope of success show an "approach tendency" (they want to perform the task), while subjects motivated by fear of failure show an "avoidance tendency" (they do not want to perform the task)". The perception of a task is the result of the conflict between these two motivational drives. Anxiety occurs when fear of failure is the dominant drive.

Factors influencing the conflict between hope of success and fear of failure are the subjective probability of success or failure at that task and the incentive value of success or the negative incentive value of failure. Hope of success results when the forecast of the adopted plan is positive; fear of failure when the forecast is negative and no alternative plan is available. In other words, expectations play a major role in learning. It is argued that the effort an individual spends on an activity is related to the expectations of the outcome [3].

In a learning task, the preferred learning style is also relevant. Although students' strategies will vary to some extent from task to task, Pask argues that these are influenced by their underlying, and relatively stable, learning styles [15].

### 2.3.2. Teacher characteristics

The teacher has a significant influence on many aspects of the student-teacher interaction. These are primarily influenced by his or her personality characteristics. When a teacher follows the rule that new knowledge should be related to previous knowledge, the expectation about students' prior knowledge and ability will primarily influence the choice of course contents and assessment. Expectations about level of outcome play an important role too. "Formal teachers see their role in education in terms of a narrow view of education, in which examination results and vocational training are dominant. Informal teachers stress pupils' enjoyment of school and opportunities for self-expression" [15].

Informal teachers can extend the level of participation of the students in the learning task to a degree in which even task contents and method are determined through dialogue. However, "facilitators who attempt to encourage collaborative modes of learning in which a genuine effort is made to prompt learners to take control of their learning, run the real risk of being perceived either as unwilling to undertake their pedagogic responsibilities in a professional manner or as refusing to inform learners of the real rules of the game" [12].

In adult education, it is argued that "adults resist learning when they are told they must learn something" [34]. Therefore, teachers should regard themselves as facilitators of learning, as "resources for learning, rather then didactic instructors who have all the answers" [12]. Therefore, in adult education, there is a plea for informal teachers. Characteristics of "ideal" teachers in this sense are [12]:

- "They are warm, loving, accepting of the learners".
- "They have a high regard for learners' self-planning competencies and do not wish to trespass on these".
- "They view themselves as participating in a dialogue between equals with learners".
- "They are open to change and new experiences and seek to learn from their helping activities".

In other words, they should possess both enthusiasm and empathy for both the task and the students. Like students who have a preferred learning style, teachers have a preferred teaching style. Matching students learning styles with corresponding learning environments seems an easy and practical way to improve the learning process [21]. This is only possible when the education is individual or when the group is homogeneous where the preferred learning style is concerned learning style. Therefore, somehow the teacher's approach to teaching must take into account of the variety of styles of learning among the learners, not just their own preference [15].

### 2.3.3. *Learning task*

The learning task is that what has to be learnt. Task content and assessment are part of the learning task, as is the way knowledge is presented. Various theorists have considered the effect of various forms of organizing and presenting knowledge [15]. Skinner's ideas were based on stimulus-response training and propagate to learning in series of small steps and to reinforce each correct response immediately by indicating its correctness. Others argued that these principles, based on conditioning, were only applicable to the simplest forms of learning (such as stimulus-response training). They considered learning not as establishing links between small units of knowledge, but rather as relating new ideas to previous knowledge.

Ausubel puts great emphasis on meaningful learning: "potentially meaningful learning tasks are, by definition, relatable and anchorable to relevant established ideas in cognitive structure ..."[15]. In his view, knowledge is acquired through the interaction between incoming information and existing ideas. Important issues in meaningful learning are the presence of relevant anchoring ideas, the extent to which ideas are discriminated from related concepts (these can be similar or different but confusing) and the stability and clarity of anchoring ideas.

Pask describes learning as a conversation between two representations of knowledge. Learning takes place through a dialogue between the two and understanding implies the ability to apply the knowledge to an unfamiliar situation. "Learning need not ... involve an interaction between the cognitive structure of two people. The student may converse silently with himself in trying to understand a topic, or he may interact with a formal description of the knowledge structure and supplementary learning materials" [15]. He argues that, "thorough understanding normally involves both description building and operation building — a use of the overall picture and a careful examination of details" [15].

### 2.3.4. *Perception of a task*

Students have a certain perception of a task, which results from their personal characteristics and the characteristics of the task. This perception is expected to have an important impact on task execution. The perception is the student's framework for the actual execution of that task. The elements that make up this frame will be discussed subsequently.

In education, a task is perceived, among others, in terms of its requirements. These requirements are concerned with required previous knowledge and skills, on which the task proceeds. To support the integration between new material and previous knowledge, the central question is, "is there sufficient *will* or *interest* in the individual to continue to learn what is expected of him or her?" [3]. To achieve this level of will, noticeable is that, "adults value information which is meaningful and useful to them; information related to their expectations and previous experience and that they seek to learn what can be applied; they are generally problem-oriented learners" [34]. The degree of relevance of new information to needs and interests can be expressed by the perceived importance of the task. The basis of the perceived importance is the relative importance of the goal for which the student expects the learning task to offer a new strategy.

Perceived difficulty is also important to determine whether a learning task is executed or not. "Success in accomplishing, a task with a higher difficulty level is more satisfying than success on an easier task ... The following is also assumed: failure at an easier task is more shameful than failure at a difficult task ... Where hope for success is the dominant motive, moderate risks provide the greatest satisfaction ... Where fear of failure is stronger, situations will be preferred in which failure is either almost impossible, or inevitable" [34]. When the expectation of failure is high, there is the risk of the student perceiving a feeling of threat from the learning task to be accomplished.

### 2.3.5. Approach/style

A learning approach is the strategy applied in the learning task. This approach is related to the achievement orientation, which, in its turn, is associated with the motivational drives. Three motivations are discerned:

- Intrinsic (interest in what is being learned).
- Extrinsic (need for qualifications or fear of failure).
- Achievement (need for success).

Intrinsic motivation implies that the new material has personal relevance and can be related to existing knowledge. Extrinsic motivations limit the activities to those necessary. Achievement-motivated students organize their work to meet deadlines and "play the game" (to win).

The learning approach is also dependent upon the learning style of the student. A learning style is, "the general tendency to adopt a particular (learning) strategy. Approaches to learning are closely linked to levels of understanding" [15]. The approaches to learning can be divided in four categories [15]:

- deep active: learning by integrating details and meaning;
- deep passive: learning by summarizing the meaning of details;
- surface active: learning by listing details; and
- surface passive: learning by memorizing details.

The way a learning process is carried out has a strong relation to the aspects *approach and style*. A 5th approach that can be discerned is a strategic one, in which an approach is adopted from which high achievement is expected.

### 2.3.6. *Level of outcome*

The level of outcome is a particular degree of understanding. The perception of the outcome is important to this extent that if the actor can attribute an outcome to an internal cause (such as ability or effort) than the outcome valence is greater than when it is attributed to an external cause (such as task difficulty, time or energy required for a task, support or hindrance).

Short-term and long-term influences can be discerned. Short-term influences modify the perception of the task. "A likely outcome may be recognized by the student early enough to modify his perceptions of the task and hence his learning strategy" [15]. Resulting from this modified approach, the level of outcome may also be influenced. Success-oriented subjects show an increase in performance if they receive feedback about their previous performance, while performance of failure-oriented subjects does not differ in conditions with and without feedback. The positive influences of performance feedback are regarded as resulting from three factors: it indicates the correct solution to a task, it facilitates ability assessment and self-evaluation and it gives information about the causes of success and failure.

The long-term influences may modify the student's characteristics. Here we consider that these long-term influences are the learning effect: previous knowledge is extended and skills are developed. Another influence is motivation. Knowledge of the results of the task has a positive influence on motivation. However, *too much success for the self-confident and too much failure for the anxious are both likely to diminish motivation* [15].

## 3. Conceptual Model of Enabling Factors

Based on the above theory, we developed a conceptual model that contains the most prominent enabling factors for learning in software development. This chapter does not leave sufficient space to clarify the complete construction process of this conceptual model, which is mainly based on the learning enablers described in [16, 24, 26] and [28]. For details on this construction process, we refer to [32].

In Fig. 3, a conceptual model is depicted. In the center, the three main and interacting stakeholders are positioned: software developers, management, and the learning support team (Goal/Question/Metric team or GQM team [30]). Several learning enablers influence the learning process of these three groups of people. The

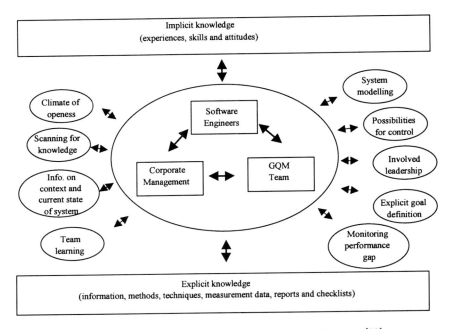

**Fig. 3.** Conceptual model of enabling factors for learning [32].

learning processes use and change both implicit and explicit knowledge. For more information on the interaction between these stakeholders and the influences on their learning processes, we refer to [30]. The learning enablers will subsequently be described, together with what the enabler means within the context of software development.

### 3.1. *Enabler* 1 : *Climate of openness*

A climate of openness addresses the establishment of an environment in which free flow of information, open communication, sharing problems and lessons learned, and open debate of ways to solve problems, is a common practice. Such a climate or "learning culture" may seem a simple concept, however, is difficult to establish in practice. Research has indicated that current structures for control and management in organizations tend to disable such climates of openness and in that way decrease the commitment of their employees [1, 35]. Especially the intrinsic motivation of people is crucial for establishing a creative and learning-oriented environment. Practical actions that managers can take to increase the intrinsic motivation of people are grouped in six categories [1]:

- *"Challenge"*: match the right people with the right job assignments in such a way that employees do not feel bored, but are not overwhelmed or threatened by a loss of control either.

- *"Freedom"*: give people autonomy concerning the processes they use. The management needs to set the goals, preferably as clear as possible, but the decision in which way these goals are to be achieved should be left to the people themselves.
- *"Resources"*: carefully allocate time and money. Time pressure can increase motivation unless deadlines are for real and not too tight. Money should be assigned properly to prevent that people have to try to find extra money themselves instead of doing their work.
- *"Work-group features"*: carefully design teams that are diverse, excited about the goal, willing to support team-mates through difficult periods, and where each member contributes a unique significant amount of knowledge.
- *"Supervisory encouragement"*: praise creative initiatives of employees. Appraisals are not considered effective when they are given in extrinsic rewards such as financial bonuses. Freely and generously recognizing creative work by employees already encourages largely. Managers should not be skeptical towards new and rigorous ideas.
- *"Organizational support"*: establish sufficient organizational support for the people in the organization. This organizational support should enable learning efforts and support learning processes. Furthermore, the value of learning should be emphasized by the procedures and systems in the organization.

A climate of openness appears to be one of the most crucial prerequisites for organizational learning. It requires a context in which people are willing to learn from their mistakes and willing to discuss underlying causes and models for these mistakes.

## 3.2. *Enabler 2 : Scanning for knowledge*

In the broadest sense scanning for knowledge means that there should be a continuous search for knowledge that could be relevant or applicable in the specific learning situation. Scanning for knowledge from previous products, competitor products, similar products, or new methods is an important input for the requirements phase of a software project. The main point is that this loop does not always build software product requirements every time from scratch, but attempts to learn from previous experiences. Furthermore, knowledge can be acquired from previous projects that created similar products. Carrying out a post-mortem analysis to find out whether a certain process model was adequate is a good way to increase learning effects. Double-loop learning also requires scanning for knowledge. Reading publications on achievements in software engineering by software developers is a way to scan for knowledge. Experiences from other organizations are in that way fed into the own organization. Sending people to conferences, seminars and training is another approach.

### 3.3. *Enabler 3 : Information on context and current state of the system*

Learning adds knowledge to an existing situation and is influenced by the state of external influences. Information is needed on the context and current state to learn appropriately, and to select the best-suited additions. The retrieval of information on the context and the current state of the product and the project are essential. Making processes explicit, measuring the performance of processes, or the current state of the product and its quality is a useful source of information for this learning enabler.

For example, carrying out frequent software process assessments is a good way to make current processes explicit. Knowing explicitly what the capabilities of an organization are and making explicit which process actions they can use contributes to this learning enabler. If for example, process assessments indicate that configuration management is a weakness in the organization, managers of projects that have high product maintainability targets will know that they need to take some specific action.

### 3.4. *Enabler 4 : Team learning*

Team learning is an important part of an organizational learning process. It means that learning is established within groups that work together towards a shared vision and mutual objectives. Joint formulation of learning objectives, information sharing, discussion, and drawing conclusions together take place within team learning.

Team learning can be used to find out a good way in which product requirements need to be specified to let the final product comply with them. It is also important that development teams learn the effects of different development processes. A specific process may not always have the same effect for different projects, different products, or different team members. These differences and their causes should be determined. Measurement is a powerful mechanism to enable such group learning. Discussing measurement results within a project team and challenging a team's interpretations is also a means to establish team learning [30].

### 3.5. *Enabler 5 : Modeling of the system under control*

In order to control a system, one needs to create a model of this system and the factors that influence it. This can be done through process modeling, and by modeling the relationship between the product requirements and this process. Another example of useful modeling is the modeling of user groups and their mutual relationships to support the identification of all stakeholders [22].

A real-life example is the explicit models of development processes or models of the expected impact of a certain process action. In one of the companies for example, they introduced "incremental development", by which the product was developed in three sequential increments, each expanding on the previous one with a specific functionality. The expectations of this change were modeled by making them explicit. The measurements showed that these expectations were indeed legitimate.

### 3.6. *Enabler 6 : Possibilities for control*

In order to steer a process towards the required outcomes, one needs possibilities for control. This implies that during a software project, (corrective) action can be taken whenever necessary. For example, when it becomes likely that it will not be possible to reach the intended product reliability level, it should be possible to take action to remedy that situation. In a double-loop fashion, the available set of process actions can be expanded with new ones that suit the specific organization.

### 3.7. *Enabler 7 : Involved leadership*

Managers should articulate vision, take part in the implementation of ideas, and be actively involved in the learning processes. The role of a manager in the establishment of organizational learning and in motivating the people in the organization is crucial [28, 16, 1]. In a learning organization managers and the role of the manager has changed drastically compared to traditional management styles. The largest differences are that [28]: the manager is a designer of the learning organization, a teacher of the view on reality, and a steward for the people he/she manages.

Practical implementation of such a different management style is not easy, because both the manager and the people that are managed might be used to a different style. If a manager who always defines the procedures that are to be used suddenly gives the employees an entire free hand in choosing these procedures it is likely that people will not be able to cope. Such a change in management style should therefore be planned carefully and a smooth transition should be made. In creative intellectual work such management styles are, however, often already present.

### 3.8. *Enabler 8 : Explicit goal definition*

In order to have clear targets regarding learning, particular goals should be defined and made explicit. Learning processes benefit if it is clear what the goals are and in which area learning is required to attain such goals. Both product and process goals should be stated explicitly. For the process, measurement goals are set to monitor the performance of specific process actions, and the measurements are analyzed explicitly to learn the effects of such a process action. For double-loop learning, explicit learning goals are defined to learn effects of process actions with which no experience exists. The expectations (hypotheses) regarding the attainability of these learning goals must be specified, because then expectations can be compared to actual values, and reasons for differences can be identified.

An example of the use of explicit goals for learning is the identification of reuse effects in one of the case-study organizations [30]. The project team defined as its explicit goal to measure the effects of software re-use on product reliability. Their expectation was that this contribution was high. The measurements indeed showed that the number of defects in fully re-used modules was remarkably low. An important learning point from this project was the indirect effect of re-use on system reliability. The project team learned that they were more strictly reviewing and testing re-used modules, because they did not "trust" them as much as the one they had developed themselves. As a consequence these modules were much more reliable, because the existing reliability problems were already identified before release. The project team learned that both direct and indirect effects of re-use largely influence product reliability, and learned what these affects are.

### 3.9. *Enabler* 9 : *Monitoring performance gap*

Monitoring the differences between target and actual situations is an important prerequisite for learning. It helps to identify what is going well and what needs improvement. Through this performance monitoring, people get feedback on the way they work and learn what to improve. Monitoring a possible performance gap is not only done for the product, but also for the development process. The performance of process actions should be monitored, and if differences exist between the expected and real effects of process actions, corrective action can be taken. For example, one of the case-study companies had a structural organizational problem. Due to the large number of countries being supplied and the large differences in government regulations across the countries, it was difficult to address all country-specific requirements. This caused many "change requests" to the national representatives in the various countries after products had been released. The performance gaps between wanted and actual product quality could be made explicit for this organization, and corrective action was defined. One example solution was to develop the country-specific requirements in close cooperation with the national representatives and use these requirements as input to the product architecture design. As a result a product architecture was designed that allowed the adding of product-specific software customizations after the release of the product.

### 4. Conclusions and Recommendations

As stated earlier in this chapter, the importance and impact of human factors on the success of software development is commonly accepted. Establishing an eager and learning-orientated environment is, therefore, essential. However, the learning theory described in this chapter illustrates that facilitating learning is a difficult and delicate process. A conceptual model including nine "learning enablers" has been presented in this chapter to facilitate learning in software development programs. This conceptual model is based on learning theory and based on experiences in various case studies. A first validation of this model has taken place [32].

This chapter has explicitly listed nine practical points of attention for software managers. By making the learning factors explicit, this chapter hopefully contributes to improving the learning conditions in software organizations. We recommend that software development line managers and project managers consider these learning enablers in daily practice so they can increase the learning effectiveness of their developers, however difficult this may be. After all, it is the people that make the product.

## Acknowledgments

The authors wish to acknowledge Erik Kooiman, Rob Kusters, Jos Trienekens, Theo Bemelmans and Aarnout Brombacher for their contributions to the work presented in this chapter.

## References

1. T. M. Amabile, "How to kill creativity", *Harvard Business Review* (September/October, 1998) 77–87.
2. R. Agarwal, G. Krudys and M. Tanniru, "Infusing learning into the information system organisation", *European Journal of Information Systems*, no. 6 (1997) 25–40.
3. F. Analoui, "Training and transfer of learning", Avebury (1993).
4. J. R. Anderson, *Cognitive Psychology and its Implications*, 3rd edn. (Freeman and Company, 1990).
5. C. Argyris and D. A. Schön, *Organizational Learning: A Theory of Action Perspective* (Addison-Wesley, 1978).
6. C. Argyris, On organizational learning (1992).
7. K. Ayas, *Design for Learning for Innovation* (Eburon Publishers, Delft, The Netherlands (1997).
8. V. R. Basili and D. M. Weiss, "A methodology for collecting valid software engineering data", *IEEE Transactions on Software Engineering* **SE-10**, no. 6 (November 1984) 728–738.
9. V. R. Basili, G. Caldiera and H. D. Rombach, "Experience factory", *Encyclopedia of Software Engineering* **1** (John Wiley & Sons, 1994) 469–476.
10. V. R. Basili, G. Caldiera and H. D. Rombach, "GQM paradigm", *Encyclopedia of Software Engineering* **1** (John Wiley & Sons, 1994) 528–532.
11. L. R. Beach, *Image Theory: Decision Making in Personal and Organizational Contexts* (John Wiley & Sons, 1990).
12. S. D. Brookfield, *Understanding and Facilitating Adult Learning* (Jossey-Bass Publishers, 1986).
13. CEMP Consortium, Customised Establishment of Measurement Programs, Final Report (1995). *http://www.iese.fhg.de/Services/Projects/Public-Projects/Cemp.html.*
14. D. L. De Vries, A. M. Morrison, S. L. Shullman and M. L. Gerlach, *Performance Appraisal on the Line* (John Wiley & Sons, 1981).
15. N. Entwistle, *Styles of Learning and Teaching* (John Wiley & Sons, 1981).
16. D. A. Garvin, "Building a learning organization", *Harvard Business Review* (July-August, 1993) 81–91.
17. G. P. Huber, "Organizational learning: The contributing processes and the literatures", *Organization Science* **2**, no. 1 (February 1991) 88–115.
18. W. S. Humphrey, *Managing the Software Process, SEI Series in Software Engineering* (Addison-Wesley, 1989).

19. Index Foundation Research Report 90, "Quality Management in the Systems Department", CSC Index, London (1992).
20. M. Jelinek, *Institutionalizing Innovation* (Praeger, 1979).
21. D. A. Kolb, *Experiential Learning* (Prentice-Hall, 1984).
22. R. Kusters, R. van Solingen and J. Trienekens, "Identifying embedded software quality: Two approaches", *Quality and Reliability Engineering International* (John Wiley & Sons, November/December, 1999) 485–492.
23. F. van Latum, M. Oivo, B. Hoisl and G. Ruhe, "No improvement without feedback: Experiences from goal oriented measurement at Schlumberger", *Proceedings of the 5th European Workshop on Software Process Technology (EWSPT'96)*, Nancy, France, *Lecture Notes in Computer Science 1149* (Springer-Verlag, October 1996) 167–182.
24. A.C.J. de Leeuw, *Organizations, Management, Analysis, Design and Change: A Systems Perspective* (van Gorcum Publishers, 1986) (in Dutch).
25. J. G. March, "Exploration and exploitation in organizational learning", *Organization Science* **2**, no. 1 (February 1991) 71–87.
26. E. Nevis, A. DiBella and J. Gould, "Understanding organizations as learning systems", *Sloan Management Review* (Winter, 1995).
27. I. Nonaka and H. Takeuchi, *The Knowledge-Creating Company* (Oxford University Press, New York, 1995).
28. P. M. Senge, *The Fifth Discipline: The Art and Practice of the Learning Organization* (Doubleday, New York, 1990).
29. P. van Solingen, F. van Latum, M. Oivo and E. Berghout, Application of software measurement at Schlumberger RPS: Towards enhancing GQM, *Proceedings of the Sixth ESCOM Conference*, May 1995.
30. R. van Solingen, E. W. Berghout and E. Kooiman, "Assessing feedback of measurement data: Schlumberger practices with reflection to theory", *Proceedings of the 4th International Symposium on Software Metrics (Metrics'97)*, Albuquerque, New Mexico, USA (IEEE Computer Society Press, November 1997) 152–164.
31. R. van Solingen and E. W. Berghout, *The Goal/Question/Metric Method: A Practical Guide for Quality Improvement of Software Development* (McGraw-Hill Publishers, 1999), ISBN 0077095537, http://www.gqm.nl/.
32. R. van Solingen, "Product focused software process improvement: SPI in the embedded software domain", BETA Research Series, No. 32, Eindhoven University of Technology (February 2000), ISBN 90-386-0613-3, Downloadable from http://www.gqm.nl/.
33. J. Swieringa and A.F.M. Wierdsma, "On the way to a learning organization: On learning and education in organizations", Wolters Noordhoff Management, (1990) (in Dutch).
34. A. M. Tuijnman and M. van der Kamp, *Learning Across the Lifespan* (Pergamon Press, 1992).
35. D. Ulrich, "Intellectual capital = competence x commitment", *Sloan Management Review* (Winter, 1998) 15–26.
36. M. Weggeman, "Knowledge management", *Scriptum Management* (1997) (in Dutch).
37. F. van Wijnhoven, "Organizational learning and information systems" (1995).
38. H. Wohlwend and S. Rosenbaum, "Schlumberger's software improvement program", *IEEE Transactions on Software Engineering* (November 1994).

# WEB-BASED LEARNING ENVIRONMENTS: TOOLS AND ENGINEERING ISSUES

BERND J. KRÄMER

*Faculty of Electrical and Information Engineering,*
*FernUniversität, 58084 Hagen, Germany*
*E-mail: Bernd.Kraemer@FernUni-Hagen.de*

This chapter will address the development of Web-based multimedia learning applications using computerized tools and systematic techniques. They include software development, knowledge modeling, and information management methods and tools. In addition, navigation, interaction, adaptation, communication, and collaboration facilities are of concern. Software development and knowledge modeling tools allow authors of multimedia learning materials to design meaningful learning tasks and to explicate and organize the information and multimedia content learners need to construct subject knowledge. Well-designed navigation facilities let learners explore an information space at their own pace and orientation. Interaction facilities provide learners with opportunities for experimentation, context-dependent feedback, and constructive problem solving. Adaptation mechanisms render it possible to select, organize and present information depending on predefined user profile settings or through monitoring of user behavior and diagnosis of learning status. Asynchronous and synchronous communication and collaboration facilities help to bridge geographical distance between teachers and students.

Research on Web-based learning environments is still at its infancy and far from mature. The following discussion will therefore be biased and selective. It will put emphasis on issues that lie in the intersection of software engineering and knowledge engineering, including domain modeling, adaptation and adaptivity of learning environments, and synchronous collaboration.

## 1. Introduction

As we get deeper in the information age, traditional ways of learning and knowledge acquisition are challenged with rapidly changing technologies and a fast growing knowledge base requiring competencies and skills to be renewed frequently. The growing entanglement of work and education imposes pressure on universities, too. They are pushed to provide custom self-instructional course material and flexible tutorial support that give learners maximum control over both the place and time of learning because:

- absence times of qualified personnel and travel costs to attend seminars and courses are expensive;
- waiting times for adequate courses may delay projects; and
- courses are usually not custom-designed to the actual needs of an enterprise or organization.

Many educational institutions are responding to this challenge by developing on-line courses and distance education programs.[a] They can rely on novel digital learning infrastructure and have information and communication technologies at their hands to build global learning infrastructures [26]. These developments promise to overcome some of the limitations of traditional distance education models by:

- delivery of interactive multimedia course materials and access to digital libraries;
- new modes of remote administration, communication and tutoring; and
- modularization and personalization of courses.

Besides apt models of instructional design including new pedagogic functions, Web-based multimedia learning environments play a crucial role for the development of instructional materials and activities, especially for distance teaching scenarios. Emerging environments also support the effective tryout and evaluation of computer mediated instruction and computer supported learner activities.

The possibilities offered by the new information and communication technologies (ICT) for reconstructing education and learning are manifold:

- Contents can be presented differently by using all the types of media available (text, two- and three-dimensional graphics, sound, image sequences, simulations).
- Different media can be synchronized into multi-modal presentations, e.g. in order to explain the sequence of a complex process visualized through an animation with a spoken commentary.
- The most suitable presentation elements can be combined to hyper-media applications, i.e., collections of multimedia components that are networked through logic, didactic or navigational relationships.
- With the help of flexible navigation and search mechanisms, the learner can move freely in the information space, following her personal learning style and interests.
- Operation sequences and preferred learning paths can be recorded, evaluated and reactivated if needed. The students can add their own reference structures and personal notes to the course material.

These and other technologies are currently being explored by a growing number of online learning projects in universities and enterprises world wide. They are too many and too diverse to come to a focused conclusion here.

The topic of this chapter is rather the investigation and illustration of generic features of *engineering environments* that support the process of hypermedia development for learning scenarios. This process covers more than just Web page design.

---

[a]We are not interested in reflecting the ongoing debate on the virtues and difficulties of online learning. Our experience builds on a long practice of distance education serving adult professionals who are stationary, have a limited time budget, and are — in most cases — highly motivated.

It includes knowledge modeling; content creation; information structuring; design of navigation structures and user interface; and program development. The engineering environment and processes should allow the production of a variety of *learning applications* in different subject domains. To misuse an overly simple analogy, we could say that an HTML editor corresponds to what we call an environment, while a Web site produced with this editor is an application.

Viewed from the learner's perspective, multimedia learning applications should provide qualities such as:

- a good mixture of orientation and freedom in navigating through information spaces;
- interactivity that supports construction and learner-controlled activities beyond the mere selection of answers to presented stimuli;
- didactic cues that help the learner to organize learning processes and environments and take decisions on learning situations and means [22]; and
- integrated communication and collaboration facilities.

Further distinguishing features of multimedia learning applications, which largely build on knowledge engineering practices and the field of computer supported collaborative work (CSCW), are:

- knowledge modeling and knowledge communication, which include the design of meaningful learning tasks and the explication and organization of the information as learners need it to acquire subject related knowledge;
- modeling and monitoring student behavior to reason about the student's learning status and appropriately control information presentation; and
- synchronous collaboration.

These three issues will be discussed in Secs. 3 to 5, respectively, after having briefly reviewed a selection of existing hypermedia development methods in Sec. 2. Section 4 will include a brief account of instructional design to the extent that the functionality and architecture of learning environments are concerned.

In our presentation, we deliberately omit other challenging themes and features such as pedagogic modeling, assessment and usability. Usability of multimedia learning applications is presumably as important for the effectiveness of the learning process as is usability of Web sites for the success of Internet economy. As we don't know good ways of measuring usability of learning applications, as yet, we would have been presumptuous if we tried to add anything to Nielsen's recent book "Designing Web Usability" [18].

Other important facets of Web-based learning environments include sharing and reuse of content, computer-aided assessment, and tools for class management, course delivery, and student assistance. They will be briefly discussed in Sec. 6. We will conclude with an outlook on an ongoing European project, which aims to build a portal to higher education through federation and intelligent course brokering.

## 2. Hypermedia Application Development

Research in hypermedia application development aims at finding effective methods and tools to organize multimedia data as associative networks of information components and retrieve multimedia information by traversing such networks within the limits of the given navigational models. In the early 90's, first approaches addressing the task of hypermedia application design have evolved.

OOHDM, the object-oriented hypermedia design method, is one of the better known research prototypes for building complex hypermedia applications [23]. It provides a framework for describing complex information and navigation structures and specifying user interfaces. The design rationale underlying the OOHDM approach was to adapt traditional software engineering methods and tools to the needs of hypermedia applications. More recently, OOHDM has been extended with a system of design patterns for solving recurrent design problems in navigation and interface design [21]. Application development with OOHDM proceeds in four steps:

— *conceptual modeling*,
— *navigational design*,
— *abstract interface design*, and
— *implementation*.

Conceptual modeling consists of finding proper topic classes and relationships modeling the semantics of the application domain. This step yields a conceptual model described in a UML-like notation in terms of classes and relationships between classes. A further outcome of this step can be use cases that describe the application's services from a user perspective.

Navigational design concentrates on the construction of one or more navigation models. Each navigation model provides a particular view on the conceptual model and specifies how the classes in the model can be accessed. OOHDM provides a small collection of predefined navigation classes, such as nodes, links, anchors, and access structures. The latter represent different ways of accessing nodes, e.g. through indices or guided tours.

The step "abstract interface design" builds on primitive interface classes such as text, image, or button. These classes serve to design the application's user interface in terms of objects that can be mapped into instances of navigation classes. Other conceptual models known from software engineering, such as state charts and Petri nets (cf. **Chapter 11, N. Juristo**) are used to specify the application's reaction on external events (e.g. a mouse click) and the synchronization of concurrent activities, respectively.

OOHDM has its strengths when the application exposes a lot of regularity in terms of similar content elements, navigational structures, and interface components. Typical examples of this type include virtual museums, online product catalogs, or interactive kiosks. These applications can be modeled as collections of art pieces, products, or announcements, respectively, whose members are similarly structured and are accessed through the same set of navigation models. In many learning applications, the modeling overhead required by OOHDM would not pay off because of the diversity of information structures and associations between content elements.

The hypermedia design model HDM [8], the predecessor of OOHDM, separates hypermedia application development activities into global and local tasks. Global tasks generate the hypermedia structure in the large, i.e., nodes and associations between them. Local tasks serve to develop the content represented by nodes. HDM provides three building blocks: entity, unit, and component. They form a hierarchy in which entities are composed of components and components are built from units. Correspondingly, HDM knows three types of links: structural, perspective and application. They connect components, units and entities, respectively. Structural and perspective links are implicitly defined in terms of the composition hierarchy, while application links must largely be constructed by the application designer.

Multimedia learning environments evolved from programmed instruction, computer-based training, hypertext systems towards intelligent tutoring systems, and simulation-based learning environments. Multimedia learning environments are software systems and as such they should be developed according to accepted software engineering practices.

Although accepted design principles and operational guidelines in Web-based learning application development are still lacking, the book "Hypermedia and the Web" [14] represents the first serious attempt to overcome this deficit for the more general field of hypermedia engineering. This book defines principle concepts, quality attributes of hypermedia, and defines a development process in analogy to software engineering processes. We are not going to review this work and neither report on well-known software engineering practices in the sequel.

In [14], Lowe and Hall discuss a number of further hypermedia research developments not mentioned here, including Microcosm [HDH96] and Hyperwave [16], which both separate management of content from management of links and provide rich data models similar to HDM.

The book authors' conclusion about the state of development is that there is still little support for the process of hypermedia authoring. Deficits include process automation, collaboration support for groups of authors, and integration and coverage of different phases of development from requirements elicitation to content development. Important principles and design goals known from software engineering such as reuse, interoperability, and portability, which translates into platform-independence, are also lacking in hypermedia application development.

## 3. Knowledge Modeling and Media Design

An important facet of multimedia learning application engineering concerns the entire process of identifying learning objectives and course goals, designing a course ontology, developing suitable expository and active learning media.

Ontologies are knowledge modeling techniques that provide a way to formalize a common vocabulary characterizing a domain of discourse [**Chapter 36, Y. Kalfoglou**]. An ontology associates concepts with the objects in the domain of discourse and specifies their meaning in terms of relationships with other domain objects [25]. An ontology represents the author's view about some universe of discourse and allows a community such as a class or learning group to share knowledge.

Carefully designed learning media provide the motivation and context students need to recognize the information content in the data presented to them in order to build up the knowledge intended by the teacher [14]. Widely accepted didactic functions of animations include [19]: the demonstration of processes and procedures; the simulation of causal models of behavioral systems; the representation of invisible functions and behavior; the illustration of tasks that are difficult to describe verbally; and a visual analogy for abstract and symbolic concepts.

Constructivist views of learning emphasize that knowledge cannot simply conveyed to learners but must be constructed by learners. This process can be supported by teachers who explicate knowledge in terms of suitable ontologies, who design useful learning tasks and teach suitable problem solving techniques. The resulting information collection can be mapped into data. They are the collected symbols humans use to represent information. Data can be communicated with the help of physical media. Their receiver interprets these data in a particular context to detect useful information and finally construct her own knowledge by performing meaningful learning tasks. Figure 1 illustrates this process of coaching knowledge modeling and acquisition through digital learning infrastructures.

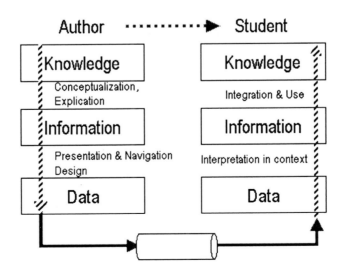

**Fig. 1.**   Data-Information-Knowledge Hierarchy (adapted from [14]).

Externalization of knowledge forces the author to move away from vague mental concepts and ideas to their concrete representations. It provides a means for the learner to interact with, react to, and build upon it.

### 3.1. *Knowledge engineering for multimedia learning environments*

The knowledge engineering process includes the structuring of concepts and information fragments according to their semantic, didactic; and presentational coherence. It produces descriptions that can be separated in three levels of abstraction:

- conceptual;
- presentation; and
- component level.

The conceptual level spans a concept space defining the domain knowledge in terms of an ontology. The ontology comprises a vocabulary of declarative and procedural knowledge of the subject domain and an organization of this domain through semantic relationships. The ontology is presented to the content author as a concept graph that provides a systematic way to analyze and explicate core concepts and relationships in the concept domain of interest.

Figure 2 shows the prototype of a concept space authoring tool that is currently under development in the Multibook project.[b] The editor's tool bar provides a list of predefined semantic relationships such as "superconcept", "has part" or "references" that were found useful in the structuring of a concept space covering the field of multimedia technology. The concept space designer is, however, free to chose her own relationships and make them accessible through the editor interface. These relationships are represented as edges in the visual presentation of a concept space. Content authors can use the concept nodes to zoom into the details of a concept, which consists of other concepts and relationships between them.

The relationships between concepts in the concepts space can be used to suggest desirable navigation paths and generate different lessons for different user types and support thematic adaptation. It can generate guided tours [24], and drive the composition of meaningful presentation units [3], e.g. Web pages. It can also be used for monitoring and diagnosing user behavior in order to provide dynamic adaptation [9] (see also next section).

The presentation level refers to a visual presentation space. It corresponds to a user interface in OOHDM, which comprises a spatial and temporal dimension for presenting textual and graphical objects, animation, sound, simulations and other programmed micro-worlds on a computer screen, through loud speakers, headphones, tactile or other interfaces. Conversely, the presentation level also responds to user interaction.

---

[b]http://www.multibook.de

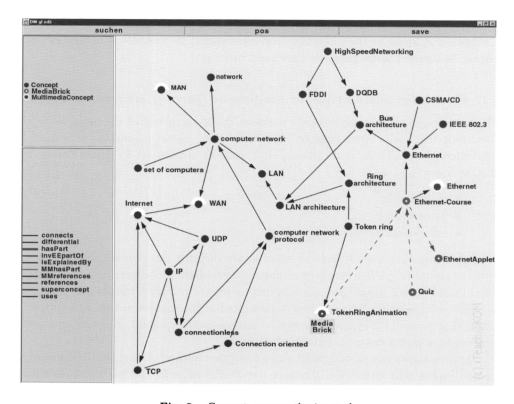

**Fig. 2.**   Concept space authoring tool.

The component level comprises individual information fragments, possibly including alternative presentation types, from which the presentation level is composed.

## 3.2. Presentation mapping

To model the presentation layer, the Multibook project chose to use a separate knowledge base, called MediaBrickSpace, which supports presentation adaptation. In the MediaBrickSpace knowledge is represented in finegrained presentation components, or media bricks, such as images, text fragments, or applets. Media bricks implement possible explanations of the subject domain under consideration. Media bricks are not only linked to the concepts they represent but are also interconnected among each other by rhetorical relations based on the Rhetorical Structure Theory [15]. Rhetoric relations such as "deepen", "explain", or "illustrate" define a conceptual structure of how information is conveyed to the learner.

Figure 3 illustrates the organization of the concept space (grey area, circle shaped nodes) and the MediaBrickSpace (rectangular nodes) and their interconnection.

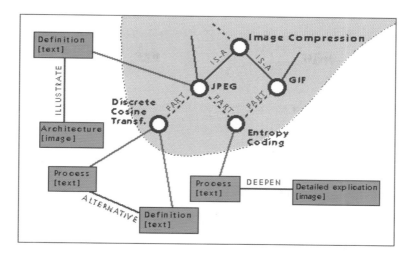

**Fig. 3.** Concept and Mediabrickspace.

Another alternative to organize the component level has been explored in [12] with the implementation of a multimedia component catalogue.[c] The catalogue aims to provide an open market place for reuse and sharing of multimedia components. Apart from the proper multimedia data, each catalogue entry includes meta data to facilitate search and reuse. Meta data provide information about a multimedia component in terms of significant keywords, a short description of the component's intended purpose and function, technical data, usage constraints, language and other attributes. These meta data rely on standards like RDF and the Dublin Core. Recently the meta data model of the catalogue has been adapted to the upcoming Learning Object Meta data (LOM) standard.[d]

The catalogue has been implemented on top of Hyperwave [16] according to the three-tier architecture depicted in Fig. 4. This architecture separates storage and maintenance of data representing information components from their structuring to meaningful composites and their presentation in terms of media matching the user's needs and constraints.

The overall structure of the catalogue complies to XML, XLink, and XSL templates used at the implementation level. These templates determine how users can navigate structured components and how individual and composite components are organized hierarchically.

The rationale underlying the catalogue was to support content authors in learning from previous work stored in the catalogue. Authors can select and adapt available media bricks to their own needs and contribute their modification to the catalogue for further reuse.

---

[c]http://gehtnix.fernuni-hagen.de:8000/catalogue
[d]http://ltsc.ieee.org/doc/wg12/LOM-WD3.htm

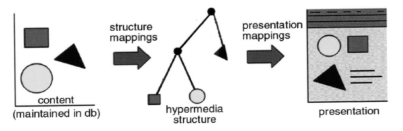

**Fig. 4.**   Three-tier hypermedia architecture.

### 3.3. *Navigation modeling*

Specifying desired navigation paths is an important part of the hypermedia application development. Navigation means traversing in information spaces by means of link hopping and touring along predefined trails. Navigation strategies have been subject to long debates and produced opinions ranging from strict learner guidance to relatively unconstrained discovery learning. The latter accepts a certain degree of disorientation of the learner to enhance depth of learning and encourage explorative behavior.

As there is no empirical evidence, yet, as to which navigation model is best suited for which type of learner and content, designers have to find their own model based on reported experiences and their specific conditions.

To complete the picture, we shall review a few approaches to navigation design based on adaptive techniques in Sec. 4. But before going on, we want to present a state-transition model of navigation behavior that has been used to develop a course module[e] describing the Ethernet protocol with all its facets. The states in Fig. 5, which are labeled by screenshots of Web pages of this course, denote different states students can pass through in their knowledge acquisition process.

The entry page labeled 1 represents a knowledge level sufficient to study this learning module. Students should have some basic knowledge about communication protocols, computer networks, and core phenomena of distributed systems such as concurrency and non-determinism. On the entry page the student is confronted with a problem and a choice of possible answers. When choosing a specific answer, the student is brought to a new interactive Web page, which picks up the student's partial or wrong answer and presents additional hints to support the student's insight into the whole range of problems addressed by this protocol. In the end, the student should arrive at Page 5, which represents a satisfactory knowledge state and provides the basis for tackling the next concept. Alternatively, the student could have used the forward/backward buttons on each Web page to follow a predefined visiting sequence (in our example Page 1–5).

---

[e]We are grateful to Abdulmotaleb El-Saddik for developing this learning module with passion and competency.

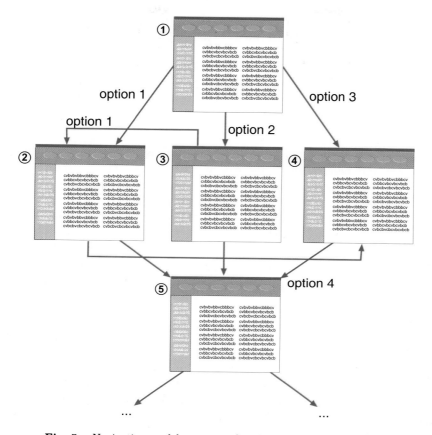

**Fig. 5.**  Navigation model represented as state-transition diagram.

Currently, we are experimenting with prototype tools that allow the content designer to specify similar navigation models and automatically derive the navigation cues. Further tests will show whether such a tool provides effective help for content designers. A second question we try to answer is, whether students may obtain a better orientation in a hypermedia course offering this degree of navigational freedom when having access to some form of a state-transition view.

## 4. Adaptation and Adaptivity

Personalization is a long-term goal of hypermedia systems research, which has led to different solutions to adaptation, which [3] classifies into *adaptable*, *adaptive* and *dynamic*.

### 4.1. *Adaptable hypermedia learning systems*

Adaptable systems rely on user profile information that can be set by the learner prior to accessing learning materials. Typical profile attributes include study objectives, background knowledge, and learning strategy. Values for study objectives might range from basic learning, to getting an overview or just consulting a specific concept. Background knowledge might extend from beginner to expert in the field. The preferred learning mode could be hierarchical — leading from concepts and definitions to examples — or problem-oriented, a strategy which would pose concrete problems to a learner and motivate her to work out own solutions and thereby understand the underlying concepts and difficulties.

In [4], Fakher proposes another definition of adaptation by presenting a learning environment, ALIS.[f] It organizes learning materials as an open system that learners can modify and personalize. They can add their own content, insert additional links, annotations and associations, and open their personal bookmark register in the navigation tree. Besides direct navigation in the browser window, Fakher's environment provides additional navigational cues in a separate window including an Explorer-like hierarchy representing a table of contents, a concept map [10] and an indication of the actual "semantic depth" of the concept at hand (see Fig. 6).

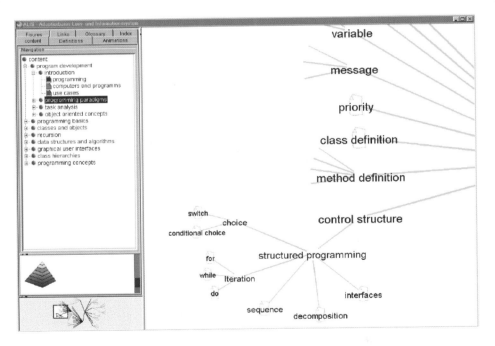

**Fig. 6.** ALIS' navigation tool for students.

To be more precise, ALIS represents structural knowledge through a mind map, a diagrammatic notation that some educational psychologist considers a useful study aid [2]. Their advantages for the learner are described in [17].

---

[f]Adaptable learning and information system, http://www.fernuni-hagen.de/ALIS.

In a programming course, for instance, which is presented in Fig. 6, the explanation of the semantics and use of a while loop might be accessed by clicking on the terms "structured programming" or "iteration" used in the mind map. Alternatively, this topic can be selected through the hierarchically ordered navigation pane. Finally, the learner can use the navigation buttons in the course pages to step through the networked material in a linear fashion. The first form of navigation derives from a concept model, while the latter follow from the author's didactic model of sequencing instruction.

ALIS' multi-dimensional navigation interface for students is illustrated in Fig. 6. Color codes in the hierarchical view indicate whether a single page or a collection of pages has been visited, learned or has not yet been looked at. Only the "learned" attribute has to be set by the student explicitly. The color bar in the middle left pane provides a percentage-wise overview of this status information.

Figure 7 illustrates the integration and filtering function of mind maps as used in ALIS.

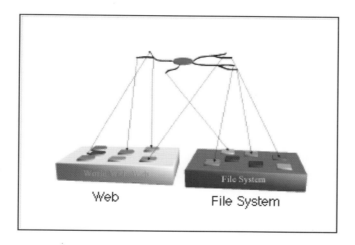

**Fig. 7.**  Integration different learning resources through mind maps.

## 4.2. *Adaptive hypermedia learning systems*

Adaptive hypermedia systems are an area of active research with the majority of applications pursuing educational purposes. Based on a user model, the system generates links to content pages that the students are supposed to study to achieve a desired learning goal.

Adaptive systems include monitoring and diagnosis capabilities to observe the student's behavior and provide appropriate guidance and presentations. The student's learning status is typically deduced from explicit student feedback and monitored page access.

An example for a feedback approach was given in Sec. 4.1 when a learner confirms that he has understood a certain topic. The KBS Hyperbook System [9] relies on semantic links between "knowledge items" whose labels carry information about the student's progress ("already known", "suggested", "too difficult") and are modified by the student herself. The system uses this information to build up a student model, which helps the system to find out whether the learner's goal and the problem she selected match. In addition, the system is able to generate sequential trails through the hyperbook.

In an earlier Version of KBS, user guidance was determined by monitoring student behavior and constructing belief about the student's learning status in terms of a Bayesian network.

The Multibook project chose to use the concept space of a subject domain together with user profile information to derive tables of contents defining guided tours through a hypermedia system dynamically [24]. Recent research results have demonstrated that Multibook's concept space also provides a foundation for generating exercises automatically [5]. A crucial aspect here is that no options are generated that are obviously false and can be easily recognized as such. For example, learners can easily recognize that the option "Ethernet" is likely to be wrong besides other options such as "Jpeg" and "Tiff" in a multiple choice question asking for still image compression techniques. Based on a notion of semantic closeness the algorithm in [5] is able to create wrong answers that bear some probability of truth.

Adaptivity plays an important role in a large number of intelligent tutoring and hypermedia systems. Some of these systems go even a step further than adaptive systems by generating presentations from information components dynamically rather than just affecting a predefined presentation.

## 5.  Synchronous Collaboration, Information Sharing and Awareness

The traditional distance education model is not without shortcomings. Remote teachers find it hard to verify that a student has actually learned the subject in the same way teachers in a classroom can gauge progress and clear up misunderstandings. For students, there is little regular hands-on experimentation and limited access to physical objects, models, simulations, and instruments in computer and engineering labs. There is also little support for cooperative learning and joint problem solving, which are considered important functions of social learning.

A key factor for the success of collaborative learning and problem solving for distributed groups lies in the use of Web-based technology not only for the presentation of material but also in the design of networked simulation environments enabling highly motivating hands-on experiences for learners [27]. This includes the technical ability to exchange information, but also to support social aspects like the feeling of "belonging" to a group and to share a focus of interest in a joint working session.

Ignoring these social and pedagogical aspects accounts for some of the sad failures of the electronic media in the past. Computer Aided Learning in the 60's and 70's, which fell far short of expectations, come to mind. Most educators today will agree that it is naive to assume that the computer (networked or not) becomes the sole mediator of knowledge and that it offers the primary interface for the knowledge acquisition process.

## 5.1. *Collaboration awareness through fingers*

To support awareness, facilitate communication, foster creativity and establish some form of social contact, two techniques occur almost universally within today's synchronous collaboration environments: video transmissions with talking head transmissions or stage views on one side and shared whiteboards for free drawing or annotating pre-existing material on the other side.

If shared authoring of a document or shared synchronous editing of a spreadsheet are involved, screen or window sharing can be added. However, like with sharing the whiteboard, problems arise in keeping views consistent in real-time and synchronizing change. Furthermore, display broadcasts increase the already high bandwidth requirements stemming from the video distribution.

Of course, the main reason for the dominance of shared whiteboards, video conferencing and chat tools in the domain of synchronous CSCW is the relative lack of collaboration-enabled application software. When existing applications are ported into this domain, they usually are collaboration transparent. This means they are either single-user applications wrapped into some distribution layer or they are multi-user transaction-based systems, which, by definition, implies isolation from concurrency. Both cases are poor platforms for collaboration awareness.

As a supplement, we suggested an interaction paradigm, called a *finger*, which highlights objects of interest within a shared information space [13]. Fingers act like cursors pointing to (selected components of) a complex structure. Figure 8 shows a representation of a programming course in the form of a relational table that combines the very learning resource, or media brick, with different categories of meta data describing the resource. In this example, we assume that two different fingers are currently pointing at two different substructure of the shared information space.

Locations of fingers, their movements, and changes inflicted on information fragments can be signaled by means of operation broadcasting to remote collaborators who need to be aware of such actions. Current techniques for collaboration support, like whiteboard or telepointer, are representation-dependent and insensitive to the structure of the item in focus, while fingers are representation-independent.

Fingers exploit the fact that many applications have users navigate within highly structured information spaces consisting of documents, multimedia courseware, graphs or nested tables. To remain independent of particular representations and to be applicable across a wide area of collaboration domains, we proposer graph based

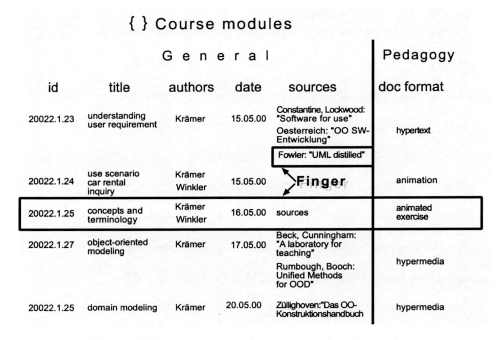

**Fig. 8.**    Table representation of course materials and meta data.

data model, where nodes represent objects and edges express whole-parts relations and links to shared subobjects.

The finger concept also assumes that the information shared among remote sites can be distributed asynchronously prior to finger manipulation. Where parts are missing or need updates, they are fetched on demand from a server and are inserted into the partial information space at the client site. Demand is created when a user navigates into territory not available locally. This can happen in two ways: a user (a) points to an object or (b) looks at an object. The first move establishes something like a new residency of a finger, which at any time points to a single object. We should also mention that a user may have several fingers opened but only one of them is the active one and can be used for manipulating objects. At the presentation level, an active finger is depicted by highlighting the object a user points to. On the conceptual level, a finger corresponds to a node in the graph. On the implementation level, a finger corresponds to the address of the node.

The second move occurs when a user slides his window to other parts of the object space, which usually is much larger than what will fit onto a screen. This is independent of where the user has placed a finger. It rather corresponds to a situation where someone has picked and reserved a seat but is looking for another possibly better suited place. The interaction between different clients, which is mediated via a shared information server, is depicted in Fig. 9.

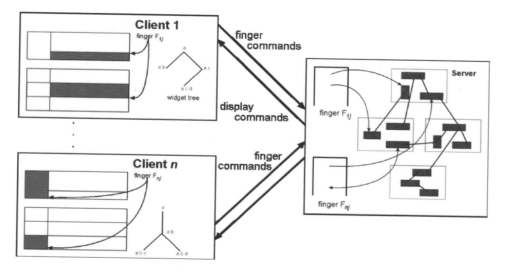

**Fig. 9.**   Broadcast of finger operations.

## 5.2. *Example*

Consider a scenario involving two students M and J, and a tutor T, who are engaged in an argument over some details in the design of a software controlled production cell that must obey strict safety requirements to prevent injuries or loss of human lives.[g] We assume they are connected through a low bandwidth network of workstations and the argument is about the safety requirements. We also assume that M, J, and T possess electronic course material and additional formal and informal specifications of the case (see, e.g. Fig. 10). Learner M asks about a detail of the inner working of a particular machine component, say a press, of the production cell and places her active finger on this component.

The pointing process involves a sequence of steps from a small set of basic operations, which are associated directly with certain key strokes: In, Out, Next, and Back. Going into a complex object means moving a finger to its first constituent sub-object: in a set or list to the first element, in a paragraph to the first word, in the production cell to the first sub-component.

Finger operations next and back move from one sibling in a tree structured document to the next, provided one has not reached the last or first child of a node, respectively.

Alternatively, fingers may be placed with cursor movements and clicks with the mouse. A mouse click always positions the finger on the atomic element whose representation (rectangular bounding box) currently encompasses the cursor co-ordinates. A mouse drag with button 1 depressed makes the finger follow the drag

---

[g]This example is actually taken from a Web-based distance course on Software Engineering offered by the author to his students at FernUniversität.

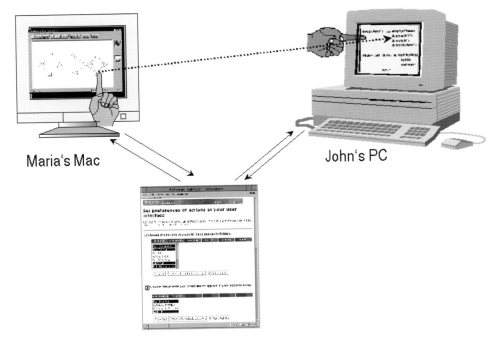

Shared Information Server

**Fig. 10.**   Shared collaboration scenario.

(in real time, at least in our table representation) to the smallest complex object, which has starting and current end position within its bounding box. The new finger position and any other navigational operations are transmitted to the collaboration server. Within the existing instructional material on T's client, the operations are performed with a finger marked as belonging to M and its new position appears as a high-lighted artifact in T's representation of the cell.

Figure 10 suggests that Mary and John are pointing at different components in the shared information space and now want to save the semantic relationship between the two components that was identified in their dialog. Subsequent update operations finally map the distributed relationship into a local relationship in each client's copy of the shared information space.

### 5.3. *Implementation layer*

A prototype implementation of the finger concept operating in distributed, Web-based environments, can be accessed over the Web.[h] A special problem we have

---

[h] http://www.db.informatik.uni-kassel.de/ escher/tcldbTclet/Welcome.de.html

to cope with lies in the fact that the Web mode of information supply is stateless. It follows the connect-get-close paradigm of information interchange and provides mostly pre-compiled pages where contents are possibly fetched from a DBMS. Thus the Web is not directly geared towards synchronous collaboration. As Fielding *et al* put it with regard to HTTP and the Web: although this simple model of communication scales well for simple retrieval tasks, it is not sufficient for the complex interactions in software engineering or in any collaborative work process [7].

Luckily, through the use of applet technologies, i.e., small mobile code loaded from a server and executed at the client side in a so-called plug-in, we can establish a connection with a server database through which updates can flow in a bi-directional way. Another solution, which we used in the prototype version, is John Ousterhout's Tcl/Tk, where applets are called Tclets.

## 5.4. *Applicability*

As we aim at minimal requirements, we target for "penetrable" as opposed to sealed documents including:

- objects that know their structure and can provide identities (addresses) of their nodes;
- objects that don't know their structure but allow a shadow object to be created and stored; and
- objects that don't have a stored structure and don't guarantee creating one but come with a filter, which understands the structure and can create relevant portions of it on the fly.

Hypermedia systems whose components are stored in object-oriented or object-relational databases satisfy the first criterion. Addresses would be URLs, values of attributes, which have key property, record or object identifiers. Some graph formats including some PostScript tools have the ability to recognize substructures like polygons and polylines, or frames. A structure can be extracted and stored as a graph in a shadow document with links into the actual graph.

Clickable maps might also fit into this area. The shadow documents give object identities to the collaboration software that wants to position fingers on certain objects but maintains an internal mapping to the recognized subobjects. The third case would be poorly structured data, e.g. pixel pictures or text streams. Although it would be too costly to store an id with each miniature object, a filter can easily identify each of them and positioning fingers on any of them is not a problem.

So far we have implemented the object database and distributed table representations and were able to integrate a limited number of multimedia types. However, much of the collaboration issues presented here are still part of active research. In the long run, immersed navigation will tie into virtual reality environments.

## 6. Web Based Course Management and Delivery Platforms

The implementation of a virtual university in which the different participants including students, professors, academic and administrative staff are ubiquitously networked requires a common technical infrastructure supporting the:

- electronic distribution of the electronic course material;
- information and tutoring of students via electronic means of communication;
- processing of administrative services such as enrolment, registration for and canceling of exams;
- integration of electronic catalogues and libraries; and even the
- distributed oral exams, seminars, and labs.

Indeed, a growing number of ambitious research projects are working toward improvements in different areas. FernUniversität's own Virtual University platform[i] is designed as a distributed client-server-architecture [11]. It is based on Internet standards, such as Java, HTML, PHP and other technologies freely available on the Internet like Web browsers, software plugins, and professional database systems for the administration of course contents, personal data of students, and important dates for examinations, practices, enrolment, seminars and the like. Course material is protected against unauthorized access by passwords. An authentication is necessary only when accessing protected material. Digital watermarks are assigned for copyright protection. An online-assistant offers students a personal view on the virtual university by managing course-related dates and personal bookmarks, requesting exercise results, and creating a communications directory.

Other improvement areas include tools and environments that can be adapted for reuse with different content such as:

- repositories of reusable and customizable learning resources [6, 12];
- an automated exercise environment forming part of the adaptive hypermedia learning environment MultiBook [20]; and
- WebAssign, a tool for submitting and receiving electronic assignments [1].

## 7. Conclusions

This chapter has opened a biased view on selected issues of hypermedia application engineering from the perspective of learning applications, authoring support, delivery and management. These issues are subject of ongoing research and development, in some of which we are personally involved.

In our detailed discussion we focussed on important tasks on the development of learning applications including domain modeling, navigational design and their interrelationship to instructional design. We addressed different forms of adaptation

---

[i]http://uni-online.fernuni-hagen.de/welcome_en.html

as it evolves in different approaches to adaptive hypermedia systems and intelligent tutoring environments. The need for synchronous collaboration tools that can be smoothly embedded in Web-based multimedia learning applications was another focal point in the main body of this chapter.

The motivation for developing our own collaboration awareness techniques relies on our belief that new media can simulate some of the social processes, which are underdeveloped in traditional distance teaching situations. To achieve a relaxed "What You See is What I See" model, it is sufficient to broadcast the finger operations to all those collaborators whose window presently intersects with the affected subspace of the finger movement. This is considerably easier and cheaper to achieve than display broadcasting.

In a recent EU-funded project, CUBER,[j] we are pursuing the attempt to:

- support learners searching for higher education courses matching their specific needs;
- make courses comparable through standardized meta data descriptions;
- allow the combination of courses from heterogeneous resources to coherent packages; and thus
- build the grounds for a Federated Virtual University,

through the provision of an effective course broker and portal to higher education. Technically, the CUBER broker will consist of a customizable dialogue oriented search engine, a knowledge base of standardized course descriptions and domain knowledge, and an authoring interface to enter and maintain course meta data.

## References

1. J. Brunsmann, A. Homrighausen, H.-W. Six and J. Voss, "Assignments in a Virtual University — The webassign-system", *19th World Conference on Open Learning and Distance Education*, Vienna/Austria (June 1999).
2. T. Buzan, *The Mind Map Book: Radiant Thinking — The Major Evolution in Human Thought* (BBC Publications, 1993).
3. P. De Bra, "Design issues in adaptive web-site development", *2nd Workshop on Adaptive Systems and User Modeling on the WWW* (1999).
4. S. Fakher, "ALIS: An adaptable learning and information system", *EdMedia and EdTelecom* (2000).
5. S. Fischer and R. Steinmetz, "Automatic creation of exercises in adaptive hypermedia learning systems", *ACM Hypertext 2000* (2000).
6. E. N. Forte, M.H.K. Wentland-Forte and E. Duval, "The ARIADNE project: Knowledge pools for computer-based and telematics-supported classical, open and distance education", *European Journal of Engineering Education* **22**, no. 1 (March 1997) 61–74.
7. R. T. Fielding, E. J. Whitehead, K. M. Anderson, G. A. Bolcer, P. Oreizy and R. T. Taylor, "Web-based development of complex information products", *Communications of the ACM* **41**, no. 8 (1998) 84–92.

[j]http://www.cuber.net

8. F. Garzotto, P. Paoli and D. Schwabe, "HDM — A model-based approach to hypermedia application design", *ACM Transactions on Information Systems* **11**, no. 1 (1993) 1–23.

9. N. Henze and W. Nejdl, "Adaptivity in the KBS hyperbook system", *2nd Workshop on Adaptive Systems and User Modeling on the WWW* (1999).

10. D. H. Jonassen, K. Beissner and M. A. Yacci, *Structural Knowledge: Techniques for Representing, Conveying, and Acquiring Structural Knowledge* (Lawrence Erlbaum, 1993).

11. F. Kaderali and A. Rieke, "The Virtual University — FernUniversität online", *For the Library of the Future — Improving the Quality of Continuing Education and Teaching* (Deutsches Bibliotheksinstitut, 1998) 108–114.

12. B. J. Krämer and U. Steinmann, "A market place for multimedia components", *19th World Conference on Open Learning and Distance Education*, Vienna/Austria (1999).

13. B. J. Krämer and L. Wegner, "Beyond the whiteboard: Synchronous collaboration in shared object spaces", *7th Workshop on Future Trends of Distributed Computing Systems*, IEEE Computer Society (1999) 131–136.

14. D. Lowe and W. Hall, *Hypermedia and the Web: An Engineering Approach* (Wiley, 1999).

15. W. C. Mann and S. A. Thomson "Rhetorical structure theory: A theory of text organization", Technical Report RS-87-190, Information Science Institute, USC ISI, USA (1987).

16. H. Maurer, *Hyper-G Now Hyperwave: The Next Generation Web Solution* (Addison-Wesley, 1996).

17. R. McAleese, "The knowledge arena as an extension to the concept map: Reflection in action", *Interactive Learning Environments* **6**, no. 3 (1998) 251–272.

18. J. Nielsen, *Designing Web Usability: The Practice of Simplicity* (New Riders, 2000).

19. O. C. Park and R. Hopkins, "Dynamic visual displays in media based instruction", *Educational Technology* **34**, no. 4 (1994) 21–25.

20. N. Poerwantoro and B. J. Krämer, "An XML-based approach for web-based self assessment", *EdMedia and EdTelecom* (2000).

21. G. Rossi, D. Schwabe and F. Lyardet, "Designing hypermedia applications with objects and patterns", *International Journal of Software Engineering and Knowledge Engineering* **9**, no. 6 (1999) 745–766.

22. R. Schulmeister, *Grundlagen hypermedialer Lernsysteme*, Oldenbourg (1997) (in German).

23. D. Schwabe, G. Rossi and G. Barossa, "The object-oriented hypermedia design model", *Communications of the ACM* **38**, no. 8 (1995) 45–46.

24. A. Steinacker, C. Seeberg, K. Reichenberger, S. Fischer, R. Steinmetz, "Dynamically generated tables of contents as guided tours in adaptive hypermedia systems", *EdMedia and EdTelecom* (June 1999).

25. A. Stutt and E. Motta, "Knowledge modelling: An organic technology for the knowledge age", Chap. 13, eds. M. Eisenstadt and T. Vincent, *The Knowledge Web* (Kogan Page, London, 1998).

26. C. Twigg and M. Miloff, "The global learning infrastructure", Chap. 9, eds. D. Tapscott, A. Lowy and D. Ticoll, *Blueprint to the Digital Economy* (McGraw-Hill, 1999).

27. P. Whalley, "Collaborative learning in networked simulation environments", Chap. 3, eds. M. Eisenstadt and T. Vincent, *The Knowledge Web* (Kogan Page, London, 1998).

# SOFTWARE ENGINEERING AND KNOWLEDGE ENGINEERING ISSUES IN BIOINFORMATICS

JASON T. L. WANG, QICHENG MA and KATHERINE G. HERBERT

*Department of Computer and Information Science,*
*New Jersey Institute of Technology, University Heights,*
*Newark, New Jersey 07102, USA*

In this chapter we address several SE and KE issues in bioinformatics. We review and compare two most widely used bioinformatics tools for sequence alignment and searches. Then, we address the need of background knowledge for processing biomolecular data. Next, we discuss the design and status of a bioinformatics infrastructure, called Genome Mining, developed in our laboratory. Finally, we conclude the chapter by pointing out some future research directions.

*Keywords*: Software development, machine learning, neural networks, biomolecular data processing.

## 1. Introduction

Bioinformatics, or computational biology, refers to an emerging, interdisciplinary field in which computer technology, including software, hardware and algorithms, is applied to solving problems arising in biology. One subject, of particular interest in the field, is to develop tools for processing biomolecular data [3, 18, 19, 20]. These data include DNA (deoxyribonucleic acid), RNA (ribonucleic acid), protein sequences, and their two-dimensional (2D) and three-dimensional (3D) structures.

DNA has a twisted double helical structure. Each strand of the DNA double helix is a polymer built from four components, called *nucleotides*: A, T, C, and G (the abbreviations for adenine, thymine, cytosine, and guanine). The two strands of DNA are complementary: whenever there is a T on one strand, there is an A in the corresponding position on the other strand; whenever there is a G on one strand, there is a C in the corresponding position on the other. DNA can be represented by a sequence of these four letters, or *bases*.

Like DNA, RNA is a long molecule but is usually single stranded, except when it folds back on itself. It differs chemically from DNA by containing ribose sugar instead of deoxyribose and containing the base uracil (U) instead of thymine. Thus, the four bases in RNA are A, C, G, and U.

A protein is also a polymer, constructed by hundreds or thousands of amino acids. The most popular representation model for biologists to describe a protein is to use the sequence. A protein sequence is made up of 20 amino acids, each represented by a letter: alanine (A), cysteine (C), aspartic acid (D), glutamic acid (E), phenylalanine (F), glycine (G), histidine (H), isoleucine (I), lysine (K), leucine (L), methionine (M), asparagine (N), proline (P), glutamine (Q), arginine (R), serine (S), threonine (T), valine (V), tryptophan (W), and tyrosine (Y).

As a result of the Human Genome Project and other initiatives, biomolecular data accumulate at an accelerating rate. For example, the Protein Information Resource (PIR) database [2], maintained at the National Biomedical Research Foundation of Georgetown University Medical Center and accessible at `http://pir.georgetown.edu/`, now contains 190,392 sequences (release 65, as of September 1, 2000).[a] It is therefore essential to have effective tools for processing these data. Data processing in this context includes classifying and aligning sequences, detecting similarities, finding protein coding regions in DNA sequences, and predicting molecular structure and function. Computational tools designed to improve these processes contribute to our understanding of life as well as to the discovery of drugs.

In examining the tools developed in the past, we can roughly classify them into two categories:

- Algorithm based — Tools belonging to this category embody a deterministic or statistical algorithm, some of which are equipped with visualization and Web interfaces
- Knowledge based — Tools of this category are implemented with background or domain knowledge, and usually borrow techniques developed from the neural networks and machine learning community.

While the techniques underlying these tools are of interest, our goal here is to address some software engineering (SE) and knowledge engineering (KE) issues in bioinformatics; we refer the reader to other introductory texts [1, 21] for algorithmic details of the tools. Table 1 (Table 2, respectively) summarizes the SE (KE, respectively) issues and explains why they arise. In addressing the SE issues, we will survey and compare two most prominent tools for sequence alignment and searches (Sec. 2). In addressing the KE issues, we point out the need of background knowledge and review a tool built using neural networks and machine learning techniques (Sec. 3). As described in these two sections, the most effective computational framework is based on incorporating and combining different tools together, as the tools often complement each other. Section 4 then presents the design of **Genome Mining**, an infrastructure built in our lab for biomolecular data processing. Finally, Sec. 5 concludes the chapter and points out some future research directions.

---

[a]In release 40 of 1995, the database has 24,569 sequences. In release 29 of 1992, the database has 8309 sequences.

**Table 1.** Software engineering issues in bioinformatics.

| SE Issues | Reason |
|---|---|
| Effective tool development | Biologists use tools to perform data analysis. |
| Internet-based access | Biologists access data and tools via ftp, email, and World Wide Web. |
| Scalable visualization interface | It allows for biological relationships to be modeled in an expressive format. |

**Table 2.** Knowledge engineering issues in bioinformatics.

| KE Issues | Reason |
|---|---|
| The need of machine learning tools | The amount of biomolecular data is enormous and no theory exists for processing the data. |
| Data encoding and knowledge representation | Good representations are crucial to the success of machine learning. |
| Feature and knowledge extraction | This allows for automating the machine learning process. |
| The need of background knowledge | One should exploit the biological characteristics of the data as much as possible. |

## 2. SE Issues in Bioinformatics

The focus of software engineering research has been shifted from system-oriented tools to user-oriented tools for problem solving [17]. Software tools in bioinformatics, for example, are targeted toward solving problems arising in biology. Among them, BLAST and FASTA are two most eminent tools, both being freely accessible on the Internet. Essentially, the two tools are "sequence alignment programs". Using local alignment algorithms [1, 21], they try to find the best alignment between a query sequence and every sequence in a database. Using various heuristics, they try to keep the search time within a reasonable time frame. While BLAST and FASTA perform essentially the same tasks, each tool has particular searches that it is better suited to perform [8].

## 2.1. *BLAST tool*

BLAST, or Basic Local Alignment Search Tool, was first developed in 1990 using Altschul's method to search for similarities between a query and all the sequences in a database. It is a set of five similarity search programs designed to explore

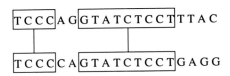

**Fig. 1.** An alignment between two sequences produced by BLAST. Matched regions are highlighted and connected by an alignment line.

all of the available sequences in a database regardless of whether the query is protein or nucleic acid. BLAST's algorithm essentially looks for matches by first looking for small segments of the input sequence to match with other sequences. It then builds from those matched regions to the largest ungapped regions it can find, (cf. Fig. 1). Often, a score is assigned to a matching sequence that rates its possibility as a match. These scores are then interpreted statistically. This statistical interpretation makes it easier to determine what is a valid match and what is not a valid match.

The most recent version of BLAST can be accessed at the Web site of the National Center for Biotechnology Information (NCBI). The URL is http://www.ncbi.nlm.nih.gov/BLAST/. At this Web site, a scientist has a choice of four different methods for accessing BLAST. The most popular and easiest way to access BLAST is through the World Wide Web interface. At the BLAST Web site, there is an easy-to-use Web page that guides the scientist through the search. Through drop-down boxes, the scientist can choose which program he or she would like to use and then which database he or she would like to search. Then the scientist can enter a protein or nucleic acid sequence in a text box. If the scientist is unfamiliar with the BLAST search programs, BLAST will revert to a default setting for the search. For more precise searches, one can customize a search. Besides the World Wide Web interface, there is also a Network BLAST. This program allows the scientist to run remote searches from his or her computer with his or her computer as a client. However, when using this option of BLAST, one should be aware that some security problems can arise, especially if one is using confidential sequences.

Another way to use BLAST is to download a stand-alone version. This version allows the scientist to implement searches on private databases. Finally, for the scientist who does not have Internet access, there is an EMAIL BLAST. Essentially, the scientist sends a specially formatted email to NCBI with the query sequence. The scientist then receives an email back from NCBI with the results of the search.

### 2.2. *FASTA tool*

FASTA is a set of programs initially developed in 1988 using Pearson and Lipman's method to search for similarities between one sequence and any group of sequences of the same type [15]. FASTA searches through databases by initially choosing very small portions of the input sequence to match exactly against sequences in the database. It then begins to work out from those exact matches to find larger ungapped alignments. Finally, FASTA joins these alignments into gapped alignments and calculates a possible score and statistical representation of that score. The output usually is first represented in a histogram followed by an analysis of the search results.

There are many executions of FASTA located on the World Wide Web. The primary site for FASTA is William Pearson's Web site at the University of Virginia. The URL is `http://www.med.virginia.edu/medicine/basic-sci/biochem/faculty/pearson.html`. At this site, the scientist can access a Web-based interface for FASTA. It provides over 20 databases for search as well as an option to search specific proteomes and genomes. Furthermore, the scientist can use default search settings as well as customize his or her searches. Also, there is a version of FASTA one can download for one's own use [15].

Besides the FASTA Web site at the University of Virginia, other groups have developed their own FASTA interface. The interface at the European Bioinformatics Institute's Web site, `http://www.ebi.ac.uk/fasta3/`, is one such example. The interface is highly interactive and allows the user to just use default settings or to specify many variables as well as offering about 30 different databases for search. Also, the scientist can specify whether he or she wants the results emailed to him or her or would like them interactively displayed at the Web site. Moreover, it allows the scientist to choose whatever format he or she would like to input the query sequence in (see Fig. 2 for some different input formats). Once the scientist begins the query, the site maintains a clock as to how long the query has been running and instructions to email the query if the search takes too long. The output is displayed in a traditional FASTA output format.

There are other Web sites that maintain versions of FASTA. Most of these sites can be found by doing a simple search from any Web search engine. Most of the

```
>carAB-P1, promoter
AAAAAAATCCCGCCATTAAGTTGACTTTTAGCGCCCATATCTCCAGAATG
GCCGCCGTTTGCCA
```

(a)

```
>JC4383 3 ' -phosphoadenosine-5 '-phosphosulfate synthetase - spoonworm (Urchis caupo)
MAFLPNGQLATNVTFQTQHVSRAKRGQVLGQRGGFRGCTVWFTGLSGAGKTTISFALE
EYLVSQGIPTYSLDGDNVRHGLNKNLGFTQEDREENIRRISEVAKLFADGGIVCLTSFISP
```

(b)

```
JC4383
```

(c)

**Fig. 2.** Different formats for inputting a query sequence; (a) inputting a DNA sequence; (b) inputting a protein sequence; (c) inputting a sequence using its ID in an existing protein database.

differences in these Web sites are just how user friendly the interfaces are. When looking for a FASTA tool to use, it would help to first check Pearson's Web site for the most recent version of the tool — this would help to choose the best possible tool for a search. Also, Bioinformatica, located at `http://www.bioinformatica.com/`, provides many tools and resources for anyone doing research in the bioinformatics field.

### 2.3. *Comparison of BLAST and FASTA*

While BLAST and FASTA essentially perform the same tasks, each tool performs better in certain queries than in others. The decision is ultimately determined by what kind of search the scientist is looking to do, time constraints, and what database the scientist wishes to search. One of the biggest differences between BLAST and FASTA is time. BLAST was specifically designed to be a speedy search without sacrificing sensitivity. Generally, BLAST is much faster than FASTA. BLAST searches usually take a few minutes while FASTA searches can take significantly longer. Therefore, if time is an important concern while doing a search, then BLAST is the better tool to use.

Another big difference between the two tools is the database access each provides. BLAST can use the non-redundant databases provided by NCBI. For a similar search, FASTA would have to access multiple databases. Moreover, BLAST offers various search modes that allow the scientist more flexibility in his or her search. FASTA doesn't offer this flexibility in some searches and it may require another computer program to translate an input into a form FASTA can read. This makes FASTA very unwieldy to use in certain searches and can add a lot of time and overhead to a search. Also, when using default settings, BLAST tends to be more sensitive than FASTA in protein searches. BLAST's algorithm allows for gapped matches. This allows BLAST to include sequences that, while not being a perfect match, may be a significant match for the query. FASTA's algorithm requires a perfect match during the first stage of the search that can force the tool to overlook some significant matches.

However, when working with nucleic acids, FASTA tends to be more sensitive than BLAST. Since FASTA allows for smaller word searches in the first phase of the search, it is more inclined to find more precise matches. However, this type of search does take time and BLAST can be adequately sensitive for most nucleic acid searches. In the latest version of BLAST, the developers included the ability to search only portions of the databases. This feature has been available for a while on FASTA. If one plans to do a partial database search (such as searching GenBank for mammals), one may want to keep in mind that this type of search is new for the BLAST tool and use the FASTA tool as well to get comprehensive search results.

Table 3 summarizes the comparison of BLAST and FASTA. In general, most users implement a BLAST search using default settings as a first step in a database search. After viewing the results from this search, he or she then decides on whether

**Table 3.**   Comparison of BLAST and FASTA.

|  | BLAST | FASTA |
|---|---|---|
| speed (using GenBank) | a few minutes | several hours |
| protein similarity searches | more sensitive | less sensitive |
| DNA similarity searches | less sensitive | more sensitive |
| database access | can access more non-redundant databases through NCBI | must access multiple databases to perform searches |
| search modes | provides facilities to make searches more flexible | may use another program to translate input |
| partial database searches | feature recently included in tool | feature available for a long period of time |

the information is reliable enough for what they need or if they need to obtain more sensitive data through customized BLAST searches or default or customized FASTA searches.

It is worth pointing out that BLAST/FASTA searches can help to do data mining in biomolecular sequences. For example, a typical data mining problem is to perform classifications. One approach for protein sequence classification is to compare an unlabeled sequence $S$ with the sequences in the target class and the sequences in the non-target class using BLAST or FASTA. One then assigns $S$ to the class containing the sequence best matching $S$. A similar approach could also be used for DNA sequence classification and recognition [20].

## 2.4.  Summary

In reviewing the two most widely used bioinformatics tools, BLAST and FASTA, we conclude that a successful tool must be user-friendly, flexible, usable, and accessible. This tool should be widely available through ftp, email, and the World Wide Web. There is often a tradeoff between time and precision. For example, FASTA is more time consuming but yields more precise results than BLAST. Performance is often data dependent. For example, BLAST is better for protein searches while FASTA is better for nucleic acids sequences. In many cases, tools complement each other. Therefore, the best result can be achieved by combining multiple tools in different ways as suggested by Gaeta [8].

One shortcoming of many of the existing alignment tools is the lack of a visualization interface. Visualization [4, 5], or icon-based navigation and browsing, has been an active research area in software development and engineering. In bioinformatics, only a few areas, such as sequence classification, exploit visualization technology. The most common way to visualize the biomolecular data is to use dendrograms (rooted trees) [9]. Essentially, in this method, the comparisons are performed, the information clustered, and then organized meaningfully into the dendrogram structure. The key advantage to the dendrogram structure is that it allows for biological relationships to be modeled in an expressive format.

While this approach provides methods for representing biological information meaningfully, there are also drawbacks. If the comparison relation is symmetric, then isomorphisms occur. Moreover, the structure cannot be scaled up for large amounts of data. Therefore, different visualization techniques are being investigated to avoid such problems. Current methods being explored involve using three-dimensional space to visualize distances between sequences directly. These methods essentially design distance measures, take these measures and map the sequences to points in 3D space, locate points accordingly, and then visualize these points. As far as the alignment tools are concerned, some sites of FASTA have implemented a rudimentary interface for displaying histograms and search results. However, how to apply advanced visualization technology to building more user-friendly bioinformatics tools with classification and clustering dendrograms remains to be an open research problem.

## 3. KE Issues in Bioinformatics

Many of the knowledge-based bioinformatics tools are built using neural networks and machine learning techniques. One important issue in applying neural networks to biosequence analysis is how to encode the biosequences, i.e., how to represent the biosequences as the input of the neural networks. Good input representations make it easier for the neural networks to recognize the underlying regularities. Thus, good input representations are crucial to the success of the neural network learning [10].

One of the encoding methods is *orthogonal encoding* [14]. In orthogonal encoding, nucleotides or amino acids in a biosequence are viewed as unordered categorical values, and are represented by $C$ dimensional orthogonal binary vectors, where $C$ is the cardinality of the 4-letter DNA alphabet $\mathcal{D} = \{A, T, G, C\}$, or the cardinality of the 20-letter amino acid alphabet $\mathcal{A} = \{A, C, D, E, F, G, H, I, K, L, M, N, P, Q, R, S, T, V, W, Y\}$. That is, we use $C$ binary (0/1) variables, among which only one binary variable is set to 1 to represent one of the $C$ possible categorical values and the rest are all set to 0. For instance, we represent the nucleotide A by "1000", and amino acid Y by "00000000000000000001". The orthogonal encoding was frequently used in the early 90's [6, 11]. Figure 3 shows an example of the orthogonal encoding of a DNA sequence.

The orthogonal encoding requires that the biosequences be equal in length, or one must sample the biosequences of variable lengths by a window of fixed size. Another disadvantage is that it wastes a lot of input units in the input layer of a neural network. For instance, for a protein sequence of 100 amino acids, 2000 input

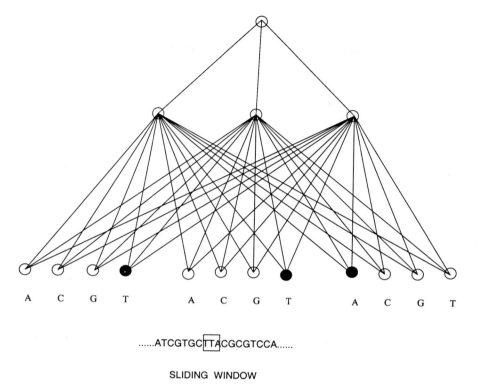

**Fig. 3.** An example of the orthogonal encoding of a DNA sequence.

units are required to represent the protein sequence. This requires many neural network weight parameters as well as many training data, making it difficult to train the neural network.

An alternative encoding method is to use high-level features extracted from biosequences. The high-level features should be relevant and biologically meaningful. By "relevant", we mean that there should be high mutual information between the features and the output of the neural network, where the mutual information measures the average reduction in uncertainty about the output of the neural network given the values of the features. By "biologically meaningful", we mean that the features should reflect the biological characteristics of the sequences. These characteristics are often referred to as the background knowledge in the development of bioinformatics tools.

### 3.1. Background knowledge

We use E. Coli promoter recognition to illustrate what is meant by background knowledge. The E. Coli promoter is located immediately before the E. Coli gene. Thus, successfully locating the E. Coli promoter conduces to identifying the E. Coli

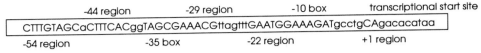

**Fig. 4.** An example promoter sequence. Regions are highlighted by upper case letters. The −54 region, −44 region, −35 box, −29 region, −22 region, −10 box, and +1 region are CTTTGTAGC, CTTTCAC, TAGCGA, AACG, GAATGG, AAAGAT and CA, respectively. Particularly important regions (binding sites) are discussed in the text.

gene. The uncertain characteristics of the E. Coli promoters contribute to the difficulty in the promoter recognition. The E. Coli promoters contain two binding sites to which the E. Coli RNA polymerase, a kind of protein, binds [12]. The two binding sites are the −35 hexamer box and the −10 hexamer box, respectively. Each binding site consists of 6 bases (nucleotides). The central nucleotides of the two binding sites are roughly 35 bases and 10 bases, respectively, upstream of the transcriptional start site. The transcriptional start site is the first nucleotide of a codon where the transcription begins; it serves as a reference point (position +1). The consensus sequences, i.e., the prototype sequences composed of the most frequently occurring nucleotide at each position, for the −35 binding site and the −10 binding site are TTGACA and TATAAT, respectively. But none of the promoters can exactly match the two consensus sequences. The average conservation is about 8 nucleotides, meaning that a promoter sequence can match, on average, 8 out of the 12 nucleotides in the two consensus sequences. Figure 4 shows an example promoter sequence with the −35 binding site being TAGCGA and the −10 binding site being AAAGAT. The conservation here includes only 6 nucleotides.

The two binding sites are separated by a spacer. The length of the spacer has an effect on the relative orientation between the −35 region and the −10 region. A spacer of 17 nucleotides is most probable. The promoter sequence in Fig. 4 has a spacer of 17 nucleotides. Another spacer between the −10 hexamer box and the transcriptional start site also has a variable length. The most probable length of this spacer is 7 nucleotides. The promoter sequence in Fig. 4 has a spacer of 6 nucleotides. In general, the distance between the −10 binding site and the transcriptional start site varies from 3 to 11 bases. The distance between the −35 binding site and the −10 binding site varies from 15 to 21 bases. These varying distances render promoter recognition difficult, as both the contents and positions of the binding sites are uncertain.

Many promoter sequences have the pyrimidine (C or T) at the position −1 (one nucleotide upstream of the transcriptional start site), while the purine (A or G) is at the transcriptional start site (position +1). The +1 region includes the nucleotides at the position −1 and the transcriptional start site. The promoter sequence in Fig. 4 has a nucleotide C at the position −1 and a nucleotide A at the transcriptional start site. To develop bioinformatics tools for recognizing promoters, one has to exploit the characteristics of the E. Coli promoters.

## 3.2. *Knowledge extraction and representation*

Knowledge extraction and representation is an important process in developing knowledge-based bioinformatics tools. We use our recently developed tool for E. Coli promoter recognition [13] to illustrate this process. Our knowledge of the nucleotide probability distributions in the two binding sites of promoter sequences is represented in the Position Weight Matrix (PWM) [16]. We use a machine learning technique, more precisely the expectation-maximization (EM) algorithm [7], to extract the knowledge of the nucleotide probability distributions in the two binding sites. Based on the knowledge, we are able to precisely locate the binding sites of the promoter sequences. We also develop feature extraction algorithms to represent a DNA sequence as a vector of high-level features extracted from the sequence. The feature values are then fed into a neural network (NN).

By considering different combinations of features, we develop three basic programs for promoter recognition. We found experimentally that a combination of the three basic programs outperforms each individual program. This result is consistent with the observation in Sec. 2.4, where we pointed out that bioinformatics tools often complement each other, and a combination of the tools usually achieves the best result.

## 4. The Genome Mining Project

The purpose of the Genome Mining project, accessible at http://www.cis.njit. edu/~eservice, is to apply data mining and knowledge engineering techniques to genome data processing. The project is to develop a Web-based server, with an advanced visualization interface, that allows the user to perform common genome mining activities, including sequence classification and clustering as well as pattern discovery. The user can run the programs provided by the Genome Mining toolbox remotely on the Web or can download these programs to a local site. The toolbox is connected to major genome data processing centers around the world.

Currently the Genome Mining toolbox has two components. The first component is the NN promoter recognition tool described in Sec. 3.2. The second component is a protein sequence classification tool, which takes as the input a protein sequence, extracts features from the protein sequence, and feeds these feature values to a trained neural network. The neural network can classify the input protein sequence and tell if it belongs to one of the globin, kinase, ras or ribitol superfamilies in the PIR protein database [2] at the National Biomedical Research Foundation of Georgetown University Medical Center.

Figure 5 illustrates the design of the Genome Mining toolbox. In the figure, a user submits a query sequence to the toolbox through the World Wide Web. Our Web server accepts the sequence, which is processed by the protein classification tool or the promoter recognition tool. Both tools have access to the underlying database containing training sequences and users' profiles. After processing, the result is sent to the Web server, which then returns the result to the user.

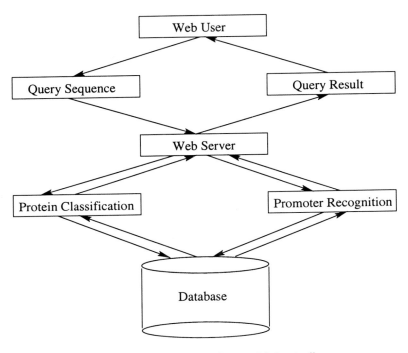

**Fig. 5.**   The design of the Genome Mining toolbox.

In addition to the promoter recognition tool and protein sequence classification tool, we are developing new tools for gene detection and for phylogenetic analysis in plants. These tools will be integrated into the Genome Mining toolbox in the near future.

## 5.  Conclusion

In this chapter we have addressed several SE and KE issues in bioinformatics. Besides topics mentioned in the chapter, new research directions, such as DNA chips, DNA probe arrays, gene expression, genome warehousing, protein synthesis, RNA processing and structure prediction, are emerging. These areas have recently gained significant attention from both computer and natural scientists. As the bioinformatics era is starting, we anticipate that SE and KE technologies are becoming increasingly important in developing complex, intelligent, and large-scale software for biological information processing.

## Acknowledgments

We thank the anonymous reviewers for their thoughtful comments, which helped to improve the presentation and quality of the paper.

# References

1. P. Baldi and S. Brunak, *Bioinformatics: The Machine Learning Approach* (The MIT Press, Cambridge, MA, 1998).

2. W. C. Barker, J. S. Garavelli, D. H. Haft, L. T. Hunt, C. R. Marzec, B. C. Orcutt, G. Y. Srinivasarao, L. S. L. Yeh, R. S. Ledley, H. W. Mewes, F. Pfeiffer and A. Tsugita, "The PIR-international protein sequence database", *Nucleic Acids Research* **26**, no. 1 (1998) 27–32.

3. C.-Y. Chang, J. T. L. Wang and R. K. Chang, "Scientific data mining: A case study", *International Journal of Software Engineering and Knowledge Engineering* **8**, no. 1 (1998) 77–96.

4. S. K. Chang (ed.), *Principles of Visual Programming Systems* (Prentice-Hall, 1990).

5. S. K. Chang (ed.), *Visual Languages and Visual Programming* (Plenum Publishing Corporation, 1990).

6. M. W. Craven and J. W. Shavlik, "Machine learning approaches to gene recognition", *IEEE Expert* **9**, no. 2 (1994) 2–10.

7. A. Dempster, N. Laird and D. Rubin, "Maximum likelihood from incomplete data via the EM algorithm", *Journal of the Royal Statistical Society*, Series B **39** (1977) 1–38.

8. B. A. Gaeta, "Database similarity searching using BLAST and FASTA", *Australasian Biotechnology*, 1995.

9. D. Gilbert, M. Schroeder and J. van Helden, "Interactive visualization and exploration of biological data", *Proceedings of the 2nd International Workshop on Biomolecular Informatics*, 2000.

10. H. Hirsh and M. Noordewier, "Using background knowledge to improve inductive learning of DNA sequences", *Proceedings of the 10th Conference on Artificial Intelligence for Applications* (1994) 351–357.

11. J. D. Hirst and M. J. E. Sternberg, "Prediction of structural and functional features of protein and nucleic acid sequences by artificial neural networks", *Biochemistry* **31**, (1992) 7211–7218.

12. S. Lisser and H. Margalit, "Compilation of E. Coli mRNA promoter sequences", *Nucleic Acids Research* **21**, no. 7 (1993) 1507–1516.

13. Q. Ma, J. T. L. Wang and C. H. Wu, "Application of Bayesian neural networks to biological data mining: A case study in DNA sequence classification", *Proceedings of the 12th International Conference on Software Engineering and Knowledge Engineering* (2000) 23–30.

14. D. W. Opitz and J. W. Shavlik, "Connectionist theory refinement: Genetically searching the space of network topologies", *Journal of Artificial Intelligence Research* **6** (1997) 177–209.

15. W. R. Pearson, FASTA programs at the University of Virginia, 1997. URL: *http://alpha10.bioch.virginia.edu/fasta/*.

16. R. Staden, "Computer methods to locate signals in nucleic acid sequences", *Nucleic Acids Research* **12**, no. 1 (1984) 505–519.

17. J. E. Urban and P. O. Bobbie, "Software productivity: Through undergraduate software engineering education and CASE tools", *The Impact of CASE Technology on Software Processes*, ed. D. Cooke (World Scientific Publishing Co., Inc., 1994) 327–347.

18. J. T. L. Wang, T. G. Marr, D. Shasha, B. A. Shapiro and G.-W. Chirn, "Discovering active motifs in sets of related protein sequences and using them for classification", *Nucleic Acids Research* **22**, no. 14 (1994) 2769–2775.

19. J. T. L. Wang, T. G. Marr, D. Shasha, B. A. Shapiro, G.-W. Chirn and T. Y. Lee,

"Complementary classification approaches for protein sequences", *Protein Engineering* **9**, no. 5 (1996) 381–386.

20. J. T. L. Wang, S. Rozen, B. A. Shapiro, D. Shasha, Z. Wang and M. Yin, "New techniques for DNA sequence classification", *Journal of Computational Biology* **6**, no. 2 (1999) 209–218.
21. J. T. L. Wang, B. A. Shapiro and D. Shasha (eds.), *Pattern Discovery in Biomolecular Data: Tools, Techniques and Applications* (Oxford University Press, New York, 1999).

# CONCEPTUAL MODELING IN SOFTWARE ENGINEERING AND KNOWLEDGE ENGINEERING: CONCEPTS, TECHNIQUES AND TRENDS

OSCAR DIESTE, NATALIA JURISTO, ANA M. MORENO and JUAN PAZOS

*Facultad de Informática Universidad Politécnica de Madrid,*
*Campus de Montegancedo, 28660-Boadilla del Monte, Madrid, Spain*
*E-mail: {odieste,natalia,ammoreno,jpazos}@fi.upm.es*

ALMUDENA SIERRA

*Escuela Superior de Ciencias Experimentales y Tecnología,*
*Universidad Rey Juan Carlos C/ Tulipán s/n, 28933-Mostoles, Madrid, Spain*
*E-mail: asierra@escet.urjc.es*

Conceptual modeling is a crucial software development activity for both Software Engineering and Knowledge Engineering. Each discipline, however, has developed its own techniques for conceptual modeling, and there is no agreement about a common set of techniques that can be used in both disciplines. This chapter will describe such techniques, paying special attention to the more recent and innovative ones, as well as to the concepts shared by the techniques used in the two disciplines.

The chapter will, therefore, outline the field of conceptual modeling within these two disciplines. Although the situation in the field is satisfactory, as can be inferred from the review conducted, there is still a lot of work to be done. Indeed, a series of shortcomings besetting the different techniques will be identified and an alternative perspective will be described, which points to a way of quieting such objections.

*Keywords*: Conceptual modeling, software engineering, knowledge engineering.

## 1. Introduction

The software development process is a kind of problem-solving process. Problem, here, means a context, environment or situation where a software system shall be developed and operated. For a successful software system development, Software Engineers (and Knowledge Engineers) shall understand all problem components, relations, rules, constraints, etc. Such an understanding is a hard and time-consuming process, which requires specialized tools for being performed. These tools, which allow the Software/Knowledge Engineer to understand the problem to solve, are known as conceptual models (CMs).

The process of creating CMs in software development is generally referred to as conceptual modeling, although it may be given other pet names depending on the actual discipline in which it is performed; for example, **problem analysis** in Software Engineering (SE) [1] or **conceptualization** in Knowledge Engineering (KE) [2] (there are specific materials about Knowledge Engineering in

*"The Knowledge Modeling Paradigm in Knowledge Engineering"*, by E. Motta, in this same volume).

The design of CMs is a crucial activity in traditional and intelligent software development. CMs are essential for:

- Making real-world concepts and relationships tangible [3].
- Recording parts of reality that are important for performing the task in question, and downgrading other elements that are insignificant [4].
- Supporting communication among the various "stakeholders" (customers, users, developers, testers, etc) [5].
- Detecting missing information, and errors or misinterpretations, before going ahead with system construction [6].
- Providing an orientation on how the software should meet a need [7].
- Providing a specification of the behaviour of the system under construction [8].

Taking into account the above citations, it can be said that CMs are critical in the problem identification and solution proposal activities of any development project. As software systems become more complex and the problem domain moves further away from knowledge familiar to developers, conceptual modeling is gaining in importance. The reason is that modeling acts as the starting point for understanding and, thus, being able to solve customer and/or user problems. This is clear from the work of several researchers in the disciplines of both SE and KE, who claim that proper conceptual modeling is crucial for the future development of software. So, for example, the papers by McGregor [9], Bonffati [10] or Høydalsvik [11] concerning SE stress how important conceptual modeling is in ensuring that CMs faithfully represent the problem to be solved in the user domain. Similarly, researchers in the field of KE, like Schreiber [6], Hoppenbrouwers [12] and Adelman [13], underscore the fact that the quality of the resulting expert system is critically dependent on the CM produced, because the CM contains the knowledge to be implemented in the future software system.

SE and KE have developed their own conceptual modeling techniques. Nevertheless, techniques in each discipline have been developed in isolation, with little or no relationship among them. Although interactions between SE and KE are becoming stronger [14, 15], practitioners in each discipline do not know which techniques are available to solve problems in the other discipline.

Moreover, this lack of knowledge makes difficult an interchange of experience between SE and KE, and much more a possible integration of techniques from both disciplines into a common toolkit, which could be used for developing traditional and intelligent systems [16]. As will be discussed in this chapter, some common ideas and principles, which have gone beyond the boundaries of their discipline and influenced the CMs used in the other, can be identified.

In this chapter, the general state of conceptual modeling in SE and KE will be reviewed, with the following objectives:

- Systematically examine the state-of-the-practice of conceptual modeling in SE and KE.
- Show the relationship between the ideas and principles used by different modeling techniques in both disciplines.
- Identify common principles and concepts in both SE and KE disciplines.
- Discuss how well adapted conceptual modeling and the existing techniques are to the functions that they should perform and the goals they should achieve in the development process.

For this purpose, this chapter will be structured as follows. Section 2 will discuss the concept of **model** within software development and will go on to stress the usefulness of the different sorts of models, typifying a special type of models called **conceptual models**, which will be specifically addressed in Sec. 3. Sections 4 and 5, introduce the major models in SE and KE, respectively. Once having explained such models, Sec. 6 discusses the interchange of some principles and ideas between the models of the two disciplines. Section 7 then analyses the models described from the viewpoint of how good they are as CMs, according to the definition given in Sec. 3. It will be concluded that the existing models generally fail to attain the established goals, and these shortcomings will be described. Finally, an approach to the conceptual modeling process will be proposed in Sec. 8, which could possibly help to solve the problems discussed in the preceding section.

## 2. Types of Models In Software Development

The term *model* is extremely polysemic in colloquial speech. As a representative sample of the diversity of meanings of the term model, take look at the definitions given by Webster's dictionary [17]:

(1) A small but exact copy of something (for instance, a ship model).
(2) A pattern or figure of something to be made (for instance, clay models for a statue).
(3) A description or analogy used to help visualize something that cannot be directly observed (for instance, a model of the atom).
(4) A system of postulates, data and inferences used to describe mathematically an object or state of affairs.
(5) A theoretical projection of a possible or imaginary system.

Each of the above definitions, and probably any other possible suggestion, refers to a particular purpose of models, that is, what they are useful for, what results their application will yield, etc, answering the question "what do we want to build a model for?" Now, let's take a look at the circumstances surrounding software development and the use to which models are put during development.

In the case of software development, there are two, clearly distinct reasons for using models. Firstly, models are used *to describe the problem raised by the user* and to be solved by the software system. Secondly, models are used *to describe what the software system* that solves this problem *will be like.* This means that the term *model* is used twice during software construction, for two different purposes [18]:

- **Descriptive or conceptual model.** The CM describes an existing part of the world, and is the output of the conceptual modeling activity. The CM matches Webster's definitions (3) and (4); that is, a model is derived from reality for the purpose of gaining an understanding of such reality.
- **Prescriptive or computational model** (CpM). The CpM is the definition of a software product, and is the output of requirements specification and design activities. CpM matches Webster definitions (1) and (2); that is, a reality, the software system, is built from the model.

Blum [19] gives a very clear view of this distinction, indicating that software development can be seen as two successive and separate moments. Figure 1 shows Blum's approach (the box in the figure symbolize the whole development process, and arrows the flow of activities):

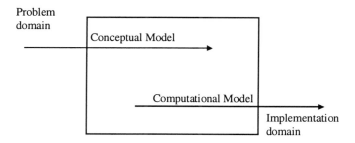

**Fig. 1.**    Software development process from the viewpoint of the types of models used.

- A first problem-oriented phase. This is the phase where CMs are used to record the important concepts of the problem domain.
- A second system-oriented phase. This is the phase where CpMs are used to univocally determine the structure and functionality of the software system for implementation.

This chapter focuses on the first group of models, that is, on CMs. In the following section, it will describe how this term emerges and how it is gaining in importance within the development process.

## 3.  Conceptual Models in Software Development

The term CM originally emerged in the field of DataBases. CMs were used to represent data and relations, which were to be managed by an information system, irrespective of any implementation feature [20]. The scope of the term CM has gradually broadened since the approval of the ISO conceptual modeling standard [21], where its goal was to represent the *domain of discourse*. The domain of discourse is the set of data involved in the problem to be solved and the operations that affect the above data. In this context, only the operations that represented domain rules or, in other words, specific integrity constraints of the problem to be solved were represented in the CM.

CMs are used in the field of SE for more than is acknowledged by the above definition. The following citations show how CMs are considered in SE:

- Describe the universe of discourse in the language and in the way of thinking of the domain experts and users [22].
- Formally define aspects of the physical and social world around us for the purposes of understanding and communication [23].
- Help requirements engineers understand the domain [24].

Generally, the meaning of CM in SE is representation of the problem domain performed for the purpose of understanding and communication between developers and users.

CMs are also used in KE, where their goal is to model the expert knowledge without referring to any implementation mechanism. Newell [25] termed the level of abstraction at which CMs are located as *knowledge level*. Clancey [26] said that the knowledge level "accounts for behaviour in terms of interaction between agents and their environment". Importance of CMs in KE is crucial, because they facilitate the understanding of the problem, and represent the knowledge needed by the software system to solve this problem [6, 27].

Despite their slightly different meanings in each discipline, the main characteristics of any CM are *description* and *understanding*; that is, the CM can be used by developers to:

(1) Understand the needs raised by users.
(2) Reach agreement with users on the scope of the system and how it is to be built.
(3) Use the information represented in the model as a basis for building a traditional or intelligent software system to meet this need.

## 4. Conceptual Models in Software Engineering

Conceptual modeling takes a pre-eminent place in the discipline of SE. This has heightened in recent years, as the importance attached to the software development requirements specification phase has grown [28].

A wide variety of markedly different CMs has been defined in the discipline of SE. Firstly, the underlying *ontology* of all these CMs is very diverse. Ontology means the type of problem domain concepts that each CM is capable of representing [29]. In this respect, the CMs in SE range from models like the state transition diagram [1], which can represent only changes of state over time, to models like KAOS [30], which can represent a huge amount of both static (entities, relations, etc) and dynamic (goals, processes, etc) aspects of the problem domain.

Secondly, the intermediate representations, also known as *builders*, used by the different CMs, that is, the set of notations and symbols used by each CM to describe a given domain, is also very diverse. There are graphic-type models, such as are used by the object diagrams [31–33]; languages, such as are used by TELOS [34]; or models that combine graphic and informal representations, like the DFD [35], for which process specifications have to be created, normally using natural language text.

Taking into account the diversity of the approaches to conceptual modeling in SE, this section will be divided into two parts to assure a clearer discussion of the different models.

The first part will refer to what can be termed "classical" CMs. The oldest and most widely used models in SE, like SADT [36], DFD [35], object diagrams [31–33] or state transition diagrams [1], were termed classical models. The main characteristic of this type of models is how limited their ontologies are, that is, the fact that they can be used to represent a relatively small number of concepts about the problem domain. Individual classical CMs will not be discussed, as they are very well known. Instead, a description of groups of models will be given, classified according to the similarity of their respective ontologies.

The second part of this section will be devoted to a set of models developed during the 90's, which, unlike the classical CMs are characterized by having powerful ontologies that can be used to describe novel aspects, like goals, agents, etc. This set of models, called "advanced" CMs, include TELOS [34], KAOS [30], EM [37] and $i^*$ [38]. They will be discussed according to the strategy they have used to extend their capability of representation beyond the classical CMs.

There are no good reviews of the CMs which will be discussed. Therefore, readers are referred to the original references for more details. However, the papers by Wieringa [39], which investigates the structured, that is, functional, and object-oriented methods, and by Davis [1], which explains at length the classical approaches to conceptual modeling in SE and offers several illustrative examples, are recommended reading.

## 4.1. *Classical conceptual models in Software Engineering*

As discussed earlier, a wide variety of CMs have been used in the discipline of SE, most of which belong to the set termed classical CMs. The best way of examining the models belonging to this set is to group them according to their orientation, as Davis [1] did, or using the terminology of this chapter, depending on the similarity of their ontologies. The groups defined thus are as follows:

- *Functional* CMs, whose paradigm is the DFD [35]. This kind of models describes the transformations of the data used in the problem domain.

The transformations are described by means of the *process* concept, which receives an input data-set and generates an output data-set.

- *Object-oriented* CMs, whose utmost representatives are object diagrams [31–33] and use cases [40]. However, use cases should, strictly speaking, be considered as functional CMs. Object-oriented CMs describe the objects or object classes and the interrelations between them in the problem domain.
- *State-oriented* CMs, including state transition diagrams [1]. These CMs describe the configuration of objects, facts, phenomena, etc on the problem domain, and the changes produced in this configuration along time.

Classical CMs have several advantages and serious drawbacks. This kind of models allows the modeler to express many things about the problem to solve, but they allow expressing only a partial view of the problem domain, that is, each kind of CMs is specialized in representing a set of facts about the problem domain. For example, let's consider the (canonical) problem of organizing a conference (this example will be used in further sections). We can model this problem using the utmost representatives of each above-mentioned group, that is, DFD, object diagrams and state-transition diagrams, as it is shown in Figs. 2, 3 and 4, respectively.

Functional models (in the case of Fig. 2, DFD) show the processes that transform input data into output data (for example, the generation of the "Conference program" using the "Papers" and "Sessions" data). Nevertheless, this kind of

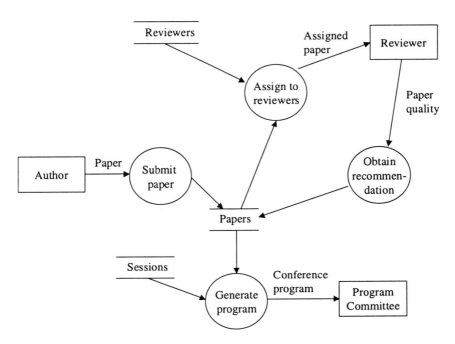

**Fig. 2.** DFD for the conference problem.

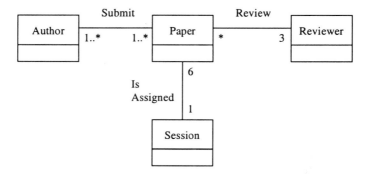

**Fig. 3.**   Object diagram for the conference problem.

models cannot express any other information, as the data structure, or the ordered sequence of events that occur in the conference organization.

For representing data, entity-relationship [41], object-role [42] or object-oriented CMs can be used (although it is not very strict, several authors, as Davis [1], consider that entity-relationship and object-role models belong to the object-oriented CMs group). Figure 3 shows an object-oriented CM built using the UML notation. It is clear that, using object diagrams, it is impossible to express something like a data transformation (for doing this, it is needed to include *methods* in the object diagram, which is a controversial topic due to such an introduction makes the model harder to understand). Object-oriented cannot express time-ordered sequences of events, as DFD cannot either.

The sequence of events in time can be expressed by means of a state transition diagram, as show in Fig. 4. Nevertheless, this model provides a partial view of the problem again, because data structure or data transformations are hidden behind

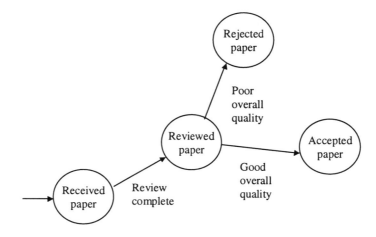

**Fig. 4.**   State-transition diagram for the conference problem.

the states and transitions of the diagram. In short, classical CM, as it was shown in the examples, possess enough power to express situations they are intended to, but it is impossible to improve their representation capabilities far from their frame of validity. For obtaining better results in the modeling activity, it was needed to define new CMs, which are introduced in next section.

## 4.2. *Advanced conceptual models in software engineering*

As specified earlier, the characteristic of a classical CM is that it can describe a given set of concepts in the client and/or user domain. For example, a DFD can be used to describe only the transformations that take place in the domain, whereas an object diagram can be used to describe the types of objects, as well as their interrelations.

Such a process of conceptual modeling has two drawbacks. Firstly, only a small set of domain concepts can be described, where the limit is established by each individual CMs capability of representation. Taking all the CMs used in SE as a whole, for example, the most important concepts that they can be used to describe are: inputs, outputs, processes, agents, data, objects, relations, states and transitions.

Secondly, as a result of the above, more than one CM, each of which describes partial aspects of the domain, has to be used at the same time to faithfully describe the problem domain. For example, structured approaches are characterized by using three CMs together [43]: a process model, built using DFD; a data model, usually described by means of a entity-relationship model, and a control model, based on the state transition diagram. Although the structured approach is a paradigmatic example, the joint use of different CMs is also a common feature of other approaches, like object-oriented methods, for example. Thus, object diagrams, DFD and state transition diagrams are all used together in OMT [31], whereas UML employs use case diagrams, object diagrams and other type of representations like interaction diagrams [44]. Nevertheless, CMs can be used together when it is not possible joining them in just one CM. For example, light is described in two ways in physics: as particles or as waves. Both representations are incompatible, that is, one of them excludes the other. Therefore, it is not possible to join them in just one single model, but they both are needed for understanding the essence and behaviour of light.

The advanced CMs emerged as a means of surmounting the above-mentioned drawbacks. For this purpose, these models include richer and more powerful mechanisms of representation. Advanced CMs employ two different strategies to improve their capability of representation:

- Enriching the CM ontology, that is, increasing the number of concepts covered by the above models. This means that they can represent novel concepts, which the classical CMs could not represent, like goals, dependencies, constraints, rules, etc.

- Defining extendible ontologies, that is, allowing the user of the CM to define the type of concepts to be represented. This means that the CMs can be extended and adapted depending on the domain and problems in question.

These two improvements do not operate simultaneously, that is, advanced CMs use only one of the two strategies. Indeed, the possibility of extending and adapting concepts that a CM can represent makes it possible to simulate any other model type, irrespective of the number of concepts covered. The two strategies and the advanced CMs that implement them are described below.

### 4.2.1. *Enriching the ontology*

There are two possible mechanisms for enriching the ontology underlying a CM. The first is to broaden the concepts that can be represented by a CM, defining special-purpose builders that represent the above concepts. The second is to define a *meta-model*, that is, a generic structure on the basis of which to build individual CMs. The following two sections describe each of the above mechanisms.

### 4.2.1.1. Definition of special-purpose builders

The first of the above-mentioned mechanisms has been the most commonly used for defining new CMs. This mechanism entails increasing the number of concepts that can be described by a model by adding new builders to the model. Each new builder represents a given concept. Also, semantics, that is, an interpretation, must be defined for each new builder by means of which its meaning can be unambiguously understood.

By way of an example, suppose that we want to represent processes in an entity-relationship diagram. The easiest, albeit not a very strict, solution would be as follows.

(1) Define a new builder, called "process".
(2) Define a graphic notation for the above builder. For example, a pentagon could symbolize the "process" builder.
(3) Define semantics for the builder. The semantics could be similar to the process semantics in a DFD. The semantics would involve the "process" transforming the data. The necessary input data are obtained from the entities or model attributes. The output data are also entities or attributes.

Figure 5 shows an example of the entity-relationship model, modified as described above, which shows how the process "Assign session to paper" would be described in a conference or workshop domain. In this figure, the static perspective has been described by means of the classical symbols of entity-relationship models. Using this diagrammatic convention, we can express that each session

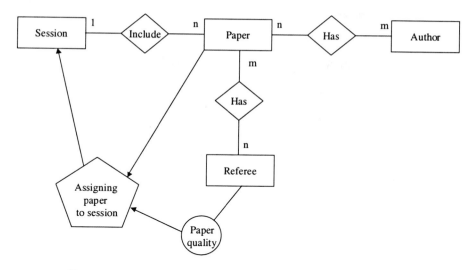

**Fig. 5.** Entity-relationship model modified to represent processes.

includes several papers, and each paper is written by several authors and has several reviewers. The new builder, symbolized by a pentagon, allows us to express a dynamic perspective, that is, the process of assigning a paper to a session once we assure it has the required quality.

Introduction of new concepts and builders has been the mechanism used in the $i^*$ advanced CM. $i^*$ (which stands for Distributed Intentionally) was originally defined in [38]. This CM can be used to describe how different actors in a domain depend on others to achieve their objectives, as well as to specify the internal motivations by which they are guided. The actors are obviously not people — they are entities that operate autonomously and have their own internal dynamics. $i^*$ is composed of two different and complementary sub-models: the Strategic Dependency Model (SDM) and the Strategic Rationale Model (SRM).

SDM can be used to describe a set of *dependencies* among actors. When there is a dependency between two actors, one depends on the other to achieve a goal, perform a task or get a resource. The actor that provides the means for satisfying the dependency is termed *depender*. The actor that is benefited when the dependency is satisfied (or harmed, otherwise) is termed *dependee*.

$i^*$ makes a distinction between four types of dependencies: *goal dependency*, where one actor depends on another to reach a given state or assure that a given condition is met [45]; *task dependency*, where one actor depends on another to be able to perform a given activity; *resource dependency*, where one actor depends on another to get any physical utility, like a tool, or logical utility, like information of some kind; and, finally, *soft-goal dependency*, which is similar to a goal dependency, except that there is no "*a priori*" procedure for determining whether or not the goal is attained.

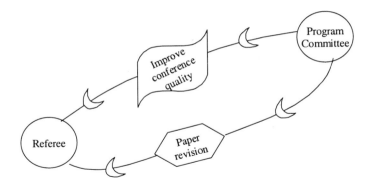

LEGEND

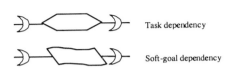   Task dependency

Soft-goal dependency

**Fig. 6.**   Example of the use of soft goals in $i^*$.

For example, soft-goal dependency arises when a conference programme committee asks referees to select the best papers. "Select the best papers" is a goal that can be attained to a greater or lesser extent rather than in absolute terms. Figure 6 shows how the above example would be represented in $i^*$, using its associated graphic notation.

SRM can be used to describe the reasoning or internal motivation of each actor. The above description is carried out in relation to the dependencies of each actor on other actors, albeit from the private viewpoint. This means that the description is made within the internal province of each actor, which is called *actor boundary* and is not shared with the other actors. The SDM and SRM are, therefore, strongly interrelated: SDM describes the goals shared by a set of actors, whereas SRM describes which mechanisms are brought into play by each actor to achieve its own goals.

### 4.2.1.2. Definition of meta-models

The second mechanism for enriching the ontology of a CM involves explicitly defining a meta-model. A meta-model is the description of the concepts that can be represented by a CM. Figure 7, for example, presents a simple meta-model for the DFD.

As shown in Fig. 7, the meta-model is (usually) described similarly to the entity-relationship diagram. This sort of description can be used to specify what the model

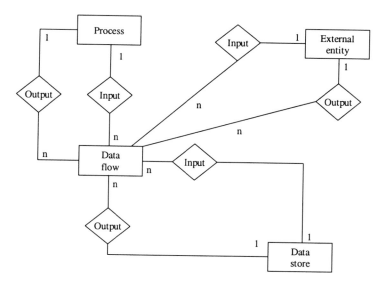

**Fig. 7.** DFD meta-model.

components (diagram entities), and the relations between these builders (relations between diagram entities) are. The meta-model shown in Fig. 7 briefly indicates that data flow diagrams are composed of "processes", "data stores", "external entities" and "data flows". Additionally, it also indicates, using the relations "input" and "output", that the processes, stores and external entities generate (output relation) and receive (input relation) data flows. Nevertheless, Fig. 7 does not include all the aspects for describing DFDs, such as, for example, the permitted connections (an external entity cannot be directly linked with a data store) or the decomposition of processes into subprocesses.

If a meta-model is defined, it is possible to distinguish between the levels at which modeling takes place, which are used unconsciously in practice. These are the *meta-level*, which defines the concepts that a given CM is capable of recording; the *domain-level*, at which the concepts of the meta-level are instantiated using specific information about a domain; and, finally, the *instance-level*, at which a distinction is made between each of the possible domain-level occurrences [46].

These three levels are shown graphically in Fig. 8, using a DFD. As above, this DFD represents the organization of a hypothetical conference. In the upper side of the figure, the META-level symbols and rules appear. These symbols and rules are the highest level of model abstraction, and they state what facts, at the domain level, the model can express. The DOMAIN-level, in the middle of Fig. 8, is what we usually know as a "model", that is, a meaningful combination of symbols with meaning, which follows the rules defined at the META-level. The INSTANCE-level, in the bottom side, is the lowest level of abstraction and it is never considered in practical modeling.

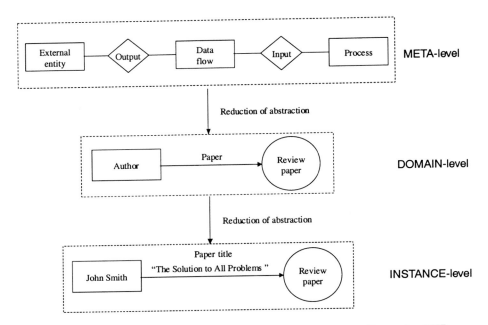

**Fig. 8.**   Meta, domain and instance levels for the conference problem using DFD.

Two advanced CMs that explicitly use the meta-model concept are: KAOS (Knowledge Acquisition in autOmated Specification), originally defined by Lamsweerde [30] and described at length by Dardenne [47], and EM (Enterprise Modeling), described by Kirikova [37]. Figure 9 presents a simplification of the KAOS meta-model, which is described with more or less evident adaptations of entity-relationship diagrams. Although it introduces different concepts, the EM meta-model is also defined as a complex network of interrelations similar to the KAOS meta-model.

KAOS and EM can be used to represent both static and dynamic aspects of a domain. This is achieved by explicitly including builders for entities and relations in the meta-model, for example, apart from builders for processes or activities. Additionally, both models introduce novel concepts, like goal, agent or constraint, which did not exist in the classical models and are very useful in the CM. This becomes perfectly clear from comparing the meta-model shown in Fig. 9 with the meta-model for the data flow diagram presented in Fig. 7.

The notation used by the two CMs is complex, and a complex algebraic definition can even be provided for KAOS. Therefore, it is a better idea to illustrate the use of these CMs with an example rather than giving the notation. The example again models a conference using KAOS. This model is illustrated in Fig. 10.

For the sake of clarity, Fig. 10 shows the meta-level, plus the domain-level, making it easier to interpret. A more extensive example using KAOS is given in [48], where it is also shown how this CM can co-exist with $i^*$.

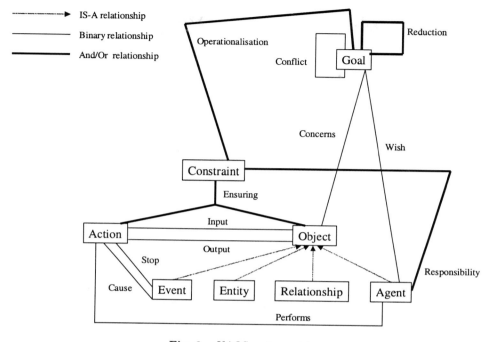

**Fig. 9.** KAOS meta-model.

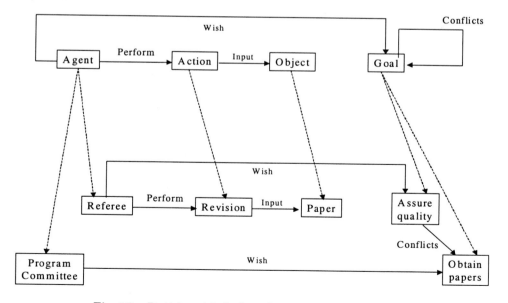

**Fig. 10.** Partial model of a hypothetical conference in KAOS.

### 4.2.2. *Extendible ontologies*

The use of fixed ontologies, even especially rich ones, always has the drawback of them not being able to encompass the wealth of concepts and shades of meaning that actually exist in the real world. For example, suppose that we need to model the control of an industrial furnace. Suppose, also, that control involves keeping the furnace within a temperature range, above which there is a danger of explosion. Again using KAOS, the set of concepts discussed could be modeled as indicated in Fig. 11.

There is no doubt that an important concept in the above problem definition is *risk*. This is due to the fact that an explosion of the furnace, for example, could lead to financial losses or even to the loss of human lives. However, as KAOS does not explicitly account for the concept of risk, there are only two possible actions during modeling:

(1) Obviate the above concept, as we did in Fig. 11.
(2) Ascribe the concept of risk to a pre-existing model builder. It would be ascribed on the basis of some relationship of similarity between the concept to be represented and the meaning of the model builder.

Generally, most classical or advanced models that have fixed ontologies take action (2). Ascribing domain concepts to model-specific builders involves creating

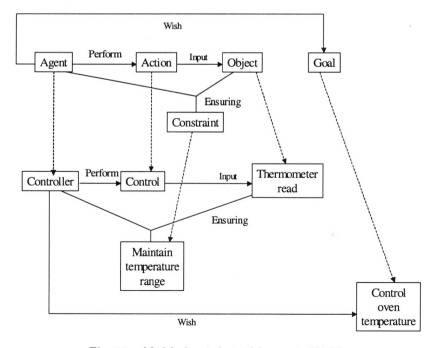

**Fig. 11.**   Model of an industrial furnace in KAOS.

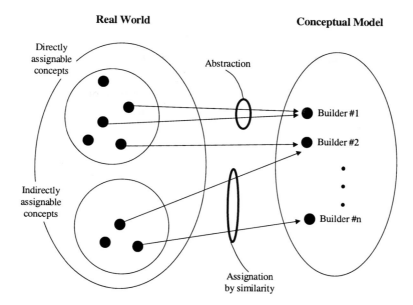

**Fig. 12.** Modeling using a CM having a fixed ontology.

an injection rather than a bijection from the real world to the CM. Some shades of the real-world meaning are inevitably lost in this way, as shown in Fig. 12.

This loss of knowledge is not due to an abstraction, as one might think at first glance. Abstraction means that two (or more) different objects, facts, phenomena, etc of real world are considered in the model as similar, due to the important properties to the modeler are perceived as similar. Nevertheless, when there exists objects, facts, phenomena, etc in the real world that the modeler cannot assign univocally to a concept in the model, but these objects, are important to the problem in question, modeler should decide how to register such information. This decision is a trade-off among several alternatives, any of them losing some information (perhaps important) about the real world. The trade-off usually ends in assigning the object, fact, phenomena, etc to the more similar concept available in the model.

One mechanism for solving the above-mentioned problem is to make provision for defining the type of builders to be used for each individual problem. This means that the CM is "reinvented" in each modeling process and adapted to the problem in question.

TELOS (from the Greek $\tau\epsilon\lambda o\varsigma$, which means purpose, end) [34] falls within this group. TELOS is a model whose main builder is the class. As in object orientation, a class is an abstraction by means of which to group a set of real-world elements under one name.

TELOS permits the classical object-oriented operations on classes: aggregation, classification and inheritance. Additionally, rules and constraints, which represent

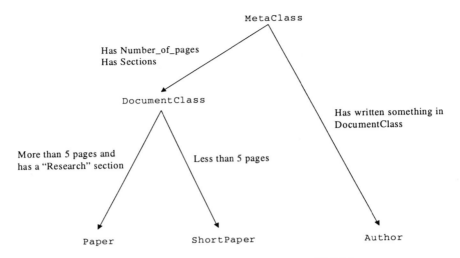

**Fig. 13.**   Definition of a new ontology in TELOS.

invariants, preconditions, postconditions or deductive rules that are applied to the instances of different classes, can also be specified in predicate logic.

Extendibility is determined by the possibility of building a specific model, using predefined classes of TELOS, including the predefined class `MetaClass`. The mechanism used is similar to the creation of a specialization hierarchy. The root of the hierarchy is the class `MetaClass`, whereas the terminal classes provide the concepts for modeling. An example of the above hierarchy is illustrated in Fig. 13.

Unlike a specialization hierarchy, however, the child classes are instances rather than a refinement of the parent classes. This is an important difference, as the child classes can be defined by entering the constraints on parent class attributes. Defined thus, classes can be used as first-order objects to model individual problems.

Any sort of CM can be defined by means of a mechanism for creating extendible ontologies. A definition of SADT [36], for example, is given in [34], and TELOS was used in practice to build some models within the ESPRIT-II NATURE project [49].

## 5. Conceptual Models in Knowledge Engineering

As discussed above, conceptual modeling plays just as an important role in KE as it does in SE, since it is the activity by means of which to define expert problem-solving behaviour and is the essential starting point for entering the above behaviour into a knowledge-based system (KBS).

There are several approaches to modeling knowledge: Problem-Solving Methods (PSM), ontologies and Knowledge-Based Systems (KBS) development methodologies. In this chapter, all we address are methodologies, since PSMs cannot be considered as techniques for building CM, the main goal of this chapter.

Additionally, the CMs for ontologies can be regarded as part of the CMs for KBS, whose construction is covered by the development methodologies.

KBS development methodologies explicitly address the definition of CMs [50–52]. Unlike SE, where, as discussed in the preceding section, the most commonly used CMs are relatively simple, the CMs in KE are fairly rich and complex, recording a huge number of concepts about the problem domain. All the methodologies described divide the CM into three different representation levels, aimed at proposing an order in which concepts should be acquired. These CM representations, or knowledge levels, are referred to slightly differently depending on the methodology in question. We will use the following terminology in this chapter:

- **Strategy models.** Strategy models identify and describe the task performed by the expert in order to carry out a given job. Additionally, they identify the (sub)tasks resulting from the decomposition of each main task, as well as the order in which the above (sub)tasks have to be performed, when they have to be executed and under what conditions. Although, owing to the slight differences between the methodologies, it is risky to generalize, the goal of this sort of models could be said to be to describe the task hierarchy, which, at a given level of decomposition, is simple enough to be implemented by a PSM or an *ad hoc* method, built especially for the case in question. This strategic level is called *task level* in other papers.
- **Reasoning models.** Reasoning models are used to represent the reasoning that the system is to carry out to perform the (sub)tasks represented in the task model, specifying which sorts of domain knowledge are required for each reasoning step and what knowledge is gained as a result of the above reasoning. This level is also sometimes termed *inference level*.
- **Domain models.** Domain models represent the domain structure, which has to be known to make inferences and execute tasks. Domain models are the static part of the CM, whereas the strategy and reasoning levels make up the dynamic part of the model.

In the following, we will analyze the CMs used by the KE methodologies, focusing attention on how each knowledge level of the expertise model is described. We will actually describe the following modeling languages: CML [53, 54], linked to CommonKADS [50], KARL [55, 56], linked to MIKE [52], and MODEL [57], linked to PROTÉGÉ-II [51]. These languages have special builders for each knowledge level.

## 5.1. *Domain level*

All the above methodologies describe the structural aspects of the problem domain at the domain level. These methodologies structure this knowledge level around the concepts of classes of objects and relations, like SE object-oriented models do. However, the syntax and nomenclature varies from KE to SE and even from one

KBS development methodology to another. Thus, for example, classes are called *concepts* in CML [53, 54], whereas they are termed *frames* in MODEL [57] and are referred to as *classes* only in MIKE [55, 56]. Each of these languages also presents other builders for modeling other aspects of reality. Although the aspects they aim to model are basically the same, there are, as for classes, some differences in the nomenclature and representation methods.

Apart from concepts and relations, CML has the following builders [6].

- Attributes that define concepts.
- Structures that are concepts that the modeler does not want to describe in detail at any given time.
- Expressions that can be used to define domain constraints and axioms. These expressions can be used to define set membership, set inclusion, relationships of order or equality between attribute values, etc. For example, one cannot be one's own supervisor.

Apart from classes and relations, MIKE also includes the following for defining the domain level [55].

- Attributes to define concepts.
- Formulas by means of which to define any constraints there are in the domain, like expressions in CML.

MODEL can be used to represent the domain concepts by means of a builder called frame [57]. A series of slots can be defined for each frame, which describe the attributes that describe the concept. Constraints on the values of the attributes can also be defined by means of a builder, called facet. The relations in MODEL must be defined as frame-type attributes; that is, a definition closer to the symbolic than the conceptual level.

Both CML and KARL [54, 55] have a graphic notation that is very similar to the one used by object languages, such as shown in Fig. 14. Rectangles symbolize classes of object, and lines symbolize relations (inheritance relation is allowed, and it is symbolized by a triangle, as show in Fig. 14).

Note that the three languages represent classes and their attributes, relations between them and constraints, although each has its particularities. Only CML has an additional element, structure, by means of which to indicate when a class has not yet been fully defined.

### 5.2. *Reasoning level*

The static domain concepts are not enough to define how an expert behaves when solving problems, as they do not include the reasoning required to yield new facts, conclusions, etc, on the basis of the existing knowledge represented at the domain level. Therefore, the goal of the reasoning level is to explicitly define the reasoning to be pursued to solve the KBS target problem, that is, the inferences can be made

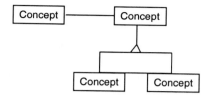

**Fig. 14.** Graphic notation used by CML and KARL.

using the domain knowledge and the knowledge roles that model inference input and output.

CML has two builders for modeling the reasoning level [6], which are as follows.

- The basic inferences, known as sources of knowledge. CML sets apart a group of special basic inferences: transfer functions. These inferences represent the operations of communication with the outside of the system.
- The metaclasses or roles that participate in the inferences as inference input or output.

MIKE has the same builders, but makes a distinction between several types of roles [56]:

- Views: supply an inference with domain knowledge.
- Stores: model the data flow dependencies among inferences.
- Terminators: are used to give the final results.

An example of the diagram of the two languages is given in Fig. 15, where roles or metaclasses are symbolized as rectangles, and inferences or knowledge sources as ovals. The rationale behind this figure is to show that in CommonKADS and MIKE roles (note that terminology is different in both approaches) are the inputs required and outputs generated by the inference process.

The problem-solving method is composed of the inferences and roles, as well as the data flow dependencies between inferences, in both CommonKADS and

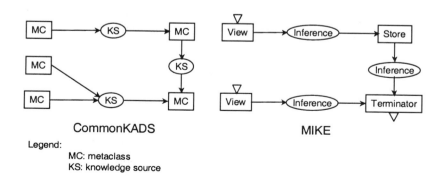

**Fig. 15.** Structure of inferences in CML and KARL.

MIKE [52]. At the conceptual level, these two languages define which inferences and which knowledge roles are required to solve the problem. However, they do not specify how this reasoning is done. This means that they specify what PSM to use. However, a PSM is not detailed at the conceptual level. It is a design or computational model, as mentioned above.

In PROTEGE-II, the reasoning level has a slightly different structure than in CommonKADS or MIKE. In these two methodologies, the reasoning level contains the allowed inferences. These inferences are related to domain knowledge, in one side, and to a PSM, in the other. In PROTEGE-II, there exists not the "inference" concept. The relationship between domain knowledge and PSM is implemented using the "mapping relations" concept [58], instead. A mapping relation is a translation that makes possible the PSM to use the knowledge of the domain level.

### 5.3. *Strategy level*

The basic inferences represented at the reasoning level along with their input and output knowledge are not enough to solve the KBS target problem. The basic inferences indicate the reasoning to be carried out. However, they make no reference to the control of this reasoning, that is, how the above basic inferences are to be sequenced to solve the problem. There are several courses of action and several inferences applicable at any one time in a somewhat complex domain, which means that they have to be controlled to arrive at the right solution.

The goal of the strategy level, therefore, is to identify and define the sequence of valid actions in the problem domain, controlling the number and type of inferences that are to be made.

The structure of the strategy level of the three languages is illustrated similarly using a decomposition tree [6, 58, 59]. The tasks that appear at the bottom of the tree are basic inferences in CML and KARL and mechanisms in MODEL, as shown in Fig. 16. They are described at the reasoning level. This is all as far as task decomposition is concerned.

As far as the sequence in which these basic inferences or mechanisms are executed is concerned, that is, task control, this is defined in all three languages using similar builders to 3rd generation programming languages (selections, repetitions, sequences and assignations), although each language has its own syntax.

### 5.4. *Relationship between the knowledge levels*

The languages described may appear to represent different facets of reality separately, but this is not the case. The elements or, better still, knowledge that is represented at the domain level is used to define the inferences. The roles of the reasoning level are covered by domain level concepts or classes. The strategy level is also related to the inference level, as the subtasks are no longer divided. They are basic inferences and are described at the reasoning level. This relationship is illustrated in Fig. 17.

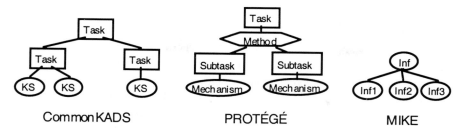

Legend:
Inf: inference
KS: knowledge source

**Fig. 16.** Decomposition of the task in each language.

The above sections discussed the CMs used in the disciplines of SE and KE. In the following, we will discuss several issues that generally affect all the above-mentioned CMs. The common features of all the methods of conceptualization will be discussed in Sec. 6, and a series of problems pointed out by several researchers concerning the above methods of conceptualization will be specified in Sec. 7. This chapter will conclude by discussing an approach to conceptual modeling that can solve the above-mentioned problems in Sec. 8.

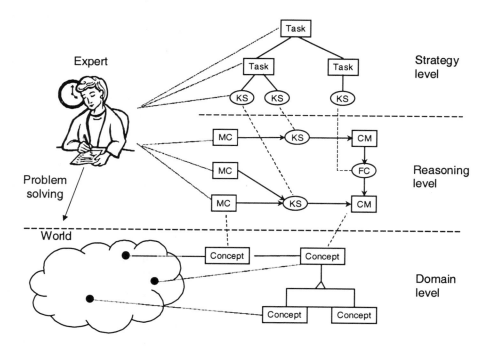

**Fig. 17.** Interrelationship of the CM knowledge levels.

## 6. Similarities between Software Engineering and Knowledge Engineering Conceptual Models

The classical and advanced models used in the disciplines of SE and KE were described above. Taken as a whole, the general impression we get is that the CMs used by the two disciplines have things in common. Indeed, as we said earlier, the disciplines of SE and KE have influenced each other, and some of the concepts created in one discipline have been absorbed to a greater or lesser extent by the other.

Generally, all the approaches described, except for the oldest methods used in SE, that is, function models and state-oriented models, can be said to have two common characteristics:

- As a general rule, the ontology underlying the set of formalisms and languages is based on the concepts of classes and relations. This is only logical considering that they have to represent the structure of the real world.
- Concepts like agent, goal, rule or constraint are used extensively. These concepts can be used to model many aspects of the problem domain.

These concepts are much more patent in some models than in others. For example, the object-oriented models explicitly include objects and relations as builders, as do TELOS and all the KE languages described. However, the representation formalism used by each individual model can make the above concepts more or less apparent. It is very easy to identify the objects and relations in TELOS, for example, and a bit more difficult in MODEL. As far as the concepts of goal, agent, rule or constraint are concerned, their use is confined to the KE languages and advanced SE models, and it is more difficult to identify the above concepts in the classical SE models. There are exceptions, however: the concept of agent or "actor" is used in use cases, whereas some constraints can be specified by means of pre- and post-conditions in some object-oriented approaches, as is advocated by Eiffel [33].

There are several reasons for the existence of the above-mentioned characteristics. The first is the need to represent the problem domain more objectively and in more detail to ease its understanding and make for a more efficient development process. The above need is felt in both SE and KE and is causing the CMs to evolve, gradually becoming more powerful and having greater capability of representation.

The second reason is the realization that the CMs used in each discipline are insufficient and that it can be beneficial to include concepts from other disciplines. This is especially patent in SE, which has borrowed concepts from other disciplines for its CMs. Some have been added directly and without adaptation, as was the case of data models. Others, like the concepts of goal, agent or constraint, were adopted only partially.

The fact that there are influences and common characteristics indicates that all the disciplines are converging, as the use of common concepts implies that there is some uniformity between the methods of conceptual modeling. Nonetheless, it is clear that we still have not reached the point of developing CMs that can be shared by disciplines and we are even further away from single formalisms, which could be used simultaneously in SE and KE.

Despite the mutual influence of one method on another, the dearth of such "interchangeable" models indicates that any sort of total unification of conceptual modeling concepts between the disciplines of SE and KE is still a long way off. Indeed, each discipline is like an island, whose only means of communication are glass bottles thrown into the water.

Nonetheless, the reasons for this isolation are not to be found in the individual characteristics of each discipline, the particular problems they solve or the methods and tools they use. The reason underlying the diversity of conceptualization methods is due to each one being linked to a given software development approach. This approach or computational paradigm restricts the possibility of using the conceptual modeling method in other settings apart from the one for which it was specifically designed. The following section addresses this idea in more detail.

## 7. Limitations of the Current Approach to Conceptual Modeling

The CMs now used in SE and KE are conditioned by computational constraints proper to given development approaches, that is, they are more like prescriptive or computational models (CpM) than CM, which, as mentioned above, are characterized by being user oriented.

The criticisms of the conceptualization methods go in two directions. The first refers to the orientation of the conceptualization methods, stressing the fact that most CMs are oriented to getting a computational solution to the problem or need raised and not to easing the understanding of the user need. The second point refers to the association between CMs and specific approaches to software development. Here, the use of a given CM during the early phases of the development process limits the number of possible implementation alternatives and means that only the options that are compatible with the CM used originally are feasible. The above-mentioned problems are discussed in more detail below.

### 7.1. *Computational orientation of the methods of conceptual modeling*

Many of the CMs are oriented to providing a computational solution to the problem raised in the user domain. This orientation to the solution is necessitated by the fact that the representations of the different CMs include computer-related concepts. Several researchers have pointed out that conceptualization methods suffer from this limitation, mainly in the object-oriented community, as the following:

- It is argued that object-oriented methods are a "natural" representation of the world. Nevertheless, this idea is a dangerous over-simplification [60].

- Object-oriented analysis has several shortcomings, most important in being target-oriented rather than problem oriented [11].
- Object-oriented analysis techniques are strongly affected by implementative issues [10].

There are authors that extend the critics to other models, too. For example, M. Jackson argues that:

- DFD's are vague pictures suggesting what someone thinks might be the shape of a system to solve a problem, but they do not say what the problem is [61].
- There exists no theory of how a model relates to the real world [62].

Thus, for example, the data flow diagrams are clearly guided by functions, key components of structured software and, likewise, the models used in object-oriented analysis lead directly towards software developed by means of classes, objects, messages, polymorphism, etc — basic concepts of object-oriented software. On the other hand, the CMs used in KE are oriented to heuristic problem solving, proper to experts. The problem with including computational considerations within the CM is that the software or knowledge engineer is forced to make a solution-oriented decision during the early development phases, when the problem to be solved is still not well enough understood. This means making design decisions when not all the variables relevant to the problem are known. Engineers thus run the risk of making the wrong decision because they are not in possession of all the information. This has quality-related implications for the final software product [63].

### 7.2. *Association between conceptual models and development approaches*

If computational characteristics are included in CMs, these are linked to a particular implementation approach, that is, once a given conceptualization method has been selected to describe the problem domain, it is practically impossible to change the above method "*a posteriori*" without having to re-analyze the problem. This has also been stressed by several researchers:

- The use of a CM during analysis defines nearly univocally how the design shall be done [64].
- Perhaps the most difficult aspect of problem analysis is avoiding software design [1].
- It is sometimes mistakenly believed that the structures produced during analysis will and should be carried through in design [65].
- The boundaries between analysis and design activities in the object-oriented model are fuzzy [66].
- The software system development approach is preconditioned by the CM used [67].

Owing to this limitation, for example, if data flow diagrams have been used to model the problem domain, it will almost certainly be necessary to use the structured method in later development phases; a method of object-oriented development will have to be used following upon an object-oriented analysis. Similarly, if the problem has been conceptualized in KE, it will be practically impossible to use a SE development method if it is discovered that the knowledge level does not call for a knowledge-based system.

Therefore, if we intended to switch development paradigms, that is, for example, pass from a data flow diagram to an object-oriented design, this transformation would lead to an information gap very difficult to fill. This gap between CMs and CpMs is caused by the fact that each CM acts like a pair of glasses used by the engineer to observe the domain and user reality. These glasses highlight certain features, tone down others and hide others. Once the real world has been filtered through the CM, it is difficult to retrieve anything that has been lost or condensed, even if this information is required by the CpM. The only way of recovering the features lost in the CM filter is to reanalyze reality using a different pair of glasses; that is, to repeat the operation using another CM. This situation has already been discussed by authors like Coleman [68], Champeaux [69] or Wieringa [70], who address the incompatibility between the CMs used in the structured approach and object-oriented CMs, owing to the conceptual difference between the elements used in the two approaches.

Despite this limitation, some attempts have been made to derive object-oriented models from structured models [71–73]. However, the guidelines proposed are confined to mere heuristics, which are not applicable in all cases. Moreover, Henderson-Sellers [64] claims that the reverse transformation is impossible and even that any transformation of structured models to object-oriented models would be partial and indirect.

Additionally, these switches from a CM of one approach to a CpM of another paradigm, even if they were possible, are not usually feasible in practice in view of the time and cost constraints and size of projects nowadays. Mostly, the CMs used are those with which developers are familiar, called for by individual standards or even, as specified by Mylopoulos [74], the models that are "in fashion". So, in the era when the structured approach was in vogue, techniques such as DFDs were used for conceptual modeling, whereas, today, with the rise of object-oriented programming and design, techniques like object diagrams, interaction diagrams, etc are employed.

Finally, the software system development approach can be said to be preconditioned from the very start, when the CMs are built. Moreover, excepting trivial problems, this precondition means that the development approach is chosen before the user need has been understood, which is the job of conceptual modeling.

## 7.3. *An alternative solution*

Due to all the above-mentioned conceptual modeling problems, it can be said that, on the one hand, CMs have to be brought closer to users, using a language that they can understand, which will improve validation. On the other, they need to include all the information required about the problem for developers to later address the software system that is to solve the problem. Indeed, it is necessary to define conceptualization methods that meet the following formal criteria of adjustment:

(1) Understanding the need raised by the user before considering an approach for developing a software system that meets this need.
(2) The understanding of the need must be independent of the chosen problem-solving approach, that is, it must not precondition the use of any development approach.
(3) Having criteria for deciding which is the best development approach once the user need has been understood.

These criteria can only be met by redefining the conceptual modeling process as now carried out in SE and KE. The only way of redefining this process is by taking into account that, as specified earlier, the software development process is related to both the user needing space and the machine space of the software, that is, to meet the need raised by the above user, as shown in Fig. 18.

This double relationship means that first it is not feasible to build any sort of CM without always taking into account the fact that the end purpose of the development is to build a software product. Second, and as mentioned earlier, it is not advisable to bring design-related issues into the conceptual modeling stage.

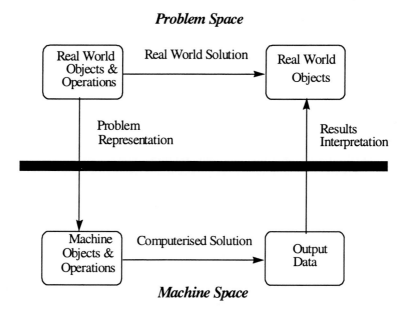

**Fig. 18.** Problem space vs machine space.

Therefore, the only solution is to redefine what are considered to be two different moments in conceptual modeling. The first moment is oriented to the problem, where the attention focuses on customer and/or user needs. The second moment is oriented to the system, where implementation alternatives must start to be considered. These two moments define the conceptual modeling approach presented in the following section.

## 8. Conceptual Models as Separate From Computational Models

Traditionally, as mentioned above, conceptualization methods have been conditioned by computational constraints. The proposed solution seeks to bring the conceptual modeling process closer to the user domain. Figure 19 shows this approach, where conceptual modeling is composed of two activities: need-oriented modeling and software system-oriented modeling. The need-oriented modeling process is directly linked to the user need and is independent of the chosen development approach. On the other hand, the software system-oriented modeling is dependent on the development approach and is, therefore, further removed from the user need.

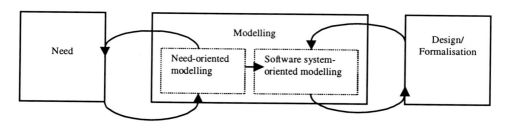

**Fig. 19.** Tasks of a development process with generic CMs.

The goal of need-oriented modeling is to give the software or knowledge engineer an understanding of the procedure used by an expert to solve a problem, and/or, the needs of the users. The software or knowledge engineer, therefore, needs to know what the need is and how it is satisfied in the user's world. So, this need will have to be outlined in a CM, which does not precondition the use of any development approach. This model will be termed generic CM to distinguish them from the CMs used today. Generic CMs would benefit the development process as follows [10]:

- Independence between conceptual modeling and subsequent development phases, that is, the possibility of carrying out analysis before choosing a given development approach.
- Independence from the computer system, that is, the possibility of using conceptual modeling results for developing software using any of the possible development approaches.

- Independence from evolving technology, that is, the possibility of the same modeling approach being valid even if the form of software development is modified.

During the software system-oriented modeling process, the software engineer has to select the best current development approach (structured, object-oriented, knowledge-based, database, etc), or any other approach that could be discovered in the future, for building the software that is to meet the above need, depending on the features of the generic model. The software engineer may opt to adopt different approaches for different parts of the system. Therefore, a set of heuristics have to be defined to determine what would be the best approach for computationally solving a specific need.

Having selected the best suited development approach, the traditional models used by each approach (data flow diagrams, object models, rules, etc) have to be derived, models which, as mentioned above, are characterized by their computational bonds. In order to promote this process of transformation, a set of rules will be required for deriving each of the most commonly used CpMs, like object-oriented or structured development models, from the generic CM. Figure 20 describes the possible products to be outputted during problem analysis.

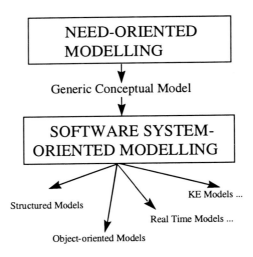

**Fig. 20.** Proposed conceptual modeling process.

## 9. Conclusions

In this chapter, we have outlined the state of the art in the field of conceptual modeling in SE and KE. Although there are considerable differences in the number and type of CMs in each discipline, the underlying concepts they use all clearly converge. These are: first, object-oriented concepts from the discipline SE; and second, goal, belief or intention, from the discipline of KE. Obviously, the above-mentioned convergence is not due to any effort at standardization, but to the permeability of the different disciplines, which have managed to take the best from the others.

However, although the current state of the field could be rated as satisfactory, owing to the number and wealth of formalisms used, quite a few researchers who point out a series of shortcomings in all the CMs used. These shortcomings can be divided into two types. Firstly, the modeling formalisms and languages still include too many computational, that is, implementation-related, considerations concerning the concepts they handle, artificially limiting how the problem domain can be described. Secondly, the use of a given representation formalism obliges software or knowledge engineers to adopt a given development approach, as ensues precisely from the inclusion of the above-mentioned implementation-related considerations.

Therefore, apart from outlining the state of the field of conceptual modeling, an approach has been proposed in this chapter, whose goal is to overcome the shortcomings of the conceptual modeling methods. The main characteristic of this approach is the division of modeling (called analysis in SE or conceptualization in KE) into two different and separate phases. The first phase is problem oriented and is characterized by the use of a generic CM. The second phase is solution oriented, and the formalisms to be used are prescriptive, including the computational considerations proper to a given development approach.

# References

1. A. M. Davis, *Software Requirements: Objects, Functions and States* (Prentice-Hall International, 1993).
2. B. J. Wielinga, A. Th. Schreiber and J. A. Breuker, "KADS: A modeling approach to knowledge engineering", *Knowledge Acquisition* **4**, no. 1 (1992).
3. R. Motschnig-Pitrik, "The semantics of parts vs aggregates in data/knowledge modeling", *Proceedings of the CAiSE'93, Lecture Notes in Computer Science 685* (Springer-Verlag, Paris, France, June 1993).
4. A. Borgida, "Knowledge representation, semantic modeling: Similarities and differences", *Entity-Relatioship Approach: The Core of Conceptual Modeling*, ed. H. Kangasalo (Elsevier Science Publishers B.V., 1991).
5. J. Mylopoulos, A. Borgida and E. Yu, "Representing software engineering knowledge", *Automated Software Engineering*, no. 4 (1997).
6. G. Schreiber, H. Akkermans, A. Anjewierden, R. de Hoog, N. Shadbolt, W. van de Velde and B. Wielinga, *Knowledge Engineering and Management: The CommonKADS Methodology* (MIT Press, 1999).
7. J. Ares and J. Pazos, "Conceptual modeling: An essential pillar for software quality development", *Knowledge-based Systems*, no. 11 (1988).
8. M. Boman, J. A. Bubenko, P. Johannesson and B. Wangler, *Conceptual Modeling* (Prentice Hall Series in Computer Science, 1997).
9. J. D. McGregor and T. Korson, "Object oriented design", *Communications of the ACM* **33**, no. 9 (1990).
10. F. Bonfatti and P. D. Monari, "Towards a general purpose approach to object-oriented analysis", *Proceedings of the International Symposium of Object Oriented Methodologies and Systems*, Palermo, Italy (1994).

11. G. M. Høydalsvik and G. Sindre, "On the purpose of object oriented analysis", *Proceedings of the Conference on Object Oriented Programming, Systems, Languages and Applications*, New York, USA (1993).

12. J. Hoppenbrouwers, B. van der Vos and S. Hoppenbrouwers, "NL structures and conceptual modeling: Grammalizing for KISS", *Data and Knowledge Engineering* **23**, no. 1 (1997).

13. L. Adelman and S. L. Riedel, "Handbook for evaluating knowledge-based systems", *Conceptual Framework and Compendium of Methods* (Kluwer Academics Publisher, Boston, 1997).

14. B. Biébow and S. Szulman, "Acquisition and validation of software requirements", *Knowledge Acquisition*, no. 6 (1994).

15. A. Aadmodt and M. Nygård, "Different roles and mutual dependencies of data, information and knowledge — An AI perspective on their integration", *Data and Knowledge Engineering*, no. 16 (1995).

16. N. Juristo, "Guest editor's view", *Knowledge-Based Systems*, no. 11 (1998).

17. *Webster's New Encyclopedic Dictionary* (Könemann, Cologne, 1994).

18. R. Wieringa, *Requirements Engineering: Frameworks for Understanding* (Wiley, Chichester, 1995).

19. B. I. Blum, *Beyond Programming. To a New Era of Design* (Oxford University Press, New York, 1996).

20. ANSI/X3/SPARC, "Study group on data base management systems", Interim Report 75-02-08 (1975).

21. J. J. van Griethuysen, "ISO — concepts and terminology for the conceptual schema and the information base", N695, ISO/TC9/SC5/WG3 (1982).

22. D. Beringer, "Limits of seamless in object oriented software development", *Proceedings of the 13th International Conference on Technology of Object Oriented Languages and Systems (TOOLS)*, Versailles, France (1994).

23. P. Loucopoulos and V. Karakostas, *Systems Requirements Engineering* (McGraw-Hill, Berkshire, 1995).

24. H. Kaindl, "Difficulties in the transition from OO analysis to design", *IEEE Software* **16**, no. 5 (1999).

25. A. Newell, "The knowledge level", *Artificial Intelligence*, **18**, no. 1 (1982).

26. W. J. Clancey, "The knowledge level reinterpreted: Modeling socio-technical environments", *International Journal of Intelligent Systems* **8**, no. 1 (1993).

27. M. Kolp and A. Pirotte, "An aggregation model and its C++ implementation", eds. M. E. Orlowska and R. Zicari, *Proceedings of International Conference on Object Oriented Information Systems (OOIS'97)* (Springer-Verlag, Australia, 1997).

28. J. Siddiqi, "Challenging universal truths of requirements engineering", *IEEE Software* **11**, no. 2 (1994).

29. Y. Wand, "A proposal for a formal model of objects", eds. W. Kim, F. H. Lochovsky, *Object-Oriented Concepts, Databases, and Applications* (ACM Press and Addison-Wesley, 1989).

30. A. Lamsweerde, A. Dardenne and F. Dubisy, "The KAOS project: Knowledge acquisition in automated specification of software", *Proceedings of the AAAI Spring Symposium Series*, Stanford University (March 1991).

31. J. Rumbaugh, *Object-oriented Modeling and dDesign* (Prentice-Hall, 1991).

32. P. Coad and E. Yourdon, *Object Oriented Analysis* (Yourdon Press, 1990).

33. B. Meyer, *Object Oriented Software Construction* (Prentice-Hall, 1988).

34. J. Mylopoulos, A. Borgida, M. Jarke and M. Koubarakis, "TELOS: Representing knowledge about information systems", *ACM Transactions on Office Information Systems* **8**, no. 4 (1990).

35. T. DeMarco, *Structured Analysis and System Specification* (Prentice-Hall, 1979).
36. D. T. Ross, "Structured analysis: A language for communicating ideas", *IEEE Transactions on Software Engineering* **3**, no. 1 (1977).
37. M. Kirikova and J. A. Bubenko, "Enterprise modeling: Improving the quality of requirements specification", Information Systems Research Seminar in Scandinavia, IRIS-17, Oulu, Finland (1994).
38. E. Yu, "Modeling strategic relationships for process reengineering", PhD Dissertation, Department of Computer Science, University of Toronto (1995).
39. R. Wieringa, "A survey of structured and object-oriented software specification methods and techniques", *ACM Computing Surveys* **30**, no. 4 (1998).
40. I. Jacobson, *Object-oriented Software Engineering: A Use Case Driven Approach* (Addison-Wesley Object Technology Series, 1994).
41. P. Chen, "The entity-relationship model: Towards a unified view of data", *ACM Transactions on Database Systems* **1**, no. 1 (1977).
42. J. R. Abrial, "Data semantics", *Data Base Management* (North-Holland, Amsterdam, 1974).
43. E. Yourdon, *Structured Analysis* (Yourdon Press, 1989).
44. G. Booch, I. Jacobson and J. Rumbaugh, *The Unified Modeling Language* (Addison-Wesley, 1999).
45. G. Agha, *Actors: A Model of Concurrent Computation in Distributed Systems* (MIT Press, Cambridge, MA, 1986).
46. H. Nissen, M. Jeusfeld, M. Jarke, G. Zemanek and H. Huber, "Managing multiple requirements perspectives with metamodels", *IEEE Software* **13**, no. 2 (1996).
47. A. Dardenne, A. Lamsweerde and S. Fickas, "Goal-directed requirements acquisition", *Science of Computer Programming* **20** (1993).
48. E. Dubois, E. Yu and M. Petit, "From early to late requirements: A process-control case study", *Proceedings 9th Int. Workshop on Software Specification and Design*, Isobe, Japan (1998).
49. M. Jarke, J. Bubenko, C. Rolland, A. Sutcliffe and Y. Vassiliou, "Theories underlying requirements engineering: An overview of NATURE at genesis", Technical Report NATURE-93-01 (1993) (*ftp://ftp.informatik.rwth-aachen.de/pub/NATURE/*).
50. A. Schreiber, B. J. Wielinga, R. de Hoog, H. Akkermans and W. van de Velde, "CommonKADS: A comprehensive methodology for KBS development", *IEEE Expert* **9** (1994).
51. W. E. Grosso, H. Eriksson, R. W. Fergerson, J. H. Gennari, S. W. Tu and M. A. Musen, "Knowledge modeling at the millennium (The design and evolution of Protege-2000)", SMI-1999-0801 Report (1999).
52. J. Angele, D. Fensel and R. Studer, "Domain and task modeling in MIKE", *Domain Knowledge for Interactive System Design* (Chapman & Hall, 1996).
53. A. Anjewierden and G. Schreiber, *CML2 syntax* (2.2.1).
    *http://www.swi.psy.uva.nl/projects/kads22/cml2doc.html*.
54. B. J. Wielinga and A. T. Schreiber, "Conceptual modeling of large reusable knowledge bases", eds. K. von Luck and H. Marburger, *Management and Processing of Complex Data Structures* (Springer-Verlag, Berlin, Germany, 1994).
55. D. Fensel, *The Knowledge Acquisition and Representation Language KARL* (Kluwer Academic, 1995).
56. D. Fensel, J. Angele and R. Studer, "The Knowledge acquisition and representation language KARL", *IEEE Transactions on Knowledge and Data Engineering* **10**, no. 4 (1998).
57. J. H. Gennari, "A brief guide to MAÎTRE and MODEL" (1993) (http://smi-web.stanford.edu/projects/protege/nextstep/maitre/MaitreIntro/MaitreIntro.html).

58. J. H. Gennari, S. W. Tu, T. E. Rothenfluh and M. A. Musen, "Mapping domains to methods in support of reuse", *International Journal of Human-Computer Studies* **41**, no. 3 (1994).

59. J. Angele, D. Fensel and R. Studer, "Developing knowledge-based systems with MIKE", *Journal of Automated Software Engineering* **5**, no. 4 (1998).

60. S. McGinnes, "How objective is object-oriented analysis?" *Proceedings of the CAISE'92 Advanced Information Systems Engineering* (1992).

61. M. Jackson, *Software Requirements and Specifications. A Lexicon of Practice* (Addsion-Wesley, 1995).

62. M. Jackson, "Will there ever be software engineering?" *IEEE Software* **15**, no. 1 (1998).

63. A. Davis, K. Jordan and T. Nakajima, "Elements underlying the specification of requirements", *Annals of Software Engineering* (Balzer Engineering Publishers, 1997).

64. B. Henderson-Sellers and J. Edwards, "The object oriented systems life cycle", *Communications of the ACM* **33**, no. 9 (1990).

65. P. Jalote, *An Integrated Approach to Software Engineering* (Springer-Verlag, 1997).

66. L. M. Northrop, "Object-oriented development", *Software Engineering* (IEEE Computer Society Press, Los Alamitos, USA, 1997).

67. N. Juristo and A. M. Moreno, "Introductory paper: Reflections on conceptual modeling", *Data and Knowledge Engineering*, no. 33 (2000).

68. D. Coleman, P. Arnold, S. Bodoff and C. Dollin, *Object-Oriented Development: The Fusion Method* (Prentice-Hall, 1994).

69. D. Champeaux, D. Lea and P. Faure, *Object Oriented System Development* (Addison-Wesley, New York, 1993).

70. R. Wieringa, "Object-oriented analysis, structured analysis, and Jackson system development", eds. F. van Assche, B. Moulin and C. Rolland, *Proceedings of the IFIP WG8.1 Working Conference on the Object-Oriented Approach in Information Systems* (North-Holland, 1991).

71. P. Ward and S. Mellor, "How to integrate object orientation with structured analysis and design", *IEEE Software* **6**, no. 2 (1989).

72. F. Y. Kuo, "A methodology for deriving an entity relationship model based on a data flow diagram", *Journal of Systems and Software* **24**, no. 2 (1994).

73. J. George and B. Carter, "A strategy for mapping from function-oriented software models to object oriented software models", *Software Engineering Notes* **21**, no. 2 (1996).

74. J. Mylopoulos, L. Chung and E. Yu, "From object-oriented to goal-oriented requirements analysis", *Communications of the ACM* **42**, no. 1 (1999).

# PATTERN-BASED SOFTWARE RE-ENGINEERING

WILLIAM C. CHU

*Department of Computer Science and Information Engineering,*
*TungHai University, Taichung, Taiwan, ROC*
*E-mail: chu@csie.thu.edu.tw*


CHIH-WEI LU, CHIH-HUNG CHANG and YEH-CHING CHUNG

*Department of Information Engineering, Feng Chia University,*
*Taichung, Taiwan, ROC*
*E-mail: {cwlu, chchang}@soft.iecs.fcu.edu.tw*

Most of legacy systems were designed in traditional way with inflexible architecture. Due to improper representations or designs, they are very difficult to understand and maintain. As a result, maintaining these legacy systems is very costly. The objective of software re-engineering is to re-structure or re-write legacy systems into new systems with better maintainability, flexibility, and scalability. Design patterns (DPs) have integrated successful standard design practices and expert experiences into a set of components that exhibit known behaviors with better structures. Re-engineering legacy systems into pattern-based systems not only decreases the cost of further software evolution but also increases their reusability. In this paper, pattern-based technologies will be surveyed. The problems of re-engineering legacy systems into pattern-based systems will then be discussed. The evaluation of the effectiveness of our re-engineering approach through real case studies will be presented.

*Keywords*: Re-engineering, legacy system, design pattern, reuse, maintainability.

## 1. Introduction

There still exist many *legacy systems* in organizations. These organizations rely on the "legacy systems" to provide critical information and support business operations. Most of the legacy systems were designed in traditional way with inflexible architecture. Due to improper representations or designs, they are very difficult to understand and maintain. As a result, maintaining these legacy systems is very costly. Studies have shown that nearly 80% of all software resources were allocated to maintaining existing systems [12]. Software maintenance and software evolution involve the identification or discovery of program requirements and design specifications which are helpful in understanding, modifying, and adding features to the old programs. The tasks of software re-engineering include the recovery and the recording of high level information about the system structure, functionality, dynamic behavior, and design rationale. Besides, software re-engineering reconstructs a better model and re-implements a system with improved maintainability.

767

Therefore, maintaining well re-engineered software systems is much more cost effective.

*Patterns* facilitate reuse of well-established solutions when known problems are encountered. They support higher abstraction levels of reuse than traditional object-oriented individual classes and instances [10]. Design patterns (DPs) [10] have integrated successful standard design practices and expert experiences into a set of components that exhibit known behaviors with better structures. DPs are considered as one of the most forward-looking methods for the modern system analysis and design [5, 25]. They provide not only a common base for better communication among software engineers, but also increase the reusability and productivity for both forward engineering and re-engineering. Instead of continually maintaining legacy systems in their original architecture and design at high cost, re-engineering them to new systems with good design and architecture can significantly improve their understandability, reusability and maintainability. Therefore, re-engineering legacy systems into pattern-based systems not only decreases the cost of further software evolution but also increases their reusability.

Software re-engineering is a systematic way of "examination and alteration of a subject system to reconstitute it in a new form and the subsequent implement of the new form" [11]. The objective of software re-engineering is to re-structure or re-write legacy systems into new systems with better maintainability, flexibility and scalability [16].

The rest of this article is organized as follows. Section 2 gives an overview about pattern-based software technologies. The issues of re-engineering legacy systems into pattern-based systems will be discussed in Sec. 3. Section 4 shows the experiments of our proposed approach. Comparison and evaluation of the proposed approach are described in Sec. 5. Section 6 summarizes the conclusions and future work.

## 2. Pattern-based Software Engineering

Like component reuse, pattern reuse covers the process of representation, retrieval, adaptation and integration of reusable patterns.

*Patterns* are recognizable traces or blocks found in a series of observations or in a system. We can observe familiar usages and constructions during a system design, which are called *"Design Patterns (DPs)"*. What is a design pattern precisely? Alexander *et al* [2] described, "Each pattern describes a problem which occurs over and over again in our environment, and then describes the core of the solution to that problem, in such a way that you can use this solution a million times over, without ever doing it the same way twice". The objective of DPs is to enable designers to easier reuse well-known and successful designs and architectures from experts' experience. Expressing proven techniques as design patterns makes them more accessible to developers of new systems. DPs help you choose design alternatives that make a system reusable and avoid alternatives that compromise reusability. DPs can even improve the documentation and maintenance of existing systems by furnishing an explicit specification of class and object interactions and their underlying intent. Put simply, design patterns help a designer get a design "right" faster [10].

## 2.1. *The representation and classification of design patterns*

Properly documenting, representing and classifying design patterns can improve the effectiveness of their usages. In 1992, Coad [25] stated seven patterns applied in OOA and OOD. Gamma *et al* [10] collected 23 design patterns and categorized these patterns into three classes: *Creational Patterns, Structural Patterns* and *Behavioral Patterns*. Their works provide a very handy reference book for software designers, particularly for beginners.

Other researchers have tried to enhance the classification and their semantic relationships of DPs. Zimmer [33] identified three semantically different layers: (1) basic design patterns, (2) design patterns for typical software problems, and (3) application domain specific patterns. Tichy [33] categorized over 100 general-purpose DPs into nine catalogues: *decoupling, variant management, state handling, control, virtual machines, convenience patterns, compound patterns, concurrency* and *distribution*.

Grand [10] presented 41 DPs that help users create more elegant and reusable designs and categorized these DPs into six classes: *Behavioral, Structural, Concurrency, Creational, Fundamental* and *Partitioning Patterns*. In 1999, he presented other 50 new patterns immediately [11], and differentiated those into six categories: *GRASP* [4] *Patterns, GUI Design Patterns, Organizational Coding Patterns, Code Robustness Patterns* and *Testing Patterns*. Agerbo and Cornils [9] presented a new design patterns classification method to discriminate Gamma's DPs into three kinds: *Fundamental Design Patterns* (FDP), *Language Dependent Design Patterns* (LDDP) and *Related Design Patterns* (RDP). Noble [18] classified DPs using two level relationships, the primary relationships are: *uses, refines and conflicts*, and secondary relationships are: *used by, refined by, variant uses, similar, combines, requires, tiling* and *sequence of elaboration*. Mikkonen [28] presented a formal design patterns description and tried to compose existing DPs and describe DP interrelationships in behavioral level formally.

## 2.2. *The retrieval of design patterns*

The effectiveness of retrieving design patterns is strongly related to their representation and classification. Unfortunately, not many researches have been focused on this area. The retrieval of design pattern involves the selection of a set of components, which is much more complicated than the traditional software components retrieval. However, this is an important issue that needs to be studied.

## 2.3. *The adaptation and integration of design patterns*

Most of the design patterns contain generic structures/behavior that need to be adapted to different applications. Each application may involve more than one design pattern at different levels of the system. Most of the approaches to solve the problems of adaptation and integration of design patterns are manual approaches. Cooper [20] showed how to use DPs in Object-Oriented programming. In [7], Nguyen implemented a data structure like binary search tree and a linked list using design patterns. Riehle [8] used class diagrams and role diagrams to help designers focus on the collaborations and distributions of objects using DPs. Mikkonen [28] tried to formalize DPs so that rigorous reasoning can be applied to ensure the consistency of behavior during the adaptation and integration.

## 2.4. *The higher-level of design patterns*

In most researches for *pattern-based engineering*, DPs only play a partial supporting role in the development process. It is suggested that DPs not only should be treated as an assistant wizard on the data-level, code-level, and design-level, but also should be extended to the architecture-level. For instance, the *Model/View/Controller* (*MVC*) triad of classes is used to build user interfaces in Smalltalk-80 [13]. The MVC model is a framework that contains high level DPs that handle the similar problem domain dealing with multiple views applications. Lacking global consideration, DPs can only offer limited assistance within system re-engineering.

## 3. Pattern-based Re-engineering

*Re-engineering* [11] has been treated as an effective solution for software maintenance. Compared with re-designing a system from scratch, re-engineering legacy systems can reduce the risk of malfunctions of original systems and the cost of maintenance.

In OO technologies, classes and objects provide basic building blocks for the software development. In this paradigm, *component reuse* usually focuses only on *data-levels* or *code-levels*. This low level reuse limits the software reusability and also creates the complexity of the components integration. For example, two integrated components may be syntactically consistent but semantically inconsistent which will cause an extra overhead to the reuse process.

On the other hand, as combining successful standard design practices and expert experiences into a set of inter-related components that exhibit known behaviors with better flexible structures, DPs can provide more high-level design semantics than segments of codes. Software development with DPs provides easier understanding and standardization that make the system evolution much more effective. DPs can be treated as a *design-level* reuse which offers a higher-level reuse by encapsulating related architecture or algorithm. However, they are still lacking in *architecture-level* reuse.

To apply pattern-based re-engineering into legacy systems, three questions must be considered. The first one is *how to recover DPs from program segments* (*semantics*). Identifying DPs from source codes or architecture is not easy because programming styles vary with different programmers. Although there are some studies [3, 17, 19, 26] about identifying design patterns from source codes automatically, most of them only work on special cases or on structural levels.

The second question is *the DP mapping problems*, i.e., reverse engineering source codes into corresponding DPs. Currently most of automatic or semi-automatic tools only offer very limited functionality on this problem [17]. Manual approaches are still the main stream. However, the results come out very promising [30].

The last question is *to define a suitable target architecture*, which is aimed to be re-engineered into. The properties of the target system should be predefined before the re-engineering, e.g. whether it should contain the attributes of flexibility, scalability or high reusability, etc. To make sure the flexibility, scalability and substitutability on both horizontal and vertical layers of the system, our target system uses the *Horizontal and Vertical N-tier* (*HVN-tier*) *architecture*, as shown in Fig. 1. N-tier architecture is to overcome the not enough flexibility of 2/3 tier models [1, 24, 27], such as CORBA [24], when they are applied at higher degree of complexity and heterogeneity computing [15]. As an extension of 3-tier architecture, N-tier architecture can model more complex relationships of cooperative components than 2/3 tier models.

### 3.1. *Pattern-based re-engineering process*

The approach in our pattern-based re-engineering is described by the following steps:

(1) Recover the system architecture and object model from a legacy system. This recovery may involve collecting information from documents, domain experts and source codes; the reverse engineering may be required in this step.

(2) Define the target framework or architecture with good patterns that the legacy system plans to re-engineer into.

(3) Decompose, restructure, and classify components in the legacy system into *behavior*, *structure*, and *creation* classes, where each component is classified into either behavioral, structural, or creational pattern categorized in Gamma, *et al*'s book [10].

(4) Map function/object components in the object model of the legacy system into patterns.

(5) Re-engineer components in the legacy system into patterns. In order to demonstrate and confirm the promises made by pattern based re-engineering, a set of comparative experiment cases will be discussed in the next section.

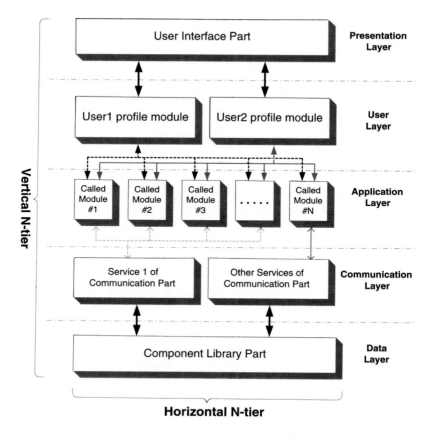

**Fig. 1.**  The horizontal and vertical *N*-tier (HVN-tier) architecture.

## 4. Experiments of Pattern-based Re-engineering

In order to experiment the design pattern based re-engineering, we have selected
the Parallel Program Generation Environment (PPGE) [29] as the experiment system. PPGE was designed to offer a semi-automatic environment to the generation
of parallel programs for solving partial differential equations (PDEs) on distributed
memory computing environments, especially for clusters of workstations and parallel machines with wormhole-routed interconnection networks. The PPGE consists
of the Graphical User Interface (GUI) package, the algorithm package and a set
of different parallel computation models. However, it is costly in maintenance and
is difficult to extend with third party solutions and algorithms. Furthermore, it
lacks the run-time reconfiguration capability which is necessary to optimize the
parallel solution. Moreover, PPGE is a standalone system, not a web-based system,
which keeps PPGE from offering services to multiple users and multiple domains.
Re-engineering PPGE into a system with the above missing features and a better
model can greatly improve the process of parallel programming.

## 4.1. *The design recovery of PPGE*

Process modeling and conceptual modeling are initial and crucial software development activities for both software engineering and knowledge engineering [34, 36]. In this experiment, the design recovery of PPGE is mainly based on documents, knowledge from designers and related papers [29], and source codes. In this phase, first of all, PPGE is decomposed into subsystems, then the behavior, architecture, and properties of each subsystem are reverse engineered and recorded. However, our pattern based reverse engineering is required to be *pattern-minded*, i.e., the recovery of DP related information is the major focus. Fortunately, the guideline of DP related information could be found from Gamma, *et al*'s book [10]. And the most of PPGE information can be collected from published papers [29] or technical reports, while incomplete information can be revealed from source codes. The more DP related information is collected, the easier the re-engineering process become. In this case study, our implementation is mainly manual. The recovery of the PPGE system architecture is shown in Fig. 2.

## 4.2. *A target architecture — CCCD*

In this experiment, a 3-tier architecture, CCCD (Control, Communication, and Component library with Dynamic packing) is introduced. CCCD, which is a primitive of the HVN-tier architecture, exhibits the features of high reusability, easy

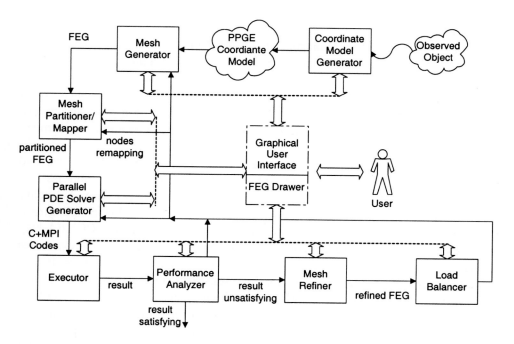

**Fig. 2.**   The system architecture of PPGE.

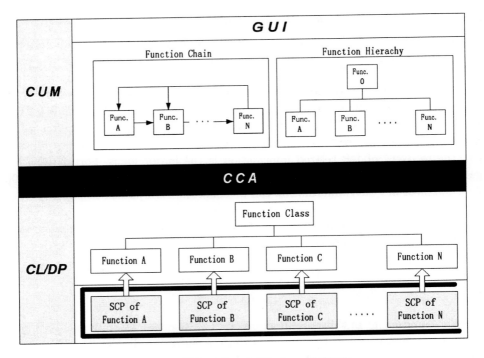

**Fig. 3.**   The system architecture of CCCD.

evolution and design-pattern based architecture. CCCD contains three major parts: Control and User-interface Management (CUM), Communication and Component Agent (CCA) and Component Library with component Dynamic Packing (CL/DP). Figure 3 shows the system architecture of CCCD. This specific architecture intends to isolate the application process and data so that the components have a low coupling and dependency among each other. Another intention is to accomplish the features of dynamic reconfiguration of software components and reuse through wrapping of legacy resources.

The implementation of CCCD is based on well-known design patterns, and this ensures the horizontal scalability while easily adding/updating modules in a tier in the future. CCCD is a 3-tier architecture that sets up a clear boundary between application processes and data resources, so they have low coupling relationships. CCCD can be figured as the integration of MVC [13] and CORBA [24]. MVC (Model/View/Controller) addresses the advantage of independency between interfaces, processes and data models. CORBA (Common Object Request Broker Architecture) is a three-tier architecture that establishes the standard for the client-server remote-accessing services. CCCD provides a higher level of abstraction than MVC by adopting the characteristics of a design pattern construction. Compared to CORBA, CCCD contains the features of an active component agent and run-time reconfiguration capability. These features greatly promote the scalability and flexibility of the re-engineered system and can be easily enhanced into an idea DNA architecture as necessary.

### 4.3. *Design pattern discovery and mapping*

The mapping/selection of right patterns to use in re-engineering is a leery and complicated task. Gamma, Helm, Johnson, and Vlisside [10] have offered a well-organized guidebook to DPs. The mapping between patterns and PPGE behavior of each subsystem is based on mapping the applicability description of patterns in Gamma, *et al*'s book [10] to the appropriate behavior characteristics that we understand and extract from PPGE.

The performance of this mapping process is quite dependent on the familiarity of design patterns. We have found the process becomes much more efficient when the process continues. We believe if these patterns have been taught in the class according to a well-defined architecture, e.g. CCCD, the re-engineering process could be very efficient and cost effective. CCCD has clearly defined the characteristics and functionalities in each layer. We try to establish mapping relationships in the layers of CUM, CCA, CL/DP with the corresponding candidate patterns. This mapping is currently accomplished with manual efforts. Table 1 shows the mapping result from our experiment in this case study.

### 4.4. *The re-implementation of the PPGE into patterns*

PPGE was implemented in C on the UNIX system which did not support interoperability and run-time configuration. The target language of this re-engineering is JAVA which has the run-time configuration capability and cross-platform interoperability. Besides, the underlined OO technologies in JAVA make the implementation of our concept and design much simpler. The most difficult task in this experiment is the actual re-engineering of codes to a new target language, in particular, the restructuring of old and bad structures in PPGE into patterns. However, the experiences from our experiments show that the process can be gradually speeded up when more and more components have been re-engineered. This also indicates that a well-structured system is much easier to re-engineer. We believe that, for a long lasting system that requires continual maintenance, the one time re-engineering cost will be easily paid back from the later maintenance. Besides, the adaptation of new functionality into a pattern-based system is much easier. For example, adding web accessibility to PPGE is very difficult before the re-engineering but becomes very easy after the re-engineering — which will be shown in the later discussion — because the implementation of new features can be done through the reuse by integrating with reusable components.

### 4.5. *The re-implementation of the CUM portion of the PPGE*

The typical process of writing parallel programs in the PPGE is similar to a transformational process. An FEG is transformed phase by phase, like a transaction, until

**Table 1.** The mapping analysis of functional features and candidate patterns in re-engineering.

| Functional/ Behavioral Features | Descriptions | Candidate Patterns | Implementations of CCCD |
|---|---|---|---|
| GUI interacting design | The complicated interactions should be eliminated with the isolation between GUI and the processing | Mediator, Builder, Observer | CUM |
| Event switching and controlling | To lower the coupling of events and the corresponding handlers | Chain of Responsibility | CUM |
| State control | To control and monitor the states of transitions of processes and the whole system | State | CUM |
| Function chain | To lower the coupling within a complex system which consists of a set of sequential subfunctions | Mediator, Command | CUM |
| Function hierarchy | To lower the coupling within a system which consists of a set of structural subfunctions | Mediator, Façade | CUM |
| Process-to process | Interactions between processes | Mediator | CUM |
| Process-to-interface | An accordant interface of processes | Template | CUM, CCA |
| Communication | To provide different communication requests with a unique interface | Mediator, Strategy, Template | CUM, CCA |
| Dynamic biding | Run-time re-configuration | Mediator, Chain of Responsibility | CCA |
| Agent services | Hide the detail of implementation and location of objects from the clients | Decorator, Adapter, Proxy | CCA |
| Process-to-data | To provide a gateway and interface for remote/local data accessing | Strategy, Proxy, Bridge | CCA |
| SCP & component management | SCP dynamic packing of components | Composite, Factory Method, Builder | CCA, CL/DP |
| A family or class of algorithms | Requests of run-time reconfigurable objects | Builder, Factory Method | CCA, CL/DP |
| Component wrapping | Provides an identical access manner to all the individual components | Command | CL/DP |

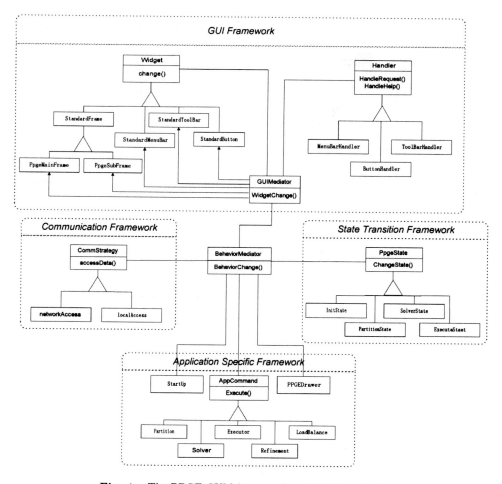

**Fig. 4.** The PPGE CUM frameworks with UML notation.

the desired optimal MPI code derived. The implementation and design of the current PPGE has tightly coupled a set of components with heavy interactions among themselves. For example, the GUI components were mixed with the components of Mesh Generator, Partitioner/Mapper, Solver, ... etc. The Mediator pattern is applied to re-construct the CUM. As shown in Fig. 4, the CUM contains a GUI Mediator and a Behavior Mediator, taking care of the GUI components interaction and the PPGE behavior respectively. To set up a clear boundary between communication tasks, processes, and service components, three frameworks are implemented — the Communication Framework, the State Transition Framework, and the Application Specific Framework.

The *Strategy* pattern is used in the Communication Framework since different parallel and distributed models of the PPGE may be used, which usually require different communication strategies. Based on the user's selection on different algorithms in each phase during the run-time, the *State* pattern is used to achieve the run-time configuration and to keep track of the status of each phase. In the Application Specific Framework, the *Command*, the *Adapter*, and the *Strategy* patterns are used. The *Command* pattern supports *undo* capability during the transaction (process). The *Adapter* pattern is applied to adapt the algorithms with unmatched interfaces. The PPGE adopts many algorithms, which were developed by many other researchers. These algorithms may require different interfaces with different formats of data. The *Adapter* pattern can bridge the differences among different algorithms. The *Strategy* pattern is used to construct a family of alternative algorithms in each phase of parallel programming in the PPGE. For some low-level implementation, the *Chain of Responsibility* pattern is also used, some examples are given in the next section. The descriptions of the applicability of the selected patterns can be found in Gamma, *et al*'s book [10].

### 4.6. *The re-implementation of CCA and CL/DP of PPGE*

While the CUM models the interaction and the process of high-level components, the CCA coordinates the services of low-level components. The most noteworthy

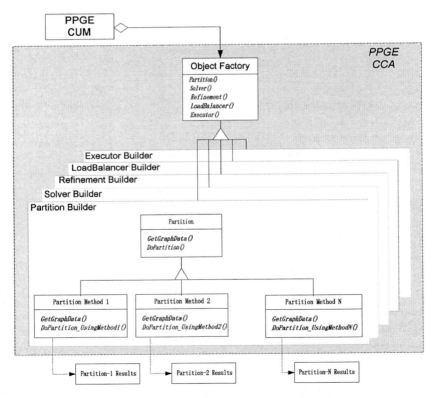

**Fig. 5.**   The PPGE CCA system model.

patterns used in the CCA are the *Factory* and the *Builder* patterns. The *Factory* pattern helps define a uniform interface for algorithms in each phase of the PPGE parallel programming process and let subclasses to decide which classes to instantiate. The *Builder* pattern is used to separate the construction of a complex object like partitioner, solver, ..., *et al*, as shown in Fig. 5, such that the components and their assembly become independent.

The CCA also provides the registration entries to the CL/DP for service index and listing. When adding new CL/DP classes or CL/DP parts into the library, or discarding some inappropriate parts, the library sends messages to update the registration of the content on the CCA. The CCA provides the transparency of dynamic re-configuration from the lower layer to the upper layer CUM. The CCA increases the independency between the CUM and the CL/DP of the PPGE.

The lowest layer of the CCCD architecture is the CL/DP. Serving as general component repository, the CL/DP offers the configurable components for the PPGE. However, it organizes these components into a set of family components where members in the same family can be substituted with each other during run-time.

## 5. Comparison and Evaluations

To evaluate the effectiveness of re-reengineering, three systems have been applied to the experiment — the original legacy PPGE, which was designed and implemented in a traditional way, UMPAL (Unstructured Mesh Partitioner and Load Balancer) [6], which is a *non-pattern-based* re-engineered subsystem from the original legacy PPGE with the feature of WWW accessibility using CGI programs, and the *pattern-based* re-engineered PPGE.

The re-engineering steps of UMPAL are as follows: (1) recover the system architecture and object model from documents, domain experts, and source codes, (2) extract reusable components from the legacy system, (3) re-implement the system into a web-based system.

Tables 2 and 3 show the detailed lines of codes (LOC) of each function in the original PPGE as well as its corresponding brief functional descriptions. The total size of the original PPGE integration programs is about 1800 LOC, which consists of seven sub-functions. Table 4 shows the detailed sizes of UMPAL.

After the pattern-based re-engineering process, the architecture of CCCD, CUM and CCA layers is independent from the integration programs. In our re-implementation, the CUM layer of PPGE is designed as a sub system consisting of seven functional modules.

Tables 5, 6 and 7 itemize the details of each module in CUM, CCA and CL/DP respectively, including their functional descriptions; sizes (LOC); the adopted design patterns; and the degree of reuse level. The degree of reuse level is an estimated value of how much code and design are being reused from the original system while implementing the target module. If the reuse value is zero, it means a new function has

**Table 2.**  The size of the integration programs of the original PPGE.

| Integration Programs | |
|---|---|
| Sub-function & Description | Size (LOC) |
| X1. Basic user interface | 488 |
| X2. Flow control | 202 |
| X3. File I/O | 93 |
| X4. Script generation | 207 |
| X5. Component algorithm dialog interface and algorithm executor | 463 |
| X6. Graphic drawer | 231 |
| X7. Environment setup | 86 |

**Table 3.**  The size of the called-component set of the original PPGE.

| Called-Component Set | |
|---|---|
| Algorithm Category & Algorithm Name | Size (LOC)* |
| Y1. Refinement | 1578 |
| Y2. Partition | 8832 |
| Y3. Load balancing | 8961 |
| Y4. Solver | 7896 |

**Table 4.**  The size of the integration programs of the original UMPAL.

| UMPAL Integration Programs | |
|---|---|
| Sub-function & Description | Size (LOC) |
| a1. Basic user interface | 485 |
| a2. Flow control | 585 |
| a3. File import/export | 383 |
| a4. Online help | 375 |
| a5. Algorithm executor | 558 |
| a6. Graphic drawer | 385 |

**Table 5.** The sizes of the CUM of the pattern-based re-engineered PPGE.

| CUM of the Pattern-based Re-engineered PPGE | | | |
|---|---|---|---|
| Sub-function & Description | Size (LOC) | Design Patterns Adopted | Reuse Level (%) |
| A1. Static user interface | 320 | • Mediator | 0 |
| A2. Flow control | 583 | • Mediator<br>• State<br>• Chain of Responsibility | 40% |
| A3. Environment setup | 112 | • Mediator | 30% |
| A4. Parser (for parsing to parameter definition of new components) | 553 | • Iterator | 0 |
| A5. Network manager | 140 | • Bridge | 0 |
| A6. Dynamic user interface | 546 | • Builder<br>• Observer | 0 |
| A7. Graphic drawer | 300 | | 80% |

**Table 6.** The sizes of the CCA of the pattern-based re-engineered PPGE.

| CCA of the Pattern-based Re-engineered PPGE | | | |
|---|---|---|---|
| Sub-function & Description | Size (LOC) | Design Patterns Adopted | Reuse Level |
| B1. Component loader | 184 | • Strategy<br>• Proxy | 0 |
| B2. Dynamic binding | 288 | • Mediator<br>• Chain of Responsibility | 0 |
| B3. SCP & component manager | 642 | • Composite<br>• Factory Method<br>• Builder | 0 |
| B4. Network access | 144 | • Bridge | 0 |

**Table 7.** The sizes of the CL/DP of the pattern-based re-engineered PPGE.

| CL/DP of the Pattern-based Re-engineered PPGE | | | |
|---|---|---|---|
| Sub-function & Description | Size (LOC) | Design Patterns Adopted | Reuse Level |
| C0. Component wrapper & SCP management | 335 | • Command | 0 |
| C1–C4 (the same as Y1–Y4 in Table 3) | — | | 100% |

been implemented from scratch. The total sizes of CUM and CCA layers are about 2550 and 1300 LOC's respectively. The experiment results match our expectation. Most of the reuse in CUM happens at the flow-control and graphical-interface re-design. On the other hand, most of modules in CCA must be re-implemented from scratch. On the contrary, the algorithm components in the lower layer are almost adopted without any changes. The notable device in this CL/DP layer is the design of *component wrapper*, which provides an identical access manner to all the individual components and this makes the features of dynamic-packing and run-time reconfiguration feasible.

Although the total cost and effort spent to construct both CUM and CCA seems to be higher than the original design, we believe that there should be even more pay back from the continual maintenances thereafter.

In order to take on the evaluation of these systems, two features are set as the criteria: *scalability* and *adaptivity*. The former is shown as the capability of range extension of services and operations. We observe this feature from the PPGE series by comparing the impact degrees raised while adding a new component option to the original and the two re-engineered versions. Table 8 shows the comparison results. In UMPAL, since it is implemented by the CGI program, a designer needs to change the flow control and algorithm executor when adding a new component. In the re-engineered PPGE in CCCD, a new component can be imported by the application; the component agent in CCA should then detect this new lodger automatically and serve it in the index through dynamic binding. We are comfortable about this cost-free advantage on the scalability promised earlier by the CCCD architecture.

The latter feature, adaptability, stands for the power of a system to evolve and/or change in order to meet future requirements. While evaluating the adaptability of adding a new subfunction into PPGE, we tried to extend PPGE into an Internet ready system. Table 9 also shows us an encouraging outcome. The

**Table 8.**   The impact analysis for system *Scalability*.

| | Adding a New Component | |
| --- | --- | --- |
| Versions | Modules that Need to be Changed | Impact Degree |
| Original PPGE | X1. Basic user interface | 65% |
| | X2. Flow control | (X1+X2+X5)/ |
| | X5. Component algorithm dialog interface and algorithm executor | (X1+X2+X3+X4+X5+X6+X7) |
| UMPAL | a2. Flow control | 41% |
| | a5. Algorithm executor | (a2+a5)/ |
| | | (a1+a2+a3+a4+a5+a6) |
| PPGE in CCCD | NIL | 0 |

**Table 9.**   The impact analysis for the system *Adaptability*.

| Network Ability Extension | | |
|---|---|---|
| Versions | Modules that Need to be Changed | Impact Degree |
| Original PPGE | X1. Basic user interface<br>X2. Flow control<br>X3. File I/O | 44%<br>(X1+X2+X3)/<br>(X1+X2+X3+X4+X5+X6+X7) |
| UMPAL | a2. Flow control | 21%<br>a2/(a1+a2+a3+a4+a5+a6) |
| PPGE in CCCD | Add a new network-access class<br>(about 20–30 LOC's) | < 1% |

only variation needed for the re-engineered PPGE is to add a tiny network-access class, which can be done by adopting the idea of *strategy* pattern, to provide the optional local/remote accessing to the different requests from the module *component loader*. CCA is already a well-balanced design for this internet/web trend.

## 6. Conclusion

Maintaining legacy systems to meet mutable organizational requirements is necessary, though usually very costly. It is impractical to discard a legacy and too risky to redesign a new replacement hastily. Re-engineering a legacy into a better system is an applicable solution. The traditional system re-engineering focuses mostly on bug fixing and new function supplement. It is less concerned about architecture restructures. However, re-engineering a legacy without the architecture refinement can only provide a partial improvement and it wouldn't last long for further environment alternations.

In this article, the concept of Design Pattern embedded software re-engineering is discussed. Design pattern is regarded as a noteworthy methodology to extend the contents of software re-engineering, from the data-level and code-level component reuse to the higher level of reuse like design-level and architecture-level. The pattern-based re-engineering reduces time of re-engineering and makes the system architecture into identical styles. It not only has the re-engineering advantages, but is also expected to reduce the total cost and increase the legacy system software life cycle.

In order to achieve a global view of pattern-based re-engineering, we introduce the HVN-tier architecture. The HVN-tier architecture can ensure the features of scalability and flexibility. In this article, we propose the processes of pattern-based re-engineering for the illustration of feasibility. We also demonstrate the advantages the HVN-tier architecture can offer through some experiments and comparisons. It does show us an encouraging outcome. With some proper enhancement and generalization, we look forward to extending the pattern-based re-engineering to re-engineer most of the existing legacy systems in industries.

At last, there are still many issues open for our further studies. For instance, most of the available design patterns are not yet formally specified, so we can only accomplish the pattern retrieval manually. Software architecture [35] is more and more an essential role in the field of software re-engineering. On the other hand, to say nothing of the idea of architecture-level reuse, it is even less mature than the reuse of design patterns. Currently we are working on the component and design pattern formalization using networking predicates. In this phase, it is necessary to involve knowledge engineering and knowledge representation. Then the *Predicate and Transition Net* [31] would be used to solve the problems of reuse integration check. The long and short of it, a tool and total solution that offers full assistance during the process of re-engineering is the ambition for scholars.

## References

1. A. Lind, "A two-tier approach to customer service", *ACM SIGUCCS XXV* (1997) 210–222.
2. C. Alexander, S. Ishikawa, M. Silverstein, M. Jacobson, I. Fiksdahl-King and S. Angel, *A Pattern Language* (Oxford University Press, New York, 1977).
3. C. Kramer and L. Prechelt, "Design recovery by automated search for structural design patterns in object-oriented software", *Proceedings of Third Working Conference on Reverse Engineering* (IEEE Computer Society Press, 1996) 208–215.
4. C. Larman, *Applying UML and Patterns* (Prentice-Hall International, Englewood Cliffs, NJ, 1998).
5. C. Larman, *Applying UML and Patterns: An Introduction to Object-Oriented Analysis and Design* (Prentice-Hall International, Englewood Cliffs, NJ, 1997).
6. D. L. Yang, J. C. Yu, C. C. Chen and Y. C. Chung, "UMPAL — An unstructured mesh partitioner and load balancer on world wide web", *Proceeding of the Sixth National Computational Fluid Dynamics Conference* (1999) 136–143.
7. D. Nguyen, "Design patterns for data structure", *Proceedings of the Twenty-Ninth SIGCSE Technical Symposium on Computer Science Education* (ACM Press, 1998) 336–340.
8. D. Riehle, "Describing and composing patterns using role diagrams", *Proceedings of the 1996 Ubilab Conference* (1996) 137–152.
9. E. Agerbo and A. Cornils, "How to preserve the benefits of design patterns", *Proceedings of the OOPSLA'98* (ACM Press, 1998) 134–143.
10. E. Gamma, R. Helm, R. Johnson and J. Vlissides, *Design Patterns: Elements of Reusable Object-Oriented Software* (Addison-Wesley Publishing Co., Reading, MA, 1994) 1–86.
11. E. J. Chikofsky and J. H. Cross, "Reverse engineering and design recovery: A taxonomy", *IEEE Software* **7**, no. 1 (1990) 13–17.
12. E. Yourdon, "RE-3: Re-engineering, restructuring and reverse engineering", *American Programmer* **2**, no. 4 (1989) 3–10.
13. G. E. Krasner and S. T. Pope, "A cookbook for using the model-view controller user interface paradigm in Smalltalk-80", *Journal of Object-Oriented Programming* **1**, no. 3 (August/September 1988) 26–49.

14. G. Odenthal and K. Quibeldey, "Using patterns for design and documentation", *Proceedings of 11th European Conference on Object-Oriented Programming* (1997) 511–529.
15. H. Steiert, "Toward a component-based n-Tier C/S-Architecture", *Proceedings of ISAW'3* (ACM Press, 1998) 137–140.
16. I. Sommerville, *Software Engineering*, 5th ed. (Addison-Wesley Publishing Co. Inc., Wokingham, England, 1996) 660–663, 700–703.
17. J. Bansiya, "Automating design pattern identification", *Dr. Dobb's Journal of Software Tools* **23**, no. 6 (June 1998) 20–22, 24, 26, 28.
18. J. Noble, "Classifying relationships between object-oriented design patterns", *Proceedings of Australian Software Engineering Conference*, IEEE Computer Society, (1998) 98–109.
19. J. Seemann and J. W. Gudenberg, "Pattern-based design recovery of Java software", *Proceedings of the ACM SIGSOFT Sixth International Symposium on Foundations of Software Engineering* (ACM Press, 1998) 10–16.
20. J. W. Cooper, "Using design patterns", *Communication of ACM* **41**, no. 6 (1998) 65–68.
21. L. Prechelt, B. Unger and M. Philippsen, "Documenting design patterns in code eases program maintenance", *Proceedings ICSE Workshop on Process Modeling and Empirical Studies of Software Evolution* (1997) 72–76.
22. M. Grand, *Patterns in Java*, Vol. 1 (John Wiley & Sons, Inc., New York, 1998).
23. M. Grand, *Patterns in Java*, Vol. 2 (John Wiley & Sons, Inc., New York, 1999).
24. OMG, "The common object request broker: Architecture and specification", Updated July 1996, Object Management Group, Formal Document 97-02-25, *http://www.omg.org*
25. P. Coad, "Object-oriented patterns", *Communication of ACM* **35**, no. 9 (1992) 152–159.
26. P. Tonella and G. Antoniol, "Object oriented design pattern recovery", *Proceedings of the International Conference on Software Maintenance*, IEEE Computer Society (1999).
27. R. Orfali, D. Harkey and J. Edwards, *Instant Cobra* (John Wiley & Sons, Inc., 1997).
28. T. Mikkonen, "Formalizing design patterns", *Proceedings of International Conference on Software Engineering'98* (IEEE Press, 1998) 115–124.
29. W. C. Chu, C. W. Lu, C. H. Chang, C. J. Liao and Y. C. Chung, "A parallel program generation environment for solving PDEs on distributed memory computing environments", *Proceedings of Eleventh International Conference on Software Engineering and Knowledge Engineering*, SEKE (June 17–19, 1999) 267–272.
30. W. C. Chu, C. W. Lu, J. P. Shiu and X. He, "Pattern based software reengineering: A case study", *Journal of Software Maintenance* **12**, no. 2 (2000) 121–141.
31. W. C. Chu, C. W. Lu, H. Yang and X. He, "A formal approach to component retrieval and integration", *Journal of Software Maintenance* **12**, no. 5 (September/October, 2000).
32. W. F. Tichy, "A catalogue of general-purpose software design patterns", *Proceedings of Tools-23: Technology of Object-Oriented Languages and Systems* (IEEE Press, 1997) 330–339.
33. W. Zimmer, "Relationships between design patterns", *Proceedings of PloP'94* (1994).
34. O. Dieste, N. Juristo, A. M. Moreno, J. Pazos and A. Sierra, "Conceptual modelling in software engineering and knowledge engineering: Concepts, techniques and trends", *Handbook of Software Engineering and Knowledge Engineering*, Vol. 1 (World Scientific Publishing, 2001).

35. R. Kazman, "Software architecture", *Handbook of Software Engineering and Knowledge Engineering*, Vol. 1 (World Scientific Publishing, 2001).

36. S. T. Acuña, A. Antonio, X. Ferré, M. López and L. Maté, "The software process: Modelling, evaluation and improvement", *Handbook of Software Engineering and Knowledge Engineering*, Vol. 1 (World Scientific Publishing, 2001).

# RATIONALE MANAGEMENT IN SOFTWARE ENGINEERING

ALLEN H. DUTOIT

*Technische Universität München, Institut für Informatik, Munich, Germany*
*E-mail: dutoit@in.tum.de*


BARBARA PAECH

*Fraunhofer Institute for Experimental Software Engineering,*
*Sauerwiesen 6, D-67661 Kaiserslautern, Germany*
*E-mail: paech@iese.fhg.de*

In this chapter, we motivate and describe the use of rationale knowledge during software development. Rationale methods aim at capturing, representing, and maintaining records about why developers have made the decisions they have. They improve the quality of decisions through clarification of issues and their related tradeoffs. Moreover, they facilitate the understanding and reevaluation of decisions, which is an important prerequisite for managing change during software development. While there are several approaches for dealing with rationale knowledge, the systematic integration of rationale into software engineering processes and tools has yet to happen.

In this chapter, we first introduce the fundamental rationale concepts. Next, we identify the knowledge management tasks that are related to identifying, eliciting, organizing, disseminating, and using rationale knowledge. Based on this, we survey representative rationale methods and illustrate the issues involved with a more detailed example on rationale management for requirements. We conclude with a discussion of open issues and future directions in rationale research.

*Keywords*: Design rationale, software evolution, negotiation, issue model, QOC, IBIS.

## 1. Introduction

*Rationale*[a] methods aim at capturing, representing, and maintaining records about why developers have made the decisions they have [8]. Rationale includes the problems developers encountered, the options they investigated, the criteria they selected to evaluate options, and, most important, the debate that lead to making decisions. Rationale can serve two different purposes: discourse and knowledge capture. By making explicit the main decision making elements, rationale facilitates negotiation among developers by systematically clarifying the possible options and their evaluation against well-defined criteria. By capturing rationale, developers make explicit knowledge that is usually only implicit and can later examine

---

[a]Historically, much research about rationale focuses on design and, hence, the term *design rationale* is most often used in the literature. Instead, we use the term *rationale* to avoid confusion and to emphasize that rationale models can be used during all phases of development, including requirements engineering, system design, implementation, and testing.

the justification of certain decisions, for example, when changing the system as a consequence of evolving requirements or the availability of new technology.

There are several reasons for integrating rationale methods in software engineering. First, software engineering, as in other design activities, involves the collaboration of many participants from different backgrounds and requires the negotiated settlement of many issues. Rationale methods, as negotiation support, clarify issues and their related trade-offs for the involved participants. Second, software systems are complex and changing artifacts: they result from the making and reopening of many interdependent decisions. Capturing not only these decisions but also their dependencies and the justification behind them facilitates their reevaluation later in the development process. The capture and organization of rationale, while introducing an overhead during the early phases of development, is beneficial during the later and more costly phases such as maintenance [12].

The application of rationale methods to software development is not new. General methods have been proposed to capture rationale as a graph of issues [12, 23, 30]. Specific methods have successfully tackled specialized issues, for example, in the area of requirements engineering [2, 34, 40]. While research efforts have focused on specialized applications of rationale, the systematic integration of rationale into software engineering processes and tools has yet to happen. Such a systematic integration would lead to a rationale centered development process, where rationale provides critical decision making information for system modeling and project management.

In this chapter, we present and discuss the various uses of rationale management in software engineering. We describe the concepts behind rationale management (Sec. 2) and their relationship with knowledge management (Sec. 3). We provide examples of their application to software engineering and the experiences made (Sec. 4). We also illustrate them with an example process and tool in use case software development (Sec. 5). We then examine the challenges of rationale management which still need to be addressed (Sec. 6).

## 2. Rationale, Knowledge, and Software Engineering Concepts

In this section, we define the fundamental rationale management and software engineering concepts we use in this chapter. First, we distinguish between the different types of knowledge in software engineering and their use within a project and within an organization. Next, we examine the representations for rationale knowledge, and, finally, we discuss the different levels of use of rationale in development projects.

### 2.1. *Knowledge needed in software engineering*

Software engineering requires different types of knowledge depending on the activities being carried out. We distinguish between two types of knowledge:

- *System knowledge* pertains to the system under construction. This knowledge is represented by several models looking at the system from different points of view. For example, the requirements analysis model describes the system from the end users' point of view. The system design model describes the system in terms of components, boundary conditions, and global control flow. System knowledge is used by developers to design and validate the system at various stages of development. Parts of the system knowledge gained during a project can be generalized for the benefit of the organization. For example, a system architecture is a generalized system model that represents the structure of a class of systems with a common property. A design pattern represents a template solution to a common, local design problem.

- *Process knowledge* pertains to the work required to develop the system, including knowledge about roles, resources, tasks, and work products. Process knowledge makes clear the responsibilities of each participants and the tasks they are currently accomplishing. Process knowledge is used by management and developers to plan and monitor work during development. As for system knowledge, process knowledge can be generalized across projects. For example, general process models describe a class of projects with common properties (e.g. same application domain, same staff expertise). For example, [22] in this book deals with knowledge management in software engineering related to process knowledge.

We further characterize knowledge based on the scope of its use:

- *Product knowledge* includes the system and process knowledge gained and used by a specific project in the course of developing a single system or a single product line. Product knowledge includes both system and process knowledge. A product's system knowledge comprises all the system models and the information specific to the system. A product's process knowledge comprises all task plans, schedule, budget, and constraints specific to the development of the system.

- *Organizational knowledge* includes the knowledge shared among the organization by multiple projects. System generalizations, such as domain models, design patterns, and software architectures, and process generalizations, such as generic process models and company procedures, are organizational knowledge. Organizational knowledge is much more structured and long lived than product knowledge.

All four types of knowledge (project system, project process, organizational system, and organizational process) can be augmented with *rationale knowledge* (see Table 1). *Rationale* is the justification of decisions. Rationale includes the problems that were solved, options that were considered, criteria that were used when evaluating options, arguments supporting or opposing options, and the decisions that were

**Table 1.**   Knowledge needed in software engineering.

|  |  | System Knowledge | Process Knowledge |
|---|---|---|---|
| Represents |  | System | Work<br>Roles<br>Resources |
| Product<br>Knowledge | What | Specification<br>System Design<br>Object Design<br>Source code<br>Test plans and results | Project plan<br>Budget<br>Expenditures<br>Policies & Procedures |
|  | Why<br>(rationale) | Justification behind the<br>system, including<br>development goals and<br>criteria, alternatives<br>evaluated, and their<br>evaluation | Justification behind the task<br>plan, including risk<br>assessments, contigency<br>plans, management goals &<br>criteria |
| Organizational<br>Knowledge | What | Domain models<br>System architectures<br>Design patterns | Process models<br>Best practices<br>Experiences |
|  | Why<br>(rationale) | Justification behind the<br>generalized model, such as<br>forces and trade-offs | Justification behind the<br>generalized model, such as<br>success factors associated<br>with practices |

made to address problems. Rationale can be used by both management and developers to represent the justification of system or process decisions. While system and process knowledge focuses on the system and the work, rationale knowledge focuses on the decision making elements that lead to the system and process knowledge. Note that rationale can apply to both product and organizational knowledge. In this chapter, however, we focus exclusively on knowledge in the scope of a project and do not examine the implication of rationale in the organizational scope.

Table 1 summarizes the types and scope of knowledge we introduced in this section and their relationship to different roles and activities.

## 2.2. *Representation of rationale*

Rationale can be represented in several different ways [38], including as justifications in natural language, as rules in a knowledge-based system, or as arguments structured in rhetorical steps. The latter case, called argumentation-based rationale, represents rationale as a graph of nodes and edges, each node representing a decision making element or rhetorical step and each edge representing a relationship between two elements. For example, the QOC notation ([30], Fig. 1) uses four

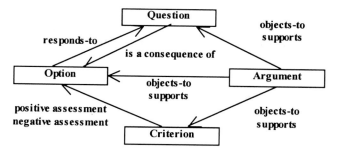

**Fig. 1.** Questions, Options, and Criteria (QOC), an argumentation-based representation of rationale [30] (UML class diagram, arrows depict association navigation paths).

rhetorical steps:

- *Questions* represent problems to be solved, such as a design issue, a need for clarification, or a disagreement.
- *Options* represent considered alternatives for answering a question. Options include designs, changes to a document, or clarifications.
- *Criteria* represent qualities that are used to evaluate options in a certain context. Criteria include design goals (e.g. reliability, cheapness, performance) and management goals (e.g. on time delivery, under budget delivery). The assessment of an option against a set of criteria is represented with assessment links between the option and the criteria nodes.
- *Arguments* represent justifications of options or criteria as expressed by the participants. Arguments can support or oppose another rhetorical node.

Consider, for example, the following argument examining the authentication mechanism in the context of the development of an Automated Teller Machine (ATM):

"We considered three possible authentication mechanisms for the ATM: (1) the user enters an account number and a personal identification number, (2) the user inserts a card and enters a personal identification number, and (3) the user inserts his finger in a finger print scanner. We found that the first option is the cheapest but the least secure. The third option offers the most flexibility to the user (no card to carry around and to lose, no personal number to forget) and is the most secure. However, the cost of the third option and the lack of security of the first option lead us to select option (2)".

Figure 2 depicts an equivalent representation of the rationale described above using QOC.

Argumentation-based representations, also called issue models, are widely used representations in rationale management [12, 23, 24]. Current research focuses on the capture of rationale, its structuring as an issue-model, its integration with other models, and the maintenance of the model. Next, we examine the different levels of use of rationale in development projects.

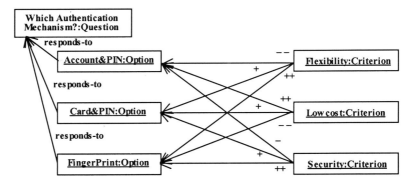

**Fig. 2.** An example of an issue model (UML object diagram).

## 2.3. Levels of rationale use

Capturing rationale represents an early investment of resources which needs to be traded off against the potential future benefits. In other words, not all types of projects may benefit from such an investment. In general, we distinguish between four levels of rationale use [6] which depend on whether the rationale is captured and organized during or after development and how much rationale should be captured:

- *No explicit rationale capture.* Resources are focused on development. No effort is invested in capturing or organizing rationale. Rationale information is present only as side effects of the development effort, such as in communication records (e.g. E-mail, faxes, meeting minutes) and developers' memories.
- *Rationale reconstruction.* Resources are spent in recovering and organizing rationale after the development is completed. Major goals, problems, and decisions are captured and justified based on records and developer knowledge. Discarded options and arguments are not captured.
- *Rationale capture.* Resources are spent in capturing rationale during development. The goal is to prevent the loss of information which occurs in the previous level. The rationale is then organized and completed after development.
- *Rationale integration.* Resources are spent to capture and organize rationale during development. This enables developers to also effectively access rationale. Rationale becomes an integral part of the development processes and tools. Rationale knowledge lives in an information base that is updated and augmented as development proceeds.

For projects in which capturing and using rationale makes sense, the benefits associated with rationale are the highest in the last level. The overhead associated with capturing and organizing rationale is lowest in the last level, assuming an integrated and pervasive process and tool support.

For example, Grudin in [18] distinguishes four different types of development: off-the-shelf product development, internal or inhouse system development, large competitively bid development contracts, and smaller customized software development project. In each development context, the opportunities and barriers for using rationale techniques are different. Two examples at opposite ends of the spectrum are the off-the-shelf product development and the customized software development:

- In *off-the-shelf product development*, project termination rates and staff turnover are high. Even though the availability of rationale records would make it easier for new developers to come on board, the constant pressure to show results frequently gives developers push ahead with coding and avoid any tasks requiring a short term overhead (including rationale techniques). Consequently, off-the-shelf product development projects are likely to fall into one of the first two levels of rationale use.
- In *customized software development* projects by consulting companies, relationships with customers are often close and with long term relationships. Moreover, consulting companies often target specific application domains and will reuse software from one customer to the next. In these context, the capture of rationale of reusable components and the system that include them can significantly lower the setup cost of a new project, thus representing a strong incentive for the consulting company. In addition, rationale can serve to capture the company's know how in the application domain and protect the company against staff turnover. We expect such development projects to fall into the last level of rationale use.

In general, the decision about when and how much rationale to capture is constrained by the short term risk associated with redirecting personpower from development to rationale capture. A project with a high risk of cancellation (e.g. an off-the-shelf product development) will capture some rationale during development and delay the organization of the rationale until the end of the project, or, most likely, delay both the capture and the organization of rationale until a later phase. A long running noncompetitive project, on the other hand, will most likely capture and organize rationale concurrently to development activities.

## 3. Rationale Management Tasks

In Sec. 2, we characterize rationale as a particular knowledge generated and used during software development. In this section, we characterize rationale management tasks as specific knowledge management tasks.

There are currently no generally accepted definitions of knowledge management. The definitions vary according to the origin within such different disciplines as economy, organizational science, information science, sociology, or psychology. Today, the most prominent driving factor to develop knowledge management techniques

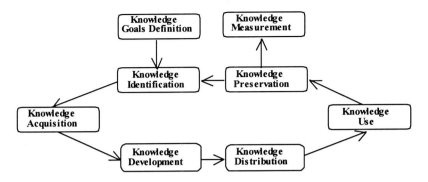

**Fig. 3.**   Knowledge management tasks (UML activity diagram).

and tools is the area of organizational learning [27]. It aims at improving the know-how transfer within and to an enterprise, at making explicit and easy-to-use documentation of the know-how, and at evaluating the return of investment of knowledge management techniques. [13] presents a study of 31 ongoing knowledge management projects in 24 enterprises which evaluates the aims and results of these projects.

In the following, we discuss the tasks to be supported by knowledge management and the specifics of rationale management.

### 3.1. *Knowledge tasks*

The task model depicted in Fig. 3 is adapted from [36]. Similar distinctions can be found in [4] who discuss the technology needed for knowledge management and in [1] who discuss the use of knowledge management of software engineering lessons learned.

Figure 3 shows two kinds of tasks:

- *Strategic tasks*: knowledge goals definition and knowledge measurement.
- *Operational tasks*: knowledge identification, knowledge acquisition, knowledge development, knowledge distribution, use of knowledge and knowledge preservation.

The two strategic tasks are important to drive and control the knowledge management process.

- *Knowledge goals definition* focuses the process on particular kinds of knowledge and their expected benefits of the process.
- *Knowledge measurement* ensures the quality of the process and its results by comparing them with the expected benefits.

The operational tasks describe the generation and handling of the knowledge.

- *Knowledge identification* aims at identifying the knowledge which is available in a specific context and important to achieve the knowledge goal together with the sources of this knowledge (internal or external, human or material).

- *Knowledge acquisition* is needed to elicit the knowledge from the identified knowledge sources. This is particularly important for implicit knowledge. The execution of this task must be sensitive to psychological issues, since human knowledge sources are not necessarily motivated to give away their knowledge.
- *Knowledge development* aims at packaging, consolidating, and enhancing the available knowledge. Typically, this is realized by communicating about the knowledge, integrating knowledge from different sources, and representing it in a specific format.
- *Knowledge distribution* is the first step for a comprehensive use of the knowledge in the relevant context. Typical technology used nowadays is the internet or intranet.
- *Knowledge use* is the key task where the return of investment of the knowledge management process is generated. Here, again, main psychological issues, such as the NIH-syndrome (Not-Invented-Here syndrome), have to be taken into account. Often, specific incentives to use the knowledge have to be given.
- *Knowledge preservation* aims at preventing uncontrolled loss of knowledge. It consists of selection and storage of new knowledge as well as adaptation of existing knowledge (including controlled deletion). This supports one of the key factors to motivate the use, namely that the knowledge is up-to-date.

## 3.2. *Rationale management tasks*

In the following, we discuss the specifics of rationale management tasks, again separating strategic from operational tasks:

Strategic rationale management tasks include:

- *Identifying rationale goals.* As described in the introduction, typical rationale goals include:

  (a) *Improve quality.* Software development involves the participation of stakeholders with different backgrounds and different objectives. Rationale improves the quality of decisions by making decision criteria and the evaluation of alternatives explicit.

  (b) *Reveal complexity.* Software systems are characterized by their high complexity. Complexity results from the making of many interdependent decisions spanning different aspects of the system. This complexity can only be handled adequately, if these decisions and their dependencies are made explicit. Rational enables the traceability of decision making for improved understanding.

(c) *Support change.* Software systems have a long life cycle or are embedded into systems with a long life cycle. Consequently, developers and maintainers often need to deal with decisions that have been taken in the past by participants who are not part of the project anymore. Rationale enables the record of decision making information for future use.

In Sec. 4, we examine more specific goals, such as the enhancement of requirements elicitation or the improvement of training support.

- *Rationale measurement* needs to define specific metrics for evaluating the rationale management process and its results according to the rationale goals. Up to now, there have been only few quantitative studies about rationale methods. Most empirical studies have focused on the feasibility or the usability of rationale [9, 17, 21].

Operational rationale management tasks include:

- *Rationale identification.* Sources of rationale knowledge include all the persons involved in decision making throughout software development. This includes the developers, managers, reviewers, users, and clients. As discussed in Sec. 2.3, the main question of rationale identification is the amount of the rationale to be captured: only the issues involved in major decisions or all issues. In both cases, identification of major issues specific to particular domains and particular knowledge goals would be helpful. Thus, for example, if the goal is to enhance the quality of the decisions, then a classification of the issues which raise the most conflicts in the given domain would help to focus the rationale process on the essential issues. Similarly, to facilitate change, it would be helpful to know beforehand which decisions are most likely to be changed.
- *Rationale acquisition.* In Sec. 2.3, we argue that there is a significant difference between rationale acquisition during or after development. In contrast to most applications of knowledge management, rationale is best captured during project execution, not after the fact. It is impossible to reveal the rationale of a development without the developers. But even with the developers the actual arguments and challenges are hard to discover after the fact, since too many issues have been discussed. However, eliciting rationale during development imposes an additional burden on software process participants during their most stressful working period. Thus, a smooth integration of rationale capture into software development is mandatory. In the example in Sec. 5, we describe some measures to alleviate this problem.
- *Rationale development.* During rationale development, the rationale is consolidated and packaged. In particular, this is based on a particular model

of how to represent and structure rationale. In Sec. 4, we give several examples of rationale models for particular applications. As for rationale acquisition, one important issue for rationale development is the facilitation during software development. Often, rationale acquisition and rationale development are intertwined. However, this imposes even more burden on the software developers. This can be alleviated by a dedicated rationale maintainer as described in the example of Sec. 5.

- *Rationale distribution.* Since rationale is secondary knowledge attached to the development decisions, rationale distribution is best achieved by easy access to rationale starting from the decisions and vice versa. Thus, rationale models needs to be intertwined with the documented decisions. One obvious, but seldom implemented, consequence is that the decisions themselves need to be identifiable within the system documentation. Another important issue is, to alleviate the access to the rationale as much as possible. This can be achieved by a user-adaptable tool to browse, view and filter the rationale and the decisions.

- *Rationale use.* As the next section shows, there is a wide variety of rationale use. It can be used throughout any software process task. For example, the rationale behind a requirements specification or a prototype can be revealed to users and serve as a basis for requirements questions. Another example is that the rationale behind the system design can be used by maintainers to make better maintenance decisions.

- *Rationale preservation:* As with any knowledge, rationale is only useful if it is up to date. Thus, there needs to be some support for maintaining the rationale as long as it might be useful. At the same time, it is important to prevent uncontrolled collection of rationale which hinders access to important rationale. As with rationale development, to some extent this can be achieved, by a rationale maintainer.

This view on rationale management as knowledge management is new. It helps to understand the differences between different applications, because it makes the different goals and solutions to the different management tasks explicit. It also makes obvious that introducing rationale management into software development is a complex process. One reason for the only partial success of rationale methods might be that so far they have only concentrated on some of the tasks, but not on a coherent process.

In the following section, the rationale management tasks identified from the knowledge management tasks are used to survey typical rationale management methods. They are also used to structure the detailed example given in Sec. 5.

## 4. Use of Rationale Management in Software Engineering

In this section, we discuss four different applications of rationale in software engineering:

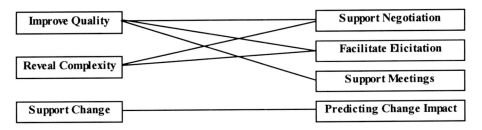

**Fig. 4.**   Relationships between high level and low level rationale goals.

- supporting negotiation during requirements (Sec. 4.1);
- facilitating the elicitation of domain knowledge (Sec. 4.2);
- structuring and capturing design meeting (Sec. 4.3); and
- predicting change impact (Sec. 4.4).

We selected these applications to provide a broad spectrum for the purpose of illustration. This list, however, is by no means complete. Other applications of rationale to software engineering include [23, 24, 34, 35, 37] and [38].

Each of these applications addresses a specific knowledge goal that refines the high-level goals we identified previously (Fig. 4). For example, supporting negotiation during requirements improves the quality of decisions made and reduces the effort spent in resolving conflicts. Predicting change impact improves the ability of maintainers to change the system without introducing new problems.

We examine each knowledge goal from the point of view of the operational rationale management tasks described in Sec. 3. These include the tasks of identifying which rationale should be captured, to elicit the rationale from users or developers, to develop rationale by representing it into models, disseminating rationale usually with the help of a tool, and its use for supporting the intended goal. None of these four applications, however, addresses the preservation of rationale knowledge. We revisit this issue in Sec. 6, when we discuss the role of rationale maintainer.

To give further evidence on the usefulness of the individual approaches, we also sketch the experiences made in their industrial or experimental application.

### 4.1. *Supporting negotiation*

By making explicit all decision making elements, including the available options and the criteria that are used to evaluate them, stakeholders solve problems by identifying conflicts and finding a commonly acceptable resolution instead of defending entrenched positions. For example, Theory W and *WinWin* [2], a process model and its corresponding tool support, leveraged off this idea in the context of negotiation among the different stakeholders of the software system.

Negotiation knowledge is acquired from the start of the WinWin development cycle. Each development cycle starts with three activities (Fig. 5):

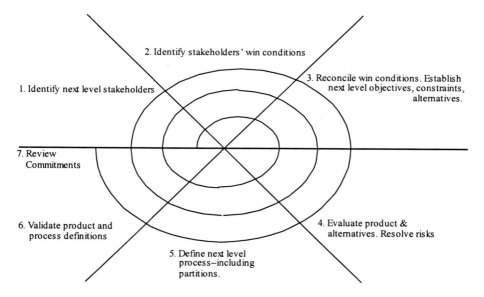

**Fig. 5.**   WinWin spiral model (adapted from [16]).

- Identification of the critical stakeholder.
- Identification of their Win conditions.
- Reconciliation of the Win conditions.

Stakeholders are participants who hold an interest in the successful development of the system, including end users, sponsors, managers, and developers. Win conditions are success criteria that a specific stakeholder uses to evaluate different options.

**Identification.** The identification of stakeholders and the definition of their Win conditions leads to the discovery of areas of agreement and of conflict. For the areas of agreement, no more actions are necessary. For the areas of conflict, however, each stakeholder needs to elicit more rationale knowledge.

**Acquisition.** Rationale knowledge for each conflict includes acceptable options, trade-offs and refined criteria. Rationale is elicited incrementally with each stakeholder entering more information using the WinWin tool as a reaction to proposals by other stakeholders. Stakeholders can explore acceptable alternatives, compromise, and arrive at a consensus.

**Development.** The knowledge acquired during negotiation is formalized in the WinWin negotiation model, which includes four types of elements (Fig. 6). In addition to Win conditions and issues (discussed in the previous paragraph), the negotiation model also includes options, which represent alternatives for resolving an issue, and agreements, which represent decisions that close a specific issue. Issues are linked to the conflicting Win conditions with "involve" links. Options are linked to the issue they address with an "address" link. Agreements are linked to the option

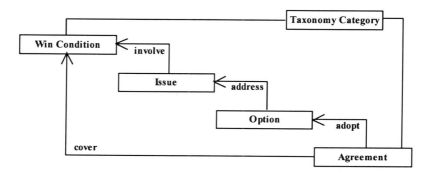

**Fig. 6.** WinWin Negotiation Model [16] (UML class diagram).

resolving the issue with a "adopt" link and to the related Win conditions with a "cover" link. Finally, the negotiation model includes a domain taxonomy which is used to classify each element of the negotiation according to application specific categories. Stakeholders are responsible for linking the negotiation elements they create with a specific category in the taxonomy. The formalization of rationale knowledge is performed at the same time as it is acquired.

**Distribution.** The elements of the negotiation model are accessible to all stakeholders via the WinWin tool. Stakeholders can browse the negotiation model either by taxonomy category or by Win condition.

**Use.** Rationale knowledge is used during the negotiation as it is being elicited. Each new piece of rationale allows stakeholders to refine their Win conditions and resolve conflicts by finding compromises. The acquisition and use tasks are tightly intertwined in this application.

**Experiences.** [2] reports from an extensive case study aiming at evaluating the feasibility of using the WinWin spiral model by graduate student development teams. The case study consisted of the development of a library multimedia archive system where WinWin was applied in four cycles. Cycle 0 focused on the feasibility of an appropriate family of multimedia applications, cycle 1 on the life-cycle objectives, prototypes, plans, specifications and architecture of each application. In cycle 3, the architecture was detailed and risks of project success handled. Cycle 4 produced an initial operational system. The study showed three main strengths of the approach: explicit negotiation enhanced flexibility in adapting to risks and uncertainties, discipline in order to maintain focus on the milestones, and trust enhancement between the project stakeholders. Overhead was mainly due to documentation overkill and to attempts to coordinate multiple views. These were reduced by more extensive training on the process and the tool.

### 4.2. *Supporting requirements elicitation*

By making the rationale of requirements decisions explicit, users are encouraged to review the reasoning behind the proposed option and participate in the decision process. Sutcliffe found that with this method, combined with a scenario-based requirements elicitation approach, requirements analysts can elicit more information and more kinds of information from end users during requirements elicitation sessions [39, 40].

In this method SCRAM, analysts elicit a first version of application domain knowledge through traditional techniques, such as interviews and questionnaires. From this knowledge, analysts build a prototype.

**Identification.** During the development of the prototype, analysts identify issues that are ambiguous and that need to be further investigated and for these issues only the analysts elicit further rationale knowledge.

**Acquisition.** Analysts elicit the rationale knowledge by describing trade-offs they made when specifying the system. In particular, they concentrate on the options they considered, the criteria they used to evaluate the options, and the selected option which is presented to the users.

**Development.** Analysts describe the proposed system in terms of scenarios and of a demonstration prototype. The scenarios capture the context in which the system is to be used, that is, the users environment and their work. Analysts formalize the requirements rationale as a QOC model, as described in Sec. 2. The QOC model explicitly lists all options that were considered and the criteria used to evaluate them. Figure 7 depicts an example QOC model used to justify the navigation features for a large information space [40]. Note that in this application the rationale is elicited and reconstructed after the fact.

**Distribution and use.** During a requirements elicitation session, an analyst describes the system by executing a scenario using the demonstration prototype. At key points, the analyst stops and describes the rationale developed in the previous point as a paper QOC model. The QOC model is then used to ask probe questions to the users. The users are encouraged to review the rationale, confirm the selected option or propose changes or clarify domain knowledge. The presence of rationale allows the users to select a different option and to clarify which decision criteria are more important from their point of view. This allows analysts to revise other decisions that depend on the same set of criteria.

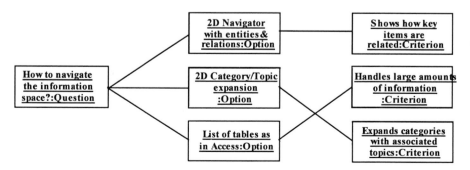

**Fig. 7.** Example of requirements rationale in QOC. (Adapted from [40], UML object diagram).

**Experiences**. [40] reports on the use of SCRAM on an European Union project, the multimedia broker. Four elicitation sessions of 1.5 hours on average with 20 users in total were held. These users gave positive feedback on SCRAM, because they thought it was helpful to see alternative designs and the demonstration was useful for discussing requirements. They all felt they had been given the opportunity to say what they wanted about the designs. Some problems encountered were the designer dominance during the session, the production of too many requirements because users were not forced to trade off judgements and session overload by discussing too many issues. The later could be reduced by filtering the more obvious and predictable requirements before hand. The effort of the designers was not further analyzed.

## 4.3. *Structuring and capturing design meetings*

By systematically enumerating options and their assessments, developers improve the quality of their decisions by discovering new options or detecting faulty assessments. In particular, issue models can be used to plan, execute, and capture design meetings [12, 14].

**Identification**. The meeting facilitator selects a number of design issues to be discussed during the meeting. The list is then circulated before the meeting among participants in the form of a meeting agenda. The participants have the opportunity to augment the agenda with additional design issues and to prioritize the agenda items.

**Acquisition**. The issues are then used to scope the discussion during the meeting. When an issues has been resolved or tabled, the facilitator moves to the subsequent issue in the agenda. A minute taker records the resulting discussion and decisions into meeting minutes.

**Development**. Both agendas and meeting minutes are structured following an issue model (Fig. 8): the list of design problems are issues, the discussion is structured in terms of proposals and arguments, the decisions are recorded as decision nodes associated with the issues. When a design problem is discussed for several design meetings, the issue model associated with the design problem is carried over and updated after each meeting. The minute taker usually concentrates on capturing content during the meeting and formalizes the rationale knowledge into an issue model after the meeting.

**Distribution**. In [12], the issues were created, stored, and retrieved using a groupware tool called gIBIS. gIBIS enabled users to access the same issue model. In [14], issue models were represented in terms of textual meeting agendas and minutes that were posted on a newsgroup.

**Use**. In addition to structuring the content of the meeting, the rationale knowledge can be used in several other ways. Participants can refer back to meeting minutes to update the project plan or the project status. Participants who did not attend the meeting can examine the discussions associated with a specific issues.

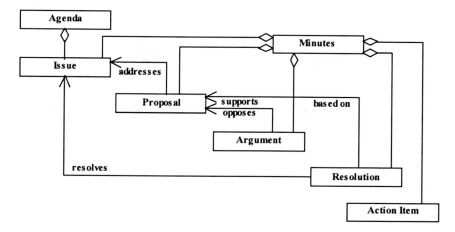

**Fig. 8.** IWEB meeting model [14] (UML class diagram).

Finally, the rationale knowledge, including the list of unresolved or tabled issues, can be used for organizing subsequent meetings.

**Experiences.** Conklin and Burgess–Yakemovic used the IBIS model for structuring design meetings in an industrial setting for 18 months [12]. This case study identified several benefits of this approach for dealing with staff turnover, reviewing and tracking problems with requirements and design documents, and otherwise improving communication among the team. This case study also identified key technology transfer issues when introducing rationale methods, such as the presence of a champion in the team, and a clear argument and supporting data of the costs and benefits of the approach. We confirmed most of these points in an experiment with senior students in the context of a software engineering project course using a similar approach for status meetings [14].

### 4.4. *Predicting change impact*

By capturing the justification of the current design, maintainers have better and more information on which to base when designing changes hence avoiding the problem of architectural erosion [5]. However, designers usually dislike making additional documentation. Also, all expansions of the software development process may affect lead-time negatively.

[5] proposes a simple approach for documenting design rationale which was used to set up a controlled experiment to study the effectiveness of rationale.

**Identification and acquisition.** Designers write down a note for each system aggregation level documenting why it is broken down into the lower aggregation levels and what the purpose of each component is. This ensures that the rationale has a strong association with the code and that the size of the rationale is limited.

**Development**. The rationale is structured according to four standardized headings: *organization of system into files, use of language constructs, main dynamic architectural principles*, and *clues to understanding the system*.

**Distribution and use**. Maintainers can access the rationale when handling change requests.

**Experiences**. The experiment was conducted with 17 participants, 7 of them from industry, the other 10 from university. All of the participants had to handle four change requests on a local telephony system modeled in SDL, but only half of them had access to the rationale. For each change request the participants were requested to indicate changes to existing components as well as the addition of new components. The maximum time allowed for each change request was 9 minutes. A similar experiment was conducted with only part of the former participants working on a cruise control system. Since this system was more complicated, only two change requests had to be handled with 30 minutes time for each of them. The analysis of the experiment data showed that for the first system there is a statistically significant difference between the two groups: the group using the design rationale on average only took 5 minutes (compared to 6 minutes for the other group) and identified more than 75% of the required change points (compared to 50% for the other group). Both groups had roughly 2 superfluous change points. The trends for the second system are similar, but not statistically significant. The reasons for this might be, that there were less data points available (due to the lower number of participants). Another reasons might have to do with the system itself. Thus, the authors conclude that rationale documentation might be a cheap, yet effective way to facilitate future system evolution, without prolonging the time to the initial system release. However, further experimentation is needed to find out what is "the best" model for various purposes.

## 5. An Example: Using Rationale in Use Case Driven Software Development

In this section, we present a particular instance of a rationale management process for requirements rationale. This section aims at complementing by a detailed process example the survey of rationale management issues and methods given in the previous sections.

Rationale management during requirements engineering is especially attractive given that requirements errors and changes are the most costly during development. Moreover, attaching rationale with requirements information, in particular with use cases, can have a high impact on all phases of development given that use cases are used throughout development.

The process is described in more details in [15]. It takes the following approach to the rationale management tasks:

**Goal**. The goal is to enhance the quality and facilitate the downstream use and change of use cases and the related requirements elements, such as scenarios, system services and non-functional requirements.

**Measurement**. The quality of the requirements elements and their rationale is measured by the number of defects found in reviews. The usefulness of the rationale is measured by the number of accesses to the rationale during design, testing and requirements change.

**Identification**. The approach aims at a very fine-grained capture of rationale. However, experiments will be carried out to evaluate the usefulness of the different rationale elements.

**Acquisition**. The rationale is provided by the requirements engineers during requirements capture. Additional rationale is elicited during discussions initiated through reviews of requirements. Acquisition is made as easy as possible through provision of a tool and a defined process.

**Development**. The rationale is formalized using the QOC model as depicted in Fig. 1. The consolidation is supported by a dedicated rationale maintainer. The rationale maintainer is a developer or a former developer with librarian skills (e.g. a person with the ability to track large amounts of loosely organized and incomplete information).

**Distribution**. Tool support for acquisition and access is provided. Currently, two implementations are under development: a dedicated web-based tool and an adaptation of the requirements management tool DOORS.

**Use**. Currently, the main emphasis is on use in dependent software development tasks like design or testing and for requirements change.

**Preservation**. The rationale maintainer is also responsible for keeping the rationale up-to-date.

In the following, we concentrate on the process for rationale acquisition, development and preservation. We briefly sketch a requirements capture process. Then, we define a rationale process intertwined with the requirements capture process. The process steps can themselves be viewed as requirements for tool support for the integrated requirements and rationale capture process.

A first generation of this process and its accompanying tool support is in use in the software engineering project course at the Technische Universität München (this project course is described in more detail in [7]). On the one hand, this approach provides us with a concrete example for teaching rationale methods to students in computer science. On the other hand, it enables us to evaluate and refine this rationale methods in a realistic (and controllable) development project.

### 5.1. *Use case-based requirements capture*

Use cases are a popular addition to object-oriented software development. They have first been proposed by Jacobson [19] and are now part of the (Rational) *Unified Software Development Process* [20].

In [15], we stipulate a detailed process of requirements capture with use cases. For the purpose of this paper it suffices to say that the main step of the requirements capture is *Propose Option* in which user tasks, use cases, example scenarios, system services and glossary entries are created as part of the requirements specification. We refer to these artifacts as requirements elements. The other steps of the requirements capture process are *Define Constraints* (on the options) and *Consolidate Requirements Elements*. The process is carried out by the requirements engineer. It is intertwined with the following rationale capture process.

### 5.2. *Issue-based rationale capture*

The rationale of requirements is captured by two processes. The first process, the capture process executed by a requirements engineer or a reviewer, focuses on rationale acquisition, whereas the second process, the maintenance process executed by the rationale maintainer, focuses on rationale development and preservation.

The capture process is composed of the following steps (see Fig. 9):

(1) *Review.* A reviewer reads some part of the requirements specification and challenges problem areas with questions.

(2) *Explore Options.* Questions can result in the discussion of possible changes in the requirements specification. A possible option that is always available is the status quo, that is, not to change the requirements. Clarification questions are addressed with options to improve the requirements specification without necessarily resulting in changes to the

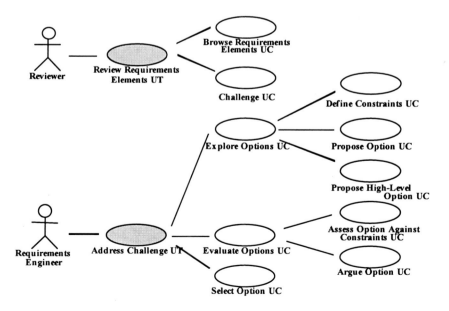

**Fig. 9.** The rationale capture process (UML use case diagram).

system. An option can be completely specified by writing out the corresponding use cases (*Propose Option*) or can be simply described as a high-level option (*Propose High-Level Option*). In both cases, the options should contain enough detail to enable the requirements engineer to evaluate and compare the proposed options (*Define Constraints*).

(3) *Evaluate Options.* Once a sufficient number of options have been proposed, requirements engineers need to evaluate them and refine them to satisfy nonfunctional constraints (*Assess Options Against Constraints*). During this step, requirements engineers also create arguments supporting and opposing options (*Argue Option*).

(4) *Select Option.* Once requirements engineers have evaluated and refined (most or) all options, requirements engineers create a decision by selecting an option which can result in minor or substantial change in the requirements specification. Note that a clarification question can be resolved without any changes. Note also that addressing a question may invalidate previous options and revisit earlier decisions.

During the capture process, requirements engineers may skip any of the above steps. Options can be generated and evaluated without an explicit question. Decisions can be taken and changes implemented without explicit discussion. It is desirable, however, that at least some of the components of the decision are recorded so that the rationale maintenance process can recover the missing parts.

The capture process can be executed at any time. Typically, it will occur when requirements engineers review the requirements specification, either when validating the requirements or in the process of executing a requirements step. The maintenance process, however, is executed by the rationale maintainer whose responsibility is to keep the content and structure of the rationale up to date. The maintenance process is composed of the following steps (see Fig. 10):

(1) *Identify Missing Questions.* Given that requirements engineers may skip steps in the capture process, there can be questions and their corresponding options that were not captured. The rationale maintainer, if involved with the development process, can document such questions, which were

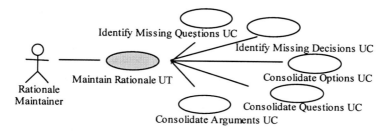

**Fig. 10.** The rationale maintenance process (UML use case diagram).

debated in meetings but not recorded online. In general, however, this task is difficult to accomplish systematically. Some important questions will occasionally fail to be recorded.

(2) *Identify Missing Decisions.* Most decisions occur during meetings or face-to-face conversations. Consequently, they may be implemented in the requirements specification but not captured in the issue model. The rationale maintainer can identify these decisions by ensuring each change is associated with a decision.

(3) *Consolidate Options.* When discussing a question, the requirements engineers may propose similar options. The rationale maintainer consolidates identical options into single nodes and restructures similar options.

(4) *Consolidate Questions.* When reviewing requirements elements, reviewers may raise similar questions. The rationale maintainer consolidates identical questions into single nodes and restructures similar options.

(5) *Consolidate Arguments.* Arguments often constitute the bulk of rationale information [31]. Arguments are usually unstructured and may apply to several options and decisions. The rationale maintainer summarizes verbose or redundant arguments and adds missing links to relevant rationale nodes.

## 5.3. *Integrating requirements and rationale*

In the previous two subsections, we described two groups of processes: one for capturing and consolidating requirements and one for capturing and maintaining rationale. The group of processes focusing on rationale represents additional overhead for developers. Capturing and maintaining rationale will yield benefits only if processes from both groups and their corresponding tool support are integrated. Indeed, the integration of rationale methods and tools with various aspects of development is a fundamental issue that has received too little attention in rationale research [26]. In this section, we describe the concepts and process steps which are related to the integration of requirements and rationale capture.

### 5.3.1. *Concepts*

There are three areas where additional associations need to be created:

*Questions/Requirements associations.* The association between a question and the requirements elements that are challenged needs to be captured. This enables a reviewer to specify which parts of the requirements are challenged and for a requirements engineer to list all questions for a given requirements element.

*Option/Requirements associations.* The association between an option (or a high-level option) and the requirements elements that the option proposes, removes, or modifies also needs to be captured. When evaluating an option, this enables the requirements engineer to assess the impact of an option. When understanding the requirements, this allows a reviewer to trace back the source option or question that lead to a specific requirement.

*Requirements elements status.* Given that requirements engineer can propose new requirements elements as part of an option but that these requirements elements can be discarded in favor of another option, each requirements element in the option base needs to include a status attribute. The requirements status can take three values:

- *current,* if the requirements element is part of the current option;
- *proposed,* if the requirements element is part of an option that has not been selected; and
- *discarded,* if the requirements element was part of the current option but has been discarded in favor of another option.

### 5.3.2. *Processes*

To integrate the requirements and rationale processes, the steps *Propose Option, Challenge,* and *Select Option,* need to be modified and three new steps, *Realize High-Level Option, Discard Current Requirement,* and *Make Proposed Requirement Current* have to be introduced.

The *Propose Option* step sets the initial value of the status attribute of each new requirement to *proposed.* This allows requirements engineers to distinguish between requirements they have just entered and those that are part of the current option.

The *Challenge* step creates associations between the question and the requirements being challenged. These associations make explicit relationships between rationale and requirements and allow reviewers and requirements engineers to trace changes to specific problems.

The *Select Option* (see Fig. 11) step can have two variations. Either an option is selected or a high-level option is selected. If a high-level option is selected, it is first realized by creating all proposed use cases and modifying existing use cases. This is accomplished using the *Realize High-Level Option* process step. At the end of this step, a new option is created and linked with the corresponding requirement. The Select Option step then invokes the *Discard Current Requirement* step to change the status of any requirement that needs to be discarded. The *Make Proposed Option*

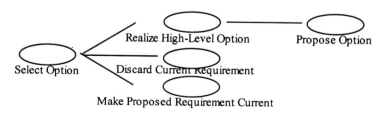

**Fig. 11.** Select option use case (UML use case diagram).

*Current* step is then invoked to change the status of the proposed requirements to *current*.

The differentiation between high-level options and options enables requirements engineer to debate several options without fully developing them *a priori*. This encourages the capture of more information about discarded options.

### 5.4. *ATM example revisited*

In the software engineering project course at TU München, the process described in this section is supported by a simple web application called REQ/QOC (Fig. 12). This tool enables the users (e.g. requirements engineer and reviewers) to examine simultaneously the requirements specification and its rationale. The requirements specification (left column in Fig. 12), is expressed in terms of requirement elements (i.e., actors, user tasks, use cases, services, nonfunctional constraints, and glossary terms). The rationale (right column in Fig. 12) is represented in terms of an issue model (i.e., questions, options, criteria, and decisions). Users collaborate by concurrently creating and modifying requirements elements, challenging them with questions, and resolving questions through argumentation.

For example in Fig. 12, a reviewer noticed that the authentication mechanism used by the ATM had not been specified. The reviewer created a question *Authentication Mechanism* and linked it with the *Deposit Money, Withdraw Money,*

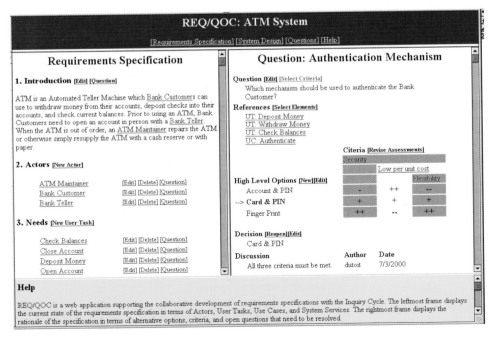

**Fig. 12.** ATM authentication question of Fig. 2 depicted in the REQ/QOC tool.

and *Check Balances* user tasks. The requirements engineering subsequently debated three possible options to this question (*Account Number & PIN, Card & PIN, Finger Print*) and assessed them against the nonfunctional constraints (*Security, Low per unit Cost,* and *Flexibility*) of the ATM system.[b] The requirements engineers discussed the question using the discussion thread at the bottom of the right column and subsequently agreed to select the *Card & PIN* option, now displayed in bold, and created an *Authenticate* use case to document this decision.

The user tasks *Deposit Money, Withdraw Money,* and *Check Balances* and the use case *Authenticate* are associated with this question and are displayed as links in the *References* section of the question. Similarly, links to open questions are listed in the left column under their corresponding requirements elements (not depicted in Fig. 12). These cross references enable users to quickly navigate between the requirements elements and their rationale.

## 6. Open Issues and Future Directions

In this chapter, we focus on the fundamental concepts behind rationale knowledge and its application to software engineering. We presented several applications of rationale as illustration of the broad range of goals that can be satisfied with rationale knowledge. Several obstacles, however, have prevented the wide-spread use of rationale in the software industry. The obstacles include:

- *Cost.* Capturing rationale introduces an initial cost. Developers need to capture more information and justify more decisions. For the organization, this is an investment, as rationale information will be most useful later in the process. However, from the developers' perspective, this is perceived as an overhead as users of the rationale are usually different persons (e.g. maintainers). If the developers do not see a short term benefit for themselves, it is likely that they will not invest sufficient effort into this task.
- *Completeness.* Rationale is lost if not captured early. Decisions can be reopened a number of times over a long period of time. If the options that were evaluated and the criteria that were used in the evaluation are not captured, it is difficult for developers to reconstruct the rationale associated with early decisions.
- *Complexity.* Rationale models are larger and more complex than system models. Given that rationale also includes discarded options and argumentation, it represents a larger body of information and is harder to search. If the access to the rationale is too cumbersome, developers will not consult it prior to reopening decisions.
- *Consistency.* Rationale is useful only if consistent with the system models. System models evolve over time. Similarly, their corresponding rationale

---

[b]Note that these nonfunctional constraints are listed as *Criteria* in the rationale window.

also evolves. If the rationale models are not kept consistent with subsequent version of the system models, the rationale quickly becomes outdated and useless.

However, recent progress in several technological areas (e.g. hypertext and hypermedia technology, search engines and natural language parsing) and organizational areas (e.g. knowledge management) promise that some of these obstacles could be overcome in specific contexts. For example:

- *Process integration.* By integrating the capture of rationale with existing activities (e.g. negotiation in Sec. 4.1, elicitation in Sec. 4.2), we can create a short term incentive for developers to capture rationale, thus reducing the perceived overhead of capture. Moreover, this increases the completeness of captured rationale since rationale is captured during development.
- *Tool integration.* Modern computer aided software engineering (CASE) tools, integrated development environments (IDEs), and groupware provide open interfaces enabling third parties to customize and integrate these tools with others. This also enables us to integrate rationale management support tools with development tools, thus providing developers easier access to rationale information. Moreover, this enables developers to capture more information during development, for example, in the form of annotations. By linking system and rationale knowledge and by providing the developers with familiar tool interfaces, we can reduce the complexity of organizing and accessing rationale knowledge. This contrasts with earlier approaches to rationale tool support in which monolithic and dedicated tools were developed (e.g. gIBIS [12]).
- *Knowledge management roles.* In knowledge management, specialized roles dedicated to knowledge acquisition and organization (e.g. knowledge brokers) are not uncommon. This stems from the realization that knowledge can become obsolete or irrelevant quickly and that only persons dedicated to maintaining this knowledge can address this issue effectively. Early efforts in rationale management assumed that developers could deal with rationale as a side effect of their work. However, preserving rationale knowledge turned out to be the most difficult challenge in rationale management. In the example, we presented in Sec. 5, the rationale maintainer, is an example of such specialized role and focuses mostly on the preservation of knowledge.

Once adequate tool and organization support exists for capturing and disseminating rationale, it then becomes possible to conduct systematic quantitative studies to identify which subset of rationale knowledge are useful and used by developers and in which applications. This would then allow further improvements in reducing the cost of introducing rationale methods in development and provide success cases for illustrating their utility, a necessary requirement before a meaningful adoption of rationale methods into everyday practice.

# References

1. A. Birk and C. Tautz, "Knowledge management of software engineering lessons learned", *International Conference on Software Engineering and Knowledge Engineering* (1998) 116–119.
2. B. Boehm, A. Egyed, J. Kwan, D. Port, A. Shah and R. Madachy, "Using the WinWin spiral model: A case study", *IEEE Computer* (July 1998).
3. G. Booch, J. Rumbaugh and I. Jacobson, *The Unified Modeling Language User Guide* (Addison-Wesley, Reading, MA, 1998).
4. U. Borghoff and R. Pareschi, *Information Technology for Knowledge Management* (Springer, 1998).
5. L. Bratthall, E. Johansson and B. Regnel, "Is a design rationale vital when predicting change impact? — A controlled experiment on software architecture evolution", *International Conference on Product Focused Software Process Improvement, Lecture Notes in Computer Science*, 1840, 2000.
6. B. Bruegge and A. H. Dutoit, *Object-Oriented Software Engineering: Conquering Complex and Changing Systems* (Prentice Hall, Upper Saddle River, NJ, 1999).
7. B. Bruegge, A. H. Dutoit, R. Kobylinski and G. Teubner, "Transatlantic project courses in a university environment", *Asian Pacific Software Engineering Conference*, Singapore (December 2000).
8. S. B. Shum and N. Hammond, "Argumentation-based design rationale: What use at what cost?" *International Journal of Human-Computer Studies* **40** (1994) 603–652.
9. S. B. Shum, "Analyzing the usability of a design rationale notation", eds. T. P. Moran and J. M. Carroll, *Design Rationale: Concepts, Techniques, and Use* (Lawrence Erlbaum, Hillsdale, NJ, 1995).
10. T. Carey, D. McKerlie and J. Wilson, "HCI design rationales as a learning resource", eds. T. P. Moran and J. M. Carroll, *Design Rationale: Concepts, Techniques, and Use* (Lawrence Erlbaum, Hillsdale, NJ, 1995).
11. A. Cockburn, "Goals and use cases", *Journal of Object-Oriented Programming* **10**, no. 5 (1997) 35–40.
12. J. Conklin and K. C. Burgess-Yakemovic, "A process-oriented approach to design rationale", *Human-Computer Interaction* **6** (1991) 357–391.
13. T. Davenport, "Successful knowledge management projects", *Sloan Management Review* **39**, no. 2 (1998) 43–58.
14. A. H. Dutoit, B. Bruegge and R. F. Coyne, "The use of an issue-based model in a team-based software engineering course", *Conference Proceedings of Software Engineering: Education and Practice (SEEP'96)* Dunedin, New Zealand (January 1996).
15. A. H. Dutoit and B. Paech, "Supporting evolution: Rationale in use case driven software development", *International Workshop on Requirements Engineering: Foundations of Software Quality (REFSQ'2000)* Stockholm (June 2000).
16. A. Egyed and B. Boehm, "Comparing software system requirements negotiation patterns", *Journal for Systems Engineering* (John Wiley & Sons, 1999).
17. G. Fischer, A. C. Lemke, R. McCall and A. I. Morch, "Making argumentation serve design", *Human Computer Interaction* **6**, no. 3 (1991) 393–419.
18. J. Grudin, "Evaluating opportunities for design capture", eds. T. P. Moran and J. M. Carroll, *Design Rationale: Concepts, Techniques, and Use* (Lawrence Erlbaum, Mahwah, NJ, 1996).

19. I. Jacobson, M. Christerson, P. Jonsson and G. Overgaard, *Object-Oriented Software Engineering — A Use Case Driven Approach* (Addison-Wesley, Reading, MA, 1992).

20. I. Jacobson, G. Booch and J. Rumbaugh, *The Unified Software Development Process* (Addison-Wesley, Reading, MA, 1999).

21. L. Karsenty, "An empirical evaluation of design rationale documents", *Conference Proceedings on Human Factors in Computing Systems* Vancouver Canada (1996) 150–156.

22. R. Kneuper, "Supporting software processes using knowledge management", to appear in *Handbook of Software Engineering and Knowledge Engineering* (World Scientific, 2001).

23. W. Kunz and H. Rittel, "Issues as elements of information systems", Working Paper No. 131, Institut für Grundlagen der Planung, Universität Stuttgart, Germany, 1970.

24. J. Lee, "A qualitative decision management system", *Artificial Intelligence at MIT: Expanding Frontiers*, eds. P. H. Winston and S. Shellard (MIT Press, Cambridge, MA) **1** (1990) 104–133.

25. J. Lee, "Extending the Potts and Bruns model for recording design rationale", *Proceedings of the 13th International Conference on Software Engineering (ICSE'13)* (IEEE Computer Society Press, Los Alamitos, CA) 114–125.

26. J. Lee, "Design rationale systems: Understanding the issues", *IEEE Expert* (May/June 1997).

27. F. Lehner, *Organizational Memory* (Hanser, 2000).

28. J. C. S. do Prado Leite, G. Rossi, F. Balaguer, A. Maiorana, G. Kaplan, G. Hadad and A. Oliveros, "Enhancing a requirements baseline with scenarios", *International Symposium in Requirements Engineering (RE'97)* (1997) 44–53.

29. R. Lougher and T. Rodden, "Supporting long-term collaboration in software maintenance", *Proceedings of the Conference on Organizational Computing Systems*, 1993.

30. A. MacLean, R. M. Young, V. Bellotti and T. Moran, "Questions, options, and criteria: Elements of design space analysis", *Human-Computer Interaction* **6** (1991) 201–250.

31. T. P. Moran and J. M. Carroll (eds.), *Design Rationale: Concepts, Techniques, and Use* (Lawrence Erlbaum Associates, Mahwah, NJ, 1996).

32. J. Mylopoulos, L. Chung and E. Yu, "From object-oriented to goal-oriented requirements analysis", *Communication of the ACM* **42** (1999) 31–37.

33. K. Pohl and P. Haumer, "Modelling contextual information about scenarios", *International Workshop on Requirements Engineering: Foundations of Software Quality (REFSQ'97)* (1997) 197–204.

34. C. Potts, "ScenIC: A strategy for inquiry-driven requirements determination", *International Symposium on Requirements Engineering (RE'99)* (1999) 58–65.

35. C. Potts and G. Bruns, "Recording the reasons for design decisions" *Proceedings of the 10th International Conference on Software Engineering (ICSE'10)* (Los Alamitos, CA, 1988) 418–427.

36. G. Probst, K. Romhardt and St. Raub, *Managing Knowledge: Building Blocks for Success* (John Wiley & Sons, 1999).

37. B. Ramesh and V. Dhar, "Representing and maintaining process knowledge for large scale system development", *IEEE Expert* **9**, no. 2 (1994) 54–59.

38. F. M. Shipman III and R. J. McCall, "Integrating different perspectives on design rationale: Supporting the emergence of design rationale from design communication", *Artificial Intelligence in Engineering Design, Analysis, and Manufacturing* **11**, no. 2 (1997).

39. A. Sutcliffe, "Requirements rationales: Integrating approaches to requirement analysis", eds. Olson G. M. and Schuon S, *Proceedings of Designing Interactive Systems, DIS' 95* (1) (ACM Press, New York, 1995).
40. A. Sutcliffe and M. Ryan, "Experience with SCRAM, a SCenario requirements analysis method", *Proceedings of the 3rd International Conference on Requirements Engineering* (April 1998).
41. K. M. Wiig, *Knowledge Management Methods* (Schema Press Ltd., 1995).

# TASK MODELS IN INTERACTIVE SOFTWARE SYSTEMS

FABIO PATERNO'

*CNUCE — C.N.R., Via V. Alfieri, 1, 56010 Ghezzano, Pisa, Italy*
*E-mail: fabio.paterno@cnuce.cnr.it*

Task models are logical descriptions of the activities to be performed in reaching user's goals. They have shown to be useful for designing, analyzing and evaluating interactive software applications. This chapter introduces the main concepts underlying task models and discusses how they can be represented and, then, used in the various phases of the life cycle.

*Keywords*: Task models, user interfaces, interactive software systems.

## 1. Introduction

Interest in design and development of interactive software applications has increased considerably over recent years. The underlying reason for this interest is the need to allow the greatest number of people access to software applications for the largest number of purposes and in the widest number of contexts. However, making systems easier to use implies taking into account many factors in the design of an interactive application, such as tasks to support, context of use, user preferences, media and interaction techniques available, and so on. It is thus important to have structured methods for allowing designers to manage such a complexity.

Despite the many direct manipulations tools currently available to designers to enable rapid building of user interfaces with graphical icons and multimedia effects, the design of interactive applications is still difficult and one of the main problems they have is to identify the interaction and presentation techniques more effective to support the possible tasks. On the other hand, end users often find interfaces difficult to understand and use in order to attain their desired ends. One of the main reasons for this is that in many cases users have trouble understanding what tasks are supported or how to associate the desired logical actions with physical actions of the user interface. Such problems could be tackled more systematically if designers had models, methods and tools to explicitly represent task models and provide indications about the most effective interaction and presentation techniques to support the possible user activities.

Task models describe how activities can be performed to reach the users' goals when interacting with the application considered. They should incorporate the requirements foreseen by all those who should be taken into consideration when designing an interactive application (designers, software developers, application domain experts, end users, and managers). They are the meeting point where the various perspectives to be considered in designing interactive applications are combined.

Wide agreement on the importance of task models has been achieved because they capture what the possible intentions of the users are and describe logically the activities that should be performed to reach their goals. These models also allow designers to develop an integrated description of both functional and interactive aspects thus improving traditional software engineering approaches which mainly focused on functional aspects.

More precisely, task models can be useful for different purposes:

- *Understanding an application domain*: as they require a precise identification of the main activities and their relationships, they help to clarify many issues that at the beginning may not be immediately recognized.
- *Recording the results of interdisciplinary discussions*: many people can be involved in the design of an interactive application — user interface designers, software developers, managers, end users, experts of the application domain. It is thus important to have a representation of the activities that can integrate all the requirements raised and supports focusing on a logical level that can be understood by all of them.
- *Designing new applications consistent with the user conceptual model*: because of the lack of structured methods often design is completely based on *ad hoc* rules or the ability of designers. If applications were designed following a task-based approach they would be usable and would incorporate the user requirements captured in the task model.
- *Analyzing and evaluating usability of an interactive systems*: task models can be useful in various ways to support the usability evaluation of an interactive application. They have been used to predict the users' performance in reaching their goals or to support analysis of user behaviour to identify usability problems.
- *Supporting the user during a session*: creating a correspondence between tasks and the interaction objects composing the user interface can be useful also at run-time, for example to provide context-sensitive, task-oriented help systems [24].
- *Documenting interactive software*: the description of how logical activities are supported by the current application is also a documentation useful for users to learn how to use it and for developers, as an abstract description of the implementation.

## 2. Basic Concepts

Tasks are activities that have to be performed to reach a goal. They can be either logical activities such as *Retrieving information about the movies projected tonight* or physical activities such as *Selecting the button in the top left corner*.

A goal is either a desired modification of the state of an application or an attempt to retrieve some information from an application. For example, *Accessing a flight's database to know what flights are available* is a goal which does not require the modification of the state of the application, whereas *Accessing a flight's database to add a new reservation* requires a modification of the state of the application.

It is evident that tasks and goals are closely connected. Each task can be associated with one goal, that is the goal achieved by performing the task. One goal can be achieved by performing one or multiple tasks. In some cases it is possible to choose among different tasks to achieve a certain goal.

We can distinguish between the task analysis and the task modeling phases. *The purpose of task analysis is to identify what the relevant tasks are.* Task analysis can be obtained using different techniques:

- interviews or workshops;
- questionnaires;
- observing users in their work place;
- considering how activities are performed in the current environment; and
- considering existing documentation and training methods.

The results of this analysis can be used to develop various types of abstractions (scenarios, domain models, task models, properties, user and system models). This analysis may have very different scopes, depending on the focus of interest. It can range from activity of a single user at work in a given environment, involving computer-supported activities as well as other types of activities, to the processes occurring in the whole environment, potentially involving several co-workers.

The result of task analysis is an informal list of tasks relevant for the application domain considered which can be supplemented with indications of possible problems, task attributes, and user preferences. The activities effectively performed by a user are sometimes complex processes which are difficult to understand fully or predict: an activity often results from a compromise between conflicting goals; goal-directed processes may be modified by opportunistic processes, the occurrence of particular conditions, exceptions, etc. It is thus important in the task analysis and modeling phases to be able to capture the main elements of such flexibility.

The task modeling phase occurs after the task analysis phase. *The purpose of task modeling is to build a model which describes precisely the relationships among the various tasks identified.* These relationships can be of various types, such as temporal and semantic relationships. The task model is usually structured in such a way as to address various logical levels. When we reach tasks which cannot be further decomposed we have basic tasks. In some cases basic tasks require one single physical action to be performed. The level of decomposition to reach in task modeling depends on its purpose. It is important that task models are rich in information and flexible so as to capture all the main activities that should be performed to reach the desired goals and the different ways to accomplish them. In terms of software engineering phases, task analysis can be particularly useful to support the requirements phase whereas task models can be mainly useful in the design and evaluation phases.

Various types of task models can be considered:

- *the system task model*, describing how the current system implementation assumes that tasks should be performed; system task models are developed when people have to understand how a system works or in usability evaluation where the purpose is to evaluate how well the system task model supports users;
- *the envisioned task model*, where designers think about a new system and how users should interact with them; usually these models are not very refined because some more-implementation dependent aspects cannot be completely defined and are used to propose or prescribe new design solutions; and
- *the user task model*, how users think that tasks should be performed in order to reach their goals. Depending on the user, this task model may not be particularly structured. Most usability problems arise when large discrepancy exists between the user and system task models.

Task models are not the only useful representation when designing interactive applications. In addition, they are sometimes hard to develop from scratch. When approaching the design of a new application or the re-design of an existing application, designers have often a lot of informal information available: documentation concerning existing applications, notes from meetings with users, requirements provided by customers, and so on. They have to refine this material to identify the task structure underlying the existing application to analyze or that corresponding to the new application to design. Scenarios are a well known technique often used during the initial informal analysis phase. They provide informal descriptions of a specific use in a specific context of an application. A careful identification of a set of meaningful scenarios allows designers to obtain a description of most of the activities that should be considered in a task model and task models can be used to identify scenarios. More generally, the main differences between a task model and a scenario are:

- a scenario indicates only one specific sequence of occurrences of the possible activities while the task model should indicate a wide set of activities and the related temporal relationships; and
- a scenario contains some detailed information that usually are not considered in abstractions such as task models.

## 3. Main Approaches to Task Modeling

A number of approaches to task modeling have been developed and it is not possible to mention all of them. In this section, some approaches, particularly interesting, are introduced and discussed.

## 3.1. *Hierarchical task analysis*

The first works on HTA (Hierarchical Task Analysis) date back to the late 60's [1]. The basic idea, to describe the set of activities to be considered logically structured in different levels, has proved to be successful, as can be seen from its application in a number of projects. However, this approach describes how the activities are related to each other in a rather rudimentary way. The representation is usually given including task names in boxes with numbers indicating the order of performance.

## 3.2. *GOMS family*

GOMS (Goals, Operators, Methods, Selection rules) [10] was the first systematic approach to the design of user interfaces. It is a method, originally introduced by Stuard Card, Thomas Moran, and Allen Newell, that has a long history and considerable influence. It is based on a cognitive model (the Human Processor Model) which is described by a set of memories and processors and a set of principles underlying their behaviour. More precisely, it is decomposed into three subsystems interacting with each other (perceptive, motor and cognitive subsystems).

GOMS provides a hierarchical description to reach goals in terms of operators. Operators are elementary perceptual, motor and cognitive acts. Actions at one level can be goals at a lower level. Methods are sequences of subgoals and operators used to structure the description of how to reach a given goal. The selection rules indicate when to use a method instead of another one. An example is when moving the cursor in a specific location of a document. If the desired position is close to the current one then it is sufficient to move the cursor by arrow keystrokes, otherwise it would be better to select the new position with the mouse support.

This notation is especially valid to describe the performance of tasks and it has been used for a number of industrial applications.

In Table 1, there is an example of a GOMS specification. It describes how a user segments the larger goal of *Access ATM* into a sequence of small, discrete operators,

**Table 1.**  Example of a GOMS specification.

---

GOAL: ACCESS ATM
        GOAL: ENABLE ACCESS
                INSERT CREDIT CARD
                INSERT PASSWORD
        GOAL: TAKE CASH
                SELECT WITHDRAW SERVICE
                SELECT AMOUNT OF MONEY
                PRESS OKAY
                TAKE MONEY
                VERIFY AMOUNT OF MONEY

---

such as *Select withdraw service* or *Select amount of money*. In this example, no
selection rule is used.

More generally, there are several different versions of GOMS in use today. In the
first proposal there was both a description of how to express a goal and subgoals
in a hierarchy, methods and operators, and how to formulate selection rules and a
simplified version of GOMS called Keystroke-Level Model (KLM). KLM uses only
keystroke-level operators, no goals, methods or selection rules. The analysis simply
lists the keystrokes, mouse-movements, and mouse-button presses that a user must
perform to accomplish a task, then uses a few simple heuristics to place a single type
of coarse "mental operator" which approximates many kinds of internal cognitive
actions. KLM models are easier to construct, but classic GOMS models provide
more information for the qualitative design. NGOMSL includes a more rigorous set
of rules for identifying the GOMS components and information such as the number
of steps in a method, how goals are set and terminated, what information needs to
be remembered while performing the task [19].

One limitation of GOMS approaches is that it considers error-free behaviour
and only sequential tasks. The latter limitation is partially overcome by one of the
extensions [18] of the GOMS approach that has been developed, CPM-GOMS [15].
In CPM-GOMS separate sequences are constructed for each category of operators
(cognitive, perceptual, and motor operators are considered). Each instance of operator is represented as a box with a name centred in it and the associated duration
in milliseconds above the top right corner. Dependencies between activities are represented as lines connecting the boxes. For example, telephone operators helping
customers cannot press the collect-call key until they hear the customer request
a collect call. Therefore, there would be a dependency line drawn between a box
representing the perception of the word *collect* and boxes representing cognitive
operators that verify the word *collect* and initiate pressing the collect-call key. The
boxes and their dependency lines are represented in a PERT chart, a common tool
used in project management. The diagrams have one row for each type of operator. Such operators are classified according to the related human resource (visual,
aural, internal cognitive, left hand, right hand, verbal, eye movement). Also system
response time is considered. The box associated with each instance of operator is
thus located in the row of the corresponding type, the position depends on when
the action should be performed whereas the size is proportional to the length of
the action. The overall diagram allows designers to easily identify the activities
that can be performed in parallel. An important concept in analyzing the total
task time for complex parallel tasks is the critical path. The critical path is the sequence of activities that takes the longest time and determines the total time for the
entire task. However, in CPM-GOMS operators for representing flexible temporal
relationships (such as dynamic disabling of activities) are not provided.

A problem in predicting time performance with GOMS-based approaches is that
when distributed applications are considered (such as Web-based applications) the
time requested by the application to respond to the user interactions is difficult to

predict because it can depend on unpredictable external factors (such as networks delays). Detailed discussion of the respective strengths and weakness of the various versions in the GOMS family can be found in [18].

## 3.3. *UAN*

One common aspect between HTA and GOMS approaches is the logical hierarchical structure. A similar structure can be found in grammar based approaches to the specification of task models such as in TAG (Task Action Grammar) [30] and ETAG (Extended Task Action Grammar) [35]. In these grammars the logical structure is defined in the production rules where high level tasks can be associated with non terminal symbols whereas basic tasks are associated with the terminal symbols of the grammar.

UAN (User Action Notation) [16] has been another successful approach, still supporting this type of logical structure. The main purpose of UAN, a notation developed by Rex Hartson and others, is to communicate design. It allows designers to describe the dynamic behaviour of graphical user interface. It combines concepts from task models, process-based notations and user actions descriptions. It is a textual notation where the interface is represented as a quasi-hierarchical structure of asynchronous tasks, the sequencing within each task being independent of that in the others. A rich set of operators to describe temporal relationships among tasks is available.

A UAN specification is usually structured into two parts:

- one part describes task decomposition and the temporal relationships among asynchronous tasks; and
- the other part associates each basic task with one table. These tables have three columns indicating the user actions, the system feedback and the state modifications requested to perform it. Some specific symbols are used in these specifications, for example to indicate button pressing or releasing.

An example of specification of a task in terms of its subtasks and their temporal relationships is:

*Task : Access ATM :*

*Enabling Access (Withdrawing Cash | Depositing Cash | Get Information)+*

This expression describes that first the *Enabling Access* task and then one or more occurrences (+ operator) of the tasks composing the expression (*Withdrawing Cash | Depositing Cash | Get Information*) should be performed (the | operator means choice).

In Table 2, we have an example of a description of a basic task. The user has to select the withdraw button. In UAN the expression ~ [object] means that the user moves the cursor to some arbitrary point on the object indicated. In our case, the

**Table 2.**    An example of a UAN specification.

*Task: Withdrawing Cash*

| User Action | Interface Feedback | Interface State |
|---|---|---|
| $\sim$ [Withdraw] V$^\wedge$ | Display (Possible amounts) | CurrentService=Withdraw |
| $\sim$ [Amount] V$^\wedge$ | Provide (AmountCash) | Account=Account-Amount |

user moves the finger on the *Withdraw* button. The selection performed by pressing and releasing an item is represented by the V$^\wedge$ symbol. Then the interface reacts by displaying the possible amounts of money to withdraw and the state of the system changes because the currently selected service becomes withdraw money. Next, the user can select one specific amount of money and the interface provides the amount requested changing the amount still available in the bank account accordingly. As can been seen, the UAN specifications should be read sequentially left-to-right and then vertically (top to bottom from line to line) when there are the tables associated with basic tasks.

The UAN notation is suitable to specifying tasks, which are the components of the specification. It also provides good support for specifying low level actions sequencing. One of the possible limitations is that it can lead to large specifications sometimes with many details not always useful for the designer (for example, often it is not important to specify all the elementary feedback provided by the user interface, for instance when the cursor is on a button then its colour changes slightly). Another limitation is that the order which has to be followed to interpret the tables of the basic tasks (left-to-right) can be rigid and inadequate. For example, when the modification of the state of the application triggers the performance of the basic task considered, it means that it is an item on the far right column that triggers events described by the other columns.

### 3.4. *ConcurTaskTrees*

The ConcurTaskTrees notation was extensively introduced in [26]. It is a notation aiming at supporting engineering approaches to task modeling. It provides a rich set of operators to describe the temporal relationships among tasks (enabling, concurrency, disabling, interruption, optionality). In addition, for each task further information can be given such as its type, the category (indicating how the performance is allocated), the objects that it requires to be manipulated and attributes, such as frequency of performance.

ConcurTaskTrees was developed after first studies [25] aimed at specifying graphical user interfaces by using the LOTOS notation [6]. LOTOS is a concurrent formal notation that seemed a good choice to specify user interfaces because it allows designers to describe both event-driven behaviours and state modifications. Markopoulos [22] provides an example of how this notation has been used to specify task models. However, LOTOS suffers from some limitations that make it unlikely to be widely used in the human-computer interaction domain. It was soon realized that there was a need for new operators to express a richer set of dynamic behaviours in human-computer interactions in a compact way and additional information useful in analyzing and representing task models. Moreover, LOTOS has a textual syntax that can easily generate complex expressions even when the behaviour to describe is quite simple. Thus, a new notation was developed, ConcurTaskTrees. Its main aim is to be an easy-to-use notation that can support the design of real industrial applications, which usually means medium to large sized applications.

The main features of ConcurTaskTrees are:

- *Focus on activities*: it allows designers to concentrate on the activities that users aim to perform, that are the most relevant aspects when designing interactive applications that encompass both user and system-related aspects avoiding low-level implementation details that at the design stage would only obscure the decisions to take.

- *Hierarchical structure*: a hierarchical structure appears quite intuitive, in fact often when people have to solve a problem they tend to decompose it into smaller problems still maintaining the relationships among the various parts of the solution. The hierarchical structure of this specification has two advantages: it provides a wide range of granularity, allowing large and small task structures to be reused, and it enables reusable task structures to be defined at both low and high semantic levels.

- *Graphical syntax*: a graphical syntax often (though not always) is more easy to interpret, in this case it reflects the logical structure so it has a tree-like form.

- *Concurrent notation*: a rich set of possible temporal relationships among the tasks can be defined. This sort of aspect is usually implicit, expressed informally in the output of task analysis. Making the analyst use these operators is a substantial change to normal practice. The reason for this innovation is that after an informal task analysis we want designers to express clearly the logical temporal relationships. This is because such ordering should be taken into account in the user interface implementation to allow the user to perform at any time the tasks that should be active from a semantic point of view.

- *Task allocation*: how the performance of the task is allocated is indicated by the related category and it is explicitly represented by using icons. There are four possibilities: user task (only internal cognitive activity such as selecting a strategy to solve a problem); application task (only system performance such as generating the results of a query); interaction task (user actions with possibility of immediate system feedback, such as editing a diagram), abstract tasks (tasks that have subtasks belonging to different categories).

- *Objects*, once the tasks are identified it is important to indicate the objects that have to be manipulated to support their performance. Two broad types of objects can be considered: the user interface objects and the application domain objects. Multiple user interface objects can be associated to a domain object (for example, temperature can be represented by a bar-chart of a textual value).

Still regarding the tasks associated with withdrawing money from an ATM, Fig. 1 presents an excerpt from the relative ConcurTaskTrees model. First there is the *EnableAccess* task composed of three sequential subtasks ($>>$ is the enabling operator). The *RequirePassword* task is performed by the system as indicated by the computer icon. The *Access* task is an iterative task (indicated by the *symbol) composed of the choice among three subtasks (*WithDrawCash*, *DepositCash, GetInformation*). *WithDrawCash* is composed of a sequence of tasks ([] $>>$ is the enabling with information passing operator). It also has a user subtask (indicated by a different icon): the *DecideAmount* task, describing the internal user cognitive activity associated with deciding the amount to withdraw. For sake of brevity, Fig. 1 does not show the decomposition of *CloseAccess, DepositCash* and *GetInformation* tasks.

Providing support for cooperative applications is important because the increasing availability and improvement of Internet connections makes it possible to use many types of cooperative applications. In ConcurTaskTrees, when there are cooperative applications the task model is composed of various parts. A role is identified by a specific set of tasks and relationships among them. Thus, there is one task model for each role involved. In addition, there is a cooperative part whose purpose is to indicate the relationships among tasks performed by different users.

The cooperative part is described in a manner similar to the single user parts: it is a hierarchical structure with indications of the temporal operators. The main difference is that it includes cooperative tasks: those tasks that imply actions by two or more users in order to be performed. For example, negotiating a price is a cooperative task because it requires actions from both a customer and a salesman.

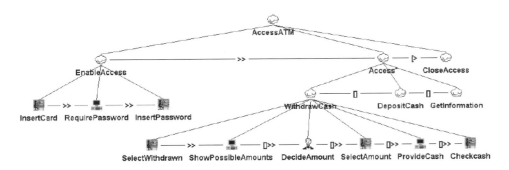

**Fig. 1.** Example of task model in ConcurTaskTrees.

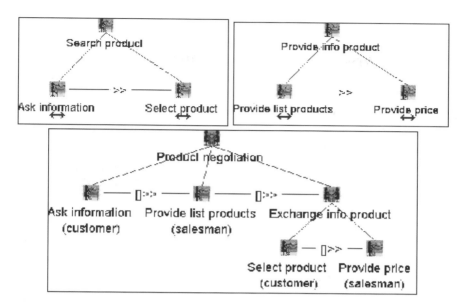

**Fig. 2.** Simplified example of cooperative task model.

Cooperative tasks are represented by a specific icon depicting two people interacting with each other.

In the cooperative part, cooperative tasks are decomposed until we reach tasks performed by a single user that are represented with the icons used in the single user parts. These single user tasks will also appear in the task model of the associated role. They are defined as *connection tasks* between the single-user parts and the cooperative part. In the task specification of a role (see for example Fig. 2, top part) we can identify connection tasks because they are annotated by a double arrow under their names.

The effect of this structure of representation is that in order to understand whether a task is enabled to be performed we have to check both the constraints in the relative single user part and the constraints in the cooperative part. It may happen that a task without constraints regarding the single user part is not enabled because there is a constraint in the cooperative part indicating another task must first be performed by another user. If we consider the example in Fig. 2, we can see the *Search Product* task performed by a Customer and the *Provide Info Product* task performed by a salesman. If we consider each part of the task model in isolation, these two tasks can be started immediately. However, if we consider the additional constraint indicated in the part below the figure we can see that the *Provide list products* task (by the salesman) needs to wait for the performance of the *Ask information* task (by the customer) first in order to be enabled.

## 4. Engineering Task Models

Despite task models have long been considered, only recently developers and designers have realized the importance of engineering approaches to task models. An engineering approach should address at least four main issues:

- availability of *flexible and expressive notations* able to describe clearly the possible activities; it is important that these notations are sufficiently powerful to describe interactive and dynamic behaviours; such notations should be readable so that they can be interpreted also by people with low formal background;
- need for *systematic methods* to support the specification, analysis, and use of task models, to facilitate their development and support designers in using the knowledge that they incorporate to address the design of the user interface and its evaluation; we note that often even designers who developed some task analysis and modeling did not use them for the detailed design of the user interface because of this lack of structured methods which should give rules and suggestions about how to use information in the task model for the concrete design;
- support for the *reuse* of good design solutions to problems which occur across many applications (using for example task patterns [26]); this is relevant especially in an industrial context where developers often have to design applications which address similar problems. Thus, it would be useful to have design solutions structured and documented in such a way as to support easy reuse and tailoring in different applications; and
- availability of *automatic tools* to support the various phases of the design cycle, including usability evaluation; for example, once structured methods for task-based design have been identified it is possible to incorporate their rules in automatic tools which can support designers giving easy to interpret representations of useful information and suggestions of possible solutions, still leaving the possibility of tailoring the criteria to the designer.

Task models have been used in various approaches and have been used to support different phases of the design cycle:

- *Requirement analysis*, where through a task analysis, designers identify requirements that should be satisfied in order to perform tasks effectively (GTA [36]).
- *Design of interactive applications* (Adept [38], Trident [5], Mobile [32]), in this case the goal is to use information contained in logical models to identify the interaction and presentation techniques best suited to support the tasks at hand and the dialogues whose temporal constraints are closest to those of the model.

- *Usability evaluation*, it can be supported in various ways: for example, identifying user efficiency in performing the tasks (such as in the KLM [10] approach) or analyzing logs of user interactions with the support of task models (see for example RemUSINE [20]).

## 5. Use of Task Models in Design of User Interfaces

A user interface is composed of two main components: the presentation, indicating how the user interface provides information to the user, and the dialogue, describing how the actions that users and system perform can be sequenced. Often the dialogue model is part of the task model and it corresponds to the most refined level. Task models can be useful for designing both aspects. The temporal relationships among tasks can be useful to identify how the dialogue should be implemented whereas the type of tasks considered is useful to select the presentation and interaction techniques more suitable.

Since design is a complex activity, it is preferable to avoid applying too rigid rules in task-based design. Rather, a set of criteria can be identified leaving the choice of what criteria should be used to the designer who may need to tailor them to the specific case study under consideration.

During a session the presentations associated with an application can change depending on user and system generated actions. Each presentation is an application-generated user interface whose elements are perceivable at the same time (this means, in a graphical user interface, that the elements are all on the screen at the same time). By analyzing the temporal relationships of a task model, it is possible to identify the enabled task sets. Each set is composed of tasks that are enabled over the same period of time according to the constraints indicated in the model. Thus, the interaction techniques supporting the tasks belonging to the same enable task set should often be part of the same presentation.

In general, when considering the tasks supported by an application there is a wide variety of possible choices in terms of the number of presentations supporting them. These choices vary from a single presentation supporting all tasks (this is possible with small, limited applications) to multiple presentations, whose maximum meaningful number is given by the number of enabled task sets. Indeed, if there are more presentations than such sets, this implies that there are tasks belonging to the same set that are being supported separately by different presentations. This means that a sequential constraint among some of them has been introduced even though it was not indicated in the task model and, thus, was not logically motivated.

Various approaches have been proposed to derive concrete user interfaces from task models. A number of criteria can be identified for this purpose. For example:

- the logical decomposition of tasks can be reflected in the presentation by explicitly grouping interaction techniques associated with tasks that share the same parent task;

- sequential tasks can be supported in various modalities such as: separate presentations for each task rendered at different times; all the interaction techniques corresponding to the sequential tasks rendered in the same presentation (this is useful when the tasks are closely linked either because the sequence of tasks is performed multiple times iteratively or because the tasks exchange information); and lastly, through separate windows for each task (still active over the same period of time but which can be iconified if they take up too much space on the screen);
- the type of task, the type of objects manipulated and their cardinality is another useful element. For example, if we have a selection task then we can immediately delimit the choice of the corresponding interaction technique to use to those supporting selection, in addition we can further limit the possibility of choice depending on the type of objects that can be selected, and, finally, if we know what the data cardinality is we can find only a few suitable interaction techniques, for example for choice among low cardinality values, we can select a radio-button; and
- disabling tasks are tasks that interrupt other activities, in some cases to activate new activities. They can be represented in the same manner (for example buttons with specific graphical attributes) and located in the same part of the layout (for example the right bottom part of the screen) for consistency.

## 6. Use of Task Models in Usability Evaluation

A number of usability evaluation techniques have been developed in recent years. They can be classified according to many dimensions: for example, the level of refinement of the user interface considered or the amount of user involvement in the evaluation. More generally, usability evaluation methods can be classified as:

- model-based approaches, where a significant model related to the interactive application is used to drive the evaluation;
- inspection-based assessment, where some expert evaluates the system or some representation of it, according to a set of criteria; and
- empirical testing, where direct use of the system is considered.

Task models have often been used [18] to produce *quantitative predictions* of how well users will be able to perform tasks with a proposed design. Usually the designer starts with an initial task analysis and a proposed first interface design. The designer should then use an engineering model (like GOMS) to find the applicable usability problems of the interface.

One important issue has been to find a method that allows designers to apply meaningful models to some empirical information. An attempt in this direction was USAGE [9] that provided tool support to a method where the user actions required to execute an application action in UIDE [13] are analyzed by the NGOMSL approach (one of the GOMS family). However this information is still limited with respect to that contained in the logs of the user actions performed during work sessions by users. More interesting results can be obtained using task models and empirical information. In [20], there is a description of how to use task models to support usability evaluation. The possible activities supported by the application described by the task model are used to analyze real user behaviour as revealed by log files obtained through automatic recording of user interactions with a graphical interface. This type of evaluation is useful for evaluating final versions of applications. Other approaches that share similar goals are described in [30].

However, task models can also be useful to support evaluation in the early phases of the design cycle when inspection-based methods are often applied to evaluate prototypes. These methods are less expensive than empirical testing. One of their advantages is that their application at least decreases the number of usability problems that should be detected by the final empirical testing. A number of inspection based evaluation methods have been proposed. Some of them do not use task models, such as heuristic evaluation [23], where a set of general evaluation criteria (such as visibility of the state of the system, consistency, avoid to provide useless information, ...) are considered and evaluators have to check whether they have been correctly applied. This method heavily depends on the ability of the evaluator. In cognitive walkthrough [31] more attention is paid to the notion of task, because the evaluators have to identify a sequence of tasks to perform and for each of them, four questions are asked: will users understand what they should do? Will users identify the interaction techniques able to support the performance of the task? Will users be able to correctly associate the interaction technique with the task to perform? After the interaction, will users receive feedback from the system? While this method is clear and can be applied with limited effort, it has a strong limitation: it tends to concentrate the attention of the evaluator on whether or not the user will be able to perform the right interactions, little attention is paid on what happens if users perform wrong interactions (interactions that are not useful for performing the current task) and on the consequences of such wrong interactions.

Methods with more systematic use of task models have been developed [12] to help designers analyze what happens if there are deviations in task performance with respect to what was originally planned. It indicates a set of predefined classes of deviations that are identified by *guidewords*. In the analysis, the system tasks model is considered: how the design of the system to evaluate assumes that tasks should be performed. The goal is to identify the possible deviations from this plan that can occur. Interpreting the guidewords in relation to a task allows the analyst to systematically generate ways the task could potentially go wrong during its performance. This then serves as a starting point for further discussion and investigation. Such analysis should generate suggestions about how to guard against deviations, as well as recommendations as to user interface designs that might either reduce the likelihood of deviations or support detecting and recovering from them. In the analysis, first basic tasks are considered. Then, evaluators analyze high level tasks, each of them identifies a *group of subtasks* and, consequently, it is possible to analyze deviations that involve more than one basic task. Such deviations concern whether the appropriate tasks are performed and if such tasks are accomplished following a correct ordering. It is important that the analysis of the deviations is carried out by interdisciplinary groups where such deviations are considered from different viewpoints and background in order to carry out a complete analysis. Since the analysis follows a bottom-up approach (first basic tasks and then high-level tasks), it allows designers first to focus on concrete aspects and then to widen the analysis to consider more logical steps. The types of deviations considered concern what happens if the task is not performed or it is performed wrongly or it is performed at the wrong time.

## 7. Tools for Task Models and Task-based Design

One of the main problems in task modeling is that it is a time-consuming, sometimes discouraging, process. To overcome such a limitation, interest has been increasing in the use of tool support [7]. Despite this wide-spread interest, tools developed for task models have been rather rudimentary, mainly research tools used only by the groups that developed them. More systematically engineered tool-support is strongly required in order to ease the development and analysis of task models and make them acceptable to a large number of designers. If we consider the first generation of tools for task models we can notice that they are mainly research prototypes aiming at supporting the editing of the task model and the analysis of the task relationships and related information. This has been a useful contribution but further automatic support is required to make the use of task models acceptable to a large number of designers. For example, the tool support provided for GOMS approaches is still far from what designers and evaluators expect from GOMS tools [4] because of limited pragmatics, partial coverage of the GOMS concepts, limited support for cognitively plausible models and lack of integration in the development process.

Thus, there is a strong need for engineered tools able to support task modeling of applications, including cooperative and multi-user ones which are on the rise, and the analysis of such models' contents which can be complex in the case of many real applications. Euterpe [37] is an example of tool for groupware task analysis based on an ontology for task models. CTTE is an engineered tool, which supports a number of possibilities, for example automatic support to improve the layout, modify the specification, furnish information on the structure of the task model, and check whether the specification is complete. The tool is publicly available at http://giove.cnuce.cnr.it/ctte.html. CTTE also supports interactive simulation of the behaviour of the task model. The tool shows the list of enabled tasks (see Fig. 3, right side) and the designer can select one of them and ask the tool to display the next enabled tasks if the selected one is performed. It is possible to identify an

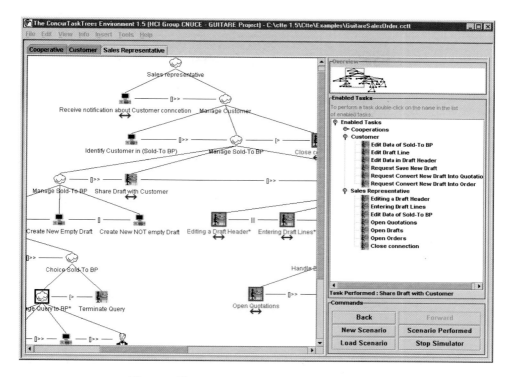

**Fig. 3.** The interactive simulator of task models.

abstract scenario by selecting a list of tasks. The scenario can be displayed by selecting the *Scenario Performed* button and can also be saved and loaded later on even from a different task model in order to check if it can still be performed.

These features are useful for designers to understand whether the dynamic behaviour described by the model corresponds to the desired behaviour. It also serves as interactive documentation of the application in question for end users.

To facilitate the development of task models a number of tools have been developed by various research groups: CRITIQUE [17] helps designers obtain KLM models from user action logs, U-TEL [34] is a knowledge elicitation system supporting the development of interface data and task structures from informal descriptions that aims mainly to identify nouns and verbs and associate them with objects and tasks in the models, and an approach to support the use of scenarios to derive ConcurTaskTrees task models is given in [28].

A number of automatic environments supporting user interface design and generation has also been proposed. A review of these approaches is in [33]. Examples of such environments are ADEPT [38], TRIDENT [5] and MOBI-D [32]. The last one is a particularly comprehensive set of tools developed because it provides a set of model editors to create relations between abstract and concrete elements, and

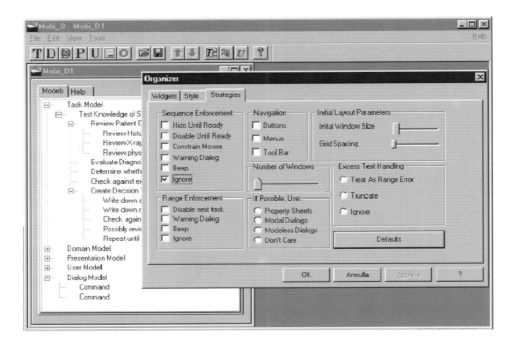

**Fig. 4.**   The Mobi-D support for model-based design.

a layout tool that can be reconfigured to reflect the decisions made at previous stages in the design process. As can be seen in Fig. 4, Mobi-D supports the development of a number of models; designers can then specify various parameters to define how the information in such models can be used to design the user interface. This enables designers to tailor general design criteria to the specific application considered.

## 8. Conclusions

Task models are entered in the current practise of design of interactive software systems. We have discussed how such models can be represented and used for analyzing an interactive application and supporting both user interface design and usability evaluation.

They can effectively complement the support given by object-oriented approaches, such as UML [8], in interactive software system design. UML is more suitable to model the internal part of an interactive software system whereas task models are more effective to indicate the activities to support and corresponding user interface interactions.

Recent years have seen the development of first engineering approaches to task models that make them suitable to be used in software companies and not only by researchers in the field.

# References

1. J. Annett and K. D. Duncan, "Task analysis and training design", *Occupational Psychology* **41** (1967) 211–221.
2. P. Barclay, T. Griffiths, J. McKirfy, N. Paton, R. Cooper and J. Kennedy, "The teallach tool: Using models for flexible user interface design", *Proceedings CADUI'99* (Kluwer Academic Publisher, 1999) 139–158.
3. R. Bastide and P. Palanque, "A visual and formal glue between application and interaction", *International Journal of Visual Language and Computing* (Academic Press) **10**, 6 (1999).
4. L. Baumeister, B. John and M. Byrne, "A comparison of tools for building GOMS Models", *Proceedings CHI'2000* (ACM Press, 2000) 502–509.
5. F. Bodart, A. Hennerbert, J. Leheureux and J. Vanderdonckt, "A model-based approach to presentation: A continuum from task analysis to prototype", *Proceedings DSV-IS'94* (Springer-Verlag, 1994) 77–94.
6. T. Bolognesi and E. Brinksma, "Introduction to the ISO Specification Language LOTOS", *Computer Network ISDN Systems* **14**, no. 1 (1987).
7. B. Bomsdorf and G. Szwillus, "Tool support for task-based user interface design", *Proceedings CHI'99*, Extended Abstracts (1999) 169–170.
8. G. Booch, J. Rumbaugh and I. Jacobson, *Unified Modeling Language Reference Manual* (Addison Wesley, 1999).
9. M. Byrne, S. Wood, P. N. Sukaviriya, J. Foley and D. Kieras, "Automating Interface Evaluation", *Proceedings CHI'94* (ACM Press, 1994) 232–237.
10. S. Card, T. Moran and A. Newell, *The Psychology of Human-Computer Interaction* (Lawrence Erlbaum, Hillsdale, 1983).
11. J. Eisenstein and A. Puerta, "Adaptation in automated user interface design", *Proceedings IUI 2000* (ACM Press, 2000) 74–81.
12. R. Fields, F. Paternò, C. Santoro and T. Tahmassebi, "Comparing design options for allocating communication media in cooperative safety-critical contexts: A method and a case study", *ACM Transactions on Computer-Human Interaction* **6**, no. 4 (December 1999) 370–398.
13. J. Foley and N. Sukaviriya, "History, results, and bibliography of the User Interface Design Environment (UIDE), an early model-based system for user interface design and development", ed. F. Paterno', *Interactive Systems: Design, Specification, Verification* (Springer-Verlag, 1994) 3–14.
14. H. Garavel, J. Fernandez, A. Kerbrat, R. Mateescu, L. Mounier, and M. Sighireanu, "CADP (C{/AE}SAR/ALDEBARAN Development Package): A protocol validation and verification toolbox", *Proceedings of the 8th Conference on Computer-Aided Verification, Lecture Notes in Computer Science 1102* (1996) 437–440.
15. W. Gray, B. John and M. Atwood, "Project Ernestine: A validation of GOMS for prediction and explanation of real-world task performance", *Human-Computer Interaction* **8**, no. 3 (1992) 207–209.
16. R. Hartson and P. Gray, "Temporal aspects of tasks in the user action notation", *Human Computer Interaction* **7** (1992) 1–45.
17. S. Hudson, B. John, K. Knudsen and M. Byrne, "A tool for creating predictive performance models from user interface demonstrations", *Proceedings UIST'2000* (ACM Press, 2000) 93–102.
18. B. John and D. Kieras, "The GOMS family of analysis techniques: Comparison and contrast", *ACM Transactions on Computer-Human Interaction* **3**, no. 4 (1996) 320–351.

19. D. E. Kieras, "Guide to GOMS model usability evaluation using NGOMSL", *The Handbook of Human-Computer Interaction*, 2nd ed. (North Holland, 1996).

20. A. Lecerof and F. Paternò, "Automatic support for usability evaluation", *IEEE Transactions on Software Engineering* (IEEE Press, October, 1998) 863–888.

21. Q. Limbourg, B. Ait El Hadj, J. Vanderdonckt, G. Keymolen and E. Mbaki, "Towards derivation of presentation and dialogue from models: Preliminary results", *Proceedings DSV-IS 2000* (Springer-Verlag, 2000).

22. P. Markopoulos and S. Gikas, "Formal specification of a task model and implications for interface design", *Cognitive Systems* **4-3**, no. 4 (1997) 289–310.

23. J. Nielsen, *Usability Engineering* (Academic Press, 1993).

24. S. Pangoli and F. Paternò, "Automatic generation of task-oriented help", *Proceedings UIST'95* (ACM Press, 1995) 181–187.

25. F. Paternò and G. Faconti, "On the use of LOTOS to describe graphical interaction", *Proceedings HCI'92* (Cambridge University Press, 1992) 155–173.

26. F. Paternò, *Model-Based Design and Evaluation of Interactive Applications* (Springer-Verlag, 1999), ISBN 1-85233-155-0.

27. F. Paternò and C. Mancini, "Designing Usable Hypermedia", *Empirical Software Engineering* **4**, no. 1 (Kluwer Academic Publishers, 1999) 11–42.

28. F. Paternò and C. Mancini, "Developing task models from informal scenarios", *Proceedings ACM CHI'99*, Late Breaking Results (ACM Press, 1999) 228–229.

29. F. Paternò, C. Santoro and V. Sabbatino, "Using information in task models to support design of interactive safety-critical applications", *Proceedings AVI'2000* (ACM Press, 2000) 120–127.

30. S. Payne and T. Green, "Task-actions grammars: A model of the mental representation of task languages", *Human-Computer Interaction* **2** (1986) 93–133.

31. P. G. Polson, C. Lewis, J. Rieman and C. Wharton, "Cognitive walkthroughs: A method for theory-based evaluation of user interfaces", *International Journal of Man-Machine Studies* **36** (1992) 741–773.

32. A. R. Puerta and J. Eisenstein, "Towards a general computational framework for model-based interface development systems", *IUI'99: International Conference on Intelligent User Interfaces* (ACM Press, January 1999) 171–178.

33. P. P. da Silva, "User interface declarative models and development environments: A survey", *Proceedings DSV-IS'2000, Lecture Notes in Computer Science, 1946* (Springer-Verlag, 2000).

34. R. C.-M. Tam, D. Maulsby and A. Puerta, "U-TEL: A tool for eliciting user task models from domain experts", *Proceedings IUI'98* (ACM Press, 1998) 77–80.

35. M. Tauber, "ETAG: Extended task action grammar — A language for the description of the user's task language", *Proceedings INTERACT'90* (Elsevier, 1990) 163–174.

36. G. van der Veer, B. Lenting and B. Bergevoet, "GTA: Groupware task analysis–modeling complexity", *Acta Psychologica* **91** (1996) 297–322.

37. M. van Welie, G. C. van der Veer and A. Eliëns, "An ontology for task world models", *Proceedings DSV-IS'98* (Springer-Verlag, 1998) 57–70.

38. S. Wilson, P. Johnson, C. Kelly, J. Cunningham and P. Markopoulos, "Beyond hacking: A model-based approach to user interface design", *Proceedings HCI'93* (Cambridge University Press, 1993).

39. M. Yvory and M. Hearst, "State of the art in automated usability evaluation of user interfaces 2000", Report available at *http://www.cs.berkeley.edu/~ivory/research/web/papers/survey/survey.html* (1999).

# PRACTICAL MACHINE LEARNING FOR SOFTWARE ENGINEERING AND KNOWLEDGE ENGINEERING

TIM MENZIES

*Department of Electrical & Computer Engineering, University of British Columbia,*
*2356 Main Mall, Vancouver, B. C., Canada V6T 1Z4*
*E-mail: tim@menzies.com*
*http://tim.menzies.com*

Machine learning is practical for software engineering problems, even in data-starved domains. When data is scarce, knowledge can be *farmed* from *seeds*; i.e., minimal and partial descriptions of a domain. These seeds can be *grown* into large datasets via Monte Carlo simulations. The datasets can then be *harvested* using machine learning techniques. Examples of this *knowledge farming* approach, and the associated technique of *data-mining*, is given from numerous software engineering domains.

## 1. Introduction

Machine learning (ML) is not hard. Machine learners automatically generate summaries of data or existing systems in a smaller form. Software engineers can use machine learners to simplify systems development. This chapter explains how to use ML to assist in the construction of systems that support classification, prediction, diagnosis, planning, monitoring, requirements engineering, validation, and maintenance.

This chapter approaches machine learning with three specific biases. First, we will explore machine learning in data-starved domains. Machine learning is typically proposed for domains that contain large datasets. Our experience strongly suggests that many domains lack such large datasets. This lack of data is particularly acute for newer, smaller software companies. Such companies lack the resources to collect and maintain such data. Also, they have not been developing products long enough to collect an appropriately large dataset. When we cannot *mine* data, we show how to *farm* knowledge by growing datasets from domain models.

Second, we will only report mature machine learning methods, i.e., those methods which do not require highly specialized skills to execute. This second bias rules out some of the more exciting work on the leading edge of machine learning research (e.g. horn-clause learning).

Third, in the author's view, it has yet to be shown empirically from realistic examples that a particular learning technique is necessarily better than the others.[a] When faced with $N$ arguably equivalent techniques, Occam's razor suggests we use

---

[a]For evidence of this statement, see the comparisons of different learning methods in [34, 17, 36].

what we learnt from old projects

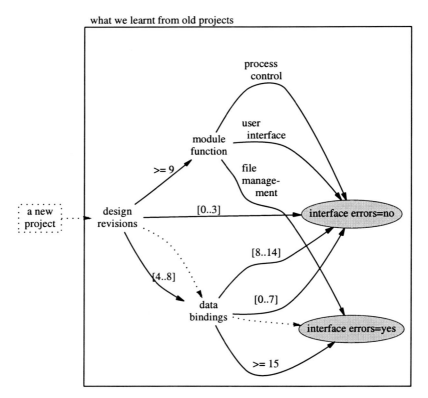

**Fig. 1.** Assessment of a new software project using knowledge learnt from some old projects. In this diagram, "data bindings" is a domain-specific metric for assessing module interrelationships. The experience summarized here declares that the number of design revisions and the large number of data bindings doom some new project into having "interface errors" (see dotted line), i.e., errors arising out of interfacing software modules. This decision tree was automatically learnt using machine learning techniques [30] using the decision tree techniques discussed in this chapter.

the simplest. We hence will explore simple decision tree learners in this chapter. Decision tree learners execute very quickly and are widely used: many of the practical SE applications of machine learning use decision tree learners like C4.5 [33] or the CART system [5]. Decision tree learners are also cheap to buy, are widely available, and are commercially supported (e.g. see http://www.rulequest.com).

In order to balance these biases, we offer the following notes:

- For an excellent theoretical discussion on a wide range of machine learning techniques, see [25].
- For examples of machine learning from naturally occurring datasets, see Figs. 1–4.
- For reviews on other kinds of learners, see the Reynolds chapter in this volume on evolutionary programming and other work on learning knowledge from data [28]; artificial neural nets [11]; an excellent review on data

mining [22]; and a recent special issue of the SEKE journal on different techniques for discovering knowledge [26].

- Looking into the future, we predict that the 2010 version of this handbook will contain many entries describing applications of horn-clause learners to the reverse engineering of software specifications from code [2, 7].

This chapter is structured as follows. Firstly, we expand on our distinction between using machine learning for *data mining* and *knowledge farming*. Secondly, we detail how to use a simple decision tree learner. Thirdly, we offer several case studies of knowledge farming. Fourthly, our discussion section describes how the above contributes to the construction of systems that support classification, prediction, diagnosis, planning, monitoring, requirements engineering, validation, and maintenance. Lastly, the appendices describe some of the lower-level technical details.

## 2. Data Mining and Knowledge Farming

Engineers often build systems without the benefit of large historical datasets which relate to the current project. For example, software development data may be scarce if the development team was not funded to maintain a metrics repository, or the collected data does not relate to the business case, or if contractors prefer to retain

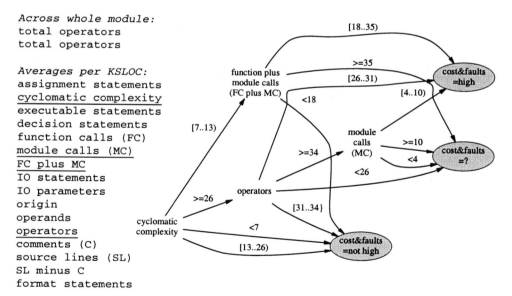

```
Across whole module:
total operators
total operators

Averages per KSLOC:
assignment statements
cyclomatic complexity
executable statements
decision statements
function calls (FC)
module calls (MC)
FC plus MC
IO statements
IO parameters
origin
operands
operators
comments (C)
source lines (SL)
SL minus C
format statements
```

**Fig. 2.** Predicting modules with high cost modules and many faults. Data from 16 NASA ground support software for unmanned spacecraft control [37]. These systems were of size 3000 to 112,000 lines of FORTRAN and contained 4700 modules. "Cyclomatic complexity" is a measure of internal program intricacy [21]. In the general case, there were not many problems with cyclomatic complexity (see [10, p. 295] and [35]). Nevertheless, in this specific domain, it was found to be an important predictor of faults. Of the 18 attributes in the dataset (listed on left), only the underlined four were deemed significant by the learner.

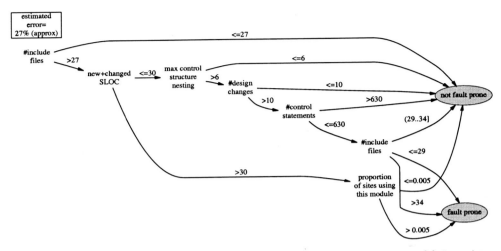

**Fig. 3.** Predicting fault-prone modules [16]. Learnt by the CART tree learner [5] from data collected from a telecommunications system with > 10 million lines of code containing a few thousand modules (exact details are proprietary confidential). Estimated error comes from 10-way cross-validation studies (explained later in this chapter). Of the 42 attributes offered in the dataset, only six were deemed significant by the learner.

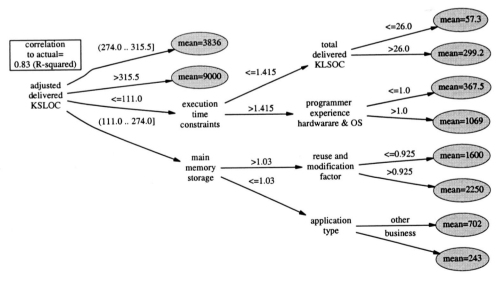

**Fig. 4.** Predicting software development time (in person months) [36]. Learnt by the CART tree learner [5] from the 63 software projects in the COCOMO database. The development times predicted by the learnt trees has a high correlation ($R^2 = 0.83$) with the actual development times in the COCOMO-1 database. For precise definitions of all attributes, see [3]. The tree shown here is just the upper-levels of the actual learnt tree (which is not shown for space reasons). Of the 40 attributes in the dataset, only six were deemed significant by the learner.

control of their own information. Machine learning that supports software engineering or knowledge engineering must therefore work when data is scarce. Hence, this chapter will focus more on *knowledge farming* than *data mining*. In *data mining*, there exists a large library of historical data that we mine to discover patterns. When such libraries exist, ML can (e.g.) infer from past projects the faults expected in new projects (see Figs. 1–3) or development times (see Fig. 4).

The power of data mining is that if the new application is built in exactly the same domain as the historical data, then the resulting predictions are tailored exactly to the local situation. For example, looking through Figs. 1–4, we see that very different attributes are available in different domains.

The drawback with data mining is that it needs the data:

(Data mining) can only be as good as the data one collects. Having good data is the first requirement for good data exploration. There can be no knowledge discovery on bad data [22].

*Knowledge farming* assumes that we cannot access a large library of historical data. When faced with a data famine, we use domain models as a *seed* to *grow* data sets using exhaustive or Monte Carlo simulations. We then *harvest* the data sets using ML. The harvested knowledge contains no more knowledge than in the original domain models. However, knowledge in the domain models can be hard to access. It may be expressed verbosely or hidden within redundant or useless parts of the model. Also, using that domain knowledge may be hard since the domain models may be slow to execute. In contrast, the harvested knowledge contains a simple and succinct record of the important knowledge. Further, the harvested knowledge can execute very quickly.

Knowledge farming can be much simpler than data mining. Naturally occurring datasets must be "cleansed" before they are useful. Data cleansing is the process of making sense of a large store of data that may be poorly-structured and contain corrupt or out-dated records. Knowledge farmers can control and understand the seed that generates the datasets. Hence, knowledge farmers rarely need to cleanse. Also, suppose a learner uses RAM storage to hold all the frequency counts of all the attribute values. Such RAM-based storage fails when data mining very large datasets, e.g. terabytes of data. However, when processing millions of examples (or less), the RAM-based leaner described here will suffice for generating the decision trees shown in (e.g.) Figs. 1–4.

## 3. Building Decision Trees

Decision tree learners such as C4.5 input classified examples and output decision trees. C4.5 is an international standard in machine learning; most new machine learners are benchmarked against this program. C4.5 uses a heuristic *entropy* measure of information content to build its trees. This measure is discussed in an appendix to this chapter.

```
golf.names
Play, Don't Play.

outlook: sunny, overcast, rain.
temperature: continuous.
humidity: continuous.
windy: true, false.

golf.data
sunny, 85, 85, false, Don't Play
sunny, 80, 90, true, Don't Play
overcast, 83, 88, false, Play
rain, 70, 96, false, Play
rain, 68, 80, false, Play
rain, 65, 70, true, Don't Play
overcast, 64, 65, true, Play
sunny, 72, 95, false, Don't Play
sunny, 69, 70, false, Play
rain, 75, 80, false, Play
sunny, 75, 70, true, Play
overcast, 72, 90, true, Play
overcast, 81, 75, false, Play
rain, 71, 96, true, Don't Play
```

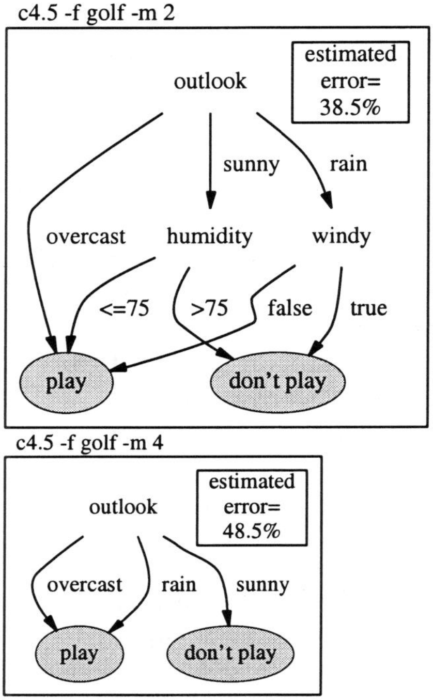

**Fig. 5.** Decision tree learning. Classified examples (bottom left) generate the decision tree (bottom right). Adapted from [32].

As an example of C4.5, suppose we want to decide when to play golf. Figure 5 shows the data we have collected by watching some golfer. The **names** file is a data dictionary describing our dataset. Line one lists our classifications and the other lines describes the attributes. Attributes are either **continuous** (i.e., numeric) or discrete. In the case of discrete values, each possible value is listed in the **names** file. Users of C4.5 should be aware that the algorithm runs faster for discrete attributes than continuous values. However, the performance on continuous variables is quite respectable. In one experiment with a dataset of 21,600 examples of nine continuous attributes, C4.5 ran in 7 seconds on a 350MHz Linux machine with 64MB of RAM.

The **data** file (bottom left of Fig. 5) shows the golf dataset. Each line contains as many comma-separated values as attributes defined in the **names** file, plus the class at the end-of-line. C4.5 supports unknown attribute values: such values may be recorded as a "?" in a **data** file. Of course if the number of unknowns is large, then the learner will have insufficient information to learn adequate theories.

C4.5 is called using the command line:

$$\texttt{c4.5 -f stem -m minobs}$$

where **stem** is the prefix of the **names** and **data** file and **minobs** is the minimum number of examples required before the algorithm forks a sub-tree (default **-m 2**).

The command "c4.5 -f golf -m 2" generates the tree shown top right of Fig. 5 (the tree is generated from the C4.5 text output shown in Appendix C). We see that we should not play golf on high-wind days when it might rain or on sunny days when the humidity is high.

C4.5 uses a statistical measure to estimate the classification error on unseen cases. In the case of "c4.5 -f golf -m 2", C4.5 estimates that this tree will lead to incorrect classifications 38.5 times out of 100 on future cases. We should expect such a large classification errors when learning from only 15 examples. In general, C4.5 needs hundreds to thousands of examples before it can produce trees with low classification errors.

If humans are to read the learnt tree, analysts must trade-off succinctness (smaller trees) vs classification accuracy. A drawback with decision tree learners is that they can generate incomprehensibly large trees. For example, we describe below cases where 10,000 node trees were generated. In C4.5, the size of the learnt tree is controlled by the minobs command-line parameter. Increasing minobs produces smaller and more easily understood trees. However, increasing minobs also decreases the classification accuracy of the tree since infrequent special cases are ignored. We can observe this effect above: the tree generated using "c4.5 -f golf -m 4" (bottom right of Fig. 5) is smaller and less accurate than the tree generated using -m 2.

## 4. Case Studies in Knowledge Farming

Having described a simple machine learner, we can now demonstrate knowledge farming. Our examples fall into two groups:

- In the first group, domains lack models and data. In these domain, knowledge farmers must first build models that we can use to grow datasets.
- In the second group, domains lack data but possess quantitative models. In these domains, we can grow datasets from these models.

### 4.1. *Knowledge farming from qualitative models*

A qualitative model is an under-specified description of a system where the range of continuous attributes are divided into a small number of symbols [13]. We can build and execute such qualitative models quicker than detailed quantitative models since we do not need precise attributes of the system, e.g. the resistance of some bulb.

For example, consider the electrical circuit of Fig. 6 (left-hand side). Suppose our goal is to build a diagnosis device that can recognize a "fault" in the circuit. In this example:

- Our "fault" will be that the circuit cannot generating "enough light".
- "Enough light" means that at least two of bulbs are working.

Ideally, we should be able to recognize this fault using the minimum number of tests on the circuit.

The qualitative model of this circuit is simple to build. We begin by replacing all quantitative numbers $x$ with a qualitative number $x'$ as follows:

$$x' = + \quad \text{if} \quad x > 0$$
$$x' = 0 \quad \text{if} \quad x = 0$$
$$x' = - \quad \text{if} \quad x < 0.$$

We can now describe the circuit in qualitative terms using the Prolog program `circuit` shown in Fig. 6 (right-hand side). In Prolog, variables start with upper case letters and constants start with lower-case letters or symbols. `Circuit`'s variables conform to the following qualitative relations shown in Fig. 7. The `sum` relation describes our qualitative knowledge of addition. For example, `sum(+,+,+)` says that the addition of two positive values is a positive value. Some qualitative additions are undefined. For example `sum(+,-,Any)` says that we cannot be sure what happens when we add a positive and a negative number.

The `bulb` relation describes our qualitative knowledge of bulb behavior. For example, `bulb(blown,dark,Any,0)` says that a blown bulb is dark, has zero current across it, and can have any voltage at all.

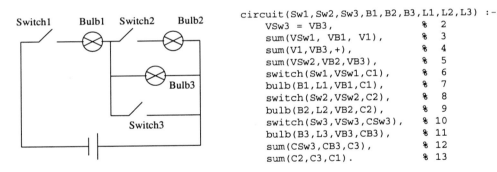

Fig. 6.   An electrical circuit. From [4].

```
%sum(X,Y,Z).            %blub(Mode,Light,Volts,Amps)   %switch(State,Volts,Amps)
sum(+,+,+).             bulb(blown,dark, Any, 0).       switch(on,    0,    Any).
sum(+,0,+).             bulb(ok,   light,+,   +).       switch(off,  Any,    0).
sum(+,-,Any).           bulb(ok,   light,-,   -).
sum(0,+,+).             bulb(ok,   dark, 0,   0).
sum(0,0,0).
sum(0,-,-).
sum(-,+,Any).
sum(-,0,-).
sum(-,-,-).
```

Fig. 7.   Some qualitative relations. From [4].

The `switch` relation describes our qualitative knowledge of electrical switches. For example `switch(on,0,Any)` says that if a switch is on, there is zero voltage drop across it while any current can flow through it.

The `circuit` relation of Fig. 6 describes our qualitative knowledge of the circuit. This relation just records what we know of circuits wired together in series and in parallel. For example:

- `Switch3` and `Bulb3` are wired in parallel. Hence, the voltage drop across these components must be the same (see line 2).
- `Switch2` and `Bulb2` are wired in series so the voltage drop across these two devices is the sum of the voltage drop across each device. Further, this summed voltage drop must be the same as the voltage drop across the parallel component `Bulb3` (see line 5).
- `Switch1` and `Bulb1` are in series so the same current `C1` must flow through both (see lines 6 and 7)

Figure 8 shows how we can learnt a decision tree for our circuit. A small Prolog program generates `circ.data`. In that program, the relation `classification` describes our recognizer for the faulty circuit: if two out of the tree bulbs are working, then the classification is `good`; else, it is `bad`. Note that the circuit's behavior can be re-classified by changing the `classification` relation. The `names` file for this example is shown top right of Fig. 8. The learnt tree is shown at bottom right. To an accuracy of 85.2%, we can detect when two of our three bulbs are blown by just watching `Bulb1`. A visual inspection of the circuit offers an intuition of why this is

*Generator, circ.data:*

```
go   :- tell('circ.data'),
        go1,
        told.
go1 :- functor(X,circuit,9),
        forall(X,example(X)).

example(circuit(
    Sw1,Sw2,Sw3,B1,B2,B3,L1,L2,L3)) :-
    classification(B1,B2,B3,Class),
    format('~a,~a,~a,~a,~a,~a,~a~n',
        [Sw1,Sw2,Sw3,L1,L2,L3,Class]).

%classification(B1, B2, B3,Class)
classification( ok, ok, B3,   good):- !.
classification( ok, B2, ok,   good):- !.
classification( B1, ok, ok,   good):- !.
classification( B1, B2, B3,   bad).

:- go, halt.
```

*circ.names:*

```
good,bad.

switch1: on, off.
switch2: on, off.
switch3: on, off.
bulb1: light, dark.
bulb2: light, dark.
bulb3: light, dark.

c4.5 -f circ -m 2
```

**Fig. 8.** Left: generation of `circ.data`. Right, top: `circ.names`. Right, bottom: learnt tree.

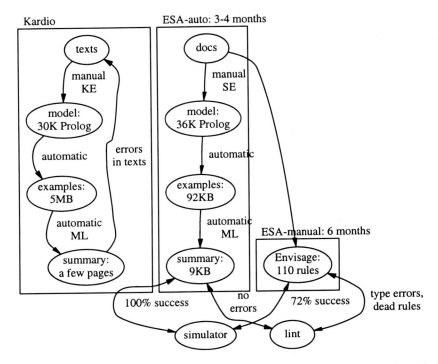

**Fig. 9.** Knowledge farming from Prolog qualitative models. Examples from [4] and [29].

so. `Bulb1` is upstream of all the other bulbs. Hence, it is a bottleneck for all the behavior in the rest of the circuit. Based on the learnt tree, we can define a minimal heuristic diagnostic strategy as follows: monitor only `Bulb1` and ignore the other 6 electrical components in the circuit.

This small example is an example of Bratko's method for understanding qualitative models:

- Build a model (which in knowledge farming is called the seed).
- Exhaustively simulate the model (which we would call growing the seed).
- Summarize the simulation results using machine learning (which we would call harvesting the seed).

Figure 9 illustrates the KARDIO and Pearce application of Bratko's technique. In the KARDIO application [4], a 30K Prolog qualitative model was built from cardiology textbooks. This model was exhaustively simulated to generated 5MB of data files. This data was summarized by a machine learner into a few pages of rules. Medical experts found differences between the learnt knowledge and the knowledge in the textbooks. On reflection, these experts preferred the learnt knowledge, arguing that the texts' knowledge was often too generalized or too specialized [Bratko, Personal Communication, 1992].

In the Pearce application [29], a 36KB Prolog qualitative model was built of the electrical circuitry in a European Space Agency satellite. This was exhaustively simulated and summarized using a machine learner. The learnt knowledge was a diagnosis device and was assessed by comparing it to a manually constructed diagnostic expert system constructed by a separate team. Note that:

- The manual system took nearly twice as long to build as the learnt system.
- The manually constructed knowledge base contained more syntactic errors (e.g. type errors and dead-end rules) than the automatically learnt knowledge base.
- When compared to a FORTRAN simulator of the circuitry, the manually constructed knowledge base could reproduce less of simulator's behavior than the automatically learnt system.

## 4.2. *Knowledge framing from quantitative knowledge*

### 4.2.1. *COCOMO*

Our next example of knowledge farming relates to assessing software development risk [23]. This study is a quintessential example of using machine learning in data-starved domains. Given a wide-range of "don't know"s, we:

- Extract variables randomly from those ranges.
- Run a model using those variables as inputs.
- Summarize the resulting behavior using machine learning.

The summaries can be very succinct. In the case study presented here, we will summarize six million "what-if"s in $\frac{1}{3}$ of a page (see Fig. 12).

Consider the software project shown in Fig. 10. The column *now*1 in Fig. 10 shows the current state of a NASA software project. Attributes in this figure come from the COCOMO-II software cost estimation model evolved by Boehm, Madachy, *et al* [3, 6, 1]. Attribute values of "2" are nominal. Usually, attribute values lower than "2" denote some undesirable situation while higher values denote some desired situation.

Note the large space of possibilities. The *changes*1 column show 11 proposed changes to that project. That is, there exist $2^{11} = 2048$ combinations of proposed changes to this project. Further, when combined with the ranges in the *now*1 column, there are $6 * 10^6$ options shown in this table.

Before a machine learner can search this space of $6 * 10^6$ options, we need to somehow classify each option. We will use the Madachy COCOMO-based effort-risk model [20]. The model contains 94 tables of the form of Fig. 11. Each such table implements a heuristic adjustment to the internal COCOMO attributes. This model generates a numeric effort-risk index which is then mapped into the classifications *low, medium, high*. Studies with the COCOMO-I project database have shown that the Madachy index correlates well with $\frac{months}{KDSI}$ (where KDSI is thousands of

| | ranges | | KC-1 (very new project) | |
| --- | --- | --- | --- | --- |
| | | | now1 | changes1 |
| Scale drives | prec = 0..5 | precedentness | 0, 1 | |
| | flex = 0..5 | development flexibility | 1, 2, 3, 4 | 1 |
| | resl = 0..5 | architectural analysis or risk resolution | 0, 1, 2 | 2 |
| | team = 0..5 | team cohesion | 1, 2 | 2 |
| | pmat = 0..5 | process maturity | 0, 1, 2, 3 | 3 |
| Product attributes | rely = 0..4 | required reliability | 4 | |
| | data = 1..4 | database size | 2 | |
| | cplx = 0..5 | product complexity | 4, 5 | |
| | ruse = 1..5 | level of reuse | 1, 2, 3 | 3 |
| | docu = 0..4 | documentation requirements | 1, 2, 3 | 3 |
| Platform attributes | time = 2..5 | execution time constraints | ? | |
| | stor = 2..5 | main memory storage | 2, 3, 4 | 2 |
| | pvol = 1..4 | platform volatility | 1 | |
| Personnel attributes | acap = 0..4 | analyst capability | 1, 2 | 2 |
| | pcap = 0..4 | programmer capability | 2 | |
| | pcon = 0..4 | programmer continuity | 1, 2 | 2 |
| | aexp = 0..4 | analyst experience | 1, 2 | |
| | pexp = 0..4 | platform experience | 2 | |
| Project attributes | ltex = 0..4 | experience with language and tools | 1, 2, 3 | 3 |
| | tool = 0..4 | use of software tools | 1, 2 | |
| | site = 0..5 | multi-site development | 2 | |
| | sced = 0..4 | time before delivery | 0, 1, 2 | 2 |

\# of what-ifs (combinations of $nowX \cup changesX$) = $\boxed{6 * 10^6}$

**Fig. 10.** The KC-1 NASA software project.

delivered source lines of code) [20]. This validation method reveals a subtle bias in the Madachy model. The model assess the *development risk* of a project, i.e., the risk that the project will take longer than planned to build. This definition is different to the standard view of risk. Standard software risk assessment defines risk as some measure of the runtime performance of the system. That is, in the standard view, risk is defined as an *operational* issue (e.g. [18, 19]). Since we are using the Madachy model, we must adopt his definitions. Hence, when we say "software risk", we really mean "development risk".

There are several sources of uncertainty when using the Madachy model. Firstly, many of its internal attributes are unknown with accuracy. Madachy's model uses off-the-shelf COCOMO and off-the-shelf COCOMO can be up to 600% inaccurate in its estimates (see [27, p. 165] and [14]). In practice, users tune COCOMO's

|  |  | rely= | | | | |
|---|---|---|---|---|---|---|
|  |  | very low | low | nominal | high | very high |
|  | very low | 0 | 0 | 0 | 1 | 2 |
|  | low | 0 | 0 | 0 | 0 | 1 |
| sced= | nominal | 0 | 0 | 0 | 0 | 0 |
|  | high | 0 | 0 | 0 | 0 | 0 |
|  | very high | 0 | 0 | 0 | 0 | 0 |

**Fig. 11.** A Madachy factors table. From [20]. This table reads as follows. In the exceptional case of high reliability systems and very tight schedule pressure (i.e., *sced=low* or very low and *rely= high or very high*), add some increments to the built-in attributes (increments shown top-right). Otherwise, in the non-exceptional case, add nothing to the built-in attributes.

attributes using historical data in order to generate accurate estimates [6]. For the project in Fig. 10, we lacked the data to calibrate the model. Therefore we generated three different versions of the model: one for each of the tunings we could find published in the literature [8, 6] plus one using the standard tunings found within the Madachy model.

A second source of uncertainty is the SLOC measures in our project (delivered source lines of uncommented code). COCOMO estimations are based on SLOC and SLOC is notoriously hard to estimate. Therefore, we run the Madachy model for a range of SLOCs. From Boehm's text *"Software Engineering Economics"*, we saw that using SLOC = 10K, SLOC = 100K, SLOC = 2000K would cover an interesting range of software systems [3].

A third source of uncertainty are the ranges in Fig. 10. There are $2^{11} = 4048$ combinations of possible changes and $10^5$ ways to describe the current situation (each "don't know" value, denoted "?", implies that we may have to run one simulation for every point in the don't know ranges). This space of uncertainty can be crippling. If we gave a manager one report for each possibility, they may be buried under a mountain of reports. Clearly, we have to explore this space of options. However, we also have to prune that space as savagely as possible.

We apply knowledge farming to this example as follows. First, we use Monte Carlo simulations to sample the $6 * 10^6$ options within Fig. 10. For every combination of attribute tunings and SLOC, we generated $N$ random examples by picking one value at random for each of the attributes from column 2 of Fig. 10. $N$ was increased till the conclusions (generated below) *stabilized*, i.e., conclusions found at sample size $N$ did not disappear at larger sample sizes. In this study, we used $N = 10,000, 20,000, 30,000, 40,000, 50,000$. This generated 45 examples of the system's behavior sorted as follows:

$$3 \text{ SLOCs} * 3 \text{ tunings} * 5 \text{ samples} = 45 \text{ samples}.$$

Secondly, we learnt an ensemble of 45 decision trees using C4.5 from each of the 45 samples. This generated 45 trees with tens of thousands of nodes in each tree. Such large trees cannot be manually browsed. With Sinsel, I have developed the TARZAN for polling ensembles of large trees. The premise of TARZAN is that when a human "understands" a decision tree, they can answer the following question:

> Here are some things I am planning to change; tell me the smallest set that will change the classifications of this system.

Note that this question can be answered by hiding the learnt trees and merely showing the operator the significant attribute ranges (SAR) that change the classifications. TARZAN swings through the decision trees looking for the SARs.

TARZAN applied eight pruning steps $P_1, P_2, \ldots, P_8$ to generate a succinct summary of the SARs. For all prunings:

- $Out_i = P_i (Out_{i-1})$.
- $Out_0$ is initialized to include all the ranges of all the variables, e.g. all of column 2 of Fig. 10.
- The SARs are $Out_8$.

$Out_1 = P_1 (Out_0)$: The entropy measure of C4.5 performs the first pruning. Attributes that are too dull to include in the trees are rejected. We saw examples of this rejection process above in Figs. 2–4.

$Out_2 = P_2 (Out_1)$: $P_2$ prunes ranges that contradict the domain constraints, e.g. $now1 \cup changes1$ from Fig. 10. Also, when applying $P_2$, we prune any tree branch in the ensemble that use ranges from $Out_2 - Out_1$ (i.e., uses ranges discarded by $P_2$).

$Out_3 = P_3 (Out_2)$: $P_3$ prunes ranges that do not change classifications in the trees. That is, $Out_3$ only contains the ranges that can change classifications. To compute $Out_3$, TARZAN finds each pair of branches in a tree that lead to different conclusions. Next, we find attributes that appear in both branches. If the ranges for that attribute in the different branches do not overlap, then we declare that the difference between these two ranges is a change that can alter the classifications in that tree.

$Out_4 = P_4 (Out_3)$: $P_4$ prunes ranges that are not interesting to the user, i.e., are not mentioned in the $changes1$ set ($Out_4 = Out_3 \wedge changes1$).

$P_1, \ldots, P_4$ apply to single trees. The remaining pruning methods collects the $Out_4$s generated from all the single trees, then explores their impacts across the entire ensemble.

$Out_5 = P_5 (Out_4)$: $P_5$ prunes ranges that do not change classifications in the majority of the members of the ensemble (our threshold is 66%, or 30 of the 45 trees).

$Out_6 = P_6 (Out_5)$: $P_6$ prunes ranges that are not stable; i.e., those ranges that are not always found at the larger samples of the random Monte Carlo simulations. In the case of Fig. 10, of the 11 changes found in $changes1$, only 4 survived to $Out_6$.

$Out_7 = P_7 (Out_6)$: $P_7$ explores all subsets of $Out_6$ to reject the combinations that have low impact on the classifications. The impact of each subset is assessed via how that subset changes the number of branches to the different classifications. For example, Fig. 12 shows how some of the subsets of the ranges found in $Out_6$ affect KC-1. In that figure, bar chart $A1$ shows the average number of branches to *low*, *medium*, and *high* risk seen in the 45 trees. For each subset $X \subseteq Out_6$, we make a copy of the trees pruned by $P_2$, then delete all branches that contradict $X$. This generates 45 new trees that are consistent with $X$. The average number of branches to each classification in these new branches is then calculated. $P_7$ would reject the subsets shown in $B1$, $C1$, and $B2$ since these barely alter the current situation in $A1$.

$Out_8 = P_8 (Out_7)$: $P_8$ compares members of $Out_7$ and rejects a combination if some smaller combination has a similar effect. For example, in Fig. 12, we see in $A2$ that having moderately talented analysts and no schedule pressure ($acap=[2]$, $sced=[2]$) reduces our risk nearly as much as any larger subset. Exception: $C2$ applies all four actions from KC-1's $Out_6$ set to remove all branches to medium and high risk projects. Nevertheless, we still recommend $A2$, not $C2$, since $A2$ seems to achieve most of what $C2$ can do, with much less effort.

$Out_8$ are the operators found by TARZAN which can effect the device. These are the significant attribute ranges (SARs). In this KC-1 study, we have found 2 significant control strategies out of a range of $6 * 10^6$ what-ifs and 11 proposed new changes. TARZAN took 8 minutes to process KC-1 on a 350MHz machine. That

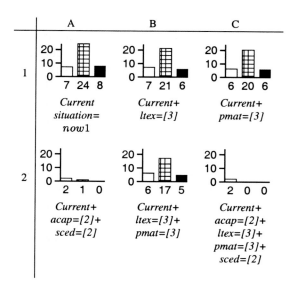

**Fig. 12.** Average number of branches to different classifications in the 45 trees in KC-1, assuming different subsets of the ranges seen in KC-1's $Out_6$ set. Legend: □ = low risk, ▦ = medium risk ■ = high risk.

time was divided equally between Prolog code that implements the tree processing and some inefficient shell scripts that filter the Prolog output to generate Fig. 12. We are currently porting TARZAN to "*C*" and will use bit manipulations for set processing. We are hopeful that this new language and smarter processing will make TARZAN much faster.

### 4.2.2. *Reachability*

Our other examples related to applications that could be useful for software engineering practitioners. This example describes an application that could be useful for theoretical software engineering researchers.

This example begins with the following theoretical characterization of testing. Testing, we will assume, is the construction of pathways that *reach* from inputs to some interesting zone of a program. This zone could be a bug or a desired feature. In this *reachability* view, the goal of testing is to show that a test set uncovers no bugs while reaching all desired features.

This theoretical view of testing can be modeling mathematically. The *reachability model* is a set of mathematical equations that computes the average case probability of finding a bug in a program using random inputs [24]. Reachability represents programs as directed graphs indicating dependencies between variables in a global symbol table; see Fig. 14 (left). Such graphs have $V$ nodes which are divided into and $f\%$ and-nodes and (or $f = 1 -$ and $f)\%$ or-nodes. These nodes are connected by yes-edges, which denote valid inferences, and no-edges, which denote invalid inferences. For the sake of clarity, we only show the yes-edges in Fig. 14 (left). To add the no-edges, we find every impossible pair and connect them; e.g. we link A=1 to A=2 with a no-edge since we cannot believe in two different assignments for the same variable at the same time. We say that, on average, each node is touched by $no_\mu$ no-edges. When inferencing across these graphs, variables can be assigned, at most $T$ different values; i.e., a different assignment for each time tick $T$ in the execution (classic propositional systems assume $T = 1$; simulation systems

```
byte a=1; byte b=1; bit f=1;
active proctype A(){ do :: f==1 -> if :: a==1 -> a=2;
                                     :: a==2 -> a=3;
                                     :: a==3 -> f=0; a=1;
                                  fi
                  od
}
active proctype B(){ do :: f==0 -> if :: b==1 -> b=2;
                                     :: b==2 -> b=3;
                                     :: b==3 -> f=1; b=1;
                                  fi
                  od
}
```

**Fig. 13.**    Two procedural subroutines from the SPIN model checker [12].

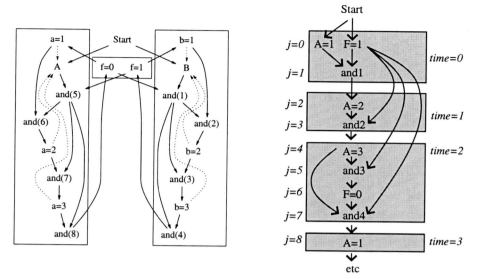

**Fig. 14.** Left: And-or links found in the SPIN model from Fig. 13. **Proctype A** and **B** are shown in the boxes on the left-hand side and right-hand side respectively. These **proctypes** communicate via the shared variable **f**. Dotted lines represent indeterminism; e.g. after **proctype A** sets **a=2**, then we can go to any other statement in the proctype. Right: Example reachability network built from the left-had-side network showing how to violate property **always not A=3** at height $j = 4$.

assume $T \geq 1$). Nodes are reached across the dependency graph using a path of height $j$ where the inputs are at height $j = 0$. For example, Fig. 14 (left) shows the network of paths of height $j = 8$ that reaches $A = 1$, then $A = 2$, then $A = 3$. Note that since four values are assigned to $A$, then time $T$ must be 4.

If we use $In$ inputs, then the odds of reaching a node at height $j = 0$ is $P[0] = \frac{In}{V}$. The odds of reaching a node at height $j > 0$ depends on the node type:

- We can't reach an and-node unless we reach all its parents at some height $i < j$.
- We can't miss an or-node unless we miss all its parents at some height $i < j$.

Based on these rules, we can compute the odds $P[j]$ of reaching a node at height $j$ (see [24] for the details). We convert these odds to the required number of tests as follows. After $N$ tests, we are $C$ certain that we will see an event of odds $P[j]$ with odds:

$$C = 1 - ((1 - P[j])^N).$$

Assuming we want to be 99% sure of reaching that node, then this equation re-arranges to:

$$N = \frac{\log(1 - 0.99)}{\log(1 - P[j])}$$

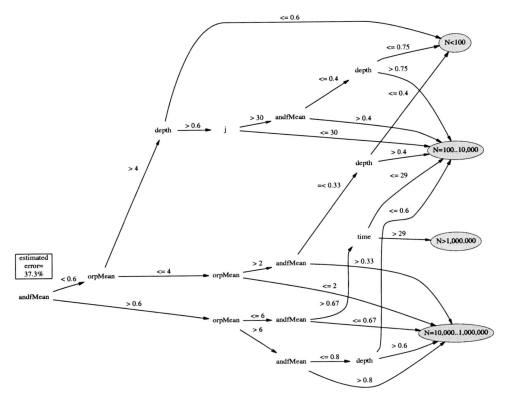

**Fig. 15.** Predicting reachability from simulations of reachability model using 1500 randomly chosen inputs. The tree was learnt using `c4.5 -m 45 -f runs1500`.

which we can use to classify each simulation run:

$$
\text{Class} = \begin{cases}
\text{fast and cheap} & \text{if } N < 10^2, \\
\text{fast and moderately expensive} & \text{if } N < 10^4, \\
\text{slow and expensive} & \text{if } N < 10^6, \\
\text{impossible} & \text{otherwise.}
\end{cases}
$$

Figure 15 shows a decision tree learnt by C4.5 using the above classifications. For reasons of readability, this tree is truncated using a large "minobs" value. From the tree, we can make many inferences about the impact of various factors on testability. For example, minor changes to the structure of a program can have massive and undesirable changes to a program's reachability and hence testability:

- We see in Fig. 15 that there are three ways to conclude that less than 100 tests are required to reach most parts of a program. The mean percentage of and-nodes appearing in all three paths is:

$$
(\text{andf}_\mu \le 0.33) \wedge (\text{andf}_\mu \le 0.4) \wedge (\text{andf}_\mu \le 0.6) = \text{andf}_\mu \le 0.6\,.
$$

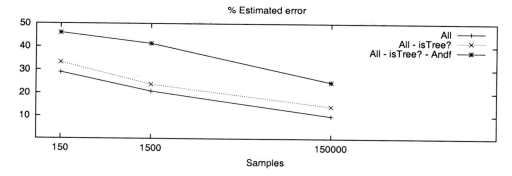

**Fig. 16.** Relative importance of andf$_\mu$ and isTree? in the reachability model.

That is, if andf$_\mu$ ever rises above 0.6, there is no way that 100 random tests will be enough to test that program.

- Figure 15 also tells us that there is only one way to show that more than 1,000,000 tests are required to reach most parts of a program. The and-node frequencies in that path are:

$$(\text{andf}_\mu > 0.6) \wedge (\text{andf}_\mu > 0.67) = \text{andf}_\mu > 0.67.$$

That is, if andf$_\mu$ rises from 0.6 to 0.67, then a system with easy reachability could suddenly transform into a system with hard reachability, hence hard testability.

Not only can we use machine learning to understand systems like the reachability model, we can also use machine learning to control the modeling process. Using a machine learner, we can recognize what portions of a model are not critical to the success of the model. Hence, machine learning can stop analysts wasting time exploring pointless issues. For example, when developing the reachability model with Singh and Cukic, we were unsure of the importance of two attributes:

Andf$_\mu$ : The frequency of conjunctions in a program.
isTree? : If this boolean is true/false, the equations of reachability returns the lower/upper estimates (respectively) on number of upstream variables used to reach a bug.

To determine the importance of these variables, we ran the reachability model by randomly selecting input values for all attributes including andf$_\mu$ and isTree? We then asked C4.5 to learn a predictor of reachability from 150, 1500, or 150,000 randomly selected outputs from the model. Three predictors were built:

(1) The first predictor was built from examples that held values for all attributes in the reachability model. This provided the baseline measure shown in All plot of Fig. 16.

(2) The second predictor was built from examples that held all values except the isTree? attribute. As we would expect, since the learner was given less information, the learnt tree was not as good as the All tree: loss of accuracy$\approx$5% (see the All-isTree? plot of Fig. 16).

(3) The third predictor was built from examples that held all values except the isTree? and andf attributes. Again, since we are giving the learner less information, the learnt tree is less accurate (see the All-isTree?-Andf$_\mu$ plot of Fig. 16).

Note that this third plot is much less accurate than the others. That is, while knowledge of isTree? is not so vital, andf$_\mu$ is clearly a crucial attribute. Therefore, if we could accept a 5% loss in the accuracy of our analysis, we could stop exploring the problems relating to the isTree? issue and focus more on issues relating to andf$_\mu$.

## 5. Discussion

When we lack sufficient data for mining, we can go farming. We can seed our knowledge with domain models, then grow and harvest decision trees. The models need not be too detailed (e.g. `circuit` in Fig. 6). Further, if we are unsure of parts of those models, we can use machine learning to identify which areas to explore and which to ignore. For example, with the reachability model, we could show that equations using the isTree? parameter were not crucial to the model.

We have seen in this chapter that machine learning can be used for many applications:

**Prediction and Classification:** In Figs. 1–3, we saw decision trees learnt to predict faults in software modules. Figure 4 showed a decision tree learnt to predict software development effort. These predictors can assess new examples, or classify old examples.

**Diagnosis:** Figure 8 showed a diagnosis tree learnt from a toy-example using qualitative modeling. Figure 9 showed how the same style of modeling could be used to build diagnosis trees for larger applications such as cardiac disease and satellite electrical malfunctions.

**Planning:** Figure 12 showed the implications of several plans for changing a software project. We can use that figure to select which plan we wish to apply.

**Monitoring:** Machine learning can rationalize metrics collection and monitoring. Figure 15 found an attribute range (andf$_\mu$ = 0.6 to andf$_\mu$ = 0.67) where some desired property of a system (testability) could degrade very sharply. Clearly, there is a strong case for monitoring at least that attribute.

**Requirements Engineering:** When conflicts arise between stakeholders, machine learning can find which decisions are crucial and which arguments do not impact the system. Debates could then be shortened to just the crucial issues.

For example, in the COCOMO KC-1 study, stakeholders need not debate the 2048 possible changes to a project. Instead, machine learning found the handful of changes that really matter (recall Fig. 12).

Machine learning can also support some crucial software processes:

**Validation:** We can validate the models used in knowledge farming by studying their behavior. For example, using TARZAN, test engineers can inspect $Out_8$ to find the effects of changing key attributes in the system. This validation scheme could fault the model used as the seed if the test engineers find that system behavior changes inappropriately when the key control attributes change. We envision that this style of validation will become very important to organizations like NASA in the near future. NASA already has hundreds of simulators of flight systems. Such simulators are used to explore alternatives in system design and flight profiles. Tools like TARZAN can be used to check if those simulators are generating sensible output.

**Maintenance:** When domain knowledge changes, we must manually change the seed. However, once that change has been made, we can then automatically generate classifiers, predictors, diagnosis engines, requirement engineering tools, planners, validation tools, and monitors.

Note that, in contrast to data mining, all the above are possible in domains that lack large datasets. For example, the Fig. 12 plans were generated in a domain where many crucial attributes were unknown.

In conclusion, we note that knowledge farming offers a natural integration of software engineering and knowledge engineering:

- Software engineers or requirements analysts develop seeds.
- Knowledge engineers grow and harvest the seeds using machine learning and tools like TARZAN.

## Appendix A: Inside a Learner

The learner described here uses a heuristic *entropy* measure of information content to build its trees. The attribute that offers the largest *information gain* is selected as the root of a decision tree. The example set is then divided up according to which examples do/do not satisfy the test in the root. For each divided example set, the process is then repeated recursively.

The information gain of each attribute is calculated as follows. A tree $C$ contain $p$ examples of some class and $n$ examples of other classes. The *information required* for the tree $C$ is as follows [32]:

$$I(p,n) = -\left(\frac{p}{p+n}\right)\log_2\left(\frac{p}{p+n}\right) - \left(\frac{n}{p+n}\right)\log_2\left(\frac{n}{p+n}\right).$$

Say that some attribute $A$ has values $A_1, A_2, \ldots, A_v$. If we select $A_i$ as the root of a new sub-tree within $C$, this will add a sub-tree $C_i$ containing those objects in $C$

that have $A_i$. We can then define the expected value of the information required for that tree as the weighted average:

$$E(A) = \sum_{i=1}^{v} \left( \frac{p_i + n_i}{p + n} \right) I(p_i, n_i) \,.$$

The information gain of branching on $A$ is therefore:

$$\text{gain}(A) = I(p, n) - E(A) \,.$$

For example, consider the decision tree learnt by C4.5 in Fig. 5. In that tree, C4.5 has decided that the weather `outlook` has the most information gain. Hence, it has placed `outlook` near the root of the learnt tree. If `outlook=rain`, a subtree is entered whose next-most informative attribute is `wind`. Attributes with little information content are not included in the final tree. Examples of numerous absent attributes can be found in Figs. 2–4.

## Appendix B: Testing a Learner

Before using the learnt trees, we should test them. When testing the trees, it is a good practice to use examples not seen during learning. A standard technique for this is *N-way cross validation*. The example set is divided into $N$ buckets, where each bucket has the same frequency distribution of classifications as the full set of examples (the `xval` script in the standard C4.5 distribution automates this task). For each bucket we place that bucket aside then learn a theory from the other buckets. The learnt tree is then assessed by classifying the examples in the bucket set aside. The average classification accuracy of these $N$ trials is then the final reported classification accuracy.

A side-effect of cross-validation is that we learn $N$ trees. Since each tree is learnt from a different sample set, each tree may be different. This is the "many oracle problem" which has been summarized as follows: a man with one watch knows the time but a man with two watches is never sure. That is, if we learn one oracle, we get one set of conclusions. However, if we learn an ensemble of $N$ oracles, they may all offer different conclusions.

The many oracle problem can be solved as follows: if 19 of your 25 watches all say that it is morning, then you could reasonably decide that it is time to get out of bed. That is, when using multiple oracles, the entire ensemble should be polled to find the conclusion(s) offered by the majority of oracles. Surprisingly, the conclusions from ensembles can be more accurate than those from any single oracle [9]. To see why, recall that cross-validation builds trees from different samples of the domain. Each such sample may explore a different part of a model. Hence, a poll of multiple samples may tell us more than a poll from a single sample.

Various systems support the polling of an ensemble of oracles. For example:

- Refinements of C4.5 offer automatic support for *boosting* (see *http://www.rulequest.com*), i.e., datasets are generated with greater emphasis for examples mis-classified in previous learning trials [9, 31].
- The TARZAN package (described above) searches ensembles of decision trees for attribute value changes that usually alter classifications [23].

## Appendix C: Output from C4.5

Many of the decision trees shown in this chapter are pretty-printed from the C4.5 text output using some awk scripts [15] and the dot package (*http://www.research.att.com/sw/tools/graphviz/examples/*) C4.5's text output look like this:

```
C4.5 [release 8] decision tree generator
Sun Jun 25 17:33:55 2000
------------------------------------------

    Options:
File stem <circ>

Read 378 cases (6 attributes) from circ.data

Decision Tree:

light3 = light: good (8.0)
light3 = dark:
|   light1 = light: good (13.0/4.0)
|   light1 = dark: bad (357.0/45.0)

Simplified Decision Tree:

light1 = light: good (21.0/5.9)
light1 = dark: bad (357.0/50.0)

Tree saved

Evaluation on training data (378 items):

 Before Pruning            After Pruning
----------------     --------------------------
Size      Errors    Size      Errors   Estimate

   5    49(13.0%)      3    49(13.0%)    (14.8%)    <<
```

Note that two trees may be generated. Sometimes C4.5 will prune subtrees if that pruning has little impact on the classification accuracy.

Within a tree, sub-trees are denoted by indentation. Every level of indentation is marked with a "|" symbol. Each final classifications is followed by two numbers in brackets: the number of cases that fell into this branch and the number of cases that fell incorrectly into this branch ("incorrect" means that the case's classification was different to the case shown at the end of this branch).

C4.5 shows classification errors on the last line of the report. Three numbers are generated: one for the unpruned tree, one for the pruned tree, and one that is an estimate of the tree's classification accuracy on future cases. All the estimated errors reported in this chapter come from this third figure (shown bottom right — in this example, it is 14.8%).

It is a simple matter to write awk or perl scripts to convert C4.5's decision trees into dot format. In writing such a conversion tool, the following tips may be useful:

- Re-compile C4.5 after setting the #define Width value in the file trees.c to a large number (e.g. 10,000). This will stop C4.5 breaking up the tree into 80-character wide subtrees which can complicate the conversion process.
- The shell script shown below will automatically strip away the header and footer of the C4.5 output, leaving just the decision tree.
- In the stripped-out tree, it is easy to recognize a line with a classification. Each such line contains a "(" character.

```
#report2tree- extract tree text from C4.5 output file
#author: tim@menzies.com, June 2000
#usage: c4.5 -f stem -m M > c45.out; report2tree c45.out > c45.tree

getTree() {
    gawk 'BEGIN{flag=0}
        NR> 3 && $0~/Decision tree:/      {flag=1; next}
        $0~/Tree saved/                   {exit}
        flag==1                           {print $0}' $1
}
getSimpleTree() {
    gawk 'BEGIN{flag=0}
        NR > 3 && $0~/Simplified Decision Tree:/ {flag=1; next}
        $0~/Tree saved/                          {exit}
        flag==1                                  {print $0}' $1
}
if    grep "Simplified Decision Tree:" $1 >> /dev/null
then getSimpleTree $1
else getTree        $1
fi
```

# References

1. C. Abts, B. Clark, S. Devnani-Chulani, E. Horowitz, R. Madachy, D. Reifer, R. Selby and B. Steece, COCOMO II model definition manual, Technical Report, Center for Software Engineering, USC, 1998. *http://sunset.usc.edu/COCOMOII/cocomox.html#downloads*.
2. F. Bergadano and D. Gunetti, *Inductive Logic Programming: From Machine Learning to Software Engineering* (The MIT Press, 1995).
3. B. Boehm, *Software Engineering Economics* (Prentice Hall, 1981).

4. I. Bratko, I. Mozetic and N. Lavrac, *KARDIO: A Study in Deep and Qualitative Knowledge for Expert Systems* (The MIT Press, 1989).
5. L. Breiman, J. H. Friedman, R. A. Olshen and C. J. Stone, "Classification and regression trees", Technical Report (Wadsworth International, Monterey, CA, 1984).
6. S. Chulani, B. Boehm and B. Steece, "Bayesian analysis of empirical software engineering cost models", *IEEE Transaction on Software Engineering* **25**, no. 4, July/August 1999.
7. W. W. Cohen, "Inductive specification recovery: Understanding software by learning from example behaviors", *Automated Software Engineering* **2** (1995) 107–129.
8. R. Cordero, M. Costamagna and E. Paschetta, "A genetic algorithm approach for the calibration of cocomo-like models", *12th COCOMO Forum*, 1997.
9. T. G. Dietterich, "Machine learning research: Four current directions", *AI Magazine* **18**, no. 4 (1997) 97–136.
10. N. E. Fenton and S. L. Pfleeger, *Software Metrics: A Rigorous and Practical Approach* (International Thompson Press, 1997).
11. G. E. Hinton, "How neural networks learn from experience", *Scientific American* (September 1992) 144–151.
12. G. J. Holzmann, "The model checker SPIN", *IEEE Transactions on Software Engineering* **23**, no. 5 (May 1997) 279–295.
13. Y. Iwasaki, "Qualitative physics", eds. P. R. Cohen, A. Barr and E. A. Feigenbaum, *The Handbook of Artificial Intelligence* **4** (Addison Wesley, 1989) 323–413.
14. C. F. Kemerer, "An empirical validation of software cost estimation models", *Communications of the ACM* **30**, no. 5 (May 1987) 416–429.
15. B. W. Kerningham and C. J. Van Wyk, "Timing trials, or, the trials of timing: Experiments with scripting and user-interface languages, 1998", From Lucent Technologies Inc. Available from *http://netlib.bell-labs.com/cm/cs/who/bwk/interps/pap.html*.
16. T. M. Khoshgoftaar and E. B. Allen, "Model software quality with classification trees", ed. H. Pham, *Recent Advances in Reliability and Quality Engineering* (World Scientific, 1999).
17. F. Lanubile and G. Visaggio, "Evaluating predictive quality models derived from software measures: Lessons learned", *Journal of Software and Systems* **38** (1997) 225–234.
18. N. Leveson, *Safeware System Safety and Computers* (Addison-Wesley, 1995).
19. M. R. Lyu, *The Handbook of Software Reliability Engineering* (McGraw-Hill, 1996).
20. R. Madachy, "Heuristic risk assessment using cost factors", *IEEE Software* **14**, no. 3 (May 1997) 51–59.
21. T. J. McCabe, "A complexity measure", *IEEE Transactions on Software Engineering* **2**, no. 4 (December 1976) 308–320.
22. M. Mendonca and N. L. Sunderhaft, "Mining software engineering data: A survey, September 1999", A DACS State-of-the-Art Report, Available from *http://www.dacs.dtic.mil/techs/datamining/*.
23. T. Menzies and E. Sinsel, "Practical large scale what-if queries: Case studies with software risk assessment", *Proceedings ASE 2000*, 2000, Available from *http://tim.menzies.com/pdf/00ase.pdf*.
24. T. Menzies, B. Cukic, H. Singh and J. Powell, "Testing nondeterminate systems", *ISSRE 2000*, 2000, Available from *http://tim.menzies.com/pdf/00issre.pdf*.
25. R. S. Michalski, "Toward a unified theory of learning", eds. B. G. Buchanan and D. C. Wilkins, *Reading in Knowledge Acquisition and Learning* (Morgan Kaufmann, 1993) 7–38.

26. S. Morasca and G. Ruhe, "Guest editors' introduction of the special issue on knowledge discovery from software engineering data", *International Journal of Software Engineering and Knowledge Engineering*, October 1999.

27. T. Mukhopadhyay, S. S. Vicinanza and M. J. Prietula, "Examining the feasibility of a case-based reasoning tool for software effort estimation", *MIS Quarterly* (June 1992) 155–171.

28. M. J. Pazzani, "Knowledge discovery from data?" *IEEE Intelligent Systems* (2000) 10–13.

29. D. Pearce, "The induction of fault diagnosis systems from qualitative models", *Proceedings of the AAAI'88*, 1988.

30. A. A. Porter and R. W. Selby, "Empirically guided software development using metric-based classification trees", *IEEE Software* (March 1990) 46–54.

31. J. R. Quinlan, "Boosting first-order learning", eds. S. Arikawa and A. K. Sharma, *Proceedings of the 7th International Workshop on Algorithmic Learning Theory, Lecture Notes in Artificial Intelligence, 1160* (Springer, Berlin, October 23–25, 1996) 143–155.

32. R. Quinlan, "Induction of decision trees", *Machine Learning* **1** (1986) 81–106.

33. R. Quinlan, *C4.5: Programs for Machine Learning* ISBN: 1558602380 (Morgan Kaufman, 1992).

34. J. W. Shavlik, R. L. Mooney and G. G. Towell, "Symbolic and neural learning algorithms: An experimental comparison", *Machine Learning* **6** (1991) 111–143.

35. M. Shepped and D. C. Ince, "A critique of three metrics", *Journal of Systems and Software* **26**, no. 3 (September 1994) 197–210.

36. K. Srinivasan and D. Fisher, "Machine learning approaches to estimating software development effort", *IEEE Transaction on Software Engineering* (Feburary 1995) 126–137.

37. J. Tian and M. V. Zelkowitz, "Complexity measure evaluation and selection", *IEEE Transaction on Software Engineering* **21**, no. 8 (August 1995) 641–649.

# EXPLORING ONTOLOGIES

YANNIS KALFOGLOU

*AKT Research Fellow,*
*Knowledge Media Institute (KMi), Milton Keynes MK7 6AA, UK*
*E-mail: y.kalfoglou@open.ac.uk*

Ontologies are studied by many scholars with diverse backgrounds and are applied in a variety of contexts and application areas. Despite the numerous reviews published there are many issues which still remain unclear with respect to their cost-effective deployment, identification of tradeoffs, maintenance strategies and ways of integration. Furthermore, there is no report which refers to all those issues along with the basic information in order to be used as a road-map. This survey article aims to provide such information in a manner which will help the interested software practitioner to comprehend the basic principles in ontology design, understand their strengths and weaknesses, be aware of a variety of areas where ontologies have been successfully applied, and identify tradeoffs and potential solutions.

*Keywords*: Ontologies, knowledge sharing and reuse, knowledge management, software design.

## 1. Introduction

In this survey article, we are exploring ontologies with emphasis on their deployment in a wide variety of areas ranging from software design to knowledge management and information retrieval. We are not interested to provide an in-depth analysis of the field of ontologies in an isolated manner nor to provide a methodological approach for guiding the software design processes. Rather, we scrutinize the ontologies field as practised, mainly, in the knowledge engineering community over the last decade, and report on their impact in software design through example application cases, worked projects, and emerging experimental results.

Before we proceed with our survey, however, we look closer at software design. Software design is still a young field, and we are far from having a clear articulation of the relevant principles. Winograd offers a parallelism of the phrase with software engineering (hereafter, SE): "... is often used to characterize the discipline that is also called software engineering — the discipline concerned with the construction of software that is efficient, reliable, robust, and easy to maintain" [108]. Although work has begun in engineering software design with the emergence of methodological approaches [78], guidelines, and bringing in rationale [68], there is still an area that remains unexplored: bringing into the design process explicit knowledge regarding the domain on which the system to be developed will operate.

The study and modeling of that knowledge is a core theme in artificial intelligence (hereafter, AI) research. Having their roots in knowledge representation, knowledge engineering methods and techniques gave AI researchers a powerful tool for transforming contextual knowledge into machine-readable form to enable mechanized reasoning about a domain of interest. Ontologies are such a form of domain knowledge. We should also note the similarity of this topic with such areas as domain analysis [4] and engineering (this volume, J. L. Diaz-Herrera's Chap. 14), object oriented patterns [30], etc. In this chapter, however, we are interested in ontologies as practiced, mainly, in the AI community.

Nowadays, they are studied by many scholars who belong to different communities. Hence, a plethora of articles and field reviews are available for the interested practitioner. However, each of them is focussed on a specific area: for example, the Uschold and Gruninger review — one of the first comprehensive reviews published — is concerned with design principles and methodological ways of construction with selective references to exemplar applications [93]; the Fridman-Noy and Hafner review further explores and compares design methods [29], the Chandrasekaran and colleagues article provides a general overview of the field [13]; and Gomez-Perez and Benjamins devote half of their report to give a catalogue-style information on ontologies research [34]. Despite the bulk of resources available it is still difficult for practitioners, especially those with a SE background, to locate and elicit the right information with respect to engineering, application, and cost-effective issues. Most of the times this information is found in different resources.

This survey aims to fill-in this gap. In order to do this effectively, we explore the field from the following angles: design, deployment, and tradeoffs. We explore design issues in Secs. 2 to 6 where we describe what an ontology stands for, ways of design, the role of ontological commitment, methodologies to follow when building ontologies, and explain the various types reported in the literature. Deployment issues are described in Secs. 7 to 8 with emphasis on uses of ontologies, ways of deployment, and references to applications and influential projects from both industry and academia. Lastly, we conclude our survey by discussing potential problems, tradeoffs and solutions proposed and used, in Sec. 9, followed by list of pointers to resources for further reading, in Sec. 10.

## 2. Definitions

We start our review by explaining what an ontology stands for. Although a single definition will usually suffice, ontologies have a peculiar characteristic: there are a number of different definitions proposed and used. Even nowadays there are people who argue about the actual meaning of the term. A reason for this is, probably, the fact that ontologies are studied, developed and applied by people with diverse backgrounds and interests. We do not subscribe to this pointless debate over the meaning of the term in this article nor we will introduce yet another definition.

Rather, we briefly review the most commonly used definitions found in the literature in order to explain what an ontology stands for.

One of the early definitions appeared in [72]. The authors define an ontology as: "the basic terms and relations comprising the vocabulary of a topic area as well as the rules for combining terms and relations to define extensions to the vocabulary". This definition introduced the idea that ontologies can be viewed linguistically, as extensible vocabularies regarding a topic area. In the context of knowledge sharing, Gruber offered a short definition which became the most widely cited in the literature: "an ontology is an explicit specification of a conceptualization" [37]. This definition was further enriched by Borst and his colleagues in [10], where they argued that the specification is actually formal and the conceptualization is shared. Studer and colleagues analyzed the terms used in the definition and provide the following explanation: "Conceptualisation refers to an abstract model of some phenomenon in the world by having identified the relevant concepts of that phenomenon. Explicit means that the type of concepts used, and the constraints on their use are explicitly defined. Formal refers to the fact that the ontology should be machine-readable. Shared refers to the notion that an ontology captures consensual knowledge, that is, it is not primitive to some individual, but accepted by a group" [85]. Uschold offers a working definition which hints at the purpose of having ontologies: "An ontology is virtually always the manifestation of a shared understanding of a domain that is agreed between a number of agents. Such agreement facilitates accurate and effective communication of meaning, which in turn leads to other benefits such as inter-operability, reuse and sharing" [90]. Others, consider ontologies as domain theories [25], as vocabularies [83], as standards [58], etc. In [43], the authors offer a clarification of terminological issues regarding the various definitions founded in the literature. In [88], the authors relate an ontology to a knowledge base in their definition: "An ontology provides the basic structure or armature around which a knowledge base can be built".

Based on the definitions quoted above we summarize what an ontology stands for: an explicit representation of a shared understanding of the important concepts in some domain of interest. The role of an ontology is to support knowledge sharing and reuse within and among groups of agents (people, software programs, or both). In their computational form, ontologies are often comprised by definitions of terms organized in an hierarchy lattice along with a set of relationships that hold among these definitions. These constructs collectively impose a structure on the domain being represented and constrain the possible interpretations of terms.

## 3. Design Principles

A number of design criteria have been proposed, originally analyzed in [38]. For a thorough analysis of these criteria we point the interested reader to the afore-mentioned citation whereas here we briefly recapitulate them. The criteria proposed are: *clarity, coherence, extendibility, minimal encoding bias,* and *minimal ontological commitment.* *Clarity* means that the intended meaning should be communicated effectively. This means that ambiguity should be minimized, distinctions should be motivated, and examples should be given to help the reader understand definitions that lack necessary and sufficient conditions. When a definition can be stated in logical axioms, it should be. Where possible, a complete definition (a predicate defined by necessary and sufficient conditions) is preferred over a partial definition (defined by only necessary or sufficient conditions). All definitions should be documented with natural language. *Coherence* means that the ontology should be internally consistent. At the least, the defining axioms should be logically consistent. Coherence should also apply to the concepts that are defined informally, such as those described in natural language documentation and examples. *Extendibility* means that one should be able to extend the existing terms in a way that does not require the revision of existing definitions. The next two criteria help to achieve that. The *encoding bias* and *ontological commitment* should be minimal. An *encoding bias* results when representation choices are made purely for the convenience of notation or implementation. Encoding bias should be minimized, because knowledge-sharing agents may be implemented in different representation systems and styles of representation. *Minimal ontological commitment* means that the ontology should make as few claims as possible about the world being modeled, allowing the parties committed to the ontology freedom to specialize and instantiate the ontology as needed. While making too many ontological commitments can limit extensibility, making too few can result in the ontology being consistent with incorrect or unintended worlds (i.e., models). For this reason, it is beneficial to make ontological commitments with respect to aspects intrinsic to a domain.

We should note that the above criteria are not always possible to meet by ontology designers. A number of tradeoffs have been identified [38], and ways of compromising between well designed ontologies and applicability have been investigated [10]. We will not expand on this issue in this article because it is peripheral to our topic: uses of ontologies. To support this we shift our attention to the notion of ontological commitment which plays an important role in using ontologies in software systems.

## 4. Ontological Commitment

Ontological commitment refers to agreement on the use of the shared vocabulary by the agents commited to the ontology in question. When we say that an agent commits to an ontology we mean that its observable actions are consistent with the definitions in the ontology [38]. It has been said that commitment to a common ontology is a guarantee for consistency but not for completeness, with respect to queries and assertions using the vocabulary defined in the ontology [38].

Guarino describes the role of ontological commitment in software: "ontological commitment should be made explicit when applying the ontology in order to facilitate its accessibility, maintainability, and integrity. This will lead to an increase of transparency for the application software which based on that ontology" [40]. These commitments are often encoded as axioms that enforce the syntactic consistency of the definitions used. Practically, an ontological commitment is an agreement to use a vocabulary (i.e., ask queries and make assertions) in a way that is consistent with respect to the theory that specifies the ontology. We build agents that commit to ontologies and we design ontologies so we can share knowledge with and among these agents. With a declarative specification, we can explicitly reason about different ontological commitments. For example, we can compare two different proposals for an ontology with respect to the classes of objects that they require and the properties and relations among these objects that they postulate [93].

Guarino and colleagues argue for a greater role of ontological commitment. In [42], the authors continue, an ontological commitment should capture and constrain a set of conceptualizations. They propose a formalization of ontological commitments which: "offers a way to specify the intended meaning of [a logical language] vocabulary by constraining the set of its models, giving explicit information about the intended nature of the modeling primitives used and their *a priori* relationships". The work of Guarino and colleagues is focussed on the design phases of ontology. Other scholars' work aim on the deployment of ontological commitments in applications. We will describe this work in Sec. 8 where we summarize uses of ontologies in software design.


## 5. Methodologies

The construction of an ontology is a time-consuming and complex task. Although there are no standards to obey when building an ontology, various design guidelines and methodological approaches have been proposed and used. In particular, in a comprehensive review of the field [93], the authors report on two methodologies used in the context of the *Enterprise* ontology [97] and the TOVE project [20]. In the former, a skeletal methodology has been proposed [98] which identifies five main steps: (a) identify purpose and scope, (b) build the ontology, (c) evaluation, (d) documentation, and (e) guidelines for each phase. Step (b) is further divided into ontology capture, coding, and integration of existing ontologies. This skeletal methodology was used in the construction of the *Enterprise* ontology but does not explicitly deploy a formal evaluation procedure. This was the main focus of the methodology used in the context of the TOVE project [20]. In particular, Gruninger and Fox used a formal methodology that supported evaluation of the ontology using the notion of *competency questions* [39]. The underlying philosophy is to define a set of queries that the ontology can answer. These queries help to assess the ontology's competence. They evaluate the expressiveness of the ontology which is required to represent these questions and characterize their solutions. These queries are drawn from a number of motivating scenarios which are story problems or examples which are not adequately addressed by existing ontologies.

Apart from the work on evaluation and construction methodologies by Uschold, Gruninger and colleagues, others have focussed on the preliminary phases of construction. In [24], the authors presented a system, called *METHONTOLOGY*, which provides support for the entire life-cycle of ontology development. A distinguishing characteristic of the METHONTOLOGY framework is that it is tailored to support the early phases of development by employing the notion of *intermediate representations*. These are representations independent of the implementation language in which the ontology will be developed. The system that support the use of these representations is the Ontology Development Environment(ODE) [9]. An overview of methodologies used in AI projects along with a comparison with standards from SE literature is given in [23].

## 6. Types

The development methodologies reported above were used in some of the ontologies which will be described in Secs. 7 and 8. Before we proceed to survey actual implementations of ontologies we describe various types of them as reported in the literature. Ontologies can be classified in terms of genericity. For example, broad ontologies like CYC [57], model generic notions that forms the foundations for knowledge representation across various domains. These are also called top-level ontologies [13], like Sowa's ontology [84]. On the other hand, small-scale, domain-specific ontologies are carefully tailored to the domain at question. Examples of this type are the *PhysSys* ontology [10] which captures knowledge regarding physical system processes, the *AIRCRAFT* ontology [100] used to represent air-campaign planning knowledge, the *PIF* ontology [55] used for business process modeling, etc.

Another classification of ontologies is concerned with their purpose. There exist *task* ontologies [67] that capture task-related knowledge independently of the domain that the task is defined. Complementary to these are the *method* ontologies [12] which provide definitions of the relevant concepts and relations used to specify a reasoning process to achieve a particular task. A specific type of ontologies is the *knowledge representation* ontologies. The most representative example is the Frame ontology [37] which captures the representation primitives used in frame-based languages. It allows other ontologies to be specified using frame-based conventions, as implemented by the Knowledge Interchange Format(KIF) [33].

Most ontologies, however, are placed under the tag *domain* ontology. These are designed to support a specific domain and applications defined within that domain. For example, the *PIF* ontology is concerned with the business process modeling domain and supports the exchange of information among a variety of business process modeling applications.

There is another type of ontology, the *linguistic* ontologies. The most illustrative examples are the Generalised Upper Model (GUM) [7], WordNet [66], and SENSUS [54]. However, these usually have the form of a vast collection of terms which led to another classification with regard to the level of formality. These sort of ontologies are often called "terminological" ontologies whereas ontologies like TOVE are called "axiomatized" ontologies.

In their overview of the field, Uschold and Gruninger identified the following types with respect to the degree of formality: *highly informal, semi-informal, semi-formal, rigorously formal* [93]. In the informal cluster we see definitions in natural language or at most in a structured form of natural language. In the formal cluster we have ontologies implemented in an artificial formal language (i.e., *Ontolingua*), or in first order theories with formal semantics, theorems and proofs of such properties as soundness and completeness (i.e., TOVE).

## 7. Engineering

Although many argue that engineering of ontologies is still in its infancy, the first comprehensive reports covering all aspects of ontology construction and deployment began to emerge few years ago. We selectively report here some of these efforts by highlighting their contributions to the field. In an experiment of ontology reuse [92], researchers working at Boeing were investigating the potential of using an existing ontology for the purpose of specifying and formally developing software for aircraft design. The application problem addressed was to enhance the functionality of a software component used to design the layout of an aircraft stiffened panel. They describe a start-to-finish process that used an existing ontology, residing on the Ontolingua [21] server, the *EngMath* [36] ontology, which was then translated to the target specification language and integrated to an engineering software component. They then executed that component and demonstrated the benefits of reusing an existing knowledge component in the development process. The lessons learned from that experience is that ontology reuse can be pursued on a large scale and, under certain circumstances, it can be a cost-effective approach. We will revisit the tradeoffs identified by Uschold and colleagues in their experiment in Sec. 9 while we continue here by reporting two studies that were focussed on the whole spectrum of engineering ontologies: the *AIRCRAFT* project, and the *PhysSys* project.

In [100], the authors describe how they achieved reuse among ontologies themselves. The resulted ontology, *AIRCRAFT*,[a] contains knowledge about types of US military aircraft, including data about the engines, PODs, and fuel tanks that these aircraft can carry. The distinguishable feature of this ontology is how it has been developed in the first place. The process, which is described in [87], was based on the use of a large-scale, linguistic ontology, the *SENSUS* [54]. A characteristic of *SENSUS* is that it is actually constructed from extracting and merging information from existing electronic resources (like the *WordNet*, dictionaries, GUM ontology). The authors, used this broad coverage ontology and then devised a

---

[a]A demonstration version is electronically available from the URL:
http://www.isi.edu/isd/ontosaurus.html

semi-automatic method which made it possible to identify terms in the original ontology that were relevant to their particular domain, and then pruned the ontology so that it included only those terms. In addition, they enhanced the newly emerged ontology with terms tailored to the domain of air campaign planning. These were military terms. The resulting ontology, *AIRCRAFT*, is accessible through an ontology development environment, the *ontosaurus* browser which supports the idea of "ontology developed collaboratively by the system developers themselves" ([87]).

In [10], a general and formal ontology, called *PhysSys* is presented. It covers the domain of dynamic physical systems and it is composed of seven different ontologies. This work explored a new idea in ontology engineering, that is *ontology projections*: "a flexible mechanism to link and configure ontologies into larger ones." Three kinds of projections demonstrated in the paper, *include-and-extend*, *include-and-specialise*, and *include-and-project*. The latter was used to link an ontology developed by the group of *PhysSys* authors to an outsourced ontology, the *EngMath*. The *PhysSys* ontology was used as the foundation for the conceptual database schema of a library of reusable engineering model components, the *OLMECO* library. The library was evaluated by modeling and numerically simulating the existing heating system of a general hospital in Schiedan, the Netherlands [10].

In the context of the *Plinious* project [101], the bottom-up method in ontology development is discussed [102]. In contrast with the majority of approaches in ontology construction which fall into two categories, top-down and middle-out (analyzed in [93]), the bottom-up way "proposes to lay down the meaning of complex concepts by means of primitive meaning constituents". It has been applied to the domain of ceramic materials and covers their properties and the processes to make them. It was found that this approach was suitable for such a domain because, the authors continue, it is impossible to exhaustively predict in advance which concepts will be needed to express the knowledge found in the texts. As this domain covers chemical substances, it was argued that listing all these substances is an open-ended task. As such, keeping track of the regular updates in a top-down designed ontology was impractical since it requires substantial effort and is error-prone. Consequently, the approach used supports reasoning along two orthogonal hierarchies: "the partonomy formed by substances and their constituents and the taxonomy formed by concepts and superconcepts" [102].

Other projects which provide an insight in the engineering process are the re-engineering effort of implemented ontologies, described in [35], and the collaborative effort in developing a common ontology for the knowledge acquisition community [8]. In particular, Gomez-Perez and Amaya describe a re-engineering process of retrieving and transforming a conceptual model of an existing ontology into a new one. The work of Benjamins and Fensel describes the *Knowledge Annotation Initiative of the Knowledge Acquisition Community* ontology (in short,

$KA^2$), which models the knowledge acquisition community and forms the basis to annotate its documents on the Web[b] in order to enable intelligent access.

## 8. Applications and Projects

A complete listing of applications of ontologies is impossible. The literature references are huge and citing lengthy lists is not practical. However, we provide pointers to various resources in Sec. 10 whereas here we selectively report the most representative ones. To do this effectively, we cluster them according to their application domain.

We start with the area of *enterprise modeling*. In this area, we found the *Enterprise* ontology [97], which captures the organizational structure of an enterprise with emphasis to activities and processes. The ontology is developed in a structured text form and a translation in *Ontolingua* is also available. In the same line is the TOVE ontologies set [20] which shares the same aims with *Enterprise*, but has been developed in a formal computational form and uses different underlying principles [28]. The differences between these two representative ontologies for enterprise modeling are highlighted in [93].

A relevant application area is that of *business process modeling*. The Process Interchange Format (PIF) [55] is among the best known in this area. The aim of PIF is to develop an interchange format to help automatically exchange process descriptions among a variety of business modeling and support systems such as workflow software, flow charting tools, planners, process simulation systems and process repositories. The core of PIF consists of the minimal sets of constructs necessary to translate simple but non-trivial process descriptions. In addition, PIF can be extended to represent local needs of individual groups with the use of Partially Shared Views (PSV) described in [56]. The PIF framework has been applied in a *supply chain scenario* [77] which was adopted from the Workflow Management Coalition (WfMC) [107]. An example of an interchange format is illustrated in Fig. 1.

Ontologies have also been applied to *medical applications*. For example, a methodology for integrating medical terminologies was presented in [31]. This is the aim of the *ONIONS* methodology [32] developed by the same group. In the same context, the European project *GALEN*[c] [80] which aims at capturing information from the clinical domain. In [1], the authors present a system, called *Sophia* which acts as a knowledge server for web-based medical applications. An ontology for bioinformatics (*TAMBIS*) is presented in [6]. Most of the applications in this area are based on terminological resources like the *GUM* ontology [7], the *CYC* ontology [57], the *Unified Medical Language System* (*UMLS*) [71], etc.

---

[b]The ontology is accessible online from the following URL: http://www.aifb.uni-karlsruhe.de/WBS/broker/KA2.html
[c]The project is electronically accessible from the URL: http://www.cs.man.ac.uk/mig/galen

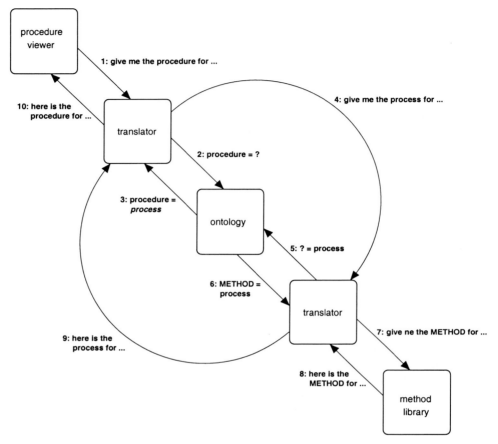

**Fig. 1.**   Ontology as inter-lingua: Example taken directly from [93]. This illustrates the use of an ontology as an inter-lingua to integrate different software tools. The term procedure, used by one tool is translated into the term, *method* used by the other via the ontology, whose term for the same underlying concept is *process*.

Another area to which ontologies have been applied is that of *ontology-based brokering*. These are specifically designed agent systems which serve as brokers between heterogeneous systems. They use ontologies to facilitate the information brokering task. Representative applications are: the *Ontobroker* [17] which was used, among others, in the $KA^2$ project [8]; the *onto2agent* [5] used to select publicly available ontologies on the web for a given application based on a *Reference Ontology* developed by the same group to classify candidate ontologies; the *OBSERVER* [63] system used to provide semantically rich information to a user who subscribes to an information management system on the web which supported by selected ontologies; the *IMPS* (*Internet-based Multi-agent Problem Solving*) [16] system which uses software agents to conduct knowledge acquisition on-line using distributed resources. Terminological ontologies (like *WordNet*) were used to underpin the whole process.

A related area of applications is that of *knowledge retrieval*. A representative application in this area is the *PlanetOnto* which provides an integrated set of tools to support news publishing based on ontology-driven document enrichment [19]. To support this project two ontology-specific tools were developed: the *Tadzebao* and *WebOnto* both described in [18]. The former aims to support a dialectical approach in ontology design and maintenance while the latter provides editing and browsing facilities. The goal of *Tadzebao* is to provide guidance for knowledge engineers around ongoing dialogues for designing ontologies. This can be used as a negotiation tool for proposed changes in an ontology with the additional flexibility that *Tadzebao* offers: the integration of discussion about an artefact and its representation in the same visual metaphor. Another application in this area is the *knowledge-enhanced search* approach used in the *FindUR* project [62]. McGuinness describes a search tool, deployed at the AT&T research labs, which uses ontologies to improve the search experiences from the perspectives of recall and precision as well as ease of query formation. A similar approach which deploys *content matching* techniques is described in [44] where the authors present the *OntoSeek* system designed to support content-based access to the web.

In the broader context of *knowledge management* (hereafter, KM) ontologies are useful to support crucial KM tasks and activities. For an overview of the field with emphasis on the role of AI in KM we point the interested reader to O'Leary's review in [74]. Here, we will use O'Leary's thesis that the goal of KM is to create valuable information by employing the so called, *converting and connecting* processes [75], in order to identify the role of ontologies in KM. The processes identified were: convert (i) individual to group knowledge, (ii) data to knowledge, (iii) text to knowledge, and connect (iv) people to knowledge, (v) knowledge to knowledge, (vi) people to people, and (vii) knowledge to people. We argue that ontologies could be used in most of these processes, either by playing a major role or by supplying the supporting infrastructure that helps an organization to implement them. In the following paragraph we mention indicative examples from the ontology research literature to justify this claim.

In particular, ontologies provide part of the infrastructure for conversion processes (i to iii as listed above) and help in the connection activities (iv to vii as listed above). Conversion processes (i) seem to benefit more from the presence of ontologies as this is the underlying principle in their construction. Methodological [93] and collaborative approaches [87, 8] in ontology building, convert individual to group knowledge in the form of an ontology. Processes (ii) and (iii) use other AI technology like data and text mining techniques with ontologies being the guide to the "right" data or text repository [17]. Ontologies seems to be more helpful in the connecting processes. Process (iv) is concerned with the so called, "pull" technology, which aims at pulling knowledge residing in vast repositories to people. The means which used to pull that knowledge are, mainly, search engines and intelligent agents. Examples of ontology use in this area are given in [62, 44]. Process (v) actually highlights the main contribution of ontologies: enabling communication

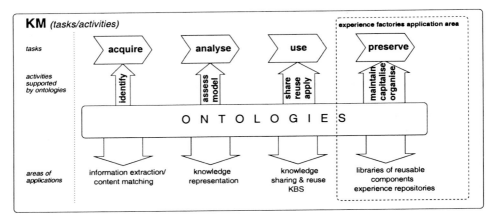

**Fig. 2.** Ontologies in knowledge management: Activities supported by ontologies help to achieve knowledge management tasks resulting in a range of application areas.

and interoperability between systems. The best way to cite indicative work here is to point to reviews and collections such as [93, 41]. Process (vi) is not directly related to ontologies as it is more concerned with technological means such as Intranets. However, we should mention the work on collaboration and discussion aided by ontologies [86]. In contrast with process (iv), process (vii) is concerned with "push" technology. Means to achieve this are designated systems that focus on content and push knowledge to the user instead of waiting for the user to pull out that knowledge. As in (iv), ontologies play a major role here since they are concerned with content and semantically enriched information. Example uses are described in [22, 17].

Finally, after having presented the processes that help to achieve the goal of KM we close this section on KM by describing main KM tasks and activities and how ontologies are related to them. These are summarized in Fig. 2 and described in the following paragraph.

On the right hand side of Fig. 2, we illustrate the main KM tasks and activities. We identify four main KM tasks: *acquiring, analyzing, using,* and *preserving* knowledge. We argue that these tasks are accomplished by activities which are supported by ontologies. In particular, the knowledge acquisition task, is accomplished by *identifying* activities which are supported by ontologies. This results in the application area of information extraction and/or content-matching. In the same manner, ontologies in the area of knowledge representation are used to *model* and *assess* the environment, which are activities employed in the *analyzing* knowledge task. The *using* knowledge task, includes the *apply, share,* and *reuse* activities, which are supported by ontologies with such application areas as knowledge sharing and reuse, and KBSs. The last task of the KM tasks/activities diagram is *preserving* knowledge. It is accomplished by activities such as *organizing, maintaining,* and *capitalizing* which are partially aided by ontologies. The resulting application area is that of libraries of reusable knowledge components and experience repositories. The knowledge preservation task and its accompanying activities along with the relevant ontologies are the area of overlap with experience factories[d] as denoted by the box surrounding the task in Fig. 2.

The last area to report is that of *systems engineering*. In Sec. 7, we already described systems like the *AIRCRAFT* and the *Boeing* experiment with the use of the *EngMath* ontology which was also used in the construction of the *PhysSys* ontologies set. Other representative applications are the *ATOS* (*Advanced Technology Operations System*) [47] system which was designed to meet specific needs of *spacecraft operations* such as the need for coordination of different agent applications who had to commit to a common ontology. In [26], the authors describe the *Integrated Development Support Environment* (*IDSE*), a commercial computational environment that supports the integration of enterprise models. The integration is underpinned by axioms representing semantic constraints and relationships between different tools which are interpreted and enforced semi-automatically. This information is contained in a method ontology, the *IDEF1X*,[e] accessed by a truth maintenance system that enforces rules and constraints defined in the method.

The use of ontological axioms has been inspirational and many researchers are investigating the practicality of deploying ontologies in *software design*. Gruber hints the role of these axioms in ontology deployment:

> "Ontologies are often equated with taxonomic hierarchies of classes, class definitions, and the subsumption relation, but ontologies need not be limited to these forms. Ontologies are also not limited to conservative definitions, that is, definitions in the traditional logic sense that only introduce terminology and do not add any knowledge about the world. To specify a conceptualization one needs to state axioms that do constrain the possible interpretations for the defined terms" [37].

A working example for the use of ontological axioms in software design is described in [53]. The authors point out that the role anticipated by ontological axioms is rarely delivered: to restrict the possible interpretations ontological constructs could have. To operationalize this role and enforce it in an integrated development environment they invented a **multi-layered** architecture in which ontological axioms are separated from other ontological constructs included in a system that uses the underlying ontology. These are enforced to comply to the axiomatization in order to verify the consistency of the system with respect to domain knowledge as explicitly represented in the underlying ontology [50]. Ultimately, this layered metaphor can be extended to check the ontological axioms themselves against another set of axioms, meta-axioms, which could come from another ontology. This facilitates the conformance check of an application to ontology and can be extended

---

[d]Kalfoglou and Robertson investigate the overlap of ontologies and experience factories in [52].
[e]Electronically accessible from the URL: http://www.idef.com/overviews/idef1.html

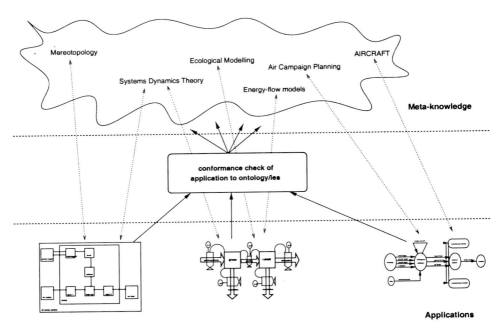

**Fig. 3.** The multi-layer approach: It enforces the conformance check of an application to ontology/ies. Applications are using meta-knowledge constructs from various ontologies (mereotopology, system dynamics theory, etc) in an integrated environment which enables checks on the use of those constructs against their axiomatized definitions.

to check dependencies among ontologies themselves [51]. Moreover, it supports the integration of ontologies in applications while preserving their identity as being a separate layer in the multi-layer architecture. The approach is illustrated in Fig. 3.

One of the early contributions that used ontological commitments was that of the Comet [61] and Cosmos [60] systems. Both systems aim at developing knowledge bases by capturing the set of ontological commitments that define the interdependencies among key terms in the ontology. Their role is to assess the impact of changes in their world and provide context-specific guidance to their users on what modules may be relevant to include in the design, and what design modifications will be required in order to include them [59]. The key idea behind this work was to make use of the ontological commitment expressed by the underlying ontology in the system's development process.

Similarly, in the **DISCOVER** project [106], the role of ontological commitment was further analyzed and operationalized. The authors state that ontological commitment is a key issue for knowledge sharing and reuse and they applied existing verification techniques from the KBSs literature to check the commitment of a knowledge base to an ontology. In that project the role of the ontology was to act as a background body of knowledge against which a knowledge base can be validated.

There are also a number of applications related with projects undertaken by various organizations involving academic and industrial partners. We already mentioned some of them in the previous sections. We complete our coverage here by describing one of the first projects in this area which was the *Knowledge Sharing Effort (KSE)* [72] aimed to realize the benefit of sharing and reusing large knowledge bases. The distinguishable contribution of this project was the Knowledge Interchange Format (KIF) framework. Other projects are the *High Performance Knowledge Bases (HPKB)* programme [15] which aims at fostering the development of technologies that can increase the rate at which we can write knowledge bases. The *Intelligent Brokering Service for Knowledge-Component Reuse on the World-Wide Web (IBROW³)* project investigates means for supporting comprehensive reuse. The idea behind this project is to provide a brokering service that plays the role of a mediator between customers and PSM providers to support the configuration of customized knowledge systems that solve customers' problems. A library of reusable components [70] has been constructed based on the work of Motta in parametric design [69]. The *Knowledge Reuse and Fusion/Transformation (KRAFT)* [79] aimed to enable the sharing and reuse of information contained in heterogeneous databases and knowledge bases. In the area of planning the *SPAR* [89] project draws on the range of previous work in planning activity ontologies to create a practically useful *Shared Planning and Activity Representation*.

## 9. Problems, Tradeoffs, and Solutions

Despite the fact that ontologies have been applied with success in a variety of fields there are reported problems and attempts have been made to identify tradeoffs and find potential solutions. We report on the problems first. In [73], the author discusses impediments in the use of ontologies. He points out the difficulty in library ontologies, scale-up, interfacing and raises the issue of formality in ontology development. O'Leary argues also for the difficulty in establishing a consensus: "ontologies are chosen after a political decision had been made, therefore it is impossible to choose an ontology that maximizes the utility of all agents in process and the group" [73]. Research in the area of studying the experts' behaviour provides an evidence of the apparent lack of consensus. For example, many researchers argue that experts disagree about even well-established features of their domain (see [27, 65]). Others studied the behaviour of experts [82] and found that they often held different views about a supposedly standard terminology in their field. Furthermore, in [2], the authors state: "expert knowledge is comprised of context-dependent, personally-constructed, highly-functional but fallible abstractions". This suggests that we should routinely expect evolution of experts' views, especially in domains where there is disagreement on used terms. However, we have to point out here that in situations where there is a lack of consensus among the experts regarding the domain of interest then the principle of ontology does not apply by definition: an ontology represents consensual and commonly agreed terminology about a domain of interest. In that respect we agree with O'Leary's thesis and as a rule of thumb we can say that in domains where there is literally no consensus among the domain experts then building an ontology is pointless. This, however, should not be interpreted as a guideline to build ontologies only when experts agree: this will rarely happen, as the studies described above suggest, therefore we have seen the most successful ontology stories coming from domains where the "majority" of experts agree on used terms. The issue here is to find the right balance between commonly agreed terminology and usability of ontology. This is actually one of the ontology design principles: minimal ontological commitment [38]. We should also mention that experience with task models in the KBS community indicates a broad degree of consensus with respect to the structure of KBS tasks, like diagnosis, parametric design, scheduling, etc. The key factor here is the effective support for KBS development rather than achieving community-wide consensus, a goal of generic ontologies.

Other problematic areas have been identified: Uschold and colleagues raise the issue of lack of translators when the representation formalisms used are not the same in the context of their experiment for ontology reuse [92]. They argued that, "the translation activity involved was an intensive one and lack of automatic support is an important disadvantage". The issue of ease of reuse was also the focal point of an empirical study performed in the context of the *HPKB* project. In [14], the authors report that ease of reuse is closely related to the type of ontology: it was found that very generic ontologies provide less support and are less useful than domain-specific ones. The latter scored a constant 60% rate of reuse in the *HPKB* study in contrast with the poor 22% rate of reuse scored by broad ontologies. However, as the authors argue, these results should not undermine their role in structuring ontologies: "Although the rate of reuse of terms from very general ontologies may be significantly lower, the real advantage of these ontologies probably comes from helping knowledge engineers organize their knowledge bases along sound ontological lines" [14].

Another important drawback is the lack of rigorous evaluation techniques for ontologies. For example, in an experiment of extending the *HPKB* upper ontology [3] the author states: "... validation remains an important issue, i.e., the *PhysSys*, *EngMath* and *topology* ontologies are capable of being validated by reference to literature in their application fields... but ontologies such as the *HPKB* upper level and *SPAR* do not capture knowledge in such well understood fields, therefore this form of validation is not possible". The issue of maintenance has also been acknowledged and studied by many. Robertson neatly summarizes the points made: "the cost of producing an ontology is not just in inventing the domain-specific formal language but in maintaining it once the system is deployed, since perfect ontologies cannot be guaranteed. Over-commitment to perfecting an ontology causes failure either during development (through irreconcilable arguments over what the ontology should be) or after deployment (through inappropriate human interpretation of inference system inputs or outputs)" [81]. In the long run this cost might hinder further deployment of ontologies. However, it is not easily predictable and quantifiable since there are various angles of viewing this problem. For instance, if we accept that ontology rarely stabilizes then we should expect to include in our budget along with the cost of constructing, costs for maintaining the ontology we use as well as the system which uses it. How common is ontology instability? We don't know since we have very little experience with the long-term use of large libraries of ontologies. However, this is a debatable point [64] and we find projects where ontology was deployed on the rationale that it was stable (i.e., in parametric design ontology: [69]), and projects where this is not taken for granted as ontology is expected to change over time (i.e., Aitken's HPKB experiment [3]).

We now shift our attention to potential solutions to some of the problems mentioned above. With respect to the problem of library ontologies, made by O'Leary, the online libraries of ontologies (i.e., *Ontolingua*) are a potential solution especially when the maintenance and update facilities that are envisaged [25] will be fully integrated. To facilitate the familiarization task, systems like *OntoSaurus* and *WebOnto* [18] aim to help the engineer accomplishing this task. The issue of interfacing has attracted a lot of attention by the community. It is seen from different angles: "integration", "merging", "mapping", are some of the terms used. A summary of these approaches is given in [76] whereas Visser and colleagues analyze the nature of the problem in [104]. Some of the solutions proposed and applied are the *ontological mediation algorithms* [11], the *ontology clustering* [105], as well as the approaches used in projects like the creation of the *AIRCRAFT* ontology and in [94]. In addition to these, the *OBSERVER* [63] and *ONIONS* [31] systems, the *Partially Shared Views* (*PSV*) scheme [56], the *encapsulation and composition* technique [46] in the context of the *Scalable Knowledge Composition* (*SKC*)[f] project provide alternative solutions.

Even with this plethora of techniques the situation remains unsettled. There is no comparative analysis which identifies potential advantages and important drawbacks and no common practices to be followed. This has started to change with the proposal of frameworks that characterize ontologies, like the one originally presented by Uschold in [91] which was further analyzed in [95]. These frameworks can be used to share experiences, discuss tradeoffs, and disseminate knowledge regarding attempts to apply ontologies. A small example of this is the instantiation of Uschold's framework, made by Kalfoglou and Robertson in the context of the *PhysSys* ontologies set [52]. Another source of information is from comparative analyses. For example, in [29], the authors compare and analyze the state-of-the-art in ontology design. Ushcold and Jasper present a cost-benefit analysis of three commonly used approaches in knowledge sharing [96]. In a larger context, Kalfoglou and colleagues, compare various meta-knowledge types, analyze their cost-benefits, and identify pragmatic aspects in using meta-knowledge [49]. In similar fashion

---

[f]Electronically accessible from the URL: http://www-db.stanford.edu/SKC/

Menzies and colleagues analyze issues with meta-knowledge in [64] and Kalfoglou speculates on the role of formal ontologies in knowledge maintenance in [48].

We close this section by summarizing the points made and speculating on the future of ontology applications. We observe a shift of interest by the community from very generic, broad ontologies to domain-related ones tailored to serve particular applications. We also saw evidence in the reported systems above that ontologies can improve systems design in such areas as knowledge sharing and reuse and contribute to enhance their reliability by consistency checking. This could have an impact by reducing production costs, shortening development times and communicating context among applications and across organizations. It also improves the quality of the resulted systems with respect to verification of their correctness against domain knowledge. However, there are serious obstacles to overcome. The most important being, the considerably high cost of constructing an ontology from scratch, the lengthy learning curve which has to be traversed in order to become familiar with an ontology before integrating it in the system, the lack of rigid maintenance strategies, and the dearth of metrics for assessing ontology.

## 10. Resources

As we stated earlier, an exhaustive review of the ontologies field is impractical and overwhelming for the reader. However, for the sake of disseminating up-to-date information on ontologies we have selected and include here pointers to publicly available online resources. These are:

- a comprehensive collection of ontology-related research in alphabetical order, maintained by Peter Clark:
  http://www.cs.utexas.edu/users/mfkb/related.html
- a similar collection maintained by Enrico Franconi:
  http://www.cs.man.ac.uk/franconi/ontology.html
- a list maintained by Adam Farquhar:
  http://ksl-web.stanford.edu/kst/ontology-sources.html
- a catalogue with classified information on ontologies prepared by Yannis Kalfoglou for a panel debate that took place in the SEKE'99 conference:
  http://www.dai.ed.ac.uk/daidb/people/homes/yannisk/seke99panelhtml.html

In addition to these periodically updated online resources there are several overviews in the literature. These are, the Uschold and Gruninger review [93], the comparative review of Fridman-Noy and Hafner in [29], the survey of ontology research in [13], an overview of ontologies and PSMs in [34], and a review of planning ontologies by Tate in [89]. There are also special issues in referred journals devoted to ontology research: with respect to their role in IT [45], their involvement in KBSs [103], and their uses [99]. In addition, we should mention the volume edited by Guarino in [41].

## Acknowledgments

The research described in this paper is supported by a European Union Marie Curie Fellowship (programme: Training and Mobility of Researchers).

## References

1. N. F. Abernethy, J. F. Wu, M. Hewett and R. B. Altman, "Sophia: A flexible, web-based knowledge server", *IEEE Intelligent Systems* **14**, no. 4 (July 1999) 79–85.
2. N. M. Agnew, K. M. Ford and P. J. Hayes, "Expertise in context: Personally constructed, socially elected, and reality-relevant?", *International Journal of Expert Systems* **7**, no. 1 (1993).
3. S. Aitken, "Extending the HPKB-upper-level ontology: Experiences and observations", eds. A. Gomez-Perez and R. Benjamins, *Proceedings of Workshop on Applications of Ontologies and Problem Solving Methods, ECAI'98*, Brighton, England (August 1998).
4. G. Arango, *Software Reusability/Domain Analysis Methods* (Ellis Horwood, Chichester, England, 1994) 17–49.
5. J. Aspirez, A. Gomez-Perez, A. Lozano and S. Pinto "(onto)2agent: An ontology-based www broker to select ontologies", *Proceedings of the Workshop on Applications of Ontologies and Problem-Solving Methods, ECAI'98*, Brighton, England (August 1998) 16–24.
6. P. Baker, C. Goble, S. Bechhofer, N. Paton, R. Stevens and A. Brass, "An ontology for bioinformatics applications", *Bioinformatics* **15**, no. 6 (1999) 510–520.
7. J. Bateman, B. Magnini and G. Fabris, "The Generalized Upper Model (GUM) knowledge-base: Organization and use", N.J.I. Mars, *Proceedings of the 2nd International Conference on Knowledge Building and Knowledge Sharing (KB & KS'95)*, Twente, The Netherlands, Amsterdam, NL (IOS Press, 1995) 60–72.
8. R. Benjamins and D. Fensel, "The ontological engineering initiative-KA2", ed. N. Guarino, *Proceedings of the 1st International Conference on Formal Ontologies in Information Systems, FOIS'98*, Trento, Italy (IOS Press, June 1998) 287–301.
9. M. Blazquez, M. Fernadez, J. M. Garcia-Pinar and A. Gomez-Perez, "Building ontologies at the knowledge level using the ontology design environment", *Proceedings of the 11th Knowledge Acquisition, Modeling and Management Workshop, KAW'98*, Banff, Canada (April 1998).
10. P. Borst, H. Akkermans and J. Top, "Engineering ontologies", *International Journal of Human-Computer Studies* **46** (1997) 365–406.
11. A. E. Campbell and S. C. Shapiro, "Algorithms for ontological mediation", Technical Report 98-03, Department of Computer Science and Engineering, State University of New York at Buffalo (January 1998).
12. B. Chandrasekaran, J. R. Josephson and R. Benjamins, "The ontology of tasks and methods", *Proceedings of the 11th Knowledge Acquisition Modeling and Management Workshop, KAW'98*, Banff, Canada (April 1998).
13. B. Chandrasekaran, R. Josephson and R. Benjamins, "What are ontologies, and why do we need them?", *IEEE Intelligent Systems* **14**, no. 1 (January 1999) 20–26.
14. P. Cohen, V. Chaudhri, A. Pease and R. Schrag, "Does prior knowledge facilitate the development of knowledge-based systems?", *Proceedings of the Sixteenth National Conference on Artificial Intelligence, AAAI'99*, Orlando, FL, USA (July 1999) 221–226.

15. P. Cohen, R. Schrag, E. Jones, A. Pease, A. Lin, B. Starr, D. Gunning and M. Burke, "The DARPA high performance knowledge bases project", *AI Magazine* **19**, no. 4 (1998) 25–49.

16. L. Crow and N. Shadbolt, "Acquiring and structuring web content with knowledge level models", eds. R. Studer and D. Fensel, *Proceedings of the 11th European Workshop on Knowledge Acquisition, Modeling and Management (EKAW'99)*, Dagstuhl, Germany (Springer-Verlag, May 1999) 83–101.

17. S. Decker, M. Erdmann, D. Fensel and R. Studer, "Ontobroker: Ontology based access to distributed and semi-structured information", ed. R. Meersman *et al*, *Proceedings of DS-8, Semantic Issues in Multimedia Systems*, Boston, MA, USA (1999) 351–369.

18. J. Domingue, "Tadzebao and webOnto: Discussing, browsing, and editing ontologies on the web", *Proceedings of the 11th Knowledge Acquisition, Modeling and Management Workshop, KAW'98*, Banff, Canada (April 1998).

19. J. Domingue and E. Motta, "Planet-Onto: From news publishing to integrated knowledge management support", *IEEE Intelligent Systems* no. 3 (2000) 26–32.

20. Enterprise Integration Laboratory, EIL. TOVE Project, University of Toronto, Canada, Available from *http://www.ie.utoronto.ca/EIL/tove/ontoTOC.html* (July 1995).

21. A. Farquhar, R. Fikes and J. Rice, "The ontolingua server: A tool for collaborative ontology construction", *International Journal of Human-Computer Studies* **46**, no. 6 (June 1997) 707–728.

22. D. Fensel, V. R. Benjamins, E. Motta and B. Wielinga, "UPML: A framework for knowledge system reuse", *Proceedings of the 16th International Joint Conference on Artificial Intelligence, IJCAI'99*, Stockholm, Sweden (August 1999) 16–21.

23. M. Fernandez, "Overview for methodologies for building ontologies", *Proceedings of the IJCAI'99 Workshop on Ontologies and Problem-Solving Methods (KRR5)*, Stockholm, Sweden (August 1999), Available from *http://sunsite.informatik.rwth-aachen.de/Publications/CEUR-WS/Vol-18/*.

24. M. Fernandez, A. Gomez-Perez and N. Juristo, "METHONTOLOGY: From ontological arts towards ontological engineering", *Proceedings of the AAAI'97 Spring Symposium Series on Ontological Engineering*, Stanford, CA, USA (March 1997) 33–40.

25. R. Fikes and A. Farquhar, "Distributed repositories of highly expressive reusable ontologies", *IEEE Intelligent Systems* **14**, no. 2 (March 1999) 73–79.

26. F. Fillion and C. Menzel, "Using ontologies to enable enterprise model integration", in Appendices of the paper: "Ontologies: principles, methods and applications", eds. M. Uschold and M. Gruninger, *The Knowledge Engineering Review* **11**, no. 2 (1996) 130–136.

27. A. Finkelstein, D. Gabbay, A. Hunter, J. Kramer and B. Nuseibeh, "Inconsistency handling in multi-perspective specifications", *IEEE Transactions on Software Engineering* **20**, no. 8 (1994) 569–578, Also as a Research Report DoC 93/2.

28. M. S. Fox and M. Gruninger, "On ontologies and enterprise modeling", *Proceedings of International Conference on Enterprise Integration Modeling Technology'97* (Springer-Verlag, 1997).

29. N. Fridman-Noy and C. D. Hafner, "The state of the art in ontology design: A survey and comparative review", *AI Magazine* **18**, no. 3 (1997) 53–74.

30. E. Gamma, R. Helm, R. Johnson and J. Vlissides, *Design Patterns: Elements of Reusable Object-Oriented Software* (Addison-Wesley, 1995).

31. A. Gangemi, D. Pisanelli and G. Steve, "Ontology integration: Experiences with medical terminologies", ed. N. Guarino, *Proceedings of the 1st International Conference on Formal Ontology in Information Systems, FOIS'98*, Trento, Italy (June 1998) 163–178.

32. A. Gangemi, G. Steve and F. Giacomelli, "ONIONS: An ontological methodology for taxonomic knowledge integration", ed. P. van der Vet, *Proceedings of the Workshop on Ontological Engineering, ECAI'96*, Budapest, Hungary (August 1996).

33. R. Genesereth and R. Fikes, "Knowledge interchange format", Computer Science Department, Stanford University, 3.0 ed., 1992. Technical Report, Logic-92-1.

34. A. Gomez-Perez and R. Benjamins, "Overview of knowledge sharing and reuse components: Ontologies and problem-solving methods", *Proceedings of the IJCAI-99 Workshop on Ontologies and Problem-Solving Methods (KRR'5)*, Stockholm, Sweden (August 1999). *http://sunsite.informatik.rwth-aachen.de/Publications/CEUR-WS/Vol-18/*.

35. A. Gomez-Perez and MD. Royas-Amaya, "Ontological reengineering for reuse", *Proceedings of the 11th European Workshop on Knowledge Acquisition, Modeling and Management (EKAW'99)*, Dagstuhl, Germany (May 1999) 139–157.

36. T. Gruber and G. Olsen, "An ontology for engineering mathematics", eds. J. Doyle, P. Torasso and E. Sandewall, *Proceedings of the Fourth International Conference on Principles of Knowledge Representation and Reasoning*, San Mateo, CA, USA (1994) 258–269.

37. T. R. Gruber, "A translation approach to portable ontologies", *Knowledge Acquisition* **5**, no. 2 (1993) 199–220.

38. T. R. Gruber, "Towards principles for the design of ontologies used for knowledge sharing", *International Journal of Human-Computer Studies* **43** (1995) 907–928.

39. M. Gruninger and M. S. Fox, "Methodology for the design and evaluation of ontologies", *Proceedings of the IJCAI'95 Workshop on Basic Ontological Issues in Knowledge Sharing*, Montreal, Quebec, Canada (August 1995).

40. N. Guarino, "Formal ontology and information systems", ed. N. Guarino, *Proceedings of the 1st International Conference on Formal Ontologies in Information Systems, FOIS'98*, Trento, Italy (IOS Press, June 1998) 3–15.

41. N. Guarino, "Formal ontology in information systems", *Frontiers in Artificial Intelligence and Applications* (IOS Press, June 1998) ISBN 90-5199-399-4.

42. N. Guarino, M. Carrara and P. Giaretta, "Formalizing ontological commitments", *Proceedings of the 12th National Conference on Artificial Intelligence (AAAI'94)*, Seattle, Washington, USA (1994).

43. N. Guarino and P. Giaretta, "Ontologies and knowledge bases: Towards a terminological clarification", *Proceedings of the 2nd International Conference on Knowledge Building and Knowledge Sharing (KB & KS'95)*, Twente, The Netherlands (April 1995).

44. N. Guarino, C. Masolo and G. Vetere, "OntoSeek: Content-based access to the web", *IEEE Intelligent Systems* **14**, no. 3 (May 1999) 70–80.

45. N. Guarino and R. Poli, "The role of ontology in the information technology", *International Journal of Human-Computer Studies* **43**, nos. 5–6 (1995) 623–965.

46. J. Jannink, S. Pichai, D. Verheijen and G. Wiederhold, "Encapsulation and composition of ontologies", *Proceedings of the AAAI'98 Workshop on Information Integration*, Madison, WI, USA (July 1998).

47. M. Jones, J. Wheadon, D. Whitgift, M. Niezatte, M. Timmermans, R. Rodriquez and R. Romero, "An agent-based approach to spacecraft mission operations", ed. N.J.I. Mars, *Proceedings of 2nd International Conference on Knowledge Building*

and *Knowledge Sharing* (*KB & KS'95*), Twente, The Netherlands (IOS Press, April 1995) 259–269.

48. Y. Kalfoglou, "The role of formal ontologies", *Proceedings of the 11th International Conference on Software Engineering and Knowledge Engineering, SEKE'99*, Kaiserslauten, Germany (June 1999) 401–405. Position paper presented at the Panel: Knowledge Maintenance. Also as Research Paper No. 952, Department of Artificial Intelligence, University of Edinburgh.

49. Y. Kalfoglou, T. Menzies, K.-D. Althoff and E. Motta, "Meta-knowledge in systems design: Panacea ... or undelivered promise?", *The Knowledge Engineering Review* **15**, no. 4 (2000) 381–404.

50. Y. Kalfoglou and D. Robertson, "A case study in applying ontologies to augment and reason about the correctness of specifications", *Proceedings of the 11th International Conference on Software Engineering and Knowledge Engineering, SEKE'99*, Kaiserslauten, Germany (June 1999) 64–71. Also as Research Paper No. 927, Department of Artificial Intelligence, University of Edinburgh.

51. Y. Kalfoglou and D. Robertson, "Managing ontological constraints", *Proceedings of the IJCAI'99 Workshop on Ontologies and Problem-Solving Methods* (*KRR5*), Stockholm, Sweden (August 1999), http://sunsite.informatik.rwth-aachen. de/Publications/CEUR-WS/Vol-18/. Also as Research Paper No. 948, Department of Artificial Intelligence, University of Edinburgh.

52. Y. Kalfoglou and D. Robertson, "Applying experienceware to support ontology deployment", *Proceedings of the 12th International Conference on Software Engineering and Knowledge Engineering, SEKE'2000*, Chicago, IL, USA (July 2000) 266–275.

53. Y. Kalfoglou, D. Robertson and A. Tate, "Using meta-knowledge at the application level", Research Paper No. 956, Department of Artificial Intelligence, University of Edinburgh.

54. K. Knight and S. Luk, "Building a large knowledge base for machine translation", *Proceedings of the American Association of Artificial Intelligence Conference AAAI'94*, Seattle, USA (July 1994).

55. J. Lee, M. Gruninger, Y. Jin, T. Malone, A. Tate, G Yost and other members of the PIF working group, "The PIF process interchange format and framework", *Knowledge Engineering Review* **13**, no. 1 (February 1998) 91–120.

56. J. Lee and T. Malone, "Partially shared views: A scheme for communicating between groups using different type hierarchies", *ACM Transactions on Information Systems* **8**, no. 1 (1990) 1–26.

57. D. B. Lenat and R. V. Guha, *Building Large Knowledge-based Systems. Representation and Inference in the Cyc Project* (Addison-Wesley, Reading, MA 1990).

58. W. Mark, "Ontologies as representation and re-representation of agreement", *Proceedings of the 5th International Conference on Principles of Knowledge Representation and Reasoning, KR'96*, MA, USA, 1996. Position paper presented on the panel: Ontologies: What are They and Where's the Research.

59. W. Mark, J. Dukes-Schlossberg and R. Kerber, "Ontological commitment and domain-specific architectures: Experience with comet and cosmos", ed. N.J.I. Mars, *Proceedings of the 2nd International Conference on Knowledge Building and Knowledge Sharing* (*KB & KS'95*), Twente, The Netherlands (April 1995) 33–45.

60. W. Mark, J. Schlossberg, S. Tyler and J. McGuire, "Cosmos: A system for supporting engineering negotiation", *Concurrent Engineering: Research and Applications* **2**, (1994) 173–182.

61. W. Mark, S. Tyler, J. McGuire and J. Schossberg, "Commitment-based software development", *IEEE Transactions on Software Engineering* **18**, no. 10 (October 1992) 870–884.

62. L. D. McGuinness, "Ontological issues for knowledge-enhanced search", ed. N. Guarino, *Proceedings of the 1st International Conference on Formal Ontology in Information Systems (FOIS'98)*, Trento, Italy, (IOS Press, June 1998) 302–316.

63. E. Mena, V. Kashyap, A. Illarramendi and A. Sheth, "Domain specific ontologies for semantic information brokering on the global information infrastructure", ed. N. Guarino, *Proceedings of the 1st International Conference on Formal Ontology in Information Systems (FOIS'98)*, Trento, Italy (IOS Press, June 1998) 269–283.

64. T. Menzies, K. D. Althoff, Y. Kalfoglou and E. Motta "Issues with meta-knowledge", *International Journal of Software Engineering and Knowledge Engineering* **10**, no. 4 (August 2000) 549–555.

65. T. Menzies and B. Clancey, "Special issue on situated cognition", *International Journal of Human-Computer Studies* **49** (1998) (editorial).

66. G. A. Miller, "WORDNET: An online lexical database", *International Journal of Lexicography* **3**, no. 4 (1990) 235–312.

67. R. Mizoguchi, J. van Welkenhuysen and M. Ikeda, "Task ontology for reuse of problem-solving knowledge", ed. N.J.I. Mars, *Proceedings of the 2nd International Conference on Knowledge Building and Knowledge Sharing (KB & KS'95)*, Twente, The Netherlands (IOS Press, Amsterdam, NL 1995) 46–57.

68. T. P. Moran and J. M. Carroll, *Design Rationale: Concepts, Techniques, and Use* (Lawerence Erlbaum Associates, 1996) ISBN 0-8058-1567-8.

69. E. Motta, "Reusable components for knowledge models: Case studies in parametric design problem solving", *Frontiers in Artificial Intelligence and Applications*, Vol. 53 (IOS Press, 1999), ISBN 1-58603-003-5.

70. E. Motta, D. Fensel, M. Gaspari and R. Benjamins, "Specifications of knowledge components for reuse", *Proceedings of the 11th International Conference on Software Engineering and Knowledge Engineering, SEKE'99*, Kaiserslauten, Germany (June 1999) 36–43.

71. National Library of Medicine, Bethesda, Maryland, USA, *UMLS Knowledge Sources*, (1997).

72. R. Neches, R. E. Fikes, T. Finin, T. R. Gruber, T. Senator and W. R. Swartout, "Enabling technology for knowledge sharing", *AI Magazine* **12**, no. 3 (1991) 36–56.

73. D. O'Leary, "Impediments in the use of explicit ontologies for KBS development", *International Journal of Human-Computer Studies* **46**, no. 2 (1997) 327–337.

74. D. O'Leary, "Knowledge management systems: Converting and connecting", *IEEE Intelligent Systems* **13**, no. 3 (June 1998) 30–33.

75. D. O'Leary, "Using Artificial Intelligence in knowledge management: Knowledge bases and ontologies", *IEEE Intelligent Systems* **13**, no. 3 (June 1998) 34–39.

76. S. Pinto, A. Gomez-Perez and J. Martins, "Some issues on ontology integration", *Proceedings of the IJCAI'99 Workshop on Ontologies and Problem-Solving Methods (KRR5)*, Stockholm, Sweden (August 1999), *http://sunsite.informatik.rwth-aachen.de/Publications/CEUR-WS/Vol-18/*.

77. S. T. Polyak, "A supply chain process interoperability demonstration using the process interchange format (PIF)", Research Paper No. 917, Department of Artificial Intelligence, University of Edinburgh (February 1998).

78. C. Potts, "Supporting software design: Integrating design methods and design rationale", eds. P. T. Moran and M. J. Carroll, *Design Rationale: Concepts, Techniques, and Use*, Chap. 10 (Lawrence Erlbaum Associates, 1996) 295–321.

79. A. Preece, K. Hui, P. Gray, P. Marti, T. Bench-Capon, D. Jones and Z. Cui, "The KRAFT architecture for knowledge fusion and transformation", *Proceedings of the 19th SGES International Conference on Knowledge-based Systems and Applied Artificial Intelligence (ES'99)*, Cambridge, England (Springer-Verlag, December 1999). Best Technical Paper Award.

80. A. L. Rector, W. A. Nowlan and the GALEN Consortium, "The GALEN project", *Computer Methods and Programs in Biomedicine* **45** (1995) 75–78.

81. D. Robertson, "Pitfalls of formality in early system design", *Proceedings of the 1998 ARO/NSF Monterey Workshop on Increasing the Practical Impact of Formal Methods for Computer-Aided Software Development*, Carmal, California (1998).

82. M. Shaw, "Validation in a knowledge acquisition system with multiple experts", *Proceedings of the International Conference on 5th Generation Computer Systems* (1988) 1259–1266.

83. D. Skuce, "Viewing ontologies as vocabulary: Merging and documenting the logical and linguistic views", *Proceedings of the IJCAI'95 Workshop on Basic Ontological Issues in Knowledge Sharing*, Montreal, Quebec, Canada (August 1995).

84. J. Sowa, *Knowledge Representation: Logical, Philosophical and Computational Foundations* (Brooks Cole Publishing Co., Pacific Grove, CA, USA, 2000), ISBN: 0-534-94965-7.

85. R. Studer, V. R. Benjamins and D. Fensel, "Knowledge engineering, principles and methods", *Data and Knowledge Engineering* **25**, nos. 1–2 (1998) 161–197.

86. T. Summer and S. Buckingham-Shum, "From documents to discourse: Shifting conceptions of scholarly publishing", *Proceedings of the CHI'98: Human Factors in Computing Systems*, Los Angeles, CA, USA (ACM Press, 1998) 95–102.

87. B. Swartout, R. Patil, K. Knight and T. Russ, "Toward distributed use of large-scale ontologies", *Proceedings of the 10th Knowledge Acquisition, Modeling and Management Workshop (KAW'96)*, Banff, Canada (November 1996).

88. W. Swartout and A. Tate, "Ontologies — Guest editors' introduction", *IEEE Intelligent Systems* **14** no. 1 (January 1999) 18–19.

89. A. Tate, "Roots of SPAR — Shared planning and activity representation", *The Knowledge Engineering Review* **13**, no. 1 (1998) 121–128.

90. M. Uschold, "Knowledge level modeling: concepts and terminology", *The Knowledge Engineering Review* **13**, no. 1 (February 1998) 5–29.

91. M. Uschold, "Where are the Killer Apps?", ed. A. Gomez-Perez and R. Benjamins, *Proceedings of Workshop on Applications of Ontologies and Problem Solving Methods, ECAI'98*, Brighton, England (August 1998).

92. M. Uschold, P. Clark, M. Healy, K. Williamson and S. Woods, "An experiment in ontology reuse", *Proceedings of the 11th Knowledge Acquisition Workshop, KAW'98*, Banff, Canada (April 1998).

93. M. Uschold and M. Gruninger , "Ontologies: Principles, methods and applications", *The Knowledge Engineering Review* **11**, no. 2 (November 1996) 93–136.

94. M. Uschold, M. Healy, K. Williamson, P. Clark and S. Woods "Ontology reuse and application", ed. N. Guarino, *Proceedings of the 1st International Conference on Formal Ontology in Information Systems (FOIS'98)*, Trento, Italy (IOS Press, June 1998) 179–192.

95. M. Uschold and R. Jasper, "A framework for understanding and classifying Ontology Applications", *Proceedings of the IJCAI'99 Workshop on Ontologies and Problem-Solving Methods (KRR'5)*, Stockholm, Sweden (August 1999), *http://sunsite.informatik.rwth-aachen.de/Publications/CEUR-WS/Vol-18/*.

96. M. Uschold, R. Jasper and P. Clark, "Three approaches for knowledge sharing: A comparative analysis", *Proceedings of the 12th Knowledge Acquisition, Modeling and Management Workshop, KAW'99*, Banff, Canada (October 1999).

97. M. Uschold, M. King, S. Moralee and Y. Zorgios, "The enterprise ontology", *The Knowledge Engineering Review* **13**, no. 1 (February 1998). Also available as AIAI-TR-195 from AIAI, University of Edinburgh.

98. M. Uschold and M. King, "Towards a methodology for building ontologies", *Proceedings of the IJCAI'95 Workshop on Basic Ontological Issues in Knowledge Sharing*, Montreal, Canada (1995).

99. M. Uschold and A. Tate, "Putting ontologies to use", *The Knowledge Engineering Review* **13**, no. 1 (1998) 1–128.

100. A. Valente, T. Russ, R. MacGrecor and W. Swartout, "Building and (re)using an ontology for air campaign planning", *IEEE Intelligent Systems* **14**, no. 1 (January 1999) 27–36.

101. P. van der Vet and N. Mars, "Structured system of concepts for storing, retrieving, and manipulating chemical information", *Journal of Chemical Information and Computer Science* **33** (1993) 564–568.

102. P. van der Vet and N. Mars, "Bottom-up construction of ontologies", *IEEE Transactions on Knowledge and Data Engineering* **10**, no. 4 (1998) 513–526.

103. G. van Heijst, A. Schreider and B. Wielinga, "Using explicit ontologies in KBS development", *International Journal of Human-Computer Studies* **46**, nos. 2–3 (1997) 183–292.

104. P.R.S. Visser, D. M. Jones, T.J.M. Bench-Capon and M.J.R. Shave, "Assessing heterogeneity by classifying ontology mismatches", ed. N. Guarino, *Proceedings of 1st International Conference on Formal Ontologies in Information Systems, FOIS'98*, Trento, Italy (IOS Press, June 1998) 148–162.

105. P.R.S. Visser and V.A.M Tamma, "An experiment with ontology-based agent clustering", *Proceedings of the IJCAI'99 Workshop on Ontologies and Problem-Solving Methods (KRR5)*, Stockholm, Sweden (August 1999). *http://sunsite.informatik.rwth-aachen.de/Publications/CEUR-WS/Vol-18/*.

106. A. Waterson and A. Preece, "Verifying ontological commitment in knowledge-based systems", *Knowledge-based Systems* **12** (April 1999) 45–54.

107. WfMC, "Workflow management coalition: Abstract specification", WFMC-TC 1012, WfMC (October 1996). Interoperability demonstration presented at the 1996 Business Process and Workflow Conference in Amsterdam.

108. T. Winograd, *Bringing Design to Software* (Addison-Wesley, 1996), ISBN 0-201-85491-0.

# ON THE USE OF LOGICAL ABDUCTION IN SOFTWARE ENGINEERING

ALESSANDRA RUSSO and BASHAR NUSEIBEH

*Department of Computing, Imperial College of Science,*
*Technology and Medicine, London SW7 2BZ, UK*
*E-mail: {ar3,ban}@doc.ic.ac.uk*

In this paper, we survey recent work on the use of abduction as a knowledge-based reasoning technique for analyzing software specifications. We present a general overview of logical abduction and describe two abductive reasoning techniques, developed from the logic and expert system communities. We then focus on two applications of abduction in software engineering, namely, analysis and revision of specifications. Specifically, we discuss and illustrate, with examples, how the above two abductive reasoning techniques can be deployed to reason about specifications, detect errors, such as logical inconsistencies, provide diagnostic information about these errors, and identify (possible) changes to revise incorrect specifications. We then conclude with a discussion of open research issues.

*Keywords*: Abductive reasoning, analysis, revision, specification, inconsistency, logic programming.

## 1. Introduction

Specifications are key products of the development process of a software system. Requirements engineering focuses on the development of requirements specifications that model real-world goals and environmental constraints of a system[a] under construction [55]. Design is concerned with the development of specifications of software architectures and their constituent components [33].

Independently of the underlying software development process, specifications are continuously subject to change and evolution. In the case of requirements specifications, for instance, inconsistencies may arise during the requirements elicitation process, and changes may be necessary in order to handle such inconsistencies [14, 40]. System requirements might also evolve because of environmental changes or to handle unforseen problems in a system. This leads to changes in the requirements specifications that describe such requirements. Changes in requirements specifications cause changes in design specifications, which themselves lead to changes in the implementation. Analysis and maintenance of specifications are therefore key activities in software engineering.

---

[a]Throughout the chapter we will not make any distinction between a system and a software system; these terms are used interchangebly.

Various techniques for analyzing specifications have been developed [26] and recently an increasing research effort has been dedicated to investigate the use of formal methods at different stages of the software development process, e.g. [1, 4, 27, 52]. The rigour and precision of formal techniques, such as model checking, theorem proving and logic-based reasoning mechanisms like abduction [35, 41, 45], facilitate a better understanding of the system to be developed by uncovering errors, inconsistencies, incompletenesses, which might otherwise go undetected. The formal techniques differ from each other in various ways and have advantages and limitations. Theorem proving techniques have been shown to be successful in supporting verification of software specificiations [42], model checking techniques were initially used in hardware verification and have started to become more widely used to support the analysis and validation of (requirements) specifications [10, 34]. More recently, logic-based reasoning techniques such as goal-regression [53] and abduction [37, 45, 48] have also been shown to be valuable techniques for analyzing and managing (requirements) specifications [41, 47, 53]. This chapter is a survey of recent work on the use of one of these formal techniques — *abduction* — in software engineering.

In Artificial Intelligence (AI) abduction is one of three common modes of reasoning (the other two being deduction and induction). In general terms, abduction is a useful constructive technique for generating "explanations" or "plans" for given "observations" or "goals". In AI, abduction has been shown to be suitable for automating tasks such as diagnosis [12], planning [15], and theory and database updates [11, 25, 28]. Recent research results have shown its applicability and utility in software engineering, as a technique for supporting knowledge-based software development [35], and for facilitating analysis and revision of specifications [41, 45, 47].

This chapter will provide an overview of these results, present a critical analysis of why and when abductive reasoning is effective in software engineering, and illustrate how to make use of such techniques. For the purposes of this paper, we assume specifications to consist of system descriptions (e.g. system requirements or system designs) and system properties (e.g. required system's invariants, safety properties, deadlocks). In this context, analysis of a specification means consistency checking to verify the satisfaction of system properties over a system description. Revision refers to the process of identifying changes (i.e., additions or deletions) to a specification that would re-establish the correctness of the specification.

The chapter is structured as follows. In Sec. 2, we define the notion of logical abduction. In Sec. 3, we describe two examples of abductive reasoning techniques. The first is an abductive proof procedure that uses logic programming [23] as the underlying rule-based reasoning engine. The second is an abductive technique that uses a graph-based approach [38] for reasoning about specifications. Sections 4 and 5 describe two main applications of abduction in software engineering, namely, analysis and revision of specifications. Illustrative examples will be given throughout the chapter. We will then conclude with a discussion of directions for future work.

## 2. Overview of Abduction

Abduction is commonly defined as the problem of finding a set of hypotheses (an "explanation" or a "plan") of a specified form that, when added to a given (formal) specification, allows an "observation" or "goal" sentence to be inferred, without causing contradictions. We consider here an example taken from [30].

### Example 1

Consider a specification $D$ composed of the following rules:

$$rained\text{-}last\text{-}night \rightarrow grass\text{-}is\text{-}wet$$

$$sprinkler\text{-}was\text{-}on \rightarrow grass\text{-}is\text{-}wet$$

$$grass\text{-}is\text{-}wet \rightarrow shoes\text{-}are\text{-}wet$$

Now suppose that we observe that our shoes are wet, and we want to know why this is so. A possible explanation is {*rained-last-night*} — if we add it to the above explicit domain-specific description $D$ it implies the given observation. Another alternative explanation is {*sprinkler-was-on*}. Abduction is then the process of computing such explanations for the given observation.

From the point of view of knowledge-based reasoning, the philosopher Pierce first introduced the notion of abduction as one of three fundamental forms of reasoning, the others being induction and deduction [43]. Informally, given a rule-based domain-specific description $D$ (e.g. a system description), some particular cases $\alpha$ (e.g. instances of system behaviors), and a result $\beta$ (e.g. a system property), deduction is the analytic process of applying the general rules to the particular cases in order to infer the result (i.e., $D \wedge \alpha \Rightarrow \beta$). Within the same context, induction is "learning" some new rules $D_i$ after having seen numerous examples of $\beta$ and $\alpha$ (i.e., $\alpha \wedge \beta \Rightarrow D_i$), and abduction is using the result and the general rules to infer the particular cases that explain such results (i.e., $\beta \wedge D \Rightarrow \alpha$).[b]

Abduction is therefore a reasoning process that computes explanations for given observations. This reasoning process is in general *non-monotonic*,[c] because the explanations generated are strictly dependent on the state of the domain-specific description $D$. If new information is added to $D$, new explanations, possibly different from those generated previously can be identified. A formal definition of abduction in logical terms is as follows.

---

[b]The symbol $\Rightarrow$ denotes the particular reasoning process: deduction, induction or abduction.
[c]Recall that a reasoning mechanism is *non-monotonic* if the addition (or deletion) of new information to (from) a specification does not necessarily preserve the set of derivable information (e.g. [5, 41]).

## Definition 1

Given a domain description $D$ and a sentence (goal/observation) $G$, abduction is the process of identifying a set $\Delta$ of assertions such that

(1) $D \wedge \Delta \models G$
(2) $D \wedge \Delta$ is consistent.

The set $\Delta$ is required to satisfy two main criteria: (1) it is restricted to belong to a domain-specific set of sentences, called *abducibles*, and (2) it is minimal. The set of abducibles are defined *a priori* to reflect some notion of causality with respect to the given observations. For instance, in Example 1, {*grass-is-wet*} is also an explanation for the observation *shoes-are-wet*. However, such assertion would explain one effect in terms of another effect, since *grass-is-wet* could itself be explained in terms of the cause {*rained-last-night*}. To draw an analog example within the context of requirements specifications, system behaviors can be seen as caused by system states and events in the environment. Observations, such as violation of a system property, should therefore be explained in terms of specific environmental events and states in which the system is when such events occur, rather then any other intermediate system state. The notion of abducibles helps, therefore, tailor the notion of explanation to the particular application domain, as well as formalize the given domain knowledge. From the knowledge representation viewpoint, in fact, abducible facts should never appear as consequence of rules. For instance, if Example 1 had also included the information *shoes-are-wet→rained-last-night*, then *rained-last-night* would not have been considered to be an abducible fact.[d] The minimality property means that the abduced explanations should not be subsumed by other explanations. For instance, in Example 1, the explanation {*rained-last-night, sprinkler-was-on*} for the observation {*shoes-are-wet*} is not minimal, since there are two other explanations {*rained-last-night*} and {*sprinkler-was-on*} that subsume it.

The abductive reasoning process can be further refined by means of *integrity constraints* [30]. In general, integrity constraints are used to define the class of legal models of a given specification. For instance, in the case of requirements specifications, integrity constraints could be the natural physics laws of the environment in which the system is supposed to operate. In the presence of integrity constraints, abductive reasoning has to generate legal explanations, namely, explanations that satisfy the given constraints. To take this into account, the definition of abduction needs to be modified sligthly. Given a set $I$ of integrity constraints, condition 2 of Definition 1 needs to be replaced by the following stronger condition:

$$2'. \ D \wedge \Delta \text{ is consistent, and } D \wedge \Delta \models I.$$

This alternative condition has the effect of further reducing the collection of alternative explanations generated by the abductive reasoning process. If, for instance,

---

[d]In this specific case, the domain description would also cause the resoning process to loop. Techniques for addressing loop problems in abduction can be found in [30].

in Example 1, we had the integrity constraint that the sprinkler can never be on, then the abductive process would only have generated the explanation {*rained-last-night*}.

The applications of abduction illustrated in Sections 4 and 5 take into account this notion of integrity constraints.

## 3. Abductive Techniques

The above overview of abduction is independent of any particular computational technique used to implement abductive reasoning. In this section, we illustrate two different computational techniques for performing abductive reasoning. The first one is based on logic programming, and the second uses reasoning on dependency-graphs. The choice of these two techniques aims to provide the reader with two different viewpoints of abduction, developed by two different knowledge engineering communities, the logic-based and the expert system communities.

### 3.1. *An abductive proof procedure using logic programming*

Abductive logic programming focuses on the development of formal frameworks and techniques for performing abductive reasoning within the (implemetation) context of logic programming [23]. Informally, a logic program is a specific logic-based form of implementation of a given specification, expressed in terms of Horn clauses extended with negation as failure [7]. Horn clauses are rules of the form

$$A \leftarrow L_1, \ldots, L_n$$

where each $L_i$ is either an atomic piece of information $B_j$ or its negation $\sim B_j$. The connective $\sim$ is called *negation as failure*, and should be read as "not provable" from a given logic program. The underlying reasoning engine is based on resolution [22].

An abductive proof procedure for logic programs with negation as failure was first developed by Eshghi and Kowalski [16] and subsequently extended for different types of (extended) logic programs (e.g. logic programs with classical negation). We will describe here the basic structure of such procedure, which still remains at the core of all existing abductive proof procedure for logic programming [30]. This procedure assumes, without loss of generality, that it is convenient to define the set of abducibles among those predicates that are not conclusions of any clause in a given logic program, and that the rules define only positive literals. The first condition automatically ensures that the explanations generated by the procedure are "basic" explanations, i.e., they are not definable in terms of other explanations.

An abductive proof procedure for logic programming consists of two phases, an *abductive phase* and a *consistency phase*, which interleave with each other. The abductive phase is an extension of standard resolution. In standard resolution, selected (sub)goals are unified and resolved with the conclusions of any rules. If this process fails, then the proof fails. In the abductive phase, when a selected (sub)goal fails to resolve with the conclusion of any of the given rules, then it is *abduced.* Each abduced assertion is temporarily added to a set of abducibles that have already been generated. The entire new set of abducibles is then checked for consistency with the specification, using the consistency rules $(CC1)$ and $(CC2)$[e]:

$$(A \wedge \sim A) \rightarrow \perp \qquad (CC1)$$
$$(A \vee \sim A) \qquad (CC2).$$

The consistency checking consists of verifying that (a) it is not the case that for some atomic fact $A$, both $A$ and $\sim A$ can be proved from the specification and a given current set of abducibles, and (b) for each atomic fact $A$, it is either the case that $A$ is proved or $\sim A$ is proved. Because of the close world assumption of logic programs and the type of logic programs considered, where negation does not appear in the consequence of any rule, the two types of consitency checking will only need to be performed on the abduced facts. For more details, the reader is referred to [30]. If the consistency checking succeeds, the temporary assertion added to a current set of abducibles is permanently accepted in the set of abducibles, otherwise it is discharged. The consistency phase may itself invoke the abductive phase, in order to verify the inference of some intermediate sub-goals.

In the presence of domain-specific integrity constraints, the consistency checking has to guarantee that the generated abducibles also satisfy those constraints. We illustrate such a procedure in more detail via an example also taken from [30].

## Example 2

Consider the following (logic program) specification:

$$s \leftarrow \sim p$$
$$p \leftarrow \sim q$$
$$q \leftarrow \sim r.$$

We want to discover the possible explanations for the given observation $s$. The computation is shown in Fig. 1, using the box notation adopted in [30]. The proof in single line boxes belong to an abductive phase, whereas the proofs in double line boxes to a consistency phase. It succeeds, generating the set $\Delta = \{\sim p, \sim r\}$. The abductive phase starts as a standard resolution step; e.g. the goal $s$ resolves with the conclusion of the first rule generating the new subgoal $\sim p$. At this point, since there is no rule with conclusion $\sim p$, this subgoal is temporally added to the set of generated abducibles, that so far is just given by $\{\sim p\}$. Once an assertion is abduced, the consistency phase begins. In this case, we check that the abduced information satisfies $(CC1)$. This means checking that the assertion $p$ is not provable. This checking succeeds if all possible ways (i.e., rules) of proving $p$ fail. In this

---

[e]These consistency rules reflect, respectively, the standard notion of classical inconsistency and the property of "completion", which is typical of the logic programming semantics. Note that abductive proof procedures for other types of logic with different underlying semantics may not necessarily need to include such consistency constraints.

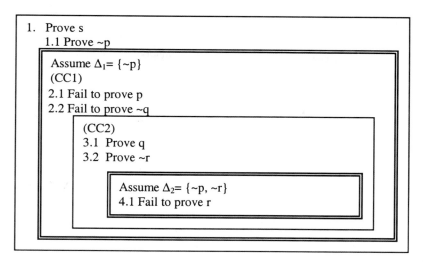

**Fig. 1.** Abductive computation for Example 2.

case we have only one rule. To make it fail, we check that $\sim q$ is not provable. At this point, no rule with conclusion $\sim q$ exists, but the integrity constraint $(CC2)$ implies that failure of $\sim q$ is only allowed provided that $q$ is provable. The abductive phase is therefore again called to compute the provability of this subgoal. By standard resolution, the subgoal $q$ unifies with the third rule and the new subgoal $\sim r$ is generated. Since there is no rule with conclusion $\sim r$, this is added to the set of abducibles and a new consistency phase is called. This point is similar to the abduction step of $\sim p$. In this case however, the consistency checking with $(CC1)$ is immediate. The failure of $r$ is guaranteed by the fact that $\sim r$ is (abductively) assumed.

If the (logic program) description includes also some integrity constraints, then the consistency phase has to check their satisfiabilty each time a new assertion is abduced. For instance, if in the Example 2, there was also an integrity constraint of the form $\sim (\sim p \wedge a)$, having assumed $\sim p$, the consistency should also check that $a$ fails. This would imply, by $(CC2)$, $\sim a$ succeeds, which means also abducing $\sim a$. The final set of abducibles would have also included some additional abduced assertions needed in order to verify the integrity constraints.

To summarize, the abductive proof procedure based on logic programming described above has the following characteristics:

(1) It can be applied to logic program representations of given (system) descriptions. Therefore, a mapping of such descriptions into a logic program is first needed. Similarly, for any domain-specific constraint.

(2) A notion of abducibles needs to be defined. This can be done by simply adding to the logic program clauses of the form abducible-predicate $(X)$, for each propositional letter or predicate $X$ that can be abduced.

(3) Any existing implementation of abductive logic programming proof procedure can be applied. Examples are given in [29].

## 3.2. *Graph-based abduction and the HT4 approach*

We now describe a second abductive technique, based on dependency-graph representations of specifications. The technique was proposed by Menzies [35], within the context of a knowledge level modelling approach to expert system design [39, 54]. Here, the knowledge base of an underlying system is assumed to be composed of domain-specific knowledge and a model of the underlying problem-solving inference process. For instance, Clancey's knowledge level modeling approach [6] assumes a "qualitative model" (essentially a first-order theory) of the underlying domain knowledge, and a full network of possible proof trees that could be generated from this qualitative model. This network is the model of the inference process. A similar approach is adopted by Menzies in his abductive framework HT4 [35, 36]. This framework uses a graph-theoretic approach, rather than a logic-based approach described in the previous section. A theory, about certain domain knowledge, is given. This is essentially a dependency graph, whose vertices are propositions that can take one of the three values {UP, DOWN, STEADY}, and the edges are labelled with "++" or "−−". An example taken from [35] is given in Fig. 2. An edge from a vertex $X$ to vertex $Y$, labelled with "++", means that the proposition $Y$ being UP/DOWN can be explained by the proposition $X$ being UP/DOWN. An edge from a vertex $X$ to a vertex $Y$, labelled with "−−", means that the proposition $Y$ being UP/DOWN can be explained by the proposition $X$ being DOWN/UP. To draw an analogy between this representation of domain knowledge and the logic-based approaches, we can think of the value UP being equal to the Boolean value TRUE, the value DOWN being equal to the Boolean value FALSE, and the value STEADY being equal to TRUE∧FALSE.[f]

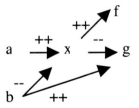

**Fig. 2.**  An example of a qualitative theory.

The HT4 algorithm generates from a given qualitative theory a complete dependency-graph, called a "super-theory", which expresses the above meaning

---

[f]Note that in the super-theory given in Fig. 3 the STEADY vertices are essentially end points, points of inconsistencies, and therefore cannot be used to explain other information (i.e., they don't have any children in the dependency-graph representation).

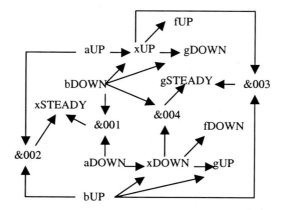

**Fig. 3.** The dependency graph generated from Fig. 2.

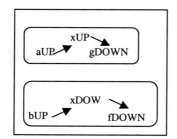

**Fig. 4.** Two possible abductive answers.

of the "++" and "−−" edges in terms of binary dependency relations between the three values that each vertex could have. Figure 3, describes the super-theory generated from the qualitative theory given in Fig. 2. The HT4 framework uses this super-theory to generate abductive proofs. The abductive reasoning is performed within a user-supplied task. A task is defined in terms of a collection IN of input vertices (a subset of the vertices in the quality theory), a collection OUT of outputs (data to be proved), and a notion of BEST. The latter is an operator that selects from alternative abductive proofs a preferred one. Of course the notion of pre-ferred one is application-dependent. Different BEST operators are discussed in [35] corresponding to applications such as prediction, qualitative reasoning, planning and monitoring.

Given a task, HT4-style abduction is the search for all possible proofs (i.e., paths in the dependency-graph) from a subset of vertices included in IN to a subset of vertices included in OUT, such that no vertices in these proofs have contradic-tory values.[g] For instance, given the super-theory described in Fig. 3 and the sets

---

[g]This feature corresponds to the notion of a consistent abductive explanation, which is stated in condition 2 of Definition 1.

IN = {aUP, bUP}, and OUT = {gDOWN, fDOWN}, an abductive answer would be the separate collections of proofs shown in Fig. 4. Note that, for instance, the path bUP → xDOWN → fDOWN is not included in the first collection because it contains the vertex xDOWN which contradicts the vertex xUP in other identified paths, and so vice-versa. The two collections of abductive proofs are called *worlds* [35].

To summarize, the HT4 abductive procedure proposed by Menzies and described above has the following characteristics:

(1) It can be applied to specifications represented as qualitative theories, since these can be transformed into full, extended dependency-graphs. Therefore, a mapping of any given specification into the dependency-graph syntax is first needed. Note that the vertices in the graph are propositions. The approach is therefore applicable to propositional representation of system specifications. First-order theories could be represented only to the extent that they can be partially evaluated into equivalent ground theories.

(2) There is no notion of abducible. The explanation generated in this approach includes both basic information as well as intermediate information inferred during the reasoning process.

(3) Different definitions of the BEST operator facilitate the use of the same abductive reasoning engine for supporting different types of reasoning: prediction, qualitative reasoning, planning and validation.

(4) The HT4 tool has gone through various phases of improvements and a description of the underlying algorithm can be found in [35].

## 4. Application of Abduction in Software Engineering

As mentioned in the introduction, two crucial problems in software engineering are the analysis and maintenance of specifications. Recent results have shown how abduction can successfully be applied to software engineering in order to address these problems [35, 45, 47, 48]. The next two sections illustrate two different applications of abduction: abduction for analyzing specifications and abduction for revising specifications. Specifically, we will illustrate how abductive reasoning allows: (a) detection of inconsistencies and/or property violations, and identification of related diagnostic information, and (b) reasoning about possible change(s) to perform on a given specification in order to resolve detected errors, or to support consistency management in evolving specifications.

### 4.1. *Analyzing specifications*

Specifications can be seen as (formal) descriptions that model an underlying system, within a specific context. For instance, requirements specifications model a system in terms of its interaction with the environment and user-goals. Specification analysis is therefore a means of performing analysis of a model of the system rather than of the system itself. Assuming that such a model is a faithful representation of the system, analyzing specifications helps identify problems in the system. For the purpose of this chapter, we focus on two particular types of specification analysis, namely, analysis for (a) detecting inconsistencies and violation of system properties, and for (b) identifying diagnostic information about detected errors as a debugging aid for engineers.

### 4.1.1. *Detecting inconsistencies*

Inconsistency detection can be seen as detection of a property violation, where the property is a domain-independent rule of the form "for any sentence $A$ (denoting either any system variable or any environmental entity), it cannot be the case that both $A$ and $\neg A$ are inferable from a given specification". The validation of this property is computationally equivalent to evaluating the satisfability of the overall specification, taken as a conjunction of formulae. For first-order representations, this is an NP-hard problem. We will therefore restrict our attention to propositional specifications or to first-order representations over finite domains that can be instatiated and grounded down to propositional level.

Abductive reasoning can, in general, be used to detect inconsistencies by considering, as an observation (goal), atomic instantiations of the form $P(X) \wedge \neg P(X)$, for each predicate symbol and ground term used in the specification. If the abductive reasoning process succeeds, i.e., it is able to identify a set of abducibles $\Delta$ that satisfies conditions (1) and (2) of Definition 1, then the specification is inconsistent since $P(X) \wedge \neg P(X)$ can be derived from it. Moreover, the set $\Delta$ would provide (consistent) diagnostic information for the inconsistency $P(X) \wedge \neg P(X)$ in terms of parts of the specification that lead to this inconsistency. However, if the abductive reasoning technique fails to find such a $\Delta$, it is either the case that $P(X) \wedge \neg P(X)$ is not inferable from the specification or there is no consistent way of constructing such an explanation $\Delta$. In that case we would not be able to conclude that the given specification is consistent with respect to the predicate $P(X)$.

The abductive approach developed by Menzies [35, 36] provides an alternative way of identifying inconsistent information in a given specification. Instead of considering ground individual inconsistencies as properties to validate, the HT4 abductive algorithm [35, 36] identifies inconsistent facts in a given specification as side effects of an abductive reasoning process for a given task. For instance, given a set of INputs and a set of OUTputs of a specification (qualitative theory), the HT4 abductive reasoning process identifies all consistent paths within the network of all possible proof trees that link the INput to the OUTput. Paths that include contradictory propositions are separated in different worlds. Therefore, in order to identify these different worlds, the HT4 abductive process identifies the set of contradictory information. For instance, in the example illustrated in Fig. 4 the only contradictory information is the proposition $x$, since it can assume both values UP and DOWN. Of course the set of contradictions identified by the HT4 abductive algorithm depends on the task under consideration. However, considering a task whose set of INputs is the entire set of inputs of a given specification, and whose set of OUTputs covers all possible outputs of a specification, the HT4 abductive reasoning process is able to identify all possible contradictory information that is included in a given specification. This is possible because the HT4 algorithm records as abductive answers all possible proof trees, separating the ones which are inconsistent with each other in different worlds. In the abductive proof procedure for logic programming, on the other hand, abductive information which is inconsistent with the given specification is simply rejected. The final abductive answers are only those Δ (parts of the specification) that are consistent with the specification itself.

An additional advantage of using the HT4 algorithm for analyzing specifications is the possibility of reasoning in the presence of inconsistencies. As illustrated in [37], given some (possibly inconsistent) specification and some reasoning task, HT4 is still able to generate abductive answers for the task despite the presence of inconsistencies. These answers are simply collected in different worlds, and the algorithm will generate as many worlds as there are inconsistencies in the specification. This is in particularly useful for analyzing multi-viewpoint specifications, which may be in conflict with each other. For examples and further details on this topic the reader is referred to [37].

### 4.1.2. *Using abduction to validate system properties*

Another type of specification analysis is validation of system properties. The work in [45] provides an example of the application of abduction for this purpose. Specifically, it shows how abductive reasoning mechanisms can be used to detect violation of properties like system invariants in event-based specifications. The basic idea and methodology described in [45] is, in principle, applicable to any type of specifications and system properties. Given a specification composed of a system description and some system invariants, the abductive reasoning mechanism can be used to check if the system invariants are satisfied by the specification. For each system invariant the abductive reasoning mechanism is able to identify a complete set of counterexamples, if any exist, to the invariant. The information included in the counterexample depends on the type of specification under consideration. For instance, in the case of event-driven specifications, such counterexamples are expressed in terms of a symbolic current state of the system and associated event-based transition. If the abductive reasoning mechanism fails to find an answer, this establishes the validity of the invariant with respect to the system description. More specifically, this application of abduction to specification analysis employs the standard notion of abduction, specified in Definition 1, in refutation mode. As illustrated in Fig. 5, the goal for the abductive reasoning mechanism is the negation of a given system invariant. If the abductive proof procedure succeeds in identifying a set of abducibles Δ, then the invariant is violated, since its negation can be inferred

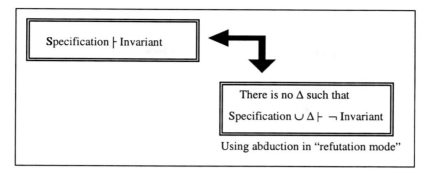

**Fig. 5.** Using abduction to analyze system invariants.

from the specification. The $\Delta$ provides the "faulty" behaviours of the system that contradict the given invariant. Therefore, the set $\Delta$ can be considered to be a set of counterexamples for the given system invariant.

Whereas the theoretical framework of abduction can in principle be applied to any type of system invariant, existing abductive proof procedures only accept instantiated sentences[h] as observations. This provides some constraint on the practicality of the abductive-based analysis process — only invariants that can be reduced *a priori* to some equivalent ground representation can be analyzed using the existing abductive techniques illustrated in Sec. 3. An example of application of abduction for analyzing system invariants is given below.

**Example 3.** Using abduction to analyze invariants in SCR specifications

The results shown in [45], illustrate how abductive logic programming techniques can be used to analyze single-state system invariants in Software Cost Reduction (SCR) specifications [21]. These are properties of the form $\forall t.\ I(t)$, which states that a required system invariant $I$ must always hold. This is typical for safety-critical system properties, where an invariant $I$ states some logical expression of system/environment properties as a function of specific system states (e.g. $\forall t.[\text{system\_state}(t) \rightarrow \text{expression}(t)]$). Examples of such properties in SCR specifications are mode invariants [19]. For instance, in the case of a cruise control system specification [2, 20], a system invariant $I$ would be:

$$system\_cruise \rightarrow system\_ignited \wedge system\_running \wedge \neg brake\,.$$

Within the logical representation of SCR specifications adopted in [45], the above invariant can be formalized as:

$$\forall t.Holds(cruise, t) \rightarrow \tag{I}$$
$$Holds(ignited, t) \wedge Holds(running, t) \wedge \neg Holds(brake, t)\,.$$

---

[h]This is the main reason why existing abductive reasoning mechanisms are proof procedures that always terminate.

where $t$ denotes the real-life time of the system. The results shown in [45], illustrate that the analysis task for verifying if a given invariant is satisfied in a given SCR specification can be reduced to a ground propositional level in the following way. Given a (first-order) logic representation of an SCR description of a required system behavior (i.e., a mode transition table), denoted with $EC(N)$, where $N$ is an underlying time structure, and given, for instance, the above invariant $I$, the analysis problem:

$$EC(N) \models I$$

can be reduced to the following two simpler tasks:

(1) $EC(N) \models I(0)$
(2) $EC(S) \wedge I(Sc) \models I(Sn)$

where $EC(S)$ is a ground instantiation of the $SCR$ description with respect to two symbolic time points "$Sc$" and "$Sn$", representing a "current time" and a "next time" respectively. The first task is a simple theorem proving problem. The second task is supported by the application of abductive reasoning in refutation mode. So, to show that $EC(S) \wedge I(Sc) \models I(Sn)$ it is equivalent to show that the abductive proof procedure for logic programming fails to find a $\Delta$ such that $EC(S) \wedge I(Sc) \wedge \Delta \models \neg I(Sn)$. Note that in this case the observation (goal) given to the abductive technique is $\neg I(Sn)$; which is the ground formula:

$$[Holds(cruise, Sn) \wedge$$
$$[Holds(ignited, Sn) \vee Holds(running, Sn) \vee \neg(Holds(brake, Sn)].$$

If, on the other hand, the abductive proof procedure produces a set $\Delta$ such that $EC(S) \wedge I(Sc) \wedge \Delta \models \neg I(Sn)$, then this $\Delta$ is an explicit indicator of where in the $SCR$ description there is a problem. Detailed results of a case study using abduction to $SCR$ specifications is given in [45].

The advantage of applying such an abductive approach to analyze system invariants is that it provides a formal technique for verifying properties and detecting errors that (a) does not rely on complete descriptions of the system specification and domain knowledge, and (b) provides diagnostic information about the detected errors (e.g. violation of safety properties) as a debugging aid for the engineer. It is the integration of these two features that distinguishes this (logic-based) abductive approach from other existing formal techniques such as those based on model checking or theorem proving [10]. The current limitation is that results so far have only shown the applicability of abduction to specific types of invariants. The authors have, however, argued in [45] that the same approach can be extended to cover other types of system properties such as liveness, deadlock, etc.

## 4.2. Revising specifications

One application of abduction is "theory change" [28]. This is particulary useful because it can support automated generation of simple changes of system specifications, in order to either resolve some detected inconsistencies or re-establish some violated system properties. A theory update problem is the problem of identifying changes (e.g. transactions) to be performed on a given theory so that some change request is satisfied (i.e., can consistently be performed). Examples of update requests are, for instance, addition (respectively deletion) of information, which in logic terms means requesting that the information should or should not be inferable from a given specification. Using abduction for performing such tasks means essentially interpreting the update request as an observation to be explained, and the explanation of the observation as changes (transactions) to be performed.

More specifically, using Inoue and Sakama's definition [25], given a specification $S$ and a pre-defined collection of abducibles Ab, if the change request is of the form "add $R$" (respectively "delete $R$"), the abductive reasoning generates a pair $(\Delta^+, \Delta^-)$, where $\Delta^+$ and $\Delta^-$ are ground instances of elements from Ab. The abduced facts in $\Delta^+$ are information to be added to the specification, whereas the abduced facts in $\Delta^-$ are information to be deleted from the specification. The pair $(\Delta^+, \Delta^-)$ has therefore to satisfy the following two conditions[i]:

$$(S \cup \Delta^+) \backslash \Delta^- \models R \qquad \text{(respectively } (S \cup \Delta^+) \backslash \Delta^- \not\models R)$$
$$(S \cup \Delta^+) \backslash \Delta^- \text{ is consistent}.$$

The change transaction is then given by the addition of each abduced fact in $\Delta^+$ and the deletion of each abduced fact in $\Delta^-$. The new specification is given by $(S \cup \Delta^+) \backslash \Delta^-$. A diagrammatic representation illustrating the use of abduction for revising specifications is shown in Fig. 6. As an example, consider the specification $S$ given by $\{p(x) \leftarrow \sim q(x), q(x) \leftarrow b(x), b(a)\}$ and the change request *insert p(a)*. The abductive proof procedure is applied, treating $p(a)$ as the observation to explain, and generating a $\Delta = (\Delta^+, \Delta^-)$, with $\Delta^+ = \emptyset$ and $\Delta^- = \{\sim b(a)\}$. The resulting revision change is then simply to delete $b(a)$, leading to the new specification $S' = \{p(x) \leftarrow \sim q(x), q(x) \leftarrow b(x)\}$. For more examples the reader is referred to [28].

The use of a logic programming abductive proof procedure for reasoning about change has the following characteristics. As shown in the example, the theory (specification) is composed of some fixed knowledge; e.g. a set of rules that is not subject to change, and explicit knowledge in terms of atomic facts that can be changed. The abductive procedure takes the update request as its observation to explain, and generates an abduced explanation $\Delta$. The negated facts in $\Delta$ give the $\Delta^-$ used in the above definition and the positive facts in $\Delta$ give the $\Delta^+$. This set $\Delta$ is then mapped onto a transition operation: negated facts are deleted from the given specification and positive facts are added.

In order to apply such a technique for reasoning about change in software specifications, we need to define what are the fixed and modifiable parts of our given description. The fixed part can either be domain-specific knowledge about

---

[i]The symbol $\backslash$ denotes the standard operation of subtraction between sets. Note that either $\Delta^+$ or $\Delta^-$ can be empty sets, and that $\Delta^+ \cap \Delta^- = \emptyset$.

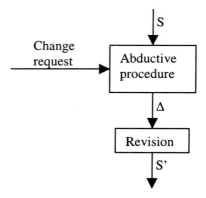

**Fig. 6.**   How to use abduction for changing specifications.

change for a given type of specification, so considering the whole specification modifiable, or a part of the specification that we can safely assume not to be subject to change, for instance the set of system's properties or some domain knowledge. Changes can be detected using only the fixed part of the specification. However, the only changes that abduction can help identify are single assertions and not more complex information such as new rules. This is somewhat restrictive, since, in a real-setting, changes to specifications can have different levels of complexity. However, as shown in [41, 47], this kind of abduction does begin to address the difficult problem of specification management. Two example applications of abduction for revising specifications are described in more detail in [41, 47].

### 4.2.1. *Using abduction to evolve inconsistent (requirements) specifications*

The work in [41] shows how abduction can be used for handling inconsistencies in (requirements) specifications. The approach provides an inconsistency handling mechanism that supports incremental evolution of specifications, by identifying changes that address some specification inconsistencies, while leaving others [17]. Specifications are assumed to be composed of many partial specifications (typically developed by different stakeholders), related to each other by means of pre-defined "consistency rules". Each partial specification may or may not contain logical inconsistencies. However, the overall specification is defined to be inconsistent[j] whenever at least one of the pre-defined rules is violated. If a particular consistency rule is violated, the abductive reasoning mechanism identifies (evolutionary) changes to perform on the specification, such that the particular consistency rule is no longer violated. In order to facilitate incremental evolution of specifications, the partial specifications and consistency rules are assumed to be represented in quasi-classical

---

[j]The word inconsistency means in this case violation of consistency rules. Of course if the consistency rule is of the form $A \wedge \neg A \rightarrow \perp$, then inconsistency means also logical inconsistencies.

(QC) logic [24] — an adaptation of classical logic that allows reasoning in the presence of inconsistencies without trivialization.[k] The novelty of this work is in applying existing abductive techniques for logic programming but within the more realistic setting of inconsistent specifications. An example of a library system case study is described in [41]. A simplified version is given here.

## Example 4

The requirements of a library system include the following partial specification:

> "... individuals should be allowed to borrow books from a library if they need these books and if the books are available. A book is available if there is one copy in the library. Once a book is borrowed, it is no longer available for others to borrow. Moreover, a book copy is needed and it is in the library".

It includes the consistency rule that "if a book is borrowed then it is no longer available". The full specification given in [41] violates such rule. This means that a QC logical representation of the negation of this rule, i.e., *BorrowingBook* ∧ *BookAvailable* is derivable from the QC representation of the specifications. Resolving this inconsistency means eliminating one of the above two literals, *BorrowingBook* or *BookAvailable* from the set of consequences of the specification.

The abductive approach developed in [41], uses an algorithm for mapping QC specifications into logic programs, and then uses existing abductive techniques for logic programming to identify changes that would resolve the detected inconsistency. Part of the logic program generated for this example is given below, where the predicate *HoldsS* provides a reified representation of the QC formulae.[l] The set of abducibles is given by the atomic predicate *HoldsS* whose content are names for single atomic QC formulae, and they are not in the left-and-side of any logic program rule. The set of rules given below correspond to the fixed part of the specification, whereas the single atomic *HoldsS* predicate is that part of the specification that can be modified.

HoldsS(BookAvailable) ←

    HoldsS(BookInLibrary),

    HoldsS(BookInLibrary → BookAvailable).

HoldsS(BookAvailable) ←

HoldsS(BookCopy),

    HoldsS(BookCopy → BookAvailable).

---

[k]Trivialization in classical logic is the inference of arbitrary information from an inconsistent specification.
[l]The content of the predicate *HoldsS* should be read as a constant name.

HoldsS(BookInLibrary → BookAvailable) ←

    HoldsS(BookCopy),

    HoldsS((BookCopy ∧ BookInLibrary) → BookAvailable).

HoldsS(BookCopy → BookAvailable) ←

    HoldsS(BookInLibrary),

    HoldsS((BookCopy ∧ BookInLibrary) → BookAvailable).

HoldsS((BookCopy ∧ BookInLibrary) → BookAvailable).

HoldsS(BookCopy).

HoldsS(BookInLibrary).

HoldsS(BookNeeded).

To apply the abductive technique for logic programming to the above logic program to resolve the detected inconsistency, the deletion of *BookAvailable* should be treated as the change request, since this will resolve the violation of the given consistency rule. Part of the abductive reasoning performed in this case is described in Fig. 7. The abductive proof identifies two alternative changes $\Delta^- = \{\sim HoldsS(BookCopy)\}$ and $\Delta^- = \{\sim HoldsS(BookInLibrary)\}$, which lead to two change transitions, *delete BookCopy* or *delete BookInLibrary* from the given specification.

For futher details on this application of abduction for inconsistency handling the reader is referred to [41].

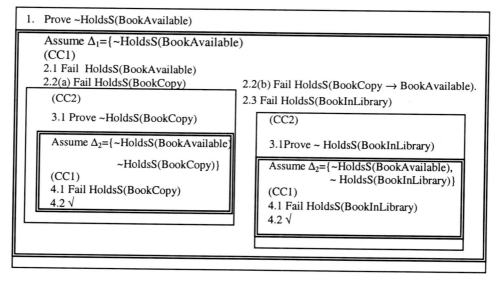

**Fig. 7.** A partial abductive proof for managing the change request "delete (BookAvailable)".

### 4.2.2. *Using abduction to manage consistency in specifications*

The work described in [46–48] takes a different perspective on the problem of specifications revision. In particular, it follows the more traditional line of research on formal techniques for analyzing and managing the impact of changes, where the starting point is a consistent specification, and the revision process is a process of re-stablishing consistency in order to accommodate a given change request. Abduction in this case is used to identify additional changes on the given specification so as to re-establish consistency.

In [46], Satoh describes a logic approach based on abductive reasoning for adding and deleting "pollution markers" from a given specification in order to manage consistency after a change has been performed. The idea of pollution markers for inconsistency handling was first introduced by Balzer [3] as a technique for treating inconsitencies as exceptions and adding or deleting such markers in order to isolate these exceptions (and therefore the inconsistencies) from the rest of the data. Satoh, on the other hand, proposes an abductive technique (a) to help identify these exceptions and the associated pollution markers to add/delete, and (b) to define a revision operator that defines the new specification after an update has been performed. We illustrate the approach via an example taken from [46].

### Example 5

Consider a specification which includes the following constraint:

> "Required working hours, $R$, for a day, for an employee $P$, must be equal to actual total working hours, $T$, of all the projects for a day, $D$".

Now suppose that the specification states that the total working hours is calculated as the sum of the hours for two projects $A$ and $B$, and that for a particular employee "Bob", his required hours are 60 and his hours for project $B$ are 30. This specification can be implemented by the following logic program:

$$th(P, D, T) \leftarrow pA(P, D, X), pB(P, D, Y), T = A + B,$$
$$rh(\text{bob}, 10, 60),$$
$$pB(\text{bob}, 10, 30),$$
$$\bot \leftarrow (rh(P, D, R), th(P, D, T), R \neq T,$$

where $th(P, D, T)$ expresses that the total hours for an employee $P$ for a day $D$ is $T$, $pA(P, D, X)$ that the hours for an employee $P$ for a day $D$ on the project $A$ is $X$, and similarly for $pB(P, D, Y)$ and $rh(P, D, R)$ that the required hours for an employee $P$ for a day $D$ is $R$. Note that the last rule is an integrity constraint that defines the constraint given in the specification. Each constraint is then rewritten into a new constraint, following a procedure defined in [46], to include information about possible pollution markers. For instance, the above constraint is rewritten as follows:

$$\perp \leftarrow rh(P, D, R), th(P, D, T), R \neq T,  \tag{I1}$$
$$\sim pm(rh(P, D, R), th(P, D, T)), \sim add^*(pm(rh(P, D, R), th(P, D, T))).$$

where $pm$ expresses a predicate for the pollution marker and $add^*$ is abducible information.

Suppose now that the leader of project $A$ updates the date with $pA(bob, 10, 40)$. This update violates the constraints in the specification since it makes the total hours for $Bob$ equal to 70 for day 10, while his required hours for day 10 are 60. The abductive proof procedure for logic programming then considers the above integrity constraint as the goal to be satisfied. Therefore, since $rh(bob, 10, 60), th(bob, 10, 70), 60 \neq 70$ are provable it must be the case that either the predicate $\sim pm(rh(P, D, R), th(P, D, T))$, or $\sim add^*(pm(rh(P, D, R), th(P, D, T)))$ should fail, for the particular instance values $P = Bob, D = 10$, $R = 60$ and $T = 70$. Since $add^*$ is a pre-defined abducible predicate, the abductive procedure tries to fail the antecedent $\sim add^*(pm(rh(bob, 10, 60), th(bob, 10, 70)))$. This means trying to prove $add^*(pm(rh(bob, 10, 60), th(bob, 10, 70)))$. This predicate can then consistently be added to the set of abducibles $\Delta$, giving the answer $add^*(pm(rh(bob, 10, 60), th(bob, 10, 70)))$. The transaction operation on the given specification will then add to the specification the pollution marker:

$$pm(rh(bob, 10, 60), th(bob, 10, 70))$$

and the following two constraints:

$$\perp \leftarrow \sim (rh(bob, 10, 60), \sim del^*(pm(rh(bob, 10, 60), th(bob, 10, 70)))).  \tag{I2}$$

$$\perp \leftarrow \sim (th(bob, 10, 70), \sim del^*(pm(rh(bob, 10, 60), th(bob, 10, 70)))).  \tag{I3}$$

This is because the pollution marker states that there is an exception given by the atomic predicates $rh(bob, 10, 60)$ and $th(bob, 10, 70)$, and that if subsequently there are other changes to the specification for which the constraint in the specification is no longer violated, we will need to delete the pollution marker corresponding to the previous violation. So, for instance, suppose that the leader of the project $B$ deletes $pB(bob, 10, 30)$ and replaces it with $pB(bob, 10, 20)$. Then the violation of the constraint no longer exists because the total number of hours is now equal to 60. In this case, the abductive proof procedure tries to satisfy each of the above integrity constraints. Constraint (I1) is satisfied because it is not the case that $60 \neq 60$, and constraint (I2) is also satisfied because $\sim rh(bob, 10, 60)$ fails since $rh(bob, 10, 60)$ is in the specification. The important step is now in the analysis of constraint (I3). The new total number of hours for bob is now 60, so the predicate $\sim th(bob, 10, 70)$ succeeds, therefore it must be the case that the predicate $\sim del^*(pm(rh(bob, 10, 60), th(bob, 10, 70)))$ fails to make the constraint satisfied. Since $del^*$ is also another pre-defined abducible predicate, to fail $\sim del^*(pm(rh(bob, 10, 60), th(bob, 10, 70)))$ the abductive proof procedure can consistently assume the predicate $del^*(pm(rh(bob, 10, 60), th(bob, 10, 70)))$. This abducible states that the pollution marker regarding $rh(bob, 10, 60)$ and $th(bob, 10, 70))$ can be deleted. Hence the transaction operation will then delete $pm(rh(bob, 10, 60), th(bob, 10, 70))$ and the above two integrity constraints (I2) and (I3).

A similar approach has been presented in [48], where the abductive proof procedure for logic programming is also used for consistency management in order to accommodate changes in a specification that can violate required constraints. Specifications are translated into logic programs, as shown above, and constraints rewritten as special integrity constraints, where some auxiliary predicate like $add^*$ and $del^*$ are appropriately added in order to keep trace of the particular instances that violate these integrity constraints. Such instances are then mapped onto assertions to be added or deleted from the specification in order to re-establish consistency, in a similar way as addition and deletion of pollution markers to/from specifications. The difference between the last two lines of research work is that the addition and deletion in the latter case is for information already included in the specification, rather then some external artifact like pollution markers. For further details the reader is referred to [48].

## 5. Conclusion and Future Work

In this paper, we have surveyed a number of research results and formal approaches for using abduction in software engineering. We have seen how two different abductive reasoning techniques, based on logic programming and dependency graphs, can facilitate both analysis and revision of specifications. In particular, abductive logic programming has been shown to be suitable for detecting violation of system properties and for identifying diagnostic information as a debugging aid for engineers. This diagnostic capability, typical of abduction, is indeed common to both techniques described in this paper, making them also suitable for supporting automated generation of explanations for a given domain related property. For instance, in the case of graph-based abduction, proof trees can be constructed from some given qualitative theory description of a specifications that provides models or descriptions of how certain OUTput information can be achieved given certain INput data. These descriptions can be seen as explanations for the given OUTput within a pre-defined context (drawn by the given INput). As an additional benefit, because of the ability to construct such explanations consistently the graph-based abductive approach can at the same time identify all or part of the inconsistencies included in the given specification, thereby providing automated support for inconsistency detection.

As a second application of abductive reasoning, we have illustrated the use of abduction for revising specifications, both in the case of evolving inconsistent specifications, and for managing consistency after performing an update. The first type of application is motivated by the fact that, in practice, inconsistency is inevitable in real large-scale specifications [3, 13, 49]. Therefore, living with inconsistency during evolutionary development is a fact of life, and *inconsistency handling* mechanisms need to support incremental evolution of specifications (i.e., identifying changes that address some specification inconsistencies, while leaving others). The second application on the other hand proposes abduction as a technique for reasoning about how to re-establish consistency in a given specification, once this has been broken by performing some (possibly evolutionary) changes.

A variety of other techniques have been developed for analyzing and managing requirement specifications. These range from informal but structured inspections [18], to more formal techniques such as data mining, machine learning, and case-based reasoning. An example of inspection techniques is perspective-based reasoning [50]. This is a scenario-based technique that provides procedural guidance on how to inspect requirements documents written in English. The identification of faulty requirements in this technique is based on answering specifically tailored questions during the development of the specifications. These questions are themselves based on a predefined taxonomy of errors such as ambiguous information. Abductive reasoning is a much more general analyzis technique, which can be appropriately tailored to analyze any type of specific domain-dependent system property. Moreover, the rigor of the underlying reasoning process guarantees a complete description of existing errors. Data mining [31] and machine learning [51] are known as techniques for *knowledge discovery*. This means, given a sample of data (in the case of data mining) or positive/negative examples (in the case of machine learning), these techniques are able to abstract such data into new rules. These can subsequently, and if necessary, be added to the given knowledge base. Abduction does not generate new rules. It only defines how to instantiate the truth value of a special set of propositions, so that the resulting model of the specification would satisfy a given observation/goal. Hence, machine learning and data mining are in their nature unsound reasoning processes, whereas abduction is a fully sound and consistent reasoning technique. Case-based reasoning [32] is another example of a (semi-)formal technique used for understanding problems and proposing solutions. This technique differs, however, from abduction in the fact that it assumes the existence of a large library of past-cases; these cases are then used either to generate solutions or as examples to illustrate an existing problem. Abduction, on the other hand, requires only the specification and the invariants of a system to perform its analysis.

Finally, abductive reasoning also differs from other formal techniques like those based on model checking or theorem proving [10] or logic-based approaches (e.g. [35, 47, 52]). The results illustrated in this paper therefore provide some valuable foundations for the use of abduction in software engineering, as well as raising some interesting and challenging research issues for future work. The ability to perform automated analysis and generation of counterexamples when errors are detected makes abduction comparable to other existing formal techniques such as those based on model checking [1, 8–10], and also highlights some interesting differences. Model checking techniques often require complete description of the initial state(s) of the system in order to compute successor states, and the application of abstraction techniques to reduce the size of the state space. In contrast, abduction doesn't necessarily rely on a complete description of some initial system state, as shown in the case study given in [45]. Moreover, because of the goal- or property-driven characteristic of the abductive techniques it does not require abstraction and it can support reasoning about specifications of systems whose state-spaces may be infinite. However, the practical application of abduction to specification analysis in software engineering is still at an early stage of development. Further research is needed to extend existing results in order to cover a wider spectrum of specification analyzes that take into account various forms of system properties as well as different types of specifications. This will consolidate the existing theoretical foundations for the development of efficient, logic-based methods for automated analysis of specifications using abduction. Their practicality will then need to be measured using a wide range of case studies.

As far as specification handling is concerned, the use of abduction is still at its initial stages of development. A variety of future directions can be taken from the existing results shown in this chapter. In particular, the development of a framework that combines abduction with induction might be useful. The identification of possible changes on a specification by abduction can only be related to single assertion. However, the counterexamples provided by abductive reasoning could be used by some inductive reasoning process in order to identify, by means of a learning process, more elaborate changes to perform on a given specification. Appropriate interleavings between abductive and inductive reasoning could provide a sound, logic-based approach to the specification management process.

## Acknowledgments

Many thanks to Tim Menzies and Ken Satoh for providing useful insights about their respective abductive approaches, to Tony Kakas for useful discussions about abduction and abductive tools, and to Jeff Kramer for useful feedback and suggestions about earlier drafts of this paper. This work was partially funded by the UK EPSRC projects MISE (GR/L 55964) and VOICI (GR/M 38582).

## References

1. R. Anderson, *et al*, "Model checking large software specifications", *ACM Proceedings of 4th International Symposium on the Foundation of Software Engineering* (1996).
2. J. M. Atlee and J. Gannon, "State-based model checking of event-driven system requirements", *IEEE Transactions on Software Engineering* **19**, no. 1 (1993) 24–40.
3. R. Balzer, "Tolerating inconsistency", *Proceedings of ICSE13* (1991) 158–165.
4. R. Bharadwaj and C. Heitmeyer, "Model checking complete requirements specifications using abstraction", Technical Report No. NRL-7999, Naval Research Laboratory (1997).

5. G. Brewka, *Non-monotonic Reasoning: Logical Foundations of Commonsense* (Cambridge University Press, Cambridge, Great Britain, 1991).
6. W. J. Clancey, "Model construction operators", *Artificial Intelligence* **27** (1992) 289–350.
7. K. Clark, "Negation as failure", *Logic and Data Bases*, eds. H. Gallaire and J. Minker (Plenum, New York, 1978) 293–322.
8. E. M. Clarke, O. Grumberg and D. E. Long, "Model checking and abstraction", *ACM Transactions on Programming Languages and Systems* **16**, no. 5 (1994) 1512–1542.
9. E. M. Clarke, O. Grumberg and D. E. Long, "Model checking", *Deductive Program Design, Proceedings, NATO ASI Series F*, ed. M. Broy (Springer, 1996).
10. M. Clarke and M. Wing, "Formal methods, state of the art and future directions", *ACM Computing Surveys* **28**, no. 4 (1996) 626–643.
11. L. Console, M. L. Sapino and D. T. Dupre, "The role of abduction in database", View Updates, *Journal of Intelligent Systems* (1994).
12. L. Console, L. Portinale and D. T. Dupre, "Using compiled knowledge to guide and focus abductive diagnosis", *IEEE Transaction on Knowledge and Data Engineering* **8**, no. 5 (1996) 690–706.
13. G. Cugola, E. Di Nitto, A. Fuggetta and C. Ghezzi, "A framework for formalising inconsistencies and deviations in human-centred systems", *ACM Transactions on Software Engineering and Methodology* **5**, no. 3 (1996) 191–230.
14. S. Easterbrook and B. Nuseibeh, "Inconsistency management in an evolving specification", *Proceedings of the 2nd International Symposium on Requirements Engineering* (1995) 48–55.
15. K. Esghsi, "Abductive planning with the event calculus", *Proceedings of International Conference on Artificial Intelligence* **1** (1988) 3–8.
16. K. Eshghi and R. A. Kowalski, "Abduction compared with negation as failure", *Proceedings of the 6th International Conference on Logic Programming* (Lisbon, 1989) 234–255.
17. A. Finkelstein, *et al*, "Inconsistency handling in multi-perspective specifications", *IEEE Transaction on Software Engineering* **20**, no. 8 (1994) 569–578.
18. T. Gilb and D. Graham, *Software Inspection* (Addison-Wesley, 1993).
19. C. L. Heitmeyer, B. Labaw and D. Kiskis, "Consistency checking of SCR-style requirements specifications", *Second International Symposium on Requirements Engineering* (York, 1995) 27–29.
20. C. L. Heitmeyer, *et al*, "Using abstraction and model checking to detect safety violations in requirements specifications", *IEEE Transaction on Software Engineering* **24**, no. 11 (1998) 927–947.
21. C. L. Hietmeyer, *et al*, "SCR: A toolset for specifying and analyzing software requirements", *Computer-Aided Verification*, Canada (1998).
22. C. Hogger, *Essentials of Logic Programming* (Clarendon Press, Oxford, 1990).
23. C. Hogger and R. A. Kowalski, "Logic programming", *Encyclopedia of Artificial Intelligence*, 2nd ed., ed. S. C. Shapiro (John Wiley & Sons, New York, 1991).
24. A. Hunter and B. Nuseibeh, "Managing inconsistent specifications: Reasoning, analysis and action", *ACM Transactions on Software Engineering and Methodology* (October 1998).
25. K. Inoue and C. Sakama, "Abductive framework for non-monotonic theory change", *International Joint Conference on Artificial Intelligence* **1** (1995) 204–210.
26. D. Jackson and M. Rinard, "Software analysis: A roadmap", *The Future of Software Engineering*, ed. A. Finkelstein (ACM Press, 2000).
27. J. Jacky, "Specifying a safety-critical control system in Z", *IEEE Transactions on Software Engineering* **2** (1995) 99–106.

28. A. C. Kakas and P. Mancarella, "Database updates through abduction", *Proceedings of 16th International Conference on Very Large Database*, Brisbane, Australia (1990).

29. A. C. Kakas, "Abductive constraint logic programming" (1998), <*http://www.cs.ucy.ac.cy/aclp/index.html*>

30. A. C. Kakas, R. A. Kowalski and F. Toni, "The role of abduction in logic programming", *Handbook of Logic in Artificial Intelligence and Logic Programming*, eds., D. M. Gabbay, C. J. Hogger and J. A. Robinson (Oxford University Press, 1998) 235–324.

31. A. Silberschatz, H. F. Korth and S. Sudarshan, *Database System Concepts*, 3rd ed. (McGraw Hill Companies Inc.).

32. D. Leake, *Case-Based Reasoning* (AAAI Press/ The MIT Press, 1996).

33. J. Magee and J. Kramer, *Concurrency: State Models & Java Programs* (John Wiley & Sons Ltd., 1999).

34. K. L. McMillian, *Symbolic Model Checking* (Kluwer Academic Publishers, 1993).

35. T. Menzies, "Applications of abduction: Knowledge level modeling", *International Journal of Human Computer Studies* **45** (1996) 305–355.

36. T. Menzies, and P. Compton, "Applications of abduction: Hypothesis testing of neuroendocrinological qualitative compartmental models", *Artificial Intelligence in Medicine* **10** (1997) 145–175.

37. T. Menzies, S. Easterbrook, B. Nuseibeh and S. Waugh, "An empirical investigation of multiple viewpoint reasoning in requirements engineering", *Proceedings of 4th IEEE International Symposium on Requirements Engineering* (Limerick, June 1999).

38. T. J. Menzies, *Principles of Generalised Testing of Knowledge Bases* PhD Thesis, University of New South Wales (1995).

39. A. Newell, "The knowledge level", *Artificial Intelligence* **18** (1982) 87–127.

40. B. Nuseibeh, "To be and not to be: On managing inconsistency in software development", *Proceedings of the 8th International Workshop on Software Specifications and Design* (1996) 164–169.

41. B. Nuseibeh and A. Russo, "Using abduction to evolve inconsistent requirements specifications", *Austrialian Journal of Information Systems*, Special Issue on Requirements Engineering, ISSN 1039-7841 (1999) 118–130.

42. S. Owre, J. Rushby and N. Shankar, "PVS: A prototype verification system", *Proceedings of the 11th Conference on Automated Deduction, Lecture Notes in Artificial Intelligence* **607** (1992) 748–752.

43. C. S. Pierce, *Collected Papers of Charles Sanders Pierce*, Hartshorn *et al* (Harvard University Press).

44. R. Reiter, *On Closed World Databases* (Plenum Press, New York, 1978).

45. A. Russo, *et al*, "An abductive approach for handling inconsistencies in SCR specifications", *Proceedings of International Workshop on Intelligent Software Engineering (ICSE'2000)* (Limerick, 2000).

46. K. Satoh, "Adding and deleting pollution marker by abductive logic programming", *Proceedings of the Asia and Pacific Rim Workshop on Intelligent Software Engineering* (1998) 48–53.

47. K. Satoh, "Computing minimal revised logical specification by abduction", *Proceedings of International Workshop on the Principles of Software Evolution* (1998) 177–182.

48. K. Satoh, "Consistency management in software engineering by abduction", *Proceedings of International Workshop on Intelligent Software Engineering (ICSE'2000)* (Limerick, 2000).

49. R. W. Schwanke and G. E. Kaiser, "Living with inconsistency in large systems", *Proceedings of the International Workshop on Software Version and Configuration Control*, Grassau, Germany (1988).

50. F. Shull, I. Rus and V. Basili, "How perspective-based reading can improve requirements inspections", *IEEE Computer* (July 2000) 73–79.

51. A. van Lamsweerde, "Learning machine learning", *Introducing a Logic Based Approach to Artificial Intelligence*, ed. A. Thayse (Wiley, 1991) 263–356.

52. A. van Lamsweerde, R. Darimont and E. Letier, "Managing conflicts in goal-driven requirement engineering", *IEEE Transactions on Software Engineering*, Special Issue on Managing Inconsistency in Software Development (1998).

53. A. van Lamsweerde and E. Letier, "Handling obstacles in goal-oriented requirements engineering", *IEEE Transactions on Software Engineering*, Special Issue on Exception Handling **26** (2000).

54. G. R. Yost and A. Newell, "A problem space approach to expert systems", *Proceedings of the International Joint Conference on Artificial Intelligence* (1989) 621–627.

55. P. Zave and M. Jackson, "Four dark corners of requirements engineering", *ACM Transactions on Software Engineering and Methodology* **6**, no. 1 (1997) 1–30.

# INDEX